Introduction to
PSYCHOLOGY

5th Edition

Introduction to
PSYCHOLOGY

5th Edition

Rod Plotnik
San Diego State University

Brooks/Cole • Wadsworth

I⟨T⟩P® An International Thomson Publishing Company

Belmont • Albany • Bonn • Boston • Cincinnati • Detroit • Johannesburg • London • Madrid
Melbourne • Mexico City • New York • Pacific Grove • Paris • Singapore • Tokyo • Toronto • Washington

Executive Editor: *Vicki Knight*
Marketing Team: *Lauren Harp & Margaret Parks*
Editorial Associate: *Shelley Tweddell*
Production Editor: *Nancy L. Shammas*
Manuscript Editor: *Shirley Simmons*
Proofreader: *Susan Pendleton*
Permissions Editor: *Linda Rill*
Interior Design: *Rod Plotnik*
Interior Illustration: *PC&F, Inc.*

Concept Illustrators: *Phillip Dvorak & Bill Ogden*
Cover Design: *Vernon T. Boes*
Cover Illustration: *Tana Powell/Conrad Represents*
Photo Researcher: *Linda Rill*
Indexer: *James Minkin*
Typesetting: *PC&F, Inc.*
Cover Printing: *Phoenix Color Corporation*
Printing and Binding: *R. R. Donnelley & Sons/Willard*

For more information, contact:

WADSWORTH PUBLISHING COMPANY
10 Davis Drive
Belmont, CA 94002
USA
http://www.wadsworth.com

International Thomson Publishing Europe
Berkshire House 168-173
High Holborn
London WC1V 7AA
England

Thomas Nelson Australia
102 Dodds Street
South Melbourne, 3205
Victoria, Australia

Nelson Canada
1120 Birchmount Road
Scarborough, Ontario
Canada M1K 5G4

International Thomson Editores
Seneca 53
Col. Polanco
11560 México D. F. México

International Thomson Publishing GmbH
Königswinterer Strasse 418
53227 Bonn
Germany

International Thomson Publishing Asia
60 Albert Street
#15-01 Albert Complex
Singapore 189969

International Thomson Publishing Japan
Hirakawacho Kyowa Building, 3F
2-2-1 Hirakawacho
Chiyoda-ku, Tokyo 102
Japan

Printed in the United States of America

10   9   8   7   6   5   4   3   2   1

Library of Congress Cataloging-in-Publication Data
Plotnik, Rod.
    Introduction to psychology / Rod Plotnik. -- 5th ed.
        p.   cm.
    Includes bibliographical references and index.
    ISBN 0-534-35611-7 (hardcover)
    1. Psychology.   I. Title.
BF121.P626 1998
150--dc21   98-37913
                                                        CIP

Dedication

To All Students Everywhere:

There were many times during the two years of revising this text when I would be a moment away from saying, "I quit. I've had enough. I can't write another word. I'd rather walk across the freeway than turn on my computer."

And then, as if by magic, I'd receive a student comment that was so wonderful it made me smile, forget my complaints, and gave me the motivation to turn on my computer and keep on going.

This 5th edition is dedicated to all those students who sent in such great comments as well as to all future students, whom I hope will also enjoy reading this text.

Here's a sample of the students' comments for which I am eternally grateful.

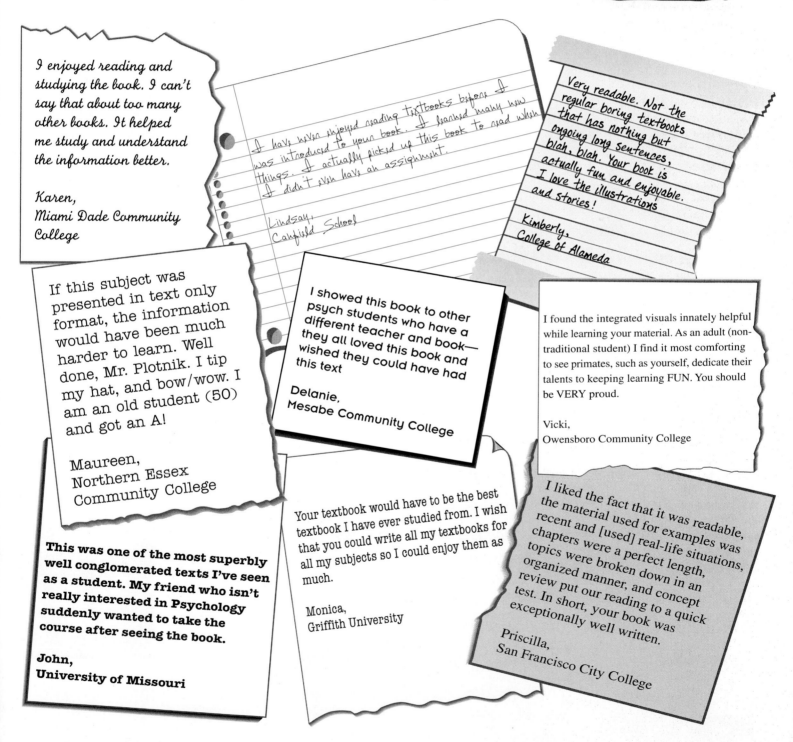

I enjoyed reading and studying the book. I can't say that about too many other books. It helped me study and understand the information better.

Karen,
Miami Dade Community College

I have never enjoyed reading textbooks before I was introduced to your book. I learned many new things. I actually picked up this book to read when I didn't even have an assignment.

Lindsay,
Canfield School

Very readable. Not the regular boring textbooks that has nothing but ongoing long sentences, blah, blah. Your book is actually fun and enjoyable. I love the illustrations and stories!

Kimberly,
College of Alameda

If this subject was presented in text only format, the information would have been much harder to learn. Well done, Mr. Plotnik. I tip my hat, and bow/wow. I am an old student (50) and got an A!

Maureen,
Northern Essex Community College

I showed this book to other psych students who have a different teacher and book—they all loved this book and wished they could have had this text

Delanie,
Mesabe Community College

I found the integrated visuals innately helpful while learning your material. As an adult (non-traditional student) I find it most comforting to see primates, such as yourself, dedicate their talents to keeping learning FUN. You should be VERY proud.

Vicki,
Owensboro Community College

This was one of the most superbly well conglomerated texts I've seen as a student. My friend who isn't really interested in Psychology suddenly wanted to take the course after seeing the book.

John,
University of Missouri

Your textbook would have to be the best textbook I have ever studied from. I wish that you could write all my textbooks for all my subjects so I could enjoy them as much.

Monica,
Griffith University

I liked the fact that it was readable, the material used for examples was recent and [used] real-life situations, chapters were a perfect length, topics were broken down in an organized manner, and concept review put our reading to a quick test. In short, your book was exceptionally well written.

Priscilla,
San Francisco City College

Contents

Module 3: Brain's Building Blocks

Module 4: Incredible Nervous System

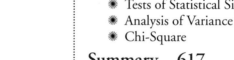

Figure A.1
A normal curve.

Number of subjects

Measurements

Choosing a Textbook

Each time I walk into my class at the beginning of every term, I realize that for the next many months my success in the classroom depends on just three things: my teaching skills, my students' abilities, and the textbook that I have chosen. Of these three things, I have control over only two, my teaching skills and the textbook.

It took me a few years of teaching Introductory Psychology to discover how important it was for me to choose a textbook that was appropriate for my students. Like some of you, I initially chose textbooks that I liked but that were not exactly right for my students. Some of the textbooks that I liked were too long, too difficult, or so uninteresting that my students did not read them. I gradually realized that since most Introductory Psychology texts cover the same material, what I wanted most was a text that motivated students to read it.

Motivating students to read a printed page in a textbook becomes more difficult since today's students have been raised in a multimedia world which presents information by integrating words and images, something unheard of when I taught my first Introductory Psychology course 30 years ago. This means that, in light of how today's students get information, my challenge in writing a textbook is how to present traditional concepts in ways that will grab my students' attention, engage their interest, and motivate them to read the material. This task would have been overwhelming except that I had one big advantage. In my role as supervisor of our department's 16 graduate assistants who teach Introductory Psychology to more than a thousand students each semester, I received an enormous amount of feedback about the kind of textbook features their students found interesting. In our weekly meetings we identified three elements that especially interested students:

1. Reading about interesting examples and real-life cases that help make traditional concepts relevant.

2. Applying psychological principles to everyday issues, people, and problems.

3. Presenting traditional information by integrating text with clever graphics.

In the 3rd and 4th editions of the text, I have tried to incorporate these three elements. In some cases I succeeded, but in other cases these elements needed more thought and development. Thus, in response to comments by more than 50 reviewers and thousands of students, I set the following goals for revising the 5th edition.

5th Edition—Goals & Changes

■ *Modular format:* One of the features liked best by both professors and students is the organization of all the material usually included in an introductory psychology course in small readable units called modules. In the fifth edition, there are 25 stand-alone modules that can be organized in any order.

■ *New information:* I have revised, rewritten, and added new information to each module. I accomplished this by reducing the size of the graphics, and using the entire page instead of leaving wide margins. Unlike traditional textbooks, which follow a fixed design for all pages, I created the fifth edition entirely on computer, which meant that I could design each page independently for maximum effectiveness.

■ *Research emphasis and references:* Because many of us want our students to understand and appreciate the experimental basis for the field of psychology, I have added over 700 new references, of which

more than 400 were published in either 1997 or 1998. I also have revised another very popular feature, the Research Focus. Each module contains a Research Focus, which uses an interesting study to explain how psychologists answer questions through surveys, experiments, and case studies. Finally, I made it a point to identify and explain the classic experiments in psychology, such as Watson's conditioning of Little Albert, Bandura's Bobo doll study, and Schachter-Singer's experiment on emotions.

■ *Better integration of text and graphics:* According to reviewers, one of the best-liked features in the 5th edition is the integration of text and graphics, which spark interest as well as explain concepts that tend to be complex and slightly boring. In the previous editions, some professors thought that there was too much emphasis on illustrations. I solved this problem in the 5th edition by reducing the size of the images so that they become part of and explain the concepts rather than overwhelm them. Because I was able to design each page, I made sure that the content and not the design was the central feature.

■ *Built-in study aids, Critical Thinking activities, and Web sites:* Students' comments indicated that they especially liked the built-in study aids. To help students organize and develop outlines, each module now opens with an outline of the eight to nine major concepts, along with their subtopics. To help students test their knowledge, each module contains a Concept Review and Summary Test. To help students develop critical thinking skills, each module contains two Critical Thinking activities. To help students easily obtain additional information on major topics, each module contains related Web addresses.

I'll let you be the judge of whether I reached my goals in revising the 5th edition by showing actual pages and explaining their features.

Modular Approach

When I have to read a long 40- to 45-page chapter, I usually run out of intellectual steam by page 20 and have to fight to read on. My problem with long chapters is shared by many instructors, students, and reviewers, who report difficulty in maintaining interest throughout a long chapter. This is why one of the most popular features of the previous editions was the modular approach. Like the 4th, the 5th edition has 25 relatively short modules rather than more traditional 40-page chapters.

What's the advantage of shorter modules?

I developed the modular approach in response to the needs of both students and instructors. Students said that they preferred shorter modules because it made the material less overwhelming, more manageable, and easier to review before going on to new material.

Instructors said that they preferred the modular approach because it allowed them to select, rearrange, or delete individual modules and thus have great flexibility in planning and personalizing their courses.

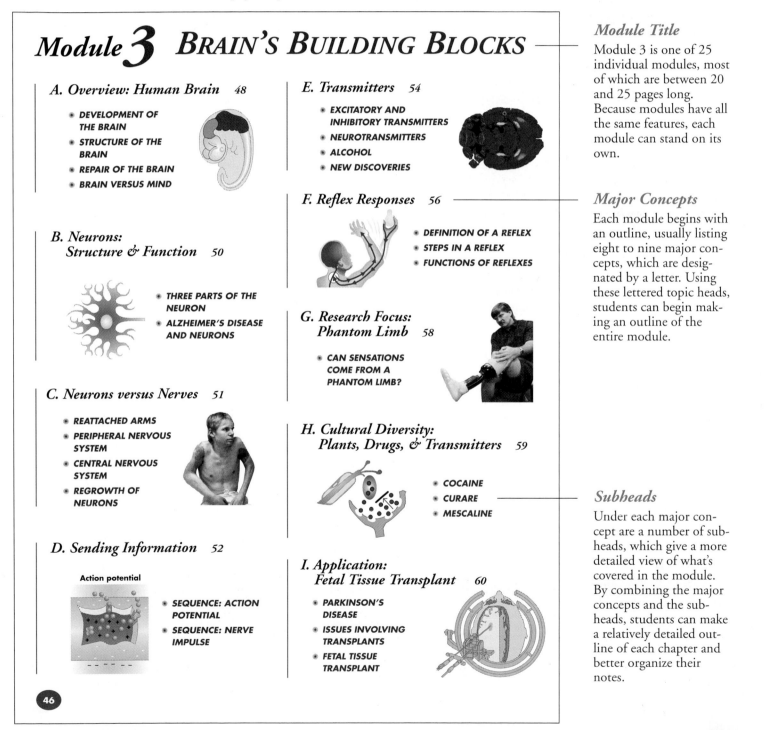

Module 3 BRAIN'S BUILDING BLOCKS

A. Overview: Human Brain 48
* DEVELOPMENT OF THE BRAIN
* STRUCTURE OF THE BRAIN
* REPAIR OF THE BRAIN
* BRAIN VERSUS MIND

B. Neurons: Structure & Function 50
* THREE PARTS OF THE NEURON
* ALZHEIMER'S DISEASE AND NEURONS

C. Neurons versus Nerves 51
* REATTACHED ARMS
* PERIPHERAL NERVOUS SYSTEM
* CENTRAL NERVOUS SYSTEM
* REGROWTH OF NEURONS

D. Sending Information 52

Action potential
* SEQUENCE: ACTION POTENTIAL
* SEQUENCE: NERVE IMPULSE

E. Transmitters 54
* EXCITATORY AND INHIBITORY TRANSMITTERS
* NEUROTRANSMITTERS
* ALCOHOL
* NEW DISCOVERIES

F. Reflex Responses 56
* DEFINITION OF A REFLEX
* STEPS IN A REFLEX
* FUNCTIONS OF REFLEXES

G. Research Focus: Phantom Limb 58
* CAN SENSATIONS COME FROM A PHANTOM LIMB?

H. Cultural Diversity: Plants, Drugs, & Transmitters 59
* COCAINE
* CURARE
* MESCALINE

I. Application: Fetal Tissue Transplant 60
* PARKINSON'S DISEASE
* ISSUES INVOLVING TRANSPLANTS
* FETAL TISSUE TRANSPLANT

46

Module Title

Module 3 is one of 25 individual modules, most of which are between 20 and 25 pages long. Because modules have all the same features, each module can stand on its own.

Major Concepts

Each module begins with an outline, usually listing eight to nine major concepts, which are designated by a letter. Using these lettered topic heads, students can begin making an outline of the entire module.

Subheads

Under each major concept are a number of subheads, which give a more detailed view of what's covered in the module. By combining the major concepts and the subheads, students can make a relatively detailed outline of each chapter and better organize their notes.

To the Instructor

Each module begins with an interesting story or case study about a person (and one bear) who has achieved something remarkable or has had an interesting problem or experience. Openers set the stage for the main module subject and show how the material is relevant to real-life experiences. Each opener ends with a paragraph titled, "What's Coming," which alerts students to the concepts that will be covered in the module.

What's the purpose of the module's opening stories?

In teaching Introductory Psychology, it soon becomes clear that students are most interested in real-life examples. The real-life examples used in the module's opening stories, which range from surviving a shark attack to being treated for a manic attack, catch students' attention, raise questions, and stimulate discussions. It's no surprise that students especially remember those concepts associated with the modules' opening stories.

Openers—Real Lives and Real Cases

Module 20 has two openers. One discusses Nelson Mandela's lifelong struggle for equal rights in South Africa and the other asks why an African American woman was not appointed head of a major police force until 1994. Here's a sample of some of the other openers and the questions they raise:

Module 1: A young boy is diagnosed as autistic. How do psychologists study this problem?

Module 10: A bear is trained to act in a movie. What psychological principles were involved in the bear's training?

Module 14: A man who never graduated from high school directs motion pictures. What is creativity?

Module 17: Three-year-old Jessica is taken from her foster home and returned to her biological parents. What effect will this enormous change have on her development?

Introduction

Power of Beliefs

> **What kept him going for 27 years in prison?**

Nelson Mandela had been born into a royal tribal African family, but he lost his father at an early age and was raised by a guardian in the tribe. According to tradition, Mandela became a man at 16, when he went through an elaborate public circumcision ceremony. When he was 21, he ran away to the big city. In Johannesburg, he entered college, received his law degree, and began his lifetime struggle to free the black people of South Africa (Ransdell & Eddings, 1994).

In 1964, Nelson Mandela (left photo) was found guilty of plotting against the all-white South African government and sentenced to prison for life. In his defense he said: "During my lifetime I have dedicated myself to this struggle of the African people. I have fought against white domination, and I have fought about black domination. I have cherished the ideal of a democratic and free society in which all persons live together in harmony and with equal opportunities. It is an ideal which I hope to live for and to achieve. But, if need be, it is an ideal for which I am prepared to die" (Bernstein, 1994, p. 11).

While in prison, he slept on a narrow bed in a barren cubicle, seven feet wide and nine feet long. He ate corn porridge, with a piece of meat every other day. He was allowed to write one letter and have one visitor every six months. Mandela endured these long, terrible years because he believed that one day he would be free to continue his fight against oppression. Many times he was offered his release from prison provided that he make no public speeches and cease his freedom-fighting activities. Mandela refused these conditional releases and remained in prison.

Finally, in 1990, at the age of 71, he was released from prison. His time had indeed come, and he repeated the moving speech that he had spoken 27 years earlier (quoted above). Mandela lost no time in resuming his fight against white domination and for equal opportunities for blacks. For these efforts, Mandela was awarded the Nobel Peace Prize in 1993.

The fulfillment of his life's dream finally came in 1994. At the age of 76, Mandela was elected the first black president of South Africa. His election marked the end to the horrible and discriminatory practice of apartheid, which had been in effect for almost 300 years and had permitted the white minority to dominate and suppress the black majority.

What were the forces that shaped Mandela's personality and gave him the strength and motivation to persist in the face of overwhelming adversity? In this module, we'll discuss three forces that shape and mold our personalities.

In a different nation, an ocean away, Beverly Harvard was waging her own personal struggle against forces that said no African American woman should be doing what she wanted to do.

Determination

> **What's unusual about this woman?**

In the 1970s, Beverly Harvard, an African American woman in a southern city (Atlanta, Georgia), was trying to become a police officer. In those days, female police recruits, black or white, faced rejection, discrimination, and harassment by their male peers, who believed strongly that women had neither the physical strength nor mental toughness to be police officers (Fletcher, 1995). From the 1970s through the 1980s, there were intense legal and political battles in the United States, in which women had to prove that they have what it takes to be good cops. Their struggle is slowly paying off: by the early 1990s, about 10% of this country's police officers were women.

With incredible determination, Beverly Harvard (photo below) worked her way up through the Atlanta police ranks. She put up with the male officers' sarcastic, hurtful, and discriminatory comments and concentrated on doing the best possible job. Finally, after struggling for almost 20 years, she was appointed head of the Atlanta police department. Her appointment in 1994 marks the first time an African American woman has headed a police department in a major city. She has 1,700 police officers under her command, and her motto is "You can talk about what's wrong with the world or help fix it" (Eddings, 1994, p. 87).

Beverly Harvard, like thousands of female police officers around the country, has shown that women make good cops, partly because of their particular personality traits: women are less authoritarian, more open, better listeners, and less likely to trigger showdowns than are their male counterparts (Fletcher, 1995; Nazario, 1993). Apparently, what women may lack in sheer muscle power, they make up for in a winning combination of personality traits.

In this module, we'll discuss personality traits, which are powerful motivating forces that we all have, cannot live without, like to talk about, may be critical of, and are often asked to change but find it difficult to do so.

What's Coming

We'll discuss two theories of personality, each with a different emphasis. The first is social cognitive theory (previously called social learning theory), which stresses the influences of cognitive, learning, and social processes on personality development. The second is trait theory, which focuses on measuring traits and describing how traits make up our different personalities and influence our behaviors.

We'll begin with three social cognitive forces that helped shape Nelson Mandela's personality.

457

Step-by-step Approach

When we teach complex subjects, such as classical conditioning, we usually divide the material into smaller units or steps, which makes it easier for students to understand. This idea of breaking down complex material into smaller steps cannot be done in most traditional texts because the text is literally in one big chunk. However, unlike traditional textbooks, the 5th edition was created entirely on the computer and that allowed me to break down complex material, such as the procedure for classical conditioning, into smaller steps.

What is the procedure for classical conditioning?
The procedure for classical conditioning is difficult for many students to grasp until they see it broken down into smaller steps. As shown in the page below, the 5th edition uses this step-by-step approach to explain difficult or complex concepts. Notice also how this step-by-step approach integrates text and graphics and helps make difficult concepts come alive.

B. Procedure: Classical Conditioning

Pavlov's Experiment

What's the procedure? Imagine that you are an assistant in Pavlov's laboratory and your subject is a dog named Sam. You are using a procedure that will result in Sam's salivating when he hears a bell, a response that Pavlov called a *conditioned reflex*. Today, we call Pavlov's procedure *classical conditioning*, which involves the following three steps.

Step 1. Selecting Stimulus and Response

Terms. Before you begin the procedure to establish classical conditioning in Sam, you need to identify three critical terms: *neutral stimulus, unconditioned stimulus,* and *unconditioned response.*

Neutral stimulus. You need to choose a neutral stimulus. A *neutral stimulus* is some stimulus that causes a sensory response, such as being seen, heard, or smelled, but does not produce the reflex being tested. Your neutral stimulus will be a tone (bell), which Sam the dog hears but which does not normally produce the reflex of salivation.

Unconditioned stimulus. You need to choose an unconditioned stimulus, or UCS. An *unconditioned stimulus,* or *UCS,* is some stimulus that triggers or elicits a physiological reflex, such as salivation or eye blink. Your unconditioned stimulus will be food, which when presented to Sam will elicit the salivation reflex; that is, will make Sam salivate.

Unconditioned response. Finally, you need to select and measure an unconditioned response, or UCR. The *unconditioned response,* or *UCR,* is an unlearned, innate, involuntary physiological reflex that is elicited by the unconditioned stimulus. For instance, salivation is an unconditioned response that is elicited by food. In this case, the sight of food, which is the unconditioned stimulus, will elicit salivation in Sam, which is the unconditioned response.

Step 2. Establishing Classical Conditioning

Trial. A common procedure to establish classical conditioning is for you first to present the neutral stimulus and then, a short time later, to present the unconditioned stimulus. The presentation of both stimuli is called a *trial.*

Neutral stimulus. In a typical trial, you will pair the neutral stimulus, the tone, with the unconditioned stimulus, the food. Generally, you will first present the neutral stimulus (tone) and then a short time later, present the unconditioned stimulus (food).

+

Unconditioned stimulus (UCS). Some seconds (but less than a minute) after the tone begins, you present the unconditioned stimulus, a piece of food, which elicits salivation. This trial procedure is the one most frequently used in classical conditioning.

→

Unconditioned response (UCR). The unconditioned stimulus, food, elicits the unconditioned response, salivation, in Sam. Food and salivation are said to be unconditioned because the effect on Sam is inborn and not dependent on some prior training or learning.

Step 3. Testing for Conditioning

Only CS. After you have given Sam 10 to 100 trials, you will test for the occurrence of classical conditioning. You test by presenting the tone (conditioned stimulus) without showing Sam the food (unconditioned stimulus).

Conditioned stimulus. If Sam salivates when you present the tone alone, it means that the tone has become a conditioned stimulus. A *conditioned stimulus,* or *CS,* is a formerly neutral stimulus that has acquired the ability to elicit a response that was previously elicited by the unconditioned stimulus. In this example, the tone, an originally neutral stimulus, became the CS.

→

Conditioned response. When Sam salivates to the tone alone, this response is called the conditioned response. The *conditioned response,* or *CR,* which is elicited by the conditioned stimulus, is similar to, but not identical in size or amount to, the unconditioned response. One thing to remember is that the conditioned response is usually similar in appearance but smaller in amount or magnitude than the unconditioned response. This means that Sam's conditioned response will involve less salivation to the tone (conditioned stimulus) than to the food (unconditioned stimulus).

Predict. One question you may ask about classical conditioning is What exactly did Sam learn during this procedure? One thing Sam learned was that the sound of a bell predicted the very likely occurrence of food (Rescorla, 1988). Classical conditioning helps animals and humans predict what's going to happen and thus provides information that may be useful for their survival (Hollis, 1997). Next we'll use the concepts of classical conditioning to explain how Carla was conditioned to her dentist's aftershave.

B. *PROCEDURE: CLASSICAL CONDITIONING* **197**

Definitions

Students need never search for definitions because they are always **bold-faced and printed in blue**. Because definitions are so clearly identified in the text, students can easily find them and use them to review important terms in a module.

Integrating Text and Graphics

This page shows how text and graphics are integrated into the step-by-step approach that is used here to explain the difficult and complex procedure for classical conditioning. By integrating text and graphics, students are better able to understand complex and difficult information.

To the Instructor

In a traditional textbook, the text often refers you to a distant figure that you must hunt for and examine before returning to your place in the text. This process usually disrupts your train of thought and makes you less likely to consult a graphic in the future. This text neither needs nor uses explanatory figure captions.

Why no figure captions?

Because of the way the 5th edition was composed, I could integrate text and graphics on each page and thus eliminate the need to send the reader off to locate distant figures. On the page below, you'll see how Schachter and Singer's classic experiment is explained by combining text and illustrations so that the information is presented naturally, step by step.

Definition

Notice how the bold-face term, *cognitive appraisal theory,* along with its definition, clearly stands out on this page. These bold-faced-printed-in-blue definitions take the place of a running glossary.

No Figure Captions

When I was a student, one of the things that I disliked about my textbooks was how I was always told to refer to a figure that was placed somewhere else on the page. In this text, the reader never has to hunt for figures referred to in the text or read figure captions because figures and text are totally integrated. For example, many students have difficulty understanding the classic Schachter-Singer experiment because of its different treatments and conditions. On this page, their experiment is clearly explained in a series of four steps that completely integrate text and figures.

B. Cognitive Appraisal Theory

Can thoughts cause emotions?

You have arranged to meet your girlfriend at 7 P.M. at the movie theater. You arrive a few minutes early and are shocked to see her in the arms of a stranger. Feeling very angry and jealous, you rush over to confront them. Just as you arrive, she turns and says, "I want you to meet my brother, whom I haven't seen in years." Her explanation immediately changes your anger and jealousy into relief and happiness. Your girlfriend's explanation flip-flopped your emotional state and illustrates the cognitive appraisal theory of emotions.

The *cognitive appraisal theory* says that your interpretation or appraisal of a situation, object, or event can contribute to, or result in, your experiencing different emotional states.

For example, believing that your girlfriend is being hugged by an attractive stranger, triggers jealousy, but hearing that the stranger is her brother changes your jealousy to relief and happiness.

Current cognitive appraisal theories can be traced back to the original work of Stanley Schachter and Jerome Singer (1962). We'll focus on one part of their famous experiment that shows the importance of cognitive interpretation, or appraisal, in emotions.

Schachter-Singer Experiment

Throughout this text, we have pointed out classic experiments, so called because these studies challenged and dramatically changed how we think about something. The Schachter-Singer study was the first to show that thoughts are important in generating and identifying emotional feelings. Here's what they did in their ground-breaking experiment.

1 PHYSIOLOGICAL AROUSAL
First, Schachter and Singer injected some of their subjects with a hormone, epinephrine (adrenaline), that caused physiological arousal, such as increased heart rate and blood pressure.

Injections with hormone . . .

. . . cause physiological arousal.

However, subjects were told that the injections were vitamins and were not told that they would experience physiological arousal.

2 INTERPRETATION OF CUES
Second, after the injections, subjects were placed in different situations—a happy one or an angry one.

In the **happy situation,** a confederate of the researchers created a happy atmosphere by laughing and throwing paper airplanes around.

In the **angry situation,** another confederate created an angry atmosphere by complaining about filling out a long questionnaire.

3 EMOTIONAL FEELING

Those subjects in the happy situation often reported feeling happy, and their observable behaviors were smiles. However, those in the angry situation often reported feeling angry, and their observable behaviors were angry facial expressions. Schachter and Singer explained that subjects did not know that their physiological arousal was caused by hormone injections and looked for other causes in their environment. Subjects interpreted environmental cues, such as being in a happy or angry situation, as the cause of their arousal and thus reported feeling happy or angry.

4 SEQUENCE FOR EMOTIONS
The Schachter-Singer explanation assumes that our interpretation or appraisal of a situation is the primary cause of emotions. This sequence is shown below:

Schachter-Singer sequence of emotional components

A. Physiological arousal → B. Cognitive interpretation of cues → C. Emotional feeling → D. Show observable behavior

5 CRITICISMS
The Schachter-Singer cognitive theory led to a classic study that was the first to show that cognitive factors, such as one's interpretation of events, could trigger and give rise to emotional feelings. However, their explanation has undergone two general revisions.

First, researchers recognize that emotions may occur without first experiencing physiological arousal (Cacioppo et al., 1993). For example, suppose a friend walked up to you and said, "I just saw somebody back into your car and drive away." Your appraisal of that situation would trigger feelings of anger before your physiological arousal kicked in.

Second, researchers argue that emotions may result not only from situational or environmental cues but also from your own cognitive processes, such as thoughts, interpretations, and appraisals (Ellsworth, 1994; Sinclair et al., 1994). For example, your friend's explanation of who the stranger was changed your jealous anger into feelings of happy relief.

Schachter and Singer's cognitive theory triggered a number of other cognitive appraisal theories that were developed independently in the 1980s (Frijda, 1986; Ortony et al., 1988; Smith & Ellsworth, 1985; Weiner, 1986). The cognitive appraisal theory of emotions points to thoughts, interpretations, and appraisals as being some of the primary ways that emotions are triggered and develop (Ellsworth, 1994; Kitayama & Markus, 1994).

Next, we'll explain the current cognitive appraisal theory.

362 **Module 16** *EMOTION*

To the Instructor

New Material

Each module in the 5th edition contains new and exciting material. For example, one of the newer theories discussed is evolutionary psychology. So that students can understand this theory, I have updated and revised the section on the evolution of the brain.

What's new in psychology?

In every module you'll find current research, discussion of new ideas, and more than 700 new references, of which 400 were published in 1997 or 1998. I have also added new material on Attention-Deficit/Hyperactivity Disorder (Module 2), phantom limb (Module 3), new neurotransmitters (Module 3), anencephaly (Module 4), using virtual reality (Module 6), master sleep switch (Module 7), and nonintellectual factors in IQ tests (Module 13). These are only samples of the new and revised materials in the 5th edition.

Evolution of the Human Brain

What is evolution?

In 1859, Charles Darwin stunned much of the Western world by publishing *The Origin of Species*, a revolutionary theory of how species originate—his theory of evolution (Darwin, 1859).

The *theory of evolution* says that different species arose from a common ancestor and that those species that survived were best adapted to meet the demands of their environments.

Although Darwin's theory of evolution is just that—a theory—it has received broad scientific support from both fossil records and more recent examination of genetic similarities and differences among species (Gore, 1997). The fact that many scientists hold to the theory of evolution clashes with deeply held religious beliefs that place humans on a family tree of their own. We don't have the space to discuss the pros and cons of evolution here but rather will look at three supposed human ancestors and see how their brains are thought to have evolved.

Australopithecus afarensis   *Homo erectus*   *Homo sapiens*

Definitions

Notice how the boldface term, *theory of evolution,* along with its definition, stands out on the page for easy recognition.

Perhaps the First Human Brain

Of the three skulls shown above, the smallest one (far left) is thought to have belonged to one of our earliest ancestors, who lived about three million years ago. This proposed ancestor has been given a common name, Lucy, and a scientific name, *Australopithecus afarensis.* Lucy's brain weighed about 500 grams, which is about the size of a chimpanzee's brain and about one-third the size of our brains. Lucy's brain size and skeleton suggest a closer resemblance to apes than to humans. She had long powerful arms and short legs and is thought to have lived mainly on leaves and fruit.

Anthropologists conclude, on the basis of Lucy's rather limited brain size, that her species did not make tools, did not have language, knew nothing of fire, and thus represents the most primitive kind of human (Kurten, 1993; Gore, 1997). Lucy's line died out about a million years ago. Anthropologists believe that another line branched out from Lucy's and gave rise to our genus, which is called *Homo;* this process was accompanied eventually by a threefold increase in brain size.

Brain Doubles in Size

The skull in the middle, which is almost twice as large as Lucy's, belongs to a species named *Homo erectus.* (*Homo* means "man" and *erectus* means "upright.") *Homo erectus,* who lived about one and a half million years ago, is thought to be part of the genus from which modern humans eventually evolved. *Homo erectus* developed a thick-boned skeleton designed for walking upright and was about as tall as modern humans. They are thought to have added meat to their diets.

With a brain size of about 1,000 grams, which was twice as large as Lucy's, *Homo erectus* had increased abilities, and made a wide variety of stone tools. The finest was a tear-shaped hand ax, whose production required much more extensive work than any previous tools. There is considerable debate about whether tool-making or the development of language was the main pressure for the doubling in brain size in *Homo erectus* (Lewin, 1993; Gore, 1997). Descendants of *Homo erectus* evolved a still larger brain; these individuals were called *Homo sapiens.*

Brain Triples in Size

The largest skull, on the far right, comes from a modern human, who is called *Homo sapiens* (*sapiens* means "wise"). Our species began about 400,000 years ago and continues to the present day. *Homo sapiens* evolved a brain that weighs about 1,350 grams, or about 3 pounds, which is the average size of our brains today and almost three times the size of Lucy's. With such a significant increase in brain size came four dramatic changes: *Homo sapiens* began growing crops instead of relying on hunting; started to live in social communities instead of roaming the country; developed language, which was a far better way to communicate compared to grunts and gestures; and painted beautiful and colorful representations of animals and humans.

Two forces are thought to be responsible for the evolution of the human brain and its tripling in size: genetic changes or mutations, which are accidental changes in genetic instructions; and natural selection, which means that only those best fitted to their environments will survive (Kurten, 1993).

Anthropologists believe that it took millions of years for our brains to evolve to their current size. Next, we'll describe how researchers study our modern brains.

Comparison of Ideas

Often in our lectures, we compare ideas or theories, such as the difference between classical and operant conditioning, the nature nurture question, or evolution of the brain. One way this is done in the 5th edition is to present such information in side-by-side comparisons. This format provides visual cues that allow students to easily spot similarities or differences among ideas or theories. For example, in the page on the left, three giant steps in evolution are discussed by presenting them in a side-by-side format.

A. *GENES & EVOLUTION* **69**

To the Instructor

One controversial issue in psychology has been the accuracy of repressed memories, especially those involving sexual abuse. In some cases additional evidence of childhood sexual abuse showed repressed memories to be true while in other cases, 300 individuals have retracted their charges of childhood sexual abuse and indicated their repressed memories to be false.

What are the controversial issues?

In addition to repressed memories, the 5th edition discusses a number of controversial topics in psychology: fetal tissue transplants (Module 3), extrasensory perception (Module 6), implanting false memories (Module 12), IQ and racial issues (Module 13), IQ and genetic factors (Module 13), language in animals (Module 14), accuracy of lie detection (Module 16), genetic influences on personality and behavior (Modules 17 and 20), and biological factors in aggression (Module 25). Below is one of two pages that discusses repressed memories.

Case Study

Throughout the 5th edition, I have increased the use of case studies, which spark student interest and show how concepts apply to real-life situations. For example, on this page, the concept of repressed memories is introduced with a lawsuit brought by a father who was accused of earlier sexual abuse by his daughter.

Definition

The term, *repression,* along with its definition, is bold-faced and printed in blue for easy recognition.

Step-by-Step Approach

The complex and controversial topic of repressed memories is broken down into four issues: definition, therapist's role (shown on this page), implanting false memories, and accuracy. As each issue is discussed, students understand that there are no easy answers and why the topic of repressed memories will remain a controversial issue.

G: Repressed Memories

Sexual Abuse

Did he do it?

At the beginning of this module, we discussed the case of Holly (left photo), who had accused her father (right photo) of sexual molestation beginning when she was 6 years old. Holly's memories of sexual abuse first surfaced during therapy sessions 13 years later, when she was 19. The father sued Holly's therapists for implanting false memories. The jury partly agreed with the father in deciding that Holly's memories were probably false and that the therapists had not implanted the memories but had negligently reinforced them (Butler, 1994). More recently, a state appeals court dismissed Holly's case against her father because some of her testimony about sexual abuse was obtained under sodium amytal, the so-called truth serum, which was administered by her therapist. Because testimony

taken under sodium amytal is often unreliable, it has been barred in California's courts since 1959 (*Los Angeles Times,* August 21, 1997).

Holly's case illustrates perhaps the most explosive psychological issue of the early 1990s, the problem of repressed memories. Almost every major newspaper and national magazine carried stories with headlines such as "When can memories be trusted?" (*Time,* October 28, 1991); "How the brain forms false memories" (*Newsweek,* March 14, 1994); or "Repressed memory of abuse questioned" (*San Diego Union-Tribune,* December 20, 1993). We'll divide this broad problem into four separate but related issues: definition, therapist's role, implantation of false memories, and accuracy.

1 Definition

What is a repressed memory?

The idea of repressed memories is based on Sigmund Freud's theory of repression, which underlies much of his psychoanalytic theory of personality (discussed in Module 21).

Repression is the process by which the mind pushes a memory of some threatening or traumatic event deep into the unconscious. Once in the unconscious, the repressed memory cannot be retrieved at will and may remain there until something releases it and the person becomes aware of it.

The phenomenon of repression and repressed memories is supported by numerous clinical reports. For example, therapists describe a woman who entered therapy with sexual problems and uncovered memories of incest committed by her father; another woman entered therapy with problems of insomnia, low self-esteem, and other difficulties and recovered memories of her father sexually assaulting her (Rieker & Carmen, 1986; Schuker, 1979).

If people have repressed memories, how often do they report them? Researchers found that 18–59% of adult clients with a history of sexual abuse said that they had either forgotten or recently uncovered repressed memories of sexual abuse (Briere & Conte, 1993; Loftus et al., 1994). In her reviews of repressed memories, Elizabeth Loftus (1994; 1997b) cautions that, although these percentages are disturbingly high, it is difficult to interpret their accuracy because the formulation of questions about repressed memories can lead to misleading or biased results.

While clinical cases support the idea of repressed memories, their increased occurrence in the early 1990s has partly been blamed on the practices of some therapists (Loftus, 1993b; 1997b).

2 Therapist's Role

What is the danger?

Therapists who treat survivors of incest and other traumatic situations maintain that repressed memories are so completely blocked that it may take deliberate suggestion and effort to release them, sometimes using hypnosis or so-called "truth serum," sodium amytal. Whatever the therapists' good intentions, Loftus (1993b; 1997b) wonders if some therapists are suggesting or implanting traumatic memories in their clients rather than releasing repressed ones. Most often, repressed memories and resulting accusations of sexual abuse were reported by women (87%) who were in therapy for depression or eating disorders (Gudjonsson, 1997).

For example, in one case a client recalls that her therapist insisted that she showed signs of having been sexually abused during childhood and probably had terrible memories buried in her unconscious. The client was dubious at first but, wanting to please her therapist, finally admitted to being raped at the age of 4. However, after leaving the hospital and enlisting help from new therapists, she concluded that the sexual assaults had never happened (Bower, 1993a).

There are also many examples of therapists who have helped clients recover and deal with terrible repressed memories (Gold et al., 1994). Thus, therapists are in the difficult position of trying to distinguish accurate accounts of repressed memories from those that may have been shaped or reinforced by the suggestions or expectations of the therapist (Byrd, 1994).

Questions about whether repressed memories can be influenced by a therapist's suggestions bring up the related and important question of whether false memories can be implanted.

Concept Review

How many times have students asked, "What should I study for the test?" You can answer this question by telling students to complete the two built-in study aids that appear in each module. One study aid is the Concept Review (shown here) and the second is the Summary Test (shown on page xxxi).

What's unique about the Concept Review?

The Concept Review appears about two-thirds of the way through each module and tests students on their knowledge of the major concepts covered up to that point. What's unique about the Concept Review is that each concept has previously been associated with an appropriate graphic that provides a visual cue for the concept. These graphics reappear next to their appropriate questions in the Concept Review. Thus, the Concept Review is unique in that it facilitates encoding and remembering by repeating visual cues for major concepts. Students report really liking this feature.

CONCEPT REVIEW

1. An emotion is defined in terms of four components: you interpret or (a)_____ some stimulus, thought, or event in terms of your well-being; you have a subjective (b)_____, such as being happy or fearful; you experience bodily responses, such as increased heart rate and breathing, which are called (c)_____ responses; and you often show (d)_____ behaviors, such as crying or smiling.

2. One theory says that emotions result from specific physiological changes in our bodies and that each emotion has a different physiological pattern. This theory, which says that we feel fear because we run, is called the (a)_____ theory. Two major criticisms of this theory are that researchers have not identified a different (b)_____ response pattern to match each emotion and that individuals with severed spinal cords, which prevents feedback from the body's physiological responses, still experience (c)_____.

3. A second theory says that feedback from the movement of facial muscles and skin is interpreted by your brain as an emotion; this theory is called the (a)_____ theory. Researchers found that emotions do occur without feedback from facial muscles and skin. However, facial feedback may initiate the occurrence of emotions and contribute to the (b)_____ of an emotion, as well as to our mood.

4. A third theory of emotions, which grew out of the work of Schachter and Singer, says that you interpret or appraise a situation as having a positive or negative impact on your life and this results in a subjective feeling that you call an emotion; this is called the _____ theory.

5. The fourth theory of emotions, which says that in some situations you feel an emotion before you have time to interpret or appraise the situation, is called the (a)_____. This theory says that, for some emotions, you (b)_____ before you think. In comparison, the cognitive appraisal theory says that you (c)_____ before you feel. This question about which comes first, feeling or thinking, is called the (d)_____.

6. Specific inherited facial patterns or expressions that signal specific feelings or emotional states across cultures, such as a smile signaling a happy state, are called _____. These emotions are thought to have evolved because they had important adaptive and survival functions for our ancestors.

7. According to one theory, we inherit the neural structure and physiology to express and experience emotions and we evolved basic emotional patterns to adapt to and solve problems important for our survival; this is called the (a)_____ theory. Facial expressions that accompany emotions communicate the state of our personal or subjective (b)_____ and provide (c)_____ signals that communicate with, and elicit responses from, those around us.

8. Your performance on a task depends on the amount of physiological arousal and the difficulty of the task. For many tasks, moderate arousal helps performance; for new or difficult tasks, low arousal is better; and for easy or well-learned tasks, high arousal may facilitate performance. This relationship between arousal and performance is known as the _____.

9. According to one theory, big events in your life, such as doing well on final exams, getting a car, obtaining a degree, or winning the lottery, do not produce long-lasting increases in happiness, because in a relatively short period of time you become accustomed to your good fortune and it contributes less to your level of happiness; this theory is called the (a)_____. The kinds of events that contribute most to your overall level of happiness are regularly occurring, simple (b)_____.

10. Specific cultural norms that regulate when, where, and how much emotion we should or should not express in different situations are called _____. These rules explain why the expression and intensity of emotions differ across cultures.

Answers: *1. (a) appraise, (b) feeling, (c) physiological, (d) observable; 2. (a) James-Lange, (b) physiological, (c) emotions; 3. (a) facial feedback, (b) intensity; 4. cognitive appraisal; 5. (a) affective-primacy theory, (b) feel, (c) think, (d) primacy question; 6. universal emotions; 7. (a) psychoevolutionary, (b) feelings, (c) social; 8. Yerkes-Dodson law; 9. (a) adaptation level theory, (b) pleasures; 10. display rules.*

368

Major Concepts

Each module contains a Concept Review that allows students to test their knowledge of ten to fifteen major terms. Notice that each concept is also linked to its appropriate graphic, which first appeared earlier in the text and now provides a visual cue for remembering the concept.

Reading versus Knowing the Material

One reason for the Concept Review is that students often think they know material because they have a general idea of what they have read. However, studies show that students can't accurately judge how well they know the material unless they have a chance to test themselves on specifics. The Concept Review lets students accurately check their knowledge by having them fill in terms that correctly match their definitions.

To the Instructor: Cultural Diversity

Cultural Diversity

Students are often tempted to think that their cultural values are the norm and that other cultures are strange, or that their culture is advanced and that other cultures need to catch up. One goal of Introductory Psychology is to broaden students' viewpoints with material from other cultures. To meet this goal, each module has a feature called Cultural Diversity.

Do cultural values affect our view of the mind-body interaction?
Although the mind-body interaction has a long history in psychology, it has gradually achieved new importance from recent findings. New findings indicate that thoughts influence physiological and immune functions (Module 21) and play a major role in the placebo response (Module 5). Although Westerners have been reluctant to accept the mind-body connection, Easterners have a long tradition of practicing mind control, which is discussed in the Cultural Diversity page shown below.

Cultural Diversity

Each of the 25 modules includes a Cultural Diversity feature, which presents worldwide viewpoints on issues that will broaden and challenge the cultural views and values of your students.

Cultural Diversity Topics Such As:

Module 1: Early Discrimination
Module 2: Use of Placebos
Module 4: Brain Size and Racial Myths
Module 6: Different Perceptions
Module 7: Incidence of SAD
Module 8: Rates of Alcoholism
Module 9: Dental Fears
Module 11: Oral versus Written
Module 15: Female Circumcision
Module 17: Gender Roles
Module 19: Unexpected High Achievement
Module 20: Resolving Conflicts
Module 22: An Asian Disorder
Module 23: Interpreting Symptoms
Module 24: Different Healer

G. Cultural Diversity: Tibetan Monks

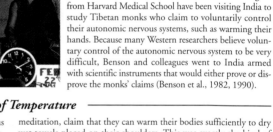

Mind-Body Interaction

Can you control your breathing?

There are only two responses of the autonomic nervous system—breathing and eye blinking—that you can voluntarily control. All other responses of the autonomic nervous system, such as increasing or decreasing blood pressure, heart rate, secreting hormones, dilating or constricting blood vessels, and increasing or decreasing oxygen consumption, are not usually under voluntary control. Normally, the responses of the autonomic nervous system are involuntary and occur automatically.

The *autonomic nervous system* has two divisions that are not normally under voluntary control: the sympathetic division causes physiological arousal by increasing heart rate, breathing, blood pressure, and secretion of stimulating hormones; the parasympathetic division calms and relaxes the body by decreasing physiological responses and stimulating digestion.

For example, try warming your hands by voluntarily dilating the blood vessels in your fingers. Try as you might, you cannnot warm your hands because blood vessels are not usually under voluntary control (I bet students that they can't do it, and I've never lost). However, for about a dozen years, Western researcher Herbert Benson and his colleagues from Harvard Medical School have been visiting India to study Tibetan monks who claim to voluntarily control their autonomic nervous systems, such as warming their hands. Because many Western researchers believe voluntary control of the autonomic nervous system to be very difficult, Benson and colleagues went to India armed with scientific instruments that would either prove or disprove the monks' claims (Benson et al., 1982, 1990).

Control of Temperature

If you wish to voluntarily control some of your autonomic nervous system's responses, such as dilating blood vessels to warm your hands, sit quietly in a chair, close your eyes, and think relaxing thoughts. If your thoughts are truly relaxing, they will activate your parasympathetic division, which will dilate blood vessels and result in warm hands. I have only been able to do this a few times (because it's very difficult to think truly relaxing thoughts), but it is a most remarkable experience to feel your hands becoming warmer.

The reason that I and most Westerners find this warming task extremely difficult is that we usually spend little time practicing relaxation exercises and thus are unfamiliar with how to concentrate on thoughts or images that will result in hand warming. Those Western individuals who have used biofeedback training have managed to raise their finger temperatures by only about 0.25–2°F, on average (Freedman, 1991). In comparison, certain Tibetan monks, through various forms of

meditation, claim that they can warm their bodies sufficiently to dry wet towels placed on their shoulders. This was exactly the kind of claim that excited and puzzled Benson's group of researchers.

Benson's group obtained permission from three monks at a monastery in Upper Dharamsala, India, to measure skin temperature during heat meditation, or g Tum-mo yoga. The monks sat in the lotus position, closed their eyes, and began meditating. As shown in the left graph, within a short period of time, one monk had raised his finger temperature as much as 7–9°C with no change in heart rate (Benson et al., 1982). The monks' success at warming their hands (9–12°F) was about five times as great as Westerners had managed (0.25–2°F). One reason monks can learn to voluntarily control their autonomic nervous systems (dilating blood vessels to warm their hands) is that they practice this task daily for many years.

Explanation and Application

Westerner Benson explains that monks are able to raise hand temperature by activating the parasympathetic division, which dilates tiny blood vessels that lie near the surface of the skin. The monks' explanation is much more interesting: during meditation, they gather winds scattered in consciousness and focus the winds into a "central channel" that generates internal heat (Benson et al., 1982).

The reason researchers studied these monks was because the ability to voluntarily control physiological responses has great application in preventing or decreasing a number of psychosomatic symptoms, including headaches, teeth-grinding (bruxism), intestinal and stomach problems, and cardiovascular symptoms (high blood pressure).

One of the major themes of health psychology is how your thoughts, beliefs, and emotional feelings influence and interact with your body's physiological and immune responses. For example, your mind's fearful or stressful thoughts can trigger the body's fight-flight response; your mind's fearful or stressful thoughts can weaken the body's immune system and increase the risks of getting infections or viruses; your mind can influence the body's immune responses (allergic reactions) through classical conditioning; and monks' minds can voluntarily control their autonomic nervous systems. All these examples illustrate how the mind and body interact, which must be considered in developing a stress management program.

G. *CULTURAL DIVERSITY: TIBETAN MONKS* **501**

To the Instructor: Research Focus

 Research Focus

One important but difficult goal in teaching Introductory Psychology is to explain how psychologists use a variety of research methods and techniques to answer questions about human and animal behaviors. To help instructors reach this goal there is a Research Focus in each module that explains how psychologists answer questions through experiments, case studies, self-reports, and surveys.

Do male and female brains process information differently?
The Research Focus shown below is from Module 4 and explains how psychologists answered this question by using and combining two research techniques: behavioral measures from paper and pencil tests and more recent neurological findings from PET scans on the living brain. Each Research Focus integrates text and graphics to help students understand exactly what researchers did, what they found, and what the findings mean.

G. Research Focus: Sexual Differences
Are There Sex Differences in the Brain?

Science and Politics

 Is this kind of research sexist?

Throughout history, politicians have either criticized or misused research depending on what was "politically correct" (Azar, 1997). For example, in the 1920s, United States politicians misused research on IQ scores to justify passing discriminatory immigration quotas (Gould, 1981) (see page 296). In the 1980s, many politicians were critical of homosexuality and denied federal money for AIDS research until the virus became a threat to the heterosexual population (Shilts, 1988). In the 1980s and 1990s, research on sex differences was criticized as "sexist" because it went against the "politically correct" belief that male and female brains are essentially equal (Azar, 1997).

Sex, or gender, differences refer to structural or functional differences in cognitive, behavioral, or brain processes that arise from being a male or a female.

Using PET scans, researchers have reported a number of interesting sex differences in the structure and function of the human brain. It is important to remember that such differences are neither good nor bad nor sexist but simply ways in which males and females differ. We'll begin with how performance on certain tasks differs according to sex.

Differences in Solving Problems

The rotating figure problem is a rather difficult spatial problem, as follows. First, study the target figure on the left. Then, from the three choices at the right, identify the same figure, even though it has been rotated.

The key to solving this problem is the ability to rotate the target figure in your mind until it matches the rotation of one of the three choices. Researchers consistently report faster or more accurate performance by males than by females in solving rotating figure problems (Kimura, 1992). (Correct answer is 1.)

There are other tasks at which women perform better than men.

For example, look at the house outlined in black (figure above) and find its twin among the three choices. Women are generally faster on these kinds of tests, which measure perceptual speed. In addition, women usually score higher on tests of verbal fluency, in which you must list as many words as you can that begin with the same letter, as in the figure below (Kimura, 1992).

One explanation for these sex differences in skills is that they result from differences in

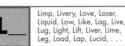
Limp, Livery, Love, Laser, Liquid, Low, Like, Lag, Live, Lug, Light, Lift, Liver, Lime, Leg, Load, Lap, Lucid, . . .

socialization and learning. Another explanation is that these sex differences have evolved from different skills needed by early humans. Males with good spatial skills had an advantage in hunting, and females with good communication skills had an advantage in child-rearing (Springer & Deutsch, 1997).

Researchers have now begun to look for sex differences in how the brain itself functions.

Differences in Brains

Researchers used PET scans, which are a measure of neural activity, to look for sex differences in brain functioning. PET scans of female and male brains were taken while subjects were resting or solving rotating figure problems. When subjects were resting, PET scans indicated that female brains did not differ in their pattern of neural activity from male brains. However, when subjects were solving rotating figure problems, PET scans showed a significant difference between male and female brains.

For male brains, PET scans (upper right figure) taken during problem-solving showed that maximum neural activity occurred in the right frontal area.

In contrast, PET scans of female brains (lower right figure) taken during problem-solving showed that maximum neural activity occurred in the right parietal-temporal area. Researchers concluded that solving rotating figure problems showed a significant sex difference in terms of which brain areas were activated and that these brain differences may underlie the basis for sex differences in performance (Alivisatos & Petrides, 1997; Deutsch & Halsey, 1991). Besides differences in cognitive tasks, researchers are also finding sex differences in emotional tasks.

Because women are consistently reported to be more sensitive, concerned, and nurturing, is it possible that women process emotional information differently than men (Halpern, 1992)? Researchers took PET scans while subjects induced emotional states (happy, sad). PET scans showed that while inducing emotional states, women used more of their limbic structures (involved in emotions) than men. Researchers speculate that these kinds of sex differences in the brain may underlie other male-female emotional behaviors (George et al., 1996).

As researchers continue to find sex differences in the brain, they warn against using such differences as the basis for promoting discriminatory practices or furthering someone's political agenda (Azar, 1997; Nishizawa et al., 1997).

 84 Module 4 *INCREDIBLE NERVOUS SYSTEM*

Research Question
Each module has a Research Focus, which begins with an interesting question. In answering the research question, students are introduced to the research methods and techniques that psychologists use.

Research Focus Topics Such As:

Module 2: ADHD Questions
Module 3: Phantom Limb
Module 5: Pain and Placebos
Module 7: Circadian Preference
Module 8: Drug Prevention
Module 9: Little Albert
Module 10: Noncompliance
Module 12: False Memories
Module 16: Emotions in the Brain
Module 17: Temperament
Module 19: Shyness
Module 20: 180-Degree Change
Module 22: School Shootings
Module 23: Brain Imaging
Module 24: EMDR—New Therapy

To the Instructor: Application

Application

Another feature that was well-liked by students and instructors was the Application, which demonstrates how psychologists use basic principles to answer relevant questions or treat real-life problems. Students like this feature because it shows how many psychological principles are relevant to their lives. Instructors like it because it generates discussion and provides an opportunity to generalize concepts to other settings.

How do learning principles help autistic children?
In the Application from Module 10 shown below, students learn how basic principles of operant conditioning were used to develop a program that helped autistic children overcome many of their problems with language and social interactions. The second page of this Application (not shown here) goes on to discuss how learning principles are also used in biofeedback and disciplining children. Each Module in the 5th edition contains a two-page Application section.

Application

Each of the 25 modules contains an Application that discusses how psychologists use basic psychological principles and methods to solve and treat real-world problems.

Application Topics Such As:

Module 1: Study Skills
Module 3: Fetal Tissue Transplant
Module 5: Artificial Senses
Module 7: Sleep Problems and Treatments
Module 9: Conditioned Fear and Nausea
Module 10: Behavior Modification
Module 11: Unusual Memories
Module 14: Do Animals Have Language?
Module 16: Lie Detection
Module 17: Child Abuse
Module 18: Suicide
Module 20: Assessment— Objective Tests
Module 21: Stress Management Program
Module 22: Treating Phobias
Module 23: Dealing with Mild Depression
Module 25: Controlling Aggression

I. Application: Behavior Modification

Definition

What is behavior modification?

Throughout this module, we have given you many specific examples of behavior modification: toilet training 3-year-old Sheryl and decreasing food refusal in young children (p. 216), stopping Walt from eating paint chips (p. 218), stopping Suzanne from injuring herself (p. 219), and decreasing noncompliance (refusal) in Morgan (p. 230).

Behavior modification is a treatment or therapy that changes or modifies problems or undesirable behaviors by using principles of learning based on operant conditioning, classical conditioning, and social cognitive learning.

For over 35 years, psychologist and researcher Ivar Lovaas of the University of California at Los Angeles has used behavior modification or, more colloquially, behavior mod, to treat autistic children (Lovaas & Buch, 1997). Lovaas's work is especially impressive because he was one of the first to adapt behavior mod procedures to treat serious problems of autistic children. We discussed autism throughout Module 1 and here will only refresh your memory with the kinds of problems that autistics may have.

Autism is marked by especially abnormal or impaired development in social interactions, such as hiding to avoid people, not making eye contact, not wanting to be touched. Autism is marked by difficulties in communicating, such as grave problems in developing spoken language or in initiating conversations. Autistics are characterized by having very few activities

and interests, spending long periods in repeating the same behaviors, such as flipping fingers (this drawing), or following rituals that interfere with more normal functioning. Signs of autism begin in the child's first 3 years (American Psychiatric Association, 1994).

Mental health experts know that, without treatment, many autistic children will remain unresponsive because they lack necessary social skills and remain uncommunicative because they lack language skills. We'll describe Lovaas's behavior modification treatment program, which is based on the principles of operant conditioning and social cognitive learning.

Autistic Children

How much time is needed?

Lovaas's UCLA Young Autism Project treats 2- to 3-year-old autistic children with a 40-hour-per-week program that runs for 2 to 3 years. We'll describe part of the program.

PROGRAM

The training program that Lovaas has developed actually consists of hundreds of separate teaching programs, many of them using principles of operant conditioning: Select a specific target behavior, shape the behavior, and use positive reinforcers of praise and food that are given immediately after the child emits the desired behavior. For example, here's a program for helping autistic children make eye contact.

The **target behavior** is getting the child to make eye contact following the command, "Look at me."

Shaping the behavior involves two steps.

Step 1. Have the child sit in a chair facing you. Give the command "Look at me" every 5–10 seconds. When the child makes a correct response of looking at you, say "Good looking," and simultaneously reward the child with food.

Step 2. Continue until the child repeatedly follows the command "Look at me." Then gradually increase the duration of the child's eye contact from 1 second to periods of 2 to 3 seconds.

Using this kind of behavior modification program, therapists and parents have had success in teaching autistic children to make eye contact, to stop their incessant rocking, to respond to verbal requests such as "Wash your hands," and gradually to play with toys, interact with peers, speak, and engage in school tasks such as reading and writing (Lovaas, 1993).

RESULTS

Lovaas and his colleagues did a long-term study of 19 children diagnosed as autistic. Behavior modification training went on for at least 40 hours per week, for 2 years or more. The graph on the

47%	Normal status
40%	Mildly retarded
10%	Profoundly retarded

right shows that, at the end of training, 47% of the autistic children reached normal status (Lovaas, 1987). These children acquired sufficient language, social, play, and self-help behaviors that they could enter preschool and go on to successfully complete grades in public school. Many of the children did so well that the teachers did not know they were autistic.

However, even with such intensive training, 40% of autistic children remained mildly retarded, and 10% remained profoundly retarded and were assigned to classes for children with mental retardation. In comparison, in a control group of autistic children who received only minimal treatment, only 2% achieved normal intellectual and educational functioning, while 45% remained mildly retarded and 53% remained severely retarded (Lovaas, 1987; Lovaas & Buch, 1997; McEachin, Smith, & Lovaas, 1993).

Lovaas concluded that without intensive behavior modification treatment, autistic children will continue to show severe behavioral deficits.

Next, we'll discuss another treatment program, called biofeedback, that also uses the principles of operant conditioning.

To the Instructor: Summary Test

Summary Test

After reading and perhaps taking notes, students often think they know the material. However, researchers found that students are poor judges of how well they know material unless they test themselves on the details. For example, if students wish to test their understanding of classical conditioning they need feedback on their answers to specific questions. That's the reason for the Summary Test, which appears at the end of each module.

Why are there two study aids?

How often have you heard students say, "I read the module three times but did poorly on the test." Reading is not always knowing and that's the reason the 5th edition has two built-in study tests: the Concept Review, which I discussed earlier (page xxvii), and the Summary Test (shown below). The Summary Test serves two functions: It's a review of the entire module and it allows students to check their specific knowledge of what they have read.

SUMMARY TEST

A. OVERVIEW: HUMAN BRAIN

1. The brain is composed of a trillion cells that can be divided into two groups. One group of cells have specialized extensions for receiving and transmitting information. These cells, which are called (a)_____, are involved in communicating with other neurons, receiving sensory information, and regulating muscles, glands, and organs. The other group of cells provide the scaffolding to guide and support neurons, insulate neurons, and release chemicals that influence neuron functions. These cells are much more numerous than neurons and are called (b)_____.

2. There is a major difference between the growth of neurons in the brains of humans and in the brains of birds. A mature human brain is normally not capable of developing new (a)_____, which are almost totally present at the time of birth. In contrast, a mature (b)_____ brain has the capacity to develop new neurons.

3. The age-old question of how the brain's membranes, fluids, and chemicals are involved in generating complex mental activities, such as thoughts, images, and feelings, is called the _____ question.

B. NEURONS: STRUCTURE & FUNCTION

4. Although neurons come in wondrous shapes and sizes, they all share three structures. The structure that maintains the entire neuron in working order, manufactures chemicals, and provides fuel is called the (a)_____. The structure with many branchlike extensions that receive signals from other neurons, muscles, or organs and conduct these signals to the cell body is called a (b)_____. The single threadlike extension that leaves the cell body and carries signals to other neurons, muscles, or organs is called the (c)_____. At the very end of this structure are individual swellings called (d)_____, which contain tiny vesicles filled with (e)_____.

5. Surrounding most axons is a fatty material called the (a)_____. This material acts like (b)_____ and diminishes interference from electrical signals traveling in neighboring axons.

6. Neurons do not make physical contact with one another or with other organs. Instead, there is an infinitely small space between a neuron's end bulbs and neighboring dendrites, cell bodies, or other organs. This space is called the (a)_____. When an axon's end bulbs secrete a neurotransmitter, it flows across this space and affects the (b)_____ on the neighboring membrane.

C. NEURONS VERSUS NERVES

7. There are major differences between neurons and nerves. Cells with specialized extensions for conducting electrical signals are called (a)_____. These cells, which are located in the brain and spinal cord, make up the (b)_____ nervous system. Stringlike bundles of neurons' axons and dendrites, which are held together by connective tissue, are called (c)_____. These stringlike bundles, which are located throughout the body, make up the (d)_____ nervous system. Nerves carry information back and forth between the body and the spinal cord. If a neuron in the central nervous system is damaged, it normally does not have the capacity to (e)_____. In comparison, a nerve in the (f)_____ nervous system has the capacity to regrow or reattach if cut or damaged.

D. SENDING INFORMATION

Action potential

8. The axon membrane has (a)_____ that can be opened or closed. These gates keep some ions inside the membrane and other ions outside. If the axon is ready to conduct but not actually conducting an impulse, the axon is said to be in the (b)_____ state. In this state, most of the positively charged (c)_____ ions are on the outside of the membrane and all the negatively charged (d)_____ ions are trapped inside. In the resting state, the outside of the membrane has a (e)_____ charge compared to the (f)_____ charge on the inside. The process responsible for picking up and transporting sodium ions from the inside to the outside of the axon membrane is called the (g)_____.

9. If a stimulus is strong enough to excite a neuron, two things happen to its axon. First, the stimulus will eventually open the axon's (a)_____. Second, after the gates are opened, the (b)_____ pump is stopped, and all the positive (c)_____ ions rush inside because they are attracted to the negatively charged protein ions. The rush of sodium ions inside generates a tiny electrical current that is called the

---

Summary Test

Each module ends with a Summary Test, which both reviews the material and allows students to test their knowledge and retention of the definitions, concepts, terms, and theories that were covered in the module.

What should I study? What will be on the test?

You have probably heard these two questions more than any other as test time approached. With the 5th edition, instructors can advise students to use the two built-in study aids, the Concept Review and the Summary Test. Both include fill-in-the-blank questions that demand recall, which is more difficult than recognition (multiple-choice questions) and thus a better test of how well students know the material.

To the Instructor: Critical Thinking

Critical Thinking

The 5th edition has two new features. One new feature, called **Critical Thinking,** (shown below) includes two activities that stimulate and facilitate critical thinking. One activity asks students to read and critically evaluate an interesting newspaper article. The second activity asks students to use information they learned in the module to answer study questions, which cover each major topic in the module.

How do students learn to think critically?

In my experience, many introductory psychology students have difficulty learning to think critically because they simply do not have enough information or because they don't know how or where to start. To help students learn to think critically, the 5th edition provides an interesting format—newspaper articles and study questions—as well as suggested answers so that students can see if they are on the right track.

Newspaper Article

At the end of each module is the *Critical Thinking* feature, which contains an interesting newspaper article that relates to one of the major topics discussed in the module. Students are asked to critically evaluate the article by answering five to seven questions that are placed next to the article. Because many students have difficulty getting started in answering questions, there are always brief suggested answers at the bottom of the next page.

These newspaper articles are also a great tool for stimulating class discussions.

Study Questions

A second *Critical Thinking* activity involves asking students to answer study questions that relate to each major topic.

Questions printed in **green** are answered in the *Critical Thinking Appendix* at the back of the text.

In addition, answers to two to three other study questions appear in the *Instructor's Resource Guide.* These study questions can be used for short essay tests or to generate class discussion.

CRITICAL THINKING

Newspaper Article

QUESTIONS

1. Why is this research topic important?

2. What is the major finding?

3. Why do people disagree over the effects of spanking?

4. What are the major limitations of this study?

5. What do other studies report?

6. What is the major advantage of this study?

7. What else might a caretaker or parent be concerned about?

SPANKING BACKFIRES, THE LATEST STUDY SAYS
by Brigid Schulte

WASHINGTON—From the dawn of time, parents have been spanking their children. Sometimes brutally, with belts and hairbrushes and buckles. And sometimes in frustration, with a swat to the rear or a smack on the head.

But research being published today by the American Medical Association suggests that times may have to change. Researchers have found that the more a parent spanks a child for misbehaving, the worse—over time—that child behaves. . . . But far from settling the score, the report, being published in the AMA's Archives of Pediatrics & Adolescent Medicine, is sure to fuel the already white-hot debate over whether to spank or not to spank. On one side are anti-spanking child advocates and psychologists concerned about child abuse and future violent behavior. On the other side are pro-spanking parents and conservative Christians, such as Focus on the Family's James Dobson, who fear that undisciplined children will run wild.

The new report has its limitations. It examined the disciplining of children ages 6 to 9, but not younger children. It still leaves completely unanswered what to do with toddlers exploring their world, terrible 2-year-olds throwing tantrums, and preschoolers testing their limits. . . . Straus (study's author) overlooks at least eight other studies which show that some spanking of children, aged 18 months to 3 years, has improved behavior. . . .

What's different about this study, Straus and even some of his critics said, is that for the first time, he and his colleagues have begun to answer that question. . . . "Of the children whose mothers didn't spank, two years later, their misbehavior score was better, they had less misbehavior," Straus said. . . . "The highest of all were the kids whose mothers spanked them three or more times during the past week. They got worse."

In the 1950s, 99 percent of all parents spanked their toddlers. Today, about 90 percent of all parents do.

Source: Knight-Ridder, appeared in *San Diego Union-Tribune*, August 15, 1997.

Study Questions

A. Operant Conditioning—How do you explain why your significant other sulks every time something is wrong even though you've told him or her that it bugs you? (See answer in Critical Thinking Appendix.)

B. Reinforcers—How would you use operant conditioning to change a rude friend into a more likable and friendly person? (See answer in Critical Thinking Appendix.)

C. Schedules of Reinforcement—Which schedules of partial reinforcement best apply to the following behaviors: eating, studying, going to the movies, dating?

D. Other Conditioning Concepts—The first time you visit your 2-year-old niece, she takes one look at you and starts to cry. What happened?

E. Cognitive Learning—Why should parents be especially concerned about what they say and do in the presence of their children?

F. Biological Factors—A 14-year-old boy recently graduated from college with outstanding grades. How could he learn so much so early?

G. Research Focus: Noncompliance—Why might parents yell, threaten, or spank rather than use a time-out to deal with a child's constant refusals?

H. Cultural Diversity: East Meets West—Why do the same principles of learning work in very different cultures? (See answer in Critical Thinking Appendix.)

I. Application: Behavior Modification—How could techniques of behavior modification be used in a computer program to teach children how to do math problems?

236 **Module 10** *OPERANT & COGNITIVE APPROACHES*

Links to Learning

The second new feature of the 5th edition is called *Links to Learning*, which helps students obtain additional information and activities from two different sources: numerous Web addresses that provide additional information for related topics in the module and related psychology CD-ROMs as well as the Study Guide that accompanies this text.

Where can I find more information on . . . ?
I find that students often ask questions about topics that there simply isn't enough time to cover in great depth, such as dreams, alcoholism, comas, supplements to improve memory, or how to deal with a family member suffering from Alzheimer's disease. To help students obtain additional information or write papers, the 5th edition provides almost a dozen **Web sites** for major topics covered in each module as well as information about related activities on **psychology CD-ROMs.**

LINKS TO LEARNING

Web Sites & Learning Activities

● BROOKS/COLE ONLINE PSYCHOLOGY STUDY CENTER
   http://psychstudy.brookscole.com/student/plotnik/quiz/ch10frm.html
   This site gives students a chance to review material by taking quizzes and doing exercises and activities for this module.

● OPERANT CONDITIONING AND BEHAVIORISM—AN HISTORICAL OUTLINE
   http://www.biozentrum.uni-wuerzburg.de/genetics/behavior/learning/behaviorism.html
   This page offers a nice history of research on operant conditioning and behaviorism, including work by Thorndike, Watson, and Skinner.

● OPERANT
   http://www.science.wayne.edu/~wpoff/cor/mem/operant.html
   This site explains the theory behind operant conditioning, including behaviors, reinforcers, and schedules of reinforcement.

● POSITIVE REINFORCEMENT
   http://server.bmod.athabascau.ca/html/prtut/reinpaˑr.htm
   This site offers a tutorial designed to teach about positive reinforcement, and it includes examples, activities, and practice exercises.

● BEHAVIORISM PSYCHOLOGY
   http://andretti.iupui.edu/subjectareas/psychology/behav.html
   This site provides links to journals, reference sources, and other Web sites with information on behaviorism.

● PARENT SOUP
   http://www.parentsoup.com/
   This site is dedicated to that ongoing experiment in operant conditioning known as parenthood. There are areas for parents with children of different ages, plus special features such as how to raise moral children and achieving pregnancy after infertility.

Welcome to the WEB

Activities

● *Integrator Online™ for Introductory Psychology* CD-ROM, Plotnik, Module 10

● Study Guide to accompany *Introduction to Psychology*, 5th edition, Module 10 (choice of PC or Mac computer version or hard copy).

● *PsychNow!* CD-ROM
   Operant Conditioning
   Observational Learning

Answers to questions on page 236

1. It studies a problem every caretaker or parent must face: how best to discipline young children for misbehaving.
2. The major finding is that the more a parent spanks a child for misbehaving, the worse the child behaves over the long term.
3. Anti-spanking people, who are concerned about child abuse and future aggressive behavior, disagree with pro-spanking forces, who believe children will run wild without such discipline.
4. Although the newspaper article refers to "children," the study actually studied only children 6 to 9, and not toddlers.
5. Previous studies showed that spanking of toddlers improved behavior, but the newspaper article does not say what happened to toddlers' behaviors over the long term.

6. The study measured children's behavior over the long term: after two years, less spanking resulted in less misbehaving, while more spanking resulted in more misbehaving.
7. They might be concerned about using time-out periods instead of spanking to discipline misbehaving children; the kind of evidence that pro-spanking people use to justify spanking; how current research findings challenge the age-old concept of spanking; and the necessity of considering both the short- and long-term effects of disciplining young children.

LINKS TO LEARNING **237**

Web Addresses
Because of the increasing popularity of searching the Web, students are provided with about a dozen relevant Web sites. These Web sites allow students to explore and obtain additional information on most of the topics covered in the module.

Learning Activities
Students are given links to additional materials and interesting activities and experiments that are available on psychology CD-ROMs. Students are also reminded about getting help from the *Study Guide* by Matt Enos, which accompanies the 5th edition.

Suggested Answers to Newspaper Article Questions
These suggested answers are included to help students get started and see if they are on the right track.

To the Instructor: Supplements

Supplements

Complete Teaching and Learning Package

The 5th edition is accompanied by a complete teaching and learning package that is as carefully developed and well integrated as the text itself.

For instructors, the teaching package includes the following complementary lecture and teaching aids:

Instructor's Resource Guide

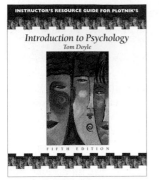

Although the *Instructor's Resource Guide* from the 4th edition was highly praised, the one for the 5th edition is even better. Tom Doyle has totally reorganized and updated an instructor's manual that facilitates an active learning environment in your classroom.

For each module, the features include: ■ numerous classroom-tested active learning exercises, many with handout masters, ■ demonstrations and individual group projects, ■ study questions with possible answers, ■ glossary, ■ an up-to-date list of films and videos for each module, each accompanied by a summary.

The friendly *Teaching Tips for New Instructors* provides support in handling typical problems that may arise.
ISBN: 0-534-36146-3.

Test Items

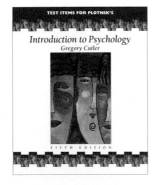

The completely revised and expanded test bank by Gregory Cutler includes approximately 3,500 test items, many of them new. Items are factual, conceptual, or applied. Page references and level of difficulty are included.

Electronic Test Items

Test item banks are also available for Windows and Macintosh computers.
ISBN: 0-534-36148-X.
Windows ISBN: 0-534-36289-3.
Macintosh ISBN: 0-534-36288-5.

Transparencies

Electronic. You can enhance your lectures with this Adobe Acrobat® slide presentation that contains the complete set of full-color transparencies that illustrate the major concepts of the text, as selected by Rod Plotnik and adapted for use in the classroom and lecture hall. (Acrobat Reader is on the disk for a quick, one-time download. Cross-platform CD for Windows® and Macintosh®: ISBN: 0-534-36286-9.)

Transparency acetates. A complete set of full-color acetate transparencies that illustrate major concepts in the text is also available. ISBN: 0-534-36147-1.

Brooks/Cole • Wadsworth Introductory Psychology Transparency Acetates

A set of 95 full-color transparencies from other sources complement the text-specific transparency acetates.
ISBN: 0-534-13013-5.

Videodisk

This videodisk was developed specifically for the Plotnik text and includes video clips and animated art. Bar codes in a separate pamphlet make it easy to integrate videodisk visuals into lectures.
ISBN: 0-534-33847-X.

Career Encounters Video

This 30-minute video produced by the APA is exclusive to APA and Wadsworth and is free to adopters.
Contact your Wadsworth representative for information.

To the Instructor: Instructor's Resource Guide

Instructor's Resource Guide

In our lectures, we often use a variety of real-life examples, interactive exercises, demonstrations, study questions, Web activities, instructional CDs, and video or movie clips. However, the task of finding and organizing these many different activities for each lecture can be overwhelming. But take heart because Tom Doyle has spent the past year organizing all these materials in his *Instructor's Resource Guide.* These interesting materials have been tested in the classroom by Tom Doyle, Katie Townsend-Merino (who wrote the *Instructor's Resource Guide* for the 4th edition), and the almost 200 teaching assistants I have supervised during the past 20 years. I strongly recommend trying these materials, especially the Active Learning Exercises. What sets this resource guide apart from all others is that Tom has made it very comprehensive and has cleverly organized all the materials so that the guide is very user friendly.

Module 4: Incredible Nervous System

A. Genes & Evolution   68
* Genetic Instructions
* Evolution of the Human Brain

B. Studying the Living Brain   70
* New Techniques
* MRI Scans
* PET Scans
* Specific Thoughts

C. Organization of the Brain   72
* Divisions of Nervous System
* Major Parts of the Brain

D. Control Centers: Four Lobes   74
* Overall Cortex
* Frontal Lobe
* Parietal Lobe
* Temporal Lobe
* Occipital Lobe

E. Limbic System: Old Brain   80
* Structures and Functions
* Autonomic Nervous System

F. Endocrine System   82
* Definition
* Control Center: Hypothalamus
* Key Player: Pituitary
* Other Glands

Resources

IN: Involvers

SQ: Study Questions

CD: PsychNow!—Brain

CD INTG: The Integrator—Brain

T: Transparencies

ALE: Active Learning Exercise I

ALE: Active Learning Exercise II

Student Projects

Web Connections

Study Question Answers

Videos and Films

Outline of Each Module
The outline on the far left shows major topics.

Resources for Each Topic
This lists and describes activities for a single module—in this case, Module 4.

Involvers and Study Questions
The Involvers create student interest. The Study Questions stimulate discussion and can be used for brief essay tests.

PsychNow! and The Integrator
These two CDs contain many activities and exercises, some of which you can integrate into your lecture and some of which students can do on their own.

Transparencies
Many are new for the 5th edition.

Active Learning Exercises
Students love these exercises because they motivate learning by creating a very active classroom environment.

Student Projects and Web Connections
These two activities are ideal for involving students in the material.

Study Question Answers
These provide great ideas for short essay questions.

Videos and Films
To help you choose, there is a content summary for each video and film.

To the Instructor: Supplements

The Wadsworth Film and Video Library for Psychology

Instructors may choose from a variety of regularly updated video and film options that currently include the "Brain" and "Mind" teaching modules; "Seeing Beyond the Obvious," a 46-minute video on sensation and perception; videos from the Annenberg "Discovering Psychology" series; and film rentals from Pennsylvania State University's project, "PCR: Films and Videos in the Behavioral Sciences." Adopters can choose from a variety of film and video options. For more information contact your Wadsworth representative.

World Wide Web Psychology Study Center: http://www.psychstudy.brookscole.com

When you adopt this text, you and your students will have access to the Brooks/Cole • Wadsworth Psychology Study Center, which features a full range of Web-based services including module-by-module online quizzes, interactive Internet activities, links to psychology-related sites on the Web (including live links from the "Links to Learning" pages that appear at the end of each module) as well as Hot Topics, Research and Teaching Showcase, Teaching Tips and Ideas, and Bulletin Boards.

Thomson World Class Learning™ Course

Using *World Class Course,* you can quickly and easily create and update a World Wide Web page specifically for a course or class. If you can fill out a form on your computer, you can use *World Class Course.* Post your own course information, office hours, lesson information, assignments, sample tests, *and* link to rich Web content, including student review and enrichment material from Brooks/Cole • Wadsworth. Customer support is available 24 hours a day, seven days a week. *For more information, drop by:* www.worldclasslearning.com

Integrator Online™ for Introductory Psychology (Instructor's Edition)

You can deliver your course over the Web quickly and easily. Ideal for use in any teaching and learning situation—from standard lecture to full Internet delivery—*Integrator Online,* by Arthur J. Kohn and Wendy Kohn, is designed for use with this text and is directly linked to the content of each module. The instructor's edition of *Integrator Online* includes *CourseWeaver Online™,* which allows you to deliver course materials via local lecture, individual computers, or the Internet. Using *CourseWeaver Online,* you can deliver individual lessons or an entire course with embedded Internet links, interactive activities, study sessions, and simulations. Alternately, students can use the CD-ROM on their own to explore activities, complete homework, or practice for quizzes. ISBN: 0-534-36590-6.

CNN Video

Professors who adopt any Brooks/Cole • Wadsworth introductory psychology text are eligible to receive this *exclusive,* 45-minute video consisting of recent CNN news segments. Each segment focuses on relevant introductory psychology topics and how psychologists study them. Please contact your local ITP sales representative to order your copy. ISBN 0-534-36634-1.

For Students, the Teaching Package Includes:

Study Guide

This fully revised and updated study guide by Matthew Enos includes short summaries and outlines of modules, as well as many multiple-choice, matching, and true–false questions and answers. Integrated language enrichment tools by Arlene Zide in each chapter provide grammar and vocabulary assistance for students who need additional help or who are non-native English speakers. ISBN: 0-534-36145-5.

Interactive Electronic Study Guide

Questions and answers are provided in an interactive format, reinforcing students' correct answers and providing helpful cues in response to incorrect answers. Windows ISBN: 0-534-36142-0, Macintosh ISBN: 0-534-36143-9.

Integrator Online™ for Introductory Psychology (Student Edition)

For each module of this text, students can interact with linked review and testing modules: the Glossary Module, the Study Module, and the Quiz Module (which provides randomized quizzes on any topic). With a click of the mouse, students can call up interactive experiments, animations, homework assignments, video clips, transparencies, audio clips, dynamic images, demonstrations, study pages, and more. ISBN: 0-534-35746-6.

PsychNow!™: Interactive Experiences in Psychology

This CD-ROM provides students with a dynamic, multimedia experience. Stunning graphics and animations, interesting video clips, and interactive exercises bring the theories of psychology to life. *PsychNow!* contains 39 fully interactive modules designed to pique students' curiosity and enhance their understanding of core concepts. ISBN: 0-314-07220-9.

Psychology Resources on the World Wide Web

This concise guide to psychology-related resources on the World Wide Web by Edward Kardas is organized by topic and designed to serve as a directory for students who may be conducting research via the Internet. The author presents an up-to-date, comprehensive book that is organized to match most introductory psychology textbooks and includes a chapter on how to perform research on the Web. ISBN: 0-534-35941-8.

Psychology/Careers for the Twenty-First Century Booklet

(Available shrinkwrapped free with Plotnik's text.) This 30-page pamphlet produced by the American Psychological Association is exclusive to APA and Brooks/Cole • Wadsworth. It describes the field of psychology, as well as the "how to" for career preparation in the many areas of psychology. Career options and resources are also discussed.

To the Student

Introductory Psychology Course

What will I learn?

The course you are about to begin is one of the most popular on campus because it is concerned with so many aspects of your life. For example, in Introductory Psychology you will learn how your brain functions, what happens when you sleep, how you learned to be anxious during exams, what an IQ score means, why you develop psychosomatic symptoms, how your personality changes, what abnormal behaviors are, how you perceive others, and many more things that affect your life. This course also

What kind of course is this?

covers many techniques that psychologists have developed to deal with relatively common problems: how to improve study habits, reduce stress, overcome insomnia, relieve mild depression, treat phobias, improve memory, and reduce anger. As you can see, this course will help you better understand your own behaviors as well as those of others.

Not Common Sense

Can you answer these questions?

I can guarantee that if you use just common sense you will never pass this course. That's because much of our common sense about human behavior is just plain wrong. For example, using your common sense, decide whether the following statements are true (T) or false (F):

Where did you put the answers?

T	F	You use only about 50% of your brain.
T	F	IQ tests measure natural intelligence.
T	F	The most common cause of colds is exposure to a draft.
T	F	The first five years of your life are critical to the development of your personality.
T	F	Eyewitness testimony is the most accurate.
T	F	You can learn a foreign language by listening to a recording during sleep.
T	F	Psychosomatic problems are imaginary.
T	F	The best way to get over an intense fear is always to avoid the feared thing.

Using common sense, you may decide that some of these statements are true. However, psychologists have discovered through systematic investigation that all the statements are false. This course will introduce you to a system of discovery that psychologists use to understand behavior. Learning all the terms, concepts, and theories will be difficult but it will also be challenging and rewarding and will improve your common sense.

Textbook

How will I ever learn all this?

As you examine this book, you will immediately notice that it doesn't look like traditional textbooks. That's because each page has been custom-designed to present information in visually exciting ways.

I'll point out some major features, such as modules, the Concept Review, the use of graphics, the Study Questions, and the Summary Test, and explain how they will help you understand and remember the material.

As you check the contents, you'll find that this textbook is divided into 25 relatively short chapters, called modules. Because each module is about half the length of a traditional textbook chapter, you have less material to read and master at any one time. In addition, each module has two built-in study aids so that you can review and test your under-

Why is this textbook so different?

standing and memory of the material. You'll also notice that each module begins with a real-life example and that interesting cases are used throughout the text to make the concepts more relevant.

You'll see that on each page the material is broken down into small, understandable units and that all the figures, illustrations, and graphs are integrated into the text. This means that you never have to hunt for a distant figure and caption. For example, on the sample page shown on the following page, notice how the material is presented in a series of eight steps, and how each step is accompanied by an interesting graphic that provides a visual cue for remembering the material.

To the Student

How do I find a definition?

Every definition of a term, concept, or theory is bold-faced and printed in blue so that you can identify it easily. In addition, about two-thirds of the way through each module, you'll discover the first study aid, the Concept Review. This feature gives you a chance to check your understanding of the key concepts you have just studied. As you fill in the blanks of the Concept Review, you'll be making a list of what's important in that module. To help you remember these important terms, each one is linked to a graphic. By combining a definition with a visual cue you will have a better chance of remembering the term.

How can I test myself?

After finishing a module you may wonder how much you have learned and will remember. A good way to answer this is to use the second study aid, the Summary Test, at the end of each module. As you read and fill in the blanks of the Summary Test, you can review the information as well as test your memory of the major concepts and terms. If you find that you have forgotten some material, you can go back and restudy it until you are able to answer all the questions in the Summary Test.

Students often ask whether they should buy the separate *Study Guide,* by Matthew Enos. If you would like additional help in mastering a module, the *Study Guide* is a useful tool. It contains outlines of each module, plus a variety of questions (multiple-choice, true–false, matching) that give you many chances to test your mastery of the material.

If you have a computer, you can buy the *Electronic Study Guide,* which presents questions, rewards correct answers, and prompts you to try again if you make an error.

C. Stimulants

Definition

What are stimulants?

"Two pills beat a month's vacation."

This marketing slogan was used to sell amphetamines in Sweden in the 1940s. It resulted in epidemic usage that peaked in the mid-1960s.

In the 1940s, American doctors prescribed amphetamines as safe energizers, mood enhancers, and appetite suppressors. By the 1960s, billions of doses of amphetamines were being used in the United States and their usage had become a serious problem.

In the 1940s, Japanese workers used amphetamines to keep factory production high during World War II. After the war, many students, nightworkers, and people displaced by the war began to use "wake-amines." Amphetamine use spread until, in 1954, two million Japanese had become abusers and addicted.

By the early 1970s, most countries had brought amphetamine usage under control through a combination of measures, including regulation of prescriptions, decrease in supply, and stiffer penalties. However, at present, amphetamine-like stimulants, such as methamphetamine (crystal) and cocaine, are widely available on the black market.

All *stimulants,* including cocaine, amphetamines, caffeine, and nicotine, increase activity of the central nervous system and result in heightened alertness, arousal, euphoria, and decreased appetite and fatigue. Dose for dose, cocaine and amphetamines are considered powerful stimulants because they produce a strong effect with a small dose; caffeine and nicotine are considered mild stimulants.

We'll discuss the more widely used stimulants—amphetamines, cocaine, caffeine, and nicotine.

Amphetamines

Why is it still a problem?

During the 1960s, amphetamine pills were heavily prescribed to treat a wide range of problems, including fatigue, depression, and being overweight. This was also the time that young adults, called "flower children," took heavy doses of amphetamines that resulted in their having true paranoid psychotic symptoms, which resulted in their being called "speed freaks." Amphetamine usage peaked in the mid-1960s when over 31 million prescriptions were written for dieting and about 25 tons of legitimately manufactured amphetamines were diverted to illegal sales (Hanson & Venturelli, 1998). Finally, in 1971, the Food and Drug Administration (FDA) outlawed the prescription of amphetamines for everything except attention deficit hyperactivity disorder (ADHD) and narcolepsy.

However, following a "war" on cocaine in the late 1980s and early 1990s, there has been a dramatic upsurge in the use of a form of amphetamine, called methamphetamine, which is manufactured in illegal home laboratories (Howlett, 1997). The possession or use of methamphetamine is illegal.

Drug

In 1996, authorities raided over 800 illegal methamphetamine laboratories in California and 450 in the Midwest, where the drug has recently increased in popularity (Howlett, 1997).

Methamphetamine (D-methamphetamine) is close to amphetamine in both its chemical makeup and its physical and psychological effects. Unlike amphetamine, which is taken in pill form, methamphetamine (speed, crank, crystal, ice) can be smoked or snorted and produces an almost instantaneous high. Both amphetamine and methamphetamine cause marked increases in blood pressure and heart rate and feelings of enhanced mood, alertness, and energy.

"It's the ultimate high. . . . It makes you feel so powerful. You have tons of energy. . . . I loved it. I craved it" (Witkin, 1995, p. 50). So said 23-year-old Tara who developed a $200-a-day habit and lost her apartment, job, and infant daughter. Her euphoria from methamphetamine soon turned into a terrible nightmare.

Nervous System

The primary affect of amphetamines and related drugs (methamphetamine) is to increase the release of the neurotransmitter, dopamine, and secondarily, to block its reuptake (Stahl, 1996). Researchers are learning that the release of dopamine occurs during a wide range of pleasurable activities, such as sex (Schuster, 1997). Thus, drugs like methamphetamine are both so desirable and dangerous because they increase release of dopamine, which causes very pleasurable feelings.

Dangers

"I couldn't get high. No matter how much I did, no matter who I was with, nothing made me happy. I was so depressed. I wanted to die," said 23-year-old Tara, who was a heavy methamphetamine user (Witkin, 1995, p. 50). At first, users of methamphetamine or ice (a concentrated form) have periods of restless activity and perform repetitious behaviors. Later, the initial euphoria is replaced with depression, agitation, insomnia, and development of true paranoid feelings. Because of its risk for addiction and dependency, as well as physical and psychological problems, methamphetamine/ice is a very dangerous drug.

Because of a crackdown on amphetamines in the 1970s, there was an enormous increase in cocaine usage, which we'll discuss next.

How can I learn to think critically?

At the end of each module are several Critical Thinking activities that include answering questions about an interesting newspaper article or answering study questions about major topics in the module. To help you get started, many questions have suggested answers that appear on the next page or in the Critical Thinking Appendix in the back of this text.

Now that I've told you a little about the course and the textbook, you're ready to begin. Here's your chance to use 100% of your brain.

Acknowledgments and Many Thanks

In developing the 5th edition, I worked with a remarkable group of creative people, each of whom deserves a special thanks.

Executive Editor: Vicki

The development of the 5th edition required energy from two thousand Dove bars (dark chocolate with almonds), more than two years of work, and most important, the best editor in publishing, Vicki Knight. I have been working with Vicki for almost 10 wonderful years and she is one of the guiding hands behind the success of this text. She always has great advice and, best of all, understands what this book is about and how to make it happen. I have been writing textbooks for most of my adult life and fully realize how lucky I am to have an editor like Vicki.

Editorial Associate: Shelley

Shelley Tweddell, editorial assistant, had the difficult task of making sure that all the modules were sent to reviewers, which for the 5th edition numbered over 100. Shelley has the attitude of a saint and if I wanted someone to run my life, I would choose Shelley.

Cover Designer: Vernon

As always, Vernon Boes came up with a great design for the cover. Developing a cover is absolutely the hardest thing since each of us has a very strong opinion about the design. I'm not sure how Vernon does it but I think it has something to do with deep breathing.

Concept Illustrators: Bill & Philip

Many ideas and concepts simply cannot be expressed well in photos. In these cases we used the creative talents of Philip Dvorak and Bill Ogden. In every module you'll discover their clever creations, which range from Sigmund Freud's head to a trash can full of memories. Their wonderful illustrations help make the book visually exciting.

Photo Researcher: Linda

Once again, Linda Rill was in charge of photo research and permissions, and there is no one as good at this as Linda. She always gets the best photos, some requiring months to track down.

Manuscript Editor: Shirley

My worst fear is that I will send my pages off to a manuscript editor who will send them back with a billion changes. Thankfully, I avoided this nightmare by having the best manuscript editor ever. Her name is Shirley Simmons and although we wrote each other some very fierce notes, in the end it worked out beautifully. Shirley's editorial skills really did improve the book, even though she made me change some of my favorite sentences.

Production: Nancy & Vena

For just a minute, think of Nancy Shammas' desk. It is piled high with 25 first-draft modules, 25 revised modules, 25 final modules, and the task of keeping everything on a diabolically impossible schedule. I am recommending Nancy for battle pay.

Vena Dyer made sure that we had paper and a printer and would end up with a real book.

Marketing: Lauren & Margaret

There is no better marketing person than Lauren Harp, who came up with great ideas for slogans, postcards, and hundreds of ways to explain what the 5th edition is all about. No matter how many other books she had to think about, Lauren gave my text the necessary attention and creativity to help make it a success in the textbook market.

When you read the great advertising copy, think of Margaret Parks. Margaret and I talk only once every three years and we always begin our conservation with, "Well, is it that time already?"

Supplements: Tom, Matt & Greg

Many talented people worked on a variety of supplements. Tom Doyle has written and designed the best *Instructor's Resource Guide* that I have ever seen. The reason Tom could develop such an exciting guide is because Tom is such a dedicated and talented teacher.

Matthew Enos once again used his friendly and helpful teaching skills to write the *Study Guide,* whose previous edition was so highly praised by students.

Once again Greg Cutler used his critical thinking skills to write the *Test Bank* for the 5th edition. What is amazing about Greg's questions is that they received not a single criticism for the previous edition's test banks.

Teaching Assistants

Many of my ideas for the 5th edition came from regular meetings with my enthusiastic and highly motivated teaching assistants. I wish to thank my current group: Helena, Mario, Michelle, Neil, Liana, Sylvia, Gabriel, Haig, Jamy, Julia, Alanna, Kristen, Susan, Jill, and Sofia and Steve. They are wonderful teachers full of great ideas.

Research Assistants

Special thanks goes to my three extremely competent research assistants. Amy Goodman worked long and hard without so much as a grumble. Also helping out were Farnez Yadeh and Herman Chambers, who copied hundreds of articles and thought about grumbling but didn't.

Production Company: Louise

The person who made sure the individual pages were turned into a complete book is "geeze" Louise Gelinas of PC&F. She kept track of a record number of photos and art work (probably more than 2000 pieces), and kept the pages rolling out. Louise did a Herculean job and truly deserves a raise.

Special Colleague: Sandy

While working on the 5th edition I alternated between "It's wonderful," and "I quit." Through it all, my friend and colleague Sandy Mollenauer provided emotional support, encouragement, and understanding.

To the Reviewers: Many Thanks

I especially want to thank the many reviewers who put in an amazing amount of time and energy to consider and comment on materials for this textbook.

I would like to explain why I was not able to include all your valuable suggestions. Sometimes your suggestions were great but required inserting material for which there simply was no room. Other times, your suggestions contradicted each other and I tried to work out the best compromise. Still other times, reviewers argued with such force for entirely different points that I felt like the proverbial starving donkey between two stacks of hay, trying to decide which way to turn. Thus, I may not have included all your suggestions, but I did give them a great deal of thought and used as many as I possibly could.

It is important that all the reviewers know that your efforts are simply invaluable to revising and developing a textbook. If it were within my power, I would triple your honorariums and give you each a sabbatical.

Glen Adams, Harding University

Nelson Adams, Winston-Salem State University

Marlene Adelman, Norwalk Community Technical College

George Bagwell, Colorado Mountain College-Alpine Campus

Roger Bailey, Southwestern College

Beth Barton, Coastal Carolina Community College

Beth Benoit, University of Massachusetts-Lowell

John B. Benson, Texarcana College

Kristen Biondolillo, Arkansas State University

Linda Brunton, Columbia State Community College

Lawrence Burns, Grand Valley State University

Ronald Caldwell, Blue Mountain Community College

James Calhoun, University of Georgia

Peter Caprioglio, Middlesex Community-Technical College

Donna M. Casperson, Harrisburg Area Community College

Hank Cetola, Adrian College

Larry Christensen, Salt Lake Community College

Saundra K. Ciccarelli, Gulf Coast Community College

Gerald S. Clack, Loyola University

J. Craig Clarke, Salisbury State University

Richard T. Colgan, Bridgewater State College

Laurie Corey, Westchester Community College

Sandy Deabler, North Harris College

Paul H. Del Nero, Towson University

Jean Edwards, Jones County Junior College

Tami Eggleston, McKendree College

Nolen U. Embry, Lexington Community College

Charles H. Evans, LaGrange College

Melissa Faber, Lima Technical College

Mike Fass, Miami-Dade Community College, North Campus

Mary Beth Foster, Purdue University

Jan Francis, Santa Rosa Junior College

Grace Galliano, Kennesaw State College

John T. Garrett, Texas State Technical College

Philip Gray, D'Youville College

Charles M. Greene, Florida Community College at Jacksonville

Lynn Haller, Morehead State University

Sheryl Hartman, Miami Dade Community College

Debra Lee Hollister, Valencia Community College

Donna Holmes, Becker College

Lucinda Hutman, Elgin Community College

Terry Isbell, Northwestern State University

Eleanor Jones, Tidewater Community College

Stan Kary, St. Louis Community College at Florissant Valley

Paul Kasenow, Henderson Community College

Don Kates, College of Dupage

Mark Kelland, Lansing Community College

Richard Kirk, Texas State Technical College

John C. Koeppel, University of Southern Mississippi

Jan Kottke, California State University-San Bernardino

Joan Krueger, Harold Washington College

Doug Krull, Northern Kentucky University

Diane J. Krumm, College of Lake County

Raymond Launier, Santa Barbara City College

Eamonn J. Lester, St. Philips College

John Lindsay, Georgia College & State University

Alan Lipman, Georgetown University

Karsten Look, Columbus State Community College

Jerry Lundgren, Flathead Valley Community College

Frank MacHovec, Rappahannock Community College

Mary Lee Meiners, San Diego Miramar College

Diane Mello-Goldner, Pine Manor College

Laurence Miller, Western Washington University

Alinde Moore, Ashland University

John T. Nixon, SUNY-Canton

Art Olguin, Santa Barbara City College

Carol Pandey, Pierce College

Christine Panyard, University of Detroit-Mercy

Jeff Parsons, Jersey City State College

Bob Pellegrini, San Jose State University

James Previte, Victor Valley College

Joan Rafter, Hudson Community College

Robert R. Rainey, Jr., Florida Community College at Jacksonville

Lillian Range, University of Southern Mississippi

S. Peter Resta, Prince George's Community College

Bret Roark, Oklahoma Baptist University

Ann E. Garrett Robinson, Gateway Community Technical College

Alan Schultz, Prince George's Community College

Robert Schultz, Fulton Montgomery Community College

Harold Siegel, Rutger's University

N. Clayton Silver, University of Nevada, Las Vegas

James Spencer, West Virginia State College

Deborah Steinberg, Jefferson Community College

Julie Stokes, California State University-Fullerton

Ted Sturman, University of Southern Maine

Clayton N. Tatro, Garden City Community College

Annette Taylor, University of San Diego

Andy Thomas, Tennessee Technical University

Larry Till, Cerritos College

Susan Troy, Northeast Iowa Community College

Jane Vecchio, Holyoke Community College

Randy Vinzant, Hinds Community College

Benjamin Wallace, Cleveland State University

James Ward, Western New England College

Mary Scott West, Virginia Intermont College

Fred W. Whitford, Montana State University

John Whittle, Northern Essex Community College

Ellen Williams, Mesa Community College

Matthew J. Zagumny, Tennessee Technological University

Gene Zingarelli, Santa Rosa Community College

Module *1* DISCOVERING PSYCHOLOGY

A. Definition & Goals 4

* **DEFINITION OF PSYCHOLOGY**
* **GOALS OF PSYCHOLOGY**

B. Modern Approaches 5

* **BIOLOGICAL**
* **COGNITIVE**
* **BEHAVIORAL**
* **PSYCHOANALYTIC**
* **HUMANISTIC**
* **CROSS-CULTURAL**

C. Historical Approaches 12

* **STRUCTURALISM**
* **FUNCTIONALISM**
* **GESTALT APPROACH**
* **BEHAVIORISM**
* **SURVIVAL OF APPROACHES**

D. Cultural Diversity: Early Discrimination 14

* **WOMEN IN PSYCHOLOGY**
* **MINORITIES IN PSYCHOLOGY**
* **RIGHTING THE WRONGS**

E. Research Focus: Class Notes 16

* **BEST STRATEGY FOR TAKING CLASS NOTES?**

Average Score on Exam

Review notes 34
Summarize notes 45
Answer questions 51

F. Careers in Psychology 17

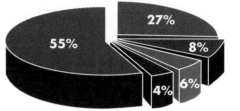

27%
55%
8%
4% 6%

* **PSYCHOLOGIST VERSUS PSYCHIATRIST**
* **MANY CAREER SETTINGS**

G. Research Areas 18

* **SOCIAL AND PERSONALITY**
* **DEVELOPMENTAL**
* **EXPERIMENTAL**
* **BIOLOGICAL**
* **COGNITIVE**
* **PSYCHOMETRICS**

H. Application: Study Skills 20

* **IMPROVING STUDY HABITS**
* **SETTING GOALS**
* **REWARDING YOURSELF**
* **TAKING NOTES**
* **STOPPING PROCRASTINATION**

Growing Up in a Strange World

When Donna was about three years old, she ate lettuce because she liked rabbits and they ate lettuce. She ate jelly because it looked like colored glass and she liked to look at colored glass.

She was told to make friends but Donna had her own friends. She had a pair of green eyes named Willie that hid under her bed, and wisps, which were tiny, transparent spots that hung in the air around her.

When people spoke, their words were strange sounds with no meaning, like mumble jumble. Donna did learn the sounds of letters and how they fit together to make words. Although she didn't learn the meanings of words, she loved their sounds when she said them out loud. As a child she was tested for deafness because she did not use language like other children. She did not learn that words had meaning until she was a teenager.

When people talked to Donna, especially people with loud or excited voices, she heard only, "blah, blah, blah." Too much excited talk or over-stimulation caused Donna to stare straight ahead and appear to be frozen. Donna later called this state, "involuntarily anesthetized."

Donna was in and out of many schools because she failed her exams, refused to take part in any class activities, walked out of classes she didn't like, and sometimes threw things. Because of her strange behaviors, other students called her "Zombie."

When Donna did make a friend, she tried to avoid getting a friendly hug, which made her feel as if she were burning up inside and going to faint. Eventually she learned to tolerate being hugged but never liked it (Williams, 1992).

Donna Williams has all the symptoms of autism, which is a relatively rare problem that occurs about once in 1,000 births, affects 2 to 4 times as many boys as girls, and is found in all parts of the world (Bristol et al., 1996).

Autism is marked by especially abnormal or impaired development in social interactions, such as hiding to avoid people, not making eye contact, not wanting to be touched. Autism is marked by difficulties in communicating, such as grave problems in developing spoken language or in initiating conversations. Autistics are characterized by having very few activities and interests, spending long periods repeating the same behaviors (flipping fingers), or following the same rituals. Signs of autism begin in the child's first 3 years (American Psychiatric Association, 1994).

Among autistic individuals, about 1–2% possess a special skill at which they excel. These individuals, called savants, may create intricate drawings with no instruction, play a song on a musical instrument after hearing the song only once, do mathematical calculations as fast as a hand calculator, or solve calendar puzzles, such as figuring out the day of the week for a date ten years ago.

Donna Williams (1992) is an example of a savant who developed exceptional language skills. At age 25, in four almost-nonstop weeks, she wrote a 500-page book that described what it was like to be autistic. In this and her more recent book (D. Williams, 1994), Donna describes how common sights, sounds, and images become strangely distorted, which makes getting through an ordinary day like finding one's way out of a terribly complex maze.

As we describe Donna's experiences, you'll see how psychologists try to answer questions about complex behaviors, such as autism, as well as countless other questions that come up in the 25 modules of this text.

One question that psychologists have some answers to involves a problem that many students have—test anxiety.

Test Anxiety

If you're like many other students, you probably experience some degree of test anxiety.

Test anxiety refers to a combination of physiological, emotional, and cognitive components that are caused by the stress of taking exams and that may interfere with one's ability to think, reason, and plan.

For some students, test anxiety is an unpleasant experience but doesn't necessarily interfere with exam performance. For other students, test anxiety is not only an unpleasant experience but also seriously interferes with exam performance. We'll discuss the components of test anxiety, why students differ in how much test anxiety they feel, and, probably most important, how to decrease test anxiety.

What's Coming

In this module, we'll explore the goals of psychology, the major approaches that psychologists use to understand behavior and answer questions, the historical roots of psychology, current research areas, and possible careers in the broad field of psychology. Let's begin with how psychologists study complex problems, such as Donna's autistic behaviors.

A. Definition & Goals

Definition of Psychology

What do psychologists study?

When you think of psychology, you may think of helping people with mental problems. However, psychologists study a broad range of behaviors, including Donna's autistic behaviors and students' test anxiety, as well as hundreds of other behaviors. For this reason, we need a very broad definition of psychology.

Psychology is the systematic, scientific study of behaviors and mental processes.

What's important about this definition is that each of its terms has a broader meaning. For example, *behaviors* refers to observable actions or responses in both humans and animals. Behaviors might include eating, speaking, laughing, running, reading, and sleeping. *Mental processes,* which are not directly observable, refer to a wide range of complex mental processes, such as thinking, imagining, studying, and dreaming. The current broad definition of psychology grew out of discussions and heated arguments among early psychologists, who defined psychology much more specifically, as we'll discuss later in this module.

Although the current definition of psychology is very broad, psychologists usually have four specific goals in mind when they study some behavior or mental process, such as Donna's autistic experiences.

Goals of Psychology

What are some of Donna's unusual behaviors?

Donna (photo below) knows that she has some unusual behaviors. For example, she says that she doesn't like to be touched, held, or hugged, doesn't like to make eye contact when speaking to people, hates to talk to someone who has a loud voice, and really dislikes meeting strangers. If you were a psychologist studying Donna's unusual behaviors, you would have the following four goals in mind: to describe, explain, predict, and control her behavior.

1 Describe

Donna says that, when she was a child, she wondered what people were saying to her because words were just lists of meaningless sounds. When people or things bothered her, she would endlessly tap or twirl her fingers to create movements that completely held her attention and helped her escape from a world that often made no sense.

The first goal of psychology is to describe the different ways that organisms behave.

As psychologists begin to describe the behaviors and mental processes of autistic children, such as difficulties in learning language, they begin to understand how autistic children behave. After describing behavior, psychologists try to explain behavior, the second goal.

2 Explain

Donna's mother believed that autism was caused by evil spirits. Donna thinks her autism may result from metabolic imbalance.

The second goal of psychology is to explain the causes of behavior.

The explanation of autism has changed as psychologists learn more about this complex problem. In the 1950s, psychologists explained that children became autistic if they were reared by parents who were cold and rejecting (Frith, 1993). More recently, researchers have discovered that autism is caused by genetic and biological factors, such as a maldeveloped brain (Cook et al., 1997; Waterhouse et al., 1996). Being able to describe and explain behavior helps psychologists reach the third goal, which is to predict behavior.

3 Predict

Donna says that one of her biggest problems is being so overloaded by visual sensations that she literally freezes in place. She tries to predict when she will freeze up by estimating how many new stimuli she must adjust to.

The third goal of psychology is to predict how organisms will behave in certain situations.

However, psychologists may have difficulty predicting how autistic children will behave in certain situations unless they have already described and explained their behaviors. For example, from the first two goals, psychologists know that autistic children are easily overwhelmed by strange stimuli and have difficulty paying attention. Based on this information, psychologists can predict that autistic children will have difficulty learning in a school environment because there is too much activity and stimuli in the classroom (Happé & Frith, 1996). However, if psychologists can predict behavior, then they can often control behavior.

4 Control

Donna knows one reason she fears meeting people is that social interactions cause a tremendous sensory overload that makes her freeze up. She controls her social fear by making a rule to meet only one person at a time.

For some psychologists, the fourth goal of psychology is to control an organism's behavior.

The idea of control has both positive and negative sides. The positive side is that psychologists can help people, such as Donna, learn to control undesirable behaviors (Howlin, 1997). The negative side is that people's behaviors might be controlled without their knowledge or consent. In Module 2, we'll discuss the strict guidelines that psychologists have established to prevent potential abuse of controlling behavior and to protect the rights and privacy of individuals, patients, and subjects in experiments.

Because many behaviors, such as autism, are enormously complex, psychologists use a combination of different approaches to reach the four goals of describing, explaining, predicting, and controlling behavior. To reach these goals, psychologists may use one or a combination of the following six approaches.

More Approaches, More Answers

How do psychologists answer questions?

Psychologists have many questions about Donna's unusual behaviors. For example, why did Donna believe that objects were alive and made their own sounds? "My bed was my friend; my coat protected me and kept me inside; things that made noise had their own unique voices, which said vroom, ping, or whatever. I told my shoes where they were going so they would take me there" (Blakely, 1994, p. 14).

Why did Donna initially hear words as meaningless sounds that people were constantly saying to her? Why did she develop her own signaling system, such as raising two fingers or scrunching her toes to signal that no one could reach her? Why did she freeze up when staring at soap bubbles in the sink? In trying to answer questions about Donna's strange and intriguing behaviors, psychologists would use a combination of different approaches.

Approaches to understanding behavior include the biological, cognitive, behavioral, psychoanalytic, humanistic, and cross-cultural. Each approach has a different focus or perspective and may use a different research method or technique.

We'll summarize these six commonly used approaches and then discuss them in more detail on the following pages.

1 As a child, was Donna unable to learn that words had meaning because of some problem with the development of her brain?

The *biological approach* focuses on how our genes, hormones, and nervous system interact with our environments to influence learning, personality, memory, motivation, emotions, and coping techniques.

2 How was Donna able to develop her own signaling system that involved gestures instead of words?

The *cognitive approach* examines how we process, store, and use information and how this information influences what we attend to, perceive, learn, remember, believe, and feel.

3 Why did Donna make it a rule to avoid leaving soap bubbles in the sink?

The *behavioral approach* studies how organisms learn new behaviors or modify existing ones depending on whether events in their environments reward or punish these behaviors.

4 Why did Donna believe her shoes were alive and took her places and that things made unique and unusual sounds?

The *psychoanalytic approach* stresses the influence of unconscious fears, desires, and motivations on thoughts, behaviors, and the development of personality traits and psychological problems later in life.

NOBODY NOWHERE

The Extraordinary Autobiography of an Autistic

Donna Williams

5 How was Donna able to overcome her early language problems and write a book in four weeks?

The *humanistic approach* emphasizes that each individual has great freedom in directing his or her future, a large capacity for personal growth, a considerable amount of intrinsic worth, and enormous potential for self-fulfillment.

6 Why did her mother believe that autism was caused by evil spirits? What do other peoples and cultures believe causes it?

The *cross-cultural approach* examines the influence of cultural and ethnic similarities and differences on psychological and social functioning of a culture's members.

By using one or more of these six different approaches, psychologists can look at autism from different viewpoints and stand a better chance of reaching psychology's four goals: to describe, explain, predict, and control behavior. We'll use the problems of autism and test anxiety to show how each approach examines these problems from a different perspective.

B. Modern Approaches

Biological Approach

Are their brains different?

As Donna explains, autism greatly affects all parts of her life. "Autism makes me feel everything at once without knowing what I am feeling. Or it cuts me off from feeling anything at all" (Williams, 1994, p. 237). Donna's description of how autism so changes her life leads researchers to question whether her brain has not developed normally or perhaps functions differently. To answer this kind of question, researchers would use the biological approach.

The *biological approach* examines how our genes, hormones, and nervous system interact with our environments to influence learning, personality, memory, motivation, emotions, coping techniques, and other traits and abilities.

Researchers who use the biological approach, called psychobiologists, use a number of different methods, including taking computerized photos of living brains. For example, the photo above is a side view of the living brain of an autistic child. Psychobiologists have discovered that in autistic children, one area of the brain, the cerebellum (shown in red), is abnormally developed. In 75% of autistic children the cerebellum is abnormally small and in 10% it is abnormally large (Courchesne et al., 1994). The cerebellum is normally involved in many behaviors, such as coordinating body movements, paying attention, feeling, and planning (Courchesne et al., 1996; Happé & Frith, 1996). So, we would expect a child with an abnormal cerebellum to be impaired in feeling, learning, moving, or attending, which is exactly what is observed in autistic children.

In the last 10 years, psychobiologists have shown that genetic factors influence a wide range of human behaviors, which we'll discuss throughout this text. Think of genes, which look like a twisted ladder (figure below), as a chemical alphabet for writing instructions that involve development of the brain and body as well as the manufacture of chemicals that affect everything we do, such as mental health, learning, emotions, and personality traits (Miles & Carey, 1997; Saudino & Plomin, 1997). For example, researchers found that autistic children share a genetic defect in regulating a chemical (serotonin) that has an important role in brain functioning (Cook et al., 1997). This finding illustrates the biological approach to answering questions.

Using very modern methods, psychobiologists are studying one of the oldest puzzles in psychology: how do the mind, brain, and body interact?

This very old puzzle—how the mind, brain, and body interact—reappears each time you take an exam and experience what many students know as test anxiety.

Test Anxiety

Why do my hands sweat?

You've probably experienced one component of test anxiety, called the emotional component. This component includes a variety of physiological responses, such as increased heart rate, dry mouth, and sweaty palms. An interesting feature of sweaty palms, called palmar sweating, is that it is caused by stressful feelings and is not related to changes in room temperature (Kohler & Troester, 1991). In fact, palmar sweating is one of the measures used in the lie detection test, which we'll discuss in Module 16.

As you take an exam—or even think about taking one—your stressful thoughts trigger the emotional component, which can interfere with processing information and increase your chances of making mistakes (Kleijn et al., 1994).

The figure on the right shows how easily your stressful thoughts can trigger palmar sweating, which is one measure of the emotional component of test anxiety.

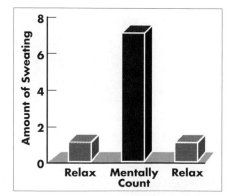

As subjects did mental arithmetic, which involved counting backward from 2007 in steps of 7, there was a significant increase in this palmar sweating. If this simple task of counting backward produced increased palmar sweating, a sign of physiological and emotional arousal, imagine the increased arousal that occurs while taking an exam!

One way to reduce the emotional and physiological component of test anxiety is through stress-reducing activities. For example, students who completed a stress-reduction program that included relaxation exercises and soothing imagining reported less test anxiety than students who were on a waiting list for the program (Register et al., 1991; Sapp, 1994). In Module 21, we'll describe several methods of reducing stress that will be especially useful in reducing the emotional component of test anxiety.

Cognitive Approach

Although autistic individuals often have difficulty developing language abilities, Donna learned to both speak and write. This demonstrates the wide range of cognitive abilities in autistic individuals, who can be divided into three groups (Koegel et al., 1994).

The first group is made up of individuals whose intellectual functioning is in the retarded range, which means their IQs are below 50, less than half of the average IQ of 100. These individuals develop no language skills, are often handicapped, and need special care.

The second group, made popular in the movie "Rain Man," is characterized by individuals who have some amazing skills. These individuals are termed autistic savants, or just savants. They have phenomenal abilities, such as performing complex mathematical calculations, memorizing vast quantities of data, and excelling at musical or artistic feats (Welling, 1994).

Individuals in the third group have IQs above 70 and develop relatively fluent speech, but they do not do well in academic subjects and have impaired social skills. These individuals, called high-functioning autistics, make up the largest group (Minshew et al., 1995).

Donna Williams is said to be a high-functioning autistic, or savant (Blakely, 1994). Although Donna did not understand words until she was an adolescent, she has learned to speak and write, has written two very creative books (Williams, 1992, 1994), and has learned French and German. To discover why autistic individuals differ in development of language and social skills, psychologists use the cognitive approach.

The *cognitive approach* focuses on how we process, store, and use information and how this information influences what we attend to, perceive, learn, remember, believe, and feel.

For example, Donna writes, "Autism makes me hear other people's words but be unable to know what the words mean. Autism stops me from finding and using my own words when I want to. Or makes me use all the words and silly things I do not want to say" (Williams, 1994, p. 237).

While psychobiologists are working to identify how brains of autistic individuals may be impaired, cognitive psychologists are studying cognitive and social problems that go with autism. For example, how is Donna able to write two books but unable to make eye contact, bear to be touched, or change her plans? Why does she begin tapping or making buzzing sounds to escape changes in her environment?

Cognitive psychologists suggest that autistic individuals may have a basic problem in processing information; specifically, they have great difficulty in imitating others and thus cannot easily learn new behaviors (Happé & Frith, 1996).

Cognitive psychologists also study many other aspects of human behavior, including learning and remembering, social interactions, development of stereotypes, and forming attitudes. In recent years, the cognitive approach has proven very useful in answering questions about human behavior (Andreasen, 1997; Wickelgren, 1997).

For example, the cognitive approach has much to say about test anxiety, especially about worrying too much.

Test Anxiety

Students who experience test anxiety must deal with two components. The first component, which we already described, is increased physiological arousal that makes up the emotional component. Cognitive psychologists have identified a second component, the cognitive component, which is excessive worrying, usually about doing poorly on exams.

Excessive worrying about your performance will interfere with your ability to read accurately, understand what you are reading, and identify important concepts (Everson et al., 1994). Considering these results, it is easy to see how excessive worrying can impair performance and result in lower grades. An interesting finding, shown in the graph on the right, was that female college freshmen reported significantly more anxiety and worry than did males (Everson et al., 1991). However, it's possible that men felt as anxious as women but neither admitted it nor reported it.

Reported Anxiety

7	Men
18	Women

In related studies, researchers found that the cognitive component could either help or hinder performance. Students who channeled their worry into complaining rather than studying performed poorly, because their worry interfered with their reading the exam material and caused them to make more reading errors (Calvo & Carreiras, 1993). In contrast, students who channeled their worry into studying performed better and achieved higher grades because they were better prepared (Endler et al., 1994).

These studies indicate that the cognitive component of test anxiety—excessive worrying—may either help or hinder cognitive performance, depending on how students channel their worries.

B. Modern Approaches

Behavioral Approach

NO LEAVING SOAP SUDS IN THE SINK!

Why have a "no-soap-suds" rule?

If Donna happened to leave soap suds in the sink, she might see a rainbow of colors reflected in the bubbles. She would become so completely absorbed in looking at the brilliant colors that she could not move; she would be in a state of temporary paralysis. Donna made her no-soap-suds rule to prevent the environment from triggering an autistic behavior—temporary paralysis. Donna and her husband, who is also autistic, have developed many rules to control some of their unwanted behaviors. Here are some of their rules: *No lining feet up with furniture; No making the fruit in the bowl symmetrical; No reading newspaper headlines in gas stations or at newsstands* (Blakely, 1994, p. 43). These rules, which help Donna and her husband avoid performing repetitive and stereotyped behaviors, illustrate the behavioral approach.

The ***behavioral approach*** analyzes how organisms learn new behaviors or modify existing ones, depending on whether events in their environments reward or punish these behaviors.

Donna and her husband's rules are examples of a basic behavioral principle: rewards or punishments can modify, change, or control behavior. Psychologists use behavioral principles to teach people to be more assertive or less depressed, to toilet train young children, and to change many other behaviors. Psychologists use behavioral principles to train animals to press levers, to use symbols to communicate, and to perform behaviors on cue in movies.

Largely through the creative work and original ideas of B. F. Skinner (1989), the behavioral approach has grown into a major force in psychology. Skinner's ideas stress the study of observable behaviors, the importance of environmental reinforcers (reward and punishment), and the exclusion of mental processes. His ideas, often referred to as strict behaviorism, continue to have an impact on psychology. In Module 10, we'll explain how Skinner's ideas were integrated into a program that taught autistic children new social behaviors that enabled them to enter and do well in public grade schools.

However, some behaviorists, such as Albert Bandura (1989b), disagree with strict behaviorism and have formulated a theory that includes mental or cognitive processes in addition to observable behaviors. According to Bandura's *social learning approach,* our behaviors are influenced not only by environmental events and reinforcers but also by observation, imitation, and thought processes. In Module 10, we'll discuss how Bandura's ideas explain why some children develop a fear of bugs.

Behaviorists have developed a number of techniques for changing behaviors. As we mentioned earlier, they used relaxation exercises to reduce the emotional component of test anxiety. Next, you'll see how they have used self-management skills to reduce the cognitive component of test anxiety.

Test Anxiety

Can I channel my worrying?

We discussed how excessive worrying, which is the cognitive component of test anxiety, can improve test performance if you can channel your worry into studying for exams. One method to channel worry into studying more is to use a system of *self-management* based on a number of behavioral principles (Kondo, 1997).

Researchers found that the following self-management practices are related to increasing studying time and achieving better grades: (1) select a place that you use exclusively for study; (2) reward yourself for studying; (3) keep a record of your study time; (4) establish priorities among projects; (5) specify a time for each task; (6) complete one task before going on to another (Long et al., 1994). Notice that each of these self-management practices derives from our basic behavioral principle: Events in your environment can modify your behaviors through rewards and punishments. As the graph on the right shows, 53% of freshmen who learned and used self-management practices survived into their sophomore year compared to the survival rate of only 7% of freshmen who did not learn self-management practices.

In later modules, we'll give many examples of how behavioral principles can be used to modify a wide range of behaviors and thought patterns.

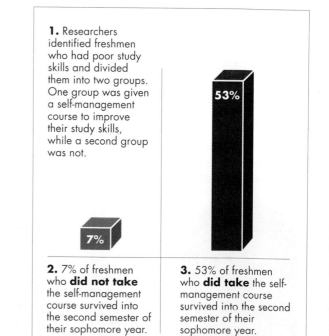

1. Researchers identified freshmen who had poor study skills and divided them into two groups. One group was given a self-management course to improve their study skills, while a second group was not.

53%

7%

2. 7% of freshmen who **did not take** the self-management course survived into the second semester of their sophomore year.

3. 53% of freshmen who **did take** the self-management course survived into the second semester of their sophomore year.

Psychoanalytic Approach

Her mother was an alcoholic and thought Donna was possessed by evil spirits. Her father was rarely around, and when he was, he and her mother had fierce arguments. Donna once cut her face with a piece of broken glass and then presented herself to her father. She felt that if she made her pain visible, her father would listen to her and see what no one else seemed to notice or be able to fix (from a personal communication). Donna's negative childhood experiences are considered very important in the psychoanalytic approach.

The *psychoanalytic approach* is based on the belief that childhood experiences greatly influence the development of later personality traits and psychological problems. It also stresses the influence of unconscious fears, desires, and motivations on thoughts and behaviors.

In the late 1800s, Sigmund Freud, a physician, treated a number of patients with psychological problems. On the basis of insights from therapy sessions, Freud proposed a number of revolutionary ideas about the human mind and personality development. For example, one hallmark of Sigmund Freud's psychoanalytic approach is the idea that the first five years have a profound effect on later personality development. According to the psychoanalytic approach, Donna's first five years with an unsympathetic mother and mostly absent father would profoundly affect her later personality development.

In addition, Freud reasoned that thoughts or feelings that make us feel fearful or guilty, that threaten our self-esteem, or that come from unresolved sexual conflicts are automatically sent deep into our *unconscious*. In turn, these unconscious, threatening thoughts and feelings give rise to anxiety, fear, or psychological problems. Because Freud's patients could not uncover their unconscious fears, he developed several techniques, such as *dream interpretation,* to bring hidden fears to the surface. Freud's idea of an unconscious force that influenced human thought and behavior was another of his revolutionary ideas.

Many of Freud's beliefs, such as the existence of unconscious feelings and fears, have survived, while other ideas, such as the all-importance of a person's first five years, have received less support. Many of Freud's terms, such as *id, ego, superego,* and *libido,* have become part of our everyday language. We'll discuss Freud's complete theory of personality in Module 19.

Unlike the biological, cognitive, and behavioral approaches, the psychoanalytic approach would search for hidden or unconscious forces behind test anxiety.

Test Anxiety

We discussed two components of test anxiety—excessive worrying and increased physiological responses—that can impair a student's performance on exams. Researchers also found that students with high test anxiety are much more likely to procrastinate than students with low test anxiety (Milgram et al., 1992a).

Procrastination refers to the tendency to always put off completing a task to the point of feeling anxious or uncomfortable about one's delay.

Researchers estimate that from 30 to 70% of students procrastinate—that is, deliberately delay completing assignments or studying for exams (Senécal et al., 1995). Some of the more common reasons students give for procrastinating include being lazy, or undisciplined, lacking motivation, or not knowing how to organize their time (Senécal et al., 1995).

However, the psychoanalytic approach would look beneath these obvious reasons and try to find personality problems that underlie the student's procrastination. Because unconscious reasons for procrastination are difficult to uncover, psychologists studied the personality of procrastinators by giving them standard paper-and-pencil personality tests.

Based on personality tests, researchers concluded that students who are regular procrastinators may have low self-esteem, be too dependent on others, or have such a strong fear of failure that they do not start the task (Ferrari, 1994). Thus, the psychoanalytic approach would point to underlying personality problems as the real cause of procrastination.

The psychoanalytic approach would also study how childhood experience may have led to being a procrastinator. For instance, researchers find that procrastinators tend to be raised by parents who stress overachievement, set unrealistic goals for their children, or link achievement to getting parental love and approval. A child who is raised by parents like these may feel very anxious when he or she fails at some task and will be tempted to put off such tasks in the future (Ferrari et al., 1997).

Psychologists know that ingrained personality characteristics, such as procrastination, remain relatively stable and persist across time unless a person makes a deliberate effort to change them. In Modules 21, 23, and 24, we'll discuss several effective methods that psychologists have developed to change personality characteristics.

B. Modern Approaches

Humanistic Approach

Can Donna develop her true potential?

Donna says that one reason she wrote her books was to escape her prison of autism. Autism has trapped her in a world where she sometimes blinks compulsively, switches lights on and off for long periods of time, rocks back and forth, freezes up, stares off into space without being able to stop herself, hates to be touched, cannot stand to enter public places, and hates to make eye contact with others (Williams, 1992).

When Donna and her husband were dating, they confided to each other that they didn't feel sexual attraction or sexual feelings like other couples. Something had been left out of their lives and made them asexual (Williams, 1994).

Donna's struggle to free herself from autism, develop close personal relationships, and reach her true potential, characterizes the humanistic approach.

The *humanistic approach* emphasizes that each individual has great freedom in directing his or her future, a large capacity for achieving personal growth, a considerable amount of intrinsic worth, and enormous potential for self-fulfillment.

Donna echoes the humanistic approach when she writes, "Autism tried to rob me of life, of friendship, of caring, of sharing, of showing interest, of using my intelligence . . . it tries to bury me alive. . . ." The last words in her book are "I CAN

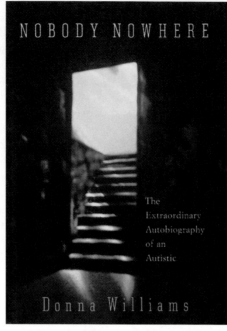

NOBODY NOWHERE

The Extraordinary Autobiography of an Autistic

Donna Williams

FIGHT AUTISM. . . . I WILL CONTROL IT. . . . IT WILL NOT CONTROL ME" (Williams, 1994, p. 238).

Humanists believe that, like Donna, we may have to struggle to reach our potential, but we have control of our fate and are free to become whatever we are capable of being. The humanistic approach emphasizes the positive side of human nature, its creative tendencies, and its inclination to build caring relationships. This concept of human nature—freedom, potential, creativity—is the most distinctive feature of the humanistic approach and sets it far apart from the behavioral and psychoanalytic approaches (DeCarvalho, 1990).

The humanistic approach officially began in the early 1960s with the publication of the *Journal of Humanistic Psychology.* One of the major figures behind establishing the journal and the humanistic approach was Abraham Maslow, who had become dissatisfied with the behavioral and psychoanalytic approaches. To paraphrase Maslow (1968), the humanistic approach was to be a new way of perceiving and thinking about the individual's capacity, freedom, and potential for growth. Many of humanism's ideas have been incorporated into approaches for counseling and psychotherapy.

Because of its free-will concept of human nature and its lack of rigorous experimental methods, many behaviorists regard the humanistic approach as more of a philosophy of life than a science of human behavior.

The humanistic approach also applies to dealing with a student's problems, such as test anxiety and procrastination.

Test Anxiety

How do students explain a poor test grade?

We've all had the experience of getting exams back and looking at the grades. Researchers wanted to know if you would give different reasons for earning high scores than earning low scores. For example, researchers asked children to explain why they performed well or poorly on reading and math exams. Children who performed well said that their good performance resulted from their effort and ability. Children who performed poorly said it was primarily because the task was too difficult and they lacked the ability (Bell et al., 1994). Based on these findings, researchers suggested that teachers be especially encouraging and supportive to children who do poorly, so that they will not give up but rather try to develop their academic potential. This advice to teachers is a good example of applying the humanistic approach to help individuals reach their highest potential.

Psychologists have also studied students whose academic performance ranged from poor to very good in order to develop a profile of a successful student. Studies showed that successful students share a number of similar characteristics: they feel competent about meeting the demands of their classes; they believe they can handle test situations; they are very good at organizing their study time and leisure time; they prepare themselves for tests and do not procrastinate (Kleijn et al., 1994). The humanistic approach would add that since successful students have found ways to reach their academic potential, all students should search for ways to reach their own potential.

Cross-Cultural Approach

Suppose you changed cultures?

When Berenice, her sister, and her mother arrived in New York from Haiti, they were poor and had to live in a cramped apartment in a very dangerous neighborhood. Her mother, a nurse, worked long hours to make ends meet. Berenice found school to be a torture since Berenice first had to learn English, as well as endure constant taunts from both Blacks and Whites.

But Berenice took her mother's advice to work extra hard and concentrate on her studies. Her efforts paid off; she got good grades. Gradually, other students recognized Berenice's ability, stopped picking on her, and even asked her to help them in their classes.

Within two years Berenice was speaking English and doing well in all her classes. The payoff came in Berenice's senior year, when she was selected class valedictorian and was accepted by the prestigious Massachusetts Institute of Technology (adapted from *Newsweek*, August 9, 1993).

Berenice's problems with changing countries and cultures and her eventual accomplishments demonstrate the concerns of one of the newer approaches in psychology, the cross-cultural approach.

*The **cross-cultural approach** studies the influence of cultural and ethnic similarities and differences on psychological and social functioning.*

In the early 1990s, about 3.7 million immigrants entered the United States, 34% coming from Mexico, 30% from Asia, 13% from Europe, 11% from Central and South America, and 2% from Africa (data from the U.S. Immigration and Naturalization Service). By the year 2000, four ethnic groups—African American, Asian, Latino, and Native American—will make up about one-third of all citizens in the United States under the age of 17. Psychologists are currently studying the attitudes, values, beliefs, social norms, and roles of different ethnic groups as well as ways to reduce intolerance and discrimination in the United States (Hall, 1997; Mays et al., 1996; Triandis, 1996).

Besides studying the impact and integration of millions of immigrants into the United States, psychologists also study cognitive and emotional factors of cultures in other parts of the world (Rogoff & Chavajay, 1995). For example, how do students in other cultures deal with test anxiety?

Test Anxiety

How do other cultures deal with test anxiety?

In several studies on test anxiety, researchers found that Mexican, Chilean, and African American inner-city grade-school children report higher levels of test anxiety than do White American students (Guida & Ludlow, 1989). Researchers suggest that higher test anxiety in Black inner-city children results from their special environmental and educational problems and that higher test anxiety in Mexican and Chilean students results from having fewer educational opportunities than their White American counterparts.

Researchers also discovered that how students evaluate success depends on their cultural values. For example, students in Chile admired successful students, whether or not they thought the success resulted from expending great effort or having natural ability. In contrast, students in America admired successful students much more if they thought the success resulted from expending great effort rather than having natural ability (Betancourt & Lopez, 1993). This study shows how the cross-cultural approach provides different and interesting answers to the same question (Gergen et al., 1996).

Many Approaches, Many Answers

Of the six approaches that we have discussed, the cross-cultural approach is the most recent. This approach began in the early 1970s with the publication of the *Journal of Cross-Cultural Psychology* and has grown in popularity (Fowers & Richardson, 1996; Gergen et al., 1996). In each module, we will highlight a cross-cultural study, which will be indicated by the symbol of multicultural people shown here on the left.

The reason modern psychology uses many different approaches to study the same behavior is that the different viewpoint of each approach serves to provide additional information. By combining information from the biological, cognitive, behavioral, psychoanalytic, humanistic, and cross-cultural approaches, psychologists stand a better chance of reaching their four goals of describing, explaining, predicting, and controlling behavior.

This symbol indicates a cultural diversity topic.

We have first discussed the approaches used by modern psychologists so that you can compare them with the different approaches used by early psychologists. As you compare early and modern approaches, you'll be able to appreciate how much psychology has changed in the past 100 years.

C. Historical Approaches

How did psychology begin? Imagine living in the late 1800s and early 1900s, when the electric light, radio, and airplane were being invented and the average human life span was about 30 years. This was the time when psychology broke away from philosophy and became a separate field of study. As they developed this new area, early psychologists hotly debated its definition, approach, and goals. We'll highlight those early psychologists whose ideas and criticisms shaped the field. We'll begin with the person considered to be the father of psychology, Wilhelm Wundt.

Structuralism: Elements of the Mind

Who established the first lab?

**WILHELM WUNDT
1832–1920**

There were no bands or celebrations when Wilhelm Wundt established the first psychology laboratory in 1879, in Leipzig, Germany. In fact, his laboratory was housed in several rooms in a shabby building that contained rather simple equipment, such as platforms, various balls, telegraph keys, and metronomes. The heavily bearded Wundt, now considered the father of psychology, would ask subjects to drop balls from a platform or listen to a metronome (figure below) and report their own sensations. Wundt and his followers were analyzing their sensations, which they thought was the key to analyzing the structure of the mind. For this reason they were called structuralists and their approach was called structuralism.

Structuralism was the study of the most basic elements, primarily sensations and perceptions, that make up our conscious mental experiences.

Just as you might assemble hundreds of pieces of a jigsaw puzzle into a completed picture, structuralists tried to combine hundreds of sensations into a complete conscious experience. Perhaps Wundt's greatest contribution was his method of introspection.

Introspection was a method of exploring conscious mental processes by asking subjects to look inward and report their sensations and perceptions.

For example, after listening to a beating metronome, the subject would be asked to report whether their sensations were pleasant, unpleasant, exciting, or relaxing. However, introspection was heavily criticized for being an unscientific method because it was solely dependent on subjects' self-reports, which could be biased, rather than on objective measurements. Although Wundt's approach was the first, it had little impact on modern psychology. The modern-day cognitive approach also studies mental processes, but with different scientific methods and much broader interests than those of Wundt.

It wasn't long before Wundt's approach was criticized for being too narrow and subjective in primarily studying sensations. These criticisms resulted in another new approach, called functionalism.

Functionalism: Functions of the Mind

Who wrote the first textbook?

**WILLIAM JAMES
1842–1910**

For twelve years, William James labored over a book called *Principles of Psychology*, which was published in 1890 and included almost every topic that is now part of psychology textbooks: learning, sensation, memory, reasoning, attention, feelings, consciousness, and a revolutionary theory of emotions.

For example, why do you feel fear when running from a raging wolf? You might answer that an angry wolf (figure below) is a terrifying creature that causes fear and makes you run—fear makes you run. Not so, according to James, who reasoned that the act of running causes a specific set of physiological responses that your brain interprets as fear—running makes you afraid. According to James, emotions were caused by physiological changes; thus, running produced fear. You'll find out if James's theory of emotions was correct in Module 16.

Unlike Wundt, who saw mental activities as composed of basic elements, James viewed mental activities as having developed through ages of evolution because of their adaptive functions, such as helping humans survive. James was interested in the goals, purposes, and functions of the mind, an approach called functionalism.

Functionalism, which was the study of the function rather than the structure of consciousness, was interested in how our minds adapt to our changing environment.

Functionalism did not last as a unique approach, but many of James's ideas grew into current areas of study, such as emotions, attention, and memory (Hunt, 1993). In addition, James suggested ways to apply psychological principles to teaching, which had a great impact on educational psychology. For all these reasons, James is considered the father of modern psychology.

Notice that James disagreed with Wundt's structural approach and pushed psychology toward looking at how the mind functions and adapts to our ever-changing world. About the same time that James was criticizing Wundt's structuralism, another group also found reasons to disagree with Wundt; this group was the Gestalt psychologists.

Gestalt Approach: Sensations versus Perceptions

MAX WERTHEIMER
1883–1943

When you see a road hazard sign like the one in the photo below, you think the lights forming the arrow are actually moving in one direction. This motion, however, is only an illusion; the lights are stationary and are only flashing on and off.

The illusion that flashing lights appear to move was first studied in 1912 by three psychologists; Max Wertheimer, Wolfgang Köhler, and Kurt Koffka. They reported that they had created the perception of movement by briefly flashing one light and then, a short time later, a second light. Although the two bulbs were fixed, the light actually appeared to move from one to the other. They called this the *phi phenomenon;* today it is known as *apparent motion.*

Wertheimer (on left) and his colleagues believed that the perception of apparent motion could not be explained by the structuralists, who said that the movement resulted from simply adding together sensations from two fixed lights. Instead, Wertheimer argued that perceptual experiences, such as perceiving moving lights, resulted from analyzing a "whole pattern," or, in German, a *Gestalt.*

The ***Gestalt approach*** emphasized that perception is more than the sum of its parts and studied how sensations are assembled into meaningful perceptual experiences.

In our example, Gestalt psychologists would explain that your experience of perceiving moving traffic lights is much more than and very different from what is actually happening—fixed lights flashing in sequence. These kinds of findings could not be explained by the structuralists and pointed out the limitations of their approach (Hunt, 1993).

After all these years, many principles of the Gestalt approach are still used to explain how we perceive objects. We'll discuss many of the Gestalt principles of perception in Module 6.

Behaviorism: Observable Behaviors

JOHN B. WATSON
1878–1958

"Give me a dozen healthy infants, well-formed, and my own special world to bring them up in and I'll guarantee to take any one at random and train him to become any type of specialist I might select—doctor, lawyer, artist . . ." (Watson, 1924).

These words come from John B. Watson, who published a landmark paper in 1913 titled "Psychology as a Behaviorist Views It." In it, he rejected Wundt's structuralism and its study of mental elements and conscious processes. He rejected introspection as a psychological technique because its results could not be scientifically verified by other psychologists. Instead, John Watson very boldly stated that psychology should be considered an objective, experimental science, whose goal should be the analysis of observable behaviors and the prediction and control of those behaviors. It is a small step from these ideas to Watson's famous boast, "Give me a dozen healthy infants . . . ," which illustrates the behavioral approach.

The ***behavioral approach*** emphasized the objective, scientific analysis of observable behaviors.

From the 1920s to the 1960s, behaviorism was the dominant force in American psychology. Part of this dominance was due to the work of B. F. Skinner and other behaviorists, who expanded and developed Watson's ideas into the modern-day behavioral approach, which is fully discussed in Module 10. However, beginning in the 1970s and continuing into the present, behaviorism's dominance was challenged by the cognitive approach, whose popularity in the 1990s may be surpassing behaviorism (Friman et al., 1993).

Survival of Approaches

The survival of each approach—structuralism, functionalism, Gestalt, and behaviorism—depended on its ability to survive its criticisms. Criticisms of Wundt's structural approach gave rise to the functional approach of James and the Gestalt approach of Wertheimer, Köhler, and Koffka. Criticisms of all three approaches—structural, functional, and Gestalt—gave rise to Watson's behavioral approach. Another approach, Sigmund Freud's psychoanalytic approach (see page 9), that emphasized the influence of unconscious processes, disagreed with Watson's strict behavioral approach, and developed largely in parallel to these other approaches. These disagreements in approaches resulted in heated debates among early psychologists, but they helped psychology develop into the scientific field it is today.

Although early American psychologists differed in their approaches, they shared one underlying theme that was a sign of their times. They discriminated against women and minorities in both academic and career settings. Such discriminatory practices were widespread, and we'll examine that issue next.

D. Cultural Diversity: Early Discrimination

Because psychologists focus on studying and understanding human behavior, you would expect them to be among the first to recognize the mistreatment of and discrimination against other groups. However, psychologists are human and being human they knowingly or unknowingly adopted and carried out the discriminatory practices that were operating at the time. This means that, for the first 75 of its more than 100 years of existence, the academic policies and career opportunities of American psychology were determined by white males, who both intentionally and unintentionally discriminated against women and people of color. Here are just a few examples.

Women in Psychology

Why couldn't she enter graduate school?

The reason Mary Calkins (on right) could not enter graduate school was that she was a woman, and many universities (Johns Hopkins, Harvard, Columbia) would not admit women. Since Calkins was a faculty member and had established a laboratory in psychology at Wellesley College in 1891, she petitioned and was allowed to take seminars at Harvard. There, she completed all requirements for a Ph.D. and was recommended for a doctorate by her professors, but the Harvard administration declined to grant it because she was a woman (Furumoto, 1989). It was not until 1908 that a woman, Margaret Washburn, was awarded a Ph.D. in psychology.

Even after women began obtaining doctorates, the only positions open to them were teaching jobs at women's colleges or normal schools, which trained high-school teachers (Furumoto & Scarborough, 1986). During the past 25 years, women have made great progress in the field. However, even though women currently earn more Ph.D.s in psychology than men, in 1991 there were more full-time male psychologists (39,180) than women (20,100). In addition, female psychologists earn less than male psychologists, and few women are editors of psychology journals (Martin, 1995). Not only did women face discrimination in psychology, but so did people of color.

Minorities in Psychology

Why so few minority students?

In psychology's early days, only a few Northern White universities accepted and encouraged Black students, while all Southern White universities denied admission to Black students.

The first African American to receive a Ph.D. in psychology was Ruth Howard (photo below) who graduated from the University of Minnesota in 1934. She had a successful career as a clinical psychologist and school consultant.

Between 1920 and 1966, only eight Ph.D.s were awarded to Black students, compared to 3,767 doctorates to Whites (Guthrie, 1976). As late as 1994, only about 200 Ph.Ds were awarded to African Americans in all the social sciences, which include psychology, sociology, and several other areas (Holden, 1996).

During the early 1900s, few degrees were awarded to Hispanics. One early exception was George Sanchez (photo below), who conducted pioneering work on the cultural bias of intelligence tests given to minority students. Sanchez criticized the claim that Mexican Americans were mentally inferior, saying that this claim was based solely on intelligence tests. Sanchez showed that intelligence tests contained many questions that were biased against minorities and thus resulted in their lower scores (Guthrie, 1976).

From the founding of the American Psychological Association in 1892 up until 1990, its cumulative membership was 128,000. Of those members, only 700 were African American, 700 were Latino, and 70 were Native American. This limited minority membership indicates how much further psychology must go to remedy its earlier discriminatory practices (Barinaga, 1996).

Righting the Wrongs

How much success?

Almost every major university and college now has a program to recruit, aid, and help minority students complete degrees in psychology. The American Psychological Association has recognized the need to recruit minority members and has formed a special group to carry out this goal. An increasing number of journals *(Psychology of Women Quarterly, Hispanic Journal of Behavioral Science, and Journal of Black Psychology)* are promoting the causes of women and minorities and are fighting discriminatory practices (DeAngelis, 1966).

However, in 1997, California and Texas passed state laws banning affirmative action programs. As a result, university enrollments of Hispanic and African American students in different programs dropped from 3 to 80% in these states (Barinaga, 1997). These disappointing decreases question whether all affirmative action programs will be dropped and whether other programs can be developed to help disadvantaged students (Goldsborough, 1997).

Next, check your memory by taking the Concept Review.

CONCEPT REVIEW

1. The systematic, scientific study of behaviors and mental processes is called _____.

2. The four goals of psychology are to (a)_____ what organisms do, to (b)_____ the causes of behavior, to (c)_____ behavior in new situations, and to (d)_____ behavior, which has both positive and negative aspects.

3. The approach that focuses on how one's nervous system, hormones, and genes interact with the environment is called the _____ approach.

4. The approach that studies how people think, solve problems, and process information is called the _____ approach.

5. The approach that analyzes how environmental rewards and punishments shape, change, or motivate behavior is called the _____ approach.

6. The approach that stresses the influence of unconscious feelings, fears, or desires on the development of behavior, personality, and psychological problems is called the (a)_____ approach. This approach also emphasizes the importance of early (b)_____ experiences.

7. The approach that emphasizes freedom of choice, self-fulfillment, and attaining one's potential is called the (a)_____ approach. Many of this approach's concepts have been taken up and used in (b)_____.

8. The newest approach, which focuses on cultural and ethnic influences on behavior, is called the _____ approach.

9. Wundt studied the elements that made up the conscious mind and called this approach (a)_____. Subjects were asked to observe the workings of their minds, a technique that Wundt called (b)_____. Modern-day psychologists who study mental activities with a more objective and scientific methods are said to use the (c)_____ approach.

10. William James disagreed with Wundt's structuralism and instead emphasized the functions, goals, and purposes of the mind and its adaptation to the environment; he called this approach (a)_____. James also applied the principles of psychology to teaching, so his approach had a great effect on the field of (b)_____ psychology.

11. Some psychologists disagreed with Wundt's approach of structuralism and instead believed that perceptions are more than the sum of many individual (a)_____. These psychologists called their approach the (b)_____ approach, which studied how sensations were assembled into meaningful (c)_____.

12. John Watson disagreed with Wundt's approach, which was called (a)_____ and disagreed with Wundt's technique of studying the mind, which was called (b)_____. Instead, Watson emphasized the objective, scientific analysis of observable behaviors, which was known as the (c)_____ approach. Later, this approach became a dominant force in psychology through the work of behaviorist (d)_____.

Answers: 1. psychology; 2. (a) describe, (b) explain, (c) predict, (d) control; 3. biological; 4. cognitive; 5. behavioral; 6. (a) psychoanalytic, (b) childhood; 7. (a) humanistic, (b) counseling or psychotherapy; 8. cross-cultural; 9. (a) structuralism, (b) introspection, (c) cognitive; 10. (a) functionalism, (b) educational; 11. (a) sensations, (b) Gestalt, (c) perceptions; 12. (a) structuralism, (b) introspection, (c) behavioral, (d) B. F. Skinner.

E. Research Focus: Class Notes
Best Strategy for Taking Class Notes?

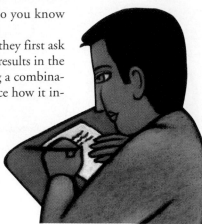

How good are your class notes?

As you listen to lectures in class, you will probably be taking notes. But do you know how to take the best notes?

When psychologists study some particular behavior, such as note-taking, they first ask a very specific research question: Which method or strategy for taking notes results in the best performance on exams? One researcher answered this question by using a combination of behavioral and cognitive approaches (King, 1992). As we describe this interesting study, notice how it involves the four goals of psychology, beginning with the first goal, describing behavior.

1st Goal: Describe Behavior

The researcher divided college students into three different groups. Each group was given a different method or strategy for taking notes. As described below, students practiced three different strategies for taking notes: review notes, summarize notes, and answer questions about notes.

A. REVIEW NOTES

The strategy that most students use is to try to write down as much as possible of what the professor says. Then, before exams, students review their notes, hoping they took good class notes.

B. SUMMARIZE NOTES

Students took notes as usual but, after the lecture, used their notes to write a summary of the lecture in their own words.

Students were shown how to identify a main topic and, in their own words, write a sentence about it. Then they identified a subtopic and wrote a sentence that related it to the main topic. When linked together, these sentences created a summary of the lecture, written in the student's own words.

C. ANSWER QUESTIONS ABOUT NOTES

Students took notes as usual but, after the lecture, used their notes to ask and answer questions about the lecture material. Students were given a set of 13 general questions, such as: **What is the main idea of . . . ? How would you use . . . to . . . ? What is a new example of . . . ? What is the difference between . . . and . . . ?** Students answered each of these questions using their class notes.

After practicing one of these three note-taking strategies, students watched a videotaped lecture and used their particular strategy for taking notes.

2nd Goal: Explain Behavior

A week after each group had watched a videotaped lecture, they were given an exam. The graph on the right shows that the group who used the strategy of taking notes plus answering questions scored significantly higher than the other two groups. The researcher explained that students who took notes and then answered questions about their notes retained more information than students who employed the other two strategies (King, 1992).

Average Score on Exam

34	Review notes
45	Summarize notes
51	Answer questions

3rd Goal: Predict Behavior

On the basis of these results, the researcher predicts that students who use the strategy that combines note-taking with answering questions are likely to retain more information and perform better on exams than students who use traditional note-taking methods, such as writing as much as they can and then reviewing their notes before exams.

4th Goal: Control Behavior

Students can increase their chances of getting better grades by taking the time to learn a better note-taking strategy. This new strategy involves taking notes and then answering, in their own words, a series of general questions about the lecture material. Although this new note-taking strategy takes a little time to learn, the payoff will be better performance on exams. Thus, this study demonstrates how students can gain control over their test-taking performance by adopting a better strategy of preparing for exams.

This study is an example of how psychologists answered a very practical and important question about how best to take lecture notes. We'll use the Research Focus to show how psychologists use different approaches and research techniques to answer a variety of questions.

Each time you see the "lightning bolt," it will indicate a Research Focus, which occurs in each module.

Although a large percentage of psychologists engage in research, you'll see next how many others work in a variety of career settings that may or may not involve research.

Psychologist versus Psychiatrist

What's a psychologist?

Many students think that psychologists are primarily counselors and therapists, even though advanced degrees in psychology are awarded in a dozen different areas. Obtaining an advanced degree in psychology requires that one finish college and spend about two to three years in postgraduate study to obtain a master's degree or four to five years in postgraduate study to obtain a Ph.D. Some careers or work settings require a master's degree, while others require a Ph.D.

Many students are confused about the difference between a psychologist, a clinical psychologist, and a psychiatrist.

A *psychologist* is usually someone who has completed four to five years of postgraduate education and has obtained a Ph.D. in psychology.

Some states permit individuals with master's degrees to call themselves psychologists.

A *clinical psychologist* has a Ph.D., has specialized in a clinical subarea, and has spent an additional year in a supervised therapy setting to gain experience in diagnosing and treating a wide range of abnormal behaviors.

Clinical psychologists do not assess physical or neurological causes of mental problems or prescribe drugs.

A *psychiatrist* is a medical doctor (M.D.) who has spent several years in clinical training, which includes diagnosing possible physical and neurological causes of abnormal behaviors and treating these behaviors, often with prescription drugs.

If you become a psychologist, you will have to decide which of the following career settings to choose.

Many Career Settings

Are psychologists usually therapists?

As you can see in the pie chart below, the majority (55%) of psychologists are therapists, while the remaining work in four other settings. In the United States and Canada, most psychologists have a Ph.D., which requires four to five years of study after college. In many other countries, most psychologists have a college degree, which requires four to five years of study after high school (Rosenzweig, 1992). Since the 1950s, there has been an increase in psychologists who provide therapy/health services and a decline in those who work in academic/research settings.

The U.S. Department of Labor predicts that employment opportunities for psychologists will grow much faster than the average for other occupations through the year 2005 (Burnette, 1994). Here's a breakdown of where psychologists in the United States currently work.

55% The largest percentage (55%) of psychologists work as clinical psychologists in either a *private practice or therapy setting,* such as a psychological or psychiatric clinic; a mental health center; a psychiatric, drug, or rehabilitation ward of a hospital; or a private office. The duties of clinical psychologists might involve doing individual or group therapy; helping patients with problems involving drugs, stress, weight, sleep, or chronic pain; designing programs for healthier living; or testing patients for psychological problems that developed from some neurological problem.

27% The second largest percentage (27%) of psychologists work in the *academic settings* of universities and colleges. Academic psychologists often engage in some combination of classroom teaching, mentoring or helping students, and doing research in their areas of interest.

8% The third largest percentage (8%) of psychologists work in a variety of other kinds of jobs and career settings.

6% The fourth largest percentage (6%) of psychologists work in *industrial settings,* such as businesses, corporations, and consulting firms. These psychologists, often called industrial/organizational psychologists, may work at selecting personnel, increasing production, or improving job satisfaction and employer-employee relations.

4% The smallest percentage (4%) work in *secondary schools and other settings.* For example, secondary school psychologists conduct academic and career testing and provide counseling for minor psychological problems.

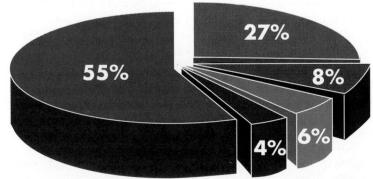

If you are thinking of entering the field of psychology today, you have a wide and exciting range of career choices. If you do decide to engage in research, we'll next discuss seven of the more popular research areas that psychologists choose.

G. Research Areas

Areas of Specialization

Which area should I choose?

If you enter graduate school in psychology, you will be expected to specialize in one of the seven areas into which psychology has been divided. Students often find it difficult to choose only one area, since they may be interested in two or three. However, the reason for choosing one is that each area includes such an enormous amount of information that it takes great effort to master even one. As you read about each research area, think about which one you might prefer. (Percentages given below do not add up to 100% because some miscellaneous areas are not included.)

Social and Personality

How important are first impressions?

How does one develop certain personality traits?

Why do we use stereotypes?

What causes aggression?

These questions come from two different and sometimes overlapping areas of social psychology and personality psychology.

Social psychology involves the study of social interactions, stereotypes, prejudices, attitudes, conformity, group behaviors, and aggression.

Personality psychology involves the study of personality development, personality change, assessment, and abnormal behaviors.

Many social/personality psychologists work in academic settings, but some work as consultants and personnel managers in business. About 22% of psychologists choose social psychology and 5% choose personality.

Developmental

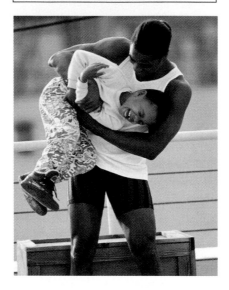

When does a newborn recognize his or her parents?

What happens to teenagers at puberty?

When does a child know he or she is a boy or girl?

You would be asking these kinds of questions if you were a developmental psychologist.

Developmental psychology examines moral, social, emotional, and cognitive development throughout a person's entire life.

Some developmental psychologists focus on changes in infancy and childhood, while others trace changes through adolescence, adulthood, and old age. They work in academic settings and may consult on day care or programs for the aging. About 25% of psychologists choose this specialty.

Experimental

Why does an animal press a bar to obtain food?

Can learning principles be used to treat a phobia?

Why do we feel fear when we see a snake?

What is taste aversion?

These kinds of questions interest experimental psychologists.

Experimental psychology includes areas of sensation, perception, learning, human performance, motivation, and emotion.

Experimental psychologists conduct much of their research under carefully controlled laboratory conditions, with both animal and human subjects. About 16% of psychologists specialize in experimental psychology. Most work in academic settings, but some also work in business, industry, and government.

Biological

How do brain cells change during Alzheimer's disease?

Do people have predispositions for mental disorders?

Does coffee improve your memory?

Do genes affect your intelligence and personality?

Physiological psychologists or psychobiologists study the biological basis of learning and memory; the effects of brain damage; the causes of sleep and wakefulness; the basis of hunger, thirst, and sex; the effects of stress on the body; and the ways in which drugs influence behavior.

Biological psychology or *psychobiology* involves research on the physical and chemical changes that occur during stress, learning, and emotions, as well as how our genetic makeup and nervous system interact with our environments and influence our behaviors.

Psychobiologists work in academic settings, hospitals, and private research laboratories. About 8% of psychologists choose this area.

Cognitive

What was unique about Einstein's thought processes?

Can you learn something but not remember it?

Does memory get worse with age?

What are repressed memories?

If these questions interest you, think about being a cognitive psychologist.

Cognitive psychology involves how we process, store, and retrieve information and how cognitive processes influence our behaviors.

Cognitive research includes memory, thinking, language, creativity, and decision making. Newer areas, such as artificial intelligence, combine knowledge of the brain's functions with computer programming in an attempt to duplicate human thinking and intelligence. About 5% of psychologists select this area.

Psychometrics

What do college entrance tests prove?

What career best fits my abilities?

How do tests assess abnormal behaviors?

These questions introduce an area called psychometrics, which involves the construction, administration, and interpretation of tests.

Psychometrics focuses on the measurement of people's abilities, skills, intelligence, personality, and abnormal behaviors.

To accomplish their goals, psychologists in this area must develop a wide range of tests, which must be continually updated and checked for usefulness and cultural biases. Some of these tests are used to assess people's abilities, as well as to predict their performance in certain situations—for example, in college. About 5% of psychologists select this area.

Decisions

If you decide to become a psychologist, you will need to make a series of decisions. Should I obtain a master's degree or Ph.D.? Where do I prefer to work—private practice or clinic, academic, industry/business, or school setting? Which of the seven research areas should I specialize in—social, personality, developmental, experimental, biological, cognitive, or psychometrics? After making all these decisions, you are on your way to having a very interesting career.

Now, we're going to take findings from several research areas, including personality, experimental, and cognitive, and give you tips on how to improve your study skills.

H. Application: Study Skills

Improving Study Habits

Which problems do over 50% of freshmen report?

In a survey of college freshmen, 57% reported that they had poor study habits, and 54% said that they had problems managing their time (Thombs, 1995). We'll discuss ways to deal with both of these problems, beginning with methods to improve study habits.

Common complaint. The most common student complaint that I hear after exams is, "I read the book and went over my notes three times and still got a C." This complaint points to the most common mistake students make in studying for exams. Because students do read the material and go over their notes several times, they may have a general feeling that they know the material. For example, you have just read about the six modern approaches, the historical approaches, and the differences between a psychologist, clinical psychologist, and psychiatrist. Having read this material, you may generally feel that you know it. However, researchers have discovered a startling fact: There is almost no relationship between how well students think they know material and how well they perform on an exam (Cull & Zechmeister, 1994; Mazzoni & Cornoldi, 1993).

Poor judges. The reason students tend to be poor judges of what they know is that they base their judgments more on what they *generally* know rather than on what they *specifically* remember (Glenberg et al., 1987). For example, you might generally remember the six approaches. However, on an exam you will be asked for specific information, such as names and definitions. One of the best ways to judge how prepared you are for an exam is to test yourself and get feedback from answering specific questions. For instance, can you list the six approaches and define each one? Because answering specific questions is one way to judge your learning, we have built specific questions and answers into this text. You can test yourself by answering the questions in the Concept Review in each module and by answering questions in the Summary Test at the end of each module.

Time management. A common problem that students have involves managing their time—specifically, underestimating how long it will take to study all the material. For example, researchers found that about 50% of college students repeatedly anticipated finishing a task earlier than they actually did (Buehler et al., 1994). Part of the problem is that students do not allow enough time for studying more difficult items. Researchers found that students who plan to set aside extra time for studying more difficult items increase their chances of remembering the material (Nelson, 1993). One way to achieve better time management involves setting the right kinds of goals.

> **REMEMBER:**
> *To judge how well prepared you are for an exam, ask yourself specific questions about the material. You can do that by taking the tests built into each module—the Concept Review and the Summary Test.*

Setting Goals

What's the best kind of goal to set?

Another way to better manage your study time is to set the right goals, which can vary from studying for a certain period of time to studying until you feel you are well prepared. Which of the following goals do you think would make your study time more efficient and improve your test performance?

1 Set a **time goal,** such as studying 10 hours a week or more, and then keep track of your study time during the semester.

2 Set a **general goal,** such as trying to study hard and stay on schedule; then, try to reach this goal during the semester.

3 Set a **specific performance goal,** such as answering at least 80% of the Summary Test questions correctly for each module.

To determine which of these three goals leads to more effective studying, researchers told three different groups of students to follow time goals, general goals, or specific performance goals when they studied on their own. The researchers found that students who set specific performance goals did significantly better on the final exam than students who set time or general goals (Morgan, 1985). Thus, if you want to improve your study skills, you should think less about the total time you study and concentrate more on reaching a specific performance goal every week. For example, the first week your goal might be to correctly answer 80% of the Summary Test questions. Once you have reached this goal, you could aim to answer 90% of the questions correctly. Setting performance goals rather than time goals is the key to better time management (Barling et al., 1996).

One way to motivate yourself to reach your performance goals is to reward yourself at the right times.

> **REMEMBER:**
> *One way to make your study time more efficient is to set a specific performance goal and keep track of your progress.*

Rewarding Yourself

What if you reach a goal?

One problem many students have is getting and staying motivated. One reliable solution is to give yourself a reward when you reach a specific goal, such as answering 80% of the questions correctly. The reward may be a special treat (such as a record, meal, movie, or time with friends) or a positive statement (such as "I'm doing really well" or "I'm going to get a good grade on the test"). Giving yourself a reward (self-reinforcement) is an effective way to improve performance (Hayes et al., 1986).

> *REMEMBER:*
> *Immediately after you reach a specific goal, give yourself a reward, which will both maintain and improve your motivation.*

Taking Notes

What are two big mistakes?

Another way to improve your performance is to take great notes. Students generally make two kinds of mistakes in taking notes. One is to try to write down everything the instructor says, which is impossible and leads to confusing notes. The other is to mechanically copy down terms or concepts that they do not understand but hope to learn by sheer memorization, which is difficult. Researchers have several suggestions for taking good notes:

1 Write down the information in your own words. This approach will ensure that you understand the material and will increase your chances of remembering it.

2 Use headings or an outline format. This method will help you better organize and remember the material.

3 Try to associate new lecture or text material with material that you already know. It's easier to remember new information if you can relate it to your existing knowledge. That is the reason we have paired terms in the Concept Review section with illustrations, drawings, and photos that you are familiar with from earlier in the text.

4 As we discussed in Research Focus (p. 16), you can improve your note-taking by asking yourself questions, such as: What is the main idea of . . . ? What is an example of . . . ? How is . . . related to what we studied earlier? Writing the answers in your own words will give you a better chance of remembering the material for exams (King, 1992).

Even though you may take great notes and set performance goals, if you procrastinate and put off getting started, as 30 to 70% of students report doing, your best-laid plans will come to nothing (Senécal et al., 1995). We already discussed some of the reasons behind procrastination (page 9) and here we'll look at ways to overcome it.

> *REMEMBER:*
> *Go through your lecture notes, ask questions, and write down answers in your own words.*

Stopping Procrastination

How to get started?

Some students find the task of reading assignments, studying for exams, or writing papers so difficult that they cannot bring themselves to start. If you have problems with procrastinating, here are three things you should do to get started (Peterson, 1997).

1 *Stop thinking about the final goal*—reading 30 pages or taking two midterm exams—which may seem too overwhelming.

2 Break the final assignment down into a number of *smaller goals* that are less overwhelming and easier to accomplish. Work on the first small goal; and when you finish it, go on to the next small goal. Continue until you have completed all the small goals.

3 Write down a *realistic schedule* for reaching each of your smaller goals. This schedule should indicate the time and place for study and what you will accomplish that day. Use a variety of self-reinforcements to stay on your daily schedule and accomplish your specific goals.

Everyone procrastinates a little, but it becomes a problem if you continually put off starting important projects with deadlines, such as exams and papers (Harriott & Ferrari, 1966). Take the advice of professionals on stopping procrastination: get organized, set specific goals, and reward yourself (Zane, 1996).

If you adopt these tested methods for improving your study skills, you'll greatly increase your chances of being a successful student (Pressley et al., 1997; Tice & Baumeister, 1997).

> *REMEMBER:*
> *One of the most effective ways to start a large assignment is to break it down into a series of smaller goals and work on each goal separately.*

Unusual Excuses for Missing Exams

✔ I missed the exam because of my uncle's funeral, and I can't take the make-up tomorrow because I just found out my aunt has a brain tumor.

✔ I can't be at the exam because my cat is having kittens and I'm her coach.

✔ I want to reschedule the final because my grandmother is a nun.

✔ I can't take the exam on Monday because my mom is getting married on Sunday and I'll be too drunk to drive back to school.

✔ I couldn't be at the exam because I had to attend the funeral of my girlfriend's dog.

✔ I can't take the the test Friday because my mother is having a vasectomy. (Bernstein, 1993, p. 4)

A. DEFINITION & GOALS

1. The broad definition of psychology is the systematic, scientific study of (a)_____ and (b)_____. The term in (a) refers to observable responses of animals and humans, and the term in (b) refers to processes that are not directly observable, such as thoughts, ideas, and dreams.

2. All psychologists agree that the first three goals of psychology are to (a)_____ what organisms do, to (b)_____ how organisms behave as they do, and to (c)_____ how they will respond in the future and in different situations. Some psychologists add a fourth goal, which is to (d)_____ behavior and thus curb or eliminate psychological and social problems.

B. MODERN APPROACHES

3. Because behavior is often so complex, psychologists study it using six different approaches. The approach that focuses on how a person's genetic makeup, hormones, and nervous system interact with the environment to influence a wide range of behaviors is called the _____ approach.

4. The approach that studies how organisms learn new behaviors or change or modify existing ones in response to influences from the environment is called the (a)_____ approach. There are two versions of this approach. One that primarily studies observable behaviors and excludes mental events is called (b)_____ and is best expressed by the ideas of B. F. Skinner; the other, which includes observable behaviors plus cognitive processes, is called the (c)_____ approach and is expressed by the ideas of Albert Bandura and his colleagues.

5. An approach that examines how our unconscious fears, desires, and motivations influence behaviors, thoughts, and personality and cause psychological problems is called the _____ approach. Sigmund Freud developed this approach, as well as the technique of dream interpretation to bring unconscious ideas to the surface.

6. The approach that investigates how people attend to, store, and process information and how this information affects learning, remembering, feeling, and believing is called the _____ approach.

7. An approach that emphasizes people's capacity for personal growth, freedom in choosing their future, and potential for self-fulfillment is called the _____ approach. One of the founders of this approach was Abraham Maslow.

8. The approach that studies how cultural and ethnic similarities and differences influence psychological and social functioning is called the _____ approach.

C. HISTORICAL APPROACHES

9. Considered the father of psychology, Wilhelm Wundt developed an approach called (a)_____. This approach studied the elements of the conscious mind by using a self-report technique, called (b)_____. Wundt's approach was the beginning of today's cognitive approach.

10. Disagreeing with Wundt's approach, William James said that it was important to study functions rather than elements of the mind. Accordingly, James studied the functions of consciousness as well as how mental processes continuously flow and adapt to input from the environment. This approach is called _____. James's ideas contributed to the modern area of psychology and has also influenced educational psychology.

11. Also disagreeing with Wundt's approach was a group of psychologists, led by Wertheimer, Köhler, and Koffka, who stated that perceptions cannot be explained by breaking them down into individual elements or sensations. Instead, they believed that perceptions are more than the sum of individual sensations, an idea called the _____ approach.

12. Another psychologist who disagreed with Wundt's approach was John B. Watson. He stated that psychology should use scientific principles to study only observable behaviors and not mental events, an approach called _____. Watson's approach gave rise to the modern behavioral approach.

D. CULTURAL DIVERSITY: EARLY DISCRIMINATION

13. During the first 75 of its more than 100 years of existence, the field of psychology discriminated against (a)_____ and (b)_____, as indicated by the very limited number of these individuals who were granted Ph.D.s or offered positions in major universities. During the past 25 years, the

American Psychological Association, minority organizations, and most universities and colleges have been actively recruiting minorities and helping them enter the field of psychology.

E. RESEARCH FOCUS: CLASS NOTES

14. Three different strategies for note-taking were studied: note-taking plus review, which means writing down almost everything the instructor says; note-taking plus questions, which means asking and answering questions about the lecture material; and note-taking plus summary, which means writing a summary of the lecture in your own words. The note-taking strategy that resulted in the highest exam grades involved (a)_____ and the note-taking strategy that resulted in the lowest exam grades involved (b)_____.

F. CAREERS IN PSYCHOLOGY

15. There are five major settings in which psychologists work and establish careers. The largest percentage of psychologists work in private practice or (a)_____ settings, where they diagnose and help clients with psychological problems. The second largest group work in (b)_____ settings, doing a combination of teaching and research. The third largest group work in a (c)_____ of settings. The fourth largest group work in (d)_____ settings, where they are involved in selecting personnel, increasing job satisfaction, and improving worker-management relations. The fifth largest group work in other settings, such as (e)_____, where they do academic testing and counseling.

G. RESEARCH AREAS

16. There are six common subareas in which psychologists specialize. Those who are interested in prejudice, attitudes, and group behaviors or in personality development and change specialize in (a)_____ psychology. Those interested in social, emotional, and cognitive changes across the life span specialize in (b)_____ psychology. Those interested in studying sensation, perceptions, learning,

and motivation, often under laboratory conditions, specialize in (c)_____ psychology. Those interested in the interaction among genes, the nervous system, and the environment choose (d)_____. Those interested in how people process, store, and retrieve information choose (e)_____ psychology, and those who are interested in the measurement and testing of skills, abilities, personality, and mental problems specialize in (f)_____.

H. APPLICATION: STUDY SKILLS

17. A common mistake that many students make is that, when they plan their study schedules, they often _____ the time it will take to complete a task.

18. Another common mistake that students make is that they think they know the material after reading the text and reviewing their notes. A better way to judge how prepared you are for an exam is to ask yourself specific (a)_____ rather than to trust your judgment about what you think you know. A good way to make your study time more efficient is to set specific (b)_____ and keep track of your progress. Immediately after you reach a specific performance goal, give yourself a (c)_____, which will both maintain and improve your motivation. To improve your lecture notes, try to associate new lecture material with what you already know, and use your notes to ask and answer (d)_____ in your own words. One of the most effective ways to overcome a strong tendency to delay starting a task, known as (e)_____, is to stop thinking about the final goal. Instead, break down a large assignment into a series of smaller goals and work on each goal separately. Finally, it's best to set a realistic (f)_____ in order to accomplish each of the smaller goals.

Answers:
1. (a) behaviors, (b) mental processes; 2. (a) describe, (b) explain, (c) predict, (d) control; 3. biological; 4. (a) behavioral, (b) strict behaviorism, (c) social learning; 5. psychoanalytic; 6. cognitive; 7. humanistic; 8. cross-cultural; 9. (a) structuralism, (b) introspection; 10. functionalism; 11. Gestalt; 12. behaviorism; 13. (a) women, (b) minorities; 14. (a) answering questions, (b) reviewing notes; 15. (a) therapy or clinical, (b) academic, (c) variety, (d) industrial, (e) schools; 16. (a) social and personality, (b) developmental, (c) experimental, (d) biological or physiological psychology, (e) cognitive, (f) psychometrics; 17. underestimate; 18. (a) questions, (b) performance goals, (c) reward, (d) questions, (e) procrastination, (f) schedule.

CRITICAL THINKING

QUESTIONS

WHEN RESEARCH IS SWEPT UNDER THE RUG
by Beth Azar

1. Why have people throughout history opposed scientific findings that make them uncomfortable?

2. Why might psychological research be a prime target for such scrutiny?

3. What is the author's point of view on this topic?

4. Do you agree that "science is basically a conservative enterprise"?

5. Are there reasons other than ideological disagreement that might lead someone to question research findings?

6. What arguments could be made that it is appropriate to question controversial research?

Since the time of Copernicus, theories and findings that contradict traditional wisdom have been met with skepticism and scorn. Politicians, the public, and even some scientists themselves have railed against data that defy current thinking or are not "politically correct."

Behavioral research is particularly rife with controversial topics that people would rather sweep under the carpet, researchers say. Studies that hint at problems with child care could lead people to believe women belong at home with their children. Intelligence research often brings up uncomfortable questions about racial differences. Research findings that tout more comprehensive sex education in schools offend some traditional moral and religious beliefs. Some researchers in these fields have had their work derided, ignored, or censored because of their findings.

Yet while such research ignites emotions, it is essential for developing well-informed public policy. Most researchers argue that no line of research should be banned if it's well done and peer reviewed. However, some scientists admit that certain studies don't deserve the highest priority from funding agencies or journals if they address topics that have the potential to hurt certain populations with little promise of helping them.

"Science is basically a conservative enterprise," says psychologist Brian Gladue, PhD, of the University of Cincinnati, who studies the relationship between hormone levels and behaviors such as aggression and sexuality. "The people who control funding, tenure, and publishing tend to stick with what they know. And those who want to break out and create new knowledge do so at their own risk."

Psychologist Jay Belsky, PhD, of Pennsylvania State University, was labeled a sexist by women's groups and other psychologists when, based on his own research and a review of others' work, he concluded that more than 20 hours of day care during the first year of life was associated with insecure infant-mother attachments and elevated levels of aggression and noncompliance in preschool and early elementary school.

He's just one example of how scientists who conduct research on politically hot topics risk being labelled based on what their data say, not what their personal beliefs are.

Source: *APA Monitor,* August 1997.

Study Questions

A. **Definition & Goals**—How would you rank the four goals of psychology in terms of importance? (See answer in Critical Thinking Appendix)

B. **Modern Approaches**—How would psychologists use the six modern approaches to study whether alcoholism runs in families?

C. **Historical Approaches**—Do any of these historical approaches match your stereotype of what psychology is all about?

D. **Cultural Diversity: Early Discrimination**—Why would discriminatory practices exist in psychology, an area devoted to studying human behavior? (See answer in Critical Thinking Appendix)

E. **Research Focus: Class Notes**—What could you do to improve your note-taking skills?

F. **Careers in Psychology**—If you're thinking about a career in psychology, what setting would you choose?

G. **Research Areas**—Which of the six subareas of psychology would you study to help people manage stress?

H. **Application: Study Skills**—What changes would you make to study most efficiently? (See answer in Critical Thinking Appendix)

Web Sites & Learning Activities

● BROOKS/COLE ONLINE PSYCHOLOGY STUDY CENTER

http://psychstudy.brookscole.com/student/plotnik/quiz/ch03frm.html

● AMERICAN PSYCHOLOGY ASSOCIATION'S PSYCHNET

http://www.apa.org/

The American Psychological Association's Web site is a good place to start Web surfing. Services include documents on psychology, information about undergraduate and graduate education in psychology, and much more.

● PSYCH WEB

http://www.gasou.edu/psychweb/psychweb.htm

This megasite of psychology resources for students, instructors, and professionals offers a special collection of information for students, including tips for applying to graduate school, an APA style crib sheet, and tips on writing research papers.

● MEGAPSYCH HOME PAGE

http://members.gnn.com/user/megapsych.htm

This site contains an extensive list of Internet resources for psychology students and faculty, including mailing lists, newsgroups, and Web pages.

● PSYCHINFO

http://www.apa.org/

APA members can search the huge PsychINFO database online.

● CYBERPSYCHLINK

http://cctr.umkc.edu/user/dmartin/psych2.html

This index of psychology sites includes listservs, newsgroups, electronic journals, self-help links, software for psychologists, and information on the teaching and history of psychology.

Welcome to the WEB

● PSYCOLOQUY

http://www.princeton.edu/~harnad/psyc.html

Psycoloquy is an electronic journal sponsored by the American Psychological Association on an experimental basis. There is no hard-copy version. It publishes articles, brief reports, book reviews, and commentary in almost all areas of psychology.

● THE PSYCHGRAD PROJECT

http://aix1.uottawa.ca/~simpson/psychgrad.html

The Psychgrad Project is a group of resources for graduate students in psychology. It features a listserv discussion forum, an electronic forum for publishing original articles, and a gateway to many Internet-based resources of interest to psychology graduate students.

● THE HISTORY OF PSYCHOLOGY

http://www.guam.net/home/bmarmie/history.html

This site contains information on many leading figures in the history of psychology, plus links for more information.

Activities

● *Integrator Online™ for Introductory Psychology* CD-ROM, Plotnik, Module 1

● Study Guide to accompany *Introduction to Psychology,* 5th edition (choice of PC or Mac computer version or hard copy)

● PsychNow! CD-ROM
  Study Skills
  Psychology and Its History
  Critical Thinking in Psychology

Answers to questions on page 24

1. People often oppose anything that seems to threaten their current system of belief.
2. Psychologists study human behavior, which may be open to many more interpretations and taken more personally than other areas of science.
3. The author seems to believe that controversial research is "essential for developing well-informed public policy."

4. One response might be that science is not conservative, because it is constantly expanding our knowledge and causing us to re-examine our beliefs.
5. Yes—the research could be flawed in some way.
6. One could argue that much controversial research is flawed by problems with methodology or researcher bias.

Module 2 PSYCHOLOGY & SCIENCE

26

Several Controversies

What is Dusty's problem?

It was 5 in the morning when Dusty began throwing a fit. As if driven by an inner motor, all 50 pounds of him was flying around the room, wailing and kicking. This raging activity went on for about 30 minutes; then he headed downstairs for breakfast. While his mother was busy in the kitchen, Dusty grabbed a box of cereal and kicked it around the room, spreading cereal everywhere. When his mother told him to clean up the mess, he got the plastic dustpan but began picking it apart, piece by piece. Next he grabbed three rolls of toilet paper and unraveled them around the house. By then, it was only 7:30. Dusty had not been given his pill, because he was seeing his doctor at 4 o'clock that day (adapted from *Time,* July 18, 1994).

Seven-year-old Dusty has a behavioral problem that has been surrounded with controversy. Dusty was diagnosed as being hyperactive, a problem that is officially called attention-deficit/hyperactivity disorder, or ADHD (American Psychiatric Association, 1994).

Attention-deficit/hyperactivity disorder, or *ADHD,* is not diagnosed by any medical tests but on the basis of the occurrence of certain behavioral problems. A child must have six or more symptoms of inattention, such as making careless mistakes in schoolwork, not following instructions, and being easily distracted; and six or more symptoms of hyperactivity, such as fidgeting, leaving classroom seat, running about when should not, and talking excessively. These symptoms should have been present from an early age, persisted for at least six months, and contributed to maladaptive development.

One controversy surrounding ADHD involves diagnosis. Since ADHD is not based on medical tests but rather on the occurrence of certain behavioral problems, how can children with ADHD be distinguished from those who are naturally outgoing and rambunctious (Barkley, 1997; Edwards, 1995; Rapport, 1994)?

To help control his ADHD, Dusty is given a drug that is a relatively powerful stimulant, called Ritalin (*WRIT-ah-lin*). Ritalin's effects are similar to another stimulant, amphetamine. For reasons researchers do not understand, stimulants, such as Ritalin and amphetamine, decrease activity in children, whether or not they are hyperactive (Rapoport et al., 1980).

Perhaps the biggest controversy surrounding the use of Ritalin concerns questions about it's being overprescribed, whether it is the most effective treatment, and how long a child with ADHD should remain on the drug. In addition, Ritalin, especially in larger doses,
does have side effects that may include loss of appetite and problems with sleeping. A related question is whether children with ADHD should be kept on a diet free of artificial dyes, sweeteners, or sugar, which some parents claim worsen the symptoms.

We're going to use Dusty's problem with ADHD to show how researchers pursue the four goals of psychology that we discussed in Module 1. In Dusty's case, the four goals are (1) to describe Dusty's symptoms, (2) to explain their causes, (3) to predict their occurrence, and (4) to control Dusty's behavior through some behavioral therapy or drug treatment.

Rhino Horn and Vitamin C

Can beliefs be as strong as real medicine?

One interesting aspect of trying to control unwanted symptoms with a drug treatment is that sometimes the drug is not really a drug because it has no proven medical effects. For example, in many parts of Asia, people take powdered rhino horn because they believe that it is a medicine for treating hundreds of physical and mental problems. Similarly, in the United States, many people take relatively large doses of vitamin C because they believe that it is a medicine for avoiding or curing the common cold. The use of rhino horn and vitamin C, both questionable medical treatments, raises the interesting question of how much one's mind or one's beliefs contributes to the development and disappearance of physical symptoms. We'll discuss methods that researchers use to decide whether the effectiveness of a treatment is due to a drug's medical effect or the person's beliefs.

What's Coming

Our main focus in this module is to explore the methods that researchers use to answer questions, such as how to treat ADHD and why placebos work. Specifically, we'll discuss the advantages and disadvantages of three major research methods—surveys, case studies, and experiments. We'll explain which research procedures can identify cause-and-effect relationships and which cannot. We begin with an overview of the three major research methods that psychologists use to answer questions.

A. Methods for Answering Questions

How do researchers study ADHD?

As you look at the photo of Dusty on the right, you see a young boy ready to explode into an uncontrolled burst of activity, a major symptom of ADHD. However, 25 years ago, ADHD was a relatively small problem in the United States, while today it is the most commonly diagnosed behavioral problem in children. ADHD is surrounded with controversy. For example, its name has been changed from hyperactivity to minimal brain damage to attention deficit disorder and most recently to attention deficit hyperactivity disorder (ADHD). The diagnosis of ADHD is not straightforward, since it is based on behavioral symptoms rather than medical tests. The proposed causes of ADHD

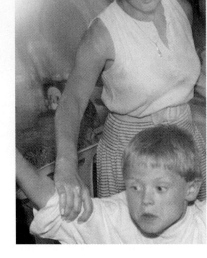

are many, including various genetic, hormonal, neurological, and dietary factors. Finally, the most popular treatment of ADHD involves giving children a stimulant drug.

In the middle of these controversies are parents like Dusty's mother, who after dealing with a hyperactive and impulsive child from an early age, have little doubt that ADHD exists and that Ritalin decreases hyperactivity and impulsivity. At the same time, critics warn that ADHD may be misdiagnosed or overdiagnosed and that while Ritalin may reduce activity it may fail to improve academic performance (Buitelaar et al., 1996; Rapport et al, 1994).

As researchers work to resolve all the controversies surrounding ADHD, they are using three major research methods—survey, case study, and experiment.

Survey

Suppose you wish to know how many children have ADHD, whether it occurs more in boys or girls, which treatment is the most popular, and how many children continue to have problems when they become adults? Researchers obtain this information with surveys.

A *survey* is a way to obtain information by asking many individuals—either person to person, by telephone, or by mail—to answer a fixed set of questions about particular subjects.

The disadvantage of a survey is that such information can contain errors or be biased because people may not remember accurately or answer truthfully. The advantage of a survey is that it is an efficient way to obtain much information from a large number of people.

But if researchers wanted to know more about a particular person, they would use a case study.

Case Study

Suppose you wish to know in greater detail about how a single child, such as Dusty, developed ADHD, performs in school, makes friends, plays team sports, and deals with everyday problems? Or suppose you wish to know about how a family copes with a child who has ADHD? For example, one mother said, "Ritalin doesn't take away the problems at all. It just helps him focus on what he's doing. You can talk to him; he can get his school work done. It still takes him a long time to get things done. He's still behind, emotionally and socially" (*San Diego Tribune,* November 27, 1989). When another mother was told that sugar doesn't increase activity, she replied, "I say, they're nuts! Where were they last Christmas when my sons ate candy canes and green frosting for days and never slept!" (*Los Angeles Times,* February 9, 1994). Researchers gather in-depth data about a particular individual with a case study.

A *case study* is an in-depth analysis of the thoughts, feelings, beliefs, experiences, behaviors, or problems of a single individual.

One disadvantage of a case study is that its detailed information about a particular person, such as Dusty, may not apply to other children with ADHD.

One advantage of a case study is that its detailed information allows greater understanding of a particular person's life.

But if researchers wanted to establish whether sugar really increases activity in children with ADHD, they would use an experiment.

Experiment

Suppose you thought that sugar or artificial dyes caused hyperactivity in your child and you wondered if this were true. For example, based on case studies and parents' reports, one researcher thought that certain artificial dyes, chemicals, and sweeteners increased the activity and impulsive behavior of children diagnosed with ADHD (Feingold, 1975). When researchers want to identify a cause-and-effect relationship, such as whether sugar increases activity, they would use an experiment.

An *experiment* is a method for identifying cause-and-effect relationships by following a set of rules and guidelines that minimize the possibility of error, bias, and chance occurrences.

A disadvantage of an experiment is that information obtained in one experimental situation or laboratory setting may not apply to other situations. An experiment's primary advantage is that it has the greatest potential for identifying cause-and-effect relationships with less error and bias than either surveys or case studies.

Very often, researchers use all three research methods—survey, case study, and experiment—because each provides a different kind of information. Surveys provide information about fixed questions from a large number of people. Case studies give in-depth information about a single person. Experiments point to cause-and-effect relationships. We'll discuss the advantages and disadvantages of each of the three methods, beginning with surveys.

Kind of Information

What do surveys tell us?

Almost every day the media report some new survey. Although surveys tell us what others believe or how they behave, survey questions can be written to bias the answers; moreover, people may not always answer truthfully. For example, how many people do you think always wash their hands after going to the bathroom? We'll sample some surveys and then discuss their problems.

Do you wash your hands?

Although 94% of the people surveyed by telephone said that they always washed their hands after going to the bathroom, direct observation of 6,333 people in five major cities found that only 68% really do and that women (74%) washed their hands more often than men (61%) (Manning, 1996).

What's your biggest worry?

A survey of 251,323 college freshmen (class of 2000) reported that 66% are worried about not having the money to finish college, 30% frequently feel overwhelmed by all they have to do, and 15% of women and 13% of men consider themselves frequent smokers (Weiss, 1997).

How many are diagnosed with ADHD?

Recent surveys report that about 3–5% of school-age children are diagnosed with ADHD and are taking Ritalin (Barkley, 1994, 1997); about 20–50% of children with ADHD continue to have symptoms as adults (Biederman et al., 1996); the rate of ADHD in China is about the same as in the United States, but France and England have one-tenth that of the United States, and Japan is just beginning to study ADHD (Leung et al., 1996).

These examples show that surveys provide a great deal of useful information. However, surveys have potential problems with accuracy (hand-washing survey) as well as with wording of questions and who asks the questions.

Disadvantages

How questions are worded

You may be surprised to learn that surveys may get very different results depending on how questions are worded. Here are two examples:

QUESTION: "Would you say that **industry** contributes more or less to air pollution than **traffic?**"
Traffic contributes more: **24%**
Industry contributes more: 57%

QUESTION: "Would you say that **traffic** contributes more or less to air pollution than **industry?**"
Traffic contributes more: **45%**
Industry contributes more: 32%

These two examples indicate that the way questions are phrased and the way the possible answers are ordered can greatly influence people's responses and, in this case, produce opposite results (Reported in *U.S. News and World Report,* Dec. 4, 1995, p. 55).

Who asks the questions

You may also be surprised to learn that the sex or race of the questioner can also affect how people answer the questions.

QUESTION: "The problems faced by blacks were brought on by blacks themselves."
When the interviewer was **white, 62%** of whites who were interviewed agreed.
When the interviewer was **black, 46%** of whites who were interviewed agreed.

These two examples indicate that when asked about sensitive or emotional issues, people take into account the race of the interviewer and tend to give socially acceptable rather than honest answers (*U.S. News and World Report,* Dec. 4, 1995, p. 55).

We can conclude that surveys may be biased because people may not answer questions truthfully, may give socially acceptable answers, or feel pressured to answer in certain ways. Also, surveys can be biased by how questions are worded and by interviewing a group of people who are not representative of the general population (Semin & De Poot, 1997). Despite these potential problems, surveys do have advantages.

Advantages

While guarding against error and bias, surveys can be a useful research tool to quickly and efficiently collect information on behaviors, beliefs, experiences, and attitudes from a large sample of people and can compare answers from various ethnic, age, socioeconomic, and cultural groups.

For example, surveys suggest that ADHD interferes with performance in school settings, decreases the chances of graduating from high school, and may lead to conduct disorder problems in adolescence as well as continued problems in adulthood (Biederman et al., 1996).

Because surveys indicate that children with ADHD have major problems in school settings, psychologists are developing methods for improving performance. These methods include: teaching ADHD children how to organize their work; giving them constant feedback on reaching their goals; and starting programs that train teachers and families to work together to help ADHD children control their disruptive behaviors (DuPaul & Eckert, 1997). Thus, another advantage of surveys is their ability to identify problems and evaluate treatment programs.

However, if researchers wish to focus on a particular individual rather than a group, they would use a case study.

C. Case Study

Kind of Information

What's a case study?

Sometimes researchers answer questions by studying a single individual in great detail. This method is called a case study.

A *case study* is an in-depth analysis of the thoughts, feelings, beliefs, or behaviors of a single person.

We'll use a different case study, this time focusing on Nick, who is now 11 years old and diagnosed as having ADHD. From the age of 3, Nick has had problems paying attention and completing tasks. Because he was so easily distracted, Nick needed to be called as many as 19 times before he answered, couldn't seem to finish tying his shoes, couldn't pay attention in school, and alternated between bouts of frustration and being an angel. In the first grade, Nick was put on Ritalin, and it made an immediate difference. He called it a "concentrating medicine," and although he still has academic problems, he can better focus on and complete a project (Leavy, 1996). This case study tells us that Ritalin helped Nick concentrate but only partially solved his academic problems. Sometimes case studies help answer questions, but as you'll see next, case studies can also result in wrong or biased answers.

Personal Case Study: Testimonial

Why did parents make a mistake?

Observations from case studies may be misinterpreted if the observer has preconceived notions of what to look for. For example, beginning in the mid-1970s, parents were told that food with artificial additives, dyes, and preservatives could cause hyperactivity in children (Feingold, 1975). Shortly after, parents reported that, yes indeed, artificial additives caused a sudden increase in restlessness and irritability in their hyperactive children (Feingold, 1975). The parents' reports and beliefs that additives cause hyperactivity are examples of another kind of case study, called a testimonial.

A *testimonial* is a statement in support of a particular viewpoint based on detailed observations of a person's own personal experience.

However, contrary to the parents' testimonials, researchers have generally found that amounts of artificial additives within a normal range did not affect hyperactivity (Kinsbourne, 1994). More recently, there are testimonials from parents that children with attention deficit disorder who ate foods with an artificial sweetener, aspartame (Nutrasweet), showed noticeable increases in symptoms.

To test the accuracy of these recent testimonials, researchers asked teachers and parents to evaluate the behaviors and cognitive functions of children who were given a capsule containing either ten times their normal daily intake of aspartame or a placebo. Neither parent, child, nor teacher knew if the capsule contained aspartame or the placebo. As the figure on the left shows, there was little or no difference between the effect of aspartame and that of the placebo on the behaviors or cognitive functions of children with attention deficit disorder (Shaywitz et al., 1994). Although testimonials from parents, friends, or peers can be very convincing, we'll point out two problems that make testimonials especially susceptible to error.

Average Ratings of Parents and Teachers

13.5	Placebo
13	Aspartame

Error and Bias

What's the problem with testimonials?

One of the major problems with testimonials is that they are based on our personal observations, which have great potential for error and bias. For example, if parents reported that sweeteners increased their son's activity, we would have to rule out personal beliefs and self-fulfilling prophecies.

Personal beliefs. If parents hear that artificial sweeteners may cause physical or psychological problems, they may interpret their child's problems as caused by artificial sweeteners. Because of biased perceptions, parents may overlook other potential causes, such as frustration, anger, or changes in the child's environment, and make the error of focusing only on artificial sweeteners. If we believe strongly in something, it may bias our perception and cause us to credit an unrelated treatment or event as the reason for some change.

Self-fulfilling prophecy. If parents believe that artificial sweeteners cause problems, they may behave in ways—being more strict or less sympathetic—that cause the problems to occur. This phenomenon is called self-fulfilling prophecy.

A *self-fulfilling prophecy* involves having a strong belief or making a statement (prophecy) about a future behavior and then acting, usually unknowingly, to fulfill or carry out the behavior.

If we strongly believe that something is going to happen, we may unknowingly behave in such a way as to make it happen (Madon et al., 1997). Self-fulfilling prophecies reinforce testimonials and thus keep our biased beliefs alive.

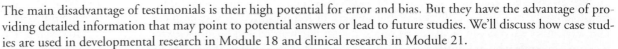

The main disadvantage of testimonials is their high potential for error and bias. But they have the advantage of providing detailed information that may point to potential answers or lead to future studies. We'll discuss how case studies are used in developmental research in Module 18 and clinical research in Module 21.

Next, we'll discuss how testimonials are a popular source of information, especially when talking about placebos.

D. Cultural Diversity: Use of Placebos

Remarkable Treatments

Can your beliefs reduce pain?

If you happen to take a prescription drug, read its brochure, which discusses what the drug does, its side effects, and, most interesting, how its effectiveness has compared to a placebo.

A *placebo* is some intervention, such as taking a pill, receiving an injection, or undergoing an operation, that resembles medical therapy but that, in fact, has no medical effects.

A *placebo effect* is a change in the patient's illness that is attributable to an imagined treatment rather than to a medical treatment.

For example, a brochure for a new drug to treat migraine headaches reported that, after drug injection, 82% of those treated reported reduced pain and 81% reported reduced nausea (Imitrex, product information, 1994). However, the same brochure also reported that 39% of individuals suffering migraine headaches reported less

pain and 63% reported less nausea after receiving an injection that was actually a placebo (salt water). None of the migraine sufferers knew whether they were receiving drug or placebo injections.

Researchers have proposed that placebos work by reducing tension and distress and by creating powerful self-fulfilling prophecies so that individuals think and behave as if the drug, actually a placebo, will work (Dodes, 1997; Montgomery & Kirsch, 1996). Self-fulfilling prophecies are strongest and placebos are most effective when they are administered by trusted and sincere professionals who convince their patients of the drugs' effectiveness, even though the "medications" are actually placebos (Turner et al., 1994).

Perhaps the most convincing evidence for the effectiveness of placebos comes from testimonials, which claim that taking various vitamins, animal parts, or herbs cures a wide variety of symptoms. We'll review some of the more common placebos in use worldwide.

Rhino Horn

Millions of people in China, Thailand, South Korea, and Taiwan claim that rhino horn is an aphrodisiac, will increase sexual desire and stamina, and is a cure for everything from headaches and nosebleeds to high fevers and typhoid. However, the basic ingredient of rhino horn is compacted hair (keratin), which has no proven medicinal powers (*Sierra*, November/December, 1989). A single rhino horn weighing about 4 to 5 pounds will bring from $25,000 to $50,000 on the black market. In the early 1900s, there were about 1 million rhinos. By 1994, poachers had reduced the total number of rhinos to about 10,000, as the desire for rhino horns continued (Berger & Cunningham, 1994).

Bear Gallbladders

In parts of Asia, a very popular "medicine" to treat many kinds of physical problems is a tablet made from bear gallbladders. Some traders are substituting pig gallbladders for bears' and customers are no more the wiser, since bear or pig gallbladders are nothing more than placebos (*Time*, November 4, 1991). The price of a single bear gallbladder has risen to an amazing $18,000, and there is now an illegal global trade in animal parts. Poachers threaten some endangered species of bears, such as the grizzly bear in the United States.

Tiger Bones

In the early 1900s, there were 100,000 tigers in Asia, but by 1994 there were fewer than 5,000. The chief reason for this precipitous decline is the use of tiger bones to treat ulcers, typhoid, malaria, dysentery, and burns, to increase longevity, to guard newborn babies from infection, and to cure devil possession (Friend, 1997). In addition, wealthy Taiwanese pay $320 for a bowl of tiger penis soup that is thought to increase flagging libidos (Nagarahole, 1994). Tiger bones and tiger penises function as powerful placebos in traditional Asian medicine.

Vitamin C

In the United States, people spend millions of dollars each year to take large doses of vitamin C to ward off colds. Researchers found that very large doses (above 400 milligrams) have no evident value and even larger doses may be hazardous (Brody, 1996). More interestingly, evidence shows that taking large doses of vitamin C (up to 1,000 milligrams) year-round does not prevent colds and may only slightly reduce the severity of colds (Barrett, 1995).

Role of Testimonials

Why are placebos so popular?

One reason placebos are used worldwide, even threatening the extinction of certain animals, is that they are backed by testimonials. Compared to surveys, testimonials are much more convincing because they are based on real-life experiences of friends, peers, and parents who are honest and believable. However, without realizing it, even honest people may misinterpret their experiences, draw the wrong conclusions, and give testimonials that are untrue.

One reason a person may misinterpret a testimonial is because it is based on experiencing two events, such as taking a pill and feeling better. However, as you'll see next, that person has no way of knowing what caused what.

E. Correlation

Definition

What's a correlation?

The photo on the left shows Dusty running wild in a supermarket. Researchers would like to know if Dusty's hyperactivity has a genetic basis. One way to identify genetic factors is to study genetic twins, since they share 100% of their genes in common. Suppose you were studying the occurrence of ADHD in identical male twins and found that, about 70% of the time, if one identical twin had ADHD so did the second twin (Eaves et al., 1993). This strong relationship among behaviors in identical twins suggests a genetic basis for ADHD. Such a relationship is called a correlation.

A *correlation* is an association or relationship between the occurrence of two or more events.

For example, if one twin has hyperactivity, a correlation will tell us the likelihood that the other twin also has hyperactivity. The likelihood or strength of a relationship between two events is called a correlation coefficient.

A *correlation coefficient* is a number that indicates the strength of a relationship between two or more events: the closer the number is to −1.00 or +1.00, the greater is the strength of the relationship.

We'll explain correlation coefficients in more detail because they can be confusing.

Correlation Coefficients

What are these numbers?

There are two major points to understand about correlations:

First, a correlation means there is an association between two or more events. For example, there is an association, or correlation, between the sex of a child and the occurrence of ADHD; two to three times more boys are diagnosed with ADHD than girls.

A second point to understand about correlations is that the strength of the relationship or association is measured by a number called a correlation coefficient. Because the correlation coefficient ranges from +1.00 to −1.00, its meaning can be confusing. In the table on the right, we'll describe what correlation coefficients mean, beginning at the top of the table with a +1.00.

+1.00

+0.05

0.00

−0.50

−1.00

If each of 20 identical pairs showed equal levels of hyperactivity, the correlation coefficient would be positive and perfect and would be indicated by a +1.00 correlation coefficient.

A **perfect positive correlation coefficient** of +1.00 means that an increase in one event is always matched by an equal increase in a second event.

That is, a coefficient of +1.00 means that if one twin of an identical pair has hyperactivity, the other twin always has hyperactivity.

If some identical pairs but not all 20 pairs were similar in hyperactivity, the result would be a positive correlation coefficient, which can range from +0.01 to +0.99.

A **positive correlation coefficient** indicates that as one event tends to increase, the second event tends to, but does not always, increase.

As the coefficient increases from +0.01 to +0.99, it indicates a strengthening of the relationship between the occurrence of two events.

If one twin of 20 pairs showed hyperactivity while the other twin sometimes did and sometimes did not show hyperactivity, the result would be no association, or zero correlation (0.00).

A **zero correlation** indicates that there is no relationship between the occurrence of one event and the occurrence of a second event.

If, in some identical pairs, one twin showed an increase while the other showed an equivalent decrease in activity, the result would be a negative correlation coefficient, which can range from −0.01 to −0.99.

A **negative correlation coefficient** indicates that as one event tends to increase, the second event tends to, but does not always, decrease.

As the coefficient increases in absolute magnitude from −0.01 to −0.99, it indicates a strengthening in the relationship of one event increasing and the other decreasing.

If one twin of 20 identical pairs showed hyperactivity and the second twin always showed decreased activity, the correlation coefficient would be negative and perfect and would be indicated by a −1.00 correlation coefficient.

A **perfect negative correlation coefficient** of −1.00 means that an increase in one event is always matched by an equal decrease in a second event.

That is, a coefficient of −1.00 means that if one twin of an identical pair has hyperactivity, the other twin always has decreased activity.

Advantages and Disadvantages

The media often headlines interesting findings: Thin people live longer than heavier ones; overweight people earn less money than their peers; school uniforms decrease violence. Before you assume that one event causes the other, such as thinness causing one to live longer, you must check to see what researchers did. If researchers only measured the relationship between two events, such as thinness and length of life, then it's a correlation. In fact, all three findings reported above are correlations. The reason you should check whether some finding is a correlation is that correlations have one very important limitation: They do not identify what causes what. For example, let's look closely at the finding about school uniforms.

CORRELATION VERSUS CAUSATION

The biggest mistake people make in discussing correlations is assuming that they show cause and effect. For instance, many school districts are considering the adoption of mandatory school uniforms, because wearing uniforms was related to decreased problems with students' behavior. The graph on the right shows that wearing school uniforms was related to or correlated with a large decrease in carrying weapons, fighting, assaults, and vandalism. Since an increase in wearing uniforms (left photo) was associated with a drop in problems, this is a negative correlation.

Although the correlation between wearing uniforms and decreased problems was impressive, you must keep in mind that correlations, no matter how impressive, cannot indicate a cause-and-effect relationship. To make the point that correlations do not indicate cause and effect, just remember that over

Wearing Uniforms and Decrease in Problems

−52%	Weapons
−51%	Fighting
−34%	Assault
−18%	Vandalism

Source: Long Beach, CA, Unified School District; 1993-94 versus 1994-95.

the past 26 years, there is a +0.88 correlation between which professional football team (American or National League) wins the Super Bowl and whether the stock market rises or falls. Although +0.88 is a very high positive correlation, it indicates only a relationship; winning a Super Bowl could not possibly cause a winning or losing stock market.

Although correlations do not indicate cause-and-effect relationships, they do serve two very useful purposes: Correlations help predict behavior and also point to where to look for possible causes, as has happened in the case of lung cancer.

CORRELATIONS AS CLUES

Although cigarette smoke was positively correlated with lung cancer (right graph), it was unknown whether smoking was the *cause* of cancer. Acting on the clue that some ingredient of cigarette smoke might trigger the development of lung cancer, researchers rubbed tar, an ingredient of cigarette smoke, on the skin of animals. After repeated applications over a period of time, the animals developed cancerous growths. This research proved that tar could cause cancer. More recently, researchers discovered that one particular ingredient of cigarette smoke (benzo[a]pyrene) turns off a gene that normally suppresses tumors. When that particular gene is turned off by cigarette smoke, lung cancer develops (Sozzi et al, 1996). In this case, correlations told researchers where to look for causes of lung cancer. In other cases, correlations help predict behavior.

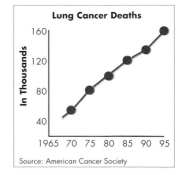

Lung Cancer Deaths

In Thousands

Source: American Cancer Society

CORRELATION AND PREDICTIONS

One way to predict how well students will do in academic settings is by looking at their IQ scores. For example, there is a reasonably high correlation, from +0.60 to +0.70, between IQ scores and performance in academic settings (Anastasi & Urbina, 1997). Thus, we would predict that individuals who score high on IQ scores have the skills to do well in college. However, IQ scores are only relatively good predictors for any single individual because doing well in college involves not only academic skills but many other motivational, emotional, and personality factors that we'll discuss in Module 13.

So far, we have discussed the advantages and disadvantages of two major research methods—surveys and case studies—that psychologists use to answer questions. We have also explained a statistical procedure—correlation—that shows the strength of relationships and points to possible causes. Next, we'll describe the other kinds of research decisions that psychologists make as they try to understand and explain behavior.

F. Decisions about Doing Research

Choosing Research Techniques

What's the best technique for answering a question?

Rarely does a day pass without your asking some question about human behavior, such as, "Why did she say that?" or "Why did he behave that way?" Similarly, rarely does a day pass without psychologists asking questions, such as "How many students believe in psychics?" or "Is there a relationship between how many hours students study and how they do on exams?" or "Do drugs improve the academic performance of children with ADHD?" After asking a question, psychologists must decide which research technique or procedure best answers it. We'll describe four different techniques for finding answers.

Questionnaires and Interviews

What percentage of the population is gay? This question is often answered by doing a survey using interviews or questionnaires.

An *interview* is a technique for obtaining information by asking questions, ranging from open-ended to highly structured, about a subject's behaviors and attitudes, usually in a one-on-one situation.

A *questionnaire* is a technique for obtaining information by asking subjects to read a list of written questions and check off specific answers.

You might think this question about what percentage of the population is gay would be relatively easy to answer. But three different surveys have reported three different answers: 2.3%, 10%, and 22% (Billy et al., 1993; Kinsey et al., 1948; Janus & Janus, 1993). These different answers resulted from surveys using differently worded questions, different groups of people, and different kinds of interview techniques. As we discussed earlier, when it comes to surveys on personal issues—such as, Did you vote? Do you wear seat belts? Do you go to church? or What is your sexual preference?—people may give the desirable rather than the honest answer.

Standardized Tests

Of what use are SAT scores? The standardized test that you may be most familiar with is the SAT (Scholastic Assessment Test), which is given to many high school seniors to help predict how they will perform in college. Each year only 0.05% of students who take the SAT score a perfect 1600, a feat accomplished for the first time in 1997 by twins, Courtney and Chris (photo on left).

A *standardized test* is a technique to obtain information by administering a psychological test that has been standardized, which means that the test has been given to hundreds of people and shown to reliably measure thought patterns, personality traits, emotions, or behaviors.

One disadvantage of standardized tests, such as the SAT, is that they may be biased toward a certain group of people. One advantage of standardized tests is that they allow comparisons to be made across schools, states, and groups of people (Anastasi & Urbina, 1997). Another well-known standardized test is the IQ test, which we'll discuss in Module 13.

Laboratory Experiment

Does hypnosis help smokers quit? Many smokers know that continued smoking is one of the most serious threats to their health. Yet, many smokers find it difficult if not impossible to quit. You may have heard many claims for hypnosis, including that it helps people stop smoking. This claim can best be evaluated with a laboratory experiment.

A *laboratory experiment* is a technique to gather information about the brain, genes, or behavior with the least error and bias by using a controlled environment that allows careful observation and measurement.

SURGEON GENERAL'S WARNING: CIGARETTE SMOKING CAUSES LUNG CANCER

For example, in laboratory experiments, researchers found that hypnosis was no more effective in helping smokers stop than were other treatments, such as health education or behavior therapy (Rue et al., 1994). Laboratory experiments are excellent ways to evaluate claims and identify cause-and-effect relationships.

Animal Models

Does a specific gene cause obesity? Over one-third of the adult population in the United States is now overweight, which may lead to serious medical problems, such as heart disease and high blood pressure. To understand the physiological causes of obesity, researchers are using animal models (Foster et al., 1997).

An *animal model* involves examining or manipulating some behavioral, genetic, or physiological factor that closely approximates some human problem, disease, or condition.

For example, researchers have identified a gene in mice that is involved in obesity (Gura, 1997). In the photo, an obese mouse on the left without the gene is compared to a normal mouse on the right. One advantage of the animal model is that it answers questions about physiological factors that cannot be investigated in humans.

Deciding which one or combination of these four research techniques to use is based on the kind of question being asked. As you'll see next, the kind of question also influences which research setting to use.

Choosing Research Settings

What kind of problems do children with ADHD have?

In trying to understand the kinds of problems faced by children with ADHD, psychologists study these children in different research settings, which may include observing them in the home, in the classroom, on the playground, or at their individual work. In addition, researchers may try to find the causes of ADHD by using different research settings, which may include studying children in the laboratory, hospital, or clinic. All these research settings can be grouped under either laboratory or naturalistic environments. We'll explain each setting and compare their advantages and disadvantages, beginning with more naturalistic environments.

Naturalistic Setting

Parents and teachers want to know if ADHD children have different problems at home than in school. Reseachers answer this question by studying ADHD children in naturalistic settings, such as their home and school environments.

A *naturalistic setting* is a relatively normal environment in which researchers gather information by observing individuals' behaviors without attempting to change or control the situation.

For example, observations of children with ADHD in school settings (left photo) indicate that they have difficulty remaining in their seats, don't pay attention to the teacher, don't complete their projects, can't sit still, get into trouble, are rude to other students, and get angry when they don't get their way. Parents report that, at home, ADHD children do not respond when called, throw tantrums when frustrated, and have periods of great activity (Hancock, 1996; Henker & Whalen, 1989). Based on these naturalistic observations, psychologists developed a list of primary symptoms of ADHD (Barkley, 1997). Similarly, psychologists study how normal people behave in different naturalistic settings, including schools, workplaces, college dormitories, bars, sports arenas, and homeless shelters. One problem with naturalistic observations is that the psychologists' own beliefs or values may bias their observations and cause them to misperceive or misinterpret behaviors. One advantage of naturalistic observations is the opportunity to study behaviors in real-life situations and environments, which cannot or would not be duplicated in the laboratory.

Case studies. As we discussed earlier, a single individual may be studied in his or her natural environment, and this is called a case study. The case study approach is often used in clinical psychology to understand the development of a personality or psychological problem or, in developmental psychology, to examine a person's behavior across his or her life span.

One disadvantage of a case study is that the information obtained is unique to an individual and may not apply to, or help us understand, the behaviors of others. One advantage of a case study is that psychologists can obtain detailed descriptions and insights into many aspects of an individual's complex life and behaviors that cannot be obtained in other ways.

As you can see, naturalistic settings are very useful for observing how individuals behave in relatively normal environments. However, since naturalistic settings are uncontrolled and many things happen, researchers find it difficult to identify what causes what. For this reason, researchers may have to answer some questions in a more controlled setting, such as a laboratory or clinic.

Laboratory Setting

Is there something different about the brains of children with ADHD? Questions about the brain are usually answered under very controlled conditions, such as in a laboratory setting.

A *laboratory setting* involves studying individuals under systematic and controlled conditions, with many of the real-world influences eliminated.

For example, researchers used special techniques (described in Module 4) that actually took pictures of the living brain of boys with and without ADHD. Researchers focused on an area called the corpus callosum (shown below in blue), which is the major pathway connecting the two halves of the brain. Boys with ADHD had significantly smaller corpus callosums, which may make communication between the two halves of the brain more difficult and thus contribute to some of the boys' troubling behaviors (Giedd et al., 1994, 1995).

Corpus callosum

Front

Back

Researchers use laboratory settings to study and identify a wide range of psychological and biological factors involved in motivation, emotion, learning, memory, drug use, sleep, intelligence, and mental disorders.

One disadvantage of laboratory settings is that they may be so controlled or artificial that their results are not always transferable to, or meaningful for, real-life situations. However, one advantage of the laboratory setting is that psychologists can carefully control and manipulate one or more treatments while reducing error or bias from other situational or environmental factors.

Psychologists may use both naturalistic and laboratory settings to obtain a broader understanding of some behavior or problem, such as ADHD.

Sometimes researchers combine the advantages of naturalistic and laboratory settings to identify cause-and-effect relationships. Such was the case when psychologists asked the interesting question: Does Ritalin help children with ADHD? Here's how researchers answered this question.

G. Scientific Method: Experiment

Advantage of Scientific Method

How do researchers reduce error and bias?

There have been many different treatments, including diets, vitamins, drugs, and behavior therapy, that claimed to help children with ADHD, such as Dusty (right photo). To discover which of these claims were valid, researchers followed a general approach called the scientific method.

The *scientific method* is an approach of gathering information and answering questions so that errors and biases are minimized.

Remember that information from surveys, case studies, and testimonials has considerable potential for error and bias. Remember too that information from correlations can suggest, but not pinpoint, cause-and-effect relationships. One way to both reduce error

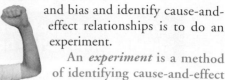

and bias and identify cause-and-effect relationships is to do an experiment.

An *experiment* is a method of identifying cause-and-effect relationships by following a set of rules and guidelines that minimize the possibility of error, bias, and chance occurrences.

An experiment, which is an example of using the scientific method, is the most powerful method for finding what causes what. We will divide an experiment into seven rules that are intended to reduce error and bias and identify the cause of an effect.

Conducting an Experiment: Seven Rules

Why seven rules?

Some researchers and parents claimed that diets without sugar, artificial colors, and additives reduced ADHD symptoms, but most of these claims proved false because the rules to reduce error had not been followed (Kinsbourne, 1994). Here are seven rules that reduce error and bias and that researchers follow when conducting an experiment.

Rule 1: Ask

Every experiment begins with one or more specific questions that are changed into specific hypotheses.

A *hypothesis* is an educated guess about some phenomenon and is stated in precise, concrete language to rule out any confusion or error in the meaning of its terms.

HYPOTHESIS:
Ritalin will improve negative classroom behaviors of children with ADHD.

Researchers develop different hypotheses based on their own observations or previous research findings. Following this first rule, researchers will change the general question—Does Ritalin help children with ADHD?— into a very concrete hypothesis: Ritalin will improve the negative classroom behaviors of children with ADHD.

Rule 2: Identify

After researchers have made their hypothesis, they are ready to identify a treatment that will be administered to the subjects. This treatment is called the independent variable.

The *independent variable* is a treatment or something that the researcher controls or manipulates.

The independent variable may be a single treatment, such as a single drug dose, or various levels of the same treatment, such as different doses of the same drug.

Ritalin

Independent Variable:

Drug treatment

In our experiment, the independent variable was administering three different doses of Ritalin and a placebo.

After researchers choose the treatment, they next identify the behavior(s) of the subjects, called the dependent variable, that will be used to measure the effects of the treatment.

Dependent variable:
Child's negative classroom behaviors

The *dependent variable* is one or more of the subjects' behaviors that are used to measure the potential effects of the treatment or independent variable.

The dependent variable, so called because it is dependent on the treatment, can include a wide range of behaviors, such as observable responses, self-reports of cognitive processes, or recordings of physiological responses from the body or brain. In the present experiment, the dependent variable is the teacher's rating of the child's disruptive classroom behaviors.

Rule 3: Choose

After researchers identify the independent and dependent variables, they next choose the subjects for the experiment. Researchers want to choose subjects who are representative of the entire group or population, and they do this through a process called random selection.

Random selection means that each subject in a sample population has an equal chance of being selected to participate in the experiment.

Random Selection

There are many ways to select randomly, such as taking every tenth child from a list of children with ADHD.

The reason researchers randomly select subjects is to avoid any potential error or bias that may come from their knowingly or unknowingly wanting to choose the "best" subjects for their experiment.

Rule 4: **Assign**

After randomly choosing the subjects, researchers then randomly assign subjects to different groups, either an experimental group or a control group.

The *experimental group* is composed of subjects who receive the treatment.

The *control group* is composed of subjects who undergo all the same procedures as the experimental subjects except that the control subjects do not receive the treatment.

In this study, some of the children will be assigned to the experimental group and will receive Ritalin; the other children will be assigned to the control group and receive a similar-looking pill that is a placebo.

The reason subjects are randomly assigned to either experimental or control groups is to take into account or control for other factors or traits, such as intelligence, social class, economic level, age, personality variables, sex, and genetic differences. Randomly assigning subjects reduces the chances that these factors will bias the results.

Rule 5: **Manipulate**

After assigning subjects to experimental and control groups, researchers manipulate the independent variable by administering the treatment (or one level of the treatment) to the experimental group. Researchers give the same conditions to the control group but give them a different level of the treatment, no treatment, or a placebo.

For example, in this study, researchers gave the experimental group a pill containing Ritalin, while the control group received a placebo. Drugs and placebos are given with special care, called a double-blind procedure.

A *double-blind procedure* means that neither the subjects nor the researchers know which group is receiving which treatment.

A double-blind procedure is essential in drug research to control for self-fulfilling prophecies, placebo effects (see page 31) or possible influences or biases of the experimenters.

Rule 6: **Measure**

By manipulating the treatment so that the experimental group receives a different treatment than the control group, researchers are able to measure how the independent variable (treatment) affects those behaviors that have been selected as the dependent variables.

For example, the hypothesis in this study is: Ritalin will improve classroom behaviors of children with ADHD. Researchers observed whether treatment (Ritalin or placebo) changed negative behaviors of ADHD children in the classroom. Negative behaviors, whose frequencies were counted for 30-minute periods, included: getting out of seat, engaging in destructive behavior, disturbing others, swearing, teasing, and not following instructions. As the graph below indicates, ADHD children given placebos showed 9.8 negative behaviors per 30-minute period, compared with 4.8 for the children given Ritalin (Pelham et al., 1985). Thus, compared to placebos, Ritalin de-

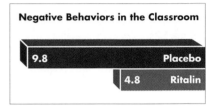

Negative Behaviors in the Classroom

9.8 — Placebo
4.8 — Ritalin

creased negative behaviors in ADHD children in the classroom. However, to be absolutely sure, researchers must next analyze the results more carefully.

Rule 7: **Analyze**

Although there appears to be a large decrease in negative behaviors, from 9.8 for the placebo control group to 4.8 for the Ritalin experimental group, researchers must analyze the size of these differences with statistical procedures.

Statistical procedures are used to determine whether differences observed in dependent variables (behaviors) are due to independent variables (treatment) or to error or chance occurrence.

Using statistical procedures, which are described in the Appendix, researchers compared the effect of placebo with that of Ritalin on negative behaviors. They concluded that, compared with placebo, Ritalin significantly reduced negative behaviors. In this case, *significantly* means that there was a 95% likelihood that it was Ritalin and not some error or chance occurrence that decreased negative behaviors (Pelham et al., 1985).

These significant findings support the original hypothesis that Ritalin improves classroom behaviors of children with ADHD.

Conclusion

What does an experiment tell you?

By following these seven rules for conducting an experiment, researchers reduced the chances that error or bias would distort the major finding, which was that Ritalin reduced negative behaviors of children in the classroom. This example shows that when an experiment is run according to these seven rules, it is a much more powerful method for identifying cause-and-effect relationships than are surveys, testimonials, correlations, or case studies. Even so, researchers usually repeat experiments many times before being confident that the answers they found were correct. That's why a newly reported finding, no matter how significant, is usually regarded as questionable until other researchers have been able to repeat the experiment and replicate the finding.

After the Concept Review, we'll discuss why, after 20 years of research, there are still controversies surrounding ADHD.

CONCEPT REVIEW

1. If psychologists obtain information through an in-depth analysis of the thoughts, beliefs, or behaviors of a single person, this method is called a (a)_____. If a method is used that minimizes error and identifies cause-and-effect relationships, it is called an (b)_____. If individuals are asked a fixed set of questions, it is called a (c)_____. If individuals make statements in support of a particular viewpoint on the basis of personal experience, it is called a (d)_____.

2. Some intervention that is designed to look like a medical treatment but that has no actual medical effect is called a (a)_____. A change in a patient's illness that is due to a supposed treatment and not to any medical therapy is called a (b)_____.

3. Psychologists describe the association, relationship, or linkage among two or more events as a (a)_____. They describe the strength of such a relationship by a number called the (b)_____, which may vary from −1.00 to +1.00. If an increase in one event is associated with an increase in a second event, this relationship is called a (c)_____ correlation. If an increase in one event is associated with a decrease in a second event, this relationship is called a (d)_____ correlation. Finding that two or more events are linked together does not prove that one event (e)_____ the other.

4. Psychologists use at least five common research techniques. They can ask subjects oral or written questions by using (a)_____ and (b)_____. They might ask subjects to answer questions on established tests, which are called (c)_____ tests. They might observe and measure behaviors, brains, or genes with the least error and bias by using a controlled environment, called a (d)_____. They could study some question or problem in animals by developing an (e)_____ that closely approximates the human condition.

DOES HYPNOSIS HELP PEOPLE STOP SMOKING?

5. If psychologists study individuals in their real-life environments, without trying to control the situation, they are using a (a)_____ setting. A variation of this approach is to study a single individual in great depth in his or her own environment, which is called a (b)_____. If psychologists study individuals under carefully controlled conditions, they are using a (c)_____ setting.

Corpus callosum
Front   Back

6. One example of searching for cause-and-effect relationships by following the rules and guidelines of the scientific method is to answer questions by conducting an _____, which has seven rules.

7. If you are conducting an experiment, you would follow seven rules.

Rule 1 is to *ask* specific questions in very concrete terms: these statements are called (a)_____.

Rule 2 is to *identify* the treatment, which is called the (b)_____; and to choose the behaviors or responses that will be observed to judge the effectiveness of the treatment. These behaviors or responses are called the (c)_____. Rule 3 is to *choose* subjects through a process called (d)_____, which gives everyone in a sample population an equal chance of being selected.

Rule 4 is to *assign* subjects to different groups by random selection. The group that will receive the treatment is called the (e)_____, and the group that undergoes everything but the treatment is called the (f)_____.

Placebo

Rule 5 is to *manipulate* the (g)_____ by administering it to the experimental group but not the control group.

Rule 6 is to *measure* the effects of the independent variable on behaviors that have been selected as the (h)_____. Rule 7 is to *analyze* the difference between the experimental and control groups by using (i)_____.

8. Researchers usually repeat experiments many times to make sure that their _____ are correct.

Answers: 1. (a) case study, (b) experiment, (c) survey, (d) testimonial; 2. (a) placebo, (b) placebo effect; 3. (a) correlation, (b) correlation coefficient, (c) positive, (d) negative, (e) causes; 4. (a) questionnaires, (b) interviews, (c) standardized, (d) laboratory experiment, (e) animal model; 5. (a) naturalistic, (b) case study, (c) laboratory; 6. experiment; 7. (a) hypotheses, (b) independent variable, (c) dependent variable, (d) random selection, (e) experimental group, (f) control group, (g) independent variable, (h) dependent variables, (i) statistical procedures; 8. answers or results.

Why do questions still remain?
You might ask why, after 20 years of research, there are still controversies over how best to diagnose and treat ADHD. Although researchers have reached the first goal of psychology, which is to describe ADHD, they have not reached the second goal, which is to explain the causes of ADHD, which will lead to better treatment. Explaining the causes of ADHD means combining biological, psychological, and behavioral factors, which is a slow, ongoing process. We'll review the current controversies to show how far researchers have come and how far they have to go.

Controversy: Diagnosis

About 3 to 7% of children are diagnosed with ADHD, with three times as many boys having ADHD as girls. Currently, the diagnosis of ADHD is based on behavioral symptoms rather than medical tests. Through the years, psychologists have tried to identify which symptoms give the best diagnosis. Initially, hyperactivity was considered the major symptom, but having poor attention and acting impulsively were added, along with seeking immediate reward. Currently, the two major symptoms of ADHD are considered to be hyperactive-impulsive and inattentive behaviors (Barkley, 1997).

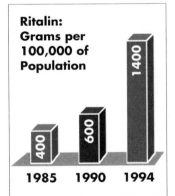

Because the behavioral symptoms may be more or less severe, there is the potential for misdiagnosis. For example, parents or teachers may label a child as having ADHD when the child is simply outgoing, rambunctious, or difficult to discipline (Edwards, 1995). A child may feel anxious or overwhelmed by the demands of school, act hyperactive or distracted, and become labeled as ADHD. There is also a relatively new concern about whether adults have ADD (without hyperactivity). Since this condition may resemble other mental health problems, an accurate diagnosis is difficult (Downey et al., 1997). Thus, the controversy regarding diagnosis of ADHD continues because, currently, there is no medical diagnostic test and the behavioral symptoms are not always clear cut.

Controversy: Treatment

As we discussed earlier, researchers found that, used in the normal range, artificial flavors or colors, preservatives, artificial sweeteners, or sugars do not contribute to or trigger hyperactive behaviors (Kinsbourne, 1994; Shaywitz et al., 1994; Wolraich et al., 1994).

Although some parents and educators have had success in helping ADHD children with behavioral programs, the graph on the right shows that the most popular treatment for ADHD is Ritalin (methylphenidate) (Hancock, 1996).

We'll review the advantages and disadvantages of using stimulant drugs to treat ADHD (Swanson et al., 1993; Mannuzza et al., 1993).

Ritalin: Grams per 100,000 of Population

1985	1990	1994
400	600	1400

STIMULANTS—ADVANTAGES

a. They decrease the child's activity, physical and verbal-aggression, and impulsive and negative behaviors (such as teasing and swearing) and generally make the child more manageable.

b. They increase the child's ability to concentrate and increase the amount and accuracy of schoolwork.

STIMULANTS—DISADVANTAGES

a. They cause side effects—most frequently, problems with eating and sleeping.

b. Even during treatment, there were no significant improvements in reading skills, athletic or game skills, or social skills in grade school.

c. Young adults with a history of ADHD may continue to have difficulty in academic settings, are less likely to graduate from high school or attend college, and are at risk for showing antisocial behaviors, such as fighting, trouble with the law, or drug abuse.

Obviously, Ritalin is not the total answer, since it doesn't always work, and when it does, its advantages must be weighed against its disadvantages.

Conclusions

One reason Ritalin is so popular is that it can produce relatively immediate and impressive decreases in hyperactivity and increases in attention so that the child is easier to manage in home and school (Buitelaar et al., 1996). However, there are numerous cases of children who were diagnosed with ADHD and given Ritalin but who did not improve because they had been misdiagnosed and actually had various other kinds of learning problems or disabilities (Hancock, 1996; Murray, 1997).

Even when Ritalin does reduce activity, it is not the entire solution, since these children continue to have academic and social problems (Wilens et al., 1997). For that reason, researchers encourage parents and teachers to use behavioral programs such as setting goals, establishing rules, and rewarding performance to help children deal with ADHD (Burcham et al., 1993). Finally, 30 to 70% of ADHD children continue to have problems through adolescence and adulthood, so it is a continuing problem (Barkley, 1997).

The story of ADHD and Ritalin points out how difficult it is to explain and treat complex human disorders. The long history of using Ritalin to treat ADHD also raises questions about the rights and concerns of using subjects, both human and animal, in research.

Concerns about Being a Subject

What's it like to be a subject?

Each time you hear about a new research finding—such as a drug to control weight or treat depression, or the discovery of a gene related to happiness, or ways to improve memory—you rarely think about the treatment of subjects, humans and animals, used in these experiments.

For example, if you were asked to volunteer to be a subject, you would certainly be concerned about whether someone has checked to ensure that the experiment is safe, that there are safeguards to protect you from potential psychological or physical harm, and that you won't be unfairly deceived or made to feel foolish. These are all real concerns, and we'll answer each one in turn.

Additionally, a separate and controversial question concerns the use of animals in research. We'll answer this question in some detail since there are many misconceptions about the use and misuse of animals in research.

We'll begin by considering the concerns of human subjects.

Code of Ethics

If you are a college student, there is a good possibility that you will be asked to participate in a psychology experiment. If you are considering becoming a subject, you may wonder what kinds of safeguards are used to protect subjects' rights and privacy.

The American Psychological Association has published a code of ethics and conduct for psychologists to follow when doing research, counseling, teaching, and related activities (American Psychological Association, 1992). This code of ethics spells out the responsibilities of psychologists and the rights of subjects participating in research.

Besides having to follow a code of ethics, psychologists must submit the details of their research programs, especially those with the potential for causing psychological or physical harm, to university research committees. These research committees carefully check the proposed experiments for any harmful procedures (Rosenthal, 1994).

Experiments are not approved unless any potentially damaging effects can be eliminated or counteracted. Counteracting potentially harmful effects is usually done by thoroughly describing the experiment, a process called debriefing.

Debriefing includes explaining the purpose and method of the experiment, asking the subjects their feelings about having been in the experiment, and helping the subjects deal with possible doubts or guilt arising from their behaviors in the experiment.

During the debriefing sessions, researchers will answer any questions or discuss any problems that subjects may have. The purpose of debriefing is to make sure that subjects have been treated fairly and have no lingering psychological or physical concerns or worries that come from being a subject in an experiment (Gurman, 1994).

Role of Deception

When recruiting subjects for their experiments, psychologists usually give the experiments titles, such as "Study of eye-witness testimony" or "Effects of alcohol on memory." The reason for using such general titles is that researchers do not want to create specific expectations that may bias how potential subjects will behave. It is well known that an experiment's results may be biased by a number of factors: by subjects' expectations of how they should behave, by their unknowingly behaving according to self-fulfilling prophecies, or by their efforts to make themselves look good or to please the experimenter.

One way that researchers control for subjects' expectations is to use bogus procedures or instructions that prevent subjects from learning the experiment's true purpose. However, before bogus or deceptive methodology can be used, researchers must satisfy the American Psychological Association's (1992) code of ethics. For example, the deceptive techniques must be justified by the scientific, educational, or applied value of the study and by giving subjects a sufficient explanation of the study as soon as possible (Fisher & Fryberg, 1994).

Another way to avoid bias from subjects' expectations is to keep both the researcher and subjects in the dark about the experiment's true purpose by using a double-blind procedure. As discussed earlier (page 37), a double-blind procedure means that neither the subjects nor the researcher are aware of the experiment's treatment or purpose.

Thus, researchers must be careful not to reveal too many details about their experiments lest they bias how potential subjects may behave.

Ethics of Animal Research

How many animals are used in research?

An estimated 20 to 30 million animals are used each year in biomedical research, which includes the fields of psychology, biology, medicine, and pharmaceutical companies (Herzog, 1993). Although these numbers seem large, they are small in comparison to the 5 billion chickens eaten annually by citizens in the United States. However, it is the use of animals in research that has generated the most concern and debate.

In the field of psychology, about 90% of the nonhuman animals used by researchers are rats and mice, while 10% are cats, dogs, monkeys, and birds (Mesirow, 1984). We'll examine the justification for using animals in research and how their rights are protected.

Are research animals mistreated?

You may have seen a disturbing photo or heard about a laboratory animal being mistreated. The fact is that, of the millions of animals used in research, only a few cases of animal mistreatment have been confirmed. That is because scientists know that proper care and treatment of their laboratory animals is vital to the success of their research. To abolish the use of all laboratory animals because of one or two isolated cases of mistreatment would be like abolishing all medical practice because of isolated cases of malpractice. Instead, researchers suggest balancing the rights of animals with the needs for advancing the medical, physiological, and psychological health of humans.

Is the use of animals justified?

Adrian Morrison, director of the National Institute of Mental Health's Program for Animal Research Issues, recently wrote,

"Because I do experimental surgery, I go through a soul-searching every couple of months, asking myself whether I really want to continue working on cats. The answer is always yes because I know that there is no other way for medicine to progress but through animal experimentation and that basic research ultimately leads to unforeseen benefits" (Morrison, 1993).

According to Frederick King, the former chair of the American Psychological Association's Committee on Animal Research and Experimentation, animal research has resulted in major medical advances, the discovery of treatments for human diseases, and a better understanding of human disorders (King et al., 1988).

In the field of psychology, animal research and animal models have led to better understanding of how stress affects one's psychological and physical health, mechanisms underlying learning and memory, and effects of sensory deprivation on development, to mention but a few (Domjan & Purdy, 1995).

Researchers are currently using animals to study epilepsy, Alzheimer's disease, fetal alcohol syndrome, schizophrenia, AIDS, and transplantation of brain tissue, none of which is possible with human subjects.

Who checks on the use of animals in research?

Numerous government and university regulations ensure the proper care and humane treatment of laboratory animals. For example, the U.S. Department of Agriculture conducts periodic inspections of all animal research facilities to ensure proper housing and to oversee experimental procedures that might cause pain or distress. Universities hire veterinarians to regularly monitor the care and treatment of laboratory animals. Finally, universities have animal subject committees with authority to decide whether sufficient justification exists for using animals in specific research projects.

How to strike a balance?

One of the basic issues is how to strike the right balance between animal rights and research needs. Based on past, present, and potential future benefits of animal research, many experts in the scientific, medical, and mental health communities believe that the conscientious and responsible use of animals in research is justified and should continue. This is especially true in light of recent rules that regulate the safe and humane treatment of animals kept in laboratories or used in research (Cork et al., 1997; Domjan & Purdy, 1995; Herzog, 1993).

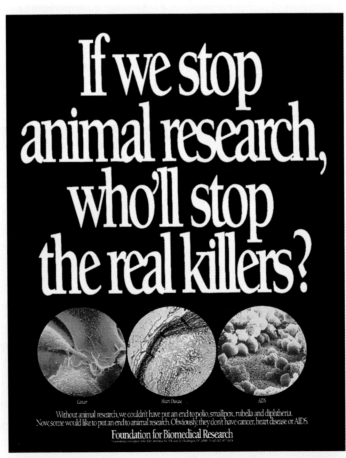

The small print in poster reads, "Without animal research, we couldn't have put an end to polio, smallpox, rubella and diphtheria. Now, some would like to put an end to animal research. Obviously, they don't have cancer, heart disease or AIDS."

SUMMARY TEST

A. METHODS FOR ANSWERING QUESTIONS

1. Psychologists use at least three methods to answer questions or obtain information. An in-depth analysis of a single person's thoughts and behaviors is called a (a)_____. One advantage of this method is that researchers obtain detailed information about a person, but one disadvantage is that such information may not apply to others. Asking a large number of individuals a fixed set of questions is called a (b)_____. Gathering information in a controlled laboratory setting is called an (c)_____.

B. SURVEYS

2. Measuring the attitudes, beliefs, and behaviors of a large sample of individuals by asking a set of questions is called a _____. One advantage of this method is that psychologists can quickly and efficiently collect information about a large number of people. One disadvantage is that people may answer in a way that they think is more socially acceptable.

C. CASE STUDY

3. A statement that supports a particular viewpoint and is based on a person's own experience is called a (a)_____, which has several potential sources of error and bias. First, strongly held personal beliefs may bias an individual's (b)_____ of events. Second, believing strongly that something will happen and then unknowingly acting in such a way as to make that something occur is a source of error called (c)_____. This source of error is one of the major reasons that people believe that their (d)_____ are true.

D. CULTURAL DIVERSITY: USE OF PLACEBOS

4. The use of some intervention that resembles a medical therapy but that, in fact, has no medical effects is called a (a)_____. If a person reports an improvement in some medical condition that is due to a supposed treatment rather than some medical therapy, that is called a (b)_____. One reason people around the world believe in placebos is that people give (c)_____ to their effectiveness.

E. CORRELATION

5. If two or more events are associated or linked together, they are said to be (a)_____. The strength of this association is indicated by a number called the (b)_____, which has a range from −1.00 to +1.00.

6. If there were a perfect association between two events—for example, when one increased, the other did also—this would be called a (a)_____. If an increase in one event is usually but not always accompanied by an increase in a second event, this would be called a (b)_____. If an increase in one event is always accompanied by a decrease in a second event, this is called a (c)_____. If an increase in one event is usually, but not always, accompanied by a decrease in a second event, this is called a (d)_____.

7. Although a correlation indicates that two or more events are occurring in some pattern, a correlation does not identify which event may (a)_____ the other(s). Although correlations do not identify cause-and-effect relationships, they do provide (b)_____ as to where to look for causes and they help to (c)_____ behavior.

F. DECISIONS ABOUT DOING RESEARCH

8. Psychologists may answer some question by using one or more of five commonly used research techniques. Asking questions about people's attitudes and behaviors, usually in a one-on-one situation, is using an (a)_____. Asking subjects to read a list of questions and indicate a specific answer is using a (b)_____. Asking subjects to complete established tests that measure personality, intelligence, or other behaviors is using (c)_____. If psychologists study subjects' behaviors under carefully controlled conditions that allow manipulation of the treatment, they are conducting a (d)_____. Psychologists can study a problem using animals by developing an (e)_____, which closely approximates the human's disease or condition.

9. Psychologists conduct research in two common settings. If psychologists obtain information by observing an individual's behaviors in his or her environment, without attempts to control or manipulate the situation, they would be using a _____. The *advantage* of this method is that it gives information that would be difficult to obtain or duplicate in a laboratory. The *disadvantage* of this method is that the psychologists' own beliefs or values may bias their observations and cause them to misinterpret the behaviors under observation.

10. If psychologists study a single individual in considerable depth in his or her own environment, they are using a _____. The *advantage* of this method is that it results in detailed descriptions and insights into many aspects of an individual's life. The *disadvantage* is that the information obtained may be so unique that it does not apply to others.

11. If psychologists want to study individuals under controlled and systematic conditions, with many of the real-life factors removed, they do the study in a _____. The *advantage* of this setting is that it permits greater control and manipulation of many conditions while ruling out possible contaminating factors. The *disadvantage* of this setting is that it may be too artificial or controlled, so that the results may not necessarily apply to real-life situations.

G. SCIENTIFIC METHOD: EXPERIMENT

12. The scientific method offers a set of rules or guidelines on how to conduct research with a minimum of error or bias. We have divided these guidelines into seven rules. **Rule 1** is to make a statement in precise, concrete terms. Such a statement is called a (a)_____, which researchers often develop based on previous observations or studies. **Rule 2** is to identify the treatment or something the experimenter manipulates, which is called the (b)_____. In addition, the experimenter also selects behaviors that are to be used to measure the potential effects of the treatment. These selected behaviors are called the (c)_____, and they may include a wide range of behaviors, such as cognitive processes, observable behaviors, or measurable physiological responses. **Rule 3** is to choose subjects so that each one in a sample has an equal chance of being selected. One procedure for doing so is called (d)_____.

Rule 4 is to assign subjects randomly to one of two groups. The group that will receive the treatment is called the (e)_____ and the group that will undergo everything but the treatment is called the (f)_____. **Rule 5** is to manipulate the (g)_____ by administering it (or one level of it) to the experimental group but not to the control group. The procedure for preventing researchers or

Ritalin

subjects from knowing who is getting the treatment is called the (h)_____. **Rule 6** is to measure the effects of the independent variable on behaviors that have been selected as the (i)_____. **Rule 7** is to analyze differences between behaviors of subjects in the experimental group with those in the control group by using various (j)_____, which determine whether differences were due to the treatment or to chance occurrences. By following these seven rules, researchers reduce the chances that (k)_____ caused their results.

H. RESEARCH FOCUS: ADHD QUESTIONS

13. The reason for the controversy over who has ADHD is that, as of this writing, there is no (a)_____ diagnostic test. As a result, the diagnosis of ADHD must be based on the occurrence of (b)_____ symptoms, some of which may be unclear. The reason for the controversy over how to treat ADHD is that stimulants produce a short-term improvement in management of some ADHD symptoms without necessarily resulting in (c)_____ improvements or gains.

I. APPLICATION: CONCERNS ABOUT RESEARCH

14. One method of counteracting potential harmful effects to experimental subjects is by thoroughly _____ them. This includes explaining the purpose and method of the experiment, asking subjects about their feelings, and helping subjects deal with possible doubts or problems arising from the experiment.

15. The justification for using _____ in research is that it has resulted in major medical advances, treatments for diseases, and understanding of human disorders.

Answers: 1. (a) case study, (b) survey, (c) experiment; 2. survey; 3. (a) testimonial, (b) perceptions, (c) self-fulfilling prophecy, (d) testimonials; 4. (a) placebo, (b) placebo effect, (c) testimonials; 5. (a) correlated, (b) correlation coefficient; 6. (a) perfect positive correlation, (b) positive correlation, (c) perfect negative correlation, (d) negative correlation; 7. (a) cause, (b) clues, (c) predict; 8. (a) interview, (b) questionnaire, (c) standardized tests, (d) laboratory study or experiment, (e) animal model; 9. naturalistic setting; 10. case study; 11. laboratory setting; 12. (a) hypothesis, (b) independent variable, (c) dependent variables, (d) random selection, (e) experimental group, (f) control group, (g) independent variable, (h) double-blind procedure, (i) dependent variables, (j) statistical procedures, (k) error or bias; 13. (a) medical, (b) behavioral, (c) long-term; 14. debriefing; 15. animals.

Newspaper Article

FREQUENT SEXUAL ACTIVITY MAY HELP MEN LIVE LONGER, STUDY FINDS

by Lawrence K. Altman

1. Was the original research question to study sex, or was this "sex" finding unexpected?

2. What are the three major methods for answering questions, and which method was used in this study?

3. Does the major finding indicate a cause-and-effect relationship or only a correlation?

4. Why couldn't this study show a cause-and-effect relationship between more sex and living longer?

5. What is the advantage and the disadvantage of this study?

Men who have more orgasms seem to live longer, a statistical study of Welsh villagers in *The British Medical Journal* has found. . . . "Sexual activity seems to have a protective effect on men's health," Dr. George Davey-Smith's team concluded after analyzing death rates of nearly 1,000 men from 45 to 59 in Caerphilly.

Davey-Smith's team assessed the existence of heart disease in the men when they entered the study from 1979 to 1983. After explaining the purpose of their question, they asked the men about the frequency of sexual activity. The answers were put into categories ranging from "never" to "daily." . . . The participants' names were flagged in the British national health service's central registry and the researchers were automatically notified if they died. The death rate was analyzed 10 years after the participants entered the study.

Men who said they had sex twice a week had a risk of dying half that of the less passionate participants who said they had sex once a month, Davey-Smith's team said. . . . Further studies of both sexes are needed to confirm their findings, the authors said.

Two other scientists added a few drops of cold water, cautioning that because of its design (use of surveys), the epidemiological study might not have been able to identify a number of factors that could have inadvertently influenced the findings. One possibility is that the link could be reversed—ill people may be less likely to have sex, according to the critics who commented in the same issue.

The authors said that they had tried to adjust the study's design to account for a factor that might explain the findings—that healthier, fitter men with more healthy life styles engaged in more sex. Even so, they could not explain the differences in risk. Hormonal effects on the body resulting from frequent sex could be among other possible explanations for the findings, Davey-Smith said.

Source: New York Times News Service, appeared in *San Diego Union-Tribune*, December 23, 1997.

Study Questions

A. Methods for Answering Questions—Which method would you use to find out if caffeine improves memory? (See answer in Critical Thinking Appendix.)

B. Surveys—How believable is a recent survey that reported that people never lie to their best friends?

C. Case Study—Why do some people put more faith in testimonials than in proven research?

D. Cultural Diversity: Use of Placebos—Why do Americans think it strange that Asians use rhino horn as medicine? (See answer in Critical Thinking Appendix.)

E. Correlation—How would you explain the positive correlation (0.60) researchers found between drinking coffee and being sexually active after age 60?

F. Decisions about Doing Research—Which research techniques and settings would you use to study mental problems in the homeless? (See answer in Critical Thinking Appendix.)

G. Scientific Method: Experiment—How would you determine whether taking vitamin B reduces stress?

H. Research Focus: ADHD Questions—If you had a child who might have ADHD, what would you do?

I. Application: Concerns about Research—What concerns might a student have about volunteering to be a subject in an experiment?

Web Sites & Learning Activities

● BROOKS/COLE ONLINE PSYCHOLOGY STUDY CENTER

http://psychstudy.brookscole.com/student/plotnik/quiz/ch02frm.html

● PSYCHOLOGICAL RESEARCH ON THE INTERNET

http://psych.hanover.edu/APS/exponnet.html

Sponsored by the American Psychological Society, this site indexes many psychology-related experiments currently being conducted using the Internet.

● INTERNET PSYCHOLOGY LAB

http://kahuna.cogsci.uiuc.edu/ipl/

This multimedia, interactive system for laboratory instruction in psychology allows students to get the science lab experience on the Internet.

● INTRODUCTORY STATISTICS

http://www.psychstat.smsu.edu/sbk00.htm

This Web site is an online statistics textbook, which includes many topics from simple to complex, illustrations, and interactive exercises.

● TWENTY SCIENCE ATTITUDES

http://psg.com/~ted/bcskeptics/ratenq/Re3.3-Attitude.html

This article from *Rational Inquirer* outlines 20 traits of a good scientist.

Welcome to the WEB

● APA SCIENCE INFORMATION FOR STUDENTS

http://www.apa.org/science/infostu.html

Interested in knowing what scientific opportunities are available to psychology students? This site is a great place to start.

● PSYCHOLOGY IN DAILY LIFE

http://www.apa.org/pubinfo/pubinfo.html

How does psychology research apply to our everyday lives? This American Psychological Association site provides some examples for the lay reader.

Activities

● *Integrator Online™ for Introductory Psychology* CD-ROM, Plotnik, Module 2

● Study Guide to accompany *Introduction to Psychology,* 5th edition (choice of PC or Mac computer version or hard copy)

● PsychNow! CD-ROM

Research Methods

Critical Thinking in Psychology

Answers to questions on page 44

1. The original purpose of this study was to assess heart disease in men. However, in answering the original research question, researchers found another interesting link between sexual activity and length of life, which raised new questions.

2. The three major methods for answering questions are survey, case study, and experiment. In this study, researchers asked men questions about their health and sexual activity, so this study primarily used the survey method.

3. Surveys cannot show cause-and-effect relationships but only associations or correlations between events: men who had sex more often lived longer than men who had sex less often.

4. To show a cause-and-effect relationship, this study must have been designed as an experiment in which an experimental group got one treatment (more sex) while a control group got no or different treatment (less sex). For ethical reasons, such an experiment could not be conducted on humans, so it would be difficult to demonstrate this cause-and-effect relationship.

5. The advantage of this survey study is that it suggests an unexpected cause or explanation of why men live longer (having more sex). One disadvantage of this survey study is that it cannot identify cause-and-effect relationships because many other factors (hormones, different life styles) cannot be ruled out.

Module 3   BRAIN'S BUILDING BLOCKS

Losing One's Mind

Why does 71-year-old Ina think the baby is hers?

Her children had always called their mother, Ina, "the Rock of Gibraltar." Ina (right photo) could fix the plumbing, hang wallpaper, and prepare a full dinner from scratch every night, while keeping her six children out of trouble. She could swim faster than anyone, she wanted to be a basketball player, and her late husband called her the most beautiful woman he had ever seen.

But that was before she started to forget things and repeat herself, which could just be part of getting old. But how to explain her mopping the kitchen floor at 2 in the morning and refusing to go to bed? Or wearing the same dirty clothes day after day, something she had never done in her entire life? Or being confused at housework?

Because Ina had always been so healthy, her six grown children thought she must have suffered a stroke or be depressed. When they took Ina in for a checkup, a neurologist confirmed their worst fears. Ina had Alzheimer's (*ALTS-hi-mers*) disease.

In 10% of the cases, *Alzheimer's disease* begins after age 50, but in 90% of the cases, it begins after age 65. Its initial symptoms are problems with memory, such as forgetting and repeating things, getting lost, and mild confusion. There are also cognitive deficits, such as problems with language, difficulties in recognizing objects, and inability to plan and organize tasks. Over a period of five to ten years, these symptoms worsen and result in profound memory loss, lack of recognition of family and friends, deterioration in personality, and emotional outbursts. There is widespread damage to the brain, especially the hippocampus, which is involved in memory. At present, there is no cure for Alzheimer's, which is always fatal (American Psychiatric Association, 1994).

In the United States, Alzheimer's is the fourth leading cause of death among adults. In 1997, approximately four million people—or 5% of adults over age 65—

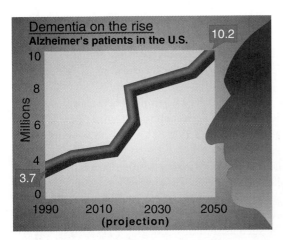

Dementia on the rise
Alzheimer's patients in the U.S.

Millions

10.2

10

8

6

4

3.7

0

1990   2010   2030   2050
(projection)

had Alzheimer's disease, and the number of patients is projected to rise dramatically in the coming decades (graph on left) as people are expected to live longer (Morrison-Bogorad et al., 1997).

Ina's condition worsened through the coming months. She had trouble completing even the simplest tasks, and the day after having a big Thanksgiving celebration with her family, she asked where she had spent the holiday. At times, she recognized her grown children; at other times, she thought they were her cousins. Ina loves her granddaughter (above right photo) but sometimes thinks the baby is hers. Ina must now be watched almost every minute so that she does not hurt herself or wander off (adapted from *Newsweek,* December 18, 1989).

For Ina, the worst is yet to come. Her memory will totally disintegrate, she will be completely bedridden, and she will not know who she is or recognize the family she has lovingly raised. When she dies—for Alzheimer's has, at present, no cure—Ina will have lost her memory, her wonderful personality, and all signs of humanity.

Diagnosis and Causes

In Ina's case as well as all cases of individuals with memory and cognitive difficulties, Alzheimer's is diagnosed by looking at a combination of behavioral symptoms and by eliminating the possibility of other physical problems. At the time of this writing, the only absolute test now available for Alzheimer's involves examination of the brain after death (Alexander et al., 1997).

In searching for the possible causes of Alzheimer's disease, researchers have suggested viruses, environmental toxins (aluminum), and genetic factors. Currently, researchers believe the most likely cause of Alzheimer's arises from genetic factors that interact differently in different people (Lendon et al., 1997; Weiner, 1997). For example, the malfunction of some genes results in making too much of a gluelike substance that eventually destroys brain cells (Selkoe, 1997). The malfunction of other genes interferes with the cells' chemical engines so that cells lose energy and die (Barinaga, 1997). Researchers are trying to identify the specific genes and determine how they interact to cause Alzheimer's disease.

What's Coming

The reason Alzheimer's gradually destroys a person's memory, personality, and humanity is that it progressively breaks down the building blocks that make up the brain's informational network. We'll explain the two groups of brain cells—glial cells and neurons—that make up this network. We'll discuss how the cells in one group—neurons—have a remarkable ability to transport information. You'll discover that brain cells communicate with chemicals that have the ability to start or stop the flow of information. Finally, we explain a remarkable new treatment of implanting neurons to treat brain diseases. We'll use the story of Ina and Alzheimer's disease to illustrate the brain's building blocks.

A. Overview: Human Brain

The fact that Alzheimer's disease is slowly destroying Ina's brain and simultaneously causing her to slowly lose her mind raises four basic questions: How does the brain become a brain? What is in the brain? Can the brain repair itself? Are the brain and the mind the same or different things? We'll answer each of these questions in order.

1 Development of the Brain

Why isn't your brain a nose? The fact that your brain does not develop into a nose is because of instructions contained in your genes.

Genes are chains of chemicals that are arranged like rungs on a twisting ladder (right figure). There are about 100,000 genes that contain chemical instructions that equal about 1,000,000 pages of written instructions. The chemical instructions in the genes program the development of millions of individual parts into a complex body and brain.

An amazing feature of the 100,000 genes is that they are contained in a fertilized egg, which is a single cell about the size of a grain of sand. We'll explain more about the genes and their chemical instructions in the next module.

In the brain's early developmental stages, it looks nothing like the final product. For example, the figure below looks more like some strange animal than what it really is, a six-week-old human embryo.

SIX-WEEK-OLD BRAIN. This drawing represents a greatly enlarged six-week-old human embryo. The 3 labeled areas (in 3 colors) will eventually develop into the 3 major divisions of the mature human brain that is shown below.

MATURE BRAIN. The 3 labeled areas represent the 3 major divisions of the mature brain that we'll discuss in the next module. The mature human brain (side view) weighs almost 3 pounds, and contains about one trillion cells (Fischbach, 1992).

In the case of Ina, who developed Alzheimer's disease, researchers think that some of her genetic instructions were faulty. The faulty instructions resulted in the excessive formation of a glue-like substance that builds up in the brain and gradually destroys brain cells (Morrison-Bogorad et al., 1997). Next, we'll explain the two different kinds of brain cells and which ones are destroyed by Alzheimer's disease.

2 Structure of the Brain

What's in your brain? Your brain (top view shown on left) has a pinkish-white color, is a relatively small, melon-shaped structure, weighs about 1,350 grams (less than 3 pounds) and has the consistency of firm Jell-O. Your brain is fueled by sugar (glucose), and has about one trillion cells that can be divided into two groups—glial cells and neurons.

GLIAL CELLS. The most numerous brain cells, about 900 billion, are called glial (*GLEE-all*) cells.

Glial cells have at least three functions: they provide scaffolding to guide the growth of developing neurons and support mature neurons; they wrap themselves around neurons and form a kind of insulation to prevent interference from other electrical signals; and they release chemicals that influence a neuron's growth and function (Travis, 1994).

A star-shaped glial cell (astrocyte) is shown above. Glial cells grow throughout one's lifetime. If something causes the uncontrolled growth of glial cells, the result is brain cancer. Alzheimer's disease does not usually destroy glial cells, but it does destroy the second kind of brain cells, which are called neurons.

NEURONS. The second group of brain cells, which number about 100 billion, are called neurons (*NER-ons*); one is shown on the right.

A *neuron* is a brain cell with two specialized extensions. One extension is for receiving electrical signals, and a second, longer extension is for transmitting electrical signals.

Depending upon their size, neurons receive and transmit electrical signals at speeds up to 200 miles per hour over distances from a fraction of an inch to over 3 feet.

Neurons form a vast, miniaturized informational network that allows us to receive sensory information, control muscle movement, regulate digestion, secrete hormones, and engage in complex mental processes such as thinking, imagining, dreaming, and remembering.

Ina's brain was constructed from two kinds of building blocks—glial cells and neurons. However, it is the neurons that Alzheimer's disease gradually destroys; the result is that Ina's brain is losing its ability to transmit information and is causing memory and cognitive difficulties. Why neurons do not repair or replace themselves is our next topic.

Repair of the Brain

'an your brain repair itself?

The two red dots show two areas of the mature canary's brain that can increase by 50% or more, on account of the growth of new neurons.

In trying to answer this question, one researcher studied song patterns of canaries (Nottebohm, 1989). A mature male canary learns to sing a breeding song in the spring, but when breeding season is over, this ability to sing the song disappears. However, come breeding season next year, the canary relearns the breeding song. As the canary relearns the song, there is a 50% or more increase in two areas of the canary's brain that control singing. This significant increase in brain size results from the formation of new neurons in the mature brain (Doupe, 1996).

ATE BRAINS. If neurons can grow in adult canary brains, as well mice and rats, can neurons also grow in the mature brains of pri- (humans, chimpanzees, and monkeys)? Another researcher stud- eural growth in monkeys' brains, which are similar in structure to n brains. However, there is almost no evidence that new neurons in the mature primate brain, which has developed the vast major- ity of its neurons by birth (Rakic, 1985). In addition, researchers discovered that neurons do not usually regrow after damage because their genetic program that regu- lates regrowth turns off when the neurons are fully grown (Schneider, 1995).

In the mature primate brain, the vast majority of neurons are present at birth. Only a tiny minority of neurons can regrow in the mature brain.

Knowing that the vast majority of neurons in the mature primate brain are present at birth and that they are not replaced if dam- aged explains why Alzheimer's disease is so devastating. Since Ina's brain cannot replace the neurons oyed by Alzheimer's disease, her behavioral symptoms will progres- worsen until her brain is mostly destroyed and death follows.

lthough mature brains do not have the capacity to regrow and ce damaged neurons, mature brains have a limited capacity to er after injury. For instance, after the brain is accidentally injured, hy neurons have the ability to send out very short extensions to e new connections with neurons whose normal connections were aged (Barinaga, 1992b). This limited ability to form some new ections explains why people may recover some of the functions lly lost after brain damage.

ecause Ina seems to be losing her mind as Alzheimer's disease oys her brain, the question arises of whether the mind and the are one and the same.

4 Brain versus Mind

Is your brain the same as your mind?

This centuries-old problem is called the mind-body question.

The *mind-body question* asks how complex mental activities, such as feeling, thinking, learning, imag- ining, and dreaming, can be generated by the brain's physical membranes, fluids, and chemicals.

Through the centuries, philosophers and scientists have answered the mind-body question differently, some believing the mind and brain are separate things and others saying the mind and brain are one and the same (Crick & Koch, 1997).

For example, Nobel Prize winner and geneticist Francis Crick (1994) believes the mind *is* the brain: "You, your joys and your sorrows, your memories and your ambition, your sense of personal identity and free will, are in fact no more than the behavior of a vast assembly of nerve cells and their associated molecules." Although some agree with Crick's answer, that the mind and brain are one and the same, others reply that mental activities cannot be reduced to the physical activities of the brain (Cole, 1997).

Another answer comes from Nobel Prize winner and neurophysiologist Roger Sperry (1993), who said that the brain is like a coin with two sides. One side consists of physical reactions, such as making chemicals that neurons use for communicating. The other side consists of all of our men- tal functions, such as thinking, imagining and deciding. According to Sperry, the brain's chemicals (physical side) influence consciousness and mental activities, which, in turn, influence the production of more or different brain chemicals. There is consid- erable support for Sperry's idea that there is an intense and con- tinuous interaction between the physical and mental sides.

For example, it is well established that your beliefs alone can reduce pain, such as happens after you take a pill that, without your knowing, turns out to be a placebo or sugar pill (Dodes, 1997). It is also well known that your thoughts or emotions can make you physically ill, such as giving you headaches or nausea, or reducing blood flow to the heart (Gullette et al., 1997). Finally, in Ina's case, as Alzheimer's disease destroys her brain, she also loses more and more of her mind. Thus, there is little ques- tion that the brain and mind are closely linked, and researchers are currently studying how this links occurs (Benson, 1997).

Knowing now how important neurons are to your mental and physical functions, we next examine them in more detail.

B. Neurons: Structure & Function

Three Parts of the Neuron

Why could Ina think, move, and talk?

Before Ina developed Alzheimer's disease, she was able to engage in an incredible variety of cognitive and physical behaviors. She was able to think, remember, walk, smile, and speak—all because of the activity of millions of microscopic brain cells called neurons. We'll examine the neuron, which comes in many wondrous shapes and sizes and has only three basic structures—cell body, dendrites, and axon.

Signals travel away from cell body, down the axon.

3 The *axon (AXE-on)* is a single threadlike structure that extends from, and carries signals away from, the cell body to neighboring neurons, organs, or muscles.

4 The *myelin (MY-lin) sheath* looks like separate tube-like segments composed of fatty material that wraps around and insulates an axon. The myelin sheath prevents interference from electrical signals generated in adjacent axons.

1 The *cell body* (or soma) is a relatively large, egg-shaped structure that provides fuel, manufactures chemicals, and maintains the entire neuron in working order.

In the center of the cell body is a small oval shape representing the nucleus, which contains genetic instructions (in the form of DNA) for the manufacture of chemicals and regulation of the neuron.

2 *Dendrites (DEN-drites)* are branchlike extensions that arise from the cell body; they receive signals from other neurons, muscles, or sense organs and pass these signals to the cell body.

At the time of birth, a neuron has few dendrites. After birth, dendrites undergo dramatic growth that accounts for much of the increase in brain size. As dendrites grow, they make connections and form communication networks between neurons and other cells or organs.

Here the axon is indicated by an orange line inside the tube composed of separate gray segments. Axons vary in length from less than a hair's breadth to as long as 3 feet (from your spinal cord to your toes). An axon conducts electrical signals to a neighboring organ (heart), a muscle, or another neuron.

The axons of most large neurons, including motor neurons, have myelin sheaths. You may have heard the brain described as consisting of gray and white matter. Gray is the color of cell bodies, while white is the color of myelin sheaths.

5 *End bulbs,* which look like tiny bubbles, are located at the extreme ends of the axon's branches. Each end bulb is like a miniature container that stores chemicals called neurotransmitters, which are used to communicate with neighboring cells.

End bulbs reach right up to, but do not physically touch, the surface of a neighboring organ (heart), muscle (head), or another cell body.

6 The *synapse (SIN-apse)* is an infinitely small space (20–30 billionths of a meter) that exists between an end bulb and its adjacent body organ (heart), muscles (head), or cell body.

When stimulated by electrical signals from the axon, the end bulbs eject neurotransmitters into the synapse. The neurotransmitters cross the synapse and act like switches to turn adjacent cells on or off. We'll explain this switching process a little later.

Alzheimer's Disease and Neurons

Why is Ina losing her mind?

A major result of Alzheimer's disease is an excessive buildup of a gluelike substance, which gradually interferes with and then destroys neurons. In Ina's case, this substance will destroy more and more of her neurons, causing more and more cognitive problems and, eventually, her death. Researchers are searching for ways to stop the buildup of this killer substance.

We have discussed the structure and function of neurons, but it is important not to confuse neurons with nerves, which are not in the brain but are located throughout your body.

Reattached Arms

What's unusual about John's arms?

Sometimes a tragic accident can tell us much about the human nervous system. Such an accident happened to 18-year-old John Thomas when a farm machine ripped off both of his arms just below his shoulders. Since he was home alone, he had to walk to the farmhouse, kick in the front door, and with a pencil clenched in his teeth, dial the phone for help. Because he was worried about bleeding on his mother's nice carpet, he waited in the bathtub for the ambulance. When paramedics arrived, he reminded them to get his two arms, which were still stuck in the farm equipment.

By the time John reached the hospital, he had lost half of his body's blood. However, doctors were able to keep John alive and, after many hours of surgery, reattached both arms.

Three months later, John could raise his arms up in the air but could not move them below his elbows. After a year and a half and hundreds of hours of occupational therapy, John could bend his elbows but not rotate his arms, and his fingers were curled into claws. After three years and 15 operations, John could raise both of his reattached arms over his head, make fists and grip with his hands. Surgeons believe that John will recover additional movement and feelings in his arms, but that may require 2–5 years of physical therapy (*USA Today,* January 12, 1995).

The scars on John's arms (photo on right) mark the areas where they were reattached. Notice that in John's case some movement and sensation has returned to his arms. In Ina's case, however, the neurons destroyed by Alzheimer's disease did not regrow. These two examples illustrate that the peripheral and the central nervous systems differ.

Peripheral Nervous System

Why could John's arms be reattached?

The reason John's arms could be reattached and regain movement is that arms have nerves, which are part of the peripheral nervous system.

The *peripheral nervous system* is made up of nerves, which are located throughout the body except in the brain and spinal cord.

Nerves (shown in red in the figure) are stringlike bundles of axons and dendrites that come from the spinal cord and are held together by connective tissue. Nerves carry information from the senses, skin, muscles, and the body's organs to and from the spinal cord. Nerves in the peripheral nervous system have the ability to regrow, regenerate, or reattach if severed or damaged.

Because nerves can regrow, severed limbs can be reattached, as they were in John's case. However, the amount of feeling and movement that returns depends upon several factors, such as the amount of damage to the nerves, the patient's age (the younger the better), and the length of physical therapy. The remarkable ability of nerves to regrow and be reattached distinguishes them from neurons, which can do neither and which make up the central nervous system.

Central Nervous System

Why won't Ina's neurons regrow?

The reason Ina's neurons do not regrow or repair themselves is because they are in the central nervous system.

The *central nervous system* is made up of neurons located in the brain and spinal cord (shown in blue in the figure). Neurons in the central nervous system normally have almost no capacity to regrow or regenerate if damaged or diseased.

Because neurons do not normally regrow, Ina's brain will actually shrink in size as Alzheimer's disease continues to destroy her neurons. Because neurons do not normally reattach themselves, people who have a damaged spinal cord experience some loss of sensation and motor movement, depending upon the severity of the damage. If the damage to the spinal cord is severe, a person may lose all movement and sensations below the neck (quadriplegic) or below the waist (semiplegic). Although neurons do not usually regrow, researchers are developing new methods to stimulate the regrowth of neurons in the central nervous system.

Regrowth of Neurons

Currently one of the most exciting areas of research is on regrowing and transplanting neurons. For example, after being damaged, axons normally wither and die. However, if axons are provided with tubes made from peripheral nerves to guide their growth or are injected with growth-producing chemicals, axons can regrow and make new connections (Olson et al., 1997). Another approach is to replace damaged neurons by transplanting fetal neurons, which has great potential for treating fatal brain diseases, such as Alzheimer's (Winkler et al., 1995). We'll discuss fetal tissue transplants in the Application section. Stimulating the growth of neurons in the central nervous system provides hope for treating individuals with brain or spinal cord injury.

Now that you know the structure of the neuron, we'll explain one of its amazing functions: sending information throughout the brain and body at speeds approaching 200 miles per hour.

D. Sending Information

Sequence: Action Potential

> **What happens when you step on a tack?**

1 Feeling a Sharp Object

When you step on a sharp object, you seem to feel the pain almost immediately because neurons send signals at speeds approaching 200 mph. To feel the pain involves the following series of electrochemical events:

A. Some stimulus, such as a tack, causes a change in physical energy. The tack produces mechanical pressure on the bottom of your foot.

B. Your skin has sensors that pick up the mechanical pressure and transform it into electrical signals. (We'll discuss various kinds of sensors in Module 5.)

C. The sensor's electrical signals are sent by the neuron's axon to various areas in the spinal cord and brain.

D. Finally, your brain interprets these electrical signals as "pain."

We're going to focus on step C and explain how axons send electrical signals by using the analogy of a battery. We'll begin by enlarging the inside of an axon.

2 Axon Membrane: Chemical Gates

Just as a battery has a protective covering, so too does the axon. Think of an axon like a long tube that is not only filled with fluid but also surrounded with fluid. The axon's tube is formed by a thin membrane, similar to a battery's outside covering, which keeps the fluid separate and also has special gates.

The axon membrane has chemical

gates (**shown in red**) that can open to allow electrically charged particles to enter or can close to keep out electrically charged particles.

Just as a battery's power comes from its electrically charged chemicals, so does the axon's power to send information. In fact, the axon's electrically charged particles are the key to making it a living battery.

3 Ions: Charged Particles

The fluid inside and outside the axon contains ions.

Ions are chemical particles that have electrical charges. Ions follow two rules: Opposite charges attract (figure below), and like charges repel.

SODIUM (NA+) IONS   **OPPOSITE CHARGES ATTRACT**   **PROTEIN⁻ IONS**

The fluid contains several different ions, such as sodium, potassium, chloride, and protein. The axon's function is often explained by discussing sodium and potassium ions. However, it is simpler and easier just to focus on sodium ions, which have positive charges and are abbreviated Na^+, and large protein ions, which have negative charges and are labeled protein⁻. Because they have opposite charges, Na^+ ions will be attracted to protein⁻ ions (figure above).

Because the axon's membrane separates the positive sodium ions from the negative protein ions, we have the makings of a living battery, as shown in section 4 on the facing page.

Sequence: Nerve Impulse

> **Is it like a gunshot or a fast-burning fuse?**

6 Sending Information

One mistake students make is to think that the axon has ONE action potential, similar to the bang of a gunshot. However, unlike a gunshot, the axon has numerous individual action potentials that move down the axon, segment by segment; this movement is called the nerve impulse.

The *nerve impulse* refers to the series of separate action potentials that take place segment by segment as they move down the length of an axon.

Thus, instead of a single bang, a nerve impulse goes down the length of the axon very much like a lit fuse. Once lit, a fuse doesn't go off in a single bang but rather burns continuously until it reaches the end. This movement of a nerve impulse all the way down to the end of an axon is actually a natural law.

7 All-or-None Law

Why does a nerve impulse travel down the axon's entire length? The answer is the all-or-none law.

The *all-or-none law* says that, if an action potential starts at the beginning of an axon, the action potential will continue at the same speed, segment by segment, to the very end of the axon.

You'll see how the all-or-none law works in the next figure.

8 Nerve Impulse

Notice in this drawing, which continues on the next page, the nerve impulse is made up of a sequence of six action potentials, with the first action potential occurring at the beginning of the axon.

1. Action potential

BATTERY

4 Resting State: Charged Battery

The axon membrane separates positively charged sodium ions on the outside from negatively charged protein ions on the inside. This separation produces a miniature chemical battery that is not yet discharging and, thus, is said to be in its resting state.

SODIUM (NA+) IONS

PROTEIN⁻ IONS

BATTERY

The *resting state* means that the axon has a charge, or potential; it resembles a battery. The charge, or potential, results from the axon membrane separating positive ions on the outside from negative ions on the inside (left figure).

The axon membrane has a charge across it during the resting state because of several factors, the primary one being the sodium pump. (To simplify our explanation of the resting state, we won't discuss other pump or transport systems.)

The *sodium pump* is a transport process that picks up any sodium ions that enter the axon's chemical gates and returns them back outside. Thus, the sodium pump is responsible for keeping the axon charged by returning and keeping sodium ions outside the axon membrane.

In the resting state, the axon is similar to a fully charged battery. Let's see what happens when the resting state is disrupted and the battery discharges.

5 Action Potential: Sending Information

If a stimulus, such as stepping on a tack, is large enough to excite a neuron, two things will happen to its axon. First, the stimulus will eventually open the axon's chemical gates by stopping the sodium pump. Second, when the stoppage of the sodium pump causes the gates to open, thousands of positive sodium ions will rush inside because of their attraction to the negative protein ions. The rush of sodium ions inside the axon is called the action potential.

The *action potential* is a tiny electrical current that is generated when the positive sodium ions rush inside the axon. The enormous increase of sodium ions inside the axon causes the inside of the axon to reverse its charge. The inside becomes positive, while the outside becomes negative.

Action potential

5a Just as a current flows when you connect the poles of a battery, current also flows when sodium ions rush through the opened gates of the axon membrane.

5b During an action potential, the inside of the axon changes to positive and the outside changes to negative. Immediately after the action potential, the sodium pump starts up and returns the axon to the resting state.

At this point, imagine that an action potential has started at the beginning of an axon. How action potentials whiz at race-car speeds down the entire length of an axon is what we'll examine next in the section below, Sequence: Nerve Impulse.

8a According to the all-or-none law, once a nerve impulse begins, it goes to the end of the axon. This means that when action potential 1 occurs, it will be followed in order by potentials 2, 3, 4, 5, and 6. After the occurrence of each action potential, the axon membrane at that point quickly returns to its resting state.

8b Notice that the *myelin sheath* has regular breaks where the axon is bare and uninsulated. It is at these bare points that the axon's gates open and the action potential takes place.

9 End Bulbs and Neurotransmitters

Once the nerve impulse reaches the end of the axon, the very last action potential, 6, affects the end bulbs, which are located at the very end of the axon. This last action potential triggers the end bulbs to release their neurotransmitters. Once released, neurotransmitters cross the synapse and, depending upon the kind, they will either excite or inhibit the function of neighboring organs (heart), muscles (head), or cell bodies.

As you can now see, neurotransmitters are critical for communicating with neighboring organs, muscles, and other neurons. We'll examine transmitters in more detail and show you how they excite or inhibit.

BREAKS IN MYELIN

2. Action potential **3.** Action potential **4.** Action potential **5.** Action potential **6.** Action potential

E. Transmitters

Excitatory and Inhibitory Transmitters

What makes your heart pound?

There's no doubt that you have felt your heart pounding when you are afraid, stressed, or angry. One reason for your pounding heart has to do with transmitters.

A *transmitter* is a chemical messenger that transmits information between nerves and body organs, such as muscles and heart.

Everything you do, including thinking, deciding, talking, and getting angry, involves transmitters. For example, imagine seeing someone back into your brand new car and then just drive away. You would certainly become angry and your heart would pound. Let's see why getting angry can increase your heart rate from a normal 60 to 70 beats per minute to over 180.

1 In the figure on the left, you see the end of an axon with 3 branches. At the very end of the bottom branch is a greatly enlarged *end bulb.* Inside the bulb are 4 colored circles that represent transmitters.

2 When the action potential hits the *end bulb,* it causes a miniature explosion, and the transmitters are ejected outside. Once ejected, transmitters cross a tiny space, or synapse, and, in this case, reach the nearby heart muscle. Think of transmitters as chemical keys that fit into chemical locks on the surface of the heart muscle. End bulbs usually hold either excitatory or inhibitory transmitters, which have opposite effects.

Transmitters

3 Strong emotions cause the release of *excitatory transmitters*, which open chemical locks in the heart muscle and cause it to beat faster (left figure). When you get very angry, excitatory transmitters may cause your heart rate to double or even triple its rate. When you start to calm down, there is a release of *inhibitory transmitters*, which block chemical locks in the heart muscle and decrease its rate (right figure). Think of transmitters acting like chemical messengers that either excite or inhibit nearby body organs (heart), neurons, or muscle fibers. One special class of transmitters that are made in the brain are called neurotransmitters.

Excitatory

Inhibitory

Neurotransmitters

What makes your brain work?

Writing a paper on a computer requires your brain to use millions of neurons that communicate with one another by using chemicals called neurotransmitters. *Neurotransmitters* refer to about a dozen different chemicals that are made by neurons and then used for communication between neurons during the performance of mental or physical activities.

Since billions of neurons that are packed tightly together use different neurotransmitters for eating, sleeping, talking, thinking, and dreaming, why don't neurotransmitters get all mixed up? The answer is that neurotransmitters are similar to chemical keys that fit only into specific chemical locks.

1 The figure on the left again shows the end of an axon with 3 branches. We have again enlarged one *end bulb* to show that it contains neurotransmitters (4 colored circles).

Neurotransmitters

2 The action potential causes the end bulbs to eject their neurotransmitters (colored circles), which, in turn, cross the synapse and, in this case, land on the surface of nearby dendrites. The surface of one dendrite is enlarged (right figure) to show its *receptors* (yellow ovals), which are special areas that function like chemical locks.

Receptors

3 Although there are many different neurotransmitters, each one has a unique chemical key that fits and opens only certain chemical locks, or receptors. Thus, billions of neurons use this system of chemical keys that open or close matching locks to communicate and to participate in so many different activities. Also, remember that some neurotransmitters are *excitatory*—they open receptor locks and turn on neurons, while others are *inhibitory*—they close locks and turn off neurons.

Since neurons use neurotransmitters to communicate, any drug that acts like or interferes with neurotransmitters has the potential to change how the brain functions and how we feel, think, and behave. For example, here's what alcohol does.

Alcohol

What does alcohol do?

Drinking alcoholic beverages usually raises the level of alcohol in the blood, which is measured in terms of blood alcohol content (BAC). For example, at low to medium doses (0.01–0.06 BAC), alcohol causes friendliness, loss of inhibitions, decreased self-control, and impaired social judgment; after 3–4 drinks, the average person's BAC will range from 0.08 to 0.1, which meets the legal definition of drunkenness in most states. (Alcohol is discussed more fully in Module 8.)

Alcohol (ethyl alcohol) is a psychoactive drug that is classified as a depressant, which means that it depresses the activity of the central nervous system.

Although alcohol has been around for 3,000 years, it is only recently that researchers have determined its effects on the brain. The effects of alcohol have proved difficult to pin down since it has so many. We'll discuss one of its major effects on the brain.

GABA Neurons

Alcohol affects the nervous system in a number of ways, blocking some neural receptors and stimulating others. For example, some neurons are excited by a neurotransmitter called GABA *(GAH-bah)*, which the brain normally manufactures. This means that GABA neurons (figure above) have chemical locks that can be opened by chemical keys in the form of the neurotransmitter GABA (Tsai et al., 1995).

GABA Keys

Now here's the interesting part. Alcohol molecules so closely resemble those of the GABA neurotransmitter that alcohol can function like GABA keys and open GABA receptors (figure below right). Opening GABA receptors excites GABA neurons.

When GABA neurons are excited, they decrease neural activity and overall produce inhibitory effects, such as reduction in anxiety and tension, loss of inhibitions and self-control, and often an increase in friendliness. Thus, one reason alcohol is such a popular drug is that it reduces tension and anxiety (Stritzke et al., 1996).

Alcohol mimics neurotransmitter

GABA Receptor

One way that alcohol affects the brain is by imitating a naturally occurring neurotransmitter, GABA. Other drugs have different effects on the brain's neurotransmitters, several of which have been recently discovered.

New Discoveries

What are the newest neurotransmitters?

There are a number of well-known neurotransmitters, such as acetylcholine, GABA, norepinephrine, epinephrine, dopamine, and serotonin. However, researchers continue to discover new ones to add to the list of neurotransmitters.

Endorphins. In the 1970s, researchers discovered that the brain makes its own painkiller, very similar to morphine. They called this neurotransmitter endorphin, which is secreted to decrease the effects of pain during great bodily stress, such as an accident (Hughes et al., 1975). We'll discuss endorphins in Module 5.

Anandamide. In the early 1990s, researchers discovered a somewhat surprising neurotransmitter, called anandamide, which is similar in chemical makeup to THC (tetrahydrocannabinol), the active ingredient in marijuana (Fackelmann, 1993). The figure on the right shows a horizontal section of a rat brain that has been treated with a radioactive version of anandamide. The areas most affected by anandamide, which are shown in yellow, are involved in memory, motor coordination, and emotions (Herkenham, 1996). Researchers speculate that anandamide may help humans deal with stress and pain (Fackelmann, 1993).

Nitric oxide. In the middle 1990s, researchers discovered that a gas, nitric oxide, functions like a neurotransmitter and may be involved in regulation of emotions. For example, mice genetically altered to lack nitric oxide were six times more likely to pick a fight (right figure) compared to normal mice (Nelson et al., 1995). Based on these results, researchers think that nitric oxide may be involved in turning off aggression in mice and perhaps in humans.

Researchers have identified about a dozen chemicals that have all the characteristics of neurotransmitters and another 40 to 50 chemicals that influence communication between neurons but do not have all the characteristics of true neurotransmitters (Bear et al., 1996). The important point to remember about neurotransmitters is that their system of chemical keys and locks permits very effective communication among billions of neurons.

Now that you are familiar with the structure and function of the neuron and the importance of neurotransmitters, we'll use this knowledge to explain a response that many of you have experienced—the almost instant withdrawal of your hand after touching a hot object.

F. Reflex Responses

Definition of a Reflex

Can you move without thinking?

If you accidentally touched a hot light bulb, your hand would instantly jerk away, without any conscious thought or effort on your part. This is an example of a reflex.

A *reflex* is an unlearned, involuntary reaction to some stimulus. The neural connections or network underlying a reflex are prewired by genetic instructions.

In some cases, such as when a doctor taps your knee, the knee-jerk reflex is controlled by the spinal cord. In other cases, such as when someone shines a bright light into your eye, the pupillary reflex causes the pupil to constrict. We are all born with a number of programmed reflexes, and all reflexes share the same two or three steps, depending upon how they are wired in the nervous system.

Steps in a Reflex

One reason reflexes occur so quickly is that they are genetically programmed and involve relatively few neural connections, which saves time. Here are the steps in a reflex:

1 **Sensors.** The skin of your fingers has specialized sensors, or receptors, that are sensitive to heat. When you touch a hot light bulb, these skin sensors trigger neurons that start the withdrawal reflex.

2 **Afferent neuron.** From the receptors in your skin, long dendrites carry "pain information" in the form of electrical signals to the spinal cord. These dendrites are part of sensory, or afferent, neurons (red arrows).

Afferent (AFF-er-ent), or *sensory, neuron*s carry information from the senses to the spinal cord.

Sensory neurons may have dendrites 2 to 3 feet long, to reach from the tips of your fingers to the spinal cord. When the pain information enters the spinal cord, it is transmitted to a second neuron.

3 **Interneuron.** Once the afferent neuron reaches the spinal cord, it transmits the pain information to a second neuron, called an interneuron.

An *interneuron* is a relatively short neuron whose primary task is making connections between other neurons.

In this example, an interneuron transmits the pain information to a third neuron, called the efferent, or motor, neuron.

4 **Efferent neuron.** Inside the spinal cord, an interneuron transfers information to a third neuron, called an efferent, or motor, neuron (blue arrows).

Efferent (EFF-er-ent), or *motor, neurons* carry information away from the spinal cord to produce responses in various muscles and organs throughout the body.

From the spinal cord, an efferent (motor) neuron sends electrical signals on its 2- to 3-foot-long axon to the muscles in the hand. These electrical signals contain "movement information" and cause the hand to withdraw quickly and without any thought on your part.

In addition, an interneuron will send the pain information to other neurons that speed this information to different parts of the brain. These different parts interpret the electrical signals coming from your hand as being hot and painful. At this point your brain may direct motor neurons to move your facial and vocal muscles so that you look pained and yell "Ouch!" or something much more intense.

Figure labels

Afferent or sensory neuron

Efferent or motor neuron

3. Interneuron makes connections between neurons which carry message to the brain.

4. Efferent or motor neuron carries neural messages from spinal cord to hand.

2. Afferent or sensory neuron carries neural messages from hand to the spinal cord.

Functions of Reflexes

The primary reason you automatically withdraw your hand when touching a hot object, turn your head in the direction of a loud noise, or vomit after eating tainted food has to do with survival. Reflexes, which have evolved through millions of years, protect body parts from injury and harm and automatically regulate physiological responses, such as heart rate, respiration, and blood pressure. One primitive reflex that is no longer useful in our modern times is called piloerection, which causes the hair to stand up on your arms when you are cold. Piloerection helped keep heat in by fluffing hair for better insulation, but clothes now do a better job.

After the Concept Review, we'll discuss a very strange neural phenomenon that you may have heard of—phantom limb.

CONCEPT REVIEW

1. The structure that nourishes and maintains the entire neuron is the (a)_____. Branchlike extensions that receive signals from senses and environment are called (b)_____. A single threadlike extension that speeds signals away from the cell body toward a neighboring cell is the (c)_____. A tubelike structure that insulates the axon from interference by neighboring signals is the (d)_____. Tiny swellings at the very end of the axon are called (e)_____, which store neurotransmitters.

2. Chemicals that have electrical charges are called (a)_____. They obey the rule that opposite charges attract and like charges repel. Although the fluid of the axon contains a number of ions, we have focused on only two, a positively charged (b)_____ ion whose symbol is Na⁺ and a negatively charged (c)_____ ion.

3. If an axon membrane has a potential similar to a charged battery, the axon is in the (a)_____. During this state, the ions outside the membrane are positively charged (b)_____ ions; the ions inside the membrane are negatively charged (c)_____ ions.

4. If an axon membrane is in a state similar to a discharging battery, the axon is generating an (a)_____. During this potential, the chemical gates open and positively charged (b)_____ rush inside, changing the inside of the membrane to a (c)_____ charge, while the outside of the membrane has a (d)_____ charge. As the action potential moves down the axon, it is called an (e)_____. Once it is generated, the impulse travels from the beginning to the end of the axon; this phenomenon is referred to as the (f)_____.

5. The end bulbs of one neuron are separated from the dendrites of a neighboring neuron by an extremely small space called the (a)_____. Into this space, end bulbs release chemicals, called (b)_____, which open/excite or block/inhibit neighboring receptors.

6. From end bulbs are secreted chemical keys or (a)_____ into the synapse. These chemical keys open matching locks called (b)_____, which are located on the surface of neighboring dendrites, muscles, or organs. Neurotransmitters that open a receptor's lock are called (c)_____; neurotransmitters that block a receptor's lock are called (d)_____.

7. Neurons in the brain and spinal cord make up the (a)_____. If this nervous system is damaged, neurons have little ability to (b)_____. Information from the body's senses, skin, organs, and muscles is carried to and from the spinal cord by nerves that make up the (c)_____. If this nervous system is damaged, (d)_____ in this system have a remarkable ability to regrow and make new connections. If your finger were accidentally cut off, it could be (e)_____ and there is a good chance that your finger would regain most of its sensory and motor functions.

8. If you touch a sharp object, your hand automatically withdraws because of a prewired reflex response. Neurons that carry "pain information" into the spinal cord are called (a)_____ neurons. Once inside the spinal cord, there are short neurons, called (b)_____ that make connections between other neurons that carry information to the brain. Neurons that carry information away from the spinal cord to muscles or organs are called (c)_____ neurons.

Answers: *1. (a) cell body or soma, (b) dendrites, (c) axon, (d) myelin sheath, (e) end bulbs; 2. (a) ions, (b) sodium, (c) protein; 3. (a) resting state, (b) sodium, (c) protein; 4. (a) action potential, (b) sodium ions, (c) positive, (d) negative, (e) impulse, or nerve impulse, (f) all-or-none law; 5. (a) synapse, (b) neurotransmitters; 6. (a) neurotransmitters, (b) receptors, (c) excitatory, (d) inhibitory; 7. (a) central nervous system, (b) regrow, (c) peripheral nervous system, (d) nerves, (e) reattached; 8. (a) sensory, or afferent, (b) interneurons, (c) motor, or efferent.*

G. Research Focus: Phantom Limb
Can Sensations Come from a Phantom Limb?

Case Study

Why did Donald cut off his leg?

Each research focus is about some interesting and puzzling question that researchers are trying to answer. This particular question, "How can you feel a phantom limb?" was first raised in 1866 and is closer now to being answered.

Donald Wyman was a bulldozer driver working in a remote forest when a giant oak tree accidentally fell and pinned him to the ground. All alone and with no one close enough to hear his shouts for help, Donald realized his only hope to get out from under the tree and survive was to cut off his leg, which he did with a 3-inch pocket knife. Although bleeding badly, he dragged himself to his truck and drove a mile and a half to get help. Even though his leg was recovered, it was too damaged to be reattached. Donald is now learning to walk with an artificial leg (photo left) that is fitted to the stump.

Donald's recovery is proceeding very well, but he says, "The toughest part since the accident is dealing with phantom pain. It feels like somebody's holding an electrical shock to your foot that's not there. It makes you jump around" (*USA Today*, August 31, 1993, p. 2A). Donald's case introduces you to the strange phenomenon of phantom limb.

Definition and Data

What is phantom limb?

Very few symptoms have so surprised doctors as when patients reported feeling strange sensations or movements in arms or legs that had been amputated, a phenomena called phantom limb.

Phantom limb refers to feeling sensations or movements coming from a limb that has been amputated. The sensations and movements are extremely vivid, as if the limb were still present.

As the figure on the right shows, the vast majority of individuals felt sensations ("pins and needles") or intense pain coming from their removed limbs. Patients insist that the phantom limb pain is real pain and not merely memories of previous pain (Hill et al., 1996).

Patients' Reports after Removal of Limbs

| 80–100% | Report sensations |
| 70–80% | Report pain |

In other cases, amputees felt that their removed limbs were not only still present but stuck in certain positions, such as straight out from their bodies, so they felt they had to be very careful not to hit their phantom limbs when going through doorways (Katz, 1992).

From 1866 to the present, there have been at least four answers for what causes the feelings of sensations and movements coming from phantom limbs.

Answers: Proposed and Rejected

1 **Sensations come from cut nerves in the stump.**
Early researchers thought that the phantom limb sensations come from cut nerves remaining in the stump. However, when these nerves were cut near the spinal cord, phantom limb should have been prevented; but the sensations still remained, so this early answer has been rejected (Melzack, 1997).

2 **Sensations come from the spinal cord.**
If sensations from phantom limbs do not come from the stump, perhaps they originate in the spinal cord. However, even individuals whose spinal cords have been severed above the stump report phantom limb sensations. Since a severed spinal cord prevents sensations (electrical signals) from reaching the brain, this answer too has been rejected (Melzack, 1997).

3 **Sensations come from the brain itself.**
Researchers now have enough data to indicate that the origin of phantom limb sensations must be the brain itself (Melzack, 1997). But having said that, researchers are puzzled about how the brain generates sensations from phantom limbs.

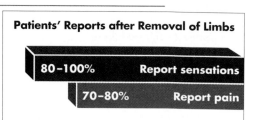

4 **Sensations come from a body image stored in the brain.**
This newest and most creative answer to the origin of phantom limb sensations comes from researcher Ronald Melzack, who has been studying this problem for about 40 years (Melzack, 1989, 1992, 1997). A simplified version of his theory is that each of us has a genetically programmed system of sensations that results in our knowing where are body parts are and in our developing an image of our body. Based on sensations from body parts, the brain pieces together a complete body image. Thus, having a body image, the brain itself can generate sensations as coming from any body part, even if that part is a phantom limb (Melzack, 1997).

Melzack admits that some of his theory must still be tested, but many researchers agree that it is so far one of the best answers to the 30-year-old question involving phantom limbs (Flor et al., 1995).

The phantom limb phenomenon points out that the brain sometimes functions in mysterious ways. Less mysterious is how certain drugs affect the functioning of the brain and the body.

H. Cultural Diversity: Plants, Drugs, & Transmitters

Where did the first drugs come from?

The very first drugs that affected neurotransmitters came from various plants, which people used long before researchers knew what those plants contained. We'll discuss three such drugs—cocaine, curare, and mescaline—which come from plants found in different parts of the world. We'll explain what these plants contain and their actions on the nervous systems.

1 Cocaine: Blocking reuptake

For almost 3,500 years, South American Indians have chewed leaves of the coca plant. Following this ancient custom, adult Indians habitually carry bags of toasted coca leaves, which contain cocaine. Throughout the day, they chew small amounts of coca leaves to relieve fatigue and hunger. Let's see how cocaine affects neurotransmitters.

Cocaine blocks reuptake

The drawing on the left shows a neuron's end bulb containing the neurotransmitter dopamine *(DOPE-ah-mean)*. Once released, dopamine (colored circles) reaches the dendrite's receptors, opens their chemical locks, and activates the neuron. However, after a short period of time, the neurotransmitter is normally removed by being transported back into the end bulb through a process called reuptake.

Reuptake is a process through which some neurotransmitters, such as dopamine, are removed from the synapse by being transported back into the end bulbs.

If reuptake did not occur, dopamine would remain in the synapse, continually activating the neuron, and causing potential problems, such as overarousal.

The effect of cocaine is to block reuptake so that dopamine remains longer in the synapse (Balter, 1966). Because of this blockage, neurons are stimulated longer, resulting in the physiological arousal and feelings of euphoria that are associated with cocaine usage. Thus, researchers now understand that cocaine relieves the fatigue and hunger of South American Indians by blocking the reuptake of dopamine.

2 Curare: Blocking receptors

When hunting animals, the Indians of Peru and Ecuador coat the ends of blowdarts with the juice of a tropical vine that contains the paralyzing drug curare.

Curare (cure-RAH-ree) is a drug that enters the bloodstream, reaches the muscles, and blocks receptors on muscles. As a result, the neurotransmitter that normally activates muscles, which is called acetylcholine, is blocked, and muscles are paralyzed.

Once hit by a curare-tipped blowdart, an animal's limb muscles become paralyzed, followed by paralysis of chest muscles used to breathe.

Curare is an example of a drug that stops neural transmission by blocking the muscles' receptors. Today, the purified active ingredient in curare (tubocurarine chloride) is used to induce muscle paralysis in humans, such as when doctors insert a breathing tube down a patient's throat. Curare doesn't easily enter the brain because the body's blood must go through a filtering system before it can enter the brain. This filtering system, called the *blood-brain barrier,* prevents some, but not all, potentially harmful substances in the body's blood supply from reaching the brain.

3 Mescaline: Mimicking a neurotransmitter

A golf-ball-sized, gray-green plant (photo right) called peyote cactus grows in Mexico and southwestern United States. Peyote contains mescaline.

Mescaline (MESS-ka-lin) is a drug that causes physiological arousal as well as visual hallucinations. Mescaline's chemical keys are similar to those of the neurotransmitter norepinephrine *(nor-epee-NEFF-rin)*.

Because mescaline's chemical keys open the same chemical locks (receptors) as norepinephrine, mescaline produces its effects by mimicking the actions of norepinephrine.

In 1965, an estimated 250,000 members of the Native American Church in the United States and Canada won a Supreme Court case that permits them to be the only group legally authorized to use peyote in their religious services. To enhance meditation, members may eat from 4 to 12 peyote buttons, which results in visual sensations, euphoria, and sometimes nausea and vomiting.

These plant-drugs illustrate three different ways of affecting the nervous system.

Researchers understand much about the brain's neurotransmitter system and how some diseases, such as Alzheimer's, result from the lack of certain neurotransmitters. However, researchers have been only moderately successful in developing drugs to replace neurotransmitters to treat such diseases. Now, there is a promising new treatment for brain diseases.

I. Application: Fetal Tissue Transplant

Parkinson's Disease

Why does Bob's arm shake?

Part of Bob's job was to climb poles and make electrical repairs. He was good at his job until he began to notice that, for no apparent reason, his hands would shake or become rigid. The shakes and tremors in his arms grew worse until he couldn't hold his tools. When his symptoms forced him to stop working, his tremors were so bad that he was too embarrassed to eat out or be seen in public. Many days he had trouble walking because his legs would suddenly become stiff and rigid and he couldn't move. It was like being frozen in space.

Bob had all the symptoms of Parkinson's disease.

Parkinson's disease includes symptoms of tremors and shakes in the limbs, a slowing of voluntary movements, and feelings of depression. As the disease progresses,

patients develop a peculiar shuffling walk and may suddenly freeze in space for minutes or hours at a time. Parkinson's is caused by a destruction of neurons that produce the neurotransmitter dopamine *(DOPE-ah-mean)*.

Like most Parkinson's patients, Bob was placed on a medication called L-dopa, which boosts the levels of dopamine in the brain. However, patients must take ever-increasing amounts of L-dopa, until the drug itself causes involuntary jerky movements that may be as bad as those produced by Parkinson's. Thus, L-dopa controls but does not cure the symptoms of Parkinson's, and after prolonged use, L-dopa's beneficial effects may be replaced by unwanted jerky movements.

In spite of taking L-dopa, Bob's symptoms were getting worse. He had heard about an experimental treatment in which fetal brain tissue that contained dopamine-producing neurons was transplanted into an area of the brain called the basal ganglia.

The *basal ganglia* are a group of structures located in the center of the brain and are involved in regulating movements. To function properly, neurons in the basal ganglia must have a sufficient supply of the neurotransmitter dopamine.

The reason Bob's symptoms had worsened was that neurons in his basal ganglia were running out of dopamine. After Bob reached what he called the "point of no return," he chose to have an experimental treatment, a fetal tissue transplant *(Los Angeles Times,* November 26, 1992).

In the United States, about 500,000 adults, usually over age 50, have Parkinson's disease (Chisholm, 1996). Researchers recently analyzed the genes of 400 Parkinson-prone family members and identified a shared genetic component that contributes to causing Parkinson's disease (Polymeropoulos et al., 1996). To date, Parkinson's has no known cure.

Issues Involving Transplants

Why not just use drugs?

The majority of patients, like Bob, have found that using L-dopa for 10 years or more to treat Parkinson's disease produces unwanted side effects, such as involuntary movements, as well as the return of some of the original symptoms described above (Olanow et al., 1996).

Because of the disappointing long-term results of using L-dopa to treat Parkinson's disease, a search has begun for alternative treatments, such as the use of fetal brain tissue transplants.

Although other countries, including Sweden and England, had allowed the use of fetal tissue transplants, the president of the United States, George Bush, banned fetal tissue transplants prior to 1993. However, in 1993, newly elected president Bill Clinton lifted the federal ban, which meant that federal

A neuron from a 12-week-old fetus has almost no dendritic branches but is primed for development. After being transplanted, a fetal neuron develops extensive dendritic branches.

A neuron from an adult human brain has developed elaborate dendritic branches. Thus, if a mature neuron is transplanted, it develops few, if any, new branches.

granting agencies could begin funding the experimental and very expensive research on fetal transplants.

Previously, researchers had shown that when fetal rat brain tissue was transplanted into older rats, the fetal neurons lived, grew, functioned, and allowed brain-damaged older rats to relearn the solutions to mazes (Shetty & Turner, 1996). Following successful fetal transplants in rats and monkeys, researchers began to transplant human fetal brain tissue into patients who were suffering from Parkinson's disease.

The primary reason for using 7- to 12-week-old fetal tissue for transplants is that this fetal tissue has a unique ability to survive and make connections in a patient's brain or body. For example, the figure on the left shows that dendrites of fetal neurons are barely developed compared to the well-developed dendrites of adult neurons. Because fetal brain tissue is primed for growth, it has a far greater chance of survival after transplantation than does tissue from mature brains (Shetty & Turner, 1996).

Fetal Tissue Transplant

Procedure. The neurosurgeon takes nervous tissue from a 6- to 12-week-old aborted human fetus and transplants the tissue into the basal ganglia of Bob's brain.

The method used to transplant fetal cells into a precise location in either animal or human brains is called the stereotaxic procedure.

The *stereotaxic procedure* involves fixing a patient's head in a holder and drilling a small hole through the skull. The holder has a syringe that can be precisely guided into a predetermined location in the brain.

As shown on the right, Bob's head has been fixed in the stereotaxic holder. (A large part of the skull has been removed to show the brain.) A long syringe extends from the holder into the basal ganglia of his brain. The surgeon will slowly inject human fetal cells into Bob's basal ganglia.

The advantages of the stereotaxic procedure are that a thin syringe can be placed in precise locations in the brain and that it causes relatively little damage to the brain. The stereotaxic procedure can be used to either inject solutions or destroy diseased brain tissue.

Results. Before surgery, Bob had suffered severe tremors and rigidity. About a year after surgery, Bob and a friend drove a motor home across country. Bob said, "I was able to take care of myself for the first time in a long time—buying groceries, filling the car with gas, and driving. I tried golf and played nine holes several times." Bob says that he still has ups and downs but that his symptoms are much more controllable (*Los Angeles Times,* November 26, 1992).

To date, about 150 Parkinson's patients worldwide have been treated with fetal tissue transplants. About 30 to 60% of these patients showed substantial improvement, but none have been completely cured (Chisholm, 1996). However, a number of questions remain to be answered: Which kind of Parkinson's patients (younger, older, less or more impaired) benefit most, how much fetal tissue should be implanted, and what are the best areas for implantation (Olanow et al., 1996)? Researchers believe that answering these questions will lead to better rates of success (Kordower et al., 1996). One way to determine how well the transplanted neural tissue is functioning is by doing brain scans.

Fetal brain cells were transplanted into this area, part of a group of neurons called the basal ganglia.

The stereotaxic procedure allows the precise placement of transplant fetal brain tissue into a host brain. In this illustration, a large portion of the skull and brain have been cut away to show the left basal ganglia. With modern techniques, only a small area of the skull need be opened, and the fetal tissue transplant can be injected with very little damage to the brain.

Before transplant: Few dopamine-producing neurons in basal ganglia, as indicated by mostly white areas, small yellow areas, and no red areas.

33 months after transplant: Many more dopamine-producing neurons in basal ganglia, as indicated by larger yellow areas and presence now of red areas.

Brain Scans. The critical question is: Once transplanted, does fetal tissue survive and produce neurotransmitter? One way to answer this question is with brain scans, which take pictures of the living brain and show the activity of neurons. For example, a brain scan before transplant (upper left), shows low activity level of dopamine-producing neurons, as indicated by the small sizes of the red and yellow areas. However, a brain scan 33 months after transplant (lower left) shows that the red and yellow areas have increased significantly, which indicates that transplanted neurons are producing dopamine. These scans offer dramatic evidence that fetal tissue does survive and produce dopamine when transplanted into other brains (Freed et al., 1992).

Significance of Fetal Tissue Transplant. Since diseased or damaged neurons do not usually regrow, the use of fetal tissue transplants is currently the only treatment for replacing diseased neurons. Researchers hope that fetal tissue transplants will become a new treatment for currently incurable brain diseases, such as Parkinson's.

We began this module with Ina, who suffered from Alzheimer's disease. Currently, researchers are studying fetal transplants in animals that may soon result in methods to treat Alzheimer's disease (Winkler et al., 1995; Shetty & Turner, 1996).

A. OVERVIEW: HUMAN BRAIN

1. The brain is composed of a trillion cells that can be divided into two groups. One group of cells have specialized extensions for receiving and transmitting information. These cells, which are called (a)_____, are involved in communicating with other neurons, receiving sensory information, and regulating muscles, glands, and organs. The other group of cells provide the scaffolding to guide and support neurons, insulate neurons, and release chemicals that influence neuron functions. These cells are much more numerous than neurons and are called (b)_____.

2. There is a major difference between the growth of neurons in the brains of humans and in the brains of birds. A mature human brain is normally not capable of developing new (a)_____, which are almost totally present at the time of birth. In contrast, a mature (b)_____ brain has the capacity to develop new neurons.

3. The age-old question of how the brain's membranes, fluids, and chemicals are involved in generating complex mental activities, such as thoughts, images, and feelings, is called the _____ question.

B. NEURONS: STRUCTURE & FUNCTION

4. Although neurons come in wondrous shapes and sizes, they all share three structures. The structure that maintains the entire neuron in working order, manufactures chemicals, and provides fuel is called the (a)_____. The structure with many branchlike extensions that receive signals from other neurons, muscles, or organs and conduct these signals to the cell body is called a (b)_____. The single threadlike extension that leaves the cell body and carries signals to other neurons, muscles, or organs is called the (c)_____. At the very end of this structure are individual swellings called (d)_____, which contain tiny vesicles filled with (e)_____.

5. Surrounding most axons is a fatty material called the (a)_____. This material acts like (b)_____ and diminishes interference from electrical signals traveling in neighboring axons.

6. Neurons do not make physical contact with one another or with other organs. Instead, there is an infinitely small space between a neuron's end bulbs and neighboring dendrites, cell bodies, or other organs. This space is called the (a)_____. When an axon's end bulbs secrete a neurotransmitter, it flows across this space and affects the (b)_____ on the neighboring membrane.

C. NEURONS VERSUS NERVES

7. There are major differences between neurons and nerves. Cells with specialized extensions for conducting electrical signals are called (a)_____. These cells, which are located in the brain and spinal cord, make up the (b)_____ nervous system. Stringlike bundles of neurons' axons and dendrites, which are held together by connective tissue, are called (c)_____. These stringlike bundles, which are located throughout the body, make up the (d)_____ nervous system. Nerves carry information back and forth between the body and the spinal cord. If a neuron in the central nervous system is damaged, it normally does not have the capacity to (e)_____. In comparison, a nerve in the (f)_____ nervous system has the capacity to regrow or reattach if cut or damaged.

D. SENDING INFORMATION

Action potential

8. The axon membrane has (a)_____ that can be opened or closed. These gates keep some ions inside the membrane and other ions outside. If the axon is ready to conduct but not actually conducting an impulse, the axon is said to be in the (b)_____ state. In this state, most of the positively charged (c)_____ ions are on the outside of the membrane and all the negatively charged (d)_____ ions are trapped inside. In the resting state, the outside of the membrane has a (e)_____ charge compared to the (f)_____ charge on the inside. The process responsible for picking up and transporting sodium ions from the inside to the outside of the axon membrane is called the (g)_____.

9. If a stimulus is strong enough to excite a neuron, two things happen to its axon. First, the stimulus will eventually open the axon's (a)_____. Second, after the gates are opened, the (b)_____ pump is stopped, and all the positive (c)_____ ions rush inside because they are attracted to the negatively charged protein ions. The rush of sodium ions inside generates a tiny electrical current that is called the (d)_____. When this current is generated, the inside of the axon membrane changes to a (e)_____ charge and the outside changes to a (f)_____ charge.

10. Once an action potential starts in the axon, it continues, segment by segment, down the entire length of the axon, creating the (a)_____. Once an action potential is triggered in the segment at the beginning of the axon, other action potentials will be triggered in sequence down the entire length of axon; this phenomenon is called the (b)_____.

E. TRANSMITTERS

11. Once started, the action potential will reach the end bulbs at the end of the axon. The action potential excites the end bulbs and causes them to secrete (a)_____ that were stored in the end bulbs. Neurotransmitters function like chemical keys that unlock chemical locks or (b)_____, which are located on neighboring neurons, muscles, or other organs. If neurotransmitters open the receptors' locks on neighboring cells, they are said to be (c)_____. If neurotransmitters block the receptors' locks, they are said to be (d)_____. Because of these different actions, neurotransmitters can cause different and even opposite responses in neurons, muscles, or organs. There are about a dozen well-known neurotransmitters. One of the newly discovered neurotransmitters that has a chemical makeup similar to THC in marijuana is called (e)_____ and is involved in emotions and motor coordination.

F. REFLEX RESPONSES

12. The movement of automatically withdrawing your hand after touching a hot object is called a (a)_____, which involves several or more neurons. Information is carried to the spinal cord by the (b)_____ neuron. Information is carried from the spinal cord to the muscle by the (c)_____ neuron. Connections between efferent (motor) and afferent (sensory) neurons are made by relatively short (d)_____, which also send signals to the brain. The functions of reflexes include protecting body parts from (e)_____ and automatically regulating the (f)_____ responses of the body.

G. RESEARCH FOCUS: PHANTOM LIMB

13. The experience of sensations from a limb that as been amputated is called the (a)_____ phenomenon. About 70–80% of patients report sensations of intense pain coming from limbs that have been amputated. A recent explanation of phantom limb sensations is that they arise from the brain's genetically programmed system of sensations that allows the brain to know the locations of all the body's (b)_____.

H. CULTURAL DIVERSITY: PLANTS, DRUGS, & TRANSMITTERS

14. One of cocaine's effects on the nervous system is to block the process of (a)_____ so that the neurotransmitter remains longer in the synapse, which causes physiological arousal. A drug that blocks receptors on muscles and causes muscle paralysis is (b)_____. A drug that mimics the naturally occurring neurotransmitter norepinephrine and can produce visual hallucinations is (c)_____.

I. APPLICATION: FETAL TISSUE TRANSPLANT

15. The tremors and rigidity of Parkinson's disease result when a group of structures that regulate movement, called the (a)_____, lose their supply of dopamine. In an experimental operation, fetal brain cells are transplanted into a precise location of a patient's brain by a technique called the (b)_____ procedure. By this procedure, fetal transplants have been used with considerable success to treat (c)_____ disease, which destroys neurons that produce dopamine.

Answers: *1. (a) neurons, (b) glial cells; 2. (a) neurons, (b) bird; 3. mind-body; 4. (a) cell body, or soma, (b) dendrite, (c) axon, (d) end bulbs, (e) neurotransmitters; 5. (a) myelin sheath, (b) insulation; 6. (a) synapse, (b) receptors; 7. (a) neurons, (b) central, (c) nerves, (d) peripheral, (e) regrow, (f) peripheral; 8. (a) chemical gates, (b) resting, (c) sodium, (d) protein, (e) positive, (f) negative, (g) sodium pump; 9. (a) chemical gates, (b) sodium, (c) sodium, (d) action potential, (e) positive, (f) negative; 10. (a) nerve impulse, (b) all-or-none law; 11. (a) neurotransmitters, (b) receptors, (c) excitatory, (d) inhibitory, (e) anandamide; 12. (a) reflex, or reflex response, (b) sensory, or afferent, (c) motor, or efferent, (d) interneurons, (e) injury or harm, (f) physiological; 13. (a) phantom limb, (b) parts; 14. (a) reuptake, (b) curare, (c) mescaline; 15. (a) basal ganglia, (b) stereotaxic, (c) Parkinson's.*

Newspaper Article

UPSETTING OUR SENSE OF SELF
by K. C. Cole

1. Do you believe the self resides in the body, the brain, or somewhere else, such as the soul?

Imagine that you've been fatally injured in a car wreck, and your doctor offers to implant your brain in another perfectly healthy body. When you wake up from the operation, who will you be? Yourself, with a new body? Or the person whose body you inhabit—with memories of being someone else?

Your answer will depend on whether you think the self is embodied in the body or is mainly in the brain.

Many people believe it is neither, but some overarching personal essence that ties body and soul together. But even scientists can't put a finger on it.

2. Why does cloning present a threat to our sense of self?

Ever since Scottish researchers cloned a sheep from an adult cell, everyone from the president to the guy next door has been wringing their hands over what such a technology might mean for the cherished human sense of "self." Thinking about clones seems to plunge people into identity crises far worse than anything brought on by adolescence or midlife.

After all, if identity is written into genes, and those genes can be copied, then what becomes of the self as a unique creation?

3. What can identical twins teach us about where the self might lie?

"It (cloning) scares people because it makes people worry about what it is about themselves that is their own," said scholar Hillel Schwartz, author of "The Culture of the Copy." "If what is unique about us is not the body, then what is it? That's a terrifying question."

4. How can the study of the human brain help answer questions about our individual identities?

As creepy as human clones may seem, they would be far less alike than identical twins. Both clones and twins share the same genetic blueprint. But twins also grow side by side in the same maternal juices, listening to the gurglings of the same maternal gut and the regular rhythms of the same maternal heart.

And yet they manage to emerge as intact, independent individuals. So identity crises are unlikely to arise in the real world.

5. In what other ways might psychologists research questions related to the self?

Still, philosophers have long worried about the essence of the self, and concerns about identity and soul preoccupy thinkers from theologians to mathematicians.

- What does it mean to be the same as something or someone else?
- How much of who we are is contained in our DNA, and how much is shaped by forces outside ourselves?
- Is a copy of a person an individual in his or her own right?

Source: *Los Angeles Times,* April 28, 1997.

Study Questions

A. **Overview: Human Brain**—Why is it really smart to drive a car only if it is equipped with driver- and passenger-side airbags? (See answer in Critical Thinking Appendix.)

B. **Neurons: Structure & Function**—How would you decide if a piece of tissue came from the brain or from a muscle?

C. **Neurons versus Nerves**—Headline—"Chimp Brain Transplanted into Human Skull." Is this possible?

D. **Sending Information**—How are the structure and function of the axon like those of a battery? (See answer in Critical Thinking Appendix.)

E. **Transmitters**—What are some of the ways that nerve gas could cause death?

F. **Reflex Responses**—How might the reflexes of professional tennis players differ from those of amateurs?

G. **Research Focus: Phantom Limb**—What problems might you have after your hand was amputated?

H. **Cultural Diversity: Plants, Drugs, & Transmitters**—What are the different ways that drugs can affect neurotransmitters? (See answer in Critical Thinking Appendix.)

I. **Application: Fetal Tissue Transplant**—Would you recommend that a family member with Parkinson's be treated with a fetal transplant?

Web Sites & Learning Activities

● BROOKS/COLE ONLINE PSYCHOLOGY STUDY CENTER

http://psychstudy.brookscole.com/student/plotnik/quiz/ch03frm.html

● BASIC NEURAL PROCESSES TUTORIALS

http://psych.hanover.edu/Krantz/neurotut.html

This site features online interactive tutorials related to neural processes and is designed for undergraduate students.

● NEUROSCIENCE-NET

http://www.neuroscience.com/

Neuroscience-Net is an electronic journal offered only on the Web, and a subscription is free. Started in 1996, it takes advantage of the Web's advanced graphics and search capabilities.

● NEUROSCIENCE WEB SEARCH

http://www.acsiom.org/nsr.neuro.html

This comprehensive site allows you to search an index of over 121,000 Web pages related to all areas of neuroscience.

● NEUROANATOMY AND NEUROPATHOLOGY ON THE INTERNET

http://www.dote.hu/%7Ehegedus/index.html#Anatomy

Sponsored by the University Medical School in Hungary, this site provides links to tutorials, images, case studies, and much more.

● JOEL'S MEDICAL PAGES: NEUROLOGY

http://s.psych.uiuc.edu/~jshenker/neuropage.html

This page includes dozens of links to journal articles, associations, and other Web sites related to neurology.

Welcome to the WEB

● NEUROSURGERY AT NEW YORK UNIVERSITY

http://mcns10.med.nyu.edu

This fascinating site shows fully illustrated examples of neurosurgery and case studies highlighting a full range of nervous system disorders.

● ALZHEIMER WEB

http://dsmallpc2.path.unimelb.edu.au/ad.html

What are the symptoms of Alzheimer's disease? What drugs are used to treat it? What research is currently being done on possible treatments? These and other questions are answered at this research-oriented site.

Activities

● *Integrator Online™ for Introductory Psychology* CD-ROM, Plotnik, Module

● Study Guide to accompany *Introduction to Psychology*, 5th edition, Module 3 (choice of PC or Mac computer version or hard copy).

● PsychNow! CD-ROM
Neurons and Synaptic Transmission

Answers to questions on page 64

1. There is no correct answer. Do you think the body and mind are separate entities? Where might the soul reside?
2. Most people feel that they are unique, but the idea of cloning threatens us with the idea of another, identical self.
3. Identical twins, like clones, start out with identical genetic material, yet they develop as distinctly separate selves. This may be a hint that the self is more than just our DNA.

4. We can look at how the structure and function of the brain correspond to different aspects of personality and identity, and how changes in the brain correspond to changes in self-perception.
5. Psychologists might look at the relative influence of heredity, biology, and environment on the self, or at how the self is perceived in different cultures.

Module 4   INCREDIBLE NERVOUS SYSTEM

Lucy's Brain: Earliest Ancestor

Although Lucy was fully grown, she was short and slightly built, standing a little under 4 feet tall and weighing about 55 pounds. She had an ape-like head, and her face (left drawing) had a large brow above her eyes and a protruding jaw that held big, uneven front teeth. Lucy had a lot of hair, was very muscular, walked upright on slightly bent legs, and had powerful arms for climbing trees to search for fruits and nuts.

Anthropologists think that Lucy did not make tools, knew nothing of fire, and conversed with hand gestures, waves, and grunts. Lucy's small skull held a brain that was only about the size of a chimpanzee's, which is about one-third the size of ours. The males of her species were about a foot taller than Lucy and at least two-thirds heavier.

Anthropologists believe that Lucy's species, formally named *Australopithecus afarensis* lived about 3,000,000 years ago and may be the earliest ancestor of modern humans (Johanson, 1996).

We'll use Lucy's brain as an example of how the human brain is thought to have evolved and increased in size over three million years.

Baby Theresa's Brain: A Fatal Problem

The press called her Baby Theresa. She was one of about 1,000 babies born each year in the United States with a disorder that is always fatal.

Baby Theresa (left photo) had almost no brain and therefore would never develop the functions we associate with being human, such as thinking, talking, reasoning, and planning. She survived for 9 days because a very primitive part of her brain was still functioning. This small, primitive brain area lies directly above the spinal cord and regulates vital reflexes, such as breathing, blood pressure, and heart rate. These vital reflexes kept her alive for a little over a week.

We'll use Baby Theresa's tragic case to illustrate some of the different structures and functions of the brain.

Steve's Brain: A Cruel Twist of Fate

When Steve walked into the hotel he felt an incredible pain in his head. He was 28 years old, a successful journalist, and in excellent health, but something terrible was happening.

He could barely talk to the hotel clerk, who said that Steve's room wasn't ready. He slowly walked to a chair and sat down to wait. He glanced at the clock on the wall to check the time. He could clearly see the hands of the clock, but he could not figure out the time. Like a small child, he said out loud, "The big hand is on twelve and the little hand is on eight." When he heard the words, he knew it was 8 o'clock and wondered why he could tell time by sound but not by sight (Fishman, 1988).

We'll use Steve's unsettling experience to show some of the symptoms of brain damage and how neurologists can examine the living brain.

Scott's Brain: Wrong Genetic Instructions

"As a very young baby, Scott seemed okay," said his mother, Cindy. "He cooed and smiled at the right times. He babbled at the right times. He seemed normal" (LaFee, 1996, p. E-1). But it was his constant crying that scared her. Scott would walk outside and burst into tears, and no one could comfort him.

As Scott (right photo) got older, other problems developed. He couldn't sit up, he refused to play with other children, and often was off in a world of his own. Finally an examination of Scott's genetic makeup revealed that he had inherited fragile X syndrome, which is the most common genetic disorder in America (Fisch et al., 1996).

We'll use Scott's problem to explain how genetic instructions are written and what happens if the instructions have errors.

What's Coming?

The brains of Lucy, Baby Theresa, Steve, and Scott raise a number of questions. Lucy's brain brings up the question of evolution, which says that modern brains have been evolving for 3 million years. Baby Theresa's brain raises the question of what it means to be human. Steve's brain brings up the questions of what happens when brains are damaged and whether doctors can look inside living brains. Finally, Scott's brain raises the questions of how brains develop and why things go wrong. We'll answer these questions as well as discuss all the major structures and functions of the human brain.

Let's begin with how genetic instructions are written.

A. Genes & Evolution

Why are brains and bodies so different?

Genetic Instructions

Your brain and body developed according to complex chemical instructions that were written in a human cell no larger than a grain of sand. The reason brains and bodies have different shapes, colors, and abilities is that they develop from different instructions, which are written at the moment of fertilization.

1 Fertilization. Human life has its beginnings when a father's sperm, which contains 23 chromosomes, penetrates a mother's egg, which contains 23 chromosomes. The result is a fertilized cell called a zygote, which is shown in the figure below.

Sperm + Egg = Zygote

2 Zygote. A zygote (above figure), which is about the size of a grain of sand, is the largest human cell.

A *zygote* is a cell that results when an egg is fertilized. A zygote contains 46 chromosomes arranged in 23 pairs.

A zygote contains the equivalent of 1,000,000 pages of type-written instructions. For simplicity, the zygote shown above has only one pair of chromosomes instead of the usual 23 pairs.

3 Chromosomes. Inside the very tiny zygote are 23 pairs of chromosomes, which contain chemical instructions for development of the brain and body.

A *chromosome* is a hairlike strand that contains tightly coiled strands of the chemical DNA, which is an abbreviation for deoxyribonucleic (*dee-ox-ee-RYE-bow-new-CLEE-ick*) acid. Each cell of the human body (except for the sperm and egg) contains 46 chromosomes, arranged in 23 pairs.

For the sake of simplicity, the cell shown here contains only 4 pairs of chromosomes instead of the usual 23 pairs.

4 Chemical alphabet. Each chromosome is made up of long strands of DNA. A long strand of DNA resembles a ladder (left figure) that has been twisted over and over upon itself.

Each rung of the DNA ladder is made up of four chemicals. The order in which the four different chemicals combine to form rungs creates a microscopic chemical alphabet. The 23 pairs of chromosomes contain the equivalent of one million pages of specific instructions for making such things as a nose, finger, brain, or toe.

Thus, a chemical alphabet is used to write instructions for the development and assembly of billions of parts that make up the brain and body.

5 Genes and proteins. Each chromosome has specific segments that contain particular instructions. In the chromosome on the right, each segment is represented by a green band, which represents the location of a gene.

A *gene* is a specific segment on the long strand of DNA that contains instructions for making proteins. Proteins are chemical building blocks from which all the parts of the brain and body are constructed.

For example, one or more genes determines your eye color, how much your ear lobes are attached, and if you will become obese (Gura, 1997). There are a total of about 100,000 human genes located on the 23 pairs of chromosomes. When researchers discover a new gene, it means they have identified the exact location of the gene on its chromosome.

Researchers are currently working on project Genome, whose goal is to identify or locate all 100,000 human genes by the year 2005. At the end of 1996, researchers had discovered the location of almost 50,000 genes (Schuler et al., 1996).

6 Scott's brain: An error in instructions. Earlier, we told you about Scott, who had unusual physical and behavioral problems. Scott has the most common inherited genetic disorder, which is called fragile X syndrome.

Fragile X syndrome is caused by a defect in the X chromosome. This defect (shown here as the pinched end of the X chromosome) can result in physical changes, such as a relatively large head with protruding ears, as well as mild to profound levels of mental retardation.

Fragile X syndrome, which can include changes in both physical features and brain development, illustrates what happens when there is an error in genetic instructions (Fisch et al., 1996). We'll discuss other problems caused by errors in genetic instructions in Module 17.

In the last 10 years, researchers have shown the importance of genetic instructions in the development of physical traits, personality characteristics, mental disorders, and various cognitive abilities (Goldman, 1996; Slutske et al., 1997).

Next we'll discuss how changes in genetic instructions are thought to have influenced brain development across millions of years.

Evolution of the Human Brain

What is evolution?

In 1859, Charles Darwin stunned much of the Western world by publishing *The Origin of Species*, a revolutionary theory of how species originate—his theory of evolution (Darwin, 1859).

The *theory of evolution* says that different species arose from a common ancestor and that those species that survived were best adapted to meet the demands of their environments.

Although Darwin's theory of evolution is just that—a theory—it has received broad scientific support from both fossil records and more recent examination of genetic similarities and differences among species (Gore, 1997). The fact that many scientists hold to the theory of evolution clashes with deeply held religious beliefs that place humans on a family tree of their own. We don't have the space to discuss the pros and cons of evolution here but rather will look at three supposed human ancestors and see how their brains are thought to have evolved.

Australopithecus afarensis   **Homo erectus**   **Homo sapiens**

Perhaps the First Human Brain

Of the three skulls shown above, the smallest one (far left) is thought to have belonged to one of our earliest ancestors, who lived about three million years ago. This proposed ancestor has been given a common name, Lucy, and a scientific name, *Australopithecus afarensis*. Lucy's brain weighed about 500 grams, which is about the size of a chimpanzee's brain and about one-third the size of our brains. Lucy's brain size and skeleton suggest a closer resemblance to apes than to humans. She had long powerful arms and short legs and is thought to have lived mainly on leaves and fruit.

Anthropologists conclude, on the basis of Lucy's rather limited brain size, that her species did not make tools, did not have language, knew nothing of fire, and thus represents the most primitive kind of human (Kurten, 1993; Gore, 1997). Lucy's line died out about a million years ago. Anthropologists believe that another line branched out from Lucy's and gave rise to our genus, which is called *Homo;* this process was accompanied eventually by a threefold increase in brain size.

Brain Doubles in Size

The skull in the middle, which is almost twice as large as Lucy's, belongs to a species named *Homo erectus*. (*Homo* means "man" and *erectus* means "upright.") *Homo erectus,* who lived about one and a half million years ago, is thought to be part of the genus from which modern humans eventually evolved. *Homo erectus* developed a thick-boned skeleton designed for walking upright and was about as tall as modern humans. They are thought to have added meat to their diets.

With a brain size of about 1,000 grams, which was twice as large as Lucy's, *Homo erectus* had increased abilities, and made a wide variety of stone tools. The finest was a tear-shaped hand ax, whose production required much more extensive work than any previous tools. There is considerable debate about whether tool-making or the development of language was the main pressure for the doubling in brain size in *Homo erectus* (Lewin, 1993; Gore, 1997). Descendants of *Homo erectus* evolved a still larger brain; these individuals were called *Homo sapiens*.

Brain Triples in Size

The largest skull, on the far right, comes from a modern human, who is called *Homo sapiens* (*sapiens* means "wise"). Our species began about 400,000 years ago and continues to the present day. *Homo sapiens* evolved a brain that weighs about 1,350 grams, or about 3 pounds, which is the average size of our brains today and almost three times the size of Lucy's. With such a significant increase in brain size came four dramatic changes: *Homo sapiens* began growing crops instead of relying on hunting; started to live in social communities instead of roaming the country; developed language, which was a far better way to communicate compared to grunts and gestures; and painted beautiful and colorful representations of animals and humans.

Two forces are thought to be responsible for the evolution of the human brain and its tripling in size: genetic changes or mutations, which are accidental changes in genetic instructions; and natural selection, which means that only those best fitted to their environments will survive (Kurten, 1993).

Anthropologists believe that it took millions of years for our brains to evolve to their current size. Next, we'll describe how researchers study our modern brains.

B. Studying the Living Brain

New Techniques

Can we look inside the human skull?

We have explained how genetic instructions guide the development and assembly of billions of parts that make up the human brain. We have discussed the anthropologists' belief that the human brain tripled in size through three million years of evolution. Now we begin the exploration of the structure and function of our own brain.

But how is it possible to see or study the brain since it is essentially sealed in a hard, half-inch-thick skull? To understand how this is possible, imagine placing a globe of the world inside a box made

of half-inch-thick wood. Now imagine being able to look through the half-inch-thick wood and see the great blue oceans and read the names of the continents. What you have just imagined doing is what doctors can actually do with amazing techniques developed in the past ten years. With astonishing clarity, doctors can use these techniques to look through the thick skull and see the brain's size and shape and study its landscape of miniature peaks and valleys.

And even though brain cells, especially neurons, are extremely fragile, they are not harmed by these new techniques. We'll discuss the two major techniques used today—MRI and PET brain scans.

MRI Scans

Why would Steve have an MRI?

At the beginning of this module, we told you about Steve, who was a successful journalist in excellent health. As he walked into his hotel, he felt a sudden searing pain in his head. As he waited for his room, he looked up at the clock and suddenly felt fear because he could see the numbers but not tell the time.

Later, the neurologist told Steve that a blood vessel had burst and blood had flowed into the surrounding area of the brain. And, in fact, it would be possible to identify the location and extent of the damaged area by having Steve take a MRI (photo below).

MRI, or *magnetic resonance imaging,* involves passing nonharmful radio frequencies through the brain. A computer measures how these signals interact with brain cells and transforms this interaction into an incredibly detailed image

of the brain (or body). MRIs are used to study the structure of the brain.

During an MRI procedure (right photo), Steve would lie with his head in the center of a giant donut-shaped machine that makes a dull drumming sound as it emits radio waves. Reflections from the radio waves are computer analyzed and developed into very detailed pictures of the living brain, as shown in the figure below on the left.

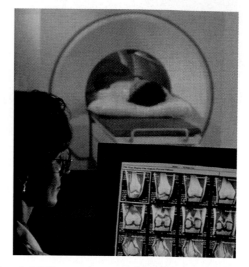

Brain damage. During Steve's MRI scan, images of his brain—slice by slice—appeared on a television screen. Suddenly, standing out from the normal grayish image of a brain slice, was an unusual area that indicated dead brain cells (small red area on right of MRI scan). Because the damaged neurons were located in a brain area involved with processing visual information, Steve had experienced visual problems, such as being unable to tell the time by looking at a clock, even though he could see the hands of the clock. However, since only a small part of his visual area was affected, most other functions, such as walking, feeling, speaking, and hearing, were normal. The reason Steve could figure out the time by saying aloud where the big and little hands of the clock were located was because his hearing areas were undamaged.

Advantage. The advantage of MRI scans is that they use nonharmful radio frequencies and give the most detailed views of the structures inside the living brain (left figure). MRI scans are used primarily to study the structure of the brain as well as to identify tumors and other types of brain damage.

When researchers want to investigate the function of the brain, such as identifying which neurons are active, they use another recently developed method known as the PET scan.

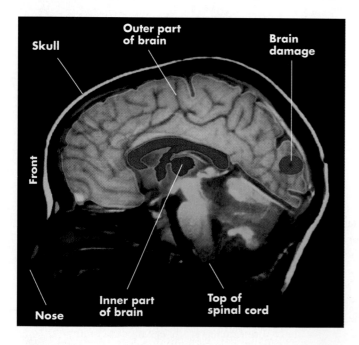

Skull — Outer part of brain — Brain damage

Front

Nose — Inner part of brain — Top of spinal cord

PET Scans

What do PET scans show?

Currently, one of the most exciting advances in biological psychology (specifically, the area of cognitive neuroscience) involves using a relatively new imaging technique that literally lights up your thoughts. This imaging technique is called the PET scan.

PET scan, or *positron emission tomography,* involves injecting a slightly radioactive solution into the blood and then measuring the amount of radiation absorbed by brain cells. Very active brain cells—neurons— absorb more radioactive solution than less active ones. A computer transforms the different levels of absorption into colors that indicate activity of neurons. The colors red and yellow indicate maximum activity of neurons, while blue and green indicate minimal activity.

For example, which parts of the brain are active when you "look at a word" compared to when you "speak a word"? Subjects were asked to either "look at a word" or "speak a word" while researchers took PET scans of their brains.

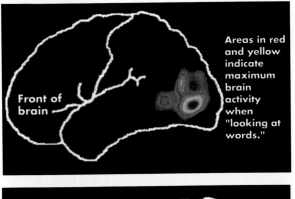

Areas in red and yellow indicate maximum brain activity when "looking at words."

Front of brain

Looking at words. PET scans in the top left figure show that when subjects were "looking at words" but not speaking them, most neural activity occurred near the back of the brain, which is involved in processing visual information.

Speaking words. PET scans in the bottom left figure show that when subjects were "speaking words" instead of just thinking about them, most neural activity occurred near the front-middle part of the brain, which is involved in speaking (Raichle, 1994).

Areas in red and yellow indicate maximum brain activity when "speaking words."

Back of brain

Mapping areas. By using PET scans, researchers can map the brain's activity as we perform complex cognitive tasks, such as thinking and speaking. Researchers recently drew an interesting map of brain activity that shows which areas are involved in something we do every day—name animals and objects (Martin et al., 1996).

Specific Thoughts

Is it possible to see your thoughts?

Using PET scans, researchers were even able to identify brain areas that are activated when we silently think very specific thoughts, such as names of tools and animals.

Naming animals. As shown at top right, the thoughts of subjects as they silently named animals (camel), activated an area in the back of the brain, which is involved in processing visual information. Researchers think this visual area helps us distinguish sizes, shapes, and colors, such as distinguishing a camel from a horse.

Naming tools. As shown at bottom right, the thoughts of subjects as they silently named tools (pliers) activated an area in the front of the brain. Researchers think this frontal area helps us think about how we use tools (Martin at al., 1996).

Researchers concluded that the brain has two separate systems: one for thoughts about naming animals, which involves distinguishing between sizes, shapes and colors; and another for thoughts about naming tools, which involves thinking about how tools are used (Martin et al., 1996).

This study is an example of a relatively new area, called *cognitive neuroscience,* which maps the paths of cognitive processes as they travel through the brain (Barinaga, 1997; Wickelgren, 1997; Seidenberg, 1997). Throughout this text, we'll include many experiments that show how cognitive processes, emotions, memories, and mental disorders are being studied using MRI and PET scans.

Now that you are familiar with ways to study the living brain, we can begin to examine the brain's specific structures and interesting functions.

C. Organization of the Brain

How many nervous systems do you have?

Divisions of the Nervous System

Because you have one brain, you may think that means you have one nervous system. In fact, your brain is much more complex: It has two major nervous systems, one of which has four subdivisions. We'll explain the overall organization of the brain's several nervous systems, beginning with its two major divisions, the central and peripheral nervous systems.

1. Major Divisions of Nervous System

CENTRAL NERVOUS SYSTEM—CNS

You are capable of many complex cognitive functions—such as thinking, speaking, and reading, as well as moving, feeling, seeing, and hearing—because of your central nervous system.

The *central nervous system* is made up of the brain and spinal cord. From the bottom of the brain emerges the spinal cord, which is made up of neurons and bundles of axons and dendrites that carry information back and forth between the brain and the body.

We'll discuss the major parts of the brain throughout this module.

PERIPHERAL NERVOUS SYSTEM—PNS

You are able to move your muscles, receive sensations from your body, and perform many other bodily responses because of the peripheral nervous system.

The *peripheral nervous system* includes all the nerves that extend from the spinal cord and carry messages to and from various muscles, glands, and sense organs located throughout the body.

The peripheral nervous system has two subdivisions, the somatic and autonomic nervous systems.

2. Subdivisions of PNS

SOMATIC NERVOUS SYSTEM

The *somatic nervous system* consists of a network of nerves that connect either to sensory receptors or to muscles that you can move voluntarily, such as muscles in your limbs, back, neck, and chest. Nerves in the somatic nervous system usually contain two kinds of fibers. Afferent, or sensory, fibers carry information from sensory receptors in the skin, muscles, and other organs to the spinal cord and brain. Efferent, or motor, fibers carry information from the brain and spinal cord to the muscles.

For example, this dancer controls his muscles, knows where his arms and legs are located in space, and maintains his coordination and balance because the somatic nervous system sends electrical signals back and forth to his brain.

AUTONOMIC NERVOUS SYSTEM—ANS

The *autonomic nervous system* regulates heart rate, breathing, blood pressure, digestion, hormone secretion, and other functions. The autonomic nervous system usually functions without conscious effort, which means that only a few of its responses, such as breathing, can also be controlled voluntarily.

The autonomic nervous system also has two subdivisions.

3. Subdivisions of ANS

SYMPATHETIC DIVISION

The *sympathetic division,* which is triggered by threatening or challenging physical or psychological stimuli, increases physiological arousal and prepares the body for action.

For example, the sight of a frightening snake would trigger the sympathetic division, which, in turn, would arouse the body for action, such as fighting or fleeing.

PARASYMPATHETIC DIVISION

The *parasympathetic division* returns the body to a calmer, relaxed state and is involved in digestion.

For example, when you are feeling relaxed or digesting food, your parasympathetic system is activated.

Now that you know the overall organization of the nervous system, we'll focus on major parts of the brain.

Major Parts of the Brain

What are the three major divisions?

A human brain, which can easily be held in one hand, weighs about 1,350 grams, or 3 pounds, and has the consistency of firm Jell-O. (Top view of brain is shown in right figure.) The brain is protected by a thick skull and covered with thin, tough, plasticlike membranes. Let's begin our exploration of the brain by looking at its three major divisions—forebrain, midbrain, and hindbrain.

1 Forebrain

When you look at the brain, what you are actually seeing is almost all forebrain (figure above).

The *forebrain,* which is the largest part of the brain, has right and left sides that are called hemispheres. The hemispheres, which are connected by a wide band of fibers, are responsible for an incredible number of functions, including learning and memory, speaking and language, emotional responses, experiencing sensations, initiating voluntary movements, planning, and making decisions.

The large structure outlined below in yellow shows only the right hemisphere of the forebrain. Both of the forebrain's right and left hemispheres are shown in the figure above. The forebrain is very well developed in humans, and we'll discuss its many functions later in this module.

2 Midbrain

If a boxer is knocked unconscious, part of the reason lies in the midbrain.

The *midbrain* is involved in visual and auditory reflexes, such as automatically turning your head toward a noise. Extending down from the top of the midbrain to the spinal cord is a long column of neurons called the reticular formation. The reticular formation alerts and arouses the forebrain so that it is ready to process incoming information from the senses.

If the reticular formation were seriously damaged—by a blow to the head, for example—a person would be unconscious and might go into a coma because the forebrain could not be aroused (Steriade, 1966).

3c Cerebellum

A person suspected of drunken driving may fail the test of rapidly touching a finger to the nose because of alcohol's effects on the cerebellum.

The *cerebellum,* which is located at the very back and underneath the brain, is involved in coordinating movements but not in initiating voluntary movements. New findings indicate that the cerebellum is also involved in learning to perform timed motor responses, such as those required in playing games or sports (Allen et al., 1997).

Because alcohol is a depressant drug and interferes with the functions of the cerebellum, an intoxicated person would experience decreased coordination and have difficulty rapidly touching a finger to the nose, which is one of the tests for being drunk.

3 Hindbrain

The structures and functions of the hindbrain, which are found in very primitive brains, such as the alligator's, have remained constant through millions of years of evolution. The *hindbrain* has three distinct structures: the pons, medulla, and cerebellum.

3a Pons

If someone has a serious sleep disorder, it may involve the pons. In Latin, *pons* means "bridge," which suggests its function.

The *pons* functions as a bridge to interconnect messages between the spinal cord and brain. The pons also makes chemicals involved in sleep (Cirelli et al., 1996).

3b Medulla

If someone dies of a drug overdose, the cause of death probably involved the medulla.

The *medulla,* which is located at the top of the spinal cord, includes a group of cells that control vital reflexes, such as respiration, heart rate, and blood pressure.

Large amounts of alcohol, heroin, or other depressant drugs suppress the functions of cells in the medulla and cause death by stopping breathing.

Of the brain's three parts—forebrain, midbrain, and hindbrain—it is the forebrain that is the most evolved, by far the largest, and most responsible for our enormous range of personal, social, emotional, and cognitive behaviors. For those reasons, we'll examine the forebrain in more detail.

D. Control Centers: Four Lobes

Overall Cortex

How do you package one trillion cells?

How would you design a container (brain) to hold one trillion cells (100 billion neurons and 900 billion glial cells) and be no bigger than a small melon? First, the cells need to be microscopic in size, which they are. But the second part of the solution might not have occurred to you: Give the container (brain) a very wrinkled surface. Here's why.

CORTEX

The photo below shows an adult human brain with its characteristic wrinkled surface that is called the cortex (in Latin, *cortex* means "cover"). The *cortex* is a thin layer of cells that essentially covers the entire surface of the forebrain. The vast majority of neurons are located in the cortex, which folds over on itself so that it forms a large surface area.

To understand the significance of the brain's wrinkled surface, just imagine having to put a large sheet of paper that is 18 inches square into a small match box that is three inches square. One solution is to crumble the sheet of paper until it easily fits into the tiny match box. Similarly, imagine many billions of neurons laid on a sheet of paper about 18 inches square. If this large sheet of neurons were wrinkled, it could fit snugly into our much smaller rounded skulls. The only other solution to having a brain as big as ours without a wrinkled surface is to have heads shaped like large boxes.

Early on, researchers found that the cortex could be divided into four different areas, or lobes (marked on the brain above by green lines).

LOBES

As you look at the brain's cortex, you see a wrinkled surface of peaks and valleys with very few distinguishing features. However, the cortex's appearance is deceiving because its hundreds of different functions are organized into four separate areas called lobes.

The cortex is divided into four separate areas, or *lobes,* each with different functions: the *frontal lobe* is involved with personality, emotions, and motor behaviors; the *parietal (puh-RYE-it-all) lobe* is involved with perception and sensory experiences; the *occipital (ock-SIP-pih-tull) lobe* is involved with processing visual information; and the *temporal (TEM-purr-all) lobe* is involved with hearing and speaking.

The one brain structure that most clearly distinguishes you from animals, is your well-developed cortex, which allows you to read, understand, talk about, and remember the concepts in this text. To understand what life would be like without a cortex, we'll return to the case of baby Theresa, who was born without any lobes and thus no cortex.

BABY THERESA'S BRAIN: A FATAL DEFECT

At the beginning of this module, we told you about Baby Theresa, who was one of the 1,000 babies born each year in the United States with almost no brain. This rare condition, caused by errors in genetic instructions, is called anencephaly (Chen et al., 1996).

Anencephaly (an-in-CEPH-ah-lee) refers to the condition of being born with little or no brain. If some brain or nervous tissue is present, it is totally exposed and often damaged because the top of the skull is missing. Survival is usually limited to days; the longest has been two months.

Anencephaly is always fatal because it also includes other serious physical defects, such as damage to the heart (Stumph et al., 1990). Baby Theresa (photo above), who survived only nine days, had almost no brain tissue and almost no skull (bandaged area above eyes). Lacking most of a brain means that she would be incapable of perceiving, thinking, speaking, planning, or making decisions.

The figure below right shows a skull without a forebrain, such as occurs in anencephaly (but without the skull). One reason babies with anencephaly may survive for days or weeks is that they may have parts of their hindbrain. As discussed earlier, the hindbrain contains the pons (blue) and medulla (red). The medulla controls vital reflexes, such as breathing, heart rate, and blood pressure, which together can maintain life for a period of time.

No forebrain

Medulla

This example of anencephaly shows that without the forebrain, a baby may be physiologically alive but show no signs of having a mind or possessing cognitive abilities associated with being human. In a real sense, it is the functions of the forebrain's four lobes that define us as human and distinguish us from all other creatures.

Because of the importance of the four lobes to our existence as humans, we'll discuss each lobe in turn. We'll begin with the frontal lobe, which became famous for very tragic reasons.

Frontal Lobe

What does the biggest lobe do?

The frontal lobe (right figure), which is the largest and most noticeable of the brain's four lobes, has a number of important functions.

The *frontal lobe*, which is located in the front part of the brain, includes a huge area of cortex. The frontal lobe is involved in many functions: performing voluntary motor movements, interpreting and performing emotional behaviors, behaving normally in social situations, maintaining a healthy personality, paying attention to things in the environment, making decisions, and executing plans. Because much of the frontal lobe is involved in decision making, planning, and carrying out behaviors, it is said to function similarly to an executive.

Our first clue about the functions of the frontal lobe came from an unusual accident in 1848, while our more recent knowledge comes from research using PET scans. Let's first go back in time and meet Phineas Gage, whose accident led to the discovery of one of the frontal lobe's important functions.

A Terrible Accident

The accident occurred at about half past four on the afternoon of September 13, 1848, near the small town of Cavendish, Vermont. Railroad crewmen were about to blast a rock that blocked their way. Foreman Phineas Gage filled a deep narrow hole in the rock with powder and rammed in a long iron rod to tamp down the charge before covering it with sand. But the tamping iron rubbed against the side of the shaft, and a spark ignited the powder. The massive rod—$3\frac{1}{2}$ feet long, $1\frac{1}{4}$ inches in diameter, and weighing 13 pounds—shot from the hole under the force of the explosion. It struck Phineas just beneath his left eye and tore through his skull. It shot out the top of his head and landed some 50 yards away.

Phineas survived, but, following the accident, his personality changed: He went from being a popular, friendly foreman to acting impatient, cursing his workers, and refusing to honor his promises.

AN IRON ROD THAT WAS A LITTLE OVER AN INCH THICK WAS ACCIDENTALLY DRIVEN THROUGH THE FRONT PART OF THE FRONTAL LOBE OF PHINEAS GAGE.

Researchers recently used Phineas's preserved skull to reconstruct the site and extent of his brain damage. As the figure above shows, the iron rod had passed through and extensively damaged Phineas's frontal lobe. Researchers concluded that Phineas had suffered a crude form of frontal lobotomy, which caused deficits in processing of emotion and decision making that result after damage to the frontal lobe (Damasio et al., 1994).

Beginning in the 1930s, doctors performed thousands of lobotomies to treat various mental and behavioral problems.

Frontal Lobotomy

In 1936, Egas Moniz, a Portuguese neurologist, used an untested surgical treatment, called frontal lobotomy, to treat individuals with severe emotional problems.

A *frontal lobotomy* was a surgical procedure in which about one-third of the front part of the frontal lobe (figure below) was cut away from the rest of the brain.

Moniz first reported that frontal lobotomies did reduce emotional problems in about 35% of severely agitated human patients, although he did no controlled or follow-up studies to check long-term effects (Weinberger et al., 1995). Based on Moniz's reports of success, about 18,000 frontal lobotomies were performed in the 1940s and 1950s on emotionally disturbed patients who were primarily confined to state mental hospitals, which had no other treatments.

Results of Lobotomies

Initially, neurologists reported good short-term effects, but better controlled, long-term studies on frontal lobotomies found mixed results: Some patients did become less violent, but others showed no improvement and some became worse (Swayze, 1995). Even those whose social-emotional behaviors improved were often left with serious problems in other areas, such as having difficulty in making and carrying out plans, adjusting to new social demands, or behaving with appropriate emotional responses in social situations (Valenstein, 1986).

Two things happened in the early 1950s that ended the use of frontal lobotomies to treat social-emotional problems. First, follow-up research indicated that lobotomies were no more successful in relieving social-emotional problems than doing nothing. Second, antipsychotic drugs were discovered and showed greater success in treating serious social-emotional problems (Swayze, 1995).

From using frontal lobotomies as treatment, researchers learned two things: (1) careful follow-up work is essential before declaring a treatment successful and (2) the frontal lobe has many different, important functions, which we'll look at next.

D. Control Centers: Four Lobes

Frontal Lobe: Functions

RIGHT **LEFT**

RIGHT **LEFT**

> **How do you move your right hand?**

The organization of the frontal lobe is somewhat confusing because it has such a wide range of functions, from motor movements to cognitive processes. We'll first focus on motor movements, which have a very unusual feature.

In the figure on the right, notice that nerves from the right hemisphere (blue) cross over and control the movements of the left hand and left side of the body; and nerves from the left hemisphere (red) cross over and control the movements of the right hand and right side of the body. The ability to move your hand or any other part of your body depends on the motor cortex in the right and left frontal lobes.

1 Location of Motor Cortex

To move your right hand, you will use the motor cortex in your left frontal lobe.

The *motor cortex* is a narrow strip of cortex that is located on the back edge of the frontal lobe and extends down its side. The motor cortex is involved in the initiation of all voluntary movements. The right motor cortex controls muscles on the left side of the body and vice versa.

The reason you can move any individual part of your body at will is because of how the motor cortex is organized.

Frontal lobe

Little · Ring · Middle · Index · Thumb · Neck · Hand · Wrist · Elbow · Shoulder · Trunk · Hip · Knee · Ankle · Toes

Brow · Eyelid and eyeball · Face · Lips · Jaw · Tongue · Swallowing

Vocalization · Swallowing · Mastication

MOTOR HOMUNCULUS

2 Organization of Motor Cortex

The large figure (upper right) shows an enlarged part of the motor cortex, which is very cleverly organized.

First, notice the different sizes of the body parts drawn on top of the motor cortex. A larger body part (notice huge hand area) indicates relatively more area on the motor cortex and thus more ability to perform complex movements. A smaller body part (notice small knee area) indicates relatively less area on the motor cortex and thus less ability to perform complex movements. This unusual drawing, which uses sizes of body parts to show the ability to perform complex movements, is called the *motor homunculus (ho-MONK-you-luss)*.

Second, notice that each body part has its own area on the motor cortex. This means that damage to one part of the motor cortex could result in paralysis of that part yet completely spare all other parts.

Third, notice that the motor cortex makes up only a small part of the frontal lobe. Next, we'll explain its other functions.

3 Other Functions of Frontal Lobe

Brain damage. Much of our knowledge of other frontal lobe functions comes from individuals who had damage to that area. By studying patients like Phineas Gage, researchers found that damage to frontal lobes may result in disruption of personality as well as emotional swings. Patients with damage to frontal lobes also have problems paying attention, remembering things, making good decisions, planning and organizing events, and carrying out a sequence of behaviors, such as following a set of instructions to operate a computer. And even though patients with frontal lobe damage can see their errors in carrying out some set of instructions, they are unable to change or modify their behaviors (Bechara et al., 1997; Rao et al., 1997; Wheeler et al., 1997).

PET scans. Researchers have also identified many cognitive functions of the frontal lobe by taking PET scans while subjects perform various tasks. For example, subjects were shown a noun, such as *hammer,* and asked to think of an appropriate

Frontal lobe

Maximum activity

Back of brain

verb, such as *hit.* PET scans, such as the one shown below, indicated that maximum activity (red and yellow areas) occurred in the frontal lobe. This means that the frontal lobe is involved in our thinking processes (Fiez & Petersen, 1993).

Other researchers asked subjects to search for a certain shape hidden among many other shapes. During this search, PET scans again indicated increased activity in the frontal lobes, which indicates their involvement in searching and paying attention (Posner & Dehaene, 1994).

Because of all these functions, frontal lobes are often said to have an executive function, meaning that they are involved in organizing, planning, deciding, and carrying out many different kinds of behaviors (West, 1996).

Immediately behind the frontal lobe is the parietal lobe, which keeps track of your body's limbs.

Parietal Lobe: Functions

How do you know where your feet are?

Every second of every minute of every day, your brain must keep track of what's touching your skin, where your feet and hands are, and whether you're walking or running. All this is automatically and efficiently done by your parietal lobe (right figure).

The *parietal lobe* is located directly behind the frontal lobe. The parietal lobe's functions include: processing sensory information from body parts, which includes touching, locating positions of limbs, and feeling temperature and pain; and carrying out several cognitive functions, such as attending to and perceiving objects.

For example, the ability to know what you're touching involves the parietal lobe's somatosensory cortex.

1 Location of Somatosensory Cortex

Knowing what you're touching or how hot to make the water for your shower involves the somatosensory cortex.

The *somatosensory cortex* is a narrow strip of cortex that is located on the front edge of the parietal lobe and extends down its side. The somatosensory cortex processes sensory information about touch, location of limbs, pain, and temperature. The right somatosensory cortex receives information from the left side of the body and vice versa.

The reason your lips are much more sensitive than your elbows is because of the way the somatosensory cortex is organized.

2 Organization of Somatosensory Cortex

The large figure (upper right) shows an enlarged part of the somatosensory cortex, which is also cleverly organized.

First, notice the different sizes of the body parts drawn on top of the somatosensory cortex. A larger body part (notice large area for lips) indicates relatively more area on the somatosensory cortex and thus more sensitivity to external stimulation. A smaller body part (notice small nose area) indicates relatively less area on the somatosensory cortex and thus less sensitivity to external stimulation. This unusual drawing, which uses sizes of body parts to indicate amount of sensitivity to external stimulation, is called the *sensory homunculus (ho-MONK-you-luss)*. In Latin, *homunculus* means "little man."

Second, notice that each body part has its own area on the somatosensory cortex. This means that damage to one part of the somatosensory cortex could result in loss of feeling to one part of the body yet completely spare all others.

Third, notice that the somatosensory cortex makes up only a small part of the parietal lobe. Next, we'll explain its other functions.

3 Other Functions of Parietal Lobe

Brain damage. When you put your hand in your pocket, you can easily tell a key from a nickel from a stick of chewing gum because your parietal lobe digests information about texture, shape, and size and "tells you" what the object is. However, patients with damage to the back of their parietal lobes cannot recognize common objects by touch or feel (Bear et al., 1996). Evidence that the parietal lobes are involved in other cognitive processes comes from studies using PET scans.

PET scans. Researchers asked subjects to remember letters they saw on a screen by repeating them over and over in their minds.

PET scans, such as the one shown here, indicated that maximum activity during this task occurred in the parietal lobe. Researchers concluded that the parietal lobe is involved when we try to remember things (Paulesu et al., 1993). Other PET studies on chess players indicated that the parietal lobe was involved in perceiving and analyzing the positions of chesspieces on the board (Nichelli et al., 1994).

Thus, case studies and PET scans indicate that the parietal lobe is involved in several cognitive functions, including recognizing objects, remembering items, and perceiving and analyzing objects in space.

Immediately below the parietal lobe is the temporal lobe, which we'll examine next.

D. Control Centers: Four Lobes

Temporal Lobe: Functions

You recognize your name when you hear it spoken; because of the way sound is processed in the temporal lobe, you know it's not just some meaningless noise.

The *temporal lobe* is located directly below the parietal lobe and is involved in hearing, speaking coherently, and understanding verbal and written material.

As you'll see, the process of hearing and recognizing your name takes two steps that involve two different areas in the temporal lobe. The first step involves the primary auditory cortex.

1a Primary Auditory Cortex

The first step in hearing your name occurs when sounds reach specific areas in the temporal lobe called the primary auditory (hearing) cortex—there is one in each lobe.

The *primary auditory cortex (shown in red)*, which is located on the top edge of each temporal lobe, receives electrical signals from receptors in the ears and transforms these signals into meaningless sound sensations, such as vowels and consonants.

At this point, you would not be able to recognize your name because the primary auditory cortex only changes electrical signals from the ears into basic sensations, such as individual sounds, clicks, or noises. For these meaningless sound sensations to become recognizable words or music, they must be sent to another area in the temporal lobe, called the auditory association area.

Temporal lobe

1b Auditory Association Area

The second step in recognizing your name is when the primary auditory cortex sends its electrical signals to the auditory association area—there is one in each lobe.

The *auditory association area (shown in blue)*, which is located directly below the primary auditory cortex, transforms basic sensory information, such as noises or sounds, into recognizable auditory information, such as words or music.

It is only after auditory information is processed by the auditory association areas that you would recognize the sounds as your name, or words, or music. So, you really hear with your brain, not your ears.

Besides being involved in hearing, the temporal lobe has other areas that are critical for speaking and understanding words and sentences.

2 Broca's Area—Frontal Lobe

Just as hearing your name is a two-step process, so is speaking a sentence. The first step is putting words together, which involves an area in the frontal lobe called Broca's *(BROKE-ahs)* area.

Broca's area, which is usually located in the left frontal lobe, is necessary for combining sounds into words and arranging words into meaningful sentences. Damage to this area results in *Broca's aphasia (ah-PHASE-zz-ah)*, which means a person cannot speak in fluent sentences but can understand written and spoken words.

Frontal lobe

Temporal lobe

The reason saying words and putting words into sentences comes naturally to small children is that Broca's area is genetically programmed to do this task. If it is damaged, people with Broca's aphasia have difficulty putting words into sentences. For example, a patient was asked, "What have you been doing in the hospital?" The patient answered, "Yes, sure. Me go, er, uh, P.T. non o'cot, speech . . . two times . . . read . . . wr . . . ripe, er, rike, er, write . . . practice . . . get-ting better" (Gardner, 1976, p. 61). The patient was trying to say, "I go to P.T. (physical therapy) at one o'clock to practice speaking, reading, and writing, and I'm getting better."

The reason a patient with Broca's aphasia cannot speak fluently but can still understand words and sentences is because of a second area in the temporal lobe—Wernicke's area.

3 Wernicke's Area—Temporal Lobe

The first step in speaking is using Broca's area to combine sounds into words and arrange words into sentences. The second step is to understand sentences, which involves Wernicke's *(VERN-ick-ees)* area.

Wernicke's area, which is usually located in the left temporal lobe, is necessary for speaking in coherent sentences and for understanding speech. Damage to this area results in *Wernicke's aphasia*, which is a difficulty in understanding spoken or written words and a difficulty in putting words into meaningful sentences.

For example, a patient with Wernicke's aphasia said: "You know, once in a while I get caught up, I mention the tarripoi, a month ago, quite a little, I've done a lot well" (Gardner, 1976, p. 68). As this gibberish shows, Wernicke's area is critical for combining words into meaningful sentences and speaking coherently (Just et al., 1996).

In almost all right-handed people (95%) and the vast majority of left-handed people (70%), Broca's and Wernicke's areas are in the left hemisphere; the remaining percentages of people have these two areas in the right hemisphere.

Compared to many other animals, humans rely more heavily on visual information, which is processed in the occipital lobe, our next topic.

Occipital Lobe: Functions

Do you see better than dogs?

Dogs have very poor color vision and rely much more on their sense of smell. In comparison, all primates, which includes monkeys, apes, and humans, have a relatively poor sense of smell and rely much more on vision for gathering information about their environments.

If you have ever been hit on the back of the head and saw "stars," you already know that vision is located in the occipital lobe.

The *occipital lobe* is located at the very back of the brain and is involved in processing visual information, which includes seeing colors and perceiving and recognizing objects, animals, and people.

Although you see and recognize things with great ease, it is actually a complicated two-step process. Here, we'll give only an overview of that process; we'll go into more detail in Module 5.

Occipital lobe

1 Vision

When you look in the mirror and see your face, you don't realize that seeing your face involves two steps and two different areas in the occipital lobe (Maldonado et al., 1997). The first step in seeing your face involves the primary visual cortex.

The *primary visual cortex*, which is located at the very back of the occipital lobe, receives electrical signals from receptors in the eyes and transforms these signals into meaningless basic visual sensations, such as lights, lines, shadows, colors, and textures.

Since the primary visual cortex produces only meaningless visual sensations (lights, lines, shadows), you do not yet see your face. Transforming meaningless visual sensations into a meaningful visual object occurs in the visual association area (Miyashita, 1995).

The *visual association area*, which is located next to the primary visual cortex, transforms basic sensations, such as lights, lines, colors, and textures, into complete, meaningful visual perceptions, such as persons, objects, or animals.

If there are problems in the second step, such as damage to the visual association area, the person can still see parts of objects but has difficulty combining the parts and seeing or recognizing the whole object (Bower, 1996). We'll discuss two unusual visual problems that result from damage to association areas.

2 Visual Agnosia

Since the visual association area is critical for recognizing objects, it follows that damage to this area results in difficulties of recognition, a condition called visual agnosia (*ag-NO-zee-ah*).

In *visual agnosia*, the individual fails to recognize some object, person, or color, yet has the ability to see and even describe pieces or parts of some visual stimulus.

Here's what happens when patients with damage to the visual association area were asked to simply copy an object.

A patient who has visual agnosia was asked to make a copy of this horse, something most everyone can do.

The patient drew each part of the horse separately and could not combine individual parts into a meaningful image.

Patients with visual agnosia can see individual parts of an object but, because of damage to visual association areas, have great difficulty combining parts to perceive a complete and recognizable image (Maratsos & Matheny, 1994). Damage to association areas can also result in seeing only half of one's world.

3 Neglect Syndrome

Individuals who have damage to association areas, usually in occipital and parietal lobes, and usually in the right hemisphere, experience a very strange problem called the neglect syndrome.

The *neglect syndrome* refers to the failure of a patient to see objects or parts of the body on the side opposite the brain damage. Patients may dress only one side of their body and deny that opposite body parts are theirs ("that's not my leg").

Here's how a patient with neglect syndrome drew an object.

A patient with neglect syndrome caused by right-sided brain damage was asked to copy this clock.

The patient drew only the right side of the clock because he did not see or recognize things on his left side.

After a stroke or other damage, usually to the occipital and parietal association areas in the right hemisphere, patients may behave as if the left sides of objects and their own bodies no longer exist. This is a dramatic example of the important function of association areas (Springer & Deutsch, 1997).

Now we'll journey beneath the cortex and explore a group of structures that existed in evolutionarily very old, primitive brains.

E. Limbic System: Old Brain

Structures and Functions

Your cortex is involved in numerous cognitive functions, such as thinking, deciding, planning, and speaking, as well as other sensory and motor behaviors. But what triggers your wide range of emotional experiences, such as feeling happy, sad, fearful, and angry? If we peeled away the cortex, you would be looking deeper inside the brain at a number of structures that are involved in emotions and that make up the limbic system.

The *limbic system* refers to a group of about half a dozen interconnected structures that make up the core of the forebrain. The limbic system's structures are involved with many motivational behaviors—such as obtaining food, drink, and sex; with organizing emotional behaviors such as fear, anger, and aggression; and with the storing of memories.

The limbic system is often referred to as our primitive, or animal, brain because its same structures are found in the brains of animals that are evolutionarily very old, such as alligators. The alligator's limbic system, which essentially makes up its entire forebrain, is primarily involved in smelling out prey, defending territory, hunting, fighting, reproducing, eating, and remembering. The human limbic system, which makes up only a small part of the human forebrain, is involved in similar behaviors.

We'll discuss many of the major structures and functions of the limbic system. In the drawing below, the left hemisphere has been cut away to reveal the inner part of the brain. Notice that the limbic structures are surrounded by the forebrain, which helps regulate the limbic system's activities.

1 One limbic structure that is a master control for many emotional responses is the hypothalamus *(high-po-THAL-ah-mus).*

The *hypothalamus* regulates many motivational behaviors, including eating, drinking, and sexual responses; emotional behaviors, such as arousing the body when fighting or fleeing; and the secretion of hormones, such as occurs at puberty.

In addition, the hypothalamus controls the two divisions of the autonomic nervous system discussed on the right-hand page.

The next limbic structure, the amygdala, is also involved in emotions but more so in the forming and remembering of them.

2 The *amygdala (ah-MIG-duh-la),* which is located in the tip of the temporal lobe, is involved in forming, recognizing, and remembering emotional experiences and facial expressions.

For example, researchers found that patients with amygdala damage had difficulty recognizing personal facial expressions, and animals that have had their amygdalas removed do not learn to fear dangerous situations (LaBar & LeDoux, 1996; Scott et al., 1997). Researchers found that the amygdala is especially involved in recognizing dangerous situations (Zald & Pardo, 1997).

3 This limbic structure, which is like a miniature computer that gathers and processes information from your senses, is called the thalamus *(THAL-ah-mus).*

The *thalamus,* located in the middle of the forebrain, is involved in receiving sensory information, doing some initial processing, and then relaying the sensory information to areas of the cortex, including the somatosensory cortex, primary auditory cortex, and primary visual cortex.

For example, if the thalamus malfunctions and slows down the processing of auditory information, the result can be difficulty in learning to read, which is one sign of dyslexia (Begley, 1994).

Our last limbic structure, the hippocampus, is involved in saving your memories.

4 The *hippocampus,* which is a curved structure inside the temporal lobe, is involved in saving many kinds of fleeting memories by putting them into permanent storage in various parts of the brain.

For example, humans with damage to the hippocampus have difficulty remembering new facts, places, faces, or conversations because these new events cannot be placed into permanent storage (Risold & Swanson, 1996; Squire & Zola-Morgan, 1991). Think of the hippocampus as functioning like the "Save" command on your computer.

One advantage of our larger and newer cortex is that it regulates the motivational and emotional functions of the smaller and older limbic system. One structure of the limbic system, the hypothalamus, has an important role in regulating the autonomic nervous system, which we'll examine next.

Autonomic Nervous System

Why don't you worry about breathing?

You are unaware of how or what regulates your breathing, heart rate, hormone secretions, or body temperature. The reason you can forget about these vital functions is because they are usually controlled by a separate nervous system, called the autonomic nervous system, which, in turn, is regulated by the master control center, the hypothalamus (discussed on the previous page).

The autonomic nervous system, which regulates numerous physiological responses, has two divisions, the sympathetic and parasympathetic nervous systems. The sympathetic division is activated when you suddenly see a snake; then, the parasympathetic division helps you relax. Here are some of the specific and automatic functions of the sympathetic and parasympathetic divisions.

Sympathetic Nervous System

If you were on a nature hike and suddenly saw a snake, your cortex would activate the hypothalamus, which in turn triggers the sympathetic division of the autonomic nervous system (Jansen et al., 1995).

The *sympathetic division,* which is one part of the autonomic nervous system, is triggered by threatening or challenging physical stimuli, such as a snake, or by psychological stimuli, such as the thought of having to give a public speech. Once triggered, the sympathetic division increases the body's physiological arousal.

All of the physiological responses listed in the left column under "Sympathetic," such as increased heart rate, increased blood pressure, and dilated pupils, put your body into a state of heightened physiological arousal, which is called the fight-flight response.

The *fight-flight response,* which is a state of increased physiological arousal caused by activation of the sympathetic division, helps the body cope with and survive threatening situations.

You have no doubt experienced the fight-flight response many times, such as when you felt your heart pound and your mouth went bone dry. We'll discuss the major role played by fight-flight response during all kinds of stressful situations in Module 21.

Parasympathetic Nervous System

After you have been physiologically aroused by seeing a snake, it is usually some time before your body returns to a calmer state. The process of decreasing physiological arousal and calming down your body is triggered by the hypothalamus, which activates the parasympathetic division.

The *parasympathetic division,* which is the other part of the autonomic nervous system, decreases physiological arousal and helps return the body to a calmer, more relaxed state. It also stimulates digestion during eating.

As shown in the right column under the heading "Parasympathetic," the parasympathetic division, once activated, decreases physiological arousal by decreasing heart rate, lowering blood pressure, and stimulating digestion, all of which leads to a calmer state.

In Module 21, we'll discuss many relaxation techniques, such as the relaxation response, various forms of meditation, and biofeedback, which are intended to increase parasympathetic activity, decrease body arousal, and thus help you calm down after stressful experiences.

Sympathetic		Parasympathetic
Pupils dilated, dry; far vision	Eyes	Pupils constricted, moist; near vision
Dry	Mouth	Salivation
Goose bumps	Skin	No goose bumps
Sweaty	Palms	Dry
Passages dilated	Lungs	Passages constricted
Increased rate	Heart	Decreased rate
Supply maximum to muscles	Blood	Supply maximum to internal organs
Increased activity	Adrenal glands	Decreased activity
Inhibited	Digestion	Stimulated
Climax	Sexual functions	Arousal

Homeostasis

One problem that some students face is becoming too stressed or upset by life's events. Because it is potentially harmful to your body to stay stressed or aroused, the autonomic nervous system tries to keep the body's level of arousal at optimum levels, a state called homeostasis.

Homeostasis (ho-me-oh-STAY-sis) means that sympathetic and parasympathetic systems work together to keep the body's level of arousal in balance for optimum functioning.

For instance, your body's balance, or homeostasis, may be upset by the continuous stress of final exams or

a difficult relationship. Such stress usually results in continuous physiological arousal and any number of physical problems, including headaches, stomachaches, tight muscles, or fatigue. These physical symptoms, which are called psychosomatic problems, may result in real pain. We'll discuss these problems in Module 21.

Besides triggering your autonomic nervous system, the hypothalamus is also involved in regulating a complex hormonal system, which we'll examine next.

F. Endocrine System

Definition

What is your chemical system?

You have two major systems for sending signals to the body's muscles, glands, and organs. We have already discussed the nervous system, which uses neurons, nerves, and neurotransmitters to send information throughout the body. The second major system for sending information is called the endocrine system.

The *endocrine system* is made up of numerous glands that are located throughout the body. In turn, these glands secrete various chemicals, called *hormones,* which affect organs, muscles, and other glands in the body.

The location and function of some of the endocrine system's glands are shown in the figure below.

Control Center

In many ways, the *hypothalamus,* which is located in the lower middle part of the brain, controls much of the endocrine system by regulating the pituitary gland, which is located directly below and outside the brain. The hypothalamus is often called the control center of the endocrine system.

The drawing below shows how the hypothalamus is connected to the pituitary gland.

Hypo-thalamus

Posterior pituitary

Anterior pituitary

Other Glands

The *pituitary gland,* a key component of the endocrine system, hangs directly below the hypothalamus, to which it is connected by a narrow stalk. The pituitary gland is divided into anterior (front) and posterior (back) sections.

Posterior pituitary. The rear portion of the pituitary regulates water and salt balance.

Dysfunction: Lack of hormones causes a less common form of diabetes.

Anterior pituitary. The front part of the pituitary regulates growth through secretion of growth hormone and produces hormones that control the adrenal cortex, pancreas, thyroid, and gonads.

Dysfunction: Too little growth hormone produces dwarfism; too much causes gigantism. Other problems in the pituitary cause problems in the glands it regulates.

Pancreas. This organ regulates the level of sugar in the bloodstream by secreting insulin.

Dysfunction: Lack of insulin results in the more common form of diabetes, while too much causes hypoglycemia (low blood sugar).

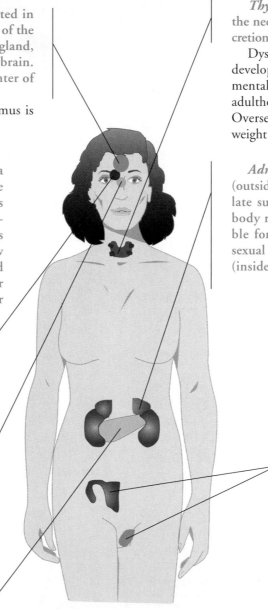

Thyroid. This gland, which is located in the neck, regulates metabolism through secretion of hormones.

Dysfunction: Hormone deficiency during development leads to stunted growth and mental retardation. Undersecretion during adulthood leads to reduction in motivation. Oversecretion results in high metabolism, weight loss, and nervousness.

Adrenal glands. The adrenal cortex (outside part) secretes hormones that regulate sugar and salt balances and help the body resist stress; they are also responsible for growth of pubic hair, a secondary sexual characteristic. The adrenal medulla (inside part) secretes two hormones that arouse the body to deal with stress and emergencies: epinephrine (adrenaline) and norepinephrine (noradrenaline).

Dysfunction: With a lack of cortical hormones, the body's responses are unable to cope with stress.

Gonads. In females, the ovaries produce hormones that regulate sexual development, ovulation, and growth of sex organs. In males, the testes produce hormones that regulate sexual development, production of sperm, and growth of sex organs.

Dysfunction: Lack of sex hormones during puberty results in lack of secondary sexual characteristics (facial and bodily hair, muscles in males, breasts in females).

Up to this point, we have examined many of the structures and functions that make up the incredible nervous and endocrine systems. After the Concept Review, we'll discuss a question that students often ask: Do the brains of males differ from those of females?

1. A hairlike structure that contains tightly coiled strands of the chemical DNA (deoxyribonucleic acid) is called a (a)_____. A specific segment on the strand of DNA that contains instructions for making proteins is called a (b)_____. A theory that different species arose from a common ancestor and that those species survived that were best adapted to meet the demands of their environments is called the theory of (c)_____.

2. There are several techniques for studying the living brain. One method for identifying structures in the brain involves measuring nonharmful radio frequencies as they pass through the brain; this is called a (a)_____ scan.

Another method that is used to study functions of the brain involves measuring amounts of low-level radioactive substances absorbed by brain cells; this is called a (b)_____ scan.

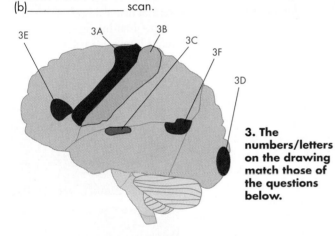

3. The numbers/letters on the drawing match those of the questions below.

3A. The cortical area that controls voluntary movements is called the (a)_____ and is located in the (b)_____ lobe.

3B. The cortical area that receives input from sensory receptors in the skin, muscles, and joints is called the (a)_____ and is located in the (b)_____ lobe.

3C. The cortical area that receives input from sensory receptors in the ears is called the (a)_____ and is located in the (b)_____ lobe.

3D. The cortical area that receives input from sensory receptors in the eyes is called the (a)_____ and is located in the (b)_____ lobe.

3E. The cortical area that is necessary to produce words and arrange them into sentences is called (a)_____ and is located in the (b)_____ lobe.

3F. The cortical area that is necessary for understanding spoken and written words and putting words into meaningful sentences is called (a)_____ and is located in the (b)_____ lobe.

4. The two major divisions of the nervous system include the (a)_____ and the (b)_____. In turn, the peripheral nervous system has two parts: one part is a network of nerves that are connected either to sensory receptors or to muscles that you can move voluntarily and is called the (c)_____; another part regulates heart rate, breathing, blood pressure, digestion, secretion of hormones, and other functions and is called the (d)_____. The brain itself is divided into three major parts: (e)_____, _____, and _____.

5. The old brain that is involved with many motivational and emotional behaviors is called the (a)_____. One structure of the limbic system, the hypothalamus, controls the autonomic nervous system, which has two divisions. The division that responds by increasing the body's physiological arousal is called the (b)_____. This division triggers an increased state of physiological arousal so that the body can cope with threatening situations; this state is called the (c)_____. The other division of the autonomic nervous system that is primarily responsible for returning the body to a calm or relaxed state and is involved in digestion is called the (d)_____. These two divisions work together to keep the body in physiological balance so that it remains or returns to a state of optimal functioning; this state is called (e)_____.

6. A system made up of numerous glands that are located throughout the body and that secrete various hormones is called the (a)_____. The brain area that can be considered the master control for this system is the (b)_____. This brain area is connected to and controls one of the major glands that has an anterior and posterior part and is collectively called the (c)_____.

G. Research Focus: Sexual Differences
Are There Sex Differences in the Brain?

Science and Politics

Is this kind of research sexist?

Throughout history, politicians have either criticized or misused research depending on what was "politically correct" (Azar, 1997). For example, in the 1920s, United States politicians misused research on IQ scores to justify passing discriminatory immigration quotas (Gould, 1981) (see page 296). In the 1980s, many politicians were critical of homosexuality and denied federal money for AIDS research until the virus became a threat to the heterosexual population (Shilts, 1988). In the 1980s and 1990s, research on sex differences was criticized as "sexist" because it went against the "politically correct" belief that male and female brains are essentially equal (Azar, 1997).

Sex, or gender, differences refer to structural or functional differences in cognitive, behavioral, or brain processes that arise from being a male or a female.

Using PET scans, researchers have reported a number of interesting sex differences in the structure and function of the human brain. It is important to remember that such differences are neither good nor bad nor sexist but simply ways in which males and females differ. We'll begin with how performance on certain tasks differs according to sex.

Differences in Solving Problems

The rotating figure problem is a rather difficult spatial problem, as follows. First, study the target figure on the left. Then, from the three choices at the right, identify the same figure, even though it has been rotated.

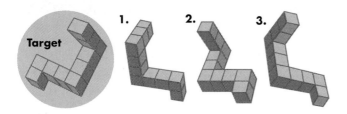

The key to solving this problem is the ability to rotate the target figure in your mind until it matches the rotation of one of the three choices. Researchers consistently report faster or more accurate performance by males than by females in solving rotating figure problems (Kimura, 1992). (Correct answer is 1.)

There are other tasks at which women perform better than men.

For example, look at the house outlined in black (figure above) and find its twin among the three choices. Women are generally faster on these kinds of tests, which measure perceptual speed. In addition, women usually score higher on tests of verbal fluency, in which you must list as many words as you can that begin with the same letter, as in the figure below (Kimura, 1992).

One explanation for these sex differences in skills is that they result from differences in

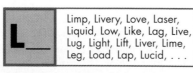

Limp, Livery, Love, Laser, Liquid, Low, Like, Lag, Live, Lug, Light, Lift, Liver, Lime, Leg, Load, Lap, Lucid, . . .

socialization and learning. Another explanation is that these sex differences have evolved from different skills needed by early humans. Males with good spatial skills had an advantage in hunting, and females with good communication skills had an advantage in child-rearing (Springer & Deutsch, 1997).

Researchers have now begun to look for sex differences in how the brain itself functions.

Differences in Brains

Researchers used PET scans, which are a measure of neural activity, to look for sex differences in brain functioning. PET scans of female and male brains were taken while subjects were resting or solving rotating figure problems. When subjects were resting, PET scans indicated that female brains did not differ in their pattern of neural activity from male brains. However, when subjects were solving rotating figure problems, PET scans showed a significant difference between male and female brains.

For male brains, PET scans (upper right figure) taken during problem-solving showed that maximum neural activity occurred in the right frontal area.

In contrast, PET scans of female brains (lower right figure) taken during problem-solving showed that maximum neural activity occurred in the right parietal-temporal area. Researchers concluded that solving rotating figure problems showed a significant sex difference in terms of which brain areas were activated and that these brain differences may underlie the basis for sex differences in performance (Alivisatos & Petrides, 1997; Deutsch & Halsey, 1991). Besides differences in cognitive tasks, researchers are also finding sex differences in emotional tasks.

Because women are consistently reported to be more sensitive, concerned, and nurturing, is it possible that women process emotional information differently than men (Halpern, 1992)? Researchers took PET scans while subjects induced emotional states (happy, sad). PET scans showed that while inducing emotional states, women used more of their limbic structures (involved in emotions) than men. Researchers speculate that these kinds of sex differences in the brain may underlie other male-female emotional behaviors (George et al., 1996).

As researchers continue to find sex differences in the brain, they warn against using such differences as the basis for promoting discriminatory practices or furthering someone's political agenda (Azar, 1997; Nishizawa et al., 1997).

H. Cultural Diversity: Brain Size & Racial Myths

Skull Size and Intelligence

Which race had the biggest brain?

When he died in 1851, The *New York Times* proudly said that Samuel George Morton, scientist and physician, had one of the best reputations among scholars throughout the world. Morton had spent his lifetime collecting skulls of different races to determine which race had the biggest brain. During Morton's time, it was generally accepted that a bigger brain meant greater intelligence and innate mental ability.

Results. Morton estimated the size of a brain by pouring tiny lead pellets (the size of present-day BBs) into each skull and then measuring the number of pellets. Using this procedure, he arrived at the following ranking of brain size in different races, from biggest to smallest (see skulls on right): 1, White (Caucasian); 2, yellow (Mongolian); 3, brown (American Indian); and 4, Black (Negro). Along with his racial ranking of decreasing brain size, Morton noted a corresponding decrease in behavioral and cognitive skills. For instance, Morton wrote that Mongolians were close in feeling and action to the monkey race, that American Indians were incapable of reasoning on abstract subjects, and that Negroes were the nearest approximation to animals (Morton, 1839, cited in Gould, 1981).

Reanalyzed. A hundred and thirty years later, Stephen Jay Gould, a renowned evolutionary biologist, reanalyzed Morton's data on brain size and found no significant difference in brain size among the four races. Furthermore, Gould concluded that Morton's strong biases about which races should have the biggest brains had unknowingly swayed his scientific judgment to fit the discriminatory racial notions of the time (Gould, 1981). Morton's biggest error was to include skulls that matched his personal expectations and to omit skulls that did not support his beliefs.

Morton's elevation of the White or Caucasian race to the pinnacle of human perfection agreed with the notions of German naturalist Johann Blumenback, who in 1795 wrote that Caucasians were the nearest to perfection (Gould, 1994).

Although Morton was asking a legitimate research question, he was unable to prevent his strong personal beliefs from biasing his research. One way current researchers guard against this problem is by having scientists in other laboratories repeat their studies. If the original findings are repeated in other laboratories, then they can be reasonably confident that their original results are valid.

1839: Morton's ratings of race and brain size

1. White: Caucasian

2. Yellow: Mongolian

3. Brown: American Indian

4. Black: Negro

Brain Size and Intelligence

Is a bigger brain more intelligent?

Currently, researchers are again studying the relationship between brain size and intelligence with MRI scans (discussed on p. 70), which can measure more precisely the size of the human brain. In four different studies, researchers found a moderate correlation of about +0.40 between brain size and intelligence (Wickett et al., 1994). These results suggest a positive relationship between brain size and intelligence, meaning that, generally, the larger the brain the higher the IQ.

Female brains. If there is a positive relationship between brain size and intelligence, then women should generally be less intelligent than men because their brains, as well as their heads, are about 10% smaller than men's (Holden, 1995). Since there is no evidence that women are less intelligent than men, how do we explain this contradiction?

Although women's brains may be smaller, perhaps their brain cells are more tightly packed together. This idea received considerable support when the brains of men and women were examined after death. Researchers reported that, in some areas of the women's brains, there were 11–17% more neurons than in corresponding parts of men's larger brains (Witelson, et al., 1995). Researchers think that women's brains are not simply scaled-down versions of men's brains but rather that neurons in women's brains are more densely packed.

Correlations. Since studies report a positive correlation between brain size and intelligence, we'll briefly review what *correlation* means. A correlation indicates only the existence of a relationship between two events but does not identify cause and effect. For example, being in a stimulating environment may promote brain growth and result in higher IQ scores, or being born with a larger brain may allow one to absorb more from one's environment and score higher on IQ tests.

Thus, at this point in time, a positive correlation between brain size and intelligence may be scientifically interesting but has little practical application.

Before we complete our journey through the brain, we'll take you on one last trip, perhaps the most interesting of all. We'll see what happens when the brain is literally cut in two.

I. Application: Split Brain

Definition

Why did Victoria choose a split brain?

Since about the age of six, Victoria had seizures (also called epileptic seizures). During the seizures, she would lose consciousness, fall to the floor, and although her muscles would jerk uncontrollably, she felt no pain and would remember nothing of the experience. She was given anticonvulsant medicine, which prevented any further seizures until she was 18.

Split-brain operation. When Victoria was 18, for some unknown reason, her seizures returned with greater intensity. And to her dismay, anticonvulsant medication no longer had any effect. The seizures continued for ten years. Finally, when she was 27, she decided that her best chance of reducing her frightening, uncontrollable seizures was to have an operation that had a high probability of producing serious side effects. In this operation, a neurosurgeon would sever the major connection between her right and left hemispheres, leaving her with what is called a split brain (figure below).

Having to choose between a future of uncontrollable seizures and the potential problems of having a split brain, Victoria chose the operation (Sidtis et al., 1981).

In addition to Victoria (identified as V.P. in published reports), dozens of other individuals have also chosen to have a split-brain operation when they found that medicine no longer prevented their severe, uncontrollable seizures.

In a split-brain operation, the neurosurgeon opens the patient's skull and separates the two hemispheres by cutting the corpus callosum.

After cutting the corpus callosum the right and left hemispheres function relatively independently.

A *split–brain operation* involves cutting the wide band of fibers, called the corpus callosum, that connects the right and left hemispheres (figure above). The corpus callosum has 200 million nerve fibers that allow information to pass back and forth between the hemispheres.

A split-brain operation not only disrupts the major pathway between the hemispheres but, to a large extent, leaves each hemisphere functioning independently. In many split-brain patients, severing the corpus callosum prevented the spread of seizures from one hemisphere to the other and thus reduced their frequency and occurrence (Gazzaniga, 1996).

Major breakthrough. It was 1961 when researcher Michael S. Gazzaniga and his colleagues tested the first split-brain patient, known as W.J. in the literature. Researchers first flashed on a screen a number of colors, letters, and pictures of objects. These stimuli were flashed so that they went only to W.J.'s left hemisphere, and he had no difficulty naming them. Then researchers flashed the same stimuli so that they went only to W.J.'s right hemisphere, and W.J. seemed to see nothing, to be blind (Gazzaniga et al., 1962). Gazzaniga calls the discovery that W.J.'s right hemisphere was saying nothing "one of those unforgettable moments in life." Was it true that W.J.'s left hemisphere could talk but not his right?

Testing a patient. To determine what each hemisphere can and cannot do, we can watch as Gazzaniga tests Victoria after her split-brain operation.

Victoria is asked to stare at the black dot between *HE* and *ART* as the word *HEART* is displayed on a screen. Because Victoria's hemispheres are split, information from each side of the black dot will go only to the opposite hemisphere (figure below). This means that Victoria's left hemisphere will see only the word *ART* and her right hemisphere will see only the word *HE*.

Severed corpus callosum

When asked, "What did you see?" Victoria says that she saw the word "ART," because it was projected to the left hemisphere, which has the ability to speak.

Although Victoria's right hemisphere saw the word *HE*, the right hemisphere turns out to be mute, meaning that it cannot say what it saw. However, Victoria can point with her left hand to a photo of a man (HE), indicating that the right hemisphere understood the question and saw the word *HE*. (Victoria points with her left hand because her right hemisphere controls the left side of the body.) Although the effects of having a split brain are obvious under special testing, the effects are not so apparent in everyday life.

Behaviors Following Split Brain

How does a split brain affect behavior? Initially, after her operation, Victoria reported that when she would choose clothes from her closet, her right hand would grab a blouse but then her left hand would put it back. However, examples of obvious conflicts between hemispheres are rare and disappear over the coming months.

Four months after her operation, Victoria was alert and talked easily about past and present events. She could read, write, reason, and perform everyday functions such as eating, dressing, and walking, as well as carry on normal conversations. For Victoria with her split brain, as well as for most of us with normal brains, only the left hemisphere can express itself through the spoken word (Springer & Deutsch, 1997). If the speech area is in the left hemisphere, then the right hemisphere is usually mute. (For a small percentage of left-handers, the speech area is in the right hemisphere and the left hemisphere is usually mute.) Thus, one reason a split-brain person appears normal in casual conversation is that only one hemisphere is directing speech. After testing split-brain patients, researchers discovered that each hemisphere is specialized for performing certain tasks.

Different Functions

Before observing split-brain patients, researchers knew very little about how each hemisphere functioned. Thus, quite by chance, an experimental treatment for seizures led to a whole new understanding of what each hemisphere does well or does poorly.

Left hemisphere

Verbal. Left hemisphere is very good at all language-related abilities: speaking, understanding language, carrying on a conversation, reading, writing, spelling.

Mathematical. Left hemisphere is very good at mathematical skills: adding, subtracting, multiplying, dividing, solving complex problems in calculus, physics, and so on. Generally, the right hemisphere can perform simple addition and subtraction but not more complex mathematics (Sperry, 1974).

Analytic. Left hemisphere appears to process information by analyzing each separate piece that makes up a whole. For example, the left hemisphere would recognize a face by analyzing piece by piece its many separate parts: nose, eye, lips, cheeks, and so on—a relatively slow process (Levy & Trevarthen, 1976).

Right hemisphere

Nonverbal. Although usually mute, the right hemisphere has a childlike ability to read, write, spell and understand speech (Gazzaniga, 1983). For example, when spoken to, the right hemisphere can understand simple sentences and read simple words.

Spatial. Right hemisphere is very good at solving spatial problems, such as arranging blocks to match a geometric design. Because hemispheres control opposite sides of the body, the left hand (right hemisphere) is best at arranging blocks, a spatial task.

Holistic. Right hemisphere appears to processes information by combining parts into a meaningful whole. For this reason the right hemisphere is better at recognizing and identifying whole faces (Levy et al., 1972). The right hemisphere is also good at making and recognizing emotional facial expressions (Springer & Deutsch, 1997).

Because each hemisphere has different skills, how are they organized? Does that mean that I'm primarily right-brained or left-brained?

Right-Brained or Left-Brained?

How is my brain organized?
Michael Gazzaniga (1994, 1996), a cognitive neuroscientist, believes that each hemisphere of the brain has many different mental programs, such as sensing, thinking, learning, feeling, and speaking, all of which can function simultaneously. For example, when you see someone smile, your brain uses dozens of mental programs from each hemisphere to receive, interpret, and respond to this relatively simple facial expression.

Thus, the organization of the brain appears to include many separate but interconnected mental programs that function together and that are vitally important in carrying out high-level cognitive tasks (Hoptman & Davidson, 1994).

Am I "left-brained" or "right-brained"?
The popular press has exaggerated the idea that we are either "right-brained"—creative, intuitive, and artistic—or "left-brained"—reasonable, logical, and rational.

According to Jerre Levy (1985), who has devoted her career to studying how the brain's hemispheres interact, these distinctions are much too simple. She believes that we are constantly using both hemispheres, since each hemisphere is specialized for processing certain kinds of information. For example, when you read a novel, you are probably using programs in the left hemisphere that allow you to understand language in written form. But at the same time, you are using programs in the right hemisphere to keep track of the overall story, appreciate its humor and emotional content, and interpret any illustrations. Although hemispheres may sometimes work alone, they share much of their information by passing it quickly back and forth through the corpus callosum (Hellige, 1993; Grabowska & Nowicka, 1996).

Does the brain get better with use?
You have about 100 billion neurons, which you can think of as forming an extremely powerful living computer. Just as you get better at using a computer, there is increasing evidence that your brain improves as you use it. For example, one researcher measured the length of dendrites in 20 deceased adults. The length of dendrites is thought to be one measure of how much information can be received and processed. Dendrite lengths varied by 40%: the longest were found in college-educated adults and the shortest in high school dropouts (Jacobs, 1993). Thus, the old saying "use it or lose it" may also apply to the brain (Gage, 1997).

SUMMARY TEST

A. GENES & EVOLUTION

1. A fertilized egg, which is called a
(a)_____, contains 46 chromo-
somes arranged in 23 pairs. A hairlike structure that contains tightly coiled strands of the
chemical DNA (deoxyribonucleic acid) is
called a (b)_____. A specific seg-
ment on the strand of DNA that contains instructions for making proteins is called a (c)_____.

2. In 1859, Charles Darwin published a revolutionary theory of
(a)_____, which said that different species arose from a
common (b)_____ and that those species survived that
were best adapted to meet the demands of their (c)_____.

B. STUDYING THE LIVING BRAIN

3. There are several recently developed
techniques for studying the living brain.
One technique, which measures nonharmful
radio frequencies as they pass through the
brain, is called an (a)_____
and is used to identify structures in the living brain. Another technique
measures how much of a radioactive substance is taken up by brain
cells and is called a (b)_____. This kind of scan is used
to study brain function and identify the most and least active parts.

C. ORGANIZATION OF THE BRAIN

4. The human nervous system is divided into
two major parts. The brain and spinal cord
make up the (a)_____. The net-
work of nerves outside the brain and spinal
cord make up the (b)_____.

5. The peripheral nervous system is further divided into two parts.
One part is made up of a network of nerves that either carry messages to muscles and organs throughout the body or carry input
from sensory receptors to the spinal cord; this is called the
(a)_____. The second part of the peripheral nervous system, which regulates heart rate, breathing, digestion, secretion of
hormones, and related responses, is called the (b)_____.

6. The human brain is divided into three major parts. The largest
part is involved in cognitive responses that we characterize as most
human. This part is called the (a)_____, which is divided
into right and left hemispheres. The part that is involved in controlling vital reflexes, sleeping, and coordinating body movements, is
called the (b)_____. The part that is involved in visual

and auditory reflexes, as well as alerting the brain to incoming sensations, is called the (c)_____.

7. Beginning in the midbrain and extending downward is a long
column of cells called the _____ that alerts the forebrain
to incoming sensory information.

8. The hindbrain consists of three structures. The structure that serves
as a bridge to connect the brain and body and also manufactures
chemicals involved in sleep is called the (a)_____. The
structure that controls vital reflexes, such as heart rate, blood pressure, and respiration, is called the (b)_____. The structure that was assumed to be involved primarily in coordinating body
movements but has recently been found to have a role in cognitive
functions, such as short-term memory, following rules, and carrying
out plans, is called the (c)_____.

D. CONTROL CENTERS: FOUR LOBES

9. The thin outside layer of cells that
has a wrinkled look and covers almost
the entire forebrain is called the
(a)_____. This layer of
cells is divided into four separate areas
or lobes: (b)_____,
_____, _____,
and _____.

10. The lobe that is involved in social-emotional behaviors, maintaining a healthy personality, and making and carrying out plans is
called the _____ lobe.

11. At the back edge of the frontal lobe is a continuous strip called
the _____, which controls the movement of voluntary
muscles. Body parts that have greater capacity for complicated muscle movement have more area on the motor cortex devoted to them.

12. Along the front edge of the parietal lobe is a continuous strip
that receives sensations from the body and is called the
_____. Body parts with greater sensitivity have more
area on the somatosensory cortex devoted to them.

13. An area on the upper edge of the temporal lobe that receives
signals from receptors in the ears and changes them into basic auditory sensations is called the (a)_____. For most individuals, an area in the left temporal lobe is involved in understanding
and speaking coherently; it is called (b)_____ area.
Damage to this area results in inability to understand spoken and
written speech or to speak coherently, a problem called
(c)_____. An area in the frontal lobe, called
(d)_____, is necessary for producing words and

arranging them into fluent sentences. If this area is damaged, the result is a speech problem called (e)_____.

14. An area at the very back of the occipital lobe that receives signals from receptors in the eyes and changes them into basic visual sensations is called the _____.

15. The vast majority of the cortex making up the four lobes is involved in adding meaning, interpretations, and associations to sensory stimuli, as well as in many cognitive functions. Together, these areas are called _____ areas.

E. LIMBIC SYSTEM: OLD BRAIN

16. Inside the forebrain is a central core of interconnected structures known as the primitive, or "animal," brain or, more technically, the (a)_____. Four of the areas that make up the limbic system are the (b)_____, _____, _____, and _____, which are all involved in motivational and emotional behaviors.

17. One structure of the limbic system, the hypothalamus, controls the autonomic nervous system, which has two divisions. The one that arouses the body, increases physiological responses (such as heart rate and blood pressure), and prepares the body for the fight-flight response is called the (a)_____. The division that calms down the body and aids digestion is called the (b)_____. These two divisions work together to keep the body's internal organs in a balanced physiological state, which is called (c)_____.

F. ENDOCRINE SYSTEM

18. Besides the nervous system, a network of glands regulates organs through the secretion of hormones. This chemical system is called the (a)_____. A major gland that controls other glands in this system is the (b)_____ gland, which has an anterior and posterior part.

G. RESEARCH FOCUS: SEXUAL DIFFERENCES

19. Structural or functional differences in the brain that arise from being male or female are called _____. One example of sex differences in the brain is that males primarily use the frontal area to solve spatial problems, while females use the parietal-temporal area.

H. CULTURAL DIVERSITY: BRAIN SIZE & RACIAL MYTHS

20. In the 1800s, one scientist measured skull size and concluded that a larger brain indicated more intelligence and that the races could be ranked by brain size. However, further analysis of this researcher's data indicated that there was no basis for ranking races by (a)_____. More recent experiments that precisely measured brain size with MRI scans found a modest correlation between brain size and (b)_____. However, we do not know if a stimulating environment causes the brain to grow more or if a larger brain is able to absorb more from the environment.

I. APPLICATION: SPLIT BRAIN

21. The two hemispheres are connected by a major bundle of fibers that is called the _____. Severing this structure produces a condition called a split brain. Study of such patients reveals that each hemisphere generally processes information in a different way.

22. For most individuals, mental programs for language, speech, and mathematics are located in the (a)_____; mental programs for solving spatial problems and processing emotional responses are located in the (b)_____. In addition, the hemispheres process information in different ways. The left hemisphere processes information in a more piece-by-piece fashion or (c)_____ way. In comparison, the right hemisphere processes information as a meaningful whole; that is, it uses a more (d)_____ approach.

23. One theory of brain organization says that your brain has many separate but interconnected _____ programs that function and work together so that you can perform many cognitive skills.

Answers: 1. (a) zygote, (b) chromosome, (c) gene; 2. (a) evolution, (b) ancestor, (c) environment; 3. (a) MRI scan, (b) PET scan; 4. (a) central nervous system, (b) peripheral nervous system; 5. (a) somatic nervous system, (b) autonomic nervous system; 6. (a) forebrain, (b) hindbrain, (c) midbrain; 7. reticular formation; 8. (a) pons, (b) medulla, (c) cerebellum; 9. (a) cortex, (b) frontal, parietal, temporal, occipital; 10. frontal; 11. motor cortex; 12. somatosensory cortex; 13. (a) primary auditory cortex, (b) Wernicke's, (c) Wernicke's aphasia, (d) Broca's area, (e) Broca's aphasia; 14. primary visual cortex; 15. association areas; 16. (a) limbic system, (b) hippocampus, hypothalamus, thalamus, amygdala; 17. (a) sympathetic division, (b) parasympathetic division, (c) homeostasis; 18. (a) endocrine system, (b) pituitary; 19. sex differences; 20. (a) brain size, (b) intelligence; 21. (a) corpus callosum; 22. (a) left hemisphere, (b) right hemisphere, (c) analytic, (d) holistic; 23. mental

CRITICAL THINKING

Newspaper Article

QUESTIONS

1. What method of brain imaging did Dr. Hopkins use to study ape brains?

2. What theory does the Living Links project rely on?

3. What will the scientists be focusing on in comparing chimp DNA to human DNA?

4. What might the fact mean that chimps are left-brained while monkeys are not?

5. How are Dr. de Waal's theories about the roots of complex cognition different from those of other scientists in this article?

RESEARCHERS MONKEY AROUND WITH ORIGINS OF THE MIND
by Lauren Neergaard

Bill Hopkins put 10 species of monkeys and apes into an MRI scanner and came to a startling conclusion: apes share a brain feature thought to make humans unique.

Fellow scientist Frans de Waal sees the roots of cognition in a bonobo named Kakowet, who spotted zookeepers turning on water valves and realized they would flood a nearby moat where infant apes were playing. Kakowet warned the zookeeper and helped rescue the babies.

The nation's largest primate research center is bringing together neuroscientists, geneticists, and behavior experts to shed new light on human evolution: using our closest living relatives—the apes—to explain how human cognition and behavior evolved.

"By understanding chimps, maybe we'll understand ourselves a wee bit better," said Tom Insel, chief of Yerkes Regional Primate Center, which is setting up the Living Links project on human evolution.

So-called evolutionary psychology is hot—and if early work is any indication, human mental traits may not be so unique. It's a controversial field, but one that should help generate new insights into "why the mind was organized the way it was," said Marc Hauser, a Harvard University evolutionary neurobiologist.

One chief project will be identifying ape genes to match with the neurologic and behavior findings. Human DNA is 98.4 percent identical to the DNA of chimps and bonobos, a lesser-known chimp-like ape.

"What is it in that other 1.6 percent that makes us different from them? That's the critical question," said de Waal, a renowned primatologist who will direct the project.

Language is one critical difference. Humans are "left brained"—the planum temporale that controls language is much larger on the left.

Hopkins' brain scans found that orangutans, gorillas, chimps, and bonobos all were left-brained too. Monkeys, lower on the evolutionary scale, were not. "We were able to pinpoint in evolutionary time when this evolved," said Hopkins.

In addition, bonobos gesture almost exclusively with their right hands—harking back to that right-hand, left-brain connection in humans. "Maybe language came from gesticulation," de Waal suggested.

De Waal's own research is more controversial: he sees roots of complex cognition and even morality in the behavior of both apes and monkeys.

Source: Associated Press, appeared in *Monterey County Herald,* May 11, 1998.

Study Questions

A. **Genes & Evolution**—If a species of humans with 5-pound brains was discovered, would their behavior differ from ours? (See answer in Critical Thinking Appendix)

B. **Studying the Living Brain**—How would you know if a professional boxer had brain damage? (See answer in Critical Thinking Appendix)

C. **Organization of the Brain**—If you had to give up one part of your brain, which one would you sacrifice?

D. **Control Centers: Four Lobes**—Which brain functions would computers be the best and worst at imitating?

E. **Limbic System: Old Brain**—What would happen if your limbic system were replaced with one from an alligator?

F. **Endocrine System**—What is one reason for the different bodies of football players, soccer players, and jockeys?

G. **Research Focus: Sexual Differences**—What's the danger of identifying sex differences in the brain?

H. **Cultural Diversity: Brain Size & Racial Myths**—Why is there a continuing interest in whether a bigger brain is more intelligent? (See answer in Critical Thinking Appendix)

I **Application: Split Brain**—If you were supposed to act like a person with a split brain, what would you do differently?

Web Sites & Learning Activities

● BROOKS/COLE ONLINE PSYCHOLOGY STUDY CENTER

http://psychstudy.brookscole.com/student/plotnik/quiz ch04frm.html

This site gives students a chance to review material by taking quizzes, and doing exercises and activities for this module.

● THE WHOLE BRAIN ATLAS

http://www.med.harvard.edu:80/AANLIB/ home.html

This amazing site from Harvard University features a complete atlas of the human brain in health and illness, featuring dozens of actual brain scan images.

● THE BRAIN IN HEALTH AND DISEASE

http://www.unihohenheim.de/~rebhan/rp.html

What are the latest scientific developments in the understanding, diagnosis, and treatment of brain disorders? This site answers those questions, and provides links to online journals and discussion groups.

● SHUFFLEBRAIN

http://www.indiana.edu/~pietsch/home.html#sample

This site is devoted to issues of brain damage and split-brain research. It provides popular science articles on these subjects as well as links to hypertext journals, images, and other Web sites.

Welcome to the WEB

● THE LIMBIC SYSTEM

http://thalamus.wustl.edu/course/limbic.html

This site contains labeled figures and text explaining the anatomy and function of the olfactory cortex, the amygdala, and the hippocampus.

● ABOUT BRAIN INJURY

http://www.waiting.com/waitingabouttbi.html

This site contains a wealth of information related to brain injury, including brain anatomy, intercranial pressure and its consequences, coma, neurosurgery, and a glossary of terms.

Activities

● *Integrator Online™ for Introductory Psychology* CD-ROM, Plotnik, Module 4

● Study Guide to accompany *Introduction to Psychology,* 5th edition, Module 4 (choice of PC or Mac computer version or hard copy).

● PsychNow! CD-ROM
The Brain and Behavior

Answers to questions on page 90

---

1. He used MRI scans, which show the structure of the brain.
2. It is based on Darwin's theory of evolution, that humans evolved from apes.
3. They will focus on the 1.6 percent of DNA that is different in chimps and humans, to try to discover what the actual differences are.

4. It could mean that language and other higher cognitive functions that humans have started to evolve with chimps.
5. Dr. de Waal based his theory on observing bonobo behavior, instead of on brain scans or DNA studies. All these methods of study could be describing the same phenomenon.

Module 5 SENSATION

An Electric Billboard in the Brain

Can Katie see without her eyes?

Katie was looking at an electric billboard made up of 36 dots of blue, purple, red, and yellow light. The billboard wasn't on the front of a store or sports stadium; it was in her own head.

When Katie was 22, she lost her eyesight to glaucoma and lived in total darkness for the next 20 years. At the age of 42, she volunteered to have experimental surgery in which 36 tiny gold wires were implanted into the occipital lobe in the back of her brain, which is the area that processes visual information. When researchers pushed a switch, a low-level, nonharmful electrical current passed through these gold wires and activated brain cells. When the brain cells in Katie's visual area were activated, she reported seeing flashes of colored light. By adjusting the amount of electrical current, researchers could vary brightness and size of the flashes from a tiny dot to the size of a nickel.

Because the implanted gold wires formed a rectangular grid of 36 dots (see figure above), researchers could apply current to particular wires in the grid to form patterns of flashing dots. For example,

when the flashing dots formed the pattern shown in the figure, Katie reported seeing the letter "S" (adapted from *Los Angeles Times*, October 30, 1992).

Although Katie is officially blind because her eyes are not functioning, she can still "see" flashes of colored lights when the visual area of her brain is electrically stimulated. This fact raises an interesting question: How is it possible to see without using one's eyes? As we answer this question, you'll discover that the eye, ear, nose, tongue, and skin are smaller, more complicated, and better recorders than any of the newest, miniaturized, high-tech video cameras, recorders, or digital disks on the market.

What's Coming

We'll discuss six major human senses—vision, hearing, balance (vestibular system), taste, olfaction, and touch. We'll also explain how you see color, why many rock-and-roll musicians may become partially deaf, why you get motion sickness, and why your sense of taste decreases when you have a cold. Although your sense organs look so different, we'll begin with three things they share in common.

Three Characteristics of All Senses

Your eyes, ears, nose, skin, and tongue are complex, miniaturized, living sensors that automatically gather information about your environment. Although they look very different, all senses share the following three characteristics.

1 Transduction. The first thing each sense organ must do is to change or transform some physical energy, such as molecules of skunk spray, into electrical signals, a process called transduction.

Electrical signal

Transduction refers to the process in which a sense organ changes, or transforms, physical energy into electrical signals that become neural impulses, which may be sent to the brain for processing.

For example, transduction occurs when a skunk's molecules enter your nose, which transforms the molecules into electrical signals, or impulses, that are interpreted by your brain as the very unpleasant odor of a skunk.

2 Adaptation. A short period of time after putting on glasses, jewelry, or clothes, you no longer "feel" them, a process called adaptation.

Adaptation refers to the decreasing response of the sense organs, the more they are exposed to a continuous level of stimulation.

For example, the continuous stimulation of glasses, jewelry, or clothes on your skin results in adaptation; soon you no longer feel them. Some sense organs adapt very quickly, and some very slowly. However, sense organs do not adapt to intense forms of stimulation, because such stimulation may cause physical damage. Instead, intense stimulation, such as from a very hot shower, may cause pain, which warns us of possible injury.

3 Sensations versus perceptions. Gathering information about the world involves two steps. In the first step, electrical signals reach the brain and are changed into sensations.

Sensations are relatively meaningless bits of information (left figure) that result when the brain processes electrical signals that come from the sense organs.

Usually, we are not aware of sensations because the brain immediately changes sensations into perceptions.

Perceptions are meaningful sensory experiences (right figure) that result after the brain combines hundreds of sensations.

For example, visual sensations would resemble the top figure, showing meaningless lines, colors, and shapes. Visual perceptions would be like the bottom figure, showing a complete "sad-happy" face.

While all sensations begin with step 1, transduction, sense organs use different mechanisms to do it. We'll start with how the visual system does it.

A. Eye: Vision

Stimulus

Why can't you see radio waves?

Each sense organ has a different shape and structure; it can receive only a certain kind of stimulus, or physical energy. For instance, the reason you cannot see radio waves is that their waves are not the right length. Although radio waves, along with light waves from the sun, are all forms of electromagnetic energy, they vary in wavelength. For example, the figure below shows that X rays are very short and AM radio waves are very long. Notice that only a small, specific range of wavelengths that come from the sun, called the visible spectrum, is able to excite receptors in your eyes.

Short wavelength   Long wavelength

Gamma rays	X rays	Ultraviolet rays		Radar	FM	TV	Shortwave	AM
10^{-14}	10^{-10}	10^{-8}		10^{-2}			10^{2}	10^{4}

Wavelength in meters (m)

Invisible—too short. On this side of the electromagnetic energy spectrum are shorter wavelengths, including gamma rays, X rays, and ultraviolet rays. These waves are invisible to the human eye because their lengths are too short to stimulate our receptors. However, some birds (such as hummingbirds) and insects can see ultraviolet rays to help them find food.

Violet Blue   Green   Yellow   Red

400   500   600   700
Wavelength in nanometers (nm)

Visible—just right. Near the middle of the electromagnetic spectrum is a small range of waves that make up the visible spectrum.

The *visible spectrum* is one particular segment of electromagnetic energy that we can see because these waves are the right length to stimulate receptors in the eye.

The reason you can see a giraffe is because its body reflects light waves from the visible spectrum back to your eyes. One function of the eyes is to absorb light waves that are reflected back from all the objects in your environment.

Invisible—too long. On this side of the electromagnetic spectrum are longer wavelengths, such as radio and television waves. These waves are invisible to the human eye because their lengths are too long to stimulate the receptors in the eye. Imagine the awful distraction of seeing radio and television waves all day long!

Stimulus. Thus, the most effective stimulus for vision is energy (light waves) from the visible spectrum. However, for you to see anything, reflected light waves must be gathered and changed into electrical signals, and for that process—transduction—we must look inside the eye itself.

Structure and Function

What if you see a giraffe?

For you to see a 16-foot-tall giraffe, your eyes perform two separate processes. First, the eyes gather and focus light waves into a precise area at the back of your eyes. Second, this area absorbs and transforms light waves into impulses, a process known as transduction. We'll follow the path of light waves from the giraffe to the back of your eyes in a series of 8 steps.

2 Light waves. The problem with light waves is that after they strike an object, such as a giraffe, they are reflected back in a broad beam. You cannot see the giraffe unless your eyes change this broad beam of light waves into a narrow, focused one. Your eye has two structures, the cornea and the lens, that bring an image into focus, much as a camera does.

1 Image reversed. Notice that, at the back of the eye, the giraffe appears upside down. Even though the giraffe is focused upside down in the eye, somehow the brain turns the giraffe—and all other objects we see—right side up so that we see the world as it really is.

3 Cornea. The broad beam of light reflected from the giraffe passes first through the cornea.

The *cornea* is the rounded, transparent covering over the front of your eye. As the light waves pass through the cornea, its curved surface bends, or focuses, the waves into a narrower beam.

4 Pupil. After passing through the cornea, light waves next go through the pupil.

The *pupil* is a round opening at the front of your eye that allows light waves to pass into the eye's interior.

The reason your pupil grows larger or smaller is because of a muscle called the iris.

5 Iris. The opening of the pupil is surrounded by the iris.

The *iris* is a circular muscle that surrounds the pupil and controls the amount of light entering the eye. In dim light, the iris relaxes, allowing more light to enter—the pupil dilates; in bright light, it constricts, allowing less light to enter—the pupil constricts. The iris muscle contains the pigment that gives your eye its characteristic color.

If you look in a mirror in bright light, you will see that the iris is constricted and that your pupil—the black dot in the center of your eye—is very small.

6 Lens. After passing through the cornea and pupil, light waves reach the lens.

The *lens* is a transparent, oval structure whose curved surface bends and focuses light waves into an even narrower beam. The lens is attached to muscles that adjust the curve of the lens, which, in turn, adjusts the focusing.

For the eye to see distant objects, light waves need less bending (focusing), so muscles automatically stretch the lens so that its surface is less curved. To see near objects, light waves need more focusing, so muscles relax and allow the surface of the lens to become very curved. Making the lens more or less curved ensures that light waves are focused into a very narrow beam that must be projected precisely onto an area at the very back of the eye, called the retina.

7 Retina. Although light waves have been bent and focused, transduction hasn't yet occurred. That is about to change as light waves reach the retina.

The *retina,* located at the very back of the eyeball, is a thin film that contains cells that are extremely sensitive to light. These light-sensitive cells, called photoreceptors, begin the process of transduction by absorbing light waves.

On the following page, we'll describe the two kinds of photoreceptors, how they absorb light waves, and how they carry out the process of transduction. For some people, light waves cannot be focused precisely on the retina because of a problem with the shape of their eyeballs.

8 Eyeball. Some of us are born with perfectly shaped eyeballs, which contributes to having almost perfect vision. Others, however, are born with eyeballs that are a little too long or too short, resulting in two common visual problems: nearsightedness or farsightedness.

8a Normal vision. If light waves reflected from a crowd of people are perfectly focused on the back of your retina, both the near and distant faces will appear clear and sharp. If this is the case, you have good vision.

8b Nearsighted. Some of us inherit an eyeball that is too long, and we are nearsighted.

Nearsightedness may result when the eyeball is too long, and objects are focused at a point slightly in front of the retina. The result is that near objects are clear, but distant objects appear blurry.

8c Farsighted. Some of us inherit an eyeball that is too short, and we are farsighted.

Farsightedness occurs when the eyeball is too short, and objects are focused at a point slightly behind the retina. The result is that distant objects are clear, but near objects are blurry.

Common treatments for being nearsighted or farsighted are to correct the faulty focusing with glasses or contact lenses, or with newer laser treatments (photo-refractive keratectomy and LASIK) that permanently change the shape of the cornea (Olmos, 1997; Stone, 1997).

Next, we'll examine the retina more closely and see exactly how transduction occurs.

A. Eye: Vision

Retina: A Miniature Camera-Computer

How do light waves become impulses?

Some miniaturized electronic cameras can record amazingly detailed video pictures. But they are primitive compared to the retina, whose microscopic cells can transform light waves into impulses that carry detailed information to the brain about all kinds of shapes, shadows, sizes, textures, and colors. Think of the retina as a combination of a video camera and a computer whose batteries never run out as it transforms light waves into impulses—the process of transduction. And here's how transduction occurs.

1 You already know that an object, such as a giraffe, reflects light waves that enter the eye and are bent, focused, and projected precisely on the retina, at the very back of the eyeball.

The *retina* contains two kinds of photoreceptors that begin the process of transduction, changing light waves into electrical signals. One kind of photoreceptor with a rodlike shape is called a rod and is primarily located in the periphery of the retina. The other photoreceptor with a conelike shape is called a cone and is primarily located in the center of the retina in an area called the *fovea (FOH-vee-ah).*

We have enlarged a section of retina (small box on right) to show that it has three layers. We'll explain the function of each layer by starting with 2, located below the figure on the far right, and moving left to 5.

Fovea

Optic nerve sends signals to the brain.

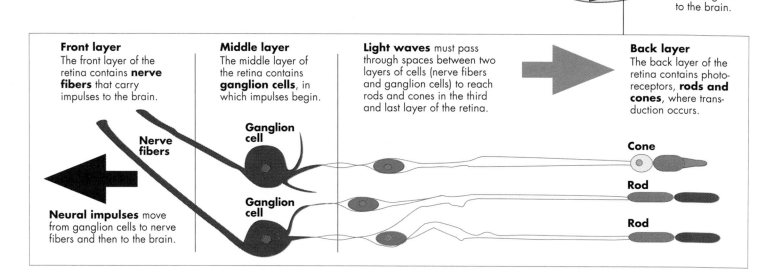

Front layer
The front layer of the retina contains **nerve fibers** that carry impulses to the brain.

Nerve fibers

Neural impulses move from ganglion cells to nerve fibers and then to the brain.

Middle layer
The middle layer of the retina contains **ganglion cells**, in which impulses begin.

Ganglion cell

Ganglion cell

Light waves must pass through spaces between two layers of cells (nerve fibers and ganglion cells) to reach rods and cones in the third and last layer of the retina.

Back layer
The back layer of the retina contains photoreceptors, **rods and cones**, where transduction occurs.

Cone

Rod

Rod

5 *Nerve impulses* generated in ganglion cells exit the back of the eye through the *optic nerve*, which carries impulses toward the brain. The point where the optic nerve exits the eye has no receptors and is called the *blind spot.* We don't notice the blind spot, however, because our eyes are continually moving.

What's surprising about the eye is that it does not "see" but rather is a sophisticated instrument for transduction, for changing light waves into impulses. In order to "see something," impulses must reach the visual areas in the brain, our next stop.

4 The process of *transduction* begins when chemicals in the rods and cones break down after absorbing light waves. This chemical breakdown generates a tiny electrical force that, if large enough, triggers *nerve impulses* in neighboring *ganglion cells;* now, transduction is complete.

3 There are about 3 million cones, most located in the retina's fovea.

Cones are photoreceptors that contain three chemicals called opsins *(OP-sins),* which are activated in bright light and allow us to see color. Unlike rods, cones are wired individually to neighboring cells; this one-on-one system of relaying information allows us to see fine details.

Next, we finally get to transduction, which begins in the rods and cones.

2 There are about 60 million rods, most located in the retina's periphery.

Rods are photoreceptors that contain a single chemical, called rhodopsin *(row-DOP-sin),* which is activated by small amounts of light. Because rods are extremely light sensitive, they allow us to see in dim light, but to see only black, white, and shades of gray.

To see color, we need the cones.

Visual Pathway: Eye to Brain

How do light waves turn into rock stars?

There is a lot of truth to the old saying, "Seeing is believing," but most people don't realize that the "seeing" takes place in the brain, not in the eye. So far, we have traced the paths along which light waves enter the eye, are focused on the retina, are changed into impulses, and leave the eye on the optic nerve. Now we will follow the optic nerve as it reaches its final destination in the occipital lobe, at the back of the brain. There, the occipital lobe changes light waves into colorful rock stars.

1 Optic nerve. Nerve impulses flow through the optic nerve as it exits from the back of the eye and creates a blind spot that the constant movements of our eyes cover up.

The optic nerves partially cross over and make a major stop in the *thalamus*, which does some initial processing. The thalamus relays the impulses to the back of the occipital lobe in the right and left hemispheres.

2 Primary visual cortex. At the very back of each occipital lobe lies a primary visual cortex, which transforms nerve impulses into simple visual sensations, such as texture, lines, and colors. At this point, you would report seeing only these basic sensations (left figure), not the complete figure of a rock star.

Researchers estimate that about a quarter of the entire cortex is devoted to processing visual information, more area than to any other sensory input (Van Essen, 1997). In fact, the visual cortex contains many different cells that respond to many different kinds of visual stimulation.

3 Specialized cells. From the Nobel Prize–winning research of David Hubel and Torsten Wiesel (1979), we know that different cells in the *primary visual cortex* respond to specific kinds of visual stimuli. For example, some cortical cells respond to lines of a particular width, others to lines at a particular angle, and still others to lines moving in a particular direction. These specialized cortical cells transform different stimuli into simple visual sensations, such as shadows, lines, textures, or angles.

Because these many different kinds of cells are involved in processing visual information, damage to the visual cortex can result in blindness, though stimulation of neurons can result in visual sensations.

4 Stimulation or blindness. At the beginning of this module, we told you about Katie, who had 36 tiny wires implanted into her primary visual cortex. When electricity was passed through these wires to stimulate neurons, Katie reported seeing flashes of colored light. She did not see meaningful images, such as a singer, because neurons in the primary visual cortex produce only simple visual sensations.

If part of your primary visual cortex were damaged, you would have a blind spot in the visual field, similar to looking through glasses with tiny black spots painted on the lens. Damage to the entire primary visual cortex in both hemispheres would result in almost total blindness; the ability to tell night from day might remain.

Normally, nerve impulses go on to neighboring visual association areas.

5 Visual association areas. The primary visual cortex sends simple visual sensations (actually, impulses) to neighboring association areas, which add meaning or *associations* (Van Essen et al., 1992). In our example, the association area receives sensations of texture, line, movement, orientation, and color and assembles them into a meaningful image of a complete rock star. There are visual association areas in each hemisphere.

If part of your visual association area were damaged, you would experience *visual agnosia,* which is difficulty in assembling simple visual sensations into more complex, meaningful images (Zeki, 1993). For instance, a person with visual agnosia could see pieces of things but would have difficulty combining pieces and recognizing them as whole, meaningful objects.

You see not only objects with your brain but also colors. We'll next explain how your visual system transforms light waves into the rock stars' red and blue outfits.

Thalamus

A. Eye: Vision

Color Vision

Debra was born with opaque films over her lenses (cataracts) that made her almost totally blind. For her first 28 years, she could tell night from day but see little else. When a newly developed operation restored much of her vision, she cried with delight as she looked around her hospital room and saw things she had only imagined. "Colors were a real surprise to me," Debra said. "They were so bright. You can't conceive what colors are until you've seen them. I couldn't imagine what a red apple looked like and now I can hold one and actually see red" (*San Diego Tribune*, April 3, 1984).

Making Colors from Wavelengths

Like Debra, you might assume that a red apple is really red, but you are about to discover otherwise. Objects, such as a red apple, do not have colors. Instead, objects reflect light waves whose different wavelengths are transformed by your visual system into the experience of seeing colors. Let's see how light waves of different lengths are turned into millions of colors.

1. A ray of sunlight is called white light because it contains all the light waves in the visible spectrum.

2. As white light passes through a prism, it is separated into light waves that vary in length. Nature creates prisms in the form of raindrops, which separate the passing sunlight into waves of different lengths, creating a spectrum of colors that we call a rainbow.

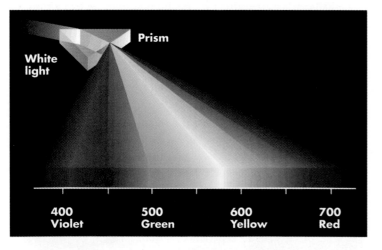

3. Our visual system transforms light waves of various lengths into millions of different colors. For example, in the figure above, notice that the numbers, which vary from about 400 to 700 (nanometers, or nm), indicate the length of light waves. We see shorter wavelengths as shades of violet, blue, and green, and longer wavelengths as shades of yellow, orange, and red (Abramov & Gordon, 1994).

The reason you see an apple as red is because the apple reflects longer light waves, which your brain interprets as red.

Actually, how our visual system transforms light waves into color is explained by two different theories—the trichromatic and opponent-process theories—which we'll examine next.

Trichromatic Theory

The explanation of how you see this native's colorful face began over 200 hundred years ago. It was the early work of an American chemist, John Young, that laid the basis for the trichromatic *(TRI-crow-MAH-tic)* theory of color.

The *trichromatic theory* says that there are three different kinds of cones in the retina, and each cone contains one of three different light-sensitive chemicals, called opsins. Each of the three opsins is most responsive to wavelengths that correspond to each of the three primary colors, blue, green, and red. All other colors can be mixed from these three primary colors.

According to this recent version of the trichromatic theory, you see the red around the man's eyes because this area reflects light waves of a longer wavelength. These particular long-length light waves are absorbed by the opsin in a cone that is most sensitive to longer wavelengths and corresponds to seeing the color "red" (Nathans et al., 1986a).

Until recently, color vision was believed to involve only three genes, one each for red, green, and blue opsin. Now, however, researchers discovered that men with normal color vision had anywhere from two to nine genes and some men had as many as four genes, and thus four cones, for longer wavelengths involved in seeing red (Neitz & Neitz, 1995).

This means that seeing a particular color, such as red, depends on how many color genes you have. Thus, one person may see "red" as deep scarlet and another as pale red. The presence of varying numbers of cones means that people have the potential to see colors very differently and explains why people may adjust the color on their televisions sets very differently (Lipkin, 1995). This new finding will significantly change the 200-year-old trichromatic theory.

The trichromatic theory explains how cones in the retina transform light waves into colors. To understand how color coding occurs in the brain, we need to examine the second theory of color vision, the opponent-process theory.

Opponent-Process Theory

If you stare at a red square for about 20 seconds and then immediately look at a white piece of paper, you'll see a green square, which is called an afterimage.

An *afterimage* is a visual sensation that continues after the original stimulus is removed.

And if you stare at a blue square, you'll see a yellow afterimage. On the basis of his work with afterimages, physiologist Ewald Hering suggested that the visual system codes color by using two complementary pairs—red-green and blue-yellow. Hering's idea became known as the opponent-process theory.

The *opponent-process theory* says that ganglion cells in the retina and cells in the thalamus of the brain respond to two pairs of colors—red-green and blue-yellow. When these cells are excited, they respond to one color of the pair; when inhibited, they respond to the complementary pair.

For example, some ganglion and thalamic cells use a *red-green* paired combination: they signal red when excited and green when inhibited;

Other ganglion and thalamic cells use a *yellow-blue* paired combination: they signal blue when excited and yellow when inhibited;

Thus, different parts of the visual system use different methods to code different colors.

Theories Combined

Because we see colors so automatically and naturally, we don't realize it involves both the opponent-process and trichromatic theories. Here's what happens when we combine the two theories to explain color vision.

First, the trichromatic theory says that there are usually three different kinds of cones (there may be as many as nine) in the retina. Each cone absorbs light waves of different lengths, which correspond to the three primary colors of blue, green, and red. Second, when electrical signals (color information) reach the ganglion cells in the retina and neurons in the thalamus, they use the opponent-process theory, which involves a pair of colors: Activation results in one color of a pair, and inhibition results in the other color. Third, nerve

impulses carry this color information to the visual cortex, where other neurons respond and give us the experience of seeing thousands of colors, which can be made by combining the three primary colors of red, green, and blue.

Although most of us have good color vision, some individuals have varying degrees of color blindness.

Color Blindness

The vast majority of us have normal color vision. We see man on the left with a pinkish face, pale yellow scarf, purple hat, blue coat with orange trim, brown pipe giving off yellow smoke, all against a two-toned orange background. However, about 1 out of 20 men in the United States see this same man in different shades of greens (photo below right) because they have inherited the most common form of color blindness.

Color blindness is the inability to distinguish two or more shades in the color spectrum. There are several kinds of color blindness.

Monochromats (MOHN-oh-crow-mats) have total color blindness; their worlds look like black-and-white movies. This kind of color blindness is rare and results from individuals having only rods or only one kind of functioning cone (instead of three).

Dichromats (DIE-crow-mats) usually have trouble distinguishing red from green because they have just two kinds of cones. This is an inherited genetic defect, found mostly in males, that results in seeing mostly shades of green (photo right) but differs in severity (Neitz et al., 1996).

People don't always realize they have color blindness. For example, a little boy came home complaining about being chased by a green dog. The dog really looked green to the little boy; he did not know he had a form of color blindness.

People in some occupations, such as electrical technicians, are screened for color blindness because they must identify differently colored wires.

Below, you'll see two circles filled with colored dots that are part of a test for color blindness. An individual taking this test is asked to look at each circle and identify what, if any, number is formed by the colored dots.

Individuals with normal vision see the number 96, while people with red-green color deficit find this number difficult or impossible to see.

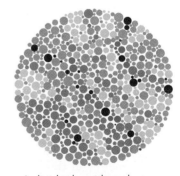

Individuals with red-green color deficits see the number 2, while those with normal vision see nothing.

From our discussion of the eye's structure and function, you can see that the eye is an engineering marvel that makes even the most sophisticated video camera seem like an expensive toy.

Next we'll examine an equally astonishing sense organ, the ear.

Stimulus: Sound Waves

How does she make a yell?

When a cheerleader gives a big yell, she is actually producing the yell by letting out air so that it is alternately compressed and expanded into traveling waves, called sound waves.

Sound waves, which are the stimuli for hearing (audition), resemble ripples of different sizes. Similar to ripples on a pond, sound waves travel through space with varying heights and speeds. Height, which is the distance from the bottom to the top of a sound wave, is called amplitude. Speed, which is the number of sound waves that occur within one second, is called frequency.

The best way to understand the concept of amplitude is to compare the sound waves of a cheerleader's yell with a child's whisper.

Amplitude and Loudness

Yell. As a cheerleader yells, she lets out an enormous amount of air that is compressed and expanded into very large traveling waves (shown below). Large sound waves are described as having high amplitude, which the brain interprets as loud sounds.

Whisper. As a child whispers a secret to his friend, he lets out a small amount of air that is compressed and expanded into very small traveling waves. Small sound waves are described as having low amplitude, which the brain interprets as soft sounds.

Relationship: amplitude and loudness. You have no difficulty distinguishing between a cheerleader's yell and a child's whisper because your auditory system automatically uses the amplitude of the sound waves to calculate loudness (Zeng & Shannon, 1994).

Loudness is your subjective experience of a sound's intensity. The brain calculates loudness from specific physical energy, in this case the amplitude of sound waves.

A whisper, which results in low-amplitude sound waves, is just above our threshold of hearing. The loudest yell on record, which resulted in high-amplitude sound waves, was about as loud as sound heard near speakers at a rock concert.

If the brain uses amplitude to calculate loudness, what does it use to calculate a sound's low or high pitch?

Frequency and Pitch

Screech or boom. As you listen to someone playing the scales on a piano, you can easily follow the progression from low notes to high notes because your brain distinguishes between different kinds of notes, or pitches.

Frequency of highest note is 4,000 cycles per second.

Frequency of lowest note is 27 cycles per second.

High note. Striking the top key on a piano produces sound waves that travel rapidly and are described as having fast frequency (above left in figure). The brain interprets fast frequency as a high note or high pitch.

Low note. Striking the bottom key on a piano produces sound waves that travel slowly or are described as having slow frequency (above right in figure). The brain interprets slow frequency as a low note or low pitch.

Relationship: frequency and pitch. When you hear a sound, your auditory system automatically uses frequency to calculate pitch.

Pitch is our subjective experience of a sound being high or low, which the brain calculates from specific physical stimuli, in this case the speed or frequency of sound waves. The frequency of sound waves is measured in cycles, which refers to how many sound waves occur within one second.

For example, the shortest string on a piano produces sound waves with a fast frequency (4,000 cycles per second), which results in high sounds (high pitch); the longest string on a piano produces sound waves of slower frequency (27 cycles per second), which results in low sounds (low pitch).

Hearing range. Humans hear sounds only within a certain range of frequencies. Infants have the widest range of hearing, from frequencies of 20 to 20,000 cycles per second. For college students, it is perhaps 30 to 18,000 cycles per second. Thereafter, the hearing range decreases with age. By age 70, many people have trouble hearing sounds above 6,000 cycles.

Next, we'll see how loud a jet plane is compared to a whisper.

MEASURING SOUND WAVES

How loud is the library?

If the sign on the right were posted in the library, you might not know that it refers to loudness, which is measured in decibels (dB).

A *decibel* is a unit to measure loudness, just as an inch is a measure of length. Our threshold for hearing ranges from 0 decibels, which is absolutely no sound, to 140 decibels, which can produce pain and permanent hearing loss.

The following table contains common sounds with their decibel levels. Notice especially those sound levels that can cause permanent hearing loss.

Please Do Not Talk Above 30 Decibels

Decibel (dB) level	Sounds and their decibel levels	Exposure time and permanent hearing loss
140	Jet engine, gun muzzle blast	Any exposure to sounds this loud is painful and dangerous. That's why aircraft ground personnel should wear ear protectors.
120	Rock concert near speakers, thunderclap, record-setting human yell (115 dB)	Fifteen minutes or less of exposure can produce hearing loss. Rock musicians and fans who do not use ear plugs risk hearing loss.
100	Chain saw, jackhammer, baby screaming, inside of racing car, firecracker	Exposure for 2 hours or more can cause hearing loss. Workers using loud power tools who do not use ear protectors risk hearing loss.
80	Heavy city traffic, alarm clock at 2 feet, subway, personal tape recorders	Constant exposure for 8 hours can produce hearing loss. Music lovers should know that stereo headphones can produce sounds from 80 to 115 dB.
60	Conversation, air conditioner at 20 feet, typewriter	Aging decreases hearing sensitivity, and that's why older adults may ask, "What did you say?" indicating that they may not easily hear normal conversations.
30	Whisper, quiet library, car idling in neutral (45 dB)	Today's cars are engineered for quietness. At idle, many cars are almost as quiet as a library; and at 65 mph (70 dB), they are not much louder than a conversation.
0	Threshold of hearing	We might say, "This is really quiet" when standing in the middle of a nature preserve. That's because most of us are accustomed to relatively noisy city environments.

CONCERN ABOUT DECIBELS

It is now well known that continuous exposure to sounds with higher decibel levels can produce permanent hearing loss (Nousaine, 1996). For example, rock musicians, rock fans, hunters, drivers of heavy machinery, airplane workers, and stereo headphone listeners who take no precautions against high dB levels may suffer significant and permanent hearing losses later.

Later on we'll discuss different causes of deafness, but now we'll take you inside the ear and explain how it turns sound waves into wonderful sounds.

B. Ear: Audition

Outer, Middle, and Inner Ear

Is that the Rolling Stones or a barking dog?

Most of us think that we hear with our ears and that's how we tell the difference between, for example, the music of the Rolling Stones and the barking of a dog. But nothing is further from the truth. What really happens is that both music and a dog's barks produces only sound waves, which are just the stimulus for hearing (audition). Your ears receive sound waves, but it is your brain that actually does the hearing, distinguishing the difference between the Stones' song, "(I Can't Get No) Satisfaction" and a dog's barks. It's a complicated journey; the first step begins in the outer ear.

1 Outer Ear

The only reason your ear has that peculiar shape and sticks out from the side of your head is to gather in sound waves. Thus, sound waves produced by the Rolling Stones are gathered by your outer ear.

The *outer ear* consists of three structures: external ear, auditory canal, and tympanic membrane.

The *external ear* is an oval-shaped structure that protrudes from the side of the head. The function of the external ear is to pick up sound waves and send them down a long, narrow tunnel called the auditory canal.

2 Middle Ear

The the middle ear functions like a radio's amplifier; it picks up and increases, or amplifies, vibrations.

The *middle ear* is a bony cavity that is sealed at each end by membranes. The two membranes are connected by three small bones.

The three tiny bones are collectively called *ossicles (AW-sick-culls)* and, because of their shapes, are referred to as the hammer, anvil, and stirrup. The first ossicle—hammer—is attached to the back of the tympanic membrane. When the tympanic membrane vibrates, so does the hammer. In turn, the hammer sends the vibrations to the attached anvil, which further sends the vibrations to the attached stirrup. The stirrup makes the connection with the end membrane, the oval window. The three ossicles act like levers that greatly amplify the vibrations, which, in turn, cause the attached oval window to vibrate.

Thus, the function of the middle ear is to pick up vibrations produced by the tympanic membrane, amplify these vibrations, and pass them on to the oval window, which marks the end of the middle ear and beginning of the inner ear.

1a The *auditory canal* is a long tube that funnels sound waves down its length so that the waves strike a thin taut membrane—the eardrum, or tympanic membrane.

In some cases, the auditory canal may become clogged with ear wax, which interferes with sound waves on their way to the eardrum. Ear wax should be removed by a professional so as not to damage the fragile eardrum.

Sound waves

1b The *tympanic (tim-PAN-ick) membrane* is a taut, thin structure commonly called the eardrum. Sound waves strike the tympanic membrane and cause it to vibrate. The tympanic membrane passes the vibrations on to the first of three small bones to which it is attached.

The tympanic membrane marks the boundary between the outer ear and middle ear described below left in 2.

3 Inner Ear

The inner ear contains two main structures that are sealed in bony cavities: the cochlea, which is involved in hearing, and the vestibular system, which is involved in balance. We'll discuss the vestibular system on page 105; now, we'll focus on the cochlea.

The *cochlea* (KOCK-lee-ah), located in the inner ear, has a bony coiled exterior that resembles a snail's shell. The cochlea contains the receptors for hearing, and its function is transduction—transforming vibrations into nerve impulses that are sent to the brain for processing into auditory information.

Researchers liken the cochlea to an exquisite miniature box that is made of bone and contains precious jewels, which in this case are miniature cells that are the receptors for hearing.

On the next page, we have enlarged and opened the cochlea so you can see the auditory receptors.

3 Inner Ear (continued)

3a If you were to take two drinking straws, hold them side by side and then wind them around your finger, you would have a huge imitation of a cochlea. The cochlea consists of two long narrow tubes (straws) separated by membranes (basilar and tectorial) but joined together and rolled up, or coiled. The beginning of the coiled compartments is sealed by a membrane, the oval window. So when the ossicles vibrate the oval window, the oval window vibrates the fluid in the cochlea's tubes, where the auditory receptors are located.

3b The auditory receptors, called *hair cells,* are miniature hair-shaped cells that stick up from the cochlea's bottom membrane, called the *basilar (BAZ-ih-lahr) membrane.* Vibration of fluid in the cochlear tubes causes movement of the basilar membrane, which literally bends the hair cells. The mechanical bending of the hair cells generates miniature electrical forces that, if large enough, trigger nerve impulses (transduction). Nerve impulses leave the cochlea as explained above right in 3c.

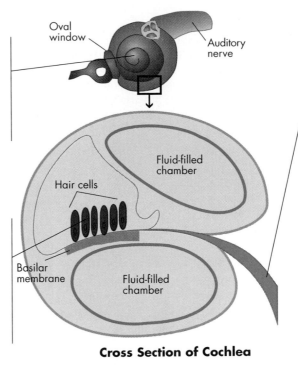

Cross Section of Cochlea

3c The *auditory nerve* is a band of fibers that carry nerve impulses (electrical signals) to the auditory cortex of the brain for processing.

Now the cochlea has completed its role of transduction —transforming vibrations into nerve impulses. However, you won't report hearing anything until the impulses reach your brain.

Brain Areas

Is it noise or music?

Just as your eye does not see, your ear does not hear. Rather, sense organs, such as the ear, perform only transduction—transform physical energy into nerve impulses. You don't hear or recognize sound as noise, music, or words until nerve impulses are processed by various auditory areas in the temporal lobes of your brain.

4 Sensations and Perceptions

After nerve impulses reach the brain, a two-step process occurs in which nerve impulses are first transformed into meaningless bits of sounds and then into meaningful sounds. The first step occurs in the primary auditory area, explained in 4a.

4a The *primary auditory cortex*, which is located at the top edge of the temporal lobe, transforms nerve impulses (electrical signals) into basic auditory sensations, such as meaningless sounds and tones of various pitches and loudness.

Next, the primary auditory cortex sends impulses (sensations) to the auditory association areas.

4b The *auditory association area* receives meaningless auditory sensations in the form of neural impulses from the neighboring primary auditory area. The auditory association areas combine meaningless auditory sensations into perceptions, which are meaningful melodies, songs, words, or sentences.

It takes only a moment from the time that sound waves enter your ear until you say, "That's the Stones' song, '(I Can't Get No) Satisfaction'." But during that amazing moment, sound waves were changed into impulses, impulses into sensations, and finally, sensations into perceptions.

Next, we'll look at three other things the brain calculates from nerve impulses, including telling you where the sound is coming from, whether it is a high or low sound, and whether it is loud or soft.

B. Ear: Audition

Auditory Cues

What do sound waves tell us?

If someone calls your name, you immediately turn your head toward the source of the sound because your brain automatically calculates the source's location. Not only does the brain calculate the source of the voice but also whether the voice calling your name is high or low or loud or soft. Thus, sound waves contain an amazing amount of information. We'll begin with how your brain calculates the direction of where a sound is coming from.

Calculating Direction

If someone yelled "Watch out!" you would automatically turn toward the source of the yell, because your brain instantly calculated the direction or source.

The brain determines the *direction of a sound* by calculating the slight difference in time (see 1 in right figure) that it takes sound waves to reach the two ears, which are about six inches apart (see 2 in right figure) (Middlebrooks et al., 1994).

If you have difficulty telling where a sound is coming from, the sound is probably arriving at both ears simultaneously. To locate the direction, you can turn your head from side to side, causing the sound to reach one ear before the other.

The brain uses other cues to calculate a sound's high or low pitch.

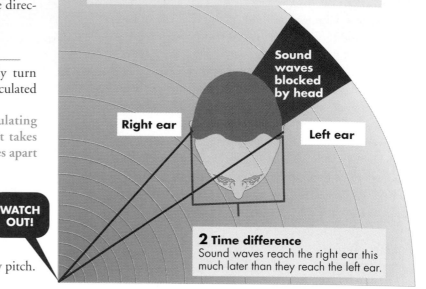

1 Source
A sound coming from the left reaches your left ear a split second before it reaches your right ear. The brain automatically interprets this difference in timing as a signal that the source of the sound is to the left. You will automatically turn your head left, to the source of the sound.

Sound waves blocked by head

Right ear

Left ear

WATCH OUT!

2 Time difference
Sound waves reach the right ear this much later than they reach the left ear.

Calculating Pitch

Imagine the low, menacing growl of a lion and then the high screech of fingernails on the chalkboard. Your subjective experience of a sound being high or low is referred to as pitch. Exactly how the cochlea codes pitch and the brain interprets the code is rather complicated. We'll focus on two better known theories of pitch, the frequency and place theories.

The *frequency theory*, which applies only to low-pitched sounds, says that the rate at which nerve impulses reach the brain determines how low the pitch of a sound is.

For example, the brain interprets a frequency rate of 50 impulses per second as a lower sound than one with a frequency rate of 200 impulses per second. Hearing the low-pitched roar of a lion involves the frequency theory. Hearing higher-pitched sounds, however, such as the screech of fingernails on a chalkboard, involves another theory, the place theory.

The *place theory* says that the brain determines medium- to higher-pitched sounds on the basis of the place on the basilar membrane where maximum vibration occurs.

For example, lower-pitched sounds cause maximum vibrations near the beginning of the cochlea's basilar membrane, while higher-pitched sounds cause maximum vibrations near the end of the membrane. Our auditory system combines the frequency and place theories to transform sound waves into perceptions of low- to high-pitched sounds (Dallos & Evans, 1995).

The brain does one more thing: It calculates how loud a sound is.

Calculating Loudness

You can easily tell the difference between a yell and a whisper because your auditory system transforms the intensity of sound waves into the subjective experiences of a soft whisper or a loud yell. This transformation occurs inside the cochlea.

Compared to a yell, a whisper produces low amplitude sound waves that set off the following chain of events: fewer vibrations of the tympanic membrane, less movement of fluid in the cochlea, less movement of the basilar membrane, fewer bent hair cells, less electrical force, and finally, fewer nerve impulses sent to the brain, which interprets these signals as a soft sound.

The brain calculates *loudness* primarily from the frequency or rate of how fast or how slowly nerve impulses arrive from the auditory nerve.

For example, the brain interprets a slower rate of impulses as a softer tone (whisper) and a faster rate as a louder tone (yell) (Bear et al., 1996).

Earlier, we said that there are two structures in the inner ear, the cochlea and the vestibular system. If you have ever stood on your head, you have firsthand experience with the vestibular system, our next topic.

C. Vestibular System: Balance

Position and Balance

What else is in the inner ear?

I guarantee that this is one question you never ask: "Where is my head?" Even though your head is in a hundred different positions throughout the day, you rarely bang it into a door, forget to duck it as you enter a car, or forget whether you're standing on your feet or your hands. That's because the position of your head is silently and automatically kept track of by another sense, called your vestibular system.

The *vestibular system*, which is located above the cochlea in the inner ear, includes three *semicircular canals*, resembling bony arches, which are set at different angles (right figure). Each of the semicircular canals is filled with fluid that moves in response to movements of your head. In the canals are sensors (hair cells) that respond to the movement of the fluid. The functions of the vestibular system include sensing the position of the head, keeping the head upright, and maintaining balance.

Vestibular system

Cochlea

The vestibular system indicates which end is up (head or feet) by providing information on the position of your head. If a person has an inner ear infection, it can affect the vestibular system and result in dizziness, nausea, and the inability to balance. And as you'll see next, the vestibular system is also involved in motion sickness.

Motion Sickness

Why am I getting sick?

One of my terrible childhood memories is sitting in the back seat of a moving car and after 30 minutes of curving roads feeling a cold sweat followed by nausea, dizziness, and an extreme desire to lie down anywhere—stationary. Along with about 25% of the United States population, I experienced moderate to severe signs of motion sickness. About 55% of people experience only mild symptoms, while the remaining 20% are lucky and rarely experience any. Researchers think that motion sickness results when information provided by the vestibular system doesn't match information coming from other senses (Gannon, 1995).

Motion sickness, which consists of feelings of discomfort, nausea, and dizziness in a moving vehicle, is thought to develop when there is a sensory mismatch between the information from the vestibular system—that your head is physically bouncing around—and the information reported by your eyes—that objects in the distance look fairly steady.

Infants below age 2 rarely have motion sickness, but susceptibility increases from 2 to about 12. After 12, susceptibility decreases in both men and women. Researchers suspect that genetic and not personality factors determine susceptibility to motion sickness (Stern & Koch, 1996).

A number of drugs reduce the symptoms of motion sickness (Attias et al., 1987). As an alternative to drugs, fliers reported a significant reduction in motion sickness after completing a behavioral training program that taught them to perform relaxation responses, think positive thoughts, or use calming images at the first sign of symptoms. Of 53 fliers who had been grounded because of chronic, severe motion sickness, 49 were able to overcome their problem and start flying again after completing the behavioral program (Jones et al., 1985).

Malfunctioning of the vestibular system can cause terrible symptoms.

Meniere's Disease and Vertigo

Why did he cut off his ear?

Researchers believe that the famous Dutch artist Vincent van Gogh cut off his ear and was driven into an asylum partly because he suffered from Meniere's disease (Milstein, 1993).

Meniere's (main-YERS) *disease* results from a malfunction of the semicircular canals of the vestibular system. The symptoms include sudden attacks of dizziness, nausea, vomiting, spinning, and head-splitting buzzing sounds.

Sufferers report ringing in their ears like Niagara Falls, walking into their bathrooms to find the toilet spinning out of range, or vomiting more than 30 times a day. About seven million Americans suffer from Meniere's disease, which is thought to be caused by a viral infection of the inner ear (Milstein, 1993).

The vestibular system is also involved in vertigo.

Vertigo, whose symptoms are dizziness and nausea, results from malfunction of the semicircular canals of the vestibular system.

For example, a friend of mine slipped in a bathtub, fell and struck the side of his head. He had severe vertigo for about a week, most likely because he temporarily damaged his vestibular system.

Meniere's disease and vertigo, which have no known cures, indicate what happens if the vestibular system malfunctions.

If you are reading this book in a car or on a plane and feel a little queasy, relax before reading the next section, which is about tasting and smelling food.

D. Chemical Senses

Taste

How does your tongue taste?

You rarely think about the thousands of chemicals that you put into your mouth every day but you do know when something tastes very good or very bad. You also know that if you burn your tongue on hot foods or liquids, your sense of taste can be markedly decreased.

Taste is called a chemical sense because the stimuli are various chemicals. On the surface of the tongue are receptors, called taste buds, for four basic tastes: sweet, salty, sour, and bitter. The function of taste buds is to perform transduction—transform chemical reactions into nerve impulses.

As you imagine biting into a slice of lemon, we'll explain how your tongue tastes.

1 Tongue: Four Basic Taste Areas

Imagine sucking on a piece of lemon and tasting its sourness, which is one of the four basic tastes: *sweet, salty, sour, and bitter.* The right figure shows that particular areas on the tongue respond most to each of the four basic tastes. Overlapping areas result in combinations, such as sweet-salty.

The reason many of us have a sweet tooth comes from the fact that, as newborns, we inherited an innate preference for sweet and salt (Harris et al., 1990; J. Williams, 1994). Like most animals, humans avoid bitter-tasting substances, presumably because many poisonous substances taste bitter. If you are one of those who likes sour lemonade, you know that people can learn to like bitter substances. Tasting begins with what happens in the trenches on the surface of your tongue.

2 Surface of the Tongue

As you chew the lemon, its chemicals, which are the *stimuli* for taste, break down into molecules. In turn, these molecules mix with saliva and run down into narrow trenches on the surface of the tongue. Once inside the trenches, the molecules stimulate the taste buds.

3 Taste Buds

Buried in the trenches on the surface of the tongue are many hundreds of bulblike taste buds.

Taste buds, which are shaped like miniature onions, are the receptors for taste. Chemicals dissolved in the saliva activate the taste buds, which produce nerve impulses that eventually reach areas in the brain's parietal lobe. The brain transforms these nerve impulses into sensations of taste.

Taste buds live in a relatively toxic environment and are continually exposed to heat, cold, spices, bacteria, and saliva. As a result, taste buds wear out and are replaced about every ten days. The human tongue can have as many as 10,000 taste buds and as few as 500; the number remains constant throughout life (Fackelmann, 1997).

1 Tongue: Four basic taste areas

Bitter

Sour · Sour

Salty · Salty

Sweet

2 Surface of tongue

Trench contains buried taste buds

3 Taste bud

4 All Tongues Are Not the Same.

In rare cases, individuals are born without any taste buds and cannot taste anything, because they have a genetically determined disorder (Bartoshuk & Beauchamp, 1994). In contrast, about 25% of the population are supertasters, which means they may have two to three times more taste buds than normal, which results in increased sensitivity to sweet, bitter, sour, and salty. For example, supertasters taste sugar to be twice as sweet as most people and get more intense oral burning sensations from the chemical (capsaicin) in chili peppers. Supertasters find grapefruit juice too bitter and don't like broccoli because it also contains a bitter chemical (Drewnowski, 1997).

Researchers found that being a supertaster is an inherited trait and speculate that it may have had some evolutionary advantage. For example, supertasters would be better able to judge whether fruits or berries were poisonous (Bartoshuk, 1997). Today, supertasters work for food manufacturers and rate the taste of new food products.

But for all of us, our ability to taste is greatly affected by our ability to smell.

5 Flavor: Taste and Smell

If taste receptors are sensitive to only four basic tastes, how can you tell the difference between two sweet tastes, such as a brownie and vanilla ice cream, or between two sour tastes, such as lemon juice and vinegar? The truth is that a considerable percentage of the sensations we attribute to taste are actually contributed by our sense of smell.

We experience *flavor* when we combine sensations of taste and smell.

You have no doubt experienced the limitations of your taste buds' abilities when you had a cold, which blocks the nasal passages and cuts out the sense of smell. Without smell, foods we usually love now taste very bland.

Since our taste of foods is greatly enhanced by the sense of smell, we'll examine olfaction next.

Smell, or Olfaction

Every year people in the United States spend about 5 billion dollars on perfumes to make themselves smell better. You may have been impressed that your tongue has up to 10,000 taste buds, but that number pales in comparison to the nose's 6 million receptor cells (Silver, 1997). That's why the sense of smell, more properly called olfaction, is 10,000 times more sensitive than taste (Reyneri, 1984).

Olfaction is called a chemical sense because its stimuli are various chemicals that are carried by the air. The upper part of the nose has a small area that contains receptor cells for olfaction. The function of the olfactory receptors is transduction, to transform chemical reactions into nerve impulses.

We'll explain the steps for olfaction by having you imagine crossing paths with an angry skunk.

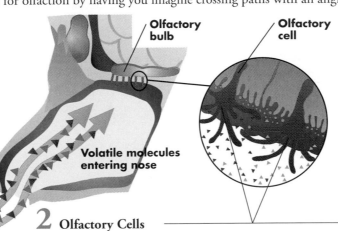

Olfactory bulb

Olfactory cell

Volatile molecules entering nose

1 Stimulus

An angry skunk protects itself by spraying thousands of molecules, which are carried by the air and drawn into your nose as you breathe. The reason you can smell substances such as skunk spray is because these substances are volatile. A volatile substance is one that can release molecules into the air at room temperature. For example, volatile substances include skunk spray, perfumes, and warm brownies, but not glass or steel, for example. We can smell only volatile substances, but first they must reach the olfactory cells in the nose.

2 Olfactory Cells

Olfactory cells, which are the receptors for smell, are located in two 1-inch-square patches of tissue in the uppermost part of the nasal passages. Olfactory cells are covered with mucus, a thick, gluey film into which volatile molecules dissolve. As molecules dissolve in the mucus, they stimulate the underlying olfactory cells, which trigger nerve impulses that travel to the brain.

As you breathe, a small percentage of the total air entering your nose reaches the uppermost surface of your nasal passages, where the olfactory receptors are located. People can lose their sense of smell in several ways. For example, a virus or inflammation can destroy olfactory receptors in their nose, or a blow to the head can damage the neural network that carries impulses to the brain (Bartoshuk & Beauchamp, 1994). Even though the olfactory cells change volatile molecules into impulses, you do not really smell anything until neural impulses reach the brain.

3 Sensations and Memories

Nerve impulses from the olfactory cells travel first to the olfactory bulb, which is a tiny grape-shaped area (green structure in diagram of nose) that lies directly above the olfactory cells at the bottom of the brain. From here, impulses are relayed to the primary olfactory cortex, (also called piriform cortex) located underneath the brain. This cortex transforms nerve impulses into the olfactory sensations of a skunk's spray or a sweet perfume (Firestein et al., 1996).

Although we can identify as many as 10,000 different odors, we soon stop smelling our deodorants or perfumes because of adaptation in the olfactory cells (Kurahashi & Menini, 1997).

Smell, in terms of evolution, is a very primitive sense; it has three important functions.

4 Functions of Olfaction

One function of smell is to intensify the taste of food. For example, you could not tell a licorice from an orange jelly bean with your nose held closed. A second is to warn us of potentially dangerous foods; the repulsive odor of spoiled or rotten food does this very effectively. A third and more recently discovered function is that smells elicit strong memories, often associated with emotional feelings; for example, the smell of pumpkin pie may remind you of a festive family gathering (Miltner et al., 1994; Silver, 1997). For many animals, such as cats and dogs, smell also functions to locate food, mates, and territory.

Next, we examine the sense of touch and explain what happens when you pet a cat.

Sophia Grojsman is one of only a dozen master perfumers in the United States who are responsible for creating some of the best-known perfumes (Calvin Klein, Estée Lauder). Known in the trade as a "nose," she

earns over $100,000 a year because there is no scientific/computer substitute for her nose and brain's ability to identify, remember, and mix fragrances that elicit pleasant memories and moods. One reason a computerized nose has not yet replaced a human nose is that scientists are only now beginning to understand which molecular qualities (weight, shape) determine which of the thousands of different odors humans can identify (Shipley & Ennis, 1996).

E. Touch

Definition

Why can you feel soft fur?

If you were to draw your hand across the surface of a cat, you would have the sensations of touching something soft and furry. These sensations are part of the sense of touch.

The sense of *touch* includes pressure, temperature, and pain. Beneath the outer layer of skin are a half-dozen miniature sensors that are receptors for the sense of touch. The function of the touch sensors is to change mechanical pressure or changes in temperature into nerve impulses that are sent to the brain for processing.

We'll examine several miniature mechanical sensors and explain how they function.

Receptors

If you were to closely examine the surface of your skin, you would see a relatively smooth membrane covered in some places with hair. Some "touch" sensors are wound around hair follicles (the backs of your arms) and are slightly different from sensors in skin without hair (your palms). However, before we discuss three major touch receptors, we need to examine the three different layers of the skin.

1 Skin. The skin, which is the body's largest organ, has three layers. The *outermost layer* of skin is a thin film of dead cells containing no receptors. Immediately below the dead layer are the first receptors, which look like groups of threadlike extensions. In the *middle and fatty layers* of skin are a variety of receptors with different shapes and functions. Some of the major sensors in the middle layer of skin are hair receptors.

2 Hair receptors. In the middle layer are free nerve endings that are wrapped around the base of each hair follicle; these are called *hair receptors.* Hair receptors respond or fire with a burst of activity when hairs are first bent. However, if hairs remain bent for a period of time, the receptors cease firing, an example of *sensory adaptation.* When you first put on a watch, it bends hairs, causing hair receptors to fire; your brain interprets this firing as pressure on your wrist. If you keep the watch on and it remains in place, keeping the hairs bent, the hair receptors adapt or cease firing, and you no longer feel pressure from your watch, even though it is still there. Your skin contains some receptors that adapt rapidly (hair receptors) and others that adapt slowly. Adaptation prevents your sense of touch from being overloaded.

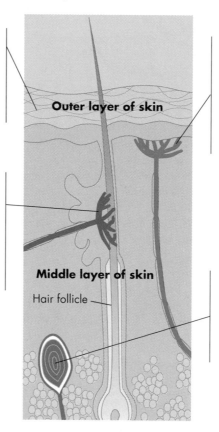

Outer layer of skin

Middle layer of skin

Hair follicle

3 Free nerve endings. Near the bottom of the outer layer of skin is a group of threadlike extensions; these are called *free nerve endings,* because they have nothing protecting or surrounding them. One question about free nerve endings is how the same receptor can transmit information about both temperature and pain. Researchers think that different patterns of neural activity may signal different sensations—for example, slow bursts of firing for temperature and fast bursts for pain (Ferster & Spruston, 1995).

4 Pacinian corpuscle. In the fatty layer of skin is the largest touch sensor, called the *Pacinian corpuscle* (*pa-SIN-ee-in core-PUS-sole*). This receptor, which has distinctive layers like a slice of onion, is highly sensitive to touch, is the only receptor that responds to vibration, and adapts very quickly.

All these receptors send their electrical signals to the brain.

Brain Areas

Did I touch my nose or my ear?

When pressure (touch), temperature, or pain stimulate the skin's receptors, they perform transduction and change these forms of energy into nerve impulses. The impulses go up the spinal cord and eventually reach the brain's somatosensory cortex.

The *somatosensory cortex,* which is located in the parietal lobe, transforms nerve impulses into sensations of touch, temperature, and pain. You know which part is being stimulated because, as we explained earlier (p. 77), different parts of the body are represented on different areas of the somatosensory cortex.

Somato-sensory cortex **Parietal lobe**

Compared with touch and temperature, the sense of pain is different because it has no specific stimulus and can be suppressed by psychological factors. We'll discuss these interesting aspects of pain, along with acupuncture, later in this module. We'll also discuss later how psychological factors can make foods that we think are truly disgusting become delicacies in other parts of the world. But first, try out your memory on the Concept Review.

CONCEPT REVIEW

EYE: Numbers on the eye match the numbers of the questions.

1. A transparent, curved structure at the front of the eye, called the _____, focuses or bends light waves into a more narrow beam.

2. A round opening at the front of the eye that allows varying amounts of light to enter the eye is called the _____.

3. A circular, pigmented muscle that dilates or constricts, thus increasing or decreasing the size of the pupil, is called the _____.

4. The function of the transparent, oval structure called the _____ is to bend light waves into a narrower beam of light and focus the beam precisely on a layer of cells in the very back of the eye.

5. Lining the back of the eye is a filmlike layer called the (a)_____, which contains several layers of cells. The back layer of cells has two kinds of photoreceptors, called (b)_____ and (c)_____.

6. This band of nerve fibers, called the (a)_____, exits from the back of the eye and carries impulses to the brain. The point at which this nerve exits is called the (b)_____ because it contains no rods or cones.

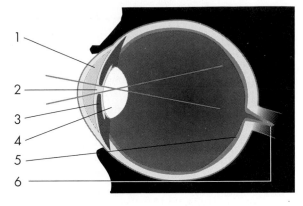

EAR: Numbers on the ear match the numbers of the questions.

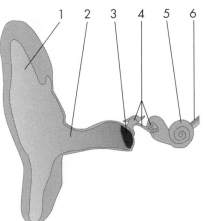

1. The funnel-like structure called the _____ gathers in sound waves from the environment.

2. The short tunnel called the _____ carries sound waves that strike a membrane.

3. The thin, taut membrane at the end of the auditory canal, called the _____, transforms sound waves into vibrations.

4. The three small bones (hammer, anvil, and stirrup) called the (a)_____ are part of the middle ear. They transform vibrations of the tympanic membrane into mechanical movements, which in turn vibrate a second membrane, called the (b)_____.

5. The coiled, fluid-filled structure called the (a)_____ is one part of the inner ear. It contains auditory receptors called (b)_____ that are attached to the basilar membrane.

6. The band of fibers called the _____ carries nerve impulses from the cochlea to the brain.

7. The inner ear contains a group of structures shaped like three tiny arches set at different angles. These structures signal body movement and position and are called the _____ system.

9. Substances give off volatile molecules that are drawn into the nose, dissolve in mucus, and activate the (a)_____. The function of these cells is to produce (b)_____ that are sent to the olfactory bulb and brain for processing.

8. Various areas of the tongue respond most to one of the four basic tastes, which are (a)_____, _____, _____ and _____. The receptors for taste are called (b)_____.

Hair follicle

10. There are several kinds of touch receptors: the (a)_____ is fast adapting; the (b)_____ is also fast adapting; the (c)_____ responds to both touch and vibration.

F. Cultural Diversity: Disgust versus Delight

Sensations and Psychological Factors

Would you eat a worm?

We have discussed how senses transform physical energy into impulses, which eventually become sensations and then perceptions. However, your perceptions are usually influenced by psychological factors, such as learning, emotion, and motivation, so that you never perceive the world exactly like someone else. For example, when offered a fish eye to eat, many of us would react with great disgust. The facial expression to express disgust (right photo) is similar across cultures.

Disgust is a universal facial expression involving closing of the eyes, narrowing of the nostrils, downward curling of the lips, and sometimes sticking out the tongue. Researchers generally agree that the purpose of the disgust expression is to indicate rejection of foods (Haidt et al., 1994).

Children begin to show this disgust expression between the ages of two and four, a time when they are learning which foods in their culture are judged edible and which are considered repugnant (Farb & Armelagos, 1980). Besides an innate preference for sweet and salty tastes and an avoidance of bitter substances, most other tastes are learned.

Cultural influence. Your particular culture has a strong influence on which foods you perceive as disgusting or delicious. Here are three examples of delicious foods from other cultures. Notice your reactions to these foods.

Plump Grubs

For most U.S. citizens, the thought of eating a round, soft, white worm would be totally unthinkable. For the Asmat of New Guinea, however, a favorite delicacy is a plump, white, 2-inch larva—the beetle grub. The natives harvest dozens of the grubs, put them on bamboo slivers, and roast them. A photographer from the United States who did a story on the Asmat tried to eat a roasted grub, but his American tastes would not let him swallow it (Kirk, 1972).

Fish Eyes and Whale Fat

Although some Americans have developed a taste for raw fish (sushi), a common dish in Japan, most would certainly gag at the thought of eating raw fish eyes. Yet for some Inuit (Eskimo) children, raw fish eyes are like candy. Here you see a young girl using the Inuits' all-purpose knife to gouge out the eye of an already-filleted Arctic fish.

Eskimos also hunt a type of whale (the narwhal) that provides much of their protein. They consider the layer of fat under the skin (*mukluk*) a delicacy, and they eat it raw or dried.

Blood

Several tribes in East Africa supplement their diet with fresh blood that is sometimes mixed with milk. They obtain the blood by puncturing a cow's jugular vein with a sharp arrow. A cow can be bled many times and suffer no ill effects. The blood-milk drink provides a rich source of protein and iron.

WHAT TASTES GOOD AND WHAT TASTES BAD

How much would someone have to pay you to eat the white, plump grub (actual size) in the photo on the right? Answers from my students vary from "1,000 dollars" to "all the money in the world." The reactions of U.S. college students to eating white, plump grubs or cold, glassy fish eyes or having a warm drink of blood mixed with milk are almost universally of disgust and not delight. These graphic examples

illustrate how much psychological factors, such as cultural values, can influence and bias perceptions so that the same things taste good in one culture but taste awful in another. We'll discuss further the interesting idea of how psychological factors influence perceptions in Module 6.

Just as psychological factors are involved in perceiving taste, they are also involved in experiencing pain.

G. Research Focus: Pain & Placebos
Can the Mind Make Pain Go Away?

Mind or Medicine?

Are sugar pills painkillers?

One of the truly amazing research findings is how sugar pills or placebos can somehow "trick" us into feeling or getting better. About one third of the population believe so strongly in placebos that they report having less pain or feeling much better after taking a pill, not knowing that it was only a sugar pill—a placebo.

A *placebo* is some intervention, such as taking a pill, receiving an injection, or undergoing an operation, that resembles medical therapy but that, in fact, has no medical effects.

REAL MEDICINE? SUGAR PILL?

A *placebo effect* is a change in the patient's illness that is attributable to an imagined treatment rather than to a medical treatment.

For example, you may think that the pain coming from a bruised toe or cut finger depends solely on the amount of physical injury. However, there is solid evidence that your expectations and beliefs themselves can either increase or decrease your perception of the pain's intensity. Somehow placebos "trick" you into *believing* that you are taking real medicine, and therefore you perceive less pain. To separate the power of your expectations from the effects of real medicine, researchers must use a very clever research method called the double-blind design.

Method: Double-Blind Design

Because researchers know that your beliefs and expectations can greatly affect your body, they separate the effects of medical treatment from the patients' expectations by using a double-blind design.

In a *double-blind design,* neither the researchers nor the subjects know who is receiving what treatment. This design makes it possible to separate the effects of medical treatment from the participants' beliefs or expectations about the treatment.

For example, in a double-blind design, headache sufferers would be told that they will be given two different pills to decrease pain. Unknown to them and the researcher, one of the pills is aspirin and one is placebo. Over the past 25 years, in double-blind experiments such as this, researchers have found that about 30% or more of people report decreased pain and get better faster after taking placebos (Brown, 1997; Dodes, 1997). These surprising findings show very convincingly that placebos are powerful "medicine" for changing something you might think unchangeable—your perception of pain.

Results: Placebos Change Perceptions of Pain

Here are four convincing examples of pain reduction that involved placebos and double-blind procedures (Turner et al, 1994).

98% of patients originally reported marked or complete relief of pain from ulcers after medical treatment (gastric freezing). However, in a later double-blind procedure, this treatment was shown to be ineffective.

85% of patients originally reported a reduction in pain from *Herpes simplex* (cold sores and genital sores) after a drug treatment. However, in a later double-blind procedure, this drug was proved to be ineffective.

56% of patients reported a decrease in heart pain (angina pectoris) after being given a medical procedure that, unknown to the patient, involved only a skin incision.

35% (range 15–58%) of patients reported that placebos reduced pain following major surgical procedures in hospitals.

Conclusions

Based on findings like those given above, researchers have reached three conclusions (Brown, 1997; Dodes, 1997; Turner et al., 1994).

First, potentially very powerful placebo effects, such as reducing pain, getting over colds, or speeding recovery from medical procedures, have been greatly underestimated.

Second, both medication (pills, injections) and fake surgeries can produce significant placebo effects, such as reducing pain, in 15% to 98% of patients.

Third, and of great interest to psychologists, placebos indicate a powerful mind-over-body interaction. This mind-over-body interaction also explains why people may really experience health benefits from tak-

ing new or medically unproven dietary supplements, such as taking vitamins to have more energy.

Researchers suggest that placebos may work by creating positive expectations and beliefs that reduce anxiety and stress. In turn, the reduction of anxiety results in perceiving less pain. And the reduction in stress improves functioning of the immune system so that the body can better fight off toxins and make a quicker recovery from some problem (Brown, 1997; Turner et al., 1994). Thus, there is no question that our minds have powerful effects on our bodies.

Next we'll examine pain in more detail and see how mental factors can affect the perception of pain.

H. Pain

Definition

What causes pain?

Many of us can relate to the pain that comes with a bad headache. However, you may not know that pain differs from the other senses in two ways. First, pain results from many different stimuli, while each of the other senses responds primarily to a single stimulus. For example, besides intense pressure or tissue damage, pain can be produced by very loud noises, bright lights, chemicals (in peppers), and intense heat or cold, which may or may not cause tissue damage (Talbot et al., 1991). Second, the intensity of the painful sensation depends not only on the intensity of the physical stimulus but also on a number of psychological factors, including attentional or emotional states (Novy et al., 1995). Here's a working definition of pain.

Pain arises when stimuli of various kinds activate free nerve endings, the receptors for pain. Nerve impulses from pain receptors are relayed to the somatosensory and limbic areas of the brain, where impulses are changed into two kinds of pain sensations. Immediately after injury, there is a sharp, localized pain, which is shortly replaced by a dull, more generalized pain. Pain is essential for survival: it warns us to avoid or escape dangerous situations or stimuli and makes us take time to recover from injury.

In most cases, pain lasts for relatively short periods of time and is called short-acting, or *acute,* pain. In other cases, when pain lasts for six months or more, it is called long-acting, or *chronic,* pain. What is true for both acute and chronic pain, but especially for chronic pain, is that the physical sensations of pain interact with *psychological factors,* such as emotions, to either lessen or increase the experience of pain (Keefe & Lefebvre, 1997; Novy et al., 1995). For example, in treating chronic pain, researchers found that they must also treat various psychological factors, such as patients' feelings of having little control over their lives or little social support (Turk, 1996).

Let's examine how our perception of pain can be influenced by psychological factors.

Gate Control Theory

How does the mind stop pain?

Although a headache is painful, the pain may come and go as you shift your attention or become absorbed in some project. Why shifting attention lessens pain is explained by the gate control theory of pain (Melzack & Wall, 1983).

The *gate control theory of pain* says that nonpainful nerve impulses (shifting attention) compete with pain impulses (headache) to reach the brain. This competition creates a bottleneck, or neural gate, that limits the number of impulses that can be transmitted. Thus, shifting one's attention or rubbing an injured area may increase the passage of nonpainful impulses and thereby decrease the passage of painful impulses; as a result, the sensation of pain is dulled. The neural gate isn't a physical structure but rather refers to the competition between nonpainful and painful impulses as they try to reach the brain.

The gate control theory explains that you may not notice pain from a headache or injury while thoroughly involved in some other activity, because impulses from that activity close the neural gate and block the passage of painful impulses (right figure above). However, when you become less involved, there are fewer nonpainful impulses, the neural gate opens, (left figure above) and you again notice the pain as painful impulses reach the brain (Brownlee & Schrof, 1997).

1. With gate open, we feel pain. | **PAIN** | Gate | open

2. Pain signals coming from spinal cord reach the brain.

3. With gate closed, we feel no pain. | **NO PAIN** | Gate closed

4. Pain signals coming from spinal cord do not reach the brain.

An extreme example of the gate control theory in action is the football player who plays for hours with a broken bone but doesn't feel any pain (Warga, 1987). According to the gate control theory, a football player's intense attentional and emotional involvement in the game causes the brain to send nonpainful impulses that close neural gates in the spinal cord. The closed neural gates block pain impulses from reaching the brain and thus prevent feelings of pain. Later, when the game is over and the player's attentive and emotional states calm down, neural gates open, impulses from the broken bone reach his brain, and he feels pain.

PAIN: PHYSICAL AND PSYCHOLOGICAL

As the gate control theory explains, our perception of pain depends not only on a physical stimulus but also on a variety of psychological factors, such as our focus of attention, emotional state, and social support, which can either decrease or increase our perception of pain (Novy et al., 1995, Turk, 1996).

Besides the effects of psychological factors, our initial perception of pain from a serious injury can also be reduced by our brain's ability to secrete its own pain-reducing chemicals called endorphins.

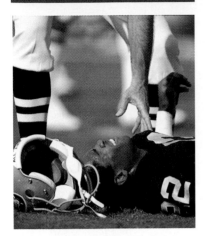

Does the brain make its own painkillers?

Someone who has experienced a serious injury—in football, for example—will usually report that initially the pain was bearable but with time the pain became much worse. One reason pain seems less intense immediately after injury is that the brain produces endorphins.

Endorphins (*en-DOOR-fins*) are chemicals produced by the brain and secreted in response to injury or severe physical or psychological stress. The pain-reducing properties of endorphins are similar to those of morphine, a powerful painkilling drug.

The brain produces endorphins in situations that evoke great fear, anxiety, stress, or bodily injury, as well as after intense aerobic activity (Tripathi et al., 1993). For example, subjects showed increased levels of endorphins after being stressed by receiving painful electric shocks or by holding their hands in ice water (Millan, 1986). Patients showed increased levels of endorphins after their teeth nerves were touched or their bandages were removed from badly burned areas of the body (Szyfelbein et al., 1985). These studies indicate that the brain produces endorphins to reduce pain during periods of intense physical stress. Endorphins and other painkillers (heroin, morphine, codeine) act mostly to stop receptors from signaling severe, persistent pain but do not stop receptors from signaling quick, sharp pain as from a pinprick (Taddese et al., 1995).

Researchers have recently identified the genetic code responsible for the development of the endorphin-morphine receptor in the brain. This receptor, which is activated by morphine, heroin, or endorphin, is the key to both reducing pain and causing addiction (Chen et al., 1993). Researchers hope that, as they better understand how this receptor works, they can develop drugs that reduce pain but are not addicting.

ADRENAL CELL TRANSPLANTS

Not only does the brain make endorphins, but so too do the body's adrenal glands (see page 82), which make an endorphin-like chemical that reduces pain. Recently, researchers removed pain-reducing adrenal gland cells from individuals who were brain-dead and transplanted these cells into the spinal cords of patients suffering from chronic and severe cancer pain. Four of five patients who received transplanted cells reported dramatic decreases in pain (Pappas et al., 1997). Researchers were very encouraged and suggested that transplants of adrenal gland cells that make an endorphin-like chemical represents a promising approach to treating chronic pain.

Endorphins may also be involved in explaining how acupuncture reduces pain.

Can an ancient technique reduce pain?

Initially, scientists trained in the rigorous methods of the West (in particular, the United States) expressed great doubt about an ancient Chinese pain-reducing procedure called acupuncture.

Acupuncture is a procedure in which a trained practitioner inserts thin needles into various points on the body's surface and then manually twirls or electrically stimulates the needles. After 10–20 minutes of needle stimulation, patients often report a reduction in pain.

The mysterious part of this procedure is that the points of insertion—such as those shown in the photograph on the right—were mapped over a thousand years ago and, as researchers now know, are often far removed from the site of painful injury.

Today, however, modern scientists have explained some of the mystery surrounding acupuncture. First, the points of needle insertion, which seem unrelated to the point of injury, are often close to known pathways that conduct pain (Chen et al., 1986). Second, there is some evidence that stimulation of these points causes secretion of endorphins, which we know can reduce pain (Lin, 1996). If patients are first given a drug (naloxone) that blocks secretion of endorphins, acupuncture does not reduce pain.

Studies on the effectiveness of acupuncture in reducing pain of headaches and back pain indicate that 50 to 80% of patients reported short-term improvement. However, the very few long-term studies indicate that, after 6 months, about 50% of the patients reported a return of their painful symptoms (Hsu, 1996). Thus, there is some evidence that acupuncture relieves certain kinds of chronic pain in the short term but not necessarily in the long term. Recently, the National

Institutes of Health concluded that acupuncture is effective for nausea (from chemotherapy or morning sickness) and some kinds of pain (after dental treatment) (Holden, 1997). However, there is little convincing evidence that acupuncture is effective in treating either heroin or cocaine dependency (McLellan et al., 1993).

Next we turn to a very practical question: Can a sense be replaced if damaged? Of the five major senses—vision, audition, taste, olfaction, and touch—damage to vision and audition is especially disastrous to the quality of life. For that reason, researchers are trying to develop artificial eyes and ears.

I. Application: Artificial Senses

Artificial Visual System

Is an artificial eye possible?

The cause and degree of blindness depends upon which part of the visual system is affected. For example, a person would be totally blind if the photoreceptors (rods and cones) in the retina were destroyed (retinitis pigmentosa) or if the entire retina or optic nerve were damaged. First, we'll look at a microchip that could be implanted into the retina to replace photoreceptors damaged by disease.

1 Artificial photoreceptors. Some individuals are blind because the front part of the eye is functioning but the photoreceptors (rods and cones) in the retina are damaged by accident or disease. For these individuals, researchers are developing a microchip the size of a match head (black square with white "E") that would be implanted in the back of the retina. This microchip would change light waves into electrical signals that would activate the middle layer of ganglion cells, which are undamaged. The ganglion cells would then make impulses

Glasses   Microchip implanted in retina

Ganglion cells make impulses

Microchip

that travel on to the brain for processing. Although this microchip would not restore full vision, it would allow people now totally blind to see shades of light. Researchers must still develop a power supply before the microchip can be tested (Liu & McGucken, 1997).

For individuals who are blind because their entire eye or optic nerve is damaged, researchers are developing a complete artificial eye that would send impulses directly to the brain.

2 Artificial eye and retina. Some individuals are blind because their eyes and retinas are damaged by accident or disease. For these individuals, the task is to develop an artificial eye and retina.

An eye can be replaced by a miniature video camera (below right figure), which changes light waves into electrical signals. In turn, those signals would be passed on to an artificial retina, which would then send electrical signals into the optic nerve. The optic nerve would carry the impulses to the brain for processing. Researchers have, in fact, developed an artificial retina and are currently testing it in animals (Zimmer, 1993). At the very least, researchers hope that artificial retinas will allow blind people to see the outlines of objects and allow them to walk around without using canes. In the near future, researchers hope to implant artificial retinas into humans and restore some of their lost vision.

Other individuals are blind because their optic nerves are damaged and impulses cannot reach their brains. In these cases, the only solution is to implant tiny wires into the brain's visual area.

3 Brain implant. If a person were blind because of damage to the entire eyes, retinas, or optic nerves, tiny wires could be implanted directly into the primary visual cortex, which is located in the occipital lobe. At the beginning of this module, we told you about Katie, who was completely blind because both her eyes were damaged. In Katie's case, only 36 tiny wires were implanted directly into her visual cortex. Her vision was restricted to only 36 dots of light, which is far less than needed for something as simple as avoiding objects while walking.

In the diagram below, you see an array of 100 wires implanted into the primary visual cortex of the occipital lobe.

4 Functional vision. Below, you see the red letter S, formed by stimulating 26 of 100 wires implanted into the primary visual cortex. However, researchers found that about 625 wires, which equal 625 dots of light, need to be implanted into the primary visual cortex for people to avoid objects and to read at about 150 words a minute (Hambrecht's data, Zimmer, 1993).

Researchers have developed an implant with 64 wires, which is far from their goal of 625 wires. Thus, there is at present no artificial visual system that can restore enough vision to enable a blind person to avoid objects while walking, much less to be able to read. However, development of a useful artificial visual system comes closer each year.

Researchers are also working on developing an artificial cochlea for the inner ear.

Kinds of Deafness

There are two major kinds of deafness that have different causes and treatments. One is caused by problems in the middle ear (conduction deafness) and one by damage to the inner ear (neural deafness).

Conduction Deafness

It is not uncommon to see older people wearing hearing aids, which are often used to treat conduction deafness.

Conduction deafness can be caused by wax in the auditory canal, injury to the tympanic membrane, or malfunction of the ossicles. All of these conditions interfere with the transmission of vibrations from the tympanic membrane to the fluid of the cochlea.

Conduction deafness can usually be treated with a hearing aid, which essentially replaces the function of the middle ear. Hearing aids pick up sound waves, change them to vibrations, and send them through the skull to the inner ear.

Neural Deafness

Hellen Keller, who was born deaf and blind, said, "To be deaf is a greater affliction than to be blind." Hellen Keller had neural deafness, which is not helped by hearing aids.

Neural deafness can be caused by damage to the auditory receptors (hair cells), which prevents the production of impulses, or by damage to the auditory nerve, which prevents nerve impulses from reaching the brain. Since neither hair cells nor auditory nerve fibers regenerate, neural deafness was generally untreatable until the development of the cochlear implant.

The *cochlear implant* is a miniature electronic device that is surgically implanted into the cochlea. The cochlear implant changes sound waves into electrical signals that are fed into the auditory nerve, which carries them to the brain for processing.

If the auditory nerve is intact, the cochlear implant can be used to treat neural deafness caused by damaged hair cells, which is the problem for about 90% of those with hearing impairment. As you proceed step by step through the figure below, notice that the cochlear implant first changes sound waves into electrical signals (1, 2 & 3), and then sends the electrical signals into the auditory nerve (4), which sends impulses to the brain (5).

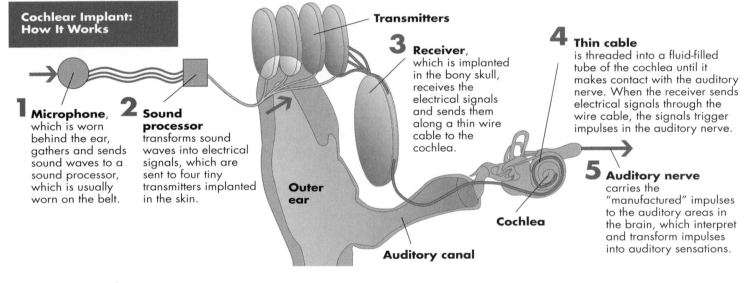

Cochlear Implant: How It Works

1 Microphone, which is worn behind the ear, gathers and sends sound waves to a sound processor, which is usually worn on the belt.

2 Sound processor transforms sound waves into electrical signals, which are sent to four tiny transmitters implanted in the skin.

Transmitters

3 Receiver, which is implanted in the bony skull, receives the electrical signals and sends them along a thin wire cable to the cochlea.

4 Thin cable is threaded into a fluid-filled tube of the cochlea until it makes contact with the auditory nerve. When the receiver sends electrical signals through the wire cable, the signals trigger impulses in the auditory nerve.

5 Auditory nerve carries the "manufactured" impulses to the auditory areas in the brain, which interpret and transform impulses into auditory sensations.

Outer ear

Auditory canal

Cochlea

Cochlear Implants

The child in the photo has been deaf from birth and is reacting to hearing his first sounds after receiving a cochlear implant. Worldwide, about 12,000 adults and children with severe neural deafness have received cochlear implants since they were approved in 1957 (NIH, 1995).

Using the newest cochlear implants, adults who had learned to speak before they became deaf were able to understand about 80% of sentences without any facial cues and from 90 to 100% of sentences when watching the speaker's face and lips (speechreading) (NIH, 1995).

The results are more complicated for very young children (up to age 2) who did not learn to speak before becoming deaf. Some clinicians believe that with cochlear implants they can easily learn sign language but may have a very difficult time learning to speak (Lane, 1997). However, long-term studies reported that cochlear implants in young children (deaf before learning to speak) were able to understand about 4% of spoken words and sentences after one year, 31% after two years and 74% after four years (Mondain et al., 1997). But clinicians warn that very young children with cochlear implants need intensive speech rehabilitation after cochlear implants (Te et al., 1996). Thus, cochlear implants are most effective in adults, adolescents, and children who spoke before becoming deaf and less effective in young children who became deaf before learning to speak (Clay, 1997).

As we end this module, you may have noticed that we mostly discussed how senses transform energy into impulses. Next, in Module 6, we'll focus on how sensations turn into meaningful perceptions.

SUMMARY TEST

A. EYE: VISION

1. Waves in about the middle of the electro-magnetic spectrum are visible because they can be absorbed by the human eye. These waves make up the _____ and can be absorbed by receptors at the back of the eye.

2. Upon entering the eye, light waves pass first through a curved, thin, transparent structure called the (a)_____, whose function is to bend or focus light waves into a narrower beam. Next, light waves pass through an opening in the eye called the (b)_____. Around this opening is a circular, pigmented muscle called the (c)_____; its function is to dilate or constrict, thus increasing or decreasing the amount of entering light. Finally, light waves pass through a transparent, oval structure called the (d)_____, whose function is to further focus light waves precisely on the photosensitive back surface of the eye, which is called the (e)_____.

3. The retina has several layers of cells, but only the very back layer contains photoreceptors. The photoreceptors that are used to see in dim light and transmit only black, white, and shades of gray are called (a)_____. Photoreceptors that are used to see in bright light and transmit colors are called (b)_____.

4. When rods absorb light waves, a chemical called (a)_____ breaks down and in turn generates tiny electrical forces that trigger (b)_____ in neighboring cells. Similarly, when cones absorb light waves, chemicals called (c)_____ break down and generate tiny electrical forces.

5. Nerve impulses generated in the eye travel along fibers that combine to form the (a)_____ nerve. This nerve carries nerve impulses to an area in the back of each occipital lobe called the (b)_____, which transforms impulses into simple visual (c)_____, such as lines, shadows, colors, and textures. If the primary visual cortex were totally damaged, the person would be essentially blind. Simple, meaningless sensations are transformed into complete, meaningful images when nerve impulses reach an area of the brain known as (d)_____.

6. We see color because our eyes absorb light waves of different (a)_____, which are transformed by the visual system into our experience of seeing colors. One theory of color applies to how the cones function; this is the (b)_____ theory. A second theory of color applies to how the ganglion and thalamic cells function; this is called the (c)_____ theory of color.

B. EAR: AUDITION

7. The stimuli for hearing, or audition, are sound waves, which have several physical characteristics. The physical characteristic of amplitude or height of sound waves is transformed into the subjective experience of (a)_____, which is measured in units called (b)_____. The frequency of sound waves (cycles per second) is transformed into the subjective experience of (c)_____, which for humans ranges from about 20 to 20,000 cycles per second.

8. The outer ear is composed of a funnel-like shape, called the external ear, whose function is to gather (a)_____. These waves travel down a short tunnel called the (b)_____, and strike a thin, taut membrane called the (c)_____, whose function is to transform sound waves into (d)_____.

9. The middle ear has three tiny bones (hammer, anvil, and stirrup), which together are called (a)_____. Vibrations in the tympanic membrane produce mechanical movements in the ossicles, the third of which is attached to another thin membrane, called the (b)_____, which is made to vibrate.

10. Of several structures in the inner ear, one is a coiled, fluid-filled, tubelike apparatus called the (a)_____, which contains the auditory receptors, called (b)_____. Movement of the fluid in the tube causes movement of the basilar membrane, which in turn causes bending of the hair cells, generating a tiny (c)_____. If this is large enough, it will trigger nerve impulses, which leave the cochlea via the (d)_____ and travel to the brain.

11. Nerve impulses are transformed into rather simple, meaningless auditory sensations when they reach the (a)_____, which is located in the temporal lobe. These sensations are transformed into meaningful and complete melodies, songs, words, or sentences by the auditory (b)_____.

12. To tell the direction of a sound, the brain analyzes the differences in time and intensity between (a)_____ arriving at the left and right ears. The brain determines degrees of loudness by using the (b)_____ of the arriving impulses. The discrimination of different tones or pitches is explained by the (c)_____ and _____ theories.

C. VESTIBULAR SYSTEM: BALANCE

13. Besides the cochlea, the inner ear contains three arch-shaped, fluid-filled structures called _____. The movement of fluid in these organs provides signals that the brain interprets in terms of the movement and position of the head and body. The vestibular system is also involved in motion sickness, Meniere's disease, and vertigo.

D. CHEMICAL SENSES

 14. Particular areas on our tongues respond most to each of the four basic tastes: (a)_____, _____, _____, and _____. The receptors for taste, which are called (b)_____, trigger nerve impulses that travel to the brain, which then transforms them into the sensations of taste.

15. Volatile airborne substances are drawn into the upper part of the nose, where they dissolve in a thin film of mucus. Underneath the mucus are layers of receptors for olfaction (smell), which are called (a)_____. These receptors trigger impulses that travel to an area underneath the brain called the (b)_____. This area transforms impulses into hundreds of different odors.

E. TOUCH

16. The sense of touch actually provides information on three different kinds of stimuli: (a)_____, _____, and _____. The various layers of skin contain different kinds of touch receptors that have different speeds of adaptation. Receptors for the sense of touch trigger nerve impulses that travel to an area in the brain's parietal lobe, called the (b)_____. This area transforms impulses into sensations of pressure, temperature, and pain. The more sensitive the area of the body is to touch, the larger is its area on this cortex.

Hair follicle

F. CULTURAL DIVERSITY: DISGUST VERSUS DELIGHT

 17. A universal facial expression that indicates rejection of food is called (a)_____. Besides our innate preferences for sweet and salty foods and avoidance of bitter substances, most of our tastes are (b)_____ and particular to our culture. The fact that foods in one culture may seem disgusting to people in another culture indicates how much psychological factors influence taste.

G. RESEARCH FOCUS: PAIN & PLACEBOS

18. In order to control for the placebo effect, researchers use an experimental design in which neither the researchers nor subjects know who is receiving what treatment. This is the _____ design, which controls for the expectations of both researchers and subjects.

H. PAIN

19. After an injury, you feel two different kinds of pain sensations: at first, there is sharp, localized pain, which is followed by a duller, more generalized pain. The receptors for pain are (a)_____, which send impulses to two areas of the brain, specifically the (b)_____ and _____. If you rub an injured area or become totally absorbed in another activity, you may experience a reduction of pain, which is explained by the (c)_____. Immediately following a serious injury or great physical stress, the brain produces pain-reducing chemicals called (d)_____.

I. APPLICATION: ARTIFICIAL SENSES

20. There are two basic causes of deafness. If the cause is wax in the auditory canal, injury to the tympanic membrane, or malfunction of the ossicles, it is called (a)_____ deafness. If the cause is damage to hair cells in the cochlea or to the auditory nerve, it is called (b)_____ deafness. One treatment for neural deafness is to use a (c)_____, which is more effective if individuals have learned to speak before becoming deaf.

Answers: 1. visible spectrum; 2. (a) cornea, (b) pupil, (c) iris, (d) lens, (e) retina; 3. (a) rods, (b) cones; 4. (a) rhodopsin, (b) impulses, (c) opsins; 5. (a) optic, (b) primary visual cortex, (c) sensations, (d) association areas; 6. (a) lengths, (b) trichromatic, (c) opponent-process; 7. (a) loudness, (b) decibels, (c) pitch; 8. (a) sound waves, (b) auditory canal, (c) eardrum or tympanic membrane, (d) vibrations; 9. (a) ossicles, (b) oval window; 10. (a) cochlea, (b) hair cells, (c) electrical force, (d) auditory nerve; 11. (a) primary auditory cortex, (b) association areas; 12. (a) sound waves, (b) rate, (c) frequency, place; 13. vestibular organs; 14. (a) bitter, sour, salty, sweet, (b) taste buds; 15. (a) olfactory cells, (b) primary olfactory cortex; 16. (a) pressure, temperature, pain, (b) somatosensory cortex; 17. (a) disgust, (b) learned; 18. double-blind; 19. (a) free nerve endings, (b) somatosensory area, limbic system, (c) gate control theory, (d) endorphins; 20. (a) conduction, (b) neural, (c) cochlear implant.

CRITICAL THINKING

Newspaper Article

1. What is tinnitus?

2. How did scientists use PET scans to determine the cause of tinnitus?

3. What is the source of the "noise" of tinnitus?

4. What do the similarities between tinnitus and phantom limb pain tell us?

5. Why do many people with severe tinnitus also have emotional problems?

6. How might this research contribute to finding a cure for tinnitus?

7. What group of people might be at high risk for tinnitus, and what might they do to avoid it?

Tinnitus Study Offers Hope for Treatment
by Thomas H. Maugh II

Researchers have for the first time identified the source of tinnitus, the constant and debilitating ringing in the ears that afflicts as many as 50 million Americans. The discovery could lead to the first effective treatment for the disorder, Buffalo researchers report today in the journal *Neurology*.

Tinnitus results from damage to the inner ear caused by loud noises, medications, blows to the head, and other factors. But researchers have never known precisely which parts of the ear are generating the disturbing sounds.

Using positron emission tomography scans to image the brains of a small group of tinnitus patients, Dr. Alan H. Lockwood of the Buffalo Veterans Affairs Medical Center concluded that the noise originates not in the ear, but in the auditory cortex, a portion of the brain in the temporal lobe opposite the affected ear.

When the ear is damaged, he said, the brain rewires itself, perhaps in an attempt to compensate for the loss of function. That rewiring generates electrical signals that the brain interprets as noise. Intriguingly, other researchers report today in the journal *Nature* that a similar type of rewiring occurs in people who have lost a limb. That rewiring process produces the phantom pain caused by many amputees. "Tinnitus may be the auditory counterpart to phantom limb pain," said Lockwood. The researchers on phantom limb pain were able to surgically implant microelectrodes into the brain to control the phantom pain. If implanted electrodes can control the pain of phantom limbs, perhaps they might also be able to control the intensity of phantom noises.

Estimates vary, but between 20% and 35% of Americans suffer tinnitus at some time in their lives, particularly in their later years. It may appear as buzzing, roaring, whistling, hissing, high-pitched screeches, or other sounds and is often accompanied by hearing loss. The condition is usually permanent.

The current research showed that tinnitus activated the hippocampus, a portion of the brain that controls the limbic system—which is associated with emotions and feelings. That link to the hippocampus, Lockwood said, may explain why some people with severe tinnitus also have emotional problems.

Source: *Los Angeles Times,* January 22, 1998.

Study Questions

A. **Eye: Vision**—What kinds of problems in the visual system could result in some forms of blindness? (See answer in Critical Thinking Appendix)

B. **Ear: Audition**—What kinds of problems in the auditory system could result in some form of deafness? (See answer in Critical Thinking Appendix)

C. **Vestibular System: Balance**—How do placebos help about 40–60% of people who suffer from motion sickness?

D. **Chemical Senses**—How might a master chef's chemical senses differ from yours? (See answer in Critical Thinking Appendix)

E. **Touch**—What would happen if touch receptors did not show adaptation?

F. **Cultural Diversity: Disgust Versus Delight**—Why do people often show disgust when offered a new but edible food?

G. **Research Focus: Pain & Placebos**—Why are some drugs initially reported to be effective but later proven to be worthless?

H. **Pain**—Why can some individuals stand more pain than others?

I. **Application: Artificial Senses**—Why is it so difficult to build an artificial eye or ear that duplicates the real one?

LINKS TO LEARNING

Web Sites & Learning Activities

● BROOKS/COLE ONLINE PSYCHOLOGY STUDY
CENTER

**http://psychstudy.brookscole.com/student/plotnik/quiz/
ch05frm.html**

This site gives students a chance to review material by taking
quizzes and doing exercises and activities for this module.

● SENSATION AND PERCEPTION

http://www.guam.net/home/bmarmie/sandp.html

This site provides links to interactive tutorials,
3-D pictures, auditory examples, and interactive
demonstrations of sensation and perception for the
psychology student.

● SEEING, HEARING, AND SMELLING
THE WORLD

http://www.hhmi.org/senses

How do we see colors and movement? How can
we locate a thing by its sound? How are smells a sexual signal? This site explores these and many other
topics related to sensation.

● AUDITORY EDUCATIONAL

http://www.neurophys.wisc.edu/www/aud/aud_educ.html

This site examines every aspect of the ear by way of interactive
tutorials, demonstrations, and research covering auditory perception and many other topics.

● VIRTUAL TOUR OF THE EAR

http://ctl.augie.edu/perry/ear/hearmech.htm

This comprehensive site contains information on the anatomy
of the ear, speech perception, disorders of hearing, and audiology.

Welcome to the WEB

● THE CHEMORECEPTION WEB

http://moe.csa.com/crw/neuro.html

This Web site explores many aspects of our senses of taste and
smell. There are interactive tutorials, color images, textual information, and a search engine.

● THE INTERNATIONAL ASSOCIATION FOR THE
STUDY OF PAIN

**http://weber.u.washington.edu:80/~crc/
IASP.html**

This site is a comprehensive index to pain issues,
including postsurgical pain, chronic pain, pediatric
pain, pain treatments, and more.

Activities

● *Integrator Online™ for Introductory Psychology*
CD-ROM, Plotnik, Module 5

● Study Guide to accompany *Introduction to Psychology,* 5th
edition, Module 5 (choice of PC or Mac computer version or
hard copy).

● PsychNow! CD-ROM
Vision and Hearing
Chemical and Somesthetic Senses

Answers to questions on page 118

---

1. Tinnitus is a constant and debilitating buzzing or ringing in the
ears resulting from damage to the ears.
2. They used PET scans to image the brain activity of people with
tinnitus.
3. The damaged auditory cortex rewires itself, which generates electrical signals that are interpreted by the brain as noise.
4. Perhaps the healing, or rewiring, the brain does in response to
injury is similar across different senses and body systems.

5. Tinnitus activates the hippocampus, a part of the brain that controls the limbic system, which controls the emotions.
6. Finding the cause of the condition is the first step in finding a
cure. For example, researchers might develop a drug that changes
the activity of neurotransmitters in the affected area.
7. People who are subjected to loud noises are at increased risk.
They should protect their ears by wearing earplugs or limiting
exposure.

Module 6 PERCEPTION

Helpful Messages

How can I be more confident?

Although it seemed like an ordinary week, Maria and her seven-year-old daughter, Gabrielle, would be involved in three relatively normal events that could change their lives forever.

On Tuesday, Maria's new boss unfairly criticized her work and made her feel insecure and unsure of herself. During her lunch hour, she browsed through a bookstore to find something on building confidence. She was intrigued by an audiotape titled "Improve Self-Esteem." The instructions read, "The listener hears only relaxing music, but the unconscious hears and automatically processes sub-

IMPROVE SELF-ESTEEM

liminal messages that boost self-esteem. In a few short weeks, the listener is guaranteed to have more confidence and self-esteem. If you're not completely satisfied, return the tape for a full refund." Maria had heard about tapes with subliminal messages from a friend who claimed that she used a weight-reduction tape that helped her lose 20 pounds. When Maria asked about the effectiveness of subliminal tapes, the salesperson said that he had a friend who increased his motivation to study by listening to one of these tapes. Maria smiled and said, "Well, it's guaranteed, so what have I got to lose?" She bought the tape, put it in her purse, and as she walked out the door, she was already feeling a little more confident.

Nice Dog, Mean Dog

How does "nice" become "mean"?

On Saturday afternoon, Maria took her daughter, Gabrielle, to play at the local park, which had slides, swings, ropes, and even a small trampoline. As Gabrielle was walking toward the trampoline, she saw a beautiful brown dog was sitting by its owner. Gabrielle loved animals, and she ran toward the dog. The dog's owner was deep in conversation and did not notice the cute little girl running toward the beautiful Doberman. As Gabrielle came closer, she thrust out her hands to pet the dog's smooth black nose. The movement of Gabrielle's hands startled the dog, who reflexively snarled and then snapped at the hands coming at its nose. Gabrielle felt the pain as the dog's teeth nipped two of her fingers, which immediately started to bleed. The owner turned to see what had happened and quickly pulled the dog away as Maria came running. Maria took Gabrielle in her arms, soothed her, and then examined the small cuts on her fingers. Gabrielle looked at her bleeding fingers and then at the big, ugly, brown dog that had bit her and said in a tearful voice, "I hate dog. Bad dog." Seeing her daughter's reaction, Maria began to have doubts about her plans to surprise Gabrielle with a cute little puppy for her birthday.

A White Spot

Can the doctor be sure?

On Friday, Maria had to take time from work for her annual physical exam, which included a mammogram. In the past, the doctor had simply said that the results of her mammogram were negative. This time, the doctor brought in her mammogram, which looked like an X ray. He pointed to a small white spot and said in a concerned voice, "I'm afraid that this tiny white dot may be a cancerous tumor." The doctor's words took her breath away. Finally, Maria asked in a terrified whisper, "Are you absolutely sure that spot is cancer?" The doctor paused for a minute, looked again at the mammogram, and said, "I can't be absolutely sure the spot is cancerous until we do a biopsy. All I can say is that there is a good possibility that it is." As Maria scheduled her biopsy, she would never forget seeing that white spot on the mammogram.

Perceptions

What do these situations have in common?

At first glance, these three events—buying a subliminal tape, being bitten by a dog, and seeing a spot on a mammogram—seem to have nothing in common. In fact, these events raise three basic questions about how we perceive things.

Maria's subliminal tape raises the first question: Are there things that we perceive but are not aware of, and can these things influence our behaviors (Kihlstrom, 1996; Shevrin et al., 1996)?

Maria's mammogram raises the second question: How large or unusual must things be before our senses can detect them? This is a very important question since the answer may have serious health consequences (Begley, 1997; Taubes, 1997).

Finally, Gabrielle's painful experience with a dog raises the third question: How much are the things we perceive influenced or biased by our cultural, learning, emotional, and personal experiences (NAMHC, 1996)? These three questions are the key to understanding how we perceive our world.

What's Coming

We'll discuss what perceptual thresholds are, how sensations differ from perceptions, how sensations are combined to form perceptions, how objects can undergo great changes yet appear the same to us, how our senses are fooled by illusions, how cultural experiences change perceptions, whether there is good evidence for ESP (extrasensory perception), and whether the newest kind of perceiving, called virtual reality, can fool our senses into believing we're in a three-dimensional world.

Let's start with our first perceptual question: At what point do we become aware of some stimulus or event?

A. Perceptual Thresholds

Aware of a Stimulus

When do you know something is there?

Imagine suddenly becoming deaf or blind, unable to hear what people are saying or to see where you are going. Only then would you realize that your senses provide a continuous stream of information about your world. Your senses tell you that something is out there, and your perceptions tell you what that something is. However, there are some sounds and objects you may not be aware of because the level of stimulation is too low and does not exceed the threshold of a particular sense.

Threshold refers to a point above which a stimulus is perceived and below which it is not perceived. The threshold determines when we first become aware of a stimulus.

For example, the reason Maria is not aware of, or does not hear, subliminal messages recorded on tape is that these messages are below her absolute threshold for hearing. To understand how the absolute threshold is determined, imagine that Maria is presented with a series of auditory messages that slowly increase in intensity. Maria is asked to press a button when she first hears a message. You may think that there will be a certain level or absolute value of intensity (loudness) at which Maria will first report hearing a tone. The idea that there is an absolute threshold was initially proposed by Gustav Fechner (1860), an important historical figure in perceptual research. However, as you'll see, Fechner had difficulty in identifying the absolute threshold as he defined it.

1 At first, *Gustav Fechner* (*FECK-ner*) defined the absolute threshold as the smallest amount of stimulus energy (such as sound or light) that can be observed or experienced.

According to Fechner's definition, if Maria's hearing could always be measured under exactly the same conditions, her absolute threshold would always remain the same. Although Fechner tried various methods to identify absolute thresholds, he found that an individual's threshold was not absolute and, in fact, differed depending on the subject's alertness and the test situation. Because of this variability in measurement, researchers had to redefine absolute threshold.

2 The graph below shows how the absolute threshold was redefined.

Absolute threshold is the intensity level of a stimulus such that a person will have a 50% chance of detecting it.

According to this updated definition, Maria's absolute threshold is the point on the graph where she has a 50% chance of hearing the message.

Once we have determined Maria's absolute threshold for hearing messages, we can define a subliminal message.

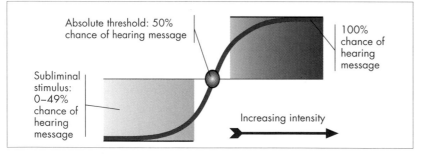

Absolute threshold: 50% chance of hearing message

100% chance of hearing message

Subliminal stimulus: 0–49% chance of hearing message

Increasing intensity

3 The graph above shows that a subliminal stimulus can occur at any point below the absolute threshold.

A *subliminal stimulus* has an intensity that gives a person a less than 50% chance of detecting it.

Because subliminal messages can occur in a wide range (0–49%), Maria may or may not report hearing

them. For example, Maria would never report hearing messages of very low intensity (0% level) but may sometimes report hearing messages of higher intensity (49%).

We'll discuss the interesting question of whether subliminal messages can change behaviors or attitudes, such as increasing self-esteem, in the Research Focus (p. 135).

Possible cancerous breast tumor stands out as a white spot

4 Although the concept of an absolute threshold may seem very abstract, it has very real consequences in detecting breast cancer.

After lung cancer, breast cancer is the second most frequently occurring cancer in American women, with approximately 200,000 new cases each year (Mah & Bryant, 1997).

When doctors read mammograms (X rays), they look for white spots that usually stand out on a black background; these white spots indicate tumors (photo above). The problem is that about 40% of women have so much connective breast tissue, which also appears white, that tiny white tumors go undetected. For this reason, doctors fail to detect about 25% of tumors on mammograms (Hager, 1997).

The task is to increase the accuracy of mammograms. Researchers found that if two mammograms were taken and read independently by two doctors, the accuracy of identifying cancerous tumors was significantly improved (Thurfjell, 1994). In addition, other techniques (digital X rays, MRI scans) are being developed to detect tumors better than current mammograms can. Thus, mammogram testing is a practical example of needing to find ways to lower the threshold for detecting cancerous tumors and thus save patients' lives.

Besides being involved in subliminal messages and mammogram tests, the problem of determining thresholds is also involved in the question of how we know a stimulus has decreased or increased in intensity. We'll discuss this next.

Weber's Law

Suppose someone is playing music too loud and you ask them to turn down the volume. Even after they turn it down, it may still seem just as loud as before. The explanation for this phenomenon can be found in the work of another historical figure in perception, E. H. Weber *(VEY-ber)*.

Weber worked on the problem of how we judge whether a stimulus, such as loud music, has increased or decreased in intensity. This problem involves measuring the difference in thresholds between two stimuli, such as very loud music and not-quite-so-loud music. To solve this problem, Weber (1834) developed the concept of a just noticeable difference.

A *just noticeable difference*, or *JND*, refers to the smallest increase or decrease in the intensity of a stimulus that a person is able to detect.

For example, to measure a just noticeable difference in weight, Weber asked people to compare stimuli of varying intensities and indicate when they could detect a difference between them. He discovered that if he presented two stimuli with very low intensities, such as a 2-ounce weight versus a 3-ounce weight, people could easily detect small differences between them. However, if he presented stimuli with high intensities, such as a 40-pound weight versus a 41-pound weight, people could no longer detect small differences. For higher-intensity stimuli, such as heavy weights, a much larger difference in intensity was required for the difference to be noticed.

Weber's observations on what it takes to detect just noticeable differences was the basis for what became known as Weber's law.

Weber's law states that the increase in intensity of a stimulus needed to produce a just noticeable difference grows in proportion to the intensity of the initial stimulus.

Weber's law (right figure) explains that if someone is playing the stereo very loud, it must be turned down a great deal, usually more than the person prefers to turn it down, for you to detect a just noticeable decrease in volume.

Another practical application of Weber's law is the detection of the softness in towels.

Weber's Law Explained

Weber's law explains that, at lower intensities, small changes between two stimuli can be detected as just noticeable differences (JNDs); however, at higher intensities, only larger changes between two stimuli can be detected as JNDs.

Stimulus: Lighter ⟶ **Heavier**

1 JND. The same height of each step illustrates your ability to detect "one sensory unit" of a *just noticeable difference* between two weights.

2 Lower intensities. The small width of this step indicates that, at lower intensities, you need only a *small difference* in weight in order to detect a just noticeable difference between two weights. This statement follows from Weber's law, which says that only a small difference in intensity is required for you to detect a just noticeable difference when judging stimuli of lower intensity.

3 Higher intensities. The considerable width of this step indicates that, at higher intensities, you need a *larger difference* in weight in order to detect a just noticeable difference between two weights. This statement follows from Weber's law, which says that a larger difference in intensity is required for you to detect a just noticeable difference when judging stimuli of higher intensity.

Just Noticeable Difference (JND)

Every year, industry and business spend billions of dollars to make sure that consumers can detect just noticeable differences between this year's and last year's cars, shampoos, cereals, and fashions. For example, consumers spend millions of dollars each year on fabric softeners, which are added during washing and are claimed to make clothes feel softer. To test such claims, researchers asked subjects to feel towels washed with and without softener and rate the softness of the towels on a scale from 1 (hard) to 30 (very soft). Subjects gave an average softness rating of 5 to towels washed repeatedly without softener

and an average rating of 18 to towels washed with softener. Researchers concluded that fabric softeners worked, since subjects could easily detect a just noticeable difference in softness (Ali & Begum, 1994). This is but one application of Weber's law and JNDs in industry.

So far, we've focused on how you detect stimuli and distinguish between their intensities. Next, we'll discuss one of the most interesting questions in perception: How do you change meaningless bits of sensations into meaningful and complete perceptions?

B. Sensation versus Perception

Basic Differences

Much of your success in being happy and successful depends on your ability to respond intelligently and adapt appropriately to changes in your environment (NAMHC, 1996). The first step in responding and adapting involves gathering millions of meaningless sensations and changing them into useful perceptions. Because your brain changes sensations into perceptions so quickly, automatically, and with very little awareness, you might assume that what you see (sense) is what you perceive. However, the process of changing sensations into perceptions is influenced by whether you are alert, sleepy, worried, emotional, motivated, or affected by the use of a legal or illegal drug. For example, drinking alcohol causes perceptions in social situations to be less rational and more uninhibited, causing people under its influence to act aggressively, make terrible decisions, create problems, or say really dumb things (Carey & Correia, 1997; Ito et al, 1966; Stritzke et al., 1996). As you are about to discover, sensing and perceiving are as different as night and day.

For example, quickly glance at the black-and-white figure on the left and then look away and describe what you saw.

Sensations

Initially, the figure on the left appears to be a bunch of meaningless lines, spaces, and blobs, which, for the sake of simplicity, we'll take the liberty of calling visual sensations. In real life, we rarely if ever experience sensations because, as we'll explain on the next page, they are immediately turned into perceptions.

A *sensation* is our first awareness of some outside stimulus. An outside stimulus activates sensory receptors, which in turn produce electrical signals that are transformed by the brain into meaningless bits of information.

You can approximate how visual sensations may look by placing half of a ping-pong ball over your eye. As you look through this nearly opaque ping-pong ball, you'll see shadows, textures, and dark shapes, but nothing meaningful; these are similar to sensations.

Another example that illustrates the difference between sensations and perceptions is the photo below. Your first impression consists of meaningless shapes, textures, and blotches of color, which we'll again take the liberty of calling visual sensations. However, you can turn these meaningless sensations into a meaningful image—a perception—by using the following clues. This photo is an ultra-

sound image of a fetus in the womb. The fetus is lying on his back with his rounded tummy on the left and his large head on the right. Above his head is the right arm and hand, and you can even count the five tiny fingers. You can also see that the fetus is sucking on his thumb. Once you know what to look for, you automatically change the random blotches of colors and shapes into the perception of a fetus.

Obviously, it would be impossible to respond, adapt, and survive if you had to rely only on sensations. You can now appreciate the importance of changing sensations into perceptions.

Perceptions

As you look at the stimulus on the right, your brain is processing many thousands of visual sensations involving lines, curves, textures, shadows, and colors. Then, instantaneously, automatically, and without awareness, your brain combines these thousands of sensations into a perception—an orange tiger's face against a green background.

A *perception* is the experience we have after our brain assembles and combines thousands of individual, meaningless sensations into a meaningful pattern or image. However, our perceptions are rarely exact replicas of the original stimuli. Rather, our perceptions are usually changed, biased, colored, or distorted by our unique set of experiences. Thus, perceptions are our personal interpretations of the real world.

If you now look at the black-and-white drawing on the upper left, your brain will automatically combine the formerly meaningless shapes and blobs into a tiger's face. This is an approximate example of how meaningless sensations are automatically combined to form meaningful perceptions.

One important feature of perceptions is that they are rarely exact copies of the real world. To study how experience can bias our perceptions, researchers asked 20 college students who liked rock music and 20 who disliked it to listen to a 10-second sample of rock music. Then, the subjects in each group were asked to adjust the volume of the rock-music sample to match different levels of intensity, ranging from very soft to extremely loud. Researchers reported that subjects who liked rock music consistently set the volume louder than the reference level, while subjects who disliked rock music consistently set the volume lower (Fucci et al., 1993). This study shows how our experiences can bias our perceptions, usually without our awareness.

To show that no two individuals perceive the world in exactly the same way, we'll explain how your personal experiences change, bias, and even distort your perceptions.

Changing Sensations into Perceptions

How does a "nice" doggie become a "bad" doggie?

It is most unlikely that you have ever experienced a "pure" sensation, because your brain automatically and instantaneously changes sensations into perceptions. Despite what you may think, perceptions do not exactly mirror events, people, situations, and objects in your environment. Rather, perceptions are interpretations, which means that your perceptions are changed or biased by your personal experiences, memories, emotions, and

motivations. For example, at the beginning of this module we told you how seven-year-old Gabrielle's perception of a dog was changed from "nice" to "bad" by her personal experience of being bitten. The next time Gabrielle sees a dog, she won't just see a four-legged creature with ears, nose, and tail; she will see a "bad" four-legged creature. To understand how sensations become perceptions, we have divided the perceptual process into a series of discrete steps that, in real life, are much more complex and interactive.

1 Stimulus. Since normally we only experience perceptions, we are not aware of many preceding steps. The first step begins with some stimulus, which is any change of energy in the environment, such as light waves, sound waves, mechanical pressure, or chemicals. The stimulus activates sense receptors in the eyes, ears, skin, nose, or mouth. In Gabrielle's case, the stimuli are light waves reflecting off the body of a large, brown dog.

2 Transduction. After entering Gabrielle's eyes, light waves are focused on the retina, which contain photoreceptors that are sensitive to light. The light waves are absorbed by the photoreceptors, which perform transduction, that is, changing physical energy into electrical signals. The electrical signals are changed into impulses that travel to the brain. Remember that all sense organs, such as the eye, do not produce sensations but simply transform energy into electrical signals.

3 Brain areas. Impulses from different sense organs go to different parts of the brain. For example, impulses from the ear go to the temporal lobe, from touch to the parietal lobe, and from the eye to areas in the occipital lobe. When impulses reach the primary visual area in the occipital lobe, the impulses are first changed into sensations. However, Gabrielle would not report seeing sensations.

Occipital lobe

4 Sensations. Each sense sends its particular impulses to a different area of the brain where impulses are changed into sensations, which are meaningless bits of information, such as the shapes, colors, and textures shown here. The "sensation" impulses are then sent to the appropriate association area in the brain. The association areas change meaningless bits of information into meaningful and complete images, called perceptions.

In Gabrielle's case, impulses from her eyes would be changed into visual sensations by the primary visual cortex and into perceptions by the visual association areas. However, Gabrielle's perception of a dog would be changed, biased, and even distorted by a number of psychological factors.

5 Personalized perceptions. Each of us has a unique set of personal experiences, emotions, and memories that are automatically added to our perceptions by other areas of the brain. As a result, our perceptions are not a mirror but a changed, biased, or even distorted copy of the real world (Niedenthal & Setterlund, 1994). For example, the visual areas of Gabrielle's brain automatically assembles many thousands of sensations into a meaningful pattern, which in this case is a dog. Now, however, Gabrielle doesn't see just an ordinary brown dog, because other brain areas add her emotional experience of being bitten. Thus, Gabrielle perceives this brown four-legged creature to be a "bad dog." For this same reason, two people can look at the same dog and have very different perceptions, such as cute dog, great dog, bad dog, smelly dog, or friendly dog. Thus, your perceptions are personalized interpretations rather than true copies of objects, animals, people, and situations in the real world.

The process of assembling and organizing sensations into perceptions was of great interest to early psychologists, who disagreed on how perceptions were formed. As you'll see next, their debate resulted in a very interesting perceptual controversy.

C. Rules of Organization

Structuralists versus Gestalt Psychologists

What was the great debate?

In the early 1900s, two groups of psychologists engaged in a heated debate over how perceptions are formed. One group, called the structuralists, strongly believed that we added together thousands of sensations to form a perception. Another group, called the Gestalt psychologists, just as strongly believed that sensations were not added but rather combined according to a set of innate rules to form a perception. One group won the debate and you might guess which one before you read further.

Structuralists

As you look at the scene in the middle of this page, you perceive a fountain at the bottom with shrubs and palm trees on the sides, all topped by a large dome of glass windows. Is it possible that your brain combined many thousands of individual sensations to produce this complex perception? If you answer yes, you agree with the structuralists.

The *structuralists* believed that you add together hundreds of basic elements to form complex perceptions. They also believed that you can work backward to break down perceptions into smaller and smaller units, or elements.

Structuralists spent hundreds of hours analyzing how perceptions, such as a falling ball, might be broken down into basic units or elements. They believed that once they understood the process of breaking down perceptions, they would know how basic units are recombined to form perceptions. Thus, structuralists believed that you add together basic units to form perceptions much as you would add a column of numbers to get a total.

For example, structuralists would say that you add together hundreds of basic units, such as colors, bricks, leaves, branches, tiles, pieces of glass, and bits of steel to form the perception of the scene above. However, the structuralists' explanation of adding bits to form a perception was hotly denied by Gestalt psychologists.

Gestalt Psychologists

The Gestalt psychologists said that perceptions were much too complex to be formed by simply adding sensations together; instead, they believed that perceptions were formed according to a set of rules.

Gestalt psychologists believed that our brains followed a set of rules that specified how individual elements were to be organized into a meaningful pattern, or perception.

Unlike the structuralists, the Gestalt psychologists said that perceptions do not result from adding sensations. Rather, perceptions result from our brain's ability to organize sensations according to a set of rules, much as our brain follows a set of rules for organizing words into meaningful sentences.

So how would Gestalt psychologists explain your perception of the scene on the left? They would say that your perception was not formed by simply adding bits of tile, steel, and foliage into a whole image. Rather, your brain automatically used a set of rules to combine these elements to form a unified whole. To emphasize their point, Gestalt psychologists came up with a catchy phrase, "The whole is more than the sum of its parts," to mean that perceptions are not merely combined sensations. The Gestalt psychologists went one step further; they came up with a list of organizational rules.

Evidence for Rules

Who won the debate?

Gestalt psychologists won their debate with the structuralists for two reasons. The first reason comes from our own personal perceptual experiences. For example, as you look again at the beautiful scene above, we must reveal that it is entirely fake. The scene, which looks so realistic and three-dimensional, is actually painted on a flat wall. It seems impossible that we could have such a complex, three-dimensional perceptual experience from simply combining bits and pieces of bricks, branches, leaves, and steel. This fake but truly realistic scene makes the Gestalt motto come to life: "The whole is more than the sum of its parts."

Equally convincing evidence that the whole is greater than the sum of its parts came from a remarkably detailed series of studies in which Gestalt psychologists presented stimuli to subjects and then asked them to describe what they perceived (Rock & Palmer, 1990). On the basis of subjects' reports, Gestalt psychologists discovered that forming perceptions involved more than adding and combining individual elements. They discovered that our brains actually did follow a set of rules for forming perceptions. We'll explain these rules for organizing perceptions next.

Organizational Rules

It is very hard to believe that the scene on the previous page (repeated here on the right) was actually painted on a flat wall. One reason you perceive this scene as complex and 3-dimensional is because the painter followed many of the Gestalt rules of organization.

Rules of organization, which were identified by Gestalt psychologists, specify how our brains combine and organize individual pieces or elements into a meaningful perception.

As you look at the this scene, your brain automatically organizes many hundreds of visual stimuli, including colors, textures, shadows, bricks, steel, glass, leaves, and branches, according to one or more of the six perceptual rules of organization described below. We'll use a relatively simple figure to illustrate each rule.

Figure-ground

One of the most basic rules in organizing perceptions is picking out the object from its background. As you look at the figure on the left, you will automatically see a black object standing out against a white background, which illustrates the figure-ground principle.

The *figure-ground rule* states that, in organizing stimuli, we tend to automatically distinguish between a figure and a ground: The figure, with more detail, stands out against the background, which has less detail.

There is some evidence that our ability to separate figure from ground is an innate response. For example, individuals who were blind from an early age and had their sight restored as adults were able to distinguish between figure and ground with little or no training (Senden, 1960). The figure-ground rule is one of the first rules that our brain uses to organize stimuli into a perception (Peterson & Gibson, 1994).

This particular image is interesting because, as you continue to stare at it, the figure and ground will suddenly reverse and you'll see profiles of two faces. In the real world, the images we usually perceive are nonreversible because they have more distinct shapes (Driver & Baylis, 1996).

Similarity

As you look at this figure filled with light and dark blue dots, you see a dark blue numeral 2.

The *similarity rule* states that, in organizing stimuli, elements that appear similar are grouped together.

The similarity rules causes us to group the dark blue dots together and prevents us from seeing the figure as a random arrangement of light and dark blue dots.

Closure

Although the lines are incomplete, you can easily perceive this drawing as a cat or dog.

The *closure rule* states that, in organizing stimuli, we tend to fill in any missing parts of a figure and see the figure as complete.

For example, the closure rule explains why you can fill in letters missing on a sign or pieces missing in a jigsaw puzzle.

Proximity

Notice that although there are exactly eight circles in each horizontal line, you perceive each line as formed by a different number of groups of circles.

The *proximity rule* states that, in organizing stimuli, objects that are physically close to one another will be grouped together.

You automatically group circles that are close together and thus perceive the first line as composed of three groups (Kubovy & Wagemans, 1995).

Simplicity

Look at figure A and then decide if it is made up of the pieces shown in figures B, C, or D. Almost everyone sees figure A as made up of the pieces in figure B—an oval with an overlapping square.

The *simplicity rule* states that stimuli are organized in the simplest way possible.

For example, almost no one sees figure A as having been formed from the complicated pieces shown in figure C or figure D. This rule says that we tend to perceive complex figures as divided into several simpler figures (Shimaya, 1997).

Continuity

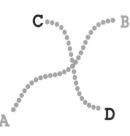

As you scan this figure, keep track of the path that your eyes follow. If you are like most people, your eyes will move from left to right in a continuous line, following the path from A to B or from C to D.

The *continuity rule* states that, in organizing stimuli, we tend to favor smooth or continuous paths when interpreting a series of points or lines.

For example, this rule predicts that you do not see a line that begins at A and then turns abruptly to C or to D.

These figures demonstrate the Gestalt rules of organizing stimuli into perceptions. Very young children slowly learn these perceptual rules and are able to use them around the age of two (Spelke et al., 1993). As adults we constantly use these rules to organize thousands of stimuli into perceptions, especially stimuli in print and advertisements (NAMHC, 1996).

Next, we turn to another interesting perceptual question: How can objects change yet appear to remain the same?

D. Perceptual Constancy

Size, Shape, Brightness, and Color Constancy

Why don't cars shrink?

Perception is full of interesting puzzles, such as how cars, people, and pets can constantly change their shapes as they move about yet we perceive them as remaining the same size and shape. For example, a car doesn't grow smaller as it speeds away, even though its shape on your retina grows smaller and smaller. A door doesn't become a trapezoid as you walk through it, even though that's what happens to its shape on your retina. These are examples of how perceptions remain constant, a phenomenon called perceptual constancy.

Perceptual constancy refers to our tendency to perceive sizes, shapes, brightness, and colors as remaining the same even though their physical characteristics are constantly changing.

We'll discuss four kinds of perceptual constancy—size, shape, brightness, and color.

Size Constancy

Imagine a world in which you perceived that every car, person, or animal became smaller as it moved away. However, we are spared from coping with so much stimulus change by perceptual constancy, one type of which is size constancy.

Size constancy refers to our tendency to perceive objects as remaining the same size even when their images on the retina are continually growing or shrinking.

As a car drives away, it projects a smaller and smaller image on your retina (left figure). Although the retinal image grows smaller, you do not perceive the car as shrinking because of size constancy. A similar process happens as a car drives toward you.

As the same car drives closer, notice in the right figure how it projects a larger image on your retina. However, because of size constancy, you do not perceive the car as becoming larger.

Size constancy is something you have learned from experience with moving objects. You have learned that objects do not increase or decrease in size as they move about. For example, an individual who was blind since birth and had his vision restored as an adult, looked out a fourth story window and reported seeing tiny creatures moving on the sidewalk. Because he had not learned size constancy, he did not know the tiny creatures were full-size people (Gregory, 1974).

We also perceive shapes as remaining the same.

Shape Constancy

Each time you move a book, its image on your retina changes from a rectangle to a trapezoid. However, you see the book's shape as remaining the same because of shape constancy.

Shape constancy refers to your tendency to perceive an object as retaining its same shape even though when you view it from different angles its shape is continually changing its image on the retina.

The figure below shows that when you look down at a rectangular book, it projects a rectangular shape on your retina.

However, if you move the book farther away, it projects trapezoidal shapes on your retina, but you still perceive the book as rectangular because of shape constancy.

Brightness and Color Constancy

If you look into your dimly lit closet, all the brightly colored clothes will appear dull and grayish. However, because of brightness and color constancy, you still perceive colors and have no trouble selecting a red shirt.

Brightness constancy refers to the tendency to perceive brightness as remaining the same in changing illumination.

Color constancy refers to the tendency to perceive colors as remaining stable despite differences in lighting.

For example, if you looked at this young girl's sweater in bright sunlight, it would be a bright yellow.

However, if you looked at her same yellow sweater in dim light, you would still perceive the color as a shade of yellow, although it is duller. Because of color constancy, colors seem about the same even when lighting conditions change.

However, if the light is very dim, objects will appear mostly gray because you lose color vision in very dim light.

Perceptual constancy is important because it transforms a potentially ever-changing, chaotic world into one with stability and comforting sameness.

Our next perceptual puzzle is how our eyes can see only two-dimensional images but our brain can transform them into a three-dimensional world.

Binocular Depth Cues

How can you see in three dimensions?

Normally, movies are shown in only two dimensions, height and width. But if you have ever seen a movie in 3-D (three dimensions: height, width, and depth), you know too well the feeling of watching objects or animals come leaping off the screen so realistically that you duck or turn your head. Although 3-D movies are very exciting, they are relatively rare because they are costly to produce and usually require the audience to wear uncomfortable glasses. You may not have realized that your eyes automatically give you a free, no-glasses, 3-D view of the world. And the amazing part of seeing in 3-D is that everything projected on the retina is in only two dimensions, height and width, which means that your eye and brain somehow add the third dimension—depth.

Depth perception refers to the ability of your eye and brain to add a third dimension, depth, to all visual perceptions, even though images projected on the retina are in only two dimensions, height and width.

The object on the left has been given a three-dimensional look by making it seem to have depth. It is impossible for most sighted people to imagine a world without depth, since they rely heavily on depth perception to move about and locate objects in space. The cues for depth perception are divided into two major classes: binocular and monocular.

Binocular depth cues depend upon the movement of both eyes (*bi* means two: *ocular* means eye).

We'll start with two binocular cues, convergence and retinal disparity.

Convergence

When you have an eye exam, the doctor usually asks you to follow the end of her finger as she holds it a few feet away and then slowly moves it closer until it touches your nose. This is a test for convergence.

Convergence refers to a binocular cue for depth perception based on signals sent from muscles that turn the eyes. To focus on near or approaching objects, these muscles turn the eyes inward, toward the nose. The brain uses the signals sent by these muscles to determine the distance of the object.

The woman in the photo at right is demonstrating the ultimate in convergence as she looks at the fly on her nose. You can experience convergence by holding a finger in front of your nose and slowly bringing it closer to your nose. The reason your finger appears to move closer to your nose is because the muscles that are turning the eyes inward produce signals corresponding to convergence. The more your eyes turn inward or converge, the nearer the object appears in space. The woman in the photo knows the fly is on her nose because of convergent clues from her turned-in eyes.

The second binocular cue comes from having an eye on each side of your face.

Retinal Disparity

One reason it's an advantage to have an eye on each side of your face is that it gives each eye a slightly different view of the world and thus provides another binocular cue for depth perception called retinal disparity.

Retinal disparity refers to a binocular depth cue that depends on the distance between the eyes. Because of their different positions, each eye receives a slightly different image. The difference between the right and left eyes' images is the retinal disparity. The brain interprets a large retinal disparity to mean a close object, and a small retinal disparity to mean a distant object.

The figure at the left shows how retinal disparity occurs: The difference between the image seen by the left eye (1) versus the one seen by the right eye (2) results in retinal disparity (3).

1. Left eye sees a slightly different image of the fly.

3. Brain combines the two slightly different images from left and right eyes and gives us a perception of depth.

2. Right eye sees a slightly different image of the fly.

Another example of retinal disparity occurs when viewers wear special glasses to watch a 3-D movie, which has width, height, and depth. Standard 3-D glasses have two different-colored lenses—a red lens and a green lens. The brain receives two slightly different images of a scene: The right eye sees the scene through a red lens, and the left eye sees the same scene through a green lens. The brain automatically combines the slightly different red and green images to give us the feeling of depth—for example, seeing a mad dog jump out at us from the movie screen.

Individuals having only one eye still have depth perception because there are a number of one-eyed, or monocular, cues for depth perception, which we'll explain next.

E. Depth Perception

Monocular Depth Cues

Could a cyclops land an airplane?

A mythical creature called the Cyclops had only one eye in the middle of his forehead. Although a Cyclops would lack depth perception cues associated with retinal disparity, he would have depth perception cues associated with having one eye, or being monocular (*mon* means one). This means that a Cyclops or an individual with one good eye could land an airplane because of monocular depth cues.

Monocular depth cues are produced by signals from a single eye. Monocular cues most commonly arise from the way objects are arranged in the environment.

We'll show you seven of the most common monocular cues.

1 Linear Perspective

As you look down a long stretch of highway, the parallel lines formed by the sides of the road appear to come together, or converge, at a distant point. This convergence is a cue for distance and is called linear perspective.

Linear perspective is a monocular depth cue that results as parallel lines come together, or converge, in the distance.

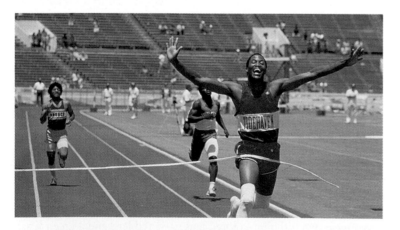

2 Relative Size

You expect the runners in the photo above to be the same size. However, since the runner on the right appears larger, you perceive him as closer, while the runner on the left appears smaller and, thus, farther away. The relative size of objects is a cue for distance.

Relative size is a monocular cue for depth that results when we expect two objects to be the same size and they are not. In that case, the larger of the two objects will appear closer and the smaller will appear farther away.

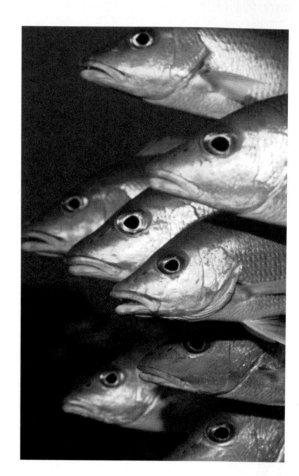

3 Interposition

Even though the fish in the photo above are all about the same size, you have no difficulty perceiving which fish are in front and which are in back. You can identify which fish are closest to you and which are farthest away by using the depth cue of overlap, which is called interposition.

Interposition is a monocular cue for depth perception that comes into play when objects overlap. The overlapping object appears closer and the object that is overlapped appears farther away.

4 *Light and Shadow*

Notice how the brightly lit edges of the footprints appear closer, while the shadowy imprint in the sand appears to recede. Also, the sunny side of the sand dune seems closer while the back side in shadows appears farther away. The depth cues shown here involve the interplay of light and shadows.

Light and shadow make up monocular cues for depth perception: Brightly lit objects appear closer, while objects in shadows appear farther away.

5 *Texture Gradient*

You can't help but notice how the wide, detailed surface cracks in the mud seem closer while the less detailed and narrower cracks appear farther away. These sharp changes in surface details are depth cues created by texture gradients.

Texture gradient is a monocular depth cue in which areas with sharp, detailed texture are interpreted as being closer, and those with less sharpness and poorer detail are perceived as more distant.

6 *Atmospheric Perspective*

One of the depth cues you may have overlooked is created by changes in the atmosphere. For example, both the man sitting on the chair and the edge of the cliff appear much closer than the fog-shrouded hills and landscape in the background. These depth cues are created by changes in the atmosphere.

Atmospheric perspective is a monocular depth cue that is created by the presence of dust, smog, clouds, or water vapor. We perceive clearer objects as being nearer and perceive hazy or cloudy objects as being farther away.

7 *Motion Parallax*

In this photo taken from a moving train, notice how the objects that appear to be speeding by—blurry telephone poles, tracks, dry grass, and railroad ties—seem to be much closer, while objects that appear to be barely moving— the large tree and the apartment house—seem much farther away. These depth cues come from the way we perceive motion.

Motion parallax is a monocular depth cue based on the speed of moving objects. We perceive objects that appear to be moving at high speed as closer to us than those moving more slowly or appearing stationary.

Now you can understand how a Cyclops could land a plane. Although people with only one good eye lack binocular depth cues, they have all these monocular cues to perceive depth and distance accurately.

We turn next to occasions where our perceptual system is fooled, and we see things that are not there. Welcome to the world of illusions.

F. Illusions

Perceptions versus Illusions

What is an illusion?

There are two reasons why much of the time our perceptions of cars, people, food, trees, animals, furniture, and professors are reasonably accurate reflections (not copies) of reality. First, we inherit similar sensory systems whose information is processed and interpreted by similar areas of the brain. However, damage to sensory areas of the brain can result in very distorted perceptions, such as the neglect syndrome (p. 79), in which people do not perceive one side of their body or one side of their environment. Another reason our perceptions are reasonably accurate is that we learn from common experience about the sizes, shapes, and colors of objects. But we've already discussed how perceptions can be biased or distorted by previous emotional and learning experiences such as perceiving dogs differently after being bitten by one. Another way that perceptions can be distorted is to change the actual perceptual cues so that you perceive something improbable, which is called an illusion.

An *illusion* is a perceptual experience in which we perceive an image as being so strangely distorted that, in reality, it cannot and does not exist. An illusion is created by manipulating the perceptual cues so that our brains can no longer correctly interpret space, size, and depth cues.

For example, if you look at the right end of this tuning fork, it appears to have two prongs but it you look at the left end, it appears to have three prongs. You're looking at a figure that most of us cannot draw, because it seems impossible.

An *impossible figure* is a perceptual experience in which a drawing seems to defy basic geometric laws.

One reason the tuning fork appears impossible to figure out and almost impossible to draw has to do with your previous experience with line drawings in books. Because you have seen many three-dimensional objects drawn in books, you tend to perceive the left side of the tuning fork as being three-dimensional (three forks) but you tend to perceive the right side as being two-dimensional (two forks). Later on in the Cultural Diversity feature, you'll learn why Africans can easily draw this impossible figure while most college professors cannot (Coren & Ward, 1993).

In this example, we perceive an illusion because the tuning fork is drawn to confuse our previous experiences with two- and three-dimensional objects.

One of the oldest illusions that has proven very difficult to explain is the moon illusion.

Moon Illusion

The moon illusion has intrigued people for centuries because it is so impressive. The left photo shows that when a full moon is near the horizon, it appears (or gives the illusion of being) as much as 50% larger than when it is high in the sky (right photo). Here's the interesting part: You perceive this 50% increase in size even though the size of both moons on your retinas is exactly the same.

For the past 50 years, researchers have proposed different explanations for the moon illusion and no one explanation seems accepted by all. One current explanation is that the moon illusion involves several perceptual cues. Distance cues make the moon on the horizon look larger because it appears to be farther away. Size cues make the moon on the horizon appear larger because of contrast with one high in the sky. Atmospheric perspective makes the moon high in the sky appear smaller because of surrounding clouds or haze (Plug & Ross, 1994). However, other researchers suggest that the moon illusion also depends partly on our experience of watching the moon seem to shrink in size as it rises into the heavens (Reed, 1996). As of this writing, there are several theories to explain the moon illusion.

Besides naturally occurring illusions, there are others that humans have created. One of the most interesting illusions comes from looking inside the Ames room.

In the Ames room (left photo) you perceive the boy on the right to be twice as tall as the woman on the left. In fact, the boy is smaller than the woman but appears larger because of the design of the Ames room.

The *Ames room*, named after its designer, Albert Ames, shows that our perception of size can be distorted by changing depth cues.

The reason the boy appears to be twice as tall as the woman is that the room has a peculiar shape and you are looking in from a fixed peephole. To see how the Ames room manipulates your depth cues, look at the diagram of the Ames room in the drawing on the right. If you view the Ames room from the fixed peephole, it appears rectangular and matches your previous experience with rooms, which are usually rectangular. However, if you view the Ames room from above, you discover that it is oddly shaped: the left corner is twice as far away from the peephole as the right corner. This means that the woman is actually twice as far away from you as the boy. Since you expect the room to be rectangular, you misperceive the distance cues and, thus, misperceive the size of the boy and woman.

The next two illusions either manipulate our perceptual cues or rely too much on our previous perceptual experiences.

Ponzo Illusion

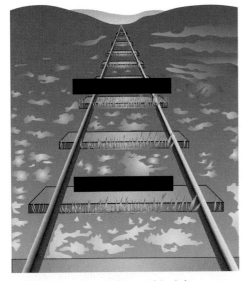

In the figure above, the top black bar appears to be much wider than the bottom black bar. However, if you measure these two bars you will discover that they are exactly the same size. This is the *Ponzo illusion*, which I clearly remember measuring the first time I saw it because I couldn't believe the bars were the same size. You perceive the top bar as being farther away, and you have learned from experience that if two objects appear to be the same size but one is farther away, the more distant object must be larger; thus, the top bar appears wider.

Müller-Lyer Illusion

The figures at the left and right illustrate the *Müller-Lyer illusion.* Notice that the length of the left arrow appears noticeable shorter than the right arrow. However, if you measure them, you'll prove that the arrows are of equal length.

One explanation for this illusion is that you are relying on size cues learned from your previous experience with corners of rooms. You have learned that if a corner of a room extends outward, it is closer; this experience distorts your perception so that the left arrow appears to be shorter. In contrast, you have learned that if a corner of a room recedes inward, it is farther away, and this experience makes you perceive the right arrow as longer. Illusions are fun, but what have we learned?

Learning from Illusions

Illusions teach us that in order to perceive the world reasonably accurately, we rely heavily on a set of proven perceptual cues for size, shape, and depth. However, if these perceptual cues are manipulated, our otherwise reliable perceptual processes can be deceived; the result is an illusion. Also, illusions emphasize that perception is a very active process, in which we continually rely on and apply previous experiences with objects when perceiving new situations. For example, you'll discover later how the current billion-dollar entertainment industry manipulates the perceptual rule of closure to create movies, whose motion is a brilliant illusion. After the Concept Review, we'll discuss a form of perception that the United States Congress almost outlawed.

CONCEPT REVIEW

1. This figure illustrates the concept of the _____, which is defined as the intensity level of a stimulus such that a person will have a 50% chance of detecting it.

2. The smallest increase or decrease in the intensity of a stimulus that a person can detect is called a (a)_____. The increase in intensity of a stimulus needed to produce a just noticeable difference grows in proportion to the intensity of the initial stimulus; this is called (b)_____ law.

3. Our first awareness of sensory information, in the form of meaningless bits of information, is called a (a)_____. When many bits of sensory information have been assembled into a meaningful image, it is called a (b)_____, which can be biased or distorted by our unique set of experiences.

4. Early psychologists discovered a set of rules or principles that our brains use to automatically group or arrange stimuli into perceptual experiences. These early researchers, who were called _____ psychologists, disagreed with other early psychologists, who were called structuralists.

5. You automatically separate an image into a more dominant, detailed figure and a less detailed background according to the _____ rule.

6. You fill in missing parts to form a complete image as a result of the _____ rule.

7. You see this image as formed by an oval and an overlying square because of the _____ rule.

8. You divide each line of this figure into separate groups of objects according to the _____ rule.

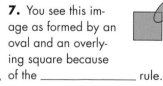

9. In this figure, you see a blue numeral 2 instead of light and dark blue circles because of the _____ rule.

10. In this figure, you see a continuous line from A to B, rather than a line from A to C, following the _____ rule.

11. Although physical qualities of stimuli may change, you may perceive them as remaining the same because of (a)_____. For example, as a car drives away from you, its image on your retina becomes smaller but you know that the car does not shrink in size because of (b)_____ constancy. When you close a door, its shape on your retina changes from a rectangle to a trapezoid, but you perceive the door as remaining the same because of (c)_____ constancy. If you had a bright red car, it would appear red in bright light and still appear to be red in dimmer light because of (d)_____ constancy.

12. Cues for depth perception that depend on both eyes are called (a)_____ cues. Cues for depth perception that depend on a single eye are called (b)_____ cues. The binocular cue that occurs when your eyes move inward to track a fly landing on your nose is called (c)_____. The binocular cue that occurs when each eye receives a slightly different image is called (d)_____.

13. Monocular cues for depth perception include: cues from overlapping objects, called (a)_____; cues from two parallel lines converging, called (b)_____; cues from larger and smaller images, called (c)_____; cues from the presence of dust and smog, called (d)_____; and cues from nearer and farther objects moving at different speeds, called (e)_____.

14. If perceptual cues are so changed that our brains can no longer interpret them correctly, we perceive a distorted image of reality, called an (a)_____. Such a distorted perception illustrates that perception is an active process and that we rely on previous (b)_____ when perceiving new situations.

Answers: *1. absolute threshold; 2. (a) just noticeable difference, (b) Weber's; 3. (a) sensation, (b) perception; 4. Gestalt; 5. figure-ground; 6. closure; 7. simplicity; 8. proximity; 9. similarity; 10. continuity; 11. (a) perceptual constancy, (b) size, (c) shape, (d) color; 12. (a) binocular, (b) monocular, (c) convergence, (d) retinal disparity; 13. (a) interposition, (b) linear perspective, (c) relative size, (d) atmospheric perspective, (e) motion parallax; 14. (a) illusion, (b) experiences.*

G. Research Focus: Subliminal Perception Can "Unsensed Messages" Change Behavior?

Why did people buy more popcorn?

Sometimes research questions come from unusual places—in this case, a movie theatre. In the late 1950s, moviegoers were reported to have bought 50% more popcorn and 18% more Coca-Cola when the words "Eat popcorn" and "Drink Coca-Cola" were projected subliminally (1/3000 of a second) during the regular movie (McConnell et al., 1958). The concern that advertisers might change consumers' buying habits without their knowledge prompted the United States Congress to consider banning any form of subliminal advertising. Congress did not take legislative action, because subliminal advertising proved to be ineffective (Pratkanis, 1992). However, history seems to be repeating itself as advertisers now claim that subliminal tapes can change specific behaviors (Harmon, 1995).

Changing Specific Behaviors

At the beginning of this module, we told you about Maria, who, like millions of other Americans, purchased an audiotape because it claimed to contain subliminal messages that would effortlessly change her behavior.

Subliminal messages are brief auditory or visual messages that are presented below the absolute threshold, which means that there is less than a 50% chance that they will be perceived.

To answer the research question, "Can subliminal messages change specific behaviors?" researchers conducted a well-designed experiment that used a double-blind procedure.

Method. For several weeks, subjects listened to two different tapes titled either "Improve Self-Esteem" or "Improve Memory." Then they rated any improvement in these behaviors.

Double-blind procedure. Researchers had to control for any possible placebo effects, such as subjects' showing improvement because they believed they were hearing powerful subliminal messages. Therefore, subjects were not told which subliminal messages the tapes contained. For example, some tapes labeled "Improve Memory" contained subliminal messages for improving memory, while others contained subliminal messages for improving self-esteem. Thus, by using a double-blind procedure, subjects never knew if the tapes' subliminal messages actually matched the tapes' labels.

Results. About 50% of the subjects reported improvements in either self-esteem or memory. However, subjects reported improvements in behavior based on what the *tape's label promised* rather than on what the subliminal messages were. For example, a subject who listened to a tape labeled "Improve Self-Esteem" reported improvements in self-esteem even though the tape contained subliminal messages for improving memory. These results suggest a self-fulfilling prophecy at work.

Self-fulfilling prophecies involve having strong beliefs about changing some behavior and then acting, unknowingly, to change that behavior.

Researchers concluded that subliminal messages in self-help tapes did not affect the behavior they were designed to change. Instead, any changes in behavior resulted from listeners' beliefs that the tapes would be effective (Greenwald et al., 1991).

Although subliminal messages are ineffective in changing specific behaviors (Harris et al., 1996), there is evidence that your emotional state can unknowingly or subliminally influence perception.

Changing Perceptions

When you're in a happy mood, do you unknowingly or subliminally notice more smily faces? This is similar to the question that researchers asked: Would subjects who were in a happy mood perceive "happy" words faster than "sad" words and vice versa (Niedenthal & Setterlund, 1994)?

Method. Subjects were put into happy or sad moods by listening to music known to induce the desired emotional states.

After being put into a sad or happy mood, subjects sat in front of a screen that projected strings of words, such as joy, habit, hurt, code, comedy, and weep. As each word appeared, subjects rated it as happy (joy, comedy), sad (hurt, weep), or neutral (habit, code). We have simplified the results by reporting only a representative sample of the data.

Time in Milliseconds to Recognize Words

530	Happy words
592	Sad words

Results. As shown in the graph above, researchers found that subjects in *happy moods* perceived *happy words* significantly faster than subjects in sad moods. Not shown is that subjects in *sad moods* also perceived *sad words* faster than subjects in happy moods.

Researchers concluded that, without awareness and at a subliminal level, the particular emotional states that we are in may affect our perceptions. Researchers suggested that these findings may explain what occurs in real life: When we are in a happy state, we are more likely to notice and perceive the things that bring us joy rather than things that make us sad. These studies indicate that our perceptions can be influenced by psychological factors, such as emotional states, at a subliminal level and often without our awareness (Niedenthal, 1992; Niedenthal & Setterlund, 1994).

Not only can emotional states unknowingly affect our perceptions, but so can cultural values and experiences, which we'll examine next.

H. Cultural Diversity: Different Perceptions
How Does Culture Influence Perceptions?

CULTURAL INFLUENCES

If you visit ethnic sections of large U.S. cities, such as Chinatown or Little Italy, or visit foreign countries, you become aware of cultural differences and influences.

Cultural influences are persuasive pressures that encourage members of a particular society or ethnic group to conform to shared behaviors, values, and beliefs.

No one doubts that cultural influences affect the way people eat, dress, talk, and socialize. But you are less likely to notice how cultural influences also affect how we perceive things in our environments.

For example, cultural anthropologists, who travel to villages or towns to study behaviors in other cultures, have reported many intriguing examples of how cultural experiences influence perceptual processes. We'll begin with an intriguing finding of natives' being unable to perceive common objects in photos.

PERCEPTION OF IMAGES

A cultural anthropologist showed African natives a black-and-white photo of a cow and a dog, two animals the natives were very familiar with. But when the natives looked at the photos, they seemed very puzzled, Their expressions suggested that the anthropologist was lying about the photos showing a cow and dog. The anthropologist then showed the natives a color photo of the same two animals.

The natives smiled and nodded in recognition and pointed to the cow and dog (Deregowski, 1980).

Because the people of this tribe had never seen black-and-white photos, they had no experience in recognizing animals in this format. But when they were shown color photographs, which presented a world more similar to the one they experienced, they immediately recognized the cow and dog. Presumably, they drew on their everyday experiences with objects in full color and could relate what they saw in the photo to what they saw in the real world. This is an example of how cultural experiences can influence relatively basic perceptual skills, such as the ability to recognize familiar images presented in different pictorial formats.

Another example of how culture influences perception is what happens if you are raised in a dense jungle.

PERCEPTION OF CONSTANCY AND DEPTH

A researcher was studying a tribe of African pygmies who lived in a dense jungle that limited their visual experiences to relatively short distances. One day the researcher took Kenge, one of the pygmies, out of the forest for the first time. As they were driving across a broad plain, Kenge looked into the distance, where a herd of about a hundred buffalo were grazing, and asked what kind of insects they were. The researcher replied that they were not insects but very large buffalo (Turnbull, 1961).

If we assume that the hardware or wiring of Kenge's visual system is virtually identical to ours, then the most likely reason for his poorly developed size constancy and depth perception was his limited visual experience with objects in the far distance. If you had spent your entire life in a dense jungle, where vision is limited to distances measured in feet, you, too, would be perplexed by your first sight of objects miles away.

Let's turn to a common example in our culture to show that what you take for granted people in other cultures find strange.

PERCEPTION OF MOTION

For just a moment, look at the cartoon drawings of the dog (below left) and notice what its tail is doing. Then look at the female figure (right) and describe what the figure is doing. Most people immediately perceive what is happening: the dog is wagging its tail and the figure is spinning.

Because of our Western cultural experience with cartoon drawings, we have learned to recognize that certain kinds of repeated images (the dog's tail) and certain lines and circles (the figure) indicate movement. We have become so accustomed to seeing these kinds of cartoon drawings that the tail and the dancer really do seem to be in motion.

However, people from non-Western cultures, who have no experience with these cartoon drawings, do not perceive the dog's tail or the figure as moving. Non-westerners see only an unusual dog who has three tails and a strange figure that is surrounded by circles; they do not perceive any indication of movement in these drawings (Friedman & Stevenson, 1980). This is a perfect example of how Western cultural influences shape our perceptions, often without our realizing it.

If part of your cultural experience involves seeing 3-dimensional objects in books, you won't be able to draw the next figure.

Perception of 3 Dimensions

Can you draw this figure?
This is the same impossible figure that you saw earlier and that changes almost magically back and forth between a two-pronged and three-pronged tuning fork. The illusion is that the middle fork is impossible because it seems to come out of nowhere.

When people from industrialized nations try to draw this figure from memory, they almost surely fail. What is interesting is that Africans who have no formal education do not see any illusion but perceive only a two-dimensional pattern of flat lines, which they find easy to draw from memory. In contrast, people with formal education, who have spent years looking at three-dimensional repre-sentations in books, perceive this object as having three dimensions, a pattern that is almost impossi-ble to draw (Coren & Ward, 1989).

Perception of Beauty

Do you think she's attractive?
In the past, when Burmese girls were about 5 years old, they put a brass coil one-third-inch wide around their necks. As they grew older, girls added more brass coils until they had from 19 to 25 wrapped around their necks. The appearance of long necks caused by the brass coils was perceived as being very attractive by Burmese peo-ple, who live in southeast Asia. This custom eventually declined because neck coils were no longer considered beautiful, just cruel and uncomfort-able. Recently, however, the custom has been revived because now tourists come and pay $12.00 to see and take photos of women with brass neck coils (Stevens, 1994).

This example illustrates how cul-tural values influence our perceptions of personal beauty.

Perceptual Sets

Do you think this body is beautiful?
From our previous cultural experiences with images and objects, we develop certain expec-tations about how things should be; these expectations are called perceptual sets.

Perceptual sets are learned expectations that are based on our personal, social, or cultural experiences. These expectations automatically add information, meaning, or feel-ings to our perceptions and thus change or bias our perceptions.

For example, as you look at this bodybuilder, you auto-matically add personal feelings, such as like/dislike, approve/disapprove, as well as impressions of physical characteristics: height, about 6 feet; and weight, about 225 pounds. Be-cause of your perceptual set for bodybuilders, you expect them to be large, and so you will be sur-prised to learn that this bodybuilder is only 5 feet 2 inches tall and weighs 182 pounds. One function of perceptual sets is to automatically fill in infor-mation or add feelings that can greatly modify our perceptions.

These examples show that we rarely perceive the world exactly as it is. Rather, our perceptions can be changed, biased, or distorted by experiences, such as cultural influences and perceptual sets.

Next, we'll discuss a controversial kind of per-ception that goes by the initials ESP.

I. ESP: Extrasensory Perception

Definition and Controversy

What are psychic powers?

No one doubts your ability to receive information through one or more of your major senses—seeing, hearing, tasting, smelling, and touching—because this ability has been repeatedly demonstrated and reliably measured. In comparison, most research psychologists do not believe that you can receive information outside normal sensory channels, which is called extrasensory perception, because this phenomenon has neither been repeatedly demonstrated nor reliably measured (Bem & Honorton, 1994).

Extrasensory perception (ESP) is a group of psychic experiences that involve perceiving or sending information (images) outside normal sensory processes or channels. ESP includes four general abilities—telepathy, precognition, clairvoyance, and psychokinesis. Telepathy is the ability to transfer one's thoughts to another or to read the thoughts of others. Precognition is the ability to foretell events. Clairvoyance is the ability to perceive events or objects that are out of sight. Psychokinesis is the ability to exert mind over matter—for example, by moving objects without touching them. Together, these psychic powers or extrasensory perceptions are called psi phenomena.

The term *psi* refers to the processing of information or transfer of energy by methods that have no known physical or biological mechanisms and that seem to stretch the laws of physics.

According to a Gallup survey of over 1,200 adult Americans, 49% reported believing in ESP, and 36% reported believing in communication between minds without using regular senses. In addition, from 25% to 50% of American adults claim to have had one or more extrasensory experience (Gallup & Newport, 1991). The reason so many Americans but so few research psychologists believe in ESP is that researchers demand hard, scientific evidence rather than testimonials based on personal beliefs or experiences.

When we discussed testimonials earlier (p. 30), we pointed out that they seem convincing because they are based on personal experiences. However, there are many examples of firmly held beliefs that, when evaluated with scientifically designed experiments, were found to be unproven. For example, researchers found that 35% to 98% of individuals who gave testimonials about becoming ill or getting well after taking a pill, dietary supplement, or herb had unknowingly taken a placebo, a medically useless treatment (Dodes, 1997; Turner et al., 1994). Scientists know that testimonials are too prone to error and bias to be accepted as evidence for something as unusual as ESP. Because psi phenomena are outside normal senses, defy physical and biological explanations, and stretch the laws of physics, researchers demand hard, scientific evidence as proof of its existence (Alcock, 1995; Kurtz, 1995).

Another reason researchers demand reliable and repeatable evidence to prove the existence of ESP is because some demonstrations of psi phenomena have involved trickery or questionable methodology. For example, at least one well-known researcher has used trickery and magic to duplicate many of the better-known demonstrations of ESP, such as mentally bending spoons, starting broken watches, moving objects, and reading messages in sealed envelopes. This researcher's name is the Amazing Randi.

Trickery and Magic

According to James Randi, known as the Amazing Randi (on the left in the photo), and others acquainted with magic, much of what passes for extrasensory perception is actually done through trickery (Steiner, 1989; Ybarra, 1991). For example, to show how easily people may be fooled, Randi sent two young magicians (also in the photo) to a lab that studied psychic phenomena. Instead of admitting they were magicians, the pair claimed to have psychic powers and to perform psychic feats, such as mentally bending keys and making images on film. After 120 hours of testing, the lab's researchers, who had carefully conducted and supervised the ESP demonstrations, concluded that the two did indeed have genuine psychic abilities. The lab's researchers were not expecting trickery, had not taken steps to prevent it, and were thus totally fooled into believing they were witnessing ESP.

Several years ago, a two-hour television show under the supervision of James Randi offered $100,000

to anyone who could demonstrate psychic powers. Twelve people claimed to have psychic powers, such as identifying through interviews the astrological signs under which people were born, seeing the auras of people standing behind screens, and correctly reading Zener cards (showing five symbols: square, circle, wavy lines, plus sign, or a star). Of the 12 people who claimed psychic powers, none scored above chance on any of these tasks (Steiner, 1989). Although people may claim psychic powers, most cannot demonstrate such powers under controlled conditions, which eliminates trickery, magic, and educated guessing.

James Randi has repeatedly shown that people untrained in recognizing trickery cannot distinguish between psychic feats and skillful tricks. To eliminate any trickery, claims of psychic abilities must withstand the scrutiny of scientific investigation. Let's see how a controlled ESP experiment is designed and conducted.

ESP Experiment

How do researchers study psychic abilities?

One of the more common demonstrations of psychic ability is to use the Zener cards, which are five symbols—circle, wave, square, plus sign, and star (on right). A researcher would hold up the back of one card and ask the subject to guess the symbol on the front. If there were a hundred trials, the subject could correctly identify 20 symbols simply by guessing (chance level). However, if a subject correctly identified 25 symbols, which is above chance level, does that mean the subject has psychic powers? This is a simplified example of a very complicated statistical question: How can we determine whether a person has psychic powers or is just guessing correctly? Therefore, to solve one major problem in psi research—how to eliminate guesswork and trickery—researchers use a state-of-the-art method called the Ganzfeld procedure.

The *Ganzfeld procedure* is a controlled method for eliminating trickery, error, and bias while testing telepathic communication between a sender—the person who sends the message—and a receiver—the person who receives the message.

In the Ganzfeld procedure, the receiver is placed in a reclining chair in an acoustically isolated room. Translucent ping-pong ball halves are taped over the eyes, and headphones are placed over the ears. The sender, who is isolated in a separate soundproof room, concentrates for about 30 minutes on a target, which is a randomly selected visual stimulus, such as a photo or art print (right figure). At the end of this period, the receiver is shown four different stimuli and asked which one most closely matches what the receiver was imagining. Because there are four stimuli, the receiver will guess the target correctly 25% of the time. Thus, if the receiver correctly identifies the target more than 25% of the time, it is above chance level and indicates something else is occurring, perhaps extrasensory perception (Bem & Honorton, 1994).

We have described the Ganzfeld procedure in great detail to illustrate the precautions that researchers must take to rule out the potential for trickery, error, and bias. The next question is perhaps the most interesting of all: What have researchers learned from the recent Ganzfeld experiments?

Status of ESP

What is the scientific status of ESP?

Several years ago, one of psychology's most prestigious academic journals (*Psychological Bulletin*) published an article on ESP for the very first time. This article, whose data supported the occurrence of mental telepathy, had been carefully scrutinized for any methodological errors by four prominent researchers before acceptance for publication. The article's two noted researchers, Daryl Bem and Charles Honorton (1994), acknowledge that most academic psychologists do not accept the existence of psi phenomena, such as mental telepathy. However, Bem and Honorton claim that by using the Ganzfeld procedure, which we described above, they have adhered to rigid scientific methodology and found evidence for mental telepathy, which they call an "anomalous process of information transfer." In the Ganzfeld procedure, a receiver usually chooses between four stimuli, so the chance of correctly guessing is one out of four, or 25%. As shown in the graph above, in 11 Ganzfeld experiments the subjects guessed correctly 35% of the time, which Bem and Honorton argue is large enough to be of both theoretical interest and potential practical importance.

Their study, however, has been criticized because the four stimuli may not have been truly randomized, which increased their chances of being correctly guessed (Hyman, 1994). Another critic (Blackmore, 1994) adds that Bem and Honorton's work is a good start but suggests we wait and see if these results can be replicated by other researchers. Science has a powerful weapon called replication, which simply says, if results can't be repeated, they probably aren't so. Psychologists will wait and see if these psi results can be replicated. As of this writing, there were no new reports of these results being replicated. However, there was a report on ESP research supported by the Central Intelligence Agency (CIA).

In 1970, the CIA supported a research program on paranormal phenomena that was later supported by the Defense Intelligence Agency and went on until it was terminated in 1995. Researchers who evaluated this lengthy research program concluded that evidence for psychic abilities had not been demonstrated because of problems in the way research was conducted (Hyman, 1996a, 1996b; Mumford et al., 1995). These researchers said that more and better studies were needed to prove that there is any hard scientific evidence that psi phenomena exist. And so we must wait for more and better studies.

Next we'll discuss several other forms of perception, one that involves using illusions to make movies and one that involves creating a new kind of perception called virtual reality.

J. Application: Creating Perceptions

Can we create new perceptions?

About 20,000 years ago, early humans (Homo sapiens) created some of the earliest perceptions by using earth pigments to paint prancing horses and dueling rhinos on the sides of their caves (Fritz, 1995). About 3,000 years ago, Egyptians created some of the most impressive perceptions with their enormous and long-lasting pyramids. Today, computer researchers are developing new perceptions that create a three-dimensional world with virtual reality. We'll discuss how the more common perceptual experiences are created, beginning with one used in lights on billboards.

Phi Movement

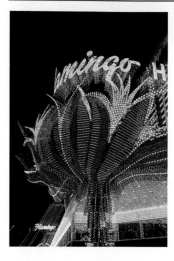

The father of the flashing lights used later in billboards, movie marquees, and traffic arrows was a distinguished Gestalt psychologist named Max Wertheimer. In the early 1900s, Wertheimer spent a considerable amount of time in a darkened room, where he experimented with flashing first one light and then a second light that was positioned some distance away. He discovered that if the time between flashing one light and then the other was adjusted just right, the two flashes were actually perceived as a moving spot of light rather than as two separate flashes. He called this illusion *phi movement*.

Phi movement refers to the illusion that lights that are actually stationary seem to be moving. This illusionary movement, which today is called apparent motion, is created by flashing closely positioned stationary lights at regular intervals.

Each time you pass a traffic arrow composed of flashing lights or perceive a moving string of lights used in an advertising sign, you are seeing a practical application of Wertheimer's phi movement. This phi movement was one of the first examples of how ordinary visual stimuli could be adjusted to create an illusion.

Another example of creating wonderful moving illusions with stationary visual stimuli came from the remarkable genius of Thomas Edison, who invented motion pictures in 1893.

Movies and Illusions

If you attend a track meet and watch a 100-meter race and then, minutes later, watch a videotaped replay of the same race, you would perceive motion produced in two very different ways. One kind of motion is real, while the other is an illusion.

Real motion refers to your perception of any stimulus or object that actually moves in space.

As you watch a live 100-meter race, you are perceiving real motion. However, when you watch a replay of that same race, you are seeing apparent motion.

Apparent motion refers to an illusion that a stimulus or object is moving in space when, in fact, the stimulus or object is stationary. The illusion of apparent motion is created by rapidly showing a series of stationary images, each of which has a slightly different position or posture than the one before.

The principle for creating apparent motion is deceptively simple and can be easily discovered by examining the positions of the runner's body in each frame of the time-lapse photo shown above.

Beginning on the left side of the photo, notice that each frame shows only a slight change in the position of the runner's body. However, if these frames were presented rapidly—for example, at the movie standard of 24 frames per second—you would perceive the illusion of an athlete running down the track.

In a series of ingenious experiments, researchers discovered that several complex mechanisms built into our visual system detect cues that produce the illusion of motion (Ramachandran & Anstis, 1986). One such cue is the closure principle, which means that our brains fill in the motion expected to occur between images that vary only slightly in position and are presented in rapid sequence. Without apparent motion, there would be no movies, television, or flip books.

Currently, researchers have developed a procedure that creates a three-dimensional perceptual experience of walking through a house, dissecting a frog, or doing complicated human surgery. This is the brave new world of virtual reality.

Virtual Reality

How can a surgeon practice?

The invention of the movie camera was revolutionary because it created a new perceptual experience: the illusion that still pictures moved. Currently, another perceptual revolution is underway, and it's called virtual reality.

Virtual reality refers to a perceptual experience of being inside an object, moving through an environment, or carrying out some action that is created or simulated by computer.

In a game-entertainment application of virtual reality, players wear special gloves that serve as pointers and look through special goggles that produce three-dimensional images, all of which are connected to a powerful computer program. By pointing at various images, moving a manipulator, or changing body posture, a person has the feeling of actually moving around in a three-dimensional computer-created space.

In a medical application of virtual reality, researchers are developing programs that will allow surgeons to practice their skills in surgical simulators on virtual cadavers

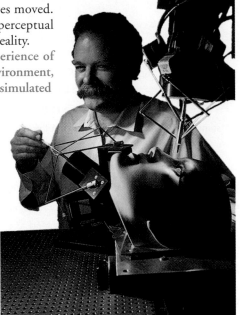

generated by computers. Such virtual reality programs will permit surgeons to operate with mechanical limbs on patients hundreds of miles away (Taubes, 1994). The photo shows a robotic arm that mimics everything the surgeon does while he or she manipulates a joy stick while looking through cameras that provide a three-dimensional view inside the model's (patient's) eye (Cowley et al., 1995). Currently, there are several robotic virtual reality devices under development that will allow surgeons to operate on microscopic body tissues or difficult-to-see areas in the brain (Rose et al., 1996; Rosenfeld, 1996).

In a psychological application of virtual reality, clients with phobias of spiders, flying, or heights are exposed to feared stimuli in a three-dimensional environment where everything appears very real. Therapists have reported good success in treating phobias with virtual reality therapy (Carlin et al., 1997).

Another area in which we spend a great deal of time, effort, and money to create perceptions involves our personal appearance.

First Impressions

Can you name these faces?

Social psychologists have discovered that facial features have a significant effect on our first impressions and perceptions of people. For example, researchers found that we perceive an attractive person as being more interesting, sociable, intelligent, outgoing, and kind (Eagly et al., 1991). Similarly, first impressions are also influenced by racial stereotypes, both positive and negative, based on physical features such as skin color and hair style. Hollywood hair stylists know that the kind, amount, color, and style of actors' hair can radically change their appearance and our impressions of them. In fact, they use different hair styles to match different roles. For example, look at the first three photos above and try to correctly identify each one of these famous personalities (answers at end).

Besides hair color and style, skin color has a considerable impact on first perceptions and impressions. To illustrate how skin color can greatly change your perceptions of people, look at the two photos above on the right and try to correctly identify these two famous

people. You may have guessed correctly that the two people are the actor Arnold Schwarzenegger of the United States and Queen Elizabeth of England. The editors of *Colors, the Multicultural Magazine*, published these computer-colored images to ask their readers: What percentage of your understanding of someone is formed by race? After looking at Queen Elizabeth with the skin color of an Indian and at Arnold Schwarzenegger with the skin color of an African American, you can judge for yourself how much race influences your impressions and perceptions of others. We'll discuss further how we perceive people and form impressions in Module 25.

The factors involved in forming first impressions as well as in creating moving lights, movies, and virtual reality illustrate an important, underlying principle of perception: Our perceptions, which may be changed or biased by personal experiences, are interpretations rather than exact copies of reality.

(Correct answers left to right: actress Marilyn Monroe, radio personality Howard Stern, actress Julia Roberts.)

SUMMARY TEST

A. PERCEPTUAL THRESHOLDS

1. We discussed three basic questions that psychologists ask about perception. Our first question—At what point are we aware of a stimulus?— can be answered by measuring the threshold of a stimulus, which is a point above which a stimulus is perceived and below which it is not. The intensity level at which a person has a 50% chance of perceiving the stimulus is called the _____.

2. Our second question—At what point do we know a stimulus intensity has increased or decreased?—can be answered by measuring the smallest increase or decrease in the intensity of a stimulus that a person can detect; this is called a (a) _____. It has been found that the increase in stimulus intensity needed to produce a just noticeable difference increases in proportion to the intensity of the initial stimulus; this is called (b) _____ law.

B. SENSATION VERSUS PERCEPTION

3. Our third question—How are meaningless sensations combined into meaningful perceptions?—can be answered by analyzing our own perceptual experiences. Our first awareness of some outside stimulus is called a (a) _____. This awareness results when some change in energy activates sensory receptors, which produce signals that, in turn, are transformed by the brain into meaningless sensory experiences. When many individual sensations are assembled into a meaningful experience, image, or pattern, it is called a (b) _____. The latter is not an exact replica of the real world but rather a copy that has been changed, biased, or distorted by our unique set of (c) _____. Our brain transforms sensations into perceptions instantaneously, automatically, and without our awareness.

4. The (a) _____ argued that we can explain how perceptions are formed by dividing perceptions into smaller and smaller elements. They believed that we combine basic elements to form a perception. In contrast, the (b) _____ psychologists replied that the formation of perceptions cannot be understood by simply breaking perceptions down into individual components and then studying how we reassemble them. They argued that "the whole is more than the sum of its parts," by which they meant that perceptions are more than a combination of individual elements. The Gestalt psychologists believed that the brain has rules for assembling perceptions, which they called principles of (c) _____.

C. RULES OF ORGANIZATION

5. Many of the rules of perceptual organization involve ways of grouping or arranging stimuli. According to one of these rules, the first thing we do is automatically separate an image into two parts: the more detailed feature of an image becomes the (a) _____ and the less detailed aspects become the (b) _____. According to the (c) _____ rule, stimuli tend to be organized in the most basic, elementary way. According to the (d _____ rule, stimuli that appear the same tend to be grouped together. According to the (e) _____ rule, stimuli that are near one another tend to be grouped together. According to the (f) _____ rule, stimuli that are arranged in a smooth line or curve tend to be perceived as forming a continuous path. According to the (g) _____ rule, we tend to fill in the missing parts of a figure and perceive it as complete.

D. PERCEPTUAL CONSTANCY

6. Although the size, shape, brightness, and color of objects are constantly changing, we tend to see them as remaining the same, a phenomenon that is called (a) _____. A person walking away does not appear to grow smaller, even though the image on the retina is decreasing in size, because of (b) _____ constancy. Even though the image of a door that is opened and closed changes on the retina from a rectangle to a trapezoid, we see it as retaining its rectangular outline because of (c) _____ constancy. Even though the color and brightness inside a car are altered when we drive from bright into dim light, we tend to see little change because of (d) _____ and _____ constancy.

E. DEPTH PERCEPTION

7. The visual system transforms the two-dimensional image (height and width) of stimuli projected onto the retina into a three-dimensional experience by adding depth. Cues for depth that are dependent on both eyes are called (a) _____; cues for depth that are dependent only on a single eye are called (b) _____. The binocular cue for depth that arises when muscles turn your eyes inward is called (c) _____. The binocular cue for depth arising because the two eyes send slightly different images to the brain is called (d) _____.

8. There are a number of monocular cues for depth. When an object appears closer because it overlaps another, the cue is called (a) _____. When parallel lines seem to stretch to a point at the horizon and create a sense of distance, the cue is called (b) _____. When two figures are expected to be of the same size but one is larger and thus appears closer, the cue is called (c) _____. If dust or smog makes objects appear hazy and thus farther away, the cue is called (d) _____. As texture changes from sharp and detailed to dull and monotonous, it creates the impression of distance; this cue is called (e) _____. The play of light and shadow gives objects a three-dimensional look, a cue that is called (f) _____. As you ride in a car, the impression that near objects are speeding by and far objects are barely moving is called (g) _____.

F. ILLUSIONS

9. For much of the time, our perceptions are relatively accurate reflections of the world (except for anything added by our attentional, motivational, or emotional filters). However, if perceptual cues that we have learned to use and rely on are greatly changed, the result is a distorted image, called an _____. Although illusions are extreme examples, they illustrate that perception is an active, ongoing process in which we use past experiences to interpret current sensory experiences.

G. RESEARCH FOCUS: SUBLIMINAL PERCEPTION

10. Brief auditory or visual messages that are presented below the absolute threshold, which means that their chance of being heard or seen is less than 50%, are called (a) _____. Researchers have concluded that any behavioral changes attributed to subliminal messages actually result because listeners' strong belief that a behavior will change leads them to act, unknowingly, to change that behavior; this is called a (b) _____.

H. CULTURAL DIVERSITY: DIFFERENT PERCEPTIONS

11. Experiences that are typical of a society and shared by its members are called _____ influences. These influences have significant effects on the perception of images, constancy, depth, and motion.

12. Expectations that are based on previous experiences, thoughts, or feelings are called _____; without our knowledge, they can change or bias our perceptions.

I. ESP: EXTRASENSORY PERCEPTION

13. The perception and transmission of thoughts or images by other than normal sensory channels are referred to as psychic experiences or (a) _____ phenomena. ESP, which stands for (b) _____, includes four psychic abilities. The ability to transfer one's thoughts to another or read another's thoughts is called (c) _____. The ability to foretell events is called (d) _____. The ability to perceive events or objects that are out of sight is called (e) _____. The ability to move objects without touching them is called (f) _____. Two reasons many researchers are skeptical of psychic abilities is that some supposedly psychic phenomena were actually accomplished with (g) _____ and some previous studies that supported ESP had questionable (h) _____. Although a recent study supported the occurrence of psi phenomena, many researchers are waiting for these positive results to be (i) _____.

J. APPLICATION: CREATING PERCEPTIONS

14. When you view objects moving in space, it is called (a) _____ motion. When you view images of stationary objects that are presented in a rapid sequence, it is called (b) _____ motion, which is the basic principle used to create movies. The illusion that stationary lights are moving can be traced to the work of Max Wertheimer, who called this phenomenon (c) _____ movement. A perceptual experience that is created by allowing the viewer to enter and participate in computer-generated images is called (d) _____; it breaks down some of the traditional boundaries between reality and fantasy.

Answers: *1. absolute threshold; 2. (a) just noticeable difference, (b) Weber's; 3. (a) sensation, (b) perception, (c) experiences; 4. (a) structuralists, (b) Gestalt, (c) perceptual organization; 5. (a) figure, (b) ground, (c) simplicity, (d) similarity, (e) proximity, (f) continuity, (g) closure; 6. (a) perceptual constancy, (b) size, (c) shape, (d) color, brightness; 7. (a) binocular, (b) monocular, (c) convergence, (d) retinal disparity; 8. (a) interposition, (b) linear perspective, (c) relative size, (d) atmospheric perspective, (e) texture gradient, (f) light and shadow, (g) motion parallax; 9. illusion; 10. (a) subliminal messages, (b) self-fulfilling prophecy; 11. cultural; 12. perceptual sets; 13. (a) psi, (b) extrasensory perception, (c) telepathy, (d) precognition, (e) clairvoyance, (f) psychokinesis, (g) trickery, (h) methodology, (i) replicated; 14. (a) real, (b) apparent, (c) phi, (d) virtual reality.*

CRITICAL THINKING

Newspaper Article

QUESTIONS

PREDICTABLY, PSYCHICS BOTCH '97 FORECASTS

Associated Press

Had the psychics been right, 1997 would have gone down in history as the year rocker Mick Jagger became a member of Parliament and former television anchorman Walter Cronkite a critically acclaimed lounge singer. O. J. Simpson would be a big star on French television as the host of a "whodunit" show, and actor John Travolta a hero for landing a commercial jetliner when its crew came down with food poisoning.

There was little—make that nothing—that the psychics got right in their predictions for the *National Enquirer, National Examiner,* and other tabloids. So says the *Skeptical Enquirer.*

The magazine, published in the Buffalo suburb of Amherst, said it applied scientific method to claims of the paranormal. The psychics' collective strikeout came as no surprise to Gene Emery, who has been checking the forecasts for the magazine since 1979. "They are consistent," he said. Since 1979, Emery has found only one prediction that came half-true.

That was in 1993, when a *National Enquirer* psychic said that Florida would be hit hard by an earthquake weeks after being devastated by the worst hurricane in state history. The timing of the forecast was right for Hurricane Andrew, but there was no temblor.

Among other predictions for 1997:

- Barbra Streisand was to convert Rush Limbaugh into a liberal Democrat.
- Pamela Anderson Lee was to either become a Washington lobbyist or star with Howard Stern in a rock musical version of "Gone With the Wind."
- Madonna was to revive the Mickey Mouse Club and cast herself as its star.

Emery, who also writes a column for the *Skeptical Enquirer,* said he keeps track of the psychic flops to prove a point. "I do this as an annual reality check to people who really want to know whether these folks have any talent," he said, "and it's become clear over the years that they don't."

Undaunted by their 1997 misses, the psychics already are polishing their crystal balls for 1998. Look for a cure for the common cold, a drink for nighttime joggers that will make their skin glow in the dark, and the need to kill all cats to stop the spread of a virus that blinds humans.

And then look for Emery's column.

Source: Associated Press, appeared in *Los Angeles Times,* January 2, 1998.

1. How many of the psychics' predictions came true in 1997?

2. How does the *Skeptical Enquirer* apply the scientific method to psychics' claims?

3. What point do *Skeptical Enquirer* writers make with their annual survey?

4. Does this prove that there is no such thing as ESP?

5. Why do you think people read psychic predictions even though they are almost always wrong?

Study Questions

A. **Perceptual Thresholds**—How does Weber's law apply to how old you perceive someone to be? (See answer in Critical Thinking Appendix.)

B. **Sensation versus Perception**—What would your life be like if your brain could receive sensations but could not assemble them into perceptions? (See answer in Critical Thinking Appendix.)

C. **Rules of Organization**—Why can you still read the message on a faded and torn billboard sign?

D. **Perceptual Constancy**—If you suddenly lost all perceptual constancy, what specific problems would you have?

E. **Depth Perception**—Would a one-eyed pitcher have any particular problems playing baseball?

F. **Illusions**—What has to happen to our perceptual processes before we see an illusion?

G. **Research Focus: Subliminal Perception**—Could advertisers make any honest claims for subliminal tapes?

H. **Cultural Diversity: Different Perceptions**—When foreigners visit the United States, what do you think they perceive differently? (See answer in Critical Thinking Appendix.)

I. **ESP: Extrasensory Perception**—How could you test your friend's claim of having had a psychic experience?

J. **Application: Creating Perceptions**—What do illusions add to our perceptions of the world?

LINKS TO LEARNING

Web Sites & Learning Activities

● BROOKS/COLE ONLINE PSYCHOLOGY STUDY CENTER

http://psychstudy.brookscole.com/student/plotnik/quiz/ch06frm.html

This site gives students a chance to review material by taking quizzes and doing exercises and activities for this module.

● SENSATION AND PERCEPTION TUTORIALS

http://psych.hanover.edu/Krantz/sen_tut.html

This site contains several online tutorials on sensation and perception, including receptive fields, Fourier analysis, and visual information in art.

● PERCEPTION, ILLUSIONS, AND THEIR NEURONAL CORRELATES

http://www.klab.caltech.edu/~seckel.index.html

This fun site contains hundreds of illusions, including interactive visual and auditory illusions.

● SUBLIMINAL PERCEPTION

http://weber.u.washington/edu/

Can subliminal messages influence our behavior? This page tackles this controversial issue, with sections on back-masking in music and commercial applications.

● SAN FRANCISCO EXPLORATORIUM EXHIBITS

http://www.exploratorium.edu/exhibits/exhibits.html

Many of these digital versions of exhibits from San Francisco's Exploratorium involve auditory and visual perception and the tricks our senses sometimes play on us.

● PERCEPTION ONLINE

http://www.pion.co.uk/perception

This online journal reports experimental results and theoretical ideas on human, animal, and machine perception.

● EXTRASENSORY PERCEPTION

http://www.hope.edu/academic/psychology/myerstxt/esp/esp.html

This site presents a critical and skeptical view of ESP, including an exploration of whether there can be perception without sensation.

Activities

● *Integrator Online™ for Introductory Psychology* CD-ROM, Plotnik, Module 6

● Study Guide to accompany *Introduction to Psychology*, 5th edition, Module 6 (choice of PC or Mac computer version or hard copy).

● PsychNow! CD-ROM
Perception

Answers to questions on page 144

1. None of them.
2. They count the number of psychic successes versus failures to quantify the data and interpret the results.
3. They hold that tabloid psychics actually have no real predictive powers.
4. This survey does not prove that there is no such thing as ESP, only that the tabloid psychics surveyed don't have it.
5. One reason might be that people like the illusion that the future can be predicted. Or the prediction may just have entertainment value.

Module 7 CONSCIOUSNESS, SLEEP, & DREAMS

Living in a Cave

Would you answer this ad?

The advertisement read: "We are looking for a hardy subject to live alone in an underground cave for four months. We'll provide board, room, and a monthly allowance. It will be necessary to take daily physiological measurements, measure brain waves, and collect blood samples."

Twenty people answered this ad, but researchers selected Stefania because she seemed to have the inner strength, motivation, and stamina to complete the entire four months. On the chosen day, Stefania crawled 30 feet underground with her favorite books into a 20-by-12-foot Plexiglas module, which had been sealed off from sunlight, radio, television, and other time cues.

During her first month underground, Stefania's concentration seemed to come and go. She appeared depressed, and she snapped at researchers when they asked her to do routine measurements. She had strange dreams—for example, that her computer monitor had turned into a TV that was talking to her. After several months, however, she became more comfortable with her underground isolation. She followed a regular routine of taking her body temperature, heart rate, and blood pressure and typing the results into a computer monitor, her only link with the outside world.

Without clocks, radio, television, or the sun, Stefania found it difficult to keep track of time, which seemed to have slowed down. When told she could leave her underground cave (photo below) because her 130 days were up, she felt certain she had been underground only about 60 days. Her time underground, which was a women's record (the men's record is 210 days), allowed researchers to closely monitor her sleeping and waking behaviors in the absence of all light and time cues (adapted from *Newsweek*, June 5, 1989).

Asking Stefania to live in a cave for many months was not a publicity stunt but a way to answer questions about how long a day is and how much one sleeps when there are no light cues. To answer these questions, researchers used a case study approach, which meant studying Stefania's behaviors and physiological responses in great detail and depth and doing so in a reasonably naturalistic setting. Researchers discovered that the preferred length of a day is not 24 hours and that during a particular kind of sleep Stefania's eyes moved back and forth as if she were watching a ping-pong game. The significance of these eye movements emphasize the fact that some major discoveries in science occur quite by accident.

Chance Discovery

Why are our eyes moving?

In the early days of sleep research, psychologists were observing changes in sleeping subjects and noticed that during a certain stage of sleep a person's eyes suddenly began to move rapidly back and forth. This back-and-forth eye movement can actually be seen under the eyelids in

the photo above. Even more interesting, when subjects were awakened during rapid eye movement they usually reported that they had been dreaming. This chance observation of rapid eye movement and its high association, or correlation, with dreaming gave researchers a reliable method to identify and study dreaming in the laboratory (Dement & Kleitman, 1957).

These examples show how researchers study waking, sleeping, and dreaming in different settings, including underground caves and sleep laboratories, and also how they were helped along by a chance discovery.

What's Coming

We'll discuss the preferred length of a day, how you know when to sleep and wake up, what happens to your body and brain during sleep, how much sleep you need, why you sleep, and common sleep problems and their treatment. We'll also discuss the one question students always ask: "What do dreams mean?" All these areas fit neatly under a much broader phenomenon that we call awareness, or consciousness, and that is where we'll begin.

A. Continuum of Consciousness

Different States

Are you conscious now?

One curious feature of consciousness is that, at some point, the person is actually observing himself or herself (Nelson, 1996). For example, how do you know that at this very moment you are conscious?

Consciousness refers to different levels of awareness of one's thoughts and feelings. It may include creating images in one's mind, following one's thought processes, or having unique emotional experiences, all of which are part of consciousness.

One way you know that you are conscious is that you are aware of your own thoughts and existence (Chalmers, 1995). You may think that when awake you are conscious and when asleep you are unconscious, but there is actually a continuum of consciousness.

The *continuum of consciousness* refers to a wide range of experiences, from being acutely aware and alert to being totally unaware and unresponsive.

We'll summarize some of the experiences that make up the continuum of consciousness.

Controlled Processes

One secret to a perfect tennis serve is the ability to focus all of your attention on the ball, which is an example of controlled processes.

Controlled processes are activities that require full awareness, alertness, and concentration to reach some goal. The focused attention required in carrying out controlled processes usually interferes with the execution of other ongoing activities.

A controlled process, such as serving a tennis ball or taking an exam, represents our most alert state of consciousness. Remember also that involvement in a controlled process disrupts other ongoing activities. For example, using a car phone, which is a controlled process, increases the chances of having a collision by 25% (Redelmeier & Tibshirani, 1997). Because of increased collisions, several countries have banned the use of car phones.

Automatic Processes

Since this woman's attention is focused primarily on reading an important report, she is almost automatically eating the donut; this is an example of automatic processes.

Automatic processes are activities that require little awareness, take minimal attention, and do not interfere with other ongoing activities.

Examples of automatic processes include eating while reading or watching television and driving a car along a familiar route while listening to the radio or thinking of something else.

Although we seem to concentrate less during automatic processes, at some level we are conscious of what is occurring. For instance, as we drive on automatic pilot, we avoid neighboring cars and can usually take quick evasive action during emergencies.

Daydreaming

Many of us engage in a pleasurable form of consciousness that is called daydreaming.

Daydreaming is an activity that requires a low level of awareness, often occurs during automatic processes, and involves fantasizing or dreaming while awake.

We may begin daydreaming in a relatively conscious state and then drift into a state between sleep and wakefulness. Usually we daydream in situations that require little attention or during activities that are repetitious or boring.

Most daydreams are rather ordinary, such as thinking about getting one's hair cut, planning on where to eat, pondering some problem, or fantasizing a date. These kinds of daydreams serve to remind us of important things in our future. Although you might guess otherwise, men's and women's daydreams are remarkably similar in frequency, vividness, and realism (Klinger, 1987).

Altered States

Over 3,000 years ago, Egyptians brewed alcohol to reach altered states of consciousness (Samuel, 1996).

Altered states of consciousness result from using any number of procedures—such as meditation, psychoactive drugs, hypnosis, or sleep deprivation—to produce an awareness that differs from normal consciousness.

For example, this woman is using a form of meditation to focus all her attention on a single image or thought, free her mind from all external restraints, and enter an altered state of consciousness.

In an interesting series of studies on himself, neuropsychologist John Lilly (1972) repeatedly took LSD (when it was legal) and reported that it caused unusual, bizarre, and sometimes frightening altered states of consciousness. For example, he described leaving his body, seeing it from above, and being afraid that he would not be able to return safely to it.

The chief characteristic of altered states, however they are produced, is that we perceive our internal and external environments in ways very different from normal perception.

Sleep and Dreams

We enter an altered state of consciousness every night when we go to sleep.

Sleep consists of five different stages that involve different levels of awareness, consciousness, and responsiveness, as well as different levels of physiological arousal. The deepest state of sleep borders on unconsciousness.

Because of decreased awareness, eight hours of sleep may seem like one continuous state. However, it is actually composed of different states of body arousal and consciousness (Kohyama et al., 1997; Maquet, 1997). One interesting sleep state involves dreaming.

Dreaming is a unique state of consciousness in which we are asleep but experience a variety of astonishing visual, auditory, and tactile images, often connected in strange ways and often in color. People blind from birth have only auditory or tactile dreams.

During the initial stage of sleep we are often aware of stimuli in our environment. However, as we pass into the deepest stage of sleep, we may sleeptalk or sleepwalk but have no awareness or memory of performing these behaviors.

Most of this module focuses on waking, sleeping, and dreaming.

The Unconscious

Earlier we told you that one of Sigmund Freud's revolutionary ideas was his idea of the unconscious.

The *unconscious,* according to Freud's theory, says that when we are faced with very threatening wishes or desires, especially if they are sexual or aggressive, we automatically defend our self-esteem by placing these psychologically threatening thoughts into a mental place that is called the unconscious, from which these thoughts cannot be voluntarily recalled.

Freud believed that we can become aware of our unconscious thoughts only through a process of free association or dream interpretation, both of which will be explained in Module 19.

Cognitive psychologists have developed a different concept, unlike Freud's theory of the unconscious, called the cognitive unconscious (Bonebakker et al, 1996; Greenwald et al., 1996; Kihlstrom, 1993).

The *cognitive unconscious* consists of mental and emotional processes that we are unaware of but that bias and influence our conscious feelings, thoughts, and behaviors.

For example, we cannot describe the complex motor movements our feet make as they walk down stairs because such motor memories lie in our cognitive unconscious, which is not accessible to our conscious mind. Kihlstrom points out that the current idea of the cognitive unconscious, which emphasizes the influence of many different kinds of motor and emotional memories, is very different from Freud's unconscious, which focused on the influence of threatening memories.

Unconsciousness

The unconscious as Freud defined it and the cognitive unconscious are usually active when we are aware of our environments. Being unconscious is entirely different.

Unconsciousness, which can result from disease, trauma, a blow to the head, or general medical anesthesia, results in total unawareness and loss of responsiveness to one's environment.

For example, a boxer's goal is to knock out the opponent with a quick blow to the head that produces a temporary state of unconsciousness. Trauma to the brain can also cause different levels of unconsciousness and result in different kinds of comas. In some comas, a person appears to be asleep and has absolutely no awareness or responsiveness; this is called a vegetative state. People in vegetative comas are unconscious and in some cases brain dead, which means they will never again regain consciousness.

Several Kinds

What is consciousness?

We know that consciousness is not one thing but a continuum of states, which range from the terrible unconsciousness of being in a coma to the keen alertness of controlled processes during a final exam. Each of us knows what it feels like to be conscious and aware of our thoughts and surroundings. Neuroscientists are working on the difficult problem of explaining how the interaction of microscopic brain cells give rise to being aware and producing thoughts, an experience often labeled as the mind (Chalmers, 1995).

Historically, Freud viewed the unconscious as an active psychological process that defended a person against threatening thoughts. The current concept of the cognitive unconscious says that we can perceive stimuli, such as words, without being aware of doing so and that these stimuli influence our thoughts, memories, and feelings. Compared with generally unreliable research of the past, current research has reliably established the existence of the cognitive unconscious (Greenwald et al., 1996).

One obvious sign of consciousness is being awake which is regulated by a clock in the brain, our next topic.

B. Rhythms of Sleeping & Waking

Biological Clocks

How long is a day?

At the beginning of this module, we discussed how sleep researchers studied Stefania, who lived in the modernized cave shown below. The reason Stefania was asked to live in a cave is that researchers wanted to study her biological clocks.

Biological clocks are internal timing devices that are genetically set to regulate various physiological responses for different periods of time.

For example, biological clocks can be set for hours (secretion of urine), for a single day (rise and fall in internal body temperature), or for many days (sequential secretion of hormones during the 28-day menstrual cycle). Here we are most interested in a biological clock that is set for about a single day and produces what is called a circadian (*sir-KAY-dee-un*) rhythm (*circa* means about; *diem* means day).

A *circadian rhythm* refers to a biological clock that is genetically programmed to regulate physiological responses within a time period of 24–25 hours (about one day).

The circadian rhythm you are most familiar with is the one that regulates your sleep-wake cycle. Because our industrialized world has standardized a day as lasting exactly 24 hours, we naturally assume that the body's circadian rhythm for the sleep-wake cycle is also 24 hours. However, when researchers removed all time cues (light, clock, radio, television) from cave dwellers like Stefania, the length of the day expanded from 24 hours to about 25 hours (Moore, 1997). However, most of us must operate on a 24-hour day and thus set back our sleep-wake circadian clock about one hour each day. Before explaining how the body's clock is reset each day, let's locate the miniature biological clock in the brain.

Interval Timing and Sleep-Wake Clocks

Where are the clocks?

Perhaps you're the type of person who can decide to take a one-hour nap and actually wake up about an hour later. The reason both humans and animals are very good at estimating time for starting and stopping activities is the existence of a recently discovered clock in the brain, which is called the interval timing clock (Gibbon, 1996).

The *interval timing clock*, which can be started and stopped like a stopwatch, gauges the passage of seconds, minutes, or hours and helps creatures time their movements, such as knowing when to start or stop doing some activity. The interval timing clock is located in a part of the brain known as the basal ganglia (see page 57).

When the interval clock was destroyed in rats, they could no longer time intervals for obtaining food (Meck, 1996). Researchers believe that, like the rat's brain, the human brain has a similar interval timer that we can start and stop. However, deciding to nap for an hour is very different from the genetically set circadian clock that regulates waking and sleeping. The waking-sleeping clock was recently located in a group of cells in the suprachiasmatic (*SUE-pra-kye-as-MAT-ick*) nucleus.

The *suprachiasmatic nucleus* is one of many groups of cells that make up the hypothalamus, which lies in the lower middle of the brain. The suprachiasmatic nucleus is a sophisticated biological clock that regulates a number of circadian rhythms, including the sleep-wake rhythm. Because this nucleus receives direct input from the eyes, the suprachiasmatic cells are highly responsive to changes in light.

The search for the circadian clock took researchers on a puzzling journey that led to hamsters with different circadian clocks. One breed of hamsters had suprachiasmatic clocks that are genetically set for a 22-hour circadian rhythm, while a second breed had a longer, 24-hour circadian clock. In a very clever switch, researchers removed a 22-hour suprachiasmatic clock from one hamster and replaced it with a 24-hour suprachiasmatic clock from a different hamster. By switching the genetically set suprachiasmatic nuclei, researchers could set the hamsters' circadian rhythms on either 22- or 24-hour sleep-wake cycles, indicating conclusively that this nucleus was the circadian clock (Ralph et al., 1990). Researchers recently discovered the genes and movement of proteins that make up suprachiasmatic nucleus's circadian clock (Kay, 1997; King et al., 1997).

Since light regulates sleep-wake circadian rhythms, the absence of light should disrupt circadian rhythms in blind people and cause sleep problems. Researchers found that many blind people do report sleep problems (Czeisler et al., 1995). However, a small percentage of completely blind people reported no sleep problems because the pathway for transmitting light from their eyes directly to the suprachiasmatic nucleus was still intact (Moore, 1997). This pathway transmits only light and has nothing to do with vision.

Walking around with a fine-tuned biological clock in your head has the potential for creating numerous physiological and behavioral problems, which we'll examine next.

Suprachiasmatic nucleus

Circadian Problems and Treatments

What if rhythms are upset?

Here's the basic problem: For most of the industrial world, a day is exactly 24 hours; but for your genetically preset sleep-wake circadian clock, a day is about 25 hours. This one-hour difference means that your sleep-wake clock must be reset about an hour each day. The resetting mechanism is the presence of morning light, which our eyes send directly to the suprachiasmatic nucleus to reset it one hour. Resetting our sleep-wake clock one hour each day usually occurs automatically, but needing to reset it by several or more hours a day can result in work-related and traffic accidents, jet lag, and sleep disorders (Moore, 1997).

Accidents

Staying awake when your sleep-wake clock calls for sleep results in decreased performance in cognitive and motor skills. For example, the graph below shows that highway

Highway Accidents

Saturday 2–3 A.M.	509
Sunday 1–2 A.M.	475
Other hours	203

Source: Data from National Highway Traffic Administration, 1992

accidents are highest in the early morning hours. Although drug usage plays a significant role in traffic accidents, another factor is that the early morning hours are a time when our bodies and brains are in a sleep rhythm. Similarly, employees who work the graveyard shift (about 1–8 A.M.) also experience the highest number of accidents, reaching their lowest point, or "dead zone," about 5 A.M., when it is very difficult to stay alert (Luna et al., 1997).

The reason shift workers and late-night drivers have more accidents is that their sleep-wake clocks have prepared their bodies for sleep, which means they feel sleepy, are less attentive and alert, and are often in a lousy mood (Boivin et al., 1997).

Circadian rhythms can also create problems for travelers.

Jet Lag

If you flew from San Diego to New York City, you would cross three time zones, experience a three-hour difference in time, and most likely have jet lag the next day.

Jet lag refers to a state experienced by travelers in which their internal circadian rhythm is out of step, or synchrony, with the external clock time at their new location. Jet lag results in fatigue, disorientation, lack of concentration, and reduced cognitive skills. The general rule for recovering from jet lag is that it takes about one day to reset your circadian clock for each hour of time change.

Because preset circadian rhythms cause problems for travelers and late-night workers, researchers have begun to find ways to more efficiently reset our biological clocks.

Resetting Rhythms

Researcher Charles Czeisler (1994) spent ten years trying to convince his colleagues that light could reset circadian rhythms. After he finally succeeded, other researchers used his and their own research to win patents for something called light therapy (Nowak, 1994).

Light therapy is the use of bright artificial light to reset circadian rhythms and so combat the insomnia and drowsiness that plague shift workers and jet-lag sufferers. It also helps people with sleeping disorders in which the body fails to stay in time with the external environment.

For example, researchers report that workers who had been exposed to bright light and then shifted to night work showed improvement in alertness, performance, and job satisfaction (Czeisler et al., 1995). Exposure to bright light (about 20 times brighter) at certain times reset the workers' suprachiasmatic nucleus and resulted in a closer match between their internal circadian rhythms and their shifted clock times. Light therapy is still a new treatment but has enormous potential for resetting our sleep-wake clocks (Skerrett, 1994).

Another factor involved in setting the sleep-wake clock is a hormone from a gland that was once thought useless.

Melatonin

One of the big scientific surprises of the mid-1990s was the discovery of a use for melatonin, which was first identified in the 1950s (Brzezinski, 1997).

Melatonin is a hormone that is secreted by the pineal gland, an oval-shaped group of cells that is located in the center of the human brain. Melatonin secretion increases with darkness and decreases with light. The suprachiasmatic nucleus regulates the secretion of melatonin, which plays a role in the regulation of circadian rhythms and in promoting sleep.

Pineal gland

Researchers found that melatonin generally reduced jet lag, but the best dosage and when to take it have not yet been determined (Arendt & Deacon, 1997). Melatonin also helped subjects go to sleep significantly sooner and stay asleep significantly longer, and it was helpful in treating patients with sleep disorders; but its beneficial effects on shift-workers is not clear (Hughes & Badia, 1997; Jan et al., 1994). Researchers recently identified the brain receptors for melatonin, which should further explain how it works (Reppert, 1997).

Next, we'll examine what happens inside the brain and body during sleep.

C. World of Sleep

Stages of Sleep

Does my brain sleep?

The first thing to know about sleep is that your brain never sleeps but is active throughout the night. To track your brain's activity during sleep, researchers would attach dozens of tiny wires or electrodes to your scalp and body and record electrical brain activity as you passed through the stages of sleep.

The *stages of sleep* refer to distinctive changes in the electrical activity of the brain and accompanying physiological responses of the body that occur as you pass through different phases of sleep.

As shown in the graph on the right, brain waves are described in terms of frequency (speed) and amplitude (height) and are recorded by a complex machine called an EEG, or electroencephalogram. Each stage of sleep can be recognized by its distinctive pattern of EEGs, which we'll explain here.

ALPHA STAGE

Before entering sleep, you briefly pass through a relaxed and drowsy state, marked by characteristic alpha waves. The *alpha stage* is marked by feelings of being relaxed and drowsy, usually with the eyes closed. Alpha waves have low amplitude and high frequency (8–12 cycles per second).

After a brief time in alpha stage, you enter stage 1 of non-REM sleep.

Alpha waves
(8–12 cycles per second)

Non-REM Sleep

What happens during sleep?

The second thing to know about sleep is that it is divided into two major categories, called non-REM and REM. We'll discuss non-REM first.

Non-REM sleep is where you spend approximately 80% of your sleep time. Non-REM is divided into sleep stages 1, 2, 3, and 4; each stage is identified by a particular pattern of brain waves and physiological responses. (REM stands for rapid eye movement.)

You begin in sleep stage 1 and gradually enter stages 2, 3, and 4 (Hirshkowitz et al., 1997).

Stage 1

This is the lightest stage of sleep.

Stage 1 sleep is a transition from wakefulness to sleep and lasts 1–7 minutes. In it, you gradually lose responsiveness to stimuli and experience drifting thoughts and images. Stage 1 is marked by the presence of theta waves, which are lower in amplitude and lower in frequency (3–7 cycles per second) than alpha waves.

Stage 1

Theta waves
(4–7 cycles per second)

Although stage 1 is usually labeled a sleep stage, some individuals who are aroused from it feel as if they have been awake.

Next, you enter stage 2 sleep.

Stage 2

This is the first stage of what researchers call real sleep.

Stage 2 sleep marks the beginning of what we know as sleep, since subjects who are awakened in stage 2 report having been asleep. EEG tracings show high-frequency bursts of brain activity called sleep spindles.

Stage 2

Sleep spindles

As you pass through stage 2, your muscle tension, heart rate, respiration, and body temperature gradually decrease, and it becomes more difficult for you to be awakened.

Stages 3 and 4

About 30–45 minutes after drifting off into sleep, you pass through stage 3 and then enter into stage 4 sleep.

Stage 4 sleep, which is also called slow wave or delta sleep, is characterized by waves of very high amplitude and very low frequency (less than 4 cycles per second) called delta waves. Stage 4 is often considered the deepest stage of sleep because it is the most difficult from which to be awakened. During stage 4, heart rate, respiration, temperature, and blood flow to the brain are reduced, and there is a marked secretion of GH (growth hormone), which controls levels of metabolism, physical growth, and brain development.

As you pass through stages 3, and 4, your muscle tension, heart rate, respiration, and temperature decrease still further, and it becomes very difficult for you to be awakened.

After spending a few minutes to an hour in stage 4, you will backtrack through stages 3 and 2 and then pass into a new stage, called REM sleep, which is associated with dreaming.

Stage 4

Delta waves
(less than 4 cycles per second)

When do you dream?

We have discussed one major category of sleep, non-REM, and now move on to the second major category, which is called REM sleep.

REM sleep makes up the remaining 20% of your sleep time. It is pronounced "rem" and stands for rapid eye movement sleep because your eyes move rapidly back and forth behind closed lids. REM brain waves have fast frequency and low amplitude

REM Sleep

~~~~~~~~~~~~~~~~~

(14–25 cycles per second)

and look very similar to beta waves, which occur when you are wide awake and alert. During REM, your body is physiologically very aroused, but all your voluntary muscles are paralyzed. REM sleep is highly associated with dreaming.

You pass into REM sleep about 5 or 6 times throughout the night with about 30 to 90 minutes between periods. You remain in each period of REM sleep for 15 to 45 minutes and then pass back into non-REM sleep.

Characteristics of REM Sleep

When REM sleep was first discovered in the early 1950s, researchers found it difficult to believe their unusual findings: Although asleep during REM, your body and brain are in a general state of arousal (Aserinsky & Kleitman, 1953). For example, during REM sleep, heart rate and blood pressure may be

twice as high as during non-REM sleep (Somers et al., 1993). Because in REM sleep you are both asleep and highly aroused, REM sleep is often called *paradoxical sleep*. (A *paradox* is something with contradictory qualities.)

Another unusual feature of REM sleep is that its brain waves are very similar to those recorded when a person is wide awake and alert. By looking at brain wave recordings alone, researchers cannot tell if a person is in REM sleep or wide awake. Only the additional recording of rapid eye movements indicates the occurrence of REM sleep.

Although many physiological responses are greatly increased, you completely lose the muscle tension (tonus) in your neck and limbs so that you are essentially paralyzed. However, involuntary muscles that regulate heart, lungs, and other body organs continue to function. Researchers think that humans evolved muscle paralysis of their limbs during REM sleep so that they would not act out violent dreams by running, fighting or jumping about and injuring themselves (Pressman & Orr, 1997). In fact, this actually happens in REM behavior disorder.

In *REM behavior disorder*, which usually occurs in older people, voluntary muscles are not paralyzed, and sleepers can and do act out their dreams. In some cases, REM behavior disorder is caused by known neurological damage, but in other cases, the causes are unknown (Plazzi et al., 1997; Rothenberg 1997).

So not only is REM a paradoxical sleep, in which you are asleep, paralyzed, yet physiologically aroused, but it is also a signal that you are dreaming.

REM and Dreaming

One of the biggest breakthroughs in dream research was the finding that about 80–90% of the times when subjects are awakened from a REM period, they report having vivid, complex, and relatively long dreams. In contrast, only about 10% of subjects awakened from non-REM sleep report similar kinds of dreams (Hirshkowitz et al., 1997).

In the late 1950s, many psychologists believed that if people were prevented from entering REM sleep and were therefore not allowed to dream, they might suffer harm to their personalities and behaviors. Since that time, many subjects have been deprived of REM sleep and dreaming by being awakened whenever their physiological signs show they are starting a REM period. Subjects deprived of REM sleep and dreaming have shown no long-term detrimental behavioral or physiological effects (Walsh & Lindblom, 1997). However, suppression of REM sleep does produce a curious phenomenon called REM rebound.

REM rebound refers to an increased percentage of time spent in REM sleep when we are deprived of REM sleep on the previous nights.

The occurrence of REM rebound suggests a need for REM sleep, but researchers have yet to identify this need.

We'll discuss the content and meaning of dreams later in this module.

Awake and Alert

A short time after awakening from sleep, you enter a state of being awake and alert. This state has distinctive brain activity called beta waves (right figure), which are characterized by high frequency and low amplitude and are very similar to those waves observed during REM sleep.

Awake and Alert

**Beta waves
(14–25 cycles per second)**

How alert you feel in the morning partly depends on whether you are a morning or night person, which we'll discuss in the upcoming Research Focus.

Although you now have an overview of the different sleep stages, you may be surprised to discover that how you go through the different stages is somewhat like riding a roller coaster.

C. World of Sleep

Sequence of Stages

Why is sleep like a roller-coaster ride?

When you go to sleep at night, you may think that you simply sleep for 8 hours, perhaps toss and turn a little, and even do some dreaming. But sleep is not one unbroken state but rather a series of recurring stages, similar to the ups and downs of a roller-coaster ride. We'll describe a typical night's pattern for George, a college sophomore, who goes to bed about 11 P.M. and gets up about 7 A.M. As we take you through the figure below, notice that non-REM sleep is indicated by the wide blue line and REM sleep is indicated by red inserts. The numbers 1 to 4 refer to sleep stages 1, 2, 3, and 4 of non-REM sleep, which we discussed earlier.

Researchers have studied hundreds of subjects and plotted systematic changes in brain waves, physiological arousal, and dreaming as subjects progressed through the stages of sleep. Here's what George will experience on a typical trip through the different stages of a night's sleep.

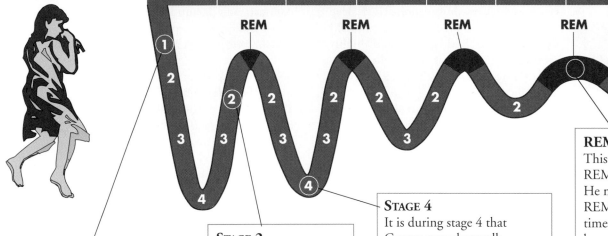

STAGE 1

As George becomes drowsy, he will enter non-REM stage 1, which is the transition between being awake and asleep.

As sleep progresses, he will continue to the next stage, non-REM stage 2, which is the first stage of real sleep. During stage 2, he may experience short, fragmented thoughts, so that if he is awakened, he may think he was dreaming.

He will continue through non-REM stage 3 and finally reach non-REM stage 4. When George enters non-REM stage 4, which is slow wave, or delta, sleep, he will be very difficult to waken. After staying in stage 4 for some minutes to an hour, he will backtrack to stage 3 and then 2.

STAGE 2

After George reaches non-REM stage 2, he does not awaken but rather enters REM sleep. He will remain in REM for 20–40 minutes and, if awakened, will likely report dreaming. When in REM, his body is in a high state of physiological arousal, but his voluntary limb muscles are essentially paralyzed. If George experiences nightmares during REM he will not act them out or injure himself because he cannot move.

After the REM period, he goes back down through non-REM stages 2, 3, and 4.

STAGE 4

It is during stage 4 that George may sleepwalk, sleeptalk, or perform other activities, such as partially awakening to turn off the alarm, pull up the covers, or get up and go to the bathroom. However, George will remember nothing of what happens in non-REM stage 4, such as sleeptalking with his roommate or walking to the kitchen and getting a snack. He will remain in stage 4 for a period of time before again backtracking up to non-REM stage 3, 2, and then to his second REM period of the night.

Children sometimes wake up terrified during non-REM stage 4. These experiences are called night terrors, but the child will have no memory of them the next day.

REM

This is George's fourth REM period of the night. He may go in and out of REM sleep five or six times, with REM periods becoming longer toward morning. If George wants to remember his dreams, he should try when he first wakes up since his last REM period may have occurred only minutes before.

When his alarm goes off at 7 A.M., he leaves whatever sleep stage he is in and slowly becomes awake and alert. If George has a difficult time awakening, it may be because he was in stage 4, the hardest stage to awaken from.

Like George, we all go through the sleep stages in about the same sequence. However, some of us like mornings while others hate them; you're about to find out why.

D. Research Focus: Circadian Preference
Are There Morning and Evening People?

Are you an early bird or a night owl?

Some students really hate morning classes, while others don't mind them. One reason for this difference is that some students are early birds and some are night owls. Researchers obtained a more accurate definition of these terms by developing and using a questionnaire.

A *questionnaire* is a method for obtaining information by asking subjects to read a list of written questions and check off or rate their preference for specific answers.

The Morning-Evening Questionnaire asked subjects to rate their preferred times for going to bed, getting up, and engaging in physical and mental activities, as well as their feelings of alertness in the morning and evening. The graph here shows the results from this questionnaire.

Score on Morning/Evening Questionnaire

Evening person — 45
Morning person — 74

Morning persons (score above 74), prefer to get up earlier, go to bed earlier, and engage in morning activities. *Evening persons* (score below 45) prefer to get up later, go to bed later, and engage in afternoon-evening activities. Those individuals who scored between 45 and 74 did not express a strong morning or evening preference (Tankova et al., 1994; Guthrie et al., 1995).

Individuals with strong preferences did not consciously decide to become morning or evening persons but rather are following a built-in genetic preference regulated by circadian rhythms. One reason a person may have a strong morning or evening preference is related to changes in body temperature, which rise and fall throughout the day.

Body Temperature

Our body has several circadian rhythms, one of them being the sleep-wake cycle, which is regulated by the suprachiasmatic nucleus in the hypothalamus. Another circadian rhythm, also thought to be regulated by the suprachiasmatic nucleus, involves body temperature, which falls as we go to sleep and rises after we get up (Boivin et al., 1997). The graph on the right shows changes in body temperature for a 24-hour period, beginning at 6 A.M.

Getting up. Body temperature is low in the morning and rises throughout the day, when we are most active. The temperature of a morning person rises much more quickly (so the person gets up earlier) than that of an evening person (so the person gets up later). In fact, body temperature in a morning person may rise 1–3 hours earlier than in an evening person (Tankova et al., 1994).

Going to bed. The body temperature of a

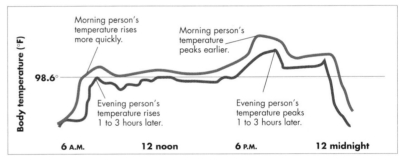

morning person peaks earlier in the evening (so the person goes to bed earlier) than the body temperature of an evening person, which peaks 1–3 hours later (so the person goes to bed later). Researchers hypothesize that the suprachiasmatic nucleus regulates the rise and fall of body temperature, which in turn determines whether we are morning or evening people.

In addition, there are some interesting behavioral differences between morning and evening people.

Behavioral Differences

Researchers found that night workers and shift workers, who must rotate through afternoon and late evening times, tend to be evening persons (Adan, 1992). Morning persons tend to eat a hearty, high-calorie breakfast, while evening persons tend either to skip breakfast or consume a light one.

Researchers found that students who were morning people took more classes in the morning (if they could get the classes), performed better in morning classes, and studied more in the morning than did students who were night people (Guthrie

et al., 1995). This means that to get better grades, you should adjust your class schedule to best fit your particular circadian rhythm.

Finally, researchers found no differences between sexes in daily circadian rhythms, but they did find that in the course of normal aging, people tend to become physiologically and behaviorally more like morning persons after the age of 50 (Tankova et al., 1994).

Although morning and night persons have interesting differences, they do share similar brain structures that either put them to sleep or awaken them. We'll discuss what causes sleep and why we spend so much time asleep.

E. Questions about Sleep

Four Major Questions

By the time you are 25 years old, you have fallen asleep over 9000 times and have spent about 72,000 hours asleep. There are usually four questions that students ask about sleep: How much sleep do I need? Why do I sleep? What happens if I go without sleep? What causes sleep? We'll discuss each of these questions in turn.

How Much Sleep?

What's the best amount for me?

According to a recent survey, 58% of adult Americans sleep 7–8 hours, 38% sleep 5–6 hours, and 4% sleep 9–10 hours (*Time,* April 19, 1993). However, if we took a survey of babies, the time spent sleeping would be dramatically different, as shown in the pie charts below.

Beginning at birth and continuing through old age, there is a gradual change in the total time we spend sleeping, the percentage of time we spend in REM sleep, and the kinds of sleep problems we experience.

INFANCY AND CHILDHOOD
From infancy to adolescence, the total amount of time spent in sleep and the percentage spent in REM gradually decline. For example, a newborn sleeps about 17 hours a day, and 50% of that time is spent in REM; a four-year-old sleeps about 10 hours, and 25–30% of that time is spent in REM.

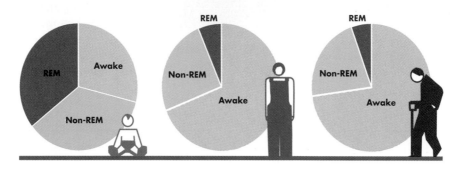

OLD AGE
Upon reaching our 60s, total sleep time drops to about 6.5 hours a day, but the percentage of REM sleep remains about the same (20%). In people over 60, about 30% report trouble getting to sleep, and 65% report difficulties staying asleep, which is partly due to daytime napping (Bliwise, 1997).

ADOLESCENCE AND ADULTHOOD From adolescence (puberty) to old age (around 60), we maintain the same amount of total sleep time, approximately 7.5 hours a day, and the same percentage of REM sleep, about 20% or less. However, compared to adults, researchers found that adolescents need more sleep (about 10 hours) and their circadian clocks favor going to bed later and getting up later (Allen & Mirabile, 1997). Based on these findings, educators suggest that the high school day should start an hour later than it does now. At about age 20, adolescents adopt sleep patterns of adults.

Why Do I Sleep?

Is my brain being repaired?

One reason we know sleep is important comes from studies of animals who are deprived of sleep. Rats can live about 16 days without food (water provided) and about 17 days without sleep (Rechtschaffen, 1997). So far, the longest a human has voluntarily gone without sleep is 11 days (discussed on next page) (Johnson et al., 1965). We'll explain two currently popular theories—the repair and adaptive theories—of why we spend about one-third of each day asleep.

The *repair theory* suggests that activities during the day deplete key factors in our brain or body that are replenished or repaired by sleep. The repair theory says that sleep is primarily a restorative process.

The repair theory is supported by several findings. First, during stage 4 sleep there is a marked secretion of growth hormone, which controls many aspects of metabolism, physical growth, and brain development (Shapiro, 1981). Second, during sleep there is increased production of immune cells to fight off infection (Born et al., 1997). Third, moderate changes in sleep schedules caused reports of decreased happiness and cheerfulness (Boivin et al., 1997). It seems the brain needs sleep to grow, repair its immune system, and maintain an optimum mood.

The *adaptive theory* suggests that sleep evolved because it prevented early humans and animals from wasting energy and exposing themselves to the dangers of nocturnal predators (Webb, 1983).

Support for the adaptive theory comes from observations that large predatory animals, such as lions, sleep a lot and wherever they wish, while smaller prey animals sleep far less and in protected areas. Also, animals (humans) that rely primarily on visual cues and have little night vision have evolved a circadian clock for sleeping at night and thus avoid becoming prey (Hirshkowitz et al., 1997).

The adaptive and repair theories are not really at odds but just focus on different reasons for why we need to sleep.

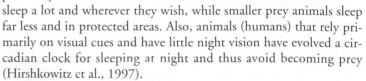

What if I Miss Sleep?

How long can you go?

One method of investigating why sleep is important is to study people or animals who are sleep deprived. The record for sleep deprivation was set by a young adult who went without sleep for 11 days, or 264 hours (Johnson et al., 1965). On his 11th day without sleep, this young man beat the researcher in a pin-ball game, which indicates he was still awake and alert. Here's what happens when people are sleep deprived.

EFFECTS ON THE BODY

Sleep deprivation, even for 264 hours, has minimal effect on a person's heart rate, blood pressure, and hormone secretions. It appears that many physiological functions controlled by the autonomic nervous system are not significantly disrupted by periods of sleep deprivation (Walsh & Lindblom, 1997).

However, sleep deprivation does affect our immune system, which is the body's defense against viruses, infections, and other toxic agents. In a recent study, men were allowed to sleep only 3–4 hours instead of their normal 8 hours. After only one night of sleep deprivation, they showed significant reductions in immune system functioning, as measured by a reduced number of killer cells (T-cells) (Irwin et al., 1994). Researchers concluded that for most people, sleep deprivation could mean increased vulnerability to some viral or bacterial infection (Everson, 1997).

EFFECTS ON THE NERVOUS SYSTEM

Sleep deprivation has consistently been shown to interfere with tasks that require vigilance and concentration, such as picking out a certain signal on a radar screen (Deaconson et al., 1988). People who are sleep deprived report an intense desire to sleep, which can interfere with attending classes or driving. Sled-dog racers who averaged 2 hours of sleep a night during the 12-day Iditarod race, reported very vivid hallucinations of rooms with beds and hot showers (Balzar, 1997). Finally, sleep deprivation causes irritability and unhappiness (Boivin et al., 1997).

Thus, depending on its extent, sleep deprivation can interfere with performance and cause moodiness.

What Causes Sleep?

Is there a master switch?

Most of us fall asleep within 5–30 minutes after going to bed and sleep an average of 8 hours. However, going to sleep is a very complicated process. One of the more dramatic and recent findings was the location of the master switch for sleep.

MASTER SLEEP SWITCH

Researchers found the master switch for sleep in a nucleus of the brain called the VPN (Sherin et al., 1996).

The *VPN—ventrolateral preoptic nucleus*—is a nucleus or group of cells in the hypothalamus that act like a master switch for sleep. When turned on, the VPN secretes a neurotransmitter (GABA) that turns off areas that keep the brain awake. When the VPN is turned off, certain brain areas become active and you wake up.

Although researchers have located the master switch for sleep, they haven't yet determined what turns it on and off.

One brain area that the VPN turns off is the reticular formation.

RETICULAR FORMATION

In order for the forebrain to receive and process information from the senses, it must be aroused and alerted by the reticular formation.

Reticular formation

The *reticular formation,* a column of cells that stretches the length of the brain stem, arouses and alerts the forebrain and prepares it to receive information from all the senses.

The reticular formation is important in keeping the forebrain alert and in producing a state of wakefulness (Munk et al., 1996). If the reticular formation is stimulated in sleeping animals, they awaken; if it is seriously damaged, in animals or humans, they lapse into permanent unconsciousness or coma.

GOING TO SLEEP

The master sleep switch and the reticular formation are but two of the factors regulating sleep. Here is the probable sequence for going to sleep (Pressman & Orr, 1997).

First, the time of day you go to sleep is regulated by circadian rhythms, which are programmed by the suprachiasmatic nucleus of the hypothalamus.

Second, something turns on your master sleep switch, which is located in the VPN (ventrolateral preoptic nucleus) of the hypothalamus. In turn, the VPN turns off areas that arouse your brain, such as the reticular formation.

Third, numerous different chemicals and neurotransmitters, some of which are manufactured in the pons, regulate when you go into and out of non-REM and REM sleep (Cravatt et al., 1995; Porkka-Heiskanen et al., 1997).

Fourth, the circadian rhythm that regulates your body temperature is tied in with sleep since you go to sleep when your temperature falls and wake up when your temperature rises.

Thus, the reasons you go to sleep and wake up involve a complex interaction between circadian rhythms, brain areas, sleep-inducing chemicals, and body temperature.

After the Concept Review, we'll describe a psychological problem whose cause seems related to decreased sunlight.

CONCEPT REVIEW

1. The various levels of awareness of one's thoughts and feelings, as well as of other internal and external stimuli, are referred to as (a)_____. This experience varies on a continuum from very aware and alert to totally unaware and unresponsive. Activities that require full awareness and alertness and may interfere with other ongoing endeavors are called (b)_____. In comparison, activities that require little awareness and minimal attention and that do not interfere with other ongoing endeavors are called (c)_____.

2. The biological clock that is set for a day of 24–25 hours is called a (a)_____. This rhythm regulates our sleep-wake cycle, which is set to a 25-hour day and must be set back by one hour to match the 24-hour day. In hamsters, and probably humans, this clock is located in a part of the hypothalamus called the (b)_____.

3. If your circadian rhythm is out of step with local time, you may feel fatigued and disoriented, a traveler's complaint called (a)_____. Workers and drivers have more accidents from 2 A.M. to 4 A.M. because their sleep-wake clock is telling them to it's time to (b)_____. Researchers have reset circadian rhythms by exposing subjects and night workers to periods of bright light; this is called (c)_____ therapy.

4. Near the center of the human brain is an oval group of cells, collectively called the pineal gland, which secrete a hormone called (a)_____. The gland secretes the hormone during dark periods and stops when it gets light. In many animals, this hormone plays a major role in the regulation of (b)_____ rhythms.

5. During a night's sleep, we gradually pass through five stages. Stage 1, which is a transition between waking and sleeping, has brain waves known as (a)_____. Stage 2 has brain waves with bursts of activity that are called (b)_____. Stage 3 and especially stage 4 are marked by high-amplitude, low-frequency (c)_____. Stage 4 is often considered the deepest stage of sleep because it is the most difficult from which to be awakened. During stage 4, heart rate, respiration, temperature, and blood flow to the brain are (d)_____. Together, stages 1, 2, 3, and 4 are referred to as (e)_____, in which we spend about 80% of our sleep time. About five or six times throughout the night, we enter a paradoxical state called (f)_____, which accounts for the remaining 20% of our sleep time. This stage is characterized by increased physiological arousal, "alert and awake" brain waves, and vivid dreaming.

6. From birth through old age, there is a decrease in total sleep time, from about 17 hours in newborns to 6.5 hours after age 60. In addition, one stage of sleep, called _____, decreases from 50% of sleep time in infancy to 20% in adulthood.

7. There are two different but not incompatible theories of why we sleep. The theory that says the purpose of sleep is to restore factors depleted throughout the day is the (a)_____. The theory that says sleep is based on an evolutionary need to conserve energy and escape nocturnal harm is the (b)_____.

8. Going to sleep is regulated by the following factors. An area in the hypothalamus that is the master sleep switch is called the (a)_____. An area in the hypothalamus that regulates circadian rhythms is called the (b)_____ nucleus. A brain area that contributes to our staying awake by sending neural signals that alert and arouse the forebrain is called the (c)_____. Several different sleep chemicals and (d)_____, some of which are made in the pons, regulate going in and out of the stages of sleep. In addition, we go to sleep several hours after a fall in body (e)_____ and get up when it starts to rise.

Answers: 1. (a) consciousness, (b) controlled processes, (c) automatic processes; 2. (a) circadian rhythm, (b) suprachiasmatic nucleus; 3. (a) jet lag, (b) sleep, (c) light; 4. (a) melatonin, (b) circadian; 5. (a) theta waves, (b) sleep spindles, (c) delta waves, (d) reduced, (e) non-REM sleep, (f) REM sleep; 6. REM sleep; 7. (a) repair theory, (b) adaptive theory; 8. (a) VPN, or ventrolateral preoptic nucleus, (b) suprachiasmatic, (c) reticular formation, (d) neurotransmitters, (e) temperature.

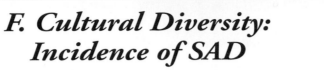

F. Cultural Diversity: Incidence of SAD

Problem and Treatment

Does light affect your mood?

Growing up in Minnesota, I remember how people (including me) complained about the cold and the gray, sunless winter days. One reason people may dislike sunless days comes from a recent and surprising finding: There is a direct nerve connection from the eye's retina to a nucleus in the brain (the suprachiasmatic nucleus in the hypothalamus). This particular nerve pathway is not involved with vision but with sensing the presence and amount of light, either sunlight or artificial light (Moore, 1997). This means that humans, like most animals, have a neural mechanism that is very responsive to the presence of light, which is critical for regulating our circadian rhythms. This neural mechanism may also be involved in the onset of a mental health problem called seasonal affective disorder, or SAD.

Seasonal affective disorder, or *SAD*, is a pattern of depressive symptoms that cycle with the seasons, typically beginning in fall or winter and going away in spring, when days are longer and sunnier. Along with depression are lethargy, excessive sleepiness, overeating, weight gain, and craving for carbohydrates (American Psychiatric Association, 1994).

SAD was recognized as a distinct mental disorder by the American Psychiatric Association in 1989. A nondrug treatment for SAD involves exposure to bright light for between 30 minutes to 1 hour, usually in the morning. Researchers reported that 69% of subjects diagnosed with SAD reported less depression after daily exposure to light while 31% experienced little or no decrease (Terman et al., 1996). Generally, exposure to light helps about 50–70% of individuals diagnosed with SAD.

Because decrease in sunlight appears to trigger SAD, we would expect the fewest cases of SAD in southern Florida, which is almost always sunny; more cases in northern New York, which has gloomy winters; and many more cases in far northern Iceland (see map), which has winters with little or no sun. Let's see if this prediction holds.

Occurrence of SAD

Where is the highest rate of SAD?

As predicted, the graph below shows that the incidence of SAD is very low (1.4%) among residents who live in sunny Florida but about five times higher (7.3%) among residents who live under the gray winter skies of New York (Rosenthal, 1993). However, residents of Iceland (see map), who live on an island in the far northern Atlantic Ocean, have only about half the incidence of SAD (3.9%) that residents of New York have, even though they experience far less sunlight during fall and winter.

When researchers try to explain any unusual or unpredicted finding, they first check the methods and procedures used to measure the dependent variables, which in this case, is the occurrence of SAD. However, Icelandic researchers used the same methods (questionnaires) and procedures that were used by researchers in the United States (Magnusson & Stefansson, 1993). If research methods and procedures were similar, what else would explain why the highest rates of SAD were reported in New York and not in Iceland?

% SAD in Florida — 1.4
% SAD in Iceland — 3.9
% SAD in New York — 7.3

Cultural Differences

What's different about Iceland?

Why did the residents of Iceland report less than half the incidence of SAD, even though they have far less daylight than residents in northeastern New York State?

Researchers concluded that differences in methods, questionnaires, and residents' lifestyles or occupations could not explain this discrepancy. Rather, there may be two other explanations—cultural differences and population density.

For 1,000 years, Icelanders have lived rather isolated in a very demanding, low-daylight environment. Because of these harsh environmental demands, Icelanders may have developed an emotional hardiness that gives them the psychological strength to deal with the gloomy winters that trigger SAD in the less hardy residents of New York State.

In addition, Icelanders experience far less crowding than do New Yorkers. The stress of living in crowded conditions, along with the lack of sunlight, may increase the occurrence of SAD (Magnusson & Stefansson, 1993).

This study shows how the occurrence of SAD, a serious mental problem, is influenced not only by changes in sunlight but also by cultural differences.

Next, we'll discuss four explanations for a phenomenon that almost everyone experiences every night—dreaming.

Iceland

Atlantic Mid Ocean

Nova Scotia

Boston

New York State

G. World of Dreams

Theories of Dream Interpretation

What do my dreams mean?

Although some people insist that they never dream, research suggests that everyone dreams during the night, even though many have forgotten their dreams by morning. In sleep laboratories, people awakened from REM periods report 80–100% of the time that they were having dreams with vivid, colorful, even bizarre images. In comparison, people awakened from non-REM sleep may also report dreams, but these usually contain dull, repetitive thoughts rather than colorful images (Gardner, 1996; Van de Castle, 1994).

For example, let's take a dream and see how others might interpret it.

I am in an elevator sitting by myself against the wall. A girl comes in, and I say, "Come sit by me," and she sits by me. (I don't even know her.) I lean over and try to kiss her, and she says, "No, don't do that." I say, "How come?" and she says something about her acne, and I say it doesn't matter and she laughs and we end up kissing and stuff on the elevator. Then these parents get on, and the elevator is real shaky, and I think that the elevator will crash or get stuck (adapted from Cohen, 1979).

Figuring out what dreams mean is a popular and scholarly activity for the more than 400 psychologists, physiologists, anthropologists, artists, "dream workers," and swamis who meet for the annual Association for the Study of Dreams. The focus of this group is to discover meaning in dreams—no easy task, since there are numerous theories. For example, some say that the young man's dream is expressing his fears of having a sexual relationship; others say that his dream is expressing his fear of being in small enclosures; while still others say that this dream is a meaningless jumble of images. We'll discuss three currently popular psychological theories of dream interpretation as well as a thousand-year-old theory of dreams from the Inuit, or Eskimo people.

We'll begin our discussion of dreams with the most controversial theory, Freud's theory of dream interpretation.

1 Freud's Theory of Dream Interpretation

In the preface to his famous book, *The Interpretation of Dreams,* Freud (1900) wrote, "This book contains, even according to my present-day judgment, the most valuable of all the discoveries it has been my good fortune to make. Insight such as this falls to one's lot but once in a lifetime." Before 1900, psychologists believed that dreams were meaningless and bizarre images (Gardner, 1995). However, Freud's theory changed all that when he said that dreams were a way ("the royal road") to reach our unconscious thoughts and desires.

Freud's theory of dreams says that we have a "censor" that protects us from realizing threatening and unconscious desires or wishes, especially those involving sex or aggression. To protect us from having threatening thoughts, the "censor" transforms our secret, guilt-ridden, and anxiety-provoking desires into harmless symbols that appear in our dreams and do not disturb our sleep or conscious thoughts.

For example, in his book, Freud (1900) discusses the meaning of symbols: male sex symbols are long objects, such sticks, umbrellas, poles, trees, knives, and pencils; female sex symbols are hollow things, such as caves, jars, bottles, shoes, drawers, and keyholes. He believed the therapist's task was to interpret these symbols and help the client discover his or her fearful and unconscious desires, needs, and childhood fears.

Many therapists agree with Freud that dreams can represent past, present, or future concerns, fears, or worries. However, many current therapists and psychoanalysts disagree with Freud's idea that a dream's contents are symbols for threatening, unconscious wishes and desires (Gardner, 1996; Reynes, 1996).

Unlike Freud, modern therapists interpret dreaming differently.

2 Extensions of Waking Life

Many therapists believe that dreams are extensions of waking life (Hill et al, 1997).

The theory that *dreams are extensions of waking life* means that our dreams reflect the same thoughts, fears, concerns, problems, and emotions present when awake.

This theory grew out of therapists' working with patients' problems. Therapist and researcher Rosalind Cartwright (1988), who is the director of Rush Sleep Disorder Service, says, "The problem most therapists face is that patients' dream material is sparse and incomplete. People simply don't remember their dreams very well. The therapist's task is often like trying to reconstruct a 500-page novel from just the last page. But dreams collected from a single night in the sleep lab read like chapters in a book. They illuminate current concerns and the feelings attached to them" (p. 36).

For example, Cartwright found that people who suffered severe traumatic emotional situations have stark nightmares that re-create the traumatic situation; people who are depressed often wake each morning feeling worse than when they went to bed and have disturbed dreams (Cartwright, 1993). Cartwright believes that patients suffering from depression or marital problems cope with their problems by repeating their fears and concerns in their dreams.

Rosalind Cartwright (1993) concludes that dreams are important because they represent another source of information, have a regular occurrence, and cannot be easily suppressed. However, she adds that this still leaves open the question of meaning and recognizes that therapists cannot always understand the dreams that patients report.

The next theory disagrees with both Freud and Cartwright.

3 Activation-Synthesis Theory

Suppose dreams resulted from the random firing of neurons in our brains and nothing more. This idea was proposed by two researchers, J. Alan Hobson and Robert W. McCarley (1977), and is called the activation-synthesis theory.

The *activation-synthesis theory of dreams* says that dreaming represents the random and meaningless activity of nerve cells in the brain. According to this theory, an area in the brain, called the pons, sends millions of random nerve impulses to the cortex. In turn, the cortex tries to make sense of these random signals by creating the feelings, imagined movements, perceptions, changing scenes, and meaningless images that we define as dreams.

Hobson (1988) has somewhat revised the original activation-synthesis dream theory to acknowledge that dreams may have deep personal significance. He now believes that the images and feelings that our cortex imposes on millions of incoming neural signals reflect our past memories, bodily states (hungry, thirsty), strong hopes and fears, and our own personal view of the world. According to this theory, there is very little need to interpret dreams because they contain little useful information (Gardner, 1996).

The three theories of dreams that we have just discussed originated with thinkers in European-Western cultures. We'll compare these three theories with one that comes from a relatively ancient hunter-gatherer culture.

4 Entering the Spiritual World

The Inuit or Eskimo people have lived for thousands of years in quiet isolation along the arctic coasts of North America. The Inuit, along with other native or indigenous people, believe that dreams are ways to enter the spiritual world (Foulks, 1992).

The *Inuit believes* that in dreaming, one enters the spiritual world, where the souls of animals, supernaturals, and departed relatives are made known. Through dreams, forces in the spiritual world help a living person reflect on some present or future event.

Although the Inuit lived in a far different time, place, and culture than did Sigmund Freud or Western therapists, there are numerous parallels between their theories of dreams. For example, the Inuit, Freud, and Western therapists all believed that past forces, wishes, or concerns could be revealed to the dreamer; that these wishes, concerns, or desires could take symbolic forms; and that Inuit shamans, who were thought to possess spiritual powers, function like Freudian-trained psychoanalysts or Western-trained therapists, who are sometimes needed to interpret dream symbols or unravel the meaning of dreams. Notice, however, that each dream theory has a unique focus: Freud says that dreams are ways to reach the unconscious; modern therapists hold that dreams represent waking problems; and the Inuit believe that dreams are ways to enter the spiritual world.

Now that you know the different theories of what dreams mean, let's examine the kind of things people dream about.

Typical Dreams

What do people dream about?

Although many animals, including bats, whales, monkeys, moles, dogs, and cats (but not snakes), have REM sleep, we do not know if they dream. We know that humans dream because they tell us. Thousands of descriptions of dreams have been obtained from people who had just been aroused from REM sleep and others who were asked to record their dreams at home. One researcher has catalogued these descriptions and found that typical dreams have the following characteristics:

- they have several characters;
- they involve motion such as running or walking;
- they are more likely to take place indoors than out;
- they are filled with visual sensations but rarely include sensations of taste, smell, or pain;
- they seem bizarre because we disregard physical laws by flying or falling without injury;
- they may be recurrent—for example, dreams of being threatened, being pursued, or trying to hide;
- they more frequently involve emotions of anxiety or fear than joy or happiness;
- they rarely involve sexual encounters and are almost never about sexual intercourse;
- rarely can we dream about something we intend to;
- they are usually in color in sighted people and are auditory or tactile in blind people.

Researchers conclude that although individual dreams represent unique experiences, the format in which we dream, such as flying, falling, or hiding, is shared by others (Van de Castle, 1994).

For many of us, dreams are interesting and we like to talk about them. In a recent study, students who volunteered for dream interpretation sessions were mostly women (77%), but not all were equally good at using dreams to make associations to their waking lives (Hill et al., 1997). Some of these students reported having nightmares, which we'll discuss next in considering sleep problems and treatments.

H. Application: Sleep Problems & Treatments

Occurrence

How big is the problem?

In the United States, about 80 million people experience some kind of sleep problem. For example, some adults stop breathing in their sleep (sleep apnea); some have trouble going to or staying asleep (insomnia); a small percentage go from being wide awake to a very deep sleep quickly and without warning (narcolepsy); and about 25% of children under age 5 have a sleep disturbance (Carskadon & Taylor, 1997). We'll discuss a number of these sleep problems as well as possible treatments, beginning with one of the more common problems, insomnia.

Insomnia

"I had a major breakdown due to insomnia, work overload, and other emotional problems. . . . The insomnia had worn me down to the point where I couldn't care for myself" (NCSDR, 1993, p. 16).

In the United States, about 17 million adults have some type of insomnia.

Insomnia refers to difficulties in either going to sleep or staying asleep through the night. Insomnia is associated with a number of daytime complaints, including fatigue, impairment of concentration, memory difficulty, and lack of well-being.

Psychological causes of insomnia may include experiencing an overload of stressful events, worrying about personal or job-related difficulties, grieving over a loss or death, and coping with mental health problems. For students, a common cause of insomnia is a change in sleep schedule, such as staying up late Saturday night and sleeping late on Sunday morning. On Sunday night you will not be tired and ready for sleep at your usual time. This Sunday night insomnia may make you irritable and grumpy on Monday morning.

Physiological causes include changing to night-shift work that upsets circadian rhythms, having medical problems or chronic pain, and abusing alcohol or other substances (sedatives), all of which disrupt the sleep stages.

There are effective nondrug (psychological) and drug treatments for bouts of insomnia.

Nondrug Treatment

Nondrug treatments for insomnia may differ in method, but all have the same goal: to stop the person from excessive worrying and reduce tension, which are major psychological causes of insomnia. One proven cognitive-behavioral method of reducing insomnia is to establish an optimal sleep pattern (Bootzin & Rider, 1997).

Establishing an Optimal Sleep Pattern

Follow the following eight steps so that sleeping becomes more regular and efficient.

1. Go to bed only when you are sleepy, not by convention or habit.

2. Put the light out immediately when getting into bed.

3. Do not read or watch television in bed, since these are activities that you do when awake.

4. If you are not asleep within 20 minutes, get out of bed and sit and relax in another room until you are tired again. Relaxation can include tensing and relaxing your muscles or using visual imagery, which involves closing your eyes and concentrating on some calm scene or image for several minutes.

5. Repeat step 4 as often as required, and also if you wake up for any long periods of time.

6. Set the alarm to the same time each morning, so that your time of waking is always the same. This step is very important because oversleeping or sleeping in is one of the primary causes of insomnia the next night.

7. Do not nap during the day, because it will throw off your sleep schedule that night.

8. Follow this program rigidly for several weeks to establish an efficient and regular pattern of sleep.

Results. People who used this or similar nondrug treatments reduced their time for going to sleep from 64 to 36 minutes. Although there were few differences between nondrug treatments, programs similar to the above were among the most effective for treating insomnia (Bootzin & Rider, 1997). More serious problems with insomnia may be treated with drugs.

Drug Treatment

Many stressful situations, such as losing a loved one, going through a divorce, or dealing with a physical injury, may result in chronic insomnia, which is defined as lasting longer than three weeks. In these cases, doctors most often prescribe one of the benzodiazepines.

Benzodiazepines (ben-zo-die-AS-ah-peens), which reduce anxiety, worry, and stress, are commonly prescribed for and effective in the short-term (3–4 weeks) treatment of insomnia. However, with increasing dosage and prolonged usage, benzodiazepines (Dalmane, Xanax, Halcion) may produce side effects that can include daytime drowsiness, loss of memory, tolerance, and dependency.

Because benzodiazepines reduce anxiety, a chief cause of insomnia, they are an effective treatment and are relatively safe when taken in moderate dosages for short periods of time (3–4 weeks) (Kuffer & Reynolds, 1997).

However, the continual use of benzodiazepines, especially at higher dosages, may lead to dependence on the drug and serious side effects, such as memory loss, and excessive sleepiness. New drugs are constantly being introduced, such as Ambien, which is not a benzodiazepine but has proved effective in treating insomnia (Priest et al., 1997). For the management of long-term insomnia, clinicians recommend a program combining nondrug (psychological) and drug treatment.

Sleep Apnea

In the United States, about 20 million adults have insomnia because they stop breathing, a problem called sleep apnea.

Sleep apnea refers to repeated periods during sleep when a person stops breathing for 10 seconds or longer. The person may repeatedly stop breathing, momentarily wake up, resume breathing, and return to sleep. Repeated awakenings during the night result in insomnia and leave the person exhausted during the day but not knowing the cause of their tiredness.

Chances of developing sleep apnea are increased if a person has a habit of intense and frequent snoring, is overweight, uses alcohol, or takes sedatives (benzodiazepines) (Ball, 1997).

The treatment for sleep apnea partly depends upon its severity. The simplest treatment is to sew tennis balls in the back of a pajama top so the person cannot lie on his or her back, which increases the chances of sleep apnea. The most popular therapy is a device that blows air into a sealed mask that the person wears over the nose. In severe cases, people with sleep apnea may have to wear a mouth device similar to a retainer or undergo surgery to remove tonsils or alter the position of the jaw (Saskin, 1997).

Narcolepsy

"I have lived with narcolepsy for 45 years. . . . I was directly responsible for several near-fatal automobile accidents. The simple joys everyone takes for granted are, for the most part denied me. I would literally sleep the rest of my life away" (NCSDR, 1993, p. 16).

Narcolepsy (NAR-ko-lep-see) is a chronic disorder that is marked by excessive sleepiness, usually in the form of sleep attacks or short lapses of sleep throughout the day. The sleep attacks are accompanied by brief periods of REM sleep, and by muscle paralysis (cataplexy) that may range from tilting head to buckling knees and falling to the ground.

Narcolepsy has a genetic component that results in a problem with the neural mechanisms that control the sleep-wake cycle (Mignot, 1997).

The photo below shows sleep researcher Dr. William Dement holding a narcoleptic dog that is an animal model for studying causes of narcolepsy.

Narcoleptics describe their sleep attacks as irresistible. They report falling asleep in very inappropriate places, such as while carrying on a conversation or driving a car. One treatment for narcolepsy is to prescribe stimulant drugs, such as amphetamine, which help prevent the onset of sleep attacks (Mindell, 1997).

Sleep Disturbances

NIGHT TERRORS

About 7% of all children experience night terrors (Mindell, 1993).

Night terrors, which occur during stage 3 or 4 (delta sleep), are frightening experiences that often start with a piercing scream, followed by sudden waking in a fearful state with rapid breathing and increased heart rate. However, the next morning the child has no memory of the frightening experience.

A child in the grip of night terrors is difficult to calm and, even if severely shaken, may need several minutes to regain full awareness. Night terrors are most common in children aged 4–12 and tend to disappear by adolescence. Caregivers should take enough time to comfort and soothe the frightened child, who usually will go back to sleep.

NIGHTMARES

Besides night terrors, about 25% of all children aged 3–6 have nightmares; about 10% of college students report having them once a month (Levin, 1994).

Nightmares, which occur during REM sleep, are very frightening and anxiety-producing images that occur during dreaming. Nightmares usually involve great danger—being attacked, injured, or pursued. Upon awakening, the person can usually describe the nightmare in great detail.

Nightmares usually stop when the person wakes, but feelings of anxiety or fear may persist for some time; it may be difficult to go back to sleep. One effective treatment for nightmares involves regular use of anxiety-reduction techniques (described in Module 21).

SLEEPWALKING

One of the more unusual sleep disturbances involves sleepwalking.

Sleepwalking usually occurs in stage 3 or 4 (delta sleep) and consists of getting up and walking while literally sound asleep. Sleepwalkers generally have poor coordination, are clumsy but can avoid objects, and can engage in very limited conversation.

Occasional sleepwalking is considered normal in children; frequent sleepwalking in adults may be caused by increased stress or mental problems. Sleepwalking can be a serious problem because of the potential of injury and harm to oneself and others (imagine sleepwalking out of the house onto the highway).

Sleep researchers and clinicians are alerting Americans to the growing number of people with sleep problems, many who don't know they have one, and the need to provide diagnostic and treatment facilities (Pressman & Orr, 1997).

A. CONTINUUM OF CONSCIOUSNESS

1. The awareness of our own thoughts and feelings, as well as of other internal and external stimuli, is called (a)_____, which occurs on a continuum from being very alert to being very unresponsive. Those activities that require our full awareness and concentration to reach some goal are called (b)_____. Those activities that require little awareness and minimal attention and that do not interfere with other ongoing activities are called (c)_____.

2. Fantasizing or dreaming while awake, which often occurs during automatic processes, is called (a)_____. If, under the influence of drugs, meditation, or hypnosis, we perceive our internal and external environments in ways that differ from normal, we may be said to have entered (b)_____ of consciousness. Sigmund Freud suggested that we push unacceptable wishes or desires into our (c)_____. A blow to the head or general anesthesia can produce complete loss of awareness, which is called (d)_____. Mental structures and processes that, although we are unaware of them, influence our conscious thoughts and behaviors are collectively called the (e)_____.

B. RHYTHMS OF SLEEPING & WAKING

3. A biological clock that is set to run on a time cycle of 24–25 hours is called a (a)_____. In animals (and probably humans) the biological clock for the sleep-wake cycle is located in a part of the hypothalamus called the (b)_____.

4. If we travel across time zones and our circadian rhythm gets out of phase with the local clock time, we experience difficulty in going to sleep and getting up at normal times, a condition known as (a)_____. Researchers have been able to reset circadian rhythms in workers by exposing them to bright light during certain times; this is called (b)_____ therapy.

5. In the center of the animal and human brain is the pineal gland, a small group of cells that secrete the hormone _____. This hormone has a major role in regulating the sleep-wake cycle in animals; its role in humans is less clear.

C. WORLD OF SLEEP

6. Researchers study sleep and wakefulness by recording the activity of brain cells and muscles. Electrical brain activity is recorded in trac-ings called an (a)_____. The height of a wave is called its (b)_____, and the number of wave cycles that occur in one second is called the (c)_____.

7. If you are awake and alert, your brain waves have a very high frequency and low amplitude and are called (a)_____ waves. If you close your eyes and become relaxed and drowsy, your brain waves remain low in amplitude but decrease slightly in frequency; these are called (b)_____ waves.

8. Researchers divide sleep into five stages. Stage 1, the transition from wakefulness to sleep, is marked by (a)_____ waves and a feeling of gradually losing responsiveness to the outside world. Stage 2 represents the first real phase of sleep and is marked by high-frequency bursts of brain activity called (b)_____. In stage 3 and especially stage 4, there are high-amplitude, low-frequency brain waves called (c)_____. Stage 4 may be considered the deepest stage of sleep, since it is the most difficult from which to wake someone. Together, stages 1, 2, 3, and 4 are referred to as (d)_____ sleep, which makes up about 80% of sleep time.

9. About every 30–90 minutes throughout sleep, you leave stage 4 (delta sleep) and progress upward to stage 2. From stage 2, you enter a new stage of sleep marked by high-frequency, low-amplitude brain waves that look identical to (a)_____ waves. This stage is called (b)_____ sleep, because your eyes move rapidly back and forth underneath closed eyelids. During this stage, you are asleep and lose muscle tension in the neck and limbs. However, your brain waves are like those when awake and alert, and there is increased arousal of many physiological responses. When awakened from this stage, people usually (80–100% of the time) report that they have been (c)_____.

D. RESEARCH FOCUS: CIRCADIAN PREFERENCE

10. People who prefer to get up earlier, go to bed earlier, and engage in morning activities and whose body temperature rises more quickly in the morning and peaks earlier at night are called (a)_____. People who prefer to get up later, go to bed later, and engage in afternoon-evening activities and whose body temperature rises more slowly in the morning and peaks later at night are called (b)_____.

E. QUESTIONS ABOUT SLEEP

11. Going to sleep is regulated by the following factors. An area in the hypothalamus that is the master sleep switch is called the (a)_____. An area in the hypothalamus that regulates circadian rhythms is called the (b)_____ nucleus. A brain area that contributes to our staying awake by sending neural signals that alert and arouse the forebrain is called the (c)_____. Several different sleep chemicals and (d)_____, some of which are made in the pons, regulate going in and out of the stages of sleep. In addition, we go to sleep several hours after a fall in body (e)_____ and get up when it starts to rise.

12. From infancy through old age, there is a gradual reduction in total (a)_____ time, from about 17 to 6.5 hours, and a reduction in the percentage of (b)_____ sleep, from about 50% to 20%.

13. The theory that says we sleep because we use up vital factors during the day that must be replaced at night is called the (a)_____ theory. The theory that says we sleep to conserve energy and avoid potential harm and injury from nocturnal predators is called the (b)_____ theory.

14. When we are sleep deprived, the next day we have difficulty performing tasks that require (a)_____. Sleep deprivation also affects the body, as measured by a decrease in killer cells, which are important in the functioning of our (b)_____ system, which fights off infections and toxic agents.

F. CULTURAL DIVERSITY: INCIDENCE OF SAD

15. The occurrence of a pattern of depressive symptoms that generally begin in the fall and winter and disappear in the spring is called (a)_____. Although the incidence of this disorder is lower in Florida and higher on the north-eastern coast of the United States, it is not higher in Iceland, which is much farther north than New York State. One reason Icelanders report lower incidence of SAD is because of their (b)_____ values.

Iceland

G. WORLD OF DREAMS

16. According to Freud's theory, dreams represent (a)_____. This involves satisfying unconscious desires, especially those involving sex and aggression, that cannot be fulfilled during waking hours because they would create too much guilt or anxiety. According to Hobson and McCarley's original theory, called the (b)_____, dreaming has no meaning because it results from the random and meaningless activity of millions of neurons. According to many therapists and sleep-dream researchers, such as Cartwright, dreams are (c)_____ of waking thoughts and concerns, especially emotional ones, and provide clues to a person's problems. According to the Inuit culture, dreams are a way to enter the (d)_____ world.

H. APPLICATION: SLEEP PROBLEMS & TREATMENTS

17. A common sleep problem that includes difficulty in going to sleep or remaining asleep throughout the night is called (a)_____. A nondrug treatment is to use a proven (b)_____ method. Drug treatment for insomnia usually involves prescribing (c)_____. Insomnia caused when the sleeper stops breathing and wakes up is called (d)_____.

18. If children wake up screaming and in a great fright, they have experienced (a)_____ but will remember nothing the next morning. When adults experience emotionally charged, frightening images during their dreams, they are having (b)_____. If a person walks or carries out other behaviors during sleep, it is called (c)_____, which may be caused by increased stress. A relatively rare condition that involves irresistible attacks of sleepiness, brief periods of REM and often muscle paralysis is called (d)_____.

Answers: *1. (a) consciousness, (b) controlled processes, (c) automatic processes; 2. (a) daydreaming, (b) altered states, (c) unconscious, (d) unconsciousness, (e) cognitive unconscious; 3. (a) circadian rhythm, (b) suprachiasmatic nucleus; 4. (a) jet lag, (b) light; 5. melatonin; 6. (a) electroencephalogram, or EEG, (b) amplitude, (c) frequency; 7. (a) beta, (b) alpha; 8. (a) theta, (b) sleep spindles, (c) delta waves, (d) non-REM; 9. (a) beta, (b) REM, (c) dreaming; 10. (a) morning people, (b) evening people; 11. (a) ventrolateral preoptic nucleus, (b) suprachiasmatic nucleus, (c) reticular formation, (d) neurotransmitters, (e) temperature; 12. (a) sleep, (b) REM; 13. (a) repair, (b) adaptive; 14. (a) concentration, (b) immune; 15. (a) SAD, or seasonal affective disorder, (b) cultural; 16. (a) wish fulfillment, (b) activation-synthesis theory, (c) extensions, (d) spiritual; 17. (a) insomnia, (b) cognitive-behavioral, (c) benzodiazepines, (d) sleep apnea; 18. (a) night terrors, (b) nightmares, (c) sleepwalking, (d) narcolepsy.*

Newspaper Article

QUESTIONS

SORRY, FREUD, DREAMS AREN'T CONFLICT RESOLVERS

by Nicholas Wade

QUESTIONS

1. According to this study, what are the purposes of REM sleep?

2. What technique did the researchers use to study the sleeping brain?

3. What phases of sleep did the researchers focus on? Why?

4. Which areas of the brain are active and which are shut down during REM sleep?

5. According to this research, why do our dreams have such bizarre, fluid plots?

6. In light of this research, do you think dreams are meaningless brain "static," or do they have meaning?

New measurements taken from sleeping people explain, at least in part, why dreams tend to have such bizarre but vivid storylines. The findings deal a blow to the Freudian interpretation of dreams but leave open the possibility that some useful personal meaning can be extracted from them. The main purpose of dreams, however, the authors of the new study believe, is to test whether the brain has had enough sleep and, if so, to wake it up.

The new results show that in sleep, the frontal lobes of the brain are shut down. In the absence of activity in these lobes, which integrate other information and make sense of the outside world, the sleeping brain's images are driven by its emotional centers. The content of these dreams may be vivid and gripping but lacks coherence.

The new results are consistent with the theory that memories are consolidated during sleep. From the pattern of activity that was recorded, "it seems that memories already in the system are being read out and filed in terms of their emotional salience, which is an extremely interesting idea," said Dr. J. Allan Hobson of Harvard Medical School.

The new measurements were made by applying the technique known as PET scanning to sleeping subjects. The biologists focused on the two forms of sleep, known as slow-wave sleep and REM sleep. REM sleep, so named because of the rapid eyeball movements that occur then, takes place about four times during the night and is the phase from which the most vivid dreams are recalled.

During REM sleep, the primary visual cortex is shut down, along with other input areas that relay information from the senses. The primary visual cortex is the area in the back of the head where information from the eyes first reaches the cortex. The sleeping brain is thus cut off from its usual stream of information from the outside world. Also off line during REM sleep are the brain's frontal lobes. These include many of the higher centers of thought and action, including working memory, the planning and executive function, and the centers that integrate data from other regions of the brain. Much of the rest of the brain, including the centers that handle emotions and the laying down of long-term memories, are highly active during REM sleep.

Source: New York Times News Service, appeared in *San Diego Union-Tribune,* January 7, 1998.

Study Questions

A. Continuum of Consciousness—How many different states of consciousness have you been in today? (See answer in Critical Thinking Appendix.)

B. Rhythms of Sleeping & Waking—If an ad promised a device to cure jet lag, what would the device do?

C. World of Sleep—How would we know whether astronauts in space were awake, asleep, or dreaming?

D. Research Focus: Circadian Preference—What kind of problems might arise if a morning person married an evening person? (See answer in Critical Thinking Appendix.)

E. Questions about Sleep—If researchers discovered the perfect sleeping pill, how might it work?

F. Cultural Diversity: Incidence of SAD—What cultural values might New York residents have that contribute to their incidence of SAD? (See answer in Critical Thinking Appendix.)

G. World of Dreams—Which of the four theories most closely matches your personal beliefs about what dreams mean?

H. Application: Sleep Problems & Treatments—If you worked in a clinic that treated sleep problems, what kinds of symptoms would your patients have?

LINKS TO LEARNING

Web Sites & Learning Activities

● BROOKS/COLE ONLINE PSYCHOLOGY STUDY CENTER

http://psychstudy.brookscole.com/student/plotnik/quiz/ch07frm.html

This site gives students a chance to review material by taking quizzes and doing exercises and activities for this module.

● ASSOCIATION FOR THE SCIENTIFIC STUDY OF CONSCIOUSNESS

http://www.phil.vt.edu/ASSC/

This site includes transcripts of seminars on various topics in consciousness research, journal articles, bibliographies, and links that cover current and historical issues in consciousness.

● NATIONAL SLEEP FOUNDATION

http://www.sleepfoundation.org/

This organization's Web site features information on sleep disorders, the latest news on sleep-related issues, publications, and links.

● SLEEPNET

http://www.sleepnet.com.

This site is an index to "everything you wanted to know about sleep but were too tired to ask," including information on sleep disorders, research, labs, and support groups.

● THE ASSOCIATION FOR THE STUDY OF DREAMS

http://www.ASDreams.org/

This interesting site includes an on-line journal, a bulletin board for dream discussion, articles, and information on graduate study in dream-related areas.

Welcome to the WEB

● *THE INTERPRETATION OF DREAMS* BY SIGMUND FREUD

http://www.psych-web.com/books/interp/toc.html

Sure, you know Freud is famous in part for his theories on dreams, but have you ever read his influential work on the subject? Now is your chance to read a complete digital version of Freud's book.

● A CHECKLIST FOR MEDITATION

http://www.sonic.net/~jotokuji/Zazen/html

Meditation is seen by many people as a safe way to access altered states of consciousness. This site offers instructions on how to meditate, plus real-time-chat meditation counseling.

Activities

● *Integrator Online™ for Introductory Psychology* CD-ROM, Plotnik, Module 7

● Study Guide to accompany *Introduction to Psychology*, 5th edition, Module 7 (choice of PC or Mac computer version or hard copy).

● PsychNow! CD-ROM
    Sleep and Dreaming

Answers to questions on page 166

1. The purposes of REM sleep are (1) to determine whether the brain has had enough sleep and, if so, to wake it up, and (2) possibly to store long-term memories.
2. They used PET scans.
3. They focused on slow-wave sleep and, especially, on REM sleep because it is the stage of sleep when the brain centers that handle emotions and the laying down of long-term memories are highly active.
4. The primary visual cortex and frontal lobes are shut down, while the centers of emotion and long-term memory are active.
5. Because the frontal lobes, which include many of the higher centers of thought and action, are shut down during dreaming, the plot doesn't unfold in a linear or logical way.
6. This research does not preclude the possibility that dreams may have meaningful personal content.

Module 8   HYPNOSIS & DRUGS

A. Hypnosis *170*

* DEFINITION
* THEORIES OF HYPNOSIS
* BEHAVIORS
* APPLICATIONS

B. Drugs: Overview *174*

* REASONS FOR USE
* DEFINITION OF TERMS
* USE OF DRUGS
* EFFECTS ON NERVOUS SYSTEM

C. Stimulants *176*

* DEFINITION
* AMPHETAMINES
* COCAINE
* CAFFEINE
* NICOTINE

303 tons

D. Opiates *179*

* OPIUM, MORPHINE, HEROIN
* TREATMENT

E. Hallucinogens *180*

* DEFINITION
* LSD
* PSILOCYBIN
* MESCALINE
* DESIGNER DRUGS

F. Alcohol *182*

* HISTORY AND USE
* DEFINITION AND EFFECTS
* RISK FACTORS
* PROBLEMS

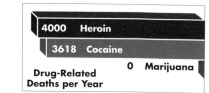

G. Cultural Diversity: Rates of Alcoholism *185*

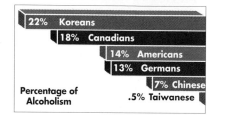

22% Koreans
18% Canadians
14% Americans
13% Germans
7% Chinese
.5% Taiwanese

Percentage of Alcoholism

* DEFINITION
* CULTURAL FACTORS

H. Marijuana *186*

* USE AND EFFECTS

4000 Heroin
3618 Cocaine
0 Marijuana

Drug-Related Deaths per Year

I. Research Focus: Drug Prevention *187*

* HOW EFFECTIVE IS THE DARE PROGRAM?

J. Application: Treatment for Drug Abuse *188*

* CASE HISTORY
* SUBSTANCE ABUSE
* TREATMENT

168

Introduction

Hypnosis

Why do people do stupid things?

One night a friend and I were sitting in the front row of one of the longest-running nightclub acts in San Diego. We are going to watch a psychologist-turned-performer who entertained locals and tourists by hypnotizing volunteers from the audience and asking them to perform funny, strange, and somewhat embarrassing acts on a stage. Before the hypnotist appeared, my friend Paul repeated for the tenth time that nothing would get him up on that stage.

Finally the lights dimmed, and the hypnotist appeared. He was a very good performer and soon had the audience laughing at his jokes and believing that he was a wonderful, trustworthy human being.

"Now we come to the interesting part," the hypnotist said in a low, soothing voice. "Just sit back and relax and, if you wish, follow my suggestions." The hypnotist slowly repeated a list of suggestions: "You cannot bend your right arm . . . you cannot close your eyes . . . your left arm will become rigid and slowly rise above your head."

As I looked around the dimly lit room, a number of rigid left arms were slowly rising. To my surprise, one of those arms was Paul's. (I could not or would not raise my arm, for fear that some of my students were in the audience and would never let me forget it.)

At the end of the show, we all filed out. Paul said nothing until we were in the car. Then he turned and asked, "Why did you let me get on that stage and be hypnotized? You better not tell anyone."

I smiled and replied, "You were terrific. That was the best imitation of Elvis Presley ever done by a reluctant friend." Then I added, "I might have been tempted to try Mick Jagger."

Although I have changed Paul's name and minor details to protect his pride and reputation, his story is essentially true and illustrates some of the strange behaviors that occur under hypnosis.

For over 200 years, psychologists have puzzled over what hypnosis really is and what it does. For example, some believe that hypnosis is a trancelike state in which people will do almost anything that is suggested by a trustworthy hypnotist. Others believe that hypnosis is just another method to induce people to comply with the demands of the situation. We'll discuss whether hypnosis is truly a trance-like state.

Many are interested in how effective hypnosis is in changing attitudes and behaviors, since our local paper carries ads claiming that hypnosis can help you stop smoking, lose weight, get rid of phobias, induce immediate relaxation, reduce pain, or increase motivation to tackle difficult projects. We'll discuss whether these claims for hypnosis are true.

Drugs

What was the first bicycle trip?

While only some psychologists believe that hypnosis may change a person's state of consciousness, most agree that there are a number of drugs, legal and illegal, that can alter consciousness. One example of how a drug greatly altered consciousness happened quite by chance and began with a bike ride.

On April 19, 1943, Albert Hofmann left his laboratory, got on his bike, and began pedaling his regular route home. As Albert pedaled, the world around him began to change into threatening, wavering forms that appeared distorted, as if he was looking into a curved mirror. Once he reached home and entered his house, the familiar objects and pieces of furniture assumed grotesque and threatening forms that were in continual motion. After a while, the threatening forms disappeared, and he began to enjoy an incredible display of visual sensations and illusions. He saw fantastic images that opened and closed in circles and spirals that seemed to explode into colored fountains. Even stranger, sounds such as the passing of a car or opening of a door were transformed into visual images with changing forms and colors (adapted from Hofmann, 1983).

The causes of Albert Hofmann's startling visual experiences during his bike ride was LSD. That day, he took LSD, which he had earlier discovered in his laboratory. However, Albert had not known about LSD's potency and had mistakenly taken a dosage that was four times the usual amount. We will discuss LSD, as well as other illegal and legal drugs that can alter consciousness.

What's Coming

We'll discuss what hypnosis is, how a person is hypnotized, what a person does and does not do under hypnosis, and the uses of hypnosis. We'll examine the use and abuse of both legal and illegal drugs, such as stimulants, hallucinogens, opiates, marijuana, and alcohol. We'll discuss how drugs affect the nervous system, their dangers, and the treatments for drug abuse.

Let's begin with an interesting and supposedly mind-altering force called animal magnetism.

A. Hypnosis

Definition

What is hypnosis?

In the late 1700s, Anton Mesmer was the hit of Paris, France, as he claimed to cure a variety of symptoms by passing a force into a patient's body; he called this force animal magnetism. So many patients testified to the success of animal magnetism as a treatment that a committee of the French Academy of Science was appointed to investigate. The committee concluded that many of Mesmer's patients were indeed cured of various psychosomatic problems. However, the committee thought it safer to ban the future use of animal magnetism because they could neither identify what it was or verify Mesmer's claims that such a force existed. Mesmer's name lives on in our vocabulary: We use the term *mesmerized* to describe

someone who is acting strangely because he or she has been spellbound or hypnotized.

Today we know that Mesmer was not creating animal magnetism but rather was inducing hypnosis. Here's the definition agreed to by the American Psychological Association's Division of Psychological Hypnosis (1993).

Hypnosis is a procedure in which a researcher, clinician, or hypnotist suggests that a person will experience changes in sensations, perceptions, thoughts, feelings, or behaviors.

We'll begin by answering three questions that are often asked about hypnosis.

Who Can Be Hypnotized?

Despite what you may have seen on television or at a stage show, not everyone can be easily hypnotized.

College Students and Hypnosis

High susceptibility	30%
Medium susceptibility	30%
Low susceptibility	40%

As shown in the graph above, about 40% of college students have low susceptibility to hypnosis, which means that they cannot be easily hypnotized. About 30% of college students have medium susceptibility, and the remaining 30% have high susceptibility to being hypnotized (Bates, 1994).

Since the time of William James (1890) and Sigmund Freud (1891), psychologists have investigated why people differ in susceptibility. They found that hypnotic susceptibility is not correlated with introversion, extraversion, social position, intelligence, willpower, sex, compliance, gullibility, weakness, or persuadability (Kirsch & Lynn, 1995). Researchers did find that positive expectations about hypnosis are related to greater susceptibility and successful treatment (Bates, 1994). Let's see how someone is tested for susceptibility to hypnosis.

Who Is Susceptible?

The standard test for susceptibility is to hypnotize a person and then give a fixed set of suggestions (Kirsch, 1997; Woody, 1997). The best-known test is the Stanford Hypnotic Susceptibility Scale, which asks the individual to carry out both simple suggestions—for example, "Your arm is moving up," and complex suggestions—for example, "Your body is heavy and you cannot stand up."

For instance, the person in the photo below is carrying out the hypnotic suggestion, "Your right arm is weightless and moving up."

Individuals who score high on the Stanford scale are usually easily hypnotized and tend to remain so across time. Compared to adults, young children, especially of ages 8–12, are more susceptible to hypnosis (Bates, 1994).

Next let's see how a person is actually hypnotized.

How Is Someone Hypnotized?

Although a number of different procedures are used, most use some the following suggestions to induce hypnosis.

Hypnotic induction refers to various methods to induce hypnosis, including asking subjects to close their eyes and go to sleep, having them fix their attention on an object (such as a watch), and instructing them to go into deep relaxation.

For example, here is a commonly used method to induce hypnosis:

1. The hypnotist establishes a sense of trust, so that the subject feels comfortable in the situation.
2. The hypnotist suggests that the subject concentrate on something, such as the sound of the hypnotist's voice, an object, or an image.
3. The hypnotist suggests what the subject will experience during hypnosis—for example, becoming relaxed, feeling sleepy, or having a floating feeling. The hypnotist may say, "I am going to count from one to ten, and with each count you will drift more and more deeply into hypnosis" (Bates, 1994).

This procedure works on both individuals and groups, provided the individuals are all susceptible to hypnosis.

Researchers have found that responsiveness during hypnosis depends more on the subject's efforts and abilities rather than on the hypnotist's skill; that hypnosis is not related to sleep; that subjects retain their ability to control their behaviors during hypnosis and are aware of their surroundings; that most hypnotized subjects are not faking their responses; and that hypnosis is not a dangerous procedure when used by an experienced researcher or clinician (Kirsch & Lynn, 1995; Orne & Evans, 1965). What actually happens when a person is under hypnosis and why hypnosis works is our next queston.

Theories of Hypnosis

Why does hypnosis work?

Explanations of hypnosis have significantly changed over the past 30 years. In the 1960s and 1970s, there were primarily two views. One view held that hypnosis was a trancelike state during which a person was more likely to carry out suggestions. The other view disagreed and held that hypnosis was not a trancelike state. After years of debate, the two views have edged more closely together and dropped the idea of a trance-like state. Currently, the explanation for hypnosis can best be thought of as on a continuum, which ranges from those who hold that hypnosis is an altered state (but not a trancelike state) to those who believe that hypnosis is not an altered state but results from a combination of social pressures and personal abilities (Kirsch & Lynn, 1995). We'll discuss both ends of the continuum and their explanations for why my shy friend got the nerve to get up on stage and imitate Elvis Presley.

Altered State Theory of Hypnosis

On one side of the hypnosis continuum are researchers and clinicians who view hypnosis as an altered state (Kirsch & Lynn, 1995).

The *altered state theory of hypnosis* holds that hypnosis is not a trancelike state but rather an altered state of consciousness, during which a person experiences different sensations and feelings.

Although this is currently a popular view, the followers of Milton Erickson (1980/1941), who was generally recognized to be the world's leading practitioner of medical hypnosis, hold to the belief that hypnosis puts clients into a trancelike state in which their conscious limitations are partially suspended, so that they can be receptive to alternative ways of thinking and behaving. Thus, at this end of the hypnosis continuum, the most extreme view, which is held by followers of Erickson, believe that hypnosis is an altered state that is also a trancelike state; the more popular, moderate view is that hypnosis is an altered state, in the same way that daydreaming is an altered state, but it is not a trancelike state (Kirsch & Lynn, 1995).

ALTERED STATE

To explain how hypnosis might produce an altered state, psychologist Ernest Hilgard (1977) has developed the hidden observer concept. So that you can experience the *hidden observer* phenomenon, we'll place you in a hypnotic experiment.

Imagine being hypnotized and told that your consciousness is divided into two parts. Your hypnotized part will feel little or no pain and can answer questions orally. Your unhypnotized part will feel normal pain sensations; it cannot answer questions orally but can answer by tapping your finger—once for yes and twice for no. Now the hypnotist asks you to plunge one hand in ice water, which is painful but not injurious, with the suggestion that you will not feel pain. When asked, "Do you feel pain?" the voice controlled by your hypnotized part answers "No." But the finger controlled by your unhypnotized, hidden part taps once, indicating "Yes" (Hilgard, 1979). Findings from such experiments support the idea that hypnosis produces an altered state in which consciousness is divided into two parts—the hidden observer and the conscious self.

However, the idea of hypnosis producing an altered state has been challenged by the sociocognitive theory of hypnosis.

Sociocognitive Theory of Hypnosis

On the other side of the hypnosis continuum are researchers who currently reject the idea that hypnosis is an altered or trancelike state and propose instead the sociocognitive theory of hypnosis (Lynn, 1997).

The *sociocognitive theory of hypnosis* says that the impressive effects of hypnosis are due to social influences and pressures as well as the subject's personal abilities.

One strong proponent of this theory is psychologist Irving Kirsch, who is currently editor of the journal *Contemporary Hypnosis* and has published more than 75 articles on hypnosis and therapeutic issues. Kirsch and other researchers have rejected the trance theory of hypnosis for three primary reasons. First, in spite of 30 years of research, no behavioral, physiological, or neurological measures have been found that distinguish hypnosis from other states of consciousness (Ray, 1997). Second, all the phenomena produced by suggestions during hypnosis, such as going back to an early age or imagining and behaving in strange ways, have also been produced by subjects who are not hypnotized. Third, increased suggestibility during hypnosis can be duplicated and even surpassed through other procedures, such as placebo pills and imagination training (Kirsch, 1994; Kirsch & Lynn, 1995).

To the question, "Does hypnosis produce an out-of-the-ordinary, trancelike, 'altered state' of consciousness?" Kirsch answers: "This was once a central question that divided hypnosis theorists into two opposing camps. However, researchers have established that one's response to hypnosis depends more on the abilities, beliefs, and interpretations of the person hypnotized than on the use of a hypnotic induction" (Kirsch & Lynn, 1995, p. 849).

EXPLAINING PAUL'S BEHAVIORS

We can now return to our earlier question of why shy Paul got up on a public stage and imitated Elvis Presley. At one end of the hypnosis continuum, researchers would answer that Paul got on stage and imitated Elvis Presley's gyrations and guitar-playing because he was in an altered state (Erickson's followers would say that he was in a trancelike state), during which he was especially likely to carry out the hypnotist's suggestions. At the other end of the hypnosis continuum, researchers would answer that Paul was motivated to get up on stage and act like Elvis because he felt social pressure from the audience and the hypnotist to carry out the hypnotist's suggestions and because Paul had the ability to imitate Elvis. Although why hypnosis works has different explanations, many clinicians agree that hypnosis has proved useful in a number of treatments and therapeutic settings—our next topic.

A. Hypnosis

Behaviors

How do people behave under hypnosis?

You have perhaps seen movies of people doing strange things, such as pretending they are chickens, after being hypnotized. However, as we describe the behaviors of people under hypnosis, keep in mind that these very same behaviors have also been performed by people who were asked to perform them without being hypnotized (Kirsch & Lynn 1995; Spanos, 1996). Thus, people who have the abilities may perform strange or unusual behaviors whether or not they are hypnotized.

Hypnotic Analgesia

Hypnosis has long been known to reduce pain; this is called hypnotic analgesia.

Hypnotic analgesia (*an-nall-GEEZ-ee-ah*) refers to a reduction in pain reported by clients after they had undergone hypnosis and received suggestions that reduced their anxiety and promoted relaxation.

Most recently, researchers used PET scans to show that hypnosis reduced the subjects' unpleasant feelings of pain though not the sensations of pain (Rainville et al., 1997). This means that when subjects put their hands in hot water they felt pain as usual but, depending on the hypnotic suggestions, reported it as either more or less unpleasant. Hypnotic analgesia has proved useful in helping patients cope with painful medical or dental treatments (Chaves, 1994).

Posthypnotic Suggestion

If subjects perform some behavior on cue after hypnosis, it's called a posthypnotic suggestion.

A *posthypnotic suggestion* is given to the subject during hypnosis about performing a particular behavior to a specific cue when the subject comes out of hypnosis.

Some believe that subjects who follow posthypnotic suggestions are acting automatically in response to some predetermined cue, such as smiling when they hear the word *student*. However, researchers have shown that subjects perform posthypnotic suggestions if they believe it is expected of them but stop performing if they believe the experiment is over or they are no longer being observed (Spanos, 1996).

Posthypnotic Amnesia

"When you wake up, you will not remember what happened." This suggestion is used to produce posthypnotic amnesia.

Posthypnotic amnesia is not remembering what happened during hypnosis if the hypnotist suggested that, upon awakening, the person would forget what took place during hypnosis.

One explanation is that the person forgets because the experiences have been repressed and made unavailable to normal consciousness. However, there is good evidence that, after coming out of hypnosis, what people remember or forget depends upon what they think or believe the hypnotist wants them to remember or forget (Spanos, 1996).

Age Regression

Could the 31-year-old woman shown at left be hypnotized and sent back to being the three-year-old child shown at the bottom? This phenomenon is called age regression.

Age regression refers to subjects under hypnosis being asked to regress, or return in time, to an earlier age, such as early childhood.

Researchers have found that during age regression, hypnotized subjects do not relive their earlier experiences as some believe but rather play the role of being a child. After an exhaustive review of more than 100 years of hypnosis research on age regression, one researcher concluded that there was no evidence that adults actually went back or regressed in time (Nash, 1987). Thus, researchers believe that, during age regression, hypnotized adults are not reliving childhood experiences but merely acting as they expect children to behave (Spanos, 1996).

Imagined Perception

When a hypnotized subject responds to a suggestion such as, "Try to swat that fly," it is called an imagined perception.

An *imagined perception* refers to experiencing sensations, perceiving stimuli, or performing behaviors that come from one's imagination.

Hypnotherapists use many forms of imagined perceptions in treating clients' problems. For example, one client imagined he was an armored knight on a great horse. After several therapy sessions, the therapist asked the client to remove the armor and discover his true self, which turned out to be a person afraid of his flaws (Eisen, 1994).

Conclusions

After spending most of his professional life studying hypnosis, this is what psychologist Nickolas Spanos concluded: "Hypnotic behavior looks unusual because hypnotized subjects are asked to do unusual things, things that in the normal course of everyday life people are rarely called on to do, such as behave as if they cannot bend their arms. . . . Excellent hypnotic subjects respond to the requests of a legitimate authority figure (the hypnotist) in the same way that most of us respond to the request of authority figures in everyday life" (Spanos, 1996, p. 39). Thus, people perform the same behaviors under hypnosis that they would perform if asked by a legitimate authority figure.

Next, we'll examine some of the therapeutic uses of hypnosis.

Applications

One use of hypnosis is entertainment: A stage hypnotist hypnotizes people in the audience, who come up on stage and perform unusual and often funny behaviors, such as Paul's wild imitation of Elvis.

However, there are also serious and legitimate uses of hypnosis in medical, dental, therapeutic, and behavioral settings. For example, the woman in the photo below is undergoing hypnosis before a potentially painful dental treatment. Here are some therapeutic uses of hypnosis.

Medical and Dental Uses

In both medical and dental settings, hypnosis can be used to reduce pain through hypnotic analgesia, to reduce fear and anxiety by helping individuals relax, or to help patients deal with a terminal disease by motivating them to make the best of a difficult situation (Erickson, 1994).

However, there is considerable evidence that clients who are highly susceptible to hypnosis are better able to respond to suggestions for pain reduction and body relaxation than are low-susceptibility clients (Bates, 1994).

For example, the graph below shows that subjects who were highly susceptible to hypnosis reported significantly lower levels of pain during hypnosis than did poorly susceptible subjects (Crawford et al., 1993). Pain was produced by putting a tourniquet, or binding, around the arm, which temporarily cuts off the blood supply and results in considerable pain. Researchers have only recently discovered what happens in the brains of subjects during hypnotic analgesia.

Average pain score in highly susceptible subjects — 0.8

Average pain score in poorly susceptible subjects — 9.3

Source: Adapted from Crawford et al., 1993

Researchers used PET scans to measure activity in different parts of the brain after subjects were hypnotized and told to place their hands in lukewarm (95°F) or "painfully hot" (115°F) water. Hypnotic suggestions to think of pain as *more unpleasant* (more painful) resulted in *decreased* brain activity in the frontal lobe (anterior cingulate cortex), while hypnotic suggestions to think of pain as *less unpleasant* (less painful) resulted in *increased* brain activity in the same area. In comparison, hypnotic instructions that pain was more or less unpleasant did not increase or decrease brain activity in the parietal lobe (somatosensory cortex), which indicates the reception of pain sensations (Rainville et al., 1997). Researchers concluded that hypnotic suggestions can change a person's *perception* of pain as more or less unpleasant, but hypnotic suggestions do not affect *receiving* pain sensations. This means that during hypnotic analgesia, subjects feel pain, but how much it bothers them depends on the kind of hypnotic suggestions.

Hypnosis is also used in helping people deal with or change their behaviors.

Therapeutic and Behavioral Uses

The use of hypnosis in therapy has a long history; Sigmund Freud (1905) used hypnosis with his patients. More recently, Milton Erickson (1980/1941), who is generally acknowledged to be the world's leading practitioner of therapeutic hypnosis, said that hypnosis made clients more open and receptive to alternative ways of problem solving. However, hypnosis is not for all clients; some people find hypnosis frightening because they fear losing control or because they believe it indicates a lack of willpower (Kirsch, 1994).

Therapists who often use hypnosis along with other techniques generally report that it is very useful in helping clients reveal their personalities, gain insights into their lives, and arrive at solutions to their problems. Research on hypnotherapy indicates that hypnosis can be a powerful tool that leads to successful outcomes when used in therapeutic settings (Coe, 1994; Dowd, 1994; Kirsch, 1994).

Clients who are highly susceptible to hypnosis generally respond better to suggestions aimed at treating a wide range of psychosomatic problems, which involve mind-body interactions. For example, hypnosis has been successfully used to reduce pain, decrease asthma attacks, remove warts, and relieve tension. But hypnosis is not as successful with problems of self-control, such as helping clients quit smoking, stop overeating, stop excessive drinking, or overcome other habits that interfere with optimal functioning (Bates, 1994).

The graph on the right shows the percentage of subjects who continued to smoke after receiving three different treatment programs. Notice that after three weeks of treatment, hypnosis was not statistically more significant in motivating people to

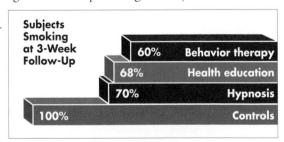

Subjects Smoking at 3-Week Follow-Up

Behavior therapy — 60%
Health education — 68%
Hypnosis — 70%
Controls — 100%

stop smoking than was health education or behavior modification.

From these results, we can conclude that all three programs were about equally effective and significantly better than controls (no treatment program) (Rabkin et al., 1984). Clinicians generally conclude that hypnosis by itself is not a miracle treatment but can be a useful technique when combined with other procedures (Rhue et al., 1994).

Although helpful in a therapeutic setting, evidence obtained under hypnosis is not allowed in most United States courts. That's because, under hypnosis, an examiner's questions or suggestions may bias or mislead witnesses and thus make their testimony unreliable (Perry, 1997).

Next, we'll discuss the use, abuse, and effects of drugs.

B. Drugs: Overview

Reasons for Use

Why do people use drugs?

Although humans have used drugs continually for the last 6000 years, worldwide usage of both legal and illegal drugs is becoming more prevalent and widespread (Hanson & Venturelli, 1998).

There is not one but many reasons people use drugs: to obtain pleasure, joy, and euphoria; to meet social expectations or give in to peer pressure; to deal with or escape stress, anxiety, and tension; to achieve altered states of consciousness; and to avoid pain (Siegel, 1989).

Americans use and spend billions of dollars on both legal drugs (right photo) and illegal drugs. One researcher, reviewing 200 years of drug use in the United States, concluded that we have gone through regular cycles of tolerant and intolerant attitudes toward illegal drug usage. Because history tends to repeat itself, the researcher warns that our society will continue to face physical

and psychological problems related to drugs (Musto, 1991). In what follows, we'll discuss stimulants, marijuana, hallucinogens, opiates, alcohol, and other commonly used psychoactive drugs.

Psychoactive drugs are chemicals that affect our nervous system and, as a result, may alter consciousness and awareness, influence how we sense and perceive things, and modify our moods, feelings, emotions, and thoughts. Psychoactive drugs are both licit (legal)—coffee, alcohol, and tobacco—and illicit (illegal)—marijuana, heroin, cocaine, and LSD.

Although all psychoactive drugs affect our nervous systems, how they affect our behaviors depends also on our psychological state and other social factors, such as peer pressure and society's values. To illustrate how drug usage involves both pharmacological and psychological factors, we describe a famous person who had a serious drug problem.

Definition of Terms

What famous therapist had a drug problem?

When this famous person was 38, his doctor told him to stop smoking because it was causing irregular heart beats. Although he tried to cut down, he was soon back to smoking his usual 20 cigars a day. When his heart problems grew worse, he stopped again. However, he experienced such terrible depression and mood swings that he started smoking to escape the psychological torture. When he was 67, small sores were discovered in his mouth and diagnosed as cancer. During the next 16 years, he had 33 operations for cancer on his mouth and jaw but continued smoking. By age 79, most of his jaw had been removed and replaced

by an artificial one. He was in continual pain and was barely able to swallow or talk. However, he continued to smoke an endless series of cigars. In 1939, at age 83, he died of cancer caused by 45 years of heavy smoking (Brecher, 1972; Jones, 1953).

Our famous person is none other than Sigmund Freud, the father of psychoanalysis. Freud had a serious drug problem most of his professional life—he was addicted to tobacco (nicotine). In spite of his great insights into the problems of others, he tried but could not treat his own drug addiction. Freud's struggle with smoking illustrates four important terms related to drug use and abuse—addicton, tolerance, dependence, and withdrawal symptoms (American Psychiatric Association, 1994).

Addiction

One reason Freud continued to smoke despite a heart condition was that he had an addiction.

Addiction means a person has developed a behavioral pattern of drug abuse that is marked by an overwhelming and compulsive desire to obtain and use the drug; and even after stopping, the person has a great tendency to relapse and begin using the drug again.

The reason Freud tried to give up smoking but relapsed each time was that he was heavily addicted to nicotine.

Tolerance

One reason Freud smoked as many as 20 cigars daily was that he had developed a tolerance to nicotine.

Tolerance means that after a person uses a drug repeatedly over a period of time, the original dose of the drug no longer produces the desired effect so that a person must take increasingly larger doses of the drug to achieve the same behavioral effect.

Becoming tolerant was a sign that Freud had become dependent on nicotine.

Dependence

Another reason Freud found it difficult to quit smoking was that he developed a dependency on nicotine.

Dependency refers to a change in the nervous system so that a person now needs to take the drug to prevent the occurrence of painful withdrawal symptoms.

Addiction and dependence combine to make stopping doubly difficult.

Withdrawal Symptoms

Being dependent on nicotine, when Freud stopped smoking he had withdrawal symptoms.

Withdrawal symptoms are painful physical and psychological symptoms that occur after a drug-dependent person stops using the drug.

Freud described his withdrawal symptoms as being depressed, having images of dying, and feeling so tortured that it was beyond his human power to bear (Jones, 1953).

Next we'll examine a number of specific drugs that people use.

Use of Drugs

Which drugs do people use?

In the United States, people spend about $91 billion yearly on legal drugs (alcohol, nicotine, caffeine) and about $50 billion on illegal drugs (cocaine, crack, marijuana, heroin) (Fineman & Pyes, 1996; Hanson & Venturelli, 1998). The graph on the right shows that two of the more popular psychoactive drugs are alcohol and nicotine, which are also the two drugs most often used by individuals who go on to use illegal drugs (Stanton et al., 1997).

To control the widespread use of illegal drugs, the U.S. government spent about $15 billion in 1996: 70% on law enforcement and 30% on treatment. Although the bulk of the money went for law enforcement, a General Accounting study concluded that even though drug agents seized 100 tons of cocaine in 1996, such efforts "... have not materially reduced the availability of drugs" (Darling, 1996). For that reason, many drug treatment professionals recommend that a better way to

Alcohol
Coffee (caffeine)
Cigarettes (nicotine)
Marijuana
Cocaine and crack
Hallucinogens
Methamphetamine
Heroin

Percentage of people who have used drugs at some time

0   10   20   30   40   50   60   70   80   90

Source: National Institute on Drug Abuse, 1993

reduce drug usage is to spend more money on drug education, counseling, and treatment (Gazzaniga, 1997). In support of this recommendation is a study by the California Department of Alcohol and Drug Programs, which concluded that drug treatment is highly cost-effective, regardless of the type of drug or treatment (Stolberg, 1994).

Because of the difficulty of controlling the use of illegal drugs, a number of prominent doctors, federal judges, and political writers have proposed legalizing such drugs (Savage, 1996). However, researchers concluded that there are so many unknowns that it is difficult to predict what effects drug legalization would have on usage or related personal and social problems (MacCoun, 1993; Rosenthal, 1994).

One reason legal and illegal psychoactive drugs are so popular is that they are a relatively quick and easy way to alter one's consciousness and emotional state. Psychoactive drugs alter consciousness by interfering with the nervous system's chemical keys and locks.

Effects on Nervous System

How do drugs work?

You may remember from Module 3 that the nervous system communicates by using chemical messengers called neurotransmitters. You can think of neurotransmitters as acting like chemical keys that open or close chemical locks on neighboring neurons (right figure). Opening chemical locks usually leads to increased neural activity, while closing chemical locks leads to decreased neural activity. We'll discuss two of the more common ways that drugs interfere with neural locks and keys and thus change a person's emotional, psychological, and physiological responses.

Neurotransmitters act like specific chemical keys.

Neurotransmitters' keys open or close chemical locks that increase or decrease neural activity.

1 Drugs Mimic Neurotransmitters

Endorphins

Your nervous system makes several dozen neurotransmitters as well as other chemicals (neuromodulators) that act like chemical messengers. After neurons release neurotransmitters, they act like chemical keys that search for and then either open or close chemical locks to either excite or inhibit neighboring neurons, organs, or muscles (top figure).

However, some drugs act like chemical keys that are so similar to neurotransmitters that these drugs can affect the same chemical locks (bottom figure). For example, morphine's chemical structure closely resembles that of the neurotransmitter endorphin. As a result of this similarity, morphine acts like, or mimics, the action of

Morphine or heroin

endorphin by affecting the same chemical locks, which decreases pain. Thus, some drugs produce their effects by mimicking the actions of neurotransmitters (Stahl, 1996).

2 Drugs Block Removal of Neurotransmitters

When excited, neurons secrete neurotransmitters (top figure) that move across a tiny space (synapse) and affect neighboring neurons' receptors (bottom figure). However, after a brief period, the neurotransmitters are reabsorbed back into the neuron. The action by which neurotransmitters are removed from the synapse through reabsorption is called *reuptake.* If reuptake did not occur, neurotransmitters would remain in the synapse, and neurons would be continually stimulated.

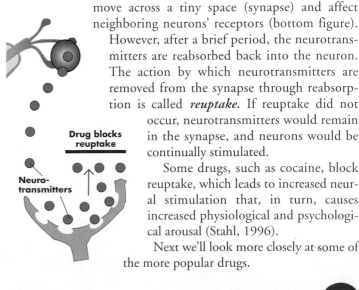

Drug blocks reuptake

Neurotransmitters

Some drugs, such as cocaine, block reuptake, which leads to increased neural stimulation that, in turn, causes increased physiological and psychological arousal (Stahl, 1996).

Next we'll look more closely at some of the more popular drugs.

B. *DRUGS: OVERVIEW* **175**

C. Stimulants

Definition

"Two pills beat a month's vacation."

This marketing slogan was used to sell amphetamines in Sweden in the 1940s. It resulted in epidemic usage that peaked in the mid-1960s.

In the 1940s, American doctors prescribed amphetamines as safe energizers, mood enhancers, and appetite suppressors. By the 1960s, billions of doses of amphetamines were being used in the United States and their usage had become a serious problem.

In the 1940s, Japanese workers used amphetamines to keep factory production high during World War II. After the war, many students, nightworkers, and people displaced by the war began to use "wake-amines." Amphetamine use spread until, in 1954, two million Japanese had become abusers and addicted.

By the early 1970s, most countries had brought amphetamine usage under control through a combination of measures, including regulation of prescriptions, decrease in supply, and stiffer penalties. However, at present, amphetamine-like stimulants, such as methamphetamine (crystal) and cocaine, are widely available on the black market.

All *stimulants,* including cocaine, amphetamines, caffeine, and nicotine, increase activity of the central nervous system and result in heightened alertness, arousal, euphoria, and decreased appetite and fatigue. Dose for dose, cocaine and amphetamines are considered powerful stimulants because they produce a strong effect with a small dose; caffeine and nicotine are considered mild stimulants.

We'll discuss the more widely used stimulants—amphetamines, cocaine, caffeine, and nicotine.

Amphetamines

Why is it still a problem?

During the 1960s, amphetamine pills were heavily prescribed to treat a wide range of problems, including fatigue, depression, and being overweight. This was also the time that young adults, called "flower children," took heavy doses of amphetamines that resulted in their having true paranoid psychotic symptoms, which resulted in their being called "speed freaks." Amphetamine usage peaked in the mid-1960s when over 31 million prescriptions were written for dieting and about 25 tons of legitimately manufactured amphetamines were diverted to illegal sales (Hanson & Venturelli, 1998). Finally, in 1971, the Food and Drug Administration (FDA) outlawed the prescription of amphetamines for everything except attention deficit hyperactivity disorder (ADHD) and narcolepsy.

However, following a "war" on cocaine in the late 1980s and early 1990s, there has been a dramatic upsurge in the use of a form of amphetamine, called methamphetamine, which is manufactured in illegal home laboratories (Howlett, 1997). The possession or use of methamphetamine is illegal.

Drug

In 1996, authorities raided over 800 illegal methamphetamine laboratories in California and 450 in the Midwest, where the drug has recently increased in popularity (Howlett, 1997).

Methamphetamine (D-methamphetamine) is close to amphetamine in both its chemical makeup and its physical and psychological effects. Unlike amphetamine, which is taken in pill form, methamphetamine (speed, crank, crystal, ice) can be smoked or snorted and produces an almost instantaneous high. Both amphetamine and methamphetamine cause marked increases in blood pressure and heart rate and feelings of enhanced mood, alertness, and energy.

"It's the ultimate high. . . . It makes you feel so powerful. You have tons of energy. . . . I loved it. I craved it" (Witkin, 1995, p. 50). So said 23-year-old Tara who developed a $200-a-day habit and lost her apartment, job, and infant daughter. Her euphoria from methamphetamine soon turned into a terrible nightmare.

Nervous System

The primary affect of amphetamines and related drugs (methamphetamine) is to increase the release of the neurotransmitter, dopamine, and secondarily, to block its reuptake (Stahl, 1996). Researchers are learning that the release of dopamine occurs during a wide range of pleasurable activities, such as sex (Schuster, 1997). Thus, drugs like methamphetamine are both so desirable and dangerous because they increase release of dopamine, which causes very pleasurable feelings.

Dangers

"I couldn't get high. No matter how much I did, no matter who I was with, nothing made me happy. I was so depressed. I wanted to die," said 23-year-old Tara, who was a heavy methamphetamine user (Witkin, 1995, p. 50). At first, users of methamphetamine or ice (a concentrated form) have periods of restless activity and perform repetitive behaviors. Later, the initial euphoria is replaced with depression, agitation, insomnia, and development of true paranoid feelings. Because of its risk for addiction and dependency, as well as physical and psychological problems, methamphetamine/ice is a very dangerous drug.

Because of a crackdown on amphetamines in the 1970s, there was an enormous increase in cocaine usage, which we'll discuss next.

Why has it been used for 3,000 years?

A drug's increase in popularity is partly due to the particular drug that enforcement agencies target for a crackdown. For example, the U.S. government's crackdown on amphetamine usage in the 1970s was largely responsible for the increased popularity of cocaine, whose usage reached epidemic proportions in the 1980s. In turn, the 1980s were marked by the government's "war" on cocaine, which was partly responsible for an upsurge in methamphetamine usage in the 1990s.

Enforcement agencies seize about 100 tons of cocaine a year and have recently used radar surveillance to detect illegal flights carrying cocaine into the United States. However, despite these efforts, government studies indicate that cocaine is still widely available (right graph) and officials estimate the market for illegal cocaine is currently about 38 billion dollars a year (Darling, 1997; Fineman & Pyes, 1996). Cocaine has a very long history of usage because it's a powerful stimulant that produces euphoria and physiological arousal.

Amount of pure cocaine consumed yearly in the USA

303 tons

Source: Health and Human Services

For 3000 years, the ancient Incas and their descendants, the indigenous Andean people of Peru, have chewed coca leaves as they made demanding journeys through the high mountains. Some minutes after chewing the leaves, which contain cocaine, they reported feeling more vigor and strength and less fatigue, hunger, thirst, and cold. Coca leaves contain very little cocaine and produce stimulation equivalent to that experienced by coffee (caffeine) drinkers (McCarry, 1996). Few psychological or physical problems are observed in those who chew coca leaves partly because they consume very little cocaine and because this activity is part of their culture. However, many problems have been observed among natives who have switched from coca leaves to more concentrated cocaine powder (Siegel, 1989).

In the United States, approximately 2.1 million people use cocaine monthly, and about 640,000 experience problems with cocaine usage (Schemo, 1997). Since the cocaine epidemic of the late 1980s, usage of cocaine is reportedly down by 10–35%. However, cocaine remains the nonalcoholic drug of abuse in ten major cities (Sanchez-Ramos, 1993). The possession or use of cocaine is illegal.

Drug

Cocaine can be sniffed or snorted, since it is absorbed by many of the body's membranes. If cocaine is changed into a highly concentrated form, which is called crack, it can be smoked or injected, and produces an instantaneous high.

Cocaine, which comes from the leaves of the coca plant, has physiological and behavioral effects very similar to amphetamine. Like amphetamine, cocaine produces increased heart rate and blood pressure, enhanced mood, alertness, increased activity, decreased appetite, and diminished fatigue. With higher doses, cocaine can produce anxiety, emotional instability, and suspiciousness.

When humans or monkeys have unlimited access to pure cocaine, they will use it continually, to the point of starvation and death. Only extreme shock will reduce an addicted monkey's use of cocaine, and only extreme problems involving health, legal, or personal difficulties will reduce an addicted human's intake.

Nervous System

Researchers have recently found that the primary effect of cocaine is to block reuptake of the neurotransmitter dopamine, which means that dopamine stays around longer to excite neighboring neurons (Balter, 1996).

Researchers also found that cocaine excites one kind of neural receptor to produce pleasure/ euphoria and another kind of receptor to produce a craving for more of the drug (Self et al., 1996). Like amphetamine, cocaine results in increased physiological and psychological arousal.

An interesting effect of cocaine is its ability to block the conduction of nerve impulses when applied to an area of the body. For this reason, cocaine is classified as a local anesthetic; this is its only legal usage.

Dangers

In *moderate doses*, cocaine produces a short-acting high (10–30 minutes) that includes bursts of energy, arousal, and alertness. Users tend to believe that they are thinking more clearly and performing better, but, in fact, they overestimate the quality of their work.

In *heavy doses,* cocaine can result in serious physical and psychological problems, which may include hallucinations and feelings of bugs crawling under the skin.

Physical problems associated with cocaine abuse can include lack of appetite, insomnia, irritation, and damage to cartilage of the nose (if snorted). Sudden death, which may result from relatively low dosages, is due to respiratory failure. Heavy usage is now known to cause physical addiction (Hammer et al., 1997).

Cocaine users often go through a vicious circle. As cocaine's effects wear off, the user experiences depression, fatigue, and an intense craving for more cocaine, which causes the user to seek another dose. Taking another dose is followed by depression and craving for more, which continues the vicious circle. Heavy users often require professional help to break out of this destructive pattern (Leshner, 1997).

Next we turn to two legal drugs that are the most widely used stimulants—caffeine and nicotine.

C. Stimulants

Caffeine

What's the most widely used drug in the world?

Caffeine, which has been used for the past 2000 years, is the most widely used psychoactive drug in the world. One 8-ounce cup of regular coffee, two cups of regular tea, one No-Doz tablet, two diet colas, or four regular-sized chocolate bars all contain about 100 milligrams of caffeine. In the United States, the average amount of caffeine consumed is 280 milligrams per person per day, compared to 400 milligrams in Sweden and England.

Drug

Many users do not consider caffeine a drug and do not realize that it is addicting. *Caffeine* is a mild stimulant that produces moderate physiological arousal. The psychological effects include a feeling of alertness, decreased fatigue and drowsiness, and improved reaction times.

Both moderate doses (200–400 milligrams or 2–4 cups of coffee per day) and especially heavy doses (500–800 milligrams or five or more cups of coffee per day) result in addiction (Schuh & Griffiths, 1997).

Nervous System

Caffeine belongs to a group of chemicals called xanthines (*ZAN-thenes*), which have a number of effects. One effect is to block certain receptors (adenosine receptors) in the brain, which results in stimulation and mild physiological and psychological arousal (Stahl, 1996).

Dangers

Researchers found that mild to heavy doses of caffeine (125–800 milligrams) can result in physical addiction and psychological dependency similar to that produced by alcohol, nicotine, and cocaine (Strain et al., 1994). Higher doses of caffeine (300–1000 milligrams) can result in feelings of depression, tension, and anxiety (DeAngelis, 1994).

Abruptly stopping the consumption of caffeine, especially medium to heavy doses, usually results in a significant number of uncomfortable withdrawal symptoms, such as increased headaches, irritability, fatigue, intense craving for caffeine, and decrease in energy (Schuh & Griffiths, 1997). These symptoms usually disappear within 5–7 days. Obviously, caffeine is a real drug.

Nicotine

What causes the most deaths?

After caffeine, nicotine is the world's most widely used psychoactive drug. In the United States, there has been a significant decline in smoking, from 42% in 1965 to 25% in 1997. Most habitual smokers begin in their teens, starting at about age 15 and becoming a daily smoker at about age 18 (Skaar et al., 1997). The graph at the right shows that, in the United States, the greatest number of deaths (400,000) results from using tobacco (McGinnis & Foege, 1993). For this reason the United States Surgeon General concluded that cigarette smoking is the single largest avoidable cause of death in our society and the most important public health issue of our time.

400,000 Tobacco	
300,000 Diet and activity patterns	
100,000 Alcohol	
Causes of Death in the United States	**35,000** Guns

Drug

In 1997, nicotine was officially labeled an addictive drug, and the U.S. Food and Drug Administration received authority to regulate tobacco as a device for delivering nicotine (Raloff, 1997).

Nicotine is classified as a stimulant because it first produces arousal but then produces calming. In low doses, nicotine improves attention, concentration, and short-term memory (Gray, 1996). Regular use of nicotine causes addiction, and stopping leads to withdrawal symptoms.

Thus, one reason smokers find it so difficult to quit is because they are addicted to nicotine.

Nervous System

Initially, nicotine stimulates certain receptors in the brain (cholinergic receptors) that cause arousal, but after a period of time, nicotine blocks these same receptors and produces calming. Recently, researchers found that nicotine activates the same brain areas (nucleus accumbens) as cocaine, which means these drugs share a common neural basis for producing arousal, pleasure, and addiction (Pich et al., 1997).

Dangers

In 1997, for the first time, an executive of an American tobacco company admitted that ". . . cigarette smoking causes health problems, including lung cancer, heart and vascular disease, and emphysema, and that . . . nicotine is addictive" (Noah, 1997, p. 29). Because researchers have long known that nicotine is addictive, a smoker will experience withdrawal symptoms if he or she quits. These symptoms range in severity and include nervousness, irritability, difficulty in concentrating, sleep disturbances, and a craving for the drug.

Researchers found that professional stop-smoking programs were all about equally effective and use of the "nicotine patch" helped smokers stop (Skaar et al., 1997). Thus, like caffeine, nicotine is a real drug that is very difficult to stop and even more difficult to stay stopped.

Unlike stimulants, which produce arousal, the next group of drugs, called opiates, produce the opposite effect.

Opium, Morphine, Heroin

How popular is heroin? From 6000 B.C. to the present, opiates have been used around the world. In the early 1800s, the active ingredient in the juice of the opium poppy (photo below) was found to be morphine, and in the late 1800s morphine was chemically altered to make heroin. Law enforcement agencies usually refer to opiates as *narcotics.*

In the early 1900s, the sale and use of narcotics (opium, morphine, and heroin) were made illegal, which gave rise to a lucrative worldwide opium black market. In spite of restrictive laws and billions of dollars spent on enforcement, the United States and many other countries have been unable to eliminate the importation and use of opiates, which are readily available in most major cities (Weatherburn & Lind, 1997).

The use of heroin peaked in the mid-1970s, dropped in the early 1980s as cocaine gained in popularity, but was rising again in the early 1990s (Friend, 1997). This increase is partly due to a crackdown on cocaine usage as well as heroin's increased availability, decreased cost, and increased purity. In 1980, heroin was about 7% pure, while current heroin is about 50% pure; this means that now, instead of being injected, it can be smoked, which appeals to new users (Maugh, 1997).

The number of Americans who use heroin regularly is estimated to be about 650,000. On the basis of visits to emergency rooms, the primary users of heroin are men over the age of 26, both Black (37%) and White (37%) (Stolberg, 1993). The graph on the

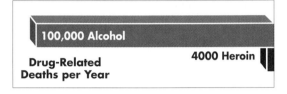

right shows that compared to 100,000 drug-related deaths a year from alcohol, there were about 4000 heroin-related deaths (Baum, 1996, Schoemer, 1996). The possession or use of opiates—opium, morphine, and heroin—is illegal.

Drug

Although all the opiates produce similar effects, users generally prefer to inject heroin because it reaches the brain more quickly and produces the biggest "rush," which is described as a whole-body pleasurable experience.

Opiates, such as opium, morphine, and heroin, produce three primary effects: analgesia (pain reduction); opiate euphoria, which is often described as a pleasurable state between waking and sleeping; and constipation. Continued use of opiates results in tolerance, physical addiction, and an intense craving for the drug.

One rock star (Steven Tyler of "Aerosmith") described using heroin as ". . . life without anxiety. It's a real floaty, godlike trip. . . . It makes you feel good" (Colapinto, 1996, p. 16). However, this rock star eventually discovered the darker side of heroin. With constant usage, his brain developed a tolerance to heroin, which means that he had to take larger and larger doses to achieve a high. Finally, he was using such large doses that getting high was almost impossible, functioning normally was out of the question, and he ended up with many personal and professional problems (Colapinto, 1996).

Nervous System

In the 1970s, researchers discovered that the brain has naturally occurring receptors for opiates (Pert et al., 1974). When morphine reaches the brain's receptors, it produces feelings of euphoria and analgesia. In addition, the gastrointestinal tract also has opiate receptors, whose stimulation results in constipation.

Researchers discovered that the brain not only has its own opiate receptors but also produces its own morphinelike chemicals. These chemicals, which function as neurotransmitters, are called *endorphins* and are found to have the same analgesic properties as morphine (Hughes et al., 1975).

Dangers

One user (Steven Tyler) said, "But all those things it [heroin] gives you it starts to take away. Soon all you care about is the drug. You'll drag yourself through hell to get it. . . . It's killing you and you don't even care" (Colapinto, 1996, p. 16).

After several weeks of regular use, a person's brain produces less of its own endorphins and relies more on the outside supply of opiates. As a result, a person becomes addicted to taking opiates and must administer one or more doses daily to prevent withdrawal symptoms. Withdrawal symptoms, which include hot and cold flashes, sweating, muscle tremors, and stomach cramps, are not life-threatening and last from 4–7 days. An overdose of opiates depresses the neural control of breathing, and a person dies from respiratory failure.

Treatment

In a 24-year study of over 500 heroin addicts, researchers found that 28% died from drug overdose, 22% were abstinent, 11% were in prison, 10% were frequent users, 7% were daily users, and 6% were in methadone treatment programs; the remaining 16% could not be located (Hsea et al., 1993). Researchers concluded that, if heroin users do not quit by age 30, they are unlikely ever to stop. The most common treatment for heroin addiction is to maintain addicts on methadone, which is a synthetic drug similar to opium. Methadone maintenance is relatively effective in preventing heroin use and reducing criminal activities (Payte, 1997; Widman et al., 1997).

Next we consider the hallucinogens, which can produce strange perceptions.

E. Hallucinogens

Definition

In many parts of the world and in many different cultures, plants and fungi (mushrooms) have long been used to produce visions or hallucinations as part of cultural or religious experiences. However, Caucasians in the United States rarely used hallucinogens until the 1950s and 1960s, when these drugs gained popularity as part of the hippie subculture. Recently, researchers have once again begun to study the potential therapeutic uses of hallucinogens, which have also gained back some of their former popularity (Strassman, 1995).

Hallucinogens are psychoactive drugs that can produce strange and unusual perceptual, sensory, and cognitive experiences, which the person sees or hears but knows that they are not occurring in reality. Such nonreality-based experiences are called hallucinations.

We'll focus on four of the more commonly used hallucinogens: LSD, psilocybin, mescaline, and a designer drug called ecstasy.

LSD

At the beginning of this module, we told you of the strange bike ride of Albert Hofmann, who in 1943 discovered LSD (lysergic acid diethylamide). However, LSD did not become popular in America until the mid-1960s. Since then, LSD has gradually fallen in popularity, but there are reports of an upsurge in usage in the 1990s (Strassman, 1995). Possession or use of LSD is illegal.

Drug

LSD is a very potent drug because it produces hallucinogenic experiences at very low doses.

LSD produces strange experiences which include visual hallucinations, perceptual distortions, increased sensory awareness, and intense psychological feelings. An LSD experience, or "trip", may last 8–10 hours.

Nervous System

LSD resembles the naturally occurring neurotransmitter serotonin. LSD binds to receptors that normally respond to serotonin, and the net effect is increased stimulation of these neurons (Aghajanian, 1994). The majority of serotonin receptors are located on neurons in the brain's outermost layer, the cerebral cortex, which is involved in receiving sensations, creating perceptions, thinking, and imagining.

Dangers

LSD's psychological effects partially depend on the setting and the person's state of mind. If a person is tense or anxious or in an unfamiliar setting, he or she may experience a bad trip. If severe, a bad trip may lead to psychotic reactions (especially paranoid feelings) that require hospitalization. Sometime after the hallucinogenic experience, users may experience frightening flashbacks that occur for no apparent reason. There have been no reports of physical addiction to LSD or death from overdose, but users do quickly develop a tolerance to LSD (Miller & Gold, 1994).

Psilocybin

The existence of "magic mushrooms" was suggested by carvings of the ancient Aztec Indians, who lived around 500 B.C. In 1957, archeologists sent samples of the supposedly magic mushrooms (*Psilocybe mexicana*) to none other than Albert Hofmann, who identified the active ingredient as psilocybin. Hofmann also tried magic mushrooms (right photo) and reported that they produced an "awake dream" that included a whirlpool of pictures rapidly changing shape and color (Hofmann, 1983). Possession or use of psilocybin is illegal.

Drug

The active ingredient in magic mushrooms is psilocybin.

Psilocybin, in low doses, produces pleasant and relaxed feelings; medium doses produce perceptual distortions in time and space; high doses produce distortions in perceptions and body image and sometimes hallucinations.

Nervous System

Psilocybin is chemically related to LSD and, like LSD, inhibits serotonin receptors. The hallucinatory effects produced by psilocybin are comparable to those from LSD, but last half as long (Stahl, 1996).

Dangers

The dangers from psilocybin come not from physical harm to the brain or body but rather from the potential for inducing psychotic states that may persist long after the experience is expected to end (Liska, 1994). In addition, accidental poisonings are common among those who eat poisonous mushrooms, mistaking them for magic mushrooms.

Mescaline

What is peyote?

In the 1500s, Spanish soldiers noted that the Aztec Indians of South America ate peyote cactus as part of their religious ceremonies. Peyote cactus contains about 30 psychoactive chemicals; one of the more potent is the drug mescaline.

In 1965, the Native American Church of North America won a battle in the U.S. Supreme Court for the legal right to use peyote as a sacrament in their Christian ritual. Participants in this ritual usually sit around a fire and eat peyote buttons. This is followed by meditation, during which the participants feel removed from earthly cares and experience unusual visual perceptions, such as seeing a vast field of golden jewels that move and change (Liska, 1994). More recently, Native American Indians in the U.S. armed forces were allowed to use peyote in religious rituals (Richter, 1997). The possession or use of mescaline is illegal for all except those who belong to the Native American Church.

Drug

Mescaline is about 2000 times less potent than LSD.

Mescaline is the active ingredient in the peyote cactus. At high doses, mescaline produces very clear and vivid visual hallucinations, such as latticework, cobweb figures, tunnels, and spirals, which appear in various colors and intense brightness. Mescaline does not impair the intellect or cloud consciousness.

As with most hallucinogens, the setting and user's psychological state influences the experience.

Nervous System

Mescaline reaches maximum concentration in the brain about 30–120 minutes after eating buttons of peyote cactus. Mescaline primarily increases the activity of the neurotransmitters norepinephrine and dopamine (Stahl, 1996). In addition, mescaline activates the sympathetic system to produce physiological arousal, such as increase in heart rate and temperature and, sometimes, vomiting.

Dangers

During a mescaline experience, which can last from 6 to 8 hours, users may experience headaches and vomiting. When street samples of mescaline were analyzed in a number of cities, researchers found that the chemical was rarely mescaline. Instead "street mescaline" was usually other hallucinogens, such as LSD or PCP (Hanson & Venturelli, 1998).

Designer Drugs

Can hallucinogens be made?

The mid-1980s marked the appearance of so-called designer drugs.

Designer drugs refer to manufactured or synthetic drugs that are designed to resemble already existing illegal psychoactive drugs and to produce or mimic their psychoactive effects.

For example, a drug designer can start with an amphetamine molecule and alter it in hundreds of ways. Because designer drugs are manufactured in home laboratories, users have no guarantees that these drugs are safe to use. Of the dozen or so designer drugs available, we'll focus on one, MDMA, whose street name is "ecstasy." Since the government has not allowed research on MDMA since 1985, there are very few reliable data on its effects. Possession or use of MDMA is illegal.

Drug

The street name of MDMA is "ecstasy," which became popular in the 1980s.

MDMA, or *ecstasy,* resembles both mescaline (hallucinogen) and amphetamine (stimulant). In anecdotal reports, users claim that MDMA causes changes in visual perceptions and increases their awareness of emotions, feelings of intimacy, and ability to interact with others. Because it lowers inhibitions, some consider it an aphrodisiac.

Nervous System

MDMA's primary action is to block receptors that normally respond to the neurotransmitter serotonin. Of more serious concern are reports that, in monkeys, high doses of MDMA produced a 30% drop in stores of serotonin and damaged serotonin neurons. Researchers concluded that using MDMA is inadvisable until its potentially toxic effects on neurons can be studied (McDowell & Kleber, 1994).

Dangers

In recreational doses, MDMA can produce jitteriness, anxiety, jaw clenching, fear, and insomnia. In addition, at higher doses, users may experience panic, with rapid heartbeat, paranoia, and psychoticlike symptoms. Prolonged use of MDMA—for a week or more—results in confusion, fatigue, depression, and nausea (Miller & Gold, 1994). However, of most concern is the possibility that MDMA damages serotonin neurons.

Unlike hallucinogens, which are the least frequently used psychoactive drugs, the drug we'll examine next is widely used, potentially very dangerous, and legal.

F. Alcohol

History and Use

What happened when alcohol was banned?

The first brewery appeared in Egypt in about 3700 B.C., making alcohol the oldest drug to be made by humans (Samuel, 1996). Through the years, alcohol has grown in popularity and its usage has been associated with a wide range of problems, including drunk driving (right figure). Because of serious personal and social problems, there was an attempt to ban alcohol.

The most drastic attempt to control the use of alcohol occurred in 1920, when the U.S. Congress passed the Eighteenth Amendment, which prohibited the sale and manufacture of alcohol. However, Americans' desire for alcohol was so deeply ingrained that a very lucrative black market developed to supply illegal alcohol. Finally, after 13 years of failure in enforcing prohibition, the U.S. Congress repealed prohibition in 1933. The lesson learned from prohibition was that it is almost impossible to ban a drug that is desired by a majority of citizens (Musto, 1996).

A similar lesson is being learned today as the U.S. government spends over $8 billion annually to control the use of illegal drugs (heroin, marijuana, cocaine methamphetamine). Despite its efforts, these drugs are readily available in an unstoppable black market in most cities.

About 100 million Americans drink alcohol, and the majority do not experience problems. However, between 10 and 15 million drinkers are alcoholics, who have significant behavioral, neurological, social, legal, or medical problems. We'll discuss alcoholism in the upcoming Research Focus. Now, we'll focus on what alcohol is and what it does to the user's brain, body, and behaviors.

The party begins.

2 drinks later.

4 drinks later.

5 drinks later.

7 drinks in all.

Definition and Effects

Although we'll use the term *alcohol,* we actually mean *ethyl alcohol,* which is safe to drink. The level of alcohol is measured in terms of percentage in the blood, which is called blood alcohol content, or BAC. For example, after 3–4 drinks in an hour, the average person's BAC will range from 0.08 to 0.1, which meets the legal definition of being drunk in most states. A

drink is defined as one cocktail, one 5-ounce glass of wine, or one 12-ounce bottle of beer. It makes no difference whether you drink hard liquor, wine, or beer, since they all contain ethyl alcohol, which affects the nervous system and results in behavioral and emotional changes.

Drug

Alcohol is not a stimulant, but a depressant.

Alcohol (ethyl alcohol) is a psychoactive drug that is classified as a depressant, which means that it depresses activity of the central nervous system. Initially, alcohol seems like a stimulant because it reduces inhibitions, but later it depresses many physiological and psychological responses.

The effects of alcohol greatly depend upon how much a person drinks. After a few drinks (0.01–0.03 BAC), alcohol causes friendliness and loss of inhibitions. After several more drinks (0.03–0.06 BAC), alcohol interferes with drinkers' ability to understand the important events going on around them. After many drinks (0.06–0.10 BAC), alcohol seriously impairs motor coordination, cognitive abilities, decision making, and speech. After very many drinks (0.5 BAC and higher), alcohol may cause coma and death. For example, a fraternity pledge died after a 7-hour drinking binge that led to a BAC of 0.58—about 24 drinks (Cohen, 1997).

Nervous System

The effects of alcohol are complex and not totally understood. Researchers found that alcohol blocks some neural receptors and stimulates others. Alcohol stimulates GABA (*GAH-bah*) neural receptors, which leads to a reduction in anxiety and loss of inhibitions (Stahl, 1996). Alcohol also interferes with NMDA neural receptors, which may result in cognitive difficulties (Tsai et al., 1995). In extremely high doses (0.5 BAC), alcohol depresses vital breathing, or respiratory, reflexes in the brain stem, and this can result in respiratory failure and death.

Dangers

The morning after a bout of heavy drinking (3–7 drinks), a person usually experiences a *hangover,* which may include upset stomach, dizziness, fatigue, headache, and depression. There is presently no cure for hangovers, which are troublesome and painful but not life-threatening.

Repeated and heavy drinking can result in tolerance and addiction. *Tolerance* means that a person must drink more to experience the same behavioral effects. *Addiction* means that a person has an intense craving for alcohol and if the person stops drinking, he or she will experience serious *withdrawal symptoms*, including shaking, nausea, anxiety, diarrhea, hallucinations, and disorientation.

Another serious problem are *blackouts*, which occur after heavy and repeated drinking. During a blackout, a person seems to behave normally but when sober cannot recall what happened. If the blackout lasts for hours or days, it is probable that the person is an alcoholic.

Repeated and heavy drinking can also result in liver damage, alcoholism, and brain damage.

Risk Factors

Whose at risk for becoming an alcoholic?

Of the 100 million people who drink alcohol, 10 to 12 million develop alcoholism. Researchers believe that certain individuals become alcoholics because they have psychological and genetic *risk factors* that make them more likely to abuse alcohol. For example, one's risk of becoming an alcoholic is 3–4 times higher if one comes from a family whose parents are alcoholic. Risk factors that increase the chances that one will abuse alcohol include both environmental and genetic factors.

Environmental Risk Factors

Children whose parents (either or both) are alcoholics, develop a number of unusual, abnormal, or maladaptive psychological and emotional traits that are called *environmental risk factors*. For example, environmental risk factors that have been identified in children of alcoholic parents include having difficulty showing trust, being overdependent in close personal relationships, and being or acting overemotional when faced with stressful and uncontrollable situations.

When children with these environmental risk factors become adults, they may have a tendency to imitate the behavior of their alcoholic parent and abuse alcohol when faced with personal, social, or work-related difficulties (Rivers, 1994). However, researchers believe that alcoholism results from a combination of environmental and genetic risk factors (Schuckit & Smith, 1997).

Genetic Risk Factors

Besides environmental risk factors, there are also *genetic risk factors*, which refer to inherited biases or predispositions that increase the potential for alcohol abuse and alcoholism. For example, researchers found that, if one identical twin was an alcoholic, there was a 39% chance that the other twin was also. In comparison, if one fraternal twin was an alcoholic, there was a 16% chance that the other twin was also. These results indicate a significant genetic risk factor in developing alcoholism (Prescott et al., 1994).

Other evidence for genetic risk factors comes from research showing that sons of alcoholic fathers reported feeling less intoxicated than did sons of nonalcoholic fathers (Schuckit & Smith, 1997). These sons, who were tested at age 20, were followed for 15 years to see who became alcoholics. Researchers found that 56% of sons who were less sensitive to alcohol became alcoholics. In contrast, only 14% of sons who were more sensitive to alcohol became alcoholics. These results indicate that a lower sensitivity to alcohol, which means that a person must drink more to feel its effects, is a genetic risk factor for future alcoholism (Schuckit, 1994b).

However, because not every child of an alcoholic parent or both members of a pair of identical twins became an alcoholic, genetic risk factors alone do not result in alcoholism. Rather, researchers believe that alcoholism results from the interaction between genetic and environmental risk factors (Buck et al., 1997).

Besides the problems associated with alcoholism, the use of alcohol is associated with a wide range of problems.

Problems

Why is alcohol so dangerous?

Here are some of the problems related to use of alcohol in the United States:

✔ 90% of all campus rapes involve drinking on the part of the assailant, victim, or both;

✔ 68% of manslaughter convictions and 63% of assaults involve alcohol;

✔ 63% of episodes in which husbands batter their wives involve alcohol;

✔ 46% of highway deaths involve alcohol;

✔ 50% of college men and 39% of college women said they had binged (consuming 4–5 successive drinks) at least once in the last two weeks;

✔ 35% of college students today drink to get drunk, whereas 15 years ago the figure was 10%;

✔ 11% of workplace accidents involve alcohol;

✔ 8–21% of suicides involve alcohol;

✔ 7% of college freshmen who drop out do so because of alcohol;

✔ alcoholism is the third leading health problem, after cancer and heart disease;

✔ alcohol is the leading cause of mental retardation due to fetal alcohol syndrome (FAS);

✔ alcohol is the most serious problem facing U.S. high schools, surpassing apathy and poor discipline by a wide margin;

✔ alcoholism and alcohol abuse cost an estimated $136 billion per year to lost production, health and welfare services, property damage, and medical expenses.

Because alcohol is significantly involved in so many social and personal problems, many consider it to be the most dangerous of all the legal or illegal drugs (Adler & Rosenberg, 1994; Rivers, 1994).

After you have had a chance to test your knowledge with the Concept Review, we'll discuss the worldwide problem of alcoholism.

CONCEPT REVIEW

1. Under hypnosis, individuals may think they return to an earlier stage in life, which is called (a)_____; they may experience a reduction in pain, which is called (b)_____; or they may experience loss of memory, called (c)_____. Hypnotized subjects may perceive stimuli that do not exist, which is called (d)_____, or they may perform some behavior after coming out of hypnosis, which is called (e)_____.

2. According to the (a)_____ theory, hypnotized subjects perform suggested behaviors because they are in a special state. According to the (b)_____ theory, hypnotized subjects perform suggested behaviors because they feel pressures to conform.

3. After using a drug repeatedly, a person must take increasingly larger doses to achieve the original behavioral effect; this is called (a)_____. A change in the nervous system that requires a person to take a drug to prevent the occurrence of painful withdrawal symptoms is called (b)_____. A behavioral pattern of drug abuse that is marked by a person's overwhelming and compulsive desire to obtain and use the drug is called an (c)_____. Painful physical and psychological symptoms that occur after a drug-dependent person stops using the drug are called (d)_____.

4. Drugs that affect the nervous system and result in altered awareness and consciousness, as well as changes in mood, cognition, and perception, are called _____.

5. There are two common ways that psychoactive drugs affect the nervous system. Some drugs act like (a)_____ keys that are so similar to neurotransmitters that these drugs open the chemical (b)_____ of nearby neurons by acting like or (c)_____ the action of regularly occurring neurotransmitters. Other drugs work by preventing the neuron's reabsorption of neurotransmitters by slowing down a process called (d)_____.

6. Those drugs that result in increased arousal, alertness, and euphoria are called (a)_____. The potent stimulant that comes from a plant, can be sniffed or smoked, and produces short-acting alertness and euphoria is (b)_____. The potent stimulant that is a form of amphetamine, is smoked, and produces longer-lasting alertness and euphoria is known on the street as (c)_____. The world's most widely used stimulant, which produces mild arousal and alertness, is (d)_____. The drug that is the single largest avoidable cause of death in the United States and has both stimulating and calming properties is (e)_____.

7. Drugs that produce unusual or distorted perceptual, sensory, and cognitive experiences that do not correspond to external reality are called (a)_____. One of the most powerful of these drugs, which can cause trips that last up to eight hours, is (b)_____. A drug that is found in certain mushrooms is (c)_____; one that is found in peyote cactus is (d)_____.

8. Synthetic drugs that are variations of known psychoactive drugs and are manufactured in illegal laboratories are called (a)_____. One designer drug that is part stimulant and part hallucinogen is (b)_____.

9. Drugs that have three primary effects—analgesia, a state of waking sleep, and constipation—are called (a)_____. Continued use of these drugs causes the user to become (b)_____; if the user stops using the drug, he or she will experience painful (c)_____.

10. The psychoactive drug that depresses the functions of the central nervous system is (a)_____. At low doses, it causes friendliness and loss of (b)_____; at medium doses, it impairs social (c)_____; and, at higher doses, it seriously impairs (d)_____ coordination.

11. Certain individuals may develop or inherit different factors that make them at risk for becoming alcoholics. For example, a child raised by alcoholic parents may develop unusual, abnormal, or maladaptive psychological and emotional traits; these are called (a)_____ risk factors. In addition, a child may inherit predispositions for abusing alcohol, such as being less sensitive to alcohol; these are called (b)_____ risk factors.

Answers: 1. (a) age regression, (b) hypnotic analgesia, (c) posthypnotic amnesia, (d) imagined perception, (e) posthypnotic suggestion; 2. (a) altered state, (b) sociocognitive; 3. (a) tolerance, (b) dependence, (c) addiction, (d) withdrawal symptoms; 4. psychoactive drugs; 5. (a) chemical, (b) locks, (c) mimicking, (d) reuptake; 6. (a) stimulants, (b) cocaine, (c) methamphetamine (crack, crystal, or ice), (d) caffeine, (e) nicotine; 7. (a) hallucinogens, (b) LSD, (c) psilocybin, (d) mescaline; 8. (a) designer drugs, (b) MDMA or ecstasy; 9. (a) opiates, (b) addicted, (c) withdrawal symptoms; 10. (a) alcohol (ethyl alcohol), (b) inhibitions, (c) judgment, (d) motor; 11. (a) environmental, (b) genetic.

G. Cultural Diversity: Rates of Alcoholism

Definition

What is alcoholism?

One question that applies to all drugs is why some can use a drug in moderation and rarely abuse it while others continually use the same drug and develop serious problems. For example, about 100 million U.S. citizens drink alcohol but rarely to excess. In contrast, 10 to 12 million drink alcohol, abuse it, and develop alcoholism.

Alcoholism involves heavy drinking (sometimes a quart a day) for a long period of time, usually many years. Alcoholics are addicted (have intense craving) and are dependent on alcohol (must drink to avoid withdrawal symptoms). They continue to use alcohol despite developing major substance-related life problems, such as neglecting family, work, or school duties, having repeated legal or criminal incidents, and experiencing difficulties in personal or social relationships (American Psychiatric Association, 1994).

One answer to why only certain drinkers become alcoholics comes from studying environmental and genetic risk factors, which we discussed earlier. Now, we'll see if these two risk factors differ across cultures.

Cultural Factors

Genetic Risk Factors

After the very first drink of alcohol, some individuals respond with a sudden reddening of the face. This reaction is called *facial flushing* and is caused by the absence of a liver enzyme involved in metabolizing alcohol.

Facial flushing from alcohol is a genetic trait and rarely occurs in Caucasians (whites) but does occur in about 30–50% of Asians (photo below). Asians who show significant facial flushing, such as Taiwanese, Chinese, and Japanese, tend to drink less and have lower rates of alcoholism than Asians who show less facial flushing, such as the

Koreans (Helzer & Canino, 1992). Thus, facial flushing is a *genetic risk factor* that influences the chances of becoming an alcoholic. There are also cultural-environmental risk factors.

Environmental Risk Factors

These factors come from different cultural values and pressures that encourage or discourage alcohol abuse. Researchers studied 48,000 adults (18 and older) in six different cultures to answer two questions: Do rates of alcoholism differ across cultures? What cultural values influence the rate of alcoholism?

The answer to the first question is shown in the graph below. Rates of alcoholism did differ across cultures, from a low of 0.5% among Taiwanese, to a high of 22% among Koreans.

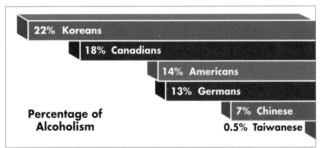

22% Koreans
18% Canadians
14% Americans
13% Germans
7% Chinese
0.5% Taiwanese
Percentage of Alcoholism

The answer to the second question—What cultural values affect the rate of alcoholism?—was also partly answered. For example, the high rate of alcoholism in Korea is almost entirely in males, who are encouraged by cultural pressures to drink heavily in certain social situations; for example, at the end of the workday, co-workers engage in drinking contests. In Germany, the U.S., and Canada, the medium rate of alcoholism is a reaction to the stress of living in heavily industrialized societies. Alcoholism is below average in China and especially Taiwan, because these societies are heavily influenced by the Confucian moral code, which has strong cultural-religious taboos against drinking or showing drunken behavior in public. These findings indicate that *environmental risk factors* can either encourage or discourage the development of alcoholism.

However, despite the different rates of alcoholism across cultures, there are some striking similarities.

Similarities

Although rates for alcoholism differed widely across cultures, from 0.5% to 22%, researchers found many similarities in how people developed alcoholism and the problems they had (Helzer & Canino, 1992; Peele, 1997). Here are some similarities that occurred across cultures:

■ the average age when the first symptoms of alcoholism appear was in the early 20s or mid-20s;

■ the average number of major life problems among alcoholics was 4–6;

■ the average duration of alcoholism was 8–10 years;

■ the average pattern of drinking involved daily heavy drinking, often a quart a day;

■ men were five times more likely to develop alcoholism than were women;

■ depression was about twice as likely to be diagnosed in alcoholics than in non-alcoholics.

■ overall mortality rate from alcoholism did not differ among cultures.

Researchers concluded that although cultural—genetic and environmental—risk factors had a significant influence on the rate of alcoholism, cultural factors had little effect on the development, symptoms, sex differences, and mental disorders associated with alcoholism.

Next, we'll focus on the most widely used illegal drug in the United States.

H. Marijuana

Use and Effects

How many people die yearly from marijuana?

The most widely used illegal drug worldwide is marijuana. In the U.S., there are about 20 million marijuana users, compared to 2.1 million cocaine users, 650,000 heroin users, and 100,000 who use ecstasy (Schlosser, 1994). Although widely used, the graph on the right shows that compared to other illegal drugs, there are few if any deaths from marijuana usage (Baum, 1996; Zimmer & Morgan, 1997).

Marijuana is one of the leading U.S. cash crops; growers make an estimated $24 billion yearly, compared to corn growers who make about $16 billion. (Top marijuana-growing states are Tennessee, Kentucky, Hawaii, California and New York.) Thus, despite billions of dollars and years of preventive efforts, marijuana is readily available, even to teenagers.

In 1997, two states (California and Arizona) passed laws allowing marijuana to be used legally for medical problems. These state laws have generated much debate since, under current federal law, it is illegal to use marijuana for any purpose. However, some resolution may be in sight since an advisory panel of the National Institutes on Drug Abuse concluded that marijuana showed promise in treating certain medical conditions: treatment of nausea and vomiting associated with chemotherapy; treatment of appetite loss in AIDS patients; and treatment of an eye disease (glaucoma) (Fackelmann, 1997). Recently, researchers reported that some of the active chemicals in marijuana (cannabinoids) are effective in relieving several kinds of chronic or long-lasting pain, such as the kind associated with arthritis (Hotz, 1997). Currently, the use or possession of marijuana is illegal (except perhaps for medical problems in California and Arizona).

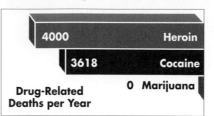

Drug-Related Deaths per Year	
4000	Heroin
3618	Cocaine
0	Marijuana

Drug

As is true of many psychoactive drugs, some of marijuana's effects depend on the user's initial mood and state of mental health. For example, patients in their 60s who were using marijuana to treat glaucoma complained about and did not like its "strange side effects," which most young adult users desire and label as "getting high."

Marijuana is a psychoactive drug whose primary active ingredient is THC (tetrahydrocannabinol), which is found in the leaves of the cannabis plant. The average marijuana cigarette ("joint") contains 2.5–11.0 mg of THC, which is a tenfold increase over the amount of THC found in marijuana in the 1970s (Schwartz, 1991). THC is rapidly absorbed by the lungs and in 5–10 minutes produces a high that lasts for several hours. The type of high is closely related to the dose: low doses produce mild euphoria; moderate doses produce perceptual and time distortions; and high doses may produce hallucinations, delusions, and distortions of body image (Hanson & Venturelli, 1998).

Depending upon the user's state of mind, marijuana can either heighten or distort pleasant or unpleasant experiences, moods, or feelings.

Nervous System

In 1964, researchers identified and synthesized THC, the main mind-altering substance in marijuana.

In 1990, researchers discovered a specific receptor for THC in the brains of rats and humans (Matsuda et al., 1990). These THC receptors are located throughout the brain, including the hippocampus, which is involved in short-term memory; the cerebral cortex, which is involved in higher cognitive functions; the limbic system, which is involved in emotions; and the cerebellum, which is involved in timing movements (Herkenham, 1996).

In 1993, researchers made an even more surprising discovery when they found that the brain makes a chemical that stimulates the THC receptors. This naturally occurring brain chemical is called anandamide, which may affect mood and emotions (Mestel, 1993).

In 1997, researchers identified a second THC-like chemical (2-AG) that the brain also makes (Piomelli, 1997). Researchers think that the new chemical (2-AG) is involved in short-term memory and appetite stimulation. Thus, the brain not only has receptors for THC but also makes two THC-like chemicals.

Dangers

Marijuana can cause changes in brain functioning, such as interfering with short-term memory (Block, 1996). However, there is no conclusive evidence that prolonged marijuana use causes permanent damage to brain, nervous system, or genetic makeup (Relman, 1982).

Marijuana causes many of the same kinds of respiratory problems as smoking tobacco, including bronchitis and asthma attacks. Because marijuana smoke contains 50% more cancer-causing substances and users hold smoke in their lungs longer, the effects of smoking 3–4 joints of marijuana are similar to those of 20 cigarettes (Tashkin, 1996).

Marijuana greatly hinders a user's ability to drive a car, boat, or plane because it impairs reaction time, judgment, and use of peripheral vision (Schuckit, 1990).

At high doses, marijuana may cause toxic psychoses, including delusions, paranoia, and feelings of terror. However, there is no evidence that marijuana use causes long-term psychosis or schizophrenia (Schuckit, 1994a).

Researchers believe that regular use of marijuana can result in addiction, and if usage is stopped, there may be mild withdrawal symptoms (Grinspoon et al, 1997; Wickelgren, 1997).

We have discussed the use and potential dangers of common legal and illegal drugs. Now we'll examine a popular program to prevent drug usage.

I. Research Focus: Drug Prevention
How Effective Is the DARE Program?

DARE Program

Psychology has four goals, one of which is to control behavior. When this goal is applied to teenage drug usage, it means that researchers want to control or prevent teenagers from using and abusing drugs. The top three reasons teens give for using drugs are peer pressure, to feel good, and to relieve stress (National Center on Addiction and Substance Abuse, *USA Today*, Oct. 22, 1996).

The graph on the right shows that, from 1991 to 1997, adolescents' use of illegal drugs has doubled (11% to 22%) (Friend, 1996). If eighth-graders start using drugs early, they are at great risk for drug-related problems and will find it more difficult to stop (Tschann et al., 1994). A popular program to prevent teenage drug use is called DARE (or D.A.R.E.).

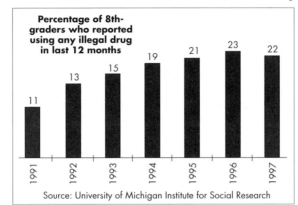

Percentage of 8th-graders who reported using any illegal drug in last 12 months

1991	1992	1993	1994	1995	1996	1997
11	13	15	19	21	23	22

Source: University of Michigan Institute for Social Research

DARE (Drug Abuse Resistance Program), is based on the idea of using social influence and role playing to discourage adolescents from starting drug use and to encourage them to refuse drugs in the future. This program is taught in grade school classrooms by trained, uniformed police officers.

Begun in 1983, DARE has become the most popular drug education school program with an annual budget of about $700 million. Currently, thousands of DARE officers speak to 5 million grade school children in 70% of the school districts in the United States (Murphy, 1996).

However, despite the widespread use of DARE's program, teenagers' use of both legal and illegal drugs has doubled since 1991. This increased drug usage was one reason researchers evaluated the effectiveness of DARE's drug prevention program.

Method and Procedure

Researchers selected 36 elementary schools in urban, suburban, and rural areas in Illinois. Schools were paired to control for ethnic differences and income levels of parents. Students in one school of a pair were the experimental group and received DARE training, while students in the other school of the pair were the control group and did not receive the DARE training. A total of 1,803 students took part in the study.

Before DARE began, students were pretested to determine their attitudes toward drugs and their use of drugs. Then students in the experimental schools began the DARE program, which consisted of educational sessions lasting 45–60 minutes that are taught in the classroom by uniformed police officers.

Immediately after the DARE program, and 1, 2, and 3 years later, students were retested on their attitudes toward drugs and their actual use of drugs.

Results and Discussion

Researchers found that going through project DARE had no statistically significant effect on whether students did or did not start smoking, drinking alcohol, or drinking to get drunk. These disappointing results were found immediately after the DARE program ended, as well as 1, 2, and 3 years later. There was a significant increase in self-esteem but this gain was short-lived and was apparently not strong enough to help students resist using drugs in the future.

Researchers concluded that, although the police officers were well trained and popular among students, there was little evidence that being in project DARE had any direct influence on adolescents' use of drugs or on attitudes and skills thought to be related to preventing drug use (Ennett et al., 1994).

Researchers who analyzed dozens of other studies involving thousands of teenagers also concluded that DARE had "a limited to essentially nonexistent effect" on drug use in teenagers (Research Triangle Institute, 1994; Sherman, 1997).

Conclusion

The DARE program has a yearly budget of $600 million and uses thousands of trained police officers who speak to millions of students in about 70% of the school districts in the United States. Despite these credentials, the program was found ineffective in preventing future drug usage in teenagers.

You may wonder how an ineffective drug prevention program became so popular. Perhaps the main reason was the glowing testimonials from police officers, school administrators, and politicians about how effective DARE was and how much good it was doing.

However, as discussed in Module 2, testimonials have great potential for error and bias and must be taken with not just a grain but at least a pound of salt. These testimonials did not stand up when DARE's program was scientifically evaluated and found lacking. This Research Focus shows the importance of checking any conclusion based on testimonials rather than on hard, scientific evidence.

We will now switch from discussing the kinds of drugs people use to examining what happens when people abuse drugs and require treatment.

J. Application: Treatment for Drug Abuse

Case History

What are the risks for drug abuse?

Earlier, we discussed the genetic and environmental risks that turn a drug user into a drug abuser. In the following case study, notice the environmental risks that pushed Martin into becoming an alcoholic.

In high school, Martin got good grades but still felt insecure, especially about his sexual abilities. His solution was to act like a "rugged, hard-drinking person." Instead of helping, drinking made him feel more insecure in relationships and made it more difficult for him to perform sexually.

When Martin entered college, he continued to have low self-esteem and feared that someone would discover that his sexual performance did not match his bragging. As he had done in high school, he buried his fears in drink, often putting down 5–10 drinks on a weekend night.

Despite his drinking bouts, Martin's knack for learning helped him finish college with good grades and even get accepted into medical school. However, between college and medical school, he took a job driving a beer truck, with the added benefit of free beer every night after work. Martin's usual quota was at least half a dozen beers.

By the time medical school began, Martin drank regularly. He wasn't worried, because he discovered that alcohol made him feel "more content" and "it made it easier to live with himself." Best of all, alcohol reduced his feelings of "self-loathing" and gave him an "instant" sense of self-worth. Despite his heavy drinking, Martin's talents for mastering academic subjects helped him finish medical school.

After medical school, Martin settled in the Midwest, developed a successful medical clinic, got married, and had a family. However, throughout this period, he continued to drink heavily and was soon unable to function without alcohol. About the same time he began having blackouts, his wife refused to put up with his heavy drinking; she took the children and left. At this point, Martin began taking painkillers, for which he wrote his own prescriptions. After 10 years of abusing drugs, Martin could not escape the vicious circle of needing more and more drugs to feed his addiction.

Finally, one cold afternoon as Martin sat home with his booze and painkillers, the police arrested him for writing illegal prescriptions. Martin was saved from himself by being forced to enter a psychiatric hospital for drug treatment (adapted from Khantzian & Mack, 1994).

Some of the environmental risks that pushed Martin to become a drug abuser are clear: for most of his life, he suffered from feelings of low self-esteem, worthlessness, and fears of not performing sexually. Hoping to solve his problems with drugs, Martin instead made them worse with substance abuse, the most common mental health problem among males (Kessler et al., 1994).

Substance Abuse

What is a drug problem?

Like Martin, about 5–15% of those who use legal or illegal drugs develop a serious drug problem called substance abuse.

Substance abuse refers to a maladaptive behavioral pattern of using a drug or medicine so frequently that significant problems develop: failing to meet major obligations, and having multiple legal, social, family, health, work, or interpersonal problems. These problems must occur repeatedly during the same 12-month period (American Psychiatric Association, 1994).

Most substance abusers need professional help and treatment to get straightened out. Martin entered a treatment program that is based on the Minnesota model, which is used in about 95% of inpatient drug treatment centers in the United States. The *Minnesota model* recognizes that the drug user has lost control when it comes to drugs, may be vulnerable to using other mood-altering substances, cannot solve the drug problem alone, must rebuild his or her life without drugs, and must strive for total abstinence (McElrath, 1997; Shorkey, 1994).

We'll follow Martin's progress as he goes through a typical drug treatment program based on the Minnesota model.

Treatment

Why don't people seek treatment?

Step 1. Admit the Problem

The fact that Martin did not seek help for his drug problem until after he was arrested points out an important difference between most individuals treated for drug problems and those treated for mental health problems.

Generally, individuals with mental health problems seek help voluntarily because they want to stop their suffering or unhappiness. In contrast, many individuals with drug problems do not recognize that they have a problem and do not seek help voluntarily. Thus, the first step in getting treatment is admitting that one has a drug problem. Although this step appears obvious, in reality it represents a hurdle that many drug abusers have a difficult time getting over. What happens is that drug users believe that drugs are the solution to their problems, fears, insecurities, and worries.

For almost ten years, Martin believed that alcohol was the solution to his sexual and social fears. In fact, the opposite was true. Heavy drug use became the problem, even though Martin and most users refuse to admit it. Convincing heavy drug users to seek treatment often requires the efforts of their family, loved ones, and employer, as well as a judge or doctor (Hodgson, 1994).

Step 2. Enter a Program

What is a drug program?

About 10 to 25% of individuals with serious drug problems do not enter a treatment program but recover on their own. However, their chances of having future drug problems are higher than individuals who seek and receive professional help (Dawson, 1996). In Martin's case, he was required to enter an in-hospital drug treatment program because he was both addicted and depressed, would not admit to having a problem, and would not seek help on his own.

After Martin was admitted to an in-hospital drug treatment program, he was given a complete medical checkup and went through a two-week period of detoxification. When he was free of drugs, a treatment team consisting of a physician, a psychologist, a counselor, and a nurse discussed the treatment program with Martin.

First goal. Help Martin face up to his drinking problem. It is not uncommon for a drug abuser to deny that he or she has a problem with drugs, even though it is obvious to everyone else.

Second goal. Have Martin begin a program of stress management, so that he could reduce his anxiety and tension without drinking. Stress management involves the substitution of relaxation exercises and other enjoyable activities (sports, hobbies) for the escape and enjoyment that alcohol has provided.

Third goal. Give Martin an opportunity to share his experiences in group therapy. Group sessions helped Martin realize that he was not suffering alone, that it was important for him to make plans for the future, and that he might have to make new, non-drinking friends once he left the program.

Fourth goal. This is perhaps the most important goal and goes to the heart of the problem: Help Martin face and overcome his environmental risk factors, which include personal and social problems such as the feelings of low self-esteem and depression that had contributed to his drug abuse.

Step 3. Get Therapy

What is the best program?

With regard to the fourth goal, a frequently asked question is Which kind of therapy is most effective in helping drug abusers?

One answer comes from a recent 27-million-dollar study that took 8 years and compared three different programs. There were over 1,700 people, all of whom were diagnosed as alcohol-dependent, which means they either drank heavily every day or went on alcohol binges that disrupted their home or work activities.

Three therapies. After volunteering for this study, individuals were randomly assigned to a 12-week treatment program that involved one of the following three therapies. *Cognitive-behavioral therapy* focuses on helping patients develop skills to control their thoughts about alcohol and learn to control their urges to drink. *Motivational therapy* helps clients recognize and utilize their personal resources and encourages them to take personal responsibil-

ity to abstain from drinking. The *12-step approach* is used in traditional Alcoholics Anonymous (AA) programs. This therapy or program is one of spiritual awakening that serves as a guide for recovery and abstinence. Here are two examples of the 12 steps: "Step 1: We admitted we were powerless over alcohol—that our lives had become unmanageable. Step 2: We came to believe that a Power greater than ourselves could restore us to sanity." AA believes that drug abuse is a disease, that a person must surrender to and ask God for help, and that total abstinence is the only solution.

Because these three therapies represent three different philosophies or approaches, many professionals believed that one therapy might be more effective than another.

Effectiveness. Researchers found that, before therapy, all individuals drank heavily on about 25 out of 30 days per month. In comparison, a year after finishing therapy, 35% reported not drinking at all, while 65% had slipped, or relapsed, into drinking again. Of the 65% who had relapsed, 40% reported periods of at least 3 consecutive days of heavy drinking.

An unexpected finding was that all three therapies were equally effective in reducing drinking (Project Match Research Group, 1997). Even though the three therapies seem to have somewhat different approaches, there was little or no difference in their effectiveness. It appears that the specific kind of therapy used is not as important as finding better ways of encouraging drug abusers to recognize and seek help for their drug problems.

Rate of success. The effectiveness of a drug treatment program is usually measured by how many clients remain abstinent (do not use drugs) for a period of one year. For most drug treatment programs, success rates range from about 30% to a high of 54% (Hodgson, 1994; Miller & Brown, 1997; Stanton & Shadish, 1997). The goal of most programs is total abstinence, because it is questionable whether individuals who once abused drugs for a long period of time can relearn to use drugs in moderate amounts (Rosenberg, 1993; Sleek, 1995).

After Martin left his in-hospital drug treatment program, he was encouraged to join an aftercare support group in his community.

Step 4. Remain Drug Free

What to do about relapse?

Recovering drug addicts are encouraged to join an aftercare support group to help fight off the temptation of returning to drugs. The most popular and successful aftercare program for alcoholics is Alcoholics Anonymous (AA); a similar program for other drug users is Narcotics Anonymous (NA). Both AA and NA provide valuable drug treatment and social support to help prevent relapse (using drugs again) (Shorkey, 1994).

Preventing relapse is a big problem; about 70% of alcoholics and other drug users relapse at some point (Vaillant, 1996). Thus, a person with a serious drug problem initially needs treatment to get off the drug and then an aftercare support program to help prevent or deal with relapse and remain drug free.

SUMMARY TEST

A. HYPNOSIS

1. Hypnosis is defined as an altered state of awareness, attention, and alertness, during which a person is usually much more open to the (a)_____ of a hypnotist or therapist. About 30% of college students are easily hypnotized, while 40% are difficult to hypnotize. The procedure used to hypnotize someone is called (b)_____.

2. Under hypnosis, subjects will experience or perform the following _____: age regression, imagined perception, posthypnotic amnesia, posthypnotic suggestions, and hypnotic analgesia.

3. According to the (a)_____ state theory, a hypnotized individual is in an altered state and experiences unusual sensations and feelings. According to the (b)_____ theory, the effects produced by hypnosis are due to powerful personal pressure and social influences as well as the abilities of the subject rather than to the process of being hypnotized.

4. In dental and medical settings, hypnosis is used to help patients deal with painful procedures by producing (a)_____. In therapeutic settings, hypnosis is used in combination with other behavioral and cognitive treatments to help clients reveal their personalities and gain insights. However, hypnosis is not very successful in dealing with problems that involve (b)_____.

B. DRUGS: OVERVIEW

5. Regular use of a drug usually results in one or more of the following. A behavioral pattern of drug abuse that is marked by an overwhelming and compulsive desire to obtain and use the drug is called an (a)_____. If the nervous system becomes accustomed to having the drug and needs the drug for normal functioning, the user is said to have developed a (b)_____. If a habitual user suddenly stops taking the drug, he or she will experience unpleasant or painful (c)_____. After using a drug over a period of time, a person must take a larger dose to achieve the original behavioral effect because this person has developed a (d)_____ for the drug.

6. Drugs that affect the nervous system to alter consciousness, awareness, sensations, perceptions, mood, and cognitive processes are called _____ drugs.

7. Some drugs act like chemical keys that are so similar to the brain's own (a)_____ that drugs can open the same chemical locks. Some drugs interfere with the reabsorption, or (b)_____, of neurotransmitters back into the neuron.

C. STIMULANTS

8. Drugs that increase activity of the nervous system and result in heightened alertness, arousal, and euphoria and decreased appetite and fatigue are called _____.

303 tons

9. In moderate doses, cocaine produces short-lived enhancement of _____. In heavy doses, it can produce addiction; serious psychological effects, such as frightening hallucinations; and serious physical problems, such as heart irregularity, convulsions, and death.

10. A form of amphetamine called _____ produces a quick high, is very addictive, and has become a major drug problem.

11. The most widely used legal psychoactive drug in the world is _____, which affects brain receptors and, depending on the dose, produces physiological arousal, a mild feeling of alertness, increased reaction time, and decreased fatigue and drowsiness.

12. The legal drug that is second to caffeine in worldwide usage is _____, which has both stimulating and calming properties.

D. OPIATES

13. All opiates produce three primary effects: a reduction in pain, which is called (a)_____; a twilight state between waking and sleeping, which is called (b)_____; and (c)_____, which permits their use as a treatment for diarrhea. With continued use of opiates, users develop tolerance, addiction, and an intense craving for the drug. The brain also produces its own morphine-like chemicals, called (d)_____.

E. HALLUCINOGENS

14. Drugs that act on the brain (and body) to produce perceptual, sensory, and cognitive experiences that do not match the external reality are called (a)_____. Sometime after using LSD, a user may suddenly have a frightening drug-related experience called a (b)_____. Examples of hallucinogenic drugs are LSD, psilocybin, and mescaline. Drugs that are manufactured or altered to produce psychoactive effects are called (c)_____; an example is (d)_____.

F. ALCOHOL

15. Alcohol is classified as a (a)_____ because it decreases the activity of the central nervous system by stimulating neural receptors called (b)_____ receptors. Heavy and repeated drinking can result in periods of seemingly normal behavior that the drinker, when sober, cannot recall at all; these periods are called (c)_____. Alcohol abuse is a major contributor to personal problems, fatal traffic accidents, birth defects, homicides, assaults, date rape, and suicide.

16. A drinker's risk of becoming an alcoholic increases 3–4 times if members of his or her family are alcoholics. The risk of developing alcoholism is increased by difficulties in showing trust and being overdependent in relationships, which are called (a)_____ factors; and also by the inheritance of predispositions for alcoholism, which are called the (b)_____ factors.

G. CULTURAL DIVERSITY: RATES OF ALCOHOLISM

17. About 10–12% of American drinkers become _____, defined as people who have drunk heavily for a long period of time, are addicted to and have an intense craving for alcohol, and have problems in two or three major life areas caused by drinking.

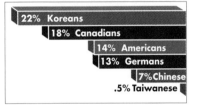

22% Koreans
18% Canadians
14% Americans
13% Germans
7% Chinese
.5% Taiwanese

18. One reason the Chinese and Taiwanese have low rates of alcoholism is that these societies are heavily influenced by the Confucian moral code, which discourages _____ in public.

H. MARIJUANA

19. After caffeine, nicotine, and alcohol, the fourth most popular psychoactive drug in the United States is (a)_____. In low

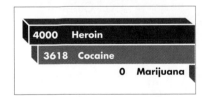

4000 Heroin
3618 Cocaine
0 Marijuana

doses it produces mild euphoria, in moderate doses it produces distortions in perception and time, and in high doses it may produce hallucinations and delusions. Researchers recently discovered that the brain has neural locks, or (b)_____, that respond to the THC in marijuana. In addition, researchers discovered that the brain makes two different chemicals that closely resemble THC and function similar to the brain's own (c)_____.

I. RESEARCH FOCUS: DRUG PREVENTION

20. The most popular program to prevent drug usage in teenagers is called (a)_____, which uses social influence and role playing to discourage adolescents from starting drug use and to encourage them to refuse drugs in the future. However, researchers found that this very popular and expensive program was not effective in preventing future drug use. One reason DARE grew in popularity was that early evidence for its effectiveness came primarily from (b)_____, which have a relatively high potential for error and bias.

J. APPLICATION: TREATMENT FOR DRUG ABUSE

21. A maladaptive pattern of continued usage of a substance—drug or medicine—that results in significant legal, personal or other problems over a 12-month period is called _____.

22. Programs that treat drug abusers have three steps: the first step is admitting that one has a (a)_____. The second step is entering a (b)_____, which has several goals. The third step is to find a support group to prevent and deal with the likelihood of future (c)_____.

23. Researchers found that three different kinds of therapy—cognitive-behavioral, motivational, and AA's 12-step approach—were about (a)_____ in helping alcoholics stop drinking. Although 35% of individuals stopped drinking, 65% started drinking again, which is called (b)_____. This is a big problem among recovering drug users, since about 70% will relapse at some time and may need some kind of (c)_____ support to once again become drug free.

Answers: *1. (a) suggestions, (b) hypnotic induction; 2. behaviors; 3. (a) altered, b) socio-cognitive; 4. (a) analgesia, (b) self-control; 5. (a) addiction, (b) dependence, (c) withdrawal symptoms, (d) tolerance; 6. psychoactive; 7. (a) neurotransmitters, (b) reuptake; 8. stimulants; 9. activity, mood, or energy; 10. methamphetamine; 11. caffeine; 12. nicotine; 13. (a) analgesia, (b) opiate euphoria, (c) constipation, (d) endorphins; 14. (a) hallucinogens, (b) flashback, (c) designer drugs, (d) MDMA, or ecstasy; 15. (a) depressant, (b) GABA, (c) blackouts; 16. (a) environmental risk, (b) genetic risk; 17. alcoholics; 18. drunkenness; 19. (a) marijuana, (b) receptors, (c) neurotransmitters; 20. (a) DARE, or D.A.R.E., (b) testimonials and surveys; 21. substance abuse; 22. (a) drug problem, (b) treatment program, (c) relapse; 23. (a) equally effective, (b) relapse, (c) social.*

CRITICAL THINKING

Newspaper Article

QUESTIONS

1. Why do you think that, until recently, little data has been collected on women's use of alcohol?

2. What research method was used in this study? What are its advantages and disadvantages?

3. Does this study prove that women are not influenced by others in their alcohol use?

4. Does this study show that women living with partners outside of marriage tend to have more alcohol problems than married women?

5. Is the only reason for the lower prevalence of alcohol dependence among older women than younger ones that they "mature out" of it?

THE FACTS ABOUT WOMEN AND ALCOHOL
by Marilyn Elias

Until recently, not much was known about patterns of alcohol use among women. But a landmark study on women and alcohol, funded by the National Institute on Alcohol Abuse and Alcoholism (NIAAA) and conducted by Sharon Wilsnack and Richard Wilsnack, helps fill in that gap. The anonymous, in-person interviews span a period of 15 years and also reflect interviews with male spouses or partners. Some common assumptions about how and why women drink were proven wrong by the new report:

- **Men influence women to become heavy drinkers.** No, it's mutual. Following women over time shows "kindred marries kindred," Wilsnack says. Women who already drink a lot marry men like themselves.
- **The stress of juggling several roles makes women heavier drinkers; a more low-key life leads to less drinking.** Actually, the more roles women play—wife, mother, worker—the less likely they are to have drinking problems.
- **Getting a divorce prompts more alcohol use for women.** It can be just the opposite. Leaving an unhappy marriage marred by problem drinking apparently improves women's chances of ending an alcohol habit. After five years, 44% of women with drinking problems who stayed married still have alcohol dependency symptoms; 31% who get divorced are still alcohol dependent.

Other findings from the survey aren't so surprising. Women of all ages who live with partners rather than marrying tend to drink more and have more alcohol-related hassles than women who choose to marry. Live-in partners are just less traditional in general than spouses are.

The survey also confirms that both sexes tend to "mature out" of serious alcohol problems. For example, 29% of women age 21 to 34 say they've had six or more drinks in a single day at least four times during the last year; only 14% who are 50 to 64 years old have binged. And 26% who are 21 to 34 report symptoms of alcohol dependency—blackouts, inability to control themselves or remember events while drinking—compared with 6% of women age 50 to 64.

Source: *USA Today,* January 5, 1998. Copyright © 1998, *USA Today.* Reprinted with permission.

Study Questions

A. **Hypnosis**—A student has great test anxiety, which is interfering with his success in college. Would hypnosis help? (See answer in Critical Thinking Appendix.)

B. **Drugs: Overview**—Keeping in mind that Americans annually spend about $50 billion on illegal drugs, what is your position on their legalization?

C. **Stimulants**—Why don't most Americans think that caffeine and nicotine are drugs that can be addictive?

D. **Opiates**—Why do you think that our brains manufacture their own morphine-like chemicals, called endorphins?

E. **Hallucinogens**—Why is there a long history of people's use of hallucinogens in religious ceremonies?

F. **Alcohol**—If researchers know who has an increased risk for alcoholism, at what age should such a person be told? (See answer in Critical Thinking Appendix.)

G. **Cultural Diversity: Rates of Alcoholism**—Why are there such striking similarities in the development of alcoholism across different cultures?

H. **Marijuana**—A regular user of marijuana says that he can drive just fine after smoking. Would you ride with him? (See answer in Critical Thinking Appendix.)

I. **Research Focus: Drug Prevention**—Can you think of reasons why a 17-week course in drug abuse prevention might not be effective for adolescents?

J. **Application: Treatment for Drug Abuse**—Why are individuals who have been successfully treated for drug abuse so often tempted to relapse and use drugs again?

Web Sites & Learning Activities

● BROOKS/COLE ONLINE PSYCHOLOGY STUDY CENTER

http://psychstudy.brookscole.com/student/plotnik/quiz/ch08frm.html

This site gives students a chance to review material by taking quizzes and doing exercises and activities for this module.

● NATIONAL INSTITUTE ON ALCOHOL ABUSE AND ALCOHOLISM

http://www.niaaa.hih.gov/

This site provides the latest news and journal articles on alcohol abuse and alcoholism. In addition, it provides links to several leading alcohol-related associations.

● HABITSMART

http://www.cts.com/crash/habtsmrt/

This site contains information about addictive behavior, including tips for managing problematic habits, a self-scoring alcohol assessment, and links to other sites.

● DRUG ENFORCEMENT ADMINISTRATION (DEA)

http://www.usdoj.gov/dea/index.htm

This government site supplies information, statistics, and photos of psychoactive drugs; it also provides information on U.S. drug enforcement activities.

● NATIONAL CLEARINGHOUSE FOR ALCOHOL AND DRUG INFORMATION

http://www.health.org/

Provides statistics, information, and publications on alcohol abuse, including resources for those who want to overcome a drug problem—their own or someone else's.

● MOTHERS AGAINST DRUNK DRIVING (MADD)

http://www.madd.org

This organization promotes efforts to develop solutions to the problems of drunk driving and underage drinking. The site provides information on many alcohol-related topics, including a guide for giving a safe party.

● HIGHER EDUCATION CENTER FOR ALCOHOL AND OTHER DRUG PREVENTION

http://www.edc.org/hec/

Sponsored by an organization that provides nationwide support for campus alcohol and drug prevention efforts, this site has information on drug use on campus and features a special area for students.

Welcome to the WEB

Activities

● *Integrator Online™ for Introductory Psychology* CD-ROM, Plotnik, Module 8

● Study Guide to accompany *Introduction to Psychology,* 5th edition, Module 8 (choice of PC or Mac computer version or hard copy).

● *PsychNow!* CD-ROM

Psychoactive Drugs

Answers to questions on page 192

1. It might be because recently most research was done on men under the mistaken belief that men and women had the same patterns of alcohol use.
2. This study was done with a survey, a good way to collect information quickly from a large population sample. The disadvantages of a survey are that results may be biased or that people may not be truthful.
3. No. This study indicates only that although women may not be influenced by male partners, they may still be influenced by family, friends, or others.
4. No. Living with a partner outside of marriage does not lead to alcohol abuse. Perhaps the link is that unmarried people who live together are likely to do other nontraditional things, such as abuse alcohol.
5. No. It is possible that older women who were formerly heavy drinkers have been in treatment. Also, young women who drink heavily may die at a younger age and so are not represented in the groups of older women.

Module 9 CLASSICAL CONDITIONING

A. Three Kinds of Learning 196

* **CLASSICAL CONDITIONING**
* **OPERANT CONDITIONING**
* **COGNITIVE LEARNING**

B. Procedure: Classical Conditioning 197

* **PAVLOV'S EXPERIMENT**
* **TERMS IN CLASSICAL CONDITIONING**

C. Other Conditioning Concepts 199

* **GENERALIZATION**
* **DISCRIMINATION**
* **EXTINCTION**
* **SPONTANEOUS RECOVERY**

D. Adaptive Value 200

* **DEFINITION**
* **TASTE-AVERSION LEARNING**
* **EXPLANATION**
* **EXAMPLES**
* **EMOTIONAL RESPONSES**

E. Three Explanations 202

* **WHAT IS LEARNED?**
* **STIMULUS SUBSTITUTION AND CONTIGUITY THEORY**
* **COGNITIVE PERSPECTIVE**

F. Research Focus: Little Albert 204

* **CAN EMOTIONAL RESPONSES BE CONDITIONED?**

G. Cultural Diversity: Dental Fears 205

* **FEAR AND PAIN**
* **CULTURAL DIFFERENCES**
* **ORIGINS OF FEAR**
* **EFFECTS OF FEAR**

H. Application: Conditioned Fear & Nausea 206

* **EXAMPLES OF CONDITIONING**
* **SYSTEMATIC DESENSITIZATION**

MOST STRESSFUL

8. Vomiting
7. Feeling nausea
6. Receiving injection
5. In treatment room
4. Smelling chemicals
3. In waiting room
2. Entering clinic
1. Driving to clinic

It's Only Aftershave

What happened to Carla?

"I've got an unusual problem and I thought you might be able to explain what happened." Carla, one of my students, looked troubled.

"I'll help if I can," I replied, and asked her to sit down.

"It all started when my dentist told me that I needed a lot of work on my teeth and gums. I spent many mornings in the dentist's chair, and even though he gave me Novocain, it was painful and very uncomfortable. But here's the strange part that I wish you would explain. I had recently bought my boyfriend a new aftershave, and as the dentist worked on my teeth, I noticed that he was using the same one. You'll think this is silly, but now when I smell my boyfriend's aftershave, I start to feel tense and anxious."

Carla stopped and waited to see if I would tell her that she was just being silly. I didn't, and she continued.

"Finally, I told my boyfriend that he would have to stop using the aftershave I had bought him because it was the same as my dentist's and the smell made me anxious. Well, we got into a big argument because he said that he was nothing like my dentist and I was just being silly. So now my teeth are great, but I feel myself getting anxious each time we get close and I smell his aftershave."

I assured Carla that she was not being silly and that many people get conditioned in the dentist's chair. In fact, patients have reported feeling anxious when they enter the dentist's office, smell the antiseptic odor, or hear the sound of the drill (Milgrom et al., 1994). I explained that, without her knowing, she had been conditioned to feel fear each time she smelled her dentist's aftershave and how that conditioning had transferred to her boyfriend. Before I explained how to get "unconditioned," I told her how after only one terrifying experience, I too had been conditioned.

It's Only a Needle

What happened to Rod?

I was about 8 years old when I had to get an injection from my local doctor, whom I really liked. He warned me in a kindly way that the injection might hurt a little. I was feeling OK until I saw the long needle on the syringe. I tried to be brave and think of my fuzzy dog, but as soon as I felt that long needle enter my little butt, everything started to spin. I remember sinking slowly to the floor, and then everything went dark. When I came to, the doctor told me that I had fainted.

Even after all these years, the sight of a needle can still strike terror into me. To prevent fainting, I always lie down when getting an injection or giving blood. But I'm not alone in my fear of needles and injections; about 10 to 20% of the general population report a similar fear (Page et al., 1997).

Besides learning to fear needles and blood, people can unknowingly learn to feel sick and nauseated, just as Michelle did.

It's Only Dish Soap

What happened to Michelle?

Michelle was nervous and afraid as the nurse put a needle into the vein in her left arm and then opened a valve that allowed chemicals to drip into her bloodstream. Michelle was in the process of receiving chemotherapy to treat her cancer. One serious side effect of chemotherapy is severe nausea, which Michelle experienced after each treatment.

What Michelle wasn't prepared for was how other things could trigger her nausea. In one case, the odor of her dishwashing liquid, which smelled similar to the chemotherapy room, made her feel nauseated. She had to change her brand of detergent because its odor made her salivate, which was the first sign of oncoming nausea (Wittman, 1994). Without her awareness, Michelle had been conditioned to feel nauseated by numerous stimuli involved in her chemotherapy (Montgomery & Bovbjerg, 1997).

The cases of Michelle, Carla, and myself show how we had been conditioned to fear relatively ordinary things, such as aftershave lotion, needles, and the smell of detergent. This conditioning illustrates one kind of learning.

Learning is a relatively enduring or permanent change in behavior that results from previous experience with certain stimuli and responses. The term *behavior* includes both unobservable mental events (thoughts, images) and observable responses (fainting, salivating, vomiting).

In all three cases, conditioning resulted in a relatively enduring change in behavior. In fact, mine has lasted almost 50 years. What happened to each of us involved a particular kind of learning, called classical conditioning, which we'll discuss in this module.

What's Coming

We'll first discuss three different kinds of learning and then focus on one, classical conditioning. We'll examine how classical conditioning is established and tested, how we respond after being classically conditioned, what we learn during classical conditioning, and how classical conditioning is used in therapy. Let's begin with a look at three different kinds of learning.

D. Adaptive Value

Definition

How useful is classical conditioning?

Pavlov believed that animals and people evolved the capacity for classical conditioning because it had an adaptive value (Hollis, 1997).

Adaptive value refers to the usefulness of certain abilities or traits that have evolved in animals and humans that tend to increase their chances of survival, such as finding food, acquiring mates, and avoiding pain and injury.

We'll discuss several examples, such as learning to avoid certain tastes, salivating at the sight of food, and avoiding pain, which support Pavlov's view that classical conditioning is useful because it has an adaptive value.

Taste-Aversion Learning

Why don't rats repeat their mistakes?

People who try to exterminate rats with bait poison see firsthand the effects of classical conditioning. That's because some rats eat sufficient bait poison to cause death, while others happen to eat only enough to become sick. Once rats get sick on a particular bait poison, they quickly learn to avoid that particular bait poison's taste or smell in the future. This is an example of taste-aversion learning (Schneider & Pinnow, 1994).

Taste-aversion learning refers to associating a particular sensory cue (smell, taste, sound, or sight) with getting sick and thereafter avoiding that particular sensory cue.

Exterminators of disease-carrying rodents find taste-aversion learning to be a real problem since they must continually change the smell and taste of bait used to lure animals into traps because animals who only get sick will avoid that particular bait.

On the other hand, taste-aversion learning can also have survival value because it warns us away from plants or poisons that cause illness or death. For example, several varieties of mushrooms contain substances that, when eaten, make humans very ill. In the future, the sight of these particular mushrooms will cause humans to avoid them. Thus, taste-aversion learning has a real adaptive value.

Taste-aversion learning can also occur from overindulgence. For example, children report taste aversions to food after overeating (left photo) and becoming sick. Similarly, the majority of college students report taste aversions after drinking too much alcohol and getting sick.

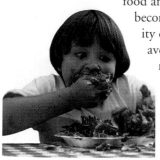

In these examples, taste aversions to food or drink developed after a single trial and lasted an average of 4 to 5 years (Logue et al., 1981; Rozin, 1986).

The study of this interesting phenomenon, taste-aversion learning, changed two long-held beliefs about classical conditioning.

Explanation

Is only one trial enough?

Psychologist John Garcia wondered how rats learned to avoid bait that made them sick, which is called *bait-shyness*. Initially, psychologists did not think that classical conditioning could be used to explain bait-shyness because of a long-held belief of how conditioning works. Most believed that classical conditioning occurred only after many trials and only if the neutral stimulus was followed closely in time (after seconds or a minute) by the unconditioned response.

Garcia showed that taste aversion could occur in one trial and, more surprising, even after long intervals (minutes to hours) between the occurrence of the neutral stimulus (smell or taste) and the unconditioned response (sickness or vomiting). At first Garcia's findings met with disbelief but, after being repeated many times, taste-aversion learning was recognized as one form of classical conditioning (Bower, 1997).

Another long-standing belief was that all stimuli have equal potential for becoming conditioned stimuli. But Garcia showed that, in taste-aversion learning, rats were easily conditioned to stimuli that involved taste cues and rarely conditioned to stimuli that involved light cues (Garcia & Koelling, 1966). From this study, Garcia concluded that all stimuli do not have the same potential for becoming conditioned stimuli. The phenomenon that some stimuli were more easily conditioned than others was called preparedness (Seligman, 1970).

Preparedness refers to the phenomenon that animals and humans are biologically prepared to associate some combinations of conditioned and unconditioned stimuli more easily than others.

For example, rats have poor vision but great taste and olfaction (smell) and thus acquire taste aversion more easily to stimuli involving smell and taste cues. In comparison, quails have poor olfaction but great vision and thus acquire taste aversion more easily to stimuli involving visual cues (Wilcoxon et al., 1971). Thus, preparedness focuses on the fact that different animals use different senses to detect stimuli that are important to their survival and adaptation.

John Garcia and his colleagues (1974) applied their knowledge of taste aversion to the problem of sheep-killing by coyotes. They baited grazing areas with pieces of sheep flesh laced with a chemical that caused coyotes to become nauseated and ill. As a result, coyotes that had acquired a taste aversion showed an estimated 30–60% reduction in sheep-killing (Bower, 1997; Gustavson et al., 1976).

Taste-aversion learning also occurs in nature.

Examples

How many things are conditioned?

It is interesting to observe how frequently classical conditioning occurs and figure out its adaptive value. For example, you're about to discover how bluejays, butterflies, and hot fudge sundaes can be involved in classical conditioning.

BLUEJAYS AND BUTTERFLIES

Some animals have evolved their own taste-aversion systems that help them survive by warning off predators.

For example, bluejays feast on butterflies, but they generally learn to avoid monarch butterflies, which have a distinctive coloring pattern. Unknown to a naive bluejay is the sad fact that monarch butterflies contain a chemical that, when eaten, will make birds sick. Through taste aversion, bluejays learn that the distinctive color pattern of monarch butterflies predicts getting sick, and so smart bluejays avoid eating monarch butterflies.

Like monarch butterflies, many animals have evolved with distinctive markings or colors that, through taste-aversion learning, have become conditioned stimuli that serve as warnings to predators. Thus, classically conditioned taste aversion has survival value for animals.

HOT FUDGE SUNDAES

The next time you enter a restaurant, read the menu, think about food, and see people eating, notice that you are salivating even though you have no food in your own mouth. Just as Pavlov's dog was conditioned to salivate at the sound of a bell, we often salivate when only thinking of, imagining, smelling, or seeing food. This is a clear example of how many different kinds of neutral stimuli (holding a menu, reading a menu, seeing people eat, looking at food, imagining food) become conditioned stimuli that elicit a conditioned response—salivation.

Salivation is a reflex response that is normally elicited when you place food in your mouth. One purpose of salivation is to lubricate your mouth and throat to make chewing and swallowing food easier. Thus, being classically conditioned to salivate when reading a menu prepares your mouth for the soon-to-arrive food. This is an example of how classical conditioning serves an adaptive value, in this case, aiding the digestive process.

Next, we'll examine how emotional responses can be classically conditioned.

Emotional Responses

Why do people fear needles?

At the beginning of this module, I told a sad but true childhood story of getting an injection that elicited such pain and fear that I fainted. Even 50 years later, I still fear injections and needles and always lie down

to avoid fainting. In my case, you can easily identify each element of classical conditioning: The neutral stimulus is the sight of the syringe; the unconditioned stimulus is injection; and the unconditioned response is pain and fear. After a painful injection, the formerly neutral stimulus, the syringe, becomes a conditioned stimulus and elicits the conditioned response, which is fear and even fainting. Because this situation involved the conditioning of an emotional response, my fear of injections and needles is called a conditioned emotional response.

A *conditioned emotional response* refers to feeling some positive or negative emotion, such as happiness, fear, or anxiety, when experiencing a stimulus that initially accompanied a pleasant or painful event.

Conditioned emotional responses can have survival value, such as learning to fear and avoid stimuli that signal dangerous situations, such as the sound of a rattlesnake or wail of a siren. Conditioned emotional responses can also signal pleasant situations, such as stimuli associated with forming parental or romantic attachments.

For example, many couples have a special song that becomes emotionally associated with their relationship. When this song is heard by one in the absence of the other, it can elicit strong emotional and romantic feelings. Similarly, stimuli associated with infants and children, such as the smell of baby powder, can elicit strong emotional feelings of attachment.

In other cases, a conditioned emotional response may develop into a very powerful, irrational fear that is called a phobia.

A *phobia* is an anxiety disorder characterized by an intense and irrational fear that is out of all proportion to the danger elicited by the object or situation. In comparison, a fear is a realistic response to a threatening situation.

About 30 to 75% of people with phobias were able to trace their phobias to fearful, painful, or traumatic situations that involved classical conditioning (Kleinknecht, 1994). For example, about 30% of victims involved in moving car accidents developed a phobia of being in cars, and 65% of individuals who experienced painful dental procedures developed a phobia of dentists (Kuch et al., 1994; Poulton et al., 1997). However, classical conditioning can also be used to reduce fears and phobias, as we'll explain in the Application section and also in Module 22 (Wolpe & Plaud, 1997).

From these many examples, you can see how classical conditioning can help animals and humans survive and adapt to their environments.

Next, we'll go to the heart of classical conditioning and examine how and why it works.

E. Three Explanations

What Is Learned?

Do you salivate when thinking of pizza?

Although most of us have had the experience of salivating when thinking about or seeing a favorite food, such as a pizza, researchers have given different explanations of what happens or what is learned during conditioning. We'll discuss three theories—stimulus substitution, contiguity theory, and cognitive perspective—that offer different explanations of why nearly all of us salivate when only thinking about or seeing a delicious pizza.

Stimulus Substitution and Contiguity Theory

Does the bell substitute for food?

The first explanation of classical conditioning came from Pavlov, who said the reason a dog salivated to a tone was that the tone became a substitute for the food, a theory he called stimulus substitution.

Stimulus substitution means that a neural bond or association forms between the neutral stimulus (tone) and unconditioned stimulus (food). After repeated trials, the neutral stimulus becomes the conditioned stimulus (tone) and acts like a substitute for the unconditioned stimulus (food). Thereafter, the conditioned stimulus (tone) elicits a conditioned response (salivation) that is similar to that of the unconditioned stimulus.

The bell becomes a conditioned stimulus by **substituting** for the food, the unconditioned stimulus.

According to stimulus substitution theory, the reason you salivate when seeing a pizza is because the act of seeing a pizza (conditioned stimulus) becomes bonded in your nervous system to the pizza itself (unconditioned stimulus). Because of this neural bond or association, the sight of pizza substitutes for the pizza, so that just the sight of a pizza can elicit salivation (conditioned response).

However, researchers discovered that the responses elicited by the unconditioned stimulus were often slightly different from those elicited by the conditioned stimulus. For example, following the unconditioned stimulus, a dog salivated and always chewed, but, following the conditioned stimulus, it salivated but rarely chewed (Zener, 1937).

As a result of this and other criticisms of Pavlov's stimulus substitution theory, researchers suggested a different explanation, the contiguity theory.

The *contiguity theory* says that classical conditioning occurs because two stimuli (neutral stimulus and unconditioned stimulus) are paired closely together in time (are contiguous). As a result of this contiguous pairing, the neutral stimulus becomes the conditioned stimulus, which elicits the conditioned response.

The contiguity theory says that because seeing a pizza is paired closely in time with eating it, the sight alone begins to elicit salivation. Contiguity theory was the most popular explanation of classical conditioning until the 1960s, when it was challenged by the creative research of psychologist Robert Rescorla (1966).

Cognitive Perspective

Does the bell predict food is coming?

To the surprise of many researchers, Robert Rescorla (1966, 1987, 1988) showed that an association between a neutral and unconditioned stimulus did not necessarily occur when the two stimuli were closely paired in time. Instead, he found that classical conditioning occurred when a neutral stimulus contained information about what was coming next; this explanation is called the the cognitive perspective.

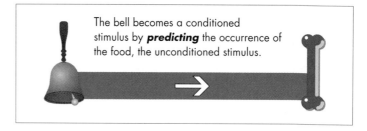

The bell becomes a conditioned stimulus by **predicting** the occurrence of the food, the unconditioned stimulus.

The *cognitive perspective* says that an organism learns a predictable relationship between two stimuli such that the occurrence of one stimulus (neutral stimulus) predicts the occurrence of another (unconditioned stimulus). In other words, classical conditioning occurs because the organism learns what to expect.

For example, the cognitive perspective theory would explain that you salivate to the sight of pizza because you have learned a predictable relationship: Seeing a pizza (conditioned stimulus) often leads to eating one (unconditioned stimulus), and your expectation causes salivation (conditioned response).

Support for the cognitive perspective comes from a number of findings. For example, classical conditioning occurs best if the neutral stimulus (tone) occurs slightly before the unconditioned stimulus (food). In this sequence, the organism learns a relationship between two stimuli: tone predicts food. However, if the sequence is reversed and the unconditioned stimulus appears before the neutral stimulus, this is called *backward conditioning* and does not usually result in classical conditioning.

The cognitive perspective would explain that backward conditioning makes it impossible to predict a relationship between the neutral and unconditioned stimuli and thus does not usually result in classical conditioning. Currently, there is widespread support for the cognitive perspective, which says that classical conditioning involves learning about predictable relationships, or learning about cause and effect (Dadds et al., 1997; Hollis, 1997).

After the Concept Review, we'll discuss a well-known study of classical conditioning that involves the famous "little Albert."

CONCEPT REVIEW

 1. In classical conditioning, one of the stimuli that is chosen has two characteristics: the stimulus, such as a tone, must cause some reaction, such as being heard, seen, tasted, or smelled, but it must not elicit the unconditioned response. A stimulus with these two characteristics is called a _____.

2. In classical conditioning, a second stimulus is chosen that can elicit an unlearned, involuntary physiological reflex, such as salivation. This stimulus is called an _____.

 3. In classical conditioning, the unconditioned stimulus elicits an unlearned, involuntary physiological reflex, such as salivation, which is called the _____.

 4. A typical trial in classical conditioning involves first presenting the (a)_____ and then, a short time later, presenting the (b)_____.

 5. On the very first conditioning trial, the neutral stimulus (tone) did not itself elicit the unconditioned response (salivation). However, on the first trial, the presentation of food, which is called the (a)_____, did elicit salivation, called the (b)_____.

6. After a dozen trials that paired the tone with the food, you noticed that as soon as the tone was presented, the dog salivated. Because the tone itself elicited a response similar to that elicited by the unconditioned stimulus (food), the tone is called the (a)_____. The salivation elicited by the tone itself is called the (b)_____.

 7. During classical conditioning there is a tendency for a stimulus similar to the original conditioned stimulus to elicit a response similar to the conditioned response. This tendency is called _____.

 8. During classical conditioning, an organism learns to make a particular response to some stimuli but not to others; this phenomenon is called _____.

9. If a conditioned stimulus is repeatedly presented *without* the unconditioned stimulus, there is a tendency for the conditioned stimulus to no longer elicit the conditioned response. This phenomenon is called _____.

 10. The tendency for the conditioned response to reappear some time later, even though there are no further conditioning trials, is called _____.

11. The kind of learning in which the cues (smell, taste, auditory, or visual) of a particular stimulus are associated with an unpleasant response, such as nausea or vomiting, is called (a)_____. This kind of learning can even occur after only a single (b)_____.

12. According to Pavlov's original explanation, classical conditioning occurs because of (a)_____, which means that the conditioned stimulus (tone) bonds to the unconditioned stimulus (food). Through this bond, or association, the conditioned stimulus (tone) elicits the conditioned response (salivation) by substituting for the (b)_____ (food). Pavlov's explanation of classical conditioning was criticized, and researchers suggested instead that conditioning occurs because two stimuli are paired closely together in time. This explanation, which is called (c)_____ theory, has been challenged, in turn, by more recent explanations.

13. The current and widely accepted explanation of classical conditioning, which is called the (a)_____ perspective, states that animals or humans learn a predictable relationship between stimuli. According to this explanation, a dog learns predictable relationships, such as a tone predicting the occurrence of (b)_____.

Answers: *1. neutral stimulus; 2. unconditioned stimulus (UCS); 3. unconditioned response (UCR); 4. (a) neutral stimulus, (b) unconditioned stimulus (UCS); 5. (a) unconditioned stimulus (UCS), (b) unconditioned response (UCR); 6. (a) conditioned stimulus (CS), (b) conditioned response (CR); 7. generalization; 8. discrimination; 9. extinction; 10. spontaneous recovery; 11. (a) taste-aversion learning, (b) trial; 12. (a) stimulus substitution, (b) unconditioned stimulus, (c) contiguity; 13. (a) cognitive, (b) food.*

F. Research Focus: Little Albert
Can Emotional Responses Be Conditioned?

Why do people fear spiders?

Why does seeing a tiny, usually harmless, many-legged spider cause many people to show great fear? One reason may be that a person has developed a conditioned emotional response to spiders. Earlier we explained how conditioned emotional responses, which can occur through classical conditioning, may be very strong, last a long time, and even result in an intense and irrational fear, or phobia (of spiders, small places, airplanes, or dentists).

However, in the 1920s, psychologists did not know if emotional responses could be conditioned. But with Pavlov's recent discovery of the conditioned reflex (classical conditioning), John Watson realized that he now had a procedure for studying emotional behaviors in an objective way. As you may remember from Module 1, John Watson was a strong advocate of behaviorism, which emphasized the study of observable behaviors and rejection of unobservable mental events. We'll discuss an important classic experiment on conditioning emotions that John Watson and his student assistant, Rosalie Rayner, published in 1920.

1. Method: Identify Terms

Watson questioned the role that conditioning played in the development of emotional responses in children. To answer his question, Watson (photo) tried to classically condition an emotional response in a young child.

Subject: Nine-month-old infant.
The subject, known later as little Albert, was described as healthy, stolid, and unemotional, since "no one had ever seen him in a state of rage and fear. The infant practically never cried" (Watson & Rayner, 1920, p. 3).

Neutral stimulus: White rat.
Watson briefly confronted 9-month-old Albert with a succession of objects, including a white rat, a rabbit, and a dog. "At no time did this infant ever show fear in any situation" (Watson & Rayner, 1920, p. 2).

Unconditioned stimulus: Noise.
Standing behind Albert, the researchers hit a hammer on a metal bar, which made a loud noise and elicited startle and crying. "This is the first time an emotional situation in the laboratory has produced any fear or crying in Albert" (Watson & Rayner, 1920, p. 3).

Unconditioned response: Startle/cry.
Startle and crying were observable and measurable emotional responses that indicated the baby was feeling and expressing fear.

After Watson identified the three elements of classical conditioning, he and his assistant, Rayner, began the procedure for classical conditioning.

2. Procedure: Establish and Test for Classical Conditioning

Establish. At the age of 11 months, Albert was given repeated trials consisting of a neutral stimulus, a white rat, followed by an unconditioned stimulus, a loud noise. During early trials, he startled at the sight of the rat and on later trials he also cried.

Test. When first presented with the rat alone (no noise), Albert startled. Then he was given additional conditioning trials and retested with the rat alone (no noise). "The instant the rat was shown the baby began to cry" (Watson & Watson, 1920, p. 5). Thus, Watson had succeeded in classically conditioning Albert's emotional response (fear).

3. Results

Watson and Rayner had shown that Albert developed a conditioned emotional response of startle and crying to the sight of a rat, which lasted about a week and then diminished, or underwent *extinction*.

After Albert was conditioned to fear a white rat, he was shown other objects to test for *generalization*. For example, he crawled away and cried at the sight of a rabbit, and he turned away and cried at the sight of a fur coat. But he showed no fear of blocks, paper, or Watson's hairy head, which indicates *discrimination*.

4. Conclusions

Watson's conditioning of Albert was more of a demonstration than a rigorously controlled experiment. For example, Watson and Rayner did not use a standardized procedure for presenting stimuli and sometimes removed Albert's thumb from his mouth, which may have made him cry. Watson was also criticized for not unconditioning Albert's fears before he left the hospital.

Although other researchers failed to replicate Watson and Rayner's results, this was the first demonstration that emotional responses could be classically conditioned in humans (Harris, 1979; Samelson, 1980). Watson's demonstration laid the groundwork for explaining how people can learn such fear of spiders.

We've discussed how emotional responses can be conditioned; next, we'll show how conditioned emotional response can influence a person's behavior.

G. Cultural Diversity: Dental Fears

Fear and Pain

How much pain can you take?

As you sit in the dentist's chair, two interesting psychological factors are at work: the possibility of being classically conditioned and the possibility of perceiving more or less pain.

Earlier, we discussed how there is a relatively good chance of being classically conditioned during dental treatment. You will be subjected to unconditioned stimuli (injection, drilling), which elicit unconditioned responses (pain, fear, and anxiety), which, in turn, can be conditioned to a variety of neutral stimuli (smells, sights, sounds, or images). At the beginning of this module we showed how Carla's anxiety was conditioned to the smell of the dentist's aftershave.

Earlier, we also discussed (in Modules 5 and 8) how a number of psychological factors, such as the ability to relax or refocus your attention, can influence whether you perceive more or less pain. Now we'll discuss how cultural factors can influence your perception of pain and fear of dentists (Milgrom et al., 1994). We'll focus on three issues: the influence of cultural differences on dental fears; the origins of dental fears; and the effects of fear.

Cultural Differences

Which citizens have most dental fears?

As the graph on the right indicates, the percentage of children reporting high levels of dental fear is considerably greater in the United States and Asia (Singapore and Japan) than in Scandinavia (Norway and Sweden) (Chellappah et al., 1990; Klingberg & Hwang, 1994; Milgrom et al., 1994; Neverlien & Johnsen, 1991).

One reason behind cultural differences in levels of dental fear is that the countries have different systems of dental care. In Scandinavian countries, dental care is part of a free, universal health care program available to all citizens. Because it is free and easily available,

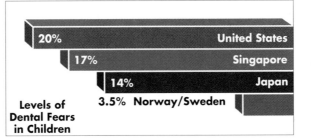

Levels of Dental Fears in Children

20% United States
17% Singapore
14% Japan
3.5% Norway/Sweden

Scandinavian children tend to receive regular dental care rather than be treated only for dental emergencies. These children view dental treatment as unpleasant but necessary.

In contrast, neither America nor Japan provide free, universal dental coverage. Consequently, some children receive treatment only when there is a dental problem and thus view dental treatment as something painful and to be avoided. Thus, cultural influences may increase or decrease the painful experiences associated with dental treatment.

Origins of Fear

When do fears develop?

American and Asian adults with high levels of dental fears were asked when their fears began. About 66% replied that they acquired their dental fears in childhood or adolescence, often after a painful treatment that was necessitated by a dental emergency (Milgrom et al., 1995; Poulton et al., 1997). As you might guess, more severe levels of pain led to higher levels of fear (Milgrom et al., 1992). Researchers concluded that the majority of dental fears are acquired in childhood or adolescence, often through classical conditioning. In addition, these fears can keep individuals from asking for or receiving dental treatment for future problems. (Portman & Radanov, 1997).

Effects of Fear

Which citizens most avoid dentists?

Once dental fears are established, about 20–40% of these individuals report avoiding regular checkups or routine dental treatment (right graph). Usually, these individuals only seek dental treatment when they have emergency problems, which tend to involve very painful procedures. As a result, painful emergency dental procedures strengthen their already high level of fears and start a new vicious cycle of avoiding dental treatment until the next emergency. From our knowledge of classical conditioning, we know that one way to reduce high levels of dental fear is to receive regular, non-painful dental checkups and treatment, which will extinguish some of the conditioned emotional responses.

Based on these data, researchers concluded that cultural differences, such as kind and frequency of dental treatment in childhood and adolescence, affect both a child's perception of pain as well as the occurrence of conditioned emotional responses—in this case, fear of dentists (Milgrom et al., 1994).

Next, we'll examine another kind of treatment—chemotherapy for cancer—that also involves classical conditioning and results in a terrible problem—conditioned nausea. We'll examine how conditioned nausea occurs and how it can be treated.

People Avoiding Dental Treatment

40% England/Wales
32% Japan
21% U.S.A.

H. Application: Conditioned Fear & Nausea

Examples of Conditioning

Why do people faint from fear?

At the beginning of this module, I related my childhood experience of receiving an injection and then fainting. This one trial of classical conditioning resulted in my fear of needles, which remains with me to this present day. My experience illustrates the powerful effect that conditioned emotional responses can have on our behavior. If you still doubt that relatively nonthreatening stimuli (needle, blood) can be conditioned to elicit such a powerful physiological response as fainting, you'll be convinced by the next study.

Conditioned Emotional Response

Just as about 10–20% of adults report a fear of needles and injections, about the same percentage report a fear of seeing blood (Locker et al., 1997). Wondering why some people feel faint at the sight of blood, researchers asked 30 such subjects to watch a movie on open-heart surgery as their heart rates were monitored. During the movie, 4 of the 30 subjects unexpectedly fainted.

For example, the graph shows that after 4 minutes of watching the open-heart surgery movie, one subject became so fearful and anxious that his body went into mild shock and he fainted. The reason this subject fainted from simply watching a movie on open-heart surgery was that he had developed a conditioned emotional response, intense fear, to the sight of blood (Steptoe & Wardle, 1988). Intense fear triggers tremendous changes in heart rate and blood pressure that can cause many physiological changes, including fainting.

Just as classical conditioning can cause people to faint at the sight of blood, it can also trigger nausea when they smell a certain odor.

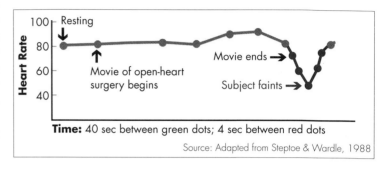

Source: Adapted from Steptoe & Wardle, 1988

Anticipatory Nausea

At the beginning of this module, we told you about Michelle, who was receiving chemotherapy treatment for breast cancer. One side effect of the powerful anticancer drugs used in chemotherapy is nausea, which may be accompanied by severe vomiting that lasts 6–12 hours.

As Michelle received additional chemotherapy injections, she experienced nausea when she smelled the treatment room or smelled her dish soap, which smelled like the treatment room. Michelle's problem is called anticipatory nausea.

Anticipatory nausea refers to feelings of nausea that are elicited by stimuli associated with nausea-inducing chemotherapy treatments. Patients experience nausea after treatment but also before or in anticipation of their treatment. Researchers believe that conditioned nausea occurs through classical conditioning.

For example, by their fourth injection, 60–70% of the patients who receive chemotherapy experience anticipatory nausea when they encounter smells, sounds, sights, or images related to treatment (Montgomery & Bovbjerg, 1997). Even 1–2 years after treatment ends, patients may continue to experience anticipatory nausea if they encounter cues associated with chemotherapy (Fredrikson et al., 1993). What makes conditioned nausea especially troublesome is that current medication does not always control it.

First we'll discuss how conditioned nausea occurs and then how it can be controlled with a nonmedical treatment.

Conditioning Anticipatory Nausea

A few weeks after beginning her chemotherapy, Michelle began to experience anticipatory nausea that was triggered by a number of different stimuli, including the smell of her dish detergent, which smelled similar to the treatment room. Now that you know her situation, perhaps you can identify the terms and explain how classical conditioning occurred.

■ **Neutral stimulus** is the smell of the treatment room and her dish detergent, which initially did not cause any nausea.

■ **Unconditioned stimulus** is the chemotherapy, which elicits nausea and vomiting.

■ **Unconditioned responses** are the nausea and vomiting, which were elicited by chemotherapy, the unconditioned stimulus.

■ **Conditioning trials** involve presenting the neutral stimuli, smell of the treatment room (same as her detergent), with the unconditioned stimulus, the chemotherapy.

■ **Conditioned stimulus** (smell of the treatment room or detergent), when presented by itself, now elicits the conditioned response (nausea).

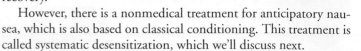

Once established, anticipatory nausea can be very difficult to treat and control with medication (Montgomery & Bovbjerg, 1997). Even after chemotherapy ends, anticipatory nausea may reappear, which is an example of spontaneous recovery.

However, there is a nonmedical treatment for anticipatory nausea, which is also based on classical conditioning. This treatment is called systematic desensitization, which we'll discuss next.

Systematic Desensitization

Can you "uncondition" fearful things?

Because of repeated chemotherapy sessions, Michelle developed anticipatory nausea (right photo), which was not relieved by medication. She is now going to try a nonmedical treatment called systematic desensitization.

Systematic desensitization is a procedure based on classical conditioning, in which a person imagines or visualizes fearful or anxiety-evoking stimuli and then immediately uses deep relaxation to overcome the anxiety. Systematic desensitization is a form of counterconditioning because it replaces, or counters, fear and anxiety with relaxation.

Essentially, systematic desensitization is a procedure to "uncondition," or overcome, fearful stimuli by pairing anxiety-provoking thoughts or images with feelings of relaxation. Systematic desensitization was developed by Joseph Wolpe in the early 1950s and has become one of the most frequently used nonmedical therapies for relief of anxiety and fears in both children and adults (Williams & Gross, 1994). Just as anticipatory nausea is based on Pavlov's classical conditioning, so to is systematic desensitization (Wolpe & Plaud, 1997).

In Michelle's case, she will try to "uncondition" or override, the anxiety-producing cues of chemotherapy, such as smells and sights, with feelings of relaxation. The procedure for systematic desensitization involves the three steps described below (Wolpe & Lazarus, 1966).

Systematic Desensitization Procedure: Three Steps

Step 1. Learning to relax

Michelle is taught to relax by tensing and relaxing sets of muscles, beginning with muscles in her toes and continuing with muscles in her calves, thighs, back, arms, shoulders, neck, and finally face and forehead. She practices doing this intentional relaxation for about 15 to 20 minutes every day for several weeks. After learning how to relax, she goes on to Step 2.

Step 2. Making an anxiety hierarchy

MOST STRESSFUL

8. **Vomiting**
7. **Feeling nausea**
6. **Receiving injection**
5. **In treatment room**
4. **Smelling chemicals**
3. **In waiting room**
2. **Entering clinic**
1. **Driving to clinic**

Michelle makes up a list of 7–12 stressful situations associated with chemotherapy treatment. As shown above, she arranges her list of situations in a hierarchy that goes from least to most stressful. For example, the least stressful situation is driving to the clinic and the most stressful is vomiting. Now she's ready for Step 3.

Step 3. Imagining and relaxing

Michelle puts herself into a deeply relaxed state and then vividly imagines the least stressful situation, driving to the clinic. She is told to remain in a relaxed state while imagining this situation. If she becomes anxious or stressed, she is told to stop imagining this situation and return instead to a relaxed state. Once she is sufficiently relaxed, she again imagines driving to the clinic. If she can imagine driving to the clinic while remaining in a relaxed state, she proceeds to the next stressful situation.

She then imagines entering the clinic, while remaining in a relaxed state. She continues up the anxiety hierarchy, imagining in turn each of the eight stressful stimuli while keeping herself in a relaxed state. At the first sign of feeling anxious, she stops and returns to a relaxed state. After returning to a relaxed state, she continues with this procedure until she reaches the most stressful situation in her anxiety hierarchy.

Effectiveness of Systematic Desensitization

As Michelle associates relaxation with each stressful situation in the hierarchy, she overcomes, or counterconditions, each stimulus in her hierarchy. Systematic desensitization can be thought of as a method of changing conditioned stimuli back to neutral stimuli.

Systematic desensitization has been found to be very effective in treating a wide variety of fearful and anxiety-producing behaviors, including conditioned nausea and fear of blood, injections, snakes, and speaking in public (Hasselt & Hersen, 1994).

We have shown you the many sides of classical conditioning, from salivation to fainting, from taste aversion to little Albert's conditioned emotional responses, from bait-shyness in rats to dental fears in humans, from anticipatory nausea to systematic desensitization. It's evident that classical conditioning has a considerable influence on many of our thoughts, emotions, and behaviors.

SUMMARY TEST

A. THREE KINDS OF LEARNING

1. A relatively permanent change in behavior that involves specific stimuli and/or responses that change as a result of experience is a definition of _____. The change in behavior includes both unobservable mental events and observable behavioral responses.

2. Psychologists have identified three different principles that are the basis for three different kinds of learning. One kind of learning can be traced to Pavlov's well-known experiment in which a bell was sounded and then food was placed in a dog's mouth. After a number of trials in which the bell and food were presented, the dog began to salivate to the bell alone. Pavlov called this kind of learning a conditioned reflex, which today is called _____.

3. A second kind of learning grew out of Thorndike's observations of cats learning to escape from a box. To explain a cat's goal-directed behavior of hitting a latch to get food, Thorndike formulated a principle of learning called the (a)_____. This law states that if certain random actions are followed by a pleasurable consequence or reward, such actions are strengthened and will likely occur in the future. Today, the law of effect has become part of the second kind of learning that is called (b)_____.

4. A third kind of learning involves mental processes, such as attention and memory; may be learned through observation or imitation; and may not involve any external rewards or require the person to perform any observable behaviors. This kind of learning is called _____.

B. PROCEDURE: CLASSICAL CONDITIONING

5. Suppose you wanted to classically condition your roommate to salivate at the sight of a psychology textbook. One procedure for establishing classical conditioning would be to present two stimuli close together in time. The presentation of the two stimuli is called a trial. In our example, a typical trial would involve first presenting a psychology textbook, initially called the (a)_____, which does not elicit salivation. A short time later, you would present a piece of brownie, called the (b)_____ stimulus, which elicits salivation. Salivation, an innate, automatic, and involuntary physiological reflex, is called the (c)_____.

6. After giving your roommate about a dozen trials, you observe that, as soon as you show him the psychology text, he begins to salivate. Because the sight of the psychology textbook itself elicits salivation, the psychology text has become a (a)_____. The roommate's salivation at the sight of the psychology book, presented alone, is called the (b)_____. You know that classical conditioning is established when the neutral stimulus becomes the (c)_____ and elicits the (d)_____. Compared to the unconditioned response, the conditioned response is usually similar in appearance but smaller in amount or magnitude.

C. OTHER CONDITIONING CONCEPTS

7. The more similar the new stimulus is to the original conditioned stimulus, the stronger or larger the conditioned response will usually be. During classical conditioning, there is a tendency for a stimulus similar to the original conditioned stimulus to elicit a response similar to the conditioned response. This tendency is called _____.

8. During classical conditioning, an organism learns to make a particular response to some stimuli but not to others; this phenomenon is called

_____.

9. If a conditioned stimulus is repeatedly presented without the unconditioned stimulus, there is a tendency for the conditioned stimulus to no longer elicit the conditioned response; this phenomenon is called (a)_____. However, if some time later you again presented the psychology text to your roommate without giving him a brownie, he would show salivation, the conditioned response. This recurrence of the conditioned response after it has been extinguished is called (b)_____.

D. ADAPTIVE VALUE

10. After receiving dental treatment, people may develop fear or anxiety in the presence of stimuli associated with the treatment. If we feel fear or anxiety in the presence of some stimulus that precedes a painful or aversive event, we are experiencing a _____.

11. A powerful form of classical conditioning occurs in real life when a neutral stimulus is paired with an unpleasant response, such as nausea or vomiting. The result of this conditioning is called _____. This form of classical conditioning is unusual in two ways: it may be acquired in a single trial and may last a relatively long period of time; and there may be a considerable lapse of time between the presentations of the two stimuli.

12. Originally researchers thought that all stimuli had about the same likelihood of becoming conditioned stimuli. However, we now know that animals and humans are biologically prepared to associate some combinations of conditioned and unconditioned stimuli more easily than others. This phenomenon is called _____.

13. Classical conditioning may produce an anxiety disorder characterized by an intense and irrational fear that is out of all proportion to its danger. This irrational conditioned fear is called a _____.

14. The occurrence of salivation in response to the thought, sight, or smell of food is helpful to digestion and shows that classical conditioning has an _____ role or value.

E. THREE EXPLANATIONS

15. According to Pavlov's explanation, classical conditioning occurs because a neural bond or association forms between the conditioned stimulus and unconditioned stimulus so that the conditioned stimulus eventually substitutes for the unconditioned stimulus. Pavlov's explanation is called _____.

16. The explanation that says that classical conditioning occurs because two stimuli (the neutral and unconditioned stimuli) are paired closely together in time is called the _____ theory. However, researchers have shown that contiguity or simply pairing stimuli closely together does not necessarily produce classical conditioning.

17. The explanation of classical conditioning that says that an organism learns a relationship between two stimuli such that the occurrence of one stimulus predicts the occurrence of the other is called the (a)_____. This theory is supported by the idea that classical conditioning is not usually learned if the unconditioned stimulus appears before the neutral stimulus, a procedure that is called (b)_____.

F. RESEARCH FOCUS: LITTLE ALBERT

18. An emotional response, fear, was classically conditioned in little Albert by presenting a white rat, which was the (a)_____, and then making a loud noise, which was the (b)_____; in turn, the loud noise elicited crying, which was the (c)_____. Albert's conditioned

emotional response, crying, also occurred in the presence of stimuli similar to the white rat, such as a rabbit; this phenomenon is called (d)_____. Albert did not cry at the sight of blocks or papers; this phenomenon is called (e)_____. Watson and Rayner were the first to demonstrate that (f)_____ responses could be classically conditioned in humans.

G. CULTURAL DIVERSITY: DENTAL FEARS

19. In the United States and Asia, the percentage of children reporting (a)_____ is considerably greater than in Scandinavia. A likely reason for this difference in dental fears is the countries' different cultures. The vast majority of people with high levels of dental fears report that these fears originated in childhood and are a primary reason for avoiding future (b)_____.

H. APPLICATION: CONDITIONED FEAR & NAUSEA

20. During chemotherapy, about 60% of the patients develop nausea in anticipation of, or when encountering stimuli associated with, the actual treatment. This type of nausea, which is called _____, cannot always be treated with drugs and may persist long after the chemotherapy ends. Researchers believe that conditioned nausea is learned through classical conditioning.

MOST STRESSFUL
8. Vomiting
7. Feeling nausea
6. Receiving injection
5. In treatment room
4. Smelling chemicals
3. In waiting room
2. Entering clinic
1. Driving to clinic

21. A nondrug treatment for conditioned nausea involves a procedure based on classical conditioning in which a person imagines or visualizes fearful or anxiety-evoking stimuli and then immediately uses deep relaxation to eliminate these stimuli. This procedure, which is called (a)_____, is a form of counterconditioning because it replaces, or counters, fear or anxiety with (b)_____.

Answers: *1. learning; 2. classical conditioning; 3. (a) law of effect, (b) operant conditioning; 4. cognitive learning; 5. (a) neutral stimulus, (b) unconditioned stimulus, (c) unconditioned response; 6. (a) conditioned stimulus, (b) conditioned response, (c) conditioned stimulus, (d) unconditioned response; 7. generalization; 8. discrimination; 9. (a) extinction, (b) spontaneous recovery; 10. conditioned emotional response; 11. taste-aversion learning; 12. preparedness; 13. phobia; 14. adaptive, or survival; 15. stimulus substitution; 16. contiguity; 17. (a) cognitive perspective, (b) backward conditioning; 18. (a) neutral stimulus, (b) unconditioned stimulus, (c) unconditioned response, (d) generalization, (e) discrimination; (f) conditioned emotional; 19. (a) dental fears, (b) dental treatment; 20. anticipatory nausea; 21. (a) systematic desensitization, (b) relaxation.*

CRITICAL THINKING

QUESTIONS

1. How would you design a study to test the effects of olestra on human subjects?

2. What advantages does a double-blind study have over testimonials like this one?

3. How do we know how many of the subjects had gastrointestinal problems? Are these results likely to be accurate?

4. Was there a significant difference in gastrointestinal problems between the two groups in this study?

5. How might classical conditioning explain how regular chips lead to gastrointestinal problems in this study?

STUDY: OLESTRA CHIPS SCORE WELL IN DIGESTIVE TEST
by Nanci Hellmich

Potato chips made with the fake fat olestra didn't cause any more digestive problems than regular chips in a study in today's *Journal of the American Medical Association.*

Olestra glides through the body without leaving any fat and calories. Chips made with the fake fat, which are being test-marketed in several cities, have been the focus of much debate since their 1996 debut.

Critics charge that the chips cause cramping and loose stools in some people who eat them. Early research by maker Proctor & Gamble showed such problems, but participants ate olestra foods at every meal for two months. Some argued that wasn't a realistic test.

In the new study, also funded by the company, Lawrence J. Cheskin, director of the gastroenterology division at Johns Hopkins University Bayview Medical Center, had 1,123 volueers ages 13–88 eat potato chips while watching a movie at a Chicago cinema. About half ate Frito-Lay Ruffles; the others ate Frito-Lay MAX Ruffles, made with olestra.

Participants could eat as much as they wanted; they didn't know which chips they were eating. The olestra group ate less, an average of 2.1 ounces vs. 2.7 for the other group. Within four days after the test, they were contacted by an independent marketing firm and asked if they had any digestive symptoms. Severity was rated for each symptom.

15.8% of those who ate the olestra chips said they had one or more gastrointestinal symptoms, such as gas and diarrhea; so did 17.6% of those who ate the regular chips. On a 9-point taste-test scale, olestra chips got a 5.6 vs. 6.4 for regular chips.

Participants knew to watch for these symptoms, which may have increased the rate of reporting, Cheskin says. But, he says, "we found no differences in (gastrointestinal) effects between olestra chips and regular potato chips."

Michael Jacobson of the Center for Science in the Public Interest, a vocal critic of olestra, says this new study is flawed. "Proctor & Gamble has done much better controlled, much larger and more sensitive studies that prove olestra causes diarrhea, cramps, and other symptoms.

"You don't give people one dose of this test compound and expect to find a problem."

Source: *USA Today,* January 14, 1998. Copyright © 1998, *USA Today.* Reprinted with permission.

Study Questions

A. Three Kinds of Learning—Can you recall situations in which you have experienced each of the three kinds of learning? (See answer in Critical Thinking Appendix.)

B. Procedure: Classical Conditioning—How do you explain why your heart pounds when you hear the words "There will be a test next class"? (See answer in Critical Thinking Appendix.)

C. Other Conditioning Concepts—If a child were bitten by a small brown dog, can you predict what other animals the child would fear?

D. Adaptive Value—Using the terms and procedures of classical conditioning, can you explain how a person might develop a fear of flying?

E. Three Explanations—How would you explain why your cat runs into the kitchen and salivates each time you open the refrigerator door?

F. Research Focus: Little Albert—What happens when you look into your rear-view mirror and see a police car's flashing lights?

G. Cultural Diversity: Dental Fears—As a parent, how can you decrease the chances that your child will become fearful of dental treatment?

H. Application: Conditioned Fear and Nausea—How would systematic desensitization be used to help reduce a student's test anxiety? (See answer in Critical Thinking Appendix.)

Web Sites & Learning Activities

● BROOKS/COLE ONLINE PSYCHOLOGY STUDY CENTER

http://psychstudy.brookscole.com/student/plotnik/quiz/ch09frm.html

This site gives students a chance to review material by taking quizzes and doing exercises and activities for this module.

● FACTORS DETERMINING THE EFFECTIVENESS OF CLASSICAL CONDITIONING

http://biozentrum.uni-wuerzburg.de/~brebs/classical/classical.html

This page outlines the factors that play a role in classical conditioning, including timing, predictability, blocking, and how associations are made.

● CONDITIONAL

http://www.science.wayne.edu/~wpoff/cor/mem/conditnl.html

This page explains classical conditioning concepts, including types of conditioning, and the generalization and extinction processes.

● HOW ADVERTISERS USE CLASSICAL CONDITIONING

http://www.psych-web.com/discuss/chap05/parallel.htm

Do advertisers use principles of classical conditioning to grab your attention? This page reviews some evidence for this idea.

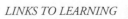

Welcome to the WEB

● BEYOND FEAR—THE DENTAL PHOBIA VIRTUAL SELF-HELP GROUP

http://www.beyondfear.org/

This group is dedicated to helping people with dental phobia overcome their fear; it features online chat and discussion groups and a usenet forum.

● SPECIFIC PHOBIAS

http://www.psyweb.com/Mdisord/AnxietyDis/specphobia.html

This site contains lots of information on specific phobias, including the criteria for their diagnosis, some types of specific phobias, and therapeutic and pharmacologic treatments.

Activities

● *Integrator Online™ for Introductory Psychology* CD-ROM, Plotnik, Module 9

● Study Guide to accompany *Introduction to Psychology*, 5th edition, Module 9 (choice of PC or Mac computer version or hard copy)

● *PsychNow!* CD-ROM
   Classical Conditioning

Answers to questions on page 210

1. The best research design for this study would be a double-blind procedure, in which neither the experimenters nor the subjects would know which kind of chips they are eating (see Module 2, page 37).

2. If we rely on testimonials to the effects of olestra, we may get biased results because eaters are warned on the package about possible gastrointestinal problems and thus may be more likely to look for such problems. A double-blind design controls for biases that would result from eaters' expectations about possible side effects.

3. This study relied on self-reports of symptoms. This method is probably reliable, because subjects did not know which kind of chips they had eaten and many subjects couldn't tell the difference.

4. The difference in gastrointestinal problems between the two groups was not statistically significant.

5. Here is how classical conditioning might explain these results. The taste of potato chips is the neutral stimulus. Olestra (fake fat) is the unconditioned stimulus, which can cause gastrointestinal upset, the unconditioned response. Through classical conditioning, the taste of any chip becomes the conditioned stimulus, and gastrointestinal upset becomes the conditioned response. Thus, because of an original bad experience (gastrointestinal upset) from eating olestra chips, a person may be classically conditioned to get stomach problems after eating any kind of chips.

Module 10 OPERANT & COGNITIVE APPROACHES

Learning 45 Commands

How did Bart become a movie star?

It was an unusual movie for two reasons. First, there was almost no dialogue: human actors spoke only 657 words. Second, the star of the movie was a nonspeaking, nonhuman, 12-year-old, 10-foot-tall, 1800-pound, enormous brown Kodiak bear named Bart (shown on the left). Bart is one of the world's largest land-dwelling carnivores and can, with one swipe of his massive 12-inch paw, demolish anything in his path. Yet, in the movie, there was big bad Bart, sitting peacefully on his haunches, cradling a small bear cub in his arms. "So what?" you might say, but what you don't know is that, in the wild, a Kodiak bear normally kills and eats any cub it encounters.

Because Bart was found as a cub and raised by a human trainer, Bart grew to act more like an overgrown teddy bear than a natural-born killer. For his role in the movie *The Bear,* Bart learned to perform 45 behaviors on cue, such as sitting, running, standing up, roaring, and, most difficult of all, cradling a teddy bear, which is not what an adult bear does in the wild.

The training procedure seems deceptively simple: Each time Bart performed a behavior on cue, the trainer, Doug Seus, gave Bart an affectionate back scratch, an ear rub, or a juicy apple or pear. For example, when the trainer raised his arms high in the air, it was the signal for Bart to sit and hold the teddy bear. After correctly performing this behavior, Doug would give Bart his reward. After Bart learned to perform all these behaviors with a stuffed teddy bear, a live bear cub was substituted and the scene was filmed for the movie (Cerone, 1989).

Bart learned to perform 45 behaviors on cue through a kind of learning called operant conditioning.

Operant conditioning, also called instrumental conditioning, is a kind of learning in which an animal or human performs some behavior, and the following consequence (reward or punishment) increases or decreases the chance that an animal or human will again perform that same behavior.

For example, if Bart performed a particular behavior, such as picking up a teddy bear, the consequence that followed—getting a rewarding apple—increased the chance that Bart would again pick up the teddy bear. Because of what Bart learned through operant conditioning, he has starred in 20 movies and is currently the highest paid animal actor, making about $10,000 a day (Brennan, 1997). That's a salary that most of us would be very happy to bear.

Operant conditioning seems rather straightforward. You perform an action or operate on your environment, such as studying hard. The consequence of your studying, such as how well you do on exams, increases or decreases the likelihood that you will perform the same behavior—studying hard—in the future.

Besides learning by having your behaviors rewarded or punished, you can also learn in a very different way.

Learning to Skateboard

What did Dusty learn from just watching?

In operant conditioning, everything is out in the open: you perform some observable response that is followed by some observable consequence. But there is another kind of learning that involves unobservable mental processes and unobservable rewards that you may give yourself. This kind of learning, called cognitive learning, is partly how Dusty (photo below) learned to skateboard.

According to his parents, 3-year-old Dusty was fascinated by skateboarders. Dusty would sit for hours watching skateboarders do spins, flips, hops, backturns, and dozens of other seemingly impossible feats on a thin board with a small fat wheel at each corner.

One day Dusty's father brought home a small skateboard to see what Dusty would do. Remembering what he had observed other skateboarders doing, Dusty put the skateboard on the floor, placed one foot on the skateboard and using his other foot, propelled himself slowly around the house, hitting a few things as he went (adapted from *Los Angeles Times,* April 14, 1990). Although Dusty had never been on a skateboard before, he was able to imitate what he had seen.

The procedure Dusty used to learn skateboarding is very different from the operant conditioning procedure used to teach Bart new behaviors. During operant conditioning, Bart performed observable behaviors that were influenced by observable consequences (apples). In comparison, Dusty's knowledge of how to get on and propel a skateboard resulted from observation and imitation, which involved unobservable mental processes. This latter kind of learning, called cognitive learning, accounts for a variety of things that we humans learn. We'll discuss cognitive learning later in this module.

What's Coming

In the first half of this module, we discuss the history and procedure of operant conditioning, how operant conditioning differs from classical conditioning, how consequences or reinforcers work, and other examples of operant conditioning. In the second half of this module, we explain the history of cognitive learning, the theory behind observational learning, and the role of insightful learning.

We'll begin with an important study that involved a cat, a puzzle box, and a smelly fish.

213

A. Operant Conditioning

Background: Thorndike and Skinner

How did Bart become a movie star?

We told you how a trainer used operant conditioning to teach Bart to perform 45 different behaviors on cue. Operant conditioning has now been applied to many different settings, such as training animals to perform, training children to use the potty, stopping retarded children from injuring themselves, and helping autistic children learn social behaviors. However, the discovery of operant behavior involved two different researchers who worked in two different laboratories on two different kinds of problems. So that you can appreciate the thinking that led to operant conditioning, we'll visit the laboratories of the two important researchers—E. L. Thorndike and B. F. Skinner.

THORNDIKE'S LAW OF EFFECT

E. L. THORNDIKE (1874–1947)

It's the late 1800s, and we're in the laboratory of E. L. Thorndike, who is interested in animal intelligence—specifically, in measuring their capacity for reasoning.

Unlike pet owners who assume from anecdotal observations that their animals are intelligent, Thorndike devised a simple but clever way to measure reasoning in a more objective way.

He built a series of puzzle boxes from which a cat could escape by learning to make a specific response, such as pulling a string or pressing a lever. Outside the puzzle box was a reward for escaping—a piece of fish.

We watch Thorndike place a cat in the puzzle box and record its escape time. After Thorndike graphs the data (graph below), we see a gradual lessening in the time needed to escape. Notice that on the first trial the cat needed over 240 seconds to hit the escape latch, but by the 21st trial, the cat hits the ecape latch in less than 60 seconds.

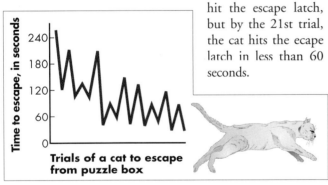

Trials of a cat to escape from puzzle box

Thorndike explains that, with repeated trials, the cat spends more time around the latch, which increases the chances of finding and hitting the latch and more quickly escaping to get the fish. To explain why a cat's random trial-and-error behaviors gradually turned into efficient goal-directed behaviors, Thorndike formulated the law of effect.

The *law of effect* states that behaviors followed by positive consequences are strengthened, while behaviors followed by negative consequences are weakened.

Thorndike's (1898) findings were significant because they suggested that the law of effect was a basic law of learning and provided an objective procedure to study it. Thorndike's emphasis on studying the consequences of goal-directed behavior was further developed and expanded by B. F. Skinner.

SKINNER'S OPERANT CONDITIONING

B. F. SKINNER (1904–1990)

It's the 1930s, and we're in the laboratory of B. F. Skinner, who is interested in analyzing ongoing behaviors of animals. Skinner explains that Thorndike's law of effect is useful since it describes how animals are rewarded for making particular responses. However, in order to analyze ongoing behaviors, you must have an objective way to measure them. Skinner's clever solution is a unit of behavior he calls an operant response (Skinner, 1938).

An *operant response* is a response that can be modified by its consequences and is a meaningful unit of ongoing behavior that can be easily measured.

For example, suppose that out of curiosity Bart picks up a teddy bear. His picking up the teddy bear is an example of an operant response because Bart is acting or operating on the environment. The consequence of his picking up the teddy bear is that he receives an apple, which is a desirable effect. This desirable effect modifies his response by increasing the chances that Bart will repeat the same response.

By measuring or recording operant responses, Skinner can analyze animals' ongoing behaviors during learning. He calls this kind of learning *operant conditioning,* which focuses on how consequences (rewards or punishments) affect behaviors.

A simple example of operant conditioning occurs when a rat in an experimental box accidentally presses a lever. If the lever press is followed by food, this consequence increases the chance that the rat will press the lever again. As the rat presses the lever more times, more food follows, which in turn increases the chances that the rat will continue to press the lever (indicated by rise of the blue line in the figure below).

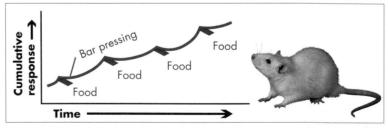

Using his newly developed procedure of operant conditioning, B. F. Skinner spent the next 50 years exploring and analyzing learning in rats, pigeons, schoolchildren, and adults.

The 1920s and 1930s gave learning a mighty jolt with the discovery of two general principles—Pavlov's classical conditioning and Skinner's operant conditioning. For the first time, psychologists had two methods to analyze learning processes in an objective way.

Now we'll examine Skinner's ingenious procedure for operant conditioning in more detail.

Principles and Procedures

Why does a rat press a lever?

A rat may initially press a lever out of curiosity, and whether it presses the lever again depends on the consequences. To show how consequences can affect behavior, imagine that you are looking over Skinner's shoulder as he places a rat into a box.

The box is empty except for a lever jutting out from one side and an empty food cup below and to the side of the lever (left figure). This box, called a **Skinner box,** is automated to record the animal's lever presses and deliver food pellets. The Skinner box is an efficient way to study how an animal's ongoing behaviors may be modified by changing the consequences of what happens after a lever press.

As you watch, Skinner explains that the rat is a good subject for operant conditioning because it can use its front paws to manipulate objects, such as a lever, and it has a tendency to explore its environment, which means that it will eventually find the lever, touch it, or even press it.

Skinner goes on to explain three factors involved in operantly conditioning a rat to press a lever, as follows.

1 The rat has not been fed for some hours so that it will be active and more likely to eat the food reward. A hungry rat tends to roam restlessly about, sniffing at whatever it finds.

2 The goal is to condition the rat to press the lever. By pressing the lever, the rat operates on its environment; thus, this response is called an **operant response.**

3 Skinner explains that a naive rat does not usually waltz over and press the lever. In conditioning a rat to press a lever, Skinner will use a procedure called shaping.

Shaping refers to a procedure in which an experimenter successively reinforces behaviors that lead up to or approximate the desired behavior.

For example, if the desired behavior is pressing the lever, here's how shaping works.

SHAPING: REINFORCING CLOSE APPROXIMATIONS

Shaping: Facing Lever

Skinner places a white rat into the experimental box, closes the door, and watches the rat through a one-way mirror. At first, the rat wanders around the back of the box, but when it turns and faces the lever, Skinner releases a food pellet into the food cup. The rat hears the pellet drop, approaches the food cup, discovers the pellet, and eats it. The rat moves away, but as soon as it again turns and faces the lever, Skinner releases another pellet.

Shaping: Touching Lever

Skinner decides to reinforce the rat only when it moves toward the lever. As soon as the rat faces and then moves toward the lever, Skinner releases another pellet. After eating the pellet, the rat wanders a bit but soon returns to the lever and actually sniffs it. A fourth pellet immediately drops into the cup, and the rat eats it. When the rat places one paw on the lever, a fifth pellet drops into the cup.

Shaping: Pressing Lever

Now the rat rears up on its back feet, sniffs the lever, and puts its front paws on it. This downward motion presses the lever and causes release of another pellet. Within a period of time, the rat is putting its paws on the lever, pressing down, and getting food pellets. Soon, the rat is pressing the lever at a fast rate and will continue for some time.

IMPORTANCE OF IMMEDIATE REINFORCEMENT

Depending on the rat and the experience of the trainer, it usually takes from minutes to an hour to shape a rat to press a lever. Skinner explains that in shaping, the food pellet, or *reinforcer,* should follow immediately after the desired behavior. In this way, the rewarding consequence will come to be associated with the desired behavior and not with some other behavior that just happens to intervene. If the reinforcer is delayed, the animal may be reinforced for some undesired or superstitious behavior.

Superstitious behavior is any behavior that increases in frequency because its occurrence is accidentally paired with the delivery of a reinforcer.

As a graduate student, while trying to condition a rat to press a lever, I conditioned my share of superstitious behaviors, such as rats turning in circles or sitting in corners, because I accidentally reinforced a rat's performance of the wrong behavior.

Humans, especially professional baseball players, report a variety of superstitious behaviors that were accidentally reinforced after getting a hit. For example, a five-time batting champion (Wade Boggs) has eaten chicken every game day since 1983, allows no one else to touch his bats, and believes each bat has a certain number of hits. Once reinforced, especially after a powerful reinforcer (major league hit), superstitious behaviors can be very difficult to eliminate.

Next, we'll discuss examples of operant conditioning in humans.

A. Operant Conditioning

Examples

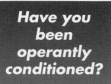
Have you been operantly conditioned?

Without realizing it, you may be performing a wide range of behaviors learned through operant conditioning. For example, operant conditioning was involved if you learned to put money into a vending machine to get a soda, drive through a yellow traffic light to avoid stopping, study for hours to get good grades, or give flowers to your honey to see him or her smile. And you may con-

tinually perform these behaviors because they are followed by reinforcers that increase the chances that you will perform these same behaviors again. To help you better understand how operant conditioning works, we'll discuss how its procedures and principles have been used by parents to solve two relatively common problems: getting young children to use the toilet and to stop refusing to eat a wide variety of healthy foods.

Toilet Training

A recent survey found that 60% of children are toilet trained by age 3 and that many parents reported not knowing how to go about training their child (Taubman, 1997).

Imagine that you are a parent of 3-year-old Sheryl, who is physically mature enough to begin toilet training. Here's how operant conditioning techniques can be applied to teach toilet training.

1. Target behavior. The target behavior or goal is for Sheryl to urinate in the toilet.

2. Preparation. Before training begins, put all of Sheryl's toys away so that she will not be distracted. Then give her a large glass of apple juice, so that she will have to urinate soon.

3. Reinforcers. Select reinforcers, which can be candy, verbal praise, or a hug. Each time Sheryl performs or emits a desired behavior, you immediately reinforce it. The reinforcer increases the likelihood that the behavior will be repeated.

4. Shaping. Just as Skinner used the shaping procedure in conditioning a rat to press a lever, you can use a similar shaping procedure in conditioning Sheryl to use the toilet. Each time Sheryl performs a behavior that leads to the target behavior (using the toilet), give her a treat, verbal praise, or a hug. For instance, when Sheryl says that she has to go potty, say, "That's great." When Sheryl enters the bathroom, say, "What a good girl." When she lowers her pants by herself, say, "You're doing really good." After Sheryl urinates into the toilet, give her a big hug and perhaps a treat.

Mothers who were supervised as they used this training procedure needed 4–18 hours to toilet train their 2- to 3-year-olds (Berk & Patrick, 1990; Matson & Ollendick, 1977).

Another difficulty parents face is when children eat only one or two favorite foods and refuse all else.

Food Refusal

Some young children who have no physiological or medical problems may develop a habit of eating a limited number of foods and refusing all else. This unhealthy diet results in their not reaching their appropriate weight (Hoch et al., 1994; Timimi et al., 1997). To overcome food refusal in young children, researchers taught parents how to use the principles of operant conditioning.

1. Target behavior. The target behavior or goal was for the child to taste, chew, and eat a food (fruits or vegetables) that she or he has persistently rejected.

2. Preparation. Researchers first showed mothers how to shape and reinforce target behaviors. Next, each mother shaped the target behavior in her child in the home setting.

3. Reinforcers. Each time the child performed or emitted a target behavior, the mother immediately reinforced the child with a positive reinforcer, such as praise, attention, or a smile.

4. Shaping. The shaping procedure consisted of having the child notice the food and let it be placed in his or her mouth, letting the child taste the food, and, finally, having the child chew and swallow the food.

The graph below shows the success of using operant conditioning to overcome food refusal (Werle et al., 1993).

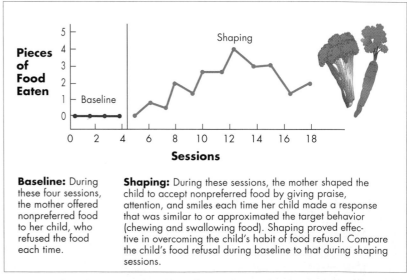

Baseline: During these four sessions, the mother offered nonpreferred food to her child, who refused the food each time.

Shaping: During these sessions, the mother shaped the child to accept nonpreferred food by giving praise, attention, and smiles each time her child made a response that was similar to or approximated the target behavior (chewing and swallowing food). Shaping proved effective in overcoming the child's habit of food refusal. Compare the child's food refusal during baseline to that during shaping sessions.

Notice that the same principles of operant conditioning apply whether the goal is to condition a child to use the potty, to overcome food refusal, or to train Bart the bear to pick up and hold a teddy bear.

Next, we'll compare the principles of operant and classical conditioning.

Comparison: Operant versus Classical Conditioning

How are they different?	At this point, you may find that the differences between classical and operant conditioning are not entirely clear. Although both kinds of conditioning lead to learning, their procedures and principles are very different. We'll use Bart and little Albert, whom you read about in Module 9, to review several important differences between classical and operant conditioning.

Operant Conditioning

1 Goal. The goal of operant conditioning is to *increase or decrease the rate* of some response, which usually involves shaping. In Bart's case, the goal was to increase his rate of holding a teddy bear.

2 Voluntary response. Bart's behavior of holding a teddy bear is a voluntary response because he can perform it at will. Bart must first perform a voluntary response before getting a reward.

3 Emitted response. Bart voluntarily performs or emits some response, which Skinner called the operant response (holding teddy bear). Skinner used the term *emit* to indicate that the organism acts or operates on the environment. In most cases, animals and humans are shaped to emit the desired responses.

4 Contingent on behavior. Bart's performance of the desired response depends on, or is *contingent* on, the consequences, or what happens next. For example, each time Bart holds the teddy bear, the consequence is that he receives an apple. The apple, which is a reward (reinforcer), increases the chances that Bart will perform the desired response in the future.

The reinforcer must occur *immediately after* the desired response. In Bart's case, the reinforcer (apple) would be given immediately after Bart holds the teddy bear. If the reinforcer occurs too late, the result may be the conditioning of unwanted or superstitious responses.

5 Consequences. An animal or human's performance of some behavior is dependent or contingent on its *consequences*—that is, on what happens next. For example, the consequences of Bart's picking up and holding a teddy bear was to get an apple.

Thus, in operant conditioning, an animal or human learns that performing or emitting some behavior is followed by a consequence (reward or punishment), which, in turn, increases or decreases the chances of performing that behavior again.

Classical Conditioning

1 Goal. The goal of classical conditioning is to create a new response to a *neutral stimulus*. In Albert's case, the new response is showing startle and crying at the sight of a white rat (neutral stimulus).

2 Involuntary response. Albert's startle response (open mouth, large eyes, tense muscles) is an example of a *physiological reflex*. Most physiological reflexes (startle, salivation, crying) must be triggered by some stimulus and, therefore, are considered involuntary responses.

3 Elicited response. A sudden loud noise triggers, or elicits, Albert's involuntary startle reflex. In this case, the loud noise is the *unconditioned stimulus*, which triggers Albert's involuntary startle reflex, the *unconditioned response*.

BANG !

4 Conditioned response. Albert was given repeated trials during which the neutral stimulus (rat) was presented and followed by the unconditioned stimulus (noise). After repeated trials, Albert learned a relationship between the two stimuli: the rat is followed by a loud noise. Finally, the rat, or neutral stimulus, became the *conditioned stimulus* because it alone could elicit the *conditioned response*, startle.

For best results, the neutral stimulus is presented slightly before the unconditioned stimulus. If the unconditioned stimulus is presented before the neutral stimulus, this is called *backward conditioning* and produces little if any conditioning.

5 Expectancy. According to the *cognitive perspective* of classical conditioning, an animal or human learns a predictable relationship between, or develops an expectancy about, the neutral and unconditioned stimuli. This means little Albert learned to expect that the neutral stimulus (rat) is always followed by the unconditioned stimulus (noise). Thus, in classical conditioning, the animal or human learns a predictable relationship between stimuli.

One major difference between operant and classical conditioning is that in operant conditioning, the performance of some response depends upon its consequence (rewards or punishment). We'll discuss the effects of different kinds of consequences next.

B. Reinforcers

Consequences

Why are consequences important?

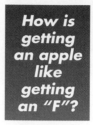

Notice where the man is sitting as he saws off a tree limb. His behavior illustrates a key principle of operant conditioning, which is that *consequences are contingent on behavior.* In this case, the man will fall on his head (consequence) if he cuts off the tree limb (behavior). Furthermore, this consequence will make the tree trimmer think twice before repeating this stupid behavior. Thus, consequences affect behavior; and in operant conditioning, there are two kinds of consequences—reinforcement and punishment.

Reinforcement is a consequence that occurs after a behavior and increases the chance that the behavior will occur again.

For example, one of the main reasons you study hard for exams is to get good grades (reinforcement). The consequence of getting a good grade increases the chances that you'll study hard for future exams.

Punishment is a consequence that occurs after a behavior and decreases the chance that the behavior will occur again.

For example, one high school used punishment to reduce students' absentee rates. Students who got more than eight unexcused absences lost very desirable privileges (no football games, no prom). In this case, punishing consequences decreased from 15% to 4% the chance of students playing hookey from school (Chavez, 1994).

Sometimes reinforcement and punishment are used together to control some behavior, as was done in treating a serious behavioral disorder called pica.

Pica is a behavioral disorder, more often seen in individuals with mental retardation, which involves eating inedible objects or unhealthy substances. This can result in serious physical problems, including lead poisoning, intestinal blockage, and parasites.

Here's an example of how both reinforcement and punishment were used to treat an adolescent who suffered from pica.

CHANGING THE CONSEQUENCES

Walt was 15 years old and suffered from profound retardation. One of Walt's problems was pica, which included eating bits of paper and clothing, metal and plastic objects, and especially paint chips, from which he had gotten lead poisoning.

To control his pica, Walt was given a tray containing nonfood items (fake paint chips made from flour) and food items (crackers). Each time Walt chose a food item, he received a reinforcement—verbal praise. Each time Walt chose a paint chip, he received a mild punishment—having his face washed for 20 seconds. The graph below shows how the consequences (reinforcement or punishment) greatly modified Walt's pica behavior (Johnson et al., 1994).

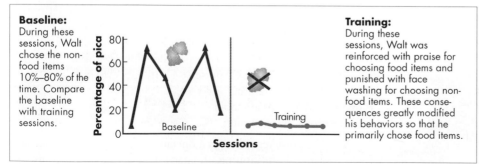

Baseline: During these sessions, Walt chose the nonfood items 10%–80% of the time. Compare the baseline with training sessions.

Training: During these sessions, Walt was reinforced with praise for choosing food items and punished with face washing for choosing nonfood items. These consequences greatly modified his behaviors so that he primarily chose food items.

In this study, reinforcement and punishment proved an effective combination to treat a potentially dangerous problem. Next, we'll discuss two kinds of reinforcements.

Reinforcement

How is getting an apple like getting an "F"?

Although getting an apple and getting a grade of "F" seem very different, they are both consequences that can increase the occurrence of certain behaviors. There are two kinds of reinforcements, or consequences—positive and negative—that increase the occurrence of behaviors.

POSITIVE REINFORCEMENT

Immediately after Bart the bear emitted or performed a behavior (holding a teddy bear), the trainer gave him an apple to increase the likelihood of his repeating that behavior. This situation is an example of positive reinforcement.

Positive reinforcement refers to the presentation of a stimulus that increases the probability that a behavior will occur again.

A *positive reinforcer* is a stimulus that increases the likelihood that a response will occur again.

Here's another example. If you ask a friend for money and get it, the money is a positive reinforcer that will increase the chances of your asking again. There's a second kind of reinforcement, called negative reinforcement.

NEGATIVE REINFORCEMENT

If you find yourself studying hard to avoid a low exam grade, your behavior is dependent on negative reinforcement.

F

Negative reinforcement refers to an aversive (unpleasant) stimulus whose removal increases the likelihood that the preceding response will occur again.

If you study hard to avoid getting a low exam grade, avoiding a low grade is a negative reinforcer because it increases the chance of your studying in the future.

Many students have difficulty remembering that both positive and negative reinforcers *increase* the frequency of the responses they follow.

Besides positive and negative reinforcers, there are also primary and secondary reinforcers, such as food and gift certificates.

Reinforcers

How are a hamburger and a certificate alike?

Sometimes we repeat a behavior because the consequence is food, a primary reinforcer, or because the consequence is money, a secondary reinforcer. Let's see how primary and secondary reinforcers could be used to increase study time and keeping quiet on a school bus.

PRIMARY REINFORCERS

If you made yourself study for 2 hours before rewarding yourself with dinner, you would be using a primary reinforcer.

A *primary reinforcer* is a stimulus, such as food, water, or sex, that is innately satisfying and requires no learning on the part of the subject to become pleasurable.

Primary reinforcers are present from birth and require no training. In our example, dinner (food) would be a primary reinforcer for studying. However, we are often reinforced by things other than food, water, or sex.

SECONDARY REINFORCERS

A school bus driver gave each child a certificate redeemable for pizza if he or she was quiet on the bus. A certificate is an example of a secondary reinforcer.

A *secondary reinforcer* is any stimulus that has acquired its reinforcing power through experience; secondary reinforcers are learned, such as by being paired with primary reinforcers or other secondary reinforcers.

Certificates, money, grades, and praise are examples of secondary reinforcers, because their value is learned or acquired through experience. For example, children learned that certificates were valuable since they could be redeemed for pizza. The certificates became secondary reinforcers that encouraged children to choose a seat quickly and sit quietly so that the driver could get rolling in 5 minutes (George, 1995). Many behaviors in our own lives are increased or maintained by secondary reinforcers.

Unlike primary and secondary reinforcers, which increase behaviors, punishment has a very different effect.

Punishment

What does punishment do?

It is helpful to distinguish between positive and negative punishment.

Positive punishment refers to presenting an aversive (unpleasant) stimulus (such as spanking) after a response. The aversive stimulus decreases the chances that the response will recur.

Negative punishment refers to removing a reinforcing stimulus (a child's allowance) after a response. This removal decreases the chances that the response will recur.

Both positive and negative punishment function as "stop signs"; they stop or decrease the occurrence of a behavior. We'll discuss negative punishment in the Application section. Here, we'll explain how positive punishment was used to treat a serious disorder called self-injurious behavior.

Self-injurious behavior refers to serious and sometimes life-threatening physical damage that a person inflicts on his or her own body; this may include body or head banging, biting, kicking, poking ears or eyes, pulling hair, or intense scratching.

About 8–14% of mentally retarded individuals who live in large residential treatment facilities engage in self-injurious behavior (Williams et al., 1993). Here's an example of a treatment program that used positive punishment.

POSITIVE PUNISHMENT

Because of the potential negative emotional and physical reactions that individuals may have to punishment, a special Task Force on Self-Injurious Behavior studied the effectiveness of using it as a treatment. This task force concluded that as a last resort, positive punishment was an effective treatment for severe self-injurious behavior that had resisted other treatments (Favell et al., 1982; Iwata et al., 1994).

In this case, a positive punishment program was used with Suzanne, who was 24 years old and profoundly mentally retarded. For many years, she engaged in such severe self-biting and eye and ear gouging that she had to continually wear a fencing mask and special gloves to prevent her from injuring herself. Since all other treatments had failed, the State Committee for Behavior Therapy approved a program of using positive punishment to treat Suzanne's problem. Essentially, the program involved giving Suzanne an electrical shock each time she bit or harmed herself. As the graph on the right shows, after a dozen sessions, the use of positive punishment decreased Suzanne's self-injurious behaviors by 99%, to almost zero. After 69 treatment sessions, Suzanne's protective face mask and gloves were removed,

Self-Injurious Behaviors per Min.	
9.3	Before treatment
0.07	After punishment

and for the first time in 15 years, Suzanne began to feed herself, perform personal care routines, and refrain from self-injury (Williams et al., 1993). Thus, as a last resort, positive punishment can be useful for stopping serious self-injurious behaviors that have resisted other treatments (Foxx, 1996).

Keep in mind that both positive and negative reinforcement *increase* the likelihood that a behavior will occur again, while both positive and negative punishment *decrease* the likelihood that a behavior will occur again.

We may not always be aware of the reinforcers in our lives because, as you'll see, they don't necessarily occur every time you perform or emit a behavior.

C. Schedules of Reinforcement

Skinner's Contributions

Why are consequences important?

On September 20, 1971, *Time* magazine recognized B. F. Skinner's influence and accomplishments in psychology and education by putting him on its cover (right photo). Just a year earlier, the *American Psychologist,* which is the official publication of the American Psychological Association, rated B. F. Skinner second, after Freud, in influence on 20th-century psychology.

Skinner is perhaps best known for his discovery of operant conditioning and how consequences or reinforcers affect behavior. He also developed a powerful method for analyzing the individual behaviors of animals and humans. Part of his method was to study how different kinds of consequences or reinforcements affected behavior, and this led to his study of different schedules of reinforcement.

B.F. Skinner 1904–1990

A *schedule of reinforcement* refers to a program or rule that determines how and when the occurrence of a response will be followed by a reinforcer.

Skinner pointed out many examples of how schedules of reinforcement both maintained and controlled behaviors. For example, slot machine players don't realize that they are paid off according to a schedule of reinforcement that encourages rapid responding. Similarly, some factories pay their workers by the piece, which is a schedule of reinforcement that results in steady and rapid work.

Skinner was able to study how different schedules of reinforcement affected behavior because he developed a clever method to record ongoing, individual behaviors. His method included the use of the now-famous "Skinner box" and something called the cumulative record.

Measuring Ongoing Behavior

Skinner showed how different schedules of reinforcement affected an animal's or a human's ongoing behavior with something called a cumulative record.

A *cumulative record* is a continuous written record that shows an animal's or a human's individual responses and reinforcements.

A rat in a Skinner box is shown on the left and a cumulative record is shown below. When the rat is not pressing the lever, a pen draws a straight line on a long roll of paper that unwinds slowly and continuously to the left. When the rat presses the lever, the pen moves up a notch. When the rat makes numerous responses, the pen moves up many notches to draw a line that resembles a stairway going up. If the rat presses the lever slowly, the pen notches up gradually,

Sloped line: series of rapid responses

Pen

Blip: reinforcement

Upward notch: one response

Blip: reinforcement

Flat line: no responses

resulting in a gentler slope. If the rat responds quickly, the pen notches up more quickly, resulting in a steeper slope. A downward blip indicates that the rat received a food pellet, or reinforcement (only two are shown). You'll see actual cumulative records on the next page. The cumulative record gives a picture of an animal's ongoing responses and reinforcements across time.

We'll first look at how two general schedules of reinforcement—continuous and partial reinforcement—affect ongoing behavior.

Basic Schedules of Reinforcement

Each time I open my front door, my dog gives me the loudest, friendliest greeting "humanly" possible. However, when I walk into my local coffee shop, I find they have my favorite coffee only about twice a week. These situations illustrate two general schedules of reinforcement—continuous and partial.

CONTINUOUS REINFORCEMENT

Getting a friendly greeting from my dog each and every time I walk through my front door means that my dog has me on a schedule of continuous reinforcement.

Continuous reinforcement means that every occurrence of the operant response results in delivery of the reinforcer.

In the real world, relatively few of our behaviors are on a continuous reinforcement schedule because very few things or people are as reliable as my dog. Continuous reinforcement is often used in the initial stages of operant conditioning because it results in rapid learning of some behavior.

PARTIAL REINFORCEMENT

Finding that my favorite coffee is available only twice a week, even though I look hopefully for it almost every day, means that my coffee shop has me on a schedule of partial reinforcement.

Partial reinforcement refers to a situation in which responding is reinforced only some of the time.

In the real world, many of our behaviors are on a partial reinforcement schedule, which is very effective in maintaining behavior over the long run. That's why I keep walking to the coffee shop and hoping that today is the day they'll have my favorite coffee.

We'll discuss the four most common schedules of partial reinforcement and show how differently they affect behavior.

Partial Reinforcement Schedules

Which schedule are you on?

Even though vending machines are unreliable and sometimes eat your money, you keep putting your money into these machines because they have you on one schedule of partial reinforcement. We'll discuss four different schedules of partial reinforcement, each of which has a different effect on controlling and maintaining your behavior.

Fixed-Ratio Schedule

Suppose a pigeon is reinforced after it pecks six times. Or a factory worker is paid after packing six boxes of carrots. These are examples of a fixed-ratio schedule.

Fixed-ratio schedule means that a reinforcer occurs only after a fixed number of responses made by the subject.

Steep slope indicates rapid response rate (reinforcers indicated by blips).

Effect. A fixed-ratio schedule is often used to pay assembly line workers because it results in fast rates of work: the more pieces of work completed, the more the worker is paid (reinforcement).

Variable-Ratio Schedule

Suppose a pigeon gets a reinforcer after 12, 6, 8, and 2 pecks, with an average of 7 pecks. Or a slot machine pays off after an average of 25 plays but with a variable number of pulls. These are examples of a variable-ratio schedule.

Variable-ratio schedule means that a subject must make a variable or different number of responses for delivery of each reinforcer.

Steep slope indicates rapid, steady response rate (reinforcers indicated by blips).

Effect. The variable-ratio schedule produces a high rate of responding because the subject (pigeon or slot machine player) doesn't know which response will finally produce the payoff.

Fixed-Interval Schedule

Suppose a pigeon gets a reinforcer for the first peck that occurs after 2 minutes. Or a surfer gets a big wave to ride (the reinforcer) every 30 seconds (waves come in regular sets). These are examples of a fixed-interval schedule.

Fixed-interval schedule means that a reinforcer occurs following the first response that occurs after a fixed interval of time.

Gradual slope indicates slower response rate with long pauses after each reinforcer (blips).

Effect. A fixed-interval schedule results in slow responding at first, but as the time for the reinforcer draws near, the response rate greatly accelerates.

Variable-Interval Schedule

Suppose a pigeon gets a reinforcer for the first response that occurs after intervals of 12, 6, 8, and 2 minutes, with an average interval of 7 minutes. Or a bus arrives (the reinforcer) at your stop an average of 7 minutes late, but at variable intervals. This reinforces your arriving just a few minutes late. These are examples of a variable-interval schedule.

Variable-interval schedule means that a reinforcer occurs following the first response after a variable amount of time has gone by.

Gradual slope indicates slower response rate without pauses after reinforcers (blips).

Effect. A variable-interval schedule results in a more regular rate of responding than does a fixed-interval schedule.

In the laboratory, Skinner demonstrated that partial reinforcement, even at a rate as low as one reinforcer for an average of 200 responses, would maintain a pigeon pecking at a key. In the real world, many of our own behaviors, such as studying for exams, working at a job, or being affectionate in a relationship, are maintained on one or more of the these four schedules of partial reinforcement.

During operant conditioning, a number of other things are happening, which we'll look at next.

D. Other Conditioning Concepts

While Bart was being operantly conditioned to pick up and hold a teddy bear, he also learned a number of other things, such as to also hold a bear cub, not to obey a stranger, and to stop holding the teddy bear if he was no longer given apples. You may remember these phenomena—generalization, discrimination, and extinction—from our discussion of classical conditioning in Module 9. We'll explain how the same terms also apply to operant conditioning.

Generalization

Why use a teddy bear?

In the movie, Bart was supposed to pick up and hold a bear cub on command. However, in the wild, adult male Kodiak bears don't pick up and hold cubs; instead, they usually kill them.

Although Bart was relatively tame, his trainer took no chances of Bart's wilder nature coming out and killing the bear cub. For this reason, the trainer started by conducting the initial conditioning with a stuffed teddy bear. Only after Bart had learned to pick up and hold the teddy bear on cue, did the trainer substitute a live bear cub. As the trainer had predicted, Bart transferred his holding the teddy bear to holding the live bear cub, a phenomenon called generalization.

In operant conditioning, *generalization* means that an animal or person emits the same response to similar stimuli.

In classical conditioning, *generalization* is the tendency for a stimulus similar to the original conditioned stimulus to elicit a response similar to the conditioned response.

A common and sometimes embarrassing example of generalization occurs when a young child generalizes the word "Daddy" to other males, who appear similar to the child's real father. As quickly as possible, embarrassed parents teach their child to discriminate between the real father and other adult males.

Discrimination

Why doesn't Bart obey other humans?

Since Bart had been raised and trained by a particular adult male, he had learned to obey and take cues only from his trainer and not from other males. This is an example of discrimination.

In operant conditioning, *discrimination* means that a response is emitted in the presence of a stimulus that is reinforced and not in the presence of unreinforced stimuli.

In classical conditioning, *discrimination* is the tendency for some stimuli but not others to elicit a conditioned response.

One problem with Bart was that he would repeatedly pick up and hold the teddy bear to receive an apple. To control this problem, the trainer used a cue—raising his arms in the air—to signal that only then would Bart receive an apple for his behavior. This is an example of a discriminative stimulus.

A *discriminative stimulus* is a cue that a behavior will be reinforced.

If you pay close attention to an animal trainer, you'll notice that discriminative stimuli, such as a hand signal or whistle, are used to signal the animal that the next behavior will be reinforced.

Young children learn to discriminate between stimuli when their parents reinforce their saying "Daddy" in the presence of their real fathers but do not reinforce their calling strangers "Daddy."

Extinction and Spontaneous Recovery

What if apples stop coming?

Even after filming ended, Bart continued to perform his trained behaviors for a while. However, after a period of time when these behaviors were no longer reinforced, they gradually diminished and ceased. This is an example of extinction.

In operant conditioning, *extinction* refers to the reduction in an operant response when it is no longer followed by the reinforcer.

In classical conditioning, *extinction* refers to the reduction in a response when the conditioned stimulus is no longer followed by the unconditioned stimulus.

After undergoing extinction, Bart may show spontaneous recovery.

In operant conditioning, *spontaneous recovery* refers to a temporary recovery in the rate of responding.

In classical conditioning, *spontaneous recovery* refers to the temporary occurrence of the conditioned response to the presence of the conditioned stimulus.

Remember that all four phenomena—generalization, discrimination, extinction, and spontaneous recovery—occur in both operant and classical conditioning.

One distinctive characteristic of operant conditioning is that it usually has an observable response and an observable reinforcer. Next, we turn to cognitive learning, which may have neither.

Three Viewpoints

How did Dusty learn?

At the beginning of this module, we told you about 3-year-old Dusty. The first time he got a skateboard, he imitated what he had observed other skateboarders doing. He put one foot on the skateboard, used his other foot to propel forward, and held his arms out for balance. Dusty had learned how to use a skateboard not from classical or operant conditioning but from another kind of learning process called cognitive learning.

Cognitive learning involves mental processes, such as attention and memory; it may be learned through observation or imitation; and it may not involve any external rewards or require a person to perform any observable behaviors.

Although interest in cognitive learning was reborn in the 1960s, its roots extend back to the work of Wundt in the late 1800s (p. 12) and that of psychologist Edward Tolman in the 1930s. Today the concepts of cognitive learning have become popular in explaining both animal and human behavior as well as the development of a new area called cognitive neuroscience (p. 71) (Cabeza & Nyberg, 1997; Domjan, 1998). We'll begin by discussing what three psychologists—B. F. Skinner, Edward Tolman, and Albert Bandura—had to say about cognitive learning.

B. F. Skinner: Against

Eight days before his death, B. F. Skinner was honored by the American Psychological Association (APA) with the first APA Citation for Outstanding Lifetime Contribution to Psychology. In his acceptance speech to over 1,000 friends and colleagues, Skinner spoke of how psychology was splitting between those who were studying feelings and cognitive processes and those who were studying observable behaviors, such as animals under controlled conditions (figure below). Repeating a thought he had expressed many times before, Skinner said, "As far as I'm concerned, cognitive science is the creationism [downfall] of psychology" (Vargas, 1991, p. 1).

Skinner's severe criticism of studying cognitive processes and mental events caused many in the audience to gasp and only a few to applaud (Vargas, 1991). Apparently, many in the audience, as well as other psychologists, believe that cognitive processes are not, as Skinner said, a terrible step backward in scientific knowledge.

Despite Skinner's disapproval, many current psychologists believe that analyzing cognitive processes is a useful and necessary approach to understanding human learning and behavior (Cabeza & Nyberg, 1997; Zeiler, 1996).

Edward Tolman: In Favor

In the 1930s, about the same time that Skinner was emphasizing observable behaviors, Tolman was exploring hidden mental processes. For example, he would place rats individually in a maze, such as the one shown below, and allow each rat time to explore the maze with no food present. Then, with food present in the maze's food box, he would test the rat to see which path it took. The rat learned very quickly to take the shortest path. Next, Tolman blocked the shortest path to the food box. The first time the rat encountered the blocked shortest path, it selected the next shortest path to the food box. According to Tolman (1948), the rat selected the next shortest path because it had developed a cognitive map of the maze.

A *cognitive map* is a mental representation in the brain of the layout of an environment and its features.

Food

Start

Tolman showed that rats, in addition to forming a cognitive map, learned the layout of a maze without being reinforced, a position very different from Skinner's. Tolman's position is making a comeback as psychologists currently study a variety of cognitive processes in animals (Domjan, 1998). Also, Tolman's study of cognitive processes has become a major focus in human learning, as shown by the current work of Albert Bandura (1995).

Albert Bandura: In Favor

Although Bandura began as a behaviorist in the Skinnerian tradition, he has gradually and almost entirely shifted to a cognitive approach. In many of his studies, Bandura (1986) has focused on how humans learn through observation. For example, Bandura would say that a child can learn to hate spiders simply by observing the behaviors of someone who exhibits a great dislike of spiders. This is an example of social cognitive learning.

Social cognitive learning results from watching, imitating, and modeling and does not require the observer to perform any observable behavior or receive any observable reward.

Just as Tolman found that learning occurred while rats were exploring, Bandura found that humans learned while observing and that much of human learning takes place through observation. Observational learning, which emphasizes cognitive processes, is 180 degrees from Skinner's position, which emphasizes observable, noncognitive behaviors.

The study of cognitive learning was revived in the 1960s and continues to increase in popularity to the present. We'll introduce you to cognitive learning by describing one of Bandura's best-known studies, which involved a doll and a considerable amount of kicking and screaming.

E. Cognitive Learning

Observational Learning

Do children learn by watching?

Perhaps a dozen experiments in psychology have become classics because they were the first to demonstrate some very important principles. One such classic experiment demonstrated the conditioning of emotional responses in "little Albert" (p. 204). Another classic is Albert Bandura (1965) and his colleagues' demonstration that children learned aggressive behaviors by watching an adult's aggressive behaviors. Learning through watching is called observational learning, which is a form of cognitive learning.

Bobo Doll Experiment

Why did children kick the Bobo doll?

One reason this Bobo doll study is a classic experiment is because it challenged the earlier idea that learning occurred either through classical or operant conditioning. You'll see that children learned to perform aggressive responses simply from watching.

Procedure. In one part of the room, preschool children were involved in their own art projects. In another part of the room, an adult got up and, for the next 10 minutes, kicked, hit, and yelled ("Hit him! Kick him!") at a large, inflated Bobo doll. Some children watched the model's aggressive behaviors while other children did not.

Sometime later, each child was subjected to a mildly frustrating situation and then placed in a room with toys, including the Bobo doll. Without the child's knowledge, researchers observed the child's behaviors.

Results. Children who had observed the model's aggressive attacks on the Bobo doll also kicked, hit, and yelled ("Hit him! Kick him!") at the doll. Through observational learning alone, these children had learned the model's aggressive behaviors and were now performing them. In comparison, the children who had not observed the model's aggressive behaviors did not hit or kick the Bobo doll after they had been mildly frustrated.

Conclusion. Bandura's point is that these children learned to perform specific aggressive behaviors not by practicing or being reinforced but simply by watching a live model perform these behaviors. Observational learning is sometimes called modeling, because it involves watching a model and later imitating the behavior.

Another interesting finding of the Bobo doll studies was that children may learn by observing but then not perform the observed behavior. This is an example of the learning-performance distinction.

Learning versus Performance

Do you learn but not show it?

Is it possible that people can learn by observing but not necessarily perform what they have learned? To answer this question, Bandura and colleagues asked a group of children to watch a movie in which someone hit and kicked a Bobo doll. However, after hitting and kicking the doll, the person in the film was punished by being soundly criticized and spanked. Next, each child was left alone in a room filled with toys, including a Bobo doll.

As the experimenters watched each child through a one-way mirror, they found that more boys than girls imitated the model and performed aggressive behaviors on Bobo. But not all the children imitated the model's aggressive behaviors. Next, each child who had not imitated the model's aggressive behaviors on Bobo was offered a reward (a sticker or some fruit juice) to imitate the model's behavior. With the promise of a reward, all of the children imitated the model's aggressive behaviors. We'll examine in more detail the girls' imitated aggressive behaviors, which were similar to the boys' but more dramatic.

As the graph below shows, girls imitated an average of 0.5 aggressive behaviors after watching a film of a model who performed aggressive behaviors on Bobo and then was punished for being aggressive.

In other words, after observing a model being punished for aggressive behaviors, girls imitated almost none of the model's aggressive behaviors. However, when the same girls were promised a reward for imitating the model's aggressive behaviors, these girls imitated an average of 3.0 aggressive behaviors (Bandura, 1965).

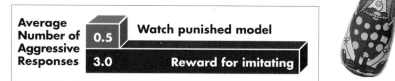

Average Number of Aggressive Responses	
0.5	Watch punished model
3.0	Reward for imitating

What does this experiment show? This experiment shows that the girls had actually *learned* the model's aggressive behaviors through observation but that some did not *perform* these behaviors until they were rewarded for doing so (Bandura, 1965). This is an example of the learning-performance distinction.

The *learning-performance distinction* means that learning may occur but may not always be measured by, or immediately evident in, performance.

Young children often demonstrate the learning-performance distinction in ways that may embarrasses their parents. For instance, a young child may overhear a "dirty" word but not repeat the word in the presence of a parent. Then, when a neighbor comes to visit, the child gleefully repeats the word, showing that the child had learned the word through observation but waited until later to say the "dirty" word.

Based on the Bobo doll study and others, Bandura developed a theory of cognitive learning that we'll examine next.

Bandura's Social Cognitive Theory

Would you hold this spider?

Just as Tolman believed that rats gather information and form cognitive maps about their environments through exploring, Bandura believes that humans gather information about their environments and the behaviors of others through observation, which is part of Bandura's (1989a) social cognitive theory of learning.

Social cognitive theory emphasizes the importance of observation, imitation, and self-reward in the development and learning of social skills, personal interactions, and many other behaviors. Unlike operant and classical conditioning, this theory says that is not necessary to perform any observable behaviors or receive any external rewards to learn.

Bandura believes that four processes—attention, memory, imitation, and motivation—operate during social cognitive learning. We'll explain how these processes operate in decreasing fear of spiders and snakes.

Social Cognitive Learning: Four Processes

1 Attention

The observer must pay attention to what the model says or does. In the photo below, a nonfrightened woman (model) holds a huge spider while another woman (observer) looks on in amazement.

2 Memory

The observer must store or remember the information so that it can be retrieved and used later. The observer in the photo will store the image of seeing a nonfrightened woman (model) holding a spider.

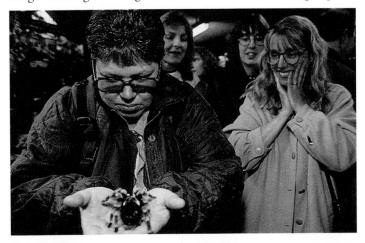

3 Imitation

The observer must be able to use the remembered information to guide his or her own actions and thus imitate the model's behavior. The observer in the photo will later try to imitate the model's nonfrightened facial expression and manner when holding a spider.

4 Motivation

The observer must have some reason or incentive to imitate the model's behavior. The observer in the photo is motivated to overcome her fear of spiders because she wants to go on camping trips.

If this observer can successfully imitate the model's calm behavior, then she will overcome her fear of spiders and be able to go camping with her friends. This example shows how Bandura's four mental processes operate during social cognitive learning.

The next study by Bandura shows how social cognitive learning, which usually takes some time and effort, decreased fear of snakes.

Social Cognitive Learning Decreases the Fear of Snakes

Background. Although most people are wary of snakes, some develop an intense fear of them. Bandura and colleagues recruited subjects who had developed such an intense fear of snakes that they avoided many normal outdoor activities, such as hiking or gardening (Bandura et al., 1969). The subjects' fear of snakes was objectively measured by noting how many of 29 steps of increasingly frightening actions they would perform. For example, step 1 was approaching a glass cage containing a snake; step 29 was putting the snake in their laps and letting it crawl around while holding their hands at their sides.

Treatment. One group of subjects watched as a model handled a live, 4-foot, harmless king snake. After watching for 15 minutes, subjects were invited to gradually move closer to the snake. Then the model demonstrated touching the snake and asked the subjects to imitate her actions. As the model held the snake, subjects were encouraged to touch the snake with a gloved hand. Another group of subjects, who also reported an intense fear of snakes, received no treatment (control group).

Results and conclusion. As the graph below shows, subjects who watched a live model handle a snake and who imitated some of the model's behaviors scored an average of 27 on the 29-step approach scale.

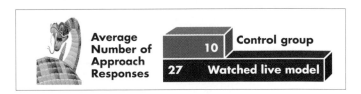

Average Number of Approach Responses | 10 Control group | 27 Watched live model

In contrast, control subjects scored an average of only 10 approach behaviors on the 29-step scale. This study clearly showed that behavior can be greatly changed through social cognitive learning, which emphasized observation and imitation.

Bandura believes that humans acquire a great amount of information about fears, social roles, discrimination, and personal interactions through social cognitive learning. We'll discuss other aspects of cognitive learning and memory in Modules 11 and 12.

Next, we'll describe another kind of cognitive learning that involves what is often described as the "ah-ha!" feeling.

E. Cognitive Learning

Insight Learning

What's the "ah-ha!" feeling?

Earlier we told you that Thorndike studied how cats learned to escape from a puzzle box to get a piece of fish. Thorndike concluded that learning occurred through a process of trial and error as cats gradually formed associations between moving the latch and opening the door. None of the cats showed any evidence of suddenly discovering the solution of how to escape the box.

About the same time that Thorndike in America was studying the trial-and-error learning of cats escaping from a puzzle box, Wolfgang Köhler in Germany was studying how chimpanzees

learned to obtain bananas that were out of reach. Köhler challenged Thorndike's conclusion that animals learned only through trial and error. Köhler suggested instead that cats and other animals that were observed under the proper circumstances could solve a problem in a sudden flash, known as insight.

Insight is a mental process marked by the sudden and expected solution to a problem: a phenomenon often called the "ah-ha!" experience.

Here's an example of Köhler's chimp, Sultan, who showed insight in getting a banana that was hanging out of reach.

Insight in Animals

How did the chimp get the banana?

Here's another classic experiment in psychology that suggested a new kind of learning.

What Köhler (1925) did was to hang a banana from the ceiling in a room that had a box placed off to one side. The banana was too high for Sultan the chimp to grab by reaching or jumping. When Sultan first entered the room, he paced restlessly for about 5 minutes. Then he seized the box, moved it toward the banana, climbed onto the box, jumped up, and seized the banana. On his second try, Sultan quickly moved the box directly beneath the banana and jumped up to get it.

What intrigued Köhler about Sultan's problem-solving behavior was that it seemed to differ greatly from the random trial-and-error behavior of Thorndike's cats. Before Sultan arrived at a solution, he might pace about, sit quietly, or vainly grasp at the out-of-reach banana. Then, all of a sudden, he seemed to hit on the solution and immediately executed a complicated set of behaviors, such as stacking boxes, to get the banana. Köhler believed that Sultan's sudden solution to a problem was an example of *insight,* a mental process quite different from what Thorndike had observed in the random trial-and-error learning of cats.

However, critics of Köhler's insight studies pointed out that he did not explain how chimps solved problems; rather, he simply described the process. Critics also noted that chimpanzees who were best at solving Köhler's problems were those who had had the most experience getting or retrieving objects. Thus, the development of insight seems to depend, to a large extent, upon previous experience.

Köhler replied that his studies on insight were more a way to study problem solving than an explanation of what was happening in the chimp's head. The significance of Köhler's work was that it represented a method for studying learning that was different from either classical conditioning or random trial-and-error learning. Since the early 1990s, there has been a renewed interest in studying the workings of the animal mind, which is currently called animal cognition (Domjan, 1998).

Let's look at an example of insight learning in humans.

Insight in Humans

Can you solve this puzzle?

Just as Sultan the chimp seemed to suddenly arrive at a solution to a problem, humans also report the experience of suddenly and unexpectedly solving a challenging or difficult problem. We call this phenomenon the "ah-ha!" experience or a flash of insight. You may have an "ah-ha!" experience if you can figure out what critical piece of information is needed to make the following story make sense.

A man walks into a bar and asks for a glass of water. The bartender points a gun at the man. The man says, "Thank you," and walks out.

Obviously, something critical happened between two events: ". . . asks for a glass of water" and "The bartender points a gun at the man." Some subjects solved this problem in a relatively short time, while others could not solve this problem in the 2-hour time limit.

I'll admit that I never solved the problem until I read the hint: The man has hiccups. Think about cures for hiccups, and, like me, you may have an "ah-ha!" experience. The man drank the water, but it didn't cure his hiccups. The bartender thought a big surprise might do the trick, so he points a gun at the man, who is frightened, and so his hiccups stop. The man says, "Thank you," and walks out.

There was a difference between nonsolvers and solvers in the cognitive strategy that they used. The nonsolvers focused mostly on the obvious elements, such as man, bartender, gun, and glass of water, and not on new concepts (hiccups, cure) that would lead to a solution. In comparison, the solvers spent more time on bringing in new information. When the solvers finally found the missing piece of information (cure for hiccups), the solution arrived suddenly, like the "ah-ha!" experience that Köhler defined as insight (Durso et al., 1994).

We have discussed three examples of cognitive learning: Tolman's idea of cognitive maps, Bandura's theory of social cognitive learning, and Köhler's study of insightful problem solving. In addition, we'll discuss cognitive learning in Modules 11 and 12.

After the Concept Review, we explain why biological factors make some things easier and some things harder to learn.

CONCEPT REVIEW

1. The kind of learning in which the consequences that follow some behavior increase or decrease the likelihood that the behavior will occur in the future is called _____.

2. In operant conditioning, the organism voluntarily performs or (a)_____ a behavior. Immediately following an emitted behavior, the occurrence of a (b)_____ increases the likelihood that the behavior will occur again.

3. Because an organism may not immediately emit the desired behavior, a procedure is used to reinforce behaviors that lead to or approximate the final, target behavior. This procedure is called _____.

4. In operant conditioning, the term *consequences* refers to either (a)_____, which increases the likelihood that a behavior will occur again, or (b)_____, which decreases the likelihood that a behavior will occur again.

5. If the occurrence of some response is increased because it is followed by a pleasant stimulus, the stimulus is called a (a)_____. An increase in the occurrence of some response because it is followed either by the removal of an unpleasant stimulus or by avoiding the stimulus is called (b)_____.

6. A stimulus, such as food, water, or sex, that is innately satisfying and requires no learning to become pleasurable is a (a)_____. A stimulus, such as grades or praise, that has acquired its reinforcing power through experience and learning is a (b)_____.

7. The various ways that reinforcers occur after a behavior has been emitted are referred to as (a)_____ of reinforcement. For example, if each and every target behavior is reinforced, it is called a (b)_____ schedule of reinforcement. If behaviors are not reinforced each time they occur, it is called a (c)_____ schedule of reinforcement.

8. When an organism emits the same response to similar stimuli, it is called (a)_____. When a response is emitted in the presence of a stimulus that is reinforced and not in the presence of unreinforced stimuli, it is called (b)_____. A decrease in emitting a behavior because it is no longer reinforced is called (c)_____. If an organism performs a behavior without its being reinforced, it is called (d)_____.

9. A kind of learning that involves mental processes, that may be learned through observation and imitation, and that may not require any external rewards or the performance of any observable behaviors is referred to as _____.

10. Tolman studied the behavior of rats that were allowed to explore a maze without any reward given. When food was present, rats quickly learned to select the next shortest path if a previously taken path was blocked. Tolman said that rats had developed a mental representation of the layout, which he called a _____.

11. Although an organism may learn a behavior through observation or exploration, the organism may not immediately demonstrate or perform the newly learned behavior. This phenomenon is known as the _____ distinction.

12. According to Bandura, one form of learning that develops through watching and imitation and that does not require the observer to perform any observable behavior or receive a reinforcer is called (a)_____ learning. Bandura believes that humans gather much information from their (b)_____ through social cognitive learning.

13. Bandura's theory of social cognitive learning involves four mental processes. The observer must pay (a)_____ to what the model says or does. The observer must then code the information and be able to retrieve it from (b)_____ for use at a later time. The observer must be able to use the coded information to guide his or her (c)_____ in performing and imitating the model's behavior. Finally, the observer must be (d)_____ to perform the behavior, which involves some reason, reinforcement, or incentive.

14. In Köhler's study of problem solving in chimps, he identified a mental process marked by the sudden occurrence of a solution, which he termed (a)_____. This phenomenon is another example of (b)_____ learning.

Answers: *1. operant conditioning; 2. (a) emits, (b) reinforcement or reinforcer; 3. shaping; 4. (a) reinforcement, (b) punishment; 5. (a) positive reinforcer, (b) negative reinforcement; 6. (a) primary reinforcer, (b) secondary reinforcer; 7. (a) schedules, (b) continuous, (c) partial; 8. (a) generalization, (b) discrimination, (c) extinction, (d) spontaneous recovery; 9. cognitive learning; 10. cognitive map; 11. learning-performance; 12. (a) social cognitive, (b) environments; 13. (a) attention, (b) memory, (c) motor control, (d) motivated; 14. (a) insight, (b) cognitive.*

Why study a single subject?

When researchers study a group of subjects, information on any single subject may be lost in the group's combined scores. One advantage of operant conditioning is that a researcher can observe, study, and modify the ongoing behavior of a single subject. The ability to focus on a single subject's behavior makes operant conditioning a powerful procedure for changing undesirable behaviors. One kind of undesirable behavior in young children can be the persistent refusal of parental requests. We'll look at 4-year-old Morgan, who is becoming unmanageable because of a problem called noncompliance.

Noncompliance refers to a child refusing to follow directions, carry out a request, or obey a command given by a parent or caregiver.

Noncompliance is one of the most common complaints of parents in general and the most frequent problem of parents who bring their children to clinics for treatment of behavioral problems (Wierson & Forehand, 1994).

When saying "NO!" becomes a big problem, parents can be trained to use operant conditioning to decrease their child's persistent refusal. Parental training may involve different kinds of operant conditioning procedures, such as using verbal praise or giving attention to increase the occurrence of positive behaviors or using negative punishment to decrease undesirable behaviors. We'll focus on one form of negative punishment—time-out.

Time-out is a form of negative punishment in which reinforcing stimuli are removed after an undesirable response. This removal decreases the chances that the response will recur.

Because Morgan persistently said, "NO!" to her mother's requests, her mother was taught how to use time-out periods.

Study: Using Time-Out to Reduce Noncompliance

The first step in parental training was for researchers to show parents how to use the principles of operant conditioning to overcome a child's persistent "NO!"

Subjects. The subjects were 4-year-old girls who were developmentally normal but had a long history of refusing requests. Their mothers had volunteered for this study because they wanted help with this problem.

Procedure. Researchers first observed mothers making typical requests and noted the children's rate of refusal, which is called the baseline. Then, mothers were trained in several procedures, but we'll focus on the most successful one, using time-out.

If Morgan's mother made a request and Morgan complied, her mother gave praise. However, if Morgan refused, her mother used the time-out procedure: She led Morgan to the corner of another room and told her to sit quietly and silently in a chair facing the wall for 1 minute. After 1 minute, Morgan was allowed to leave the room and rejoin her mother. At that point, the mother made another request of Morgan. If Morgan complied, praise was given; if she showed noncompliance, the time-out procedure was used. All procedures were conducted in the home by the mother.

Results. In the graph below you can see the changes in Morgan's behavior after her mother began using time-out periods (Rortvedt & Miltenberger, 1994).

Baseline: Remember that during baseline, the researcher only observed the number of times that Morgan refused or agreed with her mother's request. During baseline, Morgan's mother made 5–8 requests during each session. Notice that during the last five sessions, Morgan showed mostly 0% compliance, despite her mother's scolding, pleading, or reprimanding.

Time-out: During time-out training, each time Morgan refused her mother's request, she was given a time-out period. Notice that Morgan's percentage of compliance started out at 12%, reached 60% on sessions 8–11, and then reached 100%.

Six weeks later, in a follow-up session using time-out, Morgan again showed 100% compliance with her mother's requests.

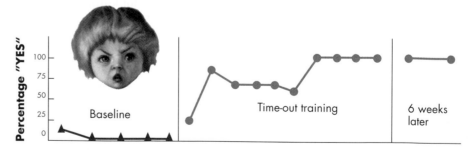

Conclusion. This study agrees with many others in showing that the time-out procedure is effective in reducing noncompliance, temper tantrums, disruptive behaviors, and other problem behaviors (Taylor & Miller, 1997). Although time-out is a form of punishment, it is generally preferable to physical punishment, which may cause negative emotional reactions as well as negative feelings toward the punisher. The time-out procedure is an example of how operant conditioning principles may be applied to modify human behavior. We'll discuss the pros and cons of punishment in the Application section.

Dealing with noncompliance is one example of how learning principles can be applied to human behavior. Another example involves learning how to play the violin.

H. Cultural Diversity: East Meets West

How to teach a 3-year-old to play a violin?

In the 1940s, Japanese violinist and teacher Shinichi Suzuki developed a remarkably successful method for teaching violin to very young children. Called the *Suzuki method,* it was brought to the United States in the mid-1960s and has generated incredible enthusiasm among children, parents, and music teachers ever since (Lamb, 1990).

It's interesting that the basic principles of the Suzuki method closely resemble Bandura's four mental processes for social cognitive learning. Suzuki developed his teaching principles from actually working with young children, while Bandura based his four mental processes on research with young children. We'll compare the principles of Suzuki and Bandura, who arrived at similar ideas although they worked in different cultures and from different perspectives.

Comparing Learning Principles: Teacher Suzuki and Researcher Bandura

1 Attention

Bandura states that the observer must pay attention to what the model says and does.

Similarly, Suzuki advises parents to teach violin information only when the child is actually looking at and watching the parent. Parents are told to stop teaching and wait if the child rolls on the floor, jumps up and down, walks backward, or talks about unrelated things.

The recommended age for starting a child with the Suzuki method is 3 for girls and 4 for boys. Parents are cautioned, however, that the attention span of the 3- to 4-year-old child is extremely limited, usually from 30 seconds to at most several minutes at a time.

2 Memory

Bandura says that the observer must code the information in such a way that it can be retrieved and used later.

Similarly, Suzuki has parents present information in ways that a young child can code. Because a 3- to 4-year-old child does not have fully developed verbal skills, little time is spent giving verbal instructions.

Instead, the child is given violin information through games and exercises. For example, children are taught how to hold the violin, use the bow, and press the strings by first playing games with their hands. Children are taught how to read music (notes) only when they have reached a certain stage of technical skill at playing the violin.

3 Imitation

Bandura says the observer must be able to use the information to guide his or her own actions and thus imitate the model's behavior.

Similarly, Suzuki suggests that children start at about 3 or 4 years old, the earliest age when they can physically perform the required movements and imitate their parents and teachers. Girls can start earlier than boys because girls physically mature earlier. For other instruments, the starting times are different—piano, 4–5 years; cello, 5 years; flute, 9 years—because these instruments require more physical dexterity. As you have probably guessed, 3- and 4-year-olds start with miniature violins and move up to bigger ones as they develop.

4 Motivation

Bandura says that the observer must have some reason, reinforcement, or incentive to perform the model's behaviors.

Similarly, Suzuki emphasizes that the most important role of the parent is to constantly reward and reinforce the child for observing and "doing what Mommy or Daddy is doing." Suzuki recommends several ways to keep motivation high in young children: Be an active and interested model for the child, play violin games that are fun for the child, avoid games or lessons that involve competition, and *never* push the child beyond the level that he or she is capable of reaching (Slone, 1985).

Conclusion. Parents and teachers who have used the Suzuki method report great success (Lamb, 1990). As you can judge, the basic principles of the Suzuki method for teaching violin are quite similar to Bandura's four mental processes for social cognitive learning. Both Suzuki and Bandura recognized the importance of modeling and how much children learn from watching and imitating models.

Suzuki's method of teaching violin is one example of how principles of learning were applied to real-world situations.

Next, we'll discuss how operant learning principles were used to develop a method for teaching autistic children.

I. Application: Behavior Modification

Definition

Throughout this module, we have given you many specific examples of behavior modification: toilet training 3-year-old Sheryl and decreasing food refusal in young children (p. 216), stopping Walt from eating paint chips (p. 218), stopping Suzanne from injuring herself (p. 219), and decreasing noncompliance (refusal) in Morgan (p. 230).

Behavior modification is a treatment or therapy that changes or modifies problems or undesirable behaviors by using principles of learning based on operant conditioning, classical conditioning, and social cognitive learning.

For over 35 years, psychologist and researcher Ivar Lovaas of the University of California at Los Angeles has used behavior modification or, more colloquially, behavior mod, to treat autistic children (Lovaas & Buch, 1997). Lovaas's work is especially impressive because he was one of the first to adapt behavior mod procedures to treat serious problems of autistic children. We discussed autism throughout Module 1 and here will only refresh your memory with the kinds of problems that autistics may have.

Autism is marked by especially abnormal or impaired development in social interactions, such as hiding to avoid people, not making eye contact, not wanting to be touched. Autism is marked by difficulties in communicating, such as grave problems in developing spoken language or in initiating conversations. Autistics are characterized by having very few activities

and interests, spending long periods in repeating the same behaviors, such as flipping fingers (this drawing), or following rituals that interfere with more normal functioning. Signs of autism begin in the child's first 3 years (American Psychiatric Association, 1994).

Mental health experts know that, without treatment, many autistic children will remain unresponsive because they lack necessary social skills and remain uncommunicative because they lack language skills. We'll describe Lovaas's behavior modification treatment program, which is based on the principles of operant conditioning and social cognitive learning.

Autistic Children

How much time is needed?

Lovaas's UCLA Young Autism Project treats 2- to 3-year-old autistic children with a 40-hour-per-week program that runs for 2 to 3 years. We'll describe part of the program.

PROGRAM

The training program that Lovaas has developed actually consists of hundreds of separate teaching programs, many of them using principles of operant conditioning: Select a specific target behavior, shape the behavior, and use positive reinforcers of praise and food that are given immediately after the child emits the desired behavior. For example, here's a program for helping autistic children make eye contact.

The **target behavior** is getting the child to make eye contact following the command, "Look at me."

Shaping the behavior involves two steps.

Step 1. Have the child sit in a chair facing you. Give the command "Look at me" every 5–10 seconds. When the child makes a correct response of looking at you, say "Good looking," and simultaneously reward the child with food.

Step 2. Continue until the child repeatedly follows the command "Look at me." Then gradually increase the duration of the child's eye contact from 1 second to periods of 2 to 3 seconds.

Using this kind of behavior modification program, therapists and parents have had success in teaching autistic children to make eye contact, to stop their incessant rocking, to respond to verbal requests such as "Wash your hands," and gradually to play with toys, interact with peers, speak, and engage in school tasks such as reading and writing (Lovaas, 1993).

RESULTS

Lovaas and his colleagues did a long-term study of 19 children diagnosed as autistic. Behavior modification training went on for at least 40 hours per week, for 2 years or more. The graph on the right shows that, at the end of training, 47% of the autistic children reached normal status (Lovaas, 1987). These children acquired sufficient language, social, play, and self-help behaviors that they could enter preschool and go on to successfully complete grades in public school. Many of the children did so well that the teachers did not know they were autistic.

47%	Normal status
40%	Mildly retarded
Profoundly retarded	10%

However, even with such intensive training, 40% of autistic children remained mildly retarded, and 10% remained profoundly retarded and were assigned to classes for children with mental retardation. In comparison, in a control group of autistic children who received only minimal treatment, only 2% achieved normal intellectual and educational functioning, while 45% remained mildly retarded and 53% remained severely retarded (Lovaas, 1987; Lovaas & Buch, 1997; McEachin, Smith, & Lovaas, 1993).

Lovaas concluded that without intensive behavior modification treatment, autistic children will continue to show severe behavioral deficits.

Next, we'll discuss another treatment program, called biofeedback, that also uses the principles of operant conditioning.

Biofeedback

The principles of operant conditioning have been applied to help people deal with a variety of psychosomatic problems—that is, problems that involve an interaction between mind and body. These problems include back pain, high blood pressure, stomach distress, and headaches. One procedure to reduce these problems is called biofeedback.

Biofeedback is a training procedure through which a person is made aware of his or her physiological responses, such as muscle activity, heart rate, blood pressure, or temperature, and then tries to increase or decrease these physiological responses.

For example, headaches may be caused or worsened by muscle tension, of which the sufferer may be unaware. The left figure shows the wide bands of muscles in the forehead and neck. Through video or audio (bio)feedback, a person can be made aware of muscle tension

As shown in the photo below, small sensors attached to the client's forehead detect activity in the large muscle that stretches across the top front part of the head. The woman is trying to relax her forehead muscle by imagining relaxing scenes, thinking relaxing thoughts, or actually tensing and relaxing the muscle itself. The target behavior is a decrease in the forehead's muscle tension. To reach this target behavior, the client practices thinking about or imagining relaxing scenes that result in a decrease in muscle tension. A decrease in muscle tension is signaled by a decrease in an audio signal, which acts as a reinforcer. After a number of these sessions, the client learns to decrease muscle tension with the goal of staying relaxed the next time she gets upset.

Biofeedback is often used in conjunction with other forms of medical treatment or psychotherapy and can help a person reduce blood pressure, decrease headaches, and reduce anxiety (Blanchard et al., 1987; Brannon & Feist, 1997; Lehrer et al., 1994). We'll discuss further methods of reducing stress and its potentially harmful effects in Module 21.

Our last example deals with concerns about using punishment to decrease undesirable behaviors.

Pros and Cons of Punishment

A recent survey of 204 mothers in New York found that, during the previous week, 42% had spanked their young children (Socolar & Stein, 1995). Although spanking remains a relatively popular form of discipline, it can have a number of negative side effects and may be a less desirable form of punishment than the time-out procedure (Geiger, 1994).

Spanking: Positive Punishment

Since spanking involves the presentation of an aversive stimulus (pain), it is an example of positive punishment. In some cases, positive punishment can decrease the occurrence of undesirable behaviors. However, a poorly chosen positive punishment, such as using harsh spanking to punish aggressive behavior, was found to have the opposite effect, increasing antisocial behavioral problems (Deater-Deckard & Dodge, 1997). In addition to increasing aggressive behaviors, studies also reported that spanking or other forms of physical punishment reduced self-esteem, made children depressed, and provided a model of aggressive behavior that the child may later imitate (Socolar & Stein, 1995). Some of the undesirable effects of positive punishment can be reduced if it is given immediately after the behavior, if it is just severe enough to be effective, if it is delivered consistently, if the child is told the reason for the punishment, and, perhaps most important, if punishment is used in combination with positively reinforcing a desirable behavior (Lieberman, 1993). One disadvantage of positive punishment is that it points out only what the child should not do, while positive reinforcers have the advantage of encouraging the child to engage in desirable behaviors.

Time-out: Negative Punishment

Another form of discipline is time-out, which was discussed earlier (p. 230). Time-out is an example of negative punishment because it involves the removal of a reinforcing stimulus (desirable reward). For example, during time-out, the child stays in a room, usually alone, without any games, books, or other amusements that could serve as rewards. Time-out is most effective when used consistently and combined with teaching the child alternative desired behaviors using positive reinforcers (Taylor & Miller, 1997; Wierson & Forehand, 1994).

Compared to punishment, time-out has fewer undesirable side effects; it does not provide a model of aggression and does not elicit severe negative emotional reactions. Thus, when it is necessary to discipline a child, care should be taken in choosing between positive punishment (spanking) and negative punishment (time-out). Although both kinds of punishment stop or suppress undesirable behaviors, spanking has more negative side effects than time-out, and time-out has been shown to be effective in eliminating undesirable behaviors. Finally, both kinds of punishment are best used in combination with positive reinforcers so that the child also learns to perform desirable behaviors.

SUMMARY TEST

A. OPERANT CONDITIONING

1. A kind of learning in which the consequences that follow some behavior increase or decrease the likelihood that the behavior will occur again is called _____.

2. To explain how random trial-and-error behaviors of cats became goal-directed behaviors, Thorndike formulated the _____, which says that behaviors are strengthened by positive consequences and weakened by negative consequences.

3. Skinner used the term *operant* (a)_____ to describe something that can be modified by its consequences. Operant responses provide one way to separate ongoing behaviors into units that can be observed and measured. Skinner believed that Pavlov's conditioning, which involves physiological (b)_____, was not very useful in understanding other forms of ongoing behaviors.

4. Suppose you wished to operantly condition your dog, Bingo, to sit up. The procedure would be as follows. You would give Bingo a treat, which is called a (a)_____, after he emits a desired behavior. Because it is unlikely that Bingo will initially sit up, you will use a procedure called (b)_____, which is a process of reinforcing those behaviors that lead up to or approximate the final desired behavior—sitting up. Immediately after Bingo emitted a desired behavior, you would give him a (c)_____.

5. Any behavior that increases in frequency because of an accidental pairing of a reinforcer and that behavior is called a _____ behavior.

6. The essence of operant conditioning can be summed up as follows: consequences or reinforcers are contingent on _____.

7. If you compare classical and operant conditioning, you will find the following differences. In classical conditioning, the response is an involuntary (a)_____ that is elicited by the (b)_____. In operant conditioning, the response is a voluntary (c)_____ that is performed or (d)_____ by the organism. In classical conditioning, the unconditioned stimulus is presented at the beginning of a trial and elicits the (e)_____. In operant conditioning, the organism emits a behavior that is immediately followed by a (f)_____.

B. REINFORCERS

8. In operant conditioning, the term *consequences* refers to what happens after the occurrence of a behavior. If a consequence increases the likelihood that a behavior will occur again, it is called a (a)_____. If a consequence decreases the likelihood that a behavior will occur again, it is called a (b)_____.

9. If a stimulus increases the chances that a response will occur again, that stimulus is called a (a)_____. If the removal of an aversive stimulus increases the chances that a response will occur again, that aversive stimulus is called a (b)_____. Both positive and negative reinforcements (c)_____ the frequency of the response they follow. In contrast, punishment is a consequence that (d)_____ the likelihood that a behavior will occur again.

10. The stimuli of food, water, and sex, which are innately satisfying and require no learning to become pleasurable, are called (a)_____. The stimuli of praise, money, and grades have acquired their reinforcing properties through experience; these stimuli are called (b)_____.

C. SCHEDULES OF REINFORCEMENT

11. A program or rule that determines how and when the occurrence of a response will be followed by a reinforcer is called a _____.

Steep slope indicates rapid response rate (reinforcers indicated by blips).

12. If you received reinforcement every time you performed a good deed, you would be on a (a)_____ schedule. This schedule is often used at the beginning of operant conditioning because it results in a rapid rate of learning. If your good deeds were not reinforced every time, you would be on a (b)_____ schedule. This schedule is more effective in maintaining the target behavior in the long run. There are four kinds of partial reinforcement schedules.

D. OTHER CONDITIONING CONCEPTS

13. The phenomenon in which an organism emits the same response to similar stimuli is called (a)_____. If a response is emitted in the presence of a reinforced stimulus but not in the presence of unreinforced stimuli, the organism is exhibiting (b)_____. If an organism's response is no longer reinforced, it will stop emitting this behavior, which is an example of (c)_____. However, even without reinforcement, an organism may perform the behavior, which is an example of (d)_____.

E. COGNITIVE LEARNING

14. The kind of learning that involves mental processes such as attention and memory, that may be learned through observation and imitation, and that may not involve any external rewards or require the person to perform any observable behaviors is called (a) _____. According to Tolman, rats developed a mental representation of the layout of their environment, which he called a (b)_____.

15. If an observer learns a behavior through observation but does not immediately perform the behavior, this is an example of the _____ distinction.

16. During his studies of problem solving in chimpanzees, Köhler used the term _____ to describe a mental process marked by the sudden occurrence of a solution.

17. Köhler's study of insightful problem solving, Bandura's theory of observational learning, and Tolman's idea of cognitive maps represent three kinds of _____ learning.

F. BIOLOGICAL FACTORS

18. Innate tendencies or predispositions that may either facilitate or inhibit learning are referred to as _____.

19. The innate tendency of newborn birds to follow the first moving object that they encounter soon after birth is called (a)_____. This kind of learning occurs best during a critical or sensitive period and is essentially (b)_____. One function of imprinting is to form social attachments between members of a species.

20. The innate tendency of animals to recognize, attend to, and store certain cues over others and associate some combinations of conditioned and unconditioned stimuli is referred to as _____. An example of this tendency is observed in Clark's nutcrackers, which are preprogrammed to bury and remember thousands of hidden stores of food.

G. RESEARCH FOCUS: NONCOMPLIANCE

21. One of the most common problems faced by parents is dealing with a child who refuses to follow directions or carry out a request or command. This refusal behavior is called _____.

22. An effective way to deal with a child's noncompliance is to use a procedure that involves placing a child in a situation where there is no chance of reinforcers. This mild form of nonphysical punishment is called _____.

Baseline | Time-out training

H. CULTURAL DIVERSITY: EAST MEETS WEST

23. Suzuki's method and Bandura's theory both emphasize observation, modeling, and imitation. Specifically, both Suzuki and Bandura focus on four concepts: paying (a)_____ to the model, placing the information in (b)_____, using the information to (c)_____ the model's actions, and (d)_____ to perform the behavior.

I. APPLICATION: BEHAVIOR MODIFICATION

24. Using principles of operant conditioning to change human behavior is referred to as (a)_____. Using these same principles to help individuals learn to control (increase or decrease) some physiological response, such as muscle activity or temperature, is called (b)_____.

25. If an aversive stimulus is presented immediately after a particular response, the response will be suppressed; this procedure is called (a)_____. If a reinforcing stimulus is removed immediately after a particular response, the response will be suppressed; this procedure is called (b)_____. A poorly chosen form of punishment, such as spanking, may have undesirable side effects, such as reducing a child's (c)_____ and serving as a model for future (d)_____ behaviors.

Answers: *1. operant conditioning; 2. law of effect; 3. (a) response, (b) reflexes; 4. (a) reinforcer, (b) shaping, (c) reinforcer; 5. superstitious; 6. behavior; 7. (a) reflex, (b) unconditioned stimulus, (c) behavior, (d) emitted, (e) unconditioned response, (f) reinforcer; 8. (a) reinforcer, (b) punishment; 9. (a) positive reinforcer, (b) negative reinforcer, (c) increase, (d) decreases; 10. (a) primary reinforcers, (b) secondary reinforcers; 11. schedule of reinforcement; 12. (a) continuous reinforcement, (b) partial reinforcement; 13. (a) generalization, (b) discrimination, (c) extinction, (d) spontaneous recovery; 14. (a) social cognitive learning, (b) cognitive map; 15. (a) learning-performance; 16. insight; 17. cognitive; 18. biological factors; 19. (a) imprinting, (b) irreversible; 20. preparedness, or prepared learning; 21. noncompliance; 22. time-out; 23. (a) attention, (b) memory, (c) imitate, (d) motivation; 24. (a) behavior modification, (b) biofeedback; 25. (a) positive punishment, (b) negative punishment, (c) self-esteem, (d) aggressive.*

Module 11 TYPES OF MEMORY

Introduction

Incredible Memory

What is possible?

Rajan Mahadevan stood before the packed house of the International Congress on Yoga and Meditation. He recited, from memory, the first 30,000 digits of pi, which is often rounded off to two decimal points or 3.14. He did not err until the 31,812th digit. This feat took 3 hours and 44 minutes and earned him a place in the *Guinness Book of World Records.*

After his record-setting memory performance, Rajan left his native India and, at age 23, entered Kansas State University. There he encountered Professor Charles Thompson, who has made the study of memory his specialty.

Thompson discovered that Rajan can quickly recall the digit at any location within the first 10,000 digits of pi. This would be equivalent to memorizing the names of 10,000 people seated in numbered seats and then recalling the name of any single person, such as the one sitting in seat 2,141. Rajan can repeat a string of 60 numbers after a single hearing, while most of us can repeat an average of ten random numbers. Rajan is one of only a half-dozen people in the world known to have such gargantuan memory powers.

Despite Rajan's unbelievable ability to memorize numbers, he seems to be worse than average at recalling faces, and he constantly forgets where he put his keys (Thompson, Cowan, & Frieman, 1993).

No one questions the accuracy of Rajan's memories, because they can be verified. However, some memories are not so easily verified, as in the case of Holly and her accused father.

Repressed Memory

How true are they?

"Holly's supposed memories are the results of drugs and quackery, not anything I did."

"I wouldn't be here if there was a question in my mind. I know my father molested me."

The man in the photo at right was accused by his daughter, Holly (photo below), for allegedly molesting her as a child. When Holly was 19, she had gone into therapy for bulimia, which is an eating disorder that involves eating a large amount of food and then inducing vomiting.

Holly's mother had asked a therapist about the causes of bulimia, and the therapist said that one of many causes was sexual molestation. Later, the mother asked Holly if she had ever been sexually molested. "Holly became very red in the face, pushed the chair out and was crying. She said, 'I don't know. I think so. Maybe,' and then 'Yes'" (Butler, 1994, p. 12). During therapy sessions, Holly reportedly told her therapist about other memories and images of her father molesting her.

Finally, about a year after first entering therapy, Holly accused her father of sexually molesting her. Holly's experience is an example of repressed memories, whose truthfulness and accuracy we'll discuss later in this module.

Definitions

What are the three memory processes?

Rajan's amazing ability to recall thousands of digits and Holly's delayed remembering of terrible but difficult-to-verify childhood experiences involve three different memory processes.

Memory is the ability to retain information over time through three processes: encoding (forming), storing, and retrieving. Memories are not copies but representations of the world that vary in accuracy and are subject to error and bias.

We'll briefly define each of the three memory processes because they are the keys to understanding the interesting and complex process of how we remember and thus create the world we live in.

1 Encoding

Rajan developed a method or code to form memories for digits, a process called encoding.

Encoding refers to making mental representations of information so that it can be placed into our memories.

For example, Rajan encoded the number 111 by associating it with Admiral Nelson, who happened to have one eye, one arm, and one leg.

2 Storing

Rajan used associations to encode information because associations are also useful for storing information.

Storing is the process of placing encoded information into relatively permanent mental storage for later recall.

New information that is stored by making associations with old or familiar information is much easier to remember, or retrieve.

3 Retrieving

Rajan was able to recall, or retrieve, 31,811 digits in order.

Retrieving is the process of getting or recalling information that has been placed into short-term or long-term storage.

Only a half-dozen people in the entire world can match Rajan's feat of encoding, storing, and retrieving thousands of digits in order. Students are familiar with the problems of retrieving information during an exam when they try but fail to retrieve information they have studied.

What's Coming

We'll discuss three kinds of memory, how memories are encoded, why emotional memories are long-lasting, the issue of repressed memories, and some unusual memory abilities. We'll start with an overview of the three kinds of memory.

A. Three Types of Memory

What are the three types? We often talk about memory as though it were a single process. In fact, a popular model of memory divides it into three different processes: sensory, short-term, and long-term memory (Atkinson & Shiffrin, 1971). To illustrate each of these processes, we'll examine what happens as you walk through a big city mall.

Sensory Memory

As you walk through a busy mall, you are bombarded by hundreds of sights, smells, and sounds, including the music of a lone guitarist playing for spare change. Many of these stimuli reach your sensory memory.

Sensory memory refers to an initial process that receives and holds environmental information in its raw form for a brief period of time, from an instant to several seconds.

For example, after reaching your ears, the guitarist's sounds are held in sensory memory for a second or two. Depending upon what you do next will determine what happens to the guitarist's sounds that are in your sensory memory.

If you pay no more attention to these sounds in sensory memory, they automatically *disappear* without a trace.

However, if you pay attention to the guitarist's music, the auditory information in sensory memory is transferred into another memory process called short-term memory.

Short-Term Memory

Because a few notes of the guitarist's song sounded interesting, you shifted your attention to that particular information in sensory memory. Paying attention to information in sensory memory causes it to be automatically transferred into short-term memory.

Short-term memory, also called *working memory,* refers to another process that can hold only a limited amount of information—an average of seven items—for only a short period of time—2 to 30 seconds.

Once a limited amount of information is transferred into short-term, or working, memory, it will remain there for up to 30 seconds. If during this time you become more involved in the information, such as humming to the music, the information will remain in short-term memory for a longer period of time.

However, the music will *disappear* after this relatively short time unless it is transferred into permanent storage, called long-term memory.

Long-Term Memory

If you become mentally engaged in humming along or wondering why the guitarist's music sounds familiar, there is a good chance that this mental activity will transfer the music from short-term into long-term memory.

Long-term memory refers to the process of storing almost unlimited amounts of information over long periods of time.

For example, you have stored hundreds of songs, terms, faces, and conversations in your long-term memory—information that is potentially available for retrieval. However, from personal experience, you know that you cannot always retrieve things you learned and know you know. In Module 12, we'll discuss reasons for forgetting information stored in long-term memory.

Now that you know what the three memory processes are, we'll explain how they work together.

Model: Three Types of Memory

1 **Sensory memory.** We'll explain how the three types of memory described above work and how attention determines what is remembered and what is forgotten.

Imagine listening to a lecture. All the information that enters your sensory memory remains for seconds or less. If you *do not pay attention* to information in sensory memory, it is forgotten. If you *do pay attention* to particular information, such as the instructor's words, this information is automatically transferred into short-term memory.

2 **Short-term memory.** If you *do not pay attention* to information in short-term memory, it is not encoded and is forgotten. If you *do pay attention* by rehearsing the information, such as taking notes, the information will be encoded for storage in long-term memory. That's why it helps to take lecture notes.

3 **Long-term memory.** Information that is encoded for storage in long-term memory will remain there on a relatively permanent basis. Whether or not you can recall the instructor's words from long-term memory depends partly on how it is encoded, which we'll discuss later. This means that poor class notes may result in poor encoding and poor recall on exams. The secret to great encoding is to make new associations, which increases chances of recall.

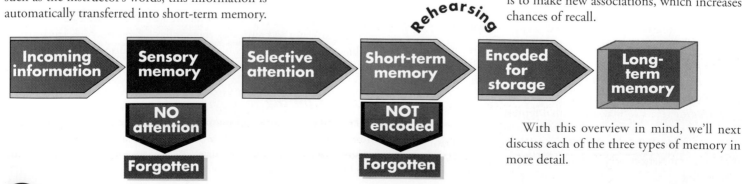

Incoming information → Sensory memory → Selective attention → Short-term memory → Encoded for storage → Long-term memory

NO attention → Forgotten

NOT encoded → Forgotten

Rehearsing

With this overview in mind, we'll next discuss each of the three types of memory in more detail.

Do you have a video recorder?

You have something like a mental video-audio recorder that automatically receives and holds incoming sensory information for only seconds or less. This brief period provides just enough time for you to decide whether some particular incoming information is important or interesting and therefore needs your further attention. We'll examine two different kinds of sensory memory: visual sensory memory, called iconic memory; and auditory sensory memory, called echoic memory.

Iconic Memory

Why do you see circles?

The woman in the photo is moving a sparkler round and round, and instead of seeing only dots of light from the end of the sparkler, you see a continuous circle of light. The reason you see a circle of light instead of separate dots is due to iconic *(eye-CON-ick)* memory.

Iconic memory is a form of sensory memory that holds visual information for about a quarter of a second or more. (The word *icon* means "image.")

For example, iconic memory briefly holds the sparkler's separate and individual images as it travels in a circle; as a result, you see a continuous circle of light rather than single dots of light.

Without iconic memory, our world would appear very jerky because our eyes normally move back and forth about four times a second as they fixate on different objects. We don't notice the darting movements of our eyes because iconic memory briefly stores visual images and thus makes objects appear stable despite the darting movements of our eyes.

To find a memory that lasts less than a second required a clever study.

IDENTIFYING ICONIC MEMORY

Here's the first study that showed the existence and length of iconic memory.

Procedure. Individual subjects sat in front of a screen upon which 12 letters (three rows of four letters) appeared for a very brief period of time (50 milliseconds, or 50/1,000 of a second). After each presentation, subjects were asked to recall a particular row of letters.

Results and conclusion. As shown in the graph below, if subjects responded immediately (0.0-second delay) after seeing letters, they remembered an average of nine letters. However, a delay of merely 0.5 seconds reduced memory to an average of six letters, and a delay of 1.0 second reduced memory to an average of only four letters (Sperling, 1960). Notice that an increased delay in responding resulted in subjects' remembering fewer letters, which indicated the brief duration of iconic memory—seconds or less.

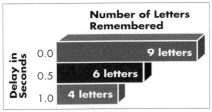

Number of Letters Remembered

Delay in Seconds	
0.0	9 letters
0.5	6 letters
1.0	4 letters

This study was the first to demonstrate the existence of sensory memory for visual information, which was called iconic memory. There is also a sensory memory for auditory information, called echoic memory.

Echoic Memory

What did you hear?

Without realizing, you have probably already experienced auditory sensory memory, which is called echoic *(eh-KO-ick)* memory.

Echoic memory is a form of sensory memory that holds auditory information for one or two seconds.

For instance, suppose you are absorbed in reading a novel and a friend asks you a question. You stop reading and ask, "What did you say?" As soon as those words are out of your mouth, you realize that you can recall, or play back, your friend's exact words. You can play

What did you say?

Oh, yes. Now I remember.

back these words because they are still in echoic memory, which may last as long as 2 seconds. In addition to letting you play back things you thought you did not hear, echoic memory also lets you hold speech sounds long enough to know that a sequence of certain sounds forms words (Norman, 1982).

Because of the importance of sensory memory, both iconic and echoic, we'll review its functions.

Functions of Sensory Memory

1 Prevents being overwhelmed. Sensory memory keeps you from being overwhelmed by too many incoming stimuli because anything you do not attend to will vanish in seconds.

Incoming information → Sensory memory → NO attention → Forgotten

2 Gives decision time. Sensory memory gives you a few seconds to decide whether some incoming information is interesting or important. Information you pay attention to will automatically be transferred to short-term memory.

3 Provides stability, playback, and recognition. Iconic memory makes things in your visual world appear smooth and continuous (see above photo of sparkler) despite frequent blinks and eye movements. Echoic memory lets you play back auditory information and gives you time to recognize sounds as words.

If you attend to information in sensory memory, it goes into short-term memory, the next topic.

C. Short-Term Memory: Working

Definition

What was that phone number?

Imagine looking up a telephone number for take-out pizza. You repeat it over and over as you dial the number. However, after giving your order and hanging up, you have forgotten the number. This example reveals two characteristics of short-term memory.

Short-term memory, more recently called *working memory,* refers to a process that can hold a limited amount of information—an average of seven items—for a limited period of time—2 to 30 seconds. However, the relatively short duration can be lengthened by repeating or rehearsing the information.

For good reason, telephone numbers and postal ZIP codes are seven numbers or fewer because that is about the limit of short-term memory. The reason we find ourselves repeating or rehearsing a new phone number is to keep it available in short-term memory, at least until we finish dialing it.

Recent studies using brain scans (PET scans) indicate that we have different working (short-term) memory systems for spatial, object, and verbal information (Smith & Jonides, 1997). This means that different parts of the brain are involved in these three functions.

We'll discuss two interesting features of working, or short-term, memory: limited duration and limited capacity.

Two Features

LIMITED DURATION

The new telephone number that you looked up will remain in short-term memory for a brief time, usually from 2 to 30 seconds, and then disappear. However, you can keep information longer in short-term memory by using maintenance rehearsal.

Maintenance rehearsal refers to the practice of intentionally repeating or rehearsing information so that it remains longer in short-term memory.

Researchers studied how long information is remembered without practice or rehearsal by asking subjects to remember a series of consonants composed of three meaningless letters, such as CHJ. Subjects were prevented from rehearsing, or repeating, these consonants by having them count backward immediately after seeing the groups of three letters.

As the graph (below right) shows, 80% of the subjects recalled the groups of three letters after 3 seconds. However, only 10% of subjects recalled the groups of three letters after 15 seconds (Peterson & Peterson, 1950).

Although this task—remembering groups of three letters—seemed easy, almost all the subjects had forgotten the groups of three letters after 15 seconds if they were prevented from rehearsing. This study clearly showed that information disappears from short-term memory within seconds unless we promptly and continually rehearse the information.

In comparison, maintenance rehearsal can considerably extend the time that information remains in short-term memory. However, during maintenance rehearsal, new information cannot enter short-term memory.

Besides having a limited duration, the second feature of short-term memory is that it has a limited capacity.

LIMITED CAPACITY

In previous modules, we pointed out several studies that are considered classic because they challenged old concepts or identified significant new information. One such classic study is that of George Miller (1956), who was the first to discover that short-term memory can hold only about seven items or bits, plus or minus two. Although this seems like too limited a number, researchers have repeatedly confirmed Miller's original finding (Baddeley, 1994; Shiffrin & Nosofsky, 1994). Thus, one reason telephone numbers worldwide are generally limited to seven digits is because that matches the capacity of short-term memory.

It is easy to confirm Miller's finding with a *memory span test,* which measures the total number of digits that we can repeat back in the correct order after a single hearing. For example, students make few errors when asked to repeat seven or eight digits, make some errors with a list of eight or nine digits, and make many errors when repeating a list that is longer than nine digits. One of the main reasons information disappears from short-term memory is because of interference (Shiffrin & Nosofsky, 1994).

Interference results when new information enters short-term memory and overwrites or pushes out information that is already there.

For example, if you are trying to remember a phone number and someone asks you a question, the question interferes with or wipes away the phone number. One way to prevent interference is through rehearsal. However, once we stop rehearsing, the information in short-term memory may disappear.

Although short-term memory has a limited capacity and duration, it is possible to increase both. For example, I use a classroom demonstration in which I guarantee that any student can learn to memorize a list of 23 digits, in exact order, in just 25 seconds. This impressive memory demonstration, which always works, is accomplished by knowing how to use something called chunking.

Chunking

How does Rajan remember 11131217 351802?

Although short-term memory can hold only an average of seven items for a brief period of time, it is possible to increase the length of each item by using a process called chunking.

Chunking is combining separate items of information into a larger unit, or chunk, and then remembering chunks of information rather than individual items.

One of the interesting things about Rajan's prodigious memory for numbers is his ability to chunk. For instance, in about 2 minutes Rajan (right photo) memorized 36 random numbers (in a block of 6 × 6) written on a blackboard. He was able to repeat the numbers forward and backward and to state those in any individual row, column, or diagonal.

When asked about his method for memorizing numbers, he replied that he automatically arranged the numbers into chunks and gave the chunks a name.

For example, here's how he chunked the first 14 numbers: 11131217351802. He chunked 111 and named it "Nelson" because Admiral Nelson had one eye, one arm, and one leg; he chunked 312 and named it the "area code of Chicago"; he chunked 1735 and named it "29" because Ben Franklin was 29 in 1735; and he chunked 1802 as "plus 2" because John Adams occupied the White House in 1800. When Rajan wants to recall the numbers, he does so by remembering a string of associations: Nelson, area code of Chicago, Ben Franklin, and John Adams. As Rajan explains, he doesn't know why he makes particular associations; they just come to him.

Sometimes we use chunking without thinking about it. For example, to remember the 11-digit phone number 16228759211, we break it into four chunks: 1-622-875-9211.

As first suggested by George Miller (1956), chunking is a powerful strategy to increase the amount of information that we can hold in short-term memory.

Here's a review of the major functions of short-term memory.

Functions of Short-Term Memory

Why is it also called working memory?

Imagine being able to store information on a mental blackboard that is automatically erased every few seconds, and you'll have a good picture of short-term memory. The name *short-term memory* is gradually being changed to *working memory* to indicate that it's an active process that has two parts. Researchers found that one part of short-term, or working, memory involves actively holding information, and that part is located in the front part of the brain; a second part for passively storing information is located in the back part of the brain (Smith & Jonides, 1997). We'll examine how paying attention transfers information into working memory, how rehearsing keeps the information there, and why some information is eventually stored.

1 Attending

Imagine driving along with your radio on while a friend in the passenger seat is talking about the weekend. A tremendous amount of information is entering your sensory memory, but you avoid stimulus overload because incoming information automatically vanishes in seconds unless you pay attention to it.

The moment you pay attention to information in sensory memory, that information enters short-term memory for further processing. For example, while your friend is talking, you don't pay attention to the radio until your favorite song comes on and enters sensory memory. As you pay attention, you hear the radio, even though it has been playing the whole time. One function of short-term memory is that it allows us *to selectively attend to information that is relevant and disregard everything else.*

Once information enters short-term, or working, memory several things may happen.

2 Rehearsing

Once information enters short-term memory, it usually remains for only seconds unless you rehearse it. For example, the announcer on the car radio gives a phone number to call for free movie tickets. But

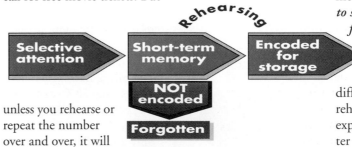

unless you rehearse or repeat the number over and over, it will probably disappear from your short-term memory because of interference from newly arriving information. Another function of short-term memory is that it allows you *to hold information for a short period of time until you decide what to do with it.*

If you rehearse the information in short-term memory, you increase the chances of storing it.

3 Storing

Rehearsing information not only holds that information in short-term memory but also helps *to store or encode information in long-term memory.*

Later, we'll discuss the two different kinds of rehearsing (p. 249) and explain why one is better than the other for storing or encoding of information in long-term memory.

Next, we'll describe the entire memory process and the features of long-term memory.

D. Long-Term Memory: Storing

Steps in the Memory Process

Is it a thing or a process? Don't think of sensory memory, short-term memory, and long-term memory as *things* but rather as on-going and interacting *processes*. To illustrate how these processes interact, we describe what happens as you hear a new song title that you want to remember.

1 Sensory memory. As you drive around with the car radio on, the incoming information is held for seconds or less in sensory memory. Some of the auditory information includes the announcer's words: "Remember this song title, 'Your Love Is Like Chocolate,' and win two movie tickets."

2 Attention. If you pay no attention to this title, it will disappear forever from sensory memory. However, if you pay attention because you want to win the tickets, the title, "Your Love Is Like Chocolate," will automatically be transferred into short-term memory for further processing.

Your love is like chocolate

3 Short-term memory. Once the song title is in short-term memory, you have a short time (2–30 seconds) for further processing. If you lose interest or are distracted by traffic, the title will likely disappear and be forgotten. However, if you rehearse the song title, it will likely be transferred to, and encoded in, your long-term memory.

4 Encoding. You place information in long-term memory through a process called encoding.

Encoding refers to the process of transferring information from short-term to long-term memory by paying attention to it, repeating or rehearsing it, or forming new associations.

For example, if a song title is catchy, unusual, or reminds you of something, such as a heart and a chocolate cake, you may easily form new associations and encode the title almost automatically and with little effort. However, if you think the title is dumb or always have trouble remembering songs, then you will have to make a deliberate effort to encode the title in long-term memory. One secret to improving long-term memory, especially for difficult items, is to make a deliberate effort to encode information by making associations (Schacter, 1996).

5 Long-term memory. Once the song title is encoded in long-term memory, it has the potential to remain there for your lifetime.

Long-term memory refers to the process of storing almost unlimited amounts of information over long periods of time with the potential of retrieving, or remembering, such information in the future.

Encoded for storage → Long-term memory "Your Love is Like Chocolate"

For example, next week, month, or year, you may try to recall the song title from long-term memory by placing it back into short-term memory. How easily and accurately you can recall, or retrieve, information depends on several factors (McDonald & Hirt, 1997).

6 Retrieving. When people talk about remembering, they usually mean retrieving.

Retrieving is the process for selecting information from long-term memory and transferring it back into short-term memory.

Your love is like _____?

It will be easier to retrieve, or recall, a song's title if you encoded it by making associations with information already stored in long-term memory. However, if you only repeated the title or did not make associations or heard a similar title that caused interference, you will have difficulty retrieving that particular song title. Later on, we'll discuss in more detail how best to encode information in long-term memory.

Features of Long-Term Memory

How big and accurate? **Capacity and permanency.** Researchers estimate that long-term memory has an almost unlimited capacity to store information. Anything stored has the potential to last a lifetime, provided drugs or disease do not damage the brain's memory circuits (Stein et al., 1997).

Retrieval and accuracy. Although all information in long-term memory has the potential to be retrieved, how much we can actually retrieve depends on a number of factors, including how it was encoded and the amount of interference from related information. In addition, researchers found that the content and accuracy of long-term memories may undergo change and distortion across time, as occurred in the following study.

College freshmen were asked to recall grades from all 4 years of high school. As the graph on the right shows, students accurately recalled 89% of grades of A but only 29% of grades of D. Thus, students were much more accurate recalling positive events, grades of A, than they were for

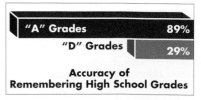

| "A" Grades | 89% |
| "D" Grades | 29% |

Accuracy of Remembering High School Grades

recalling negative events, grades of D (Bahrick et al., 1996). This study shows that we do not recall all events with the same accuracy, often inflating positive events and eliminating negative ones. The reasons we may change, distort, or forget information is discussed in Module 12.

Next, we'll explain how psychologists demonstrated the existence of two separate memory processes: a short-term and a long-term memory process.

Separate Memory Systems

What is the evidence?

Most of us have been to parties where we were introduced to people whose names we tried to remember but completely forgot 30 minutes later. This is a perfect example of the limits of short-term memory. At the same time, most of us can remember the content of many conversations that we have with our friends each day. This is a perfect example of the durability of long-term memory. Besides our personal experiences, there are two other kinds of evidence for the separate existence of short- and long-term memory. Some evidence comes from research that shows brain damage can cause serious deficits in long-term memory while completely sparing short-term memory. We'll discuss these biological memory factors a little later. Other evidence comes from research on which items in a relatively long list are best remembered. We'll give you a chance to memorize a list of items and demonstrate to yourself the separate existence of short- and long-term memory.

Primacy versus Recency

Can you remember this list?

Please read the following list only once and try to remember the animals' names.

**bear, giraffe, wolf, fly, deer,
elk, gorilla, elephant, frog, snail,
turtle, shark, ant, owl**

Immediately after reading this list, write down (in any order) as many of the animals' names as you can remember.

If you examine the list of names that you wrote down, you'll discover a definite pattern to the order of the names that you remembered. For example, here's the order in which names in the above list would most likely be remembered.

First items: Primacy effect. In studies using similar lists, subjects more easily recalled the *first* four or five items (bear, giraffe, wolf) because subjects had more time to rehearse the first words presented. As a result of rehearsing, these first names were transferred to and stored in long-term memory, from which they were recalled. This phenomenon is called the primacy effect.

The *primacy effect* refers to better recall, or improvement in retention, of information presented at the beginning of a task.

Middle items. Subjects did not recall many items from the *middle* of the list (gorilla, elephant, frog) because they did not have much time to rehearse them. When trying to remember items from the middle of the list, their attention and time was split between trying to remember the previous terms and trying to rehearse new ones. Less rehearsal meant that fewer middle names were stored in long-term memory; more interference meant that fewer names remained in short-term memory.

Last items: Recency effect. Subjects more easily recalled the *last* four or five items (turtle, shark, ant, owl) because they were still available in short-term memory and could be read off a mental list. This phenomenon is called the recency effect.

The *recency effect* refers to better recall, or improvement in retention, of information presented at the end of a task.

Together, these two effects are called the primacy-recency effect.

The *primacy-recency effect* refers to better recall of information presented at the beginning and end of a task.

As we'll explain next, the primacy-recency effect is evidence that short- and long-term memory are two separate processes.

Short-Term versus Long-Term Memory

Why didn't you remember "elephant"?

One reason you probably didn't remember the name "elephant" is because it came from the middle of the list. The middle section of a list is usually least remembered because that information may no longer be retained in short-term memory and may not have been encoded in long-term memory. Evidence for the primacy-recency effect is shown in the graph below (Glanzer & Cunitz, 1966).

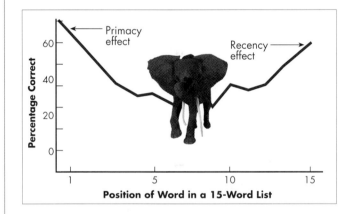

Position of Word in a 15-Word List

For example, subjects showed better recall (70%) for first items presented, which is the primacy effect. The primacy effect occurs because subjects have more time to rehearse the first items, which increases the chances of transferring these items into long-term memory. Remember that rehearsal has two functions: keeping information longer in short-term memory and promoting encoding—the transfer of information into long-term memory.

In addition, subjects showed better recall (60%) for the last items presented, which is the recency effect. Sometimes subjects say that they can still "hear these words" and usually report these items first. The recency effect occurs because the last items are still in short-term memory, from which they are recalled (Glanzer & Cunitz, 1966).

The occurrence of the primacy-recency effect suggested the existence of two separate kinds of memory processes, which we now call short-term and long-term memory (Atkinson & Shiffrin, 1968; Neath, 1998).

Next, you'll discover that instead of one, there are several different kinds of long-term memory.

D. Long-Term Memory: Storing

Declarative versus Procedural

Where do I store reading and skiing?

When I ski down a hill, I can't tell you exactly what my body does to stay upright. When I read a scientific article, I can tell you much of what I have read. These two activities, skiing and reading, use two different kinds of long-term memory. The discovery of two kinds of long-term memory is one of the newest findings, and like many discoveries in science, it happened by accident.

Researchers were testing a patient, well-known in memory circles as H. M., who suffered severe memory loss because of an earlier brain operation to reduce his seizures. H. M.'s task seemed simple: draw a star by guiding your hand while looking into a mirror. However, this mirror-drawing test is relatively difficult because looking into a mirror reverses all hand movements:

up is down and down is up. As H. M. did this task each day, his drawing improved, indicating that he was learning and remembering the necessary motor skills. But here's the strange part. Each and every day, H. M. would insist that he had never seen or done mirror-drawing before (Cohen, 1984).

How could H. M. have no memory of mirror-drawing, yet show a steady improvement in his performance as he practiced it each day? Based on H. M.'s mirror-drawing as well as data from other patients and numerous animal studies, researchers discovered that there are two different kinds of long-term memory, each involving different areas of the brain (Schacter & Tulving, 1994; Squire, 1994).

You'll understand why H. M. could improve at mirror-drawing but not remember doing it as we describe the two kinds of long-term memory: declarative and procedural.

Declarative Memory

Which bird cannot fly?
What did you have today for breakfast?

You would find the answers to these questions in one kind of long-term memory called declarative memory.

Declarative memory involves memories for facts or events, such as scenes, stories, words, conversations, faces, or daily events. We are aware of and can recall, or retrieve, these kinds of memories.

There are two kinds of declarative memory—semantic and episodic (Eichenbaum, 1997).

Semantic memory.
"Which bird cannot fly?" asks you to remember a fact, which involves semantic *(sah-MANT-ic)* memory.

Semantic memory is a type of declarative memory and involves knowledge of facts, concepts, words, definitions, and language rules.

Much of what you *learn* in classes goes into semantic memory (Ojemann et al., 1997).

Episodic memory.
"What did you have today for breakfast?" asks you to remember an event, which involves episodic *(ep-ih-SAW-dik)* memory.

Episodic memory is a type of declarative memory and involves knowledge of specific events, personal experiences (episodes) or activities, such as naming or describing favorite restaurants, movies, songs, habits, or hobbies.

Much of what you *do* in college goes into episodic memory.

Since his brain operation, H. M. cannot remember new facts (semantic memory) or events (episodic memory). Thus, H. M. has lost declarative memory, which explains why he does not remember events, such as mirror-drawing (Cohen, 1994).

However, because his motor skills improved, there must be another kind of long-term memory. And there is.

Procedural Memory

How did you learn to play tennis?
Why are you afraid of spiders?

In answering these kinds of questions, we use procedural memory.

Procedural memory involves memories for skills (playing tennis), habits (brushing teeth), and things learned through classical conditioning (fear of spiders). We are not aware of these memories and cannot retrieve them.

For example, even if you have not played tennis for years, you can pick up a racket and still remember how to serve because that information is stored in procedural memory. However, you cannot describe the sequence of detailed movements needed to serve a ball, because this sequence of movements is stored in procedural memory. Similarly, if through classical conditioning you learned to fear spiders, you may not now be able to explain why you're afraid, because the reason is stored in procedural memory. These examples indicate that although procedural memory greatly influences our behavior, we have neither awareness nor ability to recall these memories (Gabrieli et al., 1995; Mathews, 1997).

Now, we can explain H. M.'s strange behavior. He was able to improve at mirror-drawing because it involved learning a motor skill that was stored in procedural memory. But he could not talk about the skill, because no one is aware of their procedural memories. Although H. M. improved at mirror-drawing, he could not remember the event of sitting down and drawing, because that involves declarative (episodic) memories, which were damaged in his brain surgery (Hilts, 1995). The study of H. M. is a classic because it first demonstrated the existence of two kinds of long-term memory: declarative memory and procedural memory. We'll discuss the brain systems underlying these types of long-term memory in Module 12.

Next, we'll describe how strong emotions influence memories.

Animal Model

Do hormones affect memories?

Many of us have vivid memories that involve highly charged emotional situations, such as graduating from school or college, meeting someone special, getting married, attending the funeral of a loved one, or achieving a long-sought-after goal in life (Stein et al., 1997).

For example, the tennis player in the photo has just won a major tennis championship that he will likely remember the rest of his life. Does something happen during an emotional state that increases the chances of our remembering a particular situation, person, or event?

The answer to this question involved a long-term research program that began in animals. In Module 2 we explained that researchers may use an animal model (p. 32) to answer questions that for safety, moral, or ethical reasons cannot involve human subjects. Because of safety concerns, neuropsychologist

James McGaugh used an animal model to study the effects of drugs and hormones on memory. He found that certain drugs or hormones associated with emotional experiences could either increase or decrease the recall of long-term memories (Gold & McGaugh, 1975). For example, if rats were given an injection of a hormone (epinephrine) that is normally produced by the body during emotional or stressful states, rats remembered better what they had just learned (McGaugh, 1990).

Based on his animal research, McGaugh believed that one reason emotions seem to "stamp in" memories is to help species survive. For instance, if emotions stamped in memories of emotional or life-threatening situations, our early ancestors would better remember to avoid these dangers and thus increase their chances of survival.

After McGaugh's animal model established that drugs and "emotional" hormones were safe and did seem to stamp in memories, he was ready to use human subjects.

Memories of Emotional Events

Can drugs block emotional memories?

Almost 20 years of research on the animal model had shown that certain drugs and emotionally produced hormones increased or decreased recall of memories, McGaugh and his colleagues found a way to safely study this phenomenon in humans.

Subjects. Those in the experimental group received a drug (propranolol) that decreases or blocks the effects of hormones (epinephrine and norepinephrine) that are normally produced during emotional states. After taking this drug, experimental subjects would still feel emotions, but the drug would block the secretion of those emotionally produced hormones that had been shown to facilitate retention in animals. Subjects in the control group received a placebo, but because of the double-blind procedure, no subjects knew whether they were given a drug or a placebo.

Procedure. So that the drugs would have time to act, subjects were given either a placebo or drug 1 hour before seeing a series of slides. To prevent their expectations from biasing the results, subjects did not know whether they got a drug or placebo.

Each subject watched a series of 12 slides and heard an accompanying story. The beginning of the slide story was emotionally neutral and simply described a mother leaving home with her son to visit her husband's workplace. The middle of the slide story was emotionally charged and described the son having a terrible accident in which his feet were severed and his skull was damaged. The end of the slide story was emotionally neutral and described the mother leaving the hospital to pick up her other child from preschool. Subjects were tested for retention of the slide story a week later.

Hypothesis. Based on their results from the animal model, McGaugh and his colleagues guessed that if a drug blocked the effects of memory-enhancing hormones normally produced during emotional situations, subjects who took the drug should show poor retention for emotional events.

Results and conclusion. Notice in the graph below that, compared to subjects in the placebo group, subjects given a drug that blocked "emotional" hormones remembered significantly fewer emotionally charged events (Cahill et al., 1994). However, both drug and placebo subjects remembered about the same number of neutral events that were described at the beginning and end of the slide show. This study found that the hormone-blocking drug interfered with memories for emotional events but not neutral events.

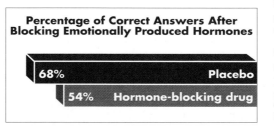

Percentage of Correct Answers After Blocking Emotionally Produced Hormones

68% Placebo

54% Hormone-blocking drug

Researchers concluded that intense feelings triggered by emotional or stressful situations are encoded, or "carved in stone," by hormones released during emotionally charged situations (Cahill et al., 1994; McGaugh, 1990). Researchers speculate that the evolution of a carved-in-stone memory system may have helped species survive by increasing retention for dangerous or life-threatening situations. This research is a good example of how an animal model laid the basis for an important study showing that emotion-produced hormones influence memory in humans.

In some cases, memories of emotionally charged situations may be encoded without effort, such as remembering a good grade. However, you'll see that in other cases, such as memorizing a definition, encoding may require great and deliberate effort.

F. Encoding: Transferring

Two Kinds

How do we store memories?

Most partners in close relationships play a conversation game that has only two rules. The first rule is that I ask about your day, and it's your turn to describe in considerable detail numerous bad and good things that happened to you. The second rule is that you then ask about my day, and then it's my turn to describe in considerable detail numerous bad and good things that happened to me. And then we both feel better. The reason we can play this game is that bad and good events are encoded in our memories, often in amazing detail, with little or no effort or awareness on our parts.

Encoding refers to placing, or storing, information, such as an object, event, or sound (music, noise, speech), in memory by making mental representations.

Although some information, such as conversations, may be encoded automatically, other information, such as memorizing terms, usually requires deliberate effort. These two kinds of processes are called automatic and effortful encoding.

Automatic Encoding

Why are some things easy to encode?

One reason the person in the illustration below can recall a list of very detailed personal activities is that this information is automatically encoded into long-term memory. In fact, many personal events (often unpleasant ones), as well as interesting facts and a wide range of skills and habits, are automatically encoded.

Automatic encoding is the transfer of information from short-term into long-term memory without any effort and usually without any awareness.

Personal events. One reason many of your personal experiences and conversations are automatically encoded is that they hold your interest and attention and easily fit together with hundreds of previous associations. Because personal experiences, which are examples of *episodic information*, are encoded automatically into long-term memory, you can easily recall lengthy conversations, movie plots, television shows, clothes you bought, or food you ate.

I bought this hat at a second-hand store for a quarter, and then I bought these shoes from a guy who said that he makes them from old tires....

Interesting facts. You may know avid sports fans or watchers of daily TV soap operas who remember an amazing number of facts and details, seemingly without effort. If these kinds of facts, which are examples of *semantic information*, are personally interesting and fit with previous associations, then they are automatically encoded into declarative long-term memory.

Skills and habits. Learning how to perform various motor skills, such as playing tennis or riding a bike, or developing habits, such as brushing your teeth, are examples of *procedural information*, which is also encoded automatically. For example, H. M. learned and remembered how to mirror-draw because mirror-drawing is a motor skill that is automatically encoded into procedural long-term memory.

On the other hand, factual or technical information from textbooks is usually not encoded automatically but rather requires deliberate, or effortful, encoding, which we'll discuss next.

Effortful Encoding

Why are some things hard to encode?

One reason the person in the illustration below is pulling his hair is that learning unfamiliar or complicated material, which involves *semantic information*, usually takes a relatively long time to encode. Such information, especially if it is uninteresting, complicated, or requires making new or difficult associations, can be encoded only with considerable concentration and effort.

Effortful encoding involves the transfer of information from short-term into long-term memory either by working hard to repeat or rehearse the information or, especially, by making associations between new and old information.

You already know that some information, such as learning a skill, habit, or personal event, is often encoded effortlessly and automatically. However, other information, such as learning hundreds of new or difficult terms, facts, concepts, or equations, usually requires effortful encoding because you must form hundreds of new associations. Forming new associations is often just plain hard work and

I've been reading and taking notes and studying these items for hours and I'm still confused!

is made even more difficult if you are simultaneously taking two or three difficult classes or have limited time because of other responsibilities, such as a part-time job.

Although there are two methods of effortful encoding—rehearsing and forming associations—the most effective method involves forming associations between the new information that you are trying to learn and the old information that you have already stored in long-term memory.

We'll next explain the two methods of effortful encoding, rehearsing and forming associations, and why the second method is more effective and results in better recall.

Methods of Effortful Encoding

The reason for spending so much time outlining, taking notes, and studying a textbook is that this is one way to encode this information in your brain (figure below). However, encoding a fact, concept, or definition does not guarantee you'll be able to retrieve this information at a later time, such as during an exam. Think of encoding as putting information into a gigantic storage place that is called long-term memory. But unless you have a good system for keeping track of where you put the information, you may have great difficulty finding and recalling it from long-term memory. One system to keep track of where information is stored is to use a process called effortful encoding, which takes two forms—maintenance rehearsal and elaborative rehearsal (Neath, 1998; Schacter, 1996).

MAINTENANCE REHEARSAL

One way people try to remember a new phone number, 926-4029, is to repeat or rehearse it. This process of encoding is called maintenance rehearsal.

Maintenance rehearsal refers to simply repeating or rehearsing the information rather than forming any new associations.

Maintenance rehearsal works best for maintaining or keeping information longer in short-term memory, such as remembering a phone number for a few seconds while dialing it. However, if you want to remember the phone number later, maintenance rehearsal is not a good encoding process because it does not include a system for keeping track of how and where that particular phone number will be stored. If you keep looking up the same phone number, it's probably because you encoded it using maintenance rehearsal rather than by making associations, which is called elaborative rehearsal.

ELABORATIVE REHEARSAL

A better method of encoding a particular phone number is to make associations between new and old information. For example, I associate this phone number, 926-4029, with age: the oldest person I know is "926," I'm "40," but I wish I were "29." To recall this number, I think of the age associations that I made. This method of encoding information is called elaborative rehearsal.

Elaborative rehearsal involves actively making meaningful associations between information to be learned with information already stored in long-term memory.

For example, researchers asked students to remember groups of three words, such as *dog, bicycle,* and *street.* Researchers found that students who used maintenance rehearsal to encode groups of three words did poorly on recall. In comparison, students who used elaborative rehearsal by making associations that grouped the three words, such as "The dog rode the bicycle down the street," had significantly better recall (McDaniel & Einstein, 1986).

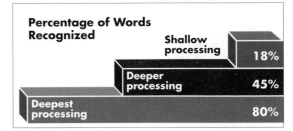

One reason elaborative rehearsal is such an effective system of encoding is that it involves making associations that help you keep track of where the new information is stored in long-term memory. Later, you can use these associations to locate the information and recall it from long-term memory.

Levels of Processing

The poorest system for encoding information is to simply repeat the information, which is maintenance rehearsal. The best encoding system is to make associations, which is elaborative rehearsal. How much effort and time you put into encoding information is the basis for the levels-of-processing theory (Craik & Lockhart, 1972).

The *levels-of-processing theory* says that remembering depends on how information is encoded. If you encode by paying attention only to basic features (length of phone number), information is encoded at a shallow level and results in poor recall. If you encode by making new associations, this information will be encoded at a deeper level, which results in better recall.

For example, students were shown a series of words, and asked a question after each one. The questions were of three types, designed to trigger three different levels of processing.

1. Shallow processing question:
"Is the word printed in capital letters?" Asks about one physical feature of the word.

2. Deeper processing question:
"Does the word rhyme with *rain?*" Asks about sound properties of the word.

3. Deepest processing question:
"Does the word fit into the sentence 'She was late for the _____'?" Asks about the meaning of the word.

After students answered these questions, they were tested to see how many of the original words they recognized.

Percentage of Words Recognized

Shallow processing	18%
Deeper processing	45%
Deepest processing	80%

As shown in the graph above, students recognized the least percentage of words after shallow processing and the most after the deepest processing (Craik & Tulving, 1975).

This study clearly demonstrates that the system you use to process or encode information has a great effect on how easily you can retrieve the information. As we'll discuss in Module 12, a major reason for forgetting is poor encoding.

Next, we discuss a kind of memory that has resulted in great controversy because of the difficulties in determining whether the event ever happened.

G: Repressed Memories

Sexual Abuse

Did he do it? At the beginning of this module, we discussed the case of Holly (left photo), who had accused her father (right photo) of sexual molestation beginning when she was 6 years old. Holly's memories of sexual abuse first surfaced during therapy sessions 13 years later, when she was 19. The father sued Holly's therapists for implanting false memories. The jury partly agreed with the father in deciding that Holly's memories were probably false and that the therapists had not implanted the memories but had negligently reinforced them (Butler, 1994). More recently, a state appeals court dismissed Holly's case against her father because some of her testimony about sexual abuse was obtained under sodium amytal, the so-called truth serum, which was administered by her therapist. Because testimony taken under sodium amytal is often unreliable, it has been barred in California's courts since 1959 (*Los Angeles Times,* August 21, 1997).

Holly's case illustrates perhaps the most explosive psychological issue of the early 1990s, the problem of repressed memories. Almost every major newspaper and national magazine carried stories with headlines such as "When can memories be trusted?" (*Time,* October 28, 1991); "How the brain forms false memories" (*Newsweek,* March 14, 1994); or "Repressed memory of abuse questioned" (*San Diego Union-Tribune,* December 20, 1993). We'll divide this broad problem into four separate but related issues: definition, therapist's role, implantation of false memories, and accuracy.

1 Definition

What is a repressed memory? The idea of repressed memories is based on Sigmund Freud's theory of repression, which underlies much of his psychoanalytic theory of personality (discussed in Module 21).

Repression is the process by which the mind pushes a memory of some threatening or traumatic event deep into the unconscious. Once in the unconscious, the repressed memory cannot be retrieved at will and may remain there until something releases it and the person becomes aware of it.

The phenomenon of repression and repressed memories is supported by numerous clinical reports. For example, therapists describe a woman who entered therapy with sexual problems and uncovered memories of incest committed by her father; another woman entered therapy with problems of insomnia, low self-esteem, and other difficulties and recovered memories of her father sexually assaulting her (Rieker & Carmen, 1986; Schuker, 1979).

If people have repressed memories, how often do they report them? Researchers found that 18–59% of adult clients with a history of sexual abuse said that they had either forgotten or recently uncovered repressed memories of sexual abuse (Briere & Conte, 1993; Loftus et al., 1994). In her reviews of repressed memories, Elizabeth Loftus (1994; 1997b) cautions that, although these percentages are disturbingly high, it is difficult to interpret their accuracy because the formulation of questions about repressed memories can lead to misleading or biased results.

While clinical cases support the idea of repressed memories, their increased occurrence in the early 1990s has partly been blamed on the practices of some therapists (Loftus, 1993b; 1997b).

2 Therapist's Role

What is the danger? Therapists who treat survivors of incest and other traumatic situations maintain that repressed memories are so completely blocked that it may take deliberate suggestion and effort to release them, sometimes using hypnosis or so-called "truth serum," sodium amytal. Whatever the therapists' good intentions, Loftus (1993b; 1997b) wonders if some therapists are suggesting or implanting traumatic memories in their clients rather than releasing repressed ones. Most often, repressed memories and resulting accusations of sexual abuse were reported by women (87%) who were in therapy for depression or eating disorders (Gudjonsson, 1997).

For example, in one case a client recalls that her therapist insisted that she showed signs of having been sexually abused during childhood and probably had terrible memories buried in her unconscious. The client was dubious at first but, wanting to please her therapist, finally admitted to being raped at the age of 4. However, after leaving the hospital and enlisting help from new therapists, she concluded that the sexual assaults had never happened (Bower, 1993a).

There are also many examples of therapists who have helped clients recover and deal with terrible repressed memories (Gold et al., 1994). Thus, therapists are in the difficult position of trying to distinguish accurate accounts of repressed memories from those that may have been shaped or reinforced by the suggestions or expectations of the therapist (Byrd, 1994).

Questions about whether repressed memories can be influenced by a therapist's suggestions bring up the related and important question of whether false memories can be implanted.

3 Implanting False Memories

Because it appeared that, in some cases, therapists' suggestions may have contributed to implanting false memories, researchers studied whether false memories could in fact be implanted.

Researchers gave 24 adults a booklet that contained descriptions of three events that occurred when each adult was 5 years old (Loftus, 1997a). Two of the childhood events had *really happened* because they were obtained from parents or relatives. One childhood event of being lost in a shopping mall, crying, being comforted by an elderly woman, and finally getting reunited with the family, had *not happened*, according to parents and relatives. After reading the three events described in the booklet, the adults (aged 18–53) were asked to write what they remembered of the event or, if they did not remember, to write, "I do not remember this."

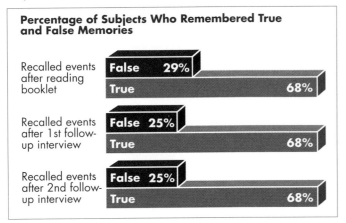

Percentage of Subjects Who Remembered True and False Memories

Recalled events after reading booklet — False 29% — True 68%

Recalled events after 1st follow-up interview — False 25% — True 68%

Recalled events after 2nd follow-up interview — False 25% — True 68%

The graph above shows that 68% of subjects remembered some or most of the two *true events* from their childhood. However, about 25% also said that they remembered having experienced the one *false event*, which was being lost in the mall at age 5. Even on followup interviews, 25% of the adult subjects continued to claim that they remembered experiencing the suggested but false event of being lost in the mall (Loftus, 1997a).

Researchers concluded that although the memory of being lost in a mall is neither as terrible nor terrifying as the memory of being abused, this study does show that false memories can be implanted through suggestion alone. Even on follow-up, subjects continued to insist that they had experienced the false event.

This and similar studies indicate that false memories can be implanted in both children and adults (Brainerd & Poole, 1997; Reyna & Lloyd, 1997). However, the fact that false memories can be implanted and later recalled as true does in no way disprove the occurrence of repressed memories. Rather, studies on implanting false memories simply show that a false suggestion can grow into a vivid, detailed, and believable personal memory (Ceci & Huffman, 1997).

But the fact that false memories can be implanted in children and adults raises the question about the accuracy of repressed memories.

4 Accuracy

From 10 to 50% of women are thought to have been sexually abused in childhood (Freyd, 1991). Some adults who were abused as children enter psychotherapy and can remember their childhood abuse. Other adults who were abused enter psychotherapy for different reasons, such as depression. During the course of therapy, their repressed memories of childhood abuse come back.

For example, a client who suffered from obesity entered a hospital weight-reduction program that also included psychotherapy. During therapy, she experienced flashbacks of being sexually abused from about age 5 by her older brother, who had since been killed in the war. When she searched through his things, she found a diary in which he had described sexual experiments with his little sister (Bower, 1993a). In this case, the woman's repressed memories of sexual abuse were proved accurate by confirming evidence, her brother's diary.

However, many individuals who recall repressed memories do not always have confirming evidence of events that happened 20–30 years earlier. When therapists have only the client's reports of repressed sexual abuse, therapists tend to believe their client's memories partly because there is little reason for their client to lie and partly because having been sexually abused as a child explains many of their client's current symptoms, such as having low self-esteem, experiencing sexual problems, or engaging in self-destructive behavior (Loftus, 1993b).

Although a significant number of psychotherapists believe that memories obtained under hypnosis are more likely to be accurate, this belief is untrue. Under hypnosis, people are more suggestible and may remember suggested or false memories as true ones (Yapko, 1994). Similarly, memories obtained under so-called truth serum, sodium amytal, are also open to suggestion and not allowed in many courts. Finally, more than 300 persons have now retracted charges of childhood sexual abuse based on "memories" recovered in therapy (de Rivera, 1997). Based on these retractions and other data, Loftus (1997a, 1997b) states that while there are examples of repressed memories that are accurate, therapists must guard against the possibility that some repressed memories may be false and arise from a person's need to explain his or her psychological problems.

Conclusions. Clinical cases provide evidence for the existence and accuracy of repressed memories. However, studies on implanting false memories show that a false suggestion can grow into a very believable, detailed experience. Because repressed memories frequently return during therapy sessions, advice to therapists includes not contaminating therapy with suggestions, guarding against personal biases, and being cautious about use of hypnosis (Byrd, 1994). All these precautions should not diminish the fact that sexual abuse is a very serious problem in our society and that repressed memories may represent one path clients take to deal with this terrible trauma (Gold et al., 1994).

After the Concept Review, we'll examine how both retrieval and encoding may be affected by cultural differences.

CONCEPT REVIEW

1. Three processes are involved in memory: the process in which information is placed or stored in memory by making mental representations is called (a)_____; the process of placing encoded information into a permanent mental state is called (b)_____; the process of getting information out of short-term or permanent storage is called (c)_____.

2. The initial step in memory is a process that holds visual and auditory information in its raw form for a very brief period of time, from an instant to several seconds; this process is called _____.

3. Memory that holds raw visual information for up to a quarter of a second is called (a)_____. Memory that holds raw auditory information for up to several seconds is called (b)_____. The process for controlling the transfer of information from sensory memory to the next memory process is (c)_____.

4. The kind of memory that has a limited capacity of about seven items (plus or minus two) and a short duration (2–30 seconds) for unrehearsed information is called either (a)_____ or _____. One way to increase this memory capacity is by combining separate pieces of information into larger units, which is called (b)_____. One way to increase the duration of this memory is by repeating the information, which is called (c)_____.

5. The kind of memory that can store almost unlimited amounts of information over a long period of time is _____, whose accuracy may undergo change and distortion across time.

6. The process for controlling the transfer of information from short-term memory into long-term memory is called _____, which may be automatic or may involve deliberate effort.

Your love is like chocolate

7. The process for selecting information from long-term memory and transferring it back into short-term memory is _____.

8. The better recall of items at the beginning of a list is called the (a)_____ effect. The better recall of items at the end of a list is called the (b)_____ effect. Evidence that there are two kinds of memory, short- and long-term, comes from the (c)_____ effect.

9. There are two kinds of encoding. Simply repeating or rehearsing the information is called (a)_____. Actively making associations between new and old information already stored is called (b)_____.

10. One kind of long-term memory that involves memories for facts or events, such as scenes, stories, words, conversations, faces, or daily events is called (a)_____ memory. We can retrieve these memories and are conscious of them. One kind of declarative memory that involves events or personal experiences is called (b)_____ memory. A second kind of declarative memory that involves general knowledge, facts, or definitions of words is called (c)_____ memory.

11. A second kind of long-term memory that involves performing motor or perceptual tasks, carrying out habits, and responding to stimuli because of classical conditioning is called _____ memory. We cannot retrieve these memories and are not conscious of them.

12. Something happens that is so threatening, shocking, or traumatic that our mind pushes that memory into the unconscious, from which it cannot be retrieved at will: this phenomenon is called _____.

13. During very emotional or stressful situations, the body secretes chemicals called (a)_____ that act to make encoding very effective, and this results in vivid, long-term memories. Researchers believe that this hormonal encoding system for stressful or emotional events has helped our species (b)_____.

Answers: 1. (a) encoding, (b) storage, (c) retrieval; 2. sensory memory; 3. (a) iconic memory, (b) echoic memory, (c) attention; 4. (a) short-term, or working, memory, (b) chunking, (c) rehearsal, or maintenance rehearsal; 5. long-term memory; 6. encoding; 7. retrieval; 8. (a) primacy, (b) recency, (c) primacy-recency; 9. (a) maintenance rehearsal, (b) elborative rehearsal; 10. (a) declarative, (b) episodic, (c) semantic; 11. procedural; 12. repression, or repressed memory; 13. (a) hormones, (b) survive.

H. Cultural Diversity: Oral versus Written

Emphasis in United States versus Africa

Do you remember better after hearing or reading?

If you went to school in the United States, you spent a considerable amount of your first 12 years learning to read and write. The U.S. culture regards these skills as very important for personal development as well as for achieving success in varied careers. For these reasons, the schools of many industrialized cultures place heavy emphasis on teaching reading and writing so that people can use these skills to encode great amounts of information in long-term memory. Similarly, much of the information you encode in college is done through reading and writing.

In contrast, if you went to school in the more rural countries of Africa, you would have spent your first dozen or so years learning through the spoken word rather than the written word. In less-industrialized countries of Africa, such as Ghana, there are fewer public or private schools, fewer textbooks and libraries. As a result, these cultures are said to have a strong *oral tradition*, which means that these people have considerable practice in passing on information through speaking and retelling, and they encode such information after hearing it rather than after reading it.

Because of these cultural differences, we would expect that African people, with a strong oral tradition, would better encode and remember information that was spoken. In comparison, we would expect that American people, who have a strong *written tradition,* would better encode and remember information that was read rather than spoken. Let's see if this hypothesis has been supported.

Remembering Spoken Information

WAR OF THE GHOSTS

One night, two young men from Egulac went down to the river to hunt seals, and while they were there it became foggy and calm. Then they heard war cries, and they thought: "Maybe this is a war party." They escaped to the shore, and hid behind a log. Now canoes came up, and they heard the noise of paddles, and saw one canoe coming up to them. There were five men in the canoe, and they said:

"What do you think? We wish to take you along. We are going up the river to make war on the people."

One of the young men said: "I have no arrows."

"Arrows are in the canoe," they said.

"I will not go along. I might be killed. My relatives do not know where I have gone. But you," he said, turning to the other, "may go with them."

So one of the young men went, but the other returned home.

And the warriors went up the river to a town on the other side of Kalama. The people came down to the water, and they began to fight, and many were killed. . . .

Who best remembered the ghost story?

On the left is part of a story called, "War of the Ghosts," which was read aloud in English to college students at Winneba Training College in Ghana and at New York University. Each group of students heard the story twice and were told to just listen to the story so that they would not take notes on their own. They were not told that they would be tested on its content.

Although English was not the native language of the Ghanaian students, they had learned English in previous schooling, and English was used exclusively in their Training College. Sixteen days after hearing "War of the Ghosts," students were asked to write down as much of the text as they could remember. Researchers scored the amount and accuracy of recalled information by counting the number of ideas or themes and the total number of words (330). The "War of the Ghosts" story has been used frequently in memory research because it can be broken down into 21 themes, or ideas, and easily scored. For example, two of the 21 themes or ideas are (1) two young men went to hunt seals, and (2) they heard war cries.

As the graph on the right shows, Ghanaian students remembered a significantly higher percentage of themes and a larger number of words than did American students. The Ghanaian students' superior performance was even more remarkable since they were tested by having to write the themes or ideas in English, which was their second language.

These results support the idea that the Ghanaian students showed superior recall of spoken information because of their long oral tradition, which involves practicing the encoding information through hearing rather than reading (Ross & Millsom, 1970). This study indicates that a culture's emphasis on how information is presented or taught can influence how information or events are encoded and how easily they can be recalled.

Next, we'll examine some unusual cases of encoding and retrieving information.

Average Number of Themes (%)

| 80% | Ghanaians |
| 57% | New Yorkers |

Average Number of Words (%)

| 70% | Ghanaians |
| 48% | New Yorkers |

I. Application: *Unusual Memories*

Photographic Memory

One kind of unusual memory that many wish they had is the ability to remember everything with little or no difficulty. Such an amazing memory is commonly called a photographic memory.

Photographic memory, which occurs in adults, is the ability to form sharp, detailed visual images after examining a picture or page for a short period of time and to recall the entire image at a later date.

There are no reports of someone developing a photographic memory and only one or two reports of adults who had a truly photographic memory (Stromeyer, 1970). Sometimes people with exceptional memories are mislabeled as having photographic memories.

For example, the photo below shows 8-year-old Jamil Moghul, who memorized all 77,934 words of the Koran, the Muslim holy book. Jamil accomplished this feat by beginning at age 5 and studying 5 to 6 hours a day. Yet neither Jamil, who memorized 77,934 words, nor Rajan, who we described earlier as having memorized 31,811 numbers,

claims to have a photographic memory. Rather, both have incredible abilities to encode information using elaborative rehearsal.

However, there is a very small percentage of children who do have photographic memories.

Eidetic Imagery

A small number of children have the ability to look at a picture for a few seconds and then describe it in great detail. This kind of remarkable memory is called eidetic *(eye-DET-ick)* imagery.

Eidetic imagery, which is a form of photographic memory that occurs in children, is the ability to examine a picture or page for 10–30 seconds and then for several minutes hold in one's mind a detailed visual image of the material.

For example, an 11-year-old girl was given the following instructions: "Look at this picture from Rudyard Kipling's *The Jungle Book* for a few minutes. Hold the details of this picture in your mind's eye for several minutes. Now, close your eyes and describe what you see."

After the picture (shown above) was removed, the young girl closed her eyes and, without hesitation, she described the picture in great detail, as follows: "Ground is dark greenish brown, then there's a mama and a little leopard and there's a native sitting against him. Then there's a pool with a crab coming out . . . with a fish in it, and I think there are turtles walking in front and a porcupine down near the right. There's a tree that separates a cow in half. The cow's brown and white, and there's something up in the tree—I can't see the bottom right-hand corner. There's a sun with a lot of rays on it near the top on the right . . . eight rays . . . the porcupine has a lot of bristles on it . . . the right is disappearing. I can still see that cow that's divided by the tree . . . Oh, there's a crocodile or alligator in the right-hand corner . . . It's very faint . . . It's gone" (Haber, 1980, p. 72).

What is unusual about her description is not only the amount of detail but the fact that she seems to be examining a vivid visual image of the actual drawing that seems to be held for a time in her mind's eye.

This girl's description is an example of eidetic imagery, which has been shown to be a real phenomenon that occurs in only about 5–8% of preadolescent children. The small percentage of children with eidetic imagery almost always lose the ability around adolescence (Neath, 1998).Why eidetic imagery drops out in adults is not known, but some suggest it may be because adults learn to use and rely more on words than on pictures (Crowder, 1992). The one or two times eidetic imagery did occur in adults it was usually called photographic memory.

Although most of us wish we had better memories, there are times when something happens that results in a very vivid and detailed image called a "flashbulb memory."

Flashbulb Memory

It was a crystal clear spring day with a deep blue San Diego sky and bright orange sun. I had driven the same route to my university so many times that I was doing it almost automatically, all the time thinking about something else. Suddenly brake lights began to flash in front of me. As I slowed down, I became alert and saw a black Toyota pickup truck about five cars in front of me swerve quickly to the outside to avoid hitting a stopping car. But the pickup driver had cut the turn too sharply. As if it happened in slow motion, I watched the pickup turn over and bounce as it hit the side of the freeway and then roll over again to land on its side. To this day, I can play back this terrible scene in great detail and vivid color as if I were watching a crash scene in a movie. Many individuals have had a similar experience, and this kind of memory event is called a flashbulb memory (Brown & Kulik, 1977).

Flashbulb memories are vivid recollections, usually in great detail, of dramatic or emotionally charged incidents that are of interest to the person. This information is encoded effortlessly and may last for long periods of time.

EMOTIONAL EVENTS

Flashbulb memories usually deal with events that are extremely surprising, emotionally arousing, or have very important meaning or consequences for the person. For example, when people were questioned about what they were doing when they heard that Presidents Kennedy or Reagan had been shot, or when the space shuttle Challenger exploded, about 80–90% could recall the exact details even 7 months later (Pillemer, 1984). Apparently, only those individuals for whom these events were personally significant developed flashbulb memories, so the personal involvement in the event is one condition for the formation of these memories (Wright & Gaskell, 1995). For example, whether or not you experienced a flashbulb memory when first hearing of Princess Diana's tragic car crash and death in the fall of 1997 will depend upon how much she meant to you.

MOST-REMEMBERED EVENTS

As you can see in the table (above right), the top five flashbulb memories of college students involved a car accident, a college roommate, high school graduation and prom, and a romantic experience, all of which are emotionally charged events (Rubin & Kozin, 1984).

Initially, flashbulb memories were claimed to represent a special kind of memory that was complete, accurate, vivid, and immune to forgetting (Brown & Kulik, 1977). Since then, several studies have investigated these claims and reported that flashbulb memories are not a separate, special kind of memory and that they are subject to inaccuracies, changes with retelling, and even forgotten over time (Bower, 1993b; Winograd & Neisser, 1992).

RECENT STUDY

In a recent multinational study of flashbulb memory, British and non-British people were asked what they were doing when they heard that the former Prime Minister Margaret Thatcher had resigned. Of the 215 British residents surveyed one year later, 86% reported having flashbulb memories, which occurred spontaneously and proved to be vivid, accurate, and full of detail. In comparison, less than 29% of 154 non-British subjects from North America and Denmark reported flashbulb memories of this event. Moreover, in non-British subjects, the flashbulb memories were characterized as being less vivid, having fewer details, and including inaccurate details (Conway et al., 1994). These researchers concluded that flashbulb memories represent a special kind of automatic encoding that occurs when events are emotionally and personally very interesting.

FLASHBULB MEMORIES AND HORMONES

Earlier, in the Research Focus, we discussed how emotionally triggered hormones encoded long-term memories as if "in stone" (Cahill et al., 1994). These emotionally triggered hormones may also explain the automatic encoding of flashbulb memories, which are vivid and detailed images of emotionally charged personal experiences (Goodman & Quas, 1997).

Although we sometimes complain about having a poor memory, the one we have is quite remarkable in its ability to encode, store, and retrieve unlimited amounts of information over long periods of time.

However, we all forget things, even things we try hard to remember. We'll discuss reasons for forgetting in the next module.

Examples of Flashbulb Memories

Cues	Percent*
A car accident you were in or witnessed	85
When you first met your college roommate	82
Night of your high school graduation	81
Night of your senior prom (if you went or not)	78
An early romantic experience	77
A time you had to speak in front of an audience	72
When you got your college admissions letter	65
Your first date—the moment you met him/her	57
Day President Reagan was shot in Washington	52
Night President Nixon resigned	41
First time you flew in an airplane	40
Moment you opened your SAT scores	33
Your 17th birthday	30
Day of the first space shuttle flight	24
The last time you ate a holiday dinner at home	23
Your first college class	21
The first time your parents left you alone for some time	19
Your 13th birthday	12

*Percentage of students in the memory experiment who reported that events on the experimenter's list were of flashbulb quality (Rubin & Kozin, 1984).

A. THREE TYPES OF MEMORY

1. The study of memory, which is the ability to retain information over time, includes three separate processes. The first process—placing information in memory—is called (a)_____. The second process, which is filing information in memory, is called (b)_____. The third process—commonly referred to as remembering—is called (c)_____.

2. Although we think of memory as a single event, it is really a complex sequence that may be separated into three different kinds of memory. The initial memory process that holds raw information for up to several seconds is called _____. During this time, you have the chance to identify or pay attention to new information.

3. If you pay attention to information in sensory memory, this information is automatically transferred into a second kind of memory process, called _____ memory.

4. If you rehearse or think about information in short-term memory, that information will usually be transferred or encoded into the third, more permanent kind of memory process, called _____.

B. SENSORY MEMORY: RECORDING

5. Visual sensory memory, known as (a)_____ memory, lasts about a quarter of a second. Auditory memory, known as (b)_____ memory, may last as long as two seconds. Sensory memory has many functions; for example, it prevents you from being overwhelmed by too much incoming information and gives you time to identify the incoming data and pay attention to it.

C. SHORT-TERM MEMORY: WORKING

6. If you pay attention to information in sensory memory, it is automatically transferred to short-term memory, which has two main characteristics. The first is

that unrehearsed information will disappear after 2–30 seconds, indicating that short-term memory has a limited (a)_____. The second characteristic is that short-term memory can hold only about seven items (plus or minus two), indicating that short-term memory has a limited (b)_____. You can increase the

length of time that information remains in short-term memory by intentionally repeating the information, which is called (c)_____. You can considerably increase the capacity of short-term memory by combining separate items of information into larger units, which is called (d)_____.

D. LONG-TERM MEMORY: STORING

7. Let's follow the progress of information from the time it enters sensory memory to its storage in long-term memory. For an instant to several seconds, incoming raw information is held in (a)_____. If you do not pay attention to this information, it disappears forever; if you pay attention, that information is automatically transferred to short-term memory. The transfer of information from sensory memory to short-term memory is controlled by the process of (b)_____.

8. If information in short-term memory is not (a)_____, it will disappear in 2–30 seconds. If you rehearse or think about information in short-term memory, it may be transferred into long-term memory. The transfer of information from short-term into long-term memory is controlled by a process called (b)_____. In some cases, information is transferred automatically; in other cases, this transfer process may require deliberate effort.

9. The process of selecting information from long-term memory and transferring it back into short-term memory is called _____. Because information has been encoded into long-term memory does not guarantee that such information can always or easily be remembered or retrieved.

10. One demonstration of the existence of, and difference between, short-term and long-term memory is observed in the order that subjects remember items from a multiple-item list. Subjects tend to have better recall of items at the beginning of a list; this tendency is called the (a)_____ effect and involves long-term memory. Subjects tend to have better recall of items at the end of the list; this tendency is called the (b)_____ effect and involves short-term memory. The order in which subjects recall items from a long list is called the (c)_____ effect.

11. There are two different kinds of long-term memory. One kind involves memories of facts or events, such as scenes, stories, words, conversations, faces, or daily events. We can retrieve these memories and are conscious of them; they constitute (a)_____ memory. There are two kinds of declarative memory. One kind consists of factual knowledge of the world, concepts, word definitions, and language rules; this is called (b)_____ memory. The second kind of declarative memory consists of knowledge about personal experiences (episodes) or activities; this is called (c)_____ memory.

12. A second kind of long-term memory involves memories for performing motor or perceptual tasks, carrying out habits, and responding to stimuli because of classical conditioning; this is called _____ memory. We cannot retrieve these memories and are not conscious of them.

E. RESEARCH FOCUS: ANIMAL MODEL

13. There are times when for safety, moral, or ethical reasons researchers cannot use human subjects but instead use an (a)_____ model. Using this model, researchers found that during emotional or stressful situations the body secretes chemicals called (b)_____, which make encoding so effective that these situations become very vivid long-term memories. One reason for the evolution of this carved-in-stone memory system is to help the species survive by remembering dangerous situations.

F. ENCODING: TRANSFERRING

14. The process of storing information in memory by making mental representations is called (a)_____. There are two processes for encoding information. Most procedural and episodic information is transferred from short-term into long-term memory without any effort, and usually without any awareness, through a process called (b)_____ encoding. Much semantic information is transferred from short-term to long-term memory by deliberate attempts to repeat, rehearse, or make associations. Together, these deliberate attempts are referred to as (c)_____ encoding.

15. There are two kinds of effortful encoding, which differ in their effectiveness. Encoding by simply repeating or rehearsing the information is called (a)_____. This method is not very effective because it involves little thinking about the information or making new associations. Encoding that involves thinking about the information and making new associations is called (b)_____.

16. One theory says that memory depends on how information is encoded in the mind. If we pay attention only to basic features of the information, it is encoded at a shallow level, and poor memory results. If we form new associations, the information is encoded at a deeper level, and good memory results. This theory is called _____.

G. REPRESSED MEMORIES

17. If something happens that is threatening, shocking, or traumatic, our minds may push that information deep into the unconscious, from which it may one day be released and enter consciousness. This phenomenon is called (a)_____ and is the theory behind the formation of (b)_____ memories. Unless there is corroborating evidence, the accuracy of repressed memories is difficult to establish.

H. CULTURAL DIVERSITY: ORAL VERSUS WRITTEN

18. There is some evidence that cultures can influence how information is encoded. For example, Ghanaian students remembered more material that was read to them than did American students. This finding supports the idea that Ghanaians' oral tradition makes them better at _____ information in sounds.

I. APPLICATION: UNUSUAL MEMORIES

19. The ability of certain children to examine a picture or page for 10–30 seconds and then retain a detailed visual image of the material for several minutes is called (a)_____ memory. In adults, the ability to form sharp, detailed visual images after a short period and recall the entire image at a later date is called (b)_____ memory. Memories that are vivid recollections, usually in great detail, of dramatic or emotionally charged incidents are called (c)_____.

Answers: *1. (a) encoding, (b) storing, (c) retrieving; 2. sensory memory; 3. short-term, or working; 4. long-term memory; 5. (a) iconic, (b) echoic; 6. (a) duration, (b) capacity, (c) maintenance rehearsal, (d) chunking; 7. (a) sensory memory, (b) attention; 8. (a) rehearsed, (b) encoding; 9. retrieval, or retrieving; 10. (a) primacy, (b) recency, (c) primacy-recency; 11. (a) declarative, (b) semantic, (c) episodic; 12. procedural; 13. (a) animal, (b) hormones; 14. (a) encoding, (b) automatic, (c) effortful; 15. (a) maintenance rehearsal, (b) elaborative rehearsal; 16. levels of processing; 17. (a) repression, (b) repressed; 18. encoding; 19. (a) eidetic, (b) photographic, (c) flashbulb memories.*

CRITICAL THINKING

Newspaper Article

QUESTIONS

BOOMER BRAIN MELTDOWN
By Anita Manning

1. What are some causes of middle-age memory problems?

The signs are all around us: a woman loads the washing machine with detergent and bleach but forgets to add the laundry. Another hides her jewelry in the house before going off on a business trip. When she returns, she has no idea where she put it. Successful, intelligent, middle-aged baby boomers seem to be losing their minds in great numbers.

Blame it on menopause? Maybe. Scientists at the National Institute on Aging report in the current issue of the journal *Neurology* that estrogen replacement therapy can help slow age-related memory decline in postmenopausal women. But men, too, are experiencing middle-age memory lapses.

2. What are some measures the article mentions that may help alleviate memory problems?

Part of the problem is that both men and women in midlife go through hormonal disruptions that cause any number of physical symptoms, from irritability to hot flashes. It's often temporary, and can be alleviated by taking hormones under a doctor's supervision—some men take testosterone supplements—and by exercise and other forms of stress reduction.

3. Are middle-age memory problems usually a function of decreased memory speed or memory power?

James McGaugh, director of the Center for the Study of Memory at the University of California-Irvine, says there's no reason to despair. You haven't lost your mind, he says; it has just slowed down a bit. "It's a speed function, not a power function," he says, and it begins at about age 25. "You'll notice that most of the people on 'Jeopardy' are young."

4. What is the "use it or lose it" theory of memory?

The "increased sludginess" of memory doesn't necessarily signal disease, he says. "It's just the natural course of events." But it can be halted and even reversed, he says, citing work of William Greenough at the University of Illinois, a proponent of the "use it or lose it" theory of memory. "He finds . . . animals can grow new synaptic connections at any age (through exercise of the brain), and can grow vascular supply for the brain at any age." In other words, just like the rest of the body, he says, the brain needs exercise.

5. What are some treatable conditions that could cause memory loss?

Neurologist David Pilgrim of Harvard Pilgrim Health Care, sounding a note of caution, says memory loss may be the result of illness or depression, and may be treatable. One way doctors tell how serious a memory problem is, he says, is "if you come to me and say your memory doesn't work anymore, most of the time it's normal, or maybe depression. But if your employer or spouse comes to me and says your memory isn't working, it's probably disease."

Source: *USA Today*, January 6, 1998. Copright © 1998 by *USA Today*. Reprinted with permission.

Study Questions

A. Three Types of Memory—Why does seeing an ambulance speed by remind you of your father's heart attack and his trip to the hospital? (See answer in Critical Thinking Appendix.)

B. Sensory Memory: Recording—Why doesn't the world disappear for the short period of time when your eyes are completely closed during blinking?

C. Short-Term Memory: Working—If you took a drug that blocked short-term memory, what would be different about your life?

D. Long-Term Memory: Storing—What would your life be like if you had declarative memory but no procedural memory?

E. Research Focus: Animal Model—Why do people who suffer traumatic situations, such as sexual abuse or job layoffs, have difficulty getting on with their lives?

F. Encoding: Transferring—Why is it important that teachers make learning interesting and meaningful? (See answer in Critical Thinking Appendix.)

G. Repressed Memories—What are some of the ways that therapists can guard against clients' reporting repressed memories that are false?

H. Cultural Diversity: Oral versus Written—How might playing video games affect a child's encoding process? (See answer in Critical Thinking Appendix.)

I. Application: Unusual Memories—If you could have one unusual memory ability, which would you choose, and how would it make your life different?

LINKS TO LEARNING

Web Sites & Learning Activities

● BROOKS/COLE ONLINE PSYCHOLOGY STUDY CENTER

http://psychstudy.brookscole.com/student/plotnik/quiz/ch11frm.html

This site gives students a chance to review material by taking quizzes and doing exercises and activities for this module.

● NEWTON'S APPLE: MEMORY

http://ericir.syr.edu/Projects/Newton/11/memory.html

This site includes an engaging explanation of memory systems, vocabulary terms, and an activity designed to explore memory.

● AMERICAN PSYCHOLOGICAL ASSOCIATION—MEMORY

http://www.apa.org/

Type "memory" into the search engine of the APA's Web site and you will find several fascinating articles on recent research, including items on memory and aging, how children form memories, and the APA's discussion of recovered memories.

● THE MAGICAL NUMBER SEVEN, PLUS OR MINUS TWO: SOME LIMITS ON OUR CAPACITY FOR PROCESSING INFORMATION

http://www.well.com/user/smalin/miller.html

George A. Miller's classic 1956 paper on memory is reproduced in its entirety on this Web page.

● FALSE MEMORY SYNDROME FOUNDATION

http://advicom.net/~fitz/fmsf/

The home page of the False Memory Syndrome Foundation provides information about and mailing lists related to false memory syndrome, plus links to other Web resources.

● RECOVERED MEMORIES OF SEXUAL ABUSE

http://www.jimhopper.com/memory

This page contains links to many sites dealing with the recovered memory debate.

Welcome to the WEB

Activities

● *Integrator Online™ for Introductory Psychology* CD-ROM, Plotnik, Module 11

● Study Guide to accompany *Introduction to Psychology,* 5th edition, Module 11 (choice of PC or Mac computer version or hard copy).

● *PsychNow!* CD-ROM Memory Systems

Answers to questions on page 258

1. Causes include hormone fluctuations, stress, and occasionally illness.
2. Some ways to alleviate memory problems are exercise, stress reduction, and intellectual stimulation.
3. They are a function of decreased memory speed.
4. This theory says that if you don't exercise your memory by staying intellectually active, you may lose some of your memory speed.
5. Illness and depression may cause memory problems, but those causes are often treatable.

Module 12 REMEMBERING & FORGETTING

A. Organization of Memories 262

* **TRASH CAN VERSUS NETWORK THEORY**
* **NETWORK THEORY OF MEMORY ORGANIZATION**
* **NETWORK HIERARCHY**

1. ANIMAL

B. Forgetting Curves 264

* **EARLY MEMORIES**
* **UNFAMILIAR AND UNINTERESTING**
* **FAMILIAR AND INTERESTING**

C. Reasons for Forgetting 265

* **OVERVIEW: FOUR REASONS**
* **INTERFERENCE**
* **RETRIEVAL CUES**
* **STATE-DEPENDENT LEARNING**

D. Biological Bases of Memory 268

* **LOCATION OF MEMORIES IN THE BRAIN**
* **MECHANISMS OF MEMORY**
* **SHORT-TERM MEMORY**
* **LONG-TERM MEMORY**

E. Mnemonics: Memorization Methods 271

* **METHOD OF LOCI**
* **PEG METHOD**
* **EFFECTIVENESS**

F. Cultural Diversity: Aborigines versus White Australians 272

* **RETRIEVAL CUES**
* **VISUAL VERSUS VERBAL RETRIEVAL CUES**

G. Research Focus: False Memories 273

* **CAN FALSE MEMORIES BE IMPLANTED?**

H. Application: Eyewitness Testimony 274

* **DEFINITION AND PROBLEMS**
* **MISLEADING THE WITNESS**
* **BIASING FACTORS**
* **SOURCE MISATTRIBUTION**
* **COGNITIVE INTERVIEW**

Watching a Crime

How much can you remember?

It was about nine at night when you entered the campus building, climbed one flight of stairs, and began walking down the long hallway. You had just finished your psychology paper and were going to slip it under the instructor's door.

Everything happened very quickly.

From about the middle of the dimly lit hallway, a man with reddish hair and wearing a brown leather jacket jumped out from behind a half-open door and ran at you. Instinctively, you threw out your hands and tried to ward off the oncoming threat. With a quick motion, the man grabbed your blue shoulder bag and pushed you down. At that instant, your eyes met. He pointed at you with a menacing gesture and said, "Don't move or make a sound." Then he checked the hallway, stepped around you, and was gone (adapted from Buckout, 1980).

A 12-second filmed sequence with a storyline similar to this one was shown on television. In the TV film, the assailant's face was on the screen for several seconds. Next, the viewers were asked to watch a lineup of six men and then to call the TV station and identify which was the assailant. Of the more than 2000 viewers who called in, only 200 identified the correct man; 1800 selected the wrong one (Buckout, 1980).

Without looking back, try to answer the following questions (answers at bottom):

1. What color was the mugger's jacket? _____

2. What color and type was the student's bag? _____

3. Besides the bag, what else was the student carrying?

   _____

4. The mugger's exact words were, "Don't make a sound." True or false?

5. When thrown down, the student yelled out, "Stop!" True or false?

6. Of the 2000 viewers who called in, 1800 identified the correct assailant. True or false?

Answers: *1. brown; 2. blue, shoulder bag; 3. psychology paper; 4. false; 5. false; 6. false.*

Recall versus Recognition

Which is easier?

You probably found the first three questions harder because they involve recall.

Recall involves retrieving previously learned information without the aid of or with very few external cues.

For example, in questions 1–3, you were asked to recall colors or objects without having any choices. Students must use recall to answer fill-in-the-blank or essay questions.

You probably thought the last three questions were easier because they involve recognition.

Recognition involves identifying previously learned information with the help of more external cues.

In questions 4–6, you have only to recognize if the information provided is correct. Students use recognition to decide which of the choices is correct on multiple-choice tests. Since multiple-choice tests involve recognition, they are generally considered easier than fill-in-the-blank and essay exams, which involve recall. Later in this module, we'll discuss why recall is more difficult than recognition.

Eyewitness Testimony

Which face did you see?

Question 6 asks about a very curious result. Although the assailant's face was on the television screen for several seconds, 90% of the viewers identified the *wrong* person in a six-man lineup. (For example, from the six faces below, can you identify the correct mugger? Answer below.) How can you clearly see someone's face and not remember it? The answer to this question comes from

studies on how eyewitness memories can be affected by suggestions, misleading questions, and false information. Although we generally assume that eyewitness testimony is the most accurate kind of evidence, you'll see that this is not always true. We'll discuss accuracy and problems of eyewitness testimony at the end of this module. (Mugger had reddish hair.)

What's Coming

We'll discuss how you organize thousands of events, faces, and facts and file this information in long-term memory. We'll explain the most common reasons for forgetting, the biological bases for memory, methods to improve memory, the creation of false memories, and the accuracy of eyewitness testimony.

I'll begin with my favorite theory of how information is organized and why I forget so many things—the trash can theory of memory.

A. Organization of Memories

Trash Can versus Network Theory

How do you store memories?

One of the great puzzles of memory is what kind of filing system stores the millions of things that it accumulates over our lifetime. Suppose that during this past year you stored the following memories: 91 faces, 2340 concepts, 251 songs, 192 names, 87 definitions, 20,987 personal events and 7 dogs. According to the "**trash can theory,**" you made mental representations of these things, which were then dumped into a huge mental trash can. If you wish to retrieve one particular item, you would need to sort through your mental trash heap until you happened upon the memory you wanted. Although I often feel that the trash can theory explains how I personally organize my memories, researchers tell us that our retrieval system is too fast and accurate to be stored in such a disorganized way.

One of the more popular theories for how we organize memories is called network theory (Neath, 1998).

Network theory says that we store related ideas in separate categories, or files, called nodes. As we make associations between information, we create links among thousands of nodes, which make up a gigantic interconnected network of files for storing and retrieving information.

Network theory may become clearer if you imagine that the mental files, or nodes, are like thousands of cities on a map and the connections or associations between them are like roads. Just as you follow different roads to go from city to city, you follow different associative pathways to go from idea to idea. Storing new events, faces, and thousands of other things would be similar to erecting new buildings in the cities and also building new roads between the cities (Schwartz & Reisberg, 1991). Here's how one cognitive psychologist, Donald Norman, used network theory to explain how he retrieved a particular memory.

Network Theory of Memory Organization

Where do the roads lead?

Just as you might follow a road map (right figure) to reach a particular city, cognitive psychologist Norman followed a network map to remember the name of a particular store in San Diego. Although the mental roads that Norman takes may seem strange, these roads represent personal associations that he created when he filed, or stored, information in long-term memory. As he follows his associations, or mental roads, he travels the cognitive network from node to node or memory to memory in search of a particular name (Norman, 1982). Please begin reading at Node 1 and continue to Node 6.

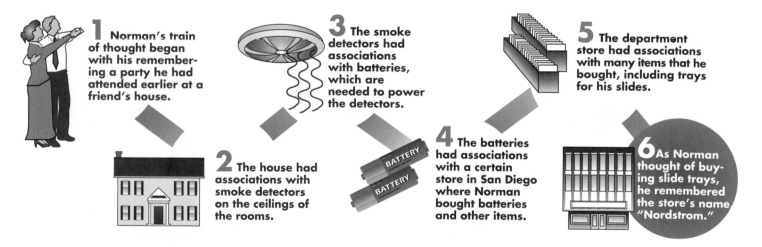

1 Norman's train of thought began with his remembering a party he had attended earlier at a friend's house.

2 The house had associations with smoke detectors on the ceilings of the rooms.

3 The smoke detectors had associations with batteries, which are needed to power the detectors.

4 The batteries had associations with a certain store in San Diego where Norman bought batteries and other items.

5 The department store had associations with many items that he bought, including trays for his slides.

6 As Norman thought of buying slide trays, he remembered the store's name "Nordstrom."

We've all shared Norman's problem of knowing we know something but having difficulty recalling it. This problem relates to how we store memories in long-term memory. According to the network theory of memory, we store memories in nodes that are interconnected by making new associations. Because the network theory is somewhat complicated, we'll review how it applied to Norman's problem of trying to recall a particular memory.

Nodes. Norman organizes or stores related ideas in separate files, or categories, called nodes. We simplified this process by showing only six nodes, but there may be dozens. Nodes are categories of related ideas, such as birds, faces, tools, friends, and store names.

Associations. Norman's nodes, or categories of ideas, were linked together by making associations or mental roads between new information and already stored information.

Network. Norman has thousands of interconnected nodes, which form an enormous mental network of files. To retrieve a particular memory, such as a store's name, he must search through this mental network to find the file in which it was stored.

How we search through our thousands of nodes to find a particular file has been an interesting research topic.

Network Hierarchy

How big is a guppy? Does a rooster have feathers? Does a bluejay have skin?

As you try to answer each of the questions on the left, the network theory says that you will search for answers in different nodes or memory files.

Nodes are memory files that contain related information organized around a specific topic or category.

For example, if you try to recall the size of a guppy, you would do so by searching for the node or memory file that contains specific information about guppies. Network theory also says that your many thousands of nodes or memory files are arranged in a certain kind of order, which is called a network hierarchy (Collins & Quillian, 1969).

A *network hierarchy* refers to the arrangement of nodes or memory files in a certain order or hierarchy: at the bottom of the hierarchy are nodes with very concrete information. These nodes are connected to ones with more abstract ideas above them, which in turn are connected to other nodes with even more abstract ideas at the top level.

For example, a partial network hierarchy for nodes or memory files containing information about animals is shown on the right. Notice that nodes containing concrete information about a specific animal (size, color), such as Bluejay, Rooster, Shark, or Guppy, are located on the bottom of the hierarchy (nodes labeled "3").

These nodes containing specific information are connected to other nodes, such as Bird or Fish, which contain more abstract or general information (has feathers or gills) that applies to all birds or all fish (nodes labeled "2").

In turn, these nodes with general information are connected to other nodes containing very general or abstract information (has skin, breathes) that apply to all animals (node labeled "1" at the very top).

Searching. According to network theory, information about an animal is organized in nodes (memory files) that are arranged in a hierarchy, with concrete or specific information located at the bottom and more abstract information located near or at the top (as shown in the figure above). For example, the answer to a very specific question, "How big is a guppy?" is found in node 3, which means searching through node 1, node 2, to get to specific information in node 3. The answer to a very general question, "Does a bluejay have skin?" would only involve searching through node 1. Network theory says that the more general the question, the farther up the network hierarchy you must search.

1. ANIMAL

This node or memory file contains information that is very abstract, and applies to all animals—has skin, can move around, eats, and breathes. This category has answers to very general questions about animals— "Does a bluejay have skin?"

2. Bird or Fish

This node, or memory file, contains information that is somewhat abstract because it applies to many fish or birds—has wings, can fly, and has feathers. This category has answers to more general questions about fish, or birds— "Does a rooster have feathers?"

3. Bluejay, Rooster, Shark, Guppy

This node, or memory file, contains very concrete information that applies only to a specific animal. This category has answers to very specific questions— "How big is a guppy?" "What color is a shark?"

Conclusion. Network theory provides one model of how you organize millions of memories. Researchers are also developing other models, some called neural networks, which try to imitate how the brain organizes millions of bits of information (Neath, 1998; Prince & Smolensky, 1997). The question of which system you use to file and organize information has not yet been answered.

Although we don't know exactly which filing systems are used to store information in the brain, we all know that sometimes we forget information that we thought we stored safely away. Next, we'll examine some of the many reasons for forgetting.

B. Forgetting Curves

Early Memories

What's your earliest memory?

Close your eyes for a moment and recall your earliest childhood memory. Researchers have found that our earliest memories are typically of events that occurred at about age 3 ½ and are often visual (Mullen, 1994). This doesn't mean that very young children have no long-term memory. Recently, researchers found that children as young as 13 months can recall visual events 8 months later. These very young children can recall a sequence of events that involves moving toys in a certain order (Bauer, 1996). However, these kinds of memories involving motor movements are not usually remembered after the age of 3 ½. That's because very young children are not yet fluent in language. For this reason, early memories cannot be verbally encoded and thus cannot be recalled verbally after the child develops language (Howe & Courage, 1997). Thus, you cannot verbally recall events before the age of 3 ½ because these events were not encoded verbally. Even though you now encode many events verbally, why do you forget these events, especially on exams?

Unfamiliar and Uninteresting

Could you remember "LUD, ZIB"?

From your experience studying for exams, you know that just because you verbally encode information by listening, reading, or writing doesn't mean that you'll automatically recall this information on exams. The kinds of events that you are more likely to remember or forget can be demonstrated with forgetting curves.

A *forgetting curve* measures the amount of previously learned information that subjects can recall or recognize across time.

We'll examine how two different kinds of information—unfamiliar and familiar—are remembered by using forgetting curves.

One of the earliest psychologists to study memory and forgetting was Hermann Ebbinghaus, who used himself as his only subject. He got around the fact that people have better memories for more familiar events by memorizing only three-letter nonsense syllables, such as **LUD, ZIB, MUC**. He made up and wrote down hundreds of three-letter nonsense syllables on separate cards and arranged these cards into sets of varying length. To the ticking of a metronome, he turned over each card and read aloud each of the syllables until he had read all the cards in the set. He used only rote memory (made no associations), and needed only one or two readings to memorize a set of seven cards (containing seven nonsense syllables). He needed about 45 readings to memorize a set of 24 cards (Ebbinghaus, 1885/1913).

The forgetting curve on the left shows that Ebbinghaus forgot about half the unfamiliar and uninteresting nonsense syllables within the first hour.

How long do we remember familiar information?

Ebbinghaus forgot the greatest number of nonsense syllables within the first hour.

LUD
ZIB
KON
MUC
SAR

His rate of forgetting leveled off and declined gradually across 31 days.

Percent Remembered

Time Between Initial Learning and Memory Test

⅓ 1   9   24   48

Hours   **Days**

Familiar and Interesting

Can you remember the names of your high school classmates?

Ebbinghaus's nonsense syllables are certainly uninteresting, so it may not be surprising that he forgot half of them within the first hour. But what about the names and faces of the members of your high school graduating class? This information is both familiar and interesting and something you were exposed to for several years.

The graph on the right shows that even after 47 years, subjects correctly matched about 80% of their high school classmates' names with faces; they correctly recalled about 25% after 47 years (Bahrick et al., 1975). Subjects did better on recognition tests (matching names to faces) because they were given clues (names). They did poorer on recall tests (seeing faces and asked to recall the names) because they were not given any clues. Similarly, students also show better memory on recognition tests (multiple-choice) than on recall tests (essay or fill-in-the blank).

Notice that even though both kinds of information (names and nonsense syllables) were encoded verbally, subjects differed greatly in their ability to remember information. Subjects correctly recalled about 60% of familiar and interesting information (names and faces) after 7 years, while Ebbinghaus forgot about 80% of the unfamiliar and uninteresting nonsense syllables after about a week.

These two studies show that remembering is partly related to how familiar or interesting the information is. Next, we'll examine four other reasons for forgetting.

Recognition test

Recall test

Percent Correct

100
80
60
40
20
0

0.3   3.8   7.4   14.5   25.8   34.1   47.6

Years Since Graduation

Overview: Four Reasons

Why can't I remember my 9th birthday?

For some reason, my sister can't remember what she did on her 9th birthday even though my brother and I can. Although researchers say that we can store enormous amounts of information for a very long time, why is it that memories of her 9th birthday seem to be missing (Schacter, 1996)? She says that she is forgetting, but what exactly does forgetting mean?

Forgetting refers to the inability to retrieve, recall, or recognize information that was stored or is still stored in long-term memory.

Although she says that she has forgotten her 9th birthday, it is possible that those memories were stored and are still in her long-term memory, but for some reason, she cannot recall, or retrieve, them. As it turns out, there are at least four good explanations for why she may have forgotten her 9th birthday.

Repression

Perhaps my sister can't remember what happened on her 9th birthday because she repressed those memories.

Repression, according to Sigmund Freud, is a mental process that automatically hides emotionally threatening or anxiety-producing information in the unconscious. Once in the unconscious, repressed memories cannot be recalled voluntarily, but something may cause them to enter consciousness at a later time.

We discussed repression, repressed memories, and implanted memories in Module 11 (pp. 250–251) and will give only a brief review here. There are clinical reports of clients who, during therapy, recovered repressed memories of very emotional or traumatic events, such as sexual abuse (Briere & Conte, 1993). However, since the early 1990s, there has been a great debate over whether some of the increasing reports of recovered repressed memories involving sexual abuse were actually implanted false memories (Bowers & Farvolden, 1996; Loftus, 1997a, 1997b; Pennebaker & Memon, 1996). Evidence that some recovered repressed memories of sexual abuse were false comes from a study of 40 women who later denied and retracted their claims of being sexually abused or being involved in satanic ritual abuse (Lief & Fetkewicz, 1996). There are also about a half-dozen court cases in which juries found therapists guilty of implanting or contributing to creating false memories (Loftus, 1997a).

On the one hand, there are clinical reports of clients who recalled repressed memories of traumatic events during the therapeutic process (Briere & Conte, 1993). On the other hand, prominent memory researchers, such as Elizabeth Loftus (1997a, 1997b), have questioned the validity of repressed memories, pointing to the possibility that such memories had been suggested or implanted during the therapeutic process. For example, false memories have been implanted in children and adults, who often insist that such memories are true (Brainerd & Poole, 1997; Loftus, 1997a). Because of new data on implanted memories and recent court rulings against therapists, there is far less discussion of repressed memories in the popular press.

As you'll soon see, my sister's forgetting her 9th birthday was not due to repressed memories but to something more concrete.

Poor Retrieval Cues

Perhaps my sister can't remember what occurred on her 9th birthday because she was ill or had received few presents, which resulted in poor retrieval cues.

Retrieval cues are mental reminders that we create by forming vivid mental images or creating associations between new information and information we already know.

Many students don't realize that retrieval cues greatly influence the remembering or forgetting of new or difficult terms. For instance, if you study primarily by cramming or rote memory, you'll form poor retrieval cues. You'll make the best retrieval cues by making associations between new information and information already learned.

Amnesia

What really happened to my sister on her 9th birthday was that she tried out her new ice skates. Wanting to show off, she tried a difficult spin, caught an edge, and fell hard on her head. She was knocked unconscious and, later, remembered nothing because the fall had caused amnesia (Mayes & Downes, 1997).

Amnesia is loss of memory that may occur after a blow or damage to the brain (temporary or permanent), after drug use, or after severe psychological stress.

Similar to my sister, people who strike their heads during car accidents usually have no memories of the events immediately before and during the accident.

Interference

If you try to recall your childhood birthdays, you may find that they begin to run together and get mixed up. This mixup leads to forgetting and is called interference.

Interference, one of the common reasons for forgetting, means that the recall of some particular memory is blocked or prevented by other related memories.

For example, the presents, parties, or people from earlier birthdays may block out or interfere with remembering what happened on a later birthday.

Of the number of reasons for forgetting, cognitive psychologists have focused primarily on interference and retrieval cues. We'll discuss these next and explain why having two exams on the same day greatly increases your chances of forgetting.

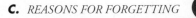

C. Reasons for Forgetting

What happens when you study for three exams?

Interference

Sooner or later, every student faces the problem of studying to take two exams on the same day. One reason this task is especially difficult is that it increases the chance for interference.

According to the theory of *interference,* we forget information not because it is lost from storage but rather because related old information or similar newer information gets in the way and mixes up or blocks its retrieval.

Students who take multiple tests on the same day often complain of studying long and hard but forgetting information that they knew they knew. In this case the culprit may be interference. Similarly, if you take two or more classes in succession, you may find that information from one class interferes with learning or remembering information from the others. We'll explain the two kinds of interference—proactive and retroactive—and how each can lead to forgetting.

Proactive Interference

The first thing to remember about interference is that it can act forward, which is called proactive, or act backward, which is called retroactive. The prefix *pro* means "forward," so *proactive* interference "acts forward" to interfere with recalling newly learned information.

Proactive interference occurs when old information (learned earlier) blocks or disrupts the remembering of related new information (learned later).

Here's how proactive interference works in studying and taking an exam.

1. Psychology information.
From 1:00 to 3:00, you study for a test in psychology. The more psychology terms that you store in memory, the more potential this psychology information has to "act forward" and disrupt whatever new and related information that you study next.

2. Psychology information acts forward.
From 3:00 to 6:00, you study for a test in sociology. You may experience difficulty in learning and remembering this new sociology information because the previously learned psychology terms can "act forward" and interfere with remembering new and related terms from sociology.

3. Proactive interference.
When you take your sociology exam, you may forget some of the sociology terms you studied because of proactive interference: Previously learned psychology terms "act forward" to interfere with or block the recall of the more recently learned and related sociology terms.

Retroactive Interference

Note that the prefix *retro* means "backward," so *retroactive* interference means "acting backward" to interfere with recalling previously learned information.

Retroactive interference occurs when new information (learned later) blocks or disrupts the retrieval of related old information (learned earlier).

Here's how retroactive interference works in studying and taking an exam.

1. Psychology information.
From 1:00 to 3:00, you study for a test in psychology. Then from 3:00 to 6:00, you study for a test in sociology.

2. Sociology information acts backward.
You may experience difficulty in remembering the psychology terms you learned earlier because the sociology terms recently put into long-term memory may "act backward" and disrupt earlier learned and related psychology terms.

3. Retroactive interference.
When you take the psychology exam, you may forget some of the psychology terms you studied earlier because of retroactive interference: Recently learned sociology terms "act backward" to interfere with or block the recall of earlier learned and related psychology terms.

Interference, both proactive and retroactive, is thought to be one of the two common reasons for forgetting. We have all experienced interference in everyday life when we mix up similar names, places, or faces. Interference may also cause serious mistakes if eyewitnesses identify or recall the wrong person, as happened in the study we discussed at the beginning of this module.

Why Did Viewers Forget the Mugger's Face?

We began this module by asking why only 200 out of 2000 viewers correctly identified a mugger's face that was shown for several seconds on television. One reason viewers forgot the mugger's face is that one or both kinds of interference were operating.

If *proactive interference* was operating, it means that previously learned faces acted forward to block or disrupt remembering of the newly observed mugger's face.

If *retroactive interference* was operating, it means that new faces learned since seeing the mugger's face acted backward to block or disrupt remembering of the mugger's face.

Thus, we may forget information that we did indeed store in long-term memory because of one or both kinds of interference.

Besides interference, the other most common reason for forgetting involves inadequate retrieval cues, our next topic.

Retrieval Cues

Have you ever parked your car in a mall and later roamed around the huge lot trying to find it? In that case, the reason for your forgetting probably involved poor retrieval cues (Lutz et al., 1994).

Retrieval cues are mental reminders that you create by forming vivid mental images of information or associating new information with information that you already know.

Retrieval cues are also important in hiding things. Researchers asked students to hide things either in common places, such as drawers or closets, or in unusual places, such as old shoes or cereal boxes. Later, when asked to locate the hidden objects, students remembered objects hidden in common places and forgot those hidden in unusual places (Winograd & Soloway, 1986). Forgetting hiding places (which I have done) and forgetting parking places (which I have done) point to the need for creating good retrieval cues.

Forming Effective Retrieval Cues

One reason we forget hiding or parking places, names, phone numbers, or concepts is that we did not take the time to create effective retrieval cues. Forming effective retrieval cues is one form of effortful encoding, which we discussed in Module 11 (pp. 248–249). For example, you can form effective retrieval cues by creating vivid mental images of the information, making associations between new and old information, or making somewhat bizarre but memorable associations.

For example, researchers wondered which types of sentences students would better remember: common sentences, such as "The sleek new train passes a field of fresh, juicy strawberries"; or bizarre sentences, such as "The sleek new train is derailed by the fresh, juicy strawberries." As a computer randomly presented 12 common and 12 bizarre sentences, students were told to form vivid mental images of the scenes. When retested later, subjects recalled significantly more bizarre than common sentences. Researchers concluded that subjects better remembered the bizarre sentences because they formed better mental images or associations, which produced better retrieval cues (Robinson-Riegler & McDaniel, 1994). Poor retrieval cues may also be a problem in eyewitness testimony.

Retrieval cues and interference. There have been cases in which eyewitnesses identified assailants who were later proven innocent based on DNA evidence (Dolan, 1995; Gerber, 1996). Even when told that their assailants, who had spent many years in prison, were innocent, the eyewitnesses insisted they had made the correct identifications. One reason eyewitnesses were mistaken is that the emotional and traumatic events prevented them from forming effective retrieval cues. Another reason the eyewitnesses made mistakes is because of interference; that is, the faces of the accused assailants somewhat resembled and interfered with their recognizing the real assailants. These examples show that forgetting can result from poor retrieval cues, no associations, or interference (Schacter, 1996).

Another example of forgetting, which involves retrieval cues and interference, usually begins with someone saying, "It's on the tip of my tongue."

Tip-of-the-Tongue Phenomenon

Most of us have had the frustrating experience of feeling we really do know a definition, term, name, movie, or song title but cannot recall it at this moment. This kind of forgetting is commonly called the tip-of-the-tongue phenomenon.

The *tip-of-the-tongue phenomenon* refers to the situation in which, despite making a great effort, we are temporarily unable to recall information that we absolutely know is in our memory. Later, in a different situation, we may recall the information.

Researchers have found that the tip-of-the-tongue phenomenon is nearly universal, occurs in daily life about once a week, most often involves names of people and objects, and about half of the time is successfully resolved minutes later (Brown, 1991).

There are two explanations for the tip-of-the-tongue phenomenon. In some cases, information was encoded with inadequate retrieval cues, and so we must think up other associations (first letter of name, where last seen) for recall. In other cases, information is being blocked by interference from similar-sounding names or objects. Once we think of something else, the interference stops and the information pops into our memory (Schacter, 1996).

An interesting feature of retrieval cues is that they can also come from our states of mind.

State-Dependent Learning

When you yell at someone for doing the same annoying thing again, why is it that a long list of related past annoyances quickly comes to mind? One answer involves state-dependent learning.

State-dependent learning means that it is easier to recall information when you are in the same physiological or emotional state or setting as when you originally encoded the information.

For example, yelling and getting angry at someone creates an emotional and physiological state that triggers the recall of other, related, past annoyances. Evidence for state-dependent learning comes from a wide range of studies in which subjects (humans, dogs, rats) learned something while using a drug and later showed better recall of this information when tested with the same drug than with a placebo (Neath, 1998). Also, subjects who learned something in a strong emotional state showed better recall if tested in the same mood (Eich, 1995). These state-dependent studies indicate that being in certain physiological or emotional states are cues for recalling information that was learned under these same conditions.

Next, we look inside the brain to see what happens during remembering and forgetting.

D. Biological Bases of Memory

Location of Memories in the Brain

Where are memories stored?

In a normal day, you are able to learn and remember many new things that must be stored somewhere in your brain. You can also remember hundreds of things that must have already been stored in there. For the past 60 years, researchers have studied normal people, brain-damaged patients, monkeys, rats, rabbits, mice, and even sea slugs to discover where memories are stored in the brain (Beardsley, 1997; Eichenbaum, 1997b).

It is only since the mid-1990s that researchers have made progress in understanding how the brain organizes and stores memories.

Part of this progress comes from recently developed methods to study and photograph the activity of the living brain while subjects are using different kinds of memory (Posner, 1997). And part of this progress comes from study of brain-damaged individuals who show deficits in some kinds of memory but not others (Vargha-Khadem et al., 1997). Based on these studies, researchers have identified areas of the brain that are involved in many different kinds of thoughts and memories. We'll discuss these interesting findings and point out where in the brain the major kinds of memories are stored.

1 Cortex: Storing Short-Term Memories

When you look up a new phone number, you can hold it in short-term memory long enough to dial the number. Your ability to hold words, facts, and events in short-term memory depends on activity in the *cortex,* which is a thin layer of brain cells that covers the surface of the fore-brain (thin red line).

People may have brain damage that prevents them from storing long-term memories, but if their cortex is intact, they may have short-term memory and be able to carry on relatively normal conversations. However, if they cannot store long-term memories, they would not later remember having those conversations.

2 Cortex: Recalling Long-Term Memories

If you learn the words to a song, these words are stored in long-term memory. Your ability to remember or recall songs, words, facts, and events for days, months, or years depends on areas widely spread throughout the cortex.

People may have brain damage that prevents them from learning or remembering any new songs. However, if they have an intact cortex, they may remember the words from songs they learned before their brain damage because such information would have already been safely stored throughout their cerebral cortex (thin red line around outside of the brain).

3 Amygdala: Adding Emotional Associations

Suppose each time you hear a particular song that was associated with your first love, you have a romantic feeling. The emotional feeling associated with this memory is provided by the amygdala, which is an almond-shaped structure lying below the surface of the cortex in the tip of the temporal lobe. Humans with damage to the amygdala may no longer have emotions associated with memories, such as hearing a loud, unpleasant horn but no longer finding it "unpleasant" (Bechara et al., 1995). Researchers conclude that the amygdala plays a critical role in adding a wide range of emotions to our memories (LeDoux, 1996).

4 Hippocampus: Transferring into Long-Term Memory

Just as the "Save" command on your computer transfers a file into permanent storage on your hard drive, the hippocampus transfers words, facts, and personal events from short-term into permanent long-term memory. The hippocampus (gold area) is a curved, finger-like structure that lies beneath the cortex in the temporal lobe.

People with damage to the hippocampus (and surrounding cortex) cannot save any declarative memories, such as new words, facts, or personal events, because the hippocampus is needed to transfer this information from short-term into long-term memory (Vargha-Khadem et al., 1997). However, people with hippocampal damage can learn and remember motor skills or procedural information but, strangely, would not remember actually doing motor skills (playing tennis) because that is a personal event (declarative memory). Thus, the hippocampus is necessary for transferring declarative information (words, facts, and events) from short-term into long-term memory but not for transferring procedural information (motor skills, habits) (Knowlton et al., 1996).

5 Memory Model

Recent findings indicate that your cortex stores short-term memories as well as long-term memories; your hippocampus transfers or saves declarative information in long-term memory but does not transfer procedural information into long-term memory; and your amygdala adds emotional associations to memories (Gabrieli et al., 1997). Now that you know which areas of the brain store, transfer, or add emotions to memories, we can examine how individual memories are actually formed.

How to study memory?

Here's one of the biggest memory puzzles that many scientists would give their right arms to solve: How do the brain's cells use physical things, such as chemicals, membranes, and neurotransmitters, to form and store mental images, thoughts, and billions of other memories? To solve this puzzle, researchers have been studying animals with simple nervous systems, such as sea snails (right photo), snails, fruit flies, mice, and tiny pieces of rat brain tissue. Because animals' nervous systems share many of the same structures and functions as humans' brains, researchers can generalize many animal findings to humans. Researchers are proposing that short-memory has a mechanism different from that of long-term memory (Johnston, 1997; Murphy & Glanzman, 1997; Tonegawa & Wilson, 1997; Tully, 1997).

Short-Term Memory

How to make a short-term memory?

Suppose you just looked up the phone number "555-9013" and repeat it as you dial. Researchers believe that your brain may store that number in short-term memory by using interconnected groups of neurons that are called neural assemblies.

Neural assemblies are groups of interconnected neurons whose activation allows information or stimuli to be recognized and held briefly and temporarily in short-term memory.

The figure on the right shows how a very simplified neural assembly might work. Some information,

or stimuli, such as repeating a phone number, activates a neural assembly that recognizes and holds the phone number in short-term memory. However, if you switch your attention to something else before encoding the number in long-term memory, this neural assembly stops and the phone number is gone and forgotten. Researchers believe that neural assemblies are one mechanism for holding information in short-term memory (Eichenbaum, 1993; Toshio et al., 1996). In comparison, permanently storing information in long-term memory involves chemical or structural changes in the neurons themselves.

Long-Term Memory

How to make a long-term memory?

One reason researchers study memory mechanisms in sea snails is that their relatively simple nervous system contains only about 20,000 neurons compared to the billions in the human brain. After the sea slug has learned a simple task, such as tensing its muscular foot in response to a bright light, researchers can dissect the sea slug's nervous system and look for chemical or physical changes associated with learning (Kandel & Abel, 1995). We'll focus on one mechanism—long-term potentiation, or LTP—that researchers believe is involved in forming long-term memories.

1 LONG-TERM POTENTIATION (LTP)

You learn the name of the large-beaked bird on the left by repeating its name, "toucan," several times. Even though you learn its odd name, you are not aware of what or how learning changed your brain. After years of research, many neuroscientists now believe that learning changes the structure and function of the neuron itself (Izquierdo & Medina, 1997; Johnston, 1997). And one way this neural change occurs is through a very complicated process called LTP.

Long-term potentiation, or *LTP,* refers to the increased sensitivity of a neuron to stimulation after it has been repeatedly stimulated.

For example, by repeating the name "toucan," you are repeatedly stimulating neurons. This repeated stimulation produces LTP, which involves complex chemical and structural changes in neurons. We'll discuss a very simple version of LTP so you can understand its importance in learning and memory.

2
Repeating the name "toucan" repeatedly stimulates neuron "A" and produces LTP in neuron "A." LTP changes the structure and functioning of neuron "A" so that it becomes more sensitive to future stimulation.

3
LTP changes the functioning of neuron "A" so that it is associated with the name "toucan." To recall the name of this bird, you activate neuron "A," which also affects other neurons (neuron "B") that form the basis for your long-term memory of the name "toucan."

4
In two recent landmark studies, researchers found that when they chemically or genetically blocked the occurrence of LTP in sea snails or mice, these animals could not learn a classically conditioned response or learn a water maze (Murphy & Glanzman, 1997; Tonegawa & Wilson, 1997). Thus, blocking the occurrence of LTP also blocked the formation of long-term memories. For this reason, many neuroscientists now believe that the LTP process may be the basis for learning and memory in animals and humans (Johnston, 1997; Tonegawa & Wilson, 1997).

CONCEPT REVIEW

1. If you retrieve previously learned information without the aid of any external cues, you are using a process of remembering called (a)_____. If you identify or match information that you have previously learned, you are using a process of remembering called (b)_____.

2. Memory files, or categories that contain related information organized around a specific topic, are called (a)_____. One theory of memory organization says that the separate memory files, or nodes, in which we file related ideas are interconnected in a gigantic system. This idea is called the (b)_____.

3. According to network theory, some nodes are arranged so that more concrete information is at the bottom and more abstract information is at the top; this order is called a _____.

4. A diagram of the amount of previously learned information that subjects can recall or recognize across time is called a _____. We tend to remember information that is familiar and interesting and forget information that is unfamiliar and uninteresting.

5. Psychologists have proposed at least four reasons for forgetting. According to Sigmund Freud, information that is threatening to our self-concept is automatically driven into our unconscious, from which we cannot retrieve it at will. This process is called _____.

6. One common reason for forgetting is that other related memories already stored in long-term memory may interfere with or block recall of some particular memory; this idea is called _____.

7. Another reason for forgetting comes from a lack of associations between new information and information we already know; this reason has to do with the quality of the _____.

8. A blow to the head may cause a form of forgetting called (a)_____, in which one loses all memories of events that occurred just before or just after being hit or after severe psychological (b)_____.

9. If we forget information not because it is lost from storage but rather because other information gets in the way and blocks its retrieval, this process is called (a)_____. If information learned earlier blocks, interferes with, or disrupts the retrieval of information that was learned later, it is called (b)_____. If information learned later blocks, interferes with, or disrupts the retrieval of information learned earlier, it is called (c)_____.

10. Mental reminders that we create by making images or associating new information with information that we already know are called _____.

11. Sometimes, despite making a great effort, we are temporarily unable to recall information that we absolutely know is in our memory. This is called the _____ phenomenon.

12. According to one memory model of the brain, short-term memories are formed and stored in different parts of the (a)_____. Long-term memories are also stored in different parts of the (b)_____, although these kinds of memories are not formed there. Declarative information is transferred by the (c)_____ into long-term memory, which is stored in different parts of the cortex. However, the hippocampus in not involved in transferring motor skill or habits, which are part of (d)_____ information, into long-term memory. Emotional associations are added to memories by an area in the temporal lobe called the (e)_____.

E. Mnemonics: Memorization Methods

At one time or another, almost everyone complains about forgetting something. Many of my students complain about forgetting information that they really knew but couldn't recall during exams. This kind of forgetting has several causes: there may be *interference (proactive and retroactive)* from information studied for related classes; there may be *poor retrieval cues* that result from trying to learn information by using rote or straight memorization; or students may not use elaborative rehearsal (p. 249), which involves making associations between new and old information.

After about age 40, adults begin to complain about forgetting things that they never forgot before. For example, memory researcher Daniel Schacter, now 45, complains, "Reading a journal article 15 years ago, I would have it at my fingertips. Now, if I don't deliberately try to relate it to what I already know, or repeat it a few times, I'm less likely to remember it" (Schacter, 1997, p. 56). This kind of forgetting is commonly caused by poor retrieval cues, which result from being busy or distracted and not having or taking the time to create meaningful associations.

If you hear about memory courses that claim to greatly improve your memory or give you a super memory, what these courses essentially teach are ways to improve encoding and retrieval cues by using mnemonic methods.

Mnemonic (ni-MON-ick) methods are ways to improve encoding and create better retrieval cues by forming vivid associations or images, which improve recall.

We'll discuss two common mnemonic methods—method of loci and peg method—that improve memory (Floyd & Scogin, 1997).

Method of Loci

If you need to memorize a list of terms, concepts, or names in a particular order, an efficient way is to use the method of loci.

The *method of loci (LOW-sigh)* is an encoding technique that creates visual associations between already memorized places and new items to be memorized.

We'll use the following three steps of the method of loci to memorize names of early psychologists: Wundt, James, and Watson.

Step 1. Memorize a visual sequence of places (loci in Latin means "places"), such as places in your apartment where you can store things. Select easily remembered places such as in your kitchen: sink, cabinet, refrigerator, stove, and closet.

Step 2. Create a vivid association for each item to be memorized. For example, picture Wundt hanging from a bridge and saying, "I wundt jump."

Step 3. Once you have created a list of vivid associations, mentally put each psychologist in one of the selected places: Wundt goes in the sink, James in the cabinet, Watson in the refrigerator.

To recall this list of early psychologists, you take an imaginary stroll through your kitchen and mentally note the image stored in each of your memorized places.

Peg Method

Another useful mnemonic device for memorizing a long list, especially in the exact order, is the peg method.

The *peg method* is an encoding technique that creates associations between number-word rhymes and items to be memorized.

The rhymes act like pegs on which you hang items to be memorized. Let's use the two steps of the peg method to memorize our three early psychologists: Wundt, James, Watson.

**one is a bun
two is a shoe
three is a tree
four is a door
five is a hive**

Step 1. Memorize a list of peg-words shown on the left, which consists of a number and its rhyming word.

Step 2. Next, associate each of the items you wish to memorize with one of the peg-words. For instance, imagine Wundt on a bun, James with two left shoes, and Watson stuck in a tree.

To remember this list of early psychologists, you recall each peg along with its image of an early psychologist that you placed there.

Effectiveness

A national magazine writer, who was 41 years old and complained about forgetfulness, decided to improve her memory by trying three different methods (Yoffe, 1997).

First, she took a 3-hour memory-enhancement class ($49). The teacher focused on the peg method and used it to memorize the names of the 11 students in the class. The magazine writer concluded the peg method was impressive and if she were back in college, she would use it to memorize the endless number of facts.

Second, she listened to an audiocassette program ($79) that promised to release the "perfect photographic memory" that everyone already had. However, memory researchers report that photographic memories are as rare as duck's teeth (Schacter, 1996). The audio program emphasized the peg method but did not describe how it could be applied to things other than remembering grocery lists, biology terms, license plate numbers, or names.

Third, she read a memory-improvement book ($10) that described the peg method, how to pay attention, and the importance of creating associations and images.

As this writer's experience illustrates, good recall depends largely on two important principles. First, good encoding involves elaborative rehearsal—creating associations and images that produce good retrieval cues and good recall. Second, good encoding requires time and effort.

Next, we'll examine possible cultural influences on whether we are more likely to use verbal or visual retrieval cues.

F. Cultural Diversity:
Aborigines versus White Australians

Retrieval Cues

How do you survive in a desert?

The left photo shows the harsh, endless, barren desert world of western Australia, where many of the native Aborigines live. For about 30,000 years, the Aborigines have followed a lifestyle of hunting and gathering in what is considered to be among the world's least hospitable habitats for humans (Gould, 1969). In this stark desert world, the Aborigines survive by remembering the locations of water, food, and game in vast stretches of unmapped country. Their survival in this barren desert is greatly dependent on their ability to store, or encode, enormous amounts of visual information by using *visual retrieval cues*.

The right photo shows the meeting of a business group in an industrialized urban area. To survive in this kind of computer-dependent and career-driven society, people need to learn a number of specific skills, especially reading and writing. In fact, success in complex urban settings is greatly dependent on the ability to store, or encode, enormous amounts of verbal information by using *verbal retrieval cues*.

You can see from these two examples that cultural needs emphasize certain ways of encoding and retrieving information. You might also predict that people from these two cultures would perform differently on tests, depending on whether the tests emphasized visual or verbal retrieval cues.

Visual versus Verbal Retrieval Cues

Psychologist Judith Kearins was not surprised to find that Aborigines scored low on Western-style intelligence tests, because these tests emphasize verbal retrieval cues and put Aborigines at a disadvantage. Considering their desert culture, she suspected that Aborigines would perform better on tests that took advantage of their ability to encode with visual retrieval cues.

USING VISUAL CUES

To see if Aborigines were better at visual encoding, Kearins developed a test that emphasized visual retrieval cues. This test consisted of looking at 20 objects that were placed on a board divided into 20 squares. Some objects were natural—stone, feather, leaf; others were manufactured—eraser, thimble, ring. Aborigines and white Australian adolescents were told to study the board for 30 seconds (sample section on right). Then all the objects were heaped into a pile in the center of the board and the children were asked to replace the items in their original locations. The 44 Aborigine adolescents had been reared for the most part in desert tribal ways, had learned a nontraditional form of English as a second language, and were now attending school. The 44 white Australian adolescents lived and attended high school in a relatively large urban area (Perth).

BETTER PERFORMANCE

Kearins tested the adolescents using four different sets of objects—all natural, all manufactured, some combined. The graph below shows that the Aborigine adolescents performed significantly better in placing objects back into their original locations than did the white Australian adolescents (Kearins, 1981). Another group of researchers essentially replicated Kearins' results using a younger population (average age of nine) of Aborigines and white Australians (Klich & Davidson, 1983).

11.6	**White Australians**
16.2	**Aborigines**

Average Correct Responses

CULTURE AND RETRIEVAL CUES

Kearins concluded that the Aborigines' survival in the harsh desert landscape encouraged and rewarded their abilities to encode information using visual retrieval cues. In comparison, the urban school setting of the white Australians encouraged and rewarded their ability to encode information using verbal retrieval cues. For example, when questioned about their strategies, many of the Aborigines said only that they remembered the look of the objects on the board. In comparison, white Australians described their strategies in great detail: "I looked at the bottom row and remembered onion, banksia nut, rock, bone, and apple core." These descriptions support the idea that the Aborigines used visual retrieval cues, while the white Australians used verbal retrieval cues. These interesting results suggest that survival needs do shape and reward a particular way of encoding information in memory.

The better performance of Aborigines on visual tasks indicates that culture does influence the encoding and recall of information. Besides culture, other things, such as the age of a child, may also influence encoding and recall, as shown next in studies on implanting false memories in young children.

G. Research Focus: False Memories
Can False Memories Be Implanted?

Is the child telling the truth?

Each year in the United States, over 10,000 children are asked to testify about sexual abuse. In some cases, the children's testimony appears truthful and believable, and the cases are settled. In other cases, especially those involving day-care centers, children may testify about unusual or bizarre sexual practices that raise questions about the reliability of their testimony. For example, in one publicized case, Margaret Kelly Michael, a 26-year-old nursery schoolteacher, was said to have played the piano while nude, made

children drink her urine, raped and assaulted children, and licked peanut butter off children's genitals. Kelly was convicted of 115 counts of sexual abuse committed against 20 children from 3 to 5 years old. After spending 5 years in prison, her conviction was overturned by a higher court because of concerns that the testimony of 19 child witnesses may have been unreliable due to improper interviewing by therapists (Ceci & Bruck, 1995). Improper interviewing refers to the possibility that the therapists, through repeated suggestions and specific questions, may have implanted false memories in the children. This very serious concern led researchers to study whether false memories could be implanted in young children.

Creating False Memories in Young Children

What happens during questioning?

When questioning young children about sexual abuse charges, therapists or officials may repeatedly suggest that certain events happened. The concern is that these repeated suggestions may eventually create false memories in young children. To test this idea, psychologist Stephen Ceci and his colleagues (1994) studied 96 children from 3 to 6 years old who came from a wide range of social and economic classes.

Procedure. To obtain a list of true and false events, researchers interviewed the children's parents about events that had occurred within the past 12 months of the child's life, such as a surprise birthday party, a trip to Disney World, injury, or death of a pet. Each child was then read a list of these events, some of which were fictitious. The children were asked "to think real hard" and identify events that had actually happened to them.

Researchers emphasized that some events on the list had not happened to the children. For example, one fictitious event was "getting one's hand caught in a mousetrap and having to go to the hospital to have it removed." This testing procedure was repeated for each child in seven to ten different interviews, which were spaced about a week apart. In the last session, children were videotaped as they described the events, true or false.

Results. As shown in the graph below, 91% of the time children correctly identified events that had happened to them, indicating that they had accurate recall. However, 34% of the time, children said that they had experienced fictitious events that had only been suggested to them (Ceci et al., 1994). Surprisingly, children remembered fictitious events in great detail.

Here's how one 4-year-old described the fictitious event of getting his hand caught in a mousetrap: "My brother Colin was trying to get Blowtorch [an action toy] away from me, and I wouldn't

Agreeing to false events 34%

91% Agreeing to true events

let him take it from me, so he pushed me into the woodpile where the mousetrap was. And then my finger got caught in it. And then we went to the hospital, and my mommy, daddy, and Colin drove me there, to the hospital in our van, because it was far away. And the doctor put a bandage on this finger."

Some believe that children's lies or made-up stories can be detected through facial features (unsure or guilty looks) and speech patterns (stammering, correcting details). To test this belief, the same researchers asked 109 professionals (clinical and developmental psychologists, law enforcement officials, social and psychiatric workers) to judge whether events described by the children were true or fictitious. Professionals who watched videotapes of the children scored no better than chance in distinguishing true from fictitious events. Thus, children were very convincing in describing fictitious events.

Conclusion. When young children were asked repeatedly "to think hard" about true and fictitious events, some children became convinced that some of the fictitious events had actually happened. In addition, children gave such detailed and convincing stories of fictitious events that their stories fooled professional judges. Although this study showed that 91% of the time young children accurately recalled information about past events, it also showed that 34% of the time they turned false memories into true and believable ones. Because very young children (aged 3 and 4 years)

were more open to suggestions than older children (aged 5 and 6 years), researchers emphasize that great care must be taken when questioning young children so that repeated suggestions do not create and implant false memories.

Just as some young children may respond to suggestions and misremember events, some adults may also misremember when giving eyewitness testimony, our next topic.

H. Application: Eyewitness Testimony

Definition and Problems

Why did she accuse the wrong man?

The woman on the witness stand was very emotional as she recalled in vivid detail the hour of terror during which two men had forced her into her car, drove away, and later raped her in the front seat. When she was asked if one of the rapists was present in the courtroom, she pointed directly at the defendant sitting at the table and said, "There is no doubt in my mind."

Eyewitness testimony refers to recalling or recognizing a suspect observed during a potentially very disrupting and distracting emotional situation that may have interfered with accurate remembering.

For example, the woman's eyewitness testimony was the major piece of evidence that sent the defendant (an accused rapist) to prison. The defendant spent 10 terrible years in prison, all the time protesting his innocence and asking for a new lawyer. Finally, a new criminal defense lawyer was appointed who was able to locate the victim's clothes, which had been left in police storage. The new lawyer asked that the victim's clothes undergo a DNA test, which had not yet been developed at the time of the initial trial. The DNA test proved that the sperm stains on the victim's jeans did not come from the man who was in prison. The man who had been sent to prison largely on the victim's eyewitness testimony was found innocent and set free (Dolan, 1995). This example raises at least three problems with eyewitness testimony.

First, many juries assume that eyewitness testimony is the best kind of evidence because it is so accurate and reliable. However, a study of people who were wrongfully convicted of crimes in the United States and England revealed that eyewitness testimony was the single most important source of evidence used to falsely convict people of crimes (Wells et al., 1994). Researchers estimate that in the United States several thousand defendants are wrongly convicted each year of a serious crime (rape, murder) (Huff, 1995).

For example, the white woman (figure above) in this rape case may have made a mistaken identification of her alleged attacker (right figure) because she was distracted by her severe emotional state and did not get a good look. Or, she may have made the wrong identification because of interference. As it turned out, the African American man whom she confidently accused did slightly resemble the real rapist.

Second, we generally assume that, the more confident an eyewitness is, the more accurate is the testimony. For example, the witness in this rape case was very confident when she said, "There is no doubt in my mind." However, six reviews of eyewitness studies concluded that there was only a weak relationship between a correct identification and how much confidence the eyewitness felt (Granhag, 1997).

Third, eyewitnesses may make errors if law enforcement officials ask misleading or biased questions. In these cases, eyewitnesses may unknowingly accept the misinformation as fact and give unreliable testimony. For example, consider the following case of mistaken identity.

Misleading the Witness

Could seven eyewitnesses be wrong?

Some years ago a series of armed robberies occurred in the Wilmington, Delaware, area. The robber was dubbed the "gentleman bandit" because of his polite manners and well-groomed appearance. The police had few leads on the gentleman bandit until a local citizen informed them that a Roman Catholic priest, Father Bernard Pagano, looked remarkably like the sketch of the robber being circulated in the media.

Seven eyewitnesses positively identified Father Pagano (left photo) as the culprit. At his trial, the case against him seemed airtight. But at the last minute, another man, Ronald Clouser (photo below), stepped forward and confessed to the robberies. He knew details about the robberies that only the true gentleman bandit could have known. The case against Father Pagano was dropped immediately, and Clouser was charged with the crimes (Rodgers, 1982).

Seven people identified Father Pagano . . .

As you look at these two photos, you will wonder how this case of mistaken identity could possibly have happened. Ronald Clouser is shorter, 14 years younger, and not nearly as bald as Father Pagano; besides, he has different facial features. Why, then, did seven eyewitnesses say with certainty that Father Pagano was the robber they had seen? One reason involves how the witnesses were questioned. Apparently, before witnesses were questioned and shown photos of the suspects, the police had suggested the possibility that the robber was a priest. After being prompted to look for a priest, the witnesses focused on the few similarities Father Pagano had to the real robber. Because Father Pagano was the only suspect wearing a clerical collar, the witnesses concluded that he must be the robber. This example is but one of many that show how eyewitness testimony may be distorted or biased. Later, we'll discuss a more reliable method of police questioning called the cognitive interview.

There is now considerable research showing that eyewitness testimony may be biased by a number of the following factors.

. . . but Ronald Clouser was the real robber.

Biasing Factors

How can witnesses be misled?

Because of concern about the reliability of eyewitness testimony, Elizabeth Loftus (1979, 1993a) studied whether people can be misled and do misremember, especially if they are given false information. We'll describe several of Loftus' experiments that demonstrate how subjects misremembered what they saw or heard.

DID THE CAR PASS THE BARN?

In one experiment, subjects watched a film of an automobile accident and then were questioned about what they saw. One of the questions contained a false piece of information: "How fast was the red sports car going when it passed the barn while traveling along the country road?" Although there was no barn in the film, 17% of the subjects said they had seen a barn, indicating that people may believe misinformation if it fits the overall scene or pattern (Loftus, 1975).

WAS THERE A STOP SIGN?

In a well-known study by Loftus and colleagues, subjects were first shown slides of a traffic accident involving a stop sign and then asked a series of questions about the accident. Some of the questions were not misleading and asked about the presence of a stop sign. Other questions were deliberately misleading and did not mention the stop sign but asked about the presence of a yield sign. Later, when subjects were asked whether they had seen a stop sign or a yield sign, those subjects who had been misled by earlier questions about a yield sign were more likely to report seeing a yield sign than subjects who were not misled (Loftus et al., 1978). These results, which show that subjects can be misled by being given false but related information, have been replicated by many other researchers (Zaragoza & Lane, 1994).

HOW DOES FALSE INFORMATION ALTER MEMORY?

Based on many such studies, Loftus and Hoffman (1989) concluded that if misleading information is introduced during questioning after an event, people may believe this misinformation and report events that they did not see.

According to Loftus, eyewitnesses believed the false information they were told, rather than what they saw, because the false information altered or overwrote their original, true memory (Loftus & Loftus, 1980). This explanation, which has generated much research and debate, says that people misremember because of a memory impairment: the true memory was erased or overwritten (Payne et al., 1994). However, other researchers argue that the original, true memory is still there but is difficult to retrieve (Zaragoza & Lane, 1994). Whatever the cause, these many studies indicate that people (witnesses) do misremember when given misleading information.

Source Misattribution

Can a suggestion become a fact?

The debate over whether false information overwrites the original memory has not been settled. However, what has been settled is that sometimes people do come to believe that they actually remember seeing things that were merely suggested to them; this phenomenon is called source misattribution.

Source misattribution is a memory error that results when a person has difficulty in deciding which of two or more sources a memory came from: Was the source something the person saw or imagined, or was it a suggestion?

For example, suppose you saw a hit-and-run accident involving a dark red car. During questioning, you are asked the color of the car that drove off. As you're thinking that the car was dark red, you remember hearing another bystander say, "The car was dark blue." Source misattribution would occur if you said that the car was dark blue (suggestion you heard) rather than dark red (something you saw). Researchers have found that false suggestions, misleading questions, and misinformation can result in source misattribution and create false memories (Hayes & Delamothe, 1997). False memories that can result from source misattribution, such as suggestions or misleading questions, are one reason that court officials may question the accuracy of eyewitness testimony.

Cognitive Interview

What's the best way to question a witness?

Suppose you had witnessed a robbery but had trouble picking the suspect out of a police lineup (photo below). To help you provide reliable information about the suspect, you might be questioned in a procedure called the cognitive interview (Fisher & Geiselman, 1992).

The *cognitive interview* is a technique for questioning people, such as eyewitnesses, by having them imagine and reconstruct the details of an event, report everything they remember without holding anything back, and narrate the event from different viewpoints.

The cognitive interview has proved very useful in police interrogation: detectives trained in cognitive interview techniques obtained 47–60% more information from victims and suspects than detectives using the standard police interrogation method (Gwyer & Clifford, 1997). The cognitive interview is an effective way to avoid making

 suggestions or giving misleading information that might create false memories and increase errors of source misattribution (Bower, 1997).

Psychologists have answered many questions about how eyewitnesses can be misled as well as how to improve the reliability of their testimony, which may result in life or death decisions. Based on this work, England has barred cases when the only evidence is an eyewitness. In the United States, many courts allow experts to testify about the reliability of eyewitnesses so that juries are made aware of the same studies and findings that you have just read (Pezdek, 1995).

SUMMARY TEST

A. ORGANIZATION OF MEMORIES

1. If you are asked to retrieve previously learned information without the aid of external cues, you are using a process of remembering called (a)_____, which is generally more difficult. If you are asked to answer multiple-choice questions, you can identify or match information and use a process of remembering called (b)_____, which is generally less difficult.

1. ANIMAL

2. According to one theory of how memory is organized, we encode or file related ideas in separate categories called _____.

3. We form links between nodes by forming associations. The idea that the interconnected nodes form a gigantic system is called the _____ theory.

4. An arrangement in which nodes are organized in a logical manner, with more concrete information at the bottom and more abstract information at the top, is called a _____.

B. FORGETTING CURVES

5. If the amount of previously learned information that subjects can recall or recognize across time is plotted, the resulting graph is called a _____. For example, Ebbinghaus demonstrated that the majority of nonsense syllables are forgotten relatively quickly—within hours. However, other studies showed that more relevant and interesting information may be remembered for many years.

C. REASONS FOR FORGETTING

6. There are at least four reasons for forgetting. One of the most common is that other memories may interfere with or prevent retrieval of some particular memory; this is called (a)_____. One kind of interference occurs when information learned earlier interferes with information learned later; this is called (b)_____. A second kind of interference occurs when information learned later interferes with information learned earlier; this is called (c)_____.

7. A second reason for forgetting is that information is poorly encoded, which means that a lack of associations or reminders makes it difficult to retrieve a memory; this is called _____.

8. A third reason, put forth by Sigmund Freud, is that information that is threatening to our self-concept is automatically driven into our unconscious, from which we cannot retrieve it at will; this is called _____.

9. A fourth reason for forgetting is the effect of a blow to the head, psychological trauma, or drugs; this is called _____.

10. To increase the chances of remembering items from long-term memory, we can create reminders that associate new information with information that we already know; these reminders are called _____.

11. There are times when you are absolutely sure that certain information is stored in memory but you are unable to retrieve it. This experience is called the _____ phenomenon.

12. Besides creating retrieval cues, it may also be easier to recall information when you are in the same physiological or emotional state as when you originally learned it; this phenomenon is called _____.

D. BIOLOGICAL BASES OF MEMORY

13. Different areas of the brain are involved in different memory processes. For example, the ability to hold words, facts, or events (declarative information) in short-term memory depends on activity in the (a)_____. The ability to transfer information about words, facts, and events (declarative information) from short-term into long-term memory depends on activity in the (b)_____. If this structure were damaged, a person could carry on a conversation but would not (c)_____ the conversation the next day.

14. The ability to recall words, facts, and events (declarative information) from the past involves activity in the outer covering of the brain, which is called the (a)_____. For example, if patients have an intact cortex they can remember past events because these events are already stored in the cortex. However, they may have difficulty remembering any new words, facts, or events (declarative information) because of damage to their (b)_____.

15. The ability to transfer motor skills and habits, which is part of _____ memory, does not involve the hippocampus. Even though a person with damage to the hippocampus can store procedural information, that person would have no memory of having engaged in that event (declarative information).

16. The area of the brain that adds emotional feelings to memories is called the _____. This area is involved in forming a wide range of happy, sad, or fearful memories.

17. Researchers believe that the brain forms and briefly stores short-term memories by using a circuit of interconnected neurons called _____. When these interconnected neurons stop being activated, the short-term memory vanishes, unless it has been encoded in long-term memory.

18. Researchers have evidence that the formation and storage of long-term memories involve the repeated stimulation of neurons, which in turn results in their becoming more sensitive to future stimulation; this phenomenon is called (a)_____. When this process was chemically or genetically blocked, animals were unable to form b)_____.

E. MNEMONICS: MEMORIZATION METHODS

19. Although we have the capacity to store great amounts of information, we may not be able to recall some of this information because of forgetting. Techniques that use efficient methods of encoding to improve remembering and prevent forgetting are called (a)_____. The major function of these techniques is to create strong (b)_____ that will serve as effective (c)_____.

20. A method that creates visual associations between memorized places and items to be memorized is called the (a)_____. With another method, one creates associations between number-word rhymes and items to be memorized; this method is called the (b)_____.

F. CULTURAL DIVERSITY: ABORIGINES

21. Data from Aborigine and white Australian children suggest that survival needs may shape and reward a particular way of (a)_____ information in memory. For example, in the industrialized world, people (white Australians) are required to store large amounts of (b)_____. However, Aborigines in the wilds of Australia need to be able to store environmental, or (c)_____, to find their way, locate watering places, and thus increase their chances of survival. Researchers found that Aborigines performed better on tests that required (d)_____ retrieval cues and performed less well on tests that required (e)_____ cues.

G. RESEARCH FOCUS: FALSE MEMORIES

22. During the past 10 years, young children have been called upon to testify in court, particularly regarding cases of sexual abuse. Because there are records of officials suggesting to young children that certain events have occurred, there is concern that children may come to believe these suggestions. Researchers found that, although young children can accurately recall past events, repeated suggestions may create _____ in young children.

H. APPLICATION: EYEWITNESS TESTIMONY

23. One reason eyewitnesses may identify the wrong suspect is because criminal situations may be emotionally very disruptive or distracting, which may cause interference that leads to (a)_____. Another reason eyewitness testimony may not be reliable is that witnesses may be influenced by officials who ask (b)_____ questions.

24. When a person has difficulty deciding which of two or more sources is responsible for a memory, it is called (a)_____. Researchers found that misleading questions and false information could cause subjects to (b)_____ events.

25. The recall of eyewitnesses may be improved by having them imagine and reconstruct the details of an event, report everything that they remember, and report things from different viewpoints. This method is called the (a)_____. By using this method, eyewitnesses remember much more information about the event than they do when asked standard questions. This questioning procedure also helps to eliminate suggestions or source misattributions, which can result in implanting (b)_____ in witnesses.

Answers: *1. (a) recall, (b) recognition; 2. nodes; 3. network; 4. hierarchy; 5. forgetting curve; 6. (a) interference, (b) proactive interference, (c) retroactive interference; 7. inadequate retrieval cues; 8. repression; 9. amnesia; 10. retrieval cues; 11. tip-of-the-tongue; 12. state-dependent learning; 13. (a) cortex, (b) hippocampus, (c) remember; 14. (a) cortex, (b) hippocampus; 15. procedural; 16. amygdala; 17. neural assemblies; 18. (a) long-term potentiation, or LTP, (b) long-term memories; 19. (a) mnemonics, (b) associations, (c) retrieval cues; 20. (a) method of loci, (b) peg method; 21. (a) encoding, (b) verbal information, (c) visual information, (d) visual, (e) verbal; 22. false memories; 23. (a) forgetting, (b) misleading; 24. (a) source misattribution, (b) misremember; 25. (a) cognitive interview, (b) false memories.*

Newspaper Article

1. Of the four reasons for forgetting, which one applies to Krickitt?

2. Krickitt's loss of many long-term memories means that which part of her brain was damaged?

3. How was Krickitt able to remember her parents but not her husband, not their apartment, and not their wedding photos?

4. Of the two kinds of long-term memory, which involves Krickitt's having to relearn to drive a car?

5. Which part of Krickitt's brain was undamaged and allowed her to store new long-term memories of Kim?

SECOND TIME AROUND
by Michael Haederle

LAS VEGAS, N.M.—Shortly after their wedding in 1993, Krickitt suffered a severe head injury in a car crash. When she emerged from a month-long coma, she no longer knew Kim (her husband), having lost all memory of the previous 18 months—including meeting and marrying her husband. . . .

Emerging from her coma around Christmas, Krickitt was as helpless as a newborn. She needed to be fed, diapered and bathed. The 5-foot-2 former college gymnast, who'd once performed back flips on a balance beam, had to learn to walk again. . . .

When quizzed by a nurse, Krickitt knew she was in Phoenix—although she thought it was 1969 (it was really 1993) and Nixon was the president. She also knew who her parents were. . . . Then the nurse asked "Who's your husband?" Krickitt said, "I'm not married." . . .

Krickitt visited their Las Vegas home, hoping the familiar surroundings might jog her memory. She wandered through the apartment she'd shared with Kim, gazing at their wedding photos and fingering her china. Nothing clicked.

"I remember asking, 'How did I do the wife thing? Did I cook for you? Did I bring you lunch?'"she says. Krickitt was unable to drive and couldn't remember directions. Kim worried she'd get lost walking the 100 yards to the grocery store. . . . It was the therapist who suggested that Kim and Krickitt start dating as a way of rebuilding their relationship. On their "date nights," they sampled everything their small town had to offer. "We'd go to Pizza Hut," Kim says. "We'd go to Wal-Mart or go bowling." Sometimes he'd bring her roses. . . .With continued therapy and the passage of time, Krickitt has accepted her new life. . . . It was Krickitt who suggested getting married again.

On Valentine's Day he went to her office with a bunch of red roses and proposed on bended knee. . . . They married (above photo) Sept. 18,1993 and honeymooned in Maui before settling into their new life together in this small northern New Mexico city.

Source: *Los Angeles Times*, May 23, 1996.

Study Questions

A. Organization of Memories—How would your memory be affected if you accidentally took a drug that prevented the formation of any new nodes? (See answer in Critical Thinking Appendix.)

B. Forgetting Curves—Why are you more likely to remember students' names than concepts from high school?

C. Reasons for Forgetting—If you wanted to change your study habits, how would you use information about why we forget?

D. Biological Bases of Memory—If a virus suddenly destroyed your hippocampus, what effect would it have on your performance in college? (See answer in Critical Thinking Appendix.)

E. Mnemonics: Memorization Methods—Can you describe a mnemonic method to remember the five reasons for forgetting?

F. Cultural Diversity: Aborigines Versus White Australians—What might be one difference between the ways in which art and English majors encode information?

G. Research Focus: False Memories—When young children are questioned, what precautions should be taken to minimize the creation of false memories?

H. Application: Eyewitness Testimony—If you were on a jury, what concerns would you have when listening to eyewitness testimony? (See answer in Critical Thinking Appendix.)

LINKS TO LEARNING

Web Sites & Learning Activities

● BROOKS/COLE ONLINE PSYCHOLOGY STUDY CENTER

http://psychstudy.brookscole.com/student/plotnik/quiz/ch12frm.html

This site gives students a chance to review material by taking quizzes and doing exercises and activities for this module.

● MINDTOOLS

http://www.psych-web.com/mtsite/memory.html

Here are several tools designed to improve your memory. The site provides techniques, such as mnemonic devices, for memory improvement.

● NOOTOPICS: COGNITIVE-ENHANCEMENT DRUGS

http://www.damicon.fi/sd/

Can so-called "smart drugs" really improve your memory, learning, and thinking? This site presents a general overview plus many specific reports.

● WHY DO WE FORGET THINGS?

http://www.bssc.edu.au/learning_areas/learning/science/wigney/tests/forgetting.htm

This fun site presents a series of quizzes involving case studies that involve common reasons for forgetting, including information decay, repression, and organic factors.

Welcome to the WEB

● THE ALZHEIMER'S DISEASE WEB PAGE

http://med-www.bu.edu/Alzheimer/home.html

This Boston University site provides lots of current information on Alzheimer's disease, including clinical research and resources for caregivers.

● BRAIN INJURY CENTER

http://www.braincenter.org/

This site offers information and support to those dealing with brain injury, one condition that can lead to memory problems.

Activities

● *Integrator Online™ for Introductory Psychology* CD-ROM, Plotnik, Module 12

● Study Guide to accompany *Introduction to Psychology,* 5th edition, Module 12 (choice of PC or Mac computer version or hard copy).

● *PsychNow!* CD-ROM
Forgetting

Answers to questions on page 278

1. Because of a car accident, Krickitt suffered a severe blow to her head that caused her to go into a coma. In addition, when she came out of her coma, the severe blow to her head also caused widespread amnesia, which is forgetting caused by loss of memory.

2. Since long-term memories are stored primarily in the cortex (surface of the brain), this means that areas of Krickitt's cortex were damaged in the accident.

3. Researchers have discovered that different kinds of long-term memories are stored in different parts of the cortex. Krickitt could remember her parents because those memories were stored in a part of her cortex that was undamaged. However, she lost all memory of her husband and being married because these memories were stored in a part of her cortex that was damaged.

4. There are two kinds of long-term memories, declarative and procedural (p. 246). Learning motor skills and habits involves storing procedural memories and does not involve the hippocampus.

5. Krickett was able to relearn who Kim was by dating him. Krickett's ability to remember that she was dating and going out with Kim means that she was able to store personal or episodic memories, which are one kind of declarative memories (p. 246). Declarative memories are transferred and stored as long-term memories by the hippocampus, which means that Krickett's hippocampus was undamaged and functioning.

Module 13 INTELLIGENCE

Supreme Court Justice

What was his background?

Clarence Thomas was born in 1948 in Pin Point, Georgia, a small backward town with dirt roads, no sewers, and about 100 residents. After the father abandoned them, the family—Clarence, his mother, older sister, and a younger brother—lived on $15 a week, wore old clothes donated by the local church, and survived on cornflakes, crabs, and grits occasionally mixed with eggs.

When Clarence was 7, the family house burned down, and he and his younger brother were sent to Savannah, Georgia, to live with his grandfather. This was the time when the South was rigidly segregated: Blacks were forced to ride in the back of buses, banned from restaurants, and made to attend segregated schools and churches.

Grandfather taught Clarence how to survive in this openly hostile environment by stressing four things: "school, discipline, hard work, and right from wrong." Clarence spent two years as the only African American student in a white Catholic boarding high school. The White students were cruel and hateful. Clarence remembers being called "coon" and "nigger," and at night, when the lights went out in the dormitory, someone would yell, "Smile, Clarence, so we can see you." Some of the students referred to Clarence as "ABC," for America's Blackest Child.

After high school, Clarence attended Holy Cross College in Worcester, Massachusetts, where he had to work doubly hard because everybody presumed "that you were dumb and didn't deserve to be there on merit." Clarence graduated from college with honors and was accepted by Yale Law School. Seventeen years later, in 1991, Clarence Thomas was confirmed to the highest court in the United States.

Older Sister

What was her background?

The story of his older sister, Emma Mae, is somewhat different, however. She attended high school in rural Georgia, but Emma chose not to attend college partly because no one encouraged her to go on. Emma had to survive some hard times; she had few job opportunities while raising two children without a husband. She currently works as a cook in a local hospital and lives in a small house in rural Pin Point, Georgia, where she was born and raised. Just as Justice Thomas needed a certain kind of intelligence to be successful in academic settings, Emma Mae needed a certain kind of intelligence to survive a hard, impoverished environment (adapted from *Newsweek*, September 25, 1991).

Justice Thomas and Emma Mae Martin (photo right), like all brothers and sisters, share 50% of their genes. However, except for their first seven years, they grew up in very different environments that offered very different educational, social, and personal opportunities. In their cases, the interaction between genetic and environmental factors resulted in different psychological abilities and traits. One of these abilities or traits is referred to as intelligence, whose measurement is part of psychometrics.

Psychometrics, which is a subarea of psychology, is concerned with developing psychological tests that assess an individual's abilities, skills, beliefs, and personality traits in a wide range of settings—school, industry, or clinic.

Psychologists developed the first tests to measure intelligence in the late 1800s. Then, as today, psychologists were concerned with three major questions: how to define intelligence, how to construct a test to measure intelligence, and how to explain intelligence (Daniel, 1997; Gardner, 1997; and Sternberg, 1997a, 1997b). Some of the early psychologists explained intelligence as being primarily an inborn trait; this theory led to the study of identical twins.

Identical Twins

Why study twins?

The reason identical twins look so similar is that they have exactly the same genetic makeup, which means that they share 100% of their genes.

In comparison, a brother and sister usually look quite different because they share only 50% of their genes. We know that because of identical genes, identical twins will have identical facial features, hair color, height, shoe size and eye color. Does this also mean that identical twins will have identical IQ scores? The answer: their IQ

scores are more similar than those of brothers and sisters. This raises another famous question: How much does nature (genes) contribute to IQ scores compared to nurture (environment) (Sternberg & Grigorenko, 1997)? Later in this module, we'll discuss this interesting question along with research from studies of identical twins.

What's Coming

We'll discuss the different theories of intelligence, how intelligence is measured, the meaning of IQ scores, the problems with intelligence tests, how genetics and environment influence intelligence, and ways to improve environmental opportunities.

We'll begin with the hundred-year-old question: How do we define intelligence?

A. Defining Intelligence

Problem

What is intelligence?

I very clearly remember bringing a report card home from grade school and being asked by my parents why I didn't get all As like my older brother had gotten. I thought about it and replied, "He must be smarter than me." From that time on I promised myself that the first chance I had I would take an IQ test and find out exactly how smart I really was. When I did take a group IQ test in high school, the counselor said it was the school's policy not to tell students their exact scores. But trying to be helpful in my case, the counselor added that I might have trouble getting through college.

The point is that someone—you, a parent, teacher, counselor, husband/wife, friend, or boss—will make a judgment about your level of intelligence. However, intelligence can be difficult to define and measure. Recently, the official journal of the American Psychological Association devoted an entire issue to discussing how to define and measure intelligence and the value and usefulness of IQ scores (*American Psychologist,* October, 1997). Although we all use the term *intelligence,* in some cases it may be difficult to define.

For example, which of these two people is more intelligent?

Clarence Thomas (left photo) graduated from highly respected Yale Law school, was a federal judge, and is now a Justice of the United States Supreme Court, the highest court in the land.

Nancy Lopez (right photo) is a professional golfer who won 47 tournaments, was in the Hall of Fame by age 30, and has earned almost 5 million dollars.

So who is more intelligent, Justice Clarence Thomas or professional golfer Nancy Lopez? The answer depends primarily on how we define intelligence. If we define intelligence in terms of cognitive abilities, we would say that Justice Thomas is more intelligent. However, if we define intelligence in

terms of motor and perceptual skills and financial earnings, we would say that Nancy Lopez is more intelligent.

Some psychologists believe that intelligence is best defined by measuring cognitive abilities. Others argue that a definition of intelligence based entirely on cognitive abilities is much too narrow. Instead, they believe that there are many kinds of intelligence, such as musical, motor (movement), creative, or practical intelligence. We'll examine three popular theories of intelligence—the two-factor, multiple-factor, and triarchic theories.

We'll begin with the oldest and most widely accepted definition of intelligence, the two-factor theory.

Two-Factor Theory

What is "g"?

In 1904, Charles Spearman reported that he had measured intelligence in an objective way; thus, he was one of the first to use the psychometric approach.

The *psychometric approach* measures or quantifies cognitive abilities or factors that are thought to be involved in intellectual performance.

Spearman (1904) reasoned that by measuring related cognitive factors he could measure intelligence. This idea led to his two-factor theory of intelligence.

Spearman's *two-factor theory* says that intelligence has two factors: a general mental ability factor, *g*, which represents what different cognitive tasks have in common; plus many specific factors, *s,* which include specific mental abilities (mathematical, mechanical, or verbal skills).

Spearman believed that factor *g*, or general mental ability, represented a person's mental energy. After almost 100 years, factor *g* has become a major force in defining and measuring intelligence. Many psychologists believe that *g* is what current intelligence tests measure, which means that Spearman's *g* has been transformed into the modern IQ score (Brody, 1997).

> **On the basis of Spearman's two-factor theory, who is more intelligent—Justice Thomas or pro golfer Lopez?**

Since Clarence Thomas graduated from college with honors, we can assume that he has the kind of cognitive abilities that are necessary for success in academic settings. Since tests of cognitive abilities form the basis for Spearman's *g*, which in turn is the basis for today's IQ score, we assume that Justice Thomas would score well on intelligence tests.

In comparison, Nancy Lopez has demonstrated exceptional motor and perceptual skills by winning 47 golf tournaments and earning millions of dollars. However, since standard IQ tests measure cognitive abilities, she would get little credit for her motor and perceptual skills and possibly score lower on IQ tests than Justice Thomas. So who do you think is more intelligent—Justice Clarence Thomas or professional golfer Nancy Lopez?

ADVANTAGES AND DISADVANTAGES

One advantage of *g* is that many assume it defines and measures general intelligence, which means that general intelligence can be represented by an IQ score. Another advantage of *g* is that it is a good predictor of performance in school and academic settings and has some success in predicting performance in certain careers (Brody, 1997), which we'll discuss later in this module.

Perhaps the major disadvantage of using *g*, or an IQ score, as the ultimate measure of intelligence is that *g* excludes and does not measure many other kinds of mental abilities, such as motor, perceptual, musical, practical, or creative abilities, which some psychologists consider to represent other kinds of intelligence (Neisser et al., 1996). For this reason, psychologists critical of *g*'s restrictive approach to measuring intelligence have proposed several other theories, definitions, and ways to measure intelligence. We'll look at those next.

Multiple-Intelligence Theory

Seven kinds of intelligence? Some psychologists reject the idea that intelligence can be reduced to *g* and expressed by a single IQ score. For example, Howard Gardner (1995, 1997) argues that there are different kinds of mental abilities that make up different kinds of intelligence, an idea he calls the multiple-intelligence theory.

Gardner's multiple-intelligence theory says that instead of one kind of general intelligence, there are at least seven different kinds, which include verbal intelligence, musical intelligence, logical-mathematical intelligence, spatial intelligence, body movement intelligence, intelligence to understand oneself, and intelligence to understand others.

Gardner states that standard IQ tests primarily measure verbal and logical-mathematical intelligence and neglect other but equally important kinds of intelligence—namely, the other five above. Gardner (1993a, 1995) arrived at his theory of seven kinds of intelligence after studying which abilities remain following brain damage, how savants and prodigies develop their specialized kinds of intelligence, and how people in different environments develop different abilities in order to adapt and be successful.

On the basis of Gardner's multiple-intelligence theory, who is more intelligent—Justice Thomas or pro golfer Lopez?

According to multiple-intelligence theory, the examples of Thomas and Lopez show evidence of different kinds of intelligence that were developed and adapted to their environments. As a successful student, lawyer, judge, and Justice, Thomas has certainly demonstrated verbal intelligence. As a successful pro golfer, Lopez has demonstrated movement intelligence. Thus, Gardner's approach, which identifies seven kinds of intelligence, is different from Spearman's *g* and *s* factors, which refer to only general or specific mental abilities.

ADVANTAGES AND DISADVANTAGES

One advantage of Gardner's multiple-intelligence approach is that it does not reduce intelligence to a single IQ score but rather credits people with different kinds of intelligence. Two disadvantages of this approach are not knowing how many kinds of intelligence there are and not having standard measuring techniques to assess all seven kinds of intelligence.

Agreeing with Gardner that *g* is too narrow a measure of intelligence, Sternberg proposed a triarchic theory.

Triarchic Theory

Three kinds of intelligence? Criticizing Spearman's *g* as being too restrictive and current IQ tests as measuring only problem-solving skills and cognitive abilities, psychologist Robert Sternberg proposed the information-processing approach, which defines intelligence by analyzing the cognitive steps that people use in solving problems. Sternberg (1985, 1997a) calls his approach the triarchic theory of intelligence.

Sternberg's triarchic theory says that intelligence can be divided into three ways of gathering and processing information (*triarchic* means three). The first is using analytical or logical thinking skills that are measured by traditional intelligence tests. The second is using problem-solving skills that require creative thinking and the ability to learn from experience. The third is using practical thinking skills that help a person adjust to, and cope with, his or her sociocultural environment.

Analytical

Problem solving

Practical

On the basis of Sternberg's triarchic theory, who is more intelligent—Justice Thomas or golfer Lopez?

According to Sternberg's triarchic theory, Clarence Thomas would probably score high on analytical thinking and problem-solving skills, as shown by his successful strategies for solving legal problems. Nancy Lopez would probably score high on problem-solving and practical skills, as indicated by her successful strategies on the golf course. Unlike Spearman's *g*, which measures general intelligence, Sternberg's theory breaks intelligence down into three different kinds: analytical, creative, and practical intelligence.

ADVANTAGES AND DISADVANTAGES

One advantage of Sternberg's triarchic theory of intelligence is that it gives people credit for being intelligent in one way measured by current intelligence tests (analytical) plus two ways not measured by intelligence tests (creative and practical). For example, a person may be "street smart" or have great practical thinking skills but may not necessarily score high on traditional intelligence tests. One disadvantage of the triarchic theory is that Sternberg has so far developed only a few tests to measure his proposed three kinds of intelligence (Sternberg, 1997b).

Current Status

Currently, the majority of psychologists assume that *g* is a measure of general intelligence and that *g* is measured by current intelligence tests and represented by an IQ score (Daniel, 1997). One reason the concept of *g* remains so popular is that most of the research on intelligence is based on the psychometric approach, from which the factor *g* was originally developed. In addition, standard intelligence tests have proved useful in predicting performance in academic settings but less so in career settings. Gardner's multiple-intelligence approach and Sternberg's triarchic approach are attempts to replace *g*'s single measure of general intelligence (IQ score). These newer approaches suggest measuring additional cognitive abilities that represent different kinds of intelligence (Sternberg & Kaufman, 1998).

How early psychologists measured intelligence is an interesting story that involved measuring skulls and brains and testing children.

B. Measuring Intelligence

Earlier Attempts

Are bigger brains better?

HEAD SIZE

In the late 1800s Francis Galton observed that intelligent people often had intelligent relatives and concluded that intelligence is, to a large extent, biological or inherited. In trying to develop a method of assessing biological intelligence, Galton measured people's heads and recorded the speed of their reactions to various sensory stimuli. However, his measures proved to be poorly related to intelligence or academic achievement (Gould, 1996). Galton also tried to correlate head size with students' grade point average. For example, he reported that the head size of Cambridge students who received As was about 3.3% larger than that of students who received Cs (Galton, 1888). However, a review of recent studies showed a very low correlation of 0.19 between head size and intelligence (IQ scores) (Brody, 1992). Such a low correlation has little practical use in measuring or predicting intelligence. For this reason, using head size as a measure of intelligence was abandoned in favor of using skull or brain size.

BRAIN SIZE

Paul Broca, a famous neurologist in the late 1800s, claimed that there was a considerable relationship between size of brain and intelligence, with larger brains indicating more intelligence. However, reanalysis of these data indicated that measures of brain size proved to be unreliable and poorly correlated with intelligence (Gould, 1996).

Advances in precise measurement of living brains—for example, using MRI scans, as discussed in Module 4—have created new interest in correlating brain size and intelligence. Two recent studies that used MRI scans reported a positive correlation of 0.32 and 0.39 between brain size and intelligence (IQ scores) (Egan et al., 1994; Wickett et al., 1994). However, such correlations indicate only that a relationship exists; they cannot tell us whether bigger brains lead to increased intelligence or whether more cognitive activity leads to bigger brains. Although these medium-sized correlations are statistically significant and indicate a positive relationship between brain size and intelligence (IQ scores), they have little practical value in actually predicting a person's intelligence.

ACHIEVEMENT AND BRAIN SIZE

Perhaps there is a relationship between brain size and personal achievement, another measure of intelligence. However, as shown in the large illustration, there is an enormous variation in brain size and achievement (Gould, 1996). Notice that Nobel Prize winner Einstein's brain (1350 grams) was of average weight and that two famous authors, poet Walt Whitman (1200 grams) and novelist Anatole France (1000 grams), achieved literary fame with brains about half the weight of Jonathan Swift's (2000 grams), one of the heaviest on record. For comparison, we have included a gorilla brain (500 grams) which is actually quite small considering the size of a gorilla head. It is difficult to test a gorilla's intelligence, but at least one is reported to have learned a vocabulary of 800 hand signs (Ross, 1991).

2000 grams—one of larger brains on record

1350 grams—average weight of human brain

1200 grams—within normal range

1000 grams—half the size of Swift's brain

500 grams

Jonathan Swift, great 18th-century British satirist who wrote *Gulliver's Travels.*

Albert Einstein, Nobel Prize–winning mathematician

Walt Whitman, 19th-century American poet

Anatole France, 19th-century French author

Gorilla learned 800 hand signs

MEASURING INTELLIGENCE

In the late 1800s, attempts to use head, skull, or brain size to measure intelligence all failed. In fact, a paper presented in 1904 to a German psychological society concluded that there was little hope of developing psychological tests to measure intelligence in an objective way (Wolf, 1973). What's interesting is that one of the authors of this paper was Alfred Binet, who went on to develop the first intelligence test.

Let's see how Binet succeeded where others had failed.

Binet's Breakthrough

Why did Binet develop an intelligence test?

In the late 1800s, a gifted French psychologist named Alfred Binet realized that Broca and Galton had failed to assess intelligence by measuring brain size. Binet strongly believed that intelligence was a collection of mental abilities and that the best way to assess intelligence was to measure a person's ability to perform cognitive tasks, such as understanding the meaning of words or being able to follow directions.

Binet was very pessimistic about developing an intelligence test. By a strange twist of fate, he was appointed to a commission that was instructed to develop tests capable of differentiating children of normal intelligence from those who needed special help. Binet accepted this challenge with two goals in mind: the test must be easy to administer without requiring any special laboratory equipment; and the test must clearly distinguish between normal and abnormal mental ability (Brody, 1992). In 1905, Binet and psychiatrist Theodore Simon succeeded in developing the world's first standardized intelligence test, the Binet-Simon Intelligence Scale (Binet & Simon, 1905).

The ***Binet-Simon Intelligence Scale*** contained items arranged in order of increasing difficulty. The items measured vocabulary, memory, common knowledge, and other cognitive abilities.

The purpose of this first Binet-Simon Intelligence Scale was to distinguish among mentally defective children in the Paris school system. In Binet's time, intellectually deficient children were divided into three groups: idiots (most severely deficient), imbeciles (moderate), and morons (mildest). These terms are no longer used today because they have taken on very negative meanings. The problems with this first test were that it classified children into only three categories (idiots, imbeciles, and morons) and that it did not have a way to express the results in a single score. However, several years later, Binet corrected both of these problems when he introduced the concept of mental level, or mental age.

MENTAL AGE: MEASURE OF INTELLIGENCE

Binet and Simon revised their intelligence scale to solve several problems in their original scale. In this revised text, they arranged the test items in order of increasing difficulty and designed different items to measure different cognitive abilities. For each test item, Binet determined whether an average child of a certain age could answer the question correctly. For example, a child at age level 3 should be able to point to various parts of the face. A child at age level 9 should be able to recite the days of the week. Because the test items were arranged for each age level (age levels 3 to 13), this new test could identify which average age level the child performed at. If a particular child passed all the items that could be

answered by an average 3-year-old but none of the items appropriate for older children, that child would be said to have a mental age of 3. Thus, if a 6-year-old child could answer only questions appropriate for a 3-year-old child, that child would be given a mental age of 3 and would be considered retarded in intellectual development. Binet's intelligence test became popular because a single score represented mental age.

Mental age is a method of estimating a child's intellectual progress by comparing the child's score on an intelligence test to the scores of average children of the same age.

At this point, the Binet-Simon scale gave its results in terms of a mental age but not an IQ score. The idea for computing an IQ score did not occur until some years later, when it was revised by L. M. Terman.

Which items could an average 9-year-old answer?

Which items could an average 3-year-old answer?

Terman's Formula for IQ

What was the big change?

The first big change was when Binet and Simon introduced the concept of mental age. The second big change occurred in 1916, when Lewis Terman and his colleagues at Stanford University in California came up with a new and better method to compute the final score. Improving on the concept of expressing the test results in terms of mental age, Terman devised a formula to calculate an intelligence quotient (IQ) score (Terman, 1916).

Intelligence quotient is computed by dividing a child's mental age (MA), as measured in an intelligence test, by the child's chronological age (CA) and multiplying the result by 100.

Remember that in Binet's test mental age was calculated by noting how many items a child answered that were appropriate to a certain age. For example, if a 4-year-old girl passed the test items appropriate for a 5-year-old, she was said to have a mental age of 5. A child's chronological (physical) age is his or her age in months and years. To compute her IQ score, we use Terman's formula, shown below.

$$IQ = \frac{MA \text{ (Mental age)}}{CA \text{ (Chronological age)}} \times 100$$

Thus, for the child in our example, we substitute 5 for MA, 4 for CA, and multiply by 100. We get: $5/4 = 1.25 \times 100 = 125$. So the child's IQ is 125. An IQ score computed in this traditional way is called a ***ratio IQ***, because the score represents a ratio of mental to chronological age. Today the ratio IQ has been replaced by the ***deviation IQ***, whose computation is somewhat too complex to explain here. The reason for the switch from ratio IQ to deviation IQ is that deviation IQ scores more accurately reflect test performance as children get older.

Since the original Binet-Simon scale in 1905, IQ tests have become very popular and have grown into a large business. We'll look more closely at one of the most widely used IQ tests.

B. Measuring Intelligence

Examples of IQ Tests

Is IQ the same as intelligence?

We are all curious to learn someone's IQ because we believe that this single score reveals a person's real intelligence. For example, try to match these IQ scores—104, 114, 228—with three famous people—John F. Kennedy, 35th president of the United States; J. D. Salinger, famous novelist *(Catcher in the Rye)*; and Marilyn vos Savant, columnist for *Parade* magazine (answers on right). Knowing the IQ scores of these individuals tells of something of their cognitive abilities, but some psychologists believe that cognitive abilities represent only one kind of intelligence. Other kinds of intelligence, such as practical, emotional, social, and creative, may be equally important, depending upon a person's goals and environment (Sternberg, 1997b). For example, would you expect Salinger, with his average IQ, to write a very creative novel? Although we'll be using the terms *intelligence* and *IQ* interchangeably, please keep in mind that IQ represents only one kind of intelligence (Neisser et al., 1996). Now, let's see how IQ scores are measured.

John F. Kennedy   **Marilyn vos Savant**   **J. D. Salinger**

Answers: Salinger, 104; Kennedy, 114; and vos Savant, 228, who has the highest IQ on record (Cowley, 1994).

Wechsler Intelligence Scales

The most widely used IQ tests are the Wechsler Adult Intelligence Scale (WAIS-III), for ages 16 and older, and the Wechsler Intelligence Scale for Children (WISC-III), for children of ages 3–16. A trained examiner administers the Wechsler scales on a one-to-one basis.

The *Wechsler Adult Intelligence Scale (WAIS-III)* and *Wechsler Intelligence Scale for Children (WISC-III)* have items that are organized into various subtests. For example, the verbal section contains a subtest of general information, a subtest of vocabulary, and so forth. The performance section contains a subtest that involves arranging pictures in a meaningful order, one that requires assembling objects, and one that involves using codes. The verbal and performance scores are combined to give a single IQ score.

Examples of the subtests for WAIS-III are shown on the right. The Verbal Scale (top right) emphasizes language and verbal skills. Because of this emphasis, a person from a deprived environment or for whom English is a second language might have difficulty on this scale because of lack of verbal knowledge rather than lack of cognitive ability.

In an attempt to measure nonverbal skills and rule out other cultural or educational problems, Wechsler added the Performance Scale (lower right). These performance subtests, which measure problem-solving abilities, require considerable concentration and focused effort, which may be difficult for individuals who are very nervous, poor test takers, or have emotional problems. Although these IQ tests carefully try to measure verbal and nonverbal abilities, you can see that part of one's success on IQ tests depends on nonintellectual factors, such as cultural, educational, or emotional factors (Kaplan & Saccuzzo, 1997). We'll discuss other problems with IQ tests later in this module.

One reason these IQ tests are widely used is that they have two characteristics of good tests: validity and reliability.

WAIS-III Verbal Scale: Subtests

Subtests for the verbal scale include information, comprehension, arithmetic, similarities, digit span, and vocabulary. These examples resemble the WAIS-III items.

Information
On what continent is France?

Comprehension
Why are children required to go to school?

Arithmetic
How many hours will it take to drive 150 miles at 50 miles per hour?

Similarities
How are a calculator and a typewriter alike?

Digit span
Repeat the following numbers backward: 2, 4, 3, 5, 8, 9, 6.

Vocabulary
What does *audacity* mean?

WAIS-III Performance Scale: Subtests

Subtests for the performance scale include digit symbol, block design, picture completion, picture arrangement, and object assembly. These sample items shown on the right resemble those given for each WAIS-III subtest.

Digit symbol

Shown: 1 2 3 4   Fill in: 1 4 3 2

Block design
Assemble blocks to match this design.

Picture completion
Tell me what is missing.

Picture arrangement
Put the pictures in the right order.

Object assembly
Assemble the pieces into a complete object.

Two Characteristics

Can you analyze handwriting?

Is there any truth to the claim that intelligence and other personality traits can be identified through analyzing handwriting? For example, which one of the four handwriting samples on the right indicates the highest IQ? (Answer at bottom of page.)

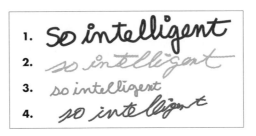

Although so-called IQ tests in popular magazines and handwriting analysis may claim to measure intelligence, research shows that their accuracy is usually no better than a good guess (Basil, 1989; Feder, 1987).

The reason so-called IQ tests in popular magazines or handwriting analysis are poor measures of intelligence (IQ) is because they lack one of the two important characteristics of a good test. These two characteristics are validity and reliability, which mark the difference between an accurate IQ test (WAIS-III) and an inaccurate test (handwriting analysis).

Validity

Handwriting analysis is fun, but it is a very poor intelligence test because it lacks validity, which is one of the two characteristics of a good test.

Validity means that the test measures what it is supposed to measure.

Although the definition of validity seems simple and short, this characteristic makes or breaks a test. For example, numerous studies have shown that handwriting analysis has little or no validity as an intelligence or personality test (Feder, 1987; Basil, 1989). Because handwriting analysis lacks the characteristic of validity, it means that this test does not accurately measure what it is supposed to measure. Thus, a test with little or no validity produces results that could be produced by guessing or by chance.

The reason the validity of handwriting analysis or tests in popular magazines are not checked for validity is that checking validity is a long, expensive, and complicated process. One way to show a test's validity is to give the new test to hundreds of subjects along with other tests whose validity has already been established. Then the subjects' scores on the new test are correlated with their scores from the tests with proven validity. Another way that the validity of intelligence tests, such as the WAIS-III, was established was to show that IQ scores correlated with another measure of intelligence, such as academic performance (Brody, 1997).

However, if IQ scores are valid measures of cognitive abilities and correlate with academic performance, why do some individuals with high IQ do poorly in college? The developer of the Head Start program, Ed Zigler, believes that academic performance depends on three factors: cognitive abilities; achievement, or the amount of knowledge that a person has accumulated; and motivation (Zigler, 1995). This means that a person may have outstanding cognitive abilities but may either lack the achievement or motivation to succeed in college.

Besides validity, a good intelligence test should also have reliability.

Reliability

If your style of handwriting remained constant over time, such as always boldly crossing your *t*'s, then this trait would be reliable.

Reliability refers to consistency: a person's score on a test at one point in time should be similar to the score obtained by the same person on a similar test at a later point in time.

For example, if boldly crossed *t*'s indicated that a person is intelligent, then this measure of intelligence would be reliable. However, there is no evidence that boldly crossed *t*'s indicates that a person is intelligent. So, in this case, handwriting analysis would be a reliable test of intelligence but since it lacks validity (doesn't measure intelligence) it is a worthless test of intelligence.

Now, suppose you took the WAIS-III as a senior in high school and then retook the test as a junior in college, you would find that your IQ score would be much the same because you would be compared with others of your same age. Because your IQ scores remains similar across time, it would mean that the Wechsler scales, like other standardized IQ tests, have reliability.

For example, the graph above shows the results of verbal IQ scores when seven different age groups of subjects were given the WAIS-III. Notice that verbal IQ scores are quite stable from ages 20 to 74, indicating that the Wechsler scales score high in reliability (Kaufman et al., 1989).

But notice that the lower graph shows that there is an overall decrease in performance IQ scores from ages 20 to 74 (Kaufman et al., 1989). However, this general decrease in performance scores across one's lifetime reflects changes in psychological and physiological functioning rather than a decrease in the test's reliability.

Researchers have shown that current intelligence tests, which primarily measure cognitive abilities, have relatively good validity and reliability (Neisser et al., 1996). Even though IQ scores can be measured with good reliability and validity, our next question to answer is "What good or use are IQ scores?"

(Handwriting answer: I wrote all four samples so that no matter which one you picked, you would think I had the highest IQ.)

C. Distribution & Use of IQ Scores

Normal Distribution

The photo on the left is of Chris Burke, who starred in the television series "Life Goes On." Burke has Down syndrome, a genetic defect that results in varying degrees of mental retardation and physical symptoms (slanting eyes, flattened nose, visual problems). Although Burke has mild or borderline mental retardation, he was able to act in the series and functions very well outside an institution. We are guessing that Burke's IQ is between 50 and 85.

In comparison, the photo on the right is of Marilyn vos Savant, who writes a column for *Parade* magazine and has a reported IQ of 228, the highest on record. To compare the IQs of Burke and vos Savant with other people, we need to look at the distribution of IQ scores. IQ scores from established intelligence tests, such as the WAIS-III, are said to have a normal distribution.

A *normal distribution* refers to a statistical arrangement of scores so that they resemble the shape of a bell and, thus, is said to be a bell-shaped curve. A bell-shaped curve means the vast majority of scores fall in the middle range with fewer scores falling near the two extreme ends of the curve.

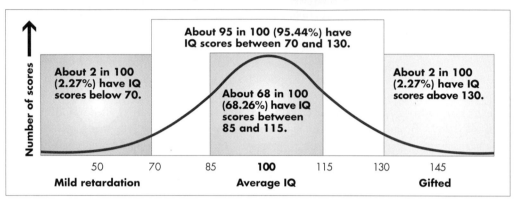

For example, a normal distribution of IQ scores is shown at the left and is bell-shaped. The average IQ score is 100, and 95% of IQ scores fall between 70 and 130. An IQ of 70 and below is one sign of mild retardation. An IQ of 145 or higher is one indication of a gifted individual. Thus, one widespread usage of IQ tests is to provide general *categories* regarding mental abilities.

Next, we'll examine these guidelines in more detail, beginning with mental retardation.

Mental Retardation: Left End of Normal Distribution

What is mental retardation?

One use of IQ scores has been to help identify individuals with mental retardation, which was Binet's original goal.

Mental retardation refers to substantial limitation in present functioning that is characterized by significantly subaverage intellectual functioning, along with related limitations in two of ten areas, including communication, self-care, home living, social skills, and safety (American Association on Mental Retardation, 1993).

Psychologists caution against using IQ scores as the sole test for mental retardation. IQ tests are usually used in combination with observations of adaptive skills, which include social, home living, and communication skills. On the basis of IQ scores and adaptive skills, three levels of retardation have been identified.

1 BORDERLINE MENTALLY RETARDED

These individuals have IQs that range from 50 to 75. With special training and educational opportunities, they can learn to read and write, gain social competency, master simple occupational skills, and become self-supporting members of society. About 70% of individuals with retardation are in this category.

2 MILDLY/MODERATELY MENTALLY RETARDED

These individuals have IQs that range from 35 to 50. With special training and educational opportunities, they can learn to become partially independent in their everyday lives, provided they are in a family or self-help setting.

3 SEVERELY/PROFOUNDLY MENTALLY RETARDED

These individuals have IQs that range from 20 to 40. With special training and educational opportunities, they can acquire limited skills in taking care of their personal needs. However, because of retarded motor and verbal abilities, they require considerable supervision their entire lives.

4 CAUSES

There are two general types of mental retardation—organic and cultural-familial.

Organic retardation results from genetic problems or brain damage. Chris Burke is an example of someone with organic retardation.

Cultural-familial retardation results from a greatly impoverished environment. There is no evidence of genetic or brain damage.

Approximately five million Americans have various degrees of mental retardation.

Next, we move to the middle of IQ's normal distribution.

Vast Majority: Middle of Normal Distribution

Since the vast majority of people, about 95%, have IQ scores that fall between 70 and 130, it is interesting to see what IQ scores can tell us.

DO IQ SCORES PREDICT ACADEMIC ACHIEVEMENT?

Because IQ tests measure cognitive abilities that are similar to those used in academic settings, it is no surprise that there is a medium-strength association, or correlation, between IQ scores and grades (0.50), between IQ scores and reading scores for grade school children (0.38 to 0.46), and between IQ scores

Middle of normal distribution

Number of scores

About 95 in 100 have IQ scores between 70 and 130.

70   85   **100**   115   130
Average IQ

and total years of education that people complete (0.50) (Brody, 1997). These medium-strength correlations mean that IQ scores are moderately good at predicting academic performance. However, based on medium-strength correlations alone, it would be difficult to predict a *specific person's academic performance* because performance in academic settings also depends on personal characteristics, such as one's interest in school and willingness to study (Neisser et al., 1996).

DO IQ SCORES PREDICT JOB PERFORMANCE?

The correlation between IQ scores and job performance is about 0.30 to 0.50. This low- to medium-strength correlation means that IQ scores are weakly related to job performance (Neisser et al., 1996). Because the correlation between IQ scores and job performance is of low to medium strength, it would be very difficult to predict a *specific person's job performance* solely on the basis of his or her IQ score. In fact, researchers argue that job performance requires not only cognitive abilities, which are measured by traditional intelligence tests, but also practical intelligence, such as how to solve problems and get the job done, which is not measured by traditional intelligence tests (Sternberg & Wagner, 1993). Thus, IQ scores alone are relatively good at predicting academic performance but less successful at predicting job performance.

Now, we'll examine the right end of the normal distribution, which contains high IQ scores.

Gifted: Right End of Normal Distribution

What if you had a very high IQ score?

Sometimes impressive cognitive abilities appear at a relatively early age. For instance, at 8 months Masoud Karkehadadi began talking; at 18 months he had memorized the top tunes on MTV; at 7 he took the high school equivalency exam and scored 100%; and at age 12 he graduated from the University of California at Irvine. Masoud's IQ, which is 200-plus, places him in the genius range and at the gifted end of the normal curve (*Los Angeles Times*, May 23, 1994). Although researchers and educators differ in how they define *gifted*, here is one definition that refers to academically gifted children.

A moderately *gifted* child is usually defined by IQ scores between 130 and 150; a profoundly gifted child has an IQ score about 180 or above.

When placed in *regular classrooms*, gifted children face a number of problems: They may be viewed as different—labeled as nerds or geeks—and are unchallenged by the material. For these reasons, one researcher recommends that gifted children be placed in special academic programs that challenge and help gifted children develop their potentials (Winner, 1997).

HOW DO GIFTED INDIVIDUALS TURN OUT?

In the early 1920s, Lewis Terman selected a sample of over 1,500 gifted children with IQs ranging from 130 to 200 (the average

Right end of normal distribution

Number of scores

Gifted

About 2 in 100 have IQ scores above 130; about 1 in a million has an IQ above 180.

130   145
Superior   **Gifted**

was 151). Over the next 65 years, researchers repeatedly tested these individuals to determine what they had achieved and how they had adjusted. Although 10–30% of the more gifted males obtained advanced degrees compared with men in the general population, 30% never finished college, and 2% actually flunked out. Although gifted individuals generally showed health, adjustment, and achievement above that of people with average IQs, about 9% had serious emotional problems, and 7% committed suicide (Holahan & Sears, 1995; Terman & Oden, 1959). As a group, these gifted individuals were generally very successful in life but not at the extraordinary level that might have been expected or predicted from their very high IQ scores (Colangelo, 1997). For example, do you think Marilyn vos Savant's (right photo) achievement as magazine writer matches her extraordinary high IQ score?

Conclusion. IQ scores have proven moderately useful in predicting academic performance, in helping to define mental retardation, and in identifying the gifted; but they have low to moderate success in predicting job performance. One reason IQ scores are not more predictive is that they do not measure numerous emotional, motivational, and personality factors that also influence behavior.

While IQ tests have proved useful, we'll next examine potential problems in taking and interpreting IQ tests.

D. Potential Problems of IQ Testing

Binet's Warnings

What problems did Binet foresee?

You may remember that Binet's original goal was to develop a test that would distinguish between normal and abnormal mental abilities and thus identify children who were mentally retarded and needed special help and education. Although previous attempts to measure intelligence had failed, Binet and Simon succeeded in developing the first scale that identified children with varying degrees of mental retardation. Binet and Simon's scale was the beginning of the modern-day IQ test. However, even in the early 1900s, Binet realized that intelligence tests could be used in two potentially dangerous ways, so he issued the following two warnings:

BINET'S WARNINGS:

1 Binet warned that *intelligence tests do not measure innate abilities or natural intelligence;* rather, they measure an individual's cognitive abilities, which result from both heredity and environment.

2 Binet warned that *intelligence tests, by themselves, should not be used to label people* (for example, "moron," "average," "genius"); rather, intelligence tests should be used to assess an individual's abilities and used in combination with other information to make academic or placement decisions about people.

History shows that neither of Binet's warnings were heeded. In the early 1900s it became common practice to treat IQ scores as measures of innate intelligence and to use IQ scores to label people from "moron" to "genius." The U.S. Congress went so far as to pass laws that restricted immigrants based on assumed levels of innate intelligence (Gould, 1996), an issue we'll discuss in Cultural Diversity.

Along with using IQ scores to label individuals came racial and cultural discrimination, some of which continue to the present. For example, a relatively recent and controversial book, *The Bell Curve* (Herrnstein & Murray, 1994), suggests that racial differences in IQ scores are primarily due to genetic factors, something we'll discuss later in this module. For now, we'll examine four issues surrounding IQ tests: racial discrimination, cultural bias, culture-free IQ tests, and nonintellectual factors.

Racial Discrimination

Are IQ tests racially biased?

There have been a number of court cases regarding the appropriate use of IQ tests. Here is one important case and the judge's ruling.

Larry was an African American child who was assigned to special classes for the educable mentally retarded because he scored below 85 on an IQ test. However, several years later an African American psychologist retested Larry and found that his IQ score was higher than originally thought. Larry was taken out of the special classes, which were considered a dead end, and placed in regular classes that allowed for more advancement. On the basis of Larry's experience, a class action suit was brought against the San Francisco school system on behalf of all African American schoolchildren in the district. The suit was based on the finding that, although African American youngsters made up 27% of all the students enrolled in classes for the mentally retarded, they composed only 4% of the entire school population (Kaplan & Saccuzzo, 1997). African American parents wanted to know why their children were so much more numerous than White children in these special classes. They felt there must be a bias against African American children in the selection process.

Although Larry's case came to trial in the early 1970s, the final decision was given in 1979 by a judge of the federal court of appeals. The judge agreed with the African American parents and found that IQ tests being used in schools (kindergarten through grade 12) to determine mental retardation were biased against people of color. The court ruled that California schools could not place children of color in classes for children with mental retardation on the basis of the IQ test alone. The schools were instructed to come up with an intelligence test that does not favor Whites or else refrain from using a standardized test to identify slow learners.

Definition of mental retardation. In other states, IQ tests are used to define mental retardation, even though these states do not always agree on the definition. For example, in Ohio, a child with an IQ below 80 is considered mentally retarded, while across the border in Kentucky, the same child is placed in a regular classroom and taught along with all the other students. In 39 states, African American students are overrepresented in special education classes,

$$IQ \text{ (Intelligence quotient)} = \frac{MA \text{ (Mental age)}}{CA \text{ (Chronological age)}} \times 100$$

especially when they are students in predominately White school districts. Critics of the special education system argue that African American students are overrepresented not because of their especially high level of disability but because of discriminatory placement procedures, such as the culturally biased IQ tests (Shapiro et al., 1993).

Educational decisions. Based on the concerns discussed above, psychologists and educators recommend that IQ tests alone not be used as the primary basis for making decisions about a child's educational future. Instead, they suggest that educational decisions, especially about placing a child in a special education class, be made only after considering a wide range of information, which may include IQ scores but also samples of the child's behavior from other situations (Detterman & Thompson, 1997).

Cultural Bias

Can the same questions be used?

One criticism of IQ tests is that they are culturally biased, especially in favor of the White middle class.

Cultural bias means that the wording of the questions and the experiences on which they are based are more familiar to members of some social groups than to others.

For example, consider the question below from an older version of the Wechsler Intelligence Scale for Children. "What would you do if you were sent to buy a loaf of bread and the grocer said he did not have any more?"

If you think the answer is "Go to another store," you are correct according to the developers of the Wechsler scale. However, when 200 minority children were asked this same question, 61 said they would go home. Asked to explain their answers, they gave reasonable explanations. Some children answered "Go home" because there were no other stores in their neighborhood. Yet the answer "Go

home" would be scored "incorrect," despite its correctness in the child's experience (Hardy et al., 1976). This example shows that children of color may have different cultural influences, experiences, and standards that may penalize them on standardized tests of intelligence (Boykin, 1996).

Researchers suggest that IQ tests are culturally biased because they measure accumulated knowledge and problem-solving strategies that depend on environmental opportunities available in a particular culture or group (Suzuki & Valencia, 1997). In addition, because IQ tests involve being asked and answering questions, children who have had such experience in their homes or schools would be better able to take these tests. However, in some cultures, parents do not engage in question-and-answer sessions with their children as parents commonly do in many Western cultures (Greenfield, 1997). This is another example of how cultural influences can affect a child's performance on standard IQ tests.

Culture-Free Tests

Is such a test possible?

Psychologists have attempted to develop culture-free tests.

A *culture-free test* does not contain vocabulary, experiences, or social situations that are very different from the cultural experiences of the individual taking the test.

However, the construction of culture-free tests has not been entirely successful, and some suggest that cultural bias in IQ tests cannot be avoided (Greenfield, 1997). One approach to developing culture-free tests is proposed by ecological psychology.

Ecological psychology says that we should measure intelligence by observing how people solve problems in their usual settings.

For instance, researchers found that dairy workers, bartenders, salespeople, and waiters regularly solved

complex problems in more efficient ways than standard IQ tests predict (Scribner et al., 1986).

In another setting, people from Micronesia demonstrate remarkable navigational skills as they sail long distances, using only information from stars and sea currents. These navigational abilities indicate a high degree of intelligence that might not show up on traditional IQ tests.

Ecological psychologists stress that intelligence should be measured by how well people adapt to and solve problems in their environments rather than answer questions on IQ tests (Ceci et al., 1997). Besides potential biases from cultural differences, another problem in taking IQ tests comes from nonintellectual factors.

Nonintellectual Factors

What if a person is nervous?

Maria is 11 years old and has been in the United States for two years. She had a hard time learning English, is not doing well in school, and is terrified about taking tests. Maria comes to take an IQ test, and the psychologist tries to put her at ease. However, Maria is so afraid of failing the IQ test that she just sits and stares at the floor. The psychologist says, "I'm going to give you a word and you tell me what it means. What is a bed?" Maria is now so anxious that she can't concentrate or think of what to say, so she remains silent.

One reason Maria will probably do poorly on this IQ test will be due to nonintellectual factors.

Nonintellectual factors refer to noncognitive factors, such as attitude, experience, and emotional functioning, that may help or hinder performance on tests.

For example, nonintellectual factors such as Maria's shyness, fear of strange situations, and anxiety about failing would certainly hinder her test performance. In comparison, a child who is more outgoing and used to taking tests has the kind of nonintellectual factors that would aid performance. It is well established that numerous nonintellectual factors can have a great influence on how a person performs on IQ tests (Kaplan & Saccuzzo, 1997).

Next, we'll discuss one of the oldest questions about intelligence, the nature-nurture question.

E. Nature-Nurture Question

Definitions

What is nature-nurture question?

We began this module with the example of Supreme Court Justice Clarence Thomas (photo below left) and his sister, Emma Mae Martin (photo at right). In an early interview, Thomas was asked why he had turned out so different from his sister. Thomas replied, "We come from the same place, have the same genes, same circumstances but were raised by different relatives" (*USA Today*, July 26, 1991, p. 2A). Although brothers and sisters share only 50% of their genes, Thomas's answer clearly emphasizes environmental factors or nurture (relatives' influences) over inherited factors or nature (genes). Without knowing it, Thomas was raising one of the oldest questions about intelligence, the nature-nurture question.

The *nature-nurture question* asks how much genetic factors and how much environmental factors contribute to the development of intelligence.

In the early 1900s, the answer to the nature-nurture question was nature because intelligence was believed to be inherited (Terman, 1916). In the 1950s, the answer changed because psychology was

heavily influenced by behaviorism, which emphasized nurture and environmental factors (Skinner, 1953). Presently, there is convincing evidence that nature and nurture contribute about equally to intelligence (Plomin & Petrill, 1997). This current answer to the nature-nurture question comes from research that compared IQ scores in siblings (brothers and sisters) and in fraternal and identical twins.

Fraternal twins, like siblings (brothers and sisters), develop from separate eggs and have 50% of their genes in common.

Identical twins develop from a single egg and thus have identical genes, which means that they have 100% of their genes in common.

If genetic factors make a significant contribution to intelligence, then IQ scores between identical twins (same genes) should be more similar than those between fraternal twins (50% of genes in common). Let's see if this is what researchers found.

Twin Studies

How much do genes contribute to intelligence?

The answer to this question about the influence of genes on intelligence can be misleading unless you keep two things in mind: how intelligence is defined and what genetic influence means.

Definition of intelligence. When researchers study genetic factors in intelligence, they commonly define intelligence as Spearman's *g* factor (see p. 282), which is measured by performance on cognitive tests and given as an IQ score. However, there are other kinds of intelligence, including practical (adjusting to one's environment), social (interacting with others), emotional (perceiving and understanding emotions), as well as creative, musical, and insightful intelligence (Mayer & Salovey, 1997; Gardner et al., 1997; Sternberg, 1997a). As discussed earlier, these kinds of intelligence are not measured by standard IQ tests.

Influence of genetic factors. When researchers report that genetic factors influence intelligence (IQ scores), it means only that genetic factors influence cognitive abilities to varying degrees (Plomin & Petrill, 1997). It does not mean that intelligence is fixed, written in stone, or predetermined solely by genetic factors.

There are now over 100 separate studies on over 10,000 pairs of twins and siblings.

Shared genes	Median correlation in IQ scores	
100%	Identical twins reared together	.85
100%	Identical twins reared apart	.72
50%	Fraternal twins reared together	.60
50%	Siblings reared together	.45
50%	Siblings reared apart	.25

Source: Adapted from Bouchard & McGue,1981; Plomin & Petrill,1997

The consistent finding from all these studies is that identical twins, whether reared apart or together, were more similar in IQ scores than were fraternal twins. In turn, fraternal twins were more similar in IQ scores than siblings.

For example, the graph below shows that the correlation between IQ scores was .85 for identical twins reared together, .60 for fraternal twins reared together, and .45 for siblings reared together (Plomin & Petrill, 1997).

Based on these kinds of studies, researchers have concluded that genetic factors (nature) contribute about 50% to intelligence (IQ scores) and environmental factors (nurture) contribute about 50% (Gottesman, 1997). Researchers believed that genetic influence on intelligence would be greatest in childhood but would decrease with increasing experience. However, a recent study of 240 twins, who were 80 years or older, found that genetic influence on intelligence remained relatively constant throughout life and did not change with increasing experience (McClearn et al., 1997).

The reason genetic factors influence but do not fix or predetermine intelligence is because genetic factors contribute 50% to intelligence (IQ scores). The other 50% comes from environmental factors, which we'll examine next.

Adoption Studies

How much does environment contribute to intelligence?

What would happen if lower-class children with limited social-educational opportunities were adopted by upper-class parents and given improved social-educational opportunities?

Researchers reasoned that if environmental factors influence the development of intelligence, then providing environmental opportunities should increase IQ scores. A group of French researchers studied children who had been abandoned as babies by their lower-class parents and adopted during the first six months of life into upper-middle-class families. The researchers found that the mean IQ of the adopted children was 14 points higher than that of similar children born and raised in lower-class settings by their natural parents. In addition, the adopted children were four times less likely to fail in school. This study suggests that by improving

environmental factors—for example, increasing social-educational opportunities—intellectual development (as measured by IQ scores) and performance in the classroom can be improved (Schiff et al., 1982).

In a similar study, African American children from impoverished environments were adopted into middle-class families, some White and some African American; all of the families provided many social-educational opportunities for the adopted children. Researchers found that the IQs of the adopted children were as much as 10 points higher than those of African American children who were raised in disadvantaged homes (Scarr & Weinberg, 1976). In a follow-up study, researchers reported that the adopted children, now adolescents, had higher IQ scores than African American children raised in their own community (Weinberg et al., 1992). Researchers concluded that data from adoption studies show the contribution of nurture or environmental factors to intellectual development (Waldman et al., 1994).

Interaction: Nature and Nurture

How do environment and genes interact?

In the last 10 years, researchers have made significant progress in answering the nature-nurture question, and one tool they have used is a number called heritability.

Heritability is a number that indicates the amount or proportion of some ability, characteristic, or trait that can be attributed to genetic factors.

For example, the graph below shows that the heritability of intelligence is 50%, which means that 50% of this general cognitive ability is contributed by genetic factors. Because IQ tests measure a number of specific cognitive abilities, researchers were able to calculate the heritability scores for spatial ability (32%), verbal ability (55%), and memory (55%) (McClearn et al., 1997). The next step in understanding genetic factors is the identification of specific genes or groups of genes that contribute to specific cognitive traits. This search has only recently begun, and its results will identify which genes are responsible for diseases, such as Alzheimer's, as well as various forms of mental retardation (Gottesman, 1997).

Notice that the heritability numbers in the graph on the left are in the 50% range, which means that genes do

not determine or fix these abilities, because the other 50% is coming from environmental factors. You can think of genetic factors as establishing a range of potential abilities or behaviors, which are shaped and molded through interaction with one's environment. This idea of how genetic factors operate is called the reaction range (Bouchard, 1997).

Reaction range indicates the extent to which traits, abilities, or IQ scores may increase or decrease as a result of interaction with environmental factors.

For example, researchers estimate that the reaction range (right figure) may vary up or down by as much as 10–15 points in one's IQ score, depending on whether one has an enriched, normal, or impoverished environment (Zigler & Seitz, 1982). Thus, the development of intelligence depends on the quality of one's environment, the kind of genes, and the reaction range, which is interaction between environmental and genetic factors (Bouchard, 1997).

One continuing question that always results in heated debate is whether and how much of the IQ differences among races are inherited or due to genetic factors. We'll discuss this issue next.

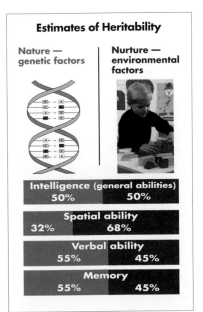

Estimates of Heritability

Nature — genetic factors   Nurture — environmental factors

Intelligence (general abilities)	
50%	50%

Spatial ability	
32%	68%

Verbal ability	
55%	45%

Memory	
55%	45%

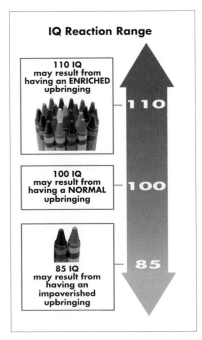

IQ Reaction Range

110 IQ may result from having an ENRICHED upbringing — **110**

100 IQ may result from having a NORMAL upbringing — **100**

85 IQ may result from having an impoverished upbringing — **85**

E. Nature-Nurture Question

Racial Controversy

What is the latest controversy?

In the early 1900s, psychologists believed that intelligence was primarily inherited. This idea reappeared in a relatively recent book, *The Bell Curve,* by psychologist Richard Herrnstein and political scientist Charles Murray (1994). But what brought these authors the greatest publicity was their statement that racial differences in IQ scores were primarily caused by genetic or inherited factors. This and other statements from Herrnstein and Murray's book set off such a heated and often misguided public debate that the American Psychological Association (APA) formed a special task force of prominent researchers. The goal of the APA task force was to summarize what is currently known about intelligence (Neisser et al., 1996). We have already discussed many of the issues raised in the APA report and will now focus on the difficult and complex question of racial differences in IQ scores.

Difference between IQ Scores

Findings. To help you understand the controversy surrounding racial differences in IQ scores, please look at the figure in the upper right. Notice that there are two distributions of IQ scores: the red bell-shaped curve shows the distribution of IQ scores for African Americans (Blacks) and the blue bell-shaped curve shows the distribution of scores for Caucasians (Whites). Although there is much overlap in IQ scores (indicated by overlapping of red and blue areas), researchers generally agree that the average or mean IQ score for African Americans is about 15 points lower than the average IQ score for Caucasians (Bouchard, 1995). This 15-point average difference in IQ scores means that although there are many African Americans with high IQ scores, they are proportionally fewer in number compared to Caucasians.

Two explanations. There are at least two possible explanations for this 15-point difference in average IQ scores. One explanation is that the differences are due to inherited or **genetic factors:** African Americans are genetically inferior to Whites. Another explanation is that the difference is due to a number of **environmental factors:** African Americans have fewer social, economic, and educational opportunities compared to Whites.

Although the authors of *The Bell Curve* emphasized the first explanation (genetic factors), you'll see that the APA task force and many other psychologists disagreed.

Cause of IQ Differences

In a careful review of *The Bell Curve,* one of the leading researchers in the area of intelligence concluded that the book offered no convincing evidence that genetic factors were primarily responsible for the 15-point IQ difference between African Americans and Caucasians (Sternberg, 1995). This conclusion is based largely on the distinction between whether genetic factors can influence the development of intelligence in an individual and whether they can influence different development of intelligence among races. The APA task force said that there is good evidence that genetic factors play a significant role in the development of an **individual's intelligence.** However, there is no convincing evidence that genetic factors play a primary role in the development of differences in intelligence **among races.** Thus, the APA task forced challenged Herrnstein and Murray's statement that IQ **differences among races** is caused primarily by genetic factors (Neisser et al., 1996).

Although no one knows exactly what causes the differences in IQ scores shown in the above graph, the APA task force as well as many other psychologists suggest the involvement of a number of environmental factors, such as differences in social-economic classes, educational opportunities, family structure, and career possibilities (Suzuki & Valencia, 1997). Thus, one of *The Bell Curve's* major conclusions—that racial differences in IQ scores are primarily based on genetic factors—is not supported by the evidence (Neisser et al., 1996; Neisser, 1997).

Another problem with *The Bell Curve* is its assumption that skin color is a meaningful way to identify different races. After a long history of racial mixing in the United States, it is next to impossible to assign people to racial groups based solely on skin color (Eberhardt & Randall, 1997; Suzuki & Valencia, 1997). For example, based on skin color, to which race would you assign the individuals in the four photos on the left? Researchers report that skin color is becoming meaningless in identifying racial makeup and the only meaningful measure is to use DNA or genetic matching, which results in an entirely different grouping of races (Diamond, 1994; Morganthau, 1995).

Two prominent researchers concluded that the *The Bell Curve's* argument for racial inferiority appeared to be based on scientific evidence, but closer examination shows that it was not (Gould, 1996; Sternberg, 1995).

After the Concept Review, we'll discuss how some of the same issues currently raised in *The Bell Curve* were originally voiced in the early 1900s and led to many discriminatory practices.

CONCEPT REVIEW

1. One approach to measuring intelligence focuses on quantifying cognitive factors or abilities that are involved in intellectual performance; this is called the (a)_____ approach. Charles Spearman used this approach to develop a two-factor theory of intelligence: one factor is **g**, or (b)_____; the second factor is **s**, or (c)_____.

2. In comparison to Spearman's two-factor approach, Howard Gardner's theory says that there are seven kinds of _____, such as verbal skills, math skills, spatial skills, and movement skills.

3 x 4 = 12

3. Another approach to measuring intelligence studies how people gather information to solve problems or acquire information; this is called the (a)_____ approach. An example of this approach is Robert Sternberg's (b)_____ theory of intelligence.

4. Alfred Binet developed an intelligence test that estimated intellectual progress by comparing a child's score on an intelligence test to the scores of average children of the same age. Binet called this concept _____.

IQ = ? ? ?

5. Lewis Terman revised Binet's intelligence test, and the most significant change he made was to develop a formula to compute a single score that represents a person's (a)_____. This formula is IQ = (b)_____ age divided by (c)_____ age, times (d)_____.

6. The most widely used series of IQ tests are the (a)_____ Intelligence Scales. These tests organize items into two subtests, which are called (b)_____ and (c)_____ scales. In an attempt to measure nonverbal skills and rule out cultural problems, Wechsler added the (d)_____ scale.

Block design
Assemble blocks to match this design.

Picture completion
Tell me what is missing.

7. A good psychological test has two characteristics. It should give about the same score over time, which is called (a)_____; and it should measure what it is supposed to measure, which is called (b)_____.

8. If IQ scores can be represented by a bell-shaped curve, the pattern is called a _____. The scores have a symmetrical arrangement, so that the vast majority fall in the middle range and fewer fall near the extreme ends of the range.

About 95 in 100 (95.44%) have IQ scores between 70 and 130.
About 68 in 100 (68.26%) have IQ scores between 85 and 115.
Average IQ

About 2 in 100 (2.27%) have IQ scores below 70.
Mild/Moderate

9. An individual who has a combination of limited mental ability (usually an IQ below 70) and difficulty functioning in everyday life is said to have some degree of (a)_____. If this condition results from genetic problems or brain damage, it is called (b)_____. If this condition results from a greatly impoverished environment, it is called (c)_____. Individuals who have above-average intelligence (usually IQ scores above 130) as well as some superior talent or skill are said to be (d)_____.

About 2 in 100 (2.27%) have IQ scores above 130; about 1 in a million has an IQ above 180.
Gifted

10. If the wording of test questions and the experiences on which they are based are more familiar to members of some social groups than to others, the test is said to have (a)_____. The approach that measures intelligence by observing how people solve problems in their usual settings is called (b)_____ psychology.

11. When we ask how much genetic factors and how much environmental factors contribute to intelligence we are asking the (a)_____ question. There is good evidence that genetic factors contribute about (b)_____ and environmental factors contribute about (c)_____ to the development of one's intelligence. The extent to which IQ scores may increase or decrease depending on environmental effects is called the (d)_____.

Intelligence (general abilities)
Spatial ability
Verbal ability
Memory

Answers: *1. (a) psychometric, (b) general intelligence, (c) specific abilities; 2. intelligence; 3. (a) information-processing, (b) triarchic; 4. mental age; 5. (a) intelligence quotient or IQ, (b) mental, (c) chronological, (d) 100; 6. (a) Wechsler, (b) verbal, (c) performance, (d) performance; 7. (a) reliability, (b) validity; 8. normal distribution; 9. (a) mental retardation, (b) organic retardation, (c) cultural-familial retardation, (d) gifted; 10. (a) cultural bias, (b) ecological; 11. (a) nature-nurture, (b) 50%, (c) 50%, (d) reaction range.*

F. Cultural Diversity: Classifying Races & Immigration

Misuse of IQ Tests

After Alfred Binet developed the first intelligence tests, he gave two warnings about the potential misuse of IQ tests. He warned that IQ tests do not and should not be used to measure innate intelligence and that IQ tests should not be used to label individuals. However, in the early 1900s the area we know as psychology was just beginning, and American psychologists were very proud of how much they had improved IQ tests. With their improved IQ tests, American psychologists not only used IQ tests to measure what they thought was innate, or inherited, intelligence but also used IQ tests to label people (as morons or imbeciles). As if that weren't bad enough, early psychologists persuaded the United States Congress to pass discriminatory immigration laws based on IQ tests. As we look back now, we must conclude that the use and abuse of IQ tests in the early 1900s was one of psychology's sorriest moments. Here's what happened.

Innate Intelligence

One name that we have already mentioned is that of Lewis Terman, who was the guiding force behind revising Binet's intelligence test (which became the Stanford-Binet test) and also developing the formula for computing a single IQ score. Terman, who became head of the Department of Psychology at Stanford University, firmly believed that intelligence was primarily inherited, that intelligence tests measured innate abilities, and that environmental influences were far less important.

One of Terman's goals was to test all children and, on the basis of their IQ scores, to label and sort them into categories of innate abilities. Terman argued that society could use IQ scores (usually of 70 or below) to restrain or eliminate those whose intelligence was too low for an effective moral life (Terman, 1916).

Terman hoped to establish minimum intelligence scores necessary for all leading occupations. For example, he believed that people with IQs below 100 should not be given employment that involves prestige or monetary reward. Those with IQs of 75 or below should be unskilled labor, and those with 75–85 IQs should be semiskilled labor. In Terman's world, class boundaries were to be set by innate intelligence, as measured by his Stanford-Binet IQ test (Gould, 1996; Hunt, 1993).

Terman's belief that IQ tests measured innate intelligence was adopted by another well-known American psychologist, Robert Yerkes.

Classifying Races

Robert Yerkes was a Harvard professor who was asked to develop a test that could be used to classify applicants for the army. Under Yerkes's direction, over 1.75 million World War I army recruits were given IQ tests. From this enormous amount of data, Yerkes (1921) and his colleagues reached three conclusions:

1. They concluded that the average mental age of White American adults was a meager 13 years, slightly above the classification of a moron (a term psychologists used in the early 1900s). The reasons they gave for this low mental age were (using the terminology then current) the unconstrained breeding of the poor and feebleminded and the spread of Negro blood through interracial breeding.

2. They concluded that European immigrants could be ranked on intelligence by their country of origin. The fair peoples of western and northern Europe (Nordics) were most intelligent, while the darker peoples of southern Europe (Mediterraneans) and Slavs of eastern Europe were less intelligent.

3. They concluded that Negroes were at the bottom of the racial scale in intelligence.

Many of Yerkes's outrageous and discriminatory views have resurfaced in the 1994 book, *The Bell Curve* (Herrnstein & Murray, 1994), which we discussed earlier. Following Yerkes's lead, IQ scores were next used for racial discrimination.

Immigration Laws

The fact that Yerkes ranked European races by intelligence eventually reached members of the United States Congress. Outraged by the "fact" that Europeans of "low intelligence" were being allowed into America, Congressmen sought a way to severely limit the immigration of people from southern and eastern Europe. In writing the Immigration Law of 1924, Congress relied, in part, on Yerkes's racial rankings and imposed harsh quotas against those they believed nations of inferior stock (people from southern and eastern Europe, Alpine and Mediterranean nations).

Stephen Jay Gould (1996), a well-known evolutionary biologist, reviewed Yerkes's data and pointed out a number of problems: poorly administered tests, terrible testing conditions, inconsistent standards for retaking tests, written tests given to illiterate recruits (guaranteeing a low score), and no control for educational level or familiarity with the English language. As a result of these problems, Gould concluded that Yerkes's data were so riddled with errors as to render useless any conclusions about racial differences in intelligence.

Looking back, it is clear that early psychologists badly misused IQ tests. They forgot that IQ tests are merely one of many tools to assess cognitive abilities, which many consider to be one of many kinds of intelligence (Gardner, 1995).

We've discussed how past IQ tests have been misused and how current IQ tests may be biased. Is there a new generation of intelligence tests on the horizon?

G. Research Focus: New Approaches
Can Bran Scans Measure Intelligence?

Some advances in science occur because of new methods to study old problems. For example, in recent years researchers have used new methods to study a very old problem: how does the brain think? As you may remember from Module 4, researchers have been using PET (positron emission tomography) scans to literally "light up" what the brain is doing. PET scans involve injecting small amounts of harmless radioactive glucose into the blood, which travels to the brain. Neurons take up the radioactive glucose, which is their major source of fuel. The more active the neurons are, the more fuel or glucose they take up, which means that PET scans are one way of recording levels of neural activity in the living brain. PET scans are color coded to show levels of neural activity: maximum activity is shown in red and yellow, and minimum neural activity is shown in blue and green (the figure below is a PET scan showing the area involved in thinking of what objects do).

During the past five years, there has been an enormous increase in using PET scans to study neural functioning. For example, researchers have used PET scans to identify areas of the brain involved in attention, memory, perception of objects and faces, and comprehension of language (Beveza & Nyberg, 1997). This increasing usage of brain scans to study cognitive processes is changing our views of brain functioning (see Module 4). In the not-too-distant future, many cognitive abilities, perhaps even some forms of intelligence, may be measured by brain scans rather than by the current paper-and-pencil intelligence tests. We'll describe several experiments that use brain scans to study cognitive abilities.

Thinking in Male and Female Brains

If you held a female brain in one hand and a similar-sized male brain in another, you could not tell which was which based on any physical traits. Even if you took PET scans while a person was in a resting state (not actively thinking or imagining), you would have a very difficult task correctly deciding if the PET scan was from a male or female brain (Mansour et al., 1996). However, if you took PET scans while subjects were trying to correctly identify the shape of a figure that had been turned around (rotated figure test), you would see a clear difference in "thinking patterns." On this task, males think primarily with the right frontal part of their brains (right frontal lobe) while females think primarily with the right middle-back part of their brains (right parietal-temporal area) (Deutsch & Halsey, 1991). This difference in "thinking patterns" suggests that although males and females may achieve similar IQ scores, they may do so by using different areas of their brains.

Researchers also reported that female and male brains may have a biological difference in how they process emotional information (Gur et al., 1995). For example, when asked to produce a sad mood, women activated a larger part of their "emotional brain" (limbic brain) than did males (George et al., 1996). This difference may be the basis for the often-reported observation that females are better at showing and recognizing emotions than are men.

Besides showing differences in thinking between male and female brains, PET scans also show differences between thinking in normal individuals and those with mental retardation.

Thinking in Normal Controls and Individuals with Mental Retardation

Intelligence tests are one of several measures that are used to evaluate the abilities of individuals with mental retardation. Researchers wondered if PET scans would also show a difference in "thinking" between individuals with normal brains and those with mental retardation (Down Syndrome, p. 288). Researchers compared PET scans from individuals with mild mental retardation (IQs between 50 and 70) with those from normal individuals (IQs of 115 or higher). Individuals with mental retardation showed 20% more neural activity when engaged in a relatively simple attention task compared to normal controls (Haier et al., 1995). Examples of their PET scans are shown on the left.

Mental retardation
Individuals with mild mental retardation showed 20% more overall brain activity (more brain areas in red and yellow) on an attention task.

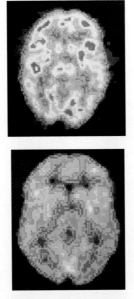

Individuals with normal intelligence showed less overall brain activity (more areas in green and blue) on an attention task.
Normal controls

Researchers concluded that individuals with mental retardation have brains that must work to full capacity on even very simple tasks. Researchers think that brains that show so much overall activity on such simple tests are less efficient than normal brains, which show reduced overall activity on simple tasks (Haier et al., 1995). This kind of research suggests that PET scans may be used to measure how efficiently a person "thinks" by identifying the number of active brain areas.

These kinds of studies give researchers hope that brain scans may lead to the development of new and better ways of defining and measuring intelligence (Haier, 1996).

Besides searching for new ways to measure intelligence, researchers are developing environmental programs to help disadvantaged children develop their intellectual potential. We'll now examine several of these programs.

H. Application: Intervention Programs

Definitions and Programs

Why does a child need a head start?

For a moment, imagine what will happen to Nancy's child. Nancy, who is in her mid-twenties, is a single mother with a 3-year-old child. Nancy lives in a lower-class neighborhood and earns less than $5,000 a year doing part-time work. She has completed only two years of high school, has no family and few friends. What effects do you think Nancy's background, educational level, and current impoverished environment will have on her child? Psychologists would predict that Nancy's 3-year-old child will not likely acquire the social, emotional, and cognitive skills and abilities needed to do well in school or society. Her child may need outside help, which may come from an intervention program (Ramey et al., 1982).

An *intervention program* creates an environment that offers increased opportunities for intellectual, social, and personality-emotional development while ensuring good physical health.

There are different kinds of intervention programs that could give Nancy training in how to be a good parent and provide her child with educational and social opportunities.

Perhaps the best-known intervention program in the United States is Head Start, which began in 1965 as a six-to-eight-week program with a budget of 96 million dollars and a goal of combating poverty. Researchers soon discovered that a longer intervention program was needed, so Head Start was lengthened to two years. Head Start enrolls almost 800,000 3- to 5-year-olds, has a budget of about 3 billion dollars and six different goals (Murray, 1997).

We'll discuss Head Start's program and goals as well as another longer and more intense intervention program for disadvantaged children called the Abecedarian Project.

ABECEDARIAN PROJECT

The project's goal was to teach youngsters from disadvantaged environments the cognitive and social skills needed for future success in school. Psychologists identified babies who were at high risk of failing in school because they were in disadvantaged settings. Most of the mothers had low IQs, were African American, young, without a high school education, and single. With the mothers' permission, 2- to 3-month-old infants were assigned to either a control group that did not receive any special treatment or to an experimental group. Children in the experimental group spent six or more hours daily, five days a week, in a carefully supervised day care center that continued for about four years until the children entered public school at the age of 5.

After four years of this intense intervention program, children in the Abecedarian Project had IQ scores 12 points higher than control children from disadvantaged environments. Once children left the program, their advantage in IQ gains gradually lessened. When these children were retested at age 12 and age 15, these children retained a small gain in IQ scores (Campbell & Ramey, 1990; Ramey et al., 1982).

These data indicate several things: first, the relatively large gains in IQ scores resulting from early intervention were not maintained in later years. However, at age 12 and 15, these children did retain small gains in IQ scores, indicating the positive influence of the intervention program. Second, once children leave the intervention program and return to their disadvantaged environments, they no longer have the personal, social, or motivational support needed to maintain all their newly acquired cognitive skills (Brody, 1997).

HEAD START

Head Start, which is a day-care program for disadvantaged children, usually lasts for two years, from ages 3 to 5, and has six goals: preschool education, health screening, mental health services, hot meals, social services for the child and family, and involvement and participation of parents in the program (Zigler & Styfco, 1994).

Head Start was initially viewed as something of a failure because two to three years after children left Head Start, few if any differences on IQ or other academic scores were found between those children and control groups (Clarke & Clarke, 1989). However, despite the fact that increased IQ scores were not maintained, the Head Start program showed other important long-term beneficial effects (Zigler & Styfco, 1994):

■ Adolescents who had been in the Head Start program were more likely to be in classes appropriate for their ages rather than to have had to repeat a class, were less likely to show antisocial or delinquent behavior, and were more likely to hold jobs.

■ Mothers whose children had been in the Head Start program reported fewer psychological symptoms, greater feelings of mastery, and greater current life satisfaction.

■ Children who had two years of Head Start and an additional two to seven years of educational help were much more successful in graduating from high school (69%) than a control group (49%).

From these data we can draw two conclusions. First, early and often rather large increases (up to 10 points) in IQ scores do not last after the child leaves the intervention program. Second, Head Start programs resulted in a number of long-term benefits, such as increased social and personal well-being, to both the participating children and mothers (Zigler, 1995; Zigler & Styfco, 1993; Zigler & Styfco, 1994). These encouraging long-term effects indicate that Head Start should not be evaluated solely on IQ scores but on other personality, motivational, and psychological benefits.

Raising IQ Scores

In the early days of Head Start, psychologists were very encouraged to find that the program initially increased disadvantaged children's IQ scores about 10 points, a very significant amount. One reason IQ scores can be raised in young children from disadvantaged homes is that these children have not been exposed to and have not acquired the kinds of skills and cultural experiences assessed by IQ tests. However, when disadvantaged children are exposed to the enriched environment of Head Start, these children quickly acquire all kinds of new skills and abilities that help them score higher on IQ tests (Spitz, 1997).

For example, researchers compared two groups of disadvantaged children, all of whom had IQ scores below 80 (100 is considered the average IQ). Some of these children, called the experimental group, were placed in a special educational intervention program from ages 3 to 5. Other children, called the control group, were given no additional training and remained in their home environments.

The figure below shows that, after only one year, children in the experimental group (intervention program) showed a significant increase in IQ scores (about 10 points) compared to the children in the control group who remained in disadvantaged home environments (Schweinhart & Weikart, 1980). However, after the children left the intervention program at the age of 5 and entered public school, their IQ scores began a slow but consistent decline. At this same time, the IQ scores of control children began a gradual increase as they benefited from attending public school. By the age of 11, when children were in the fourth grade of public school, there was no longer any difference in IQ scores.

One reason for this decline in IQ scores has to do with what happens to children after they leave an interventional program, such as Head Start, which usually lasts only two to three years. Once children leave the support of a intervention program and return to less stimulating environments, children receive less educational, social, and motivational support, which leads to a gradual decline in their IQ scores (Brody, 1997). For this reason, researchers recommend that programs like Head Start should be lengthened from three to at least five years so that the children have additional time to practice their newly acquired social, emotional, and academic skills (Zigler & Styfco, 1994).

Finally, as we discussed earlier, intervention programs should not be evaluated solely on IQ scores but rather on other social, emotional, and psychological gains that are found to be long-lasting.

Importance of Intervention Programs

Researchers make four important points about the usefulness of intervention programs such as Head Start:

1 Nearly 25% of children in the United States are growing up below the poverty line (Kassebaum, 1994). The effects of poverty include delays in young children's developmental progress, lowered aspirations and increased apathy among older children, and school failure or withdrawal (Zigler, 1994). Intervention programs help reduce the devastating effects that continuing poverty across several generations can have on families and children (Ramey & Ramey, 1998).

2 About 25 to 30% of children live in single-parent families that are below the poverty line (Kassebaum, 1994). In some cases, impoverished family environments lead to neglect or abuse, which has very negative effects on a child's social, emotional, and intellectual development. Intensive intervention programs during the first years of life are effective in reducing and preventing the significant intellectual dysfunction that may result from continuing poverty and lack of environmental support (Ramey & Ramey, 1998).

3 After studying intervention programs for 30 years, psychologists have learned that short periods of intervention, such as onc or two years, are not as effective in promoting social, emotional, and cognitive growth as programs that last six or seven years (Reynolds, 1994; Zigler, 1994).

4 Successful intervention programs are those that have a strong educational emphasis, which means that they have specially trained teachers, and have a low ratio of children to teachers. Good Head Start programs have these characteristics, but not all Head Start programs can meet these standards (Zigler & Styfco, 1994).

Psychologists concluded that Head Start and other intervention programs give children from impoverished environments a better opportunity for cognitive, social, and emotional development (Ramey & Ramey, 1998).

SUMMARY TEST

A. DEFINING INTELLIGENCE

1. A subarea of psychology that is concerned with developing psychological tests to assess an individual's abilities, skills, beliefs, and personality traits in a wide range of settings—school, industry, or clinic—is called _____.

2. Spearman's two-factor theory of intelligence says that there is a general factor, called (a)_____, which represents a person's ability to perform complex mental work, such as abstract reasoning and problem-solving. The general factor underlies a person's performance across tests. In addition, there is a second factor, called (b)_____, which represents a person's specific mental abilities, such as mathematical or verbal skills. These specific mental abilities may differ across tests.

3. Gardner says that there are seven kinds of intelligence: verbal intelligence, musical intelligence, logical-mathematical intelligence, spatial intelligence, body movement intelligence, intelligence to understand oneself, and intelligence to understand others. This is called the _____ theory.

4. Sternberg's triarchic theory says that intelligence can be divided into three ways of gathering and processing information (*triarchic* means three). The first is using (a)_____ skills that are measured by traditional intelligence tests. The second is using (b)_____ skills that require creative thinking, the ability to deal with novel situations, and the ability to learn from experience. The third is using (c)_____ skills that help a person adjust to, and cope with, his or her sociocultural environment.

B. MEASURING INTELLIGENCE

Block design
Assemble blocks to match this design.

Picture completion
Tell me what is missing.

5. In trying to measure intelligence, researchers through the years have learned that neither skull size nor brain weight is an accurate predictor of _____.

6. The first intelligence test, which was developed by (a)_____, measured vocabulary, memory, common knowledge, and other cognitive abilities. By comparing a child's score with the scores of average children at the same age, Binet was able to estimate a child's (b)_____. Thus, the Binet-Simon Intelligence Scale gave its results in terms of mental age, while the IQ score was later developed by (c)_____ who devised a formula to calculate

an individual's intelligence quotient. The formula can be written as IQ = (d)_____.

7. The Wechsler Adult Intelligence Scale (WAIS-III) and Wechsler Intelligence Scale for Children (WISC-III) have items that are organized into various subtests. Subtests for general information, vocabulary, and verbal comprehension, are some of those in the (a)_____ section. Subtests that involve arranging pictures in a meaningful order, assembling objects, and using codes are examples of subtests in the (b)_____ section. An individual receives a separate score for each of the subtests; these scores are then combined to yield overall scores for verbal and performance abilities, which, in turn, are combined into a single score, called an (c)_____ score.

8. A good psychological test must have two qualities. One quality ensures that a person's score on a test at one point in time is similar to a score by the same person on a similar test at a later date; this is called (a)_____. The other quality ensures that a test measures what it is supposed to measure; this is called (b)_____. Although the results from analyzing handwriting may be consistent from time to time, this is a poor test of personality or intelligence because handwriting analysis lacks the quality of (c)_____.

C. DISTRIBUTION & USE OF IQ SCORES

9. Suppose IQ scores are in a statistical arrangement that resembles the shape of a bell, with the vast majority of scores falling in the middle range and fewer scores falling near the two extreme ends of the curve. This arrangement is called a _____.

About 95 in 100 (95.44%) have IQ scores between 70 and 130.

About 68 in 100 (68.26%) have IQ scores between 85 and 115.

85   100   115
Average IQ

10. Substantial limitation in present functioning that is characterized by significantly below-average intellectual functioning, along with related limitations in two of ten areas, including communication, self-care, home living, social skills, and safety, is called _____.

11. There are two general causes of mental retardation: genetic problems or brain damage give rise to (a)_____ retardation; in the absence of apparent genetic or brain damage, greatly impoverished environments can give rise to (b)_____ retardation. Mental retardation is reflected in IQ scores at one end of the normal distribution. At the other end of the normal distribution of

IQ scores are those who are considered (c)_____; such people have above-average intelligence (usually IQs above 130) as well as some superior talent or skill.

D. POTENTIAL PROBLEMS OF IQ TESTING

12. Binet warned that intelligence tests should not be used to measure (a)_____ mental abilities because intelligence tests measure cognitive abilities, which are influenced by both heredity and environment. Binet also warned that intelligence tests, by themselves, should not be used to (b)_____ people—for example, a moron or a genius. Current IQ tests have been criticized for including wording or experiences that are more familiar to a particular culture, which is called (c)_____. One way to avoid bias is to measure intelligence by observing people as they solve problems in natural settings; this is called (d)_____. One reason individuals may do poorly on IQ tests is because of noncognitive factors, such as attitude, experience, and emotional functioning, which are called (e)_____.

E. NATURE-NURTURE QUESTION

13. The (a)_____ question refers to the relative contributions that genetic and environmental factors make to the development of intelligence. On the basis of twin studies, researchers generally conclude that about (b)_____ of the

Intelligence (general abilities)

Spatial ability

Verbal ability

Memory

contribution to intelligence (IQ scores) comes from genetic factors and about (c)_____ comes from environmental factors. Adoption studies support the idea that environmental factors contribute to intellectual development (as measured by IQ scores). The idea that about half of one's intellectual development is dependent on environmental factors has resulted in (d)_____ programs that give impoverished children increased social-educational opportunities. There is little or no cause-and-effect evidence that the average difference in IQ scores between African Americans and Whites is caused primarily by (e)_____ factors.

F. CULTURAL DIVERSITY: RACES AND IMMIGRATION

14. Early psychologists ignored Binet's warning about misusing IQ tests. For example, in the early 1900s, Terman believed that IQ tests did measure (a)_____ intelligence, and he wanted to use

IQ tests to sort people into categories. Terman's view was adopted by Robert Yerkes, who wanted to use IQ tests to rank the intelligence of (b)_____ entering the United States. In the 1920s, (c)_____ were written to exclude citizens from certain countries because Yerkes had ranked these individuals low in intelligence.

G. RESEARCH FOCUS: NEW APPROACHES

15. Psychologists are using new methods, such as (a)_____ scans to study the old problem of learning how the brain thinks. By using PET scans, researchers found that when identifying shapes of figures, females "think" by using a different part of their (b)_____ than do males.

Researchers also found that brains of retarded individuals showed more activity and thus were less (c)_____ in solving a simple attention task than brains of normal individuals, which showed less activity and were thus more efficient.

H. APPLICATION: INTERVENTION PROGRAMS

16. A program that creates an environment with increased opportunities for intellectual, social, and personality-emotional development is called an (a)_____ program. Although data indicate that IQ increases resulting from intervention programs may be short-lived, there are other long-term positive benefits; for example, adolescents who have passed through such programs are more likely to complete school and hold jobs, and less likely to show (b)_____ behavior. In addition, mothers involved in the Head Start program reported fewer psychological (c)_____ and had greater feelings of mastery and life satisfaction.

Answers: 1. psychometrics; 2. (a) **g**, (b) **s**; 3. multiple-intelligence; 4. (a) analytical, cognitive, or logical, (b) problem-solving, (c) practical; 5. intelligence; 6. (a) Binet & Simon, (b) mental age, (c) Terman, (d) MA/CA × 100; 7. (a) verbal, (b) performance, (c) IQ; 8. (a) reliability, (b) validity, (c) validity; 9. normal distribution; 10. mental retardation; 11. (a) organic, (b) cultural-familial, (c) gifted; 12. (a) innate, (b) label or classify, (c) cultural bias, (d) ecological psychology, (e) nonintellectual factors; 13. (a) nature-nurture, (b) 50%, (c) 50%, (d) intervention, (e) inherited, or genetic; 14. (a) innate, (b) immigrants, (c) immigration laws, or quotas; 15. (a) PET, (b) brain, (c) efficient; 16. (a) intervention, (b) antisocial or delinquent, (c) symptoms or problems.

CRITICAL THINKING

QUESTIONS

A REAL BRAIN TEASER
by Julie Marquis

What makes people smart? It is a question that scientists and philosophers have pondered for centuries, prompting complex calibrations, from head measurements to brain-bending tests.

Now, scientists are using the latest technology to peer inside the brain, producing some of the first images of how gifted, and not-so-gifted, minds think.

Scholars have long haggled over whether smarts can be summed up as a single entity, as in an intelligence quotient, or a collection of interacting capabilities, or perhaps many distinct skills

"We don't want to be evaluating people on one thing with its turning out to be a very narrow and prejudicial concept of cognition," said Harvard psychologist Howard Gardner, who goes so far as to argue that we have at least seven different "intelligences."

Proponents of a new concept called "emotional intelligence" don't necessarily consider IQ the best predictor of how one will fare in life. What about empathy, intuition, and social savvy? Certain emotional skills, they argue, seem to bring success—promotions and coveted invitations, for example.

They propose that emotion should not be considered separately from intellect. Often, feelings sharpen reason, says University of Iowa neuroscientist Dr. Antonio R. Damasio. Emotion helps reason to focus the mind, to set priorities.

UC Irvine professor Richard Haier, in a series of pioneering studies, has used positron emission tomography (PET) scanning to probe the neural underpinnings of intelligence, as traditionally assessed by IQ tests and the SATs.

Based on his continuing studies, Haier suggests that brighter people have lower brain metabolic rates because their brains are more efficient. Haier speculated that bright people might use fewer inessential, or even detrimental, circuits.

He and Iowa researcher Camilla P. Benbow compared PET scans of mathematically talented students—as determined by the SAT—to those of average students. He expected to find some measurable difference in brain activity between the gifted and not-so-blessed.

Instead, his most striking finding was overall gender differences. Among the men doing math problems, a part of the temporal lobe consistently lit up; the more it lit up, the better they scored on the math test. Among women, however, no such pattern emerged. Average and gifted women showed no significant difference in temporal lobe activity.

What gives? Haier's short answer is, "we don't know." But he suspects that men's brains are more focused in their mathematical thinking than women's. Conversely, the talented females simply may be more efficient than their average peers, rather than more focused.

Source: *Los Angeles Times,* October 17, 1996.

1. What is emotional intelligence?

2. How might emotional intelligence be important for success in the business world?

3. What technology did Dr. Haier use to probe the neurology of intelligence?

4. What do Dr. Haier's studies show about the differences in the brain processes of bright and not-so-bright people?

5. According to Dr. Haier's studies, how do the brains of men and women differ when they do math problems?

Study Questions

A. **Defining Intelligence**—How intelligent was Ray Kroc, who never finished high school but started the world-famous McDonald's hamburger chain? (See answer in Critical Thinking Appendix.)

B. **Measuring Intelligence**—Would a new test based on a very accurate count of all the cells in your brain be a good test of intelligence?

C. **Distribution & Use of IQ Scores**—If you were hiring for a large department store, would it help to know the applicants' IQ scores?

D. **Potential Problems of IQ Testing**—Should we use IQ scores to assign the growing number of students from different cultures to grade levels? (See answer in Critical Thinking Appendix.)

E. **Nature-Nurture Question**—If parents were going to adopt a child, how important would it be to know the child's genetic makeup?

F. **Cultural Diversity: Races & Immigration**—What convinced members of the United States Congress to use IQ scores as the basis for immigration laws?

G. **Research Focus: New Approaches**—Would brain scans provide a less biased, more culture-free measure of intelligence than standard IQ tests?

H. **Application: Intervention Programs**—Since Head Start fails to raise IQ scores over the long run, should its financial support be reduced? (See answer in Critical Thinking Appendix.)

Web Sites & Learning Activities

● BROOKS/COLE ONLINE PSYCHOLOGY STUDY CENTER

http://psychstudy.brookscole.com/student/plotnik/quiz/ch13frm.html

This site gives students a chance to review material by taking quizzes and doing exercises and activities for this module.

● SELF-DISCOVERY WORKSHOP

http://www.iqtest.com/

What's your IQ? This site features an online IQ test that claims to be very accurate. It takes about 20 minutes to complete the whole process.

● IQ TEST

http://www.psychtests.com/iq.html

Here's another online IQ test. This one is a bit longer—60 items.

● BRAINTAINMENT

http://brain.com/welcome.html

This commercial site offers several fun online tests, including an IQ test.

● WHAT'S YOUR EMOTIONAL INTELLIGENCE QUOTIENT?

http://www.utne.com/lens/bms/9bmseq.html

Many people now believe that emotional intelligence is as important as IQ in determining your success in life. This site contains information on emotional intelligence, plus a self-quiz.

Welcome to the WEB

● THE ARC: A NATIONAL ORGANIZATION ON MENTAL RETARDATION

http://www.TheArc.org.welcome.html

The ARC is the largest national organization devoted to helping people who are mentally retarded. Their site contains its own search engine and a wealth of information on all aspects of mental retardation.

● MENSA INTERNATIONAL

http://www.mensa.org/

Here is the home page for the famous high IQ social club. To become a member of Mensa, you must prove that your IQ is in the top 2% of the general population.

Activities

● *Integrator Online™ for Introductory Psychology* CD-ROM, Plotnik, Module 13

● Study Guide to accompany *Introduction to Psychology,* 5th edition, Module 13 (choice of PC or Mac computer version or hard copy)

● *PsychNow!* CD-ROM

Answers to questions on page 302

1. Emotional intelligence is aptitude at emotional skills such as empathy, intuition, and social savvy.
2. Emotional intelligence would be an asset in business by allowing you to get along with coworkers and clients, understand people's needs, and know your own strengths and limitations.

3. He used positron emission tomography (PET scans).
4. His studies showed that brighter people have lower brain metabolic rates because their brains are more efficient.
5. Talented men doing math problems show activity in the temporal lobe; among women, no such activity showed up.

Module 14 THOUGHT & LANGUAGE

dog (dog, dag) n.; pl. dogs, dog.

1. any of a large and varied group of domesti- animals (Canis famil...) that have four legs, a tail, ...nent nose, a hai... ...ark.

Left thalamus has fewer cells.

Concepts

What is that four-legged thing?

Jeff, who is only 14 months old, walks up to his mother and says, in a somewhat demanding voice, "Juice." Jeff's one-word sentence, "Juice," is shorthand for "Can I please have a glass of orange juice?" Even as a toddler, Jeff already knows a considerable number of words that represent a whole range of objects, such as cookie, car, bottle, bunny, baby, juice, ball, apple, and the most hated words of all for a young child, "wash up." So when Jeff points at an object and says, "ball," his one-word sentence is short for "That is my ball." Jeff's use of these single-word "sentences" indicate that he is on his way to learning a very complex system of communicating by using language.

Jeff also uses one-word "sentences" to ask questions. For instance, he'll point to a picture in his animal book and and ask, "Name?" This means "What is the name of that animal?" Jeff has already

learned that a four-legged, fuzzy-tailed, large-eared animal is a bunny; a four-legged, long-nosed animal that barks is a dog; and a four-legged, short-eared animal with a long tail that says, "meow," is a cat. Perhaps when Jeff sees an animal, such as a dog, cat or rabbit, he takes a "mental photo" that he uses for future identifications. But that would mean storing an overwhelming number of "mental photos" of all the animals, objects, and people in his environment. We'll explain a more efficient system that Jeff probably uses to identify animals, objects, and people.

Creativity

How does one become creative?

One of Jeff's most favorite things to do is to paint the animals in his picture books. Although Jeff makes a terribly wonderful mess, his parents encourage him because they hope that Jeff's early interest in painting may indicate a creative talent for painting or art. How one becomes a creative person is quite a mystery; take the case of Gordon Parks, for example.

No one thought Gordon Parks would amount to much. He was out on the streets at age 15 and never had time to finish high school, where he and his classmates were told, "Don't worry about graduating—it doesn't matter because you're gonna be porters and maids." Parks is African American and grew up in the 1920s, surrounded by segregation, discrimination, and worst of all, lynchings.

Parks was a teenager when his mother died. He was sent to live with his brother-in-law, but, Parks remembers, "That man didn't like children and didn't want to take me on, and I sensed that the minute I walked into his house." He was soon out on the street. He drifted from city to city, lived in flophouses, and worked at odd jobs. What would become of Parks (McKenna, 1994)?

Parks (right photo) is now in his eighties and looks back on what he has accomplished. With little formal schooling and little professional help, he has written five volumes of poetry and a best-selling autobiography, *The Learning Tree*. He worked as a professional photographer for *Vogue* and *Life* magazines, and directed several films (*Shaft* and *The Learning Tree*). Recently, he completed another novel, attended an exhibition of his photographs, and published a book of his incredible photos (Parks, 1997). Parks's early years showed no signs of his creativity. We'll discuss what creativity is and what makes creative people different.

Cognitive Approach

How does your mind work?

How do toddlers like Jeff learn to speak a complex language and to recognize hundreds of objects? How did Gordon Parks, with little formal schooling, develop the ability to write and express his creativity in so many ways? The answer to these kinds of questions involves figuring out how our minds work. One way to study mental processes is to use the cognitive approach.

The *cognitive approach* is one method of studying how we process, store, and use information and how this information, in turn, influences what we notice, perceive, learn, remember, believe, and feel.

We have already discussed several aspects of the cognitive approach: learning in Modules 9 and 10, and memory and forgetting in Modules 11 and 12. Here we'll explore two other cognitive processes, thinking and language.

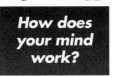

Thinking, which is sometimes referred to as reasoning, involves mental processes that are used to form concepts, solve problems, and engage in creative activities.

Language is a special form of communication in which we learn and use complex rules to form and manipulate symbols (words or gestures) that are used to generate an endless number of meaningful sentences.

In fact, thinking and using language are two things we do much better than animals (Kosslyn, 1995).

What's Coming

We'll discuss how we form concepts, solve problems, think creatively, acquire language, and reason. We'll also examine why people have difficulty recognizing words (dyslexia) and how language used by animals is different from the language used by humans.

We'll begin with the interesting question of how Jeff learned to distinguish a rabbit from a dog, and a dog from a cat.

A. Forming Concepts

Most of us have forgotten a problem that we faced as children: how to distinguish between animals, such as distinguishing a dog from a cat or a rabbit. One way we solved this problem was to form concepts.

A *concept* is a way to group objects, events, animals, or people on the basis of some characteristics they all share.

As a child, you probably learned through experience which characteristics are shared by dogs, by cats, and by rabbits. So when you saw a strange animal, such as a 9-ounce, hairless Chihuahua, or a 5-foot-tall, 110-pound Great Dane, you guessed correctly that it was a dog and not a cat or rabbit. How you formed the concept of a dog or cat or rabbit has two different explanations; the definition theory and the prototype theory.

Definition Theory

You easily recognized the animals on the left, but the question is how did you know which animal was which? Is it because your mind contains definitions of hundreds of animals?

Definition theory says that you form a concept of an object, event, animal, or person by making a mental list of the actual or essential characteristics of that particular thing.

According to definition theory, you formed a concept of a dog, cat, or rabbit by learning its essential characteristics. The essential characteristics of a dog might include its barking, a long nose, two ears, two eyes, four legs, some hair, and usually a tail. Similarly, you made mental definitions or concepts for all animals. Then, when you looked at animals, such as those on the left, you automatically sorted through your hundreds of animal definitions until you found one that included the essential properties of a dog, cat, or rabbit. Once you found the definition, you knew what the animal was. Although the definition theory seems like a reasonable method of forming concepts, it has two serious problems.

PROBLEMS WITH DEFINITION THEORY

Too many features. In reality, it is very difficult to list all the defining features of any object (Rey, 1983). For example, if your list of features to define a dog wasn't long enough, the list might also apply to wolves, jackals, coyotes, and skunks. If your list of features to define a dog included every possible feature, such a mental list would be complete but take so long to go through that it would be very slow to use. And worse, you would need a long list of defining features for each and every animal, person, and object. Dealing with such a great number of mental lists, each one defining a separate concept, would tax the best of memories.

Too many exceptions. After making a list of defining features, you would also need to list all the exceptions that do not fit into the dictionary definition of dog. For example, some dogs rarely bark, some are very tiny, some are very large, some are hairless, and some are very fuzzy.

Because of these two problems, you would need to check two mental lists—a long list that contained all the defining features and another that contained all the exceptions—before finding the concept that correctly identified the animal, person, or object.

For these reasons, the definition theory has been replaced by a different theory of how we form concepts: the prototype theory.

Prototype Theory

Please look at animals #1, #2, and #3 on the right. Despite the great differences in size, color, and facial features of these animals, prototype theory explains why you can easily recognize each one as a dog.

Prototype theory says that you form a concept by creating a mental image that is based on the average characteristics of an object. This "average" looking object is called a prototype. To identify a new object, you match it to one of your already formed prototypes of objects, people, or animals.

For example, based on experience, you have developed prototypes of many different objects, persons, and animals (Cohen & Murphy, 1984; Rosch, 1978). Your prototype of a dog would be an animal of *average* height, weight, and color, with an average-sized nose, tail, and ears. Using this prototype, you identify as dogs the large brown mutt (#1), the tiny Chihuahua (#2) and the Dalmatian (#3).

ADVANTAGES OF PROTOTYPE THEORY

Average features. The first big advantage of prototype theory over definition theory is that you do not have to make a mental list of all the defining features of an object, which is often impossible. Instead, you form a prototype by creating an image of the object, animal, or person that has only average features.

Quick recognition. The second advantage of prototype theory is that it can result in quick recognition, as happened when you identified animals #1, #2, and #3 as dogs. The more a new object resembles a prototype, the more quickly you can identify it; the less it matches your prototype, the longer it takes to identify it.

For example, what is the strange animal #4 (below right), and where is its head? Because this animal is not close to your dog prototype, it will take you some time to realize that this animal is entirely covered in "dreadlocks," its head is on the right, and it's an unusual dog (called a Puli).

Prototype theory, which explains that you form concepts by creating and using prototypes, is widely accepted and has replaced the older, more traditional definition theory.

Next, we'll discuss how early children begin forming concepts and why forming concepts or putting things into categories is relatively easy and usually automatic.

Early Formation

When do children form concepts?

At the beginning of this module, we described how 14-month-old Jeff had already learned a number of concepts, such as juice, cookie, car, ball, apple, and bunny. Like all children 10 to 16 months old, Jeff has already formed a number of concepts, such as correctly identifying animals that live on land or in the sea (Oakes et al., 1997). Researchers found that children form concepts and place things into categories as a result of experience with objects and development of the ability to use language to name things (Gershkoff-Stowe et al., 1997). For example, the child in the photo is learning the concept *block* as she plays with them. Initially a child's categories may be very broad, such as objects, people, animals, and events. However, with more experience come more concepts.

Once children form one concept—for example, place the block *up*—they easily form the concept for its opposite, place the block *down;* once they form the concept for *high,* they easily form the concept for *low.*

As children gain even more experience and better use of language (as 5-year-olds), they can form more complex concepts that deal with the qualities of objects, such as *heavy, shiny, colorful,* or *sweet.* Because experience stimulates the formation of concepts, children benefit from being in stimulating environments that provide increased opportunities to encounter and interact with a wide variety of objects, animals, and people (Kagan, 1994b).

One reason children are able to form a wide variety of concepts with relative ease and at such an early age is partly due to the way the brain processes information about categories.

Brain Ready for Processing

How does the brain form concepts?

Without thinking, you can quickly and easily recognize the three objects on the right as turtle, apple, and clown and, if asked, place them into three different categories: of animal, food, and person. Researchers explain that you were able to recognize these three things by matching each to your prototype of a turtle, apple, and clown (Squire & Knowlton, 1995). The reason you are not aware of forming prototypes or of matching things to prototypes is that these cognitive processes go on at an unconscious, or implicit, level, which means that you are unaware of and cannot recall what is happening (see Module 11). Evidence that forming prototypes and matching things to prototypes occurs at an unconscious (implicit) level comes from studies on patients who had suffered various forms of amnesia or memory loss due to brain damage. Although amnesic patients were able to form prototypes and correctly match things to prototypes, they could not explain how they did it. Researchers con-

cluded that using prototypes involves implicit processes, which we are not aware of and cannot voluntarily recall (Squire & Knowlton, 1995).

One reason children can form concepts or categories so easily and so early is because the brain is innately wired or already set up to process different concepts in different places. Based on PET scans of normal subjects and tests on brain-damaged individuals, researchers found that different concepts, such as for animals, vegetables, and faces, were processed in different parts of the brain (Martin et al., 1996, Moscovitch, 1997). These kinds of data suggest that the brain is innately wired to form prototypes or categories, which explains why children can easily and early on perform these complex cognitive tasks (Squire & Knowlton, 1995). Being able to form and use concepts has two real advantages.

Two Functions

What if you lost your concepts?

If you woke up one day to find that you had lost all your concepts, you would indeed have a very bad day because concepts perform two important functions: they organize information and allow us to avoid relearning.

1 Organize information. Concepts allow us to group things into categories and thus better organize and store information in memory. For example, instead of having to store hundreds of mental images of many different kinds of dogs, you can store a single "dog" prototype.

2 Avoid relearning. By having concepts that can be used to classify and categorize things, we can easily classify new things without having to relearn what that thing is. For example, once you have a concept for a dog, rabbit, cat, or cookie, you do not have to relearn what that thing is on each new encounter.

Without concepts, our cognitive worlds would consist of unconnected pieces of information. In fact, some forms of brain damage destroy a person's ability to form concepts, so that the person is unable to name or categorize what he or she sees (see Module 5 for a discussion of visual agnosia). By using concepts, we can identify, categorize, and store information very efficiently.

There is no doubt that concepts are useful for identifying objects and helping us make sense of our world. Next, you'll see that concepts are valuable for solving problems and thinking creatively.

B. Solving Problems

In the photo at right, world chess champion Gary Kasparov looks very glum. In 1997, for the first time, he lost a match to a computer named Deep Blue. Programmers had built Deep Blue, a 1.4-ton monster containing the equivalent of 32 powerful personal computers, for only one reason: to beat Kasparov. This match of the century, between the world's best chess players—human and machine—was all about problem solving.

Problem solving involves searching for some rule, plan, or strategy that results in our reaching a certain goal that is currently out of reach.

In previous matches, Kasparov had always beat the machine because he was the better problem solver. For Kasparov, as well as for most of us, problem solving involves three states: (1) the *initial state,* which is thinking about the unsolved problem; (2) the *operations state,* which involves trying various rules or strategies to solve the problem; and (3) the *goal state,* which is reaching the solution. One plan or strategy used by expert problem solvers, such as Kasparov, is to think in broader terms of how to solve the problem, while less successful novices become too focused on specifics (Abernethy et al., 1994; Rostan, 1994). For example, expert computer programmers look at the final goal (to write a new program) and work their way down to specific solutions. In comparison, novices become bogged down in working on specific steps of the program and never reach the final goal of writing a complete program. In other words, novices are so focused on individual trees that they lose sight of the forest.

The most interesting part of the chess match between human and machine was each one's plan, or strategy, for winning.

Two Rules for Solving Problems

The match between Kasparov and Deep Blue was essentially a match between two different ways of solving problems. Kasparov used rules based on clever mental shortcuts, or heuristics, while Deep Blue's 1.4-ton computer used rules based on logical fixed sequences or algorithms. We'll explain the difference between these two general sets of rules for solving problems—algorithms and heuristics.

ALGORITHMS

If you wanted to win at a variety of games such as chess, checkers, and bridge, you would follow a fixed set of rules that are called algorithms *(AL-go-rhythms).*

Algorithms are a fixed set of rules that, if followed correctly, will eventually lead to a solution.

For example, learning to play chess involves following algorithms that define how pieces move and the results of those moves. The reason relatively few chess players become grand masters like Kasparov is that people vary in their ability to learn and use algorithms.

Initially, Deep Blue was given little chance to beat world chess champion Kasparov. That's because playing chess by using algorithms is a slow process, similar to driving a car by reading rules from a book. You could only drive slowly and would be passed by every other driver. Instead of using algorithms, chess champion Kasparov was playing with a potentially more powerful set of rules called heuristics.

HEURISTICS

Kasparov's unique brain, together with his years of experience, allowed him to develop hundreds of clever shortcuts for playing chess. These shortcuts are called heuristics *(hyur-RIS-ticks).*

Heuristics are rules of thumb, or clever shortcuts, that reduce the number of operations and allow one to solve problems more easily and quickly.

Prior to 1997, Kasparov's clever shortcuts, or heuristics, had always given him the advantage over the fixed algorithms of computer programs. However, Deep Blue's new algorithms raised the limits on its speed of "thinking" from the old rate of 100,000 moves per second to the unbelievable rate of 200,000 moves per second. Even Kasparov's clever heuristics could not match the brute computer force of 200,000 moves per second (Peters, 1997). Computer programmers don't (can't) write chess programs based on heuristics, because they first need to understand Kasparov's complex, skilled, and intuitive thinking before they can translate it into a chess program.

Psychologists have discovered that people, in making daily decisions, use a number of different heuristics, such as the availability heuristic (Fisk & Pidgeon, 1997; Tversky & Kahneman, 1983).

The *availability heuristic* says that we rely on information that is more prominent or easily recalled and overlook other information that is available but less prominent or notable.

For example, you may think that televised newscasts contain only tragic events—floods, earthquakes, murders—since those are most prominent in your memory. However, if you were asked to think carefully about the newscast, you would recall many other events.

When we use the availability heuristic to make a decision, we are essentially using a shortcut. Although heuristics allow us to make quick decisions, they may result in bad decisions since we make them using shortcuts, which limits the amount of information we can use (Bower, 1997).

Sometimes we are not given the rules to solve problems but must develop our own. We'll explore several effective problem-solving strategies.

Three Strategies for Solving Problems

What if you get stuck?

Most of us have had the experience of getting stuck while trying to solve a problem and wondering what to do next. By studying people who are good at problem solving, such as chess players, engineers, and computer programmers, psychologists have identified a number of useful strategies for solving problems. We'll discuss three problem-solving strategies—changing a mental set, using analogies, and forming subgoals. (Solutions to the first two problems appear on page 317.)

General problem:
Write a term paper

Subgoals:

1 Do library research.

2 Take notes.

3 Make detailed outline.

4 Write paper.

Changing One's Mental Set

Problem. Connect all nine dots shown above by drawing four straight lines without lifting your pencil from the paper or retracing any lines. Try to solve it before reading any further.

If, like most people, you failed to solve this problem, it may be because of functional fixedness.

Functional fixedness refers to a mental set that is characterized by the inability to see an object as having a function different from its usual one.

For instance, you probably have a mental set that a straight line must begin and end on a dot. To solve the nine-dot problem, you need to break out of functional fixedness and think of a line as continuing past a dot.

As discussed in an earlier module (p. 226), some people solve this problem in a sudden flash known as insight.

Insight is the sudden grasp of a solution after many incorrect attempts.

You can increase your chances of solving a problem by insight if you consider the problem from many different viewpoints and unusual angles and if you decrease your anxiety and concern, which will in turn help you to overcome functional fixedness.

Using Analogies

Problem. Imagine that you have a box of matches, two candles, a piece of string, and several tacks as shown in the photo above. How would you mount a candle on the wall so that it could be used as a light?

You may solve the candle problem in a flash of insight. However, most of us have to develop a strategy to solve the problem, and a good strategy may involve using an analogy.

An *analogy* is a strategy for finding a similarity between the new situation and an old, familiar situation.

If you adopt an analogy to solve the candle problem, here's how your thinking might proceed: "I'm familiar with using a shelf to hold a candle on the wall. Which of the objects—candle, string, or box—could serve as a shelf? If I remove the matches, I can tack the box to the wall."

As you gain more experience and knowledge, you become better at using analogies to solve problems. This is one reason that businesses prefer employees with experience: these employees are more likely to use analogies to solve problems.

What about the problem every student must face—writing a paper?

Forming Subgoals

Problem. Your assignment is to write a term paper titled "Creativity and Madness."

A useful strategy for writing the paper would be to divide the assignment or general problem into a number of subgoals.

Using *subgoals* is a strategy that involves breaking the overall problem into separate parts that, when completed in order, will result in a solution.

As shown in the figure above, the first subgoal is doing library research and finding a number of articles on creativity and madness. The second subgoal is reading the articles and taking notes. The third subgoal is making a detailed outline of the whole paper. A fourth subgoal is using your outline to write the paper. By completing all four subgoals, you will have completed your paper.

The strategy of dividing a general problem into subgoals makes the overall problem seem more manageable because, at any one time, you are working on a single subgoal rather than worrying about completing the entire project.

To solve some problems, you may need to combine several of the strategies above. Another problem-solving strategy is to use creative thinking, our next topic.

C. Thinking Creatively

At the beginning of this module, we told you about Gordon Parks (photo on left). Parks grew up in the 1920s, a time of segregation, discrimination and lynchings. As a result of the way Blacks were treated in the 1920s, Parks received little formal schooling or professional help and was told that he should be happy just to look forward to a job as a porter. Despite overwhelming odds, Parks succeeded in writing two novels and five volumes of poetry, directing two movies, and, now in his 80s, having an exhibition of his photographs (photo on right) and publishing some in a recent book (Parks, 1997). This intriguing story of Gordon Parks raises four interesting questions about creativity: How is creativity defined? Is IQ related to creativity? How do creative people think and behave? Is creativity related to psychological problems? Although there are more than 60 definitions of creativity, we'll begin with the one most commonly used (Boden, 1994).

Definition

The definition of creative thinking is somewhat different from that of a creative individual.

Creative thinking is a combination of flexibility in thinking and reorganization of understanding to produce innovative ideas and solutions (Greeno, 1989).

A *creative individual* is someone who regularly solves problems, fashions products, or defines new questions that make an impact on his or her society (Gardner, 1993a).

People can show evidence of creative thinking in many different ways. For example, recognized creative individuals include Albert Einstein, who formulated the theory of relativity; Michelangelo, who painted the Sistine Chapel; Sigmund Freud, who developed psychoanalysis; Dr. Seuss, who wrote rhyming books for children (and adults); Rolling Stones, a well-known, 30-year-old rock-and-roll band; Ray Crock, who founded McDonald's worldwide hamburger chain; and Gordon Parks, who is a writer, director, and photographer.

Because there are so many different examples (and kinds) of creativity, psychologists have used three different approaches to measure creativity: the psychometric, case study, and cognitive approaches (Sternberg & Lubart, 1996).

PSYCHOMETRIC APPROACH

This approach, which uses objective problem-solving tasks to measure creativity, focuses on the distinction between two kinds of thinking—convergent and divergent (Guilford, 1967; Kitto et al., 1994).

Convergent thinking means beginning with a problem and coming up with a single correct solution.

Examples of convergent thinking include answering multiple-choice questions or solving math problems. The opposite of convergent thinking is divergent thinking.

Divergent thinking means beginning with a problem and coming up with many different solutions.

For example, the two problem-solving tasks on page 309 (nine-dot and candle-match puzzles) are used to assess divergent thinking, which is a popular psychometric measure for creativity (Amabile, 1985; Camp, 1994).

Tests of divergent thinking have good reliability, which means that people achieve the same scores across time (Domino, 1994). However, tests of divergent thinking have low validity, which means that creative persons, such as Gordon Parks, may not necessarily score high on psychometric tests of creativity (Gardner, 1993a).

CASE STUDY APPROACH

Because the psychometric approach is limited to using objective tests, it provides little insight into creative minds. In comparison, the case study approach analyzes creative persons in great depth and thus provides insight into their development, personality, motivation, and problems.

For example, Howard Gardner (1993a) used the case study approach to analyze seven creative people, including Sigmund Freud. Gardner found that creative people are creative in certain areas but poor in others: Freud was very creative in linguistic and personal areas but very poor in spatial and musical areas. Although case studies provide rich insight into creative minds, their findings may be difficult to generalize: Freud's kind of creativity may or may not apply to Gordon Parks's remarkable achievements (Freyd, 1994).

COGNITIVE APPROACH

Although case studies provide detailed portraits of creative people, the findings are very personal or subjective and not easily applied to others. In comparison, the cognitive approach tries to build a bridge between the objective measures of the psychometric approach and the subjective descriptions provided by case studies. The cognitive approach, which is also the newest, identifies and measures cognitive mechanisms that are used during creative thinking (Freyd, 1994).

For example, many individuals have reported that one cognitive mechanism vital to creative thinking is the use of mental imagery, which involves thinking in images, without words or mathematical symbols (Finke, 1993). Thus, the cognitive approach involves analyzing the workings of mental imagery and its relationship to creative thinking.

Now, let's see what these three approaches say about creativity.

Relationship to IQ

In some cases, such as those of Michelangelo, Sigmund Freud, and Albert Einstein, creativity seems to be linked to genius. However, creativity is not the same as intelligence, as best illustrated by savants.

Savants refer to about 10% of autistic individuals who show some incredible memory, music, or drawing talent.

Despite their creativity, many savants score below 70 on IQ tests (the average score is 100). For instance, the detailed drawing shown below was done by Chris, a 16-year-old savant who has little knowledge or use of language and whose IQ is 52. After finishing a painting, Chris shows no further interest in it (Sacks, 1995).

Instead of linking creativity to genius, some psychologists believe that creativity involves relatively ordinary cognitive processes that result in extraordinary products (Weisberg, 1993). This creative output would include the products of many inventors (Post-its or sticky notes), chemists (new drugs), and computer programmers.

It is true that, compared with the general population, creative scientists, writers, and artists generally score above average with IQs of 120 and higher. However, when the IQs of creative individuals are compared among themselves, there is little correlation between creativity and IQ. In other words, those who are generally recognized as creative do tend to have above-average IQ scores, but those with the highest IQs are not necessarily those who are the most creative (Gardner, 1993a).

Thinking and Behaving

Researchers have studied creative individuals to identify what is unusual about their work habits and psychological traits (Boden, 1994; Gardner, 1993a; Helson, 1996; Lubart, 1994; Simonton, 1994). Here are some of their findings.

Focus. Creative people tend to be superior in one particular area, such as dance, music, art, science, or writing, rather than many areas. For example, Einstein (drawing above) was superior in the logical-spatial area—the theory of relativity —but poor in the personal area—developing close relationships.

Cognition. Creative individuals have the ability to change mental directions, consider problems from many angles, and make use of mental images. They are also interested in solving unusual problems.

Personality. On the positive side, creative people tend to be self-confident, unconventional, risk-taking, hard-working, and obsessively committed to their work. On the negative side, they tend to have large egos that make them insensitive to the needs of others. They may pursue their goals at the expense of others, and they may be so absorbed in their work that they exclude others.

Motivation. They are driven by internal values or personal goals; this is called intrinsic motivation. They are less concerned about external rewards such as money or recognition (extrinsic motivation). They are motivated by the challenge of solving problems; their reward is the satisfaction of accomplishment. On average, creative people work on a project for about ten years before reaching their creative peaks.

One question asked about creative people is whether their creative fires are fueled by psychological problems.

Mental Health

There are numerous historical reports of a link between creativity and madness or insanity, more correctly called psychopathology. For example, Mark Twain (Samuel Clemens), Tennessee Williams, Ernest Hemingway, Charles Mingus, Cole Porter, Edgar Allan Poe, and Herman Hesse were all reported to suffer from either depression or manic-depression (swings between euphoria and depression) (Jamison, 1995).

A more formal study of 291 creative writers, artists, composers, thinkers, and scientists indicated that 17–46% suffered from severe psychopathology, especially mood disorders. As the graph below shows, writers had the highest percentage of psychopathology, especially alcoholism and depression (Post, 1994).

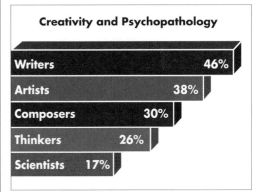

A number of studies indicate that highly creative people experience major mood disorders more often than other groups in the general population (Jamison, 1995). But does the mood disorder contribute to creativity? One researcher suggested that severe mood change could contribute to creativity by sharpening thoughts and broadening the person's emotional, intellectual, and perceptual views of the world (Jamison, 1995). One interesting finding is that those creative individuals who reported emotional problems said that such problems often began when they were teenagers (Ludwig, 1995).

Although mental disorders may provide a sense of discomfort that may motivate creative activity, there are creative individuals, such as many scientists, who have achieved creative breakthroughs without having severe emotional problems (Ludwig, 1995).

Next, we turn to a very important component of many creative activities, the development and use of language.

D. Language: Basic Rules

How many languages are there?

Of all the things that humans do, none is more impressive and distinctively human than using language. Although language requires learning a very complex set of symbols and rules, most young children have little difficulty learning to speak their parents' or caretaker's language. Currently, people of planet Earth speak some 6,000 different languages (Raloff, 1995).

Language is a special form of communication that involves learning complex rules to make and combine symbols (words or gestures) into an endless number of meaningful sentences.

The reason language is such a successful form of communication arises from two amazingly simple principles—words and grammar.

A *word* is an arbitrary pairing between a sound or symbol and a meaning.

For example, the word *parrot* does not look like, sound like, or fly like a parrot, but refers to a parrot because all of us memorized this pairing as children. Young adults are estimated to have about 60,000 such pairings or words in their mental dictionaries (Pinker, 1995). However, these 60,000 symbols or words would be rather useless unless the users followed similar rules of grammar.

Grammar refers to a set of rules for combining words into phrases and sentences to express an infinite number of thoughts that can be understood by others.

For instance, our mental rules of grammar immediately tell us that the headline, "Parrot Bites Man's Nose," means something very different from "Man Bites Parrot's Nose." It may seem surprising, but speakers of all 6,000 languages learned the same four rules.

Four Language Rules

As children, each of us learned, without much trouble, the four rules of language. Now as adults, we use these rules without being aware of how or when we use them. To illustrate the four rules of language that we all learned, take the word *caterpillar*. Perhaps as a child, you put a caterpillar on your hand and watched it slowly crawl around.

1 The first language rule governs phonology.

Phonology (FOE-nawl-uh-gee) specifies how we make the meaningful sounds that are used by a particular language.

Any English word can be broken down into phonemes.

Phonemes (FOE-neems) are the basic sounds of consonants and vowels.

For example, the various sounds of *c* and *p* represent different phonemes, which are some of the sounds in the word *caterpillar.* At about 6 months, babies begin to babble and make basic sounds, or phonemes. We combine phonemes to form words by learning the second rule.

2 The second language rule governs morphology.

Morphology (MOR-fawl-uh-gee) is the system that we use to group phonemes into meaningful combinations of sounds and words.

A *morpheme (MOR-feem)* is the smallest meaningful combination of sounds in a language.

For example, a morpheme may be
   a word, such as **cat,**
   a letter, such as the **s** in **cats,**
   a prefix, such as the **un-** in **un**breakable,
   or a suffix, such as the **-ed** in walk**ed.**

The word **caterpillar** is actually one morpheme, and the word **caterpillars** is two (**caterpillar-s**). After we learn to combine morphemes to form words, we then learn to combine words into meaningful sentences by using the third rule.

3 The third language rule governs syntax, or grammar.

Syntax, or *grammar,* is a set of rules that specifies how we combine words to form meaningful phrases and sentences.

For example, why doesn't the following sentence make sense?

Caterpillars green long and are.

You instantly realize that this sentence is nonsensical or ungrammatical because it doesn't follow the English grammar rules regarding where we place verbs and conjunctions. If you apply the rules of English grammar, you would rearrange the combination of words to read: "Caterpillars are long and green." Although you may not be able to list all the rules of grammar, you automatically follow them when you speak. One way you know whether the word *bear* is a noun or a verb is by using the fourth rule.

4 The fourth language rule governs semantics.

Semantics (si-MANT-iks) specifies the meaning of words or phrases when they appear in various sentences or contexts.

For instance, as you read "Did Pat pat a caterpillar's back?" how do you know what the word **pat** means, since it appears twice in succession. From your knowledge of semantics, you know that the first **Pat** is a noun and the name of a person while the second **pat** is a verb, which signals some action.

Somehow you knew that the same word, **pat,** had very different meanings depending on the context. How you know what words mean in different contexts is a very intriguing question.

Understanding Language

What did you pick up?

One of the greatest mysteries of language can be demonstrated by the following two sentences.

You picked up a caterpillar.
A caterpillar was picked up by you.

Despite an entirely different word order, you know instantly that these two sentences mean exactly the same thing. How you know that these different sentences mean exactly the same thing was explained by linguist Noam Chomsky (1957). Chomsky's (1957) revolutionary theory involved two fundamental principles—mental grammar and innate program—that have had the greatest impact on our understanding of language in this century (Pinker, 1994). What made Chomsky's two principles so important?

Mental grammar. Almost every sentence we speak or understand is formed from a brand-new combination of words. Chomsky pointed out that the brain does not have the capacity to contain a list of all the sentences we will ever use. Instead, Chomsky argued that the brain contains a program or *mental grammar* that allows us to combine nouns, verbs, and objects in an endless variety of meaningful sentences. Chomsky's principle of mental grammar answers the question of how we can so easily create so many different sentences. The second question that Chomsky answered was How do we acquire this mental grammar?

Innate program. How is it possible that 4-year-old children, with no formal schooling and relatively limited instruction from their parents, can speak and understand an endless variety of sentences? For example, the average 4-year-old child can already determine that the sentence "The caterpillar crept slowly across the leaf" is correct but that the sentence "The crept leaf caterpillar slowly the across" is meaningless. Chomsky's answer is that young children can learn these complex and difficult rules of grammar because our brains come with a built-in, or *innate, program* that makes learning the general rules of grammar relatively easy. The existence of the brain's innate program for learning rules of grammar explains how a child learns most of the complex and difficult rules of grammar by the age of 4 or 5. However, keep in mind that it is the interaction between the innate program with a child's range of experience and kind of environment that results in learning the complicated rules of grammar (Seidenberg, 1997).

But how would an innate grammar program, which could be used by any child in any culture, specify the rules for forming and understanding an endless number of meaningful sentences? The answer to this question is perhaps Chomsky's greatest contribution.

Different Structure, Same Meaning

One of the most difficult questions that Chomsky had to answer was how an idea can be expressed in several different ways, with different grammatical structures, yet mean the same thing.

He answered this question by making a distinction between two different structures of a sentence: surface structure and deep structure.

Surface structure refers to the actual wording of a sentence, as it is spoken.

Deep structure refers to an underlying meaning that is not spoken but is present in the mind of the listener.

We can illustrate the difference between surface and deep structure with our same two sentences.

You picked up a caterpillar.
A caterpillar was picked up by you.

Notice that these two sentences have different *surface structures,* which means they are worded differently. However, according to Chomsky, you are able to look underneath the different surface structures of the two sentences and recognize that they have the same *deep structure,* which is why you know they have the same meaning.

Chomsky argues that we learn to shift back and forth between surface and deep structure by applying transformational rules.

Transformational rules are procedures by which we convert our ideas from surface structures into deep structures and from deep structures back into surface ones.

For example, when you hear the two sentences about picking up the caterpillar, you transform the words into their deep structure, which you store in memory. Later, when someone asks what the person did, you use transformational rules to convert the deep structure in your memory back into a surface structure, which can be expressed in differently worded sentences. The distinction between surface and deep structure is part of Chomsky's theory of language.

Chomsky's theory of language says that all languages share a common universal grammar and that children inherit a mental program to learn this universal grammar.

Chomsky's theory of language, which is widely accepted today, is considered a major breakthrough in explaining how we acquire and understand language (Stromswold, 1995). However, one criticism of Chomsky's theory is that he downplays the importance of environmental influences (hearing and practicing sounds), which have been shown to influence language development (Saffran et al., 1996).

Chomsky's idea of an innate mental grammar would predict that children around the world should go through the same stages of language development. Can this be true for all 6,000 languages?

E. Acquiring Language

Four Stages in Acquiring Language

Does every child go through stages?

If Chomsky is correct that all children inherit the same innate program for learning grammar, then we would expect children from around the world to go through similar stages in developing language and acquiring the rules for using language. And in fact, all children, no matter the culture or the language, do go through the same stages (Pinker, 1994).

Language stages refer to four different periods—babbling, single words, two-word combinations, and sentences—in each of which children show new and more complex language skills. All children go through these four stages in the same order.

Here are the four stages that each of us went through in learning to speak and understand the language of our parents or caregiver.

1 Babbling

Why do babies babble?

One of the key features in human development is that infants begin to make sounds long before they can say real words. Infants repeat the same sounds over and over and these sound are commonly called babbling.

Babbling, which begins at about 6 months, is the first stage in acquiring language. Babbling refers to making one-syllable sounds, such as "deedeedee" or "bababa," which are most common across all languages.

Bababa

Babbling is an example of an innate "sound" program in the brain that is involved in making and processing sounds that will eventually be used to form words. Researchers have discovered that by 6 months of age, infants have already learned to discriminate between sounds, such as *ba* from *pa,* and to distinguish sounds in their native language from those used in a foreign language (Buonomano & Merzenich, 1995; Dehaene-Lambertz & Dehaene, 1994). These findings indicate that, at an early age, infants have already become accustomed to making and hearing sounds that make up their native languages. At about 9 months, babbling sounds begin to resemble more the vowels and consonants that children will actually use in speaking their native languages.

In children who can hear, babbling is oral. However, in deaf children who have been exposed only to the sign language of their deaf parents, babbling is manual and not oral. That is, these babies babble by repeating the same hand sign over and over (Petitto & Marentette, 1991). This means that the brain has an innate program for acquiring language, whether it is spoken or sign language.

Through endless babbling, infants learn to control their vocal apparatus so that they can make, change, and repeat sounds, and imitate the sounds of their parents or caregivers (Stromswold, 1995).

After babbling, infants begin to say their first words.

2 Single Word

When does a child say his or her first word?

Shortly before 1 year of age, an infant usually performs a behavior that every parent has been eagerly waiting for: to hear the child's first word. At about 1 year of age, infants not only begin to understand words but also to say single words.

Single words mark the second stage in acquiring language, which occurs at about 1 year of age. Infants say single words that usually refer to what they can see, hear, or feel.

An infant's ability to form sounds into words begins at about 8 months and results from an interaction between the brain's innate language program and the infant's experience with hearing sounds (Jusczyk & Hohne, 1997; Saffran et al., 1996). About half the infants' single words refer to objects (juice, cookie, doll, dada) and the other half refer to actions, routines, or motions (up, eat, hot, more) (Pinker, 1994). The infants' single words, such as "Milk" or "Go," often stand for longer thoughts such as "I want milk" or "I want to go outside."

As the infant learns to say words, parents usually respond by speaking in a specific way called parentese (motherese).

Parentese (motherese) is a way of speaking to young children in which the adult speaks in a slower and higher than normal voice, emphasizes and stretches out each word, uses very simple sentences, and repeats words and phrases.

Milk. Go.

In a recent study of mothers in United States, Russia, and Sweden, researchers found that when talking to their infants, these mothers exaggerated certain sounds (vowel sounds), which they did not do when speaking to their husbands (Kuhl et al., 1997). Another researcher, who spent ten years traveling around the world to record child-parent interactions, concludes that parentese has several functions: getting an infant's attention and stimulating infants to make sounds they will need to speak themselves (Fernald, 1992).

Next, the young child begins to combine words.

3 Two-Word Combinations

What can two words mean?

Starting around age 2, children begin using single words that they have learned to form two-word combinations.

Two-word combinations, which represent the third stage in acquiring language, occur at about 2 years of age. Two-word combinations are strings of two words that express various actions ("Me play," "See boy") or relationships ("Hit ball," "Milk gone").

All dry.   Hit ball.

Each of the two words provides a hint about what the child is saying. In addition, the relationship between the two words gives hints about what the child is communicating. For example, "See boy" tells us to look at a specific object; "Daddy shirt" tells us that something belongs to Daddy. The child's new ability to communicate by combining two words and changing their order marks the beginning of learning the rules of grammar. From about 2 years of age through adolescence, a child learns an average of a new word every two hours (Pinker, 1994).

A child's language development is partly dependent on how responsive the parent or caretaker is. A more responsive parent is one who shows more contact, awareness, and warmth during the child's verbal interactions. For example, infants whose mothers were more responsive to their speech at 13 months had significant larger vocabularies at 21 months compared to less responsive mothers (Tamis-LeMonda et al., 1996).

By the age of 2, a child may have a vocabulary of more than 50 words, many of which will be used in two-word combinations. Although children usually go through a stage of forming single words and then two-word combinations, there is no three-word stage. Instead, at a certain point the child will begin to form sentences, which gradually increase in length through the fourth year.

4 Sentences

What is telegraphic speech?

Children make a rather large language leap when they progress from relatively simple two-word combinations to using longer and more complex sentences.

Sentences, which represent the fourth stage of acquiring language, occur at about 4 years of age. Sentences range from three to eight words in length and indicate a growing knowledge of the rules of grammar.

However, a child's first sentences differ from adults' in that the child may omit the "small words" and speak in a pattern that is called telegraphic speech.

Telegraphic speech is a distinctive pattern of speaking in which the child omits articles (the), prepositions (in, out), and parts of verbs.

For example, an adult may say, "I'm going to the store." A 3- to 4-year-old child may use telegraphic speech (omit article) and say, "I go to store." However, by the time children are 4 or 5 years old, the structure of their sentences improves and indicates that they have learned the basic rules of grammar.

Basic rules of grammar are the rules for combining nouns, verbs, and adjectives to form meaningful sentences.

However, as children learn the rules of grammar, they often make errors of overgeneralization.

I goed to store.
I want blue toy.

Overgeneralization means applying a grammatical rule to cases where it should not be used.

For example, after a child learns the rule of forming the past tense of many verbs by adding a *d* sound to the end, he or she may overgeneralize this rule and add a *d* to the past tense of irregular verbs (and say, for instance, "I goed to store"). By the time children enter school, they usually have a good grasp of the general rules of their language.

Effects of Stages

How fast does a child go through the stages?

Parents or caretakers sometimes worry about whether their child is late in developing language. For instance, my older sister did not begin talking until she was almost 2, but I began talking nonstop at about 9 months. In the real world, normal children pass through the four stages of language at a pace that can differ by a year or more. However, as Chomsky's theory predicts and research has shown, all normal children pass through the four stages, even though some of the stages may last for shorter or longer periods of time (Pinker, 1994).

Even though all children initially make the same sounds and inherit the same program for learning grammar, they must still learn the words and word order for their particular language. For instance, in English phrases nouns come first, but in Japanese phrases nouns come last. The four stages of language can be thought of as a process through which a child learns to share a word code with other people.

Although all children go through the same sequence (four stages) of developing language, how rapidly and how well language skills are acquired depends on the interaction of genetic and environmental factors, which is our next topic.

E. Acquiring Language

How does each child learn his or her own language?

Learning a Particular Language

Children from Africa, Bali, China, Sweden, Japan, United States, and Chile, acquire the sounds, words, and rules of their particular native languages because of an interaction between innate and environmental factors.

Innate Factors

Children from around the world go through the same four language stages because there are innate factors that allow humans to acquire language (Pinker, 1994).

Innate language factors are genetically programmed physiological and neurological features that facilitate our making speech sounds and acquiring language skills.

We'll examine three innate language features that work together so that we can learn to speak and use language.

Innate physiological features. We have a specially adapted vocal apparatus (larynx and pharynx) that allows us to make sounds and form words. In comparison, the structures of gorillas' and chimpanzees' vocal apparatus prevent them from making the wide variety of sounds necessary to form words (Pinker, 1994). Without our specialized vocal apparatus, we humans would be limited to making "animal" sounds.

Innate neurological features. When people speak or use sign language, certain brain areas are activated. The PET scan above shows a side view of brain: red and yellow indicate most neural activity (Petitto, 1991). These findings indicate that the left hemisphere of the brain is prewired to acquire and use language, whether spoken or signed. In Module 4, we explained how damage to these same language areas (Broca's and Wernicke's areas) seriously disrupts the use and understanding of language. Although your brain is prewired for language, there is a best, or critical, time for learning a language.

Innate developmental factors. Researchers have discovered that there is a critical period when acquiring language is the easiest (Stromswold, 1995).

The *critical language period* is the time from infancy to adolescence when language is easiest to learn. Language is usually more difficult to learn anytime after adolescence.

For example, immigrant children do very well in learning English as a second language, while immigrant adults do less well (Jackendoff, 1994). The the timing of the critical period explains why, as a child, you were able to learn your native language quite easily. However, now that you have passed the critical period, you will usually find that learning a foreign language in college can be quite difficult.

Although innate factors provide all of us with the ability to acquire any one of 6,000 languages, how is it that you learned the particular language of your parents or caregiver?

Environmental Factors

Each child learns the particular or native language of his or her parents or caregivers because of environmental factors.

Environmental language factors refer to interactions children have with parents, peers, teachers, and others who provide feedback that rewards and encourages language development, as well as providing opportunities for children to observe, imitate, and practice language skills.

Operant conditioning. The strongest case for environmental factors was made by B. F. Skinner (1957), who believed that children acquire language according to the principles of operant conditioning (discussed in Module 10). However, two major criticisms have weakened Skinner's explanation. First, children understand language before they can speak or actually receive feedback and reinforcement. Second, children acquire language rules without receiving any feedback or reinforcement for speaking correctly. For these reasons, operant conditioning principles cannot easily explain language acquisition (Pinker, 1994).

Social learning approach. In contrast to Skinner's operant learning approach, many developmental psychologists take a social learning approach.

The *social learning approach* emphasizes the role of observation, exploration, and imitation in acquiring language skills.

According to the social learning approach, children have a strong desire to use language to express their needs and to interact socially with their parents, caretakers, and peers. For example, young children are constantly using language to get attention, request help, protest some apparent injustice, or make social contact (Pinker, 1994).

Parents and caregivers can stimulate and encourage language development in their children by speaking in parentese and by being very responsive to what their child says (Kuhl et al., 1997; Tamis-LeMonda et al., 1996). Researchers found that 2- and 3-year-old children who had the biggest vocabularies and performed best on developmental language tests were those who parents were the most talkative during the child's first two years (Hart & Risley, 1996). These studies illustrate how environmental and innate factors interact to influence how quickly and how well a child acquires the language skills of his or her particular culture.

Once children master their language, they have a powerful tool for thinking, as we'll discuss after the Concept Review.

CONCEPT REVIEW

dog (dog, dag) *n.; pl.* **dogs, dog.**

1. any of a large and varied group of domesticated animals (*Canis familiaris*) that have four legs, a tail, two ears, prominent nose, a hairy coat, and a bark.

1. If you form a concept of an object, event, or characteristic by making a list of the properties that define it, you are forming a concept according to _____ theory.

2. If you form a concept by putting together the average characteristics of an object and then seeing whether a new object matches your average object, you are forming a concept according to (a)_____ theory. If you develop an idea of a dog of average age, height, weight, and color, you have formed a (b)_____ of a dog.

3. If you search for some rule, plan, or strategy that results in your reaching a certain goal that is currently out of reach, you are engaging in an activity called (a)_____. During this activity, you go through three states: contemplating the unsolved problem, which is the (b)_____ state; trying out various operations, rules, or strategies to solve the problem, which is the (c)_____ state; and reaching the solution, which is the (d)_____ state.

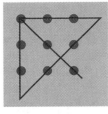

Answers to problems on page 309

4. Some problems can be solved by following certain rules. If you correctly follow rules that lead to a certain solution, you are using (a)_____. If you follow rules that reduce the number of operations or allow you to take shortcuts in solving problems, you are using (b)_____.

5. When you use a combination of flexibility in thinking and reorganization of understanding to produce innovative ideas and solutions, you are engaging in (a)_____. If you begin with a problem and come up with many different solutions, you are using (b)_____ thinking, which is one definition of creative thinking. The opposite of this type of thinking is beginning with a problem and coming up with the one correct solution; this is called (c)_____ thinking.

6. A system of symbols that we use in thinking, solving problems, and communicating with others is called (a)_____. There are four rules for learning and using language. How we make the meaningful sounds used by a particular language is covered by the rules of (b)_____. Any English word can be broken down into basic sounds of consonants and vowels, which are called (c)_____. How we group phonemes into meaningful combinations of sounds and words is covered by the rules of (d)_____. The smallest, meaningful combination of sounds in a language is called a (e)_____. How we combine words to form meaningful phrases and sentences is specified by the rules of (f)_____. How we know the meaning of words in various contexts is covered by the rules of (g)_____.

7. Chomsky explained that a sentence can be stated in different ways and yet have the same meaning. The actual wording of a sentence is called its (a)_____ structure. The underlying meaning of the sentence that is not spoken but is present in the mind of the listener is called the (b)_____ structure. To convert our ideas from surface structures into deep structures and from deep structures back into surface ones we use (c)_____ rules.

You picked up a caterpillar.
A caterpillar was picked up by you.

8. In acquiring language, all children go through the same four stages but at different rates. Beginning at about the age of 6 months, a baby begins making one-syllable sounds, such as "Bababa," which is called (a)_____. By about 1 year of age, a child forms (b)_____ words, which usually refer to what the child can see, hear, or feel. At about 2 years of age, a child makes (c)_____, which are strings of two words that express various actions ("Me play") or relationships ("Hit ball," "Milk gone"). At about 4 years of age, a child begins forming sentences, which range from three to eight words in length and indicate a growing knowledge of the rules of (d)_____.

9. One reason all children acquire a language in much the same order is because of genetically programmed physiological and neurological features in the brain and vocal apparatus. These are known as (a)_____ factors. Interactions between the child and others, which offer opportunities for feedback, reward, observation, and imitation, are called (b)_____ factors.

Answers: *1. definition; 2. (a) prototype, (b) prototype; 3. (a) problem solving, (b) initial, (c) operations, (d) goal; 4. (a) algorithms, (b) heuristics; 5. (a) creative thinking, (b) divergent, (c) convergent; 6. (a) language, (b) phonology, (c) phonemes, (d) morphology, (e) morpheme, (f) syntax or grammar, (g) semantics; 7. (a) surface, (b) deep, (c) transformational; 8. (a) babbling, (b) single, (c) two-word combinations, (d) grammar or syntax; 9. (a) innate, (b) environmental.*

F. Reason, Thought, & Language

Reasoning

If you saw a nicely dressed older man standing in the ocean, you would naturally wonder what he was doing. To figure out this man's unusual behavior, you could use the personal computer inside your brain, which has a very powerful software program called reasoning (Sloman, 1996).

Reasoning, which often means thinking, is a mental process that involves using and applying knowledge to solve problems, make plans or decisions and to achieve goals.

To figure out why this normal-looking, fully-dressed but shoeless man is standing in the ocean, you could use two different kinds of reasoning—deductive or inductive.

Deductive Reasoning

Since you rarely see a nicely dressed older man standing in the ocean, you might assume that he is drunk. The kind of reasoning that begins with a big assumption is called deductive reasoning.

Deductive reasoning begins with making a general assumption that you know or believe to be true and then drawing specific conclusions based on this assumption. In other words, reasoning from a general assumpton to particulars.

Your general assumption is that only a drunk person would gleefully walk into the ocean dressed in a suit. This man is doing so. Therefore, he must be drunk. In its simplest form, deductive reasoning follows this formula: if you are given an assumption or statement as true, then there is only one correct conclusion to draw. This formula is often referred to as "If p (given statements), then q (conclusion)." For example:

Statements ("If p"): Only people who are over 21 years of age drink alcohol. That man is drinking alcohol. Conclusion ("Then q"): That man must be over 21 years of age.

One mistake people make in deductive reasoning is that they assume but do not always know if the basic statement or assumption (p) is true. If the basic statement is false—that is, drunkenness is not the only explanation for the man's behavior—then so are the conclusions. Another way to figure out why the man is standing in the ocean is to use inductive reasoning.

Inductive Reasoning

Instead of just assuming that this man is standing in the ocean because he's drunk, you walk over and ask some specific questions. After listening to this man's answers, you reach a different explanation for why he's standing in the ocean. The kind of reasoning that starts with specific facts or observations is called inductive reasoning.

Inductive reasoning begins with making particular observations that you then use to draw a broader conclusion. In other words, reasoning from particulars to a general conclusion.

For example, when questioned, the man answers, "No" to all the following questions: Did you drink alcohol today? Do you have a job? Are you married? Do you do this often? Have you eaten today? Are you ill? Would you like me to take you home? After considering all these particulars, you reach a general conclusion: This man is either suffering from Alzheimer's disease or he is lying.

Researchers use inductive reasoning when they use past experiences or observations to form a general hypothesis (Evans, 1993). For instance, researchers observed that when some students take exams they have rapid heart rate, sweaty palms, muscle tension, and increased blood pressure. Based on these particulars, researchers reached the general conclusion that these students have test anxiety.

One big mistake people make in inductive reasoning is jumping to a conclusion before knowing all the facts (Levy, 1997).

Depending on the situation, deductive and inductive reasoning are powerful mental tools provided you're aware of their pitfalls.

Why Reasoning Fails

Many students found it very difficult to solve the problem given below.

Problem	Reasoning	Solution
If you drop one bullet off a table 3 feet high, and fire another one straight across an empty football field, which hits the ground first?	Based on experience, it seems the dropped bullet will land first because it has only 3 feet to travel.	Based on physics, both bullets hit at the same time because downward velocity is independent of horizontal velocity.

On the basis of their experiences, students believed that a dropped bullet would surely hit the ground before one fired parallel to the ground. However, physics principles say that both bullets would hit the ground at the same time, which is completely opposite to students' experiences.

According to Alan Cromer (1993), who taught introductory science classes for 32 years, the formal reasoning needed to solve science problems is very difficult to teach because it often runs counter to our experiences or intuitions. Researchers suggest that our brains are equipped or prewired for reasoning to meet real-world challenges, such as surviving, finding food, and finding mates, rather than solving physics problems, which requires a special kind of abstract reasoning (Cosmides & Tooby, 1994). One reason students may have difficulty in science classes is that their personal experiences interfere with using abstract reasoning.

Because words are so much a part of our reasoning process, we need to know if and how much words can influence or bias our thinking.

Words and Thoughts

Almost everyone has heard it said that the Inuit (Eskimos) are supposed to have dozens of words for snow because their survival depends upon knowing how to travel and hunt in different kinds of snow. This particular observation was first made by amateur linguist Benjamin Whorf (1956), who noticed that languages differed in their vocabularies depending on how much emphasis they gave to different objects and events in their environment. For example, Whorf reasoned that because the Inuit (Eskimos) have many names for snow, they must be able to perceive many more kinds of snow than Americans, for whom snow conditions are less important. On the basis of these kinds of observations, Whorf formulated the theory of linguistic relativity.

The *theory of linguistic relativity* states that the differences among languages result in similar differences in how people think and perceive the world.

For example, according to the theory of linguistic relativity, people whose language divides colors into only two categories (dark or black and bright or white) should perceive fewer colors. In comparison, people whose language divides colors into eleven categories (black, white, red, yellow, green, blue, brown, purple, pink, orange, gray) should perceive many more colors in their environment. However, researchers discovered that although languages differ in their number of color categories, all languages divide colors into the same basic categories. According to Whorf's theory of linguistic relativity, we would have expected people to perceive colors differently, depending upon whether their culture has two or eleven names, but this is not what researchers found (Davies & Corbett, 1997). Thus, people in different cultures seem to perceive colors in similar ways even if they do not have names for different colors (Pinker, 1994).

Now, let's examine Whorf's famous claim that Inuits have more words for snow than do Americans.

Inuit versus American Words for Snow

In his original article, Whorf (1940) estimated that Inuits (Eskimos) have about seven words for snow: *falling snow, snow on the ground, snow packed hard like ice, slushy snow, drifting snow, snow drift,* and *wind-driven flying snow,* while most Americans use a single word, snow. Whorf reasoned that the Inuits' larger vocabulary of snow-related words should make them think and perceive snow very differently than most Americans. Since Whorf's time, the number of snow words attributed to Inuits has ranged from two dozen to about 400 (Pullum, 1991).

More recently, another linguist did a closer examination and found that Inuits and Americans each have about eight words for snow (English words for snow include *blizzard, sleet, hail, hardpack, powder, avalanche, flurry,* and *dusting*) (Martin, 1986). So, as it turns out, Whorf was wrong about how many words Inuits and Americans have for snow. One reason Whorf's story about differences in snow words lives on is that it's a great (but untrue) story (Pullum, 1991).

Although Whorf's story about snow words was untrue, the basic question still remains: Do differences in language mean that people think and perceive the world in different ways? One way to answer this question is to examine how individuals who are bilingual—that is, fluent in two languages—think and perceive their world.

Thinking in Two Languages

Suppose your native language is Chinese but you are also fluent in English. You are asked to read descriptions in either Chinese or English of two different people and then to write impressions of these individuals. You read a Chinese and an English description of a type of person easily labeled in Chinese—"shi gu," a person with strong family ties and much worldly experience—but not easily labeled in English. You read an English and a Chinese description of a type of person easily labeled in English—an "artistic" character, a person with artistic abilities who is very temperamental—but not easily labeled in Chinese. Researchers found that when subjects were reading and thinking in Chinese, they formed a clearer impression of the shi gu person; when reading and thinking in English, they formed a clearer impression of the artistic character (Hoffman et al., 1986). This is one of the few studies that supports the linguistic relativity theory and the idea that language influences thinking (Hardin & Banaji, 1993).

Other prominent linguists argue that thoughts or ideas are not the same thing as words (Pinker, 1994, 1995). For example, sometimes we find it difficult to put a thought or idea into words, which would not be the case if every thought had a matching word. Also, how would new words be formed if thoughts depended on words that did not yet exist? For all these reasons, psychologists have generally found little or only weak support for Whorf's theory of linguistic relativity (Davies & Corbett, 1997; Pinker, 1994).

We know that words are important tools for reasoning, so what happens to an individual's thinking if he or she has great difficulty recognizing printed words? Our next topic is dyslexia.

I. Application: Do Animals Have Language?

Criteria for Language

What does my dog understand?

Most pet owners talk to their pets and believe that their pets understand. For example, my dog Bear, who is great on personality but a little short on brains, understands only "go," "food," and "bone." The obvious question is: Has Bear learned a language? The answer to this question hinges on the difference between communication and language. As do many animals, Bear has the ability to communicate.

Communication is the ability to use sounds, smells, or gestures to exchange information.

But language is something different. *Language* is a special form of communication in which an individual learns complex rules for using words or gestures to generate an endless number of meaningful sentences. Although Bear can communicate, he, like most animals, shows no evidence of meeting the following four criteria for having true language.

1 Language, which is a special form of communication, involves *learning a set of abstract symbols* (whether words for spoken language or hand signs for sign language).

2 Language involves *using abstract symbols* (words or signs) to express thoughts or indicate objects and events that may or may not be present.

3 Language involves *learning complex rules of grammar* for forming words into meaningful phrases and sentences.

4 Language involves using the rules of grammar to *generate an endless number of meaningful sentences.*

Because some animals, such as dolphins and pygmy chimps, show an amazing ability to communicate, researchers are debating whether animals can satisfy all four criteria for language (Begley, 1998; Savage-Rumbaugh & Lewin, 1994). We'll examine how close several animals come to satisfying the four criteria for language.

Dolphins

How much can dolphins understand?

In proportion to the size of its body, a dolphin's brain is smaller than the human brain but larger than that of the great apes. Because dolphins do have relatively large brains, researchers are particularly interested in how well they communicate.

In the wild, dolphins use two kinds of sounds for communication: clicks, which they use to probe the sea and "see" their environment; and whistles, which they use in dolphin-to-dolphin communication, probably to express emotional states and identify the animal to the group (Ralston, 1989). However, there is little evidence that dolphins in the wild use symbols or apply any rules of grammar in their normal communications.

In testing the ability of dolphins to communicate, psychologist Louis Herman (1989, 1993) has been training dolphins to respond to hand signals or whistles. So far, he has taught two dolphins to respond to approximately 50 such signals.

For example, in the top-right photo, Herman is raising his hands, which is part of a signal for "person over," which means "jump over the person in the pool."

The bottom-right photo shows the dolphin carrying out the command by jumping over the person and not the surfboard.

Herman found that dolphins can understand a variety of hand signals and perform behaviors in sequence. For example, the hand signal combination, "basket, right, Frisbee, fetch," means "Go to the Frisbee on the right and take it to the basket." Although Herman admits that the ability of dolphins to acquire the four rules of language is much inferior to that of humans, he insists that dolphins understand word order and can grasp concepts, such as the hoop (no matter if it is round, octagonal, or square). Thus, he argues that dolphins do have some understanding of grammar or syntax (Herman, 1993).

Some researchers reply that what may look like language in dolphins may simply be imitation, mimicry, or rote learning, which is observed in many pets (Schusterman, 1993). Thus, although dolphins understand a variety of signals, perform behaviors in sequence, and form concepts, they show minimal evidence of using abstract symbols to communicate or applying rules of grammar to generate meaningful sentences. It is these two criteria that distinguish the ability to use language from the simple ability to communicate with signs, sounds, or gestures.

Next, let's turn to the greater apes, which in terms of evolution are the animals closest to humans.

Gorilla and Chimpanzee

How much can a gorilla understand?

Gorillas and chimpanzees have relatively large and well-developed brains. A gorilla's brain weighs about 500 grams, a chimpanzee's about 400 grams, and a human's about 1,350 grams. However, because gorillas and chimpanzees lack the vocal apparatus necessary for making speech sounds, researchers have taught them other forms of language, such as American Sign Language (Ross, 1991).

Shown on the right is researcher Francine Patterson using sign language to communicate with Koko the gorilla, who has a vocabulary of about 800 signs. Similarly, Beatrice and Allen Gardner (1975) taught sign language to a chimpanzee named Washoe, who after four years of training had learned about 160 signs. The finding that gorillas and chimps can learn sign language raised the question of whether they use language in the same way as humans.

Psychologist Herbert Terrace (1981) analyzed videotapes of chimps using sign language with their trainers. He was particularly interested in the videotapes of a chimp named Nim, who has learned more than 125 signs, such as "give orange me." After observing over 20,000 of Nim's signs on videotape, Terrace concluded that Nim was using signs more as tools to obtain things than as abstract symbols or words and that Nim never learned to form combinations of more than a few words. Perhaps the most devastating criticism was that Nim had primarily learned to imitate or respond to cues from human teachers rather than learning and using rules of grammar to initiate or produce new sentences.

As a result of criticisms by Terrace and others, research monies to study language in animals mostly disappeared in the 1980s, and researchers were discouraged from pursuing studies on sign language in chimps (Gibbons, 1991; Savage-Rumbaugh & Lewin, 1994). However, in the late 1980s, new findings again raised the question of language in animals.

Bonobo: Star Pupil

How much can a bonobo understand?

The best evidence for language in animals comes from the work of psychologist Sue Savage-Rumbaugh. She reported that Kanzi, a bonobo (commonly called a pygmy chimp), has remarkable language skills that surpass previous accomplishments of common chimps (Savage-Rumbaugh, 1991; Savage-Rumbaugh & Lewin, 1994).

Instead of using sign language, Kanzi "speaks" by touching one of 256 symbols on a board (top photo), each of which stands for a word. For example, Kanzi (bottom photo) might signal "Want a drink" by touching the symbol for "drink" or signal "Want to play" by touching in sequence two symbols for "hiding" and "play biting."

By the time Kanzi was 6 years old, he had a vocabulary of 90 symbols; at age 12 he knew about 190 symbols but used about 128 regularly. Even more surprising, Kanzi understands about 200 spoken English words, something that common chimps have failed to master.

Perhaps Kanzi's greatest accomplishment is his knowledge of word order. Psychologists tested the ability of Kanzi to respond to 600 spoken English commands that he had not previously encountered, such as "Put the melon in the potty." Savage-Rumbaugh suggests that Kanzi, now 17 years old, is capable of using abstract symbols (keyboard)

BLACKBERRIES   BUTTER   VELVET PLANT

SHOT   STRING   PINE CONE

and a kind of primitive grammar (word order) for combining symbols that equals the language ability of a 2-year-old child (Savage-Rumbaugh, 1998).

One reason the findings on Kanzi's language abilities are receiving new attention is that Savage-Rumbaugh used strict control procedures. Savage-Rumbaugh used one-way mirrors to eliminate the possibility that Kanzi was simply imitating or responding to human cues, which had been the major criticism of previous research with chimps.

Doubts about the chimpanzees' ability to learn and use language was partly based on the belief that they lacked a brain area similar to the ones that humans used for language. The considerable language ability of humans comes from a specific brain area (Wernicke's area) that is larger in the left than right hemisphere. However, researchers recently reported that chimpanzees do have a similar brain area and that, as in humans, this area is larger in the left hemisphere (Gannon et al., 1998). Researchers suggest that human language originated from this brain structure in the left hemisphere and that language began more than 8 million years ago in the common ancestor of chimpanzees and humans.

Researchers who study evolution speculate that as early humans began to form social groups, the great pressure to keep track of their physical needs and enormously complex personal and social interactions led to the development of language abilities (Linden, 1993).

A. FORMING CONCEPTS

1. There are two theories of how you might have formed your concept of a bird and how you form concepts generally. If you form a concept of an object, event, or characteristic by making a list of the properties that define it, you are using (a)_____ theory. If you form a concept by constructing an idea of the ideal object and then seeing whether a new object matches that idea, you are using (b)_____ theory.

2. A concept is a way to group objects, events, or characteristics on the basis of some common property they all share. Concepts perform two important functions: they allow us to (a)_____ objects and thus better organize and store information in memory, and to identify things without (b) _____.

B. SOLVING PROBLEMS

3. The process of searching for some rule, plan, or strategy that results in reaching a certain goal that is currently out of reach is called (a)_____. We usually go through three states in solving problems: (b)_____, _____, and _____.

4. We win at games by following rules. If we correctly follow a set of rules that lead to a solution, these rules are called (a)_____. As you gain experience with solving problems, you may use rules of thumb that reduce the number of operations or allow you to take shortcuts in solving problems; these shortcuts are called (b)_____. In making everyday decisions, you rely on information that is more prominent or easily recalled and overlook other information that is available but less prominent or notable; this is an example of using the (c)_____ heuristic.

5. By studying how people eventually solve problems, psychologists have discovered a number of useful strategies, including changing our (a)_____. This often involves breaking out of a pattern called (b)_____, in which we cannot see an object as having a function different from its usual one.

6. The sudden grasp of a solution after many incorrect attempts is called (a)_____. Another kind of thinking that is useful in solving problems is to find (b)_____, which are similarities between new situations and familiar situations. Still another useful strategy for solving problems is to break the problem down into a number of (c)_____, which, when completed in order, will result in a solution.

C. THINKING CREATIVELY

7. A combination of flexibility in thinking and reorganization of understanding to produce innovative ideas and solutions is referred to as (a)_____. Psychologists distinguish between two different kinds of thinking. If you begin with a problem and come up with the one correct solution, it is called (b)_____. If you begin with a problem and come up with many different solutions, it is called (c)_____, which is another definition of creative thinking.

D. LANGUAGE: BASIC RULES

8. Our most impressive skill is thought to be a special form of communication in which an individual learns complex rules to manipulate symbols (words or gestures) and so generate an endless number of meaningful sentences; this form of communication is called _____.

9. All of the 6,000 known languages share four basic language rules, which are normally learned during childhood. The first language rule governs (a)_____, which specifies how we make meaningful sounds that are used by a particular language. The second language rule governs (b)_____, which specifies how we group phonemes into meaningful combinations of sounds and words. The third language rule governs (c)_____, which specifies how we combine words to form meaningful phrases and sentences. The fourth language rule governs (d)_____, which specifies the meaning of words in various contexts.

10. The linguist Noam Chomsky distinguished between how a sentence is worded, which he called the (a)_____ structure, and the meaning of the sentence, which he called the (b)_____ structure. Procedures for converting our ideas from surface structures into deep structures and from deep structures back into surface ones are called (c)_____.

E. ACQUIRING LANGUAGE

11. Children all around the world acquire language in the same four stages. In the first stage, generally at about the age of 6 months, the infant makes one-syllable sounds; this is called (a)_____. By about 1 year of age, a child forms (b)_____, which usually refer to what the child can see, hear, or feel. At about 2 years of age, a child makes (c)_____ to express various actions or relationships. At about 4 years of age, a child is forming sentences, which range from three to eight words in length and indicate a growing knowledge of the (d)_____.

12. A child's beginning sentences differ from adult sentences. A child's speech is called (a)_____ because it omits articles, prepositions, and parts of verbs. In learning the rules for combining nouns, verbs, and adjectives into meaningful sentences, children often apply a grammatical rule to cases where it should not be used. This type of error is called (b)_____. Although all children pass through these stages in the same order, they may go through them at different ages and speeds.

13. One reason children acquire a language with so little formal training is because of genetically programmed physiological and neurological features in the brain and vocal apparatus; these features are called (a)_____ factors. One such factor is the period of time from infancy to adolescence when language is easier to learn, called the (b)_____. One reason children acquire the sounds and rules of a particular language is because of their interactions with their surroundings; these are called (c)_____ factors. The approach that emphasizes observation, exploration, and imitation in language acquisition is the (d)_____ approach.

F. REASON, THOUGHT, & LANGUAGE

14. The process by which we use and apply knowledge to achieve certain goals that involve solving problems or making decisions is called (a)_____. This process has two different forms: if you begin with a general assumption and draw specific conclusions, you are using (b)_____ reasoning; if you begin with specific observations and then draw a general conclusion, you are using (c)_____ reasoning.

15. Whorf has suggested that language determines or influences the way people think and that people with different languages think and perceive their world differently. This is called the theory of _____. There is only weak support for Whorf's theory.

G. RESEARCH FOCUS: DYSLEXIA

16. A neurological disorder whose symptoms include reversing or skipping letters and numbers, with accompanying difficulties in reading, spelling, and writing, is called (a)_____. These

Left thalamus has fewer cells

symptoms are believed to be caused by maldevelopment in a particular part of the brain, called the (b)_____, which processes auditory information necessary for hearing differences in sounds that are used to make words. Dyslexia is not an all-or-nothing condition but rather is on a continuum that includes a wide range of reading difficulties, which may be accompanied by normal IQ scores.

H. CULTURAL DIVERSITY: POWER OF WORDS

17. Men tend to use language to express ideas, maintain their position in the group, and solve (a)_____, while women use language more to share concerns, daily experiences, and develop feelings of (b)_____.

18. MRI scans of the brain have shown that women process some words equally in both (a)_____, while men process words only in the (b)_____ hemisphere.

I. APPLICATION: DO ANIMALS HAVE LANGUAGE?

19. Many animals have the ability to use sounds, smells, or gestures to exchange information; this is the ability to (a)_____. Another question is whether animals can communicate with abstract symbols; this is called (b)_____. To decide that an animal truly uses language, researchers must show that the animal has learned complex rules of (c)_____ to manipulate symbols (words or gestures) and so generate an endless number of meaningful sentences. The best evidence for language in animals has come from a bonobo (pygmy chimp) who has matched the language ability of a 2-year-old child.

Answers: *1. (a) definition, (b) prototype; 2. (a) categorize, (b) relearning; 3. (a) problem solving, (b) initial state, operations state, goal state; 4. (a) algorithms, (b) heuristics, (c) availability; 5. (a) mental set, (b) functional fixedness; 6. (a) insight, (b) analogies, (c) subgoals; 7. (a) creative thinking, (b) convergent thinking, (c) divergent thinking; 8. language; 9. (a) phonology, (b) morphology, (c) syntax or grammar, (d) semantics; 10. (a) surface, (b) deep, (c) transformational rules; 11. (a) babbling, (b) single words, (c) two-word combinations, (d) rules of grammar; 12. (a) telegraphic, (b) overgeneralization; 13. (a) innate, (b) critical language period, (c) environmental, (d) social learning; 14. (a) reasoning, (b) deductive, (c) inductive; 15. linguistic relativity; 16. (a) dyslexia, (b) thalamus; 17. (a) problems, (b) intimacy; 18. (a) hemispheres, (b) left; 19. (a) communicate, (b) language, (c) grammar.*

Newspaper Article

QUESTIONS

1. What is the purpose of the "baby talk" we use with infants?

2. What is "parentese"?

3. Why did the researchers study English, Russian, and Swedish?

4. What were the researchers' findings?

5. Why might these findings be important?

THE LANGUAGE OF LEARNING
by Robert Lee Hotz

The singsong crooning that every adult instinctively adopts for conversation with a newborn baby is more than patronizing gibberish passing between the generations. It is a universal teaching mechanism rooted in the biology of language and the developing human brain, say neuroscientists Patricia Kuhl and her colleagues at the University of Washington in Seattle, who recently studied how native speakers of English, Swedish, and Russian talk to infants.

Linguists call the special tone adults reserve for speech with infants "parentese," and the new research indicates it is the same in every culture around the world.

To examine the role of parentese, Kuhl and her colleagues in Russia and Sweden investigated differences in how American, Swedish, and Russian mothers speak to their infants and to other adults. The three languages were chosen because each has a significantly different number of vowel sounds. Russian has five vowel sounds, English nine, and Swedish 16.

The researchers recorded 10 women from each of the three countries talking for 20 minutes to their babies, who ranged in age from 2 to 5 months. Then they recorded the same women talking to other adults. The mothers were told to talk naturally, but were given a list of words containing three common vowel sounds and instructed to work them into their conversations.

For those speaking English, the target words were "bead" for its "ee" vowel sound, "pot" for its "ah" sound, and "boot" for its "oo" sound. Similar words were chosen from Russian and Swedish.

The researchers then used a spectrograph to analyze more than 2,300 instances of how the target words were used in the conversations and discovered that, in all three language groups, the speech directed at infants was stretched out to emphasize the vowel sounds, in contrast to the more normal tone used with adults.

The researchers concluded that the exaggerated speech allowed the mothers to expand the sounds of the vowels so they would be more distinct from each other. It also appears to allow the mothers to produce a greater variety of vowel pronunciations without overlapping other vowel sounds.

Source: *Los Angeles Times,* September 18, 1997.

Study Questions

A. Forming Concepts—Why is it difficult to explain to your younger sister or brother that a whale is a mammal and not a fish? (See answer in Critical Thinking Appendix.)

B. Solving Problems—Why is it easier to win at checkers the longer you have been playing?

C. Thinking Creatively—How would you teach people to think more creatively?

D. Language: Basic Rules—To develop a secret code for sending computer messages across a network, which language rule should you break?

E. Acquiring Language—Why might students in college have more difficulty learning a foreign language than students in grade school?

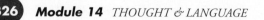

F. Reason, Thought, & Language—What problems might result when heads of government speak through translators? (See answer in Critical Thinking Appendix.)

G. Research Focus: Dyslexia—Why does dyslexia cause difficulties with reading but not with engineering and inventive abilities?

H. Cultural Diversity: Power of Words—What kinds of social problems can arise from finding differences between male and female brains? (See answer in Critical Thinking Appendix.)

I. Application: Do Animals Have Language?—When a parrot speaks perfect English and understands dozens of commands, can we conclude it is using language?

LINKS TO LEARNING

Web Sites & Learning Activities

● BROOKS/COLE ONLINE PSYCHOLOGY STUDY CENTER

http://psychstudy.brookscole.com/student/plotnik/quiz/ch14frm.html

This site gives students a chance to review material by taking quizzes and doing exercises and activities for this module.

● CREATIVITY WEB

http://www.ozemail.com.au/~caveman/creative/

This page includes resources to promote creativity, information on creativity and humor, and a mental workout center.

● THE HUMAN LANGUAGES PAGE

http://www.june29.com/HLP/

Interested in linguistics? Here is a comprehensive index to language-related Internet sites.

● ENGLISH AS A SECOND LANGUAGE HOME PAGE

http://granny.lang.uiuc.edu/r-li5/esl/

This site, sponsored by the University of Illinois-Urbana, features resources for the student of English as a second language.

● THE DOLPHIN SPEECH PROJECT

http://home.earthlink.net/~mhobson/#toc

Can animals use language? This site is maintained by researchers who are trying to use computers to communicate with dolphins.

Welcome to the WEB

● DYSLEXIA: THE GIFT

http://www.dyslexia.com/

This site offers support for people with dyslexia, as well as a newsletter, library, games, and links.

● NATIONAL APHASIA ASSOCIATION

http://www.aphasia.org/

Aphasia is a common cause of language problems, especially among older people. This site offers news, research, readings, and support to anyone interested in aphasia.

Activities

● *Integrator Online™ for Introductory Psychology* CD-ROM, Plotnik, Module 14

● Study Guide to accompany *Introduction to Psychology,* 5th edition, Module 14 (choice of PC or Mac computer version or hard copy)

● *PsychNow!* CD-ROM

Cognition and Language
Problem Solving and Creativity

Answers to questions on page 326

1. "Baby talk" helps teach infants the phonetic building blocks of language.
2. "Parentese" is the word linguists use to describe the way adults talk to infants.
3. These languages were chosen because each has a different numbers of vowel sounds.
4. The researchers found that the mothers exaggerated vowel sounds when speaking to their babies but did not when speaking to other adults.
5. The capacity to distinguish the different sounds that make up a language is the basis of speech perception.

Module 15 MOTIVATION

Motivation

Why would a paraplegic climb a mountain?

On a cool September morning, two men began to climb a nearly vertical slope rising over 2,200 feet from the floor of Yosemite National Park. Because of the slope's crumbly granite, fewer than 30 people have completed this particular route up Half Dome, Yosemite's well-known landmark. What made this particular climb very difficult and dangerous was that one of the men, Mark Wellman, is a paraplegic (left photo).

Some years ago, on a different climb, Mark fell 50 feet into a crevice, hurt his back, and was paralyzed from the waist down. Mark now climbs with his friend Mike Corbett, who takes the lead and sets the supports. Because Mark's legs are paralyzed, he climbs by using the supports to pull himself up inch by inch.

Mark figured that by doing the equivalent of 5,000 pull-ups, each of which would raise him about 6 inches, he could climb the 2,200 feet in seven days. By the end of day seven, however, Mark and Mike were only a little more than halfway up the slope and had to sleep by hanging in sleeping bags anchored to the sheer granite wall.

By day ten, Mark was becoming exhausted as his arms strained to raise his body's weight up the vertical face. By day 12, the men were almost out of food and water. Finally, on day 13, six days later than planned, Mark pulled himself up the last 6 inches and over the top of Half Dome. When Mark was asked later why he still climbed and risked further injury, he said, "Everyone has their own goals. . . . Never underestimate a person with a disability" (adapted from the *Los Angeles Times,* September 19, 1991, p. A-3).

Reporters who questioned Mark about why he risked his life to climb were really asking about his motivation.

Motivation refers to the various physiological and psychological factors that cause us to act in a specific way at a particular time.

When you are motivated, you usually show three characteristics:

1. You are *energized* to do or engage in some activity.
2. You *direct* your energies toward reaching a specific goal.
3. You have differing *intensities* of feelings about reaching that goal.

We can observe these three characteristics in Mark's behavior:

1. He was energized to perform the equivalent of 5,000 pull-ups during his 13-day climb.
2. He directed his energy toward climbing a particular slope that fewer than 30 other climbers had completed.

3. He felt so intensely about reaching that goal that even when totally exhausted he still persisted in reaching his goal, the top of Half Dome.

We'll discuss many kinds of motivation, including eating and drinking, finding a sex partner, engaging in sex, achieving good grades, underachieving, and of course, climbing mountains.

Achievement

Why did his Black friends call him a "White boy"?

Victor remembers being in the seventh grade when some of his Black buddies called him a "White boy" because they thought he was studying too hard. "You can't be cool if you're smart," says Victor, who was Mission Bay High's student body president, had a 3.7 (A–) grade point average, and will attend the University of Southern California in the fall (adapted from the *San Diego Union-Tribune,* June 17, 1994).

Victor (right photo) grew up with an obstacle that goes largely unnoticed and is rarely discussed in public: pressure from students in the same racial or ethnic group not to succeed in the classroom. Faced with this negative peer pressure, some minority students (principally Latino, African American, and Native American teenage boys) stop studying, don't do homework, avoid answering questions in class, join gangs, and even drop out of school.

Educators believe that the high dropout rates for minorities are, in part, the result of peer pressure not to succeed in school (Portillo, 1994). How Victor overcame this negative peer pressure and did succeed will be discussed later in this module.

What's Coming

We'll look at four general theories that psychologists use to explain motivation, discuss the differences between social and biological needs, and then focus on specific examples, such as hunger, sexual behavior, and achievement. We'll examine why some people are achievers and others are underachievers. We'll discuss why people become overweight and why dieting is so difficult. We'll look at two serious eating disorders that result more from psychological than from biological factors.

We'll begin with four general theories that psychologists use to explain motivation.

A. Theories of Motivation

Why does Mark climb?

For 13 days, sightseers on the Yosemite valley floor watched Mark pull himself up the granite face of Half Dome. Many asked, "Why is he doing that?" The inquisitive onlookers were asking about Mark's motivation: Why was he pulling himself up this impossibly steep mountain? To understand what motivates Mark's behavior, we'll discuss four general theories—the instinct, drive-reduction, incentive, and cognitive theories.

Instinct Theory

Was he driven by instincts?

At the beginning of the 1900s, William McDougall (1908) claimed that humans were motivated by a number of instincts. *Instincts* are innate tendencies or biological forces that determine behavior.

Initially, McDougall listed about a half-dozen instincts, such as flight, repulsion, curiosity, pugnacity, and self-abasement. By the 1920s, psychologists had proposed over 6,000 instincts to explain every kind of human motivation.

DOES MARK HAVE AN INSTINCT FOR CLIMBING?

In the 1920s, Mark's desire to climb mountains would probably have been explained in terms of an instinct for excitement or taking risks. But to label climbing or some other behavior as an instinct does nothing more than describe the behavior; it does not explain why a person engages in the behavior. Because instincts became labels rather than explanations, psychologists abandoned the use of instincts to explain human motivation. However, psychologists and ethologists—biologists who study animal behavior—have now redefined instinct as fixed action patterns (FitzGerald, 1993).

A *fixed action pattern* is an innate biological force that predisposes an organism to behave in a fixed way in the presence of a specific environmental condition.

For example, in the above photo, the baboon is innately predisposed to behave in a fixed way (opens mouth, stares, rises on hind feet) in the presence of a specific environmental condition (a cheetah, a threatening stimulus).

Ethologists observe how animals use fixed action patterns in adapting to their natural environments. In Module 10, we discussed ethologist Konrad Lorenz (1952) and his well-known work on imprinting in birds. As you may remember, soon after birth a bird usually becomes attached to, or imprinted on, the first moving object (animal, human, or basketball) it encounters, and it continues to interact with that object as if it were its parent. This is an excellent example of a fixed action pattern.

The second theory of motivation focuses on biological factors.

Drive-Reduction Theory

Does he have a need to climb?

By the 1930s, so many human instincts had been proposed that instinct was no longer a useful concept to explain motivation. In the 1940s and 1950s, psychologists developed two new concepts to explain human motivation—needs and drives (Hull, 1952).

A *need* is a biological state in which the organism lacks something essential for survival, such as food, water, or oxygen. The need produces a *drive,* which is a state of tension that motivates the organism to act to reduce that tension.

Once the need is satisfied, the body returns to a more balanced state. *Homeostasis* is the tendency of the body to return to, and remain in, a more balanced state.

By combining these three concepts—need, drive, and homeostasis—we have the key components of the drive-reduction theory.

The *drive-reduction theory* says that a need results in a drive, which is a state of tension that motivates the organism to act to reduce the tension and return the body to homeostasis.

As an example, not eating for a period of time causes a need for food, which produces a *drive,* or state of tension. In turn, the drive, or tension, energizes the person to *act,* perhaps by raiding the refrigerator, thereby reducing the tension and returning the body to *homeostasis.*

According to drive-reduction theory, drives motivate us to engage in a wide variety of behaviors to satisfy biological needs. For example, psychologists might refer to an organism as having a hunger drive or a thirst drive. However, drive-reduction theory has difficulty explaining why, after we satisfy our hunger need with a complete meal and say we are full, we then eat a dessert.

DOES MARK HAVE A NEED TO CLIMB?

Mark probably does not have a biological need for climbing, which in most cases results in fear and excitement that increases rather than decreases body arousal or tension. Drive-reduction theory cannot explain why we sometimes act to increase needs and drives (Locke & Latham, 1994). It is more likely that Mark climbs to satisfy a variety of psychological needs, including need for excitement or challenge.

Needs and drives are processes that we assume are going on inside Mark's body. Researchers have also identified motivational forces that occur in our environments or in our minds.

Incentive Theory

We can make the issue of motivation very personal by asking why you work so long and hard in college? One answer would be that part of your motivation comes from wanting to graduate and get a college degree. A college degree is considered a very big incentive (Atkinson & Birch, 1978; Skinner, 1953).

Incentives are environmental factors, such as external stimuli, reinforcers, or rewards, that motivate our behaviors.

Our behaviors can be motivated by a variety of incentives, including grades, praise, money, and a high school or college degree. Because incentives are external—in the environment—they are thought of as *pulling* us to obtain them. In comparison, because drives are internal, they are thought of as *pushing* us to reduce needs. This push-pull difference between drives and incentives explains some otherwise perplexing and seemingly unexplainable behaviors.

For instance, what motivates us to continue performing the same behavior after our need is already met? Why do we eat a dessert after complaining of being stuffed, or buy more clothes when our closet is already full? Incentive theory explains that, even though our immediate needs are met, incentives such as stylish clothes or highly desired foods continue to pull us toward them.

Why do we engage in risky behaviors that increase arousal, such as mountain climbing, or behaviors that deliberately throw homeostasis out of balance, such as vigorous sports? Incentive theory explains that when we perform arousing or life-threatening behaviors, we are motivated by positive incentives, such as praise, recognition, or rewards.

DOES MARK CLIMB TO OBTAIN INCENTIVES?

One reason Mark may climb is to obtain incentives, such as recognition in the form of national press coverage, invitations for speaking, and monies ($100,000) from corporate sponsors that he donates to help others with disabilities. However, other equally powerful reasons for Mark's climbing probably involve cognitive factors.

Cognitive Theory

Thousands of people train for months to run grueling 23-mile-long marathons, in which only the top two or three receive any prize money. What motivates people to endure such agony? Beginning in the 1960s, psychologists such as Albert Bandura (1986), Richard deCharms (1980), Edward Deci (Deci & Ryan, 1985), and Bernard Weiner (1986, 1991) began applying cognitive concepts to explain human motivation. These cognitive researchers said that one reason people run marathons, usually for no reward other than a T-shirt, has to do with the difference between extrinsic and intrinsic motivation.

Extrinsic motivation involves engaging in certain activities or behaviors that either reduce biological needs or help us obtain incentives or external rewards.

Intrinsic motivation involves engaging in certain activities or behaviors because the behaviors themselves are personally rewarding or because engaging in these activities fulfills our beliefs or expectations.

Intrinsic motivation explains that people volunteer their services, spend hours on hobbies, run marathons, or work on personal projects because these activities are personally rewarding, fulfilling, or challenging. Intrinsic motivation emphasizes that we do many things because of personal beliefs, expectations, or goals, rather than external incentives. The concept of intrinsic

motivation provides a quite different way of explaining human motivation.

DID MARK CLIMB BECAUSE OF INTRINSIC MOTIVATION?

Besides the explanations offered by the drive-reduction and incentive theories, cognitive theory's concept of intrinsic motivation suggests another reason for Mark's dangerous behavior: climbing itself was rewarding; climbing allowed him to meet his own personal goals, beliefs, and expectations. As Mark said, "Everyone has their own goals." And so does Mark.

Explaining Human Motivation

We have discussed four theories of motivation that attempt to explain what *energizes* people and what *directs* their behavior into specific actions. The theory of fixed action patterns explains the behaviors of animals. The drive-reduction theory, a pushing force, explains our actions to meet biological or physiological needs. The incentive theory, a pulling force, explains that we may do things to obtain external rewards. The cognitive theory explains that we may do things to satisfy personal beliefs or meet personal goals. For example, Mark may have undertaken the life-threatening climb, or students may work years to obtain a degree, out of strong personal beliefs (O'Neil & Drillings, 1994). One reason the cognitive theory of human motivation has grown in popularity is that it focuses on the importance of beliefs and expectations, which are primary forces in many human behaviors (Cacioppo et al., 1996; Higgins, 1997).

Two interesting questions about human motivation are how many needs do we have and in which order will we satisfy them. Next, we'll answer these questions.

B. Biological & Social Needs

How many needs do you have?

If you did nothing but watch people for a day, you would soon discover that people spend much of their time trying to satisfy numerous biological and social needs. You become aware of biological needs when you get hungry, but you may be less aware of social needs. Here's how biological and social needs differ.

Biological Needs

Why is this man in the refrigerator?

One of our most popular activities is eating, which fulfills a basic biological need.

Biological needs are physiological requirements that are critical to our survival and physical well-being.

Researchers have identified 10–15 biological needs, six of which are listed on the right (Madsen, 1973). We share the same biological needs, many of which we must satisfy daily to survive and to keep our bodies functioning optimally. In extreme cases, people may seriously interfere with meeting their biological needs. Such is the case with the eating disorder, anorexia nervosa, in which individuals may starve themselves to death. We'll discuss this disorder in the Application section. In other cases, people subject themselves to pain and injury, as happens in football, horse racing, and boxing. These examples demonstrate how psychological factors can override basic biological needs.

Although there are a limited number of biological needs, there are many social needs.

> **Biological Needs**
> Food
> Water
> Sex
> Oxygen
> Sleep
> Avoidance of pain

Social Needs

Why did they get married?

One reason 90% of adults in the United States get married is that being married satisfies a number of social needs.

Social needs are needs that are acquired through learning and experience.

Depending upon one's learning and experiences, there are dozens of social needs, some of which are listed on the right (Murray, 1938). Notice that being married can satisfy a number of these social needs, such as affiliation, nurturance, play, dominance, and achievement. The need for affiliation, or forming lasting and positive interpersonal attachments, is one of our stronger social needs and is important to maintaining physical health and psychological well-being (Baumeister & Leary, 1995).

In some cases, the distinction between biological and social needs is blurred. For example, we may eat or drink not only to satisfy biological needs but to make social contact as well. Similarly, we may engage in sex for reproduction, which is a biological need, or to express love and affection, which is a social need. Even if needs overlap, we have only so much time and energy to satisfy a relatively large number of biological and social needs. This condition leaves us with a problem: How do we decide which needs to satisfy first?

> **Social Needs**
> Achievement motive (need to excel)
> Affiliation motive (need for social bonds)
> Nurturance motive (need to nourish and protect others)
> Autonomy motive (need for independence)
> Dominance motive (need to influence or control others)
> Order motive (need for orderliness)
> Play motive (need for fun, relaxation)

Satisfying Needs

Which need gets satisfied?

As you may remember from Module 1, Abraham Maslow was one of the founders of the humanistic approach in psychology. Maslow was particularly interested in human motivation, especially in how we choose which biological or social need to satisfy. For example, should you study late for an exam and satisfy your social need to achieve, or go to bed at your regular time and satisfy your biological need for sleep? Maslow (1970) proposed that we satisfy our needs in a certain order or according to a set hierarchy.

Maslow's hierarchy of needs is an ascending order, or hierarchy, in which biological needs are placed at the bottom and social needs at the top. This hierarchy indicates that we satisfy our biological needs before we satisfy our social needs.

Maslow hypothesized that, after we satisfy needs at the bottom level of the hierarchy, we advance up the hierarchy to satisfy the needs at the next level. However, if we are at a higher level and basic needs are not satisfied, we may come back down the hierarchy. Let's examine Maslow's hierarchy of needs in more detail.

Maslow's Hierarchy of Needs

Which needs do you satisfy first?

If you were very hungry and very lonely at the same time, which need would you satisfy first, your biological need (hunger) or your social need (affiliation)? One answer to this question can be found in Maslow's hierarchy of needs, which says that you satisfy your biological needs before you can turn your attention and energy to fulfilling your personal and social needs. According to Maslow, when it comes to satisfying your needs you begin at the bottom of the needs hierarchy, with physiological needs, and then work your way toward the top. As you meet the needs at one level, you advance to the next level. For example, if your physiological needs at level 1 are satisfied, you advance to level 2 and work on satisfying your safety needs. Once your safety needs are satisfied, you advance to level 3, and so forth, up the needs hierarchy.

Maslow's hierarchy of needs is represented by a pyramid and shows the order in which you satisfy your biological and social needs. The first needs you satisfy are physiological or biological ones, so please go to the bottom of the pyramid and begin reading Level 1. Then continue reading Levels 2, 3, 4, and 5, which takes you up the pyramid.

Level 5 Self-actualization: Fulfillment of one's unique potential. If we face roadblocks in reaching our true potential, we will feel frustrated. For example, if you are majoring in business and your real interest and talent is music, your need for self-actualization may be unsatisfied. According to Maslow, the highest need is self-actualization, which involves developing and reaching our full potential as unique human beings.

Level 4 Esteem needs: Achievement, competency, gaining approval and recognition. During early and middle adulthood, people are especially concerned with achieving their goals and establishing their careers. As we develop skills to gain personal achievement and social recognition, we turn our energies to level 5.

Level 3 Love and belonging needs: Affiliation with others and acceptance by others. Adolescents and young adults, who are beginning to form serious relationships, would be especially interested in fulfilling their needs for love and belonging. After we find love and affection, we advance to level 4.

Level 2 Safety needs: Protection from harm. People who live in high-crime or dangerous areas of the city would be very concerned about satisfying their safety needs. After we find a way to live in a safe and secure environment, we advance to level 3.

Level 1 Physiological needs: Food, water, sex, and sleep. People who are homeless or jobless would be especially concerned with satisfying their physiological needs above all other needs. We must satisfy these basic needs before we advance to level 2.

Conclusion. One advantage of Maslow's hierarchy is that it integrates biological and social needs into a single framework and sets up a system of priorities for satisfying various needs. One problem with Maslow's hierarchy is that researchers have found it difficult to verify whether his particular order of needs is accurate or how to assess some of his needs, especially self-actualization (Geller, 1982). Another problem is that people give different priorities to needs: some may value love over self-esteem or vice versa (Neher, 1991). Despite the criticisms of Maslow's hierarchy, it remains a useful reminder of the number and complexity of human needs.

To give you a sample of how psychologists study human motivation, we have selected two biological needs—hunger and sex—from Maslow's level 1 and one social need—achievement—from Maslow's level 4. We consider these needs in the following sections.

C. Hunger

Optimal Weight

Why aren't there overweight wolves?

The reason you would never see a fat wolf is that they, like all animals, have an inherited biological system that regulates hunger so that they maintain their optimal, or ideal, weights.

Optimal or *ideal weight* results from an almost perfect balance between how much food an organism eats and how much it needs to meet its body's energy needs.

In the wild, animals usually eat only to replace fuel used by their bodies, and thus they rarely get fat. In addition, most wild animals use up a tremendous amount of energy in finding food. In

comparison, home pets may become fat because their owners, having the best of intentions, give the pets too much food or food so tasty that their pets eat too much. And unlike wild animals, home-bound pets may have few opportunities to run around and burn off the extra calories.

A *calorie* is simply a measure of how much energy food contains. For example, fats (cheese, hamburger, whole milk) contain twice the calories or fuel of proteins (fish, chicken) or carbohydrates (vegetables, fruits, grains). The same factors that make pets overweight also make humans overweight.

Overweight

Why are there overweight people?

Like animals, humans also have an inherited biological system that regulates hunger to keep us at our ideal weights. However, humans become overweight for the same two reasons that pets do: one reason is eating more food than required to fuel the body's energy needs; another reason is a lack of exercise (Troiano, 1997).

Overweight means that a person is 20% over their ideal body weight.

Obesity means that a person is 30% or more above their ideal body weight.

The table on the right shows that in the late 1970s about one in four, or 26%, of adult Americans were overweight; by the late 1980s, about one in three, or 34%, were overweight

Americans ages 20–74 who are overweight

1976–1980	26%
1988–1997	34%

(Troiano, 1997). Researchers found that a person's body fat typically doubles between ages 20 and 50 unless they have a program to get more exercise (Roberts, 1997).

Being overweight has become a major health problem in the United States because it doubles the risk for heart disease, stroke, high blood pressure, clogged arteries, adult-onset diabetes, and early death (National Task Force on the Prevention and Treatment of Obesity, 1994). For example, one group of Pacific Islanders have an obesity rate of 65%, and of these, 33% have diabetes (Gibbs, 1996). In 1994, almost 6% of all health problems were weight related, for a total annual bill of $39 billion (Azar, 1994a).

However, you'll see that solving the problem of being overweight is complicated by the fact that eating is influenced by three different hunger factors.

Three Hunger Factors

So, what controls your eating?

Hunger is considered a biological drive because eating is essential to our survival. However, the way in which we satisfy our hunger drive—when, where, and how much we eat—is influenced by three different kinds of factors: biological, psychosocial, and genetic.

Biological hunger factors come from physiological changes in blood chemistry and signals from digestive organs that provide feedback to the brain, which, in turn, triggers us to eat or stop eating.

If our eating were primarily regulated by biological factors, as in most animals, we would keep our weight at optimal levels. The fact that 34% of adults are overweight and some individuals suffer from serious eating problems indicates the influence of both psychosocial and genetic factors.

Psychosocial hunger factors come from learned associations between food and other stimuli, such as snacking while

watching television; sociocultural influences, such as pressures to be thin; and various personality problems, such as depression, dislike of body image, or low self-esteem.

Genetic hunger factors come from inherited instructions found in our genes. These instructions determine the number of fat cells or metabolic rates of burning off the body's fuel, which push us toward being normal, overweight, or underweight.

Our eating habits and weight result from a combination of all three hunger factors. For example, because of psychosocial hunger factors, we may eat when we're not hungry; and because of genetic hunger factors, we may eat as much as we want without gaining weight because excess calories are not stored but burned off (Gibbs 1996). We'll discuss the three hunger factors, beginning with biological factors.

Biological Hunger Factors

Why do you start or stop eating?

The Japanese sumo wrestler on the right is Konishiki, nicknamed Meat Bomb. He is 6 feet 1 inch tall and weighs 580 pounds, which is considered normal by sumo standards but obese by Western medical charts. He maintains his huge body by consuming about 10,000 calories daily, which is 3–5 times the amount required by an average-sized male. Konishiki starts or stops eating partly because of biological hunger factors that come from two different sources—peripheral and central cues.

Peripheral cues come from changes in blood chemistry or signals from digestive organs.
Central cues come from the activity of chemicals and neurotransmitters in different areas of the brain.

Peripheral and central cues are part of an elaborate biological system that evolved across millions of years to help humans and animals maintain their optimal weight.

Peripheral Cues

Signals for feeling hungry or full come from a number of body organs that are involved in digestion and regulation of blood sugar (glucose) levels, which is the primary source of fuel for the body and brain.

1 The *stomach* monitors the amount and kinds of nutrients our body needs to restore our depleted stores of fuel. In addition, after eating a meal, the stomach's walls are distended and their stretch receptors signal fullness or time to stop eating.

The stomach's signals about fullness are monitored by a particular area of the brain, the hypothalamus, which is the master control center for hunger and eating behaviors (Schwartz, 1996).

2 The *liver* monitors nutrients, especially the level of glucose (sugar) in the blood. When the level of glucose falls, the liver signals hunger; when the level of glucose rises, the liver signals fullness.

The liver's signals about being hungry or full are monitored by a certain part of the hypothalamus (Carlson, 1998).

3 The *intestines* respond to the presence of food, especially fats, by secreting a hormone called CCK (cholecystokinin), which inhibits eating.

The intestine's signals about fullness are monitored by a certain part of the hypothalamus (Carlson, 1998).

4 *Fat cells* secrete a hormone (leptin) that is monitored by the brain. In turn, the brain signals a person to eat or stop eating so that a certain level of body fat remains constant over a person's lifetime.

As fat cells secrete the hunger-related hormone (leptin), it is monitored by a certain part of the hypothalamus (Unger, 1997).

There are also central cues for hunger.

Central Cues

Located in the lower middle of the brain are groups of cells that are collectively called the hypothalamus. We have greatly simplified the hypothalamus's role in motivation by focusing only on its role in hunger.

Hypothalamus

1 The *hypothalamus* has many different groups of cells that are involved in a number of different behaviors having to do with motivation, such as thirst, sexual behavior, and regulation of hunger.

Two particular groups of cells, the lateral and ventromedial hypothalamus, affect eating in opposite ways.

2 The *lateral hypothalamus* is a group of cells that regulates hunger by creating feelings of being hungry (Winn, 1995).

For example, rats begin eating when the lateral hypothalamus is electrically stimulated. They stop eating, and may starve, if the lateral hypothalamus is destroyed. In addition, the lateral hypothalamus has cells that increase or decrease activity depending on the blood level of glucose.

3 The *ventromedial hypothalamus* is a group of cells that regulates hunger by creating feelings of satiety (*say-TIE-ah-tea*) or fullness.

For example, rats stop eating when the ventromedial hypothalamus is electrically stimulated. They greatly overeat and become obese if the ventromedial hypothalamus (and adjacent areas) is destroyed.

The hypothalamus has other groups of cells that regulate our specific appetites for foods.

4 *Galanin,* which is a chemical produced by the brain, acts on the hypothalamus and stimulates eating fat. *Norepinephrine,* which is a neurotransmitter produced by the brain, acts on the hypothalamus and stimulates eating carbohydrates. *Neuropeptide Y,* which is a chemical produced by the brain, acts on the hypothalamus and stimulates eating (Carlson, 1998; Seeley & Schwartz, 1997).

Thus, the hypothalamus has several centers involved in eating: one to start eating (lateral hypothalamus), another to stop eating (ventromedial hypothalamus), and others for eating specific foods (fats or carbohydrates).

Although each of us has a sophisticated biological system to keep us at our ideal weight, you'll see that various genetic and psychological factors can change or interfere with this system.

D. Sexual Behavior

Three Factors

Why do lions know how to do it?

Although we don't look, sound, or behave the same as lions do, we share similar biological and genetic factors that regulate sexual behavior. The sexual behavior of lions and most animals is chiefly controlled by genetic and biological factors, which means that most animals engage in sex primarily for reproduction.

Genetic sex factors include inherited instructions for the development of sexual organs, the secretion of sex hormones, and the wiring of the neural circuits that control sexual reflexes.

Biological sex factors include the action of sex hormones, which are involved in secondary sexual characteristics (facial hair, breasts), sexual motivation (more so in animals than in humans), and the development of ova and sperm.

Lions, like most animals, generally avoid sexual interactions unless the female is in heat, which means she is ovulating and can be impregnated. In comparison, humans engage in sexual behavior for many reasons, which point to psychological sexual factors.

Psychological sex factors play a role in developing a sexual or gender identity, gender role, and sexual orientation. In addition, psychological factors can result in difficulties in the performance or enjoyment of sexual activities.

For example, otherwise healthy men and women may report difficulties in sexual activities arising from stress, anxiety, or guilt, which can interfere with the functioning of genetic and biological sex factors. One reason psychological factors play such an important role in human sexual behavior is because our large forebrains have the capacity to think, reason, and change our minds and thus increase, interfere with, or completely block sexual motivation, performance, or enjoyment.

As we did for the hunger drive, we'll discuss in order the influence of genetic, biological, and psychological factors on sexual behavior.

Genetic Sex Factors

Which sex organ?

How we develop particular sex organs, male or female, is determined by a genetic program that is contained in a single human cell about the size of a grain of sand. The genetic program is contained in long strands of DNA (deoxyribonucleic acid) that make up the sex chromosomes.

SEX CHROMOSOME

Unlike the other cells of our body, which contain 46 chromosomes (23 pairs), the sperm and egg each contain half that number and are called sex chromosomes (figure on right).

The *sex chromosome*, which is either the sperm or the egg, contains only 23 chromosomes on which are genes that have the instructions for determining the sex of the child.

As we discussed in Module 4, the chromosomes contain genes, which are chemically coded instructions for the development and maintenance of our bodies. Notice that some sperms have an *X* chromosome and some have a *Y*, which will result in different instructions for development of sex organs.

1 The human egg contains one of the sex chromosomes, which is always an **X** chromosome. Thus, each human egg has a single **X** chromosome.

2 A human sperm also contains one of the sex chromosomes. However, the sperm's chromosome can be either an **X** chromosome, which has instructions for development of female sex organs and body, or a **Y** chromosome, which has instructions for male sex organs and body.

3 During fertilization, a single sperm penetrates an egg. The fertilized egg will have a pair of chromosomes: either the combination **XY,** which has the genetic instructions for a male's sex organs; or the combination **XX,** which has the genetic instructions for a female's sex organs.

Following fertilization, the human cell, which is called a *zygote,* will divide over and over during the following weeks and months and eventually develop into a female body with female sex organs or male body with male sex organs. What determines which sex organs, male or female, is an interesting story.

Genetic Sex Factors *(continued)*

DIFFERENTIATION

  Although it would seem that at fertilization you are destined to be either a male or a female, there is actually no physical difference between a male and female embryo for the first four weeks of development in the womb. During this time period, the embryos are identical and have the potential to develop into either a male or female (Federman, 1994). At about the fifth week, the embryo begins to differentiate into either a male or female because of the presence or absence of certain sex hormones.

MALE SEX ORGAN AND MALE BRAIN

In an embryo that began from an **XY** fertilized egg, the **Y** sex chromosome has instructions for the development of male testes. About the fifth week, the testes begin to grow and produce tiny amounts of male hormones or androgens, such as testosterone.

 The presence of testosterone does two things: it triggers the development of the male sexual organ (penis); and it programs a particular area of the brain, called the hypothalamus, so that at puberty it triggers the pituitary gland to secrete hormones on a continuous basis, which results in the continuous production of sperm.

FEMALE SEX ORGANS AND FEMALE BRAIN

In an embryo that began from an **XX** fertilized egg, the second **X** sex chromosome contains instructions for the development of ovaries, which do not secrete testosterone.

 The absence of testosterone in the developing embryo means two things: the automatic development of female sexual organs (clitoris and vagina); and the hypothalamus, which is normally programmed for female hormonal functions, keeps its female program. Thus, at puberty, this female-programmed hypothalamus triggers the pituitary gland to secrete hormones on a cyclic basis, which results in the menstrual cycle.

IMPORTANCE OF TESTOSTERONE

The ***presence*** of testosterone, which is secreted by fetal testes, results in male sexual organs and a male hypothalamus; the ***absence*** of testosterone results in female sexual organs and a female hypothalamus (Carlson, 1998).

When the infant is born, the doctor identifies the infant's sex organs and says those famous words, "It's a boy" or "It's a girl." At that point a hormonal clock begins ticking and its alarm will set off biological factors at puberty.

Biological Sex Factors

 What happens at puberty? You have seen how genetic sex factors influence the development and growth of the body's sex organs. The next big event to affect a person's sex organs and sexual motivation occurs at puberty as a result of biological sex factors.

PUBERTY

The sex hormones secreted during puberty either directly or indirectly affect our bodies, brains, minds, personalities, self-concepts, and mental health. Here, we'll focus on how sex hormones affect our bodies.

Sex hormones. At puberty, some yet unknown signal activates cells in the hypothalamus, which trigger a 10- to 20-fold increase in the secretion of sex hormones.

 Sex hormones, which are chemicals secreted by glands, circulate in the bloodstream to influence the brain, body organs, and behaviors. The major male sex hormones secreted by the testes are *androgens,* such as testosterone; the major female sex hormones secreted by the ovaries are *estrogens.*

Male/female difference. Because of neural programming in the womb resulting from the presence or absence of testosterone, the male hypothalamus functions differently from the female hypothalamus.

 The *male hypothalamus* triggers a continuous release of androgens, such as testosterone, from the testes. The increased level of androgens causes the development of male secondary sexual characteristics, such as facial and pubic hair, muscle growth, and lowered voice.

 The *female hypothalamus* triggers a cyclical release of estrogens from the ovaries. The increased level of estrogens causes the development of female secondary sexual characteristics, such as pubic hair, breast development, and widening of the hips. The cyclical release of hormones (estrogen and progesterone) also regulates the menstrual cycle.

SEXUAL MOTIVATION

In animals, sexual motivation is primarily regulated by the rise and fall in levels of sex hormones.

In contrast, human sexual motivation shows little correlation with levels of sex hormones, provided they are within the normal range. For example, the normal rise and fall in levels of androgens or estrogens has no clear-cut effect on sexual motivation (Schiavi & Segraves, 1995). Provided a person has a normal level of sex hormones, increases or decreases in sexual motivation are more dependent upon psychological factors, such as feelings, desires, and expectations (Tiefer & Kring, 1995).

At the same time that genetic and biological factors are guiding our bodies toward physical sexual maturity, numerous psychological factors are preparing our minds for psychological sexual maturity. Next, we'll examine these psychological sex factors.

D. Sexual Behavior

Male-Female Sex Differences

How are males different from females?

After we have acquired a gender identity, gender role, and sexual orientation, we face many and sometimes difficult decisions about when, how often, and with whom to engage in sexual behavior. A recent national sex survey by researchers from the University of Chicago involved face-to-face interviews with a random sample of 3,500 Americans, ages 18–29 (Laumann et al., 1994). As the graph below shows, this survey, along with virtually every previous survey, reported that males engage in more sexual behaviors and with greater frequency and have more sexual partners than do females (Baldwin & Baldwin, 1997). Why males consistently report more sexual desire, motivation, and activity than females is explained by two different theories—social role theory and evolutionary (sociobiology) theory.

The *social role theory*, which emphasizes social and cultural forces, states that sexual differences between males and females arise from different divisions of labor.

According to social role theory, men were traditionally providers and protectors while women were homemakers and caregivers (Eagly, 1997). Based on these different roles, society has developed a set of different norms for sexual behaviors—the double standard.

The *double standard for sexual behavior* refers to a set of beliefs, values, and expectations that subtly encourages sexual activity in males but discourages the same behavior in females.

According to social role theory, one reason males are more interested in and engage in more sexual activities is that our cultural and social standards permit greater sexual freedom for males. A different explanation comes from evolutionary (sociobiology) theory.

The *evolutionary (sociobiology) theory,* which emphasizes genetic and biological forces, says that current sexual differences are a continuation of the behaviors that evolved from early men and women who adapted these different behaviors in their attempts to survive the problems of their time (Buss, 1995, Archer, 1997).

We'll discuss how each theory explains some of the major male-female sexual differences.

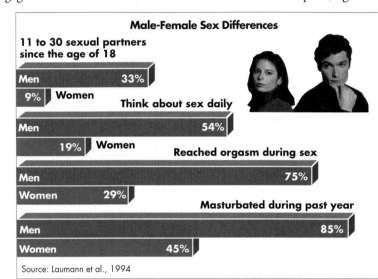

Male-Female Sex Differences

11 to 30 sexual partners since the age of 18
- Men 33%
- Women 9%

Think about sex daily
- Men 54%
- Women 19%

Reached orgasm during sex
- Men 75%
- Women 29%

Masturbated during past year
- Men 85%
- Women 45%

Source: Laumann et al., 1994

Social Role Theory

Researchers consistently find at least two male-female differences in sexual behavior. First, men consistently report greater interest in sex as shown by increased frequency of sexual activities, greater percentage of extramarital affairs, and desire for more sex partners (about 18 partners) than women (about 4–5 partners) (Buss & Schmitt, 1993). Second, in an international study of 37 cultures, 10,000 individuals were asked to state their top priorities in choosing a mate. Across all cultures and all racial, political, and religious groups, men generally valued physical attractiveness more than women, while women valued the financial resources of prospective mates twice as much as men (Buss et al., 1990).

Males: Top preference was for a physically attractive mate.

According to social role theory, these differences in sexual activities and priorities in mate selection developed from traditional cultural divisions of labor, in which women were child-bearers and homemakers while men were providers and protectors (Eagly, 1997). Because each sex performed different duties, men and women developed different sex roles. Social role theory points to different social and cultural pressures as being the basis for sex differences.

Evolutionary (Sociobiology) Theory

According to evolutionary (sociobiology) theory, men developed a greater interest in sex and desire for many attractive sex partners because it maximized their chances for reproduction. In comparison, women would not benefit from indiscriminate and frequent mating because it would place them at risk for having offspring of low quality and create an unstable environment for raising their children. Instead, women sought a good protector and provider that would increase survival during childbearing (Buss, 1994b).

Females: Top preference was for a mate with a good earning potential.

According to evolutionary theory, our current sexual differences arise from genetic and biological forces that evolved from an ancient set of mating patterns that helped the species survive (Archer, 1997).

Because social role theory emphasizes cultural forces and evolutionary theory emphasizes genetic and biological forces, some researchers suggest that by combining the two theories we could better explain the development of our current male and female sex differences (Baldwin & Baldwin, 1997; Schaller, 1997).

Next, we'll return to a controversial question in sexual behavior: Why does an individual develop a homosexual orientation?

Homosexuality

Were these brothers born gay?

As shown in the graph on the right, current national surveys estimate that about 1–3% of the American male population are homosexual (gay) and about 1.4% of the female population are homosexual (lesbian). These recent estimates are much less than Kinsey's early estimate of 10%.

National surveys in 1978 and 1994 found a little over half (53%) of adult Americans approved of homosexuality while about half disapproved for a variety of reasons (Henry, 1994). Many people say that they would be more accepting of homosexuality if it were shown to be mainly genetic, since it would be similar to inheriting other preferences, such as being left-handed (Leland, 1994). We'll discuss recent genetic/biological and psychological factors that relate to whether brothers Rick and Randy (photo at left) were born or chose to be gay.

% Male Homosexuals

10%   Kinsey et al., 1948

2.8%   Laumann et al., 1994

% Female Homosexuals

1.4%   Laumann et al., 1994

Genetic/Biological Factors

One way to study the influence of genetic factors on sexual orientation is to study twins. Three recent studies on identical male and female twins have found that, if one male or female twin of an identical pair was gay, about 48–65% of the time so was the second twin; this compared to 26–30% for fraternal twins and 6–11% for adopted brothers or sisters. One criticism of these studies is that the twins were not reared separately so it is impossible to determine the effects of similar environments on sexual orientation. Even more significant is a recent study on genetic similarities among gay men.

Researchers studied 40 families, each of which had two gay brothers (including Rick and Randy). Researchers identified an area at the end of the X chromosome that was shared by 33 out of 40 pairs of gay brothers (figure below).

X Chromosome   **Area shared by high percentage of gay brothers**

Thus, although they were not twins, Rick and Randy, who are gay, share the same section of genetic material. Researchers concluded that this was the strongest evidence to date that homosexual orientation is strongly influenced by genetic factors (Hamer et al., 1993a; Hammer, 1995). These researchers cautioned that they have not found a "homosexual gene," but only identified an area of shared genetic material that contributes to sexual orientation.

Taken together, these studies suggest that, to a certain extent, Rick and Randy were born with inherited tendencies and that these inherited factors may play a larger role in sexual orientation than previously thought (Gladue, 1994; Hammer 1995; LeVay & Hamer, 1994; Rosenberg, 1994). However, the studies on twins also indicate the influence of psychological factors, since only about half the pairs of identical twins had exactly the same sexual orientation (Byne, 1994).

Next, we'll examine the influence of psychological factors on sexual orientation.

Psychological Factors

When is a person aware of his or her sexual orientation? Most gays report becoming aware of their orientation around puberty. By the end of their teenage years, most men who eventually come out as gay have already acknowledged their homosexual orientation to themselves (Pillard & Bailey, 1995).

Do young children who develop a heterosexual orientation differ from children who develop a homosexual orientation? Researchers have consistently found that young boys who preferred girl playmates and girls' toys, avoided rough-and-tumble play, and engaged in wearing girls' clothing had a tendency to develop a homosexual orientation (Pillard & Bailey, 1995). In addition, adult gay men and lesbian women recalled engaging in more behaviors of the opposite sex as children than did heterosexual adults (Bailey & Zucker, 1995). Thus, there is evidence that psychological factors influence the development of a homosexual orientation and coming out as gay or lesbian (Bell et al., 1981).

Beginning in the early 1970s, researchers began to study homosexuals and found that homosexuals scored about the same as heterosexuals on tests of mental health (Rosenberg, 1994). On the basis of these findings, two major mental health organizations, the American Psychological Association and the American Psychiatric Association, decided that homosexuality was part of the normal range of human sexual behavior. In 1994, the American Medical Association revised its formerly discriminatory policy and now recommends that its members have a nonjudgmental attitude toward sexual orientation. Thus, the three major American health organizations have indicated that being homosexual should not result in discriminatory practices, because homosexuality is within the range of normal sexual behavior.

Next, we'll discuss common sexual problems and their treatments.

D. Sexual Behavior

Sexual Problems

What are some common sexual problems?

Clinical psychologists report that many men and women experience a sexual problem at some time in their lives (Becker & Kaplan, 1994). Some seek help for their problem, while others are ashamed or embarrassed and suffer in silence. There are two categories of sexual problems—paraphilias and sexual dysfunctions.

Paraphilias, commonly called sexual deviations, are characterized by repetitive or preferred sexual fantasies involving nonhuman objects, such as sexual attractions to particular articles of clothing (shoes, underclothes).

Sexual dysfunctions refer to problems of sexual arousal or orgasm that interfere with adequate functioning during sexual behavior.

When a person seeks help for a sexual problem, the clinician will check whether the causes are organic or psychological.

Organic causes refer to medical conditions or drug or medication problems that lead to sexual difficulties.

For example, certain medical conditions (such as diabetes mellitus), medications (such as antidepressants), and drugs (such as alcohol abuse) can interfere with sexual functioning.

Psychological causes refer to performance anxiety, sexual trauma, guilt, or failure to communicate, all of which may lead to sexual problems.

Four-stage model. To understand sexual problems, it helps to know Masters and Johnson's (1966) four-stage model of the sexual response.

1st stage: Excitement. The body becomes physiologically and sexually aroused, resulting in erection in the male and vaginal lubrication in the female.

2nd stage: Plateau. Sexual and physiological arousal continues in males and females.

3rd stage: Orgasm. Men have rhythmic muscle contractions that cause ejaculation of sperm. Women experience similar rhythmic muscle contractions of pelvic area. During orgasm, women and men report very pleasurable feelings.

4th stage: Resolution. Physiological responses return to normal.

Sexual problems can occur at different stages. For example, some individuals cannot reach stage 1, excitement, while others can reach stages 1 and 2 but not stage 3, orgasm.

There were few successful treatments for sexual problems until Masters and Johnson (1970) published their program. Their program has several stages. First, the therapist provides basic information about the sexual response and helps the couple communicate their feelings. Then the therapist gives the couple "homework," which is designed to reduce performance anxiety. Homework involves learning to pleasure one's partner without genital touching or making sexual demands. This nongenital pleasuring is called *sensate focus.* After using sensate focus, the couple moves on to genital touching and intercourse. Sex therapists have expanded and modified Masters and Johnson's program and report considerable success with many sexual problems (Wincze & Carey, 1991).

We'll discuss two common sexual problems and their treatments.

Premature Ejaculation

John and Susan had been married for three years and were both 28 years old. When the clinician asked about their problem, Susan said that sex was over in about 30 seconds because that's how long it took for John to have an orgasm. John replied that he had always reached orgasm very quickly and didn't realize it was a problem. Susan said that it was a problem for her (Althof, 1995). John's problem is called premature ejaculation.

Premature or *rapid ejaculation* refers to persistent or recurrent absence of voluntary control over ejaculation, in that the male ejaculates with minimal sexual stimulation before, upon, or shortly after penetration and before he wishes to.

Premature ejaculation is the most common male sexual problem, which is reported by 30–40% of adult men (Althof, 1995). A common treatment for it is called the squeeze technique. First, the partner stimulates the man's penis to nearly full erection. Then, the partner squeezes the head of the penis, which reduces arousal and erection. This squeeze procedure is repeated until the male develops a sense of control over arousal and ejaculation (Sarwer & Durlak, 1997). This procedure has proved successful in treating premature ejaculation.

Inhibited Female Orgasm

Greta and Bill had been married for five years and were in their late 20s. When asked about their problem, Greta said that she didn't think she had ever had an orgasm. She added that she loved Bill very much but that she was becoming less interested in sex (Barlow & Durand, 1995). Greta's problem is called inhibited female orgasm.

Inhibited female orgasm refers to a persistent delay or absence of orgasm after becoming aroused and excited.

About 5–10% of females never or almost never reach orgasm, and about 30% do not have orgasms during intercourse. Difficulty in reaching orgasm is the most common complaint of women seeking help for sexual problems (Sarwer & Durlak, 1997).

Psychological treatment begins with sensate focus, during which the couple learns to pleasure each other and the woman learns to relax and enjoy her body's sensations. The man is told how to help a woman reach orgasm, for example, by using his hand or, in Greta's case, using a vibrator (Barlow & Durand, 1995). This program has proved successful in treating inhibited female orgasm.

Next, we'll discuss a sexual problem that involves a potentially deadly transmitted disease—AIDS.

AIDS: Acquired Immune Deficiency Syndrome

What is the definition of AIDS?

On June 5, 1981, the United States Centers for Disease Control issued a brief report describing five gay men in Los Angeles with a rare form of pneumonia; eventually this pneumonia was determined to be one symptom of AIDS. By 1993, only 13 years later, between 1 and 4 million people in over 130 countries had AIDS, and about 17 million were infected with the human immunodeficiency virus (HIV), which is believed to be responsible for AIDS. As of January 1, 1993, the definition of AIDS was changed by the U.S. Centers for Disease Control and Prevention (1992).

HIV positive refers to the presence of HIV antibodies, which means that the individual has been infected by the human immunodeficiency virus (HIV).

AIDS (Acquired Immune Deficiency Syndrome) is a life-threatening condition that, by the latest definition, is present when the individual is HIV positive and has a level of T-cells (CD4 immune cells) of no more than 200 per cubic milliliter of blood (one-fifth of the level of a healthy person) or has developed one or more of 26 specified illnesses (including recurrent pneumonia and skin cancer).

The new definition of AIDS, which added the criterion of a T-cell level below 200, means that some people who were previously defined as being HIV positive will now be defined as having AIDS, even if they have not developed an illness.

In 1997, there were about 30.6 million cases of AIDS worldwide and 860,000 cases of AIDS in the United States (Freiberg, 1998). The tragedy of AIDS is brought home to us when it affects well-known individuals. In 1991, Magic Johnson, who played for the Lakers basketball team, announced that he was HIV positive. In 1995, Greg Louganis (above photo), who won four Olympic gold medals for diving, announced that he had AIDS. We'll discuss three major issues involving AIDS.

Risk for AIDS

As the graph below shows, those at greatest risk for AIDS in the United States are gay men and heterosexual intravenous drug users. In 1996, for the first time, the incidence of AIDS fell 6% in the United States, falling to second place as the leading cause of death among American men between the ages of 25 and 44 (Cimons, 1997).

The risk of AIDS among heterosexual couples has been gradually increasing, from 0.5% of couples in 1981 to 8.0% in 1996. Worldwide, AIDS is primarily spread through heterosexual intercourse (70 to 75%), and three women develop the disease for every two men (Elmer-Dewitt, 1997).

The HIV virus survives best in blood tissues and some bodily fluids, such as semen and vaginal fluids. The HIV virus cannot survive in air, in water, or on things that people touch. There are no reports of getting AIDS through casual contact, such as through touch.

How they get AIDS

7%	Gay intravenous drug users
8%	Heterosexual contact
12%	Other
25%	Heterosexual intravenous drug users
48%	Homosexual contact

Source: Centers for Disease Control and Prevention (1997)

Progression of Disease

Researchers' current concepts about how AIDS progresses are very different from their original ideas. After infection, the AIDS virus replicates rapidly and intensively. As a result, newly infected individuals are 100–1000 times more infectious than they are throughout the remainder of the disease (Koopman, 1995). In addition, newly infected individuals have no symptoms and the presence of antibodies to the HIV virus cannot be confirmed biochemically for at least 60 days. Thus, the newly infected person is regarded as a walking time bomb.

HIV destroys T-cells (CD4 cells), which are immune cells that fight off toxic agents (viruses and bacteria). It takes an average of seven years for a person infected with HIV to develop AIDS (T-count below 200) and another 2–3 years after that to develop diseases that result in death. A person with AIDS is especially susceptible to infections and diseases because the HIV virus destroys his or her immune system.

Because of yet unknown qualities of their immune systems, about 10 to 17% of HIV-infected indivuals will be AIDS-free 20 years after infection. Researchers are studying these AIDS-free individuals to find out how their immune systems can fight off AIDS.

Treatment

For the first time, in 1996 the number of AIDS-related deaths in the United States fell 23%, primarily because of several new breakthroughs—drugs that were introduced in 1995 (Cimons, 1997). A new drug treatment program has patients taking a drug "cocktail" of 10 to 20 pills daily, which include several new drugs (protease inhibitors). In many cases, these new drugs have reduced levels of HIV virus to undetectable levels for 30 months, greatly reduced life-threatening symptoms, and given AIDS patients a longer and better life (Rabkin & Ferrando, 1997).

However, researchers have found that not all patients are helped by these drugs. Also, they are very expensive ($15,000 a year); and if a patient stops taking these drugs, the HIV virus, which "hides out" in the body, returns again (Altman, 1997; Siliciano, 1997).

Next, we'll return to the social-cultural influences on sexual behavior by examining the tradition of female circumcision.

E. Cultural Diversity: Female Circumcision

Worthwhile Tradition or Cruel Mutilation?

Males have a long history of trying to control the sexual motivation of females. In many countries, men want to marry virgins and insist that women remain so until marriage, although the men do not hold themselves to the same standards. One extreme example of men controlling the sexual motivation and behavior of women is found in parts of Africa and the Arabian Peninsula, where young girls are circumcised before they become sexually mature (Caldwell et al., 1997).

Female circumcision involves cutting away the female's external genitalia, usually including her clitoris and surrounding skin (labia minora). The remaining edges are sewn together, which leaves only a small opening for urination and menstruation.

Soraya Mire (above photo) remembers the day that her mother said, "I'm going to buy you some gifts." Soraya, who was 13, obediently got into the car with her mother and driver. They didn't go

shopping but stopped at a doctor's house. Once inside, they went into an operating room where a doctor asked Soraya to lie on the operating table. He tied her feet down with a rope so she could not move. Her mother said that it was time for Soraya to become a woman and undergo female circumcision.

Like her mother and her mother's mother, Soraya underwent this ancient rite of passage. But unlike them, Soraya has decided to break the silence and fight this cruel mutilation. Now 33, Soraya has made a documentary called *Fire Eyes* to protest the current practice of female circumcision (Tawa, 1995).

Researchers estimate that currently over 100 million women have undergone circumcision, which is currently practiced in about 26 African countries by peoples of different socioeconomic classes and ethnic and cultural groups (Caldwell et al., 1997).

What Is Its Purpose?

In many of the poorer societies of Africa and Ethiopia, female circumcision is a common ritual to physically mark young girls and increase their chances for future marriage. Most recently, conservative Muslim clerics in Egypt overturned a government ban on female circumcision, which serves no hygienic or medically useful purpose (Daniszewski, 1997).

Girls are commonly circumcised before they reach puberty, usually between the ages of four and ten. The primary reason for female circumcision is the male's belief that if females are surgically deprived of receiving sexual pleasure they will remain clean and virginal until marriage. Men in these societies often refuse to marry a woman who has not been circumcised because they believe that she is unclean and not a virgin (Walker & Parmar, 1993).

The male equivalent of female circumcision would be amputation of the male's penis.

Are There Complications?

Because of the high social status of Soraya's father, who was a general, her circumcision was performed by a doctor. However, in the majority of cases, it is done by someone with no medical training who uses a razor blade and less than sterile procedures.

Because the genital area has a high percentage of nerves and blood vessels, female circumcision results in severe pain, bleeding, and even hemorrhaging, which can lead to shock and death. Because of poor surgical procedures, girls endure a number of medical complications, including infections, cysts, and permanent scarring. This procedure also makes menstruation and intercourse painful and childbirth dangerous (Caldwell et al., 1997).

Girls who live in communities where female circumcision carries a high social value submit to the fear, pain, and trauma so as to gain social status, please their parents, and comply with peer pressure. However, many circumcised women suffer chronic anxiety and depression from worry about their disfigured genitals, difficulties with menstruation, and fear of infertility (Caldwell et al., 1997).

Is There a Solution?

The United Nations health organizations have endorsed anti-circumcision laws, but such laws would not eliminate the strong sociocultural traditions that exist in many of the villages that currently practice this procedure. As one supporter of circumcision said, "This procedure helps to keep women's sexual drives at acceptable and reasonable levels" (Daniszewski, 1997). Although Westerners are horrified by this barbaric practice, many African societies consider this practice part of their culture. For example, when a newspaper in Ghana, Africa, published articles in favor of banning female circumcision, local women had great success in drumming up support for keeping this ancient practice and rejecting values from the outside world.

A number of feminists in Africa and Egypt have formed a society to fight the sexual mutilation of females, but they have encountered considerable resistance from both men and women who wish to maintain the practice (Caldwell et al., 1997). Female circumcision is an extreme example of how far human societies (men) have gone to control the sexual behavior of females.

We have discussed two biological drives, hunger and sex. After the Concept Review, we'll examine an important social need—achievement.

CONCEPT REVIEW

1. Physiological or psychological factors that cause us to act in a specific way at a particular time are included in the definition of _____.

2. Innate biological forces predispose an animal to behave in a particular way in the presence of a specific environmental condition. These ways of behaving are called _____.

3. A biological need produces a state of arousal during which the organism engages in behaviors to reduce the need. This state of arousal is called a (a)_____. Once a need is satisfied, the body returns to a more balanced state, called (b)_____. This need-drive-homeostasis sequence is described by the (c)_____ theory.

4. External stimuli, reinforcers, goals, or rewards that may be positive or negative and that motivate one's behavior are called _____.

5. When we perform behaviors to reduce biological needs or obtain various incentives, we are acting under the influence of (a)_____ motivation. When we perform behaviors because they are personally rewarding or because we are following our personal goals, beliefs, or expectations, we are acting under the influence of (b)_____ motivation.

6. Needs that are not critical to your survival but that are acquired through learning and socialization, such as the needs for achievement or affiliation, are called (a)_____ needs. Needs that are critical to your survival and physical well-being, such as food, water, and sex, are called (b)_____ needs.

7. The ascending order or hierarchy with biological needs at the bottom and social needs at the top is _____. This idea assumes that we satisfy our biological needs before satisfying our social needs.

8. There are three major factors that influence eating. Cues that come from physiological changes are called (a)_____ factors. Cues that come from inherited instructions are called (b)_____ factors. Cues that come from learning and personality traits are called (c)_____ factors.

9. Biological cues for hunger that come from the stomach, liver, intestines, and fat cells are called (a)_____ cues. Biological cues that come from the brain are called (b)_____ cues.

10. The part of the hypothalamus that is involved in feelings of being hungry is called the (a)_____; the part that is involved in feelings of being full is called the (b)_____.

11. We inherit the following genetic factors involved in weight regulation: a certain number of (a)_____ cells that store fat; a certain (b)_____ rate that regulates how fast we burn off fuel; a certain (c)_____ point that maintains a stable amount of body fat; and weight-regulating (d)_____ that influence appetite, metabolism, and hormone secretion.

12. Psychological factors that influence eating include (a)_____ associations, (b)_____ influences, and (c)_____ variables.

13. Genetic sex factors involve the 23rd chromosome, called the (a)_____, which determines the sex of the child. Biological sex factors include sex hormones, which for the male are called (b)_____ and for the female are called (c)_____. Psychological sex factors include the subjective feeling of being male or female, which is called (d)_____; adopting behaviors and traits that society identifies as male or female, which is called (e)_____; and being more sexually aroused by members of the same or opposite sex, which is called (f)_____.

14. Evidence from the sexual orientation of identical twins and the shared genetic material from gay brothers are examples of (a)_____ factors in the development of a homosexual orientation. Young boys who prefer girls' toys and girl playmates and engage in opposite-sex behaviors show a tendency to develop a homosexual orientation, which shows the effects of (b)_____ factors on sexual orientation.

% Male Homosexuals 2.8%

% Female Homosexuals 1.4%

15. A person who has been infected by the human immunodeficiency virus but has not yet developed any illnesses is said to be (a)_____. A person whose level of T-cells has dropped to 200 per cubic milliliter of blood but who may or may not have developed an illness is defined as having (b)_____.

Answers: *1. motivation; 2. fixed action patterns; 3. (a) drive, (b) homeostasis, (c) drive-reduction; 4. incentives; 5. (a) extrinsic, (b) intrinsic; 6. (a) social, (b) biological; 7. Maslow's hierarchy of needs; 8. (a) biological, (b) genetic, (c) psychosocial; 9 (a) peripheral, (b) central; 10. (a) lateral hypothalamus, (b) ventromedial hypothalamus; 11. (a) fat, (b) metabolic, (c) set, (d) genes; 12. (a) learned, (b) social-cultural, (c) personality; 13. (a) sex chromosome, (b) androgens, (c) estrogens, (d) gender identity, (e) gender role, (f) sexual orientation; 14. (a) genetic, (b) psychological; 15. (a) HIV positive, (b) AIDS.*

F. Achievement

Definition

Why did Victor succeed when his friends didn't?

At the beginning of the module, we told you about Victor, an African American high school student whose buddies called him a "White boy" because they thought he was studying too hard. "You can't be cool if you're smart," says Victor, who was Mission Bay High's student body president, had a 3.7 (A–) grade point average, and will attend the University of Southern California in the fall (adapted from the *San Diego Union-Tribune,* June 17, 1994).

Victor (right photo) grew up with an obstacle that goes largely unnoticed and is rarely discussed in public: pressure from students in the same racial or ethnic group not to succeed in the classroom (Steele, 1995). Faced with this negative peer pressure, principally from Latino, African American, and Native American teenage boys, some minority students stop studying, don't do homework, avoid answering questions in class, join gangs, or even drop out of school.

Educators believe that the high dropout rates for minorities result, in part, from peer pressure not to succeed in school or show academic achievement (Portillo, 1994). For Victor, academic achievement was one of many social needs.

Social needs are those acquired through learning and experience.

Social needs include desire for affiliation or close social bonds; nurturance or need to help and protect others; dominance or need to influence or control others; and achievement or need to excel (Murray, 1938). The fact that you are in college suggests that you are showing your social need for achievement.

The *achievement need* refers to the desire to set challenging goals and to persist in pursuing those goals in the face of obstacles, frustrations, and setbacks.

The achievement need is not only a major concern of college students but also ranks high (level 4 out of 5) in Maslow's hierarchy of needs. We'll discuss four questions related to the achievement need: How is the need for achievement measured? What is high need for achievement? What is fear of failure? What is underachievement?

How Is the Need for Achievement Measured?

You could simply ask people if they had a great need to achieve, but, depending on social pressures, their answers might be biased, untrue, or otherwise unreliable. To obtain a more reliable measure of a person's need for achievement, psychologists David McClelland and John Atkinson used the Thematic Apperception Test (TAT).

The *Thematic Apperception Test,* commonly called the *TAT,* is a personality test in which subjects are asked to look at pictures of people in ambiguous situations and to make up stories about what the characters are thinking and feeling and what the outcome will be.

For example, the TAT card on the left shows a younger woman with a concerned expression and an older woman staring out from the background. If you were taking the TAT test, you would be asked to describe what is happening in this card. In measuring the level of achievement, your stories would be scored in terms of achievement themes such as setting goals, competing, or overcoming obstacles (Atkinson, 1958; McClelland et al., 1953). The TAT test assumes that the strength of your need to achieve will be reflected in the kind of thoughts and feelings that you use to describe the TAT cards. However, TAT stories are difficult to score reliably because there is no objective way to identify which thoughts and feelings indicate level of achievement (Keiser & Prather, 1990). For that reason, achievement is often measured with more objective paper-and-pencil tests because they are easier to administer and score and have better reliability and validity than does the TAT (Kaplan & Saccuzzo, 1997).

What Is High Need for Achievement?

There is perhaps no better example of individuals with high need for achievement than Olympic athletes. One example is Shannon Miller (photo below), who from a very early age trained for hours each day, gave up the fun and games that most children take for granted, and endured the stress and frustration of competition for a dozen years to achieve her final goal, winning four medals in gymnastics at the 1992 Olympics. Shannon is a perfect example of someone with a high need for achievement (Atkinson & Raynor, 1974; McClelland, 1985).

High need for achievement is shown by those who persist longer at tasks; perform better on tasks, activities, or exams; set challenging but realistic goals; compete with others to win; and are attracted to careers that require initiative.

Although the vast majority of us will not make the Olympics or achieve an A average, most of us exhibit varying degrees of need to achieve, by doing our best, striving for social recognition, and working to achieve material rewards (Snow & Jackson, 1994). The need for achievement influences and motivates many of your behaviors.

If we consider one side of a coin to be a need for achievement, the opposite side is fear of failure.

Fear of Failure

Why do some fail to reach their goal?

Just as some individuals may be motivated by a need for achievement, others may be motivated by a fear of failure. Atkinson (1964) believed that, in order to understand fully why a person succeeds or fails in reaching a goal, we must examine not only that person's need for achievement but also his or her fear of failure.

Fear of failure is shown by people who are motivated to avoid failure by choosing easy, nonchallenging tasks where failure is unlikely or difficult.

For example, fear of failure may motivate a student to study just enough to avoid failing an exam but not enough to get a good grade or set higher academic goals. In fact, the fear of failure is a good predictor of poor grades: the greater a student's fear of failure, the poorer his or her grades (Herman, 1990). Atkinson believed that just as people vary in their need for achievement, they also vary in their motivation to avoid failure. Atkinson said that individuals who are motivated primarily by a fear of failure would never do as well, work as hard, or set goals as high as those who were motivated by a need for achievement.

Self-handicapping. If a person is motivated primarily by the fear of failure, how does this individual explain his or her poor performances yet keep a good self-image? One solution to this problem is to make up excuses, which is called self-handicapping (Jones & Berglas, 1978).

Self-handicapping refers to a tendency to do things that contribute to failure and then to use these things as excuses for failures in performance, activities, or achieving goals.

Some of the more popular self-handicapping excuses are to use concerns about health (missed sleep, have a cold), drug usage (have a hangover), or chance/fate (it was bad luck, could only happen to me). Although self-handicapping excuses help preserve our positive self-image, they interfere with taking personal responsibility to achieve our goals (Berglas, 1989).

One example of how fear of failure affects motivation is seen in underachievers.

Underachievement

Why do some underachieve?

One of my friends described his 14-year-old son, Rich, as having all the brains in the world but doing nothing with them. Although Rich is a computer wizard, he gets terrible grades in school, never does his homework, and doesn't seem to have any ambition. Rich might be called an underachiever.

Underachievers are individuals who score relatively high on tests of ability or intelligence but perform more poorly than their scores would predict.

The most common example of underachievers consists of students who score relatively high on ability or intelligence tests but perform poorly in school or academic settings (Lupart & Pyryt, 1996). Researchers found that underachievement is not related to socioeconomic class, that there are two or three male underachievers for every female, and that about 15% of students are underachievers (McCall, 1994).

Characteristics. The psychological characteristics of underachievers include having a poor self-concept, low self-esteem, and poor peer relations and being shy. The cognitive characteristics of underachievers include fear of failure, poor perceptions of their abilities, and lack of persistence. This means that underachievers are less likely to persist in getting their college degrees, holding on to jobs, or maintaining their marriages (McCall, 1994). Thus, underachievement reduces performance in academic, job, and marital settings, and its effects may last through adulthood.

The paradox of underachievement is that underachievers have the abilities but are not motivated to use them. Clinicians, counselors, and researchers are developing treatment programs to help underachievers change their psychological traits and cognitive perceptions so they will have the motivation to use their considerable abilities (McCall, 1994).

Three Components

Why is a person successful?

Explaining why a person is a successful student, parent, teacher, programmer, salesperson, or waiter involves the interaction of the three components that we have just discussed: need for achievement; fear of failure; and presence of psychological and cognitive factors, such as self-concept, self-esteem, and confidence in one's abilities. For example, researchers wondered why some minority children from low-income homes were successful in school while others were not. Those minority students who succeeded had higher self-esteem, greater confidence in their abilities, and received more support and encouragement from a parent or caregiver (Finn & Rock, 1997). In addition, successful students not only worked harder but liked what they were doing. This "enjoyment of work" is an important cognitive factor that can greatly influence motivation, which is our next topic.

Need for achievement — Fear of failure — Psychological and cognitive factors

HOW SUCCESSFUL?

F. Achievement

Cognitive Factors

Each year, over 1,600 seniors compete in the Westinghouse Science Talent Search to win the most prestigious high school science award in the United States. One winner was Ann Chen (left photo), a high school senior from California. Chen's project involved studying how genes function in the spread of cancer. When interviewed after receiving her award, Chen said that science has been a life-long love and interest for her (Balint, 1995). Chen's love of science translates into a motivating force that comes from cognitive factors.

Cognitive factors in motivation refer to how people evaluate or perceive a situation and how these evaluations and perceptions influence their willingness to work.

Ann Chen perceives science projects as interesting and enjoyable and works hard to complete them. Other students find science projects boring and tedious and complete them only because they are required. The difference between being motivated by love of science or by course requirement illustrates the difference between intrinsic and extrinsic motivation.

Competence Self-determination Curiosity Enjoyment Interest

INTRINSIC MOTIVATION

Intrinsic motivation involves engaging in certain activities or behaviors without receiving any external rewards because the behaviors themselves are personally rewarding or because engaging in these activities fulfills our beliefs or expectations.

Extrinsic motivation involves engaging in certain activities or behaviors that either reduce biological needs or help us obtain incentives and external rewards.

Being motivated because you love the work indicates intrinsic motivation, which is related to competence, self-determination, curiosity, enjoyment, and interest. Being motivated because the work is required indicates extrinsic motivation, which is related to competition, evaluation, recognition, money, and incentives, such as a nice house. The major advantage of working because of intrinsic motivation (loving what you're doing) is that you will feel powerfully motivated. Without intrinsic motivation, there would be very little charitable work or donations; very few people would volunteer their time or donate their blood.

Competition Evaluation Recognition Incentive Money

EXTRINSIC MOTIVATION

Intrinsic Motivation

What would happen if people were suddenly paid for doing something they usually did from intrinsic motivation, such as donate blood? Researchers generally thought that if people were given external rewards (money, awards, prizes, or tokens) for doing tasks (donating blood) that they formerly did from intrinsic motivation, their performance of these tasks would decrease (Cameron & Pierce, 1994).

Because the finding that external rewards decreased intrinsic motivation was widely accepted, many books advised that rewards should not be used in educational settings, hospitals, or volunteer organizations because such rewards would do more harm than good. However, researchers recently reanalyzed the past 25 years of studies on intrinsic motivation and reached two different conclusions. First, they found that any decrease in intrinsic interest resulting from an external reward was so small as to not be detected by statistical analysis of hundreds of studies.

Second, they found that verbal praise, which is a form of external reward, did not decrease intrinsic interest but rather increased it (Carton, 1996; Eisenberger & Cameron, 1996).

For a long time, it was also thought that external rewards automatically decreased creative work and interest. But researchers have found that the effects of giving children a reward for completing a creative task depends on how they perceive the reward. If they perceive the reward as a treat, it will increase their intrinsic interest, but if they see the reward as an external pressure to be creative, it will decrease their intrinsic interest (Eisenberger & Armeli, 1997).

These studies show that, unlike previously thought, external rewards do not automatically decrease intrinsic interest and that verbal praise actually increases intrinsic motivation. Research on intrinsic motivation shows how cognitive factors, such as how you perceive situations, influence your motivation and achievement (Hayamizu, 1997).

Next, we'll examine how cognitive factors have greatly influenced children's motivation and achievement in school.

G. Research Focus: Immigrant Students
How Do Immigrant Children Do In School?

Immigrant Children

Why were they doing so well?

Sometimes psychologists find a situation that is very puzzling because, according to the best educated guesses, what is happening is not what anyone expected. Here's the situation.

As you visit a junior high school, the teacher explains that some of the students have only recently immigrated to the United States while others were born here. You are asked to guess which group of children is getting better grades: the children who had recently immigrated or those who had been born in the United States.

Certainly the best guess would be that children born in the United States would be getting the better grades. That's because the newly arrived immigrant children would have a number of considerable handicaps. They would have to learn a new language, adjust to new cultural norms and expectations, and get over feeling socially isolated from the other children who had been born and raised in the United States. What researchers actually found surprised everyone.

Procedure

To answer the question, "How well do immigrant children do in school?" researchers analyzed data from a representative sample of 24,599 eighth-grade students who came from 1,052 randomly selected schools in the United States. The students were Latino, Asian, Black (mostly from the Caribbean), and White (Kao & Tienda, 1995).

Researchers compared the academic performance of three different groups of students, but we'll focus on two groups. One group was the first generation students, which meant both the student and his or her mother were foreign born. The other group was third generation students, which meant that both the student and his or her mother were native born (born in the United States).

In order to compare the performance of first and third generation students, researchers used standardized tests for math and reading. Standardized tests mean that questions were previously shown to be appropriate for eighth-grade students. At the end of the test, students were asked about their future academic plans, such as, "Do you intend to go to college?"

Results

In the graph on the right, notice that there are three pairs of bars, and each pair compares the math scores of first and third generation Asian, Latino, and Black *immigrant* students. In each case, the first generation immigrant students, who faced the most difficulties in language and social adjustment, performed better on math tests (and other tests not shown) than did the third generation students who were born in the United States.

This result was unexpected, as was the finding that first generation students intended to go to college at a higher rate than did third generation students.

Conclusions

Perhaps this difference in scores between first and third generation students was due to different socioeconomic conditions. However, after controlling (by using statistics) for socioeconomic class differences, researchers found that the major reason for the greater performance of first generation minority students was that they had adopted their parents' *hopeful values* about education.

Parental Values. The first generation immigrant mothers and fathers believed that their children would achieve social and economic advantages by obtaining a good education. The parents' hopeful values about educational opportunities translated into encouraging their children to work together, help one another, and spend a significant amount of time doing homework (three hours nightly).

In comparison, third generation parents who have lived for some years in the United States have become less hopeful about making advances through education. Because they are less hopeful about educational opportunities, they pass along a negative attitude about doing well in school. In turn, negative parental attitudes translate into their children having less motivation, spending less time doing homework, performing poorer on tests, and having less desire to go on to college (Kao & Tienda, 1995). This study shows how cognitive factors, in this case parents' optimistic or pessimistic attitudes toward education, translate into encouraging or discouraging their children, which in turn increases or decreases their children's motivation, performance, and academic achievement.

We have discussed how cognitive or psychological factors can influence social needs, such as achievement, performance, and motivation (Eaton & Dembo, 1997). Next, we'll discuss how various psychological factors also influence a basic biological need and result in serious eating disorders.

Math Scores

| 0 | 40 | 45 | 50 |

First generation Asian

Third generation Asian

First generation Latino

Third generation Latino

First generation Black

Third generation Black

A. THEORIES OF MOTIVATION

1. The combined physiological and psychological factors that cause you to act in specific ways at particular times are referred to as (a)_____. When motivated, you usually exhibit three characteristics: you are (b)_____ to do something; you (c)_____ your energies toward a specific goal; and you have different (d)_____ of feelings about reaching that goal.

2. There are four general theories to explain human motivation. One theory, which applies primarily to animal motivation, involves innate biological forces that determine behavior. This is called the (a)_____ theory. Another theory explains human motivation in terms of a need that results in a drive, by which we are motivated to engage in activities to return to a more balanced state. This is called the (b)_____ theory. Because this theory does not explain why we continue to perform after our needs are met or why we perform risky behaviors, other theories were developed. The theory that says that we are motivated by external rewards is called the (c)_____ theory. The theory that distinguishes between extrinsic and intrinsic motivations is called the (d)_____ theory. If we are motivated because we find the activities personally rewarding or because they fulfill our beliefs or expectations, our motivation is said to be (e)_____.

B. BIOLOGICAL & SOCIAL NEEDS

3. Food, water, and sleep are examples of (a)_____ needs. In comparison, needs that are acquired through learning and socialization are called (b)_____ needs. The theory that we satisfy our needs in ascending order, with physiological needs first and social needs later, is called (c)_____.

According to this theory, needs are divided into five levels: biological, safety, love and belongingness, esteem, and self-actualization.

C. HUNGER

4. If there is an almost perfect balance between how much food an organism needs to maintain the body's energy needs and how much the organism actually eats, the organism's weight is said to be (a)_____. Three different factors influence the hunger drive. Factors that come from physiological changes in blood chemistry and signals from digestive organs that provide feedback to the brain, which, in turn, triggers us to eat or stop eating, are called (b)_____ factors. Factors that come from learned associations between food and other stimuli, sociocultural influences, and various personality problems are called (c)_____ factors. Factors that come from inherited instructions contained in our genes are called (d)_____ factors.

5. Biological factors that influence eating come from two different sources. Cues arising from physiological changes in your blood chemistry and signals from your body organs are called (a)_____; cues from your brain are called (b)_____.

6. Genetic factors that influence hunger come from four different sources: the number of cells that store fat, which are called (a)_____; your rate of burning the body's fuel, which is called your (b)_____; the body's tendency to keep a stable amount of fat deposits, which is called the (c)_____; and a number of (d)_____ genes that influence appetite, metabolism, and secretion of hormones regulating fat stores.

D. SEXUAL BEHAVIOR

7. Human sexual behavior is influenced by three different factors. Inherited instructions for the development of sexual organs, hormonal changes at puberty, and neural circuits that control sexual reflexes are called (a)_____ factors. The fact that humans engage in sexual behavior for many reasons besides reproduction and the fact that humans experience sexual difficulties that have no physical or medical basis indicate the influence of (b)_____ factors on sexual behavior. Factors that regulate the secretion of sex hormones, which play a role in the development of secondary sexual characteristics, influence sexual motivation (more so in animals than humans), regulate the development of ova and sperm, and control the female menstrual cycle are called (c)_____ factors.

8. Biological sex factors include the secretion of sex hormones, which is controlled by an area of the brain called the (a)_____. The major male sex hormones secreted by the testes are called (b)_____, and the major female sex hormones secreted by the ovaries are (c)_____. Assuming that hormone levels are within the normal range, there is little (d)_____ between levels of sex hormones and sexual motivation in humans.

9. Three psychological sex factors include the individual's subjective experience and feelings of being a male or a female, which is called (a)_____; traditional or stereotypic behaviors, attitudes, and personality traits that society designates as masculine or feminine, which are called (b)_____; and whether a person is sexually aroused primarily by members of his or her own sex, the opposite sex, or both sexes, which is called (c)_____.

10. The findings that identical twins are often alike in their sexual orientation and that homosexual brothers shared similar inherited material indicate the influence of (a)_____ factors on homosexual orientation. The finding that genetic factors do not necessarily determine sexual orientation indicates the influence of (b)_____ factors on sexual orientation.

11. There are two kinds of sexual problems. Problems that are characterized by repetitive or preferred sexual fantasies involving nonhuman objects (articles of clothing) are called (a)_____. Problems of sexual arousal or orgasm that interfere with adequate functioning during sexual behavior are called (b)_____. When a person seeks help for a sexual problem, the clinician will check whether the causes are (c)_____ or

_____.

12. If a person has been infected by the human immunodeficiency virus (HIV) but has not yet developed one or more of 26 illnesses, that person is said to be (a)_____. A person whose level of T-cells (CD4 immune cells) has dropped to below 200 per cubic milliliter of blood (one-fifth the level of a healthy person) and who may or may not have any other symptoms is said to have (b)_____.

E. CULTURAL DIVERSITY: FEMALE CIRCUMCISION

13. In some cultures the female's external genitalia, usually including her clitoris and surrounding skin (labia minora), are cut away; this practice is called _____. Girls often submit to the fear, pain, and trauma of this procedure so as to gain social status, please their parents, and comply with peer pressure. A number of feminists in Africa have formed a society to fight the sexual mutilation of females.

F. ACHIEVEMENT

14. High in Maslow's needs hierarchy is a desire to set challenging goals and persist in pursuing those goals in the face of obstacles, frustrations, and setbacks. This social need is called the (a)_____. Someone who persists longer at tasks, shows better performance on tasks, activities, or exams, sets challenging

but realistic goals, competes with others to win, and is attracted to careers that require initiative is said to have a high (b)_____. Individuals who score relatively high on tests of ability or intelligence but perform more poorly than their scores would predict are called (c)_____. Individuals who either choose easy, nonchallenging tasks or challenging tasks where failure is probable and expected are said to be motivated by (d)_____.

G. RESEARCH FOCUS: IMMIGRANT STUDENTS

15. Researchers found that the major reason for the greater success of first generation immigrant students was that they had taken on their (a)_____ hopeful outlook toward advancement through education. This study shows that parents' optimistic or pessimistic attitudes toward education, which are examples of (b)_____ factors, influence their children's academic achievement.

H. APPLICATION: EATING PROBLEMS & TREATMENT

16. A healthy weight-maintenance program, which can reduce the risk of serious medical problems of (a)_____ people, involves changing (b)_____ toward food, changing (c)_____ patterns, developing an (d)_____ program, and sticking to a long-term (e)_____ program. Two serious eating disorders include a pattern characterized by bingeing, fear of not being able to stop eating, and regularly purging the body, which is called (f)_____; and another pattern in which a person starves to remain thin, has a fear of being fat, and has a disturbed body image, which is called (g)_____.

Answers: *1. (a) motivation, (b) energized, (c) direct, (d) intensities; 2. (a) instinct, (b) drive-reduction, (c) incentive, (d) cognitive, (e) intrinsic; 3. (a) biological, (b) social, (c) Maslow's hierarchy of needs; 4. (a) ideal or optimum, (b) biological, (c) psychosocial, (d) genetic; 5. (a) peripheral cues, (b) central cues; 6. (a) fat cells, (b) metabolic rate, (c) set point, (d) weight-regulating; 7. (a) genetic, (b) psychological, (c) biological; 8. (a) hypothalamus, (b) androgens, (c) estrogens, (d) correlation or association; 9. (a) gender identity, (b) gender roles, (c) sexual orientation; 10. (a) genetic, (b) psychological; 11. (a) paraphilias, (b) sexual dysfunctions, (c) psychological, physiological; 12. (a) HIV positive, (b) AIDS; 13. female circumcision; 14. (a) achievement motive, (b) need for achievement, (c) underachievers, (d) fear of failure; 15. (a) parents', (b) cognitive or psychological; 16. (a) overweight, (b) attitudes, (c) eating, (d) exercise, (e) maintenance, (f) bulimia nervosa, (g) anorexia nervosa.*

CRITICAL THINKING

Newspaper Article

CHILDHOOD OBESITY: A LURKING HEALTH RISK

by Julie Marquis

Patricia Verdugo got used to being the biggest kid in her class, her round figure dwarfing her classmates even in kindergarten. With 220 pounds on her 4-foot, 10-inch frame, the third grader is starting to feel health consequences from being overweight, such as knee problems. And she winces when her 280-pound father mentions the daily dose of insulin he takes to control diabetes, but she knows the needles she dreads may become a fixture in her own life. Doctors say she is poised on the edge of the disease herself.

American children face this ordeal in rising numbers. About 11% of 6- to 17-year-olds are obese, and twice that number are overweight. That's up from 5% who were obese and 15% who were overweight in the 1960s.

"It is an impending time bomb," said Naomi Neufeld, a UCLA pediatric endocrinologist. "It's not going to kill them tomorrow, but in terms of a threat to long-term health, it affects more children than any other disease."

In general, experts believe that there are some common causes for obesity among the young: poor nutrition education, paltry opportunities for exercise, too much TV, and the glorification and overconsumption of fast food. In addition, they cite psychological and cultural factors: the concept of food as love, for example, and the equation, particularly among disadvantaged groups, of fat with healthfulness.

Parents may be poor role models. More than a third of adult Americans are overweight, and their children tend to take after them. But why does fat run in families? And why, in particular, does it run in American families? Most experts agree that weight gain is the product of some combination of genetic and environmental factors—with genes accounting for about 25% of the variation among individuals, according to one widely cited estimate.

Research has shown that certain minority groups, especially African American and Mexican American women, are at greater risk for obesity as adults. Though the differences are not as pronounced in children, the pattern emerges as early as preschool. The reasons for greater prevalence of obesity among some minorities is not clear, but different cultural standards of beauty may be a factor, as well as the deprivations of poverty. Poor children have fewer places to burn off energy, and their parents have more limited shopping options.

Source: *Los Angeles Times,* December 14, 1997.

---

1. What explanations have been given for the increasing incidence of childhood obesity?

2. Which children are at special risk for obesity?

3. Can you use two theories of motivation to explain childhood obesity?

4. How might biological, psychosocial, and genetic hunger factors contribute to childhood obesity?

5. What would you include in a community program to reduce the incidence of childhood obesity?

Study Questions

A. **Theories of Motivation**—Which theory best explains why students work hard to get good grades? (See answer in Critical Thinking Appendix.)

B. **Biological & Social Needs**—How would your needs change if you won a $20 million lottery? (See answer in Critical Thinking Appendix.)

C. **Hunger**—As a parent, what would you do to keep you and your children from becoming overweight?

D. **Sexual Behavior**—What would happen to someone's sexual behavior if, at puberty, no sex hormones were secreted?

E. **Cultural Diversity: Female Circumcision**—Are there any American cultural traditions that are detrimental to the sexual behavior of men or women?

F. **Achievement**—Why might some students get the "sophomore blues" and feel less motivated about doing well in college?

G. **Research Focus: Immigrant Students**—What is one key to unlocking the potential of students from different cultures?

H. **Application: Eating Problems & Treatment**—Would you believe an ad that promised you could "lose weight easily and quickly without dieting or exercise by practicing self-hypnosis"? (See answer in Critical Thinking Appendix.)

LINKS TO LEARNING

Web Sites & Learning Activities

● BROOKS/COLE ONLINE PSYCHOLOGY STUDY CENTER

http://psychstudy.brookscole.com/student/plotnik/quiz/ch15frm.html

This site gives students a chance to review material by taking quizzes and doing exercises and activities for this module.

● BEING HUMAN: MOTIVATION

http://www.cmhc.com/perspectives/columns/be0596.htm

This thoughtful article addresses the interplay between intrinsic and extrinsic motivational factors in real life.

● EMPOWERMENT NOW

http://www.empowerment-now.com/

This commercial site includes a range of information to help people get motivated, including quotes, research, and articles.

● THE PROCRASTINATOR'S AID

http://www.geocities.com/SouthBeach/1915/

Warning: this page is completely silly! If you are lacking in motivation and want a variety of jokes, quizzes, and other procrastination tools, this is your site.

● THE FEMALE GENITAL MUTILATION HOMEPAGE

http://www.hollyfeld.org/fgm/index.html

This comprehensive site offers articles, a bibliography, advocacy groups, legislation, and discussion forums relating to female genital mutilation.

Welcome to the WEB

● THE CENTER FOR EATING DISORDERS

http://www.eating-disorders.com/

This site offers background information on eating disorders, how to spot them, plus a discussion group and mailing list.

● OVEREATERS ANONYMOUS

http://www.overeatersanonymous.org/

This 12-step group is dedicated to helping those who compulsively overeat. The site contains information on the organization, locations of meetings, and an on-line quiz.

Activities

● *Integrator Online™ for Introductory Psychology* CD-ROM, Plotnik, Module 15

● Study Guide to accompany *Introduction to Psychology*, 5th edition, Module 15 (choice of PC or Mac computer version or hard copy)

● *PsychNow!* CD-ROM
Motivation

Answers to questions on page 356

1. Some explanations are poor nutrition, lack of exercise, too much TV, too much fast food, and social and psychological factors, such as equating food with love.
2. Children whose parents are obese, children with poor nutritional habits, and children in some minority groups are at higher risk for obesity.
3. According to drive-reduction theory, the hunger drive might be overactive in some people. According to cognitive theory, overeating fulfills our perceived cultural expectations.
4. Biological mechanisms may be different in obese people. Psychosocial influences may include family pressures, cultural factors, and learned associations between food and other stimuli. Some people may have a genetic predisposition to obesity.
5. You might include education about nutrition, exercise, and health risks; family involvement and counseling; and positive reinforcement for healthy behavior.

Module 16 EMOTION

A. Peripheral Theories 360

* **SEQUENCE FOR EMOTIONS**
* **JAMES-LANGE THEORY**
* **FACIAL FEEDBACK THEORY**

B. Cognitive Appraisal Theory 362

* **SCHACHTER-SINGER EXPERIMENT**
* **WHICH COMES FIRST: FEELING OR THINKING?**
* **COGNITIVE APPRAISAL THEORY**
* **AFFECTIVE-PRIMACY THEORY**

C. Universal Facial Expressions 364

* **DEFINITION**
* **CROSS-CULTURAL EVIDENCE**
* **GENETIC EVIDENCE**

D. Functions of Emotions 365

* **SOCIAL SIGNALS**
* **ADAPTATION AND SURVIVAL**
* **AROUSAL AND MOTIVATION**

Difficult tasks: low arousal is optimal

Most tasks: medium arousal is optimal

Easy or simple tasks: high arousal may be optimal

Difficulty of tasks

← Level of arousal

E. Happiness 366

* **DEFINITION**
* **ADAPTATION LEVEL THEORY**
* **LONG-TERM HAPPINESS**

F. Cultural Diversity: Emotions Across Cultures 367

* **DISPLAYING EMOTIONS IN PUBLIC**
* **PERCEIVING INTENSITY OF EMOTIONS**

G. Research Focus: Emotions in the Brain 369

Middle view

Sad: increased activity

* **WHERE DOES THE BRAIN MAKE EMOTIONS?**

H. Application: Lie Detection 370

* **WHAT IS THE THEORY?**
* **WHAT IS A LIE DETECTOR TEST?**
* **HOW ACCURATE ARE LIE DETECTOR TESTS?**

Critical question: "Did you rob the liquor store?"

Subject's answer: "No."

Emotional Experience

What did Rick feel during a shark attack?

What happened to Rick at 7:30 in the morning on a warm Thursday was something he would never forget. He had paddled his surfboard about 150 feet from shore to catch the best waves. As he waited, he saw a large green sea turtle swim by and disappear under the deep blue surface. Moments later he felt the water under him start to move and saw some colors and swirls but thought it must be the turtle swimming around. It wasn't a turtle but a 14-foot tiger shark, a very dangerous killing machine. With one quick motion of its head, the shark tossed Rick and his surfboard out of the water. When the board landed, Rick was hanging on the back of the board while the shark was sinking its rows of jagged teeth into the front of the board.

As Rick hung on, he heard his heart pounding like a hammer and then a loud snapping sound as the shark broke off a piece of Rick's surfboard. Looking down into the water, Rick saw one of the shark's big eyes staring right at him, and he felt his adrenaline pumping. After what seemed like forever, the shark swam away with a big piece of Rick's surfboard stuck in its mouth.

Rick pulled himself onto what was left of his surfboard and paddled toward shore. When he reached the shallows, he stood up on still-shaking knees and walked to the beach, where a crowd had gathered. Rick showed them his board with the big piece missing (above photo) and was thankful he wasn't missing a leg or arm.

It was almost a month before Rick was able to go surfing again. As he paddled out, this time with about 20 others, he began to have a weird, terrible feeling that something bad was going to happen again (adapted from the *Los Angeles Times,* February 8, 1993).

Rick experienced a variety of different emotions during and after his shark attack. During the attack, he felt intense anxiety and fear for his life. When he reached shore safely, he felt relief and happiness for having survived with all his limbs intact. Sometime later, he felt some fright and apprehension about surfing again. Although Rick experienced a half-dozen different emotions, they all shared the same four components (Winter & Kuiper, 1997).

An *emotion* is defined in terms of four components. First, you interpret or appraise some stimulus (event, object, or thought) in terms of your well-being. Second, you have a subjective feeling, such as fear or happiness. Third, you experience physiological responses, such as changes in heart rate or breathing. Fourth, you may show observable behaviors, such as smiling or crying.

You can identify these four components in Rick's experience with the shark: First, he interpreted the stimulus, a shark attack, as a threat to his well-being. Second, he had the subjective feeling of fear and terror. Third, he experienced physiological responses, such as heart pounding and adrenaline pumping. Fourth, he showed overt behaviors, such as fearful facial expressions and frantic swimming to escape the shark. One of the interesting questions about emotions concerns the order in which these four components occur. (Ellsworth, 1994a; Winter & Kuiper, 1997). For instance, did Rick have to think about the shark before he felt fear, or did he feel fear immediately and then think how terrified he was? We'll discuss this as well as many other questions about emotions.

Staying Happy

How long do emotions last?

Being attacked by a shark results in a very different emotional experience than winning big bucks in a lottery. Since lotteries began in the late 1970s, about 4000 people have become instant millionaires. Immediately after winning, the new millionaires reported feeling intense pleasure, being ecstatic, being unbelievably happy, and living in a dream world (Angelo, 1991). But what happens when a winner finally realizes that for the next 20 years he or she will receive a large monthly check? Will the emotional high continue, or will being a millionaire become a taken-for-granted experience? Researchers have studied lottery winners to find out what effect such an enormous windfall has had on their lives (Gould, 1995). Later in this module, we'll tell you what the researchers discovered about happiness and how it applies to lottery winners.

What's Coming

To realize the importance of emotions, just imagine going through one day without them. We'll discuss how emotions occur; how much our physiological responses, facial expressions, and interpretations contribute to emotions; whether feeling or thinking comes first in experiencing an emotion; if there is a set of basic or universal facial expressions that occur across all cultures; what the functions of emotions are; how specific emotions work; and how emotions are used in lie detection.

Let's begin with how the sight of a shark causes you to feel fear.

B. Cognitive Appraisal Theory

Can thoughts cause emotions?

You have arranged to meet your girlfriend at 7 P.M. at the movie theater. You arrive a few minutes early and are shocked to see her in the arms of a stranger. Feeling very angry and jealous, you rush over to confront them. Just as you arrive, she turns and says, "I want you to meet my brother, whom I haven't seen in years." Her explanation immediately changes your anger and jealousy into relief and happiness. Your girlfriend's explanation flip-flopped your emotional state and illustrates the cognitive appraisal theory of emotions.

The *cognitive appraisal theory* says that your interpretation or appraisal of a situation, object, or event can contribute to, or result in, your experiencing different emotional states.

For example, believing that your girlfriend is being hugged by an attractive stranger, triggers jealousy, but hearing that the stranger is her brother changes your jealousy to relief and happiness.

Current cognitive appraisal theories can be traced back to the original work of Stanley Schachter and Jerome Singer (1962). We'll focus on one part of their famous experiment that shows the importance of cognitive interpretation, or appraisal, in emotions.

Schachter-Singer Experiment

Throughout this text, we have pointed out classic experiments, so called because these studies challenged and dramatically changed how we think about something. The Schachter-Singer study was the first to show that thoughts are important in generating and identifying emotional feelings. Here's what they did in their ground-breaking experiment.

1 PHYSIOLOGICAL AROUSAL

First, Schachter and Singer injected some of their subjects with a hormone, epinephrine (adrenaline), that caused physiological arousal, such as increased heart rate and blood pressure.

Injections with hormone . . .
. . . cause physiological arousal.

However, subjects were told that the injections were vitamins and were not told that they would experience physiological arousal.

2 INTERPRETATION OF CUES

Second, after the injections, subjects were placed in different situations—a happy one or an angry one.

In the **happy situation,** a confederate of the researchers created a happy atmosphere by laughing and throwing paper airplanes around.

In the **angry situation,** another confederate created an angry atmosphere by complaining about filling out a long questionnaire.

3 EMOTIONAL FEELING

Those subjects in the happy situation often reported feeling happy, and their observable behaviors were smiles. However, those in the angry situation often reported feeling angry, and their observable behaviors were angry facial expressions. Schachter and Singer explained that subjects did not know that their physiological arousal was caused by hormone injections and looked for other causes in their environment. Subjects interpreted environmental cues, such as being in a happy or angry situation, as the cause of their arousal and thus reported feeling happy or angry.

4 SEQUENCE FOR EMOTIONS

The Schachter-Singer explanation assumes that our interpretation or appraisal of a situation is the primary cause of emotions. This sequence is shown below:

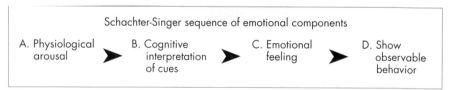

Schachter-Singer sequence of emotional components

A. Physiological arousal ➤ B. Cognitive interpretation of cues ➤ C. Emotional feeling ➤ D. Show observable behavior

5 CRITICISMS

The Schachter-Singer cognitive theory led to a classic study that was the first to show that cognitive factors, such as one's interpretation of events, could trigger and give rise to emotional feelings. However, their explanation has undergone two general revisions.

First, researchers recognize that emotions may occur without first experiencing physiological arousal (Cacioppo et al., 1993). For example, suppose a friend walked up to you and said, "I just saw somebody back into your car and drive away." Your appraisal of that situation would trigger feelings of anger before your physiological arousal kicked in.

Second, researchers argue that emotions may result not only from situational or environmental cues but also from your own cognitive processes, such as thoughts, interpretations, and appraisals (Ellsworth, 1994; Sinclair et al., 1994). For example, your friend's explanation of who the stranger was changed your jealous anger into feelings of happy relief.

Schachter and Singer's cognitive theory triggered a number of other cognitive appraisal theories that were developed independently in the 1980s (Frijda, 1986; Ortony et al., 1988; Smith & Ellsworth, 1985; Weiner, 1986). The cognitive appraisal theory of emotions points to thoughts, interpretations, and appraisals as being some of the primary ways that emotions are triggered and develop (Ellsworth, 1994; Kitayama & Markus, 1994).

Next, we'll explain the current cognitive appraisal theory.

Which Comes First: Feeling or Thinking?

Suppose you won 5 million dollars?

There's no question that thinking can trigger emotions, but the question is whether you think before you feel emotions. For example, suppose you picked the winning lottery numbers and won $5 million. At that moment, you felt incredibly happy. Did that emotional feeling occur before or after you thought about winning the lottery? This example raises the primacy question.

The *primacy question* asks whether we can experience an emotion immediately, without any thinking, or whether we must engage in some kind of thinking or appraisal before feeling an emotion.

We'll examine two different theories that propose two different answers to the primacy question.

Cognitive Appraisal Theory

One theory says that you usually think before you feel.

The *cognitive appraisal theory* assumes that your interpretation or appraisal of a situation is often the primary cause of emotions.

According to the cognitive appraisal theory, here's the sequence for feeling happy if you win a lottery.

1 The stimulus could be an event, object, or thought. In this example, the stimulus is holding a winning lottery ticket for $5 million.

2 You appraise or interpret how the stimulus affects your well-being; in this case your appraisal is extremely positive since you have won $5 million.

3 Your appraisal of having won $5 million gives rise to your emotional feelings of happiness and joy. In this example, you think or appraise before you feel an emotion.

4 Along with feeling comes a variety of bodily responses, including physiological arousal and overt behaviors, such as smiling.

Stimulus

Appraisal

Emotion

Bodily responses

5 THINKING BEFORE FEELING
The chief spokesperson for this position is Richard Lazarus (1991), who argues that, for an emotion to occur, it is necessary, at some level, to first think about or appraise the situation. There are many cases where thinking obviously precedes feelings, as in the example of jealousy changing to relief after hearing your girlfriend's explanation of the event. In other cases, such as winning a lottery, the emotion (happiness) seems to occur very quickly. However, even in these situations, researchers explain that the thinking or appraising goes on at a subconscious level, without our awareness (Ellsworth, 1994a).

Affective-Primacy Theory

Another theory says that you often feel before you think.

The *affective-primacy theory* says that, in some situations, you feel an emotion before having time to interpret or appraise the situation.

According to the affective-primacy theory, here's the sequence for feeling happy if you win a lottery.

1 The stimulus could be an event, object, or thought. In this example, the stimulus is holding a winning lottery ticket for $5 million.

2 Holding and seeing the winning lottery ticket triggers an emotional experience, feeling happy, so quickly that there seems to be little or no thinking or appraisal preceding your feeling.

3 You already feel happy, but as you appraise or think about how you will spend the $5 million, you may feel even happier. In this example, you feel an emotion before you think.

4 Along with feeling comes a variety of bodily responses, including physiological arousal and overt (observable) behaviors, such as smiling.

Stimulus

Emotion

Appraisal

Bodily responses

5 FEELING BEFORE THINKING
The chief spokesperson for this position is Robert Zajonc (1984), who believes that feelings or emotions may occur before thinking. Although Zajonc does not deny that cognition may sometimes precede emotions, he gives examples, such as reactions to winning a lottery or seeing a snake, in which emotions occur so rapidly there seems to be little time for thinking. Other researchers point out that thinking or appraising can occur quickly, automatically, and without our awareness and that some kind of appraisal precedes feelings or emotions (Ellsworth, 1994; Labouvie-Vief, 1996).

Now that you know the general theories for how we feel emotions, we'll discuss how people across cultures feel and express emotions.

C. Universal Facial Expressions

Definition

Suppose you survived a plane crash in the jungles of Borneo. After crawling out of the plane and checking for cuts, bruises, and broken bones, you look up and see two native people with blow-dart guns watching from the shadows. Not knowing their language, how would you communicate that you were friendly? Your best bet is to break into a big smile; there is good evidence that the native people will recognize that facial expression as friendly. Smiling is a sign of being happy (friendly) and is one of the universal emotional expressions (Ekman, 1994; Izard, 1994).

Universal emotional expressions refer to a number of specific inherited facial patterns or expressions that

signal specific feelings or emotional states, such as a smile signaling a happy state.

For example, notice that although the four individuals in the photos on this page come from four different countries, they display similar facial expressions—smiles—which you would interpret as showing happiness. Universal emotional expressions are thought to have evolved because they had important adaptive and survival functions for our ancestors.

The existence of universal emotions was scientifically formulated by Charles Darwin (1872/1965), and his ideas have inspired modern-day researchers to study universal emotional expressions (Ekman, 1994; Izard, 1994; Biehl et al., 1997). We'll review two kinds of evidence that support the existence of universal emotional expressions.

Cross-Cultural Evidence

How does a person from a relatively isolated culture in New Guinea, Burma, Thailand, or Borneo (photos top to bottom) know how to smile or what a smile means? One answer is that a smile is one of the unlearned, inherited universal emotional expressions. For example, suppose researchers showed photos of different facial expressions to individuals in 20 different Western cultures and 11 different primitive (illiterate and isolated) cultures. As the graph below indicates, researchers found that individuals in both Western and primitive cultures showed significant agreement on which facial expressions signaled which emotions. Most individuals in Western and primitive cultures agreed that a smile indicated happiness. However, fewest individuals in Western and primitive cultures agreed that an open-mouth and raised-eyebrows expression indicated surprise.

On the basis of these kinds of data, researchers concluded that there is evidence for innately or biologically determined universal facial emotional expressions, which most likely include happiness, surprise, fear, anger, contempt, disgust, and sadness (Ekman, 1994; Izard, 1994; Biehl et al., 1997).

Another kind of evidence for the existence of universal emotional expressions comes from observing the development of infants' emotional expressions.

Genetic Evidence

How does an infant who is born blind learn to smile? Is it possible that the programming of specific facial expressions, such as smiling, is contained in our DNA, or chemically coded genetic instructions? The answer to this question comes from observing the development of emotional expressions in infants.

Researchers found that at 4–6 weeks of age, infants begin to smile; this greatly pleases parents, who usually smile back. The question is whether the infant's smiling is biologically programmed or whether the infant has learned to smile by observing and imitating the parents' facial expressions. An ethologist studied the facial expressions of infants born blind and found that, at around 4–6 weeks, blind infants also begin to smile. This observation supports the idea of biologically programmed emotional expressions, since blind children have never seen their parents' smiling faces (Eibl-Eibesfeldt, 1973).

Additional evidence for universal emotions comes from reports that all infants develop facial expressions in a predictable order. For instance, newborns show facial expressions signaling disgust in response to foul tastes or odors; infants 3–4 months old show angry and sad facial expressions; infants 4–6 weeks old begin to smile; and infants 5–7 months old show fear. Since infants in all cultures develop these emotional expressions at about the same age, we have further evidence for the existence of universal emotions (Izard, 1993a).

Researchers conclude that evidence from studies on facial expressions across cultures and on emotional development in infants indicates strong biological influences on the development of emotional expressions (Ekman, 1994, Izard, 1994). But why should humans have an innate, genetic program for the development of facial emotional expressions?

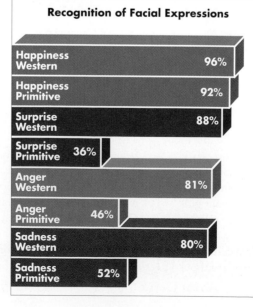

Recognition of Facial Expressions

Happiness Western	96%
Happiness Primitive	92%
Surprise Western	88%
Surprise Primitive	36%
Anger Western	81%
Anger Primitive	46%
Sadness Western	80%
Sadness Primitive	52%

What good are emotions?

To appreciate the value and worth of emotions, try living a single day without feeling or expressing any emotions. It would be one of the worst days of your life because emotions have three important functions. Emotions send powerful social signals about how you feel; emotions help you adapt and survive in your world; and emotions cause physiological arousal and motivate many of your behaviors. We'll examine each emotional function in turn.

Social Signals

As you look at the photo on the right, you immediately recognize the baby's emotional facial expression because it is a powerful social signal that the child is feeling unhappy, distressed, or in pain. In turn, this particular social signal usually elicits help, sympathy, or compassion from the parents or caregiver. This example illustrates how we send social signals through a variety of facial expressions.

Facial expressions that accompany emotions communicate the state of your personal feelings and provide different social signals that elicit a variety of

This facial expression is a social signal for_____?

responses from those around you (Frijda & Mesquita, 1994).

Facial expressions may more accurately signal a person's emotional state or mood even though a person may deny his or her feelings by saying, "Nothing's wrong," or "I'm fine." In contrast, a lack of facial expressions may signal some emotional problem. Emotional problems are one symptom of certain mental disorders, such as depression and schizophrenia, which we'll discuss in Module 23 (National Advisory Mental Health Council, 1995).

Adaptation and Survival

According to Charles Darwin (1872/1965), our early ancestors evolved the ability to smile, cry, laugh, and display other emotional expressions because such facial expressions helped the species adapt and survive. Building on Darwin's idea, current researchers have proposed the psychoevolutionary theory of emotions (Ekman, 1994; Izard, 1994).

The *psychoevolutionary theory of emotions* says that we inherit the neural structure and physiology to express and experience emotions and that we evolved emotional patterns to adapt to our environment and solve problems important for our survival.

There are many examples of emotion having survival value: expressing anger (right photo) may help

This facial expression is an adaptive response to help this person_____?

you escape or survive a dangerous situation; showing disgust may signal the presence of poisonous or rotten food; and crying may indicate the need for help. The fact that all animals have basic emotional expressions supports the idea that emotions have evolved because of their survival value (Plutchik, 1993).

Emotions also have adaptive value in dealing with basic social problems because they signal how you intend to act (McIntosh, 1996). You may smile to show you are being friendly and sociable; you may look angry to threaten or settle some conflict; or you may look hurt or jealous when competing for some goal. Besides being adaptive and helping us survive, emotions can also provide energy and motivation.

Arousal and Motivation

You may spend hours playing a challenging computer or video game because this activity arouses and motivates you to work harder. In contrast, you may have difficulty spending time studying a foreign language because this boring activity reduces your arousal and motivation. These examples show that emotions function to arouse or depress many of our behaviors (Lang, 1995). In fact, there is a relationship between emotional arousal and your performance on a task. That relationship is called the Yerkes-Dodson law (right graph).

The *Yerkes-Dodson law* says that performance on a task is an interaction between the level of physiological arousal and the difficulty of the task. For difficult tasks, low arousal results in better performance; for most tasks, moderate arousal helps performance; and for easy tasks, high arousal may facilitate performance.

Difficult tasks: low arousal is optimal

Most tasks: medium arousal is optimal

Easy or simple tasks: high arousal may be optimal

Difficulty of tasks

← Level of arousal

For example, suppose we apply the Yerkes-Dodson law to taking difficult exams. We would predict that a person with high test anxiety (high arousal) would do more poorly than someone with comparable ability but low test anxiety. Researchers tested this idea by comparing students who were highly aroused either because of high test anxiety or drinking much coffee (caffeine) with students who had low test anxiety or were given little coffee. Highly aroused students scored more poorly on difficult tasks than less aroused students (Anderson, 1994; Endler et al., 1994). The well-established fact that emotions increase physiological arousal is the basis for the so-called lie detector test, which we'll discuss in the Application section.

Another interesting aspect of emotions is that negative emotions (fear, anger, hate) seem to last longer than positive ones (happiness, joy). Why doesn't happiness last longer?

E. Happiness

Definition

Pam was unmarried, eight months pregnant, and holding down two jobs when she stopped in at Jackson's Food Store for her morning orange juice, doughnut, and one lottery ticket. She remembers praying, "Please, God, let something happen so I can afford a small studio apartment" (Reed & Free, 1995, p. 63). The next day she pulled out her lottery ticket and discovered that she had won 87 million dollars. She was very happy.

Happiness includes three components: feeling a positive emotion, being satisfied with one's life (life satisfaction), and not experiencing negative emotions (Lu & Shih, 1997).

For example, Pam's first check for $3.1 million made her experience all three components—positive emotion, great life satisfaction, and no negative feelings—and sent her on a a buying spree: new cars for herself and family, a new home, and several trips. Some months later she said, "I thought I'd drop everything and travel the world. But my idea of a good time is still to hang out at my brother's house, have dinner, or have a friend over for videos" (Reed & Free, 1995, p. 64). Like other lottery winners, Pam discovered that money helps and makes life easier but it doesn't buy long-term happiness. Why not?

Adaptation Level Theory

Why can't money buy happiness?

Researchers have interviewed hundreds of lottery winners and found that after winning they initially experience a short period of great happiness and wild euphoria, just as Pam did when she went on a spending spree. But this is often followed by a long period of mixed emotions because of indecision about what to do with one's life, job, or career, as well as potential problems with friends, relatives, or in-laws who are envious and insist on sharing the riches (Gould, 1995).

When researchers interviewed lottery winners 1 to 12 months after they had won large sums of money, the majority reported positive changes, such as financial security, more leisure time, and earlier retirement. However, when asked to rate their happiness one year after winning, lottery winners were no happier than before (Diener & Diener, 1996). This curious finding that the happiness of being a millionaire lasts a relatively short time (less than a year) is explained by the adaptation level theory.

The *adaptation level theory* says that we quickly become accustomed to receiving some good fortune (money, job, car, degree); we take the good fortune for granted within a short period of time; and as a result, the initial impact of our good fortune fades and contributes less to our long-term level of happiness.

According to the adaptation level theory, the immediate emotional high of obtaining good fortune—such as graduating from college, getting married, buying a new car, getting a much-wanted job, or winning a lottery—will fade with time and contributes less and less to our long-term happiness (Brickman et al., 1978). For example, three weeks after winning $87 million, Pam gave birth to Nicholas, and she said, "Winning the lottery was pretty exciting, but it can't compare to Nicholas. I want him to grow up caring about people and knowing the value of work" (Reed & Free, 1995, p. 64). The daily joys of raising her son will contribute more to Pam's long-term feeling of happiness than winning the lottery. The reason little bits of daily good news have more impact on long-term happiness is because they are constantly changing and are immune to adaptation (Goleman, 1996). Thus, according to adaptation theory, money cannot buy happiness because we adapt to continuous satisfaction. Instead, long-term happiness is more dependent on noticing and enjoying daily good news and little pleasures (Myers & Diener, 1996).

Long-Term Happiness

Although worldwide surveys indicate that the vast majority (84%) of people report being happy, some people report being happier on average than others (Diener & Diener, 1996). Reasons for being happy come from both environmental and inherited factors.

Genes. For example, researchers found that identical twins (share 100% of genes), who were reared together or apart, showed significantly higher correlations in their happiness ratings (0.44 to 0.52) than did fraternal twins (share 50% of their genes), who were raised together or apart (0.08 to –0.02). Based on these data, researchers estimated that about half of your level of happiness comes from inherited or genetic influences. The other half comes from environmental influences such as your unique living experiences (Lykken & Tellegen, 1996).

Environment. The kinds of environmental influences that have the greatest effect on your long-term level of happiness come from a steady diet of simple pleasures because they continually provide little highs. In comparison, influences of big environmental events (college degree, exam grade, lottery) will disappear in a relatively short time (several months to a year) (Goleman, 1996; Lykken & Tellegen, 1996).

Next we'll examine how important and powerful environmental factors—cultural influences—affect emotions.

F. Cultural Diversity: Emotions Across Cultures

Displaying Emotions in Public

Why don't grown men cry? Although many emotional expressions are shared and recognized across cultures, it is also true that each culture has unique gestures and differ in their display of emotions. For example, in the United States, it is very rare to see a grown man cry in public, while it is relatively common to see a grown woman cry. One explanation for this male-female cultural difference involves display rules (Ekman, 1993; Ekman & Friesen, 1969).

Display rules refer to specific cultural norms that regulate how, when, and where we should express emotion and how much emotion is appropriate.

There are many examples of how display rules differ across and within different cultures. For instance, in some European cultures it is acceptable and expected that males greet each other with a kiss to the cheek or lips, while such a male gesture of greeting is not observed or acceptable in most Western cultures. Among the Inuit (Eskimos), feelings of anger are strongly condemned, but among certain Arab groups, a man's failure to respond with anger is seen as dishonorable (Briggs, 1970; Abu-Lughod, 1986).

Although there is cross-cultural evidence for universal emotions, this does not mean that all individuals use exactly the same facial expressions.

For example:
1. Japanese and Chinese have more difficulty identifying facial expressions of fear and anger than do North Americans (Biehl et al., 1997; Tang, 1998).
2. North Americans were worse at identifying contempt than Japanese, Poles, or Hungarians (Biehl et al., 1997).
3. Vietnamese were worse at identifying disgust than Japanese, Poles, or North Americans (Biehl et al., 1997).

These examples illustrate how cultural influences create display rules, which in turn affect how frequently facial expressions occur and how easily specific facial expressions are identified (Ekman, 1993; Tang, 1998).

Not only do different cultures have different display rules but they also have different interpretations of what causes emotions. For example, in the United States, people interpret negative events initiated by other people (insult, automobile accident, rudeness) as evoking anger. In comparison, negative events caused by fate, change, or circumstances beyond anyone's control (earthquake, flood, or tornado) are interpreted as evoking sorrow (Ellsworth, 1994a). Thus, each culture has different ways of interpreting events, which in turn affect the kind of emotion we feel.

Cultures also influence how much emotion their inhabitants are "permitted" to display.

Surprise

Sadness

Anger

Perceiving Intensity of Emotions

Why do Japanese and Americans disagree? When I visited Japan, I noticed that the Japanese tended not to display emotions in public and often covered their mouths when they laughed. In comparison, I have never seen any of my fellow citizens use their hands to cover or hide their mouths when they laugh. These kinds of obvious cultural differences in displaying emotions led researchers to wonder if inhabitants would also differ in how they perceived or judged the intensity of emotions. Researchers showed photos of five emotional expressions—surprise, anger, happiness, disgust, and sadness (similar to photos on right)—to a group of Japanese and a group of Americans (Matsumoto & Ekman, 1989). Each group looked at two sets of photos: one depicted a Japanese showing five facial emotional expressions and the other depicted a Caucasian showing the same five expressions. The Japanese and Americans were asked to rate the intensity of each emotional expression in each set. The Japanese gave significantly lower ratings of *emotional intensity* to all five emotional expressions than did the Americans. These results indicate that the cultural display rules of Japan discourage showing emotional intensity in public while cultural display rules of America encourage the showing of emotional intensity.

Happy

Japanese rated disgust as the most intense of five emotions.

Americans rated happiness as the most intense of five emotions.

When asked to rate which of the five emotions is most intense—surprise, anger, happiness, disgust, or sadness—the Japanese rated disgust as the most intense emotion while Americans rated happiness as the most intense. This and other studies illustrate how cultural influences not only affect displaying but also perceiving the intensity of emotions in public (Biehl et al., 1997).

After the Concept Review, we'll discuss an exciting new finding showing how the brain processes different emotions.

Disgust

H. Application: Lie Detection

How did a spy twice pass a lie detector test?

From 1985 to 1994, the Russians paid or promised $4.6 million to Aldrich Ames (photo on right), who was a high-level Central Intelligence Agency official. Later, Ames pleaded guilty to espionage, which involved selling secrets to the Russians. Ames is currently serving a life sentence in prison. The Ames case brings up the issue of lie detection because he reportedly passed at least two lie detector (polygraph) tests during the time that he was selling U.S. secrets to Russia (Jackson, 1994). The publicity surrounding this case made people ask, "How could Ames be selling secrets and pass two lie detector tests?" The Ames case raises three questions: What is the theory behind lie detection? How is a lie detector test given? How accurate are lie detector tests?

What Is the Theory?

Does the test measure lying?

The lie detector test is based on the four components of an emotion that we discussed earlier. The first component of an emotion is interpreting or appraising a stimulus. In this case, Ames will need to interpret questions such as, "Have you ever sold secrets to Russia?" The second component of an emotion is a subjective feeling, such as whether Ames will feel any guilt or fear when he answers "Yes" or "No" to the question, "Have you ever sold secrets to Russia?" The third component of an emotion is the occurrence of various physiological responses (figure below). If Mr. Ames feels guilty about selling secrets, then his guilt feeling will be accompanied by physiological arousal, which includes increases in heart rate, blood pressure, breathing, and sweating of the hands. These physiological responses occur automatically and are usually involuntary, because they are controlled by the autonomic nervous system (discussed in Module 4). The fourth component of an emotion is the occurrence of some overt behavior, such as a facial expression. Mr. Ames may be able to control his facial expressions and put on a nonemotional poker face. However, neither the presence nor absence of facial expressions are critical to the theory behind lie detector tests.

Lie detector (polygraph) tests are based on the theory that, if a person tells a lie, he or she will feel some emotion, such as guilt or fear. Feeling guilty or fearful will be accompanied by involuntary physiological responses, which are difficult to suppress or control and can be measured with a machine called a polygraph.

A polygraph (lie detector) is about the size of a laptop computer (right figure) and measures chest and abdominal muscle movement during respiration, heart rate, blood pressure, and skin conductance or galvanic skin response.

The *galvanic skin response* refers to changes in sweating of the fingers (or palms) that accompany emotional experiences and is independent of perspiration under normal temperatures (Cacioppo et al., 1993).

Chest movement during respiration
Abdominal movement during respiration
Heart rate and blood pressure
Skin conductance

For example, you may remember having sweaty or clammy palms when taking exams, giving a public talk, or meeting someone important, even though the temperature was not unduly hot.

We'll focus on the galvanic skin response because its changes are often the most obvious.

What Is a Lie Detector Test?

Is the suspect lying?

Very few details have been released about how Mr. Ames, who apparently lied, passed two lie detector tests. Instead, we'll use a more detailed report of a man named Floyd, who told the truth but failed two lie detector tests.

Floyd was very surprised when two police officers came to his home. They had a warrant and arrested him for the armed robbery of a liquor store. However, the case against Floyd was weak, since none of the witnesses could positively identify him as the robber. Soon after his arrest, the prosecutor offered to drop all charges if Floyd agreed to take, and pass, a lie detector test. Floyd jumped at the chance to prove his innocence and took the test. He failed the lie detector test but insisted that he had not lied and that he be allowed to take a second one, which he also failed. Eventually Floyd was tried, found guilty, and sent to prison. He served several years behind bars before his lawyer tracked down the real robbers, which proved Floyd's innocence (*Los Angeles Times,* December 22, 1980).

Floyd was given the most commonly used procedure for lie detection in criminal investigations, which is called the Control Question Technique (Bashore & Rapp, 1993; Saxe, 1994).

The *Control Question Technique* refers to a lie detection procedure in which the examiner asks two kinds of questions: neutral questions that elicit little emotional response; and critical questions that are designed to elicit large emotional responses. The person answers only "Yes" or "No" to the questions and, if guilty, is expected to show a greater emotional response to the critical questions than to the neutral questions.

NEUTRAL QUESTIONS

These are general questions, such as "Is your name Floyd?" or "Do you live at a particular place?" These questions are designed to elicit few if any emotional responses and are used to establish a baseline for normal physiological responding.

CRITICAL QUESTIONS

These are specific questions about some particular crime or misconduct that only a person who committed the crime would know, such as "Did you rob the liquor store on 5th and Vine?" Critical questions are designed to elicit emotional responses, such as guilt or fear, if the person tells a lie.

As shown in the figure below, Floyd showed very little physiological arousal—as measured by the galvanic skin response—when asked a neutral question, "Is your name Floyd?" However, he showed great physiological arousal when asked a critical question, "Did you rob the liquor store?"

Galvanic Skin Response

Neutral question: "Is your name Floyd?"

Critical question: "Did you rob the liquor store?"

Floyd's answer "Yes" to a neutral question elicits little change in galvanic skin response.

Floyd's answer "No" to a critical question elicits a big change in galvanic skin response.

The examiner decides whether the client is lying or telling the truth by comparing differences in physiological responses between neutral and critical questions. In Floyd's case, he answered "No" to a number of critical questions, such as "Did you rob the liquor store?" But his "No" answers were accompanied by large increases in galvanic skin response (as well as other responses). For those reasons, the examiner decided that Floyd had lied and thus failed the polygraph test. However, when the real robbers were eventually caught, tried, and sentenced, it proved that Floyd had not lied even though he failed the lie detector test twice. Floyd's case, as well as the Ames case, questions the accuracy of lie detector tests.

How Accurate Are Lie Detector Tests?

Why aren't tests allowed in most courts?

If Floyd was innocent, why did he fail two lie detector exams? If Ames was lying, why did he pass two lie detector tests?

The basic problem with lie detector tests is that researchers have been unable to identify a pattern of physiological responses specific to lying. This means that a number of different emotions—such as guilt, fear, nervousness, or worry—can trigger physiological responses that make a person appear to be lying when he or she may be telling the truth (Honts, 1994; Iacono & Lykken, 1997). Because of this serious problem, researchers estimate that lie detector tests (graph below) are wrong about 25–75% of the time (Saxe, 1994).

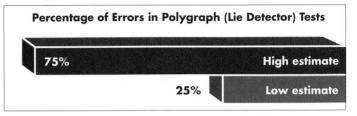

Percentage of Errors in Polygraph (Lie Detector) Tests

75% — High estimate

25% — Low estimate

Although very low error scores (5–10%) for lie detector tests have been reported, these data come from less realistic laboratory settings that use simple tasks, such as identifying some object about which the subject—often a college student—has been told to lie. The much higher error scores reported in the graph come from field studies that simulate more realistic conditions, in which subjects actually steal objects that they are told will be replaced after the test (Bashore & Rapp, 1993; Honts, 1994).

Besides high error scores, lie detector tests have two other problems: in one field study, about 40% of subjects were judged to be lying or maybe lying when they were telling the truth (Honts, 1994); and in another field study, about 50% of guilty people who were told to both press their toes to the ground and bite their tongues during control questions passed lie detector tests (Honts et al., 1994).

Because of these problems, federal law now prohibits most employers from using polygraph tests to screen employees and most state and federal courts prohibit the use of polygraph evidence (Saxe, 1994). In 1998, the United States Supreme Court ruled that polygraph evidence cannot be used in most courts.

For about the last ten years, researchers have studied the possibility of using brain waves to detect deception. One particular brain wave, called the P300, is associated with processing oddball stimuli, such as, "Do you take your coffee black or with ketchup?" The oddball pairing of coffee with ketchup would generate a P300 brain wave. Although researchers have reported that the P300 brain wave has shown promise in detecting deception, more work needs to be done to prove its validity (Bashore & Rapp, 1993; Rosenfeld, 1995).

One curious and little-known fact about lie detector tests is that they are primarily used in the United States. Lie detector (polygraph) tests are almost unknown and are not used in the rest of the industrialized world (Shenour, 1990).

A. PERIPHERAL THEORIES

1. We can define an emotion in terms of four components: we interpret or appraise a (a)_____ in terms of our well-being; we have a subjective (b)_____; we experience various (c)_____ responses, such as changes in heart rate, respiration; and we often show (d)_____ behaviors, such as crying or smiling.

2. Several theories explain what causes emotions. Theories that emphasize changes in the body are called (a)_____ theories. One such theory states that emotions result from specific physiological changes in your body and that each emotion has a different physiological basis; this is called the (b)_____ theory. The major criticism of this theory is that different emotions do not always cause different patterns of physiological arousal. However, feedback from physiological changes may increase the (c)_____ of emotional feelings.

3. According to another peripheral theory, sensations or feedback from the movement of facial muscles and skin are interpreted by your brain and result in an emotion; this is called the (a)_____ theory. One criticism of this theory is that facial skin and muscles do not initiate emotions. However, they may contribute to the (b)_____ of emotional feelings and also contribute to our mood.

B. COGNITIVE APPRAISAL THEORY

4. Theories about emotions that emphasize the importance of how you interpret a stimulus are called (a)_____ theories. One such theory is Schachter and Singer's cognitive theory of emotions. According to their theory, a stimulus causes physiological arousal, which creates a need for an explanation. To find the explanation, the person checks out the environment and (b)_____ the situational cues in order to label his or her emotional feeling. This theory has been revised to recognize that emotions may occur without prior physiological arousal and that emotions may result from our (c)_____ processes.

5. According to the current cognitive appraisal theory of emotions, here is the sequence for how you have an emotional experience: first, some stimulus (thought, event, or object) occurs; second, you (a)_____ this stimulus as to how it will affect your well-being; third, your appraisal results in an (b)_____; fourth, the emotional feeling includes (c)_____, such as changes in heart rate and blood pressure, and may include overt behaviors.

6. Some researchers believe that certain emotions, such as feeling afraid when you see a snake, involve feeling before thinking; however, other emotions, such as feeling jealous when seeing your partner with someone else, involve complex thought processes where thinking precedes feeling. The interesting question regarding the order of feeling and thinking is called the (a)_____ question. The most likely answer to this question is that some thinking or appraisal always precedes an emotional feeling, but that this appraisal may occur quickly, automatically, and without our (b)_____.

C. UNIVERSAL FACIAL EXPRESSIONS

7. Specific inherited facial patterns or expressions that signal specific feelings or emotional states, such as a smile signaling a happy state, are called (a)_____. These emotions, which are said to include happiness, surprise, fear, anger, contempt, disgust, and sadness, are thought to have evolved because they had important adaptive and survival functions for our ancestors. There are two kinds of evidence for the existence of universal emotions: people in different cultures from around the world recognize the same (b)_____ expressions; across cultures, infants show a predictable (c)_____ in developing facial expressions and even blind children, who cannot observe their parents' faces, develop smiling at the same time as sighted children.

D. FUNCTIONS OF EMOTIONS

8. We communicate the state of our personal feelings and provide social signals that communicate with, and elicit responses from, those around us with (a)_____ expressions. In some cases, the lack of facial expressions is one of the symptoms of certain mental (b)_____.

Difficult tasks: low arousal is optimal	↑
Most tasks: medium arousal is optimal	
Easy or simple tasks: high arousal may be optimal	Difficulty of tasks

← **Level of arousal**

9. According to one theory of emotions, we have inherited the neural structure and physiology to express and experience emotions and we evolved basic emotional patterns to adapt to and solve problems important for our survival; this is called the _____ theory.

10. There is a relationship between emotional arousal and your performance on a task; this relationship is called the (a)_____ law. According to this law, low arousal results in better performance on (b)_____ tasks; for most tasks, (c)_____ arousal helps performance; and for easy tasks, (d)_____ arousal may facilitate performance.

may differently influence how people perceive the (c)_____ of emotions.

E. HAPPINESS

11. Being happy involves three components: you feel a (a)_____ emotion, you are very satisfied with your (b)_____, and you are not experiencing any (c)_____ emotions. Reasons for being happy come from factors that involve both (d)_____ and _____ influences. The finding that identical twins (share 100% of genes) are significantly more similar in happiness ratings than fraternal twins (share 50% of genes) supports the influence of (e)_____ factors.

12. One theory explains that we quickly become accustomed to receiving some good fortune (money, job, car, degree) and, within a short period of time, take the good fortune for granted; as a result, it contributes little to our long-term level of happiness; this is called the (a)_____ theory. According to this theory, very positive significant events—such as graduating from college, getting married, winning the lottery, or buying a new car—have huge initial emotional impacts, but these emotional highs fade with time. Factors that have more influence on long-term happiness involve learning to notice and enjoy the small and regularly occurring (b)_____ in our lives.

F. CULTURAL DIVERSITY: EMOTIONS ACROSS CULTURES

13. Although many emotional expressions are shared and recognized across cultures, it is also true that cultures have unique rules that regulate how, when, and where we should express emotion and how much emotion is appropriate; these rules are called _____. For example, among the Inuit (Eskimos), feelings of anger are strongly condemned, but among certain Arab groups a man's failure to respond with anger is seen as dishonorable.

14. Another example of display rules is from a study in which Americans and Japanese rated the intensity of five emotions—surprise, anger, happiness, disgust, and sadness—on a scale from 1 to 10. The emotion rated most intense by the Japanese was (a)_____, while the Americans rated (b)_____ as the most intense of the five emotions. This study illustrates how cultural display rules

G. RESEARCH FOCUS: EMOTIONS IN THE BRAIN

15. Researchers are using new methods of studying the living brain to discover how the brain processes emotional information. In one of the first such experiments, researchers reported that when subjects reported feeling sad, certain structures (medial prefrontal area, anterior cingulate, thalamus, hypothalamus) showed (a)_____ activity. In contrast, when subjects reported feeling happy, certain structures (temporal-parietal and frontal cortex) showed (b)_____ activity. This study confirms that some (c)_____ system structures (hypothalamus, thalamus, cingulate and prefrontal areas) are involved in emotional behavior.

H. APPLICATION: LIE DETECTION

16. The instrument mistakenly referred to as a lie detector is correctly called a (a)_____; it measures a person's heart rate, blood pressure, respiration, and emotionally induced hand sweating, which is called the

(b)_____ response. To determine whether a person is telling the truth or a lie, the examiner compares the person's physiological responses to (c)_____ and _____ questions. The basic problem with lie detector tests is that no pattern of physiological responses has been specifically associated with lying. This means that many emotions can cause increased physiological responses that make the person appear to be lying. Because of the relatively high (d)_____ rate, evidence from lie detector tests is not admitted in most courts of law.

Answers: *1. (a) stimulus, (b) feeling, (c) physiological, (d) overt; 2. (a) peripheral, (b) James-Lange, (c) intensity; 3. (a) facial feedback, (b) intensity; 4. (a) cognitive appraisal, (b) interprets or appraises, (c) cognitive; 5. (a) interpret or appraise, (b) emotion, (c) physiological arousal; 6. (a) primacy, (b) awareness or conscious awareness; 7. (a) universal emotions, (b) facial, (c) order; 8. (a) facial, (b) disorders; 9. psychoevolutionary; 10. (a) Yerkes-Dodson, (b) difficult, (c) medium, (d) high; 11. (a) positive, (b) life, (c) negative, (d) environmental, (e) genetic; 12. (a) adaptation level, (b) pleasures; 13. display rules; 14. (a) disgust, (b) happiness, (c) intensity; 15. (a) increased, (b) decreased, (c) limbic; 16. (a) polygraph, (b) galvanic skin, (c) neutral, critical, (d) error.*

CRITICAL THINKING

Newspaper Article

QUESTIONS

SUPREME COURT WEIGHS POLYGRAPH'S LEGAL ADMISSIBILITY

by David G. Savage

1. What does a polygraph actually measure?

2. How have polygraph machines improved in recent years?

Is the polygraph a reliable "lie detector" that can convict the guilty and free the innocent, or a pseudoscientific fraud that has no place in a court of law? That is an old question, but it came before the Supreme Court for the first time Monday. The answer has the potential to reshape virtually every trial in the nation.

Polygraph testing has greatly improved in recent years, its advocates say, thanks to computer monitoring of minute changes in a person's pulse, perspiration, and breathing. Some studies have concluded that polygraphs are accurate 90% of the time.

Last year, in a major departure, the U.S. Court of Appeals for the Armed Forces ruled that a defendant has a constitutional right to tell jurors of a polygraph test that indicated he was not lying.

3. Why did the Supreme Court rule against the use of polygraphs in court?

The Supreme Court ruled that no one has the right to use a polygraph test to defend himself in court. The 8–1 decision by implication also upholds the rule in California and most other state courts that exclude the use of polygraphs.

"There is simply no consensus that polygraph evidence is reliable," wrote Justice Clarence Thomas. "To this day, the scientific community remains extremely polarized about the reliability of polygraph evidence."

4. How might polygraphy be inaccurate?

No one questions that a polygraph machine can accurately measure slight changes in a person's blood pressure or breathing. But no one can prove whether a change means the subject is lying.

A person who is fearful about being falsely accused could react noticeably to a question involving the accusation, even if he is entirely innocent, the court was told. Similarly, it is impossible to prove that a person who shows no reaction is telling the truth.

With 30 minutes of practice, determined liars can learn such techniques as biting your tongue or pressing your toes against the ground in a way that will register on a polygraph machine, fooling the examiner.

5. In light of this information, should the government continue to use polygraph tests for people applying for federal jobs?

Still, the government finds itself in an odd position fighting the use of polygraph evidence. Last year, federal agencies administered nearly 35,000 polygraph tests, primarily to people applying for jobs in the FBI, CIA, and Defense Department.

Source: *Los Angeles Times,* November 4, 1997.

Study Questions

A. Peripheral Theories—Does someone with many facial expressions experience more emotions than someone with few facial expressions? (See answer in Critical Thinking Appendix.)

B. Cognitive Appraisal Theory—Why would you get very angry if someone backed into your car but calm down as soon as you discovered your mother had done it?

C. Universal Facial Expressions—Do animals express emotions with facial expressions that are similar to humans'?

D. Function of Emotions—Why might people who are madly in love have difficulty making the right decisions? (See answer in Critical Thinking Appendix.)

E. Happiness—How might your level of happiness change after you reach a big goal in your life, such as getting a college degree, new job, or relationship?

F. Cultural Diversity: Emotions Across Cultures—Is there any truth to the stereotypes that Italians are emotional, British hide their feelings, Germans are serious, and Americans are impulsive?

G. Research Focus: Emotions in the Brain—If PET scans could identify emotions, would our criminal justice system benefit from knowing whether violent criminals felt guilt for their crimes?

H. Application: Lie Detection—Would it be fair to use lie detector tests to identify students who are suspected of cheating on exams? (See answer in Critical Thinking Appendix.)

Web Sites & Learning Activities

● BROOKS/COLE ONLINE PSYCHOLOGY STUDY CENTER

http://psychstudy.brookscole.com/student/plotnik/quiz/ch16frm.html

This site gives students a chance to review material by taking quizzes and doing exercises and activities for this module.

● EMOTION LABORATORY RESEARCH PAGE

http://www.psy.ulaval.ca/~arvid/R2e.html

This site explores the scientific study of emotions, including how emotions are displayed in the face and voice.

● WALKERS IN DARKNESS

http://www.walkers.org/

This organization of people suffering from mood disorders offers information on them, medications used in their treatment, other resources, and a chat room.

● DEPRESSION RESOURCE LIST

http://www.execpc.com/~corbeau/

This site offers information on many aspects of mood disorders, including depression, manic depression, suicide, treatment, and anxiety disorders.

Welcome to the WEB

● AMERICAN POLYGRAPH ASSOCIATION

http://www.polygraph.org:83/

This professional organization's site includes background information on polygraphy, its accuracy, professional policies, and legal and ethical issues.

● ANGER: WHAT IS IT? AND WHY?—PLUS SELF-TEST

http://cybertowers.com//selfhelp/articles/growth/anger.html

This site describes several different styles of coping with anger and offers a self-test to help you explore the role of anger in your life.

Activities

● *Integrator Online™ for Introductory Psychology* CD-ROM, Plotnik, Module 16

● Study Guide to accompany *Introduction to Psychology,* 5th edition, Module 16 (choice of PC or Mac computer version or hard copy)

● *PsychNow!* CD-ROM
   Emotion

Answers to questions on page 374

---

1. It measures small changes in pulse, perspiration, and breathing.
2. They now utilize computer monitoring to gauge minute changes.
3. Because there is no scientific consensus that polygraphs can reliably show whether a person is lying or not.

4. A person who is innocent but nervous could register as lying, or a person who is lying could fool the machine by showing no reaction.
5. There is no "right" answer. It might be appropriate to discuss the pros and cons of using polygraphy in this way.

Module 17 INFANCY & CHILDHOOD

Introduction

Nature-Nurture Question

Who should be Jessica's parents?

For the first $2\frac{1}{2}$ years of her life, Jessica's parents were Roberta and Jan DeBoer, who had raised her and tried hard to adopt her. However, the Iowa court ruled that they could not adopt Jessica and further that she must be returned to her biological parents. At Jessica's birth, her mother, Clara Clausen, was single and had put Jessica up for adoption. Later, Clara changed her mind and married Jessica's biological father, and now the biological parents wanted Jessica back.

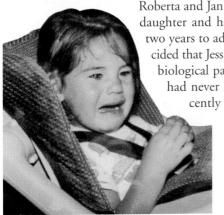

Roberta and Jan had viewed Jessica as their daughter and had legally fought for over two years to adopt her. But the court decided that Jessica must be returned to her biological parents, even though Jessica had never known them and only recently met them. On the court appointed day, a lawyer took Jessica away from the DeBoer's home, placed her in a car seat (left photo), and drove Jessica to where Dan and Clara waited. On the way, Jessica cried and said, "I want my daddy. Where's my daddy?" (Moss, 1993, p. 3A).

The baby Jessica case triggered a national debate: Why was Jessica taken from the parents who had raised and loved her and wanted to adopt her, and returned to her biological parents, whom Jessica had never known? This debate brings up an interesting question that in developmental psychology is referred to as the nature-nurture question.

The ***nature-nurture question*** asks how much nature (genetic factors) and how much nurture (environmental factors) contribute to a person's biological, emotional, cognitive, personal, and social development.

Although the nature-nurture question seems like an abstract intellectual issue, it has very practical consequences. For example, in the United States, most courts have traditionally sided with biological parents (nature) over adoptive parents (nurture) when awarding custody of an adopted child. Likewise, in Jessica's case, the Iowa court declared that the rights of her biological parents were primary and came before the rights of her adoptive parents. A number of child development experts criticized the Iowa court for basing its decision solely on nature. Professor Solnit, senior research scientist at Yale Child Study Center, argued that removing a child as young as Jessica from a loving home and placing her with strangers could have serious consequences. Solnit says, "One of the basic capacities that children develop in that period is the ability to trust an adult so that they can look ahead to a world that seems to them safe and reasonable, rather than a world that is unpredictable and unstable" (Gibbs, 1993a, p. 49).

More recently, however, some courts have begun to favor adoptive parents (nurture) over biological parents (nature). Denver juvenile court judge Dana Wakefield says that he invariably considers the child's needs over the parents' demands. "In my courtroom, they stay where they've been nurtured," he says flatly. "You have to consider who the child feels is the psychological parents. If they have a good bond in that home, I'm not about to break it" (Gibbs, 1993a, p. 49).

Developmental Psychologists

In a recent court case, State Supreme Court Justices refused to take an adopted 4-year-old boy named Michael away from his adoptive parents and return him to his biological father. In their ruling, the Justices sided with nurture when they explained that Michael, who had lived for all his four years with adoptive parents, might suffer psychological harm if taken from the only parents he has known since birth (Dolan, 1995).

These kinds of real-life decisions, which involve the psychological well-being of adopted children such as Michael and baby Jessica, illustrate the kinds of issues and questions studied by developmental psychologists.

Developmental psychologists study a person's biological, emotional, cognitive, personal, and social development across the life span, from infancy through late adulthood.

For example, developmental psychologists are interested in how young children such as Jessica adjust to adoption or divorce and whether such changes result in any long-term psychological problems. Later in this module, we'll explain how Jessica was doing at age three (she has a new name) and why she is smiling again (right photo). From the work of developmental psychologists, we have learned that the age-old question of whether nature or nurture is more important has been answered. The answer is that nature and nurture are both important and that their interaction is the key to understanding how a person develops (Plomin, 1997).

What's Coming

We'll discuss how development is affected by various prenatal factors, such as alcohol, which is the leading known cause of mental retardation. We'll explain the amazing abilities of newborns, the early appearance of a basic emotional makeup, the surprising growth of mental abilities, the different factors influencing social development, and the terrible occurrence of child abuse, which affects over a million children a year.

We'll begin with a family whose infant son's unusual musical abilities showed how nature and nurture interact.

A. Prenatal Influences

Nature and Nurture

How can one be a great violin player at age 5?

The reviewer for the *San Francisco Examiner* had listened to an inspired performance and wrote that the violinist "would one day be a master among masters" (Magidoff, 1973, p. 35).

At that point, the "master" was all of 5 years old and had been taking lessons for only six months. His name was Yehudi Menuhin. When Yehudi was 8 years old, he made his first professional appearance. The reviewer wrote, "This is not talent; it is genius!" (Magidoff, 1973, p. 46). He made his debut in New York at the age of 10, and the reviewer wrote, "What built the world in six days is what contrived the genius of Yehudi. He walks on the waves" (Magidoff, 1973, p. 52).

The amazing musical abilities of young Yehudi certainly classify him as a prodigy.

A *prodigy* is a child who shows a highly unusual talent, ability, or genius at a very early age and does not have mental retardation. A small percentage of autistic children, who have some degree of mental retardation, may also show unusual artistic or mathematical abilities; they are called savants.

Because prodigies demonstrate such unusual abilities so early, they are excellent examples of the interaction between nature (genetic influences) and nurture (learned influences).

Genetic and Environmental Factors

One reason Yehudi Menuhin was a prodigy and could give an inspiring violin performance at the age of 5 was because of the prenatal (before birth) effects of genetic influences. Prenatal influences, in the form of genetic instructions, regulated the development of Yehudi's brain and body.

Parents. The father contributed half of Yehudi's genetic instructions (23 chromosomes) and the mother contributed half of the genetic instructions (23 chromosomes).

The father and mother were teachers, and both had musical interests. The father had taken six violin lessons when he was a boy, but his grandfather had forbidden him to play any further. The mother had musical ability and took regular cello lessons. Through their chromosomes, the parents passed some of their musical talents on to their three children, Yehudi and his two younger sisters.

Daughters. The two daughters each received half of their genetic instructions from their mother and half from their father. Both daughters, who were younger than Yehudi, showed early musical abilities and began playing piano at the ages of 5 and 7. It is difficult to tell if the daughters had as much natural ability as Yehudi because in the 1930s and 1940s there were few opportunities for women in professional music. As a result, these negative environmental influences actively discouraged the two daughters from developing their considerable musical abilities.

Son. Yehudi received half of his genetic instructions from his mother and half from his father. The unique pairing of chromosomes from the mother and father results in different physical and mental traits for each of the three children. Because Yehudi and his two younger sisters showed great musical ability by age 5, we can assume that their early musical ability was primarily due to genetic or inherited instructions that came from their parents' chromosomes. However, certain environmental factors—few opportunities for women musicians—discouraged the sisters from developing their talents. Other environmental factors—many opportunities for male musicians—encouraged Yehudi to develop his musical talents.

Interaction. Yehudi Menuhin, who was universally hailed as the greatest child prodigy since Mozart, developed into a legendary violin performer (Magidoff, 1973). The development of Yehudi's musical talents is a perfect example of how nature and nurture interact. On the one hand, genetic influences (nature) played a major role in wiring his brain so that his incredible musical abilities appeared at a very early age. On the other hand, environmental influences (nurture)—being taken to concerts from age 2, being encouraged by his parents to practice and take lessons—interacted with genetic influences (nature) so that Yehudi was pushed to develop and perfect his musical talents.

Psychologists have long recognized the importance of learning influences, but it is only for about the past ten years that psychologists have also recognized the importance of genetic influences on almost every aspect of behavior, including cognitive, social, emotional, and personality development (Gottlieb et al., 1998). Today, researchers no longer focus on which is more important, nature or nurture, but rather on how nature and nurture interact to influence and regulate our behaviors (Plomin, 1997).

Genetic instructions from our parents can result in our having a wide range of abilities. Next, we'll explain what happens when genetic instructions are damaged—for example, if the mother uses drugs during the prenatal period.

Prenatal Period: Three Stages

How did you begin?

You began as a single cell about the size of a grain of sand. In this tiny cell was the equivalent of about 1,000,000 pages of instructions for the development of your brain and body. This single cell marks the beginning of the prenatal period.

The *prenatal period* extends from conception to birth and lasts about 266 days (around nine months). It consists of three successive phases: the germinal, embryonic, and fetal stages. During the prenatal period, a single cell will divide and grow to form 200 billion cells.

As we examine the prenatal period, we'll unravel one of the great puzzles of science—how a human being begins, develops, and is born. We'll start with the germinal stage.

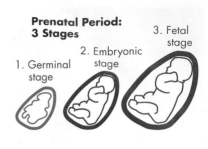

Prenatal Period: 3 Stages

1. Germinal stage
2. Embryonic stage
3. Fetal stage

---

1 GERMINAL STAGE

What is the germinal stage?

The germinal stage marks the beginning of our development into a human being.

The *germinal stage* is the first stage of prenatal development and refers to the two-week period following conception.

To understand how conception occurs, we need to back up a little and explain ovulation.

Ovulation refers to the release of an ovum or egg cell from a woman's ovaries.

In most cases, only a single ovum is released during ovulation, but sometimes two ova are released. If two separate ova are released and fertilized, the result is fraternal twins, who can be two brothers, two sisters, or a brother and sister. Because fraternal twins come from two separate eggs, they are no more genetically alike than any other two children of the same parents. In contrast, if a single ovum splits into two parts after fertilization, the result is identical twins, who share the same genes and thus are genetically alike.

How does conception take place?

If no sperm are present, there can be no fertilization, and the ovum, together with the lining of the uterus, is sloughed off in the process called *menstruation*. If, however, sperm have been deposited in the vagina (100–500 million sperm may be deposited with each act of intercourse), they make their way to the uterus and into the fallopian tubes in search of an ovum to be fertilized.

Conception, or *fertilization,* occurs if one of the millions of sperm penetrates the ovum's outer membrane. After the ovum has been penetrated by a single sperm (left photo), its outer membrane changes and becomes impenetrable to the millions of remaining sperm.

Once the ovum has been fertilized, it is called a *zygote,* which is a single cell that is smaller than the dot in the letter *i*. The zygote begins a process of repeated division and, after about a week, consists of about 150 cells. After two weeks, it has become a mass of cells and attaches itself to the wall of the uterus. Once the zygote is implanted, or attached to the wall of the uterus, the embryonic stage begins.

---

2 EMBRYONIC STAGE

What is the embryonic stage?

During this next stage, the organism begins to develop body organs. The *embryonic stage* is the second stage of the prenatal period and spans the 2–8 weeks that follow conception; during this stage, cells divide and begin to differentiate into bone, muscle, and body organs.

At about 21 days after conception, the beginnings of the spinal cord and eyes appear; at about 24 days, cells differentiate to form what will become part of the heart; at about 28 days, tiny buds appear that will develop into arms and legs; and at about 42 days, features of the face take shape.

During this stage, the embryo is very fragile, since all of its basic organs are being formed. This is the time when most miscarriages occur and when most major birth defects occur (Mortensen et al., 1991).

Toward the end of the embryonic stage, the organism has developed a number of body organs, such as the heart. The embryo is only about an inch long but already has the beginnings of major body organs and limbs and begins to look somewhat human.

In the left photo, you can see the head as the large rounded structure at the top, and the black dot on the side of the head is the developing eye. After this phase of development, the embryo enters the fetal stage.

A. Prenatal Influences

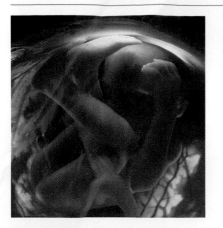

3 FETAL STAGE

The embryonic stage is followed by the fetal stage.

The *fetal stage*, which is the third stage in prenatal development, begins two months after conception and lasts until birth.

At the end of the fetal stage, usually 38–42 weeks after conception (or roughly nine months), birth occurs and the fetus becomes a newborn.

During this stage the fetus develops vital organs, such as lungs, and physical characteristics that are distinctively human. For example, at about six months a fetus has eyes and eyelids that are completely formed (left photo), a fine coating of hair, relatively well-developed external sex organs, and lungs that are beginning to function.

Infants born very prematurely will have difficulty surviving if their lungs are not yet completely formed. Usually, a six-month-gestation fetus begins to show irregular breathing and, for this reason, can survive if born prematurely.

During the fetal stage, a process called amniocentesis may be carried out.

Why don't some "premies" survive?

Birth Defects

Can genetic problems be checked?

During the fetal stage, it is possible to test for a number of genetic errors by amniocentesis *(AM-nee-oh-sen-TEE-sis)*.

Amniocentesis, which is a medical test done between weeks 14 and 20 of pregnancy, involves inserting a long needle through the mother's abdominal muscles into the amniotic fluid surrounding the fetus. By withdrawing and analyzing fetal cells in the fluid, doctors can identify a number of genetic problems.

One example of a genetic problem identified by amniocentesis is Down syndrome.

Down syndrome results from an extra 21st chromosome and causes abnormal physical traits (a fold of skin at the corner of each eye, a wide tongue, heart defects) and abnormal brain development, resulting in degrees of mental retardation.

In addition to Down syndrome, more than 450 other inherited genetic disorders can now be tested for and identified (Painter, 1997).

As the figure on the right indicates, birth defects can occur if something (toxin, drug, genetic malfunction) interferes with developing structures, especially during the embryonic stage (Lie et al., 1994). To help keep out toxins, we'll look at a natural filtering system that develops between the mother and fetus.

Source: Adapted from Moore, 1988

Placenta and Teratogens

What does the placenta do?

Because the fetus experiences rapid body growth and development of the nervous system, it is highly vulnerable to the effects of drugs and other harmful agents. However, the blood supply of the fetus is partly protected by the placenta (right illustration).

The *placenta* is an organ that connects the blood supply of the mother to that of the fetus. The placenta acts like a filter, allowing oxygen and nutrients to pass through while keeping out some toxic or harmful substances.

However, certain viruses, such as the HIV virus, and many drugs, including nicotine, caffeine, marijuana, cocaine, and heroin, pass from the placenta into the fetus's blood vessels and thus can affect fetal development. These potentially dangerous agents are called teratogens.

A *teratogen* is any agent that can harm a developing fetus (causing deformities or brain damage). It might be a disease (such as genital herpes), a drug (such as alcohol), or another environmental agent (such as chemicals).

We'll discuss several teratogens (from the Greek word *tera*, meaning monster) that can pass through the placenta and affect fetal growth and development.

Drugs and Prenatal Development

How well is the fetus protected?

In the womb, the fetus is protected from physical bumps by a wrap-around cushion of warm fluid. The fetus is also protected from various teratogens (certain chemicals and drugs) by the filtering system of the placenta. However, we'll discuss several drugs, both legal and illegal, that can reach the fetus and cause potential neurological, physiological, and psychological problems.

Multiple Drug/Cocaine Usage

In the 1980s and early 1990s, the media focused on "crack babies," who were born to mothers who had used "crack" cocaine during pregnancy. However, most of these reports had two serious problems: they were based on one or two anecdotal cases, and they didn't separate the effects of cocaine from other drugs (Lester, 1997).

Multiple drug usage. In most cases, pregnant women who had used cocaine also used other drugs, including alcohol, marijuana, heroin, or tobacco (nicotine). As a result, almost all the previous studies on crack babies were actually studies on babies exposed to multiple drugs, one of which was cocaine (Lester, 1997). For example, earlier reports said that newborns exposed prenatally to cocaine had low birth weight, were irritable, and had poor feeding habits (Richardson & Day, 1994). However, since the vast majority of these infants were also exposed prenatally to other drugs (alcohol, tobacco, marijuana), these worrisome effects likely result from a combination of drugs, rather than from cocaine alone. Thus, pregnant women who use multiple drugs can cause serious problems for their newborns, but the use of cocaine alone is a rare occurrence (Chasnoff, 1997).

Long-term effects. One of the real concerns is whether prenatal drug exposure results in long-term behavioral effects. Several recent followup studies have been done on children from 4 to 7 years old who had been exposed prenatally to multiple drugs, such as alcohol, marijuana, tobacco, or opiates, plus cocaine. Researchers reported that although children exposed to multiple drugs plus cocaine did not usually show deficits in IQ performance, they were found to be more impulsive, less able to adapt to stressful situations, and had more behavioral problems later on in life than did a control group of children whose mothers had not used drugs (Chasnoff 1997; Espy et al., 1997; Richardson, 1997). Research from animals indicates that cocaine interferes with brain development and the functioning of neurotransmitters (dopamine and serotonin) (Whitaker-Azmitia, 1997). The same problems may occur in fetuses exposed to cocaine and multiple drugs during pregnancy .

Researchers strongly recommend not using cocaine or other drugs (alcohol, marijuana, tobacco, opiates) during pregnancy because, later on, children exposed to such drugs may show behavioral problems (acting impulsively), especially in stressful situations (Harvey, 1997).

Alcohol

In the United States, alcohol is the leading known cause of mental retardation. Alcohol crosses the placenta, affects fetal development and can result in the fetal alcohol syndrome (Young, 1997).

Fetal alcohol syndrome (FAS) is caused by heavy maternal drinking during pregnancy, especially in the first 12 weeks. FAS results in a combination of physical changes, such as short stature, flattened nose, and short eye openings (right photo), and psychological deficits, such as degrees of mental retardation and hyperactivity (Jones & Smith, 1973).

Children with fetal alcohol syndrome continue to have problems into adolescence and adulthood. In two followup studies conducted 5–12 years after the original diagnosis, researchers retested adolescents and adults (age range 12–40 years). Subjects tended to remain short, their average IQ was below normal (68), and they tended to be easily distracted and to misperceive social cues (Streissguth et al., 1991; Spohr et al., 1993). Thus, many problems associated with fetal alcohol syndrome are long-lasting.

More recently, researchers found that most children born to pregnant women who abused alcohol showed a variety of behavioral impairments even though these children didn't meet the formal criteria for fetal alcohol syndrome. This problem, called Prenatal Exposure to Alcohol (PEA), is less severe than fetal alcohol syndrome but three times more prevalent. Researchers reported that children with prenatal exposure to alcohol showed deficits in a number of cognitive tasks (work comprehension), academic skills, and fine motor speed and coordination (Mattson et al. 1998).

Because of the serious and preventable effects of drinking alcohol during pregnancy, the American Academy of Pediatrics recommends abstinence from alcohol for women who are pregnant or are planning a pregnancy (Roan, 1997).

Although the fetus is vulnerable to various drugs (teratogens), over 90% of babies are normal, and many of those born with birth defects have mild, temporary, or reversible problems (Sigelman & Shaffer, 1995).

We have discussed the three stages of prenatal development, which ends with the baby's birth. After the baby gets a pat on the backside and lets out a cry, he or she is ready to take on the world. You may surprised at how many abilities a newborn has.

Why can't a newborn walk? Some animals, such as baby chicks (3 ounces) and elephants (150 pounds), can walk immediately after birth. In comparison, baby humans (7 pounds) cannot walk because neither their leg muscles nor brain areas controlling walking muscles are well-enough developed. However, human infants are born with a surprising number of sensory and motor abilities, such as hearing, grasping, sucking. How these abilities develop is explained by an inherited genetic program.

Genetic Developmental Program

Conception results in a fertilized human egg, which contains a genetic developmental program that is the equivalent of 1,000,000 pages of typed instructions for developing the body and brain. The mother contributes 23 chromosomes and the father contributes 23, so that each child receives a unique genetic program.

1. The **cell body** contains 23 pairs of chromosomes.

2. Each **chromosome** is made of a long strand of DNA. On the 23 pairs of chromosomes are about 100,00 **genes,** which are pieces of DNA that contain specific instructions.

3. A strand of **DNA** is stretched out to show that it looks like a twisted ladder with "chemical" rungs.

4. "Chemical rungs" function like a **chemical alphabet** that writes instructions (genes) for development of millions of parts for your brain and body.

Part of the genetic program involves the development of neural connections in the brain. In the figures below, notice that a 1-month-old brain has very few neural connections, while a 2-year-old brain has many thousands. The enormous increase in neural connections partly explains why the baby's brain increases from 340 grams at birth to about 900 grams at 2 years old.

1-month-old brain
Notice how neurons have very few connections.

Neurons

2-year-old brain
Notice how neurons have made many connections.

Neurons

Sensory Development

During the nine months of development in the womb, the genetic program is guiding the development of a number of motor and sensory functions that are important for the newborn's survival. For example, each newborn is equipped with a sucking reflex to ensure getting food and a very loud cry to demand attention. Here's a summary of a newborn's sensory and perceptual abilities.

Faces. At 1 month of age, an infant can distinguish his or her mother's face from that of a stranger, provided the infant also hears the mother's voice. By 3 months of age, an infant can visually distinguish his or her mother's face from a stranger's (Burnham, 1993). By 3 to 4 years of age, an infant's visual abilities are equal to those of an adult.

Hearing. One-month-old infants have very keen hearing and can discriminate small sound variations, such as the difference between *bah* and *pah*. By 6 months, infants have developed the ability to make all the sounds that are necessary to learn the language in which they are raised (Bower, 1994a).

Touch. Newborns also have a well-developed sense of touch and will turn their head when lightly touched on the cheek. Touch will also elicit a number of reflexes, such as grasping and sucking.

Smell and taste. Researchers found that 1-day-old infants could discriminate between a citrus odor and a floral odor (Sullivan et al., 1991). Six-week-old infants can smell the difference between their mother and a stranger (Macfarlane, 1975). Newborns have an inborn preference for both sweet and salt and an inborn dislike of bitter tasting things.

Depth Perception. By the age of 6 months, infants have developed depth perception, which was tested by observing whether they would crawl off a visual "cliff." (Gibson & Walk, 1960)

A *visual cliff* is a glass tabletop with a checkerboard pattern over part of its surface; the remaining surface consists of clear glass with a checkerboard pattern several feet below, creating the illusion of a clifflike drop to the floor.

An infant is placed on the area with the checkerboard pattern and is encouraged to creep off the cliff. Six-month-old infants hesitate when they reach the clear glass "dropoff," indicating that they have developed depth perception.

Although the genetic program is largely responsible for the early appearance of these sensory abilities, *environmental stimulation,* such as parental touch and play, encourages the infant to use and further develop these sensory abilities (Shatz, 1997).

Motor Development

"Gloria just took her first step." Mothers and fathers proudly relate their children's motor accomplishments, which are primarily due to the child's genetic program. As infants learn to crawl and walk, they change from passive observers into very active participants in the family's social life. The first area studied by early developmental psychologists was motor skill development (Thelen, 1995).

Motor development refers to the stages of motor skills that all infants pass through as they acquire the muscular control necessary for making coordinated movements.

Because each child has a unique genetic program, he or she will acquire motor skills at different times. The development of early motor skills, such as sitting, crawling, and walking, follows two general rules, called the proximodistal and cephalocaudal principles.

1 The *proximodistal principle* states that parts closer to the center of the infant's body (*proximo* in Latin means near) develop before parts farther away (*distal* in Latin means far).

For example, activities involving the trunk are mastered before activities involving the arms and legs. For that reason, infants can roll over before they can walk or bring their arms together to grasp a bottle.

2 The *cephalocaudal principle* states that parts of the body closer to the head (*cephalo* in Greek means head) develop before the parts closer to the feet (*caudal* in Greek means tail).

For example, infants can lift their heads before they can control their trunks enough to sit up, and they can sit up before they can control their legs to crawl. The left figure shows the head area (larger) developing before the feet area (smaller).

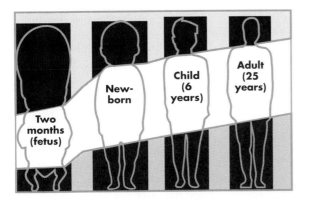

3 The cephalocaudal and proximodistal principles, which regulate the sequence for developing early motor skills, are part of a process known as maturation.

Maturation refers to developmental changes that are genetically or biologically programmed rather than acquired through learning or life experiences.

In developing motor skills (three right photos), such as sitting up alone, crawling, and walking, all infants in all parts of the world go through the same developmental stages at about the same times. However, if children are given more opportunities to practice their stepping reflex earlier in life, they will begin to walk at an earlier age than children who lack such opportunities (Thelen, 1995). Thus, the development of early motor development is heavily influenced by maturation (genetic program) but the timing can be partly slowed or speeded up by experience/learning (nurture).

4 Parents often note the major milestones in their infants' motor development, such as their first time crawling or walking, because they want to know if their children are within the developmental norms.

Sitting up alone— average 5.5 months (range 4.5–8.0 months)

Developmental norms refer to the average age at which children perform various kinds of skills or exhibit abilities or behaviors.

Some examples of developmental norms for stages in walking accompany the three photos. Because norms for motor development represent average ages rather than absolute ages, parents should not be disturbed if their infant's motor progress does not match the norms.

By the age of 2, infants have grown into toddlers who can walk up and down stairs and use their hands to hold glasses of juice, operate toys, and, of course, get into a lot of trouble.

5 The reason infants develop skills and abilities at different times is because neural connections develop at different rates. This means that infants cannot perform complex cognitive, sensory, or motor tasks, such as walking, talking and reading, until appropriate areas of their brains develop neural connections.

Crawling— average 10 months (range 7.0–12.0 months)

Walking alone— average 12.1 months (range 11.5–14.5 months)

Although we have focused on the role of the genetic developmental program (nature), it's important to remember that nature interacts with the environment (nurture) to encourage or discourage the development of various motor, sensory, and cognitive abilities (Shatz, 1997). For example, infants need appropriate *environmental stimulation* for development of their visual systems (see things), for learning to speak (hear parents speaking), for emotional development (get loving care), and for motor development (explore objects). These examples show how the genetic program needs and interacts with environmental stimulation for proper development of most of a child's sensory, motor, and cognitive abilities (Lach, 1997; Nash, 1997).

Next, we'll explain how the genetic program is involved in emotional development.

C. Emotional Development

Definition and Kinds of Temperament

Why are babies so different?

A colleague who had just had her second baby was explaining how different the new baby is. "My first baby was very fussy and required constant attention. But my new baby is a dream. He's such a good, happy baby and totally unlike how his older sister was." My colleague is actually discussing how each of her two babies has a very different temperament.

Temperament refers to individual differences in attention, arousal, and reactivity to new or novel situations. These differences appear early, are relatively stable and long-lasting, and are influenced in large part by genetic factors

Most parents with two or more children have noticed differences in their babies' temperaments. Using a more scientific approach, researchers studied differences in infants' temperaments by interviewing mothers with 2- to 3-month-old infants and then observing these same infants repeatedly over the next seven years. Researchers rated each infant on nine components of temperament, including activity level, attention span, fussiness, and mood. On the basis of these ratings, they were able to divide the infants into four categories (Thomas & Chess, 1977).

1 Easy babies, who made up 40% of the sample, were happy and cheerful, had regular sleeping and eating habits, and adapted quickly to new situations.

2 Slow-to-warm-up babies, who made up 15% of the sample, were more withdrawn, were moody, and tended to take longer to adapt to new situations.

3 Difficult babies, who made up 10% of the sample, were fussy, fearful of new situations, and more intense in their reactions. During the course of the seven-year study, difficult babies developed more serious emotional problems than the easy or slow-to-warm-up babies.

4 No-single-category babies, who made up 35% of the sample, had a variety of traits and could not be classified into one of the other three categories.

This and other studies have led researchers to conclude that the majority of infants develop distinct temperaments very early, usually in the first 2–3 months of life, and that these distinct temperaments occur largely because of genetic factors rather than learning experiences (Goldsmith et al., 1997; Martin et al., 1997).

Additional evidence that differences in temperament primarily result from a genetic developmental program comes from the finding that about 10–15% of Caucasian babies inherit an inhibited or fearful temperament. For fearful babies, novel and strange situations or people elicit great physiological arousal and distress. In comparison, about 40% of Caucasian babies inherit a fearless temperament. Fearless babies remain relaxed and calm in novel or strange situations. Although some fearful infants became less so as they grew up, most individuals retained their generally fearful or fearless dispositions from infancy into adolescence (Kagan, 1998). Other studies also report that a distinct temperament developed in infancy can have long-lasting effects. For example, babies who developed a difficult temperament (negative mood, intense crying) were found to have a negative attitude and mood and significantly more behavioral problems at age 12 (Guerin et al., 1997). Thus, temperament is a genetic influence that affects a child's level of arousal and reactivity to new situations, which, in turn, affects the development of a child's personality and social relationships (Rothbart & Bates, 1998).

15% FEARFUL

40% FEARLESS

Emotions and Temperament

When is the first smile?

Becki is describing the personalities of her sextuplets (below photo). "Brenna, the oldest by 30 seconds, is the affectionate one. Julinan, the second child delivered, is 'Mr. Smiley.' Quinn, the third, is sweet and generous and most adventurous. Claire, fourth oldest, is the boss, as charming as

she is tough. Ian, the fifth, is the smallest and loves music, drawing, and sleep. Adrian, the youngest, is the biggest and most gentle" (Reed & Breu, 1995, p. 127). Each of these 2-year-old sextuplets is already showing a distinct personality, partly a result of his or her unique emotional development.

Emotional development results from our biological capacity to produce emotional expressions (nature) which interact with the positive or negative feedback (nurture) we receive in attempting to maintain or change our environment.

For example, researchers found that newborns have a limited emotional capacity to change their environment because their repertoire of emotional expressions includes only interest, startle, distress, disgust, and neonatal smile (a sort of half-smile that appears spontaneously for no apparent reason). Over the next two years, infants develop a wide range of emotional expressions and feelings, including *social smiling* (age 4–6 weeks); *anger, surprise,* and *sadness* (age 3–4 months); *fear* (age 5–7 months); *shame* and *shyness* (age 6–8 months); and *contempt* and *guilt* (age 24 months) (Izard, 1990, 1994). As children acquire more of these specific emotions, they also acquire a greater capacity to maintain or change their environments.

A child's emotional development also interacts with his or her basic **temperament.** For instance, a child whose temperament includes being fearful, distressed, and easily aroused, will show greater emotional intensity than a child with an opposite temperament (Saarni et al., 1998). In turn, the intensity of an infant's emotional reactions influences the bond, or attachment, between parent and child.

Attachment

Do infants and parents form a special bond?

For the first $2\frac{1}{2}$ years of her life, Jessica was lovingly cared for by the only parents she ever knew, her adoptive parents, Roberta and Jan DeBoer. When the court decided that Jessica must be returned to her biological parents, whom Jessica did not know, she cried (right photo) as she was taken away. Taking Jessica away from her adoptive parents broke a special bond that she had developed with Roberta and Jan. This emotional bond is called attachment.

Attachment refers to a close fundamental emotional bond that develops between the infant and his or her parents or caregiver.

The interesting theory behind attachment comes from psychologist John Bowlby (1969), who believed that attachment behavior evolved through a process of natural selection. According to his idea, attachment evolved because of its adaptive value. Attachment gave the infant a better chance of surviving because the parent was close by to provide care and protection. Much of the research on attachment was initiated by Mary Ainsworth (1989), who asked three general questions: How does attachment occur? Are there different kinds of attachment? What are the long-term effects of attachment?

How Does Attachment Occur?

According to attachment theory, Jessica, like most babies, would have formed an attachment to her parents through a gradual process that begins shortly after birth and continues through infancy. As a newborn, Jessica has a powerful social signal, crying, which elicits care and sympathy. As a 4- to 6-week-old infant, she will begin social smiling (smiling at others), which will elicit joy and pleasure in her parents. At about 6 months, Jessica begins to give her parents a happy greeting (smiling, holding out her arms) when they reappear after a short absence. All of these behaviors contribute to building a good parent-child attachment (Thompson, 1998).

As the infant develops a closer attachment to her parents, she also shows more distress when her parents leave; this is called separation anxiety.

Separation anxiety is an infant's distress—as indicated by loud protests, crying, and agitation—whenever the infant's parents temporarily leave.

According to Ainsworth, separation anxiety is a clear sign that the infant has become attached to one or both parents. By the end of the first year, an infant usually shows a close attachment to her parents, as well as to one or more other family members.

However, depending upon the infant's temperament (easy or difficult) and the mother's attitude (caring or not responsive), different kinds of attachment occur.

Are There Different Kinds of Attachment?

Ainsworth (1979) is best known for developing a method for studying infants' reactions to being separated from, and then reunited with, their mothers. She used these reactions to indicate the kind or quality of the infants' attachment. There are now four different kinds of attachment, but we'll focus on two, which are called secure (65% of infants) or insecure attachment (20% of infants).

Secure attachment is characteristic of infants who use their parent as a safe home base from which they can wander off and explore their environments.

For example, when infants are placed in an unfamiliar room containing many interesting toys, securely attached infants tend to explore freely as long as their parent looks on. If the parent leaves, most of the infants cry. On the parent's return, securely attached infants happily greet the caregiver and are easily soothed. By contrast, some infants show insecure attachment.

Insecure attachment is characteristic of infants who avoid or show ambivalence or resistance toward their parent or caregiver.

For example, insecurely attached infants may cling and want to be held one minute but squirm and push away the next minute, apparently displaying a lack of trust in the parent or caregiver.

Researchers found that infant's sense of trust or attachment was not affected by whether or how long a child was in day care. Instead, what most affected the infant's attachment was a mother's sensitivity, caring, and responsiveness to the infant's needs (NICHD, 1997). As you'll see, attachments may affect later behaviors and relationships.

What Are Effects of Attachment?

After spending $2\frac{1}{2}$ years with her adoptive parents, Jessica was taken from them. Psychologists worried that breaking this original attachment might have long-term effects on Jessica's sense of security and trust. However, after being with her biological parents for eight months, Jessica (now called Anna) seemed to have formed a healthy attachment to them (photo below) and, as yet, shows no obvious symptoms of being insecure or untrusting.

The kind of attachment an infant forms during the first five years is thought to be associated with future behaviors. For example, a secure attachment is associated with being better at resolving conflicts, being more trusting, enjoying relationships, and dealing better with stress and anxiety; an insecure attachment is associated with being dependent, having poor social relationships, and showing more anxiety in stressful settings (Burge et al., 1997). Thus, the kind of attachment an infant forms—secure or insecure—is thought to have long-term effects, either positive or negative, on that individual's future behaviors, personality, and social relationships (Zeifman & Hazan, 1997).

The kind of attachment an infant forms is also partly dependent on the infant's temperament. We'll next discuss a classic study on kinds of temperaments.

D. Research Focus: Temperament
Are Some Infants Born Fearful?

Research Methods for Studying Developmental Changes

How can children be so different?

We're going to discuss a series of classic studies by Jerome Kagan (1998) that changed the way we think about children's temperaments. Kagan wanted to answer a question asked by many parents: Why do children raised by the same parents in the same family grow up with such different emotional makeups? For instance, Eric's parents wondered why he (similar to circled child in right photo) was more shy and fearful than his two brothers. Eric would never leave his mother's side to play with other children, was afraid to tell a story to his grade school class, and feared going into the swimming pool with other children (Elias, 1989). Kagan wondered if fearful children like Eric were born that way and if they changed as they grew up. The first problem Kagan faced was to select between two different research methods—longitudinal and cross-sectional methods—to study developmental changes. As we discuss the advantages and disadvantages of each method, you'll understand why Kagan selected the longitudinal method to study temperament.

Longitudinal Method

One method researchers use to study developmental changes, such as a child's temperament, is with the longitudinal method.

A *longitudinal method* means that the same group of individuals is studied repeatedly at many different points in time.

For example, as shown in the figure below, researchers first measure temperaments in a group of 2-year-old children, retest this same group again at age 7, then test them again at age 12, and so on.

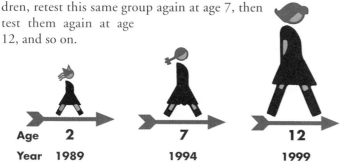

Age	2	7	12
Year	1989	1994	1999

Advantages and disadvantages. A major advantage of the longitudinal method is that it allows researchers to study the developmental patterns or changes of the same subjects across time. One disadvantage is that researchers must wait many years for their subjects to grow older and must deal with the problem of subjects dropping out of the study (due to relocation, illness, or death). However, researchers generally prefer using the longitudinal method to study developmental changes because they can track the behaviors of the same subjects across time.

Cross-Sectional Method

Another method researchers can use to study developmental changes in temperament is called the cross-sectional method.

A *cross-sectional method* means that several groups of different-aged individuals are studied at the same time.

For example, in the figure below, researchers are using the cross-sectional method because they selected a group of 2-year-olds, a group of 7-year-olds, and a group of 12-year-olds and measured their temperaments at the same time.

Age	2	7	12
Year		1999	

Advantages and disadvantages. One advantage of the cross-sectional method is that researchers can immediately compare any developmental differences, such as in temperaments, across many different age groups. A major disadvantage of the cross-sectional approach is that it cannot tell us if the same individuals remain the same or change across time. For this reason, the longitudinal method is preferable to the cross-sectional method in studying developmental differences.

Procedure

Using the longitudinal method, Jerome Kagan and his colleagues (Kagan, 1998; Kagan et al., 1991) began by studying the temperaments of 4-month-old infants. These same infants would be retested several times, at several different ages, until they turned 12. Kagan found that some 4-month-olds were shy and fearful; he called them inhibited children.

Inhibited children show avoidance, anxiety, or fear (measured by avoiding, fretting, or crying) when in a strange or novel environment; these children also show increased physiological arousal (increased heart rate) to novel or strange situations.

After identifying a group of inhibited—shy or fearful—infants, Kagan next asked if these inhibited infants would grow into inhibited children. We'll discuss some of Kagan's interesting findings.

Results

First question: How many infants are born fearful?

As shown in the graph below, Kagan and his colleagues observed several hundred 4-month-old infants, and reported that about one fourth were classified as inhibited, or highly fearful. An inhibited, or highly fearful, infant showed a high degree of avoidance, fretting, and crying in novel or strange situations. About one third of the infants were classified as uninhibited, or low-fear, individuals and the remaining infants were classified in between.

Temperament at 4 Months

23% Inhibited (fearful)

37% Uninhibited (fearless)

The vast majority of infants who showed high fear at 4 months continued to show high fear at 21 months (Kagan et al., 1988; Kagan & Snidman, 1991). Thus, the answer to our first question is that some infants are born with a tendency to develop either an inhibited (fearful) or uninhibited (fearless) temperament. Data from twin studies indicate that the influence of genetic factors on temperament ranges from 50 to 60% (Kagan, 1998). An infant's temperament may influence the kind of attachment formed with its mother. Infants who have a fearful or distressed temperament may develop an insecure attachment if raised by a rigid or less affectionate mother, but the same infant may develop a secure attachment if raised by a more flexible, affectionate mother (Kagan, 1998). This means an infant's temperament interacts with a mother's traits to result in the development of a secure or insecure attachment.

Second question: Do infants change their temperaments?

To answer this question, researchers repeatedly tested the same group of infants until they were 7 years old. As the graph below shows, between the ages of 21 months and 7 years, about half the children retained their temperaments, either remaining inhibited or uninhibited, while about one fourth showed a major change from one to the other. How do these inhibited and uninhibited children differ in behavior?

Temperament Changes Between 21 Months and 7 Years

23% Changed temperament

50% Retained temperament

Profile of inhibited child. A typical inhibited child stayed at the periphery of a large group of peers, reading a book, painting at an easel, or standing in a corner quietly watching another child. One of the best indicators of an inhibited child was that he or she spoke very little or initiated very little spontaneous conversation with unfamiliar peers or adults.

Profile of uninhibited child. A typical uninhibited child was involved in group activities, was very talkative, initiated spontaneous interactions, engaged in conversations, often with smiling and laughter, and showed enthusiasm for social interactions not observed in inhibited children.

This brings up another question: What should parents do to help an inhibited child overcome his or her fear and shyness?

Conclusions

One reason children raised by the same parents in the same family can be so different is that they inherit different temperaments. Kagan's (1994b, 1998) series of longitudinal studies showed that there are at least two distinct temperaments, which he called inhibited (shy or fearful) and uninhibited (outgoing or fearless). These two temperaments are relatively stable across time, involve both observable behaviors and physiological arousal, and probably involve the excitability of different brain areas.

The appearance of these temperaments in very young infants indicates the influence of genetic factors (nature). However, the finding that about 50% of the children's temperaments changed indicates the influence of environmental or learning experiences (nurture). Kagan estimates that about 10–15% of the general population have an inhibited (fearful) temperament while about 20–40% have an uninhibited (fearless) temperament.

Another interesting finding was that although children differed in temperament—inhibited or uninhibited—they did not differ in IQ scores, intellectual abilities, language, memory, or reasoning abilities (Kagan, 1998).

What should parents do if their child is inhibited?

Researchers advise parents with inhibited children to be very caring and supportive and to consistently help their inhibited child deal with minor stressors. With such support, inhibited children learned to control their initial urges to withdraw from strange people or situations. Additionally, researchers suggest that if parents avoid becoming too anxious, overprotective, or angry at their children's extreme fearfulness and timidity there will be a better chance that the inhibited child will become less anxious in adolescence (Kagan, 1994b).

Eric's parents followed this advice. As an infant and child, Eric (similar to right photo) showed signs of being fearful or inhibited. For example, Eric spent two weeks worrying about having to give a book report, which meant standing in front of, and speaking to, the whole class. Eric was sure he couldn't do it. His parents encouraged Eric to role-play giving his book report. Eric performed his speech over and over at home until he felt comfortable. When Eric gave his book report to the class, he did very well and felt great afterward (Elias, 1989). With support and understanding, parents can help a shy or fearful child become more expressive and outgoing.

At the same time that an infant is developing emotional behaviors, he or she is also acquiring numerous cognitive skills and abilities, which we'll discuss next.

E. Cognitive Development

Piaget's Theory

What is Sam doing?

We have already explained how an infant comes equipped with relatively well developed senses, with a temperament that influences arousal and activity, and with emotional feelings and expressions that can be used for wordless communication. The result is not a passive infant but an amazingly competent tiny person who is eager and ready to begin a process of discovering, thinking, and learning, which we call cognitive development.

Cognitive development refers to how a person perceives, thinks, and gains an understanding of his or her world through the interaction and influence of genetic and learned factors.

For example, if you gave some blocks to Sam, who is 6 months old, he would surely put one into his mouth. If you gave some blocks to Sam when he was 2 years old, he might stack them. If you gave some blocks to Sam when he was an adolescent, he might throw them or cover them with graffiti. From these examples, you can see that what Sam does with blocks depends on how he perceives and thinks about them, which in turn depends upon his cognitive development.

Jean Piaget. In the history of developmental psychology, the person who had the greatest impact on the study of cognitive development was Jean Piaget, who was both a biologist and a psychologist. From the 1920s to his death in 1980, Piaget (1929) studied how children solved problems in their natural settings, such as cribs, sandboxes, and playgrounds. Piaget developed one of the most influential theories of cognitive development. According to Piaget, infants were not just passive observers but were actively involved in making sense of what they saw and discovered. Being actively involved meant that children formed their own guesses or hypotheses about how the world works.

It is easier to understand Piaget's idea of *active involvement* if you imagine a 2-year-old playing with blocks. Piaget believed that children learn to understand things, such as whether to eat or stack blocks, through two active processes: assimilation and accommodation.

ASSIMILATION

If you gave Sam a block when he was 6 months old, he would first try to put it into his mouth because he believes that objects are for eating. This mouthing behavior is an example of assimilation.

Assimilation is the process by which a child uses old methods or experiences to deal with new situations.

At 6 months, Sam will first put a new object into his mouth because his knowledge of objects is that they are for eating or sucking. Thus, Sam will assimilate the new object as something too hard to eat but all right for sucking.

Depending on their age and knowledge, children assimilate blocks in different ways: infants assimilate blocks as something to suck; toddlers assimilate blocks as something to stack or throw; adolescents assimilate blocks as something used to play games; and adults assimilate blocks as something to give to children. The assimilation of new information leads to Piaget's next process—accommodation.

ACCOMMODATION

If you gave blocks to Sam when he was 2 years old, he would not try to eat them, but he might try to stack them: this stacking behavior is an example of accommodation.

Accommodation is the process by which a child changes old methods to deal with or adjust to new situations.

For example, because of Sam's experience with wood objects, he learns that some objects may look like chunks of food but are not food. The process of having to change existing knowledge because of new information, which is accommodation, is one way that mental growth occurs.

An infant's or child's active involvement with his or her environment provides more opportunities for assimilation and accommodation, resulting in different kinds of cognitive growth and development.

According to Piaget, children make big gains in reasoning, thinking, and understanding through active involvement and the processes of assimilation and accommodation. Using these two processes, children proceed through a series of reasoning or cognitive stages.

Piaget's Stages of Cognitive Development

What is Sam thinking?

The genius of Piaget was his ability to map out the changes or stages in cognitive development that a person goes through from infancy through adulthood.

Piaget's cognitive stages refer to four different stages—sensorimotor, preoperational, concrete operations, and formal operations stages—each of which is more advanced than the preceding stage because it involves new reasoning and thinking abilities.

1. Sensorimotor
2. Preoperational
3. Concrete
4. Formal

Although Piaget believed that all people go through the same four cognitive stages, he acknowledged that they may go through the stages at different rates.

Piaget's hypothesis that cognitive development occurs in stages and that each stage involves different kinds of thinking was one of his unique contributions to developmental psychology. We'll explain Piaget's four stages by following Sam through his cognitive development.

1. Sensorimotor

Stage 1

Imagine Sam as a newborn infant. His primary way of interacting with the world is through reflexive responses, such as sucking and grasping. By 5 months, Sam has developed enough voluntary muscle control so that he can reach out, grasp things, and put them into his mouth to discover if the thing is good to suck on. Sam is going through the sensorimotor stage.

The *sensorimotor stage* (from birth to about age 2) is the first of Piaget's cognitive stages. During this stage, infants interact with and learn about their environments by relating their sensory experiences (such as hearing and seeing) to their motor actions (mouthing and grasping).

At the beginning of sensorimotor stage, Sam has one thinking problem: remembering that hidden objects still exist. For example, notice in the top left photo that 5-month-old Sam is shown a toy dog. Sam immediately tries to grab it and put part of it in his mouth. This is another example of assimilation; Sam believes that objects are mostly for mouthing.

However, notice in the bottom left photo, when a screen is placed in front of the dog, Sam looks away. He doesn't push the screen away to get at the toy because, at this point, Sam behaves as if things that are out of sight are out of mind and simply no longer exist. Sam has not learned object permanence.

Object permanence. Beginning at around 9 months, if Sam is shown a toy dog, which is then covered by a screen, he will try to push the screen away and look for the dog. Sam has learned that a toy dog that is out of sight still exists behind the screen. This new concept is called object permanence.

Object permanence refers to the understanding that objects or events continue to exist even if they can no longer be heard, touched, or seen.

The concept of object permanence develops slowly over a period of about nine months. By the end of the sensorimotor period (about age 2), an infant will search long and hard for lost or disappeared objects, indicating a fully developed concept of object permanence.

At the end of the sensorimotor stage, 2-year-old Sam can think about things that are not present and can form simple plans for solving problems, such as searching for things.

After the sensorimotor stage, Sam enters the preoperational stage.

2. Preoperational

Stage 2

As a 4-year-old, Sam is busy pushing a block around the floor and making noises as he pretends the block is a car. The cognitive ability to pretend is a sign that Sam is going through the preoperational stage.

The *preoperational stage* (from about 2 to 7 years old) is the second of Piaget's cognitive stages. During this stage, children learn to use symbols, such as words or mental images, to solve simple problems, and to think or talk about things that are not present.

At this stage, Sam is acquiring the cognitive ability to pretend things and to talk about or draw things that are not physically present. Although Sam is learning to use words and images in speech and play, his thinking has a number of interesting limitations that make his thinking different from an adult's. During the preoperational stage, two of his cognitive limitations involve problems with conservation and engaging in egocentric thinking.

Conservation. As 4-year-old Sam watches you pour milk from a tall thin glass into a short wide glass, will he know that the amount of milk remains the same even though its shape changes? This is called the problem of conservation.

Conservation refers to the fact that even though the shape of some object or substance is changed, the total amount remains the same.

Here's what happens when 4-year-old Sam is faced with a conservation problem.

In photo #1, 4-year-old Sam watches as his mother fills two short, wide glasses with equal amounts of milk.

In photo #2, Sam sees his mother pour the milk from one short, wide glass into a tall, thin glass. Mother asks, "Does one glass have more milk?"

In photo #3, Sam points to the tall, thin glass as having more milk because the tall glass looks larger. He makes this mistake even though he just saw his mother pour the milk from a short, wide glass.

Sam, like other children at the preoperational stage, will not be able to solve conservation problems until the next stage.

Egocentric thinking. A second problem that Sam has during the preoperational stage is that he makes mistakes or misbehaves because of egocentric thinking.

Egocentric (ee-goh-SEN-trick) *thinking* refers to seeing and thinking of the world only from your own viewpoint and having difficulty appreciating someone else's viewpoint.

Piaget used the term *egocentric thinking* to mean that preoperational children cannot see situations from another person's, such as a parent's, point of view. When they don't get their way, children may get angry or pout because their view of the world is so self-centered.

E. Cognitive Development

3. Concrete

Stage 3

Sam is now 10 years old and feeling pretty good because he has learned the concept of conservation. This new cognitive skill occurs during the concrete operations stage.

The *concrete operations stage* (from about 7 to 11 years), is the third of Piaget's cognitive stages. During this stage, children can perform a number of logical mental operations on concrete objects (ones that are physically present).

Conservation. As you may remember, when Sam was 4 years old and in the preoperational stage, he had not mastered the concept of conservation. In the preoperational stage, Sam thought a tall thin glass held more milk than a short wide glass. And if 4-year-old Sam watched as a ball of clay (top left photo) was flattened into a long piece (left bottom photo), he would say the long piece was larger. However, Sam is now 10 years old and has just watched you flatten a ball of clay into a long piece. Sam now says that the long flattened piece contains the same amount of clay as the ball, even if the shape changed. Similarly, if 10-year-old Sam watched you pour cola from a short glass into a tall glass, he would correctly answer that the amount of cola remained the same. Children gradually master the concept of conservation during the concrete operations stage, and they also get better at classification.

Classification. If you gave 4-year-old, preoperational Sam some trail mix (below photo), he would be able to classify the pieces according to a single category, such as color. However, during the concrete operations stage, 10-year-old Sam has acquired the ability to classify trail mix according to two categories, such as color and size, indicating that he has learned a new cognitive skill.

New abilities. During the concrete operations stage, children learn to classify or sort objects according to more than one category and learn to solve a variety of conservation problems. The reason Piaget called this the *concrete* operations stage is because children can easily classify or figure out relationships between objects provided the objects are actually physically present or "concrete."

However, children at the concrete operations stage still have difficulty figuring out relationships among objects that are not present or situations that are imaginary. Thinking about imaginary or hypothetical situations occurs in Piaget's fourth stage.

4. Formal

Stage 4

Sam is now 15 years old and is surfing the Web for a paper he's writing on what killed the dinosaurs. This kind of abstract thinking indicates that Sam is in the formal operations stage.

The *formal operations stage* (from about 12 years old through adulthood) is Piaget's fourth cognitive stage. During this stage, adolescents and adults develop the ability to think about and solve abstract problems in a logical manner.

Piaget believed that it is during the formal operations stage that adolescents develop thinking and reasoning typical of adults. For example, 15-year-old Sam can compare several theories about why the dinosaurs died, including being destroyed by a giant asteroid, radical temperature change, or some terrible virus. In the formal operations stage, Sam will learn to solve abstract problems in a systematic, logical manner. In comparison, five years ago when Sam was in the concrete operations stage, he lacked the ability to solve abstract problems. Now that Sam is 15 and in the formal operations stage, Sam is learning to use a computer graphics program as well as solving the latest video game that involves careful planning to outthink seven layers of evil creatures.

Once adolescents reach the formal operations stage, they encounter exciting new worlds of abstract ideas and hypothetical concepts. For example, Sam can discuss abstract ideas, such as whether computer hackers should go to jail, if going steady is a good idea, and how strict parents should be. Acquiring the ability to think in a logical, systematic, and abstract way is one of the major characteristics of the formal operations stage and opens a whole new world of ideas. The cognitive skills associated with the formal operations stage are the very ones that you will need to do well in college.

KEY IDEAS

We have discussed Piaget's cognitive stages in some detail but there are at least three ideas that stand out (Flavell, 1996):

1 Children gradually and in a step-by-step fashion develop reasoning abilities through the active processes of assimilation and accommodation.

2 Children are naturally curious and intrinsically or self-motivated to explore their worlds and, in the process, develop numerous cognitive skills.

3 Children acquire different kinds of thinking and reasoning abilities as they go through different stages of cognitive development.

Because Piaget's theory and ideas have been studied and tested for about 40 years, you may be asking, "How well has his theory of cognitive development stood the test of time?"

Evaluation of Piaget's Theory

The immense influence of Piaget's theory on the field of cognitive development has been compared to the immense influence of Shakespeare on the development of English literature or of Aristotle on the development of philosophy (Flavell, 1996). We'll discuss the advantages and criticisms of Piaget's theory as well as the current directions in studying and explaining cognitive development.

Advantages and Criticisms

Four stages. A major advantage of Piaget's theory is that it describes how children go through four cognitive stages, and how at each stage they develop new and dif-

1. Sensorimotor
2. Preoperational
3. Concrete
4. Formal

ferent ways of thinking and reasoning. However, one criticism of Piaget's four stages is that they are not as rigid as he proposed. Researchers have found that children can solve certain kinds of problems at stages earlier than Piaget proposed. For example, preoperational children can solve some abstract problems, such as who is taller or shorter than someone else, provided the problems are presented simply and are repeated many times. According to Piaget (right photo), preoperational children should not be able to solve these simple abstract problems. However, researchers have found that children do show certain thinking skills earlier than would be predicted from Piaget's cognitive stages. For this reason, Piaget's stages are now viewed as being neither as rigid nor as complete as he originally proposed (Haith & Benson, 1998).

Description versus explanation. One advantage of Piaget's stages is that each stage described what a child could and could not do, such as an infant learns object permanence but not conservation during the sensorimotor stage. One problem with Piaget's theory is that it describes the kind of thinking a child can and cannot do but it does not explain how this change occurs. Thus, one criticism of Piaget's cognitive stages is that they describe rather than explain what causes children's thinking to change from one stage to another (Wellman & Gelman, 1998).

Errors and exceptions. The biggest advantage of Piaget's theory was that his four stages offered a very complete description of how cognitive development gradually changes between infancy and adulthood. However, as discussed above, researchers have found errors and exceptions in Piaget's stages of cognitive development. As a result of these criticisms, Piaget's theory is still viewed as being of great historical importance, but it is no longer the major force in guiding research in childhood cognitive development (Gopnik & Meltzoff, 1997).

Current Directions

Since Piaget developed his theory, there have been at least three major changes or advances in the study of cognitive development.

1 Genetic factors. One of the biggest changes has been in the identification of genetic factors that influence memory, learning, and cognitive skills. For example, current research on identical and fraternal twins has shown that genetic factors account for between 20–60% of the influence on verbal, spatial, and perceptual abilities as well as on memory (Petrill, 1998). In Piaget's time, the influence of genetic factors on cognitive abilities had not been as clearly established. In the last 10 years there has been an increasing number of studies showing how genetic cognitive factors (nature) influence and interact with a child's environment (nurture). Researchers conclude that genetic factors set a range for many cognitive abilities, whose growth can be either facilitated by a stimulating environment or depressed by an impoverished environment (Plomin & Rutter, 1998).

2 Basic abilities. A second major change is the discovery that infants and young children have many more basic cognitive skills and abilities than Piaget believed. For example, researchers report that infants are aware that objects continue to exist even when screened from view; that infants have a basic concept of how objects move; that infants understand the concept of addition; and that they have remarkable abilities to recognize speech sounds (Haith & Benson, 1998). The fact that infants and young children possess a relatively large number of cognitive skills means that they are even more actively involved in learning about and discovering their environments than Piaget or anyone previously believed (Haith & Benson, 1998).

3 New theories. A third major change in the field of cognitive development is that there is no longer a single grand theory, such as Piaget's theory of four cognitive stages. Although Piaget's original theory had and still has some influence on cognitive development studies, recent findings described above point out the weaknesses in his theory. For this reason, psychologists are constructing new theories; one has the unusual name of theory theory.

Theory theory says that children have innate abilities to make guesses about how things are, test their guesses through interactions with the environment, and change their guesses as they gather new or conflicting information.

According to theory theory, a child develops cognitively by acting like an everyday scientist who makes guesses about how the world works, tests these guesses by gathering new information, and changes these guesses in the face of conflicting information (Gopnik & Meltzoff, 1997). Theory theory is one example of the new theories being developed to replace Piaget's theory.

For the sake of simplicity, we have discussed cognitive development as if it proceeded independently. In fact, cognitive development is closely intertwined with social development, which we'll examine next.

F. Social Development

What will happen to baby Jessica?

At the beginning of this module we described how baby Jessica at age 2½ was taken away from the adoptive parents who had raised her from birth and returned to her biological parents, whom she had never met. Some psychologists wonder how Jessica's early emotional difficulties will affect her future social development.

Social development refers to how a person develops a sense of self or a self-identity, develops relationships with others, and develops the kind of social skills important in personal interactions.

In baby Jessica's case, we know that after eight months with her new, biological parents, she seemed to have made a very good adjustment. However, some psychologists believe that Jessica's first five years are the most important and that her early emotional troubles may lead to social problems as an adult.

Jessica's social development is a long and complicated process, which is influenced by many of the emotional and cognitive factors that we have just discussed. We'll describe three different theories of social development, each of which emphasizes a different aspect of behavior.

Freud's Psychosexual Stages

One of the best-known theories is that of Sigmund Freud (1940/1961), who said that each of us goes through five successive psychosexual stages.

The *psychosexual stages* are five different developmental periods—oral, anal, phallic, latency, and genital stages—during which the individual seeks pleasure from different areas of the body that are associated with sexual feelings. Freud emphasized that a child's first five years were most important to social and personality development.

In Freud's theory, there is often conflict between the child and parent. The conflict arises because the child wants immediate satisfaction or gratification of its needs, while the parents often place restrictions on when, where, and how the child's needs should be satisfied. For example, a child may

wish to be fed immediately, while the parent may want to delay the feeding to a more convenient time. Freud believed that interactions between parent and child in satisfying these psychosexual needs—for example, during breast-feeding or toilet training—greatly influence the child's social development and future social interactions. In addition, Freud emphasized the importance of a child's first five years in influencing future social development or future personality problems.

According to Freud, Jessica will go through five developmental stages, some of which contain potential conflicts between her desires and her parents' wishes. If her desires are over- or undersatisfied, she may become fixated at one of the first three stages. As you'll see, becoming fixated at one of these stages will hinder her normal social development.

---

1 Oral Stage

Period: Early infancy—first 18 months of life.

Potential conflict:
The *oral stage* lasts for the first 18 months of life and is a time when the infant's pleasure seeking is centered on the mouth.

Pleasure-seeking activities include sucking, chewing, and biting. If Jessica were locked into or fixated at this stage because her oral wishes were gratified too much or too little, she would continue to seek oral gratification as an adult.

2 Anal Stage

Period: Late infancy—1½ to 3 years.

Potential conflict:
The *anal stage* lasts from the age of about 1½ to 3 and is a time when the infant's pleasure seeking is centered on the anus and its functions of elimination.

If Jessica were locked into or fixated at this stage, she would continue to engage in behavioral activities related to retention or elimination. Retention may take the form of being very neat, stingy, or behaviorally rigid. Elimination may take the form of being generous or messy.

3 Phallic Stage

Period: Early childhood—3 to 6 years.

Potential conflict:
The *phallic (FAL-ik) stage* lasts from about age 3 to 6 and is a time when the infant's pleasure seeking is centered on the genitals.

During this stage, Jessica will compete with the parent of the same sex (her mother) for the affections and pleasures of the parent of the opposite sex (her father). Problems in resolving this competition (called the Oedipus complex and discussed in Module 19) may result in feelings of inferiority for women and of having something to prove for men.

4 Latency Stage

Period: Middle and late childhood—from 6 to puberty.

Potential conflict:
The *latency stage*, which lasts from about age 6 to puberty, is a time when the child represses sexual thoughts and engages in nonsexual activities, such as developing social and intellectual skills.

At puberty, sexuality reappears and marks the beginning of a new stage.

5 Genital Stage

Period: Puberty through adulthood.

Potential conflict:
The *genital stage* lasts from puberty through adulthood and is a time when the individual has renewed sexual desires that he or she seeks to fulfill through relationships with members of the opposite sex.

If Jessica successfully resolved conflicts in the first three stages, she will have the energy to develop loving relationships and a healthy and mature personality.

According to Freud, Jessica's future personality and social development will depend, to a large extent, on what she experiences during the first three psychosexual stages, which occur during her first five years. Freud's psychosexual stages are part of his larger psychoanalytic theory of personality, which we'll discuss more fully in Module 19.

Erikson's Psychosocial Stages

How important is trust?

According to well-known psychologist Erik Erikson, Jessica will encounter kinds of problems very different from the psychosexual ones proposed by Freud. Unlike Freud's emphasis on psychosexual issues, Erikson (1963, 1982) focused on psychosocial issues and said that each of us goes through eight psychosocial stages.

The *psychosocial stages* are eight developmental periods during which an individual's primary goal is to satisfy desires associated with social needs: the eight periods are associated, respectively, with issues of trust, autonomy, initiative, industry, identity, intimacy, generativity, and ego integrity.

Erikson hypothesized that from infancy through adulthood we proceed through these stages, each of

which is related to a different problem that needs to be resolved. If we successfully deal with the potential problem of each psychosocial stage, we develop positive personality traits and are better able to solve the problem at the next stage. However, if we do not successfully handle the psychosocial problems, we may become anxious, worried, or troubled and develop social or personality problems.

Unlike Freud, Erikson believed that psychosocial needs deserve the greatest emphasis and that social development continues throughout one's lifetime. Thus, Erikson would emphasize Jessica's psychosocial needs and downplay the importance of sexuality in the first five years.

We'll explain Erikson's first five stages here and discuss the remaining three stages in Module 18, which deals with social development in adolescents and adults.

Stage 1 Trust versus Mistrust	Stage 2 Autonomy versus Shame and Doubt	Stage 3 Initiative versus Guilt	Stage 4 Industry versus Inferiority	Stage 5 Identity versus Role Confusion
Period: Early infancy—birth through first year.	**Period:** Late infancy—1 to 3 years.	**Period:** Early childhood—3 to 5 years.	**Period:** Middle and late childhood—5 to 12 years.	**Period:** Adolescence.
Potential problem: Jessica comes into the world as a helpless infant who needs much care and attention. If her parents are responsive and sensitive to her needs, Jessica will develop what Erikson calls basic trust, which makes it easier for her to trust people later in life. If Jessica's parents neglect her needs, she may view her world as uncaring, learn to become mistrustful, and have difficulty dealing with the second stage. It appears that both sets of parents gave Jessica care and attention.	**Potential problem:** As Jessica begins walking, talking, and exploring, she is bound to get into conflict with the wishes of her parents. Thus, this second stage is a battle of wills between her parents' wishes and Jessica's desires to do as she pleases. If her parents encourage Jessica to explore, she will develop a sense of independence, or autonomy. If her parents disapprove of or punish Jessica's explorations, she may develop a feeling that independence is bad and feel shame and doubt.	**Potential problem:** As a preschooler, Jessica has developed a number of cognitive and social skills that she is expected to use to meet the challenges in her small world. Some of these challenges involve assuming responsibility and making plans. If her parents encourage initiative, Jessica will develop the ability to plan and initiate new things. However, if they discourage initiative, she may feel uncomfortable or guilty and may develop a feeling of being unable to plan her future.	**Potential problem:** Jessica's grade school years are an exciting time, filled with participating in school, playing games with other children, and working to complete projects. If Jessica can direct her energy into working at and completing tasks, she will develop a feeling of industry. If she has difficulty applying herself and completing homework, she may develop a feeling of inferiority and incompetence.	**Potential problem:** Adolescents need to leave behind the carefree, irresponsible, and impulsive behaviors of childhood and develop the more purposeful, responsible, planned behaviors of adults. If Jessica is successful in making this change, she will develop a sense of confidence and a positive identity. If she is unsuccessful, she will experience role confusion, which will result in having low self-esteem and becoming socially withdrawn.

According to Erikson, Jessica will encounter a particular psychosocial problem at each stage. If she successfully solves the problem, she will develop a good social trait that will help her solve the next problem. If she does not solve the problem, she will develop a bad social trait that will hinder her solving a new problem at the next stage.

Evaluation of Erikson's and Freud's theories. Many psychologists agree with Erikson that psychosocial conflicts, which are based on interpersonal and environmental interactions, do contribute to social-emotional development (Bugental & Goodnow, 1998). Erikson said that the first five years were not necessarily the most important and that social development continues throughout one's life. In fact, longitudinal studies show that personality change and development continues well into middle adulthood (McCrae & Costa, 1990).

Many psychologists also agree with Freud that childhood events are important to social development. However, they criticize Freud for emphasizing childhood sexuality while neglecting the influences

of social and cognitive factors on social development (Bugental & Goodnow, 1998). In addition, longitudinal studies show that children may overcome a variety of problems during the first five years and still have a well-adjusted personality, contrary to Freud's predictions (Werner, 1995).

The strength of Erikson's and Freud's theories is that they explain the whole of social development, from infancy through adulthood. Their weakness, however, is that many of their concepts (trust, autonomy, oral stage, fixation) are more descriptive than explanatory and very difficult to verify or test experimentally. Next, we'll examine the social cognitive theory of social development.

F. Social Development

Bandura's Social Cognitive Theory

What is this three-year-old doing?

After watching his daddy bowl, this 3-year-old boy walked up to his daddy, pointed at the ball, and said, "Me too ball." Neither Freud's nor Erikson's theory explains why this 3-year-old child wanted to learn to bowl, what motivated him to ask his daddy, or why he clapped his hands just like his daddy when the ball hit the pins. Albert Bandura (1989a) says that this little boy, like all of us, develops many of his behaviors and social skills through a variety of social cognitive processes.

The *social cognitive theory* emphasizes the importance of learning through observation, imitation, and self-reward in the development of social skills, interactions, and behaviors. According to this theory, it is not necessary that you perform any observable behaviors or receive any external rewards in order to learn new social skills because many of your behaviors are self-motivated, or intrinsic.

Social cognitive theory stresses how you learn by modeling and imitating behaviors that you observe in social interactions and situations. For example, after watching his daddy, this 3-year-old is intrinsically motivated to imitate many of his daddy's social behaviors. Social cognitive theory would emphasize that children develop social behaviors and skills by watching and imitating the social behaviors of their parents, grandparents, teachers, and peers.

In comparing Bandura's, Freud's, and Erikson's theories, notice that although the three theories are very different, they are complementary because they each emphasize a different process. Social cognitive theory emphasizes learning through modeling; Freud's theory focuses on parent-child interactions that occur in satisfying innate biological needs; and Erikson's theory points to the importance of dealing with social needs.

We'll use these theories to explain how children overcame terrible childhood experiences to develop normal social behaviors.

Resiliency

How do children survive early problems?

Based on observations of his patients, Freud concluded that social and personality development is essentially completed in the first five years. That is, even though an individual might undergo later social changes, his or her basic social and personality traits are primarily established during the first five years. One way to test Freud's hypothesis is to do a long-term study of children who are faced with major problems. One such child was Delia.

During her first year, Delia's unwed mother was withdrawn and showed little interest in Delia; her father was rarely around. But, during her second year, she was sent to live with her grandparents, who raised Delia in a warm, loving, and caring home environment and later adopted her.

Delia was part of a study of 600 children from a small rural community on the Hawaiian island of Kauai. In this study, conducted by psychologist Emmy Werner (1989), the children (right photo) were followed from birth to almost 20. Like Delia, all the children were exposed to numerous life stresses, including problems during their mother's pregnancy, family instability, parents' mental and financial difficulties, and a lower social class environment with limited stimulation. How these life stressors affect children depends on their vulnerability and resiliency.

Vulnerability refers to psychological or environmental difficulties that make children more at risk for developing later personality, behavioral, or social problems.

Resiliency refers to various personality, family, or environmental factors that compensate for increased life stresses so that expected problems do not develop.

In Delia's group of 600 children, about 200 showed increased vulnerability and later developed serious behavioral or learning problems. However, the most remarkable finding is that over 400 of the children showed resiliency and developed into competent and autonomous young adults (Werner, 1989; Werner & Smith, 1982).

Children like Delia are called resilient, or stress-resistant. These children defy expectations because they develop into well-adapted individuals in spite of serious life stressors (Masten & Coatsworth, 1998). For example, despite having an insensitive, unresponsive young mother and an absent father, Delia at age 20 had developed adequate self-esteem, high achievement motivation, a fair degree of insight into her life, and realistic plans for the future.

Researchers identified several factors that contribute to resiliency. One factor was genetic: children born with *positive temperaments,* meaning they are more smiley and socially responsive, elicited more attention and care. Another factor was related to social cognitive processes: resilient children had a *substitute caregiver* whose caring behaviors and social skills could be observed and imitated; as a result, resilient children were socially popular. Another factor involved Erikson's psychosocial stages: resilient children received *social support, care,* and *trust* from their peers and caregivers and developed well-adjusted social behaviors (Werner, 1989).

Studies on resilient children show three things. First, early traumatic emotional events do not necessarily lead to later social-emotional problems, as Freud predicted. Second, a loving, supportive caregiver can substitute for a disinterested parent. Third, children observe and imitate normal social behaviors modeled by caregivers (Masten & Coatsworth, 1998; Werner, 1995).

CONCEPT REVIEW

1. The question that asks how much genetic factors and how much environmental factors contribute to a person's biological, emotional, cognitive, personal, and social development is called the _____ question.

2. The prenatal period, which begins at conception and ends at birth, is composed of three different stages. The

 first stage of prenatal development refers to the two-week period following conception; this is called the (a)_____ stage. The second stage of the prenatal period spans the 2–8 weeks that follow conception; this is called the (b)_____ stage. The third stage of the prenatal period begins two months after conception and lasts until birth; this is called the (c)_____ stage.

3. The organ that connects the blood supply of the mother to that of the fetus is called the (a)_____, which acts as a filter. However, some agents, such as drugs, viruses, and chemicals, pass into the fetal blood supply and harm the developing fetus; these agents are called (b)_____. One example of these agents is alcohol, which if drunk heavily during pregnancy can result in a combination of physical changes and mental retardation called (c)_____.

Placenta

Umbilical cord

4. Newborns have some visual acuity, respond to touch, and are able to hear, smell, and taste. This indicates that they have relatively well-developed

_____.

Two months (fetus)

Newborn

5. The acquisition of the muscular control necessary for coordinated physical activity, which is called (a)_____ development, follows two general principles. The principle that parts of the body closer to the head develop before the parts closer to the feet is the (b)_____ principle. The principle that parts closer to the center of the infant's body develop before parts farther away is the (c)_____ principle. Development of motor skills occurs in a sequential and orderly fashion because of a genetic plan; this process is called (d)_____.

6. An individual's stable pattern of behavioral and emotional reactions that appear early and are influenced in large part by genetic factors is called his or her _____.

7. The close fundamental emotional bond that develops between the infant and his or her parent or caregiver is called (a)_____. Infants who use their parent as a safe home base from which they can wander off and explore their environments are said to have formed a (b)_____ attachment. Infants who avoid or show ambivalence toward their parents are said to have formed an (c)_____ attachment.

8. Piaget believed that children are actively involved in understanding their world through two basic processes: incorporating new information or experience into existing knowledge is called (a)_____; changing existing knowledge or experience as a result of assimilating some new information is called (b)_____.

9. Piaget's theory of cognitive development includes four stages, each of which is characterized by the development of particular kinds of reasoning. The first stage, during which infants learn about their environments by relating their sensory experiences (such as hearing and seeing) to their motor actions, is called the (a)_____ stage. The second stage, during which infants learn to use symbols to think about things that are not present and to help them solve simple problems, is called the (b)_____ stage. The third stage, during which children learn to perform a number of logical mental operations on objects that are physically present, is called the (c)_____ stage. The fourth stage, during which adolescents and adults develop the ability to think about and solve abstract problems in a logical manner, is called the (d)_____ stage.

10. According to Freud's theory of social development, children go through five developmental periods, which he called _____ stages. During these stages, a child's primary goal is to satisfy desires associated with innate biological needs.

11. According to Albert Bandura's social cognitive theory, we learn social skills through _____, _____, and self–reward.

12. According to Erik Erikson, a person goes through eight developmental periods during which the primary goal is to satisfy desires associated with social needs. Each of these eight periods is called a _____ stage, during which the person works to resolve a potential problem.

Answers: *1. nature-nurture; 2. (a) germinal, (b) embryonic, (c) fetal; 3. (a) placenta, (b) teratogens, (c) fetal alcohol syndrome; 4. senses; 5. (a) motor, (b) cephalocaudal, (c) proximodistal, (d) maturation; 6. temperament; 7. (a) attachment, (b) secure, (c) insecure; 8. (a) assimilation, (b) accommodation; 9. (a) sensorimotor, (b) preoperational, (c) concrete operations, (d) formal operations; 10. psychosexual; 11. observation, imitation; 12. psychosocial.*

F. Social Development

Review: The Big Picture

Throughout infancy and childhood, there are amazing increases in sensory abilities and motor skills, and wonderous development of emotions, cognitive skills, social interactions, and personality traits. We'll briefly review these developments so that you can appreciate the incredible changes and see the big picture.

1 Newborn's Abilities

Newborns come with more sensory and perceptual abilities than previously thought. They have a well-developed sense of touch, show an innate preference for sweet and salt, and recognize (smell) their mothers' odors. In a few more months, infants can recognize their mothers' faces, produce speech sounds, perceive depth, and have a basic concept of addition. This new and improved version of infants' abilities better explains how they discover the world.

2 Motor Development

Infants gradually acquire *coordinated movements* that they need to crawl, sit, stand, and walk. Many motor skills occur in a set sequence called *maturation* that is regulated by genetic programming. Two principles for motor development are that parts closest to the center of the body develop first—the *proximodistal* principle; and parts closer to the head develop first—the *cephalocaudal* principle. With motor development comes the ability to get up and explore.

3 Emotional Development

"Good" babies and "difficult" babies show signs of differences in temperament, which is largely influenced by genetic factors. *Temperament* refers to stable differences in attention, arousal, and reaction to new situations; it also affects level of arousal and development of emotional behaviors. Infants develop many *emotions,* which allow a wide range of wordless communication with the parent and the world. Infants form a close emotional bond with parents (caregiver). This emotional bond, which is called *attachment,* is thought to influence the development of future emotional and social behaviors.

4 Cognitive Development

One theory of cognitive development is *Piaget's theory,* which says that children play an active role in cognitive development by incorporating new information into existing knowledge *(assimilation)* or changing existing knowledge through experience *(accommodation).* Children pass through four different cognitive stages—*(1) sensorimotor, (2) preoperational, (3) concrete operations,* and *(4) formal operations*—in that order but at different rates. With each stage, the child adds a new and qualitatively different kind of thinking or reasoning skill that helps the child make better sense of the world.

5 Social Development

At the same time that children are developing emotionally and cognitively, they are also developing socially. *Freud* said that children develop socially by going through five *psychosexual stages* and that during the first three stages, the individual seeks pleasure from different areas of the body associated with sexual feelings. *Erikson* said that children develop socially by going through eight *psychosocial stages* during which an individual's primary goal is to satisfy desires associated with social needs. According to *Bandura's* *social cognitive theory,* children develop social skills through imitation, observation, and self-reward. These three theories are not mutually exclusive but rather complement each other by focusing on different factors believed to be important in social development. Freud's is the only theory that says the first five years are critical.

6 Importance of Childhood

How important are events that occur during childhood? In some cases, traumatic events (poverty, parental disinterest) result in later behavioral and social problems, but in other cases, a loving, supportive parent or caregiver compensates for early problems and results in a resilient child. Although childhood may be an important time for emotional, social, and personality development, both positive and negative personality and social changes continue into middle adulthood.

Next we'll examine an interesting and related question: Do children from very different cultures acquire similar or different gender roles and behaviors?

Oliviero Toscani for BENETTON

G. Cultural Diversity: Gender Roles

Do cultures have different gender roles?

Although we know that young boys and girls acquire different gender roles, the intriguing question is why do little boys generally grow up to be more aggressive and independent while little girls grow up to be less aggressive and more concerned? To answer this question, researchers tested hundreds of 5-, 8-, and 11-year-old children in 24 countries to find out if young children from so many different cultures developed similar or different male-female gender roles and behaviors (Williams & Best, 1990).

Identifying Gender Roles

For younger children (5- and 8-year-olds), researchers told them 32 brief stories, and then asked whether the person in the story was more like a man than a woman; an example is given at right. For older children (11-year-olds), researchers gave them a list of 300 adjectives, such as aggressive, affectionate, calm, bossy, sensitive, loud, and helpful, and asked which adjectives were more likely to be associated with males and which with females. Unlike 5- and 8-year-old children, 11-year-olds were able to understand the meanings of the adjectives and indicate their preferences by checking off adjectives that they thought best suited males or females.

1. One of these people is a very affectionate person. When they like someone, they hug and kiss them a lot. Which person likes to hug and kiss a lot?

Gender Roles Across Cultures

Similarities. Researchers found that across the 24 countries, relatively young children showed remarkable similarities in characteristics that they associated with gender roles.

For example, 57% of 5-year-old children made stereotyped responses about gender roles by associating people in the stories with a particular sex, either male or female. For example, 5-year-old children associated being strong, aggressive, and dominant with males while associating being gentle and affectionate with females. Eight-year-old children had learned even more stereotypic behaviors. They associated being weak, emotional, appreciative, excitable, gentle, softhearted, meek, and submissive with females, while they associated being disorderly, cruel, coarse, adventurous, independent, ambitious, loud, and boastful with males. By the age of 11, the percentage of children making stereotyped responses about gender roles jumped to 90%.

Differences. Researchers also found that across countries and cultures, interesting differences occurred in children's perception of gender roles. For example, in Germany, children associated being adventurous, confident, jolly, and steady with females, while in most other countries these characteristics were typically associated with males.

In Japan, children associated being dominant and steady with females, while in other countries, these characteristics were typically associated with males.

Conclusions. Researchers concluded that children in 24 different countries and cultures developed knowledge of gender roles relatively early and showed remarkable similarities in choosing different gender roles and behaviors for males and females. Although there were some differences due to cultural values, there were generally more similarities in male-female gender roles across the 24 countries (Williams & Best, 1990).

Boy with sling: Strong, aggressive, dominant, independent, coarse, loud, boastful

Girl with doll: Emotional, weak, appreciative, excitable, gentle, meek, submissive

Acquiring Gender Roles: Two Theories

We began with the question, "How do little boys grow up to be more aggressive and independent while little girls grow up to be less aggressive and more concerned?" To this we add another question, "Why do little boys and little girls from 24 different countries and cultures develop such similar male-female gender roles?" Two theories give different but somewhat complementary answers.

The **social role theory**, which emphasizes social and cultural influences, states that gender differences between males and females arise from different divisions of labor.

According to social role theory, male-female gender differences developed from traditional cultural divisions of labor, in which women were childbearers and homemakers while men were providers and protectors (Eagly, 1997). Because men and women performed different duties, men and women developed different gender roles. Social role theory says that social-cultural pressures are the basis for gender differences. The next theory gives a different answer.

The **evolutionary theory**, which emphasizes genetic and biological forces, says that current gender differences are a continuation of the behaviors that evolved from early men and women who adapted these different behaviors in their attempts to survive the problems of their time.

According to evolutionary theory, men increased their chances for reproduction by being dominant, controlling, and aggressive. In comparison, women increased their chances of raising their children by being concerned, sensitive, and nurturing. According to evolutionary theory, the current male-female gender differences arise from genetic and biological forces that evolved from an ancient set of mating patterns that had initially helped the species survive (Buss, 1995, Archer, 1996, 1997).

Because social role theory emphasizes cultural influences and evolutionary theory emphasizes genetic and biological forces, researchers suggest that by combining the two theories we could better explain the development of our current male and female gender differences (Baldwin & Baldwin, 1997; Schaller, 1997).

H. Application: Child Abuse

The family had all the trappings of being perfect, including wealth, status, and prestige.

Father. The father was a handsome, intelligent man who served as president of the Denver Area Boy Scout Council and helped establish Denver's Cleo Wallace Village for Handicapped Children. He was a millionaire socialite and a pillar of the Denver community.

Mother. The mother was a good homemaker, who spent all of her time caring for her four children, all girls.

Marilyn. Marilyn was the youngest daughter and described as a golden-haired beauty. In college she was a straight-A student and a swimming champion. At the age of 20, she was crowned Miss America (right photo).

The secret. Marilyn had been sexually abused by her father from the time she was 5 until she was 18, when she moved away to college. However, Marilyn had completely repressed any knowledge of sexual abuse by her father until she was 24. She was having a conversation with a former youth minister at her church when she broke down and told her painful secret. She made the minister promise not to tell anyone except her fiancé, who was very sympathetic and understanding, and her oldest sister, who said, "Oh, no! I thought I was the only one" (van Derbur Atler, 1991, p. 91).

Dealing with abuse. Marilyn says that she didn't tell anyone because she didn't want to destroy her family and was afraid her father would go to jail. Thus, she kept her secret and survived by splitting into a day child who seemed normal and happy and a night child who feared her father and suffered his abuse.

Facing the abuser. When Marilyn was 40 years old, the sight of her own 5-year-old daughter triggered terrible memories of her father's abuse and gave her frightening physical symptoms. She knew that her misery would remain until she confronted him. She met and talked to him for 20 minutes. He did not deny anything and said, "If I had known what this would do to you, I never would have done it" (van Derbur Atler, 1991, p. 94).

Aftermath. At 47, Marilyn van Derbur was named the Outstanding Woman Speaker in America. But she was having terrible bouts of anxiety and couldn't continue her career. Finally, she told her mother about being abused and spent the next seven years in therapy. At 54, Marilyn (right photo) stood before the Adult Incest Survivors Group and publicly revealed her secret: she had been abused for 13 years by her father. Her goal now is to help others who have been abused.

Marilyn was a victim of one kind of child abuse, sexual abuse. There are several kinds of child abuse.

Kinds of Abuse

In 1997, the National Committee to Prevent Child Abuse found that there were about 3 million reported cases of child abuse, of which almost 1 million were confirmed. Of the confirmed cases, there were about 1300 deaths and, of these, 85% were children under the age of 5. As the right graph shows, the most common abuse is neglect, followed by physical abuse and sexual abuse. The "other" category includes emotional neglect and other kinds of abuse that do not easily fit into any category.

Child abuse and neglect (physical and emotional) result from inadequate care or acts of the parent that put the child in danger, cause physical harm or injury, or involve sexual molestation.

Kinds of Child Abuse

Neglect	60%
Physical abuse	23%
Sexual abuse	9%
Other	8%

Source: National Committee to Prevent Child Abuse

The second most frequently confirmed kind of child abuse (23%) is *physical abuse.* For example, 10-year-old Karen vividly remembered how much and how often she was beaten by her mother. Her mother would get angry over the tiniest things, grab something handy (shoes, father's belt, potato masher), and start hitting her. One time her mother beat her so hard that Karen's legs turned black and blue. When Karen threatened to tell the police, her mother replied in an angry voice, "Go ahead. They won't believe you and they'll put you in the darkest prison" (*Time,* September 5, 1983).

The third most frequently confirmed kind of child abuse (9%) is *sexual abuse.* For example, Marilyn's case shows that very often the abuser is the father or stepfather and that many children are too fearful of the abuser to report their maltreatment. Surveys of sexual abuse in 21 different countries indicate that 7–36% of women and 3–29% of men have been sexually abused; females are 2–3 times more likely to suffer abuse than males (Emery & Laumann-Billings, 1998). This indicates that sexual abuse, which may result in serious long-term behavioral, social, and personality problems, is an international problem.

We'll focus on three questions related to abuse and neglect: Who abuses children? What problems do abused children suffer? How are abusive parents helped?

Who Abuses Children?

What are the parents' problems?

Parents who abuse their children are likely to have low self-esteem and a wide range of personal problems. They are apt to be impulsive, anxious, defensive, aggressive, and socially isolated. Often, serious marital problems add to their numerous life stresses (Emery & Laumann-Billings, 1998). Studies show that about 60% of *physical* abuse is committed by mothers and about 90% of *sexual* abuse is committed by fathers or stepfathers (Miller, 1995). In addition, about 30% of abused children become parents who abuse their own children (Kaufman & Zigler, 1989).

Although an abused child is at risk for becoming an abusive parent, a number of ***compensatory factors*** can prevent this from happening. These compensatory factors include having a positive attachment to a caregiver, resolving not to repeat the abuse, having an awareness of one's early abusive experiences, experiencing fewer stressful life events than the abusive parents did, and having a supportive spouse or good social support. The path from being abused to becoming an abusive parent is neither direct nor fixed and can be reversed by these compensatory factors (Belsky, 1993).

A child's characteristics can also increase or decrease the chances of being abused. For example, a fussy, irritable, dependent, sickly, or physically handicapped child is more difficult to care for if the parents have personal problems of their own (Knutson, 1995). The interaction between a difficult child and troubled parents illustrates the principle of bidirectionality (Maccoby, 1984).

The ***principle of bidirectionality*** says that a child's behaviors influence how his or her parents respond, and in turn the parents' behaviors influence how the child responds.

According to this principle, child abuse results from an interaction between a child's difficult traits, which tend to elicit maltreatment or abuse from the parents, and the parents' social-emotional and caregiving problems, which make it difficult for them to recognize and meet the needs of their child (Miller, 1995). Thus, the combination of a difficult child and parents who have their own personal or drug-related problems result in a potentially explosive parent-child interaction that increases the risk for child abuse. Abused children can develop a variety of problems.

What Problems Do Abused Children Have?

Are there long-term problems?

Children who suffer abuse may experience a number of physical and psychological problems. The **physical problems** include having more stomachaches, headaches, bedwetting, and hormonal changes that indicate their systems are trying to deal with large doses of stress (Putnam, 1995). Abused children also suffer a number of **psychological problems,** which include increased anxiety, social withdrawal, delays in social, cognitive, and emotional development, poorer school performance, attention problems, and fearful nightmares.

When abused children become teenagers, they may experience continuing problems, such as having poor self-esteem, more depression, loneliness and suicidal impulses, more conflicts with friends, and engaging in more delinquent behaviors. Thus, child abuse may result in many psychological and physiological problems, some of which may persist for some time (Howe, 1997, Tebbutt et al., 1997).

Long-term or longitudinal studies on sexually abused children report that within 12–18 months after sexual abuse stopped, 55–65% of children showed a substantial decrease in symptoms, but 10–24% appeared to get worse. Those children who showed the best recovery were those who received strong support and care from their mothers (Kendall-Tackett et al., 1993).

How Are Abusive Parents Helped?

How can abusive parents be changed?

Treatment for abusive parents focuses on solving their personal and marital problems and increasing their childrearing skills. A number of therapy programs that use some combination of cognitive-behavior therapy (Module 25) and parent-training programs (Module 10) have proven relatively successful in decreasing child abuse. In general, these programs have at least two goals (Peterson & Brown, 1994).

1. **Overcoming the parent's personal problems.** Abusive parents need help in learning about and developing social relationships, which are needed for positive bonding and attachment between parent and child. Abusive parents also need training in basic caregiving skills, which involves learning how to meet the physical, social, and emotional needs of their children. Dealing with abusive parents' personal or drug problems usually requires long-term professional therapy. As parents get their personal or marital problems under control, they can concentrate on improving the interactions with their child.

2. **Changing parent-child interactions.** Researchers have found that abusive parents are less likely to use positive behaviors such as smiling, praising, and touching and are more likely to use negative behaviors such as threatening, disapproving, and showing anger when dealing with their child (Reid et al., 1981). This means that abusive parents need to learn more positive ways of interacting with their children. Parent-training programs, which use behavior modification techniques (discussed in Module 10), are effective in helping parents learn to reduce negative interactions with their children (Kolko, 1995).

Clinicians and researchers recognize that, in many countries, neglect, physical abuse and sexual abuse are serious social problems that deserve more attention and treatment than they currently receive (Emery & Laumann-Billings, 1998).

SUMMARY TEST

A. PRENATAL INFLUENCES

1. The time from conception to birth is called the (a)_____ period, which is divided into three parts. The two-week period that immediately follows conception is called the (b)_____ period; it is marked by the zygote dividing into many cells. The period that includes the 2–8 weeks after conception, during which cells continue to divide and begin to differentiate into bone, muscle, and body organs, is called the (c)_____ period. The period of development that begins two months after conception and lasts for about seven months is called the (d)_____ period. At the end of this period, birth occurs and the fetus becomes a newborn.

Placenta

Umbilical cord

2. The development of the fetus can be interrupted or damaged by a variety of toxic agents, called (a)_____, which cause malformation of the brain or body and result in birth defects. For example, heavy drinking during pregnancy can cause a combination of physical and psychological deficits called (b)_____, which is the leading known cause of mental retardation in the United States.

B. NEWBORNS' ABILITIES

Two months (fetus)   New-born

3. The newborn comes into the world with relatively well-developed sensory and perceptual responses. For example, the newborn can see, but his or her ability to see details, which is called (a)_____, is poor. Six-month-old infants will not crawl off the visual cliff, indicating that they have developed (b)_____ perception. Newborns have good hearing, touch, and smell and an inherited preference for sweet and salt tastes.

4. Motor development, which is the acquisition of the muscle control required for coordinated physical activity, follows two general principles. The principle that parts of the body closer to the head develop before those closer to the feet is called the (a)_____ principle. The principle that parts closer to the center of the body develop before those farther away is called the (b)_____ principle.

5. Development that occurs in a sequential and orderly fashion because of a genetic plan is called (a)_____. The average age at which individuals perform various kinds of motor skills or exhibit abilities or behaviors is reflected in (b)_____.

C. EMOTIONAL DEVELOPMENT

6. Early and stable individual differences in attention, arousal, and reaction to new things refer to an infant's _____, which is greatly influenced by genetic, or inherited, factors.

7. Newborns have a limited range of emotional expressions that include interest, startle, distress, disgust, and neonatal smile. During the first two years, infants develop a wide range of _____ expressions and feelings that signal the infant's physiological needs and psychological moods.

8. The close emotional bond that develops between infant and parent (caregiver) is called (a)_____. As the infant develops a closer attachment to her parents, she also shows more distress when her parents leave; this distress is called (b)_____.

9. There are two kinds of attachment. Infants who use their caregiver as a safe home base from which they can wander off and explore their environments are said to be (a)_____ attached. This kind of attachment may contribute to better emotional bonds later in life. Infants who avoid or show ambivalence toward their caregivers are said to be (b)_____ attached. For example, these infants may cling and want to be held one minute but squirm and push away the next minute.

D. RESEARCH FOCUS: TEMPERAMENT

Age   2   7

10. Researchers use two different methods to study developmental processes. Repeatedly studying the same group of individuals at different ages is using the (a)_____ method. Studying different groups of individuals who are of different ages is using the (b)_____ method.

11. Researchers estimate that about 10–15% of the general population show reluctance, anxiety, or fear and increased physiological arousal when in a strange or novel situation. These individuals are called shy or _____. This finding supports the idea that temperaments develop early, are stable across time, and are partially under genetic control (nature).

E. COGNITIVE DEVELOPMENT

12. Piaget believed that children participate in their own cognitive development by active involvement through two different processes: incorporating new information or experience into existing knowledge is called (a)_____; and changing one's knowledge or experiences as a result of assimilating some new information is called (b)_____.

13. Piaget divided cognitive development into four stages. In the first, lasting from birth to about age 2, infants interact with and learn about their environments by relating their sensory experiences to their motor actions; this is called the (a)_____ stage. A significant development of this stage is the concept that objects or events continue to exist even if they cannot be heard, touched, or seen; this is called (b)_____.

14. In the second stage, lasting from the age of about 2 to 7, children learn to use symbols to think about things that are not present and to help them solve simple problems; this is the (a)_____ stage. A limitation in this stage is the tendency to think of the world only from one's own viewpoint, called (b)_____ thinking.

15. The third stage, which lasts from the age of about 7 to 11, is called the (a)_____ stage. During this stage, children can perform a number of logical mental operations on concrete objects (ones that are physically present). The idea that the amount of a substance remains the same even in different shapes, known as (b)_____, is mastered during the third stage.

16. During the fourth and last stage, which lasts from about age 12 through adulthood, the individual develops the ability to think about and solve abstract problems logically; this is called the (a)_____ stage. Each of Piaget's cognitive stages is thought to be qualitatively different from the previous one, because each new stage represents the development of some new (b)_____ ability.

F. SOCIAL DEVELOPMENT

17. How a person develops social relationships, develops a sense of self, and becomes a social being is called (a)_____ development. Three theories of such development each emphasize a different aspect. According to Freud, a person goes through five developmental periods, called (b)_____ stages, during which the primary goal is to satisfy innate biological needs. In contrast, Erikson divided development into eight developmental periods in which the primary goal is to satisfy social needs; he called these (c)_____ stages. Bandura emphasizes the importance of learning through imitation, observation, and reinforcement; this is called (d)_____ theory.

18. Freud's five psychosexual stages are called the (a)_____, (b)_____, (c)_____, (d)_____, and (e)_____ stages. Freud believed that the first five years left a lasting impression on the individual's personality and social development.

19. The first five of Erikson's eight stages involve the resolution of a potential social problem between the child and his or her environment. In stage 1, the infant deals with resolving issues surrounding trust versus (a)_____. In stage 2, the toddler must resolve issues surrounding autonomy versus shame and (b)_____. In

stage 3, the younger child deals with issues of initiative versus (c)_____. In stage 4, the older child deals with issues that involve industry versus (d)_____. In stage 5, the adolescent deals with issues that involve identity versus (e)_____.

20. Early psychological difficulties increase a child's (a)_____, which in turn increases the risk for developing later social or personality problems. However, certain emotional traits, family factors, and outside emotional support help a child overcome early problems and are said to help make the child (b)_____ and thus develop normal social behaviors.

21. Expectations of how we should think or behave because we are male or female are called (a)_____. One theory says that these roles develop because parents or caregivers expect, treat, and reward different kinds of behaviors depending on the child's sex; this is the (b)_____ theory. Another theory says that children learn rules for male or female behavior through active involvement with their environments; this is the (c)_____ theory.

G. CULTURAL DIVERSITY: GENDER ROLES

22. Although children's perceptions of gender roles show some variation across countries and cultures, it appears that their _____ of gender roles develops in a generally similar way at similar times.

H. APPLICATION: CHILD ABUSE

23. Inadequate care, neglect, or acts of the parent that put the child in danger or that cause physical harm or injury or involve sexual molestation compose the definition of (a)_____. According to the principle of (b)_____, the child's behaviors influence how the parents respond and the parents' behaviors influence how the child responds. Two goals of treatment to stop or prevent child abuse are to help parents overcome their (c)_____ problems and to change parent-child interactions from negative to positive.

Answers: *1. (a) prenatal, (b) germinal, (c) embryonic, (d) fetal; 2. (a) teratogens, (b) fetal alcohol syndrome (FAS); 3. (a) visual acuity, (b) depth; 4. (a) cephalocaudal, (b) proximodistal; 5. (a) maturation, (b) developmental norms; 6. temperament; 7. emotional; 8. (a) attachment, (b) separation anxiety; 9. (a) securely, (b) insecurely; 10. (a) longitudinal, (b) cross-sectional; 11. inhibited; 12. (a) assimilation, (b) accommodation; 13. (a) sensorimotor, (b) object permanence; 14. (a) preoperational, (b) egocentric; 15. (a) concrete operations, (b) conservation; 16. (a) formal operations, (b) reasoning or thinking; 17. (a) social, (b) psychosexual, (c) psychosocial, (d) social cognitive; 18. (a) oral, (b) anal, (c) phallic, (d) latent, (e) genital; 19. (a) mistrust, (b) doubt, (c) guilt, (d) inferiority, (e) role confusion; 20. (a) vulnerability, (b) resilient; 21. (a) gender roles, (b) social learning, (c) cognitive developmental; 22. knowledge; 23. (a) child abuse, (b) bidirectionality, (c) personal.*

Module 18 ADOLESCENCE & ADULTHOOD

A. Puberty & Sexual Behavior   408

* **DEFINITION**
* **GIRLS DURING PUBERTY**
* **BOYS DURING PUBERTY**
* **ADOLESCENTS: SEXUALLY MATURE**

B. Cognitive Changes   410

* **DEFINITION**
* **PIAGET'S COGNITIVE STAGES**
* **BIOPSYCHOSOCIAL MODEL**
* **KOHLBERG'S THEORY OF MORAL REASONING**
* **PARENTING EFFECTS**
* **ADOLESCENT VERSUS ADULT**
* **LIFE SPAN CHANGES**

1. Sensorimotor
2. Preoperational
3. Concrete
4. Formal

C. Personality & Social Changes   416

"Who am I?"

* **DEFINITION**
* **ADOLESCENCE: PATTERNS OF SELF-ESTEEM**
* **ADULTHOOD: ERIKSON'S PSYCHOSOCIAL STAGES**
* **PERSONALITY CHANGE**

D. Gender Roles, Love, & Relationships   418

* **DEFINITION: GENDER ROLES**
* **ISSUES**
* **KINDS OF LOVE**
* **CHOOSING A PARTNER**
* **RELATIONSHIP: SUCCESS OR FAILURE**

E. Research Focus: Happy Marriages   422

"Honey, would you help me?"

* **HOW DO COUPLES MAINTAIN HAPPY MARRIAGES?**

F. Cultural Diversity: Preferences for Partners   423

* **MEASURING CULTURAL INFLUENCES**
* **DESIRABLE TRAITS**
* **REASONS FOR MARRYING**

G. Physical Changes: Aging   424

* **DEFINITION**
* **REASONS FOR AGING**
* **WOMEN'S SEXUAL CHANGES**
* **MEN'S SEXUAL CHANGES**

H. Application: Suicide   426

* **TEENAGE SUICIDE**
* **PROBLEMS RELATED TO TEENAGE SUICIDE**
* **PREVENTING TEENAGE SUICIDE**
* **SUICIDE IN THE ELDERLY**

"I have six months to live and I'm in constant pain."

Adolescence

Will Branndi become president?

"I will eventually become President. In 2017. I think. I've figured it out. I don't want people to think, 'She's just a kid. She doesn't know what's ahead of her.' I know the presidency will not come easy to me. I'm black, first of all, and I'm a woman. I want to be a lawyer, then work my way up in politics, become like mayor, then senator, then governor . . .

"I know people will look into my past and say, 'Years ago, she did this, she did that, blah, blah blah.' The worst thing I've ever done is to steal two little five-cent Bazooka gums from a 7-Eleven when I was nine. I don't think they'll count that against me . . .

"Sometimes people just expect me to make trouble because I'm 'one of the black kids.' Do not label me as anything. Label me as individual . . .

"I want everyone to know that some 12-year-olds really do think seriously about the future. I want to be a role model. I'm glad I was born black. I want to tell others, 'Stay in there because you can do just as much good as any other person.'"

Besides talking like a philosopher, Branndi is a fun-loving adolescent who likes rap music, hanging out at the mall with her friends, and "dumb" movies. She is an above-average student, likes to write fairy tales for children, and sings in the youth choir at the neighborhood church (*Los Angeles Times*, December 22, 1991, pp. E-1, E-12).

At age 12, Branndi is just beginning adolescence.

Adolescence is a developmental period, lasting from about ages 12 to 18, during which many biological, cognitive, social, and personality traits change from childlike to adultlike.

While it is true that adolescents, like Branndi, go through dramatic changes, experts now believe that adolescence is not necessarily marked by great psychological turmoil. Psychologists have learned that the majority of teenagers, unlike the terrible adolescents portrayed in the media, do develop a healthy sense of identity, maintain close relationships with their families, and avoid major emotional disorders (Compas et al., 1995; Lerner & Galambos, 1998). After making it through adolescence, most teenagers are ready and eager to enter the adult world.

Adulthood

Did the prom queen live happily ever after?

"I remember standing on stage in front of all the students. I was thinking 'Can this really happen to me?' It was my junior year of high school, and I had been elected prom queen. It was like being in a fairy tale.

"I cried at my high school graduation, but I was excited about going away to college and being on my own. I considered myself a very sensible, logical, and levelheaded person. So what did I do? I began seriously dating a guy who was my opposite. He was a fun-loving, kidding-around, cocky-type person. I met him in January, got engaged in February, and was married in September. What had love done to my sensible head?

"As I look back over my five years of marriage, I now realize that it was okay but not great. It was great to have two wonderful children. It wasn't great to discover that my husband was having an affair when I was pregnant the second time. We got divorced soon after my daughter was born. It was hard being single again, with two children and no job. Later, my 12-year-old son developed a brain tumor and after two years of suffering, he died. How does one prepare for the death of one's child? Without help from my parents and friends, I would never have survived.

"I'm almost 40 now. My daughter and I are doing pretty well. I think about getting married again. I don't know if I will. You see, I also like my independence. Come back and see me when I'm 70 and I'll tell you what happened" (Wallechinsky, 1986).

Susan had dreamt of finishing college, getting married, and having a family, all of which she did. However, she did not figure on a divorce, having to support herself and her children, and her son's dying of a brain tumor, all before she reached 40. These are some of the joys and pains of adulthood.

Major Periods of Change

Both Susan and Branndi went through periods of great change. Each of us goes through three major developmental periods marked by significant physical, cognitive, personality, and social changes. We discussed childhood in Module 17. Now we turn to the other two periods: adolescence and adulthood. Generally, adolescents are more concerned about their physical appearance and finding their identities, while adults are more concerned with establishing a long-term relationship and finding a good job. Thus, the individual's concerns and goals undergo major changes between adolescence and adulthood.

What's Coming

We'll explain the personality, social, cognitive, and physical changes that individuals undergo from adolescence through adulthood and discuss some of the challenges and problems that adolescents and adults face during each of these periods.

We'll begin with perhaps the biggest change in adolescence—puberty.

A. Puberty & Sexual Behavior

Definition

A teenager leaves behind the mind and body of a child and begins to take on the mind and body of an adult. This great change from child to adult is full of challenge, excitement, and anxiety for both the adolescent and the parents. Perhaps the biggest event in changing from a child to an adult is the onset of puberty, which is altogether interesting, wondrous, and potentially very stressful.

Puberty refers to a developmental period, between the ages of 9 and 17, when the individual experiences significant biological changes that result in developing secondary sexual characteristics and reaching sexual maturity.

As puberty triggers dramatic changes in the structure and function of our bodies, we simultaneously experience dramatic changes in our thoughts, personalities, and social behaviors. To understand why puberty changed our minds, we first need to know how puberty changed our bodies.

Girls During Puberty

A teenage girl dreams about having the body of a woman and her dream comes true as she experiences three major biological changes during puberty. Puberty typically occurs between ages 9 and 13 and usually takes place about two years earlier than in boys (10.5 versus 12.5 years).

1 Puberty sets off a surge in *physical growth,* which is marked by an increase in height that starts on average at 9.6 years. This growth spurt begins about 6–12 months before the onset of breast development.

2 Puberty triggers a physiological process that results in a girl's reaching *female sexual maturity,* which primarily involves the onset of menarche.

Menarche is the first menstrual period; it is a signal that ovulation may have occurred and that the girl may have the potential to conceive and bear a child.

In the United States, menarche occurs on average at 12.5 years, about 2.5 years after the beginning of breast development. For reasons of diet, exercise, family stress, and genes, age of menarche varies with society and country (Graber et al., 1995).

The onset of menarche is triggered by an area of the brain called the **hypothalamus,** which stimulates the pituitary to produce hormones that travel throughout the bloodstream. These hormones stimulate the ovaries to greatly increase production of female hormones.

Estrogen is one of the major female hormones. At puberty, estrogen levels increase eightfold, which stimulates the development of both primary and secondary sexual characteristics.

3 Puberty marks a major change in the girl's body as she develops female secondary sexual characteristics.

Female secondary sexual characteristics, whose development is triggered by the increased secretion of estrogen, include growth of pubic hair, development of breasts, and widening of hips.

In girls, the onset of secondary sexual characteristics begins at 10.5 years (the range is from age 9 to age 18) and continues for about 4.5 years.

Early versus late maturing. Girls who are early maturing—that is, who go through puberty early—may be more shy and introverted, rate lower on social skills, and try cigarettes and alcohol ahead of their later-maturing classmates (Wilson et al., 1994). One reason girls who mature early physically may encounter psychological problems is that they have not yet acquired the adult personalty traits and social skills that are needed for normal and healthy functioning in their too newly developed adult bodies (Lerner & Galambos, 1998).

Boys During Puberty

A boy wants to have the body of a man so he can act grownup and independent. A boy experiences three major biological changes during puberty, which typically occur between ages 10 and 14. The onset of puberty in a boy usually occurs about two years later than in a girl.

1 Puberty triggers an increase in physical growth, especially height, generally at 13–14 years of age. The increase in height may be dramatic, and a boy may feel strange as he discovers that he is taller than his mother and as tall or taller than his father.

2 Puberty starts a physiological process that results in a boy's reaching **male sexual maturity,** which includes growth of the genital organs—testes and penis—and production of sperm. The onset of genital growth begins at around 11.5 years (the range is from age 9 to age 16) and continues for approximately three years. The production and release of sperm begins at 12–14 years of age.

The increase in genital growth and the production of sperm is triggered by the **hypothalamus,** which stimulates the male pituitary gland. The pituitary in turn triggers the testes to increase production of testosterone as much as 18 times more than before puberty.

Testosterone, which is the major male hormone, stimulates the growth of genital organs and the development of secondary sexual characteristics.

3 The increased production of testosterone triggers the development of male secondary sexual characteristics.

Male secondary sexual characteristics, which are triggered by the increased secretion of testosterone, include the growth of pubic and facial hair, development of muscles, and a change (deepening) in voice.

These changes usually occur between 12 and 16 years of age, but there is a wide range in their development.

Early versus late maturing. Generally, boys who are early maturing, which means they go through puberty earlier, are found to be more confident, relaxed, socially responsible, popular, and highly regarded by their peers. In comparison, boys who go through puberty later (are late maturing) are found lacking in self-confidence and self-esteem, more dependent on their parents, and less highly regarded by peers.

However, many of the psychological differences between early- and late-maturing girls and boys decrease and disappear with age (Sigelman & Shaffer, 1995). One interesting difference between boys and girls during puberty is that boys see themselves generally as being physically attractive, while many girls doubt their attractiveness and are constantly comparing themselves with other girls (Rodriguez-Tome et al., 1993).

During puberty, boys and girls become physically sexually mature, a brand-new body state that raises many difficult questions for adolescents.

Adolescents: Sexually Mature

Now what do I do?

In the United States, about 28 million youths between the ages of 10 and 17 are looking for answers to the question, "Now that I am sexually mature, what do I do?" A hundred years ago people married and had children soon after becoming sexually mature because life expectancy was only about 25 to 30 years. Today, young adults become sexually mature 10 to 15 years before deciding to get married or have children. Part of the problem is that adolescents receive conflicting answers about how to behave.

CONFLICTING ANSWERS

On the one hand, the media (movies, television, magazines), as well as peers, friends and classmates, often discuss or portray sex in exciting ways that stimulate and encourage adolescents to try sex, often before they are emotionally ready. For example, in a study of 174 girls, most said that they had been too young (average age was 13) at the time of their first intercourse. The reasons (in order of frequency) that they gave for engaging in sex were because they were physically attracted, curious, were alone with their partner, or knew that all their friends were having sex. Looking back, most of these girls wished they had waited longer before having sexual intercourse because they had not been ready and not appreciated the risks of pregnancy and disease (Rosenthal et al., 1997).

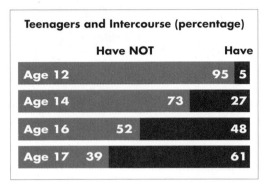

Teenagers and Intercourse (percentage)

	Have NOT	Have
Age 12	95	5
Age 14	73	27
Age 16	52	48
Age 17	39	61

On the other hand, most parents, mental health organizations, and religious groups advise adolescents not to engage in sex too early and to wait until they are more emotionally mature and involved in an intimate relationship.

Faced with conflicting pressures, many adolescents worry about becoming sexually active. For example, here's what one young female said: "My school taught us what our sexual anatomy did. But when the time came, what I really needed to know was all the dimensions of having a sexual relationship with my boyfriend. . . . What existed beyond the physical? Was I ready to make love with a man who I perceived I loved deeply?" (Minton, 1995, p. 8).

These thoughts reflect adolescents' concerns about the relationship between sex and love and introduce a new model of adolescent sexual development, called the BioPsychoSocial model (Compas et al., 1995).

The *BioPsychoSocial model* views adolescent development as a process that occurs simultaneously on many levels and includes sexual, cognitive, social, and personality changes that interact and influence each other.

According to the BioPsychoSocial approach, sexual behavior cannot be discussed independently of other cognitive, personality, or emotional behaviors. For example, it is well known that sex hormones trigger a variety of physical changes, the most obvious being the development of secondary sexual characteristics. At the same time, sex hormones also influence mood changes; adolescents experience more swings in mood and more intense feelings, whether it be happiness, loneliness, depression, or sexual desire (Buchanan et al., 1992). Thus, hormones not only dramatically change the adolescent's body but also contribute to psychological moods and desires that continually push adolescents to seek intimate relationships to satisfy these desires.

FREQUENCY OF SEXUAL BEHAVIOR

The number of adolescents becoming sexually active has generally been increasing, from 29% in 1970 to almost 60% today. A survey of thousands of adolescents found that by age 14 about 25% had engaged in sexual intercourse (left graph). By age 17 about 60% of adolescents had engaged in sex, with boys being more sexually active than girls (Leigh et al., 1994).

Girls. The survey reported that 56% of girls had had sexual intercourse by age 17, compared to 29% in 1970 and 42% in 1980. Although the median age for first intercourse was 17.4 years for girls, about half the girls (48%) said that the best age for first intercourse is between 18 and 20 years old. Almost half of girls who were sexually active reported not using contraceptives.

Boys. The survey reported that 67% of boys had had sexual intercourse by age 17. The median age for first intercourse was 16.6 years for boys, but almost half the boys (47%) said that the best age for first intercourse is between 18 and 20 years old. About 43% of boys who were sexually active reported not using contraceptives.

This and other surveys make several important points. First, the age at which teenagers actually engage in sexual activity is earlier than what they think is the best age. Second, as the graph (above left) shows, a relatively large percentage (39%) had not engaged in sex by age 17. Third, about half the boys and girls did not use contraceptives, which contributes to two major problems: the transmission of sexually transmitted diseases, including AIDS, and births among unwed teenage girls. Fourth, compared to 20 years ago, deciding whether or not to become sexually active is more difficult today because adolescents are exposed to more sex on the media, are more open about sexual matters, and report greater peer pressure to become sexually active (Koch, 1993; Leigh et al., 1994).

Just as adolescents' bodies are changing, so too are their minds. Next, we'll examine their changes in cognitive development.

B. Cognitive Changes

Definition

Why is Branndi's head spinning?

Beginning in the 1990s, developmental psychologists gathered new data on adolescents that did not support their earlier beliefs that adolescence is necessarily a time of long-lasting storm, stress, and anxiety. Instead, developmental psychologists now view adolescence as a potentially difficult time but also as a time for tremendous growth in emotional, social, and cognitive development as teenagers go from childhood to adulthood (Lerner & Galambos, 1998).

We have just discussed the changes that accompany puberty, the BioPsychoSocial model of development, and the potential problems and questions that are associated with becoming physically sexually mature. We'll now focus on another major change during adolescence—cognitive development.

Cognitive development refers to how a person perceives, thinks, and gains an understanding of his or her world through the interaction and influence of genetic and learning factors.

For example, at the beginning of this module we told you about the developmental changes that Branndi (right photo) will undergo

during adolescence. One change will be in the way she thinks about the world. Here are some examples.

"I don't believe in the Pledge of Allegiance. I don't say it, because they're telling a lie—'liberty and justice for all.' . . . My first step into politics will be mayor. I write lots of letters to Tom Bradley [former mayor of Los Angeles] about things like animal rights. But he just sent me, you know, one of those typed things. I don't think it's right . . . I'm very outspoken. I worry about things—sex, rape, and stuff like that . . . I believe in God. I believe God lets awful things happen to teach us a lesson . . ." (*Los Angeles Times,* December 22, 1991, p. E-13).

There's no question that Branndi is outspoken and holds absolute opinions on a variety of concrete and abstract issues. Her views illustrate one of the most significant changes in cognitive development during adolescence, which is the ability to think about abstract issues, such as the meaning of liberty, justice, and whether one should recite the Pledge of Allegiance. Twelve-year-old Branndi's kind of thinking indicates that she is entering Piaget's fourth cognitive stage, called formal operations. We'll discuss the formal operations stages and the kind of thinking and reasoning that it involves.

Piaget's Cognitive Stages

What's new about a teenager's thinking?

As you may remember from Module 17, the heart of Piaget's theory of cognitive development is the idea that we all go through four distinct cognitive stages (left figure). As we go through each *cognitive stage,* we acquire a new and distinct kind of reasoning and thinking that is very different from and more advanced than the reasoning abilities we possessed at our previous stage. Although we discussed Piaget's stages in Module 17, we'll review stage 4, the formal operations stage, because it is especially relevant to adolescent thinking.

STAGE 4: FORMAL OPERATIONS

The fact that 12-year-old Branndi is using abstract concepts, such as liberty, justice, animal rights, and God, is good evidence that she is entering the formal operations stage.

The *formal operations stage,* the last of Piaget's four cognitive stages, extends from about age 12 through adulthood. During this stage, adolescents and adults develop the abilities to think about abstract or hypothetical concepts, to consider an issue from another's viewpoint, and to solve cognitive problems in a logical way.

1. Sensorimotor
Birth to age 2

2. Preoperational
Ages 2 to 7

3. Concrete
Ages 7 to 11

4. Formal
Ages 12 through adulthood

Having the ability to think about and discuss abstract concepts means that adolescents can critically consider their beliefs, attitudes, values, and goals as well as discuss a wide range of topics important to their becoming adults. For instance, when adolescents were asked about their major concerns (right figure), tops on their lists were getting married, having friends, getting a good job, and doing well in school. Each of these concerns involves the ability to discuss abstract concepts, which is a cognitive skill that they are learning at the formal operations stage.

Although adolescents are developing adultlike thinking abilities, they still have a couple of problems that need to be worked out. One problem is that they believe everyone is watching and listening to them, so they have trouble thinking for themselves. A second problem is that they have a difficult time planning for the future because they are so emotionally involved in what is happening now. We'll discuss these two problems, using examples written by high school students, whose own words best illustrate their thinking.

Getting married
Having friends
Getting a good job
Doing well in school

ADOLESCENT EGOCENTRIC THINKING

Corinne: "As a high school student, I've grown up watching and listening to violence in the media. I can still remember my first horror movies and how the neighbor kids chased me around the block, screaming 'bang, bang, you're dead.' I never thought it was anything significant. Yet at the age of 12, I began watching the news, hearing of murders and kids my age being involved in acts of violence. It became hard to tell what was real and what was not" (*San Diego Union-Tribune,* October 23, 1993, p. E-4).

"What's real and what's not?"

Having difficulty in distinguishing between what is real and what isn't is an example of adolescent egocentric thinking (Elkind, 1978).

Adolescent egocentric thinking refers to difficulties in separating one's own thoughts and feelings from those of others.

There are two interesting kinds of adolescent egocentric thinking. One is that teenagers confuse their thoughts with an *imaginary audience;* for example, they might assume that everyone at a party is watching them. A second is that each teenager thinks that his or her thoughts are special or unique to him or her; for example, they might feel that no one else could possibly be so much in love. This is called a *personal fable.* Thankfully, adolescent egocentric thinking decreases as the teenager becomes an adult (Elkind, 1978). Until recently, adolescent egocentric thinking was also thought to involve a feeling of being indestructible or invulnerable, which was used to explain why teenagers had higher rates of doing all kinds of risky things.

For example, because only half of adolescents use condoms, they have about twice the rate, compared to adults, of transmitting venereal diseases. Because of drinking alcohol, speeding, and reckless driving, teenagers have 20 times the rate of automobile accidents as adults in their mid-20s (Adler, 1993b). However, in a recent study, researchers asked teenagers (11–18 years old) to judge the probability of facing various risks (being in an automobile accident, becoming alcoholic, having an unwanted pregnancy), and also asked their parents to do the same. Contrary to researchers' predictions, adolescents estimated that their chances of facing these risks were slightly less than their parents'. Researchers took this to mean that adolescents felt only slightly less vulnerable than did their parents (Quadrel et al., 1993). Researchers concluded that although adolescents do take more risks, they do not do so because they feel invulnerable but rather because they have not yet figured out what a risk is or perhaps because they value risk-taking more than adults do.

THINKING ABSTRACTLY

Carmelia: "I'm really concerned and nervous about my future because it seems like it's really hard for people to get along. People are really ignorant. There's racism, prejudice and cultural ignorance. Why do we have to categorize people as Latino, white, black? I get upset when people put up this wall around me just because of my race or gender. Just accept me for who I am" (*Los Angeles Times,* May 2, 1994, p. E-3).

"Why can't people get along?"

Carmelia's ability to discuss her fears, values, goals, and think about the future comes from her new capacity to *think abstractly,* which is characteristic of formal operations. With the development of abstract thinking, adolescents' descriptions of themselves shift from the concrete, such as things they are doing, to the more abstract, such as their feelings and psychological states (Harter, 1990). Thus, being able to think abstractly gives adolescents a new way of looking at and describing themselves.

One reason about 50% of all adolescents engage in two or more risky behaviors (drug and alcohol use, unsafe sex, school underachievement or failure, delinquency) is that they are just beginning to learn the importance of thinking about and planning for their futures (Lerner & Galambos, 1998). Especially toward the end of adolescence, young adults begin making plans for their careers, lifestyles, relationships, and families. One interesting finding is that in *planning for the future,* boys tend to be more optimistic because they have a career in mind, but girls tend to be more pessimistic because they feel a conflict between having a career and having a family.

BioPsychoSocial Model

What about sex and love?

Although we've discussed sexual and cognitive development separately, they are occurring at the same time. Earlier we explained the BioPsychoSocial model, which says that adolescent development is a process that goes on simultaneously on many levels. For example, you can see how cognitive and sexual processes develop together and interact by noticing what young girls and boys say about the first sexual experiences. Generally, both boys and girls report that they started sex too early, that the experience was OK but not great for girls, and the best time to start is between 18 and 20 years old (Rosenthal et al., 1997). Boys and girls also report that they started to have sex mostly because of physical attraction, curiosity,

"So, what's the difference?"

and peer pressure. However, toward the end of adolescence, their abilities for abstract thinking and planning are more fully developed. At this point, adolescents begin to understand and appreciate the difference between sex, which is a physical act, and love, which is a powerful emotional feeling that may be expressed by sexual behaviors within the bonds of an intimate and loving relationship. Thus, abstract thinking provides the cognitive tools to understand and appreciate the difference between sex and love (Peterson, 1998).

Being able to think abstractly means teens can discuss what is right and wrong. How adolescents develop concepts of morality is our next topic.

B. Cognitive Changes

Kohlberg's Theory of Moral Reasoning

Suppose your best friend is dying of cancer. You hear of a chemist who has just discovered a new wonder drug that could save her life. The chemist is selling the drug for $5,000, many times more than it cost him to make. You try to borrow the full amount, but can get only $2,500. You ask the chemist to sell you the drug for $2,500 and he refuses.

Later that night, you break into the chemist's laboratory and steal the drug. Should you have done that?

Did you decide that it would be all right to steal the drug to save the life of your dying friend? If you did, how did you justify your moral decision? Lawrence Kohlberg (1984) and associates presented similar dilemmas to individuals who were asked to explain their moral decisions. On the basis of such studies, Kohlberg explained the development of moral reasoning in terms of three levels.

Three Levels of Moral Reasoning

Level 1

The *preconventional level,* which represents Kohlberg's lowest level of moral reasoning, has two stages. At stage 1, moral decisions are based primarily on fear of punishment or the need to be obedient; at stage 2, moral reasoning is guided most by satisfying one's self-interest, which may involve making bargains.

For example, individuals at stage 1 might say that you should not steal the drug because you'll be caught and go to jail. Individuals at stage 2 might say that you can steal the drug and save your best friend, but in return you'll have to give up some freedom by going to jail. Most children are at the preconventional level.

Level 2

The *conventional level,* which represents an intermediate level of moral reasoning, also has two stages. At stage 3, moral decisions are guided most by conforming to the standards of others we value; at stage 4, moral reasoning is determined most by conforming to laws of society.

Individuals at stage 3 might say that you should steal the drug since that is what your family would expect you to do. Individuals at stage 4 might say that you should not steal the drug because of what would happen to society if everybody took what they needed. Many adolescents and adults are at this level.

Level 3

The *postconventional level,* which represents the highest level of moral reasoning, has one stage. At stage 5, moral decisions are made after carefully thinking about all the alternatives and striking a balance between human rights and laws of society.

Individuals at stage 5 might say that one should steal the drug because life is more important than money. (Stage 6, which appeared in earlier versions of Kohlberg's theory, has been omitted in later versions because too few people had reached it.) Some, but not all, adults reach the postconventional level.

Kohlberg's theory has two distinct features. First, he classifies moral reasoning into three distinct levels—preconventional, conventional, and postconventional. Second, he suggests that everyone progresses through the levels in order, from lowest to highest. However, not everyone reaches the higher levels of moral development.

Next, we'll evaluate Kohlberg's theory and compare it to another theory.

Evaluating Kohlberg's Theory

Stages. Kohlberg hypothesized that everyone goes through the five stages in sequence. That is, you begin at stage 1 and cannot reach stage 4 without going through stages 2 and 3. Researchers reviewed 45 Kohlberg-type studies conducted in 27 cultures. The vast majority of these studies supported Kohlberg's assumption that individuals progress through the stages in order but that not everyone reaches the higher stages (Eckensberger, 1994; Helwig, 1997).

Criticisms. There are two serious criticisms of Kohlberg's stages. The first is that Kohlberg's moral stages indicate different kinds of moral thinking that may or may not predict how an individual actually behaves. Thus, Kohlberg focused on development of moral thinking rather than on development of moral behavior (Shweder & Haidt, 1993).

The second criticism, made by Carol Gilligan (1982), is that men and women may differ in their moral thinking: men use a justice orientation and women use a care orientation.

A *care orientation* is making moral decisions based on issues of caring, on avoiding hurt, on how things affect their interpersonal relationships, and on concerns for others.

A *justice orientation* is making moral decisions based more on issues of law and equality and individual rights.

However, after 15 years of studies, Gilligan's idea that women and men differ in moral thinking has received either slight or no support (Walker, 1991). More recent studies suggest that Gilligan's difference in moral reasoning is due more to differences in gender (sex) roles, which are influenced by cultural values. For example, women used a justice orientation if their gender role was a more independent, dominant one (stereotypical male) and used a care orientation if their gender role was a more nurturing, caring one (stereotypical female) (Sochting et al., 1994). Thus, differences in moral thinking may depend more on **gender roles** and **cultural values** than on simple male-female differences (Haidt et al., 1993).

One factor that influences moral thinking is the kind of rules that your parents laid down for you. We'll discuss how different styles of parenting affect cognitive development in adolescents.

Parenting Effects

Were your parents easy or strict?

During adolescence, teenagers will go through at least three major cognitive changes. One change involves developing new cognitive skills and moral reasoning, which we have just discussed. A second change involves forming their own identities, which we will discuss later in this module. A third change involves developing a sense of independence and achievement, which may be helped or hindered by their parents' rules, standards, and codes of conduct (Baumrind, 1991; Paikoff & Brooks-Gunn, 1991). For just a minute, think about how you responded to the rules your parents laid down for you as an adolescent. Or, if you are a parent, think about how your children respond to your own rules. When teenagers were asked how they responded to their parents' rules, here's what the two in the photo below replied:

Ida (age 17)

"I live in a strict Italian home. Sometimes my parents are really, really great, but their rules for me are absolutely ridiculous. So I get around them. My friends will tell you I'm a good kid. I don't drink. I don't do drugs. I don't smoke. But my parents think that, if I've gone out on a Friday night and I ask to go on Saturday, too, I'm asking for the world . . . So I lie a lot.
. . . A lot of people know I do this, but nobody yells at me for it, because I'm a good kid, and my parents' rules are so ridiculous."

Christopher (age 18)

"My parents never make their punishments stick. Like, I'll get my Jeep taken away for a week, and I'll get it back within six hours. Why? Because my parents hate to see their kids unhappy, and I know it, so I play right into it. They'll punish me by not letting me go out, so I'll walk around the house, slam the door occasionally, this, that . . . and after a while this just plays on them, and they feel bad, and they let me out" (*Parade Magazine,* July 14, 1991, pp. 6–7. Reprinted with permission from Parade. Copyright © 1991).

After reading these two descriptions, you can see that Ida's parents are the opposite of Christopher's. How do such different styles of parenting affect adolescents' development? To answer this question, psychologist Diana Baumrind (1991, 1993) has been carrying out a series of longitudinal studies on parent-child and parent-adolescent interactions. She has identified a number of parenting styles that are associated with different kinds of adolescent development. We'll focus on three of these parenting styles: authoritarian parents, authoritative parents, and permissive parents.

Styles of Parenting

Authoritarian parents attempt to shape, control, and evaluate the behavior and attitudes of their children in accordance with a set standard of conduct, usually an absolute standard that comes from religious or respected authorities.

For these parents, obedience is a virtue, and they punish and use harsh discipline to keep the adolescent in line with their rules. This parenting style seems to describe Ida's parents. Boys from authoritarian families are found to be relatively hostile, while girls are found to be relatively

dependent and submissive. This description fits Ida, who admits to problems with being independent.

Authoritative parents attempt to direct their children's activities in a rational and intelligent way. They are supportive, loving, and committed, encourage verbal give-and-take, and discuss their rules and policies with their children.

Authoritative parents value being expressive and independent, but are also demanding. The children of such parents tend to be competent. In addition, girls are

achievement-oriented and boys are friendly and cooperative.

Permissive parents are less controlling and behave with a nonpunishing and accepting attitude toward their children's impulses, desires, and actions; they consult with their children about policy decisions, make few demands, and tend to use reason rather than direct power.

This parenting style seems to describe Christopher's parents. Girls with such parents are less socially assertive, and both boys and girls are less achievement-minded.

Conclusions

It is clear that each of the three parenting styles have different costs and benefits. Authoritarian parents, who are very demanding, benefit by preventing adolescent behavioral problems but at some cost to adolescents, who tend to be more conforming and have lower self-esteem. Authoritative parents, who state their values clearly, benefit by having loving and supportive parent-teenager interactions, which further benefits their teenagers, who tend to be more friendly, cooperative, and achievement-oriented. Permissive parents benefit by having to make fewer demands and enforcing fewer rules but at some cost to adolescents, who may be less socially assertive

COSTS ⬍ BENEFITS

and less achievement-oriented than adolescents with authoritative parents (Baumrind, 1991, 1993). The kind of parenting also influences whether and how often adolescents engage in risky behaviors (drugs, early sex). Researchers report that adolescents engage in fewer risky behaviors if they can openly communicate with at least one of the parents. Furthermore, the better the communication is between the adolescent and parent, the less likely the adolescent will engage in risky behaviors (Marta, 1997; Resnick et al., 1997). Thus, parenting styles can significantly effect the cognitive, social, and personality development of adolescents.

B. Cognitive Changes

Adolescent versus Adult

Why do teens and parents argue?

I can still remember my heated adolescent arguments with my father over staying out late. I believed that I was totally right and my father was totally wrong. Looking back, it's easy to see that adolescent minds simply lack the reasoning experience and knowledge to make the right decisions. Even though adolescents and adults are both in Piaget's fourth cognitive state— formal operations—their thinking abilities are certainly not the same.

Differences in thinking and reasoning abilities between adolescents and adults are easy to spot. For example, if you are a college student with younger brothers or sisters, you may find that they are

"Why can't I stay out late?"

impossible to reason with because they lack your experience and reasoning abilities. If you are a more mature, returning student, you'll probably find that freshmen are difficult to reason with because they think they know everything and have solutions to all the world's problems. Finally, when you reach your senior years, you'll realize that despite years of experience, there are no simple answers to life's important questions. These examples illustrate how thinking and reasoning change across the life span.

We'll discuss thinking across the life span and begin by comparing the different thinking styles of adolescents and adults.

Different Styles of Thinking

The father-son and mother-daughter photos show two adolescents who are at the beginning of Piaget's stage 4 and two adults who are well into acquiring stage 4 thinking. Remember that Piaget's stage 4, called formal operations, extends from about age 12 through adulthood. This is the period when adolescents and adults develop the abilities to think about abstract or hypothetical concepts, to solve cognitive problems in a logical way, and to plan ahead. As adolescents acquire these new thinking and reasoning abilities, they gain new insights about themselves, new ways to judge their parents, and new ways to explore their world. Because adolescents are beginning to think for themselves but lack experience, they tend to be stubborn, self-centered, and ready to argue with their parents over every little thing. Although adolescents may think they are now adults, they still do not think like adults.

"Can I tell dad my problems?"

Adolescents. Along with changing from children to young adults, adolescents not only develop physically and sexually mature bodies but also develop quite different minds. As they develop different minds, teenagers acquire a new and proud sense of independence and self-identity, which means they no longer take parental advice, no matter how good and reasonable.

Although teenagers are entering Piaget's formal operations stage, they don't realize that they lack the years of experience and knowledge that their parents have acquired. Thus, although adolescents are beginning to think on their own, you'll see that their thinking is still different from adults.

Adults. Piaget suggested that most adolescents and young adults master the formal operations stage by age 18. However, researchers found that only about half the college students they studied had mastered the problem-solving tasks that indicate a high level of abstract thinking and reasoning. Here's one way of measuring abstract thinking.

One of Piaget's best-known tasks for testing problem-solving thinking is the pendulum task. A person is given a length of string, a number of different weights, and asked to determine which factors determine the speed of the pendulum's swing. To solve this problem you must figure out a strategy for testing various hypotheses: How important is the length of the string? How critical are heavier weights? What is the best combination of string and weights? Individuals capable of problem-solving thinking are able to figure out and test different hypotheses (educated guesses). Those not capable of problem-solving thinking do not formulate a plan or develop a reasonable strategy but simply use trial and error, hoping to hit the right solution (Sigelman & Shaffer, 1995). One advantage of going to college is that the more formal education a person receives, the more likely he or she will master formal operational (problem-solving) thinking.

"Can I be good friends with mom?"

Adolescent-parent communication. We have discussed the considerable differences in thinking between adolescents and parents. However, some of this difference can be overcome if one or both parents makes the effort and takes the time to listen to their adolescents. Open lines of communication between parents and adolescents results in adolescents feeling close to their parents and being less likely to engage in risky behaviors (Marta, 1997; Resnick et al., 1997).

Once adolescents become adults, their cognitive abilities change little until they get into their 50s and 60s, when the first noticeable decreases occur (Schacter, 1996). Next, we'll discuss the kinds of cognitive changes that occur later in the life span.

Life Span Changes

What happens after 60?

After the age of 60, people usually have the following complaint. "Learning of our research on cognitive aging, a 69-year-old professor came to see us because she wanted to know if she were 'losing it.' The professor reported that she had difficulty recalling the names of new faculty she had met recently, could not remember the number of her classroom when ordering audiovisual equipment, and just this

"Am I losing it?"

morning could not think of the name for the thing you turn over eggs with. She went on to say that she had consulted a doctor who, after examining her, told her she was 'just fine'" (Powell & Whitla, 1994, p. 27).

This particular professor was worried about whether her noticeable decrease in cognitive skills was the result of normal aging or whether she was experiencing the first signs of Alzheimer's disease. The cognitive researchers reassured her that she was most likely not suffering from Alzheimer's disease but rather experiencing normal aging, which affects memory as well as a number of other cognitive skills.

Age-Related Changes in Speed of Perceiving and Responding

When I was in my 30s and 40s, I observed my parents forgetting things as they grew older, but I couldn't believe it would happen to me. That's because from about age 20 to 50, cognitive skills remain relatively stable. However, between 50 and 80, there is a general slowing of the following cognitive processes (Verhaeghen & Salthouse, 1997).

Processing speed is the rate at which we encode information into long-term memory or recall or retrieve information from long-term memory; this rate slows down after age 60.

For example, 20-year-olds can memorize and recall significantly more words than 60-year-olds. Older adults appear to have more difficulty in encoding or storing lists of information, as well as a greater difficulty in reliably retrieving or recalling specific information (Salthouse, 1994).

Perceptual speed is the rate at which we can identify a particular sensory stimulus; this rate slows down noticeably after age 60.

For instance, in a set period of time, subjects were given a list of words and were instructed to find and draw a line through all words that contained the letter *a*. On this task, 25-year-old subjects canceled significantly more words than 67-year-old subjects (52 versus 48 words). Researchers believe that slower perceptual speed in older adults results from slower encoding of information (Salthouse et al., 1990).

Reaction time is the rate at which we respond (see, hear, move) to some stimulus; this rate slows down noticeably after age 60.

For instance, 20- to 29-year-old subjects were fastest in pressing a button when a light appeared, while subjects 60 and above were slowest. Researchers are convinced that the decline in speed of performance in older adults results from slowing in mental processing rather than decreased motor (hand movements) or sensory abilities (Bashore et al., 1989; Tranel et al., 1997).

Researchers did a longitudinal study of over 5,000 subjects, who were retested at 10 different ages, beginning at age 25 and continuing through age 88. Researchers found that decreases in cognitive skills were signs of normal aging and result from the slowing down of processing speed, which affects both encoding and retrieving information (Shaie, 1994; Lindenberger & Baltes, 1997).

Behaviors. This slowing in processing, perceiving, and reacting partly explains why older people react more slowly when driving a car or playing golf and are slower to make decisions or understand and follow instructions. This slowing down in processing also affects memory.

"Why is my golf game slowing down?"

Age-Related Changes in Memory

Even people in their 40s and 50s complain about not remembering things. To study this problem, researchers asked different groups of subjects, who ranged in age from 13 to 70 years old, to read a short story, which they would later summarize. When young adults summarized the story, they essentially gave all details without talking about the story's meaning. In contrast, when older adults summarized the story, they gave few exact details but rather focused on the meaning of the story (Adams, 1991). These differences indicate that young adults excel at encoding (storing) and recalling vast amounts of detail, with little attempt at interpretation or analysis. On the other hand,

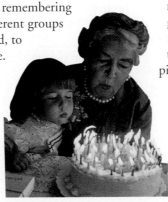

mature adults excel at interpreting information and grasping the underlying meaning, but at the cost of forgetting much of the detail. Researchers concluded that older adults have no trouble remembering the big picture but do forget most of the details. In comparison, young adults easily remember all the details but often miss the big picture (Schacter, 1996). So as people move into their 50s, 60s, and 70s, their complaints are true: they do forget details (names, places, groceries) that may be bothersome but are usually unimportant.

Next, we turn to personality and social development across the life span.

C. Personality & Social Changes

Definition

Who am I?

We began this module by letting 12-year-old Branndi describe herself. She said that she likes being who she is, dislikes being labeled, wants to be considered an individual, and thinks everyone can accomplish something good. As Branndi talks about herself, she is describing some of her personality and social development.

Personality and *social development* refer to how a person develops a sense of self or self-identity, develops relationships with others, and develops the skills useful in social interactions.

When Branndi asks, "How do I just be me?" she is bringing up perhaps the greatest challenge that she and all adolescents face, which is finding and defining her own identity.

"Who am I and who should I be?"

Identity, or *self-identity,* refers to how we describe ourselves and includes our values, goals, traits, interests, and motivations.

Adolescents often display their independence and establish their identities by wearing distinctive clothes (baggy pants, ugly shoes) or having obvious signs (tatoos, pierced ear, nose, or navel). One important component of developing a sense of identity involves establishing a sense of worth, which is called self-esteem.

Adolescence: Patterns of Self-Esteem

Branndi is proud to be Black and female, has high hopes for her future, is not afraid to speak out on important issues, and wants to be a role model. All of these beliefs indicate that Branndi has high self-esteem.

"How can I be a Black role model?"

Self-esteem is how much one likes oneself and includes feelings of self-worth, attractiveness, and social competence.

In adolescents, self-esteem is greatly influenced by two critical factors: how physically attractive and how socially competent they appear to their peers (Kernis et al., 1993). As teenagers develop sexually mature bodies, they wonder how physically attractive they are; as teenagers begin dating, they wonder how socially skilled they are. Researchers measure changes in adolescents' self-esteem by using longitudinal studies that begin in adolescence and continue through adulthood. For example, researchers might measure adolescents' self-esteem at ages 14, 18, and 23 by comparing their descriptions of themselves with descriptions of what they would ideally like to be. We'll discuss three different patterns of self-esteem development in adolescents: some develop and maintain high or low levels, while some show reversals in self-esteem (Block & Robins, 1993; Zimmerman et al., 1997).

High Self-Esteem. A large percentage of adolescents (about 60%) develop and maintain a strong sense of self-esteem through junior high. These individuals do well in school, develop rewarding friendships, participate in social activities, and are described as cheerful, assertive, emotionally warm, and unwilling to give up if frustrated.

Low Self-Esteem. A small percentage of adolescents (about 15%) develop and maintain a chronically low sense of self-esteem that continues through junior high school. These adolescents usually have continuing personal and social problems (shy, lonely, depressed), which have been present for some time and contribute to this low self-esteem.

Reversals. A moderate percentage of adolescents (about 25%) show dramatic reversals in self-esteem, either from high to low or from low to high. For example, some boys change from being stern, unemotional, and lacking social skills into being open and expressive. Researchers think that reversals in self-esteem may result from changes in their peer groups, personal attractivness, or parental relationships.

Forces shaping self-esteem. Although development of self-esteem includes many factors, such as physical attractiveness, acceptance by peers, parental support, and performance in social and academic settings, boys and girls respond to different forces.

In girls, self-esteem is especially dependent upon the ability to relate well to others. Probably the most disturbing finding is that, compared to boys, girls are more likely to be the ones showing declining or low self-esteem. In boys, self-esteem is especially dependent upon looking cool in public, which means not letting stress or anxiety make them look bad (Block & Robins, 1993). Compared to girls, boys are more likely to be the ones showing increasing or high self-esteem (Zimmerman et al., 1997).

"So, what's your problem?"

Perhaps the most encouraging finding is that many adolescent boys and girls who show lowered self-esteem during adolescence were able to recover and reach a higher level of self-esteem during their early adult years (Block & Robins, 1993).

Importance of self-esteem. Researchers are specifically interested in levels of self-esteem because high self-esteem is associated with positive outcomes, such as being cheerful, happy, and promoting personal adjustment, while low self-esteem accompanies negative outcomes, such as depression, anxiety, and poor personal adjustment (Leary et al., 1995).

One explanation of how self-esteem and self-identity develop comes from Erikson's psychosocial stages.

Adulthood: Erikson's Psychosocial Stages

At the beginning of this module, we described how Susan went from teenage prom queen to middle-aged adult. Along the way, she dealt with dating, going to college, getting married, having children, getting divorced, finding a job, and losing her son. How dealing with these life events might affect Susan's social and personality development was something that Erik Erikson (1982) tried to explain. As you may remember from Module 17, Erikson divided life into eight *psychosocial stages,* each of which contained a unique psychosocial conflict, such as intimacy versus isolation. If Susan successfully solved each psychosocial conflict, she would develop a healthy personality; if unsuccessful in solving these conflicts, she might develop an unhealthy personality and future psychological problems. In Module 17 we discussed Erikson's stages related to childhood; now, we discuss stages related to adolescence and adulthood.

"What happened to all my dreams?"

Stage 5 Identity versus Role Confusion

Period.   Adolescence (12–20)

Potential conflict.   Adolescents need to leave behind the carefree, irresponsible, and impulsive behaviors of childhood and develop the more purposeful, planned, and responsible behaviors of adulthood. If adolescents successfully resolve this problem, they will develop a healthy and confident sense of identity. If they are unsuccessful in resolving the problem, they will experience *identity confusion,* which results in their having low self-esteem and becoming unstable or socially withdrawn.

Stage 6 Intimacy versus Isolation

Period.   Young adulthood (20–40)

Potential conflict.   Young adulthood is a time for finding intimacy by developing loving and meaningful relationships. On the positive side, we can find *intimacy* in caring relationships. On the negative side, without intimacy we will have a painful feeling of *isolation,* and our relationships will be impersonal.

Stage 7 Generativity versus Stagnation

Period.   Middle adulthood (40–65)

Potential conflict.   Middle adulthood is a time for helping the younger generation develop worthwhile lives. On the positive side, we can achieve *generativity* through raising our own children. If we do not have children of our own, we can achieve generativity through close relationships with children of friends or relatives. Generativity can also be achieved through mentoring at work and in helping others. On the negative side, a lack of involvement leads to a feeling of *stagnation,* of having done nothing for the younger generation.

Stage 8 Integrity versus Despair

Period.   Late adulthood (65 and older)

Potential conflict.   Late adulthood is a time for reflecting on and reviewing how we met previous challenges and lived our lives. On the positive side, if we can look back and feel contented about how we lived and what we accomplished, we will have a feeling of satisfaction or *integrity.* On the negative side, if we reflect and see a series of crises, problems, and bad experiences, we will have a feeling of regret and *despair.*

Conclusions.   Erikson believed that achieving a personally satisfying identity was the very heart and soul of an adolescent's development (Hirsch, 1997). As adolescents developed into adults and reached middle adulthood (Stage 7), Erikson described a shift from concerns about identity to concerns about being productive, creative, and nurturing (Bradley, 1997).

Researchers have found evidence that we do go through a sequence of psychosocial stages and that how we handle conflicts at earlier stages affect our personality and social development at later stages (Van Manen & Whitbourne, 1997).

Personality Change

When Mick Jagger, lead singer of the Rolling Stones, was in his early 20s (top right), he boasted, "I'd rather be dead than sing 'Satisfaction' when I'm 45." Now in his 50s, Jagger (bottom right) has changed his tune; he and the Stones recently completed a world tour and sang "Satisfaction" dozens of times. As Jagger found out, some of the things that we say and do at 20 may seem stupid when 50. The differences in Jagger at 20 and 50 raise an interesting question: How much do our personalities change and how much do they remain the same?

Researchers answer these questions with longitudinal studies, which measure personality development across time in the same group of individuals (Whitbourne et al., 1992). One study found that from adolescence to middle adulthood, individuals became more trusting and intimate and developed a better sense of control and identity. Researchers also found that

"I'd rather be dead than . . ."

". . . sing 'Satisfaction' when I'm 45!"

possessing certain personality traits as a young adult (early 20s) led to developing related traits in middle adulthood (middle 40s). For example, individuals with a high level of identity in their early 20s showed more independence, warmth, and compassion later on in their mid 40s (Vandewater et al., 1997).

From these kinds of longitudinal studies we can draw these conclusions: First, from the end of adolescence through middle adulthood, there are less dramatic but still continuing changes in personality traits, such as becoming more trusting and intimate. Second, possessing certain personality traits in early adulthood is the foundation for developing related traits later on. Third, adults appear to pass through psychosocial stages and face conflicts in personality development similar to those proposed by Erikson (Van Manen & Whitbourne, 1997).

One of the major social and personality changes that women and men go through involves gender roles.

D. Gender Roles, Love, & Relationships

Definition: Gender Roles

Why couldn't women be firefighters?

In the 1970s, the first five female firefighter recruits flunked out of the San Diego Academy, and the local paper warned against the city's "futile exercise in trying to fit women into jobs which common sense tells us are best filled by men." After four years of lawsuits and controversy, women finally began graduating as firefighters but still faced years of harassment from male firefighters. However, in 1995, San Diego became the first city to have an all-female fire engine company (right photo) (Perry, 1995).

Perhaps the main reason male firefighters fought for 25 years to keep women out of their ranks had to do with male and female gender roles.

Gender roles refer to the traditional or stereotypic behaviors, attitudes, and personality traits that parents, peers, and society expect us to have because we are male or female.

A change in gender roles, such as allowing women to become firefighters, involved heated political, legal, and financial battles because it meant overturning strongly held traditional beliefs of how males and females are expected to think, feel, and act. For example, in the 1970s, stereotypic or traditional gender roles for women were to be homemakers, grade school teachers, waitresses, and nurses, but certainly not firefighters. After 20 years of battling to change gender roles, women can now enter careers traditionally reserved for men, such as doctors, dentists, police officers, senators, astronauts, soldiers, and perhaps one day, president of the United States. Thus, gender roles have a powerful impact on our personality and social development because they affect how we think, feel, and behave. We'll focus on two major questions about gender roles: What are current gender roles? What are the functions of gender roles?

What Are the Current Gender Roles?

Female Gender Role

Caring
Insecure
Helpful
Emotional
Social
Shy

One way researchers answered this question was to ask United States college students (males and females, about half being non-Caucasians) to describe the traits of a typical female and a typical male. Students generally agreed that female gender role included being caring, insecure, helpful, emotional, social, and shy. In comparison, students said that the male gender role included being arrogant, self-confident, aggressive, ambitious, not emotional, and dominant (Helgeson, 1994). These results are very similar to descriptions of traditional, stereotypic gender roles that other researchers have found—that females are generally concerned, sensitive, and nurturing while males are independent, controlling and dominant (Cross & Madson, 1997; Eagly, 1995a, 1995b).

During the past 10 years, women have struggled to broaden their gender role by assuming some traits, behaviors, and occupations traditionally associated with the male gender role. For example, it took 25 years of legal and political battles before women in San Diego were allowed to become firefighters, a traditionally male career. Although women have struggled to assume some of the traits traditionally associated with the male gender role (ambitious, dominant, assertive), males have been less eager to take on traits traditionally associated with the female gender role (caring, emotional, helpful) (Twenge, 1997). One reason males and females follow relatively well-defined gender roles is because society (family, peers, bosses, and colleagues) generally encourages and rewards behaviors that match expected gender roles and discriminates against behaviors that don't fit in (Wood et al., 1997).

What is the reason gender roles exist in every culture?

What Are the Functions of Gender Roles?

Male Gender Role

Arrogant
Self-confident
Aggressive
Ambitious
Not emotional
Dominant

College students from around the world agreed remarkably well on which traits were associated with which gender roles: male traits were ambitious, dominant, independent; female traits were submissive, affectionate, emotional (Williams & Best, 1990). Researchers conclude that cultures around the world exert considerable pressure on their members to conform to stereotypic male and female gender roles and that these roles have remained relatively stable for the past 20 years (Archer, 1996).

The question of why every culture has gender roles has two different answers: One answer comes from evolutionary psychology theory, which says that differences in gender roles arose because of the different evolutionary demands placed on the survival of each sex; for example, men need to be aggressive to protect their families, and women need to be caring to raise their children (Buss, 1996). A different answer comes from social psychology theory, which says that gender differences arose because men traditionally had occupational roles, and society encouraged them to be assertive, while women traditionally had family roles, and society encouraged them to be caring (Eagly, 1995a). These two theories do not disagree but rather emphasize different factors, either biological or psychological. Researchers caution that differences in gender roles do not mean that one role is better or worse and that such differences should not be used for discriminatory practices (Eagly, 1995a).

Gender roles affect not only our cognitive, social, and personality development but also our expectations about love, relationships, and marriage, which we consider next.

Did Susan recognize Mr. Right?

As each of us acquires a gender role, we automatically develop expectations about the kind of person we would like for an intimate relationship. For example, here are some of the expectations of Susan, the high school prom queen.

"When I went away to college, I was a very sensible, logical, and levelheaded person. That's probably why the first person I dated was very much like me. We had wonderful serious talks, read poetry, discussed philosophy, but never had much passion. After we broke up, a friend of mine fixed me up with Charlie, who was a fun-loving, arrogant, cocky, abrasive basketball player and my complete opposite. We dated, got engaged, and about a year later were married. Oh, yes, I knew we were complete opposites, but I passionately loved Charlie" (Wallechinsky, 1986).

Susan's first choice for someone to love was someone like her, which didn't last. Then she chose someone very different from her and decided he was the one to marry. After five years of marriage, she got divorced.

We'll focus on three big issues: different kinds of love, choosing a partner, and what makes a relationship a success or failure.

Kinds of Love

Which kind of love are you in?

Previous researchers had thought love too mysterious for scientific study, but current researchers have begun to analyze love into various components. As a starting point, researchers distinguish between passionate and companionate love (Hatfield & Rapson, 1995).

Passionate love involves continuously thinking about the loved one and is accompanied by warm sexual feelings and powerful emotional reactions.

Companionate love involves having trusting and tender feelings for someone whose life is closely bound up with one's own.

When people fall madly in love, it's usually passionate love. When mature couples talk about enjoying each other's company, it's usually companionate love, which may or may not involve sexual behaviors. Thus, love is more complex than many think. One of the better known theories of love is Robert Sternberg's (1986, 1988) triangular theory of love.

The *triangular theory of love* has three components: passion, intimacy, and commitment. *Passion* is feeling physically aroused and attracted to someone. *Intimacy* is feeling close and connected to someone; it develops through sharing and communicating. *Commitment* is making a pledge to nourish the feelings of love and to actively maintain the relationship.

What makes you feel in love is the component of passion, which rises quickly and strongly influences and biases your judgment. What makes you want to share and offer emotional and material support is the component of intimacy. What makes you want to form a serious relationship, such as getting married, and to promise support through difficult times is the component of commitment. Sternberg believes that the kind of love most of us strive for is complete or consummate love, which is a balanced combination of all three components—passion, intimacy, and commitment.

Sternberg (1988) uses his triangular theory to answer some of the most commonly asked questions above love.

Commitment • Intimacy • **Love triangle** • Passion

Is there love at first sight?

Love at first sight occurs when we are overwhelmed by passion, without any intimacy or commitment. Sternberg calls this *infatuated love,* which can arise in an instant, involves a great deal of physiological arousal, and lasts varying lengths of time. Because there is no intimacy or commitment, infatuated love is destined to fade away.

Why do some people get married after being in love for a very short time?

Sternberg calls this *Hollywood love,* which is a combination of passion and commitment but without any intimacy. In Hollywood love, two people make a commitment based on their passion for each other. Unless they develop intimacy over time, the relationship is likely to fail.

Can there be love without sex?

Sternberg calls love without sex *companionate love,* which is a combination of intimacy and commitment without any sexual passion. An example of companionate love is a married couple who are committed to each other and share their lives but whose physical attraction has waned.

Why doesn't romantic love last?

Romantic love, which is a combination of intimacy and passion, usually doesn't last because there is no commitment. As soon as the passion dies and the intimacy fades, the individuals no longer feel in love and go their separate ways.

About 90% of adults report having fallen in love, 10% report never being in love, and some individuals report finding love so painful that they will never love again (Thompson & Borrello, 1992). Researchers believe that when we first fall in love, the excitement and happiness we feel is fueled by passion, but we need to gradually develop commitment and intimacy if the relationship is to last (Hatfield & Rapson, 1995). Most often we use the term *in love* to mean emotional feelings plus sexual attraction. However, as couples age and reach their senior years, sexual attraction may lessen and give way to a different kind of love that includes feelings of tenderness, support, and commitment (Meyers & Berscheid, 1997).

Falling in love is but the first step in developing an intimate relationship and making a more permanent commitment, such as marriage. Developing a long-term relationship is our next topic.

D. Gender Roles, Love, & Relationships

Choosing a Partner

The fact that about 90% of adults in the United States marry means that most of us will eventually select a partner for a long-term relationship. However, the fact that 40 to 60% of new marriages and an even higher percentage of second marriages end in divorce means that selecting the right partner can be a very difficult, demanding, and somewhat mysterious process (Gottman, 1998).

Researchers suggest that one way we choose a partner for a long-term relationship is by finding someone who most closely matches our perfect-partner schema (Singelis et al., 1995).

A *schema* refers to an organized mental or cognitive list that includes characteristics, facts, values, or beliefs about people, events, or objects.

A perfect-partner schema would be a mental list of the most desirable characteristics that we are looking for in a prospective mate. For instance, a perfect-partner schema in order of preference for unmarried college students (averaged for men and women) is shown here

1 Kind and understanding

2 Exciting personality

3 Intelligent

4 Physically attractive (*more important for men*)

5 Healthy

6 Easygoing

7 Creative

8 Wants children

9 College graduate

10 Good earning capacity (*more important for women*)

(Buss 1994b). Researchers concluded that men and women form perfect-partner schemas with two major differences: men rank physical attractiveness as more important, and women rank good earning capacity higher (Buss, 1994a, 1995).

Perhaps the primary reason we date people is to find the Mr. or Ms. Right who best matches the list of traits on our perfect-partner schema list. But as soon as we become passionately attracted to a person, we lose the ability to rationally decide whether a person really has the traits on our list (Rossi, 1994). Even though our parents or best friends may warn us that Mr. or Ms. Right has some negative traits, we usually turn a deaf ear because in our love-blinded state the person looks perfect.

After selecting Mr. or Ms. Right, we are ready to make a commitment, such as getting married. What can we do to have a successful relationship and avoid an unhappy one?

Relationship: Success or Failure

To find out why some relationships or marriages succeed and why about 40 to 60% fail, researchers repeatedly observed the same married couples over many years, which is an example of the longitudinal method. Researchers both interviewed couples and videotaped couples' interactions in order to identify which qualities and social skills separate happy couples from distressed couples.

Unhappy relationships. About half of new marriages and a larger percentage of second marriages fail. Success or failure often depends on how couples handle conflicts and how often they share happy moments.

During a longitudinal study of 135 couples across 12 years, 21 couples either separated or divorced. In cases where couples broke up, a major sign that the relationship was failing was the couples' poor handling of conflicts. For example, in marriages that failed, husbands were more likely to either deny the conflicts or withdraw and refuse to deal with the conflicts; wives were more likely to exaggerate or escalate the conflicts, which often turned into ugly verbal fights. These unhealthy patterns of dealing with marital conflicts took their toll on the couples' relationships. In fact, researchers predicted with great accuracy (93%) which couples would eventually separate or divorce based on how they dealt with conflicts (Markman, 1995).

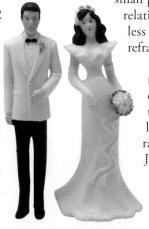

Another problem found in distressed couples is that they shared too few happy experiences. In fact, one researcher was able to predict which of 2,000 couples would get divorced by a relatively simple mathematical equation: a successful couple regularly had at least five times as many positive as negative experiences while an unsuccessful couple had about the same number of positive and negative experiences (Gottman, 1995).

Happy relationships. Couples in happy and successful marriages learn to confront and deal with disagreements in an open, straightforward way, are less defensive about negative feedback, criticize their partners less, are less emotional, and more likely to overlook small problems (Gottman, 1998). Couples make and keep relationships happy by working out their conflicts, being less critical and more supportive of their partners, and refraining from acting too defensive.

In some cases, couples in unhappy relationships may not know what's wrong or may not have the necessary social or communication skills. Couples who participated in programs on how to manage conflicts and learn effective communication skills showed lower rates of both divorce and domestic violence (Prince & Jacobson, 1997). Although falling in love is grand, it doesn't guarantee long-term success. We'll discuss ways to develop and maintain a successful relationship in the upcoming Research Focus.

1. Puberty is accompanied by a number of biological and physical changes, which are triggered by male or female (a)_____. These chemicals result in the development of male and female secondary (b)_____ characteristics and, for females, their first menstrual cycle, which is called (c)_____.

2. The idea that adolescent development consists of a number of cognitive, sexual, social, and personality changes that occur simultaneously is called the _____ model.

"What's real and what's not?"

3. Piaget hypothesized that cognitive development is made up of four distinct stages of reasoning, each of which is qualitatively different from and more advanced than the previous one. According to Piaget, from adolescence through adulthood, we are at the _____ stage, which involves the ability to think about hypothetical concepts, consider an issue from another's viewpoint, and solve abstract problems in a logical manner.

4. Adolescents typically have problems in separating their own thoughts and feelings from those of others. Piaget called this kind of adolescent thinking _____ thinking.

5. One reason about 50% of adolescents engage in two or more risky behaviors (drugs, unsafe sex) is because they have not yet learned the ability to _____ for the future.

6. The idea that moral reasoning can be classified into three distinct levels and that everyone goes through these levels in order is a theory of moral development proposed by (a)_____. The level of moral reasoning based primarily on punishment is called (b)_____; the one based on conforming to laws and society is called (c)_____; and the one based on balancing rights and laws is called (d)_____. Most research supports Kohlberg's idea that people do go through (e)_____ of moral development but that not everyone reaches the highest stage.

7. Carol Gilligan has proposed two basic approaches to moral decisions that seem to depend primarily on gender roles. Making moral decisions based on issues of caring and on how things affect interpersonal relationships is called the (a)_____ orientation. Making moral decisions based more on issues of law and equality is called the (b)_____ orientation.

COSTS ⬍ BENEFITS

8. The development of independence and achievement during adolescence is shaped by a number of different kinds of parenting styles—in particular, (a)_____, (b)_____, and (c)_____—each of which has different costs and benefits to parents and adolescents.

9. In late adulthood, individuals experience a decline in three cognitive processes: an increase in the time required to respond to some sensory stimulus, which is called the (a)_____; a decrease in the rate at which we identify some sensory stimulus as different from other stimuli, which is called the (b)_____; and a decrease in the rate at which we encode information into long-term memory or retrieve it, which is called the (c)_____ speed.

"Am I losing it?"

"Who am I?"

10. According to Erik Erikson, across our lifetimes we proceed through eight (a)_____, each of which presents a particular kind of personality or social problem. For adolescents, stage 5 is most relevant and involves (b)_____ versus role confusion. Finding one's identity has many aspects; the aspect that involves how much we like ourselves and our feelings of worth, attractiveness, and social competence is called (c)_____. Erikson believed that the most important part of personality development for an adolescent was to achieve a satisfying sense of (d)_____ while adults are more concerned about being (e)_____.

11. Males and females think, act, and behave in different ways, and these are called _____, which we are pressured into following by the expectations and rewards or punishments of parents, peers, and society.

12. One way we select a partner for a long-term relationship is by first forming a mental list of characteristics and then looking for someone who matches our mental list, which is called a _____.

13. The theory of love that has three components—passion, intimacy, and commitment—is called the _____.

14. Couples are more likely to have successful long-term relationships if they learn to deal with (a)_____ in a straightforward way and experience at least five times more positive (b)_____ than negative ones.

Answers: 1. (a) hormones, (b) sexual, (c) menarche; 2. BioPsychoSocial; 3. formal operations; 4. egocentric; 5. plan; 6. (a) Kohlberg, (b) preconventional, (c) conventional, (d) postconventional, (e) stages; 7. (a) care, (b) justice; 8. (a) authoritarian, (b) authoritative, (c) permissive; 9. (a) reaction time, (b) perceptual speed, (c) processing; 10. (a) psychosocial stages, (b) identity, (c) self-esteem, (d) identity, (e) productive, creative, nurturing; 11. gender roles; 12. schema; 13. triangular theory; 14. (a) conflicts, (b) experiences.

E. Research Focus: Happy Marriages
How Do Couples Maintain Happy Marriages?

What is the secret of a happy relationship?

Each of us would like to know the answer to this question, "What is the secret to a happy relationship?" because it's one of the most important questions in our lives. This question takes on even more importance when you realize that about half of all new relationships, which began with great love, happiness, and hope, end some years later in stress, frustration, and divorce (Karney & Bradbury, 1995).

What's difficult about maintaining a long-term relationship is that a couple must deal with a continuing series of potentially stressful events, such as raising children, having careers, and building a life with someone who may have different values, beliefs, and personality traits. How successful couples are in dealing with stressful events and conflicts determines to a large extent how happy or unhappy their relationship will be (Karney & Bradbury, 1995).

When researchers studied couples' happiness across 30 years of marriage, they found a definite pattern: newly married couples are very happy at first, but their happiness starts to decline and reaches a low point after the birth of their first child; it reaches another low point when the children are adolescents, but after the children leave home, happiness rises back to its level at the beginning of the marriage (Levenson et al., 1994). This study indicates that after the newness of marriage wears off, couples must use their wits, experience, and social skills to solve a continuing series of potentially disruptive events. Finding the secrets of how couples solve problems, resolve conflicts, and maintain successful relationships was what the following study was all about.

Method

Of the different research methods and techniques that we have discussed, you may ask yourself which one you would use to answer the question "How do couples maintain happy marriages?" If you decided on the longitudinal method, you would be right because this method lets you observe how couples interact, deal with stress, and handle conflicts across time—in this case, eight years. The advantage of the longitudinal method is that it allows you to track changes in the same couples across time and identify those behaviors that may lead to happy or unhappy relationships.

In this study, researchers recruited 130 newlywed couples and followed them for eight years. Researchers gave couples extensive interviews and questionnaires. Perhaps the most important data came from videotaping the couple's interactions. As researchers analyzed the videotaped interactions, they looked for differences between how happy and unhappy couples resolved conflicts, settled disagreements, handled fighting, and gave or took advice. During the course of this eight-year study, 17 couples developed unhappy relationships and were divorced (Gottman, 1998; Gottman et al., 1998).

"You never do anything I ask."

Results

Researchers were just as surprised by what they didn't find as by what they did. First, we'll look at what they didn't find (Gottman et al., 1998).

Didn't find. To help couples with relationship problems, therapists often advise each partner to work at becoming an active listener. Being an active listener means repeating in your own words what your partner said, such as, "So, what I hear you saying is that . . ." But researchers found that couples who used active listening techniques were no more likely to stay together than couples who did not. Researchers explain that asking couples in the middle of an emotional argument to become active listeners and rephrase their spouse's complaints seems unnatural and requires more self-control than many couples have at such a time.

Did find. Researchers found two major things that predicted a happy, long-term relationship.

First, happy marriages had **husbands** who were really good at not rejecting their wives' advice out of hand but either accepting it or finding something reasonable in it. In contrast, unhappy marriages had husbands who were autocratic, failed to listen to their wives' complaints, and dismissed their wives' advice, often with contempt.

Second, happy marriages had **wives** who were careful to express their complaints and advice in gentle, soothing ways, which were easier for their husbands to accept. In contrast, unhappy marriages had wives who phrased their complaints and advice in angry, fighting words that, in turn, triggered equally angry replies from their husbands.

"Honey would you help me?"

Conclusions

So, what can husbands and wives do to develop a happy relationship? Here's what psychologist John Gottman, lead author of the study on long-term relationships, says. "The only way to change marriage for the better is to improve the quality of friendship between a husband and wife and to help them deal with disagreements differently. There has to be a kind of gentleness in the way conflict is managed. Men have to be more accepting of a woman's position, and women have to be more gentle in starting up discussions" (Maugh, 1998, p. A20).

Along these same lines, other researchers add that successful long-term relationships depend on a couple's ability and experience to adapt to the continuing stressful events that unfold year after year (Karney & Bradbury, 1995). Those couples who develop patterns of handling stressful problems and settling conflicts in a straightforward yet considerate way are most likely to develop and maintain their happy relationship through the years.

In the United States, most people marry for love, but that's not true in other cultures.

F. Cultural Diversity: Preferences for Partners

Measuring Cultural Influences

Can 9,000 people agree?

Imagine being born and raised in a country different from your own, such as Nigeria, Germany, China, Iran, Brazil, Japan, France, or India. Now imagine being asked to list, in order, those traits that you consider most desirable in a potential partner. How much would your culture influence the order of desirable traits? To answer this

question, researchers surveyed over 9,000 young adults (males and females), all in their 20s, who lived in 37 different countries (Buss, 1994b; Buss et al., 1990). Subjects were given a list of 32 traits and asked to rank the traits from most to least desirable in a potential partner. The results indicate that 9,000 individuals from many different cultures seemed to agree reasonably well in ranking traits.

Desirable Traits

What is considered desirable in a potential partner? The list on the left shows the most desirable traits for potential partners averaged across cultures. Men and women have similar lists of desirable traits, as indicated by a high correlation of +0.87 between lists. The numerous similarities between males' and females' lists indicate similar cultural influences.

The list on the right shows that there were also some interesting differences between males and females. Males almost always ranked physical appearance in a partner higher, while females almost always ranked earning potential in a partner higher.

How much is virginity valued around the world? In two-thirds of all the cultures measured, men desired virginity or chastity (the lack of previous sexual intercourse) in marriage partners more than women; there were no cultures where women valued virginity in a prospective partner more than men (Buss, 1994b). For example, in China, virginity is indispensable in a partner; marrying a nonvirgin is simply out of the question (Buss, 1994b). In addition, people in India, Taiwan, and Iran placed great value on virginity, while people in the Netherlands, Sweden, and Norway placed little value on virginity in a prospective partner. These differences in the value placed on virginity of females indicate how cultural influences can raise or lower the desirability of certain traits in potential marriage partners.

Average ranking of desirable traits

1 Kind and understanding
2 Intelligent
3 Exciting personality
4 Healthy
5 Emotionally stable and mature
6 Dependable character
7 Pleasing disposition

Differences in desirable traits

8 Good looks (ranked higher by males)
9 Good financial prospect (ranked higher by females)
10 Virginity (ranked higher by males)

Reasons for Marrying

How much is love valued? As the figure on the right shows, cultures in different countries place different values on marrying for love. In the United States and other Western countries, marrying for love is highly valued, but it is least valued in some Middle East, Asian, and African nations.

How do women decide? Some anthropologists have argued that women, who invest more time in caring for offspring, would adopt more discriminating standards for potential mates than would men, who invest less time in rearing children. Thus, women would be more careful in deciding whom to marry. This proved true: in nearly every culture, women expressed more stringent standards across a wide range of characteristics (Buss, 1994b).

Ranking Love in Choosing a Spouse

United States: **First**

Iran: **Third**
Ranked higher: education/intelligence, ambition, chastity

Nigeria: **Fourth**
Ranked higher: good health, refinement/neatness, desire for home and children

China: **Sixth**
Ranked higher: good health, chastity, homemaker

South Africa-Zulu: **Seventh**
Ranked higher: emotionally stable, mature, dependable

How do men decide? Across cultures, men generally decide to marry younger women who are physically attractive. In those societies where men purchase their wives, younger women command a higher bride price. Also, across cultures, the most common reason that men use to dissolve marriages is infertility, or the inability to have children (Buss, 1994b).

From surveys of desirable traits in marriage partners, researchers found many similarities in cultures but found considerable differences among cultures in reasons for getting married.

We have primarily discussed development in adolescents and young to middle-aged adults. Next, we'll examine the physical changes that come with aging.

G. Physical Changes: Aging

Definition

Why do we grow old?

As you look at the photo at right, the difference you see between grandmother and granddaughter is an example of normal aging, which is very different from pathological aging.

Normal aging is a gradual and natural slowing of our physical and psychological processes from middle through late adulthood.

Pathological aging may be caused by genetic defects, physiological problems, or diseases, all of which accelerate the aging process.

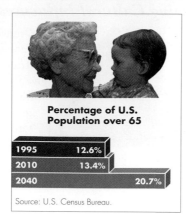

Percentage of U.S. Population over 65

Year	Percentage
1995	12.6%
2010	13.4%
2040	20.7%

Source: U.S. Census Bureau.

One goal of the study of aging, which is called *gerontology,* is to separate the causes of normal aging from those of pathological aging. The study of aging will grow in importance, because the percentage of people in the United States over 65 is expected to almost double by the year 2040 (left graph). Life expectancy in the United States was only 45 years in 1945, but it is currently 75.5 years and rising. In the 1920s, there were only 3,700 people over 100, but currently there are about 61,000 over that age (Cowley, 1997).

We'll examine two related questions about aging: Why do our bodies age? How do our bodies change with age?

Reasons for Aging

How long you will live and how fast your body will age depends about 50% on heredity (genes) and 50% on other factors (diet, exercise, lifestyle, diseases) (Finch & Tanzi, 1997). Researchers have two general theories to explain the aging process: aging by chance and aging by design.

AGING BY CHANCE

The *aging by chance theory* says that our bodies age because of naturally occurring problems or breakdowns in the body's cells, which become less able to repair themselves.

These cellular changes, which occur as a result of normal wear and tear, may include a buildup of waste products that interferes with the cell's functioning; a breakdown in the immune system, which destroys the body's defenses against toxic agents; or an increased number of errors in the genetic mechanism (DNA code), which interferes with cell structure and function (Wallace, 1997).

AGING BY DESIGN

The *aging by design theory* says that our bodies age because there are preset biological clocks that determine the number of times cells can divide and multiply; after that limit is reached, cells begin to die and aging occurs.

Researchers believe that the biological clocks may involve the nervous and immune systems and could serve as coordinators and regulators for aging (Wallace, 1997).

Evidence suggests that our bodies age from a combination of biological clocks, wear and tear, as well as environmental factors such as diet, exercise, and lifestyle (Finch & Tanzi, 1997). As we age, our bodies undergo many changes.

Early Adulthood

The finding that most athletes peak in their 20s indicates that this is a period of maximum physical ability and capacity. For example, tennis champions reach their peak at about 25 years, baseball players are best at about 27, Olympic runners at about 25, and Olympic swimmers at about 20 (Schulz & Curnow, 1988). In our early to middle 20s, our immune system, senses, physiological responses, and mental skills are most efficient.

Middle Adulthood

In our 30s and 40s, we usually gain weight, primarily because we are less active. By the late 40s, there is a slight decrease in a number of physiological responses, including heart rate, lung capacity, muscle strength, kidney function, and eyesight.

Late Adulthood

In our 50s and 60s, we may experience a gradual decline in height because of loss of bone, a further decrease in output of lungs and kidneys, an increase in skin wrinkles, and a deterioration in joints. Sensory organs become less sensitive, resulting in less acute vision, hearing, and taste. The heart, which is a muscle, becomes less effective at pumping blood, which may result in as much as a 35% decrease in blood flow through the coronary arteries. A general decrease occurs in both the number and diameter of muscle fibers, which may explain some of the slowing in motor functions that usually accompanies old age.

Very Late Adulthood

In our 70s and 80s, we undergo further decreases in muscle strength, bone density, speed of nerve conduction, and output of lungs, heart, and kidneys. More than 10% have Parkinson's or Alzheimer's disease. In 1997, the oldest living person in the world was a 117-year-old Canadian woman. At current rates, life expectancy is projected to reach 100 in the next century.

As many of the body's physical responses slow down with aging, there are corresponding decreases in related behaviors, one of which is sexual behavior.

Surveys of sexual behavior, which usually sample people between the ages 17–59, generally report that single men have more sex partners, experience orgasm more frequently, and masturbate more frequently than single women and that about one-third of married couples have sex 2–3 times a week (Laumann et al., 1994). However, people in late adulthood (60–80) are often not included in these surveys, because of the common stereotype that they no longer have any interest in sexual activity or that it is inappropriate for them to engage in sex (Masters & Johnson, 1981). However, recent surveys reported that about 30% of healthy men and women over 65 (average age was 77) were sexually active, primarily those who were married (Matthias et al., 1997). This survey indicates that adults can enjoy sexual activity well into their later years, especially if they know how sexual responses change and learn ways to deal with these changes.

Women's Sexual Changes

The single most significant effect on women's sexual behavior in later adulthood is menopause.

Menopause occurs in women at about age 50 (range 35–60) and involves a gradual stoppage in secretion of the major female hormone (estrogen), which, in turn, results in cessation of both ovulation and menstrual cycle.

In the early 1900s, only 5% of women lived beyond their 50th birthday. Over the next 20 years, approximately 40 million baby boomers will enter menopause, and most can expect to live nearly one-third of their lives after menopause (Fackelmann, 1995b). During and immediately after menopause, about 75% of women experience some physical symptoms but most do not have increased psychological problems (Laan & Lunsen, 1997).

PHYSICAL SYMPTOMS

Most women experience hot flashes, some sleep disturbance, and dryness of the vagina, which results from a decrease and eventual stoppage in the secretion of the female hormone estrogen. A lack of estrogen results in thinning of the vaginal wall and reduction of lubrication during arousal. However, there is little or no change in the ability to become sexually aroused or to reach orgasm. Potential problems with lack of lubrication or painful intercourse may be compensated for by hormone replacement therapy or the use of vaginal creams. Because researchers find no correlation between decrease in hormones and sexual activity, it means that women's continued sexual activity after menopause is due primarily to psychological rather than physiological factors (Dennerstein et al., 1997; Laan & van Lunsen, 1997).

PSYCHOLOGICAL SYMPTOMS

Researchers followed more than 400 healthy women through menopause and observed many psychological changes. They found that women did report psychological symptoms, such as moodiness, depression, anxiety, and anger. However, these symptoms were more related to other stressful issues—for example, growing older in a society that glorifies being young—rather than the physical symptoms of menopause. In addition, women's expectations greatly influence the psychological outlook during menopause. Women with positive expectations about what they hope to accomplish have few psychological symptoms, compared to women who expect their lives to be over and thus feel depressed and angry during menopause (Dennerstein et al., 1997; Neugarten, 1994).

SEXUAL ACTIVITIES

Researchers report that those women who experienced sexual activity as fulfilling and enriching before menopause will likely continue to enjoy sexual activity after menopause and into late adulthood. On the other hand, women who experienced sexual activity as just tolerable or worse before menopause may gradually discontinue sexual activity after menopause (Leiblum, 1990).

Interestingly enough, women in cultures where menopause confers increased stature look forward to menopause and have fewer symptoms than women in the United States (Richters, 1997).

Men's Sexual Changes

As men reach late adulthood (60s, 70s, and 80s) they may experience some physiological changes that decrease sexual responsiveness.

SEXUAL RESPONDING

Because many of the body's physiological responses slow down, older men may require more time and stimulation to have an erection and to reach orgasm. Upon ejaculation, there may be a reduction in the force and amount of fluid. However, in healthy men, there is usually no difficulty in becoming sexually aroused or reaching orgasm. Some men worry that their decreased ability to have an erection or reach orgasm means an end to their sexuality (Masters & Johnson, 1981). In 1998, a new drug (Viagra) was approved for the treatment of impotency, which is the inability to have an erection. Early reports are that about 80% of men with impotency can be helped by the drug (Mann, 1998).

PSYCHOLOGICAL PROBLEMS

Although older men are generally more sexually active then older women, some men see their decreased sexual abilities as a threat to their self-esteem (Matthias et al., 1997). However, any increased time and stimulation

required for erection and orgasm can usually be compensated for by longer periods of stimulation and more imaginative sexual activity by the couple.

According to one researcher, as we grow older we also learn more skills—for example, being more understanding and sensitive to our partner's needs—and these skills help maintain sexual enjoyment and activity (Rossi, 1994).

Next, we discuss a serious problem for both adolescents and seniors, a high rate of suicide.

H. Application: Suicide

Teenage Suicide

Suicides for teenagers aged 15–19 almost quadrupled from about 3.5 per 100,000 in 1960 to 11.1 per 100,000 in 1994 (Nazario, 1997). In this age group, suicide is now the third leading cause of death. White teenage boys continue to have the highest suicide rates (18 per 100,000). Based on a survey of over 11,000 teenagers, the Centers for Disease Control and Prevention estimate that about one million American teenagers attempted suicide during 1990.

We'll focus on the two most-asked questions: What are the problems related to teenage suicide? How can teenage suicide be prevented? We'll use four real-life examples to illustrate how complex the issues and causes are. In a span of five weeks, four teenage boys—one a straight-A student, one the class clown, one deeply religious person, and one very troubled boy—committed suicide in the small southern town of Sheridan, Arkansas (adapted from *People*, May 21, 1990, pp. 56–59).

1 March 28, 1990: Raymond, 17 Years Old

According to the police chief, Ray had threatened to kill himself in the past, but the threats were considered teenage histrionics. He had a drinking problem, had been arrested for drunken driving, and had been sent to a rehabilitation center for several weeks. Before Ray shot himself, however, his life seemed to be improving, and he had made plans to go to college. A suicide note to his girlfriend said, "Don't blame yourself. It's nobody's fault."

3 April 30, 1990: Thomas, 19 Years Old

Thomas was a straight-A student who liked to read, listen to oldies, and hunt and fish. He did not drink, smoke, or swear. He lived too far out of town to have many buddies. His father had died when he was nine. Two years earlier, his grandfather, who had terminal cancer, committed suicide with a pistol to his head. Tommy had shot himself in the afternoon, and that very night Thomas did the same. In his suicide note he said, "Where shall I begin? I really don't know. It's hard to say what's going on anymore. A long time now I have felt like I am on the edge and slipping fast. I guess I've finally slipped over the edge."

2 April 30, 1990: Tommy, 16 Years Old

His teenage peers considered Tommy a clown, but his best friend, Rhonda, didn't believe that. She thought Tommy's clever wit and clowning were a mask for his insecurity. On April 29, Tommy called Rhonda, which he did regularly, and told her that he was going to kill himself. Certain he would not carry out his threat, she made him promise to come to school the next day. Tommy came to school, and in one of his classes he got up and stated that he had two things to say. He said that he loved Rhonda, although they had never dated. "The other thing," he said, "is this." He pulled out a pistol and shot himself.

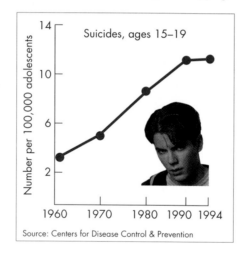

Suicides, ages 15–19

Number per 100,000 adolescents

14 / 10 / 6 / 2

1960 1970 1980 1990 1994

Source: Centers for Disease Control & Prevention

4 May 2, 1990: Jerry, 17 Years Old

Jerry's suicide was the last of the four and the most troubling. He was popular, gregarious, good-looking, and so deeply religious that he was nicknamed "preacher boy." The night after Tommy's suicide he told his mother, "I can't understand how anyone would commit suicide—that was the coward's way." That same night he called his girlfriend and said, "I love you. I'll talk to you tomorrow." The next day he stayed home from school, and around noon he shot himself in the head. The family insists that Jerry's death was accidental.

Problems Related to Teenage Suicide

Notice that in the above examples, family and friends could not believe that two of the four adolescents would ever even think of committing suicide. That's because one was a straight-A student and the other was very popular and deeply religious. In the other two cases, one adolescent had said he was thinking about suicide and one had made a previous attempt. Thus, if and when adolescents talk about committing suicide, parents and friends need to take such talk seriously. In other cases, the problems, symptoms, or events leading up to or triggering suicide may be difficult to recognize. However, clinicians find that the following problems may lead to or trigger suicide attempts.

Problems and symptoms. The most common *psychological problems* include depression, feelings of helplessness, and drug-related problems, such as Raymond's alcohol problem. Usually these problems have persisted for some time (Walter et al., 1995). The most common *behavioral symptoms* include decline in school performance; social isolation and withdrawal; intense difficulties with parents, siblings, and peers; and antisocial behavior (Patton et al., 1997). For example, Thomas' suicide note says, "A long time now I have felt like I am on the edge and slipping fast."

Precipitators. In most cases, there are *precipitators* of suicide, which may be certain events, feelings, or situations. For example, common precipitators include problems with relationships, bouts of depression, drinking problems, or relatively ordinary stressors, such as difficulties with dating, parents, or school. A high percentage of victims had either expressed the wish to die or threatened suicide, as was true for both Raymond and Tommy.

One reason parents and friends are shocked by an adolescent's suicide is that the problems or precipitators may be hard to spot.

Preventing Teenage Suicide

What can be done to help teens?

A survey by the Centers for Disease Control and Prevention found that 1 in 12 high school students have attempted suicide and about 24 out of 100 students have seriously thought about committing suicide (Nazario, 1997). Because suicide is the third leading cause of death in adolescents, therapists have proposed a three-step program for suicide prevention.

IDENTIFY RISK FACTORS

The first step is to identify risk factors, including depression, drug abuse, previous suicide attempt, recent suicide of a friend, and major life stressors, such as family turmoil or parental separation (Lewinsohn et al., 1994). A youth with one or more of these risk factors is in imminent danger of committing suicide (Berman & Jobes, 1994). Methods for identifying risk factors include special programs on suicide prevention in schools and support groups among families to deal with life and environmental stressors (Garland & Zigler, 1993).

CRISIS MANAGEMENT

The Centers for Disease Control and Prevention (1988) recommend that, following a suicide in a school or local community, a team of mental health professionals be sent to the location to screen for students who may be at risk for suicide. For example, in a questionnaire screening of 2,000 students, about 3% requested help from a counselor (Berman & Jobes, 1994).

HOTLINE SERVICES

The rationale for 24-hour hotline services is that suicidal behavior is often associated with a crisis situation during which the person may have a strong need or desire to talk to someone in a last cry for help (Garland & Zigler, 1993). Hotline services may reach adolescents, such as those in poverty or without health coverage, who would not otherwise be served by mental health facilities.

The combination of these programs in schools and communities can aid in identifying, helping, and preventing potential suicides in adolescents (Berman & Jobes, 1995). In one case, suicides decreased by 50% after an antisuicide program in schools (Kalafat, 1997).

Although adolescents have a high rate of suicide, the highest rate of any group is one you rarely hear about.

Suicide in The Elderly

Why are rates so high?

Although suicides are the third leading cause of death among adolescents, the highest suicide rate for any group is among the elderly. For individuals 65 and over, the suicide rate in the United States is almost double (20 per 100,000) that of the national average (12 per 100,000). Reasons behind the high rate of suicide in the elderly involve a number of risk factors.

The common risk factors for suicide among the elderly are depression and loneliness, but the major contributing cause in 69–85% of the cases was a serious health problem (Cattell & Jolley, 1995). Thus, the major factor leading to suicide in the elderly, which is physical illness, is very different from the major factors involved in adolescent suicide, which involve psychological problems. The question of how the elderly deal with serious physical problems brings up the question of physician-assisted suicide.

"I have six months to live and I'm in constant pain."

At the time of this writing, Dr. Jack Kevorkian has allegedly assisted at or been at the deaths of over 45 men and women. All were terminally ill, in great pain or fear of pain, had made known their wishes to die, and took their lives with Kevorkian's alleged help. Since 1991, Kevorkian has been arrested several times because his state and at least 27 others have laws banning assisted suicide by anyone, including doctors. However, suicide by one's own hand is legal in all states.

Legal suicide. In 1994, Oregon voters approved—by a vote of 51% to 49%—a measure that would allow a patient to request a lethal dose of drugs if at least two doctors determine that the person has less than six months to live. This law went into effect in 1998. Since then, at least four people have ended their lives in Oregon with a physician's help.

Besides Oregon, the Netherlands and Australia have passed laws that allow physician-assisted suicide. Should a person be allowed to end his or her own life with a doctor's help (Mydans, 1997)?

OPPONENTS OF PHYSICIAN-ASSISTED SUICIDE

Opponents say that allowing people to take their own lives opens the door to many potential abuses. For example, making assisted suicide easier may increase the chances that people who are suffering from mental problems or temporary emotional difficulties will take their own lives without exploring other possibilities for living. Some fear that the profit motive may make assisted suicide or euthanasia a lucrative business (Hendin, 1994). Others argue that when people are distressed they are unlikely or unable to make a rational decision about committing suicide (Clay, 1997).

PROPONENTS OF PHYSICIAN-ASSISTED SUICIDE

Proponents explain that each of us has the moral right to end our lives if we find that life has become unbearable for health reasons. In 1975, public opinion polls found that 41% believed that someone in great pain and with no hope of improvement has the moral right to commit suicide (euthanasia); by 1990, that figure had risen to 66% (Blendon et al., 1992). The *New England Journal of Medicine* published an article by a group of doctors who proposed a policy of legalized physician-assisted death with safeguards to protect patients, preserve the integrity of physicians, and assure that voluntary physician-assisted death occurs only as a last resort (Miller et al., 1994).

The pros and cons of euthanasia and assisted suicide in patients who have a terminal illness or chronic unbearable pain will continue to be debated, especially since the population of the elderly will almost double in the next 35 years.

SUMMARY TEST

A. PUBERTY & SEXUAL BEHAVIOR

1. Girls and boys experience three major biological changes as they go through a period called (a)_____. For both girls and boys, one of these changes is the development of (b)_____ maturity, which for girls includes the first menstrual cycle, called (c)_____, and for boys includes the production of sperm. These physical changes in girls and boys are triggered by a portion of the brain called the (d)_____. A second change is the development of (e)_____ sexual characteristics, such as pubic hair and gender-specific physical changes. A third change is a surge in (f)_____ growth, especially height. The changes for girls tend to start about a year earlier than those for boys.

B. COGNITIVE CHANGES

2. Piaget's fourth cognitive stage, which begins in adolescence and continues into adulthood, is called the (a)_____ stage. During this stage, adolescents and adults develop the ability to think about (b)_____ concepts, plan for the future, and solve abstract problems. Many adolescents have a difficult time separating their own thoughts and feelings from those of others; this is called (c)_____.

3. According to Kohlberg's theory, moral reasoning can be classified into three distinct levels, and everyone progresses through the levels in the same order. However, not all adults reach the highest levels. The first level, the (a)_____ level, has two stages. In stage 1, moral decisions are determined primarily through fear of punishment, while at stage 2 they are guided by satisfying one's self-interest. The second level, the (b)_____ level, also has two stages. In the first of these, stage 3, people conform to the standards of others they value; in stage 4, they conform to the laws of society. In the third level, the (c)_____ level, moral decisions are made after thinking about all the alternatives and striking a balance between human rights and the laws of society.

1. Sensorimotor

2. Preoperational

3. Concrete

4. Formal

4. Gender roles or gender differences seem to influence moral reasoning. Women may tend to make moral decisions based on a (a)_____ orientation, while men tend to make moral decisions based on a (b)_____ orientation.

5. Parenting styles affect many aspects of adolescents' development. Parents who attempt to shape and control their children in accordance with a set standard of conduct are termed (a)_____. Parents who attempt to direct their children's activities in a rational and intelligent way and are supportive, loving, and committed, are called (b)_____. Parents who are less controlling and behave with a nonpunishing and accepting attitude toward their children's impulses are called (c)_____.

C. PERSONALITY & SOCIAL CHANGES

6. How you describe yourself, including your values, goals, traits, interests, and motivations, is a function of your sense of (a)_____, which is part of the problem to be faced in stage 5 of Erikson's eight (b)_____ stages. Those who are unsuccessful in resolving the problems of this stage will experience (c)_____, which results in low self-esteem, and may become socially withdrawn.

7. An adolescent's feeling of worth, attractiveness, and social competence is called _____, which is influenced particularly by physical appearance, social acceptability, and management of public behaviors (anxiety and stress).

8. The challenges of adulthood are covered in the last three of Erikson's eight (a)_____ stages. According to his theory, in stage 6, young adults face the problems of intimacy versus (b)_____. In stage 7, middle adults face problems of generativity versus (c)_____. In stage 8, older adults reflect on their lives; if they feel positive and contented about how they lived and what they accomplished, they will have a feeling of satisfaction or (d)_____; if not, they will have a feeling of regret and (e)_____.

D. GENDER ROLES, LOVE, & RELATIONSHIPS

9. During childhood and adolescence, males and females experience pressures and expectations from parents, peers, and society to behave in different ways. These expected patterns called _____, influence cognitive, personality, and social development.

10. The kind of love that involves continually thinking about the loved one and is accompanied by sexual feelings and powerful emotional reactions is called (a)_____ love. The kind of love that involves trusting and tender feelings for someone whose life is closely bound up with one's own is called (b)_____ love. Sternberg has developed a triangular theory of love, dividing it into three components. Feeling physically aroused and attracted to someone is called (c)_____; feeling close and connected to someone, which develops through sharing and communicating, is called (d)_____; making a pledge to nourish the feelings of love and to maintain the relationship is called (e)_____. Sternberg believes that most of us strive for (f)_____, which is a balanced combination of these three components.

11. One way that we select a mate is by developing an organized mental list of desirable characteristics and then looking for someone who matches this mental list, which is called a _____.

E. RESEARCH FOCUS: HAPPY MARRIAGES

12. Studies on long-term relationsips indicate that in happy marriages husbands do not reject and can find something reasonable in their wives' (a)_____; and wives learn how to put their complaints or advice in (b)_____ ways so their husbands are more likely to listen and follow it. In addition, in happy marriages couples learn to adjust to a continuing series of (c)_____ events and situations.

F. CULTURAL DIVERSITY: PREFERENCES FOR PARTNERS

13. People's lists of desirable traits for a mate show remarkable similarity across cultures. However, there are some differences in ranking between the genders; for example,

United States: **First**

Iran: **Third**
Ranked higher: education/ intelligence, ambition, chastity

men rank (a)_____ higher than do women, and women rank (b)_____ higher than do men. Also, different cultures place different values on the desirability of marrying someone who is a (c)_____ and marrying somone primarily because of being in (d)_____.

G. PHYSICAL CHANGES: AGING

14. The gradual and natural slowing of physical and psychological processes from middle through late adulthood is called (a)_____ aging and is explained by two theories, each of which emphasizes a different mechanism. According to one theory, our bodies age because of naturally occurring problems or breakdowns in the cells. This theory is called aging by (b)_____. According to another theory, our bodies age because of a biological limit on the number of times that cells can divide and multiply; after

that limit is reached, cells begin to die and aging occurs. This is called aging by (c)_____.

15. The aging that may be caused by genetic defects, physiological problems, or diseases is called _____ aging, an example of which is Alzheimer's disease.

16. In later adulthood (about age 50), women experience a gradual reduction in the secretion of estrogen, which results in cessation of ovulation and the menstrual cycle; this is called (a)_____. In late adulthood (60–80) men do not stop producing testosterone, but they may experience a decrease in sexual responsiveness due to (b)_____ changes.

H. APPLICATION: SUICIDE

17. A number of factors have been found to be related to teenage suicide. Before committing suicide, adolescents usually have a number of (a)_____ problems, such as depression, feelings of helplessness, or drug-related problems; adolescents also show a number of (b)_____

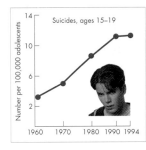

Suicides, ages 15–19

Number per 100,000 adolescents

1960 1970 1980 1990 1994

symptoms, such as falling grades, social isolation and withdrawal, difficulties with family and peers, and antisocial behavior. Usually, suicide is preceded by events or feelings called (c)_____; these may include problems with relationships or bouts of depression or drinking.

18. Among the risk factors for suicide in the elderly are depression and loneliness, but the major contributing cause is (a)_____ problems. Currently, there is considerable discussion in the United States over the right of a person with a terminal disease to end his or her life through (b)_____ suicide.

Answers: 1. (a) puberty, (b) sexual, (c) menarche, (d) hypothalamus, (e) secondary, (f) physical; 2. (a) formal operations, (b) abstract or hypothetical, (c) adolescent egocentric thinking; 3. (a) preconventional, (b) conventional, (c) postconventional; 4. (a) care, (b) justice; 5. (a) authoritarian, (b) authoritative, (c) permissive; 6. (a) identity or self, (b) psychosocial, (c) identity confusion; 7. self-esteem; 8. (a) psychosocial, (b) isolation, (c) stagnation, (d) integrity, (e) despair; 9. gender roles; 10. (a) passionate, (b) companionate, (c) passion, (d) intimacy, (e) commitment, (f) complete or consummate love; 11. schema; 12. (a) advice, (b) gentle, (c) stressful; 13. (a) good looks, virginity; (b) financial prospects; (c) virgin; (d) love; 14. (a) natural, (b) chance, (c) design; 15. pathological; 16. (a) menopause, (b) physiological; 17. (a) psychologial, (b) behavioral, (c) precipitators; 18. (a) health or medical, (b) assisted.

CRITICAL THINKING

ADULTHOOD? LATER, DUDE!

by D. James Romero

1. What attitudes does the author say young people today have about adulthood?

Adulthood has become a dirty word in America. No one, it seems, wants to live the Cleaver life. Some would just as soon be in prison as be beholden to family, job, and community. They see it as the antithesis of freedom. Others dream of suburbia and strollers, but simply don't have the means.

America, some say, has become a nation of adolescents. The nation has been transformed so that self-indulgence takes precedence over family values, some experts argue. As some people in their 30s, 40s, and 50s see no need to take charge of the world in the way their parents once did, the young—adolescents and teens—are sometimes forced to act old prematurely for lack of guiding hands.

2. What definition does the author offer of adulthood?

The grownup state of mind is coming at later and later ages, if at all. Many culture watchers and sociologists argue that true adulthood in America is postponed until at least after age 30. It comes, they say, when people master responsibilities—ethics, finances, psychological stability—worthy of parenthood, regardless of whether they have children.

3. What three theories are offered to explain delayed adulthood?

Diane Crispell, executive editor of American Demographics magazine, says there's one very good reason people are growing up at older ages: money. Higher paying jobs go to those who have better educations, so people stay in school and reach for higher degrees. Housing prices are through the roof (the Census Bureau reports that two-thirds of those ages 25 to 34 can't afford a median-priced home in their area), so twentysomethings rent. The cost of living is at an all-time high, so young people take on college-style living arrangements with roommates or stay at home with Mom or Dad.

4. What are the differences between your life and those of your parents when they were your age? To what do you attribute these differences?

Author Gail Sheehy blames expanding life spans for prolonged adolescence. Average life expectancy is 75 and rising, with some experts predicting that people will live well into the triple digits in the next few decades. That pushes all phases of life in to older years. Adolescence reaches into the 20s, midlife into the 50s.

5. Do you think you are an adult now? What is your definition of adulthood?

Yet author Neil Howe, one of the country's foremost experts on generational sociology, takes a bit different view. He says each generation has its own tempo for turning adult, and that it's not necessarily young adults who are acting like kids. In fact, people in their 20s and 30s actually grew up fast, he maintains. "They grew up at a time of massive child under-protection," Howe says, "so they raised themselves."

Source: *Los Angeles Times,* March 21, 1997.

Study Questions

A. Puberty & Sexual Behavior—How are the sexual concerns of adolescents and senior adults similar but also different? (See answer in Critical Thinking Appendix.)

B. Cognitive Changes—If you overheard an adolescent discussing politics with her grandfather, what cognitive differences would you notice?

C. Personality & Social Changes—If you become a parent, what special concerns might you have when your own children go through adolescence? (See answer in Critical Thinking Appendix.)

D. Gender Roles, Love, & Relationships—If you are beginning a long-term relationship, what two things should you and your partner do to ensure success?

E. Research Focus: Happy Marriages—What is different about the interactions of couples who are happy from those of couples who are unhappy?

F. Cultural Diversity: Preferences for Partners—What do you think are the advantages and disadvantages of having parents arrange marriages for their children?

G. Physical Changes: Aging—Although two people are both 65, why might one seem much older and the other much younger?

H. Application: Suicide—If your grandmother had incurable cancer and unbearable pain and asked you to help her commit suicide, would you help her? (See answer in Critical Thinking Appendix.)

LINKS TO LEARNING

Web Sites & Learning Activities

● BROOKS/COLE ONLINE PSYCHOLOGY STUDY CENTER

http://psychstudy.brookscole.com/student/plotnik/quiz/ch18frm.html

This site gives students a chance to review material by taking quizzes and doing exercises and activities for this module.

● COLLEGE VIEW

http://www.collegeview.com/index.html

These days, college often forms the link between adolescence and adulthood. This site provides virtual college tours, a survival guide, financial information, and more.

● AMERICAN ACADEMY OF CHILD AND ADOLESCENT PSYCHIATRY

http://www.aacap.org/

What special psychiatric risks do adolescents face? This site provides information on mental disorders, including substance abuse, research, and breaking news.

● MARRIAGE SURVIVAL GUIDE

http://www.geocities.com/Heartland/Meadows/9082/

This site explores various marriage-related topics, including affairs, flirting, money issues, and in-laws. There are funny stories as well as good advice.

Welcome to the WEB

● THE COMMISSION ON DOMESTIC VIOLENCE

http://www.abanet.org/domviol/home.html

This site deals with issues of domestic violence, including where to get help, legal issues, phone numbers, articles, and a bibliography.

● CAREGIVER SURVIVAL RESOURCES

http://www.caregiver911.com/

Caring for an aging or ill person can be one of life's biggest challenges. This site offers resources for support, a reading list, and an Ask Dr. Caregiver feature.

Activities

● *Integrator Online™ for Introductory Psychology* CD-ROM, Plotnik, Module 18

● Study Guide to accompany *Introduction to Psychology*, 5th edition, Module 18 (choice of PC or Mac computer version or hard copy)

● *PsychNow!* CD-ROM

Adolescent Development

Adult Development, Aging, and Death

Answers to questions on page 430

1. Some are hesitant to assume the responsibilities of adulthood, and others want to become adults but can't afford it.
2. He says it comes when people master the responsibilities that would make them good parents, whether or not they have children.
3. The financial instability of young people, expanding life spans, and generational style.
4. There is no "right" answer to this one—but it could be interesting to discuss your thoughts with your parents!
5. Again, no "right" answers, just food for thought.

Module 19 FREUDIAN & HUMANISTIC THEORIES

A. Freud's Psychodynamic Theory   434

* **DEFINITION**
* **CONSCIOUS VERSUS UNCONSCIOUS FORCES**
* **TECHNIQUES TO DISCOVER THE UNCONSCIOUS**

B. Divisions of the Mind   436

* **ID, EGO, AND SUPEREGO**
* **ANXIETY**
* **DEFENSE MECHANISMS**

C. Developmental Stages   438

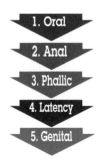

* **DEVELOPMENT: DEALING WITH CONFLICTS**
* **FIXATION: POTENTIAL PERSONALITY PROBLEMS**
* **FIVE PSYCHOSEXUAL STAGES**

D. Freud's Followers & Critics   440

* **DISAGREEMENTS**
* **NEO-FREUDIANS**
* **FREUDIAN THEORY TODAY**

E. Humanistic Theories   442

* **THREE CHARACTERISTICS**
* **MASLOW: NEED HIERARCHY AND SELF-ACTUALIZATION**
* **ROGERS: SELF THEORY**
* **APPLICATION**
* **EVALUATION**

F. Cultural Diversity: Achievement   448

* **BOAT PEOPLE: REMARKABLE ACHIEVEMENT**
* **VALUES AND MOTIVATION**
* **PARENTAL ATTITUDES**

© Jason Goltz

G. Research Focus: Shyness   449

* **WHAT IS SHYNESS AND WHAT CAUSES IT?**

H. Application: Assessment—Projective Tests   450

* **DEFINITIONS**
* **PROJECTIVE TESTS**
* **TWO CHARACTERISTICS**
* **USEFULNESS**

Personality

When he had it all, why did he end it all?

In the early 1990s, the top punk rock band was Nirvana, and their hit song "Smells Like Teen Spirit" was number one in the charts and in the hearts of millions of fans. Nirvana's founder, song writer, and lead guitar player was Kurt Cobain, whose troubled life was beginning to unravel. Just as his band and career had finally reached the top in the United States and his music was getting international acclaim, he wrote a very revealing one-page note, part of which read as follows:

"I haven't felt the excitement of listening to as well as creating music, along with really writing for too many years now. I feel guilty beyond words about these things. For example, when we're backstage and the lights go out and manic roar of the crowd goes up, it doesn't affect me the way in which it did for Freddie Mercury, who seemed to love and relish in the love and admiration from the crowd, which is something I totally admire and envy. The fact is, I can't fool you, any one of you. It simply isn't fair to you or to me. The worst crime I can think of would be pull people off by faking it and pretending as if I'm having a hundred percent fun. . . . I've tried everything that's in my power to appreciate it, and I do. God, believe me, I do. But it's not enough. . ."(Strauss, 1994, p. 40).

After writing this note, Kurt Cobain, 27 years old and at the height of his popularity, opened his wallet to his Washington driver's license and tossed it on the floor. He apparently drew up a chair to the window, sat down, took some drugs, pressed the barrel of a 20-gauge shotgun to his head, and—eventually using his thumb—pulled the trigger (Strauss, 1994).

How could someone with so much going for him—youth, a family (wife and baby daughter), the number-one band in the United States, hit records, fame, and money—turn away from all that and commit suicide? Cobain's tragic story introduces some of the most puzzling and fascinating issues about our innermost selves, our personalities.

Personality refers to a combination of long-lasting and distinctive behaviors, thoughts, motives, and emotions that typify how we react and adapt to other people and situations.

Cobain's rocket to stardom and tragic ending raise a number of questions about personality: How does personality develop? Why do personalities differ? How well do we know ourselves? These kinds of questions are answered by theories of personality.

A *theory of personality* is an organized attempt to describe and explain how personalities develop and why personalities differ.

On the one hand, personality theories try to explain why Cobain's personality put him at risk for suicide. On the other hand, personality theories also try to explain why some individuals have personalities that help them overcome horrendous problems and achieve personal success. One such individual is Charles Dutton.

Changing Personality

How did he change from a criminal to an actor?

Charles Dutton had been in and out of reform schools since he was 12 years old and was finally sent to prison for manslaughter and illegal possession of a firearm. While in prison, he got into trouble for being a ringleader of a riot and was punished with solitary confinement. To pass his time, he took along a friend's book of plays by black authors. Dutton was so moved by the plays' messages that for the first time he thought about channeling his rage and anger into acting.

At one point he spent more than 60 painful days in the prison hospital after a fellow inmate had plunged an icepick through his neck. During those long days in the hospital, he decided that it was time to put his life in order and accomplish something worthwhile during his remaining time in prison. He obtained a high school equivalency certificate and then a two-year college degree, read dozens of plays, and even started a prison theater. After his parole, he attended college and got his B.A. in drama. His high point came when he was accepted into Yale drama school.

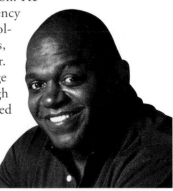

By 1992, ex-problem boy, ex-con, ex-prison terrorist Charles Dutton (right photo) had turned into a very successful actor and was starring in *Roc*, his own television series (*Los Angeles Times*, August 25, 1991). Dutton's story is an emotionally painful search for identity, culminating in the discovery and development of his acting potential. We'll discuss a theory of personality that emphasizes the development of our full potential.

What's Coming

We'll discuss two very different theories of personality: Sigmund Freud's psychodynamic theory emphasizes unconscious forces, irrational thoughts, and the lasting impressions of childhood experiences, whereas humanistic theories emphasize our rational processes and our natural striving to reach our true potentials.

We'll begin with a look at Kurt Cobain's problems and where his inner demons came from.

A. Freud's Psychodynamic Theory

Definition

What was one of Freud's key ideas?

Freud's theory of personality begins with a controversial assumption that is an important key to unlocking the secrets of personality. To understand how Freud found this key idea, we'll journey back in time to the late 1800s.

At that time, Freud was wondering why several of his women patients had developed very noticeable physical symptoms, such as losing all sensation in their hands or being unable to control the movements of their legs. What most puzzled Freud, who was a medical doctor, was that despite these obvious physical complaints, he could not identify a single physical cause for these symptoms. Somehow, Freud's brilliant mind solved this problem and in so doing, found an important key to unlocking the secrets of personality. Freud reasoned that since there were no observable physical or neurological causes of the women's physical symptoms, the causes must come from unconscious psychological forces (Westen, 1990).

In the 1800s, Freud's belief that human behavior was influenced by unconscious psychological forces was revolutionary, and it led to his equally revolutionary theory of personality.

Freud's psychodynamic theory of personality emphasizes the importance of early childhood experiences, repressed thoughts that we cannot voluntarily access, and the conflicts between conscious and unconscious forces that influence our thoughts and behaviors. (Freud used the term *dynamic* to refer to mental energy or force.)

Freud believed not only that unconscious psychological forces had a powerful influence on personality but that these forces originated

in early childhood. This means that if Freud were alive today, he would look for reasons behind Kurt Cobain's suicide at age 27 by searching through Kurt's childhood. Here's what Freud would find.

When Kurt was 8 years old, his mother filed for divorce, and his parents began their endless fighting. Now Kurt, who had been an outgoing, happy child, became sullen and withdrawn. Because he was skinny and frail, the local town bullies gave him a bad time. Kurt lived sporadically with his father, grandparents, and three sets of aunts and uncles, never finding a real home or anyone to give him love and support. Kurt developed some behavioral problems, such as trouble paying attention, and was given Ritalin (a drug similar in effect to amphetamine) because he was thought to be hyperactive. As if his own problems weren't difficult enough for him to deal with, two of his uncles committed suicide. Friends had only to look into Kurt's eyes to see his sadness and loneliness (Mundy, 1994).

According to Freud, Kurt's childhood, which was full of hurt, pain, and rejection, greatly affected his personality development and caused problems that eventually overwhelmed him. To explain the complex development of someone's personality, such as Kurt Cobain's, is such a difficult task that only a dozen or so psychologists have tried. One of the best-known attempts to explain personality is included in Sigmund Freud's (1901/1960, 1924, 1940) overall theory of psychoanalysis, which includes two related theories: a method of psychotherapy, which we'll discuss in Module 24, and a theory of personality development, which we'll focus on here.

We'll begin with Freud's controversial and revolutionary assumption that unconscious psychological forces influence behavior.

Conscious versus Unconscious Forces

What kind of forces drove Kurt Cobain?

Cobain's life was full of inconsistencies. The closer he got to the top, the less happy he became. "Sometime during the months leading up to the recording sessions for Nirvana's last album, Kurt Cobain wrote a song called 'I Hate Myself and Want To Die.' It was a phrase he used a lot at the time—ever since the band's Australian tour—as a backhanded response to people who kept asking him how he was doing. Cobain thought it was so funny he wanted it to be the title of the album" (Fricke, 1994, p. 63).

Kurt indicated that the title of his song was a joke. In doing so, he was expressing a conscious thought.

Conscious thoughts are wishes, desires, or thoughts that we are aware of, or can recall, at any given moment.

However, Freud theorized that our conscious thoughts are only a small part of our total mental activity, much of which involves unconscious thoughts or forces.

Conscious thoughts → BEHAVIOR ← Unconscious forces

Unconscious forces represent wishes, desires, or thoughts that, because of their disturbing or threatening content, we automatically repress and cannot voluntarily access.

Did Cobain write the song "I Hate Myself and Want To Die" because of some unconscious forces that he was unaware of and had repressed? According to Freud, although repressed thoughts are unconscious, they may influence our behaviors through unconscious motivation.

Unconscious motivation is a Freudian concept that refers to the influence of repressed thoughts, desires, or impulses on our conscious thoughts and behaviors.

Freud used the concept of unconscious forces and motivation to explain why we say or do things that we cannot explain or understand. Once he assumed that there were unconscious forces and motivations, Freud needed to find ways to explore the unconscious.

What was in Cobain's unconscious?

It was one thing for Freud to propose the existence of powerful psychological forces and motivations that were unconscious, but it was quite another thing for him to show that such unconscious forces actually existed. For example, were there any signs that unconscious psychological forces were making Cobain more and more unhappy as he became more and more successful and popular?

Looking back now at Kurt Cobain's suicide, perhaps there was more truth than jest to the title of his song, "I Hate Myself and Want To Die." One music critic wrote that Cobain was very clever at hiding the true meanings of his lyrics under a layer of the funny or bizarre (Fricke, 1994). The fact that he committed suicide at the height of his career puts a different and tragic light on many of his verses. For example, did Cobain hide some of his unconscious feelings in the following lyrics?

"Everything is my fault / I'll take all the blame" ("All Apologies")

"Monkey see monkey do / I don't know why I'd rather be dead than cool" ("Stay Away")

"One more special message to go / And then I'm done, then I can go home" ("On a Plain")

If Freud were to examine these lyrics, he might say that they reflected some of Cobain's repressed and unconscious thoughts, desires, and wishes about death and dying. Because neither Cobain nor any of us can easily or voluntarily reveal or talk about our unconscious thoughts and desires, Freud needed to find ways for his patients to reveal their unconscious thoughts and desires, some of which may be psychologically threatening or disturbing. From observing his patients during therapy, Freud believed that he had found three techniques that uncovered, revealed, or hinted at a person's unconscious wishes and desires.

Freud's three techniques to uncover the unconscious included free association, dream interpretation, and analysis of slips of the tongue (which are now commonly known as Freudian slips) (Macmillan, 1997).

FREE ASSOCIATION

One technique for revealing the unconscious was to encourage his patients to relax and to sit back or lie down on his now-famous couch and talk freely about anything. He called this process free association.

Free association is a Freudian technique in which clients are encouraged to talk about any thoughts or images that enter their head; the assumption is that this kind of free-flowing, uncensored talking will provide clues to unconscious material.

Free association, which is one of Freud's important discoveries, continues to be used today by some therapists (Macmillan, 1997). However, not all therapists agree that free associations actually reveal a client's unconscious thoughts, desires, and wishes (Grunbaum, 1993).

DREAM INTERPRETATION

Freud listened to and interpreted his patients' dreams because he believed that dreams represent the purest form of free association.

Dream interpretation, a Freudian technique of analyzing dreams, is based on the assumption that dreams contain underlying, hidden meanings and symbols that provide clues to unconscious thoughts and desires. Freud distinguished between a dream's manifest content—the plot of the dream at the surface level—and its latent content—the hidden or disguised meaning of the plot's events.

For example, Freud interpreted certain objects (such as sticks and knives) as symbols for male sexual organs and interpreted other objects (such as boxes and ovens) as symbols for female sexual organs. The therapist's task is to look behind the dream's often bizarre disguises and symbols to decipher clues to unconscious material. According to Freud, dreams are the "royal road" into the unconscious.

FREUDIAN SLIPS

At one time or another, most of us, according to Freud, unintentionally reveal some unconscious thought or desire by making what is now called a Freudian slip (Macmillan, 1997).

Freudian slips are mistakes or slips of the tongue that we make in everyday speech; such mistakes, which are often embarrassing, are thought to reflect unconscious thoughts or wishes.

For example, one of my colleagues was lecturing on the importance of regular health care. She said, "It is important to visit a veterinarian for regular checkups." According to Freud, mistakes like substituting *veterinarian* for *physician* are not accidental but rather "intentional" ways of expressing unconscious desires. As it turns out, my colleague, who is in very good health, was having serious doubts about her relationship with a person who happened to be a veterinarian.

Freud assumed that free association, dream interpretation, and slips of the tongue share one thing in common: they are all mental processes that are the least controlled by our conscious, rational, and logical minds. As a result, he believed that these three techniques allowed uncensored clues to slip out and reveal our deeper unconscious wishes and desires (Macmillan, 1997).

According to Freud's theory, there is a continuing battle going on in our minds between conscious thoughts and unconscious forces. How our minds fight these battles is perhaps one of Freud's best-known theories, and you'll easily recognize many of the terms.

B. Divisions of the Mind

Id, Ego, and Superego

Kurt Cobain's suicide note revealed some of his problems and internal struggles; here are some excerpts (Strauss, 1994, p. 40):

"I'm too sensitive."

"I must be one of those narcissists who only appreciate things when they're alone."

"Thank you all from the pit of my burning nauseous stomach."

"It's better to burn out than to fade away."

Cobain's final thoughts suggest that he was fighting a number of psychological and emotional battles. Sometimes his problems became public when, for no apparent reason, he would violently throw or smash his guitar during concerts. According to Freud's theory, some of Cobain's driving forces were arising from unconscious battles among three separate mental processes, which you know as the the id, ego, and superego.

To understand how the id, ego and superego interact, imagine an iceberg floating in the sea (figure below). The part of the iceberg that is above the water represents conscious forces, while those below water indicate unconscious forces. Notice that in this figure, the ego has a larger part in the iceberg above water (conscious part) and a smaller part below the water (unconscious part); the superego has a smaller portion of the iceberg above water (conscious part), but a larger part below water (unconscious part); and the id is completely below water, operating at a completely unconscious level.

C O N S C I O U S

U N C O N S C I O U S

Three Mental Processes

In his theory, Freud did something that no one had done before. He divided the mind into three separate processes, each with a different function. Then he described how these three processes interact and sometimes even fight among themselves. Please begin at the bottom with number **1**, the id.

3 Superego: Regulator

As children learn that they must follow rules and regulations in satisfying their wishes, they develop a superego.

The *superego,* which is Freud's third division of the mind, develops from the ego during early childhood; the superego's goal is applying the moral values and standards of one's parents or caregivers and society in satisfying one's wishes.

Using an iceberg analogy, think of part of the superego as above water (conscious), while the rest extends below the water (and is part of the unconscious). Through interactions with the parents or caregivers, a child develops a superego by taking on or incorporating the parents' or caregivers' standards, values, and rules. The superego's power is in making the person feel guilty if the rules are disobeyed. Because the pleasure-seeking id wants to avoid feeling guilty, it is motivated to listen to the superego. You can think of a superego as a moral guardian or conscience that is trying to control the id's wishes and impulses.

Freud believed that at times the three processes—id, ego, and superego—are in agreement on their goals but other times they are not. Next, we'll see how Freud explains what happens when the id, ego, and superego disagree about their goals.

2 Ego: Negotiator Between Id and Superego

As infants discover that parents put restrictions on satisfying their wishes, infants learn to control their wishes through the development of an ego.

The *ego*, which is Freud's second division of the mind, develops from the id during infancy; the ego's goal is to find safe and socially acceptable ways of satisfying the id's desires and to negotiate between the id's wants and the superego's prohibitions.

Freud said that a relatively large part of the ego's material is conscious (iceberg above water), such as information that we have gathered in adapting to our environments. Smaller parts of the ego's material are unconscious (below water), such as threatening wishes that have been repressed. In contrast to the id's pleasure principle, the ego follows the reality principle.

The *reality principle* has a policy of satisfying a wish or desire only if there is a socially acceptable outlet available.

You can think of the ego as an executive who operates in a reasonable, logical, and socially acceptable way in finding outlets for satisfaction. This ego executive tries to come up with compromising solutions to satisfy the needs of the id and the demands of the superego.

1 Id: Pleasure Seeker

Freud believed that mental processes must have a source of energy, which he called the id.

The *id*, which is Freud's first division of the mind to develop, contains two biological drives—sex and aggression—that are the source of all psychic or mental energy; the id's goal is to pursue pleasure and satisfy the biological drives.

Freud assumed that the id operated at a totally unconscious level, which is analogous to an iceberg's massive underwater bulk. The id operates according to the pleasure principle.

The *pleasure principle* operates to satisfy drives and avoid pain, without concern for moral restrictions or society's regulations.

You can think of the id as a spoiled child who operates in a totally selfish, pleasure-seeking way, without regard for reason, logic, or morality. Simply following the pleasure principle leads to conflict with others (parents) and this conflict results in the development of the ego.

<table>
<tr><td>**Why do you become anxious?**</td></tr>
</table>

You may feel anxious during exams, going on first dates, looking for a part-time job, asking parents for money, having to write a huge paper, going to a party the night before finals, or locking your keys in the car. One of Freud's interesting ideas about why you feel anxious, such as when going to a party when you should be studying, comes from infighting among the three divisions of the mind, the id (pleasure seeker), ego (negotiator), and superego (regulator). Freud suggested that when one of your needs is not satisfied, the id, ego, and superego are in conflict, and a sign of this inner conflict is a feeling of anxiety.

Anxiety is an unpleasant state that is associated with feelings of uneasiness, apprehension, and heightened physiological arousal, such as increased heart rate and blood pressure.

For example, what happens when you plan to study but a friend wants you to go to a movie? Here's a situation that many of us have experienced and that sets up a potential conflict among the id, ego, and superego. You can think of this situation as a conflict between your pleasure-seeking id, which wants to go to the movie and your rule-enforcing superego, which says that the right thing for you to do is stay home and study. Caught in the middle of this conflict between the id and superego is your ego, which tries to negotiate a peacekeeping solution. However, if your ego feels threatened by the id's desires, the ego creates a feeling of anxiety.

Freud suggested that you may deal with and decrease your anxiety by denying that you need to study or claiming that you can always cram before the exam. Freud called these kinds of mental methods of reducing anxiety defense mechanisms, and he described about a dozen different kinds.

Defense Mechanisms

<table>
<tr><td>**Have you ever been accused of rationalizing?**</td></tr>
</table>

I'm a great rationalizer, and I caught myself doing it the other day. I had found a new mole and was anxious about the possibility of its being cancerous. However, I heard an inner voice saying, "Don't worry, you always use sun screen, so it can't be cancerous; so it's no big deal." In the space of 30 seconds, I had just used two of Freud's defense mechanisms to reduce my anxiety.

Defense mechanisms are Freudian processes that operate at unconscious levels to help the ego reduce anxiety through self-deception.

According to Freud, my ego has two ways to reduce anxiety over finding a new mole. My ego can take realistic steps to reduce my anxiety, such as motivating me to see a doctor. Or my ego can use a number of defense mechanisms, such as denial and rationalization, which reduce my anxiety, make me feel OK, and let me put off going to a doctor. If you're like me, you may regularly use one or more of the following defense mechanisms.

Rationalization involves making up acceptable excuses for behaviors that cause us to feel anxious.

A student who feels anxious about doing poorly on a test would be rationalizing if he blamed his low test score on poorly worded test questions rather than on the fact that he did not study.

Denial is refusing to recognize some anxiety-provoking event or piece of information.

Heavy smokers would be using denial if they disregarded the scientific evidence that smoking increases the risk of lung cancer.

Repression involves pushing unacceptable or threatening feelings or impulses into the unconscious.

You would be repressing envious feelings of your sibling's academic abilities if you shoved them into your unconscious.

Projection is unconsciously transferring unacceptable traits onto others.

A worker may be projecting if she attributes a quick temper to her boss when in fact it's she herself who has the temper.

Reaction formation involves turning unacceptable wishes into acceptable behaviors.

A person who feels guilty about engaging in sexual activity may use reaction formation by joining a strict religious group that bans sex.

Displacement involves transferring feelings from their true source to another source that is safer and more socially acceptable.

If you were angry with a friend, you might displace your anger by picking an argument with a safer individual, such as a stranger.

Sublimation, which is a type of displacement, involves redirecting a threatening or forbidden desire, usually sexual, into a socially acceptable one.

For instance, a person might sublimate strong sexual desires by channeling that energy into physical activities.

Pros and cons. There are two things to remember about defense mechanisms. First, defense mechanisms are totally unconscious, which means that, if a spouse, friend, co-worker, or boss points out that we are being defensive, we will deny it. Second, according to Freud, defense mechanisms can be helpful or harmful, depending on how much we rely on them. The occasional use of defense mechanisms is normal and helps reduce anxiety so that we can continue to function as we work on the real causes of our anxiety. But the overuse of defense mechanisms may prevent us from recognizing or working on the real causes. The idea of defense mechanisms continues to be important, as growing experimental evidence indicates that we do indeed use defense mechanisms in the way that Freud theorized (Newman et al., 1997; Paulhus et al., 1997).

We have discussed the three divisions of the mind—id, ego, and superego—and how the ego may use defense mechanisms to reduce anxiety. Now we'll turn to how one's ego and personality develop.

C. Developmental Stages

Development: Dealing with Conflicts

What shaped Kurt's personality?

Imagine a theory so powerful that it is able to describe almost exactly how and why your personality developed the way it did and why you did or did not develop certain personality problems along the way. Such is the personality theory developed by Sigmund Freud, whose genius is clearly evident in his ability to weave a complex description of how each of us develops a different personality.

For example, let's return to the example of Kurt Cobain, especially his childhood. When Kurt was 5 years old, he was described as an artistic, inquisitive, and energetic child, who was the center of attention, especially at family gatherings. To the delight of all the relatives, Kurt sang, drew pictures, and acted out imaginative skits. Just three years later, when he was 8, Kurt's mother filed for divorce, which triggered years of parental fighting with Kurt caught in the middle. During this time, Kurt changed from being happy, outgoing, and energetic to becoming sullen, shy, and withdrawn (Mundy, 1994).

According to Freud, the development of Kurt's personality, such as becoming outgoing and energetic and then changing to shy and withdrawn, was primarily influenced by how he dealt with the five different kinds of conflicts that occurred at five different times or stages. According to Freud (1940), our personality develops as we pass through and deal with potential conflicts at five psychosexual stages.

Psychosexual stages are five developmental periods—oral, anal, phallic, latency, and genital stages—each marked by potential conflict between parent and child. The conflicts arise as a child seeks pleasure from different body areas that are associated with sexual feelings (different *erogenous zones*). Freud emphasized that the child's first five years were most important in personality development.

You can think of each psychosexual stage as being a source of potential *conflict* between the child's id, which seeks immediate gratification, and the parents, who place restrictions on when, where, and how the gratification can take place. For example, the child may want to be fed immediately, while the parent may wish to delay the feeding to a more convenient time. The kind of interactions that occur between parent and child in satisfying these psychosexual needs and the way a child learns to deal with psychosexual conflicts, especially during breast-feeding or toilet training, will greatly influence the personality development as well as future problems and social interactions.

One of Freud's controversial ideas is the relationship between early psychosexual stages and development of later personality and social problems. Here is Freud's clever explanation.

Fixation: Potential Personality Problems

Why did Kurt develop problems?

Freud explained that the way a person deals with early psychosexual conflicts lays the groundwork for personality growth and future problems. This means that, to a large extent, Kurt's later personality problems grew out of early childhood experiences. Freud would say that Kurt problems in finding his identity and dealing with fame and fortune began in childhood, which included being caught in the middle of parents fighting over a divorce, becoming shy and withdrawn, being sent to live with various relatives, and finally hearing about the suicides of two uncles (DeCurtis, 1994).

As an adult, there were times when Kurt was happy and smiley (right photo), but at other times he was eerily moody and withdrawn (drawing below). The problem for any theory of personality is to explain how problems and contradictions in personality occur. For example, why did Kurt continue to play on center stage and go on world tours yet complain of not enjoying it and having to pretend to be happy? Freud would explain that the development of Kurt's personality depended, to a large extent, on the way he dealt with early psychosexual conflicts. One way a child can deal with or resolve these conflicts—wanting to satisfy all desires but not being allowed to by the parents—is to become fixated at a certain stage.

Fixation, which can occur during any of the first three stages—oral, anal, or phallic—refers to a Freudian process through which an individual may be locked into a particular psychosexual stage because his or her wishes were either overgratified or undergratified.

For example, if a person were fixated at the oral stage because of *too little* gratification, he might go through life trying to obtain oral satisfaction through eating too much, boasting too much, or other oral behaviors. If fixation had occurred at the oral stage because of *too much* gratification, he might focus on seeking oral gratification while neglecting to develop other aspects of his personality.

Next, we'll briefly summarize each of Freud's psychosexual stages, pointing out the possible parent-child conflicts, problems developing from fixation, and implications for future personality and social development.

Five Psychosexual Stages

What are the potential conflicts?

According to Freud, every child goes through certain situations, such as nursing, bottle feeding, and toilet training, that contain potential conflicts between the child's desire for instant satisfaction or gratification and the parent's wishes, which may involve delaying the child's satisfaction. How these conflicts are resolved and whether a child becomes fixated at one stage because of too much or too little satisfaction greatly influences development of personality and onset of future problems.

1 Oral Stage

Time. Early infancy: first 18 months of life.
Potential conflict. The *oral stage* lasts for the first 18 months of life and is a time when the infant's pleasure seeking is centered on the mouth.

Pleasure-seeking activities include sucking, chewing, and biting. If we were locked into or fixated at this stage because our oral wishes were gratified too much or too little, we would continue to seek oral gratification as adults. *Fixation* at this stage results in adults who continue to engage in oral activities, such as overeating, gum chewing, or smoking; oral activities can be symbolic as well, such as being overly demanding or "mouthing off."

2 Anal Stage

Time. Late infancy: $1\frac{1}{2}$ to 3 years.
Potential conflict. The *anal stage* lasts from the age of about $1\frac{1}{2}$ to 3 and is a time when the infant's pleasure seeking is centered on the anus and its functions of elimination.

Fixation at this stage results in adults who continue to engage in activities of retention or elimination. Retention may take the form of being very neat, stingy, or behaviorally rigid (thus the term *anal retentive*). Elimination may take the form of being generous, messy, or behaving very loose or carefree.

3 Phallic Stage

Time. Early childhood: 3 to 6 years.
Potential conflict. The *phallic (FAL-ik) stage* lasts from the age of about 3 to 6 and is a time when the infant's pleasure seeking is centered on the genitals.

Freud theorized that the phallic stage is particularly important for personality development because of the occurrence of the Oedipus complex (named for Oedipus, the character in Greek mythology who unknowingly killed his father and married his mother).

The *Oedipus (ED-ah-pus) complex* is a process in which a child competes with the parent of the same sex for the affections and pleasures of the parent of the opposite sex.

According to Freud, the Oedipus complex presents different problems for boys and girls.

Boys. When a boy discovers that his penis is a source of pleasure, he develops a sexual attraction to his mother. As a result, the boy feels hatred, jealousy, and competition toward his father and has fears of castration. The boy resolves his Oedipus complex by identifying with his father. If he does not resolve the complex, fixation occurs and he may go through life trying to prove his toughness.

Girls. When a girl discovers that she does not have a penis, she feels a loss that Freud called penis envy. Her loss makes her turn against her mother and develop sexual desires for her father. A girl resolves her Oedipus complex, sometimes called the Electra complex (for Electra, a woman in Greek mythology who killed her mother) by identifying with her mother. If this complex is not resolved, fixation occurs and the woman may go through life feeling inferior to men.

Over the years, the idea of the Oedipus complex has waned in popularity and credibility, both within psychoanalysis and within the culture at large. That's because there's almost no way to scientifically test this idea and also Freud's assertion that the Oedipus complex occurs universally is not supported by data from other cultures (Bower, 1991b; Crews, 1997).

1. Oral
2. Anal
3. Phallic
4. Latency
5. Genital

4 Latency Stage

Time. Middle and late childhood: 6 to puberty.
Potential conflict. The *latency stage,* which lasts from about age 6 to puberty, is a time when the child represses sexual thoughts and engages in nonsexual activities, such as developing social and intellectual skills.

At puberty, sexuality reappears and marks the beginning of a new stage, called the genital stage.

5 Genital Stage

Time. Puberty through adulthood.
Potential conflict. The *genital stage* lasts from puberty through adulthood and is a time when the individual has renewed sexual desires that he or she seeks to fulfill through relationships with other people.

How a person meets the conflicts of the genital stage depends on how conflicts in the first three stages were resolved. If the individual is fixated at an earlier stage, less energy will be available to resolve conflicts at the genital stage. If the individual successfully resolved conflicts in the first three stages, he or she will have the energy to develop loving relationships and a healthy and mature personality.

Summary. Freud's psychodynamic theory of personality development made a number of assumptions that, at the time, were revolutionary. His assumptions included the influence of unconscious forces; the division of the mind into the id, ego, and superego; the importance of resolving conflicts at five psychosexual stages; the importance of fixation; and the importance of the first five years to personality development.

Next, we'll discuss what Freud's critics have had to say about his theory and assumptions.

D. Freud's Followers & Critics

Disagreements

What did they argue about?

Because Freud's theory was so creative and revolutionary for its time, it attracted many followers, who formed a famous group called the Vienna Psychoanalytic Society. However, it was not long before members of the society began to disagree over some of Freud's theories and assumptions, such as whether Freud placed too much emphasis on biological urges (sex and aggression), psychosexual stages, and importance of early childhood experience in personality development (Horgan, 1996). We'll focus on three influential followers who eventually broke with Freud's theory.

Carl Jung

Why did Freud's "crown prince" stop talking to him?

In 1910 Carl Jung, with the whole-hearted support of Sigmund Freud, became the first president of the Vienna Psychoanalytic Society. Freud said that Jung was to be his "crown prince" and personal successor. However, just four years later, Jung and Freud ended their personal and professional relationship and never again spoke to each other.

The main reason for the split was that Jung disagreed with Freud's emphasis on the sex drive. Jung believed the collective unconscious—and not sex—to be the basic force in the development of personality.

The *collective unconscious,* according to Jung, consists of ancient memory traces and symbols that are passed on by birth and are shared by all peoples in all cultures.

Jung's theory of collective unconscious and his elaborate theory of personality, called *analytical psychology,* had more influence on the areas of art, literature, philosophy, and counseling/therapy than on current areas of psychology.

Alfred Adler

Why did one of the society's presidents resign?

Alfred Adler was another contemporary of Freud's who later became president of the Vienna Psychoanalytic Society.

However, after Adler voiced his disagreement with Freud at one of the society's meetings, he was so badly criticized by the other members that he resigned as president.

Like Jung, Adler disagreed with Freud's theory that humans are governed by biological and sexual urges. Adler believed that the main factors influencing a child's development were sibling influences and child-rearing practices.

In contrast to Freud's biological drives, Adler proposed that humans are motivated by *social urges* and that each person is a social being with a unique personality. Adler formed his own group, whose philosophy became known as *individual psychology.* In contrast to Freud's emphasis on unconscious forces that influence our behaviors, Adler suggested that we are aware of our motives and goals and have the capacity to guide and plan our futures.

Karen Horney

What would a woman say about penis envy?

Karen Horney was trained as a psychoanalyst; her career reached its peak shortly after Freud's death in 1939. For many years, Horney was dean of the American Institute of Psychoanalysis in New York.

Horney strongly objected to Freud's view that women were dependent, vain, and submissive because of biological forces and childhood sexual experiences. She especially took issue with Freud's idea that penis envy affects girls' development.

In contrast to Freud's psychosexual conflicts, Horney insisted that the major influence on personality development, whether in women or men, can be found in child-parent *social interactions.* Unlike Freud, who believed that every child must experience child-parent conflicts, Horney theorized that such conflicts are avoidable if the child is raised in a loving, trusting, and secure environment. Karen Horney would now be called a feminist and is credited with founding the psychology of women.

Neo-Freudians

Karen Horney is sometimes referred to as a *neo-Freudian* because she changed and renovated Freud's original theory. One of the best-known neo-Freudians was Erik Erikson, who formulated his own theory of personality development, which we discussed in Modules 17 and 18. Erikson proposed that everyone goes through a series of *psychosocial* stages, rather than the *psychosexual* stages proposed by Freud.

Neo-Freudians generally agreed with Freud's basic ideas, such as the importance of the unconscious; the division of the

mind into the id, ego, and superego; and the use of defense mechanisms to protect the ego. However, they mostly disagreed with Freud's placing so much emphasis on biological forces, sexual drives, and psychosexual stages (Horgan, 1996). The neo-Freudians turned the emphasis of Freud's psychodynamic theory away from biological drives toward psychosocial and cultural influences.

From early on, members of the Vienna Psychoanalytic Society criticized and disagreed with many of Freud's theories. As you'll see next, this criticism has continued to the present day.

Freudian Theory Today

What are the basic questions?

In 1993, *Time* magazine's cover featured a picture of Sigmund Freud with the question, "Is Freud Dead?" Answering this question with a loud "Yes," are four scholarly books that seriously question Freud's theory and all its assumptions (Crews, 1996). Answering this question with a loud, "No," are 400 members of the American Psychology Association's psychoanalysis division who meet the attacks on Freud with equally strong defenses (Horgan, 1996). To give you a sense of where Freud's theory stands today, we'll focus on four questions: How valid is Freud's theory? How important are the first five years of childhood? Are there unconscious forces? What was the impact of Freud's theory?

1 How Valid Is Freud's Theory?

Perhaps the main reason Freud's theory is still around today is that, in spite of all its flaws, it's the only theory with a broad enough framework to describe so many puzzles and mysteries of human behavior (Horgan, 1996). In fact, Freud's theory is so comprehensive that it can explain almost every behavior—even opposite ones. For example, Freud's theory predicts that fixation at the anal stage may result in a person being at one extreme very messy and at the other extreme very neat. However, critics reply that since Freud's theory can explain almost every behavior, his theory is not very useful in explaining or predicting behaviors of specific individuals.

Critics also argue that most of Freud's concepts, such as id, ego, and superego, fixation, repression, unconscious forces, and the psychosexual stages, have proved difficult to test or verify (Horgan, 1996). In fact, recent critics charge that Freud did not develop these concepts through careful and controlled observations but rather made them up to explain the unusual behaviors of his patients (Macmillan, 1997). For example, since the id is a totally unconscious force and represents biological energy, how does one study it or know that it really exists? Critics argue that Freudian concepts either are too descriptive or involve unconscious processes that are difficult to verify through experimental methods (Crews, 1996).

Current followers reply that Freud's theory has proven useful in looking at and raising new issues and questions about human behavior. However, many psychoanalytic theorists now suggest that, if psychoanalysis is to survive, Freud's theory must adopt a more systematic and experimental basis so that it can be more adequately tested (Macmillan, 1997).

2 How Important Are the First Five Years?

Based on observations of his patients, Freud concluded that personality development is essentially complete after the first five years. However, Freud never collected any longitudinal observations that supported this hypothesis (Grunbaum, 1993). There are now several lines of evidence that challenge Freud's assumption about the importance of the first five years.

First, you may recall from our discussion of resilient children in Module 17 that the occurrence of serious psychological and physical problems during the first five years does not necessarily stunt or inhibit personality development, as Freud predicted. For example, many children who had experienced poverty, the death of or separation from their parents, or a poor home life nevertheless developed into healthy, mature adults provided the children had a loving caregiver (Werner, 1995).

Second, a number of longitudinal studies indicate that personality development is not complete in the first five years but rather continues well into middle adulthood (Costa & McCrae, 1997). For these reasons, psychologists question Freud's idea that personality development is complete in the first five years.

3 Are There Unconscious Forces?

One of Freud's major assumptions was that unconscious forces greatly influence our conscious thoughts and behaviors. According to John Kihlstrom (1993), there is now good evidence that unconscious influences do affect our conscious behaviors, but these influences are not the repressed, threatening desires proposed by Freud. To indicate that his meaning is different from Freud's unconscious forces, Kihlstrom uses the term *cognitive unconscious.*

The *cognitive unconscious* refers to mental processes of which we are unaware but that automatically and effortlessly influence our thoughts and behaviors.

Examples of what's in the cognitive unconscious include procedural memories discussed in Module 12, such as skills and motor habits (typing or tying shoes), and conditioned emotional responses (fear of spiders). Thus, there is strong evidence for a cognitive unconscious, but it is part of an information-processing system that includes procedural memories rather than a battleground for the id, ego, and superego (Westen, 1998).

4 What Was the Impact of Freud's Theory?

Freud's theory had an enormous impact on society, as can be seen in the widespread use of Freudian terms (ego, id, rationalization) in literature, art, and our everyday conversations. Freud's theory also had a great impact on psychology: many of his concepts have been incorporated into the fields of personality, development, abnormal psychology, and psychotherapy. However, many of Freud's terms have come under increasing criticism as being difficult to test or verify (Crews, 1996).

Freud's psychodynamic theory paints a picture of humans filled with irrational and unconscious forces that control our behaviors with little allowance for free choice. Next, we'll discuss a family of theories that is almost the direct opposite of Freud's theory.

E. Humanistic Theories

How did he develop his real potential?

At the beginning of this module, we told you about two very different people. One was rock musician Kurt Cobain, who struggled with numerous personal and drug-related problems. At age 27, when his band, Nirvana, had reached the peak of its fame and popularity, he committed suicide.

The other person was Charles Dutton, who had been in and out of reform schools since he was 12 years old, was sent to prison on charges of manslaughter, and spent time in solitary confinement for his ringleader role in a prison riot. Just when most people would have given up on reforming Dutton, he began to reform himself. Inspired by reading a book of plays, he began to channel his rage against society into becoming a student and then an actor. After leaving prison, Charles Dutton (right photo) worked hard to become a very successful actor and starred in *Roc,* his own television series, and a number of recent movies.

What Dutton and Cobain shared in common as young men was that neither showed particular evidence of having special talents or great potentials. Few people would have predicted that skinny, frail Cobain would discover the raw power of punk rock and take it farther than anyone had before with his band, Nirvana. No one would have predicted that angry, tough, mean Charles Dutton would discover, of all things, acting and would channel his anger into becoming a very successful professional actor. The lives of these two men demonstrate the difficulty in predicting someone's potential and whether he or she will develop it. Developing our potential is at the heart of humanistic theory.

Humanistic theories emphasize our capacity for personal growth, development of our potential, and freedom to choose our destiny.

Humanistic theories reject the biological determinism and the irrational, unconscious forces of Freud's psychodynamic theory. Humanistic theories emphasize freely choosing to go after one's dream and change one's destiny, as Kristi Yamaguchi did.

Three Characteristics

What did she do to reach her goal?

For Kristi Yamaguchi, reaching her goal of winning a gold medal meant giving her whole life to ice skating. From early childhood on, she spent thousands of hours practicing, entering grueling competitions, struggling with disappointments, and sacrificing her life to reach the final contest—the winter Olympics. After so many years of preparation, Kristi's grace, skill, and artistry (photo below) dazzled the audience and impressed the judges. She reached her lifelong dream: a gold medal in figure skating at the winter Olympics.

Kristi Yamaguchi's life illustrates the three characteristics that distinguish humanistic theory from other theories of personality. We'll describe each of the three characteristics unique to humanistic theory: having a phenomenological perspective, a holistic view, and a goal of self-actualization (Wertz, 1998).

1 Humanistic theories stress learning about the world through personal experiences, which illustrates the phenomenological *(feh-nom-in-no-LODGE-uh-cal)* perspective.

The *phenomenological perspective* means that your perception or view of the world, whether or not it is accurate, becomes your reality.

For instance, Kristi's phenomenological perspective of how she perceived her skating abilities may or may not have been accurate. However, because she believed so strongly that she had the abilities, this perception became her reality. Other examples of phenomenological perspectives are long-held beliefs that women could not perform certain jobs—for example, police officer, doctor, plumber, truck driver, or lawyer. Since women have demonstrated that they can perform these jobs, this particular perception has been proven false. As a result, people (especially men) have developed a new perspective and accepted the reality of what women can accomplish.

2 Humanistic theories emphasize looking at the whole situation or person, which illustrates the holistic *(hole-LIS-tick)* view.

The *holistic view* means that a person's personality is more than the sum of its individual parts; instead, the individual parts form a unique and total entity that functions as a unit.

For example, the holistic view would explain that Kristi outperformed her competitors because of her unique combination of many traits—discipline, ability, motivation, persistence, desire—rather than any single trait.

3 Humanistic theories highlight the idea of developing one's true potential, which is called self-actualization.

Self-actualization refers to our inherent tendency to develop and reach our true potentials.

By winning an Olympic gold medal, Kristi is a wonderful example of someone who has developed and reached her true potential and thus achieved a high level of self-actualization. According to humanistic theories, no matter what our skills or abilities, each of us has the capacity for self-actualization and can reach our potentials as whoever we are.

The beginning of humanistic theory can be traced to two psychologists—Abraham Maslow and Carl Rogers. They had surprisingly different backgrounds, but they arrived at the same uplifting ideas.

Maslow: Need Hierarchy and Self-Actualization

Why did a behaviorist become a humanist?

We can trace the official beginning of the humanistic movement to the early 1960s and the publication of the *Journal of Humanistic Psychology.* One of the major figures behind establishing this journal was Abraham Maslow. Interestingly enough, Maslow was trained as a behaviorist, but along the way he felt there was too much emphasis on rewards and punishments and observable behaviors and too little emphasis on other important aspects of human nature, such as feelings, emotions, and beliefs. For these reasons, Maslow (1968) broke away from the reward/punishment/observable behavior mentality of behaviorism and developed his humanistic theory, which emphasized two things: our capacity for growth, or self-actualization, and our desire to satisfy a variety of needs, which he arranged in an hierarchy.

Maslow's Hierarchy of Needs

Maslow's Hierarchy of Needs

Level 5
Self-actualization: fulfillment of one's unique potential

Level 4
Esteem needs: achievement, competency, gaining approval and recognition

Level 3
Love and belonging needs: affiliation with others and acceptance by others

Level 2
Safety needs: protection from harm and concern about safety and survival

Level 1
Physiological needs: hunger, thirst, sex, and sleep

For just a moment, think of all the needs that you try to meet each day: eating, having a safe place to live, talking to your friends, perhaps working at a part-time job, caring for loved ones, and studying for exams. Maslow believed that you satisfy these needs in a certain order. As you may remember from Module 15, Maslow arranged all human needs into a hierarchy of five major needs.

Maslow's hierarchy of needs arranges needs in ascending order (figure on left), with biological needs at the bottom and social and personal needs at the top. Only when needs at a lower level are met can we advance to the next level.

According to Maslow's hierarchy, you must satisfy your biological and safety needs before using energy to fulfill your personal and social needs. Finally, you can devote time and energy to reaching your true potential, which is called self-actualization, your highest need.

Maslow divided our needs into two general categories: deficiency and growth needs.

Deficiency needs are physiological needs (food, sleep) and psychological needs (safety, love, and esteem) that we try to fulfill if they are not met.

Growth needs are those at the higher levels and include the desire for truth, goodness, beauty, and justice.

According to Maslow, we must satisfy our deficiency needs before having the time and energy to satisfy our growth needs and move toward self-actualization.

Self-Actualization

One of the major characteristics of the humanistic movement is the emphasis on a process called self-actualization.

Self-actualization refers to the development and fulfillment of one's unique human potential.

Maslow (1971) developed the concept of self-actualization after studying the lives of highly productive and exceptional people, such as Abraham Lincoln, Albert Einstein, and Eleanor Roosevelt. Maslow believed that these individuals had been able to reach the goal of self-actualization because they had developed the following personality characteristics.

Characteristics of Self-Actualized Individuals

- They perceive reality accurately.
- They are independent and autonomous.
- They prefer to have a deep, loving relationship with only a few people.
- They focus on accomplishing their goals.
- They report peak experiences, which are moments of great joy and satisfaction.

Maslow believed that, although very few individuals reach the level of self-actualization, everyone has a self-actualizing tendency. This tendency motivates us to become the best kind of person we are capable of becoming.

There is no doubt that Maslow would also have considered Martin Luther King, Jr., an example of a self-

actualized person. Martin Luther King, Jr., devoted his life to achieving civil rights for all people. Here he delivers his famous "I Have a Dream" speech at a civil rights rally in Washington, D.C. He was awarded the Nobel Prize for peace at age 35. He was gunned down by an assassin's bullet at age 39. King's achievements exemplify the humanistic idea of self-actualization.

About the same time that Maslow was making this journey from behaviorism to humanism and developing the concept of self-actualization, another psychologist by the name of Carl Rogers was developing a different but related humanistic theory.

E. Humanistic Theories

Rogers: Self Theory

What are the two most important concepts?

Carl Rogers was initially trained in the psychodynamic approach, which he used in his practice as a clinical psychologist. However, Rogers began to feel that Freud placed too much emphasis on unconscious, irrational forces and on biological urges, and too little emphasis on human potential for psychological growth. As a result, Rogers gradually abandoned the psychodynamic approach in favor of a new theory of personality that he developed in the 1960s. Rogers' new humanistic theory is often called self theory because of his emphasis on the self or self-concept.

Self theory, also called *self-actualization theory,* is based on two major assumptions: that personality development is guided by each person's unique self-actualization tendency; and that each of us has a personal need for positive regard.

Rogers' first major assumption about self-actualization is similar but slightly different from Maslow's use of the term.

Rogers' self-actualizing tendency refers to an inborn tendency for us to develop all of our capacities in ways that best maintain and benefit our lives.

The self-actualizing tendency refers to *biological functions,* such as meeting our basic need for food, water, and oxygen, as well as *psychological functions,* such as expanding our experiences, encouraging personal growth, and becoming self-sufficient. The self-

actualizing tendency guides us toward positive or healthful behaviors rather than negative or harmful ones. For example, one of the two girls in the photo below has lost the use of her legs and must use a wheelchair. Part of her self-actualizing process will include learning to deal with her disability, engaging in positive healthful behaviors, and getting to know herself.

Self or *self-concept* refers to how we see or describe ourselves. The self is made up of many self-perceptions, abilities, personality characteristics, and behaviors that are organized and consistent with one another.

Because of very different experiences, the girl in the wheelchair will develop a self-concept different from that of her friend who has normal use of her legs. According to Rogers (1980), self-concept plays an important role in personality because it influences our behaviors, feelings, and thoughts. For example, if you have a *positive self-concept,* you will tend to act, feel, and think optimistically and constructively; if you have a *negative self-concept,* you will tend to act, feel, and think pessimistically and destructively.

Sometimes a person may be undecided about what is his or her real self. As we discover our real self, we may undergo a number of changes in personality.

Real Self versus Ideal Self

Who is the real David Bowie?

We all change how we see ourselves but probably not as much as rock star David Bowie, who, through the years, has radically changed his looks, clothes, and personal values. For example, Bowie's earlier looks (top photo) and behaviors might be described as having pushed society's limits. Now, however, Bowie is in his 50s and appears quite conventional in hair style and clothes (bottom photo), and he has adopted many of society's values, such as getting married. The question is "Which is Bowie's real self?"

Carl Rogers said that his clients often asked questions related to their selves: "How do I find myself?" "Why do I sometimes feel that I don't know myself?" "Why do I say or do things that aren't really me?" Rogers developed a clever answer to these relatively common and perplexing questions. He said that there are two kinds of selves: a real self and an ideal self.

The *real self,* according to Rogers, is based on our actual experiences and represents how we really see ourselves.

The *ideal self,* according to Rogers, is based on our hopes and wishes and reflects how we would like to see ourselves.

My ideal self is based on my hopes and wishes.

My real self is based on my actual experiences.

In some cases, the hopes and wishes of one's ideal self may contradict the abilities and experiences of the real self. For example, a student's ideal self may be someone who is very responsible and studies hard, but the real self may be someone who puts things off and studies less than is required. According to Rogers, a glaring contradiction between the ideal and real self can result in personality problems. Rogers suggested that we can resolve contradictions between the ideal and real self by paying more attention to our actual experiences, working to have more positive experiences, and paying less attention to the expectations of others. In working out discrepancies between our ideal and real selves, we may undergo changes in looks, clothes, and behavior.

Now that you know what the self is, here's how it develops.

Positive Regard

Why are there millions of dog owners?

One reason I am one of the millions of dog owners is that my dog Bear, like most dogs, is especially good at showing real appreciation, no matter how angry, grouchy, depressed, or sad I may feel or act. In fact, researchers found that residents in nursing homes were more alert and sociable when allowed to have a pet to play with and care for (Hendy, 1984).

The need to feel appreciated is so important that in the United States we have a number of days throughout the year that are officially designated for appreciation, such as Mother's, Father's, Grandparent's, and Secretary's days, as well as birthdays and Valentine's Day.

It's so nice you're always glad to see me.

The creation of national appreciation days and the popularity of pets illustrate the second assumption of Carl Rogers' self theory, which is that all humans have a need for positive regard.

Positive regard includes love, sympathy, warmth, acceptance, and respect, which we crave from family, friends, and people important to us.

Rogers believed that positive regard was essential for the healthy development of one's self as well as for successful interpersonal relations (Liebert & Spiegler, 1994). When we are children, positive regard comes mainly from our parents, siblings, or grandparents. But as we become adults, we learn to provide some of our own positive regard.

Conditional and Unconditional Positive Regard

What's a big problem for teenagers?

Unlike friends and family, pets never pass judgment; they provide endless amounts of positive regard no matter how their owners look, feel, dress, or talk. In contrast, friends and family can be very judgmental and may give only conditional positive regard.

Conditional positive regard refers to the positive regard we receive if we behave in certain acceptable ways, such as living up to or meeting the standards of others.

For instance, one way teenagers display their newly developed independence is by choosing different (radical, awful, outrageous) hair styles and fashions. In this case, if the teenagers receive conditional positive regard based on conforming to the more traditional fashion standards of their parents, they may develop a negative self-concept or feel bad or worthless because they displeased or disappointed their parents.

Dad, why don't you like the way I look? All my friends do.

Rogers believed that the development of a healthy and positive self-concept depends on receiving as much unconditional positive regard as possible.

Unconditional positive regard refers to the warmth, acceptance, and love that others show you because you are valued as a human being even though you may disappoint people by behaving in ways that are different from their standards or values or the way they think.

Parents who provide love and respect, even if a teenager does not always abide by their fashion standards, are showing unconditional positive regard, which will foster the development of a healthy self-concept. Nevertheless, however much we need, want, and enjoy unconditional positive regard, it appears to be more the exception; conditional positive regard appears to be more the rule (Culp et al., 1991).

Importance of Self-Actualization

What would you do to reach your potential?

In 1945, Russian leader Stalin exiled writer Aleksandr Solzhenitsyn (right photo) to Siberia for publishing essays critical of Stalin's abuse of power. In 1976, Solzhenitsyn received the Nobel Prize for his novels, such as *One Day in the Life of Ivan Denisovich,* and was allowed to come to the United States, where, he said, "you can be free."

The life of Solzhenitsyn is a case study in self-actualization. He persisted in developing his potential as a thinker and writer, despite being persecuted for years, exiled to the terrible living conditions of Siberia, and forbidden to publish his works. Rogers

I survived Siberia and prison so I could keep writing.

would explain that Solzhenitsyn persisted in writing because of the tendency for self-actualization, which provides direction and motivation to develop one's potential. Rogers recognized that our tendency for self-actualization may be hindered or blocked by situational hurdles or personal difficulties. But Rogers believed that we will experience the greatest self-actualization if we work to remove situational problems, resolve our personal problems, and receive unconditional positive regard.

Humanistic theories contain powerful positive messages, but do these messages work?

E. Humanistic Theories

Application

Unlike almost every other theory of personality, humanism holds that people are basically good and can achieve their true potentials if the roadblocks placed by society, poverty, drugs, or other evil influences are removed (Megargee, 1997). Based on this belief, one of the primary goals of the humanistic approach is to find ways of removing blocking influences so that people can grow and self-actualize. In the United States, psychologists have identified African American boys as one group of individuals whose paths are often filled with roadblocks. Some of the roadblocks that prevent African American boys from reaching their potentials include peer pressure to act out, to "take nothing from nobody," to turn down educational opportunities and to not "act white" by excelling in school, to hang out on the streets, to join gangs, and to take part in a variety of antisocial and illicit activities (Franklin, 1995).

To help remove these roadblocks to healthy personality development in African American boys, counselors are using humanistic ideas, such as providing positive regard and role models for self-actualization. For example, for the past dozen years, counselor Roland Gilbert in San Francisco has been conducting a mentoring program for African American boys who are at high risk for developing personality

I try to show these young boys that someone really cares.

problems. These boys live in neighborhoods with daily occurrences of violence and drugs; their fathers are often absent; and they have few adult male role models to help them through adolescence's difficult times. At the heart of Gilbert's program are twice-weekly meetings between young African American boys and adult men from the community. During these meetings, the African American men discuss the importance of getting regular jobs, demonstrate how to deal with anger by talking rather than hitting, and provide positive regard by showing that someone really cares (Smith, 1993).

In the United States, there are now numerous mentoring programs, such as Big Brothers/Big Sisters of America, which instill a sense of pride and self-worth and give children the motivation to achieve success (Hill, 1995). For example, children who participated in mentoring programs reported significantly higher self-concepts than children without mentors (Turner & Scherman, 1996). Thus, applying humanistic principles helped improve the self-concept of children who came from problem families or neighborhoods.

Next, we'll summarize the important humanistic concepts and discuss what critics have to say about humanistic theories.

Evaluation

Perhaps the main reason humanistic theories, such as those of Maslow and Rogers, continue to be popular is that they view people as basically good and believe that people can develop their true potentials (Megargee, 1997). However, these optimistic views of human nature have triggered a number of criticisms.

Impact

In the African-American mentoring programs described above, the self-worth of boys at risk is increased when mentors are successful role models who also provide positive regard. These programs illustrate the humanistic theories' emphasis on building self-worth through positive regard. In a real sense, the mentors are removing roadblocks so that each boy can find a path to his true potential through a process called self-actualization.

Humanistic theories have had their greatest impact in counseling, clinical settings, and personal growth programs, where ideas like self-concept, self-actualization, and self-fulfillment have proven useful in the development of healthy personalities and interpersonal relationships (Ford, 1991). Compared to Freud's idea that we are driven by unconscious irrational forces, humanism says that we are driven by positive forces that point us toward realizing our good and true selves.

Criticisms

Humanistic theories have come under considerable criticism because Rogers and Maslow provide little or no scientific evidence that an inherent (biological) tendency to self-actualization really exists. Because the major assumption of self-actualization and other humanistic concepts, such as positive regard and self-worth, are difficult to demonstrate experimentally, critics argue that humanistic theories primarily describe how people behave rather than explain the causes of their behaviors. For these reasons, critics regard humanistic theories more as a wonderfully positive view of human nature or a very hopeful philosophy of life rather than as a scientific explanation of personality development (Liebert & Spiegler, 1994). Critics note that humanistic theories have had less impact on mainstream psychology because humanistic concepts are too descriptive and limited in scope. Another major problem is that humanistic theories generally ignore research showing that 20 to 60% of the development of intellectual, emotional, social, and personality traits comes from genetic factors (McClarn et al., 1997). This means that genetic factors must be considered when discussing a person's true potential or a person's ability to achieve self-actualization.

Maslow hoped that humanistic theories would become a third major force in psychology, along with behavioral and psychoanalytic theories. Although it appears that the humanistic approach has not achieved Maslow's goal, many of humanism's ideas gave birth to the human potential movements in the 1960s and 1970s and have been incorporated into approaches for counseling and psychotherapy (Wertz, 1998).

CONCEPT REVIEW

1. The combination of long-lasting and distinctive behaviors, thoughts, and emotions that are typical of how we react and adapt to other people and situations forms our _____.

2. Freud's theory of personality, which emphasizes the importance of early childhood experiences and of conflicts between conscious thoughts and unconscious forces, is called a _____ theory.

3. Freud developed three techniques for probing the unconscious. A technique that encourages clients to talk about any thoughts or images that enter their head is called (a)_____. A technique to interpret the hidden meanings and symbols in dreams is

called (b)_____. With a third technique, the therapist analyzes the mistakes or (c)_____ that the client makes in everyday speech.

4. Freud considered the mind to have three major divisions. The division that contains the biological drives and is the source of all psychic or mental energy is called the (a)_____. This division operates according to the (b)_____ principle, which demands immediate satisfaction. The division that develops from the id during infancy and whose goal is finding safe and socially acceptable ways of satisfying the id's desires is called the (c)_____. This division operates according to the (d)_____ principle, which involves satisfying a wish only if there is a socially acceptable outlet. The division that develops from the id during early childhood and whose goal is applying the moral values and standards of one's parents and society is called the (e)_____.

5. Conflicts between the id and the superego over satisfaction of desires may cause the ego to feel threatened. When threatened, the ego generates an unpleasant state that is associated with feelings of uneasiness, apprehension, and heightened physiological arousal; this unpleasant state is called (a)_____. Freud suggested that the ego may reduce anxiety by using unconscious mechanisms that produce self-deception; these are called (b)_____.

6. Freud proposed that the major influence on personality development occurs as we pass through five developmental periods that he called the (a)_____ stages, each of which results in conflicts between the child's wishes and parents' restrictions. The result of a person's wishes being overgratified or undergratified at any one of these stages is called (b)_____.

7. Personality theories that emphasize our capacity for personal growth, the development of our potential, and freedom to choose our destinies are referred to as _____ theories.

8. These theories have three characteristics in common. They take the perspective that our perception of the world, whether or not it is

accurate, becomes our reality; this is called the (a)_____ perspective. Humanistic theories see personality as more than the sum of individual parts and consider personality as a unique and total entity that functions as a unit; this is the (b)_____ view of personality. Humanistic theories point to an inherent tendency that each of us has to reach our true potential; this tendency is called (c)_____.

9. The idea that our needs occur in ascending order, with biological needs at the bottom and social and personal needs at the top, and that we must meet our lower-level needs before we can satisfy higher ones is called (a)_____. Our physiological needs (food, sleep) and psychological needs (safety, belongingness, and esteem) are called (b)_____ needs because we try to fulfill them if they are not met. The highest need of self-actualization, which includes the desire for truth, goodness, beauty, and justice, is called a (c)_____ need.

10. Carl Rogers' self theory of personality makes two basic assumptions. The first is that personality development is guided by an inborn tendency to develop our potential; this idea is called (a)_____. The second assumption is that each of us has a personal need for acceptance and love, which Rogers called (b)_____. According to Rogers, it is important that we receive love and acceptance despite the fact that we sometimes behave in ways that are different from what others think or value; this type of acceptance is called (c)_____.

11. Rogers proposes that we have two kinds of selves: the self that is based on real-life experiences is called the (a)_____ self; the self that is based on how we would like to see ourselves is called the (b)_____ self.

Answers: *1. personality; 2. psychodynamic; 3. (a) free association, (b) dream interpretation, (c) Freudian slips or slips of the tongue; 4. (a) id, (b) pleasure, (c) ego, (d) reality, (e) superego; 5. (a) anxiety, (b) defense mechanisms; 6. (a) psychosexual, (b) fixation; 7. humanistic; 8. (a) phenomenological, (b) holistic, (c) self-actualization; 9. (a) Maslow's hierarchy of needs, (b) deficiency, (c) growth; 10. (a) self-actualization, (b) positive regard, (c) unconditional positive regard; 11. (a) real, (b) ideal.*

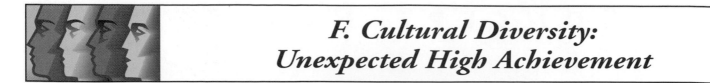

Boat People: Remarkable Achievement

What was different about these children?

I have always been puzzled by why students with similar academic skills perform so differently: some do well on my exams while others do poorly. A humanist would look at the same differences and ask, "Why are some students developing their potential while others are not?" One answer comes from studying thousands of Indochinese refugees, known as the boat people, who were allowed to resettle in the United States in the 1970s and 1980s.

On their arrival in America, the boat people's only possessions were the clothes they wore. They knew virtually no English, had almost no knowledge of Western culture, and had no one to turn to for social or financial support. In spite of horrendous difficulties, refugee children achieved such remarkable academic success that American educators were scratching their heads and asking why.

Researchers set out to discover why these refugee children had achieved astonishing scholastic success against overwhelming odds (Caplan et al., 1992). The researchers selected a random sample of 200 Indochinese refugee families with a total of 536 school-age children. The children had been in the United States for an average of

© Jason Goltz

$3\frac{1}{2}$ years. They had generally lived in low-income metropolitan areas with troublesome neighborhoods and run-down schools that were plagued with problems and not known for their high academic standards. Despite all these problems, children of the boat people performed remarkably well in school. Here's what researchers found.

The researchers computed the mean grade point average for the 536 children, who were fairly evenly distributed among grades 1 to 12. They found that 27% of the children had a grade point average (GPA) in the A range, 52% had a GPA in the B range, 17% in the C range, and only 4% had a GPA below C. Equally noteworthy was the children's overall performance in math: almost 50% of the children earned A's, while another 33% earned B's. On national math tests, the Indochinese children's average scores were almost three times higher than the national norm.

After analyzing all these data, researchers were able to identify several reasons why immigrant Indochinese students achieved such high grades.

Values and Motivation

What were their values?

Although Indochinese refugee children had been in the United States for an average of only $3\frac{1}{2}$ years, they were doing better in math than 90% of their peers. It could not be the quality of their schools, which were average, undistinguished low-income schools in metropolitan areas. But clearly there were powerful factors helping these children overcome the problems of learning a second language and adapting to a new culture. Researchers located these powerful factors in the values of the Asian family.

The *primary values* held by the Indochinese families were that parents and children have mutual respect, cooperate freely, and are committed to accomplishment and achievement. A clear example of commitment to accomplishment is the amount of time Indochinese children spend doing homework: they average about 3 hours a day, while American students average about $1\frac{1}{2}$ hours. Thus, among refugee families, doing homework, not watching television, is the main activity; the older children help the younger children.

Another primary value is that parents were very involved in their children's education: over 50% of parents read aloud and helped with homework. When children were asked, "What accounts for your academic success?" the children most often checked the category, "having a love of learning." Love of learning was one of the values nourished and passed on from parent to child. When children were asked, "How much do you choose your own destiny?" the children answered that they did not trust luck or fate but were the masters of their own destinies.

Parental Attitudes

How did parents help?

One reason Indochinese children earned great academic success was because of personal and cultural values transmitted by their parents, who were committed to help their children succeed through educational performance. After studying the immigrant parents' values and how they instilled these values in their children, researchers concluded that for American schools to succeed, parents must become more committed to the education of their children. In this case, Americans can truly learn from the values of their newest refugees.

In explaining the immigrant children's wonderful academic achievement, humanists would emphasize how parental values served to remove mental roadblocks that otherwise might have hindered their children from developing their true potentials and reaching self-fulfillment.

Next, we turn to a relatively common personality problem, shyness, and discuss how different theories of personality explain its causes.

G. Research Focus: Shyness
What Is Shyness and What Causes It?

What's it like to be shy? At some time and in some situations, we have all felt a little shy. However, there are degrees of shyness and a high degree of shyness can interfere with enjoying personal and social interactions. For example, when Alan was a child, he would walk home from school through alleys to avoid meeting any of his classmates. Although he received a perfect math score on his SAT, he dropped out of the University of Texas because he always felt like a stranger and was continually frustrated by not being able to reach out and make contact with people. He was so shy that he could not even use the Internet. Finally, feeling so lonely, Alan sought help at the Shyness Clinic, which was founded in the 1970s by well-known shyness researcher, Philip Zimbardo of Stanford University (Noriyuki, 1996).

Shyness is a feeling of distress that comes from being tense, stressed, or awkward in social situations and from worrying about and fearing rejection.

Surveys indicate that about 40% of adults report mild but chronic shyness and although they are good at hiding their shyness, internally they feel distress. About 20% report more severe shyness and are unable to hide their pain and distress (Carducci & Zimbardo, 1995). The cause and treatment for shyness depend partly on which theory of personality guides our thinking. We'll contrast answers from two different theories: Freud's psychodynamic theory and social cognitive theory.

Psychodynamic Approach

Is shyness due to unresolved conflicts? As a practicing psychoanalyst, Donald Kaplan (1972) uses his clinical experience and psychodynamic concepts to answer the question, "What causes shyness?" Kaplan traces the causes of shyness back to *unresolved conflicts* at one or more of Freud's psychosexual stages. For example, one very shy client reported that his mother constantly fed him so that he would never cry or whimper. As a result, Kaplan suggests that this client's unresolved conflict during the oral stage resulted in his feelings of inadequacy and shyness in later social interactions.

According to Kaplan, the symptoms of shyness include both conscious fears, such as having nothing to say, and unconscious fears of being rejected. Shy people may deal with these anxieties by using *defense mechanisms;* for example, one client reduced his anxiety through displacement, by changing his fears of being rejected into opposite feelings of self-righteousness and contempt.

One *advantage* of the psychodynamic approach is that it suggests that a number of causes, such as conscious and unconscious fears, as well as unresolved psychosexual conflicts, are involved in shyness.

One *disadvantage* of the psychodynamic approach is that Freudian concepts (unconscious fears, unresolved psychosexual stages) are difficult to verify by experimental methods (Macmillan, 1997). For example, saying that being fixated at the oral stage may result in a person becoming a shy adult is mostly a descriptive guess rather than testable hypothesis.

A very different account of what causes shyness comes from the social cognitive theory of personality.

Social Cognitive Theory

What are the three factors? Unlike the Freudian approach, which relies primarily on therapists' personal observations, social cognitive theory primarily uses experimental studies to answer questions about personality. Social cognitive theory breaks shyness down into three measurable or observable components—cognitive, behavioral, and environmental—which can be studied using the experimental method described in Module 2 (Carducci & Zimbardo, 1995). For example, in a series of longitudinal studies, researchers found that about 10–15% of the population have a shy personality that, to a large extent, comes from genetic factors—for example, inheriting a nervous system that is easily aroused by novel stimuli (Kagan, 1998). By observing the social interactions of shy people (the behavioral component), researchers found that shy people have too few social and communication skills and, as a consequence, they are continually punished during social interactions (Jackson et al., 1997). By giving personality tests (the cognitive component), researchers found that shy people are overly self-conscious, which leads to worrisome thoughts and irrational beliefs that interfere with social functioning (Romney & Bynner, 1997). According to social cognitive theory, which we'll discuss more fully in Module 20, shyness can be understood by analyzing the interaction among cognitive, behavioral, and environmental components (Carducci & Zimbardo, 1995).

One *advantage* of social cognitive theory is that it breaks shyness down into three measurable or observable components, each of which can be studied using the experimental method.

One *disadvantage* of this approach is that researchers may overlook certain influences that we are neither conscious or aware of, such as conditioned emotional responses, that can also trigger shy behaviors (Westen, 1998).

Our discussion of shyness raises the interesting question of how psychologists measure or assess personality traits, such as shyness.

H. Application: Assessment—Projective Tests

Definitions

How did friends describe Kurt's personality?

At the beginning of this module, we discussed Kurt Cobain, the 27-year-old singer and songwriter, who committed suicide at the height of his fame and fortune. When friends, schoolteachers, and writers described Cobain's personality, some said that he was a nice young man, very quiet, a kind sweet man, and a sincere listener (top photo). Other friends said that he was very moody, extremely intimidating, unhappy, filled with anger, never close to anyone (bottom drawing) (DeCurtis, 1994). When friends were describing Kurt's personality, they were making a kind of psychological assessment.

Psychological assessment refers to the use of various tools, such as psychological tests and/or interviews, to measure various characteristics, traits, or abilities in order to understand behavior and predict future performance or behavior.

Psychological tests are usually divided into ability tests and personality tests, which differ considerably. For example, when

Kurt entered a drug treatment program, he was most likely given personality tests to identify his personal problems.

Personality tests are used to measure both observable or overt traits and behaviors as well as unobservable or covert characteristics. Personality tests are used to identify personality problems and psychological disorders, as well as to predict how a person might behave in the future.

Although you may not have taken a personality test, you certainly have taken many ability tests, such as exams.

Ability tests include achievement tests, which measure what we have learned; aptitude tests, which measure our potential for learning or acquiring a specific skill; and intelligence tests, which measure our general potential to solve problems, think abstractly, and profit from experience (Kaplan & Saccuzzo, 1997).

The primary tools of assessment are tests of ability and personality. There are two kinds of personality tests. Here we'll focus on one kind, projective personality tests, and discuss the second kind, objective personality tests, in Module 20.

Projective Tests

In describing Cobain's personality, some listed observable behaviors, such as quiet, kind, and nice, while others hinted at unobservable behaviors, such as filled with anger, not close to anybody. In Freud's psychodynamic theory, observable behaviors reflect conscious wishes, desires, and thoughts, while unobservable behaviors may reflect unconscious forces. Freud developed three techniques for revealing unconscious forces—free association, dream interpretation, and interpretation of slips of the tongue. We now add a fourth technique to reveal hidden or unconscious forces: projective tests.

Projective tests require individuals to look at some meaningless object or ambiguous photo and describe what they see. In describing or making up a story about the the ambiguous object, individuals are assumed to project both their conscious and unconscious feelings, needs, and motives.

Although projective tests were not developed by Freud, they are assumed to reveal unconscious thoughts (Masling, 1997). We'll examine the two most widely used projective tests—Rorschach (*ROAR-shock*) inkblot test and Thematic Apperception Test (TAT).

RORSCHACH INKBLOT TEST

What do you see in this inkblot?

The Rorschach inkblot test, which was published in the early 1920s by a Swiss psychiatrist, Hermann Rorschach (1921/1942), contains five inkblots printed in black and white and five that have color (the inkblot shown on the left is similar to but is not an actual Rorschach inkblot).

The *Rorschach inkblot test* is used to assess personality by showing a person a series of ten inkblots and then asking the person to describe what he or she sees in each.

This test is used primarily in the therapeutic setting to assess personality traits and identify potential problems of adolescents and adult clients (Masling, 1997).

THEMATIC APPERCEPTION TEST (TAT)

What's happening in this picture?

A person would be shown a picture like the one on the right and asked to make up a plot or story about what the young woman is thinking and what has happened to her. This is a sample picture from the TAT.

The *Thematic Apperception Test,* or *TAT,* involves showing a person a series of 20 pictures of people in ambiguous situations and asking the person to make up a story about what the people are doing or thinking in each situation.

The TAT, which was developed by Henry Murray (1943), is used to assess the motivation and personality characteristics of normal individuals as well as clients with personality problems (Kaplan & Saccuzzo, 1997).

Before we discuss how well the Rorschach inkblot test and the TAT assess personality traits and identify potential problems, we'll look at another personality test that you have probably heard of: handwriting analysis. How much can someone learn just from your handwriting?

Two Characteristics

What does hand-writing show?

Handwriting analysts (graphologists) charge about $75 a hour to do personality assessments that they claim reveal a person's strengths and weaknesses, which are important to selecting job applicants and identifying people who may not be trusted (Scanlon & Mauro, 1992).

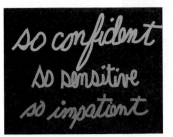

However, researchers report that handwriting analysis is no better than chance at assessing personality characteristics, rating the success of job applicants, or identifying one's profession (Basil, 1989; Ben-Shakhar et al., 1986; Feder, 1987). In order for handwriting analysis or any personality test to be an effective personality assessment tool it must have two characteristics, validity and reliability. Handwriting analysis is no better than chance in assessing personality because it lacks validity.

VALIDITY

Handwriting analysis is fun but no better than chance as a personality test because it lacks validity.

Validity means that the test measures what it says it measures or what it is supposed to measure.

For example, for a personality test to be valid, it must measure personality traits specific to the person rather than general traits that apply to almost everyone. Handwriting analysis does not measure, identify, or predict traits specific to an individual, so it has no validity as a personality test (Basil, 1989; Feder, 1987).

In addition to validity, a good personality test must also have a second characteristic, reliability.

RELIABILITY

In judging the usefulness of any personality test, the major question is always the same: How good are the test's validity and reliability?

Reliability refers to having a consistent score at different times. A person who takes a test at one point in time should receive the same score on a similar test taken at a later time.

For example, handwriting analysis may have good reliability provided your handwriting remains about the same across time. But, even if handwriting analysis has good reliability, it is still no better than chance at assessing or predicting an individual's personality traits because graphology lacks the important characteristic of validity.

This means that the usefulness of projective personality tests, such as the Rorschach and TAT tests, depends on their validity and reliability.

Usefulness

Are they valid and reliable?

Projective tests, such as the Rorschach inkblot test, have been around for over 75 years. However, there is still a debate between therapists, who report that projective tests are useful in assessing personality traits and problems, and researchers, who continue to question the reliability and validity of projective tests (Weiner, 1997). This debate involves the advantages and disadvantages of projective tests.

ADVANTAGES

Individuals who take projective tests do not know which are the best, correct, or socially desirable answers to give because the stimuli—the inkblot or the TAT picture—are ambiguous and have no right or wrong answers.

Thus, one advantage of projective tests such as the Rorschach and the TAT is that they are difficult to fake or bias since there are no correct or socially desirable answers.

When clients respond to Rorschach's meaningless inkblots or make up stories about what is happening in TAT's ambiguous pictures, clinicians assume that clients will project their hidden feelings, thoughts, or emotions on to these ambiguous stimuli. Based on this assumption, some clinicians believe that a second advantage of projective tests is that they are another method for assessing a client's hidden and unconscious thoughts and desires of which he or she is normally unaware (Weiner, 1997). However, many researchers disagree with the basic assumption of projective tests and question their reliability and, especially, their validity (Viglione, 1997).

DISADVANTAGES

Because projective tests use ambiguous stimuli, clients give a variety of answers that the clinician interprets and scores on a number of different variables, such as content, theme, or popularity (commonly given responses) (Weiner, 1997). Because there are no right or wrong answers, it is difficult to know if the interpretation and scoring of the client's responses accurately assess the client's personality traits and problems or rather reflect the biases of the interpreting clinician (Rorer, 1990).

Because there are no correct responses in projective tests, the reliability and validity of the Rorschach and TAT tests depend almost entirely on the clinician's experience and ability to accurately interpret and score the client's responses. Since clinicians differ in experience and accuracy, their interpretations and scoring may differ. These kinds of differences cause projective tests to have relatively low reliability and validity, their major disadvantages (Kaplan & Saccuzzo, 1997; Viglione, 1997).

However, experienced clinicians report that projective tests, when used in combination with other assessment techniques, provide useful information about a client's personality and problems (Anastasi & Urbina, 1997).

A. Social Cognitive Theory

Review and Definition

What shaped his personality?

How many of us would have stayed in prison for 27 years, as Mandela did, if the only condition for our release was that we not speak in public against the government? What were the forces that shaped Mandela's personality and gave him such courage, self-confidence, and perseverance? In Module 19, we discussed two answers to this question, Freud's psychodynamic theory and humanistic theories.

Freud's psychodynamic theory said that our personality is primarily shaped by our inborn biological urges, especially sex and aggression, and by how we resolve conflicts during the psychosexual stages, especially during the first five years.

Humanistic theories, such as those of Abraham Maslow and Carl Rogers, assume that we are basically good and that our personality is primarily shaped by our inborn tendency for self-actualization, or self-fulfillment, which includes both biological and psychological factors.

Now we discuss two more answers: first, social cognitive theory and, later, trait theory.

Social cognitive theory says that personality development is primarily shaped by three forces: environmental conditions (learning), cognitive-personal factors, and behavior, which all interact to influence how we evaluate, interpret, organize, and apply information.

Social cognitive theory grew out of the research of a number of psychologists, including Julian Rotter (1966), Albert Bandura (1986), and Walter Mischel (1990). According to social cognitive theory, we are neither good nor bad but primarily shaped by three influential factors.

Interaction of Three Factors

Cognitive → | Behavior → | Environmental → | Personality

For almost his entire life, Nelson Mandela has been fighting the white domination of blacks in South Africa. During this time, he suffered tremendous personal hardships, including 27 years in prison. You can't help wondering what shaped his personality and gave him the strength, determination, and character to sacrifice so much to reach his goal of freedom for his people. According to social cognitive theory, Mandela's personality was influenced and shaped by the interactions among three significant forces, namely cognitive-personal, behavioral, and environmental factors.

Cognitive-Personal Factors

Mandela was born to an African tribal royal family, and he was expected and trained to be a leader someday (right photo). Mandela's family encouraged him to be self-confident, have dignity, and, if needed, be ruthless and determined to achieve his goal (Mathews et al., 1990). Being born into a royal family and being taught to view himself as a leader are examples of cognitive-personal factors that helped shape Mandela's personality.

Cognitive factors include our beliefs, expectations, values, intentions, and social roles. *Personal factors* include our emotional makeup and our biological and genetic influences.

Cognitive factors guide personality development by influencing the way we view and interpret information. For example, Mandela viewed the world from the standpoint of someone trained to lead and help his people. These kinds of beliefs (cognitions) gave Mandela the strength and determination to fight for freedom. Thus, cognitive-personal factors influence our personalities by affecting what we think, believe, and feel, which in turn affect how we act and behave.

Behaviors

All his life Mandela spoke forcefully against oppression (photo top of page), organized political groups, and led marches against unfair domination of his people. These are examples of the kinds of behaviors that also shaped his personality.

Behaviors includes a variety of personal actions, such as the things we do and say.

In Mandela's case, the political and social behaviors that he engaged in to help his people achieve freedom, in turn, strengthened his belief that apartheid (discriminatory practices against blacks) was morally and politically wrong.

Just as behavior influences our beliefs, so too does our environment influence both.

Environmental Factors

Mandela lived in a society based on apartheid, which meant strict separation of the races, limited opportunities for nonwhites, and the fostering of intense racial hatred. These environmental factors certainly affected Mandela's personality developmenmt.

Environmental factors include our social, political, and cultural influences, as well as our particular learning experiences.

Just as our cognitive factors influence how we perceive and interpret our environment, our environment in turn affects our beliefs, values, and social roles.

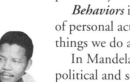

We can assume that living in such an oppressive environment strengthened Mandela's determination to get a law degree and to devote his life to obtaining freedom for all.

According to Bandura, personality development is influenced by the interactions among these three factors. He especially focused on cognitive-personal factors, which we'll discuss next.

Bandura's Social Cognitive Theory

Why are beliefs important?

Albert Bandura (1986) originally called his theory of personality development the social learning theory. However, to emphasize the importance of cognitive factors in personality development, he has recently changed the name to the social cognitive theory.

Bandura's social cognitive theory assumes that personality development, growth, and change are influenced by four distinctively human cognitive processes: highly developed language ability, observational learning, purposeful behavior, and self-analysis.

Bandura believes that these four cognitive processes reach their highest level of functioning in humans and that much of human personality and behavior is shaped by our own thoughts and beliefs.

For example, the young black men in the photo on the left are wearing T-shirts that say, "ANC LIVES." Nelson Mandela helped found a social-political organization whose initials, ANC, stand for African National Congress. For many years Mandela was the head of ANC, whose goal was freedom and equal opportunities for black Africans. According to Bandura's social cognitive theory, these young men's personalities will, to a large extent, be molded by cognitive factors such as the beliefs, values, and goals of the African National Congress. We'll briefly explain each of Bandura's cognitive factors.

Four Cognitive Factors

At the heart of Bandura's social cognitive theory is the idea that much of personality development is shaped and molded by cognitive processes that influence how we view and interpret the world (Carducci, 1998). And, in turn, how we view and interpret the world influences how we behave. Here's how Bandura's cognitive processes apply to the young black men who have joined the ANC.

1 Language ability. This is a powerful tool for processing and understanding information that influences personality development. We turn this information into ideas, beliefs, values, and goals, which shape, guide, and motivate our behaviors. For example, the ANC talks about, teaches, and values fighting for freedom. This information motivates its members to become assertive, self-confident, and determined.

2 Observational learning. Almost all of us "people watch"; we observe parents, brothers, sisters, peers, friends, and teachers; by doing so, we learn a great deal. Observational learning involves watching, imitating, and modeling. Most of the time, the observer provides his or her own reward for developing some belief or performing some behavior. For example, observational learning allows the young black men to imitate and model the personality characteristics of adult role models in the ANC.

3 Purposeful behavior. Our capacity to anticipate events, plan ahead, and set goals influences our personality development, growth, and change. For instance, in fighting for freedom, the young black men will organize, plan marches, and develop political strategies, which will encourage them to become responsible, confident, and energetic.

4 Self-analysis. This is a powerful internal process that allows us to monitor our own thoughts and actions. By deciding to change our goals or values, we can significantly affect our personality development. For instance, the young black men use self-analysis to check their personality progress as well as to reward themselves for meeting the goals of the ANC.

According to Bandura's social cognitive theory, these four cognitive processes influence our personality development, growth, and change.

To make the relationship between cognitive factors and personality more concrete, we'll focus on three specific beliefs: locus of control (this page), delay of gratification, and self-efficacy (next page).

Locus of Control

Can you control when you'll graduate?

This is the kind of question that intrigued Julian Rotter (1990), who was interested in how social cognitive theory applied to human behavior. Rotter developed a well-known scale to measure a person's expectancies about how much control he or she has over situations, which Rotter called the locus of control.

> Can you control when you will graduate?

Locus of control refers to our beliefs about how much control we have over situations or rewards. We are said to have an *internal locus of control* if we believe that we have control over situations and rewards. We are said to have an *external locus of control* if we believe that we do not have control over situations and rewards and that events outside ourselves (fate) determine what happens.

For example, if you believe that when you graduate depends primarily on your motivation and determination, then you have more of an internal locus of control. If you believe that when you graduate depends mostly on chance or things outside your control, then you have more of an external locus of control. Having more of an internal locus of control is an advantage because hundreds of studies report a positive correlation (0.20 to 0.30) between internal locus of control and mental health and psychological functioning (Smith et al., 1997). For example, people with an internal locus of control were generally higher achievers and were likely to take preventive health measures, to report less stress, and to be less depressed than were those with an external locus of control (Carducci, 1998). These findings indicate that a specific belief, such as how much control you believe you have, influences how you perceive your world; and this, in turn, affects how you behave. Next, we'll examine two other beliefs that influence behavior.

B. Trait Theory

Definition

Do women make better cops?

At the beginning of this module, we told you about Beverly Harvard (photo below), who in 1994 became the first African American woman appointed to head a police department in a major city (Atlanta, Georgia). In 1992, Elizabeth Watson was the first Caucasian woman to head a major metropolitan police force (Houston, Texas).

Throughout the 1970s and 1980s, women fought discrimination and harassment from male police officers who believed that women did not have the physical or mental stuff to be police officers (Brewer, 1991; Fletcher, 1995). However, a number of studies have shown that women do make good police officers and do the job as well as males (Bartol et al., 1992).

Peacekeeper. For example, police officer Kelly, who is female, patrols an area known for problems with street thugs. Although we may think that the best way to control thugs is with threat or force, Kelly rarely uses either. Kelly readily admits that her physical strength cannot always match that of some of the macho males she encounters. "Coming across aggressively doesn't work with gang members," Kelly explains. "If that first encounter is direct, knowledgeable, and made with authority, they respond. It takes a few more words but it works" (McDowell, 1992, p. 70). This example suggests that, in some ways, women make better cops than men because they have different personality traits (figure below).

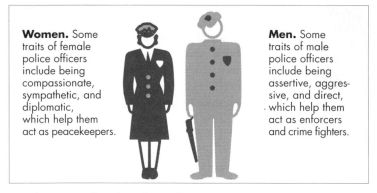

Women. Some traits of female police officers include being compassionate, sympathetic, and diplomatic, which help them act as peacekeepers.

Men. Some traits of male police officers include being assertive, aggressive, and direct, which help them act as enforcers and crime fighters.

The reason female police officers act more as peacekeepers and male police officers act more as enforcers may be explained by trait theory (Johnson, 1997).

Trait theory is an approach for analyzing the structure of personality by measuring, identifying, and classifying similarities and differences in personality characteristics or traits.

The basic unit for measuring personality characteristics is the trait.

A *trait* is a relatively stable and enduring tendency to behave in a particular way.

For example, traits of female police officers include being compassionate and diplomatic, while those of male police officers include being assertive and direct. Determining exactly how many traits are needed to describe someone's personality took psychologists almost 60 years.

Identifying Traits

Can you describe them?

How would you describe the personalities of a criminal, clown, graduating student, nun, and rock star? This seemingly impossible task was the major goal of personality researchers. They were determined to find a list of traits whose two characteristics seemed mutually exclusive: the list had to contain very few traits but at the same time be able to describe differences among anyone's and everyone's personality, from avocado grower to zookeeper. The search for this elusive list began in the 1930s with, of all things, a dictionary.

How many traits can there be?

In the 1930s, Gordon Allport and an associate went through the dictionary and selected every term that could distinguish differences among personalities (Allport & Odbert, 1936). They found about 18,000 terms that dealt with all kinds of personality differences; of these, about 4,500 were considered to fit their definition of personality traits. Allport defined *traits* as stable and consistent tendencies in how an individual adjusts to his or her environment. The advantage of Allport's list was that it was comprehensive enough to describe anyone's and everyone's personality. The disadvantage was that it was incredibly long and thus impractical to use in research.

Allport's search for a list of defining traits set the stage for future research. However, his list of thousands of traits needed to be organized into far fewer basic traits. This task fell to Raymond Cattell.

Aren't some traits related?

In the 1940s Raymond Cattell (1943) took Allport's list of 4,500 traits and used factor analysis to reduce the list to the most basic traits.

Factor analysis is a complicated statistical method that finds relationships among many different or diverse items and allows them to be grouped together.

Cattell used factor analysis to search for *relationships* among hundreds of traits on Allport's list so that the original list could be reduced to 35 basic traits, which Cattell called *source traits.* He claimed that these 35 basic traits could describe all differences among personalities. Although Cattell's achievement was remarkable, his list of 35 traits—and even his further reduction of the list to 16 traits—still proved too long to be practical for research and only moderately useful in assessing personality differences. Obviously, Cattell's list needed more reducing, but that was to take another 30 years.

Finding Traits: Big Five

Can it be done with just five?

From the 1960s to the early 1990s, about a dozen researchers in several countries were using factor analysis to find relationships among lists of adjectives that described personality differences. Doing the impossible, researchers reduced the list of 35 traits to only five, which make up the five-factor model of personality (Wiggins & Trapnell, 1997).

The *five-factor model* organizes personality traits and describes differences in personality using five categories, which are *openness, conscientiousness, extraversion, agreeableness,* and *neuroticism.*

These five factors became known as the Big Five; they are easy to remember if you note that their first letters make the acronym OCEAN. Each of the five factors actually represents a continuum of behavior, as briefly described in the figure below.

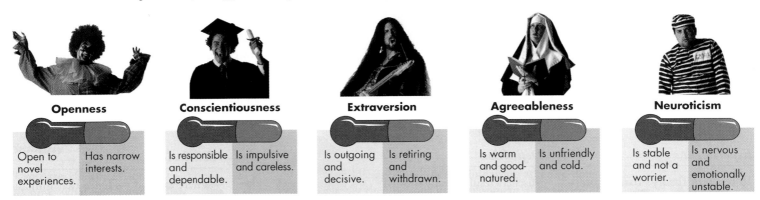

Openness	Conscientiousness	Extraversion	Agreeableness	Neuroticism
Open to novel experiences. / Has narrow interests.	Is responsible and dependable. / Is impulsive and careless.	Is outgoing and decisive. / Is retiring and withdrawn.	Is warm and good-natured. / Is unfriendly and cold.	Is stable and not a worrier. / Is nervous and emotionally unstable.

You can think of each Big Five factor as a supertrait because each factor's thermometer includes dozens of related traits at the hot and cold ends. For example, conscientiousness, at the hot end, includes the traits of being dependable, responsible, deliberate, hardworking, and precise; at the cold end are the traits of being impulsive, careless, late, lazy, and aimless. Although it took 30 years of research, coming up with the Big Five means that trait theory finally achieved its major goal, which was to describe and organize personality characteristics using the fewest number of traits (John, 1990).

Importance of the Big Five

When the Big Five factors first appeared in the early 1990s, some researchers questioned whether these five traits really could organize and describe all personality differences. However, after almost ten more years of research, there is now convincing data that the five-factor model can indeed use only five traits to describe personality differences. In addition, the five-factor model has been replicated in children and adults in the United States, as well as in six other countries (Germany, Portugal, Israel, Hong Kong, South Korea, and Japan) (McCrae & Costa, 1997; Wiggins & Trapnell, 1997).

The fact that the five-factor model has been replicated in seven different countries raises an interesting question: Is the structure of personality shaped primarily by cultural factors (child-rearing practices, religious and moral values, language similarities); or is personality structure shaped primarily by variations in basic human ways of acting and experiencing that are universal, or similar across all peoples and countries. Because support for the five-factor model was found in seven very different countries, researchers concluded that the basic structure of human personality arises from some universal living experience or biological basis rather than being shaped by individual cultures (McCrae & Costa, 1997). If basic human personality structure is universal, it means that the personalities of individuals in different countries can be described by using the Big Five traits.

Applying the Big Five

Compared with previous lists of personality traits, the five-factor model is the first to organize all personality differences under so few comprehensive categories. This means that researchers can use questionnaires based on the five-factor model to assess major personality differences among diverse individuals. In addition, the five-factor model can lead to more accurate methods for assessing personality and personality problems, which is one of the major tasks of therapists, clinicians, and psychologists. Although the five-factor model has proven very useful in describing and organizing personality traits, some critics note that this model does not explain how these traits arise or account for unusual situations (risking one's life to climb Mount Everest) (Digman, 1997).

Researchers generally agree that the five-factor model is a giant leap forward in trait theory and is a useful tool for defining personality structures and differences, predicting behaviors, and identifying personality problems (Graziano & Eisenberg, 1997; Hogan & Ones, 1997; Salgado, 1997).

For instance, the Big Five traits can be used to describe differences between male and female police officers: compared with their male counterparts, female officers are generally more agreeable (sympathetic), open (insightful), and extraverted (sociable), traits that make female police officers more diplomatic communicators (Manuel et al., 1993; Morash & Greene, 1986).

Although each of us possesses at least five relatively enduring supertraits that push us to behaving in a stable way, why do we sometimes contradict ourselves and behave differently in different situations?

E. Research Focus: 180-Degree Change
Can People Make a Major Change in a Day?

You will discover that changing parts of your personality, such as becoming more outgoing, assertive, punctual, or sympathetic, can be difficult and time consuming because these traits are relatively stable and enduring. Then what are we to make of people who claim to have totally changed their personalities in a single day? Researchers have studied these 180-degree personality changes, which they call quantum personality changes (Miller & C'deBaca, 1994).

A *quantum personality change* is a very sudden (in a single day) and radical or dramatic shift in one's personality, beliefs, or values.

For example, take the story of Bill Wilson, who cofounded Alcoholics Anonymous (AA). He was in the depths of alcoholic despair and depression when he suddenly saw his room lit with a bright light. In his mind's eye, he saw himself on a mountaintop and felt that spirit winds were blowing through him. Then, suddenly, a simple but powerful thought burst upon him: he was a free man (Kurtz, 1979). This dramatic experience changed Wilson's personality 180 degrees as he went from being a desperate and hopeless drunk to being a sober and dedicated worker who devoted his life to helping others overcome alcoholism.

This and other personal accounts of sudden, major personality changes are hard to believe because they challenge two well-established psychological findings: first, personality traits are stable and enduring tendencies that may change gradually but rarely undergo sudden and dramatic changes; and second, even when people want to change their personalities, as in therapy, it doesn't happen overnight but takes considerable time and effort. Then how can quantum personality changes occur, often in a single day? Exactly what does the person experience and feel? To answer these questions, researchers developed a method to study quantum changes.

Method

Researchers needed a method to measure quantum personality change, which meant assessing cognitive processes, which are often not observable and can be obtained only through self-reports, which may be biased or inaccurate. Researchers decided on a simple and direct approach. They used a feature story in the local paper (Albuquerque, New Mexico) to ask for volunteers who, in a relatively short period of time, had experienced a transformation in their basic values, feelings, attitudes, or actions. Out of a total of 89 people who responded, 55 were found acceptable.

Subjects were first given a series of personality tests and structured interviews (average length 107 minutes).

Structured interviews involve asking each individual the same set of relatively narrow and focused questions so that the same information is obtained from everyone.

During these interviews, subjects were asked detailed questions about the what, when, and where, of the unusual experiences that had apparently transformed their personalities so completely.

Results

Researchers first noted that their subjects (31 females and 24 males), performed within the normal range on personality tests, had no strange problems, and showed no striking or unusual things in common. In fact, on the basis of the battery of personality tests and interviews, all subjects seemed to be largely ordinary individuals who had had extraordinary experiences (Miller & C'deBaca, 1994). Here are some of the major findings:

- A majority of subjects (58%) could specify the date and time of day when the quantum experience occurred even though the experience had occurred, on average, 11 years earlier.

- A majority of subjects (75%) reported that the quantum experience began suddenly and took them by surprise. For some, the experience lasted only minutes (13%) and for most it was over within 24 hours (64%). The actual experiences varied from being struck by an intense thought, making a total commitment, hearing a voice, or hearing God's voice.
- A majority of subjects (56%) reported a high level of emotional distress and a relatively high level of negative life experiences in the year before the quantum experience.
- Most (96%) reported that the quantum experience had made their lives better and most (80%) stated that the changes had lasted.
- Most (87%) said that, during the quantum experience, an important truth was revealed to them; 78% said that they were relieved of a mental burden; and 60% said that they felt completely loved.

All of these 55 individuals reported that they had, in a single day, experienced a 180-degree change in personality that, for many, seems to have been triggered by a long period of bad times.

Conclusions

Researchers concluded that the quantum personality changes reported by the subjects were dramatically larger than are ordinarily observed, occurred in a quicker period of time than is normally reported, and lasted for years (Miller & C'deBaca, 1994). For most of the subjects, the changes represented an increased sense of meaning, happiness, and satisfaction; some reported a sense of closeness to God. This study suggests that quantum changes in personality do occur and may be one way a person solves some long-standing and stressful personal problem.

In many cases, people who experienced quantum personality changes also reported subsequent changes in behavior. How much personality affects behavior is partly dependent on culture.

Interpersonal Conflicts

One reason psychologists have been studying personality traits for over 60 years is because traits are stable and enduring tendencies to behave in certain ways. Knowing if a friend is usually on time or late will help predict your friend's behavior. Similarly, knowing a person's level of assertiveness will partly predict how he or she will handle an interpersonal conflict.

Interpersonal conflict refers to your disagreeing with another person who opposes your getting some wish, goal, or expectation.

For example, imagine that your best friend suddenly decides to get married and insists that you be at the wedding the same week you have a major paper due. You explain the problem to your professor and ask for a week's extension of the deadline. Your professor replies that if you turn your paper in late, you will receive a grade of D. How would you handle this interpersonal conflict? Most people use two different strategies for resolving interpersonal conflicts—a passive strategy or an active strategy (Hocker & Wilmot, 1991).

In a *passive strategy,* you resolve the conflict by avoiding further discussion or restating your request or opinion.

In an *active strategy*, you resolve the conflict by making compromises or persuading the other person to adopt your position.

Which strategy you choose depends partly on your personality traits (assertive, passive), which are influenced by your culture. We'll examine how two different cultures—the United States and Japan—influence personality traits that, in turn, influence how people behave to solve their interpersonal conflicts.

Cultural Differences

One of the major cultural differences between Western and Eastern countries is how citizens rate their priorities and goals. Generally, citizens in Western countries rate individual goals over group goals, while citizens in Eastern countries rate group or collective goals over individual ones.

As a Western nation, the United States is considered an individualistic culture (Triandis, 1989).

An *individualistic culture* places a high priority on attaining personal goals and striving for personal satisfaction, often by being competitive and assertive.

Since the focus in many Western cultures is on individual goals, citizens are generally encouraged to be independent, competitive, and assertive (Ohbuchi & Takahashi, 1994).

As an Eastern nation, Japan is considered a collectivistic culture.

A *collectivistic culture* places a high priority on group goals and norms over personal goals and values. Individuals in these cultures work to control their behaviors and maintain harmonious relationships with others.

Since the focus in many Asian cultures is on collective or group goals, citizens are generally encouraged to be dependent on and submissive to group values (Ohbuchi & Takahashi, 1994). Will these cultural differences result in different strategies for solving interpersonal conflicts?

Using Different Strategies

Researchers predicted that because of these cultural differences, students in the United States and in Japan would use different strategies to resolve interpersonal conflicts. College students in the United States and Japan were asked to recall their interpersonal conflicts during the past several weeks and describe what they had actually done to resolve these conflicts. Two trained raters divided students' responses into two different strategies for resolving interpersonal conflicts: passive strategy, which is to avoid further discussion; and active strategy, which is to engage in persuasion or compromise.

Different strategies. As shown in the graph at right, Japanese students usually used the passive strategy, which means they were more likely to solve interpersonal conflicts by avoiding any further discussion of the conflict. Japanese students were less likely to use the active strategy, which means that they did not try to resolve problems through persuasion, bargaining, or compromise (Ohbuchi & Takahashi, 1994).

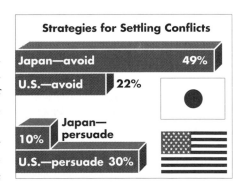

Strategies for Settling Conflicts

Japan—avoid	49%
U.S.—avoid	22%
Japan—persuade	10%
U.S.—persuade	30%

In comparison, American students used the opposite strategies: they were significantly more likely to use the active strategy and to resolve the problem through persuasion, bargaining, or compromise. American students were significantly less likely to use the passive strategy—to settle the interpersonal conflict by avoiding further discussion.

Researchers concluded that the collectivistic culture of Japan rewards personality traits that lead to avoiding the public discussion of conflicts. In comparison, the individualistic culture of the United States rewards personality traits that lead individuals to settle conflicts through public persuasion or compromise (Ohbuchi & Takahashi, 1994). This study is a good example of how culture influences the development of different personality traits, which, in turn, lead to different behaviors.

Next, we'll briefly review the four major theories of personality to give you a better overview of their similarities and differences.

G. Four Theories of Personality

Psychodynamic Theory

Freud's psychodynamic theory, which was developed in the early 1900s, grew out of his work with patients.

Freud's *psychodynamic theory of personality* emphasizes the importance of early childhood experiences, the importance of repressed thoughts that we cannot voluntarily access, and the conflicts between conscious and unconscious forces that influence our thoughts and behaviors. (Freud used the term dynamic to refer to mental energy force.)

Conscious thoughts are wishes, desires, or thoughts that we are aware of or can recall at any given moment.

Unconscious forces represent wishes, desires, or thoughts that, because of their disturbing or threatening content, we automatically repress and cannot voluntarily access.

Freud believed that a large part of our behavior was guided or motivated by unconscious forces.

Unconscious motivation is a Freudian concept that refers to the influence of repressed thoughts, desires, or impulses on our conscious thoughts and behaviors.

Freud developed three methods to uncover unconscious processes: *free association, dream interpretation*, and *slips of the tongue* (Freudian slips).

Divisions of the Mind

Freud divided the mind into three divisions: id, ego, and superego.

The first division is the *id*, which contains two biological drives—sex and aggression—that are the source of all mental energy. The id follows the pleasure principle, which is to satisfy the biological drives.

The second division is the *ego*, whose goal is to find socially acceptable ways of satisfying the id's desires within the range of the superego's prohibitions. The ego follows the reality principle, which is to satisfy a wish or desire only if there is a socially acceptable outlet available.

The third division is the *superego*, whose goal is to apply the moral values and standards of one's parents or caregivers and society in satisfying one's wishes.

Psychosexual Stages

Freud assumed that our personality develops as we pass through a series of *five psychosexual stages.*

During these developmental periods—the *oral, anal, phallic, latency,* and *genital stages*—the individual seeks pleasure from different areas of the body associated with sexual feelings. Freud emphasized that the child's first five years were the most important in personality development.

Humanistic Theories

Humanistic theories emphasize our capacity for personal growth, development of our potential, and freedom to choose our destiny. *Humanistic theories* stress three major points—phenomenological perspective, holistic view, and self-actualization.

The *phenomenological perspective* means that our perception of the world, whether or not it is accurate, becomes our reality.

The *holistic view* means that a person's personality is more than the sum of its individual parts; instead, the individual parts form a unique and total entity that functions as a unit.

Self-actualization refers to our inherent tendency to reach our true potentials.

Humanistic theories reject the biological determinism and the irrational, unconscious forces of Freud's psychodynamic theory. Humanistic theories emphasize freely choosing to go after one's dream and change one's destiny.

The beginning of humanistic theory can be traced to two psychologists: Abraham Maslow, who rejected behaviorism's system of rewards and punishment; and Carl Rogers, who rejected Freud's psychodynamic theory with its emphasis on unconscious forces.

Abraham Maslow

Maslow (1968) broke away from the reward/punishment/observable behavior mentality of behaviorism and developed his humanistic theory. *Maslow's humanistic theory* emphasized two things: our capacity for growth or self-actualization and our desire to satisfy a variety of needs.

Maslow's hierarchy of needs arranges needs in ascending order, with biological needs at the bottom and social and personal needs at the top; as needs at one level are met, we advance to the next level.

Carl Rogers' Self Theory

Carl Rogers rejected the psychodynamic approach because it placed too much emphasis on unconscious, irrational forces. Instead, Rogers developed a new humanistic theory, which is called self theory. *Roger's self theory*, also called self-actualization theory, has two primary assumptions: personality development is guided by each person's unique self-actualization tendency; and each of us has a personal need for positive regard.

Rogers said that the *self* is made up of many self-perceptions, abilities, personality characteristics, and behaviors that are organized and consistent with one another.

Social Cognitive Theory

Freud's *psychodynamic theory*, developed in the early 1900s, grew out of his work with patients. Humanistic theories were developed in the 1960s by an ex-Freudian (Rogers) and ex-behaviorist (Maslow), who believed that previous theories had neglected the positive side of human potential and fulfillment.

In comparison, *social cognitive theory*, developed in the 1960s and 1970s, grew out of a strong research background that emphasized a more experimental approach to developing and testing concepts that could be used to understand and explain personality development.

Social cognitive theory says that personality development is primarily shaped by three factors: environmental conditions (learning), cognitive-personal factors, and behavior. *Behavior* includes a variety of actions, such as what we do and say. *Environmental influences* include our social, political, and cultural influences, as well as our particular learning experiences. Just as our cognitive factors influence how we perceive and interpret our environment, our environment in turn affects our beliefs, values, and social roles. *Cognitive-personal factors* include our beliefs, expectations, values, intentions, and social roles as well as our biological and genetic influences. Thus, what we think, believe, and feel affects how we act and behave.

Bandura's Social Cognitive Theory

Perhaps the best example of the social cognitive approach is Bandura's social cognitive theory, which he developed in the 1970s. *Bandura's social cognitive theory* says that personality development, growth, and change are influenced by four distinctively human cognitive processes: highly developed language ability, observational learning, purposeful behavior, and self-analysis.

Bandura's theory emphasizes *cognitive factors*, such as personal values, goals, and beliefs. Three particular beliefs have been shown to influence personality development: *locus of control*, which refers to how much control we think we have over our environment; *delay of gratification*, which involves our voluntarily postponing an immediate reward for the promise of a future reward; and *self-efficacy*, which refers to our personal beliefs of how capable we are in performing specific tasks and behaviors.

Should I take one marshmallow now or wait and get two?

One of the *basic assumptions* of social cognitive theory is that our beliefs, values, and goals influence the development of our personalities, which, in turn, affects how we behave.

Trait Theory

For over 50 years, a *major goal* of personality researchers was to find a way to define the structure of personality with the fewest possible traits. The search for a list of traits that could describe personality differences among everyone, including criminals and nuns, began in 1930s with a list of about 4,500 traits and ended in the 1990s with a list of only five traits.

In the 1990s, trait theory developed the five-factor model, which is based on laboratory research, especially questionnaires and statistical procedures. *Trait theory* refers to an approach for analyzing the structure of personality by measuring, identifying, and classifying similarities and differences in personality characteristics or traits. The basic unit for measuring personality characteristics is the trait. *Traits* are relatively stable and enduring tendencies to behave in particular ways, but behavior is not always the same across different situations.

Trait theory says relatively little about the development or growth of personality but instead emphasizes measuring and identifying differences among personalities.

Five-Factor Model

The *five-factor model* organizes all personality traits under five categories—openness, conscientiousness, extraversion, agreeableness, and neuroticism (OCEAN). These traits, which are referred to as the *Big Five traits*, raise three major issues.

First, although traits are stable tendencies to behave in certain ways, this stability does not necessarily apply across situations. According to the *person-situation interaction*, you may behave differently in different situations because of the effects of a particular situation.

Second, personality traits are both *changeable and stable*: most change occurs before age 30, because adolescents and young adults are more willing to adopt new values and attitudes or revise old ones; most stability occurs after age 30, but adults do continue to grow in their ideas, beliefs, and attitudes.

Third, *genetic factors* have a considerable influence on personality traits and behaviors. Genetic factors push and pull the development of certain traits, whose development may be helped or hindered by environmental factors.

Traits are useful in that they provide shorthand descriptions of people and predict certain behaviors.

H. Application: Assessment—Objective Tests

Definition

Why are traits big business?

One reason traits are big business is that they are used in many kinds of personality tests. For instance, suppose you're applying for a fast-food job and your employer asks you to fill out a written questionnaire, which is really a honesty test. The employer knows that about 62% of fast-food workers steal money or give away food to friends and hopes this honesty test will help select an honest employee (Murphy, 1993). To help employers make hiring decisions, about 5,000 companies administer honesty tests to almost five million people each year (Lilienfeld, 1993). Honesty tests, which are the most frequently administered psychological tests in the United States, are examples of objective personality tests.

I've heard others do, but I would never steal from my employer.

Objective personality tests, also called *self-report questionnaires,* consist of specific written statements that require individuals to indicate, for example, by checking "true" or "false," whether the statements do or do not apply to them.

Because objective personality tests or self-report questionnaires use very specific questions and require very specific answers, they are considered to be highly *structured,* or objective. In comparison, projective tests, which we discussed in Module 19, use ambiguous stimuli (ink blots, photos), have no right or wrong answers and are considered to be *unstructured,* or *projective,* personality tests.

It is most likely that as part of a job interview, you will be asked to take a variety of self-report questionnaires. That's because employers, clinicians, researchers, and government and law enforcement agencies use self-report questionnaires to identify and differentiate personality traits.

The basic assumption behind self-report questionnaires brings us back to the definition of traits. We defined traits as stable and enduring tendencies to behave in certain ways. Self-report questionnaires identify traits, which employers use to predict how prospective employees will behave in their particular jobs or situations.

Before we discuss how valid and reliable self-report questionnaires are in predicting behavior, we'll examine two of the more popular self-report questionnaires.

Examples of Objective Tests

How honest are most employees?

Objective personality tests are used in both business and clinical settings. In business settings, self-report questionnares are often used in the hiring process. Because most employers want honest and trustworthy employees, they may give them an integrity test.

INTEGRITY TESTS

Integrity or honesty tests are supposed to assess whether individuals have high levels of the trait of honesty. Questions asked on honesty tests are similar to those below (Lilienfeld, 1993).

1. Have you ever stolen merchandise from your place of work?
2. Have you ever been tempted to steal a piece of jewelry from a store?
3. Do you think most people steal money from their workplace every now and then?
4. A person has been a loyal and honest employee at a firm for 20 years. One day, after realizing that she has neglected to bring lunch money, she takes $10 from her workplace, but returns it the next day. Should she be fired?

People strong in the trait of honesty answer: (1) no, (2) no, (3) no, (4) yes.

Notice that some self-report questionnaires, such as the integrity test, focus on measuring a single personality trait, in this case honesty. The next self-report questionnaire, called the MMPI-2, is primarily used in clinical settings and measures a number of traits and personality problems.

MINNESOTA MULTIPHASIC PERSONALITY INVENTORY–2

Suppose a parole board needed to decide if a convicted murderer had changed enough in prison to be let out on parole. To help make this decision, they might use a test that identifies the range of normal and abnormal personality traits, such as the well-known Minnesota Multiphasic Personality Inventory–2 (MMPI-2).

The *Minnesota Multiphasic Personality Inventory (MMPI-2)* is a true-false self-report questionnaire that consists of 567 statements describing a wide range of normal and abnormal behaviors. The purpose of the MMPI-2 is to help distinguish normal from abnormal groups.

The MMPI-2 asks about and identifies a variety of specific personality traits, including depression, hostility, high energy, and shyness, and plots whether these traits are in the normal or abnormal range. A few of the 567 statements used in the MMPI are given below:

- I do not tire quickly.
- I am worried about sex.
- When I get bored, I like to stir up some excitement.
- I believe I am being plotted against.

One advantage of this test is that it contains three kinds of scales: *validity scales,* which assess whether the client was lying or faking answers; *clinical scales,* which identify psychological disorders, such as depression, paranoia, or schizophrenia; and *content scales,* which identify specific areas, such as the anger scale, whose content includes references to being irritable and hotheaded and to difficulties controlling anger (Kaplan & Saccuzzo, 1997).

The MMPI-2 is commonly used to assess a wide range of personality traits, numerous behaviors, health and psychosomatic symptoms, and many well-known psychotic symptoms (Greene & Clopton, 1994). The MMPI-2 and the integrity questionnaire are examples of objective tests used to identify personality traits.

Another method that claims to identify your particular traits is astrology.

Reliability and Validity

How do horoscopes work?

About 78% of women and 70% of men read horoscopes, and many believe that they are so correct that they were written especially for them (Halpern, 1998). Horoscopes, which are carried in most newspapers (often labeled as entertainment), are a popular method of identifying traits. As you read the horoscope on the right, note how many traits apply to you. Because horoscopes contain traits that could apply to almost everyone, a majority of readers believe in horoscopes; this phenomenon is called the Barnum principle (Guastello et al., 1989; Snyder et al., 1977).

The *Barnum principle* (named after the famous circus owner P. T. Barnum) refers to the method of listing a number of traits in such a general way that almost everyone who reads the horoscope thinks that these traits apply specifically to him or her. But, in fact, these traits are so general that they apply to almost everyone.

Sagittarius: Nov. 23–Dec. 22. You are bright, sincere, likeable, and have a good sense of humor. At times you can be a little too outspoken and independent. Don't be so critical of yourself and let your warm side show itself more.

Astrologers claim they can identify your personality traits by knowing the sign under which you were born. However, researchers found that astrology is a very poor method to assess personality traits because it lacks at least one of the two characteristics of a good test—validity.

I read my horoscope every day, and it's always right on the mark.

VALIDITY

With a little practice, I have become a very good horoscope writer. Like the person on the left, students rate my horoscopes a 9 or 10 (10 being best) on how well I described their particular personality traits. Although students give my horoscopes high ratings for accuracy, they have no validity.

Validity means that the test measures what it is supposed to measure.

The reason I can write "accurate" horoscopes is that I use the *Barnum principle*, which means that I state personality traits in such a general way that they apply to everyone. Because professional astrologers essentially use the Barnum principle, their descriptions are "accurate" for almost everyone. For this reason, researchers found that the 12 zodiac signs were no better than chance at identifying traits for a *particular individual* (Crowe, 1990; Svensen & White, 1994). Because horoscopes cannot identify traits for a particular person, horoscopes lack validity. In addition to validity, a good test must also have reliability.

RELIABILITY

Even through horoscopes lack validity, they may actually have the second characteristic of a good personality test, reliability.

Reliability refers to consistency: a person's score on a test at one point in time should be similar to the score obtained by the same person on a similar test at a later point in time.

Horoscopes may be reliable if the writer remains the same. However, horoscopes are no better than chance at identifying traits of a particular person because horoscopes still lack validity.

Usefulness

Is a monk or devil more honest?

One reason self-report questionnaires are so popular and widely used is that they obtain a considerable amount of personal information in a structured way so that such information can be compared with that of others who have taken the test. For example, employers, government, and law enforcement agencies use objective tests, such as integrity tests, to compare and select certain traits in job applicants. Researchers use self-report personality questionnaires to differentiate between people's traits. Counselors and clinicians use self-report questionnaires, such as MMPI-2, to identify personality traits and potential psychological problems (Maruish, 1994). We'll examine the disadvantages and advantages of self-report questionnaires.

DISADVANTAGES

There are several major disadvantages of self-report questionnaires. First, because the questions and answers are very structured, critics from the psychodynamic approach point out that self-report questionnaires may not measure deeper or unconscious personality factors. Second, because the questions are straightforward, people may figure out how to bias the test's results by giving more socially desirable or acceptable answers—compare the devil's with the monk's response. Third, many self-report questionnaires measure specific traits, which we know may predict behavior in the same situations but not across situations. This means a person may behave honestly with his or her family but not necessarily with his or her employer.

Of course I'm a very, very honest person.

I'm not as honest as I should be.

ADVANTAGES

There are a number of advantages of self-report inventories. First, they are easily administered and can be taken individually or in groups. Second, the questions are unambiguous and highly structured and require either a true-false or yes-no answer. Third, the scoring is relatively straightforward—for example, summing marked answers according to certain directions. Fourth, many of the self-report questionnaires have good reliability. For example, the reliability of the MMPI-2 ranges from 0.68 to 0.92 (1.0 is perfect reliability) (Butcher et al., 1989). Fifth, the validity of self-report questionnaires varies with the test; it ranges from poor to good. For example, the validity of integrity tests appears to be poor: in one study, a group of monks and nuns scored "more dishonest" than a group of prisoners in jail (Lilienfeld, 1993; Rieke & Guastello, 1995). In comparison, many studies on the MMPI-2 indicate its validity to be good (Kaplan & Saccuzzo, 1997).

Because self-report inventories and projective tests (discussed in Module 19) have different advantages and disadvantages, counseling and clinical psychologists may use a combination of both to assess a client's personality traits and problems.

SUMMARY TEST

A. SOCIAL COGNITIVE THEORY

1. One theory says that personality development is primarily shaped by environmental conditions (learning), cognitive-personal factors, and behavior, which all interact to influence how we evaluate, interpret, and organize information and apply that information to ourselves and others; this is called the _____ theory.

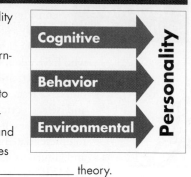

2. Albert Bandura called the version of his original social learning theory the (a)_____ theory. Bandura's theory assumes that four distinctively human cognitive processes—highly developed language ability, observational learning, purposeful behavior, and self-analysis—influence the growth, development, and change in (b)_____.

3. Our highly developed (a)_____ ability provides us with a tool for processing and understanding information, which is critical to personality development. Our capacity for (b)_____ learning allows us to learn through watching, without observable behavior or a reinforcer. Our capacity for forethought enables us to plan ahead and set goals—to perform (c)_____ behavior. Finally, the fact that we can monitor our thoughts and actions as well as set and change goals and values gives us the capacity for (d)_____.

4. The power of beliefs and ideas to change the way that we interpret situations and events is one of the basic assumptions of social cognitive theories. Rotter developed a scale to measure our belief about how much control we have over situations or rewards; he called this belief (a)_____. If we believe that we have control over situations and rewards, we are said to have an (b)_____ locus of control. In contrast, if we believe that we do not have control over situations and rewards and that events outside ourselves determine what happens, we are said to have an (c)_____ locus of control.

5. According to Bandura, our personal belief regarding how capable we are of exercising control over events in our lives is called (a)_____. According to Mischel, our voluntary postponement of an immediate reward and persistence in completing a task for the promise of a future reward is called delay of (b)_____.

B. TRAIT THEORY

6. A relatively stable and enduring tendency to behave in a particular way is called a (a)_____. An approach to understanding the structure of personality by measuring, identifying, and analyzing differences in personality is called (b)_____ theory. In attempting to pare down a list of traits by finding relationships among them, researchers have used a statistical method called (c)_____.

7. The model that organizes all personality traits into five categories is called the (a)_____. These five categories, known as the Big Five, are (b)_____, _____, _____, _____, and _____; their initial letters spell out the word OCEAN.

8. Mischel questioned the basic assumption of trait theory, saying that, if traits represent consistent behavioral tendencies, they should predict behaviors across many different (a)_____. Instead, he found that people behaved with great consistency in the same situation but behaved with low consistency across different situations. Mischel pointed out that predicting a person's behavior must take into account not only the person's traits but also the effects of the situation; this idea became known as the (b)_____ interaction.

C. GENETIC INFLUENCES ON TRAITS

9. How inherited or genetic factors influence and interact with psychological factors—for example, the ways we behave, adapt, and adjust to our environments—is the focus of the field of behavioral (a)_____. Current thinking about genetic factors is that they do not fix behaviors but rather set a range for behaviors. Researchers estimate genetic influences with a measure that estimates how much of some behavior is due to genetic influences; this measure is referred to as (b)_____.

10. Considering the various influences on personality development, researchers estimated that about 40% of the influence comes from (a)_____, which are inherited. About 27% of the influence on personality development comes from environmental factors that involve how each individual reacts and adjusts to his or her own environment; these are called (b)_____ factors. About 7% of the influence on personality development comes from environmental factors that involve parental patterns and shared family experiences; these are called (c)_____ factors. The remaining 26% of the influence on personality development cannot as yet be identified and is attributed to errors in testing and measurement procedures.

D. EVALUATION OF TRAIT THEORY

11. Trait theory assumes that differences among personalities can be described by a short but comprehensive list of traits. Critics of the current list, known as the (a)_____, point out that the data for the model may paint too simplistic a picture of human personality and may not reflect its depth and complexity. Trait theory assumes that traits are consistent and stable influences on our (b)_____ but critics argue that when traits are measured in one situation, they do not necessarily predict behaviors in other situations.

12. The biggest changes in personality occur during childhood, adolescence, and young adulthood because young men and women are somewhat more likely to be open to new ideas. Personality is less likely to change after age (a)_____. Observations from over 10,000 pairs of twins indicate that (b)_____ factors significantly influence personality traits. Critics warn that inherited factors should not be exaggerated because 50% or more of the influence on traits comes from (c)_____ influences.

E. RESEARCH FOCUS: 180-DEGREE CHANGE

13. If you were to experience a sudden and radical or dramatic shift in personality, beliefs, or values, you would be said to have experienced a (a)_____ in personality. One way researchers studied these changes in personality was to ask each individual the same set of relatively narrow and focused questions so that the same information was obtained from everyone; this method is called the (b)_____.

F. CULTURAL DIVERSITY: RESOLVING CONFLICTS

14. A culture that places a high priority on attaining personal goals and striving for personal satisfaction is called an (a)_____ culture. A culture that places a high priority on group goals and norms over personal goals and values is called a (b)_____ culture.

15. The strategy that Japanese students used most frequently to resolve interpersonal conflicts was to (a)_____ discussion of the conflict; the strategy favored by American students was to resolve the problem through (b)_____. In addition, Japanese students reported that the vast majority of their interpersonal conflicts were (c)_____, while American students reported that the vast majority of their conflicts were (d)_____.

G. FOUR THEORIES OF PERSONALITY

16. How does personality grow and develop? We discussed four different answers. The theory that emphasizes the importance of early childhood, unconscious factors, the three divisions of the mind, and psychosexual stages is called (a)_____. The theories that focus on the phenomenological perspective, a holistic view, and self-actualization are called (b)_____ theories. The theory that says that personality development is shaped by the interaction between three factors—environmental conditions, cognitive-personal factors, and behavior—is called (c)_____ theory. The theory that emphasizes measuring and identifying differences between personalities is called (d)_____ theory.

H. APPLICATION: ASSESSMENT—OBJECTIVE TESTS

17. Self-report questionnaires, which consist of specific written statements that require structured responses—for example, checking "true" or "false"—are examples of _____ personality tests.

18. A true-false self-report questionnaire containing hundreds of statements that describe a wide range of normal and abnormal behaviors is called the (a)_____. The purpose of this test is to distinguish normal from (b)_____ groups.

19. The method of listing a number of traits in such a general way that almost everyone who reads a horoscope thinks that many of the traits apply specifically to him or her is called the _____ principle.

Answers: *1. social cognitive; 2. (a) social cognitive, (b) personality; 3. (a) language, (b) observational, (c) purposeful, (d) self-analysis; 4. (a) locus of control, (b) internal, (c) external; 5. (a) self-efficacy, (b) gratification; 6. (a) trait, (b) trait, (c) factor analysis; 7. (a) five-factor model, Big Five, (b) openness, conscientiousness, extraversion, agreeableness, neuroticism; 8. (a) situations, (b) person-situation; 9. (a) genetics, (b) heritability; 10. (a) genetic factors, (b) nonshared environmental, (c) shared environmental; 11. (a) Big Five, (b) behaviors; 12. (a) 30, (b) genetic, (c) environmental; 13. (a) quantum change, (b) structured interview; 14. (a) individualistic, (b) collectivistic; 15. (a) avoid, (b) persuasion, bargaining, or compromise, (c) covert, (d) overt; 16. (a) Freud's psychodynamic theory, (b) humanistic, (c) social learning, (d) trait; 17. objective; 18. (a) Minnesota Multiphasic Personality Inventory–2, or MMPI-2, (b) abnormal; 19. Barnum.*

Newspaper Article

COMPANIES USING PERSONALITY TESTS FOR MAKING HIRES THAT FIT
by Carol Smith

1. Why do employers use personality tests to make hiring decisions?

Like a growing number of white-collar workers, Stacy McCollough discovered that an interview and a resume review are no longer the only hurdles to landing a job in today's competitive marketplace. Today, workers going for mid- and upper-level management or sales positions are increasingly likely to have to take hard-to-fool psychological exams as well.

When McCollough applied to work at a medical malpractice insurance brokerage firm, she took a two-hour test to determine how psychologically fit she was for the job. The test revealed she didn't have the aggressive traits needed to excel as a broker, but it helped the company steer her into a job that made the most of her skills.

2. If you were using the Big Five traits to design a test of potential salespeople, what might you look for?

Increasingly, companies are finding that an individual's past performance may not be the best predictor of success, because work requirements are changing so rapidly. Instead, companies are looking for new ways to assess intangible skills, such as how people work on teams, how organized they are, or how strategic they are in their thinking.

3. What are some objections to personality tests?

Although many employers like the tests, applicants aren't always as comfortable. "Some people say they think it's kind of weird—they've already made it to upper management and suddenly they're being given a test," said Barry Lawrence of the Society for Human Resource Management. "Their attitude is, 'My experience should speak for itself.'"

Most candidates, however, accept testing as part of the hiring process. And test advocates point out that sometimes testing can help a candidate overcome a lack of experience by showing he or she has the right potential for the job.

4. Why might the MMPI be ineffective in assessing job applicants?

The tests range from standard psychological profiles, or "personality tests," such as the 60-year-old Minnesota Multiphasic Personality Inventory, to specialized tests such as the Caliper Profile, which has been developed specifically for use in hiring.

While people can sometimes act their way through an interview, it's hard to fool the tests, which have built-in safeguards against cheating.

5. How would you feel if you were asked to take a personality test to land your first job after college?

They are a good reality check on how someone appears in the interview, said human resources specialist Philip Barquer. "You can't fake your character."

Source: *Los Angeles Times,* February 9, 1997.

Study Questions

A. **Social Cognitive Theory**—Why do students invest thousands of dollars and 4–6 years of hard work to obtain a college degree? (See answer in Critical Thinking Appendix.)

B. **Trait Theory**—Would knowing about the Big Five traits help you write an ad to find the perfect roommate or life mate? (See answer in Critical Thinking Appendix.)

C. **Genetic Influences on Traits**—How is it possible that, in the same family, one child may be lively and outgoing and another may be shy and withdrawn?

D. **Evaluation of Trait Theory**—Why might newlyweds discover that the person they married is not the person they thought they knew?

E. **Research Focus: 180-Degree Change**—What are some of the reasons that we should be cautious in believing self-reports of dramatic behavioral changes?

F. **Cultural Diversity: Resolving Conflicts**—What could happen when U.S. officials negotiate public trade agreements with Japanese officials? (See answer in Critical Thinking Appendix.)

G. **Four Theories of Personality**—Do you think that all four theories of personality could be or should be reduced to just one?

H. **Application: Assessment—Objective Tests**—A psychological test in a magazine promises to tell you what kind of mate is perfect for you. Can you believe it?

Web Sites & Learning Activities

- BROOKS/COLE ONLINE PSYCHOLOGY STUDY CENTER

  http://psychstudy.brookscole.com/student/plotnik/quiz/ch20frm.html

  This site gives students a chance to review material by taking quizzes and doing exercises and activities for this module.

- GREAT IDEAS IN PERSONALITY

  http://galton.psych.nwu.edu/GreatIdeas.html

  This site covers scientific research programs in personality theory, including cognitive/social learning theories and the Five-Factor Model.

- PERSONALITY THEORISTS

  http://www.wynja.com/personality/theorists.html

  This site presents papers on leading personality theorists such as Adler, Freud, Maslow, and Rogers. If you write a good paper, you can submit it for inclusion here!

- THE PERSONALITY PROJECT

  http://fas.psych.nwu.edu/personality.html

  This site includes an overview of personality research and theory, links to online articles, and a special area with advice for students interested in personality study.

- ASTROLOGY ONLINE

  http://www.astrology-online.com/zodiac.htm

  Many people believe that our personalities are determined by our astrological sign. This site describes the history of astrology and provides daily horoscopes.

Welcome to the WEB

- PERSONALITY TESTS ON THE WWW

  http://www.2h.com/Tests/personality.phtml

  This site indexes many personality tests available on the Web. While most of them have not been scientifically validated, they are fun and may give you some insight into your personality.

- A CONFLICT RESOLUTION PAGE

  http://www.geocities.com/Athens/8945/

  This site contains information on conflict resolution from psychological and political points of view, plus a bibliography and links to other references on the subject.

Activities

- *Integrator Online™ for Introductory Psychology* CD-ROM, Plotnik, Module 20

- Study Guide to accompany *Introduction to Psychology,* 5th edition, Module 20 (choice of PC or Macintosh computer version or hard copy).

- *PsychNow!* CD-ROM

Answers to questions on page 478

1. Employers use personality tests to make sure applicants have the traits necessary for the job, to avoid hiring mistakes, and to assess intangible skills.
2. They do not account for work experience, they could be flawed, and they may invade applicants' privacy.
3. Good salespeople might be high in extraversion, agreeableness, and conscientiousness.
4. The MMPI was designed to distinguish normal people from abnormal groups, and it may not produce useful information on skills and traits.
5. There is no right answer to this one—just something to think about.

A. Appraisal

Primary Appraisals

If there is no real threat to my physical survival in giving a sample of blood, why do I and millions of others overreact to the point of fainting? One answer may be obtained by questioning people about the origin of their blood fear. As was true for me, 76% reported that it began with a traumatic event (Kleinknecht, 1994). Through conditioning, this traumatic event makes the blood a powerful emotional stimulus that automatically triggers a chain of intense mental events (feelings of fear) and overactive physiological responses (changes in blood pressure to produce fainting). In my case, I was about 8 years old when I saw my father almost cut off his thumb. As I saw his hand covered with blood, I thought he was going to die. Thereafter, each time I saw blood I automatically interpreted this situation as a severe emotional threat. The initial interpretation of a potentially stressful situation is called a primary appraisal (Lazarus 1990, 1993).

Primary appraisal refers to our initial, subjective evaluation of a situation, in which we balance the demands of a potentially stressful situation against our ability to meet these demands.

For example, there can be three different primary appraisals of giving blood. If giving blood doesn't matter one way or another to your well-being, your primary appraisal is that the situation is *irrelevant* and therefore mostly nonstressful. If you're giving blood to help a friend, your primary appraisal is that the situation is *positive* and mostly nonstressful because it makes you feel good. If giving blood triggers uncontrollable fear, your primary appraisal is that the situation is *stressful,* meaning that it overtaxes your emotional and psychological recourses. Your primary appraisal that a situation is stressful involves three different interpretations: harm/loss, threat, or challenge.

Harm/Loss

If you broke your arm in a bike accident, you would know that you have suffered harm or loss.

A *harm/loss appraisal* of a situation means that you have already sustained some damage or injury.

Because a harm/loss appraisal *elicits negative emotions,* such as fear, depression, fright, and anxiety, you will feel stressed; and the more intense your negative emotions are, the more stressful and overwhelming the situation will seem.

Threat

If you have a terrible fear of giving blood and are asked to do so, you would automatically interpret giving blood as a threat to your well-being.

A *threat appraisal* of a situation means that the harm/loss has not yet taken place but you know it will happen in the near future.

Because a threat appraisal also *elicits negative emotions,* such as fear, anxiety, and anger, the situation or event may seem especially stressful. In fact, just imagining or anticipating a threatening situation, such as giving blood or taking a final exam, can be as stressful as the actual event itself.

Challenge

If you are working hard in college but find that you have to take two more classes, you might interpret taking these classes as a way to achieve a major goal—that is, you use a challenge appraisal.

A *challenge appraisal* of a situation means that you have the potential for gain or personal growth but also need to mobilize your physical energy and psychological resources to meet the challenging situation.

Because a challenge appraisal *elicits positive emotions,* such as eagerness or excitement, it is usually less stressful than a harm/loss or a threat appraisal.

Situations and Primary Appraisals

Your first reaction to potentially stressful situations, such as waiting in line, dealing with a sloppy roommate, giving blood, making a public speech, dealing with a rude salesperson, taking an exam, seeing a vicious dog, or being in a car accident, is to appraise the situation in terms of whether it harms, threatens, or challenges your physical or psychological well-being.

Making primary appraisals about complex situations, such as whether to take a certain job, get married, or go on to graduate school, may require considerable time as you think over the different ways a situation will affect you. In comparison, making primary appraisals about very emotional situations, such as taking a surprise quiz, presenting a report in class, or, in my case, giving blood, may occur quickly, even automatically (Shannon, 1994). However, not all appraisals neatly divide into harm/loss, threat, or challenge. Some primary appraisals are a combination of threat and challenge. For instance, if you are about to ask someone for a first date, you may feel threatened by the possibility of being rejected yet challenged by the chance to prove yourself. Later in this module, we'll discuss how you can change a threat appraisal into more of a challenge appraisal and thus reduce your stressful feelings. At this point, just keep in mind that making a primary appraisal is the first step in experiencing stress. Depending on the kind of primary appraisal, your level of stress may either increase or decrease.

Appraisal and Stress Level

Would it stress you to watch a bloody accident?

If you were asked to watch a film of bloody accidents caused by power-saws, how much would your primary appraisal affect your level of stress? This is exactly what researchers asked subjects to do while recording a major sign of physiological arousal, called the galvanic skin response.

The *galvanic skin response* is a measure of how much a person's hand sweats due to physiological arousal and not to normal temperature changes.

As subjects watched the accident films, they were given instructions that would result in making a primary appraisal of challenge or threat. To encourage challenge appraisals, subject were told to watch the film objectively, to consider how these accidents might be prevented, but not to identify with the injured. To encourage threat appraisals, subjects were told to put themselves in the place of men who accidentally cut off their fingers with power saws and imagine how they would feel in these situations.

As the graph below shows, subjects using threat appraisals showed significantly more physiological arousal—that is, high levels of galvanic skin responses—than subjects using challenge appraisals (Dandoy & Goldstein, 1990). Researchers concluded that in threatening or disturbing situations, your feelings of stress increase with the kind of appraisal: threat appraisals raise levels of stress more than challenge appraisals do.

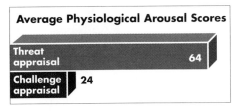

Average Physiological Arousal Scores

Threat appraisal	64
Challenge appraisal	24

However, when people are asked to identify the cause of their stressful feelings, they usually—and often incorrectly—point to a particular situation rather than to their primary appraisals. But as you'll see next, people often appraise the same situation in different ways.

Same Situation, Different Appraisals

Why isn't waiting in line always stressful?

When I ask my students, "What stresses you?" they always list a variety of situations, including many of the potentially stressful situations listed in the table below right. Notice especially how the same situation was stressful for some but not for others. For example, 65% said waiting for a late person was stressful, but 35% reported it wasn't. Similarly, 42% said looking for a parking space was stressful, but 58% said that it wasn't. Because people don't agree on which situations are stressful, researchers concluded that level of stress depends not only on the kind of situation but also on the kind of primary appraisal one makes. For example, you would appraise waiting in line to get your favorite beverage as a challenge, which elicits positive emotions. In contrast, you would appraise waiting in line to pay a parking ticket as a harm/loss or threat, which elicits negative emotions. Thus, similar situations can result in different level of stress depending upon your primary appraisals.

Situation	Percentage rating it	
	stressful	**not stressful**
Waiting for someone who is late	65	35
Being caught in traffic	63	37
Waiting in line	61	39
Waiting in a doctor's office	59	41
Waiting for the government to act	51	49
Waiting for a repair person	46	54
Looking for a parking space	42	58
Waiting for an airplane to take off	26	74

Sequence: Appraisal to Arousal

How does stress start?

The first step in feeling stress depends upon your primary appraisal, which can be one of harm/loss, threat, or challenge. In turn, harm/loss and threat appraisals elicit negative emotions, which, in turn, increase levels of stress. In comparison, challenge appraisals elicit positive emotions, which, in turn, decrease levels of stress. Thus, when you say that a situation is causing you stress, such as giving blood, taking an exam, making a public speech, changing your job, asking for a date, arguing with your boss, having to move, getting

married, or arguing with your roommate, you are forgetting that part of the stress is coming from whether you make a harm/loss or threat appraisal versus a challenge appraisal (Lazarus, 1993; Tomaka et al., 1997).

The moment after you make an appraisal, especially a harm/loss or threat appraisal, your body changes from a generally calm state into one of heightened physiological arousal as it prepares to deal with the stressor, whether it involves a car accident, a mugger, a public speech, or giving blood. We'll look inside the body and see what happens when you are stressed.

B. Physiological Responses

Psychosomatic Symptoms

What causes stomach pains?

By the end of the semester, Joan is worrying about having too many chapters to read, too many papers to write, too many tests to take, and too little time. Her worries keep her awake and make her feel anxious much of the time. But worst of all are those nagging stomach pains that don't seem to go away, even though she makes a big effort to eat healthy foods.

Joan is not too different from many students who find their psychological resources taxed to the limits by very difficult and demanding situations, such as having to work part-time, being short on funds, switching majors, taking too many units, working hard for good grades, and feeling burned out. What all these situations have in common is the potential to be appraised as threatening to one's psychological well-being and thus very stressful (Holt, 1993).

But how can worrying cause my awful stomach pains?

Each time Joan makes appraisals that cause stress, she automatically triggers the powerful fight-flight response, which transforms her body into an aroused state that is ready for action. One of the first researchers to recognize that stressful experiences trigger the fight-flight response was Hans Selye (1956, 1993). His pioneering work showed that continuing stress takes its toll on the body in the form of physical symptoms, which are called psychosomatic symptoms.

Psychosomatic (SIGH-ko-so-MAH-tik) symptoms refer to real, physical, and often painful symptoms, such as headaches, muscle pains, and stomach problems, that are caused by psychological factors, such as worry, tension, stress, and anxiety. (The word *psychosomatic* is derived from *psyche,* which means mind, and *soma,* which means body.)

In a very real sense, the constant worries going on in Joan's head were interfering with the functions of her stomach, and the result was painful digestive problems. Sometimes people think psychosomatic problems are imagined and thus not real or painful. Psychosomatic problems are real and painful because they result from the actual breakdown, damage, or irritation of body organs. Not only are psychosomatic problems real and painful, but as you'll see, they are relatively common, especially among college students whose lives are filled with worry, anxiety, and stress.

Kinds of Symptoms

Do you have any of these symptoms?

Doctors and researchers estimate that 50–80% of patients seen in general medical practice have stress-related problems (Ursin, 1997). For example, 56% of patients complaining of stomach pain were diagnosed as having psychosomatic or stress-related symptoms since no organic causes could be identified. What's interesting is that all the patients whose problems were stress-related reported that they had experienced a serious stressor (breakup of a relationship, family member leaving home) during the previous six months (Creed, 1993). Some of the more common stress-related or psychosomatic symptoms are listed below (Smith & Seidel, 1982). My students (and I) usually report having at least one of these psychosomatic symptoms.

COMMON PSYCHOSOMATIC SYMPTOMS

- **Stomach symptoms:** feelings of discomfort, pain, pressure, acid, and churning
- **Muscle pain and tension:** occurring in neck, shoulders, and back
- **Fatigue:** feeling tired or exhausted without doing physical activity
- **Headaches:** having either tension or migraine headaches
- **Intestinal difficulties:** having either constipation or diarrhea
- **Skin disorders:** exaggerated skin blemishes, pimples, oiliness
- **Eating problems:** either feeling a compulsion to eat or losing one's appetite
- **Insomnia:** having recurring bouts of being unable to get to sleep or stay asleep
- **Asthmatic** or **allergic problems:** worsening of problems
- **High blood pressure** or **heart pounding**
- **Bruxism:** grinding teeth during sleep
- **Colds or flus:** recurring problems

DEVELOPMENT OF PSYCHOSOMATIC SYMPTOMS

Researchers believe that developing a psychosomatic symptom is a three-step process.

Step 1: Genetic predisposition and lifestyle. Some of us may have a genetic predisposition for the breakdown of certain organs, such as heart, blood vessels, or stomach lining, or our lifestyle may promote poor health practices, such as smoking, being overweight, or not exercising. Either inherited predispositions or poor lifestyle practices can target certain body organs for future problems (Plomin et al., 1994).

Step 2: Prolonged stress. Some of us may be more likely than others to appraise situations as threatening, thus eliciting negative emotions and automatically triggering the fight-flight response. The continual activation of the fight-flight response produces a state of heightened physiological arousal (increased heart rate, blood pressure, and secretion of arousing hormones) that will put a strain on our body organs and immune system (Cohen, 1996).

Step 3: Psychosomatic symptoms. The interaction of body organs that are already targeted or weakened from genetic predispositions or poor lifestyle practices and prolonged physiological arousal from stressful experiences can result in a variety of psychosomatic problems (Goldberger & Breznitz, 1993).

Next, we'll examine how prolonged stressful experiences affect the body.

General Adaptation Syndrome

How can stress cause stomach pains?

One reason Joan develops psychosomatic symptoms (stomach pains) is that her continued worrying elicits fight-flight responses. The continual activation of fight-flight responses results in what Hans Selye (1993) has described as the general adaptation syndrome.

The *general adaptation syndrome* (GAS) refers to the body's reaction to stressful situations during which it goes through a series of three stages—alarm, resistance, and exhaustion—that gradually increase the chances of developing psychosomatic symptoms.

Here's how Selye's general adaptation syndrome explains Joan's problem.

1 Alarm Stage

Each time Joan worries about the two papers due next week, she appraises that situation as a terrible threat to her well-being, which in turn triggers the alarm stage.

The *alarm stage* is the initial reaction to stress and is marked by activation of the fight-flight response; in turn, the fight-flight response causes physiological arousal.

Your body may go into and out of the alarm stage (fight-flight response) many times during the day as stressful experiences come and go. Normally, you do not develop psychosomatic problems during the alarm stage because the fight-flight responses come and go. However, if stress continues for a longer period of time, your body goes into the resistance stage.

2 Resistance Stage

As the semester comes to an end, Joan's continual worries about papers and exams cause almost continual fight-flight responses, which in turn cause her body to go into the resistance stage.

The *resistance stage* is the body's reaction to continued stress during which most of the physiological responses return to normal levels but the body uses up great stores of energy.

During the resistance stage, Joan's body will use up vital reserves of hormones, minerals, and glucose (blood sugar) because her body is almost continually in the fight-flight state. Joan doesn't realize that the resistance stage is taking a toll on her stomach by interfering with digestion and causing psychosomatic symptoms—stomach pains. If her stress continues, her body will go into the exhaustion stage and her psychosomatic symptoms will increase.

3 Exhaustion Stage

As the stress of writing papers, completing assignments, and taking exams continues over many weeks, Joan's body may enter the exhaustion stage.

The *exhaustion stage* is the body's reaction to long-term, continuous stress and is marked by actual breakdown in internal organs or weakening of the infection-fighting immune system.

During the exhaustion stage, Joan's stomach problems may become more serious and painful. During extended periods of stress, such as during the final-exam period, your body may go into the stage of resistance or exhaustion. This is the time when you may come down with a variety of psychosomatic symptoms, such as colds, flu, cold sores, sore throats, allergies, aching muscles, or stomach problems. For example, researchers found that individuals with prolonged and high levels of anger were more likely to develop high blood pressure than those with normal levels (Jorgensen et al., 1996).

Next, we'll look more closely at how the mind and body interact.

Mind-Body Connection

Why do I faint?

At the beginning of this module, I told you that my fear of human blood is so intense that my just seeing or giving blood can make me faint. This is a perfect example of the mind-body connection (Benson, 1997).

The *mind-body connection* refers to how your thoughts, beliefs, and emotions can produce physiological changes that may be either beneficial or detrimental to your health and well-being.

For example, the mind-body connection explains why fearful or threatening thoughts cause about 15% of the adult population to faint at the sight of blood, needles, or injections (Kleinknecht, 1994). For these individuals (including me), fearful thoughts or appraisals trigger the fight-flight response, which greatly increases blood pressure. This is shortly followed by a rebound drop in blood pressure, which lowers blood flow to the brain and results in fainting (Roan, 1997). The mind-body connection also explains why after a prolonged period of fearful or anxious thoughts that continually trigger fight-flight responses, there may be a breakdown in body organs and development of psychosomatic symptoms (Rosch, 1994).

Continuing research on the importance and implications of the mind-body connection has given rise to a new area called mind-body therapy (Goleman & Gurin, 1993).

Mind-body therapy is based on the finding that thoughts and emotions can change physiological and immune responses. Mind-body therapy uses mental strategies, such as relaxation, meditation, and biofeedback, as well as social support groups, to help individuals change negative beliefs, thoughts and emotions to more positive ones.

At the end of this module, we'll discuss specific mind-body therapies, called stress-management programs, which help people recognize and deal with stress overload and thus prevent or get rid of painful psychosomatic symptoms.

The mind-body connection is not only responsible for the development and maintenance of psychosomatic symptoms but is also involved in the strengthening or weakening of our immune systems, which is the next topic.

B. Physiological Responses

Immune System

How often have you gotten a cold, strep throat, or some other bacterial or viral infection when final exams were over? This rather common experience of "coming down with something" when exams are over indicates how prolonged stressful experiences can decrease the effectiveness of your immune system.

The *immune system* is the body's defense and surveillance network of cells and chemicals that fight off bacteria, viruses, and other foreign or toxic substances.

As recently as ten years ago, researchers firmly believed that the immune system was a totally independent system without any input from the brain and certainly not influenced by your thoughts. In the mid-1970s, quite by chance, a psychologist and an immunologist found the first good evidence that there was a mind-body connection—that psychological factors influenced the immune system (Ader & Cohen, 1975). Their results and subsequent studies from other researchers led to the development of an entirely new area of medical science that is called psychoneuroimmunology *(SIGH-ko-nu-ro-im-you-NAWL-a-gee)*.

Psychoneuroimmunology

Researchers Ader and Cohen (1975) were trying to figure out why some of their rats were dying so young when they chanced upon one of the important scientific discoveries of the 1970s. For the previous 50 years, immunologists had believed that the immune system operated independently of outside influences. To the surprise of all and disbelief of many, Ader and Cohen reported that psychological factors influenced the immune system's functioning, a finding that challenged 50 years of thinking. Today, no one doubts their findings, which single-handedly launched the new field of psychoneuroimmunology.

Psychoneuroimmunology is the study of the relationship among three factors: the central nervous system, the endocrine system, and psychosocial factors. The central nervous system consists of the brain and spinal cord; the endocrine system is the network of glands that secrete hormones; and psychosocial factors include cognitive reactions to stressful events, the individual's personality traits, and social influences.

It is the interaction among these three factors—central nervous system, immune system, and psychosocial factors—that can suppress or strengthen the immune system and in turn make the body more or less susceptible to disease and infection (O'Leary et al., 1997). For example, researchers reported that taking exams suppressed the immune systems of medical students, which explains why students are more likely to get sick after exams (Kiecolt-Glaser & Glaser, 1989). When the immune system is not suppressed, it has several ways to kill foreign invaders. For example, in the remarkable photo above, an immune system cell actually sends out a footlike extension to engulf and destroy the small green bacterial cell (inside white oval).

What we're most interested in is how psychosocial factors, especially our reactions to stressful events, can decrease the functioning of the immune system.

Evidence for Psychoneuroimmunology

Researchers were faced with a difficult question: Why doesn't everyone who is exposed to a disease virus or bacteria actually get the disease? They tackled this question head-on by giving the same amount of cold virus to 394 subjects, all of whom were quarantined for a week. During this period, the researchers checked for symptoms of colds and related the percentage of colds to the levels of stress that subjects had reported before they received the virus. As shown in the graph below, researchers found that those individuals who reported high levels of psychological stress were significantly more likely to develop colds than were those who reported low stress levels (Cohen et al., 1997).

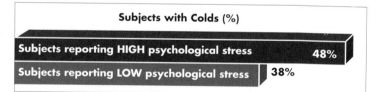

Subjects with Colds (%)

Subjects reporting HIGH psychological stress — 48%

Subjects reporting LOW psychological stress — 38%

Individuals who reported high levels of stress described their lives as somewhat unpredictable, uncontrollable, and overwhelming. Researchers concluded that, with every increase in psychological stress, there's an increased likelihood of developing a cold—provided we are exposed to the cold virus. (There is no truth to the folk wisdom that people get colds simply by being cold or damp.)

Fight-flight response. Another reason some individuals are more likely to get colds is that they are continually activating their fight-flight responses, thus decreasing the effectiveness of the immune system. When activating the fight-flight response, your body produces two groups of hormones: corticoids and catecholamines (epinephrine or adrenaline is a catecholamine.) These hormones suppress the immune system, which in turn, makes the body more susceptible to diseases, viruses, and other infections (Cohen & Williamson, 1991). Here's what happens: the more stress you feel, the more you activate your fight-flight response, the more your fight-flight response suppresses your immune system, and the more likely you are to get something (cold, virus, or other infection) (O'Leary et al., 1997). Thus, psychosocial factors can significantly increase or decrease the effectiveness of your immune system.

How psychological factors affect the immune system will become clearer as we describe a really clever experiment on animals.

There is an interesting story of a woman who was in therapy for having severe allergic reactions to flowers. The therapist was curious about what caused her allergic reaction. It could be caused either by organic factors, which refer to the physical properties of flowers, or by psychosomatic factors, which refer to thoughts, beliefs, or conditioned responses to flowers. To determine whether the cause was organic or psychosomatic, one day the therapist took a dozen red roses from under her desk, gave them to the woman, and asked her what the flowers reminded her of. The woman held them for a short time and then began to have allergic responses, including nasal congestion and tears. What the woman did not know was the flowers were artificial. Thus, the woman's allergic reaction clearly demonstrated that the cause was not organic, but psychosomatic. This

Why do artificial flowers make my nose run?

means that, through classical conditioning, flowers had become conditioned stimuli capable of eliciting a conditioned response, in this case a real allergic reaction. As the woman later explained, her husband had regularly given her flowers as a sign of affection, but now he was seeking a divorce.

Because this case study had occurred before the existence of psychoneuroimmunology, researchers seriously doubted that the independent immune system could be conditioned or influenced by purely psychological factors. Since then, many researchers have shown that the immune system, in both animals and humans, can be classically conditioned (Maier et al., 1994; O'Leary et al., 1997). We'll explain how researchers classically conditioned the immune system, which demonstrated the existence of a powerful connection between the mind and the immune system.

CLASSICAL CONDITIONING EXPERIMENT

The influence of psychological factors was cleverly shown when researchers demonstrated that the immune system could be classically conditioned in rats. As you may remember from Module 9, classical conditioning involves changing a neutral stimulus, such as a flashing light or a humming fan, into a conditioned stimulus that can elicit a conditioned response, in this case an allergic reaction in a rat. Here's how an immune response—allergic reaction—was classically conditioned in rats.

Conditioned stimuli: flashing light and humming fan.

Unconditioned stimulus: injection of a substance that produces allergy.

Unconditioned response: allergic reaction elicited by injected substance.

1 For the first three trials, each rat was first presented with two conditioned (neutral) stimuli, a light flashing and a fan humming. A short time later, each rat was given an injection of an allergic-producing substance, which was the unconditioned stimulus. In turn, the unconditioned stimulus elicited an allergic reaction, which was the unconditioned response.

2 On the fourth trial the animals were divided into two groups: control and experimental groups.

Control group received a trial with the regular sequence: flashing light and fan humming, then the injection of the substance, which elicited the allergic reaction.

Experimental group of rats received a different trial: rats were exposed only to the conditioned stimuli of flashing light and fan humming, with no injection.

3 The *experimental group* of animals showed a conditioned response, which means that just being given or exposed to the conditioned stimuli (flashing light and humming fan) caused the allergic reaction, which is the *conditioned response.*

4 **Discussion.** During classical conditioning, animals or people learn that the neutral or conditioned stimulus signals or predicts what will happen next. In this study, rats learned that the flashing light and humming fan predicted an allergic reaction. And in fact, by the fourth trial, the conditioned stimuli (light and fan) alone elicited the allergic reaction—the conditioned response. Researchers concluded that the psychological factors can trigger an allergic reaction in animals (MacQueen et al., 1989).

5 **Conclusion.** The amazing fact that immune responses can be conditioned demonstrates a method through which purely psychological or cognitive factors can affect immune function. Although the immune system was originally thought to act independently, it is now known that psychological factors influence the immune system in both animals and humans (Maier et al., 1994).

These findings in rats explain why the woman had an allergic reaction to artificial flowers: the artificial flowers had become conditioned stimuli that, by themselves, could elicit conditioned responses—in this case, allergic reactions of congestion and running eyes.

The history of psychoneuroimmunology reads like a mystery story. For 50 years, researchers had written in stone that the immune system was totally independent and only a fool would believe otherwise. In the early 1970s, Ader the psychologist and Cohen the immunologist were studying something entirely different (why animals were dying prematurely) when they discovered the reason was that the animals' immune systems had been weakened through classical conditioning (Ader & Cohen, 1975). This revolutionary finding meant the immune system could be influenced by psychological factors, and this lead to the birth of a whole new field, called psychoneuroimmunology (O'Leary et al., 1997).

We have discussed how stressful experiences trigger the fight-flight response and affect the immune system. Next, we examine which situations are the most likely to become stressful.

C. Stressful Experiences

Kinds of Stressors

What are Sandra's stressors?

We began this module with a description of Sandra's busy day as single mother and college student: she gets up at 6:30 A.M., wakes her two children, yells for them to get dressed, rushes to get her kids on the school bus, panics when she can't find her paper that's due today, and speeds out the door to make her first class. Every day of Sandra's life is filled with small annoyances that are called hassles, which can add up to make what she would probably call "a very bad day."

Besides dealing with daily hassles, Sandra has also gone through a number of major life changes: she left her husband; quit using drugs; began group therapy; did well in a community college; and went on to Wellesley College. Unlike hassles, which seem relatively small, major life events have had a significant impact on Sandra's life and can be very big stressors.

Both hassles and major life events have the potential to become stressful experiences that influence mood and development of psychosomatic problems.

Hassles

When someone asks, "And how was your day?" you usually reply with a list of hassles.

Hassles are those small, irritating, frustrating events that we face daily and that we usually appraise or interpret as stressful experiences.

The different kinds and number of hassles are usually measured with questionnaires that ask about work, time pressures, health, friends, interpersonal relationships, and financial status (Setterlind & Larsson, 1995). The reason researchers measure hassles is that the score on a hassle scale is a reasonably good predictor of a person's daily mood, perceived level of stress, and development of future psychosomatic symptoms (Miller, 1993; Sorbi et al., 1996). For example, researchers have found that an increase in number of daily hassles predict a decrease in one's daily mood, daily health, and overall health

status (Miller, 1993; Wu & Lam, 1993). The opposite of a hassle is a wonderful experience called an uplift.

Uplifts are those small, pleasurable, happy, and satisfying experiences that we have in our daily lives.

In contrast to hassles, researchers have found that increased daily uplifts are associated with less depression and better functioning (Kanner & Feldman, 1991). If you were to keep a record of your daily hassles and uplifts, you would probably discover that hassles, which put you in a bad mood, may far outnumber uplifts, which put you in a good mood. One obvious way to decrease your daily stress is to pay more attention to and enjoy the uplifts while trying to reduce hassles.

Another source of stress comes from major life events.

Major Life Events

Most would agree that events such as the death of a spouse, getting divorced or married, or being fired from work are major life events.

Major life events are potentially disturbing, troubling, or disruptive situations, both positive and negative, that we appraise as having a significant impact on our lives.

Researchers reasoned that people who face a large number of major life events would experience increasing levels of stress, which might increase the frequency of psychosomatic problems. For this reason, researchers developed a way to measure life chances, which is called the Social Readjustment Rating Scale (Holmes & Rahe, 1967). Take a moment to read the recently updated Social Readjustment Rating Scale on the right, which is a shortened version of the original 44-item list (Miller & Rahe, 1997).

As you read this list, notice any of these many major life events you may have experienced during the past year. Each number refers to the expected impact that the event would have on one's life; death of one's spouse has the maximum value (119). To obtain your score, add the numbers associated with each event you experienced in the last year. The total reflects how much life change you have experienced. In the updated scale, events in a six-month period that total

SOCIAL READJUSTMENT RATING SCALE

Life event	Mean value
Death of spouse	119
Divorce	98
Death of close family member	92
Fired at work	79
Personal injury or illness	77
Death of a close friend	70
Pregnancy	66
Change in financial state	56
Change in work conditions	51
Marriage	50
Sex difficulties	45
Change in living conditions	42
Change in residence	41
Beginning or ending school	38
Great personal achievement	37
Change in school	35
Trouble with boss	29
Revision of personal habits	27
Change in sleeping habits	26
Vacation	25
Minor violations of the law	22

over 300 and events in a one-year period that total over 500 indicate high recent life stress and a greatly increased risk of developing psychosomatic problems (Miller & Rahe, 1997). Researchers do report a modest correlation ($+0.20$ to $+0.30$) between number of major life events experienced and development of psychosomatic symptoms (Johnson & Roberts, 1995).

One problem with the Social Readjustment Rating Scale is that it makes no distinction between appraisal of positive events (getting married) and negative events (getting divorced). More recent scales found that the appraisal of negative life events was more important in predicting illnesses than were positive events (Sarason et al., 1985).

Measuring major life events as well as daily hassles are two ways of assessing your current level of stress. Researchers generally find that as your level of stress rises, so does your chance of developing psychosomatic symptoms as well as a bad mood (Kaplan & Damphousse, 1997).

One particular characteristic of major life events and hassles that makes them such potentially stressful experiences is that they are generally frustrating experiences. We'll discuss frustration and its long-term effects.

Situational Stressors

We're going to examine three situations—being frustrated, feeling burnt out, and experiencing interpersonal violence—that have the potential to be highly stressful. What can make these situations especially stressful is they can all elicit very negative emotions, which can greatly increase levels of stress.

Frustration

Don Nelson (right photo), former coach of the professional basketball team, the Golden State Warriors, checked into a hospital complaining of exhaustion. To reduce his stress, he was forced to take a month-long vacation. Los Angeles District Attorney William Hodgman was forced to take a break from the famous O. J. Simpson murder trial when he experienced chest pains after working "eighteen-hour days" (Hancock et al., 1995). These two examples illustrate the difficulties of having an occupation where success is judged by whether you win or lose, and losing can be very frustrating.

Frustration is the feeling that results when your attempts to reach some goal are blocked.

You may be blocked from reaching a goal because of *personal limitations,* such as losing your temper, making dumb mistakes on an exam, or not having the skills to pass a course.

Or you may be blocked from reaching a goal because of *social* or *environmental limitations,* such as having to work eighteen-hour days. One reason frustrating situations may seem especially stressful is because they seem to be out of your control (Goldberger & Breznitz, 1993).

Negative emotions. As soon as one of your goals is blocked, you experience frustration, which in turn elicits very negative emotions, such as anger, anxiety, or fear. In turn, these negative emotional feelings trigger the fight-flight response, which causes increased physiological arousal and further increases in stressful feelings. For all these reasons, frustrating situations take a great toll on our bodies and our moods.

Most of us experience daily frustration. If the frustration extends over a long period of time, we may experience burnout.

Burnout

Nurses, lawyers, police officers, social workers, managers, counselors, teachers, and others whose job demands intense involvement with people suffer a relatively high rate of burnout (Pines, 1993).

Burnout refers to feelings of doing poorly at one's job, physically wearing out, and becoming emotionally exhausted due to the intense involvement with people who demand too much of one's time and energy and provide too little reward or satisfaction.

Burnout is accompanied by intense feelings and negative emotions that trigger the fight-flight response, keep the body in a continual stage of heightened physiological arousal, and cause most of the psychosomatic symptoms that we have discussed: stomach disorders, frequent and

prolonged colds, headaches, sleep problems, muscular pain (especially lower back and neck), and chronic fatigue (Pines, 1993).

Idealistic people who desire to help and give are the most susceptible to burnout, while cynical people who want to succeed at whatever cost are least likely to burn out (Pines, 1993).

College counselors report that burnout often causes students to drop out of college before they obtain their degrees. Counselors suggest that before students decide to drop out they should consider ways to reduce their work and class load so that life and school seem less overwhelming and more manageable (Leafgren, 1989).

The next situation is so stressful that it leaves a terrible, lasting mark that may trigger years of problems.

Interpersonal Violence

The one situation that can produce horrible psychological after effects and nightmares involves experiencing interpersonal violence and can result in posttraumatic stress disorder.

Posttraumatic stress disorder or *PTSD* is a disabling condition that results from personally experiencing an event that involves actual or threatened death or serious injury or from witnessing such an event or hearing of such an event happening to a family member or close friend. People suffering from PTSD experience a number of psychological symptoms, including recurring and disturbing memories, terrible nightmares, and intense fear and anxiety (American Psychiatric Association, 1994).

For example, about 32% of women report having PTSD after being raped; about 15% of soldiers report having

PTSD after serving in war; and about 15% of people report having PTSD after being in a natural disaster or serious car accident (Foa & Meadows, 1997). These horrible memories and feelings of fear keep stress levels high and result in a wide range of psychosomatic symptoms, including sleep problems, pounding heart, high blood pressure, and stomach problems (Murberg, 1994).

The treatment of posttraumatic stress disorder involves providing emotional support so victims can begin the healing process, slowly eliminating the horrible memories by bringing out the details of the experience and gradually replacing the feeling of fear with a sense of courage to go on with one's life (Foa & Meadows, 1997).

We'll examine two more situations with high potential for stress because they involve conflict or anxiety.

D. Personality & Social Factors

Hardiness

How can he work 12 hours a day, every day?

The door opens. Dr. Michael DeBakey enters and walks quickly to the operating table. His assistants have already opened the patient's chest and removed the diseased heart. With the skill and precision of a master, DeBakey (below photo) transplants a healthy donor heart into the patient's chest. It takes about an hour. When DeBakey finishes, he leaves the operating suite and goes to the scrub room. He takes off his operating clothes, scrubs down, and puts on clean, sterilized clothes. In a matter of minutes, he enters another operating suite, and the whole process starts over. In a normal working day, DeBakey operates on five to nine patients. He normally spends 12–15 hours a day, seven days a week, in the hospital and performs as many heart operations in one month as most surgeons do in a year. There is one more thing you should know about DeBakey. He is over 80 years old (*San Diego Tribune,* November 27, 1987).

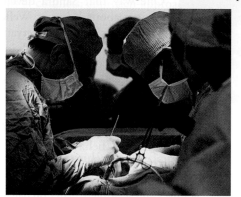

There are two primary reasons Dr. Michael DeBakey functions so successfully in such a potentially stressful environment. The first is that he appraises these situations—doing complicated heart transplants—as challenges rather than as threats. The advantage of *challenge appraisals* is that they help a person focus on making particular decisions or solving particular problems. In turn, problem-focused coping brings out positive feelings and emotions, such as excitement and eagerness, which help reduce stress levels. In contrast, *threat appraisals* elicit negative emotional feelings, such as fear or anxiety, which raise levels of stress. Because emotion-focused coping is directed at managing negative emotional feelings, the person isn't motivated to solve his or her problem.

A second reason DeBakey functions so well is that he has a winning combination of personality factors that help him perform under great stress. Specifically, he has what is known as a hardy personality.

Definition

Why is it that certain people, like Dr. DeBakey, seem to handle stressful situations better than others? This was exactly the question researchers asked as they studied the personality characteristics of middle- and upper-level executives and lawyers who had experienced considerable stress in the previous three years (Kobasa, 1982; Kobasa et al., 1982a, b). Researchers discovered that those executives and lawyers who stayed healthy in spite of stressful life situations had three personality traits, which, taken together, were labeled hardiness.

Hardiness is a combination of three personality traits—control, commitment, and challenge—that protect or buffer us from the potentially harmful effects of stressful situations and reduce our chances of developing psychosomatic illnesses.

From what we know of Dr. DeBakey, he appears to be the perfect example of a hardy person who has the three Cs—control, commitment, and challenge. For example, his world-wide medical reputation shows he has *commitment,* which means he knows and pursues his goals and values. His desire to do open-heart surgery shows he likes a *challenge,* which means he actively confronts and solves problem situations. His role as head of surgery indicates his desire to be in *control*, which means he believes that his actions directly affect how situations turn out.

Being hardy gives people a real edge in dealing with potentially stressful situations.

Function

What would happen to your heart rate if you were told that you had to listen to a 4-minute lecture and then repeat it to two professors, who would grade your performance?

This is exactly what male college students were told while their heart rates were being recorded. Researchers predicted that hardy students (those who scored higher in control, commitment, and challenge) would appraise this situation as more challenging and less threatening than would students who were less hardy.

In the graph on the right, notice that both low and high hardy subjects had similar heart rates during rest. (Heart rate changes are good indicators of physiological arousal and stress levels.) However, as soon as students were put into a potentially stressful situation, (told about repeating a lecture), low hardy subjects' heart rates shot up significantly higher than did those of high hardy subjects. And low hardy subjects' heart rates remained higher after the stressor while high hardy subjects calmed down more. These data indicate that high hardy subjects appraised the potentially stressful task as more challenging and less threatening (Wiebe, 1991).

Generally, hardiness is a personality factor that functions to decrease the chances of developing psychosomatic symptoms and to increase protection against the harmful and physiologically arousing effects of stress (Wiebe & Smith, 1997).

Researchers have especially studied control, one of the three traits composing hardiness, because feelings of being in control reduces stressful feelings.

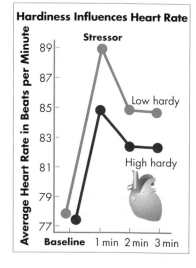

Hardiness Influences Heart Rate

Average Heart Rate in Beats per Minute

Stressor

Low hardy

High hardy

89
87
85
83
81
79
77

Baseline   1 min   2 min   3 min

Locus of Control

Why can waiting be such a hassle?

A daily hassle that most of us hate is being made to wait for something, such as a doctor's appointment, red light, salesperson, late friend, or bus. One reason we find waiting so stressful is that we have little or no control in this situation. How much psychological control you feel you have over a situation is a personal belief that is called locus of control.

Locus of control represents a continuum: at one end is the belief that you are basically in control of life's events and that what you do influences the situation; this belief is called an internal locus of control. At the other end is the belief that chance and luck mostly determine what happens and that you do not have much influence; this belief is called an external locus of control.

What's the use of studying when I do poorly on exams?

Most of us lie somewhere along the locus of control continuum, rather than being at one end or the other (Carducci, 1998). For example, when students discuss how much their studying affects their grades, they are, to a large extent, talking about their locus of control, which in turn affects their stress level.

External locus of control. "No matter how much I study, it never seems to help," says a student with an external locus of control. This student will likely appraise exams and papers as less of a challenge and more of a threat appraisal, which in turn will generate negative emotions (fear, anxiety, anger) and increase stress levels.

Internal locus of control. "If I study hard and apply myself, I can get good grades," says a student with an internal locus of control. This student will likely appraise exams and papers less as threats and more as challenges, which in turn will generate positive emotions (excitement, enthusiasm) and decrease stress levels. This means that students with internal locus of control have lower levels of stress and, as a result, report fewer psychosomatic symptoms than those with external locus of control (Wiebe & Smith, 1997).

An example of how locus of control relates to psychosomatic symptoms is shown on the right. In this study, subjects with an external locus of con-

Illness Score

High controllability	1,100
Low controllability	1,850

trol perceived situations as uncontrollable, which led to increased levels of stress that were associated with significantly more psychosomatic symptoms (they developed more physical illnesses). In comparison, subjects with an internal locus of control appraised situations as less stressful and developed fewer psychosomatic symptoms (Stern et al., 1982). From many studies on locus of control, we learn that our personality traits influence our appraisal (more or less threatening), which, in turn, increase or decrease our feelings of stress and our chances of developing psychosomatic symptoms.

Another personality trait that can influence stress levels is how much negative affect or emotion one has.

Optimism versus Pessimism

Why is it better to be an optimist?

One reason it's better to be an optimist is that you'll have more positive thoughts, which lead to making more challenging than threatening appraisals and experiencing more positive than negative emotions.

Optimism is a relatively stable personality trait that leads to believing and expecting that good things will happen (Scheier & Carver, 1992). *Pessimism* is a relatively stable personality trait that leads to believing and expecting that bad things will happen.

Optimists. Because optimistic students expect good things will happen, they are likely to use problem-focused coping, which means that they use their energy to solve rather than complain about problems (Scheier & Carver, 1992). Researchers found that optimists reported lower stress levels and decreased psychosomatic symptoms (Weibe & Smith, 1997).

Pessimists. Because pessimistic students expect bad things to happen, they are likely to use emotion-focused coping, which means they use their energy to deal with their negative emotions and avoid rather than solve the underlying problems causing their stress (Scheier & Carver, 1992).

My job has turned me into a real pessimist.

Negative emotions. Being a pessimist is also associated with negative emotions, such as anger, hostility, rage, fear or anxiety. Numerous studies associate pessimism and negative emotions with increasing stress levels, decreasing functioning of the immune system, and a wide range of psychosomatic symptoms such as high blood pressure, heart problems, headaches, allergies, and stomach problems (Arena et al., 1997; Gullette et al., 1997; Wiebe & Smith, 1997).

For example, researchers found that men with high levels of negative emotions, such as anger, were four times more likely to suffer sudden heart death. Patients were more likely to die during the next eight months if they had a pessimistic attitude toward treatment and recovery from cancer (Kawachi et al., 1994; Schulz, 1994). In comparison, optimistic patients who received heart transplants reported more positive emotions and dealt better with setbacks than patients with a pessimistic outlook (Leedham et al., 1995).

During the past 10 years, a number of personality factors, such as optimism/pessimism, locus of control, and hardiness, have been associated with increasing or decreasing stress levels and increasing or decreasing chances of developing psychosomatic symptoms (Wiebe & Smith, 1997).

Next, we'll examine one particular combination of personality traits that has been labeled Type A behavior, which has been associated with increasing the chances of having a heart attack.

D. Personality & Social Factors

Type A Behavior

What goes into Type A behavior?

In the mid-1970s, a new expression—"You're a Type A person"—was coined when two doctors published the book *Type A Behavior and Your Heart* (Friedman & Rosenman, 1974). At that time, the best-known risk factors associated with developing heart disease were diet, exercise, and smoking. This book startled the medical world by describing a combination of personality traits that made up a psychological risk factor, which was called Type A behavior. No one had ever before suggested that any psychological factor could possibly influence getting heart disease. Even though the term has remained the same, the description of exactly what makes up Type A behavior has changed during the past 25 years. We'll describe the interesting search for what makes up Type A behavior and what it means today.

1970s: Type A Behavior—Impatient, Hostile, Workaholic

Well begin with the original 1970s definition of Type A behavior (Friedman & Rosenman, 1974).

Type A behavior referred to a combination of personality traits that included an overly competitive and aggressive drive to achieve, a hostile attitude when frustrated, a habitual sense of time urgency, a rapid and explosive pattern of speaking, and being a workaholic. *Type B behavior* was characterized by being easygoing, calm, relaxed, and patient.

The reason Type A behavior made such a big scientific splash was that compared to Type B's, Type A's were found to have experienced two to three times as many heart attacks. By 1978, Type A behavior was officially recognized as an independent risk factor for heart disease by a National Institutes of Health panel.

However, at about the same time that Type A behavior was declared a risk factor, researchers began having trouble replicating earlier findings and began to seriously question the definition of Type A behavior.

1980s: Type A Behavior—Depressed, Angry, Competitive

In the late 1970s and throughout most of the 1980s, researchers ran into a number of problems with the original description of Type A behavior. In particular, a number of large-scale studies failed to replicate the earlier and revolutionary finding that Type A behavior was a risk factor for the onset of heart disease. Researchers thought the reason for this failure was that the original definition of Type A behavior wasn't quite accurate.

The 1970s definition of Type A behavior included being hurried, impatient, and a workaholic, but researchers found that coronary disease was not associated with being impatient or a workaholic, so both traits were dropped from the new definition (Booth-Kewley & Friedman, 1987; Matthews & Haynes, 1986).

Type A behavior was defined in the 1980s as being depressed, aggressively competitive, easily frustrated, anxious, and angry, or some combination of these traits.

Despite using this new and improved definition, researchers analyzed 83 relevant studies but reported only a modest association between Type A behavior and heart disease (Booth-Kewley & Friedman, 1987). These data again raised the question of whether Type A behavior is a risk factor for coronary heart disease (Miller et al., 1991). And that brings us to the 1990s.

1990s: Type A Behavior—Hostile, Angry

A review of about 100 relevant Type A behavior studies between 1983 and 1992 led one researcher to conclude that the relationship between Type A behavior and cardiac disease is so low as to have no practical meaning and that Type A behavior is no longer a valid or useful concept (Myrtek, 1995). Because of the continuing failure to replicate the original relationship, researchers have again redefined Type A behavior.

The 1990s definition of *Type A behavior* specifies an individual who feels angry and hostile much of the time but may or may not express these emotions publicly.

In support of the new definition, researchers found that behavioral ratings for hostility were reasonably good predictors of heart disease. Also, hostile people experience more stress and receive less social support (Helmers et al., 1995; Wiebe & Smith, 1997). It is too early to know if these data can be replicated.

2000s: Type A Behavior—????

Some researchers remain steadfast in the belief that there is a relationship between Type A behavior (defined as hostility and anger) and heart disease, although only a few recent studies have reported this relationship (Friedman et al., 1994; Rosenthal, 1993). Other researchers believe that different personality characteristics may be involved in Type A behavior. For example, based on animal studies, some researchers believe that the drive for social dominance may be a more reliable psychological risk factor for heart disease (Morell, 1996). At this point, researchers do not entirely agree on exactly what is Type A behavior, but many are still convinced that psychological risk factors will be found that influence the development of heart disease and other illnesses (Wiebe & Smith, 1997).

Research on Type A behavior was the first to recognize personality factors as risk factors for diseases. Now researchers are also looking at how various social factors increase or decrease the effects of stressful experiences.

Social Support

Do friends help you deal with stress?

In the small town of Roseto, Pennsylvania, people were relatively obese and ate a lot of animal fat. They smoked as much and exercised as little as residents of other neighboring towns. Despite the citizens' awful diet and lifestyle—obvious risk factors for developing heart disease—only one man in 1,000 died of a heart attack, compared with a national rate of 3.5 per 1,000, and the rates for women were even lower. Citizens of Roseto also had lower rates for ulcers and emotional problems compared with rates in the rest of the United States and their neighboring towns. This puzzling question—why the citizens of Roseto should enjoy such good physical and mental health in the face of obvious risk factors—was answered by a study of the town's social order. "One striking feature did set Roseto apart from its neighbors," says Stewart Wolf, vice president for medical affairs at St. Luke's Hospital in Bethlehem, Pennsylvania, and a principal investigator of the Roseto phenomenon. "We found that family relationships were extremely close and mutually supportive, and this wonderful social support system extended to neighbors and to the community as a whole" (Greenberg, 1978, p. 378). But the story of Roseto does not have a happy ending.

As families of Roseto prospered, they moved into larger and finer homes in the countryside, and their social support system began to break down. Families no longer had helpful friends for neighbors, which meant fewer family and friendly get-togethers and far less social support. One of the most interesting and deadly findings was that with the breakdown in social support came an increase in heart attacks, especially in younger men. This study on families in Roseto was one of the first to suggest that dealing with stress and overcoming health risks was in large part due to one's social support.

We're always helping one another.

Social support refers to three factors: having a group or network of family or friends who provide strong social attachments; being able to exchange helpful resources among family or friends; and feeling, or making appraisals, that we have supportive relationships and behaviors.

Thirty years ago, no one would have blamed loneliness and lack of social support for contributing to illness and psychosomatic symptoms. Today, study after study points to the importance of social support in helping individuals use their resources to decrease the effects of stressful situations (Ornish, 1998). We'll discuss several studies that illustrate how social support buffers us from stress and helps maintain our mental health.

Buffer Against Stress

Many of us have asked for help in solving a variety of problems, which range from feeling lonely to needing to borrow money. In these troublesome situations, social support helps us cope with stress by giving us confidence, raising our self-esteem, and increasing our feelings of self-worth, which in turn promote and maintain psychological adjustment.

For example, many of you have experienced the common psychosomatic symptom of a pounding heart while having to speak in public. Researchers wondered if the presence of a supportive person would buffer or decrease the stressful experience of college students who were asked to do public speaking. Changes in stress levels were

assessed by measuring changes in blood pressure, which increases dramatically during the fight-flight response that is triggered by stressful situations.

The graph on the left shows that students speaking in public with no supportive person present had almost double the increase in blood pressure compared to that of students who spoke in public with a supportive person present (Lepore et al., 1993). From this and similar studies, researchers concluded that social support, such as the help, advice, sympathy, and reassurance from family or friends, can decrease effects of stressful experiences (Ornish, 1998).

Change in Blood Pressure (mm Hg)

Social support — 15
No social support — 28

Maintaining Mental Health

One reason we tell a friend or family member about how our day went and the problems we had is that the telling elicits support and sympathy, which make us feel better (Kowalski, 1996). Besides making us feel better, researchers wondered if social support would also help prevent individuals who already had mild psychiatric symptoms, such as anxiety or depression, from getting worse. In a 10-year study, researchers interviewed the same individuals several times to see how social support affected levels of anxiety or depression.

The graph on the right shows that individuals with strong social support had a low chance of worsening psychiatric symptoms even if they had faced two to six stressful life events in the previous year. In comparison, individuals with a weak social support system had

a significantly greater chance of worsening anxiety or depression. Researchers concluded that a good social support system, such as having one or more close friends or neighbors, decreases the effects of stressful life events, prevents the worsening of anxiety and depression, and thus helps maintain a person's mental health (Dalgard et al., 1995).

These kinds of studies indicate that social support functions to protect or buffer us from the potentially harmful effects of stressful life events and daily hassles. Thus, in a very real sense, a good social support system facilitates our maintaining good mental health and protects us from developing illnesses and psychosomatic symptoms (Ornish, 1998).

Probability of Developing Psychiatric Symptoms

Strong social support — 0.03
Weak social support — 0.16

CONCEPT REVIEW

1. The cognitive and behavioral efforts that we use to manage a situation that we have appraised as exceeding, straining, or taxing our personal resources are referred to as _____.

2. Our initial, subjective evaluation of a situation, in which we balance environmental demands against our ability to meet them, is referred to as _____. We may appraise the situation in three ways: as irrelevant, positive, or stressful.

3. If we appraise a situation as stressful, we go on to determine whether it represents (a)_____, _____, or _____. If our primary appraisal is one of harm/loss or threat, we will experience more (b)_____ than if our appraisal is one of challenge, because harm/loss or threat appraisals elicit (c)_____ emotions.

4. A combination of physiological responses that arouse and prepare the body for action is referred to as the (a)_____ response. This response begins in a part of the brain called the (b)_____, which triggers the (c)_____ division of the autonomic nervous system. This response is especially triggered by threat appraisals.

5. Real and painful physical symptoms that are caused by psychological factors, such as our reactions to stress, are called _____ symptoms.

6. A series of three stages—alarm, resistance, and exhaustion—that the body goes through in dealing with stress is referred to as the (a)_____. The alarm stage is our initial reaction to stress and is marked by activation of the (b)_____. The resistance stage is the body's reaction to continued stress and is marked by most physiological responses returning to (c)_____ levels. The exhaustion stage is the body's reaction to long-term, continuous stress and is marked by the actual breakdown or weakening of (d)_____.

7. The body's defense and surveillance network of cells and chemicals that fight off bacteria, viruses, and other foreign matter is called the _____ system.

8. The study of how three factors—the central nervous system, the endocrine system, and psychosocial factors—interact to affect the immune system is called _____.

9. Potentially disturbing, troubling, or disruptive situations—both positive and negative—that we appraise as having considerable impact on our lives are called (a)_____ events. In comparison, those small, irritating, frustrating events that we face in our daily lives are called (b)_____ and those small, pleasurable, daily experiences that make us feel happy are called (c)_____.

10. When our attempts to reach some goal are blocked, the feeling we have is called (a)_____. The feeling of doing poorly at one's job, physically wearing out, and becoming emotionally exhausted due to intense involvement with people is called (b)_____. The problem arising from direct personal experience of an event that involves actual or threatened death or serious injury or from witnessing such an event, or hearing of such an event happening to a family member or close friend is called (c)_____.

11. There are three general kinds of conflict. A single situation that has both pleasurable and disagreeable aspects is called (a)_____ conflict; choosing between two options that both have pleasurable consequences is called (b)_____ conflict; choosing between two options that both have disagreeable consequences is called (c)_____ conflict.

12. We can become anxious in at least three different ways. If an emotional response is classically conditioned to a previously neutral stimulus, this procedure results in a (a)_____ response. If we become anxious through watching and do not perform any observable behavior or receive a reinforcer, this is called (b)_____ learning. If we become anxious because of unconscious conflicts between the id and superego, this is (c)_____ explanation of anxiety.

13. A combination of three personality traits—control, commitment, and challenge—that protect or buffer us from the potentially harmful effects of stressful situations and reduce our chances of developing psychosomatic illness is referred to as (a)_____. The belief that you are basically in control of life's events and that what you do influences the situation is called an (b)_____ locus of control. The belief that chance and luck mostly determine what happens is called an (c)_____ locus of control.

14. If we have family or friends who provide strong social attachments, if we can exchange helpful resources among friends, and if we appraise our relationships as supportive, we would be said to have strong _____.

Answers: *1. stress or stressful; 2. primary appraisal; 3. (a) harm/loss, threat, challenge, (b) stress, (c) negative; 4. (a) fight-flight, (b) hypothalamus, (c) sympathetic; 5. psychosomatic; 6. (a) general adaptation syndrome, (b) fight-flight response, (c) normal, (d) internal organs or the immune system; 7. immune; 8. psychoneuroimmunology; 9. (a) major life, (b) hassles, (c) uplifts; 10. (a) frustration, (b) burnout, (c) posttraumatic stress disorder; 11. (a) approach-avoidance, (b) approach-approach, (c) avoidance-avoidance; 12. (a) conditioned emotional, (b) observational, (c) Freud's; 13. (a) hardiness, (b) internal, (c) external; 14. social support.*

Appraisal

Sooner or later, every couple gets into an argument, as Bill and Susan did (photo right). Susan complained about a small thing—Bill's getting home late once again—but Bill was grumpy from having a bad day and said that he didn't want to talk about it. Bill's reply made Susan angrier, and she made a few more complaints that made Bill grumpier, and so it went. The reason Bill and Susan's argument became very stressful is that it involved all the things we have discussed: conflict, frustration, negative emotional feelings (anger, fear, rage, hurt, depression), and activation of the fight-flight response that increases physiological arousal and intensifies feelings. The reason Bill and Susan's argument quickly grew in intensity was that Bill's primary appraisal of Susan's complaints threatened his feelings. Because Bill's primary

appraisal of Susan's complaints was one of threat, this triggered negative emotions, increased his stress, and left him deciding what to do next, which is called secondary appraisal.

Secondary appraisal involves deciding to deal with a potentially stressful situation by using one or both of two different coping patterns: problem-focused coping means doing something about the problem, while emotion-focused coping means dealing with our emotions.

Which coping strategy Bill and Sandra adopt during their argument—that is, whether they use problem-focused or emotion-focused coping—will affect how their argument gets resolved and what happens to their levels of stress (Lazarus, 1993). We'll examine each coping strategy in more detail to show how it may increase or decrease stress levels.

Problem-Focused versus Emotion-Focused Coping

As Susan and Bill's argument begins, each makes a secondary appraisal of whether to cope with this potentially stressful situation by choosing one of two coping strategies, either problem-focused or emotion-focused coping. If Bill or Susan stopped arguing and agreed instead to try to change the situation, they would be using problem-focused coping.

Problem-focused coping means we solve the problem by seeking information, changing our own behavior, or taking whatever action is necessary.

For example, if Bill were to agree with Susan's complaint and try to find ways to avoid being late, he would be using problem-focused coping. If Susan agreed to interpret Bill's being late as something he cannot always control and something she should not get angry about, she would be using problem-focused coping. However, if they don't use problem-focused coping, their argument

is likely to end with Susan's getting angry and Bill's becoming grumpy, both of them using emotion-focused coping.

Emotion-focused coping means that we primarily do things to deal with our emotional distress, such as seeking support and sympathy, or avoiding or denying the situation.

For example, Bill may deal with his grumpiness by using emotion-focused coping, such as going to a sports bar to watch television with his friends. Susan may deal with her hurt feelings by using emotion-focused coping, such as calling her friends to get sympathy. Notice that emotion-focused coping helps Bill and Sandra deal with hurt or angry feelings in the short term but does not solve the basic problem. Only by using problem-focused coping, which means dealing with Susan's complaint, will Susan and Bill solve the problem and avoid future arguments over the same issue (Lazarus, 1993).

Choosing a Coping Strategy

Suppose you're in a relationship and your partner complains about something you do. Which coping strategy you choose depends partly upon the situation and partly on your personality (Lazarus, 1990).

One personality factor that influences whether you primarily use problem-focused or emotion-focused coping is how much *control* you believe you have over the situation. For example, if you appraise a situation such as not being late as being under your control, you can primarily use problem-focused coping to deal with the situation. On the other hand, if you appraise a situation such as dealing with your partner's complaints as being out of your control, you may first need to use primarily emotion-focused coping to manage your negative emotional state. Once you calm down, you can then use problem-focused coping to take some

direct action to solve the basic problem, which often involves changing some undesirable behavior.

The more frustrating situations are, the more likely you will need to use both emotion-focused and problem-focused coping (Lazarus, 1993). For example, in dealing with the breakup of a relationship, you may need to use emotion-focused coping to deal with your hurt feelings and problem-focused coping to keep your life going and decide on how to meet someone new. Similarly, in dealing with finals, you may need to use emotion-focused coping to deal with test anxiety and problem-focused coping to arrange time for studying. Perhaps the biggest mistake people make in dealing with stressful situations is that they primarily use emotion-focused coping, which is only a short-term solution. To get to the cause of a problem, you need to use problem-focused coping, which is a long-term solution for reducing stress levels (Wiebe & Smith, 1997).

F. Research Focus: Coping with Trauma
How Do People Cope with Severe Burns?

What can we learn from burn victims?

We have discussed stress and coping in general, and now we turn to the specific case of Harold Dennis. It was late at night, and Harold had fallen asleep in the school bus, which was returning from a trip to an amusement park. Out of nowhere came a pickup truck, traveling the wrong way on the freeway, and it drove head-on into the bus. Later, it was found that the truck driver was drunk. The bus burst into flames, and before Harold could be pulled out the back, he suffered severe burns to his face. At the young age of 13, Harold would need to cope with terrible pain, multiple surgeries, and, worst of all, the sight of his disfigured face in a mirror (photo below) (Fisher, 1995). One reason psychologists study burn victims such as Harold is to discover how they cope with traumatic and chronic stress.

1 Research Methods

In Module 2, we discussed several ways psychologists answer questions, including experiments and case studies, each of which has advantages and disadvantages.

An *experiment* is a method for identifying cause-and-effect relationships by following a set of guidelines that describe how to control, manipulate, and measure variables, while at the same time minimizing the possibility of error and bias.

Although experiments permit great control over manipulating treatments and measuring subjects' responses, it would be unethical to inflict burns on individuals to study how they cope. This brings us to situations that result from accidents, natural disasters, or cruel fate, and involve the use of a case study.

A *case study* is more of an in-depth analysis of the thoughts, feelings, beliefs, or behaviors of individuals without much ability to control or manipulate situations or variables.

For example, much of the initial information on how the brain functions came from case studies on individuals who had tumors, gunshot wounds, or accidental damage. Similarly, psychologists learn much about how people cope with traumatic events by observing the recovery and adjustment of burn victims. A case study approach would involve observing, questioning, and perhaps administering various personality tests to burn victims, such as Harold, to identify how they cope and adjust to their condition.

2 Coping with Initial Stressful Effects

Harold's face was so badly burned that he could not speak and had to communicate by writing notes. Harold kept asking for a mirror to see how he looked, but doctors had told the nurses not to give him one. A new nurse, who had not heard the doctors' orders, gave Harold a mirror, and when he looked at his terribly disfigured face, he began to scream. When his mother explained to Harold that 27 children had died in the bus crash and how lucky Harold was just to be alive, he got the courage to go on. Over the weeks and months following injury, burn patients undergo painful changes of their dressings, plastic surgery, skin grafting, and rehabilitation. Each of these procedures is stressful and elicits a variety of emotional reactions, the most common of which are confusion, anxiety, and depression. In dealing with these emotional reactions, burn victims use a number of emotion-focused coping strategies, which include complaining ("Why me?"), denying the severity of the problem (being too cheerful), rationalizing ("I'm being punished"), and trying to have a positive outlook (looking on the bright side) (Patterson et al., 1993). One emotion-focused coping strategy that Harold used to deal with his disfigured face was, "I'm just lucky to be alive."

3 Coping with Long-Term Stressful Effects

About five months after his face was severely burned, Harold started high school. He constantly worried how fellow students, especially girls, would react when seeing his disfigured face (left photo). It was Harold's quiet courage, charm, and smile that won students over and helped him find a girlfriend (Fisher, 1995).

Researchers found that both personality traits and social factors helped burn victims cope with long-term stressful effects, such as the anxiety and depression that come from being disfigured by burns. For example, burn victims with high self-esteem and strong social support are better able to cope with long-term stressful aftereffects of their burn injuries (Patterson et al., 1993). Harold kept his self-esteem high by finding a girlfriend and going out for football his sophomore year. In addition, he received strong social support from his mother and girlfriend.

4 Conclusions

Based on case studies, researchers found that the majority of people (50–80%) hospitalized for severe burns did not develop major psychological problems and showed good psychological adjustment to their physical problems. Burn victims coped better when they had high self-esteem and a good social support system. When it came to coping strategies, burn victims used problem-focused coping to deal with social, family, and job situations and used emotion-focused coping to deal with anxiety and depression that results from being disfigured (Patterson et al., 1993). By using in-depth case studies, researchers learned how burn victims cope and adjust to severe physical, personal, and emotional trauma.

Next, we'll look at how some monks develop mind-over-body control.

G. Cultural Diversity: Tibetan Monks

Mind-Body Interaction

Can you control your breathing?

There are only two responses of the autonomic nervous system—breathing and eye blinking—that you can voluntarily control. All other responses of the autonomic nervous system, such as increasing or decreasing blood pressure, heart rate, secreting hormones, dilating or constricting blood vessels, and increasing or decreasing oxygen consumption, are not usually under voluntary control. Normally, the responses of the autonomic nervous system are involuntary and occur automatically.

The *autonomic nervous system* has two divisions that are not normally under voluntary control: the sympathetic division causes physiological arousal by increasing heart rate, breathing, blood pressure, and secretion of stimulating hormones; the parasympathetic

division calms and relaxes the body by decreasing physiological responses and stimulating digestion.

For example, try warming your hands by voluntarily dilating the blood vessels in your fingers. Try as you might, you cannnot warm your hands because blood vessels are not usually under voluntary control (I bet students that they can't do it, and I've never lost). However, for about a dozen years, Western researcher Herbert Benson and his colleagues from Harvard Medical School have been visiting India to study Tibetan monks who claim to voluntarily control their autonomic nervous systems, such as warming their hands. Because many Western researchers believe voluntary control of the autonomic nervous system to be very difficult, Benson and colleagues went to India armed with scientific instruments that would either prove or disprove the monks' claims (Benson et al., 1982, 1990).

Control of Temperature

If you wish to voluntarily control some of your autonomic nervous system's responses, such as dilating blood vessels to warm your hands, sit quietly in a chair, close your eyes, and think relaxing thoughts. If your thoughts are truly relaxing, they will activate your parasympathetic division, which will dilate blood vessels and result in warm hands. I have only been able to do this a few times (because it's very difficult to think truly relaxing thoughts), but it is a most remarkable experience to feel your hands becoming warmer.

The reason that I and most Westerners find this warming task extremely difficult is that we usually spend little time practicing relaxation exercises and thus are unfamiliar with how to concentrate on thoughts or images that will result in hand warming. Those Western individuals who have used biofeedback training have managed to raise their finger temperatures by only about 0.25–2°F, on average (Freedman, 1991). In comparison, certain Tibetan monks, through various forms of

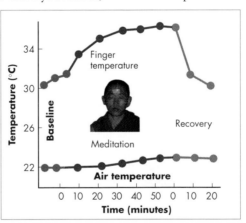

meditation, claim that they can warm their bodies sufficiently to dry wet towels placed on their shoulders. This was exactly the kind of claim that excited and puzzled Benson's group of researchers.

Benson's group obtained permission from three monks at a monastery in Upper Dharamsala, India, to measure skin temperature during heat meditation, or g Tum-mo yoga. The monks sat in the lotus position, closed their eyes, and began meditating. As shown in the left graph, within a short period of time, one monk had raised his finger temperature as much as 7–9°C with no change in heart rate (Benson et al., 1982). The monks' success at warming their hands (9–12°F) was about five times as great as Westerners had managed (0.25–2°F). One reason monks can learn to voluntarily control their autonomic nervous systems (dilating blood vessels to warm their hands) is that they practice this task daily for many years.

Explanation and Application

Westerner Benson explains that monks are able to raise hand temperature by activating the parasympathetic division, which dilates tiny blood vessels that lie near the surface of the skin. The monks' explanation is much more interesting: during meditation, they gather winds scattered in consciousness and focus the winds into a "central channel" that generates internal heat (Benson et al., 1982).

The reason researchers studied these monks was because the ability to voluntarily control physiological responses has great application in preventing or decreasing a number of psychosomatic symptoms, including headaches, teeth-grinding (bruxism), intestinal and stomach problems, and cardiovascular symptoms (high blood pressure).

One of the major themes of health psychology is how your thoughts, beliefs, and emotional feelings influence and interact with your body's physiological and immune responses. For example, your mind's fearful or stressful thoughts can trigger the body's fight-flight response; your mind's fearful or stressful thoughts can weaken the body's immune system and increase the risks of getting infections or viruses; your mind can influence the body's immune responses (allergic reactions) through classical conditioning; and monks' minds can voluntarily control their autonomic nervous systems. All these examples illustrate how the mind and body interact, which must be considered in developing a stress management program.

H. Application: Stress Management Programs

Definition

Can you deal better with stress?

As I stand in line at the college cafeteria, I hear students talking about having too many exams and assignments and classes and too little time and money and energy, which adds up to a lot of stressors. How well students cope with their major life events and daily hassles depends to a great extent on their having an effective stress management program.

A *stress management program* uses a variety of strategies to reduce anxiety, fear, and stressful experiences by changing three different aspects of our lives: thoughts (appraisals), behaviors, and physiological responses.

Psychologists have developed a number of very effective stress management programs that reduce stress levels, which in turn decrease occurrence of psychosomatic symptoms. Although stress management programs have different names, they all focus on ways to change three major contributors to stressful experiences: your thoughts and beliefs (appraisals), your behaviors, and your emotional and physiological responses (Granvold, 1994).

We'll describe several methods that psychologists have developed for effectively changing each of these three factors, beginning with changing your thoughts.

Changing Thoughts

Can you learn to think more positively?

Many daily situations—dealing with tardy friends, long lines, slow traffic, rude people, loud neighbors, and sloppy roommates—can be made more or less stressful depending on how you appraise these situations. Since your appraisal of a situation as threatening or challenging is related to increasing or decreasing your stress levels, it follows that an effective way to decrease stressful experiences is to work at changing how you initially appraise a situation. We'll explain two effective strategies for changing your appraisals: thinking of potentially stressful situations as challenging rather than threatening, and changing negative self-statements into positive ones.

USE CHALLENGE APPRAISALS

The reason you want to think or appraise potentially stressful situations as challenging rather than threatening is that threat appraisals elicit negative emotions (fear, anxiety, depression), which in turn raise stress levels, while challenge appraisals elicit positive emotions that lower stress levels. For example, students who emphasize threat appraisals of exams, such as thinking they will not have time to study or expecting to do poorly, are more likely to experience negative emotions such as anxiety and fear (Shannon, 1994). In turn, anxiety and fear trigger the fight-flight response, which raises the level of stress and often leads to emotion-focused coping, such as complaining, seeking sympathy, or avoiding studying. However, emotion-focused coping does not usually motivate actions, such as studying, that are needed to prepare students for exams.

I see life as one big challenge!

In comparison, students who emphasize challenge appraisals of exams, such as wanting to do their best or to prove themselves, are more likely to experience positive emotions, such as excitement or eagerness, which decrease levels of stress. In turn, challenge appraisals are more likely to result in problem-focused coping, which means taking direct action to deal with the situation itself, such as developing a study program.

Thus, a good way to deal with potentially stressful situations is to focus on challenging rather than threatening appraisals (Lazarus, 1993).

SUBSTITUTE POSITIVE SELF-STATEMENTS

Another way to prevent a situation, such as taking an exam, from becoming more stressful is to work at removing negative self-statements by substituting positive ones. Specifically, on one side of a sheet of paper write your negative self-statements, then next to them on the other side write the positive ones that you can substitute. The example below shows negative self-statements changed into positive ones.

Negative self-statements	Positive self-statements
"I know I'll do badly."	*"I know I can do OK."*
"I always get so anxious."	*"I'm going to stay calm."*
"I'm not smart enough."	*"I've got plenty of ability."*
"I'm never going to learn it."	*"I can learn the material."*

The reason you want to avoid making negative self-statements is that they elicit negative emotions (fear, anger, anxiety) that increase stress levels. By substituting positive self-statements, which elicit positive emotions, you can decrease stress levels. For example, each time you begin to think of a negative self-statement, stop yourself and substitute a positive one. For regularly occurring stressors, such as taking exams, waiting in lines, fighting with traffic, dealing with rude people, it is best to have prepared different lists of self-statements to go with each different situation. Researchers found that a program of substituting self-statements proved very effective in helping people change their thought patterns and reduce their stress levels (Meichenbaum & Fitzpatrick, 1993).

You better be good, better not pout, and better think positively.

Changing Behaviors

How do you get ready for an exam?

There are generally two different ways that students get ready for exams. Some students get ready for an exam by complaining about how much work there is, making excuses about not studying, or blaming the instructor for too much material. All these behaviors involve emotion-focused coping, which in the short term serves to reduce stress by reducing negative emotional feelings. However, in the long run, students may need to change these behaviors and engage in problem-focused coping, which means developing a study plan (Lazarus, 1993).

Because some students are not aware of whether they use emotion-focused or problem-focused coping, stress manage-

Maybe it's time for a change.

ment programs include an observation period of 1–2 weeks. During this time, a student observes or monitors his or her own behaviors to identify emotion-focused versus problem-focused behaviors. If a student is primarily using *emotion-focused coping* (making excuses, procrastinating, or blaming others), he or she will likely do poorly on exams. Instead, a student would need to start a program of *problem-focused coping* (making a study program, rewriting class notes) by using some of the self-reward and behavior modification techniques that we discussed in Module 10 (Granvold, 1994; Meichenbaum & Fitzpatrick, 1993). Thus, one way to reduce stress is to change your behaviors—that is, to emphasize problem-focused over emotion-focused activities.

Changing Physiological Responses

How do you learn to relax?

There are two good reasons why it is difficult for you to relax at will. First, the autonomic nervous system, which controls relaxing responses, is not normally under voluntary control (except by Tibetan monks). Second, learning to have some voluntary control over the autonomic nervous system involves learning a mind-over-body program that takes considerable effort and practice. However, learning to relax at will is an important part of a stress management program. We'll describe three techniques that have proved almost equally effective in learning to relax (Lehrer et al., 1994).

Biofeedback

You could learn a relaxing response, such as decreasing muscle tension, by having small sensors placed on your forehead. The sensors are attached to a machine that records, amplifies, and displays changes in muscle tension. Each time you think thoughts or images that increase tension, you hear a high tone; if you decrease tension, you hear a low tone. This procedure is called biofeedback.

Biofeedback refers to voluntarily learning to control physiological responses, such as muscle activity, blood pressure, or temperature, by recording and displaying these responses.

After 12–30 biofeedback training sessions (about 20 minutes per session), most individuals have some success in turning on relaxing responses. You could also learn to relax with progressive relaxation.

Progressive Relaxation

You could learn to relax your body's muscles by first tensing and relaxing your toes and then continuing up the body, tensing and relaxing the muscles of your calves, thighs, pelvis, stomach, shoulders, arms, hands, neck, face, and forehead. This procedure is called progressive relaxation.

Progressive relaxation involves practicing tensing and relaxing the major muscle groups of the body until you are able to relax any groups of muscles at will.

After several weeks of daily practice, about 20 minutes per session, you would be able to use this exercise to relax your body. You could also relax by meditating.

Meditation

There are many kinds of meditation exercises. We'll describe two of the more popular ones.

Transcendental meditation (TM) involves assuming a comfortable position, closing one's eyes, and repeating and concentrating on a sound to clear one's head of all thoughts (worrisome and otherwise).

TM is an Eastern form of meditation. A Western counterpart is the relaxation response (Benson, 1975).

The *relaxation response* involves sitting or lying in a comfortable position while silently repeating a sound over and over to rid oneself of anxious thoughts.

Meditation involves removing all stressful thoughts and replacing them with peaceful ones. Becoming competent at using meditation to relax usually requires practicing about 20 minutes a day for about six weeks.

You may hear claims that a particular form of meditation, such as Zen or yoga, is effective in reducing stress. However, researchers report that most relaxation techniques, whether biofeedback, progressive relaxation, or various forms of meditation, are about equally effective in producing relaxation and reducing stress (Clay, 1997). For example, different relaxation techniques were about equally effective in reducing anxiety and decreasing a variety of psychosomatic complaints, such as headaches, high blood pressure, insomnia, stomach pain, and

intestinal problems (irritable bowel syndrome) (Gutkin et al., 1994; McGrady et al., 1997; Meissner et al., 1997; Rokicki et al., 1997). Since methods of relaxation are about equally effective, the one you choose comes down to personal preference. More important than which relaxation technique you choose is the need for daily practice so that you will be able to relax at will. All researchers agree that continued use of relaxation techniques is a critical part of any effective stress management program (Clay, 1997).

SUMMARY TEST

A. APPRAISAL

1. The uncomfortable feeling we have when we appraise a situation as something that overloads or strains our psychological resources is called _____.

2. Our initial, subjective evaluation of a situation in which we balance various environmental demands against our ability to meet them is called _____.

3. There are three outcomes of primary appraisal. Those situations that do not matter to our well-being are called (a)_____; those that will enhance or preserve our well-being are called (b)_____; and those that overtax our resources are called (c)_____.

4. A stressful situation has the potential for three different kinds of personal experiences. If you have already sustained some damage or injury, this is referred to as (a)_____. If the injury has not yet taken place but you anticipate it in the near future, this is referred to as (b)_____. If you have the potential for gain or personal growth but need to use physical energy and psychological resources, this is referred to as (c)_____. Not all appraisals are clear-cut; some may represent a combination of threat and challenge.

B. PHYSIOLOGICAL RESPONSES

5. A combination of physiological responses that arouse and prepare the body for action is called the (a)_____ response. Although this response originally evolved to help our ancestors survive dangerous and life-threatening situations, it can also be triggered by psychological stimuli, such as our primary (b)_____ of a situation as harm/loss, threatening, or challenging.

6. Threat appraisals activate a part of the brain called the (a)_____, which triggers two responses simultaneously. It causes the (b)_____ gland to release ACTH (adrenocorticotropic hormone), which acts on the adrenal cortex to secrete hormones that regulate levels of minerals and glucose in the body. The hypothalamus also triggers the (c)_____ division of the autonomic nervous system, which causes physiological arousal.

7. Our psychological reactions to stressful situations can result in real, painful, physical symptoms called (a)_____ symptoms. According to Selye, we develop psychosomatic symptoms because the body's response to stress involves going through three stages that he called the (b)_____ syndrome. The first is called the (c)_____ stage, which is our initial reaction to stress and is marked by physiological arousal. The second is called the (d)_____ stage, in which most physiological responses return to normal levels as the body uses up great stores of energy. The third is called the (e)_____ stage, which is marked by the actual breakdown in body organs or weakening of the infection-fighting immune system.

8. The body's network of cells and chemicals that automatically fight off bacteria, viruses, and other foreign matter is known as the (a)_____. The study of the relationship between the central nervous system, the endocrine system, and psychosocial factors is called (b)_____. The interaction among these factors affects the immune system and, in turn, makes the body more or less susceptible to disease and infection.

C. STRESSFUL EXPERIENCES

9. Situations that are potentially disturbing or disruptive and that we appraise as having an impact on our lives are called (a)_____ events. Small, irritating daily events are called (b)_____ and small, pleasant daily experiences are called (c)_____. How we cope with hassles predicts our daily mood and the occurrence of psychosomatic symptoms.

10. The feeling that results when our attempts to reach some goal are blocked is called (a)_____. Feelings of wearing out or becoming exhausted because of too many demands on our time and energy are referred to as (b)_____. A direct personal experience of actual or threatened death or serious injury or witnessing such an event could result in terrible stress symptoms called (c)_____.

11. When we must decide between two or more incompatible choices, we are in (a)_____, which can include at least three possibilities. If we must choose between two options with pleasurable consequences, we experience (b)_____ conflict. If we must choose between two options that both have disagreeable consequences, we are in (c)_____ conflict. If a single situation has both pleasurable and disagreeable aspects, we are in (d)_____ conflict.

12. An unpleasant state in which we have feelings of uneasiness and apprehension as well as increased physiological arousal is called (a)_____. This feeling has at least three causes. One is classical conditioning of an emotional response to a previously neutral stimulus; the result is called a (b)_____ response. A second cause is a form of learning that develops through watching and does not require any observable behavior or reinforcer; this is called (c)_____ learning. According to Freud, anxiety arises when

the id and superego disagree, resulting in an (d)_____
conflict, which results in the ego producing a feeling of anxiety.

D. PERSONALITY & SOCIAL FACTORS

13. Three personality traits that decrease the potentially
harmful effects of stressful situations are control, commitment, and challenge, which together are called
_____.

14. If you believe that what you do influences what
happens, you are said to have an (a)_____
of control. In contrast, if you believe that chance and luck mostly
determine what happens and that you do not have much influence,
you are said to have an (b)_____ of control. People with
an external locus of control experience more negative emotions,
higher levels of stress, and more psychosomatic symptoms than do
those whose locus of control is internal.

15. Because the original association between Type A behavior
and the occurrence of cardiovascular disease was not replicated,
researchers redefined Type A behavior as having two primary traits,
_____ and _____. Even with the new
definition, researchers have questioned an association between
Type A behavior and cardiovascular disease.

16. One factor that buffers us from stressful experiences is having a
group or network of family or friends who provide strong support
and this is called _____.

E. KINDS OF COPING

17. After we make a primary appraisal, we then
must decide what action to take, which is called a
(a)_____ appraisal. This involves two
different kinds of coping. If we seek information
about what needs to be done, change our own behavior, or take whatever action will solve the problem, we use (b)_____ coping. If we use our energies to deal with emotional distress caused by a
harm or threat appraisal, we are using (c)_____ coping.
Compared to emotion-focused coping, problem-focused coping is better at reducing long-term effects of stress because it solves the problem.

F. RESEARCH FOCUS: COPING WITH TRAUMA

18. Psychologists use a number of different research methods. One method identifies cause-and-
effect relationships by following a set of guidelines
that describe how to control and manipulate variables; this is called the (a)_____
method. Another method is a more in-depth analysis of the thoughts,

feelings, beliefs, or behaviors of individuals; this is called the
(b)_____. Researchers found that burn victims use
(c)_____-focused coping to adjust to social, family, and
job situations, and (d)_____-focused coping to deal with
anxiety and depression that may result from disfigurement.

G. CULTURAL DIVERSITY: TIBETAN MONKS

19. Many of our physiological responses
involved in relaxation (heart rate, blood pressure, temperature, and secretion of hormones)
are not under voluntary control because they
are regulated by the (a)_____
system. Researchers discovered that some monks have learned a
method to voluntarily control temperature, which involves relaxation.
This demonstrates that the (b)_____ can be used to control the (c)_____ physiological responses.

H. APPLICATION: STRESS MANAGEMENT PROGRAMS

20. A program for reducing anxiety, fear, and
stressful experiences by using a variety of strategies
to change three different aspects of our lives—
thoughts, behaviors, and physiological responses—is
called a _____.

21. One component of a stress management program is learning to
relax at will, which can be accomplished with three different methods.
Recording and amplifying physiological signals from the body and
displaying these signals so that we can learn to increase or decrease
them is known as (a)_____. An exercise of tensing and
relaxing the major muscle groups is called (b)_____.
Meditation can take many forms. Sitting or lying in a comfortable
position while repeating a meaningless sound over and over to rid
oneself of anxious thoughts is called (c)_____ or the
_____ response. Researchers found that all three techniques are about equally effective in learning to relax.

Answers: *1. stress; 2. primary appraisal; 3. (a) irrelevant, (b) positive,
(c) stressful; 4. (a) harm/loss, (b) threat, (c) challenge; 5. (a) fight-flight,
(b) appraisal; 6. (a) hypothalamus, (b) pituitary, (c) sympathetic;
7. (a) psychosomatic, (b) general adaptation, (c) alarm, (d) resistance,
(e) exhaustion; 8. (a) immune system, (b) psychoneuroimmunology;
9. (a) major life, (b) hassles, (c) uplifts; 10. (a) frustration, (b) burnout,
(c) posttraumatic stress disorder; 11. (a) conflict, (b) approach-approach,
(c) avoidance-avoidance, (d) approach-avoidance; 12. (a) anxiety,
(b) conditioned emotional, (c) observational, (d) unconscious; 13. hardiness;
14. (a) internal locus, (b) external locus; 15. hostility, anger; 16. social
support; 17. (a) secondary, (b) problem-focused, (c) emotion-focused;
18. (a) experimental or scientific, (b) case study, (c) problem, (d) emotion;
19. (a) autonomic nervous or parasympathetic, (b) mind, (c) body's;
20. stress management program; 21. (a) biofeedback, (b) progressive
relaxation, (c) transcendental meditation (TM) or relaxation.*

CRITICAL THINKING

Newspaper Article

QUESTIONS

1. What defense mechanisms does the author use?

2. Does the author use problem-focused or emotion-focused coping strategies?

3. On the basis of research done on burn patients, how well do you expect the author to cope with her illness?

4. How might the author's good system of social support help her through her illness?

5. If you've ever known anyone with cancer, how did that person and his or her family cope?

THE DIAGNOSIS
by Mary Herczog

Early last year, a mammogram and an ultrasound diagnosed some lumps in my breasts as cysts. One month later, when I found another lump, I dismissed it as a cyst the doctor had certainly noticed. And continued to dismiss it for a few weeks until it grew to more than the size of a peach pit and turned very hard. When a lump turned up in my armpit, I knew.

A biopsy was taken on a Thursday and I was told to call on Monday for news that I was still almost certain would be that this lump was a fibroadenoma—totally benign. My husband, Steve, and I spent a weekend telling ourselves this would turn out to be nothing.

After all, I'm 33, way too young to have breast cancer. There is no history in my family. I never drank, smoked, did drugs, or drank coffee, tea, or soda. So how could I have breast cancer?

But on Monday I was told that the biopsy result was "suspicious for cancer." So I wasn't exactly surprised when the doctor told me the pathologist would "bet his children's lives" that this was cancer. In both lump and lymph node, the latter being the bad news as this meant the cancer had spread.

The plan was to hit me with four months of chemotherapy, remove both the lump and the lymph node, and follow up with six weeks of radiation, then four more weeks of chemo.

You can spend a week thinking, "What if I have cancer. OK, so I'm going to lose my hair, which is bad, but I love hats, and I can explore my inner drag queen by wearing wigs" and other Pollyanna things. But, actually hearing someone tell you that removing your breast is a possibility in your future—well, pass the Kleenex.

Damn, damn, damn.

The next few days passed in a haze of more biopsies and tests. In between them were phone calls. Many, many phone calls. Soon the phone lines were buzzing. The reactions poured in, and while one does not enjoy creating anguish for one's friends, the love and concern that result are as good as any medicine—in some ways better than a medicine that makes you vomit, lose your hair, and gain weight.

Source: *Los Angeles Times,* December 8, 1997.

Study Questions

A. **Appraisal**—Sue says that some situations always cause her stress, but John says it's how she thinks about them. Who's right? (See answer in Critical Thinking Appendix.)

B. **Physiological Responses**—Why are people so very reluctant to admit that some painful physical symptoms can be caused by their thoughts?

C. **Stressful Experiences**—Why does Sally always feel a little anxious when she goes to parties where she doesn't know anyone?

D. **Personality & Social Factors**—Greg did great in high school, so why is he doing poorly in his first year of college, away from home?

E. **Kinds of Coping**—How would you cope with finding out that, because of major differences, you must break off your current relationship?

F. **Research Focus: Coping with Trauma**—What can you learn from how burn victims cope with stress that would apply to dealing with stress in your own life? (See answer in Critical Thinking Appendix.)

G. **Cultural Diversity: Tibetan Monks**—Why is it so much easier for most of us to use our minds to trigger the fight-flight response than to calm or relax our body?

H. **Application: Stress Management Programs**—Why is it better to cope with stress by changing three things—thoughts, behaviors, and physiological responses—rather than just one? (See answer in Critical Thinking Appendix.)

Web Sites & Learning Activities

● BROOKS/COLE ONLINE PSYCHOLOGY STUDY CENTER

http://psychstudy.brookscole.com/student/plotnik/quiz/ch21frm.html

This site gives students a chance to review material by taking quizzes and doing exercises and activities for this module.

● THE AMERICAN INSTITUTE OF STRESS

http://www.stress.org/

This organization's home page is devoted to the field of stress and health. It includes a monthly newsletter and information about professional activities.

● STRESS, DEPRESSION, ANXIETY, SLEEP PROBLEMS, AND DRUG USE

http://www.teachhealth.com/

This informative site offers information on recognizing stress, a self-test for stress levels, the biological bases of stress, and stress-management techniques.

● TRAUMA INFO PAGES

http://www.trauma-pages.com/

This site focuses on trauma and the aftermath of stressful events. It includes general information, resources, and support groups for those affected.

● STRESS BUSTERS

http://stressbusters.com/strssbus.html

This commercial site is dedicated to reducing workplace stress and includes stress-building beliefs and stress-busting techniques.

Welcome to the WEB

● A CHECKLIST FOR MEDITATION

http://www.sonic.net/~jotokuji/Zazen.html

Daily meditation practice is a great way to reduce the effects of stress, and this site offers detailed instructions on how to get started.

● ASSOCIATION FOR APPLIED PSYCHOPHYSIOLOGY AND BIOFEEDBACK

http://www.aapb.org/

This professional organization's home page contains information on biofeedback, current research, news briefs, and links to other resources.

Activities

● *Integrator Online™ for Introductory Psychology* CD-ROM, Plotnik, Module 21

● Study Guide to accompany *Introduction to Psychology,* 5th edition, Module 21 (choice of PC or Macintosh computer version or hard copy)

● *PsychNow!* CD-ROM

Answers to questions on page 506

1. At first she denies the possibility of cancer; later she uses humor to deflect some of her anxiety.
2. She uses both. She takes action to diagnose and treat her cancer (problem-focused coping) and she also seeks support (emotion-focused coping).
3. She will probably cope well. She has good support, uses both problem- and emotion-focused coping, and she seems to have high self-esteem.
4. The author's support system might help her by buffering her against stress and by helping her maintain mental health.
5. Was the person optimistic or pessimistic? Where was the locus of control? Was social support available?

Module 22   DISORDERS I: DEFINITION & ANXIETY DISORDERS

Mental Disorder

How did a serial killer go unnoticed?

His eyes are hazel, placid, almost vacant, and his appearance is neither sinister nor scary. Until the day he was caught, his neighbors considered him an "average Joe." But over a period of three years, Jeffrey Dahmer planned and carried out the murders of 15 young men, while five more potential victims managed to escape.

In a very real sense, Dahmer led two different lives. In public, Dahmer seemed like a harmless, quiet guy who held down a job in a chocolate factory. However, in private, Dahmer would con potential victims into coming to his apartment, where he would drug them, commit sexual acts, and then kill, mutilate, and sometimes eat parts of them.

Although no two serial killers are alike, Dahmer fits the typical pattern. Serial killers are almost always young, white males who are quite intelligent and often come from broken homes; they may have been physically or sexually abused during childhood, and they have serious personality defects, such as low self-esteem and a lifelong sense of loneliness. Over half of all serial killers have mutilated their victims (Hickey, 1991). John Douglas, investigative chief at the FBI's National Center for Analysis of Violent Crime, adds that serial killers are obsessed with control, manipulation, and dominance and often con their victims into agreeing to their requests.

When Dahmer was brought to trial, his defense claimed that he was legally insane when he committed the murders. Some psychiatrists testified for the defense that Dahmer was insane; others testified for the prosecution that he was sane.

Insanity, according to its legal definition, means not knowing the difference between right and wrong.

The jury rejected Dahmer's plea of insanity and agreed with the prosecution that Dahmer was legally sane. The jury found Dahmer guilty on 15 counts of murder and characterized him as a con man who killed for his own selfish interests. On February 17, 1992, a Milwaukee County judge sentenced 31-year-old Dahmer to 15 consecutive life terms (*Newsweek*, August 5, 1992). In 1994, Dahmer was beaten to death in prison.

When mental health professionals discuss a person's sanity, they are trying to determine whether the person has a mental disorder.

A *mental disorder* is generally defined as a prolonged or recurring problem that seriously interferes with an individual's ability to live a satisfying personal life and function adequately in society.

Deciding whether a person has a mental disorder can be difficult because so many factors are involved in defining what is abnormal. As you'll learn in this module, someone's behavior may be described as abnormal but the person may or may not have a mental disorder.

Phobia

What's so scary about flying?

There is no doubt that Jeffrey Dahmer's murder and mutilation of 15 young men indicates severe mental disorder and extremely abnormal behavior. In other cases, mental disorders may involve a relatively common behavior or event that, through some learning, observational, or other process, has the power to elicit tremendous anxiety and becomes a phobia (Kleinknecht, 1994; Page, 1994).

A *phobia* (FOE-bee-ah) is an anxiety disorder characterized by an intense, excessive, and irrational fear that is out of all proportion to the danger elicited by the object or situation.

Kate Premo's phobia of flying began in her childhood, when she experienced a turbulent flight that left her scared and anxious. Later, as a young adult, her fear of flying was worsened by memories of the 1988 terrorist bombing of Pan Am flight 103, which killed several of her fellow students from Syracuse University. After that incident, her phobia of flying kept her from visiting friends and family. She would try to fly and even make reservations but always cancel them at the last minute.

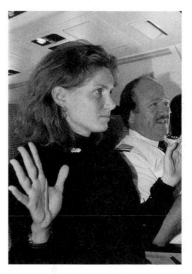

An estimated 25 million Americans have a similar irrational and intense fear of flying, which is called *aerophobia;* they refuse to get on a plane. Another 30 million Americans report moderate to high degrees of anxiety when they fly (Wilhelm & Roth, 1997). To treat her phobia, Kate Premo (photo above) took part in a weekend seminar that included actually flying in a plane. We'll tell you about Kate's phobia and treatment later in this module.

These two examples of Jeffrey Dahmer and Kate Premo raise a number of questions about mental disorders: How do they develop? How are they diagnosed? How are they treated? We'll answer these three questions as we discuss mental disorders.

What's Coming

In this module, we'll discuss three approaches to understanding mental disorders. We'll explain how mental disorders are assessed and diagnosed and go into some specific examples of mental disorders, such as generalized anxiety, phobias, obsessive-compulsive behaviors, and somatoform disorders. Finally, we'll discuss how common phobias, such as fear of flying, are treated.

We'll begin with the three approaches that are used to define, explain, and treat abnormal behaviors, such as that of Jeffrey Dahmer.

A. Three Approaches

Causes of Abnormal Behavior

Why were witches hanged?

The view of mental disorders has changed greatly through the centuries. In the Middle Ages, mental disorders were thought to be the result of demons or devils who inhabited individuals and made them do strange and horrible things. In the 1600s, mental disorders were thought to involve witches, who were believed to speak to the devil. This was the case

in Salem, Massachusetts, in 1692, where, in a short span of four months, 14 women and five men were hanged as witches on the testimony of young girls and God-fearing adults (Shapiro, 1992).

Presently, there are three major approaches to understanding and treating mental disorders: medical, cognitive-behavioral, and psychoanalytic approaches. You'll see that each approach emphasizes different factors as we discuss serial killer Jeffrey Dahmer (shown at left with photos of some of his victims).

Medical Model Approach

If you think that Jeffrey Dahmer's mental disorder results primarily from a biochemical or neurological problem in his brain, you favor the medical model approach.

The *medical model approach* views mental disorders as similar to physical diseases; both have symptoms that can be diagnosed and treated. Just as doctors use drugs to treat physical diseases, psychiatrists use psychoactive drugs to treat mental disorders.

One advantage of the medical model is that it emphasizes the role of the nervous system, genetic makeup, and chemical balance in mental disorders. For example, researchers have found that mental disorders run in families, which points to genetic factors (Alanen, 1997). In addition, researchers have reported both anatomical and chemical differences in the brains of individuals with mental disorders, which points to the importance of brain structures and neurotransmitters (Nemeroff, 1998).

One disadvantage of the medical model is that mental disorders have similar symptoms that are not always clearly defined, and they may lack identifiable physical and genetic causes. In addition, treatment with psychoactive drugs is not always effective, and in some disorders, nonmedical psychotherapy has proven equally effective (Barlow & Durand, 1995).

The medical model approach has benefited from newer brain-imaging techniques that allow researchers to analyze anatomical and chemical differences in living brains (Rauch & Renshaw, 1995; Wilde & Cinciripini, 1994).

Cognitive-Behavioral Approach

If you think that Jeffrey Dahmer's mental disorder results primarily from strange beliefs, thoughts, and behaviors, you prefer the cognitive-behavioral approach.

The *cognitive-behavioral approach* emphasizes that mental disorders result from deficits in cognitive processes, such as thoughts and beliefs, and from behavioral problems, such as deficits in skills and abilities.

The *cognitive* part of this approach grew out of research on how faulty beliefs, attitudes, and thoughts can result in serious mental and behavioral problems, such as depression and anxiety. The *behavioral* part of this approach grew out of research on how inappropriate behavior or behavioral deficits may lead to cognitive and behavioral problems such as shyness, loneliness, or helplessness. The cognitive-behavioral approach is supported by data showing that cognitive-behavior therapy can be as effective in treating depression as various antidepressant drugs (Antonuccio et al., 1997).

The cognitive-behavioral approach views mental disorders as resulting from maladaptive ways of thinking and behaving. Accordingly, treatment for mental disorders involves changing a person's maladaptive thoughts and behaviors.

Psychoanalytic Approach

If you think that Jeffrey Dahmer's mental disorder results primarily from deep, unconscious psychological conflicts that may have begun when he was a child, you favor the psychoanalytic approach.

The *psychoanalytic approach* states that mental disorders are due to unconscious conflicts or problems with unresolved conflicts at one or more of Freud's psychosexual stages.

Sigmund Freud divided the mind into three functions: the id or pleasure seeker; the superego or conscience; and the ego or rational peacekeeper. If these three divisions are in conflict, the result is anxiety. To deal with anxiety, the ego uses various defense mechanisms; overusing these defense mechanisms can create additional problems. In addition, Freud believed that various personality problems could result from the unsuccessful resolution of conflicts during the psychosexual stages of early childhood (please see Module 19). For example, reports that Jeffrey's mother did not like nursing and became withdrawn and that his parents had many fights and disagreements suggest that Jeffrey may have had an unhappy childhood, which would lay the groundwork for future personality problems (Dahmer, 1994).

According to Freud, treatment of mental disorders centers on the therapist's helping the patient identify and resolve his or her unconscious conflicts.

These three approaches emphasize different factors. In practice, it is likely that mental disorders result from the interaction of these factors.

Next, we'll examine several ways of defining abnormal behaviors.

Definitions of Abnormal Behavior

Is Mr. Thompson abnormal?

In some cases, such as Jeffrey Dahmer's murder and mutilation of 15 young men, we have no doubt that he demonstrated an extremely abnormal behavior pattern. In other cases, such as Kate Premo's phobia of flying, we would probably say that most of her life appears to be normal except for a small piece—flying in airplanes—that is abnormal. In still other cases, such as that of 54-year-old Richard Thompson (right photo), it is less clear what is abnormal behavior.

The City of San Diego evicted Thompson and all his belongings from his home. His belongings included shirts, pants, dozens of shoes, several Bibles, a cooler, a tool chest, lawn chairs, a barbecue grill, tin plates, bird cages, two pet rats, and his self-fashioned bed. For the previous nine months, Thompson had lived happily and without any problems in a downtown storm drain (sewer). Because the city does not allow people to live in sewers, Thompson was evicted from his underground storm-drain home and forbidden to return. Although Thompson later lived in several care centers and mental hospitals, he much preferred the privacy and comfort of the sewer (Grimaldi, 1986).

There are three different ways to decide whether Richard Thompson's behavior—living in the sewer—was abnormal.

Statistical Frequency

Although Thompson caused no problems to others except to violate a city law against living in a storm drain, his preferred living style could be considered abnormal according to statistical frequency.

The *statistical frequency approach* says that a behavior may be considered abnormal if it occurs rarely or infrequently in relation to the behaviors of the general population.

By this definition, Thompson's living in a storm drain would be considered very abnormal since, out of over 230 million people in the United States, only a very few prefer his kind of home. This illustrates that even though statistical frequency is a relatively precise measure, it is not a very useful measure of abnormality. By this criterion, getting a Ph.D., being president, living in a monastery, or selling a million records are abnormal, although some of these behaviors would be considered very desirable by most people. In fact, the *Guinness Book of Records* (1995) lists thousands of people who have performed some statistically very abnormal behaviors and are very proud of them. We would not consider any of these individuals to necessarily have mental disorders.

As all these examples demonstrate, the statistical frequency definition of abnormality has very limited usefulness.

Deviation from Social Norms

Thompson's behavior—preferring to live in a sewer—could also be considered abnormal based on social norms.

The *social norms approach* says that a behavior is considered abnormal if it deviates greatly from accepted social standards, values, or norms.

Thompson's decision to live by himself in a storm drain greatly deviates from society's norms about where people should live. However, a definition of abnormality based solely on deviations from social norms runs into problems when social norms change with time. For example, 20 years ago, no male would be caught dead wearing an earring, while today many males consider earrings very fashionable. Similarly, 30 years ago, a woman who preferred to be thin was considered to be ill and in need of medical help. Today, our society pressures women to be thin like the fashion models in the media.

Thus, defining abnormality on the basis of social norms can be risky, as social norms may, and do, change over time. The definition of abnormality most used by mental health professionals is the next one.

Maladaptive Behavior

The major problem with the first two definitions of abnormal behavior—statistical frequency and deviation from social norms—is that they don't say whether a particular behavior is psychologically damaging or maladaptive.

The *maladaptive behavior approach* defines a behavior as psychologically damaging or abnormal if it interferes with the individual's ability to function in one's personal life or in society.

For example, being terrified of flying, hearing voices that dictate dangerous acts, feeling compelled to wash one's hands for hours on end, starving oneself to the point of death, and committing serial murders and eating parts of the victims would all be considered maladaptive and, in that sense, abnormal.

However, Thompson's seemingly successful adaptation to living in a sewer may not be maladaptive for him and certainly has no adverse consequences to society. Of the three definitions discussed here, the most useful definition of abnormal behavior is based on the maladaptive definition—that is, whether a particular behavior or behavior pattern interferes with a person's ability to function normally (Barlow & Durand, 1995).

However, you'll see that deciding if behavior is truly maladaptive is not always so easy.

C. Diagnosing Mental Disorders

DSM-IV

How many mental disorders?

"Maybe she was just plain crazy."
"Maybe she was too depressed to know what she was doing."
"Maybe she had bad genes."

When faced with such an abnormal behavior—a mother drowning her own children—people tried to label Susan's problem. Similarly, mental health professionals use clinical assessments to label mental disorders, a process called a clinical diagnosis.

A *clinical diagnosis* is a process of matching an individual's specific symptoms to those that define a particular mental disorder.

Making a clinical diagnosis, which means matching symptoms to a specific mental disorder, was very difficult prior to the 1950s because there was no uniform diagnostic system. However, since 1952, the American Psychiatric Association (APA) has been developing a uniform diagnostic system, whose most recent version is known as the *Diagnostic and Statistical Manual of Mental Disorders*-IV, abbreviated as DSM-IV (American Psychiatric Association, 1994).

The *Diagnostic and Statistical Manual of Mental Disorders*-IV, or DSM-IV, describes a uniform system for assessing specific symptoms and matching them to almost 300 different mental disorders.

The first *Diagnostic and Statistical Manual of Mental Disorders* (1952) described about 100 mental disorders, as compared to the almost 300 in DSM-IV (table below). A major improvement in DSM-II (1968) was to give general descriptions of mental problems based on Sigmund Freud's concepts of *psychoses*

DISORDERS	
DSM-I	106
DSM-II	182
DSM-III	265
DSM-IV	297

(severe mental disorders, such as schizophrenia) and *neuroses* (less severe forms of psychological conflict, such as anxiety). Because these Freudian-based descriptions were rather general and based more on expert opinion than on research findings, there were considerable disagreements in making clinical diagnoses. To decrease such disagreements, the DSM-III (1980) dropped Freudian terminology and instead listed specific symptoms and criteria for mental disorders. However, since criteria for mental disorders were still based primarily on clinical opinion, disagreements continued over making uniform diagnoses.

A major improvement in the current DSM-IV is that it establishes criteria and symptoms for mental disorders based more on research findings than on expert clinical opinion (Clark et al., 1995). We'll discuss both the advantages and disadvantages of using the DSM-IV.

Axis I

How to make a diagnosis?

In making a clinical diagnosis, the mental health professional first assesses the client's specific symptoms and then matches these symptoms to those described in the DSM-IV. The DSM-IV has five major dimensions, called *axes,* which serve as guidelines for making decisions about symptoms. We'll first describe Axis I and show how it can be used to diagnose Susan Smith's and Kate Premo's problems. (The numbered items below and on the opposite page are based on the *Diagnostic and Statistical Manual of Mental Disorders* [1994], American Psychiatric Association.)

Axis I: Nine Major Clinical Syndromes

Axis I contains lists of symptoms and criteria about the onset, severity, and duration of these symptoms. In turn these lists of symptoms are used to make a clinical diagnosis of the following nine major clinical syndromes.

1. Disorders usually first diagnosed in infancy, childhood, or adolescence. This category includes disorders that arise before adolescence, such as attention deficit disorders, autism, mental retardation, enuresis, and stuttering (discussed in Modules 1, 2, and 13).

2. Organic mental disorders. These disorders are temporary or permanent dysfunctions of brain tissue caused by diseases or chemicals. Examples are delirium, dementia, and amnesia (discussed in Module 3).

3. Substance-related disorders. This category refers to the maladaptive use of drugs and alcohol. Mere consumption and recreational use of such substances are not disorders. This category requires an abnormal pattern of use, as with alcohol abuse and cocaine dependence (discussed in Module 8).

4. Schizophrenia and other psychotic disorders. The schizophrenias are characterized by psychotic symptoms (for example, grossly disorganized behavior, delusions, and hallucinations) and by over six months of behavioral deterioration. This category, which also includes delusional disorder and schizoaffective disorder, will be discussed in Module 23.

5. Mood disorders. The cardinal feature is emotional disturbance. Patients may, or may not, have psychotic symptoms. These disorders, which include major depression, bipolar disorder, dysthymic disorder, and cyclothymic disorder, will also be discussed in Module 23. An example of a mood disorder is that of Susan Smith.

Susan Smith: Diagnosis—Mood Disorder

From childhood on, Susan's symptoms include being depressed, attempting suicide, seeking sexual alliances to escape loneliness, drinking heavily, and having feelings of low self-esteem and hopelessness, all of which match the DSM-IV's list of symptoms for a mood disorder. In Susan's case, the specific mood disorder most closely matches that of major depressive disorder but without psychotic symptoms or serious thought disorders and delusions.

In diagnosing major depression, the DSM-IV distinguishes between early (before age 21) and late onset depression—Susan would be early; and between mild and severe depression, as judged by how many episodes of depression she had, and whether she showed a decreased capacity to function normally, such as the inability to work or care for children. Susan's ability to hold a job and care for her children suggest mild depression. This example shows how the guidelines of Axis I are used to arrive at one of nine major clinical syndromes—in this case, major depression.

6. Anxiety disorders. These disorders are characterized by physiological signs of anxiety (for example, palpitations) and subjective feelings of tension, apprehension, or fear. Anxiety may be acute and focused (phobias) or continual and diffuse (generalized anxiety disorder). An example of an anxiety disorder is that of Kate Premo.

KATE PREMO: DIAGNOSIS— SPECIFIC PHOBIA

Kate Premo's symptoms include having an intense fear of flying, knowing that her fear is irrational and that she can't control it, going out of her way to avoid flying, and making reservations that she later cancels. Kate's symptoms most closely match the DSM-IV's list of symptoms for an anxiety disorder called a specific phobia. The DSM-IV's symptoms for a specific phobia matches those of Premo—experiencing intense and irrational fear when exposed to a feared situation (flying) and having to avoid that situation at all costs, which interferes with part of her normal activities (going to meetings).

7. Somatoform disorders. These disorders are dominated by somatic symptoms that resemble physical illnesses. These symptoms cannot be accounted for by organic damage. There must also be strong evidence that these symptoms are produced by psychological factors or conflicts. This category, which includes somatization and conversion disorders and hypochondriasis, will be discussed in this module.

8. Dissociative disorders. These disorders all feature a sudden, temporary alteration or dysfunction of memory, consciousness, identity, and behavior, as in dissociative amnesia and multiple personality (discussed in Module 23).

9. Sexual and gender-identity disorders. There are three basic types of disorders in this category: gender-identity disorders (discomfort with identity as male or female), paraphilias (preference for unusual acts to achieve sexual arousal), and sexual dysfunctions (impairments in sexual functioning) (discussed in Module 15).

Axes II, III, IV, and V

Why four more? We have explained how Axis I is used to make clinical diagnoses of such mental disorders as major depression and specific phobias (flying). Now, we'll briefly describe how the other four axes are used.

Axis II: Personality Disorders

This axis refers to disorders that involve patterns of personality traits that are longstanding, maladaptive, and inflexible and involve impaired functioning or subjective distress. Examples include borderline, schizoid, and antisocial personality disorders. Personality disorders will be discussed in Module 23. An example of a personality disorder is that of Dahmer.

JEFFREY DAHMER: DIAGNOSIS—ANTISOCIAL PERSONALITY DISORDER

Jeffrey Dahmer's symptoms include sexually assaulting and killing 15 young men, in some cases eating parts of them, feeling no guilt or remorse, and exhibiting this behavior over a considerable period of time. Dahmer's symptoms may indicate a combination of mental disorders, but here we'll focus on only one from the DSM-IV, a personality disorder. According to DSM-IV, the essential features of an antisocial personality disorder are the existence of strange inner experiences that differ greatly from the expectations of one's culture, that lead to significant impairment in personal, occupational, or social functioning, and that form a pattern of disregard for, and violation of, the rights of others. This list of symptoms from DSM-IV matches those of Dahmer.

Axis III: General Medical Conditions

This axis refers to physical disorders or conditions, such as diabetes, arthritis, and hemophilia.

Axis IV: Psychosocial and Environmental Problems

This axis refers to psychosocial and environmental problems that may affect the diagnosis, treatment, and prognosis of mental disorders in Axes I and II. A psychosocial or environmental problem may be a negative life event (experiencing a traumatic event), an environmental difficulty or deficiency, a familial or other interpersonal stress, an inadequacy of social support or personal resources, or another problem that describes the context in which a person's difficulties have developed (PTSD was discussed in Module 21).

Axis V: Global Assessment of Functioning (GAF) Scale

This axis is used to rate the overall psychological, social, and occupational functioning of the individual on a scale from 10 (severe danger of hurting self) to 100 (superior functioning in all activities).

In making a clinical diagnosis of Jeffrey Dahmer, Axis II is used to match his symptoms to a list that makes up a personality disorder. (He may also have had a sexual disorder from Axis I.) Axis III is used to note any medical conditions. (Dahmer had none.) Axis IV refers to any other psychological, social, or environmental factors, such as stress, that might worsen symptoms. (He was a loner, had poor self-esteem, and poor social skills.) Axis V is used to rate a person's general functioning. (He functioned well enough to hold a job and go unnoticed in his neighborhood.) Thus, each of the five axes focuses on different factors that contribute to the overall clinical diagnosis.

ADVANTAGES OF DSM-IV

There are three advantages of using DSM-IV's uniform system to diagnose and classify mental disorders: (1) mental health professionals use the classification system to communicate with one another and discuss their clients' problems; (2) researchers use the classification system to study and explain mental disorders; (3) therapists use the classification system to design their treatment program so as to best fit their clients' problems (Clark et al., 1995). However, using the DSM-IV system of diagnosing or labeling mental disorders can also lead to other problems, which we'll examine next.

D. Anxiety Disorders

Phobias

Can fear go wild?

We all have fears of various things, such as exams, seeing blood, spiders, injections, mice, meeting new people, speaking in public, flying, or being in small places. But sometimes these common fears turn into very intense fears, called phobias.

A *phobia* (FOE-bee-ah) is an anxiety disorder characterized by an intense and irrational fear that is out of all proportion to the possible danger of the object or situation. Because of this intense fear, which is accompanied by increased physiological arousal, a person goes to great lengths to avoid the feared event. If the feared event cannot be avoided, the person feels intense anxiety.

Reseachers believe that, because 75% of individuals with phobias could trace their onset to specific traumatic events, the majority of phobias are learned through conditioning or observation (Kleinknecht, 1994; Menzies & Clarke, 1995). However, since 25% of those with phobias could not recall their onset, there may also be other causes of phobias.

We discussed blood injection phobias in Modules 9 and 21. Here we discuss three more common phobias—social phobias, specific phobias, and agoraphobia (graph above) (Kessler et al., 1994).

Common Phobias
Social phobia — 13%
Specific phobia — 11%
Agoraphobia — 5%

Social Phobia

Speech

Why didn't Billy talk up in class?
In junior high school, Billy never, never spoke up in class or answered any questions. The school counselor said that Billy would be sick to his stomach the whole day if he knew that he was going to be called on. Billy began to hide out in the restrooms to avoid going to class. Billy's fear of speaking up in class is an example of a social phobia (Barlow & Durand, 1995).

Social phobias are characterized by irrational, marked, and continuous fear of performing in social situations (right graph). The individuals fear that they will humiliate or embarrass themselves (American Psychiatric Association, 1994).

As a fearful social situation approaches, great anxiety builds up and may result in considerable bodily distress, such as nausea, sweating, and other signs of heightened physiological arousal. Although a person with a social phobia realizes that the fear is excessive or irrational, he or she may not know how to deal with it, other than by avoiding the situation.

Social Phobias
Speaking in public — 8%
Speaking to strangers — 5%
Eating in public — 4%
Source: Eaton et al., 1991.

Specific Phobias

Why couldn't Kate get on a plane?
In the beginning of this module, we told you about Kate Premo (left photo) whose traumatic childhood and adult experiences with flying turned into a phobia of flying, which is called a specific phobia.

Specific phobias, formerly called simple phobias, are characterized by marked and persistent fears that are unreasonable and triggered by anticipation of, or exposure to, a specific object or situation (flying, heights, spiders, seeing blood) (American Psychiatric Association, 1994).

Among the more common specific phobias seen in clinical practice (right) are fear of animals (zoophobia), fear of heights (acrophobia), fear of confinement (claustrophobia), fear of injury or blood, and fear of flying (Emmelkamp & van Oppen, 1994).

The content and occurrence of specific phobias varies with culture. For example, fears of spirits or ghosts are present in many cultures but become specific phobias only if the fear turns excessive and irrational (American Psychiatric Association, 1994).

Specific Phobias
Bugs, snakes, etc. — 23%
Heights — 22%
Water — 13%
Closed places — 10%
Source: Eaton et al., 1991.

Agoraphobia

Why couldn't Rose leave her house?
Fear trapped Rose in her house for years. If she thought about going outside to do her shopping, pain raced through her arms and chest. She grew hot and perspired. Her heart beat rapidly and her legs felt like rubber. She said that thinking about leaving her house caused stark terror, sometimes lasting for days. This 39-year-old mother of two is one of millions of Americans suffering from an intense fear of being in public places, which is called agoraphobia (*Los Angeles Times,* October 19, 1980).

Agoraphobia is characterized by anxiety about being in places or situations from which escape might be difficult or embarrassing if a panic attack or panic-like symptoms (sudden dizziness or onset of diarrhea) were to occur (American Psychiatric Association, 1994).

Agoraphobia arises out of an underlying fear of either having a full-blown panic attack (discussed on the previous page) or having a sudden and unexpected onset of panic-like symptoms.

After any of these phobias are established, they are extremely persistent and may continue for years if not treated (Gould et al., 1997). We'll discuss drug and psychological treatments for phobias at the end of this module, in the Application section.

Next, we'll look at another form of anxiety that can be very difficult to deal with—obsessive-compulsive disorders.

Agoraphobia
Public transport — 13%
Tunnels or bridges — 8%
Crowds — 7%
Going out by oneself — 4%
Source: Eaton et al., 1991.

Obsessive-Compulsive Disorders

Why was Shirley always late?

Shirley was an outgoing, popular high school student with average grades. Her one problem was that she was late for school almost every day. Before she could leave the house in the morning, she had to be very sure that she was clean, so she needed to take a shower that lasted a full two hours. After her two-hour shower, she spent a long time dressing, because for each thing she did, such as putting on her stockings, underclothes, skirt, and blouse, she had to repeat each act precisely 17 times. When asked about her washing and counting, she said she knew that it was crazy but that she just had to do it and couldn't explain why. She said that she had struggled against this problem for three years without success (Rapoport, 1988). Shirley's symptoms would be diagnosed as indicative of an anxiety problem called an obsessive-compulsive disorder.

An *obsessive-compulsive disorder* consists of obsessions, which are persistent, recurring irrational thoughts, impulses, or images that a person is unable to control and that interfere with normal functioning; and compulsions, which are irresistible impulses to perform over and over some senseless behavior or ritual (hand washing, checking things, counting, putting things in order) (American Psychiatric Association, 1994).

We'll discuss the symptoms and treatment of obsessive-compulsive disorder, or OCD.

Symptoms

Shirley's symptoms included both obsession—her need to be clean and careful about dressing—and compulsions—her need to take two-hour showers and to perform each act of dressing precisely 17 times. Some individuals have obsessions (irrational, reccurring thoughts) without compulsions. Because compulsions are usually very time-consuming, they often take an hour or more to complete each day. Although doing the compulsive behaviors may help individuals reduce their anxiety in the short term, in the long term the compulsive behaviors interfere with normal daily functioning.

The most common compulsions involve cleaning, checking, and counting; the less common include buying, hoarding, and putting things in order. For example, individuals obsessed with being dirty or contaminated reduce their anxiety by washing their hands until their skin is raw, while those obsessed with leaving a door unlocked may be driven to check the lock every few minutes (American Psychiatric Association, 1994). These kinds of obsessive-compulsive behaviors interfere with normal functioning and make holding a job or engaging in social interactions difficult.

Only five years ago, obsessive-compulsive disorder (OCD) was considered relatively rare, but now it is known to affect about 3% of adults in the United States (right graph) (Stanley & Turner, 1995). Worldwide, about 2% to 3% of the general population suffer from OCD (Sasson et al., 1997).

Treatment

As recently as 1987, the American Psychiatric Association viewed obsessive-compulsive disorder as a chronic, incurable disorder. Currently, however, about half the patients report being much improved after treatment with some combination of exposure psychotherapy or antidepressant drugs (Abramowitz, 1997).

Exposure therapy. Shirley's compulsive behaviors are thought to be one way that she reduces or avoids anxiety—in her case, anxiety associated with feeling dirty. The most successful treatment programs involve exposure therapy.

Exposure therapy consists of gradually exposing the person to the real anxiety-producing situations or objects that he or she is attempting to avoid and continuing exposure treatments until the anxiety decreases.

For example, Shirley would be exposed to dirt or dirty things over and over until such exposure elicited little or no anxiety. After exposure therapy, about 85% of patients reported being improved and 55% reported being much improved (Abramowitz, 1997).

Antidepressant drugs. For those clients who cannot tolerate exposure or are not motivated to undergo exposure therapy, the antidepressant drug clomipramine is often used. For example, Shirley refused to cooperate with the therapist and insisted that she had to continue her washing and counting rituals. But after taking clomipramine for about three weeks, her urges to wash and count faded sufficiently that she could try exposure therapy (Rapoport, 1988). However, about 25% of clients dislike clomipramine's side effects so much (nausea, dry mouth, diarrhea) that they drop out of therapy (Bisserbe et al., 1997). In addition, about 50% of clients with obsessive-compulsive disorder (OCD) are not helped by clomipramine or even a newer class of drugs called selective serotonin inhibitors (sertraline) (McDougle, 1997).

Thus, although for 25% to 50% of individuals with OCD drug treatment is not tolerated or effective, they can still be treated with exposure theapy.

One real advantage of using exposure therapy or cognitive-behavioral therapy to treat OCD is that these therapies have no unwanted physical side effects. In addition, researchers found that both exposure and cognitive-behavioral therapy were either equal to or more effective than antidepressant drugs or the newer selective serotonin inhibitors. However, in some cases, a combination of exposure therapy and drug treatments proved best (Abramowitz, 1997).

You have seen how irrational thoughts and compulsive rituals of OCD interfere with normal functioning. Next, we'll discuss how people create real physical symptoms that also interfere with normal functioning.

Anxiety Disorders

Social phobia	13%
Agoraphobia	5%
Obsessive-compulsive	3%

E. Somatoform Disorders

Mass Hysteria

Why did 250 students get sick?

As more than 500 students from various schools began to give a choir and orchestra concert, they suddenly began to complain of headaches, dizziness, weakness, abdominal pain, and nausea. These symptoms spread rapidly until about half the students developed one or more of the symptoms. Students who became ill were most often those who saw someone near them take ill. Students from one school, particularly girls in the soprano section, experienced the highest rate of symptoms. Younger members reported more symptoms than older ones, and girls (51%) reported more symptoms than boys (41%). At first, someone thought that a gas line had broken, but no one in the audience developed any symptoms. There was no ruptured gas line. The students' symptoms resulted from mass hysteria (Small et al., 1991).

Mass hysteria refers to a condition experienced by a group of people who, through suggestion, observation, or other psychological processes, develop similar fears, delusions, abnormal behaviors, or physical symptoms.

In this case, several of the most popular and visible girls complained of feeling dizzy and nauseous (they had been standing for hours). Soon other students were complaining about having similar physical symptoms until over 200 students eventually developed these physical symptoms.

In the Middle Ages, hysteria was attributed to possession by evil spirits or the Devil. Today, cases of mass hysteria are relatively rare but are reported in the media every 5 to 10 years. Mass hysteria always involves members of a group who, through psychological processes, develop *real physical symptoms* with no known physical causes. Mass hysteria is related to a group of psychological problems that together are called somatoform disorders.

Somatoform Disorders: Definition and Examples

What causes their physical complaints?

The same kind of painful or uncomfortable physical symptoms observed in mass hysteria are observed in individuals with somatoform disorders.

Somatoform (so-MA-toe-form) disorders are marked by a pattern of recurring, multiple, and significant bodily (somatic) symptoms that extend over several years. The bodily symptoms (pain, vomiting, paralysis, blindness) are not under voluntary control, have no known physical causes, and are believed to be caused by psychological factors (American Psychiatric Association, 1994).

Although the term *somatoform disorders* is not well known, these disorders are among the most common health problems seen in general medical practice (Kirmayer et al., 1994). The DSM-IV lists seven kinds of somatoform disorders. We'll discuss one of the more common forms—somatization disorder.

SOMATIZATION DISORDER

One kind of somatoform disorder, which was historically called hysteria, is now called somatization disorder.

Somatization disorder begins before age 30, lasts over several years, and is characterized by multiple symptoms—including pain, gastrointestinal, sexual, and neurological symptoms—that have no physical causes but are triggered by psychological problems or distress (American Psychiatric Association, 1994).

This disorder is reported in most cultures, and women are five times more likely to report it than men (Gureje et al., 1997). Those having this disorder use health services frequently and tend to have many hospitalizations and surgeries (Wool & Barsky, 1994). Researchers found that this disorder is frequently associated with a variety of personality problems, such as paranoia (Kirmayer et al., 1994). Somatization disorders are apparently a means of coping with a stressful situation, or indicating distress, or obtaining wanted attention (Janca et al., 1995).

CONVERSION DISORDER

The students at the choir concert described above probably experienced a kind of somatoform disorder called a conversion disorder.

A *conversion disorder* refers to changing anxiety or emotional distress into real physical, motor, sensory, or neurological symptoms (headaches, nausea, dizziness, loss of sensation, paralysis) for which no physical or organic cause can be identified (American Psychiatric Association, 1994).

For example, individuals have reported paralysis of a limb, lack of balance, blindness, or seizures, when in fact no physical, organic, or neurological damage could be identified. Usually the symptoms of a conversion disorder are associated with psychological factors, such as depression, concerns about health, or the occurrence of a stressful situation. The development of physical symptoms gets the person attention, effectively removes the person from threatening or anxiety-producing situations, and thus reinforces the occurrence and maintenance of the symptoms involved in the conversion disorder. Researchers found that in some cultures, bodily complaints (somatoform disorders) are used instead of emotional complaints to express psychological problems (Gureje et al., 1997; Janca et al., 1995).

After the Concept Review, we'll discuss how symptoms of mental disorders can vary between cultures, as we examine a disorder that seems to be unique to Asian cultures, especially Japan.

CONCEPT REVIEW

1. A prolonged or recurring problem that seriously interferes with the ability of an individual to live a satisfying personal life and function in society is called a _____.

2. There are three approaches to studying mental disorders. Viewing mental disorders as diseases is using the (a)_____ approach. Looking for the causes of mental disorders in unconscious conflicts or problems with unresolved conflicts is using the (b)_____ approach. Combining information from cognitive processes and learning-conditioning factors to understand mental disorders is using the (c)_____ approach.

3. There are three definitions of abnormality. A behavior that occurs infrequently in the general population is abnormal, according to the (a)_____ definition. A behavior that deviates greatly from accepted social norms is abnormal, according to the (b)_____ definition. Behavior that interferes with the individual's ability to function as a person or in society is abnormal, according to the (c)_____ definition, which is used by most mental health professionals.

4. When performed by a mental health professional, a systematic evaluation of an individual's various psychological, biological, and social factors that may be contributing to his or her problem is called a clinical (a)_____. A mental health professional who determines whether an individual's specific problem meets or matches the standard symptoms that define a particular mental disorder is doing a clinical (b)_____. One of the primary techniques used to gather an enormous amount of information about a person's past behavior, attitudes, and emotions and details of current problems is the clinical (c)_____.

5. The manual that describes the symptoms for almost 300 different mental disorders is called the (a)_____. The manual's primary goal is to provide mental health professionals with a means of (b)_____ mental disorders and (c)_____ that information in a systematic and uniform way. The DSM-IV has five major dimensions, called (d)_____, which serve as guidelines for making decisions about symptoms.

DISORDERS
DSM-I 106
DSM-II 182
DSM-III 265
DSM-IV 297

6. There are several kinds of anxiety disorders. An anxiety disorder that is characterized by excessive and/or unrealistic worry or feelings of general apprehension about events or activities, when those feelings occur on a majority of days for a period of at least six months, is called a (a)_____ disorder. An anxiety disorder marked by the presence of recurrent and unexpected panic attacks, plus continued worry about having another panic attack, when such worry interferes with psychological functioning, is called a (b)_____ disorder. Suppose a person has a period of intense fear or discomfort during which four or more of the following symptoms are present: pounding heart, sweating, trembling, shortness of breath, feelings of choking, chest pain, nausea, feeling dizzy, and fear of losing control or dying. That person is experiencing a (c)_____.

7. An anxiety disorder characterized by an intense and irrational fear and heightened physiological arousal that is out of all proportion to the danger elicited by the object or situation is called a (a)_____, of which there are several kinds. Unreasonable, marked, and persistent fears that are triggered by anticipation of, or exposure to, a specific object or situation are called a (b)_____. An anxiety that comes from being in places or situations from which escape might be difficult or embarrassing if a panic attack or panic-like symptoms were to occur is called (c)_____. Irrational, marked, and continuous fear of performing in social situations and feeling humiliated or embarrassed is called a (d)_____.

Speech

8. A disorder that consists of persistent, recurring irrational thoughts, impulses, or images that a person is unable to control and irresistible impulses to perform over and over some senseless behavior or ritual is called a (a)_____ disorder. A nondrug treatment for this disorder, which consists of gradually exposing the person to the real anxiety-producing situations or objects that he or she is attempting to avoid, is called (b)_____ therapy.

9. When something happens to a group of people so that all share the same fears or delusions, or develop similar physical symptoms, it is called (a)_____. There is a disorder that involves a pattern of recurring, multiple, and significant bodily complaints that have no known physical causes. This is called (b)_____ disorder, and one of its more common forms is somatization disorder.

Answers: *1. mental disorder; 2. (a) medical, (b) psychoanalytic, (c) cognitive-behavioral; 3. (a) statistical, (b) social norms, (c) maladaptive; 4. (a) assessment, (b) diagnosis, (c) interview; 5. (a) Diagnostic and Statistical Manual—IV, (b) diagnosing, (c) communicating, (d) axes; 6. (a) generalized anxiety, (b) panic, (c) panic attack; 7. (a) phobia, (b) specific phobia, (c) agoraphobia, (d) social phobia; 8. (a) obsessive-compulsive, (b) exposure; 9. (a) mass hysteria, (b) somatoform.*

Taijin Kyofusho, or TKS

Can a culture create a disorder?

Anxiety is a worldwide concern and is the third most common mental disorder in the United States and several Asian nations, especially Japan. We have already discussed how somatoform disorders, which come under the heading of anxiety disorders, occur in very similar form in many cultures around the world (Gureje et al., 1997). Now we look at how unique cultural values can lead to developing unique mental disorders. For example, if you had a social phobia in the United States, it would usually mean that you had a great fear or were greatly embarrassed about behaving in social situations, such as making a public speech. But if you had a social phobia in several Asian cultures, especially Japan, it might mean that you had a very different kind of fear or embarrassment, called taijin kyofusho, or TKS.

Taijin kyofusho, or TKS, is a kind of social phobia characterized by a terrible fear of offending others through awkward social or physical behavior, such as staring, blushing, giving off an offensive odor, having an unpleasant facial expression, or having trembling hands (Kirmayer, 1991).

Although many Westerners are also concerned or embarrassed about offending others through staring, having offensive body odors, or blushing, TKS is different in that it is an intense, irrational, morbid fear—in other words, a true phobia. Asians desperately try to voluntarily stop these TKS symptoms. However, since that usually fails, they try to avoid social interactions altogether. The Japanese word *taijin-kyofu* literally means "fear of interpersonal relation."

Occurrence. The top graph shows that TKS is the third most common psychiatric disorder treated in Japanese college students (Kirmayer, 1991). TKS is more common in males than in females, with a ratio of about 5:4. Most patients have a primary symptom, which has changed during the past 40 years. Initially, fear of blushing was the primary symptom, but it has currently been replaced by fear of making eye contact or staring (Yamashita, 1993). In comparison, making eye contact is very common in Western cultures; if you did not make eye contact in social interactions, you would be judged as shy or lacking in social skills.

The bottom graph shows that TKS begins around adolescence, when interpersonal interactions play a big role in one's life. TKS is rarely seen after the late 20s because, by then, individuals have learned the proper social behaviors. TKS seems to develop from certain cultural influences that are unique to Japan.

Cultural values. The Japanese culture places great emphasis on the appropriate way to conduct oneself in public, which means a person should avoid making direct eye contact, staring, blushing, having trembling hands, or giving off offensive odors. To emphasize the importance of avoiding these improper behaviors, mothers often use threats of abandonment, ridicule, and embarrassment as punishment. Through this process of socialization, the child is made aware of the importance of avoiding improper public behaviors, which result in a loss of face and reflect badly on the person's family and social group. Thus, from early on, Japanese children are strongly encouraged to live up to certain cultural expectations about avoiding certain improper public behaviors, especially staring and blushing, which are considered to be rude and disgraceful.

Percentage of Students

Psychosomatic disorders	24%
Depressive reactions	20%
TKS	19%

Clients Treated for TKS

15	10–12 years old
74	13–15 years old
55	16–18 years old
28	19–21 years old
7	22–24 years old

Social Customs

In Japan, individuals are expected to know the needs and thoughts of others by reading the emotional expressions of faces rather than asking direct questions, which is considered rude social behavior. In contrast, Westerners may ask direct questions to clarify some point and often use direct eye contact to show interest. Individuals in Japan who make too much eye contact or ask too direct questions are likely to be viewed as insensitive to others, unpleasantly bold, or aggressive. In fact, Japanese children are taught to fix their gaze at the level of the neck of people who they are talking to. This Japanese social custom that emphasizes not making eye contact, blushing, having trembling hands or offensive body odors during social interactions results in about 20% of Japanese teenagers and young adults developing an intense, irrational fear called TKS. This social phobia is so common in Japan that there are special clinics devoted only to treating TKS. The Japanese TKS clinics are comparable in popularity to the numerous weight clinics found in the United States. Interestingly, TKS is a kind of social phobia that doesn't occur in Western cultures (Kleinknecht et al., 1997; Yamashita, 1993).

Culture-Influenced Disorders

Although people in many cultures report anxiety about behaving or performing in public, the particular fears that they report may depend on their particular culture's values. For example, TKS—the fear and embarrassment of making eye contact, blushing, or having trembling hands during social interactions—is a social phobia unique to Asian cultures and unknown in Western cultures. Because of cultural differences, clinicians and researchers emphasize the importance of taking cultural values, influences, and differences into account when diagnosing behaviors across cultures (Kleinman & Cohen, 1997).

We have discussed the task of identifying symptoms and making a clinical diagnosis. However, as you'll see, making a clinical diagnosis sometimes proves very difficult.

G. Research Focus: School Shootings
What Drove Teens to Kill Fellow Students?

The boys were young (11 to 16 years old) and used rapid-firing guns. They targeted both students and teachers. Over a period of nine months, seven teenage boys took part in school shootings that left 15 people dead and 42 wounded. Everyone was shocked by the violence and wondered what had turned these adolescents into killers. In some cases, but not all, these adolescents might be clinically diagnosed with conduct disorder.

Conduct disorder refers to a repetitive and persistent pattern of behaving that has been going on for at least a year and that violates the established social rules or the rights of others. Problems may include aggressive behaviors such as threatening to harm people, abusing or killing animals, destroying property, being deceitful, or stealing.

The diagnosis of conduct disorder seems to apply to Kipland Kinkel, age 15, who was charged with firing 50 rounds from a semiautomatic rifle into the school cafeteria, killing two students and injuring 23. Those who knew him said that Kinkel had a violent temper and a history of behavioral problems, which included killing his cat by putting a firecracker in its mouth, blowing up a dead cow, stoning cars from a highway overpass, and making bombs (Witkin et al., 1998). Kinkel is also charged with killing his mother and father in their home the day before the cafeteria shootings. In trying to answer the question, "Why did these adolescents shoot their fellow students and teachers," mental health professionals have primarily used the case study approach.

A *case study* is an in-depth analysis of the thoughts, feelings, beliefs, experiences, behaviors, or problems of a single individual.

Mental health professionals have developed case studies by interviewing some of the adolescent shooters, who are listed below left. These case studies point to personal and social-emotional problems that likely contributed to the teenagers' unthinkable acts of violence. (All information and quotes below come from Egan, 1998.)

Adolescents Involved in School Shootings

Moses Lake, Washington: February 2, 1996
Barry Loukaitis, 14, confessed to firing on his algebra class, killing three and wounding one. He said that he wanted to get back at a popular boy who had teased him. Loukaitis shot the boy dead.

Bethel, Alaska: February 19, 1997
Evan Ramsey, 16, was convicted of killing a student and principal, whom he tracked down and shot with a 12-gauge shotgun. Ramsey thought it was "cool" to shoot up the school.

Pearl, Mississippi: October 1, 1997
Luke Woodham, 16, was found guilty of stabbing his mother, shooting and killing his ex-girlfriend and another student and wounding seven other students.

West Paducah, Kentucky: December 1, 1997
Michael Caneal, 14, allegedly killed three students and wounded five more when he fired on a prayer circle outside the high school. Caneal said, "It was kind of like I was in a dream."

Jonesboro, Arkansas: March 24, 1998
Andrew Golden, 11, (left) and Mitchell Johnson, 13, (right) were charged with killing five and wounding 10 when they fired on students and teachers leaving school after a fire alarm was pulled.

Problems Shared by Adolescent School Shooters

Although there are many differences among these seven teenage shooters, there are also the following similarities (Egan, 1998).

■ In almost every case, the teenage shooters felt inferior or picked on and held a grudge against some student or teacher.

■ The teenage shooters complained of normal things that bother most teens: being fat, short, unloved, or neglected. Most were of above-average intelligence, but depressed and suicidal.

■ The teenage shooters were able to obtain high-powered guns, often with the help of or through the negligence of their parents.

■ To varying degrees, many of the teenage shooters were obsessed with violent pop culture, including favorite violent rap lyrics, fantasy video games (*Mortal Kombat*), violent television, movies (*Natural Born Killers*), and violent Internet sites.

■ In almost every case, the teenage shooters gave warning signs of their intentions to kill somebody. Kinkel read a graphic journal entry to his class about killing fellow students. Loukaitis wrote a poem: "I look at his body on the floor / Killing a bastard that deserves to die / Ain't nothing like it in the world / But he sure did bleed a lot." Woodham's journal warned, "I do this to show society . . . No one truly loves me."

Mental health experts in school violence used case studies to identify the above symptoms and uncover possible reasons for these school shootings. The experts found these teenage shooters were generally depressed, insecure, lonely, and unloved. They held grudges, easily obtained guns, and surrounded themselves with violent music, video games, and movies. The experts suggest that these disturbed teenage killers saw the shootings as a way to end their sad and tortured lives in a final blast of terror (Egan, 1998).

Most of this module has focused on describing various mental disorders. Next we turn to explaining several ways of treating mental disorders—in this case, different kinds of phobias.

H. Application: Treating Phobias

Specific Phobia: Flying

At the beginning of this module, we told you about Kate Premo (left photo), who developed a phobia of flying. In some cases, people don't remember what caused their phobias, but Premo remembers exactly when her phobia began. Her fear began as a child when she was on a very turbulent and stressful flight. Her fear was further intensified by her memories of the terrorist bombing of Pan Am flight 103, which killed several of her fellow students. After that incident, her fear of flying turned into a real phobia that kept her from flying to visit friends and family. An estimated 25 million Americans have a phobia of flying called aerophobia, which may include fear of flying, crashing, heights, being in small enclosed spaces, or not having control of the situation (Van Gerwen et al., 1997).

Most phobias do not disappear without some treatment, and on the few occasions that Premo was forced to fly, she dosed herself so much with alcohol and tranquilizers that she was groggy for days. Finally, she joined a weekend seminar that helps people overcome their fears of flying (Sleek, 1994). Treatment for phobias can involve psychotherapy or drugs, or some combination of them. We'll discuss psychotherapy and drug treatment, beginning with cognitive-behavioral and exposure therapy.

Cognitive-Behavioral Therapy

Kate's intense and irrational fear of flying was fueled by two different processes involving fearful thoughts and heightened physiological arousal. These processes can be reduced or eliminated with cognitive-behavioral or exposure therapy, which may be combined or used separately and are about equally effective (Gould et al., 1997).

Cognitive-behavioral therapy involves using a combination of two methods: changing negative, unhealthy, or distorted thoughts and beliefs by substituting positive, healthy, and realistic ones; and changing limiting or disruptive behaviors by learning and practicing new skills to improve functioning.

Thoughts. Cognitive-behavioral therapy is used to help Kate control her fearful thoughts and eliminate dangerous beliefs about flying. For example, Kate had learned to fear various noises during flight, such as thumps and whines, which she believed indicated trouble, problems, or impending danger. To change these fearful thoughts, an airplane pilot explained the various functions of a plane: thumps meant the landing gear was retracting after takeoff or being put down for landing, and whines indicated movement of wing flaps. Thus, when Kate has a fearful thought, for example, "That noise must mean trouble," she immediately stops herself and substitutes a realistic thought, "That's just the landing gear."

Behaviors. Because Kate automatically gets nervous and fearful when just thinking about flying, she is instructed to do breathing, relaxation, and imagery exercises that will help her calm down. Deep and rhythmic breathing is an effective calming exercise because it distracts Kate from her fears and focuses her attention on a pleasant activity. Relaxing and tensing groups of muscles is also calming and helps to decrease physiological arousal. Finally, imagery exercises are calming because focusing on pleasant images is a very powerful way of using her mind to control (relax) her body's fight-flight response.

Cognitive-behavioral methods have proved effective in treating a variety of phobias (Gould et al., 1997). Sometimes cognitive-behavioral therapy is combined with another kind of therapy, called exposure therapy.

Exposure Therapy

Exposure therapy is the most difficult part of Kate's treatment because she must confront her most feared situation, flying.

Exposure therapy consists of gradually exposing the person to the real anxiety-producing situations or objects that he or she is attempting to avoid and continuing exposure treatments until the anxiety decreases.

Kate's weekend program provided one day for learning to control her thoughts and acquiring some basic relaxation techniques. However, the second day required that she fly on a regularly scheduled airline. As she sat in her airplane seat waiting for takeoff, she tried to fight back her tears and confront the irrational fear that she had lived with most of her life. Of the 12 people in Kate's weekend group, two backed out at the last minute because they could not overcome their terror and get on the plane.

During the entire flight, Captain Michael Freebairn (left photo) sat next to Kate and coached her. For example, as the plane began to taxi down the runway, Kate panicked but Captain Freebairn reminded her to begin her relaxation exercises (breathing and relaxing) and use pleasant images. Thus, throughout the flight, Kate was busy relaxing, breathing, and substituting positive, healthy thoughts for negative, fearful ones. When the plane landed, Kate was all smiles (left photo).

There are more than 35 fear-of-flying programs operating across the United States (Seaman, 1996). Most programs, which use some combination of cognitive-behavioral and exposure therapy, claim a success rate of about 80% (Sleek, 1994). The remaining 20%, whose fears are very intense, may require a number of treatment sessions; or they may undergo drug therapy or try computerized virtual reality programs. In this high-tech version of exposure therapy, individuals wear special goggles to view their worst fears in 3-D but do so in safety. Exposure to heights through virtual reality shows promise in helping individuals conquer their phobias (Fenly, 1996).

Social Phobia: Public Speaking

When does a fear become a phobia?

Almost everyone is somewhat anxious about getting up and speaking in public. For a fear to become a full-blown phobia, however, the fear must be intense, irrational, and out of all proportion to the object or situation. For example, individuals with social phobias have such intense, excessive, and irrational fears of doing something humiliating or embarrassing that they will go to almost any lengths to avoid speaking in public. There

are a number of very effective, nondrug programs for treating social phobias (fear of speaking, performing, acting in public) and specific phobias (fear of flying, heights, spiders, blood, needles, or small enclosed spaces). These programs involve some combination of cognitive-behavioral and exposure therapies and usually include the following four components (Gould et al., 1997; Turner et al., 1994).

1 Explain. Clinicians *explain* to the person that, since the fears involved in social phobias are usually learned, there are also methods to unlearn or extinguish such fears. The person is told how both thoughts and physiological arousal can exaggerate the phobic feelings and make the person go to any lengths to avoid the feared situation.

2 Learn and substitute. Clinicians found that some individuals needed to *learn* new social skills (initiating a conversation, writing a speech) so that they would function better in social situations. In addition, individuals were told to record their thoughts immediately after thinking about being in a feared situation. Then they were shown how to *substitute* positive and healthy thoughts for negative and fearful ones.

3 Expose. Clinicians first used *imaginary exposure,* during which a person imagines being in the situation that elicits the fears. For example, some individuals imagined presenting material to their coworkers, making a classroom presentation, or initiating a conversation with the opposite sex. After imaginary exposure, clinicians used *real (in vivo) exposure,* in which the person gives his or her speech in front of a group of people or initiates conversations with strangers.

4 Practice. Clinicians asked subjects to *practice* homework assignments. For instance, individuals were asked to imagine themselves in feared situations and then to eliminate negative thoughts by substituting positive ones. In addition, individuals were instructed to gradually expose themselves to making longer and longer public presentations or having conversations with the opposite sex.

Researchers report that programs similar to the one above resulted in reduced social fears in about 30–80% of those who completed the program (Gould et al., 1997; Turner et al., 1994).

Drug Treatment of Phobias

How effective are drugs?

Imagine being told to walk into a room and meet a group of strangers while you are stark naked. For most of us, this idea would cause such embarrassment, fear, and anxiety that we would absolutely refuse. This imagined situation is similar to the powerful kind of negative emotions that individuals with social phobia feel when they must initiate a conversation, meet strangers, or give a public presentation. Many of these individuals (30–80%) experience relief of symptoms after completing a program of cognitive-behavioral therapy (Gould et al., 1997). However, some individuals with social phobia do not choose to, or cannot, complete a cognitive-behavioral therapy program, which includes exposure to the feared situation. Instead, these individuals may choose drug therapy, which primarily involves tranquilizers (benzodiazepines) and, less frequently, antidepressants (Davidson, 1994; Davidson et al., 1994; Salzman et al., 1993).

The graphs below right show the results of a double-blind study in which individuals with social phobia were given either a placebo or a tranquilizer, in this case one of the benzodiazepines (clonazepam). After ten weeks of treatment, individuals given benzodiazepines showed a significant clinical reduction in scores on both anxiety and avoidance tests, which means they were able to function relatively well in social situations (Davidson, 1994). Although 73% of those on benzodiazepines showed a significant decrease in fear and anxiety, a remarkable 22% of those given placebos showed a similar decrease. This means that the significant decrease in the social fears of almost one out of four individuals was due only to psychological factors, such as the changes in their expectations and beliefs ("the pill will reduce my fear").

Average Score on Fear Scale

Baseline	39
Placebo	32
Baseline	41
Drug	21

Average Score on Avoidance Scale

Baseline	39
Placebo	30
Baseline	39
Drug	21

Although drug treatments are effective in reducing social phobias, there are two potential problems. First, about 50–75% of individuals relapse when drugs are discontinued, which means that their original intense social phobic symptoms return. Second, long-term maintenance on drugs can result in tolerance and increases in dosage, which, in turn, can result in serious side effects, such as loss of memory (Davidson, 1994).

Generally, similar and significant decreases in phobic symptoms (specific phobias, social phobias, and agoraphobia) have been reported using either drug therapy or cognitive-behavioral programs (Gould et al., 1997). Compared to drug treatment programs, one advantage of psychotherapy programs is that they have no unwanted physical side effects.

A. THREE APPROACHES

1. A prolonged or recurring problem that seriously interferes with an individual's ability to live a satisfying personal life and function in society is a _____. This definition takes into account genetic, behavioral, cognitive, and environmental factors, all of which may contribute to a mental disorder.

2. One approach to understanding and treating mental disorders views psychological problems as similar to diseases, and a major part of the treatment involves the use of psychoactive drugs. This approach is called the (a) _____ model. An approach that looks for the causes of mental disorders in unconscious or unresolved conflicts is the (b) _____ approach. An approach that uses a combination of information from cognitive processes and learning-conditioning factors to understand and treat mental disorders is the (c) _____ approach. According to this approach, people have learned maladaptive ways of responding to or thinking about themselves and their environments.

3. If a behavior is considered abnormal because it occurs infrequently in the general population, we are using a definition based on (a) _____ frequency. If a behavior is considered abnormal because it deviates greatly from what's acceptable, we are using a definition based on (b) _____. If a behavior is considered abnormal because it interferes with an individual's ability to function as a person or in society, we are using a definition based on (c) _____ behavior.

B. ASSESSING MENTAL DISORDERS

4. A systematic evaluation of an individual's various psychological, biological, and social factors that may be contributing to his or her problem is called a (a) _____. The primary method used in clinical assessments is to get information about a person's background, current behavior, attitudes, and emotions and also details of present problems through a (b) _____. A complete clinical assessment usually includes three major methods: (c) _____, _____, and _____.

5. Assessing mental disorders may be difficult because (a) _____ vary in intensity and complexity. The assessment must take into account past and present problems and current stressors. The accurate assessment of symptoms is important because it has significant implications for the kind of (b) _____ that the client will be given.

C. DIAGNOSING MENTAL DISORDERS

6. When mental health professionals determine whether an individual's specific problem meets or matches the standard symptoms that define a particular mental disorder, they are making a (a) _____. In trying to reach an agreement on the clinical diagnosis, mental health professionals use a set of guidelines developed by the American Psychiatric Association, which are called the (b) _____, abbreviated as DSM-IV.

7. The DSM-IV is a set of guidelines that uses five different dimensions or (a) _____ to diagnose mental disorders. The advantage of the DSM-IV is that it helps mental health professionals communicate their findings, conduct research, and plan for treatment. One disadvantage of using the DSM-IV to make a diagnosis is that it places people into specific categories that may have bad associations; this problem is called (b) _____.

D. ANXIETY DISORDERS

8. A mental disorder that is marked by excessive and/or unrealistic worry or feelings of general apprehension about events or activities, when those feelings occur on a majority of days for a period of at least six months, is called _____. This anxiety disorder is treated with some form of psychotherapy and/or drugs known as benzodiazepines.

9. One mental disorder is characterized by recurring and unexpected panic attacks and continued worry about having another panic attack; such worry interferes with psychological functioning. This problem is called a _____ disorder.

10. Suppose you experience a period of intense fear or discomfort in which four or more of the following symptoms are present: pounding heart, sweating, trembling, shortness of breath, feelings of choking, chest pain, nausea, feeling dizzy, and fear of losing control or dying. You are having a (a) _____. Panic disorders are treated with a combination of benzodiazepines or antidepressants and (b) _____.

11. Another anxiety disorder characterized by increased physiological arousal and an intense, excessive, and irrational fear that is out of all proportion to the danger elicited by the object or situation is called a _____.

12. DSM-IV divides phobias into three categories. Those that are triggered by common objects, situations, or animals (such as snakes or heights) are called (a) _____ phobias. Those that are brought on by having to perform in social situations and expecting to be humiliated and embarrassed are called (b)_____ phobias. Those that are characterized by fear of being in public places from which it may be difficult or embarrassing to escape if panic symptoms occur are called (c)_____. Once established, phobias are extremely persistent, continue for years, and may require professional treatment.

13. Persistent, recurring irrational thoughts that a person is unable to control and that interfere with normal functioning are called (a)_____. Irresistible impulses to perform some ritual over and over, even though the ritual serves no rational purpose, are called (b)_____. A disorder that consists of both of these behaviors and that interferes with normal functioning is called (c)_____. The most effective nondrug treatment for obsessive-compulsive disorder is (d)_____ therapy.

E. SOMATOFORM DISORDERS

14. The appearance of real physical symptoms and bodily complaints that are not under voluntary control, have no known physical causes, extend over several years, and are believed to be caused by psychological factors is characteristic of (a)_____ disorders. DSM-IV lists seven kinds of somatoform disorders. The occurrence of multiple symptoms—including pain, gastrointestinal, sexual, and neurological symptoms—that have no physical causes but are triggered by psychological problems or distress is referred to as (b)_____ disorder; a disorder characterized by unexplained and significant physical symptoms or deficits that affect voluntary motor or sensory functions and that suggest a real neurological or medical problem is called a (c)_____ disorder. A recent survey reported that somatoform disorders occur worldwide, although their symptoms may differ across cultures.

F. CULTURAL DIVERSITY: AN ASIAN DISORDER

15. A social phobia found in Asia, especially Japan, that is characterized by morbid fear of making eye-to-eye contact, blushing, giving off an offensive odor, having an unpleasant or tense facial expression, or having trembling hands is called _____. This phobia appears to result from Asian cultural and social influences that stress the importance of showing proper behavior in public.

Percentage of Students	
Psychosomatic disorders	24%
Depressive reactions	20%
TKS	19%

G. RESEARCH FOCUS: SCHOOL SHOOTINGS

16. A method of investigation that involves an in-depth analysis of the thoughts feelings, beliefs, experiences, behaviors, or problems of a single individual is called a (a)_____. This method was used to decide if teenage school shooters had repetitive and persistent patterns of behavior that had been going on for at least a year and involved threats or physical harm to people or animals; destruction of property; being deceitful or stealing. These symptoms define a mental disorder that is called (b)_____.

H. APPLICATION: TREATING PHOBIAS

17. There are several different treatments for phobias. A nondrug treatment combines changing negative, unhealthy, or distorted thoughts and beliefs by substituting positive, healthy, and realistic ones and learning new skills to improve functioning; this treatment is called (a)_____ therapy. Another therapy that gradually exposes the person to the real anxiety-producing situations or objects that he or she has been avoiding is called (b)_____ therapy. Individuals who are unwilling or too fearful to be exposed to fearful situations or objects may choose drug therapy.

18. Social and specific phobias have been successfully treated with tranquilizers called (a)_____. Although these drugs are effective, they have two problems: when individuals stop taking these drugs, the original fearful symptoms may return, which is called (b)_____; and, if individuals are maintained on drugs for some length of time, they may develop tolerance, which means they will have to take larger doses, which in turn may cause side effects such as loss of (c)_____. Researchers found that drug therapy was about equally effective as cognitive-behavioral or exposure therapy in reducing both social and specific phobias, including agoraphobia.

Answers: *1. mental disorder; 2. (a) medical, (b) psychoanalytic, (c) cognitive-behavioral; 3. (a) statistical, (b) social norms, (c) maladaptive; 4. (a) clinical assessment, (b) clinical interview, (c) clinical interview, psychological tests, neurological tests; 5. (a) symptoms, (b) treatment; 6. (a) clinical diagnosis, (b) Diagnostic and Statistical Manual of Mental Disorders—IV; 7. (a) axes, (b) labeling; 8. generalized anxiety; 9. panic; 10. (a) panic attack, (b) psychotherapy; 11. phobia; 12. (a) specific, (b) social, (c) agoraphobia; 13. (a) obsessions, (b) compulsions, (c) obsessive-compulsive disorder, (d) exposure; 14. (a) somatoform, (b) somatization, (c) conversion; 15. taijin kyofusho or TKS; 16. (a) case study, (b) conduct disorder; 17. (a) cognitive-behavioral, (b) exposure; 18. (a) benzodiazepines, (b) relapse, (c) memory.*

Module 23 DISORDERS II: MOOD DISORDER & SCHIZOPHRENIA

Mood Disorder

Why do his thoughts speed up?

Chuck Elliot (photo below) was checking out the exhibits at an electronics convention in Las Vegas when suddenly his mind seemed to go wild and spin at twice its regular speed. His words could not keep up with his thoughts, and he was talking in what sounded like some strange code, almost like rapid fire, "dot, dot, dot." Then he stripped off all his clothes and ran stark naked through the gambling casino of the Hilton hotel. The police were called and Chuck was taken to a mental hospital. After his symptoms were reviewed, Chuck was diagnosed with what was then called manic depression.

At one time, Chuck had a very successful career. After taking postgraduate courses, he obtained a doctor of education degree (Ed.D). He started and ran his own video production business while also designing computer software. But since that first strange episode at the computer electronics convention, Chuck has been hospitalized about twice a year when his mind races and spins wildly out of control in what are called manic episodes. He usually takes medication, but because the drug slows him down more than he likes, he stops taking his medication every so often. Without medication, his energy may come back with such force that it blasts him into superactive days and sleepless nights, and he often ends up in a psychiatric hospital.

His last regular job ended when he was in the middle of another manic attack. He was going on 100 hours without sleep when he went out to his car, grabbed a bunch of magazines, books, fruits, and vegetables and piled them all on the desk in his office. When his boss came by and found a desk piled high with junk and Chuck sitting there with his mind spinning, the boss fired him on the spot (Brooks, 1994). Since that time, despite his very good academic, computer, and business qualifications, he has not been able to hold a steady job.

More recently, Chuck married a woman he had been dating for only ten days. She understands Chuck very well because she too is a manic-depressive and has similar mental health problems. She hopes that they can care for each other. She says, "Chuck is the most brilliant man I have ever met. I am so lucky" (Brooks, 1994, p. 4).

In this module, we'll explain Chuck's illness, his treatment, and how he is currently doing.

Schizophrenia

Why was he hearing voices?

When Michael McCabe was 18 years old, Marsha, his mother, thought that he was just about over his rebellious phase. She was looking forward to relaxing and enjoying herself. But then Michael said that he was hearing voices. At first Marsha thought that Michael's voices came from his smoking marijuana. But the voices persisted for two weeks, and Marsha checked Michael into a private drug treatment center. He left the center after 30 days and seemed no better off than he had been before. Several days later, Marsha found Michael in her parents' home, a couple of miles down the road from her own house. Michael was sitting on the floor, his head back, holding his throat and making grunting sounds like an animal. Marsha got really scared and called the police, but before they arrived, Michael ran off.

Michael spent time with his grandparents, who finally called Marsha and said that they couldn't take his strange behavior anymore. Once again Marsha called the police. Just as Michael (right photo) tried to run away, the police caught him and took him to the community psychiatric hospital.

Marsha received a call from a psychiatrist at the hospital, who explained that Michael had been diagnosed as having schizophrenia, a serious mental disorder that includes hearing voices and disoriented thinking. A few days later, Michael escaped from the hospital. He was later returned by police, put into leather restraints, and given antipsychotic drugs that would also calm him down. Michael remained in the hospital and was treated with drugs for about a month, with little success.

Just about the time Marsha was at her wits' end about what to do next, Michael was put on a new antipsychotic drug, clozapine. After about a month on the new drug, Michael improved enough to be discharged back into Marsha's care (Brooks, 1994, 1995b).

In this module, we'll explain what schizophrenia is, describe the drugs Michael was given, and report how he is currently doing.

What's Coming

We'll discuss several different mental disorders and their treatments. We'll explain mood disorders and their treatments, including the treatment of last resort for depression, electroconvulsive shock therapy. We'll also examine several personality disorders and different kinds of schizophrenia, along with old and new antipsychotic drugs. We'll end with a group of strange disorders, one of which is multiple personality.

We'll begin with Chuck Elliot's problem, which is an example of one kind of mood disorder.

A. Mood Disorders

Treatment of Mood Disorders

Is there a "best" treatment? We have discussed Rod Steiger (right photo), who was diagnosed with a major depressive disorder, and Chuck Elliot, who was diagnosed with a bipolar I disorder (manic-depressive disorder). Because of their different diagnoses, they would be treated with different drugs, which are often combined with psychotherapy. We'll discuss the benefits and limitations of drug therapy and psychotherapy.

Major Depressive and Dysthymic Disorder

The reason actor Rod Steiger waited some time before seeking treatment was that he feared the public stigma that Hollywood attached to having a mental illness. He decided to fight the stigma by making his fight with depression public and seeking treatment, which involved taking an antidepressant drug.

Antidepressant drugs act by increasing levels of a specific group of neurotransmitters (monoamines, such as serotonin) that is believed to be involved in the regulation of emotions and moods.

Selective serotonin reuptake inhibitors. Currently, about 80% of prescribed antidepressant drugs, such as Prozac (fluoxetine), belong to a group of drugs called selective serotonin reuptake inhibitors (Sussman & Ginsberg, 1998). These drugs are relatively new and work primarily by raising the level of a single neurotransmitter, serotonin. When the effectiveness of several older antidepressant drugs were compared with Prozac, all the drugs proved effective, but the other drugs had more undesirable side effects than Prozac. Twice as many patients (up to 50%) dropped out of treatment due to side effects of the older antidepressants as did patients who took Prozac (Rivas-Vazquez & Blais, 1997).

Effectiveness of antidepressants. One curious feature of antidepressants is that it may be four to six weeks before they begin to work. About 70% of patients show improvement, while the remaining 30% receive little or no benefit from antidepressant drugs (Rivas-Vazquez & Blais, 1997). In addition, when patients stop taking antidepressants, about 50% relapse within three months, and more than 80% will relapse during the next three years (Fava & Kaji, 1994). Although antidepressant drugs have proved effective for the majority of patients, the question is whether drugs are more or less effective than psychotherapy.

Psychotherapy. Researchers have compared patients who received antidepressant drugs, psychotherapy, or a combination of drugs and psychotherapy to treat major depression. For patients with less severe depression, psychotherapy was as effective as antidepressant drugs. For patients with more severe depression or who were older, a combination of antidepressant drugs and psychotherapy was more effective (Elkin et al., 1989; Thase et al., 1997). When patients who had recovered were followed for 18 months, the results were discouraging. Only about 30% of patients who had received psychotherapy were still well, compared with about 20% of patients who had received antidepressant drugs and 20% who had received placebos. Researchers concluded that either the treatment did not last long enough or was not good enough to produce long-term, significant changes and prevent relapse for 70% of the patients (Shea et al., 1992).

The current treatments for depression, whether drug or psychotherapy, initially help the majority of patients. However, about 70% of patients relapse, become depressed, and require further treatment for depression during their lifetime (Solomon et al., 1997).

Bipolar I Disorder

Unlike Rod Steiger's problem, which was major depressive disorder, Chuck Elliot has bipolar I disorder, which means that he cycles between episodes of depression and mania. For example, one of Elliot's manic episodes lasted four days, during which he was in almost constant motion and did not sleep (right photo). Several times, when he lost control, he screamed at his wife and ripped the blinds from the windows. At that point, his wife called the police, whom Elliot wanted to avoid meeting at all costs. Elliot immediately left the house, but the police caught and handcuffed him and drove him to a psychiatric hospital for drug treatment. The medication that Elliot takes for his bipolar I disorder is called lithium.

Lithium (LITH-ee-um), which is a naturally occurring mineral salt, is the most effective treatment for bipolar I disorder because it reduces or prevents manic episodes.

Lithium is thought to prevent manic episodes by preventing neurons from being overstimulated (Chuang, 1998). When Elliot takes his medication, he functions well enough that he has enrolled in law school and is currently working toward his degree. The problem arises when Elliot doesn't take his lithium. Within four weeks of stopping lithium, about 50% of the patients experience a manic episode (Cookson, 1997).

In terms of effectiveness, about 30–60% of bipolar patients are greatly helped with lithium; 30–50% are partially helped; and 10–20% get little or no help (Moncrieff, 1997). Because of lithium's serious side effects (weight gain, toxic effects), about 28% of patients stop treatment on their own and may relapse (Maj et al., 1997). Because lithium prevents mania, patients may stop taking it to experience the euphoria they miss, as Elliot did several times. Lithium has also been found to be effective in treating individuals with *mania*—that is, manic episodes without the depression.

Thus, the same problem exists for treatment of major and bipolar I disorder: 10–30% receive no help from current drugs and 30–70% initially get better but may relapse. Researchers are constantly searching for new ways to treat mood disorders and prevent relapse.

For individuals with major depression who are not helped by drugs, the treatment of last resort is electroconvulsive therapy.

Definition

Can brain seizures decrease depression?

Dick Cavett (right photo) was known as a witty and clever radio and television talk show host with a great sense of humor, a boyish smile, and a Yale education. No one would ever have guessed that for most of his life Cavett suffered from major depression. He described becoming stuck in a state of depression for months, when he wouldn't do anything but brush his teeth and sleep till three in the afternoon. His episodes of depression persisted for years until his wife suggested that he get professional help. A psychiatrist prescribed antidepressants that helped to keep him from falling into depressed states. However, once he went off antidepressants, he had his most terrible depressive episode, for which he was hospitalized. While in the hospital, his depression was treated with electroconvulsive therapy, or ECT.

Electroconvulsive therapy, or *ECT,* involves placing electrodes on the skull and administering a mild electrical current that passes through the brain and causes a seizure. Usual treatment consists of a series of 10–12 ECT sessions, at the rate of about three per week.

Cavett says that, in his case, "ECT was miraculous. My wife was dubious, but when she came into my room afterward, I sat up and said, 'Look who's back among the living.' It was like a magic wand. ECT is used as a jump start to get you back. From that point on—the six weeks I was in the hospital and to this day—I've been treated with medication" (Cavett, 1992, p. 90).

Currently, Cavett appears to be functioning very well. He does radio commercials, has a program on the World Wide Web, and shows few if any of the side effects associated with ECT. We'll discuss the pros and cons of electroconvulsive therapy.

Use of ECT

If antidepressants fail to decrease depression, as they do in up to 30% of patients in the United States, the treatment of last resort is ECT. As shown in the graph, ECT's use has been increasing since 1980 and is currently estimated at between 50,000 and 100,000 patients per year (Cauchon, 1995). ECT is primarily used to treat

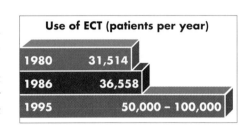

Use of ECT (patients per year)

Year	Patients per year
1980	31,514
1986	36,558
1995	50,000 – 100,000

mood disorders (84%), especially depression. The majority of ECT treatment occurs in private hospitals (64%), and the vast majority of patients have been white (90%) and female (71%) (Thompson et al., 1994). Why is ECT called the treatment of last resort?

Effectiveness of ECT

ECT is considered a treatment of last resort because it produces major brain seizures and may cause varying degrees of memory loss. However, a recent review reported that ECT was effective in reducing depressive symptoms in about 60–80% of patients. This relatively high rate is surprising, since all these patients had already tried and failed to benefit from antidepressants (Rabheru & Persad, 1997). For example, the graph on the right shows the results for eight out of nine seriously depressed patients who had received no help from antidepressants. After a series of ECT treatments, they showed a rather dramatic reduction in depressive symptoms and remained symptom-free after one year (Paul et al., 1981). Researchers suggest that ECT works by temporarily reducing blood flow to certain brain areas (Nobler & Sackheim, 1998).

Modern ECT. Unlike patients who received ECT in the movie *One Flew Over the Cuckoo's Nest*, there is no evidence that modern ECT procedures cause brain damage or turn people into "vegetables" (Salzman, 1998). Modern ECT procedures include the proper placement of electrodes on the scalp and reduced levels of electrical current. However, one serious side effect of ECT is

memory impairment, which may range from a persistent loss of memory for events experienced during the weeks of treatment, as well as events before and after treatment. Following ECT treatment, there is a gradual improvement in memory functions, and researchers have reported that long-term impairment of memory following ECT was minimal and returned to pretreatment levels within six months (Sackeim & Stern, 1997). In spite of this finding, about 50% of patients given ECT reported poor memory three years after treatment. In these cases, it is not known whether the impairment was caused by the ECT or by the long-standing depression (Squire & Slater, 1983; Sobin et al., 1995).

A National Institute of Mental Health panel of experts gave a cautious endorsement to the use of ECT as a treatment of last resort for some types of severe depression. The panel added that the patient should be informed as fully as possible of the potential risks, such as memory loss (Holden, 1985).

Next, we examine a disorder that is found in many serial killers.

C. Personality Disorders

Definition

How do people describe serial killers?

We have all heard the expression "Don't judge a book by its cover." That advice proved absolutely true when we heard what their friends and neighbors said about the following individuals.

A high school classmate of Joel Rifkin said that he was "quiet, shy, not the kind of guy who would do something like this." Rifkin confessed to killing 17 prostitutes.

His boss said David Berkowitz was "quiet and reserved and kept pretty much to himself. That's the way he was here, nice—a quiet, shy fellow." Berkowitz, known as "Son of Sam," was convicted of killing six people.

A neighbor of Westley Allan Dodd said that he "seemed so harmless, such an all-around, basic good citizen." Dodd was executed for kidnapping, raping, and murdering three small boys.

A neighbor said John Esposito "was such a quiet, caring person. He was a very nice person." Esposito was charged with kidnapping a young girl and keeping her in an underground bunker for 16 days.

A friend said Jeffrey Dahmer "didn't have much to say, was quiet, like the average Joe." Dahmer confessed to killing and dismembering 17 people (*Time*, July 12, 1993, p. 18).

Notice how their friends and neighbors judged all these cold-blooded killers to be "quiet" and "nice" and even "caring" individuals. However, while these individuals appeared very ordinary in public appearance and behavior, each was hiding a deep-seated, serious, and dangerous personality disorder (Hickey, 1991).

A *personality disorder* consists of inflexible, long-standing, maladaptive traits that cause significantly impaired functioning or great distress in one's personal and social life (American Psychiatric Association, 1994).

Personality disorders are found in about 12% of the adult population in the United States (Weissman, 1993). Of the ten different personality disorders described in DSM-IV, here are six of the more common types.

- *Paranoid personality disorder* is a pattern of distrust and suspiciousness and perceiving others as having evil motives (0.5–2.5% of population).
- *Schizotypal personality disorder* is characterized by an acute discomfort in close relationships, distortions in thinking, and eccentric behavior (3–5% of population).
- *Histrionic personality disorder* is characterized by excessive emotionality and attention seeking (2% of population).
- *Obsessive-compulsive personality disorder* is an intense interest in being orderly, achieving perfection, and having control (4% of population).
- *Dependent personality disorder* refers to a pattern of being submissive and clingy because of an excessive need to be taken care of (2% of population).
- *Antisocial personality disorder* refers to a pattern of disregarding or violating the rights of others without feeling guilt or remorse (3% of population, predominantly males) (American Psychiatric Association, 1994).

Individuals with personality disorders often have the following characteristics: troubled childhoods, childhood problems that continue into adulthood, maladaptive or poor personal relationships, and abnormal behaviors that are at the extreme end of the behavioral continuum. Their difficulties arise from a combination of genetic, psychological, social, and environmental factors (Brennan & Raine, 1997; Morey, 1997).

We'll focus on one particular personality disorder, the antisocial personality, because it is one the media is most likely to cover.

Antisocial Personality Disorder

The five "nice," "quiet" killers described above would probably be diagnosed with antisocial personality disorder or some combination of personality disorders. These individuals are more commonly called psychopaths or sociopaths, whose symptoms are on a continuum. At one end of the continuum are chronic delinquents, bullies, or lawbreakers; at the other end are the serial killers (Widiger & Costa, 1994).

Delinquent. An example of the delinquent end of the continuum is Tom, who always seemed to be in trouble. As a child he would steal items (silverware) from home and sell or swap them for things he wanted. As a teenager, he skipped classes in school, set deserted buildings on fire, forged his father's name on checks, stole cars, and was finally sent to a federal institution. After he served his time, he continued to break the law, and by the age of 21, he had been arrested and imprisoned 50–60 times (Spitzer et al., 1994).

Serial killer. At the other end of the psychopathic continuum is serial killer Jeffrey Dahmer, whom we also discussed in Module 22. Dahmer would pick up young gay men, bring them home, drug them, strangle them, have sex with their corpses, and then, in some cases, eat their flesh. As Dahmer said in an interview, "I could completely control a person—a person that I found physically attractive, and keep them with me as long as possible, even if it meant just keep a part of them" (Gleick, 1994, p. 129).

Two characteristics. One characteristic of psychopaths is their consistent pattern of disregard for or violation of the rights or properties of others; they may steal, harass or beat people, destroy property, kidnap or kill. Another characteristic of psychopaths is their dishonesty, lying, or deceitful manipulation of others. The combination of these two groups of characteristics make psychopaths potentially dangerous to deal with and, as you'll see, very difficult to treat or change into more responsible individuals.

Psychopaths: Causes and Treatment

Why are psychopaths difficult to treat?

Imagine trying to change someone who shows a complete disregard for behaving responsibly, is a habitual and very convincing liar, has no guilt or remorse, is impulsive and reckless, and fails to learn from experience (Lewis, 1991). These traits describe a psychopath, a person with an antisocial personality disorder. Psychopaths are much more likely to be men (2–4.5%) than women (0.5–1%), and they usually have a number of other related problems, including alcoholism, drug abuse, depression, anxiety, sexual deviance, and suicidal tendency (Black et al., 1995). We'll first look at the causes of this antisocial personality disorder and then the attempts to treat the disorder.

CAUSES

What makes psychopaths such puzzling and potentially dangerous individuals is a disorder that involves complex psychosocial and biological factors (Brennan & Raine, 1997).

Psychosocial factors. To identify psychosocial factors, researchers followed more than 500 cases of children who had been referred for behavioral problems (Robins et al., 1991). Many of these problem children, who later developed into full-blown psychopaths, had originally been brought to the clinic because of aggressive and antisocial behaviors, such as truancy, theft, disobeying their parents, and frequent lying with no signs of remorse. Because of the stress of dealing with constant problems, some parents became rejecting and hostile toward their children, and this hostile attitude elicited more behavioral problems. Thus, one psychosocial factor in the development of antisocial personality is the child-parent interaction: difficult children may elicit hostility from parents, which in turn makes children even more difficult and may increase their risk of developing chronic antisocial behaviors and a psychopathic personality (Morey, 1997).

Another psychosocial factor that may contribute to developing an antisocial personality is physical or sexual abuse in childhood, which is reported by 59–70% of psychopaths (Ruegg & Frances, 1995). However, many abused children do not become psychopaths, although they may develop other psychological problems (Module 17). For this reason, it is difficult to determine how much childhood abuse contributes to the development of antisocial personality disorders.

Biological factors. Many parents reported that, from infancy on, their children had temper tantrums, became furious when frustrated, bullied other children, did not respond to punishment, and were generally unmanageable. Behavioral problems that appear at such an early age and are so difficult to change suggest that there may be underlying biological factors, both genetic and neurological, that contribute to antisocial disorders.

Evidence for genetic factors comes from twin and adoption studies that show that genetic factors contribute 30–50% to the development of antisocial personality disorders (Thapar & McGuffin, 1993). Evidence for neurological factors comes from studies on neurotransmitters that indicate that individuals with antisocial personality disorders may have up to a 25% reduction in the neurotransmitter serotonin compared to control groups (Coccaro & Kavoussi, 1997).

Serotonin levels reduced by 25%

Based on all these studies, researchers suggest that genetic and neurological factors may predispose individuals to develop personality disorders and that the risk is increased by a number of psychosocial factors (Brennan & Raine, 1997).

TREATMENT

Psychotherapy has not proved very effective in treating psychopaths because psychopaths fail to see that many of their behaviors are antisocial and maladaptive, they do not hear or take their therapists' advice, and they do not speak the truth. In addition, because they are mistrusting, irresponsible, guiltless, and practiced liars who learn little from past mistakes, they constantly challenge and provoke their therapists. As a result, most therapists are pessimistic about modifying the behavior of psychopaths, whether teenagers or adults (Millon, 1981).

Because of the relative ineffectiveness of psychotherapy, clinicians have tried various drugs, including antidepressants, that act to raise levels of serotonin in the brain. Currently, researchers believe that some abnormality in the brain's serotonin system may underlie the impulsive, aggressive, and self-destructive behaviors observed in personality disorders (Coccaro & Kavoussi, 1997). Following this line of reasoning, researchers have used several relatively new drugs (sertraline, fluoxetine or Prozac) whose primary action is to raise levels of serotonin. As shown in the left graph, patients who took a serotonin-increasing drug (sertraline) reported significant decreases in their aggressive behaviors across eight weeks of treatment. However, researchers caution that aggressive behaviors may return once patients stop taking these serotonin-increasing drugs (Coccaro & Kavoussi, 1997; Kavoussi et al., 1994).

Drug That Increases Serotonin

A major question is whether psychopaths improve over time. Researchers did a 29-year followup of 71 men who had been treated for antisocial personality disorder. They found that only 31% continued to show improvement; the remaining 69% either showed no improvement or relapsed (Black et al., 1995). Researchers concluded that, for more than two-thirds of the patients, antisocial personality disorders are an ongoing, relatively stable, long-term problem that may need continual treatment.

Next, we'll examine one of the most tragic mental disorders—schizophrenia.

D. Schizophrenia

Definition and Types

What if you lose touch with reality?

At the beginning of this module, we told you about 18-year-old Michael McCabe (right photo), who said that his mind began to weaken during the summer of 1992. "I totally hit this point in my life where I was so high on life, it was amazing. I had this sense of independence. I was 18 and turning into an adult. Next thing I knew I got this feeling that people were trying to take things from me. Not my soul, but physical things from me. I couldn't sleep because they [his mother and sister] were planning to do something to me. I think there was a higher power inside the 7-Eleven that was helping me out the whole time, just bringing me back to a strong mental state" (Brooks, 1994, p. 9). Michael was diagnosed as having schizophrenia *(skit-suh-FREE-nee-ah)*.

Schizophrenia is a serious mental disorder that lasts for at least six months and includes at least two of the following symptoms: delusions, hallucinations, disorganized speech, disorganized behavior, and decreased emotional expression. These symptoms interfere with personal or social functioning (American Psychiatric Association, 1994).

Michael has a number of symptoms described in the list (right), including delusions (higher power inside the 7-Eleven), hallucinations (hearing voices), and disorganized behavior. Schizophrenia affects about 0.2–2% of the adult population or about 4.5 million people (equal numbers of men and women) in the United States (American Psychiatric Association, 1994). Of the inpatients in mental hospitals, about 30% are there because of schizophrenia, and this percentage is the highest of any mental disorder (Robins & Regier, 1991).

Subcategories of Schizophrenia

Michael's case illustrates some of the symptoms that occur in schizophrenia. In fact, no two patients have exactly the same set of symptoms, which are described in the list on the right. The DSM-IV describes five different subcategories of schizophrenia, each of which is characterized by different symptoms. We'll briefly describe three of the more common schizophrenic subcategories—paranoid, disorganized, and catatonic.

Paranoid schizophrenia is characterized by auditory hallucinations or delusions, such as thoughts of being persecuted by others or thoughts of grandeur.

Disorganized schizophrenia is marked by bizarre ideas, often about one's body (bones melting), confused speech, childish behavior (giggling for no apparent reason, making faces at people), great emotional swings (fits of laughing or crying), and often extreme neglect of personal appearance and hygiene.

Catatonic schizophrenia is characterized by periods of wild excitement or periods of rigid, prolonged immobility; sometimes the person assumes the same frozen posture for hours on end.

Differentiating between types of schizophrenia can be difficult because some symptoms, such as disordered thought processes and delusions, are shared by all types.

Do Some Schizophrenics Have a Better Chance of Recovery?

Chances of recovery are dependent upon a number of factors, which have been grouped under two major types of schizophrenia (Crow, 1985).

Type I schizophrenia includes having positive symptoms, such as hallucinations and delusions, which are a distortion of normal functions. In addition, this group has no intellectual impairment, good reaction to medication, and thus a good chance of recovery.

Type II schizophrenia includes having negative symptoms, such as dulled emotions and little inclination to speak, which are a loss of normal functions. In addition, this group has intellectual impairment, poor reaction to medication, and thus a poor chance of recovery.

According to this classification system, the best predictor of a schizophrenic's recovery is his or her symptoms: those with positive symptoms have a good chance of recovery, while those with negative symptoms have a poor chance (Andreasen et al., 1994b).

On the next page, we'll look at the causes of schizophrenia.

Symptoms of Schizophrenia

1 Disorders of thought. These are characterized by incoherent thought patterns, formation of new words (called *neologisms*), inability to stick to one topic, and irrational beliefs or delusions. For example, Michael believed that his mother and sister were plotting against him.

2 Disorders of attention. These include difficulties in concentration and in focusing on a single chain of events. For instance, one patient said that he could not concentrate on television because he couldn't watch and listen at the same time.

3 Disorders of perception. These include strange bodily sensations and hallucinations.

Hallucinations are sensory experiences without any stimulation from the environment.

The most common hallucinations are auditory, such as hearing voices. Other distorted perceptions include feeling that parts of the body are too small or too large.

4 Motor disorders. These include making strange facial expressions, being extremely active, or (the opposite) remaining immobile for long periods of time.

5 Emotional (affective) disorders. These may include having little or no emotional responsiveness or having emotional responses that are inappropriate to the situation—for example, laughing when told of the death of a close friend.

Biological Causes

What caused Michael's problems?

When Michael was in the hospital, his mother, Marsha (right photo), began going to a support group to get help and find out about schizophrenia. At one meeting Marsha said, "I haven't been doing very well with this, to be perfectly honest. How in the hell were we dealt this hand?" (Brooks, 1994, p. 8).

The psychiatrist who led Marsha's group answered that about 1 in 100 people get schizophrenia but the odds increase to 1 in 10 if it's already in the family. If a person inherits a predisposition for schizophrenia, any number of things—such as drugs, a death in the family, growing-up problems—can trigger its onset (Brooks, 1994). The psychiatrist was pointing out at least two major factors—biological and environmental—that interact in the development of schizophrenia. We'll begin with biological factors, specifically genetic causes.

Genetic Predisposition

In 1930, the birth of four identical baby girls (quadruplets) was a rare occurrence (1 in 16 million) and received great publicity. By the time the girls had reached high school, all four were labeled "different." They sometimes broke light bulbs, tore buttons off their clothes, complained of bones slipping out of place, and had periods of great confusion. By young adulthood, all four girls, who are called the Genain quadruplets and share 100% of their genes, were diagnosed with schizophrenia (Mirsky & Quinn, 1988). The finding that all four Genain quadruplets (left photo) developed schizophrenia supports the existence of a genetic factor in its development. Other support comes from twin studies.

Genetic Markers

Because researchers knew that schizophrenia might have a genetic factor, they compared rates of schizophrenia in identical twins, who share 100% of their genes, with fraternal twins and siblings (brothers and sisters), who share only 50% of their genes. The graph below shows the risk of developing schizophrenia for individuals who share different percentages of genes and thus have different degrees of genetic similarity. Notice that if one identical twin is schizophrenic, there is about a 48% chance that the other twin will also develop the disorder. In comparison, if one brother or sister (sibling or fraternal twin) is schizophrenic, there is only about a 10–17% chance that the other will develop the disorder (Gottesmann, 1991). In a recent study, researchers reported that if one identical twin was schizophrenic, there was an 83% chance that the other twin was also (Cannon et al., 1998). These twin data show that genetic factors are involved in developing schizophrenia and that the range is from 48% to 83%.

A *genetic marker* refers to an identifiable gene or number of genes or a specific segment of a chromosome that is directly linked to some behavioral, physiological, or neurological trait or disease.

During the past ten years, researchers have reported about half a dozen genetic markers for schizophrenia, but none proved valid, since none could be replicated by other laboratories (Marshall, 1995).

Currently, a group of researchers claim to have found a new genetic marker for schizophrenia that lies on a specific part of chromosome 6 (Wang et al., 1995). In this study, researchers analyzed the DNA from 186 Irish families, each having at least two members diagnosed with schizophrenia. They found that a specific part of chromosome 6 showed a significant association with those individuals who developed schizophrenia. As researchers continue to search for genetic markers, they believe that they will find not a single gene but a combination of genes that interact to produce a predisposition (a greater risk) for developing schizophrenia (Portin & Alanen, 1997). Researchers believe that genetic factors

Risk of Developing Schizophrenia

Identical twins (100% of genes in common)	48% – 83%
Offspring of two schizophrenic parents (50% of genes from each parent)	45%
Fraternal twins (50% of genes in common)	17%
Sibling (50% of genes in common)	10%
General population (0% of genes in common)	2%

The finding that increased genetic similarity is associated with increased risk for developing schizophrenia suggests that a person inherits a *predisposition* for developing the disorder. With this finding in mind, researchers have been searching for the location of specific genes involved in schizophrenia; such genes are called a genetic marker (Byerley & Coon, 1995).

act primarily during the 20th to 30th week of the fetal stage, when neurons show a fantastic rate of growth and development (Seeman, 1994).

One way that genes could produce a predisposition for schizophrenia would be to cause faulty development of certain structures in the brain. We'll examine what might go wrong in the brain to predispose one to develop schizophrenia.

D. Schizophrenia

Neurological Causes

Is the brain different?

During the past ten years, advances in studying the living brain—for example, using PET and MRI scans (discussed in Module 4)—have revealed at least three major differences between brains of schizophrenics and brains of mentally healthy individuals. As we'll explain, the brains of schizophrenics have larger ventricles, a smaller thalamus, and decreased activity in the prefrontal cortex (Lawrie & Abukmeil, 1998).

Ventricle Size

The brain contains four fluid-filled cavities called ventricles. The fluid cushions the brain against blows and also serves as a reservoir of nutriments and hormones for the brain. One early finding was that ventricles in the brains of schizophrenics were larger. Using MRI scans, researchers studied 15 pairs of identical twins, one of whom was diagnosed as schizophrenic while the other was mentally healthy (normal). Researchers found that the brains of schizophrenics had *larger ventricles* compared to brains of normals (left figures) (Suddath et al., 1990). Because more space is taken up by larger ventricles, the result is a reduction in overall brain size, which researchers have also reported (Kareken et al., 1995). However, not all brains of schizophrenics have larger ventricles or an overall decrease in brain size. Researchers conclude that some schizophrenics have abnormal brain structures but do not yet know how these abnormalities cause or contribute to the development of schizophrenia (Lawrie & Abukmeil, 1998).

Normal: Lateral ventricle

Schizophrenia: Lateral ventricle

Thalamus

Schizophrenia involves a bewildering combination of symptoms, from social withdrawal to hearing voices. Researchers have been hard put to find a single brain structure responsible for all these symptoms (Taubes, 1995). But that may change with a recent report that schizophrenic brains have an abnormally *smaller thalamus*. The

Thalamus

thalamus (shown above in blue) can be likened to a master switchboard, through which most sensory information passes on its way to other brain structures. Using MRI scans, researchers studied the brains of 40 schizophrenics and 40 normals and found that the average size of the thalamus was significantly smaller in brains of schizophrenics. Researchers concluded that the smaller thalamus may represent a defect in the neural circuitry, which underlies how we process information and may explain many of the diverse symptoms found in schizophrenia (Andreasen, 1997a).

Frontal Lobe

Another brain structure involved in many important cognitive, emotional, and personality behaviors is the prefrontal cortex

Prefrontal cortex

(shown in green), which is a thin film of neurons that covers part of the frontal lobe. Researchers report that in pairs of identical twins where one twin was schizophrenic and the other was not, the brain of the schizophrenic twin was characterized by significantly *less activation of the prefrontal cortex* (Torrey et al., 1994). This decreased prefrontal lobe activity is consistent with many of the cognitive (disorganized thinking), emotional (inappropriate emotional reactions), and personality symptoms (paranoia) observed in schizophrenics (Rajkowska et al, 1997).

All these studies point to at least three major brain abnormalities that may underlie the problems in schizophrenics. Next, we'll turn to environmental factors.

Environmental Causes: Diathesis Theory

Does stress play a role?

If biological factors alone explained why some develop schizophrenia, then the risk for developing schizophrenia in identical twins would be 100% rather than 48%. The risk for the other 50% comes from the influence of environmental factors, such as stress. For example, Michael McCabe (right photo) developed schizophrenia after the death of his father and during the stressful period between adolescence and adulthood.

Researchers believe that stressful events—such as having hostile parents, poor social relations, suffering the death of a parent or loved one, experiencing career or personal problems—contribute to the development of schizophrenia (Walker & Diforio, 1997). This relationship between stress and onset of schizophrenia is called the diathesis stress theory.

The *diathesis (die-ATH-uh-sis) stress theory* of schizophrenia says that some people have a genetic predisposition (a diathesis) that interacts with life stressors to result in the onset and development of schizophrenia.

This theory assumes that biological or neurological factors produce a predisposition for schizophrenia that interacts with environmental factors. If environmental factors include stressful events, they may increase the risk and vulnerability for developing the disorder, trigger an episode, or influence the recovery (Benes, 1997). Thus, the diathesis stress theory says that biological and environmental factors interact in the development of schizophrenia.

Now we'll examine the drugs used to treat schizophrenia.

Treatment

How is Michael treated?

After Michael (right photo) was taken to the psychiatric hospital, his symptoms were assessed and he was diagnosed as schizophrenic. Schizophrenic symptoms are commonly divided into positive and negative symptoms.

Positive symptoms of schizophrenia reflect a distortion of normal functions: distorted thinking results in delusions; distorted perceptions result in hallucinations; distorted language results in disorganized speech.

Negative symptoms of schizophrenia reflect a decrease in or loss of normal functions: decreased range and intensity of emotions, decreased ability to express thoughts, and decreased initiative to engage in goal-directed behaviors (American Psychiatric Association, 1994).

Like most individuals diagnosed with schizophrenia, Michael had both positive symptoms, such as delusions that people were going to steal from him, and negative symptoms, such as loss of emotional expression. To reduce these symptoms, he was given haloperidol, which is an example of an antipsychotic or neuroleptic (meaning "taking hold of the nerves") drug.

Neuroleptic drugs, also called antipsychotic drugs, are used to treat serious mental disorders, such as schizophrenia, by changing levels of neurotransmitters in the brain.

Currently, there are two kinds of neuroleptic drugs, typical and atypical.

Typical Neuroleptics

Typical neuroleptics were discovered in the 1950s and were the first effective medical treatment for schizophrenia.

Typical neuroleptic drugs primarily reduce levels of the neurotransmitter dopamine. Two of the more common are phenothiazines (for example, Thorazine) and butrophenones (for example, haloperidol). These drugs primarily reduce positive symptoms but have little or no effect on negative symptoms (Miller et al., 1994).

Because typical neuroleptics primarily reduce levels of dopamine, their method of action supports the dopamine theory of schizophrenia (Sanyal & van Tol, 1997).

The *dopamine theory* says that in schizophrenia the dopamine neurotransmitter system is somehow overactive and gives rise to a wide range of symptoms.

The neurons in one particular brain structure, the basal ganglia (right figure), use dopamine in communicating; these communications are significantly blocked by typical neuroleptics. However, because typical neuroleptics do not help about 20% of schizophrenics and a new group of atypical neuroleptics are proving effective, the dopamine theory is under revision (Sanyal & van Tol, 1997).

NEUROLEPTICS

| Typical: decrease dopamine | Atypical: decrease serotonin |

Basal ganglia

Atypical Neuroleptics

In Michael's case and for about 20% of all schizophrenics, typical neuroleptic drugs (haloperidol or Thorazine) have little or no effect on their symptoms. About half of these patients are now being helped by atypical neuroleptic drugs (Tamminga, 1997).

Atypical neuroleptic drugs somewhat lower levels of dopamine but, more importantly, reduce levels of other neurotransmitters, especially serotonin. One group of these drugs is the benzamides, such as clozapine. These drugs primarily reduce positive symptoms and may slightly improve negative symptoms (Bondolfi et al., 1998).

The first atypical neuroleptic, clozapine, was first approved for use in schizophrenia in 1990. Since then, a number of atypical neuroleptics have proven effective in decreasing schizophrenic symptoms, especially in patients who were not helped by typical neuroleptics.

Michael, for example, showed little improvement with typical neuroleptics (haloperidol). However, the atypical neuroleptic clozapine reduced his positive symptoms to the point that he was allowed to leave the psychiatric hospital and return home. A year later, Michael is still taking clozapine and is making slow progress in overcoming his symptoms, such as paranoia.

On most days, Michael comes home from group therapy and job-training classes, puts on a Bob Marley record, and sits and listens, afraid to do much else. As Michael explains, "I can't go out and skate or do anything because I'm afraid I'm going to have a paranoia attack" (Brooks, 1995a, p. D-3). His mother and sister (right photo) provide Michael with financial and social support but wish Michael (right photo, standing in back) would take greater initiative to improve his own life. Michael and many other patients with schizophrenia face a daily struggle to overcome their symptoms, which may last for months, years, or in some cases, a lifetime (Kane, 1997).

Clozapine—atypical neuroleptic. Many studies have found that about 50% of patients who did poorly on typical neuroleptics showed significant improvement on atypical neuroleptics, such as clozapine (Bondolfi et al., 1998). For this reason, atypical neuroleptics have been called the second major advance in the treatment of schizophrenia, the first being the discovery of typical neuroleptics (phenothiazines) in the 1950s.

Although typical neuroleptics and the newer atypical neuroleptics represent significant advances in the treatment of schizophrenia, both can produce significant and undesirable side effects, which we'll discuss next.

D. Schizophrenia

Problems with Neuroleptic Drugs

What are the side effects?

The major advantage of neuroleptic drugs is that they effectively reduce positive symptoms so that many patients can regain some degree of normal functioning. However, neuroleptics also have two potentially serious disadvantages: they may produce undesirable side effects, and they may not prevent relapse or return of the original schizophrenic symptoms. We'll first explain the side effects.

NEUROLEPTICS

| Typical: decrease dopamine | Atypical: decrease serotonin |

Typical Neuroleptics: Side Effects

One group of typical neuroleptics, called the phenothiazines *(pheen–no–THIGH–ah–zines)*, is widely prescribed to treat schizophrenia. Phenothiazines can produce unwanted motor movements, which is a side effect called tardive dyskinesia.

Tardive dyskinesia (TARD-if dis-cah-KNEE-zee-ah) involves the appearance of slow, involuntary, and uncontrollable rhythmic movements and rapid twitching of the mouth and lips, as well as unusual movements of the limbs. This condition is associated with the continued use of typical neuroleptics.

As shown in the graph below, the risk for developing tardive dyskinesia increases with use: after three months, 16% developed this side effect; after ten years, 40% developed it (Sweet et al., 1995). About 30% of patients with tardive dyskinesia will experience a reduction in symptoms if they are taken off typical neuroleptics, but the remaining 70% may experience the problem even when the drug therapy is stopped (Roy-Byrne & Fann, 1997).

The basic problem with taking patients off typical neuroleptics is that they may relapse. For example, after an average of 19 months, 53% of patients taken off typical neuroleptics experienced a relapse as compared to a relapse rate of 16% for those who were maintained on atypical neuroleptics (Gilbert et al., 1995). In treating patients with phenothiazines, clinicians must balance the dangers of a patient relapsing against those of developing tardive dyskinesia.

Risk of Developing Tardive Dyskinesia

3 months	16%
3–12 months	29%
1–10 years	30%
More than 10 years	40%

Atypical Neuroleptics: Side Effects

One advantage of atypical neuroleptics, such as clozapine, is that these drugs produce tardive dyskinesia in only about 5% of patients. However, about 15–35% of patients taking clozapine reported side effects of feeling fatigued and emotionally indifferent to what was happening around them (Gerlach & Peacock, 1994). One of the more serious side effects of clozapine is seizures, which were reported by 8% of patients, usually those on higher doses (Fleischhacker et al., 1994). But the most serious side effect of clozapine is sudden loss of infection-fighting white blood cells, which occurs in only 1–2% of patients but can result in death if not detected early. Perhaps the best news is that some of the newer atypical neuroleptics, which are similar in effectiveness to clozapine, have fewer side effects than clozapine (Roy-Byrne & Fann, 1997).

Relapse Rate and Long-Term Outcome

Typical neuroleptics. Researchers have completed several long-term followup studies on patients who were treated for schizophrenia with typical neuroleptics. They found that, 2–12 years after treatment, about 20–30% of patients showed a good outcome, which means they needed no further treatment and had no relapse; about 40–60% continued to suffer some behavior impairment and relapse, although their symptoms reached a plateau in about five years and did not worsen after that; and about 20% were not helped by these drugs and remained schizophrenic. Researchers concluded that, for the majority of patients, schizophrenia can be a chronic problem with a high risk for relapse during the person's lifetime (Davidson & McGlashan, 1997; Harding & Hall, 1997).

Atypical neuroleptics. Because atypical neuroleptics are relatively new, there are few long-term studies. In addition, only recently have atypical neuroleptics been made widely available. Previously, all patients must have been treated with, and showed no benefit from, at least three other typical neuroleptics before they could be given clozapine. This restriction was primarily because a serious side effect of clozapine was a sudden loss of white blood cells that could result in death if not quickly diagnosed. For this reason, patients are usually monitored weekly to check levels of white blood cells. Initially, clozapine treatment was not widely used because it cost $2,700 yearly versus only $1,000 for typical neuroleptics. However, researchers found that clozapine treatment was more cost effective in the long term because patients on clozapine spent less time in hospitals than did patients on typical neuroleptics (Aitchison & Kerwin, 1997).

Effectiveness. Studies on clozapine's effectiveness indicate that, after a year, 31–60% of patients who did poorly on typical neuroleptics showed significant improvement when given clozapine. In addition, after one year, only about 17% of patients who were maintained on clozapine were rehospitalized, while the percentage was almost double (31%) for patients on typical neuroleptics. The most surprising finding is that of the 50% who improve on clozapine, about 10% show very dramatic improvement, almost as if they were suddenly "awakened" from a long and silent sleep (Weiden et al., 1996). All these data support the claim that atypical neuroleptics represent a second revolution in the treatment of schizophrenia.

After the Concept Review, we'll discuss a disorder that has a very strange symptom—the person does not know who he or she is.

CONCEPT REVIEW

1. A prolonged emotional state that affects almost all of a person's thoughts and behaviors is called a _____ disorder.

2. The most common form of mood disorder is marked by at least two weeks of daily being in a bad mood, having no interest in anything, or getting no pleasure from activities and having at least four of these additional symptoms: problems with weight or appetite, sleeping, fatigue, difficulty thinking, and feeling worthless and guilty. This problem is called _____ disorder.

3. Another depressive disorder is characterized by being chronically depressed for many but not all days over a period of two years and having two of the following symptoms: poor appetite, insomnia, fatigue, low self-esteem, and feelings of hopelessness. This problem is called _____ disorder.

4. Another mood disorder is characterized by a fluctuation between a depressive episode and a manic episode that lasts about a week, during which a person is unusually euphoric, cheerful or high, speaks rapidly, feels great self-esteem and needs little sleep. This problem is called a _____ disorder.

5. The theory that underlying genetic, neurological, or physiological factors may predispose a person to developing a mood disorder is called the _____ of depression.

6. Factors such as dealing with stressors and stressful life events are believed to interact with predisposing biological factors and contribute to the development, onset, or maintenance of mood disorders. These are called _____ factors.

7. One treatment for major depression involves placing electrodes on the skull and administering a mild electrical current that passes through the brain and causes a seizure. Usual treatment consists of a series of 10–12 such sessions, at the rate of about three per week. This treatment is called _____.

8. Certain psychoactive drugs act by increasing levels of a specific group of neurotransmitters (monoamines, such as serotonin) that is believed to be involved in the regulation of emotions and moods.

These are called (a)_____ drugs. A naturally occurring mineral salt that is an effective treatment for bipolar I disorder because it reduces or prevents manic episodes is called (b)_____.

9. A person who has inflexible, long-standing, maladaptive traits that cause significantly impaired functioning or great distress in his or her personal and social life is said to have a (a)_____ disorder. Examples of this disorder include a pattern of distrust and suspiciousness and perceiving others as having evil motives, which is called a (b)_____ personality disorder; a pattern of being submissive and clingy because of an excessive need to be taken care of, which is called a (c)_____ personality disorder; and a pattern of disregarding or violating the rights of others without feeling guilt or remorse, which is called an (d)_____ personality disorder.

10. A serious mental disturbance that lasts for at least six months and that includes at least two of the following persistent symptoms—delusions, hallucinations, disorganized speech, grossly disorganized behavior, and decreased emotional expression—is called (a)_____. There are subcategories of this disorder: the one characterized by auditory hallucinations or delusions, such as thoughts of being persecuted by others or thoughts of grandeur, is called (b)_____ schizophrenia.

11. Drugs that are used to treat schizophrenia and that act primarily to reduce levels of dopamine are called (a)_____ drugs, and include phenothiazines. Drugs that are used to treat schizophrenia and that slightly reduce levels of dopamine but act primarily to reduce levels of serotonin are called (b)_____ drugs, and include clozapine. The theory that, in schizophrenia, the dopamine neurotransmitter system is somehow overactive and gives rise to many of the symptoms observed in schizophrenics is called the (c)_____ theory, which is supported by the actions of (d)_____ drugs but not by the action of (e)_____ drugs.

Answers: *1. mood; 2. major depressive or unipolar depression; 3. dysthymic; 4. bipolar I; 5. biological theory; 6. psychosocial; 7. electroconvulsive therapy, or ECT; 8. (a) antidepressant, (b) lithium; 9. (a) personality, (b) paranoid, (c) dependent, (d) antisocial; 10. (a) schizophrenia, (b) paranoid; 11. (a) typical neuroleptic, (b) atypical neuroleptic, (c) dopamine, (d) typical neuroleptic, (e) atypical neuroleptic.*

E. Dissociative Disorders

Definition

You have probably had the experience of being so absorbed in a fantasy, thought, or memory that, for a short period of time, you cut yourself off from the real world. However, if someone calls your name, you quickly return and explain, "I'm sorry, I wasn't paying attention. I was off in my own world." This is an example of a normal "break from reality," or dissociative experience, which may occur when we are self-absorbed, hypnotized, or fantasizing (Kihlstrom et al., 1994). Now imagine a continuum of dissociative experiences, with normal dissociative experiences on one end

and abnormal dissociative disorders on the other end. Although normal dissociative experiences are rather common in our lives, abnormal dissociative disorders are relatively rare and very unusual experiences.

A *dissociative disorder* is characterized by a person having a disruption, split, or breakdown in a his or her normal integrated self, consciousness, memory, or sense of identity (American Psychiatric Association, 1994).

We'll discuss three of the five more common dissociative disorders listed in the DSM-IV. These are dissociative amnesia (Who am I?), dissociative fugue (Where am I?), and dissociative identity disorder (formerly called multiple personality disorder).

Dissociative Amnesia

Mark is brought into the hospital emergency room by police. He looks exhausted and is badly sunburned. When questioned, he gives the wrong date, answering September 27th instead of October 1st. He has trouble answering specific questions about what happened to him. With much probing, he gradually remembers going sailing with friends on about September 25th and hitting bad weather. He cannot recall anything else; he doesn't know what happened to his friends, the sailboat, how he got to shore, where he has been, or where he is now. Each time he is told that it is really October 1st and he is in a hospital, he looks very surprised (Spitzer et al., 1994). Mark is suffering from dissociative amnesia.

Dissociative amnesia is characterized by inability to recall important personal information or events and is usually associated with stressful or traumatic events. The importance or extent of the information forgotten is too great to be explained by normal forgetfulness (American Psychiatric Association, 1994).

In Mark's case, you might think his forgetfulness was due to a blow to the head suffered on the sailboat in rough seas. However, doctors found no evidence of head injury or neural problems. To help Mark recall the events between September 25th and October 1st, he was given a drug (sodium amytal) that helps people relax and recall events that may be blocked by stressful experiences. While under the drug, Mark recalled a big storm that washed his companions overboard but spared him because he had tied himself to the boat. Thus, Mark did suffer from dissociative amnesia, which was triggered by the stressful event of seeing his friends washed overboard (Spitzer et al., 1994). In dissociative amnesia, the length of memory loss varies from days to weeks to years and is often associated with a series of stressful events (Eich et al., 1997).

As we'll see next, a person may forget who he or she is.

Dissociative Fugue

He got into a fight with a customer at the diner where he worked. When the police arrived, he gave his name as Burt Tate, but had no identification. He said he had drifted into town a couple of weeks ago and taken a job as a cook at the diner. Burt could not recall where he had come from, where he had worked before, whether he was married or had children, or anything from his past. When the police ran a missing persons' check on Burt, they discovered that he matched a person, Gene Saunders, who had disappeared a month before from a city 200 miles away. When Mrs. Saunders arrived, she identified Burt Tate as her husband, Gene Saunders (Spitzer et al., 1994). Gene Saunders had experienced dissociative fugue.

Dissociative fugue is a disturbance marked by suddenly and unexpectedly traveling away from home or place of work and being unable to recall one's past. The person may not remember his or her identity or may be confused about his or her new, assumed identity (American Psychiatric Association, 1994).

Before clinicians diagnosed Gene-alias-Burt as suffering from dissociative fugue, they ruled out drugs, medications, or head injuries.

Mrs. Saunders explained that, for about 18 months before Gene disappeared, he had been having great trouble at work; he had been criticized for his poor performance and passed over for promotion. The stress at work had made him difficult to live with at home. Formerly easygoing and sociable, he had become sullen and withdrawn.

As Gene's case illustrates, the onset of dissociate fugue is related to stressful or traumatic life events. Usually fugue states end quite suddenly, and the individual recalls most or all of his or her identity and past.

In other cases, a person may have several "true" identities. This condition is called dissociative identity disorder.

Dissociative Identity Disorder

The idea that one individual could possess several or more "different persons" who may or may not know one another, and who may appear at different times to say and do different things, describes one of the more remarkable and controversial mental disorders (Eich et al., 1997). Previously, this disorder was called multiple personality but now it's called dissociative identity disorder. We'll discuss a real case of dissociative identity disorder and its possible causes.

DEFINITION

Mary noticed something very peculiar about her car's gas gauge. Each night when she returned home from work, the gauge registered a nearly full tank of gas. However, when she got in to drive to work the next morning, the gauge registered about half full. Thinking that something suspicious was going on, she noted the mileage on the odometer each evening and compared it with the morning's. Someone was driving her car between 50 to 100 miles each night, and she had no idea who it was.

During a hypnotic treatment for pain, the physician asked Mary about the mileage someone was putting on her car. Suddenly a different voice answered, "It's about time you knew about me." This new voice said that her name was Marian and that she drove the car around at night to work out difficulties. Marian was as hostile and unfriendly as Mary was pleasing and sociable. During the course of therapy, six other personalities came out, some of whom were independent and aggressive while others were dependent and submissive. At times, the different personalities fought for control; each reported different memories. As a child, Mary had been physically and sexually abused by her father (Spitzer et al., 1994). The physician diagnosed Mary as suffering from dissociative identity disorder.

Dissociative identity disorder (formerly called multiple personality disorder) is the presence of two or more distinct identities or personality states, each with its own pattern of perceiving, thinking about, and relating to the world. Different personality states may take control of the individual's thoughts and behaviors at different times (American Psychiatric Association, 1994).

As in Mary's case, the personalities are usually quite different and complex, and the original personality is seldom aware of the existence of the others. After four years of psychotherapy, Mary managed to integrate the personalities into just two, which continued to fight with each other (Spitzer et al., 1994).

How common is dissociative identity disorder, and what causes it?

OCCURRENCE AND CAUSES

As shown in the right graph, the worldwide occurrence of dissociative identity disorder was very rare before 1970, with only 28 cases reported. However, an "epidemic" occurred in the 1970s and 80s, with estimates ranging from 300 to 2,000 cases (Fahy, 1988; Spanos, 1994). Reasons for the upsurge include incorrect diagnosis, renewed professional interest, the trendiness of the disorder, and therapists' (unknowing) encouragement of patients to play the roles (Hayes & Mitchell, 1994; Spanos, 1994). Whatever the reasons, the vast majority (70–80%) of mental health professionals are skeptical about the recent upsurge in occurrence of dissociative identity disorder (Hayes & Mitchell, 1994). The patients most often diagnosed with dissociative identity disorder (DID) are females, who outnumber males by 8:1. In addition, patients with DID usually have a history of other mental disorders.

Explanations. There are two opposing explanations for DID. One is that DID results from the severe trauma of childhood abuse, which causes a mental splitting or dissociation of identities as one way to defend against or cope with the terrible trauma. In one study, 89% of patients diagnosed with DID were women, and of these, 98% reported having been physically or sexually abused during childhood (Ellason & Ross, 1997). A second explanation is that DID has become so commonplace that it is now a legitimate way for people to express their frustrations or to use DID as a way to manipulate or gain personal rewards (Spanos, 1994). These opposing explanations reflect the current controversy in diagnosing patients with DID.

Treatment. Patients diagnosed with DID may also have problems with depression, anxiety, interpersonal relations, and substance abuse. As a result, treatment for DID involves helping patients with these related problems as well as helping them integrate their various personalities into one unified self, which may take years. For example, after two years of treatment, patients diagnosed with DID who showed the greatest improvement were those who showed the greatest ability to integrate or bring together and resolve the differences of their separate selves, and see themselves as a person with a single self. Clinicians concluded that treatment for DID is a long-term process but that many patients with DID were helped by psychotherapy (Ellason & Ross, 1997).

Worldwide cases of dissociative identity disorder

300 (1971–1988)

28 (1874–1920)

8 (1921–1970)

Spirit Possession

How does the world view mental disorders?

Imagine being a clinician and interviewing a 26-year-old female client who reports the following symptoms: "Sometimes a spirit takes complete control of my body and mind and makes me do things and say things that I don't always remember. The spirit is very powerful and I never know when it will take control. The spirit first appeared when I was 16 and has been with me ever since."

As a clinician, you would of course conduct a much more in-depth clinical interview and administer a number of psychological tests. But on the basis of these symptoms alone, would you say that she has delusions and hallucinations and possibly schizophrenia or that she has multiple identities and possibly dissociative identity disorder? In this case, both diagnoses would be incorrect. This female client comes from a small village in

Northern Sudan, where spirit possession is part of their culture and about 45% of married women over 15 years of age report spirit possession (Boddy, 1988). While in the United States symptoms of spirit possession would probably be interpreted as delusional and abnormal, in Northern Sudan spirit possession is interpreted as a normal behavior and an expression of the women's culture. To deal with possible cultural differences, the DSM-IV now includes an appendix that describes how to diagnose symptoms within the context of a person's culture (American Psychiatric Association, 1994).

Spirit possession is an example of how cultural factors determine whether symptoms are interpreted as normal or abnormal. Researchers are also finding that cultural factors influence the occurrence of certain other kinds of mental disorders (Kleinman & Cohen, 1997). We'll examine how cultural factors influence their occurrence.

Cultural Differences in Occurrence

Just as there is a manual to guide the diagnosis of mental disorders in the United States, *Diagnostic and Statistical Manual,* 4th edition (DSM-IV), there is also a worldwide classification system, called the *International Classification of Disease and Related Health Problems,* 10th revision (ICD-10) (World Health Organization, 1993). Since 1970, the ICD–10 has been used to make uniform, worldwide diagnoses of mental disorders. Using this worldwide diagnostic system, clinicians report remarkable differences in the frequencies of certain mental disorders.

■ Since 1970, the United States recorded the greatest increase in dissociative identity disorders (DIDs), while DIDs were rarely diagnosed in France, Great Britain, Russia, Japan, or Switzerland (Spanos, 1994).

■ Paranoid schizophrenia is 50% more common in developed countries. Catatonic schizophrenia, which has almost disappeared in developed nations, is 60% more common in developing countries (Kleinman & Cohen, 1997).

■ The suicide rate in China is about twice that of the United States and is highest among rural women. In the United States, the suicide rate is highest among white males (Kleinman & Cohen, 1997).

Although we know that biological factors play a role in the development of mental disorders, the examples above show the importance of cultural factors in the development of mental disorders.

Cultural factors influence not only the occurrence of disorders but also their rates of occurrence in males and females.

Cultural Differences in Gender Roles

Many mental disorders in the United States, such as bipolar I disorder and schizophrenia, are reported about equally by women and men. However, several disorders, such as major depression and dysthymic disorders, are reported significantly more frequently by women than by men (graph below) in the United States as well as in other countries, such as Chile, China, Taiwan, and Uganda (Kleinman & Cohen, 1997).

Major Depression and Dysthymic Disorder

Women	70%
Men	30%

Source: Kessler et al., 1994

One researcher attributes the larger percentage of women reporting depression to cultural differences in gender roles. Although gender roles have been gradually changing, the stereotypic gender role for men is to be independent and assertive and to take control, which tends to reduce levels of stress. In comparison, the stereotypic gender role for women is to be dependent, passive, and emotionally sensitive to the needs of others. This stereotypic role for women serves to reinforce women's feelings of being dependent, not having control, and being helpless, which in turn are known to increase levels of stress and thus place women at greater risk for developing emotional disorders such as depression (Barlow & Durand, 1995). These differences in reported depression between men and women point to cultural differences that influence gender roles, which in turn have the potential to increase women's risk of developing mood disorders, such as major depression (Kleinman & Cohen, 1997).

Just as cultural factors affect mental disorders, so too do neurological factors, which show what happens inside the brains of patients with mental disorders.

G. Research Focus: Brain Imaging
What Happens During Mental Disorders?

Looking Inside the Brain

How do researchers look inside the brain?

The development of new methods to look inside living brains gives researchers a way to look inside the brain of patients with mental disorders (Liddle, 1997). Earlier we discussed brain imaging methods in Module 4 and will briefly review two of them here.

When researchers wish to study the structure of the brain, they get very precise and detailed pictures by using MRI scans.

MRI or *magnetic resonance imaging,* involves passing non-harmful radio frequencies through the brain. A computer measures how these signals interact with brain cells and transforms this interaction into an incredibly detailed image of the brain (or body). MRIs are used to study the structure of the brain.

The MRI scan on the right shows a section through the middle of the brain, in which you can clearly see different areas. Remember that MRI scans show only brain structures. For example, MRI scans showed that some schizophrenics had larger ventricles (see page 540).

To study brain function, such as tracking specific brain areas that are activated during thinking, imagining, or perceiving, researchers use PET scans.

PET scan or *positron emission tomography* involves injecting a slightly radioactive solution into the blood and then measuring the amount of radiation absorbed by brain cells. Very active brain cells—neurons—absorb more radioactive solution than less active ones. A computer transforms the different levels of absorption into colors that indicate activity of neurons. The colors red and yellow indicate maximum activity of neurons, while blue and green indicate minimal activity.

The PET scan on the right shows a side view of the brain. You interpret a PET scan by looking for red and yellow areas, which show maximum neural activity. For example, researchers took PET scans of schizophrenic patients when they reported hearing voices. The PET scan above right shows that when patients reported hearing voices, maximum neural activity occurred in a primary speech center, called Broca's area. Based on PET scans, researchers concluded that when schizophrenics reported hearing voices, they really were hearing voices and not just imagining them and that the voices (auditory hallucinations) were actually coming from the patients' own speech areas (McGuire, 1993).

We'll describe some of the recent findings based on MRI and PET scans, which were taken from individuals with various mental disorders, including mood disorders and schizophrenia.

Brain Changes in Mental Disorders

How do brains differ?

Before the development of MRI and PET scans, researchers could only guess at structural and functional differences in living brains. By using MRI and PET scans, researchers have identified a number of structural and functional differences in individuals with mental disorders. The findings summarized below are the average from many brains, which means that some individuals may have greater changes, some lesser changes, and some almost none at all.

1 Frontal lobe. In some schizophrenics, MRI scans indicate a decreased size in frontal lobe area, and PET scans show less activity in the very front area, which is called the prefrontal area (Gur et al., 1997). The frontal lobe is involved in paying attention, planning, behaving emotionally, interacting socially, making decisions, and carrying out plans. Since the frontal lobe functions much like an executive, having a maldeveloped or underactive frontal lobe is much like having a disorganized executive in charge. Thus, a faulty frontal lobe may result in symptoms similar to those observed in schizophrenia.

2 Temporal lobe. In normal brains, temporal lobes are involved in perceiving reality. In brains of schizophrenics, PET scans showed that some temporal lobe areas were overactive (medial area) while others were underactive (inferior area). Researchers concluded that temporal lobes are involved in distorting reality, such as occurs during delusions or hallucinations (Liddle, 1997).

3 Thalamus, 4 Frontal lobe. MRI scans indicate that the thalamus, which filters and relays almost all sensory information to areas of the brain, is smaller than normal in brains of some schizophrenics. PET scans show that the connections between the thalamus and frontal lobe are faulty, which means that the brain's executive is receiving faulty information (Andreasen, 1997a).

5 Amygdala. PET scans of individuals with major depression show increased activity in the amygdala, which creates strong emotional memories, such as occur in major depression.

Based on brain imaging studies, researchers are developing a model of mental disorders that links mental problems with faulty brain structure and faulty brain circuitry (Andreasen, 1997b). Although this model shows the importance of biological factors, keep in mind that there is always an interaction between biological and psychological factors (stress).

SUMMARY TEST

A. MOOD DISORDERS

1. A prolonged emotional state that affects almost all of a person's thoughts and behaviors is called a _____ disorder.

2. One mood disorder is marked by being in a daily bad mood, having no interest in any-

Risk of Developing Bipolar Disorder	
Identical twins	80%
16% Fraternal twins	

thing, or getting no pleasure from activities and having at least four of the following symptoms: problems with weight, appetite, sleep, fatigue, thinking, or making decisions and having suicidal thoughts. This is called (a)_____ disorder, which is the most common form of mood disorder. Another mood disorder is characterized by being chronically depressed for many but not all days over a long period of time and having two of the following symptoms: problems with appetite and sleep, fatigue, low self-esteem, and feelings of hopelessness. This is called (b)_____ disorder.

3. A mood episode that is characterized by a distinct period, lasting at least a week, during which a person is unusually euphoric, cheerful, or high and has at least three of the following symptoms—has great self-esteem, needs little sleep, speaks rapidly and frequently, experiences racing thoughts, is easily distracted—is called a (a)_____ episode. A disorder characterized by periods of fluctuation between episodes of depression and mania is called (b)_____ disorder.

4. The theory that underlying genetic, neurological, or physiological factors may predispose a person to developing a mood disorder is called the (a)_____ theory of depression. Factors such as dealing with stressors and stressful life events are believed to interact with predisposing biological influences and contribute to the development, onset, or maintenance of mood disorders. These are called (b)_____ factors.

5. Psychoactive drugs that act by increasing levels of a specific group of neurotransmitters (monoamines, such as serotonin) believed to be involved in the regulation of emotions and moods, such as major depression, are called (a)_____. These drugs may take 4–6 weeks before they begin working, during which time up to 50% of patients drop out because of undesirable (b)_____. Currently the most popular antidepressant drug is (c)_____, which is no more effective but has fewer side effects than do previous antidepressants.

6. The most effective treatment for bipolar I depression is a natural mineral salt called (a)_____, which reduces manic episodes in about half the patients. Lithium is also used to treat euphoric episodes without depression; this disorder is called (b)_____.

B. ELECTROCONVULSIVE THERAPY

7. If antidepressant drugs fail to treat major depression, the treatment of last resort involves placing electrodes on the skull and administering a mild electrical current that passes through the brain and causes a seizure. This treatment is called (a)_____ therapy. A potentially serious side effect of this treatment is impairment or deficits in (b)_____, which usually affects events experienced during the weeks of

treatment, as well as events before and after treatment. However, following ECT treatment, there is a gradual improvement in memory functions.

C. PERSONALITY DISORDERS

8. A disorder that involves inflexible, long-standing, maladaptive traits that cause significantly impaired functioning or great distress in one's personal and social life is called a (a)_____ disorder. Ten of these disorders are listed in the DSM-IV, including: a pattern of being submissive and clingy because of an excessive need to be taken care of, which is called a (b)_____ disorder; and a pattern of disregarding or violating the rights of others without feeling guilt or remorse, which is called an (c)_____ disorder. There is evidence that personality disorders develop from an interaction of (d)_____ and _____ factors.

9. Evidence that genetic factors influence personality disorders come from studies on (a)_____, which show that genetic factors contribute 30–50% to the development of these personality disorders. Evidence for neurological factors comes from studies on (b)_____, which indicate that individuals with antisocial personality disorders may have up to a 25% reduction in serotonin.

D. SCHIZOPHRENIA

10. Schizophrenia is a serious mental disturbance that lasts for at least six months and includes at least two of the following

NEUROLEPTICS

Typical: decrease dopamine	Atypical: decrease serotonin

persistent symptoms: delusions, hallucinations, disorganized speech, grossly disorganized behavior, and decreased emotional expression. These symptoms interfere with personal or social _____.

11. DSM-IV lists five categories of schizophrenia, which include the following three. A category characterized by bizarre ideas, confused speech, childish behavior, great emotional swings, and often extreme neglect of personal appearance and hygiene is called (a)_____ schizophrenia. Another form marked by periods of wild excitement or periods of rigid, prolonged immobility is called (b)_____ schizophrenia. A third form characterized by thoughts of being persecuted or thoughts of grandeur is called (c)_____ schizophrenia.

12. Researchers have searched for an identifiable gene or a specific segment of a chromosome that is directly linked to developing schizophrenia. This genetic link is called a _____.

13. Two kinds of neuroleptic drugs are used to treat schizophrenic symptoms by changing levels of neurotransmitters in the brain. Drugs that act primarily to reduce levels of the neurotransmitter dopamine are called (a)_____ neuroleptics. An example is the phenothiazines. Drugs that somewhat lower levels of dopamine but, more importantly, also reduce levels of other neurotransmitters, especially serotonin, are called (b)_____ neuroleptics. An example is (c)_____, which is currently used when patients do not respond to the typical neuroleptics.

14. One side effect of continued use of phenothiazines is the appearance of slow, involuntary, and uncontrollable rhythmic movements and rapid twitching of the mouth and lips, as well as unusual movements of the limbs. This side effect is called _____.

15. One theory of schizophrenia says that it develops when the (a)_____ neurotransmitter is overactive. Another related theory says that some people have a genetic predisposition, called a (b)_____, that interacts with life stressors to result in the onset and development of schizophrenia.

E. DISSOCIATIVE DISORDERS

16. A dissociative disorder is characterized by a (a)_____ in a person's normally integrated functions of memory, identity, or perception of the environment. The DSM-IV lists five types of dissociative disorder, which include the following three. If a person is unable to recall important personal information or events, usually in connection with a stressful or traumatic event, and the information forgotten is too important or lengthy to be explained by normal forgetfulness, it is called (b)_____. If a person suddenly and unexpectedly travels away from home or place of work and is unable to recall the past and may assume a new identity, it is called (c)_____. If a person experiences the presence of two or more distinct identities or personality states, each with its own pattern of perceiving, thinking about, and relating to the world, it is called (d)_____ disorder.

17. One theory says that dissociative identity disorder (DID) develops as a way to cope with the severe trauma of childhood (a)_____. A second explanation is that DID has become

a legitimate way for people to express their (b)_____ or to manipulate others or gain personal rewards.

F. CULTURAL DIVERSITY: INTERPRETING SYMPTOMS

18. Spirit possession is one example of how cultural factors determine whether symptoms are interpreted as (a)_____ or _____. An example of how cultural factors may increase the risk for development of mood disorders can be traced to the differences in assigned (b)_____ roles: males are expected to be independent and in control, and females are expected to be dependent and not have control.

G. RESEARCH FOCUS: BRAIN IMAGING

19. Researchers use (a)_____ scans to identify brains structures and (b)_____ scans to identify brain-functions in the living brains of individuals with and without mental disorders. Changes in brain structure or function of individuals with mental disorders include having a underactive frontal lobe, both under- and overactive temporal lobes, and an overactive (c)_____, which is involved in creating strong emotional memories, as occurs in depression.

H. APPLICATION: DEALING WITH MILD DEPRESSION

20. Beck's cognitive theory of depression says that when we are depressed, we have automatically occurring (a)_____, which center around being personally inadequate. In turn, these negative thoughts (b)_____ how we perceive and interpret the world and thus influence our behaviors and feelings. Three factors that maintain mild depression are having poor social skills, lacking social support, and thinking negative thoughts or paying attention to negative events. Psychologists have developed effective programs to change these three behaviors.

Answers: *1. mood; 2. (a) major depressive, (b) dysthymic; 3. (a) manic, (b) bipolar I; 4. (a) biological, (b) psychosocial; 5. (a) antidepressants, (b) side effects, (c) Prozac; 6. (a) lithium, (b) mania; 7. (a) electroconvulsive, (b) memory; 8. (a) personality, (b) dependent, (c) antisocial, (d) biological, psychological; 9. (a) twins, (b) neurotransmitters; 10. functioning; 11. (a) disorganized, (b) catatonic, (c) paranoid; 12. genetic marker; 13. (a) typical, (b) atypical, (c) clozapine; 14. tardive dyskinesia; 15. (a) dopamine, (b) diathesis; 16. (a) disruption, split, breakdown, (b) dissociative amnesia, (c) dissociative fugue, (d) dissociative identity; 17. (a) physical or sexual abuse, (b) frustrations, fears; 18. (a) normal, abnormal, (b) gender; 19 (a) MRI, (b) PET, (c) amygdala; 20. (a) negative thoughts, (b) bias or distort.*

B. Questions about Psychotherapy

What do I need to know ?

If you or a family member, friend, relative, or acquaintance has a mental health problem, there are at least four questions that you might ask about seeking professional help or psychotherapy: Do I need professional help? Are there different kinds of therapists? Are there different approaches? How effective is psychotherapy? We'll answer each question in turn.

Do I Need Professional Help?

According to the American Psychological Association (1995), more than 30 million Americans each year need help in dealing with a variety of disorders, which range from those that cause some problems in daily activities to those that interfere with a person's normal functioning. A person may feel overwhelmed by a sense of sadness, depression, or helplessness so that he or she cannot form a meaningful relationship. A person may worry or expect such terrible things to happen that he or she cannot concentrate or carry out everyday activities. A person may become so dependent on drugs that he or she has difficulty functioning in personal, social, or professional situations. If these problems begin to interfere with daily functioning in social, personal, business, academic, or professional interactions and activities, then a person may need help from a mental health professional.

In the previous module, we discussed how two well-known individuals—actor Rod Steiger and television talk show host Dick Cavett—suffered from major depression for several years before they sought professional help. They delayed seeking help because of the stigma attached to having, and being treated for, a mental disorder. Similarly, most surveys report that about 40% of individuals with psychological problems do not seek professional help (Kessler et al., 1994). In part, this may be due to the cost or lack of availability of services, but a major reason why individuals avoid professional treatment is reluctance to admit to a personal failing or a psychological problem. In these cases, encouragement from a friend or loved one may be needed.

In the previous module, we also discussed the treatment of individuals with more serious mental symptoms. In one case, Michael McCabe heard voices and believed people were going to steal things from him (schizophrenia); and in another case, Chuck Elliot went sleepless for four nights and had trouble controlling his behavior (bipolar I disorder). Both of these individuals needed professional treatment but neither wanted nor asked for it. Thus, individuals with more serious mental disorders may not be able to decide what is best, and their friends or family may need to make that decision and ensure that they receive professional help.

Once a person makes a decision to seek professional help for a mental health problem, which kind of therapist should he or she select?

Are There Different Kinds of Therapists?

We'll discuss three of the more common kinds of therapists: psychiatrists, clinical psychologists, and counseling psychologists, each of whom receives a different kind of training in psychotherapy techniques.

Psychiatrists go to medical school, receive an M.D. degree, and then take a psychiatric residency, which involves additional training in pharmacology, neurology, psychopathology, and psychotherapeutic techniques.

Psychiatrists focus on biological factors and usually prescribe drugs to treat mental health disorders. Psychiatrists who receive additional training in psychoanalytic institutes are called *psychoanalysts*.

Clinical psychologists go to graduate school in clinical psychology and earn a Ph.D. This training, which includes one year of work in an applied clinical setting, usually requires five to six years of work after obtaining a college degree.

Clinical psychologists who receive additional training in psychoanalytic institutes can also use psychoanalysis. Clinical psychologists focus on psychosocial and environmental factors and use psychotherapy to treat mental health disorders.

Counseling psychologists go to graduate school in psychology or education and earn a Ph.D. This training, which includes work in a counseling setting, usually requires about four to six years after obtaining a bachelor's degree.

Counseling psychologists receive training similar to that of clinical psychologists but with less emphasis on research and more emphasis on counseling in real-world settings. Counseling psychologists, who function in settings such as schools, colleges, industry, and private practice, generally deal more with problems of living than with the mental disorders that are treated by clinical psychologists.

In addition, other mental health professionals, such as *clinical social workers* and *psychiatric nurses,* also provide mental health services.

Just as there are different kinds of therapists, there are also different kinds of therapeutic approaches from which to choose.

Are There Different Approaches?

If you were to seek professional help for a psychological or behavioral problem, you could choose from a number of different therapeutic approaches: some primarily use psychotherapy, some primarily use drugs, and others use a combination of psychotherapy and drugs. These different therapies can be divided into three groups: insight therapy, cognitive-behavior therapy, and medical therapy.

With *insight therapy,* the therapist and client talk about the client's symptoms and problems with the goal of reaching or identifying the cause of the problem. Once the client has an insight into the cause of the problem, possible solutions can be discussed with the therapist.

The classic example of insight therapy is psychoanalysis, whose goal is to help clients get insights into their problems. But because psychoanalysis requires hundreds of sessions, it is very costly; and since it is no more effective than other, briefer therapies, its popularity has significantly decreased since the 1950s. The next kind of therapy, called cognitive-behavior therapy, combines some features of insight therapy with a much more directive approach.

Here's my problem . . .

Cognitive-behavior therapy involves the application of principles of learning that were discussed in Modules 9 and 10. The therapist focuses on the client's problem, identifies specific thoughts and behaviors that need to be changed, and provides techniques based on learning principles to make desired changes.

Unlike psychoanalysis, which focuses on insight and gives little direction for change, cognitive-behavior therapy focuscs on changing specific undesirable or problematic thoughts and behaviors. This approach, which is sometimes called behavior therapy, has become very popular today.

Currently, the most popular approach, used by about 68% of therapists, is the eclectic approach (Lambert & Bergin, 1994).

The *eclectic (ee-KLEK-tik) approach* involves combining and using techniques and ideas from many different therapeutic approaches.

For example, a therapist using an eclectic approach might combine some of the nondirective techniques from psychoanalysis with more directive techniques from cognitive-behavior therapy. Unlike insight and cognitive-behavioral approaches, which focus on psychosocial factors, the next kind of therapy focuses on changing biological factors.

Medical therapy involves the use of various psychoactive drugs to treat mental disorders by changing biological factors, such as the levels of neurotransmitters in the brain.

Phenothiazines

Decrease dopamine

In Modules 22 and 23, we discussed medical therapies and how various psychoactive drugs are used to treat a wide variety of mental disorders, including anxiety, mood disorders, and schizophrenia. Unlike medical therapies, in which drugs may have undesirable physical side effects, no undesirable side effects are associated with psychotherapy. In this module, we'll focus on several psychotherapies, specifically insight and cognitive-behavioral approaches.

With so many different therapeutic approaches, is one kind of psychotherapy more effective than another?

How Effective Is Psychotherapy?

When we have problems, we sometimes say, "I'll just wait and maybe the problem will go away by itself." This kind of remark raises a major question: Is psychotherapy more effective than just waiting for problems to go away?

To answer this question and determine the effectiveness of psychotherapy, researchers used a complex statistical procedure called meta-analysis.

Meta-analysis is a powerful statistical procedure that compares the results of dozens or hundreds of studies to determine the effectiveness of some variable or treatment examined in these studies.

Researchers have done meta-analysis on over 1,500 studies that examined the effects of psychotherapy on a variety of problems, such as depression, anxiety disorders, family problems, eating disorders, and headaches (Jacobson & Christensen, 1996; Matt & Navarro, 1997; Wampold et al., 1997). There were three major findings:

■ Psychotherapy was effective in relieving a wide variety of psychological and behavioral symptoms in comparison with control groups who were on a waiting list to receive therapy or who received no systematic treatment.

■ There was little or no significant difference in effectiveness between the approaches used by different therapies. In other words, the same psychological or behavioral symptoms were, in most cases, treated effectively with different approaches.

■ The vast majority of patients (75%) showed measurable improvement by the end of six months of once-a-week psychotherapy sessions (26 sessions).

Thus, on the basis of data on thousands of patients and hundreds of therapists from the Western world, psychotherapy proved effective in treating numerous mental and behavioral problems, and the greatest improvement occurred in a relatively brief period of time (Lambert & Bergin, 1994). Generally, about 10–20% of clients who seek psychotherapy experience great improvement, 30–50% receive some improvement, and about 10–30% show little or no improvement (Bergin & Garfield, 1994; Mohr, 1995). Thus, although psychotherapy has proved to be an effective treatment, the amount of improvement varies across patients (VandenBos, 1996).

Although many different therapies seem to be about equally effective overall, we'll discuss how some approaches are preferred for certain problems. Another reason for different approaches is that some therapies better suit the personalities and expectations of the clients and therapists (Howard et al., 1996). For example, as we next discuss specific therapies, you may find that you would prefer one over another. We'll begin with one of the best-known therapy approaches—psychoanalysis.

C. Insight Therapies

Problems During Therapy

Why did clients get angry?

Freud was the first to notice that, during therapy, his clients became somewhat hostile toward him, a problem he called transference. He also found that patients became very resistant about dealing with their feelings. Freud believed that how these two problems, called transference and resistance, were handled determined how successful therapy would be. We'll explain these two concepts by using the cases of Rat Man and Wolf-Man.

Rat Man: Transference

Freud describes a patient, later labeled Rat Man, as expressing powerful, aggressive feelings toward him. For example, Rat Man refused to shake hands with Freud, accused Freud of picking his nose, called Freud a "filthy swine," and said that Freud needed to be taught some manners (Freud, 1909/1949). According to Freud, Rat Man was projecting negative traits of his own very controlling mother onto Freud, who became a "substitute mother." This process of transferring feelings to the therapist is called transference.

Transference is the process by which a client expresses strong emotions toward the therapist because the therapist substitutes for someone important in the client's life, such as the client's mother or father.

Freud believed that the main part of therapy involved working through the transference—that is, resolving the emotional feelings that the client has transferred to the therapist. Freud said that if the feelings involved in transference are not worked out, therapy would stall and treatment would not occur. For this reason, Freud believed that one of the major roles of the analyst was to help the client deal with, work through, and resolve the transferred feelings. Identifying the process of transference, which occurs in many therapeutic relationships, is considered one of Freud's greatest achievements (Ponsi, 1997).

Wolf-Man: Resistance

For most patients, working out transference and achieving insight into their problems are long and difficult processes. One reason for the difficulty is that the client has so many defenses against admitting repressed thoughts and feelings into consciousness. These defenses lead to resistance.

Resistance is characterized by the client's reluctance to work through or deal with feelings or to recognize unconscious conflicts and repressed thoughts.

Resistance may show up in many ways: clients may cancel sessions or come late, argue continually, criticize the analyst, or develop physical problems. For example, the patient named Wolf-Man constantly complained of severe constipation. Freud said that Wolf-Man used constipation as an obvious sign that he was resisting having to deal with his feelings (Freud, 1909/1949). Freud overcame Wolf-Man's resistance by promising that his constipation would disappear with continued therapy, and it did (Buckley, 1989). Freud cautioned that the analyst must use tact and patience to break down the client's resistance so that the client faces his feelings.

Thus, a necessary role of the analyst is to overcome the client's resistance so that the therapy can proceed and stay on course.

Short-Term Dynamic Psychotherapy

The cases of Rat Man and Wolf-Man illustrate that psychoanalysts must help clients do two essential things to achieve insight into the causes of their problems. First, analysts must help clients work out their strong emotional feelings involved in transference or else therapy will not succeed. Second, analysts must help clients overcome their resistance and begin dealing with threatening or undesirable feelings. However, resolving these problems of transference and resistance may take years. One reason psychoanalysis has greatly decreased in popularity is that it often requires several years of weekly sessions, while other current forms of psychotherapy are relatively short term. For this reason, a briefer version of psychoanalysis has been developed; it is called short-term dynamic psychotherapy (Della Selva, 1996).

Short-term dynamic psychotherapy, which is a shortened version of psychoanalysis, assumes that symptoms are signs of more basic underlying problems, that transference needs to

How long will it take for me to get over my fears?

be worked out, and that client's behaviors need to be interpreted. The main goal is to bring the client's underlying feelings to the surface. To do this, therapists take a more active and directive role in identifying and discussing the client's problems and suggesting solutions.

Unlike traditional psychoanalysis, which requires an average of 600 sessions over two years, short-term dynamic psychotherapy occurs in a maximum of 25–30 sessions. In addition, unlike traditional psychoanalysis, which is rarely evaluated for its effectiveness, short-term dynamic psychotherapy has proven effective for the treatment of stress and bereavement disorders, late-life depression, and adjustment, affective, and personality disorders (Della Selva, 1996; Lambert & Bergin, 1994). Short-term dynamic psychotherapy is now more popular than long-term psychoanalysis.

Next, we'll evaluate the current importance of psychoanalysis.

Psychoanalysis: Evaluation

The 50th anniversary of Sigmund Freud's death (1939) was marked by a series of articles in the *Psychoanalytic Quarterly* titled, "Is There a Future for American Psychoanalysis?" One author said that such a question was unheard of in the 1950s, when psychoanalysis was at the height of its popularity (Kirsner, 1990). However, following the 1950s, there has been a gradual decline in the popularity of psychoanalysis, which continues to the present (Henry et al., 1994). We'll examine the reasons for the decline in popularity of psychoanalysis, as well as its new directions.

1 Decline

No one factor but rather a combination of the following factors have contributed to the decline in popularity of psychoanalysis (Henry et al., 1994; Kirsner, 1990).

■ Many concepts of psychoanalysis, such as the search for unconscious conflicts, dream interpretation, working through transference, and overcoming resistance, have been incorporated into other approaches, such as the short-term psychodynamic approach and the eclectic approach.

■ A number of competing psychotherapies (discussed later in this module) have proven equally effective but have a great advantage in that they are much quicker and far less costly. Psychoanalysis may require 600 sessions versus 25 for other therapies. This last point is particularly important since most major health plans limit either the amount of money or the number of sessions (usually 23–25) for treatment of psychological problems.

■ Psychoanalysts have been very slow to analyze their own profession in terms of education—how best to train analysts—and to conduct research into what goes on during analysis and how to make it more effective. For example, during the past ten years, there have been almost no systematic, scientific studies on the effectiveness of the techniques used in psychoanalysis (Henry et al., 1994; Waldron, 1997).

■ Psychoactive drugs and briefer forms of other therapies have proved very effective, less costly, and much quicker in treating many of the problems formerly dealt with in psychoanalysis, such as anxiety and mood disorders.

These are some of the factors that have resulted in a significant decline in the use of psychoanalysis since its high point in the 1950s.

2 New Directions

While the practice of classical psychoanalysis has declined in recent years, there has been an increase in psychotherapy based on psychoanalytic principles; this is called the psychodynamic approach (Henry et al., 1994).

Psychodynamic psychotherapy shares many of the features of psychoanalysis—for example, discussing the client's feelings; breaking down the client's defenses and resistances; interpreting the client's behaviors; and working through transference problems. However, these therapists take a more directive role and thus shorten the total time in therapy.

Short-term dynamic psychotherapy, which is an example of the psychodynamic approach, has increased in popularity (Mitchell, 1996).

3 Popularity

As shown in the graph below, the most popular psychotherapy approach used by psychologists is the eclectic approach, which combines techniques and methods from many different therapies. But notice that the second most popular approach is the psychodynamic approach, which, as defined above, shares many of its methods and techniques with classical psychoanalysis (Sammons & Gravitz, 1990; Smith, 1982). Thus, while the practice of classical psychoanalysis has declined in recent years, there has been a corresponding gain in popularity of the psychodynamic approach, which makes use of several basic principles from psychoanalysis, such as tranference and resistance (Henry et al., 1994).

4 Conclusion

Freud's classical psychoanalysis has fallen on hard times, driven there by its high costs, the restrictive reimbursement policies of health plans, and the development of briefer and equally effective therapies. However, many of Freud's ideas have been incorporated into other and more popular types of therapy.

The next psychotherapy approach, client-centered therapy, is interesting because it was developed by a clinician who was displeased with Freud's psychoanalytic approach.

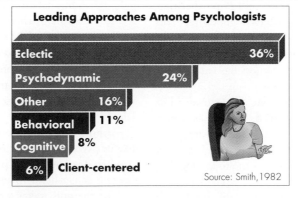

Leading Approaches Among Psychologists

Eclectic	36%
Psychodynamic	24%
Other	16%
Behavioral	11%
Cognitive	8%
Client-centered	6%

Source: Smith, 1982

C. Insight Therapies

Client-Centered Therapy

What should therapists do?

As a therapist, Carl Rogers used the most popular therapy in his time, which was Freud's psychoanalytic approach. However, it wasn't long before Rogers became dissatisfied with Freud's dark and pessimistic view of human nature. Rogers disagreed with Freud's view that human nature was dependent on biological urges and instincts—sex and aggression—and that psychological problems arose from unconscious thoughts and desires that threatened one's self-concept. Not only did Rogers become dissatisfied with the assumptions and goals of psychoanalysis, but he also disagreed with Freud's role of the analyst. Specifically, Rogers objected to the expert role that the analyst played and the assumption that the analyst—and not the client—was responsible for the client's progress. Rogers turned this assumption around and said that clients themselves have the capacity for and are responsible for change. Rogers transformed the therapist's role from that of an all-knowing expert to a helper or facilitator, whose personal characteristics would foster growth and change (Rogers, 1986). Rogers made a 180-degree change from psychoanalysis and developed client-centered therapy (Rogers, 1951, 1986).

Client-centered therapy (also called person-centered therapy) assumes that each person has an actualizing tendency, which is a tendency to develop one's full potential; the therapist's task is to show compassion and positive regard in helping the client reach his or her potential.

Therapy session. To illustrate some of the differences between psychoanalysis and client-centered therapy, here is a brief excerpt of a client-centered therapy session where a mother is talking about her problems with letting her daughter be more independent.

Client: I'm having a lot of problems dealing with my daughter. She's 20 years old; she's in college; I'm having a lot of trouble letting her go . . . And I have a lot of guilt feelings about her; I have a real need to hang on to her. And it's very hard with a lot of empty places now that she's not with me.

Rogers: The old vacuum, sort of, when she's not there.

Client: Yes, yes. I also would like to be the kind of mother that could be strong and say, you know, "go and have a good life," and it's really hard for me to do that.

Rogers: It's very hard to give up something that's been so precious in your life, but also something that I guess has caused you pain when you mentioned guilt.

Client: Yeah, and I'm aware that I have some anger toward her that I don't always get what I want. I have needs that are not met. And, uh, I don't feel I have a right to those needs. You know . . . she's a daughter; she's not my mother—though sometimes I feel as if I'd like her to mother me . . . It's very difficult for me to ask for that and have a right to it.

Rogers: So it may be unreasonable, but still, when she doesn't meet your needs, it makes you mad.

Client: Yeah. I get very angry, very angry with her. *(pause)*

Rogers: You're also feeling a little tension at this point, I guess.

Client: Yeah, yeah. A lot of conflict . . .

Rogers: A lot of pain.

Client: A lot of pain.

Rogers: A lot of pain. Can you say anything more what that's about? (adapted from Rogers, 1989).

Client-centered approach. In this brief excerpt, you can see two of the hallmarks of client-centered therapy. First, Rogers avoids giving any suggestions, advice, or disapproval and primarily shows the client that he understands what the client is feeling. Second, one technique Rogers uses for showing understanding is *reflecting* or restating the client's concerns. Reflecting the client's feelings is one of the basic techniques of the person-centered approach. In addition, humanistic therapists believe that clients have the capacity to discover and reach their true potential and it is the therapist's role to help and remove any roadblocks in their paths (Greenberg & Rice, 1997).

THERAPIST'S TRAITS

Rogers believed that personal characteristics of the therapist—empathy, positive regard, genuineness—would bring about the client's change. *Empathy* is the ability to understand what the client is saying and feeling. *Positive regard* is the ability to communicate caring, respect, and regard for the client. *Genuineness* is the ability to be real and nondefensive in interactions with the client. Rogers and his followers assumed that a therapist with these three characteristics would be able to help a client change and grow.

However, numerous studies have shown that these three characteristics are not always related to successful outcomes (Greenberg et al., 1994). The success of client-centered therapy appears to be due more to developing a good working client-therapist partnership and to the client's attitudes of wanting to and working hard to change (Greenberg & Rice, 1997).

What's blocking my path to developing my true potential?

EFFECTIVENESS

A recent review of client-centered therapy reported that it was effective in producing significant changes in clients in comparison with no-treatment control groups, but it was no more or less effective than were other forms of therapy. Although client-centered therapy has emphasized the importance of empathy in producing change, studies have generally failed to find such an association. In addition, client-centered therapists who were very reflective and gave very little direction were less effective than therapists who made more suggestions and gave more direction (Greenberg & Rice, 1997).

Although client-centered therapy is less popular today (used by 6% of psychologists), it has helped to make therapists aware of the need to develop a positive working relationship with their clients (Bergin & Garfield, 1994).

The therapist takes a much more directive role in the next kind of insight therapy, called cognitive therapy.

Cognitive Therapy

Do negative thoughts get you down?

Aaron Beck was trained in psychoanalytic techniques and used them to treat patients, many of whom were suffering from depression. When he asked them to free-associate, he noticed that depressed patients often expressed negative or distorted thoughts about themselves—"I'm a failure, no one likes me, nothing turns out right." What really caught his attention was how patients would express a string of negative thoughts almost automatically, without paying much attention. Beck reasoned that these automatically occurring negative thoughts had a great impact on the patients' lives—for example, by lowering their self-esteem and raising their self-blame and self-criticism. Beck developed his form of cognitive therapy to stop these thoughts and so treat depression and other problems (Beck, 1976, 1991).

Cognitive therapy, as developed by Aaron Beck, assumes that we have automatic negative thoughts that we typically say to ourselves without much notice. By continually repeating these automatic negative thoughts, we color and distort how we perceive and interpret our world and influence how we behave and feel.

Overgeneralization
Polarized thinking
Selective attention

EMOTIONAL PROBLEMS

Negative things we say to ourselves—for example, "Nothing ever goes right," "I'm a failure," or "Everybody criticizes me"—can bias and distort our thoughts and feelings. Cognitive therapy was developed to make a person aware of, and stop, negative self-statements.

Therapy session. To give you an idea of how negative thoughts occur, here is a brief excerpt from one of Dr. Beck's sessions.

The client is a 26-year-old graduate student who has bouts of depression.

Client: I get depressed when things go wrong. Like when I fail a test.

Therapist: How can failing a test make you depressed?

Client: Well, if I fail, I'll never get into law school.

Why do I keep thinking all those negative thoughts?

Therapist: Do you agree that the way you interpret the results of the test will affect you? You might feel depressed, you might have trouble sleeping, not feel like eating, and you might even wonder if you should drop out of the course.

Client: I have been thinking that I wasn't going to make it. Yes, I agree.

Therapist: Now what did failing mean?

Client (*tearful*): That I couldn't get into law school.

Therapist: And what does that mean to you?

Client: That I'm just not smart enough.

Therapist: Anything else?

Client: That I can never be happy.

Therapist: And how do these thoughts make you feel?

Client: Very unhappy.

Therapist: So it is the meaning of failing a test that makes you very unhappy. In fact, believing that you can never be happy is a powerful factor in producing unhappiness. So, you get yourself into a trap—by definition, failure to get into law school equals "I can never be happy" (Beck et al., 1979, pp. 145–146).

Cognitive approach. Notice how the client tries to avoid admitting that her thoughts influence her feelings. Also notice her negative self-statements, such as, "I'm just not smart enough" and "I can never be happy." Beck believes that these kinds of negative self-statements will influence this client's thoughts and feelings and contribute to her major symptom, depression.

IMPORTANT FACTORS

Beck has identified a number of specific maladaptive thoughts that contribute to various symptoms, such as anxiety and depression. Thus, thinking "I'm a failure" after doing poorly on one test is an example of *overgeneralization,* which is making blanket judgments about yourself on the basis of a single incident. Thinking "Most people don't like me" is an example of *polarized thinking,* which is sorting information into one of two categories, good and bad. Thinking "People always criticize me" is an example of *selective attention,* which is focusing on one detail so much that you do not notice other events, such as being complimented. Beck believes that maladaptive thought patterns cause a distorted view of oneself and one's world, which in turn may lead to various emotional problems. Thus, the primary goals of cognitive therapy are to identify and change maladaptive thoughts.

Cognitive techniques. Beck's approach, which is an example of cognitive therapy, works to change thought patterns, which, in turn, play a critical role in influencing behavior and emotions. In cognitive therapy, clients are told how their maladaptive thoughts and irrational beliefs can result in feelings of depression, anxiety, or other symptoms. Clients are shown how to monitor their thoughts and beliefs, recognize maladaptive thought patterns, such as overgeneralization and polarized thinking, and how to substitute rational thought patterns. In the upcoming Application section, we'll give several examples of specific techniques for stopping negative thoughts and substituting positive ones.

EFFECTIVENESS

Cognitive therapy, which is used by about 8% of therapists, has proved effective in treating a variety of symptoms. For example, it was as effective as various drugs in treating depression, general anxiety, agoraphobia, panic attacks, stopping smoking, and eating disorders (Beck & Fernandez, 1998; Richmond et al., 1997; Scott, 1997; Spangler et al., 1997). In some cases, the benefits of cognitive therapy were longer lasting than those from other forms of therapy (Hollon & Beck, 1994). Increasingly, methods of cognitive therapy are combined with those of the next approach, behavior therapy. The result is cognitive-behavior therapy, which we'll discuss after behavior therapy.

D. Behavior Therapy

Definition

At the beginning of this module, we told you about Little Albert, who initially wanted to touch and play with a white rat but, after being conditioned, came to fear it (Watson & Rayner, 1920). This demonstration, which occurred in the 1920s, showed that emotional responses could be conditioned.

But it was not until the 1950s that a clinician developed a procedure to unlearn emotional responses.

The 1950s was the time that Carl Rogers developed client-centered therapy and Aaron Beck developed cognitive therapy. Both were motivated to develop new approaches because they had become disillusioned with the techniques and results of psychoanalytic approach, which they had used in clinical practice.

This was also the time that Joseph Wolpe (1958, 1990), a physician in South Africa, became disillusioned with psychoanalysis and developed a new, quicker, and more effective procedure to reduce fear and anxiety.

In a real sense, Wolpe finished what John Watson had started: Watson had conditioned Little Albert to fear an object, while Wolpe conditioned patients to be less fearful. Wolpe's procedure was the first experimental demonstration of reducing fear through conditioning and gave a real kickstart to the development of behavior therapy (Persons, 1997).

Behavior therapy, also called behavior modification, uses the principles of classical and operant conditioning to change disruptive behaviors and improve human functioning. It focuses on changing particular behaviors rather than on the underlying mental events or possible unconscious factors.

We'll first give you an example of a behavior therapy session and then describe Wolpe's conditioning procedure to reduce fear.

Therapy session. In this session, the therapist is talking to a woman who feels bad because she has great difficulty being assertive.

Client: The basic problem is that I have the tendency to let people step all over me. I don't know why, but I just have difficulty in speaking my mind.

Therapist: So you find yourself in a number of different situations where you don't respond the way you would really like to and you would like to learn how to behave differently.

Client: Yes. But you know, I have tried to handle certain situations differently, but I just don't seem to be able to do so.

Therapist: Well maybe you tried to do too much or didn't quite know the right technique. For example, imagine yourself at the bottom of a staircase, wanting to get to the top. It's too much to ask to get there in one gigantic leap. Perhaps a better way to go about changing your reaction in these situations is to take it one step at a time.

Client: That would seem to make sense, but I'm not sure if I see how it could be done.

Therapist: Well, there are probably certain situations in which it would be less difficult for you to assert yourself, such as telling your boss that he forgot to pay you for the past four weeks.

Client (*laughing*): I guess in that situation, I would say something. Although I must admit, I would feel uneasy about it.

Therapist: But not as uneasy as if you went in and asked him for a raise.

Client: No. Certainly not.

Therapist: So, the first situation would be low on the staircase, whereas the second would be higher up. If you can learn to handle easier situations, then the more difficult ones would present less of a problem. And the only way you can really learn to change your reactions is through practice.

Client: In other words, I really have to go out and actually force myself to speak up more, but taking it a little bit at a time?

Therapist: Exactly. And it's easier and safer to run through some of these situations here because you can't really get into trouble if you make a mistake. Once you learn different ways to speak your mind, you can try them out in the real world (adapted from Goldfried & Davison, 1976).

Behavioral approach. Notice that the behavior therapist does not encourage the client to free-associate, a major technique of psychoanalysis. The behavior therapist does not repeat or reflect what the client says, which is a major technique of client-centered therapy. The behavior therapist does not discuss the client's tendency to automatically think negative thoughts, which is a major technique of cognitive therapy.

Instead, the behavior therapist quickly identifies the specific problem, which is the woman's tendency to be unassertive when she really wants to speak her mind. Next, the behavior therapist will discuss a program for behavioral change that will help this woman learn to behave more assertively.

Two goals. Behavior therapy has two goals. The first is to modify undesirable behaviors and teach the client how to perform new behaviors, which for this woman involves learning ways to be more assertive. The second goal of behavior therapy is to help the client meet specific behavioral goals through constant practice and reward. For example, this woman would be asked to practice initiating conversations and stating her opinions, perhaps beginning in the safety of the therapist's office and gradually practicing these new assertive behaviors in the more threatening situations of the real world (Fishman & Franks, 1997).

The next example of behavior therapy illustrates a specific technique that is used to help clients overcome phobias.

Why do I let people walk all over me?

Systematic Desensitization

Would Jack face his most feared situation?

Jack was a high school senior who wanted to be an ambulance driver. But he had one serious problem: he passed out at the sight or discussion of blood. He had been afraid of blood for years and had fainted about 20 times in science and biology classes. He even felt queasy when bloody accidents or operating-room scenes were shown on television. He worried that his supervisor would find out about his phobia and not let him try out for ambulance driver. Nevertheless, he was happy at school, rarely became depressed, and was generally easygoing. His only real problem was this phobia of blood (Yule & Fernando, 1980).

Some therapies for phobias might require years of treatment; for instance, a psychoanalyst would search for unconscious conflicts causing the phobia. In contrast, behavior therapists would take a direct approach to the treatment, requiring 5–30 sessions. The technique used today by behavior therapists is based on the one that Wolpe (1958) developed in the 1950s and is called systematic desensitization.

Systematic desensitization is a technique of behavior therapy in which the client is gradually exposed to the feared object while simultaneously practicing relaxation. Desensitization involves three steps: learning to relax; constructing a hierarchy with the least feared situation on the bottom and most feared situation at the top; and progressive exposure to the feared situation.

Behavior therapists assume that Jack's phobia was acquired through a conditioning process and that it can therefore be unconditioned. At the heart of the unconditioning process is exposure to the feared object, which occurs in the following systematic way.

1 Relaxation

Jack, whose phobia was a fear of blood, underwent systematic desensitization, a very effective treatment for phobias (Wolpe & Plaud, 1997). In the first step, Jack learned to relax by practicing progressive relaxation. This method involves tensing and relaxing various muscle groups, beginning with the toes and working up to the head. With this procedure, Jack learned how to put himself into a relaxed state. For most individuals, learning progressive relaxation requires several weeks with at least one 15-minute session every day.

2 Stimulus Hierarchy

The second step was for Jack to make a *stimulus hierarchy*, which is a list of feared stimuli, arranged in order from least to most feared. With the help of his therapist, Jack made the stimulus hierarchy shown on the right, which lists various situations associated with blood. A rating of 1 indicates little fear if confronted by this stimulus, while a rating of 10 indicates that he would probably pass out from this stimulus.

MOST STRESSFUL

8. **Needle drawing blood out**
7. **Own finger dripping blood**
6. **Seeing someone being cut**
5. **Needle being put into arm**
4. **Watching operation on TV**
3. **Bad cut on own finger**
2. **Small cut on own finger**
1. **Seeing the word** *blood*

3 Exposure

Systematic desensitization training means that, after successfully completing steps 1 and 2, Jack was ready for step 3, which was to systematically desensitize himself by exposing himself to the fear stimuli. Desensitization occurs through relaxing while simultaneously imagining the feared stimuli.

Jack put himself into a relaxed state and then imagined the first or least-feared item in his hierarchy, seeing the word *blood*. He tried to remain in a relaxed state while vividly imagining the word *blood*. He repeated this procedure until he felt no tension or anxiety in this situation. At this point, he went on to the next item in his hierarchy. Jack repeated the procedure of pairing relaxation with images of each feared item until he reached the last and most feared item.

Through the desensitization program described here, Jack's blood phobia was treated in five one-hour sessions. A follow-up five years later indicated that Jack was still free of his blood phobia, had not developed any substitute symptoms, and was training to be an ambulance driver (Yule & Fernando, 1980).

4 Exposure: Imagined or In Vivo

Systematic desensitization appears to be most effective if instead of just imagining the items on the list, which is called imagined exposure, clients gradually expose themselves to the actual situation, which is called *in vivo exposure* (the phrase *in vivo* is Latin for "in real life") (Emmelkamp & van Oppen, 1994). For example, in Module 22 we described the case of Kate Premo (photo below), who signed up for a treatment course that used in vivo exposure to treat her lifetime phobia of flying. In her case, a modified systematic desensitization program included in vivo exposure, which meant taking an actual flight while doing the breathing and relaxation exercises that she had learned. The in vivo exposure worked for Premo, who was able to overcome her phobia of flying.

Clinicians also found that in vivo exposure was a very effective treatment for about 55% of obsessive-compulsives, who were once viewed as having chronic, incurable problems (Abramowitz, 1997).

Thus, systematic desensitization has proved a very effective treatment for a variety of anxiety disorders, especially when combined with in vivo exposure (Gould et al., 1997).

The next therapy is actually a combination of behavior and cognitive therapies.

D. Behavior Therapy

Cognitive-Behavior Therapy

Why combine two different therapies?

As psychoanalysis reached its peak of popularity in the 1950s, a number of clinicians and researchers were becoming dissatisfied with its procedures, which were too time-consuming, too costly, and too ineffective, except in treating a very small number of people who had relatively minor psychological problems (Franks, 1994).

At this same time, there was a great increase in the popularity of learning principles that came from Pavlov's work on classical conditioning and Skinner's work on operant conditioning. Researchers and clinicians began to apply these learning principles to change human behavior with methods based on a strong experimental foundation rather than Freud's unverified beliefs about unconscious conflicts. Both behavior and cognitive therapy developed out of dissatisfaction with psychoanalysis and the belief that learning principles would provide more effective methods of changing human behavior than would the concepts of psychoanalysis.

I need to learn assertive behaviors.

One of the interesting developments in therapy has been occurring since the late 1970s as both behavior and cognitive therapies have become increasingly popular. The major difference between them is that behavior therapy focuses on identifying and changing specific behaviors while cognitive therapy focuses on identifying and changing specific maladaptive thought patterns. Beginning in the early 1990s, researchers and clinicians have been combining methods of behavior and cognitive therapies into what is now called cognitive-behavior therapy (Wilson et al., 1997).

Cognitive-behavior therapy combines the cognitive therapy technique of changing negative, unhealthy, or distorted thought patterns with the behavior technique of changing maladaptive or disruptive behaviors by learning and practicing new skills to improve functioning.

I need to stop thinking all those negative thoughts.

Currently, the difference between cognitive therapy and behavior therapy has become blurred as techniques from these two approaches are combined into what is commonly called cognitive-behavior therapy (Ellis, 1997; Hollon & Beck, 1994).

Cognitive-behavior approach. Cognitive-behavior therapists use a number of techniques to change thoughts and behaviors and thus improve functioning. These techniques include monitoring one's own thoughts and behaviors; identifying thoughts and behaviors that need to be changed; setting specific goals that increase in difficulty; learning to reinforce oneself for reaching a goal; imitating or modeling new behaviors; substituting positive for negative thoughts; and practicing new behaviors in a safe setting before performing them in the real world (Larkin & Edens, 1994). These cognitive-behavior techniques are the basis for almost all self-help programs, which may be completed without the assistance of a therapist. For more serious problems or additional support, the aid and help of a therapist may be needed (Gambrill, 1994; Marks, 1994).

Kinds of Problems

Who can be helped?

Throughout this text, we have discussed how behavior therapy, cognitive therapy, or the popular cognitive-behavior therapy have been used to treat the following problems:

■ **Insomnia:** cognitive-behavior program was as effective as drugs in helping people get to sleep (p. 162).

■ **Conditioned nausea:** individuals undergoing chemotherapy developed conditioned nausea and were treated with behavior therapy (p. 207).

■ **Noncompliance in children:** behavior therapy, also called behavior modification, was used to treat young children who refused to eat healthy foods (p. 230).

■ **Autistic children:** behavior modification helped some autistic children develop sufficient academic and social skills to enter public schools and function very well (p. 232).

■ **Psychosomatic problems:** behavior therapy (biofeedback) helped people decrease stress-related symptoms by reducing headaches and physiological arousal (p. 233).

■ **Abusive parents:** cognitive-behavior therapy that involved training in social skills helped parents deal with their own personal problems as well as daily difficulties related to caring for demanding children (p. 401).

■ **Stress management:** cognitive-behavior techniques are basic to all programs for reducing stress (p. 502).

■ **Phobias:** various phobias, such as fear of specific situations (flying) or objects (snakes, bugs) have been successfully treated with cognitive-behavior techniques (p. 524).

We'll also discuss several other examples of cognitive-behavior techniques in the upcoming Application section.

Effectiveness. Cognitive-behavior therapy is currently being used to treat a wide variety of problems, including eating disorders, marital problems, anxiety and phobias, depression, and sexual dysfunction. Programs based on cognitive-behavior therapy are widely used to help people stop smoking, become more assertive, improve communication and interpersonal skills, manage stress, and learn to control anger. Researchers report that cognitive-behavior therapy was significantly more effective in treating this wide variety of problems than were control procedures (Beck & Fernandez, 1998; Fishman & Franks, 1997; Spangler et al., 1997). And in some cases, cognitive-behavior therapy was as effective as drugs in treating some forms of anxiety, phobia, depression, and insomnia (Abramowitz, 1997; Gould et al., 1997; Thase et al., 1997).

After the Concept Review, we'll review and compare the development, techniques, and effectiveness of all the major therapies that we have discussed.

CONCEPT REVIEW

1. If you first trained as a physician and then went into a psychiatric residency, which involves additional training in pharmacology, neurology, and psychotherapeutic techniques, you would be a (a)_____. If you completed a Ph.D. program in psychology, including one year of work in a clinical setting, you would be a (b)_____. If you completed a Ph.D. program in psychology or education, including work in a counseling setting, you would be a (c)_____.

2. A process characterized by verbal interaction between therapist and client and the development of a supportive relationship, during which a therapist may analyze or suggest ways for the client to deal with and overcome his or her problems, is called _____.

3. One approach to therapy is characterized by the idea that we have an unconscious part whose activities and thoughts are hidden behind a mental barrier that we cannot voluntarily remove. Behind this barrier are repressed and psychologically dangerous thoughts that give rise to unconscious conflicts, which, in turn, can result in psychological and physical symptoms. This approach is called _____.

4. Freud developed two techniques to uncover unconscious thoughts. One was to encourage clients to talk about any thoughts or images that entered their heads, which is called (a)_____. The second technique was based on the assumption that dreams contain hidden meanings and symbols and the therapist's role was to (b)_____ these dream symbols.

5. Freud said that, during therapy, a patient may respond as if the therapist were a father or mother and project strong feelings toward the therapist. This process is called (a)_____. Also during therapy a patient may be reluctant to work through feelings or to recognize unconscious conflicts and repressed thoughts; this is called (b)_____.

6. The second most popular approach to therapy shares many of the features of psychoanalysis—for example, discussing the client's feelings; breaking down the client's defenses and resistances; and interpreting the client's behaviors—but may not necessarily use free association or agree that many problems result from unconscious sexual conflicts. This approach, which takes less time than psychoanalysis, is called _____ psychotherapy.

7. One approach to therapy assumes that each person has an actualizing tendency—that is, a tendency to develop his or her full potential. In this approach, the therapist's task is to show compassion and positive regard in helping the client reach his or her potential. This approach was developed by (a)_____ and is called (b)_____ therapy.

8. Another approach to therapy assumes that we have automatic negative thoughts that we usually say to ourselves without much notice. By continually repeating these automatic negative thoughts, we color and distort how we perceive and interpret our world and influence how we behave and feel. This approach to therapy was developed by (a)_____ and is called (b)_____ therapy.

9. One approach to therapy primarily uses the principles of classical and operant conditioning to change disruptive behaviors and improve human functioning. This approach, which focuses on changing particular behaviors rather than on the underlying mental events or possible unconscious factors, is called _____ therapy.

10. One approach combines changing negative, unhealthy, or distorted thoughts and beliefs by substituting positive, healthy, and realistic ones and changing one's undesirable or disruptive behaviors by learning and practicing new skills to improve functioning. This approach which combines two therapies is called _____ therapy.

11. There is a technique of behavior therapy in which the client is gradually exposed to the feared object while simultaneously practicing relaxation. This technique, which involves three steps—learning to relax; constructing a hierarchy with the least feared situation on the bottom and most feared situation at the top; and progressive exposure to the feared situation—is called _____.

12. Because of its effectiveness, cognitive-behavior therapy has become the basis for many self-help programs to stop smoking, reduce insomnia, as well as decrease conditioned nausea, help autistic children develop academic and social skills, and reduce intense and irrational fears, called _____.

Answers: *1. (a) psychiatrist, (b) clinical psychologist, (c) counseling psychologist; 2. psychotherapy; 3. psychoanalysis; 4. (a) free association, (b) interpret; 5. (a) transference, (b) resistance; 6. psychodynamic; 7. (a) Carl Rogers, (b) client-centered; 8. (a) Aaron Beck, (b) cognitive; 9. behavior; 10. cognitive-behavior; 11. systematic desensitization; 12. phobias.*

E. Review: Evaluation of Approaches

Assumptions, Methods, and Techniques

We have discussed five different approaches to psychotherapy, including psychoanalysis, client-centered therapy, cognitive therapy, behavior therapy, and the increasingly popular cognitive-behavior therapy. We'll briefly review the different backgrounds, assumptions, and techniques for these approaches, and then discuss their effectiveness.

PSYCHOANALYSIS

Background. Psychoanalysis, which was developed by Sigmund Freud in the late 1800s and early 1900s, marked the beginning of psychotherapy. Freud gradually developed his major assumptions from treating patients for a variety of symptoms and problems. Thus, Freud's assumptions are based on case studies rather than experimental data.

Basic assumption. Freud believed that unacceptable or threatening thoughts were repressed and unavailable to conscious recall. Repressed thoughts could produce unconscious conflicts that, in turn, could result in feeling anxious and a variety of psychological and emotional problems.

Techniques. Freud developed two techniques for uncovering and revealing unconscious thoughts: free association and dream interpretation. Freud was also the first to identify and recognize the importance of transference and resistance during therapy. He believed that patients overcame their problems by bringing up and dealing with underlying unconscious conflicts.

CLIENT-CENTERED THERAPY

Background. In the late 1940s and early 1950s, Carl Rogers became disillusioned with the psychoanalytic role of the therapist as expert and in charge of changing the client. To give the client a greater role in making decisions and changes, he developed his client-centered approach.

Basic assumption. Rogers assumed that the client has the capacity to actualize and reach his or her full potential and the client, not the therapist, is responsible for change. He believed that, although the client had the major role in making changes, there were certain characteristics of the therapist that helped the client change.

Techniques. The client-centered therapist uses the technique of repeating or reflecting what the client says and thereby showing interest and understanding. Rogers believed that therapists would be effective if they had three characteristics: empathy, positive regard, and genuineness. These characteristics produced a warm and supportive atmosphere in which the client felt comfortable and could better deal with solving his or her problems.

COGNITIVE THERAPY

Background. In the late 1960s and early 1970s, Aaron Beck became dissatisfied with the psychoanalytic assumption that unconscious conflicts were the chief cause of psychological problems. As Beck treated patients, he noticed that they would often repeat a string of negative statements, almost without notice. Beck believed that these automatic, negative self-statements played a major role in emotional problems.

Basic assumption. Beck pointed out that our automatic, irrational thoughts and beliefs can color our feelings and actions, distort our perceptions, and result in various psychological and emotional problems. He assumed that these irrational self-statements, such as polarized thinking, needed to be changed.

Techniques. The techniques of cognitive therapy include having the client monitor and identify his or her automatic, negative, irrational thoughts and replace them with positive ones. Thus, clients deal with and solve their problems by gradually substituting positive thoughts for distorted self-statements.

BEHAVIOR THERAPY

Background. Developed in the 1950s, behavior therapy was based on principles of learning from classical and operant conditioning. Behavior therapy was a reaction to psychoanalysis, whose emphasis was on unconscious and unobservable conflicts and whose concepts lacked a scientific foundation.

Basic assumption. Behavior therapy assumes that just as emotional reactions can be learned or conditioned, so too can they be unlearned using the same principles of learning. Behavior therapy focuses on observable behaviors, while cognitive-behavior therapy also emphasizes changing thought patterns.

Techniques. The behavior therapist identifies specific behaviors that need to be changed and provides the client with particular methods for carrying out the changes. Specific behavioral techniques include self-observation, self-reward, modeling, and role playing. For treatment of anxiety, fears, and phobias, systematic desensitization combined with in vivo exposure has proved effective.

Currently, techniques of cognitive and behavior therapies are combined into cognitive-behavior therapy, which has proved effective for a variety of psychological problems and self-help programs.

These four approaches differ in their assumptions and techniques. The interesting question is whether one approach is more effective than another.

Effectiveness of Psychotherapy

Imagine that you have a psychological problem that is interfering with your daily functioning, such as a phobia of going out in public, or major depression, or difficulty establishing or maintaining intimate relationships. If you were to seek professional help, you could choose between at least six major approaches (see graph), and dozens of off-shoots (Singer & Lalich, 1996). In making your decision, you need to consider two practical questions: Is psychotherapy more effective than just waiting for the problem to go away? Is one approach more effective than another?

For a small percentage (10–20%) of individuals with psychological problems, simply waiting for the problem to go away will work. However, clinicians do not know how to identify these individuals beforehand and give them the option of waiting (Eysenck, 1994). For a large percentage (80–90%) of individuals with psychological problems, simply waiting is

not effective and their problems may either continue or worsen. For these individuals with psychological problems, professional help is the better choice.

Researchers have analysed over 1,500 studies that examined the effects of psychotherapy on a variety of problems, such as depression, various kinds of anxieties, family problems, interpersonal difficulties, and eating disorders. Researchers found that psychotherapy was more effective in relieving a wide variety of psychological and behavioral symptoms than were control procedures such as being on a waiting list to receive therapy or just being in a group that received no systematic treatment. In addition, most improvement occurs in a relatively short period of time, about 25 to 40 sessions (Jacobson & Christensen, 1996; Lowry & Ross, 1997; Matt & Navarro, 1997).

Knowing that psychotherapy is an effective treatment brings us to the second question: "Is one kind of psychotherapy better than another?"

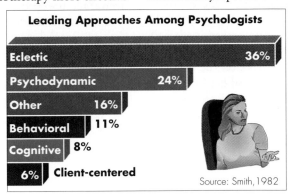

Leading Approaches Among Psychologists

Eclectic — 36%
Psychodynamic — 24%
Other — 16%
Behavioral — 11%
Cognitive — 8%
Client-centered — 6%

Source: Smith, 1982

Common Factors

Because the more popular therapies (graph above) begin with different assumptions and use different methods and techniques, you would wonder if they also differ in their effectiveness. For the past 20 years, researchers have consistently found that there is very little if any difference in effectiveness among various therapies (DeRubeis & Crits-Christoph, 1998; Howard et al., 1997; Wampold et al., 1997). However, for a small number of specific disorders, including *panic attacks, phobias, compulsions,* and *depression,* behavior, cognitive, or cognitive-behavior therapies have been generally shown to be more effective than traditional talk therapies, such as the psychodynamic approaches (Lambert & Bergin, 1994).

> I need professional help but I don't know which therapy to choose.

It may seem surprising that therapies with such different assumptions and techniques have been found to be equally effective. One reason different therapies using different techniques can achieve the same results is that they all share common factors (Arkowitz, 1997; Weinberger, 1995).

Common factors refer to a basic set of procedures and experiences that different therapies share and that explain why different approaches are equally effective. Common factors include the growth of a supportive and trusting relationship between therapist and client and the development of an accepting atmosphere, in which the client feels willing to admit problems and is motivated to work on changing.

The fact that certain common factors are basic to all approaches explains why different therapies are equally effective and why different techniques can be effectively combined into the most popular form of therapy, the eclectic approach (graph above) (Lambert & Bergin, 1994; Messer & Wachtel, 1997).

For example, one common factor—development of a warm, trusting, and accepting relationship between client and therapist—has been shown to play a major role in helping clients work out their problems and change their behaviors (Lambert & Bergin, 1994). Since the client-therapist relationship is important in influencing the effectiveness of treatment, researchers suggest that a client select a therapist to whom he or she can relate (Dawes, 1994).

> I found out that many of the therapies are about equally effective.

The use of psychotherapy to treat a wide variety of mental disorders has grown over the past ten years. In the United States in 1994, over seven million individuals (3% of the population) sought professional help; the majority made 20 or more visits at an annual cost of over four billion dollars (Docherty & Streeter, 1995). The client-consumer should know that psychotherapy is generally effective and that (except for anxiety disorders and depression) the particular therapy approach does not matter as much as do common factors.

Common factors may also explain why the next treatment, which seems very strange to Westerners, proved effective.

F. Cultural Diversity: Different Healer

Case Study: Young Woman

What was Putu's problem?

In Bali, which is a province of Indonesia, as well as in parts of Africa and China, many psychological problems that Western clinicians would diagnose as anxiety, mood disorders, or schizophrenia are believed to be caused by possession by evil spirits (Kua et al., 1993; Straker, 1994). For example, take the case of Putu, a young unmarried woman, who was about 20 years old.

Putu lived with her family in a small village on the beautiful island of Bali. Putu's family had made her break off her loving relationship with one man and become engaged to another, whom she did not want to marry. Since her new engagement, Putu had lost all interest in things around her, ate very little, and did not take part in

normal activities or conversation. Putu was taken to the local nurse, who gave an injection of multivitamins to treat her low energy level and general apathy. The injection did not help and the nurse recommended that the family take Putu to a local witchdoctor or healer, who could use special rituals to cure Putu (Connor, 1982).

In Western terminology, clinicians would say that Putu was suffering from depression, which was most certainly brought on by having to break off her loving relationship and being forced by her family to become engaged to someone she did not like. Western therapists would have treated her depression with some form of psychotherapy and, if possible, would have brought the whole family in for therapy. However, in Bali, Putu was said to be the victim of witchcraft, which could be cured by the local healer, or *balian*.

Healer's Diagnosis and Treatment

What is healing smoke?

The family took the depressed Putu to a well-respected healer, a woman named Jero. After massaging Putu's neck, Jero located a small pulsation beneath Putu's jawbone that indicated the presence of an evil wind spirit. The rejected lover had placed the evil spirit into Putu's body, and there was now a great danger that this evil spirit might travel throughout her body: if it reached Putu's ears, she would go deaf; if it reached her brain, she would become violent and insane. Jero (right photo) said that she would mix special medicine and that the family should return in two days for an exorcism of the evil wind spirit.

As part of the exorcism rites, two small human effigies, a male and a female, were made out of cooked rice and were set on the ground to the south of the girl. When the evil spirit was driven out of Putu's body by smoke, the evil spirit would be attracted to the effigies, which would then be broken to destroy the spirit.

You are possessed of an evil wind spirit.

In the morning, Jero asked Putu to stand in the middle of healing smoke. After about 40 minutes, the evil wind spirit left Putu's body and entered the small male and female rice figures, which were broken and thrown away. Then Putu's body was purified with holy water. During the course of the afternoon, Putu began to talk, show interest in food and things around her, and generally to get over her former apathy.

For two more weeks, Putu stayed with Jero, who continued to perform purification ceremonies and drive away any lingering evil wind spirits. As part of the purification ceremonies, Putu was asked to take part in everyday activities, such as gathering and making food, engaging in normal conversations, washing clothes, and doing other chores. Through this process, Putu was helped and encouraged to resume her normal duties and take part in social activities.

Healer versus Western Therapists

Is witchcraft a form of therapy?

The case of Putu shows that the beliefs and treatments used in the witchcraft of African and Asian healers are very different from those used by Western therapists to treat psychological problems. But notice that the healer's exorcism rites, purification rituals, and herbal medicines did reduce Putu's depression. In many parts of Asia, China, Africa, and Indonesia, healers use herbal medicines, exorcism, and purification rituals to successfully treat a variety of psychological problems (Kua et al., 1993; Torrey, 1986).

There are at least two explanations of why a healer's potions and rituals are effective treatments for various problems. First, studies on

Western patients find that about 10–30% of patients suffering from a variety of psychological and physical problems show remarkable improvement after receiving placebo treatments (Dodes, 1997; Turner et al., 1994). The healers' rituals and herbs may function like placebos. Second, the healer's purification ceremonies involve the development of a close relationship with the victim, and this relationship may involve common factors similar to those found effective in Western therapy. Thus, placebos and psychotherapy's common factors may be the underlying basis for treating a variety of physical and psychological problems in different cultures.

Next, we'll discuss treatment of one of the more difficult psychological problems, getting over a terrible and traumatic situation.

G. Research Focus: EMDR—New Therapy Method to Eliminate Traumatic Memories?

Definition

During the past 50 years, there have been literally hundreds of therapies that were claimed to be uniquely effective, were popular for a time, and then disappeared because their claims were not supported (Pitman, 1994). Recently, strong claims have been made for another new therapy, called Eye-Movement Desensitization and Reprocessing, or EMDR (Shapiro, 1989, 1991).

Eye-Movement Desensitization and Reprocessing (EMDR) involves focusing on a traumatic memory while visually following the back-and-forth movement of a therapist's hand or pen. One

memory may trigger another, which the client focuses on while again visually following the back-and-forth movement. This process usually continues for a 90-minute session, during which the traumatic memories are said to be reprocessed by eye movements that help replace traumatic memories with pleasant ones (Shapiro, 1991).

Francine Shapiro discovered EMDR after noticing that her own troubling thoughts had disappeared after being associated with her back-and-forth eye movements. Shapiro (1995) estimates that about 14,000 therapists in the United States have been trained in using EMDR.

Evidence from Case Studies

All of the early support for the effectiveness of EMDR came from testimonials and case studies, many of them as dramatic as the following:

After one individual lost both arms and hearing in a tragic fire and explosion, he experienced terrible flashbacks and nightmares for the next six years. When he finally consulted a psychiatrist, he was desperate and agreed to try the then-new EMDR procedure. Following the EMDR procedure, he vividly recalled the fire, the shouts of the employees, and other terrible images, while visually following the back-and-forth movement of the therapist's hand. However, as he continued imagining terrible images and following the therapist's hand movements, he began to feel a flowing sensation of peace. Following a number of sessions, he was reported to be free of flashbacks and nightmares, had taught himself to drive a car, and had joined a group that helps children who need artificial limbs (Wartik, 1994).

Dramatic cases like this suggested that EMDR was a simple but effective treatment for traumatic memories, one of the most difficult problems therapists face. Shapiro (1991) explained that EMDR somehow functions like the eye movements during rapid eye movement (REM) sleep and may help to unlock and reprocess traumatic memories. However, Shapiro provides no evidence for her neurological interpretation.

Although the effectiveness of EMDR was supported by case studies and testimonials, we must remember that such methods have great potential for error and bias and cannot demonstrate cause and effect. Thus, to evaluate the effectiveness of EMDR, researchers turned to the experimental method.

Evidence from Experiments

Method. The major question is whether eye movements are uniquely effective for the treatment of traumatic memories. To answer this question, researchers who had been trained by Shapiro recruited subjects who satisfied the DSM-IV criteria for experiencing traumatic events. The subjects were randomly divided into three groups, two of which we'll describe here. One group received EMDR treatment, in which subjects recalled traumatic events while their eyes moved back and forth as they tracked the end of a moving pen; another group recalled traumatic events while staring straight ahead at a fixed light. All subjects filled out questionnaires that evaluated their level of distress before and after treatment.

Results. As shown in the graph below, subjects who received EMDR treatment showed a significant reduction in distress. However, the treatment that involved fixed staring produced a similar significant reduction in distress. Researchers concluded that the back-and-forth eye movements used in EMDR were not necessary for effective treatment, since fixed staring produced equally good results (Renfrey & Spates, 1994).

Conclusions. There are continuing reports that EMDR, which is a relatively brief and easy-to-use therapy, was effective in reducing distress and anxiety following traumatic situations and that the beneficial effects may be long lasting (15 months) (Carlson et al., 1998; Scheck et al., 1998; Wilson et al., 1997).

Score on Distance Scale

EMDR	8	Before
Fixed	8	
EMDR	1	After
Fixed		

However, there is as yet no explanation for why or how EMDR works. For example, some studies report that fixed staring is equally effective and do not support Shapiro's claim that rapid back-and-forth eye movement is necessary for effective treatment (Feske & Goldstein, 1997; Foa & Meadows, 1997). In addition, cognitive-behavior and exposure therapies have also proved effective in treating traumatic memories but there are as yet no reports comparing the effectiveness between these different therapies (Foa & Meadows, 1997). Thus, until future experimental studies compare EMDR to other kinds of exposure therapies, we will not know if it is especially effective in treating traumatic memories.

Next, we'll review several cognitive-behavior techniques that have proven effective in treating a number of relatively common psychological problems.

H. Application: Cognitive-Behavior Techniques

Problems

What's a common problem?

When someone says, "Don't let that bother you," what they often mean is "Stop thinking about that!" The ability to stop thinking about something and drive it from your consciousness is truly a skill worth learning. Most of the time, trying not to think of something just makes you think about that unwanted thing even more because putting something out of your mind can be an almost impossible task. For example, if you do poorly on an exam, you

How do I battle crazy thoughts?

have a big fight, break up with someone, or get rejected, you often replay that scene over and over because it seems to be glued in your mind. As it turns out, clinicians have developed a number of very useful cognitive-behavior techniques, which can be used to change thought patterns. We'll explain two techniques to change thought patterns, beginning with a program to get rid of annoying thoughts.

Thought Stopping

What are intrusive thoughts?

One of the things that drives me crazy is thinking about things that I would rather forget. In fact, when people say, "Don't let that bother you," what they usually mean is "Stop thinking about that." But most us know from experience that the more you want to stop thinking about something, the more you think about it. And the reason it's so difficult to stop thinking is that most of us don't have a mental program to keep away annoying, unwanted, intrusive thoughts (Kelly & Kahn, 1994).

Intrusive thoughts are thoughts that we repeatedly experience, are usually unwanted or disruptive, and are very difficult to stop or eliminate.

Intrusive thoughts can be about a past relationship, something we should have done differently, an old argument, or negative thoughts about ourselves. Cognitive-behavior therapists have developed a program to identify and change intrusive thoughts. This program can be carried out on one's own or with the help and support of a therapist.

For example, let's take the real-life case of Carol, who was depressed because she couldn't stop thinking about her former boyfriend, Fred. Since they had broken up, she couldn't help thinking about Fred almost every day, and her thinking triggered a chain of other negative thoughts about herself: "I feel that I am a failure. I feel ugly and useless. I keep thinking about not being able to have a relationship. I feel really depressed and I don't want to do anything" (Martin, 1982).

Carol's problem involves intrusive thoughts about Fred, whom she can't stop thinking about even though it's very depressing to do so. An effective cognitive-behavior technique for stopping intrusive thoughts has three steps.

1 Self-monitoring

In all behavior-changing procedures, the first step is *self-monitoring*, which is observing one's own behavior without making any changes. In Carol's case, it meant that for one week she wrote down all depressing thoughts about Fred that lasted for more than a couple of

How do I stop thinking of my former boyfriend?

minutes. In addition, the therapist asked Carol to bring in pictures of herself that showed her in pleasurable activities. These pictures would provide cues for thinking rational thoughts.

2 Thought stopping

Each time Carol began to experience a disturbing thought, she would stop what she was doing, clasp her hands, close her eyes, silently yell "Stop!" to herself, and silently count to ten. This was the *thought-stopping procedure.*

3 Thought substitution

After counting silently to ten, she would open her eyes and take five photographs out of her purse. She would look at each photograph and read what she had written on the back. For example, one photograph showed her about to board an airplane for a trip. On the back she had written, "I'm my own boss. My life is ahead of me. I can do what I want to do." Carol would then think about the trip and how much she liked to travel. She would do the same for all five photographs.

This *thought-substituting procedure* took 1–2 minutes. After that, she would return to whatever she had been doing.

During Carol's first week of self-monitoring, she thought about Fred constantly and spent from 15 minutes to an hour each day crying. However, after using the thought-stopping and thought-substituting procedures for eight weeks, Carol had reduced the time thinking about Fred to the point that she rarely cried or was depressed. A follow-up interview four months after therapy revealed that Carol was no longer having intrusive thoughts about Fred, was no longer depressed, had developed no new symptoms, and had a new boyfriend (Martin, 1982).

If you simply try stopping an undesired thought, there is a good chance that the undesired thought may rebound or occur even more frequently (Macrae et al., 1998; Wegner & Gold, 1995). One way to prevent thought rebound is to combine thought-stopping procedures with thought-substitution techniques. Thought substitution, which we'll discuss next, is a very useful technique for a number of problems, including fear and anxiety.

Thought Substitution

For many years Rose was trapped in her house because of her intense fear, or phobia, of going out into public places, which is called agoraphobia. If she even thought about going outside to do her shopping, she felt pain in her arms and chest, she began to perspire, her heart beat rapidly, and her feet felt like rubber. However, after cognitive-behavior therapy, she overcame her agoraphobia.

As part of the overall therapy program, a cognitive therapist asked Rose a number of questions to identify her irrational thoughts. For example, she may have overgeneralized, thinking, "The last time I went out I was terrified; it's sure to happen again." Or Rose may have engaged in polarized thinking: "All my happiness is right here in this house; nothing outside could give me any pleasure." Her thinking might have been distorted by selective attention, such as remembering all those activities outside the house that terrified her and forgetting all those activities that she had once found pleasurable, such as shopping and going to movies.

Rose was asked to make a list of all her irrational thoughts on one side of a sheet of paper. Then, next to each irrational thought, she was asked to write down a rational response that could be substituted for the irrational one. Here are some examples:

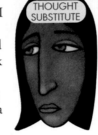

IRRATIONAL THOUGHTS

- I am much safer if I stay at home.
- I feel more protected if I do not have to walk through crowds.
- I think something awful will occur if I go to a supermarket.
- I can't bear the thought of going to a movie theater.

RATIONAL THOUGHTS

- Rarely has anything bad happened when I have gone out.
- I have never been harmed by a crowd of people.
- Thousands of people go to supermarkets and do their shopping unharmed.
- Many people enjoy going to movies.

Like Rose, you can follow the same three steps of the thought-substitution program, which is a very effective technique for changing feelings and behaviors.

1 Through self-monitoring, write down as many irrational thoughts as possible. If you are in a habit of thinking irrational thoughts, it may require special attention to identify them.

How do I change my fearful thoughts so I can go out in public?

2 Next to the column of irrational thoughts, compose a matching list of rational thoughts. The rational thoughts should be as detailed or specific as possible.

3 Begin to practice substituting rational thoughts for irrational ones. Each time you make a substitution, give yourself a mental reward for your effort.

Cognitive-behavior therapists see irrational thoughts and beliefs as the primary causes of emotional and behavioral problems. Therapeutic homework, such as thought stopping and thought substituting, helps the client practice rational living.

Worrisome, annoying, and irrational thoughts are one of the major causes of insomnia, which can also be treated with a cognitive-behavior program.

Treatment for Insomnia

There are a number of nondrug treatments for insomnia that differ in method, but all have the same goal: to stop the person from excessive worrying and tension, which are major psychological causes of insomnia. One proven cognitive-behavioral method to reduce insomnia is to establish an optimal sleep pattern (Bootzin & Rider, 1997).

Establishing an Optimal Sleep Pattern

By following the eight steps below, your sleep pattern will become more regular and efficient and help reduce insomnia.

1. Go to bed only when you are *sleepy*, not by convention (it's time for bed) or habit.

2. Put the *light out* immediately when getting into bed.

3. *Do not read or watch television* in bed since these are activities that you do when awake.

4. If you are not asleep within *20 minutes,* get out of bed and sit and relax in another room until you are *sleep tired* again. Relaxation can include tensing and relaxing one's muscles or using *visual imagery*, which involves closing one's eyes and concentrating on some calm scene or image for several minutes.

5. *Repeat step 4* as often as required, and also if you wake up for any long periods of time.

6. *Set the alarm to the same time each morning* so that your time of waking is always the same. This step is very important because oversleeping or sleeping in is one of the primary causes of insomnia the next night.

7. *Do not nap during the day* because it will throw off your sleep schedule that night.

8. *Follow this program* rigidly for several weeks to establish an efficient and regular pattern of sleep.

Results. Establishing an optimal sleep pattern by this eight-step program was a very effective nondrug method to help people overcome insomnia (Bootzin & Rider, 1997).

These are just a sample of cognitive-behavior techniques that can be used on one's own or with the aid of a therapist and have proven effective for treating a wide range of symptoms (Ellis, 1997).

SUMMARY TEST

A. HISTORICAL BACKGROUND

1. In the early 1800s, the popular belief that mental patients could be helped to function better by providing humane treatment in a relaxed and decent environment was called (a)_____. In the early 1950s, the first drugs to reduce schizophrenic symptoms were discovered. These drugs, called (b)_____, reduced the effects of the neurotransmitter (c)_____.

2. Following the use of phenothiazines, many mental patients were released from mental hospitals and returned to the community to develop more independent and fulfilling lives; this process was called (a)_____. People with mental disorders that do not require hospitalization often seek treatment in (b)_____ centers.

B. QUESTIONS ABOUT PSYCHOTHERAPY

3. If you go to medical school, receive an M.D. degree, and then take a psychiatric residency, you can become a (a)_____. If you go to graduate school in clinical psychology and complete a Ph.D. program, including at least one year of work in a clinical setting, you can become a (b)_____. If you go to graduate school in psychology or education and complete a Ph.D. program, including work in a counseling setting, you can become a (c)_____.

4. Therapy in which the therapist and client talk about the client's symptoms and problems with the goal of reaching or identifying the cause of the problem is called (a)_____ therapy. Therapy that involves the application of learning principles and focuses on identifying and changing specific behaviors is called (b)_____ therapy. Therapy that involves the use of various psychoactive drugs, such as tranquilizers and neuroleptics, to treat mental disorders is called (c)_____ therapy.

C. INSIGHT THERAPIES

5. Freud developed one of the first forms of insight therapy, which he called (a)_____. At the core of psychoanalysis is the idea that psychological and physical symptoms arise from (b)_____ that a person cannot voluntarily uncover or recall.

6. Freud developed two techniques that he believed provide clues to unconscious thoughts and conflicts: when clients are encouraged to talk about any thoughts or images that enter their heads, this is called (a)_____; when a therapist looks for hidden meanings and symbols in dreams, this is called (b)_____.

7. During the course of therapy, a patient will project conflict-ridden emotions onto the therapist; this process is called (a)_____. Working through transference is one of the two essential requirements for improvement in psychoanalysis; the other is that the patient achieves (b)_____ into the causes of his or her problem. A patient's reluctance to work through feelings or recognize unconscious conflicts and repressed thoughts is called (c)_____.

8. The second most popular approach to therapy shares many of the features of psychoanalysis—such as discussing the client's feelings and breaking down the client's defenses and resistances—but does not necessarily use free association. This approach, which greatly shortens the therapy time, is called _____ psychotherapy.

9. A form of insight therapy developed by Carl Rogers emphasizes our creative and constructive tendencies and the importance of building caring relationships. This is called (a)_____ therapy. One of its basic techniques is to restate or (b)_____ the client's concerns and feelings.

10. Rogers believed that the therapist's characteristics foster growth and change. The therapist needs to have the ability to understand what the client is saying and feeling, a trait called (a)_____; the ability to communicate caring, respect, and regard for the client, called (b)_____; and the ability to be real and nondefensive in interactions with the client, called (c)_____.

11. Another form of insight therapy is the cognitive therapy developed by Aaron Beck. The basic assumption of Beck's cognitive theory is that our (a)_____ negative thoughts distort how we perceive and interpret things, thus influencing our behaviors and feelings. For example, making blanket judgments about yourself on the basis of a single incident is called (b)_____. Sorting information into one of two categories is (c)_____. Focusing on one detail so much that you do not notice other events is using (d)_____. Beck believes that maladaptive thought patterns cause a distorted view of one's world, which in turn may lead to various emotional problems.

12. Cognitive therapy has been shown to have approximately the same effectiveness as do drugs in treating major _____ and has been used effectively to treat other psychological problems.

D. BEHAVIOR THERAPY

13. Therapy that emphasizes treatment of specific behaviors and working toward specific goals without focusing on mental events or underlying unconscious factors is known as _____ therapy. This form of therapy is based on classical and operant conditioning principles.

14. A technique of behavior therapy in which the client is gradually exposed to the feared object while simultaneously practicing relaxation is called (a)_____. As part of this technique, the client must prepare a list of feared stimuli, arranged in order from least to most feared; this is called a (b)_____ hierarchy. Another technique is for the client to be gradually exposed to the actual feared or anxiety–producing situation; this is called (c)_____ exposure.

15. One form of therapy combines two methods: changing negative thoughts by substituting positive ones; and changing unwanted or disruptive behaviors by learning and practicing new skills to improve functioning. This approach is called _____ therapy.

E. REVIEW: EVALUATION OF APPROACHES

16. Sigmund Freud developed psychoanalysis, whose basic assumption is that emotional problems are caused by underlying (a)_____. Techniques used to uncover unconscious conflicts include (b)_____ and _____.

17. Carl Rogers developed (a)_____ therapy, whose basic assumption is that the client is responsible for change and has the capacity to grow and reach his or her full potential. Techniques include (b)_____ the client's concerns; therapists must also show the characteristics of empathy, positive regard, and genuineness.

18. Aaron Beck's cognitive theory assumes that automatic, negative, and irrational (a)_____ can color our feelings and actions, distort our perceptions, and result in various problems. Its techniques include recognizing negative thoughts and (b)_____ positive ones.

19. An approach to therapy based on learning principles is called (a)_____ therapy, whose basic assumption is that emotional problems are (b)_____ and thus can be unlearned by using learning principles. Its techniques include systematic desensitization, role playing, imitation, and modeling.

20. Despite differences in approaches and techniques, the six most popular forms of psychotherapy differ little in (a)_____, except for a small number of disorders, such as phobias, panic attacks, and depression, in which (b)_____ therapy is found more effective. Most improvement in therapy occurs in a relatively short period of (c)_____.

21. One reason therapies tend to be equally effective is that they all share _____. For example, the development of a supportive and trusting relationship between therapist and client re-sults in an accepting atmosphere, in which the client feels willing to admit problems and is motivated to work on changing.

F. CULTURAL DIVERSITY: DIFFERENT HEALER

22. In many cases, the healers of Asia and Africa are as effective as Western therapists. One explanation is that these healers may rely on a (a)_____ effect, which is found to produce significant improvement in 10–30% of Western patients. Another is that the healers' ceremonies may involve some of the (b)_____ that underlie the effectiveness of Western therapy.

G. RESEARCH FOCUS: EMDR—NEW THERAPY

23. A number of studies report that eye-movement desensitization reprocessing (EMDR) therapy is an effective method to reduce distress, anxiety and depression following a (a)_____ experience. However, studies have not shown that (b)_____ movements are necessary or that EMDR is more effective than cognitive-behavior therapies.

H. APPLICATION: COGNITIVE-BEHAVIOR TECHNIQUES

24. Behavior or cognitive-behavior therapy usually involves three steps in changing thought patterns. The first step is observing one's own behavior without making any changes; this is called (a)_____. The second step is to identify those (b)_____ thoughts that need to be changed. The third step is to (c)_____ a positive thought for a negative one. Another step that is sometimes included is to actively stop (d)_____ thoughts.

Answers: 1. (a) moral therapy, (b) phenothiazines, (c) dopamine; 2. (a) deinstitutionalization, (b) community mental health; 3. (a) psychiatrist, (b) clinical psychologist, (c) counseling psychologist; 4. (a) insight, (b) behavior, (c) medical; 5. (a) psychoanalysis, (b) unconscious conflicts; 6. (a) free association, (b) dream interpretation; 7. (a) transference, (b) insight, (c) resistance; 8. psychodynamic; 9. (a) client-centered, (b) reflect; 10. (a) empathy, (b) positive regard, (c) genuineness; 11. (a) automatic, (b) overgeneralization, (c) polarized thinking, (d) selective attention; 12. depression; 13. behavior; 14. (a) systematic desensitization, (b) stimulus, (c) in vivo; 15. cognitive-behavior; 16. (a) unconscious conflicts, (b) free association, dream interpretation; 17. (a) client-centered, (b) reflecting or restating; 18. (a) thoughts, (b) substituting; 19. (a) behavior, (b) learned; 20. (a) effectiveness, (b) behavior or cognitive-behavior, (c) time; 21. common factors; 22. (a) placebo, (b) common factors; 23. (a) traumatic, (b) eye; 24. (a) self-monitoring, (b) negative or automatic, (c) substitute, (d) intrusive or annoying.

Newspaper Article

QUESTIONS

VIRTUAL THERAPY

by Jane E. Stevens

When psychologist Ralph Lamson first put on a virtual-reality helmet at an exhibition of new technology in San Jose two years ago, he unexpectedly collided with his worst fear: his terror of heights.

He found himself in a tall building looking through floor-to-ceiling windows at a panorama far below. But instead of ripping off the helmet that displayed the illusion, he took a deep breath and began inching toward the windows, reminding himself with each baby step that he was safe—and that what he was experiencing was not real.

Lamson says he walked out of the exhibit hall cured of acrophobia and thinking to himself: "I'd better research this."

Last year, with hardware and software on loan from Division Inc. of Redwood City, Lamson conducted what is believed to be the first, and perhaps only, clinical trial of virtual reality in any health care field. Lamson, a psychologist at Kaiser-Permenente Medical Group in San Rafael, used the new technology in an attempt to relieve the fears of 36 people who had a 20- to 30-year history of acrophobia.

After just one 50-minute treatment, 90% of the participants were able to complete self-assigned goals such as walking across a bridge or riding a glass-enclosed elevator, he told 700 health-care professionals who recently attended the "Medicine Meets Virtual Reality" conference in San Diego.

"It's clear that the time has come for this technology to be applied for therapeutic use," said psychiatrist Hans Sieburg, director of the Laboratory for Biological Informatics and Theoretical Medicine at UC San Diego.

"But we're still very much at the beginning. We need to know what the brain is doing, if virtual reality changes its neurophysiology. Will it help people, or will it fry their brains?"

Lamson, however, is already preparing to expand the clinical trials. "I think it can be used for a range of anxiety disorders," he said, "from public speaking to obsessive-compulsive behavior."

Source: *Los Angeles Times,* February 28, 1995.

QUESTIONS

1. What is acrophobia?

2. What therapeutic approach does Lamson's virtual-reality experiment most resemble?

3. Why might anxiety disorders be especially suitable for treatment with virtual-reality devices?

4. What are some concerns about virtual-reality therapy?

5. Can you think of other ways new technology could be used therapeutically?

Study Questions

A. Historical Background—Should our major cities spend more money to develop care and treatment programs for the homeless? (See answer in Critical Thinking Appendix.)

B. Questions about Psychotherapy—Suppose your friend or loved one has a relatively serious psychological problem. Should you suggest that he or she get professional help?

C. Insight Therapies—Several computer programs have been written to "do psychotherapy." Could a computer program be written to "do psychoanalysis"?

D. Behavior Therapy—Susan complains of having terrible test anxiety. What would a behavior therapist do to help her? (See answer in Critical Thinking Appendix.)

E. Review: Evaluation of Approaches—Janice has a phobia of going out in public. Which approach would be most effective for treating her problem?

F. Cultural Diversity: Different Healer—If a Westerner believed that he or she was possessed by the devil, would therapy or an exorcism ritual be the more effective treatment?

G. Research Focus: EMDR—New Therapy—Why do you think that people are often more convinced by dramatic case studies than by sound experimental evidence?

H. Application: Cognitive-Behavior Techniques—Frank has very little self-confidence and self-esteem. What is one way that he could work on raising them? (See answer in Critical Thinking Appendix.)

LINKS TO LEARNING

Web Sites & Learning Activities

● BROOKS/COLE ONLINE PSYCHOLOGY STUDY CENTER

http://psychstudy.brookscole.com/student/plotnik/quiz/ch24frm.html

This site gives students a chance to review material by taking quizzes and doing exercises and activities for this module.

● BEHAVIOR ON-LINE

http://www.behavior.net

This site includes discussion groups about many kinds of therapy, including cognitive, psychodynamic, Gestalt, and EMDR.

● THE PSYCHOANALYTIC CONNECTION

http://psychoanalysis.net/

Covering all aspects of psychoanalysis, this site includes information on both history and current applications.

● GROUP PSYCHOTHERAPY FOR THE LAYMAN

http://freud.tau.ac.il/~hairmw/group1.html#group1

Ever wondered about group therapy? This site covers the basics, including how to choose a group, different kinds of groups, and what is expected of participants.

● AMERICAN ASSOCIATION FOR MARRIAGE AND FAMILY THERAPY

http://www.aamft.org/

The AAMFT is a professional organization of marriage and family therapists. Their site includes lots of information, including a clinical update and resources.

● COGNITIVE THERAPY AND RESEARCH

http://www.sci.sdsu.edu/CAL/CTR/CTR.html

This journal is now available online and includes scholarly articles related to the clinical applications of cognitive therapy.

● NON-MAINSTREAM PSYCHOTHERAPY AND COUNSELING RESOURCES

http://ourworld.compuserve.com/homepages/selfheal.nonmain.htm

Alternative therapies are popular but controversial. This site lists many resources for both well-known and obscure non-mainstream approaches to therapy.

Welcome to the WEB

Activities

● *Integrator Online*™ *for Introductory Psychology* CD-ROM, Plotnik, Module 24

● Study Guide to accompany *Introduction to Psychology,* 5th edition, Module 24 (choice of PC or Mac computer version or hard copy).

● *PsychNow!* CD-ROM

Major Psychological Therapies

Answers to questions on page 578

1. Acrophobia is a fear of heights.
2. It is similar to systematic desensitization, a behavioral approach.
3. Anxiety disorders involve fears and compulsions that have been successfully treated with behavioral therapies.
4. How does it affect the brain? Could people be harmed by this therapy? For whom might it be effective, and who should not use it? What does it cost?
5. Some people are experimenting with online psychotherapy. What other possibilities can you think of?

Module 25 SOCIAL PSYCHOLOGY

Stereotypes

Why did he take a $90,000 pay cut?

Lawrence Graham wanted to get a job at a country club and had phoned numerous clubs to set up personal interviews. Here's what happened when he arrived for one of his interviews.

"We don't have any job openings— and if you don't leave the building, I will have to call security," the receptionist said at the first club Graham visited.

"But I just spoke to Donna, your dining manager, and she said to come by and discuss the waiter job."

"Sorry, but there are no jobs and no one here named Donna" (Graham, 1995, p. 4).

Graham finally got two job offers and decided on the exclusive Greenwich Country Club. This club had been in existence for 100 years, and was *the* country club in the very affluent, prestigious, and white town of Greenwich, Connecticut. The Club's members included a former president, a number of high-ranking government officials, and dozens of *Fortune* 500 executives, bankers, and Wall Street lawyers.

Although Graham wanted a job as a waiter, he was hired to be a busboy. Except when one of the members wanted something and deliberately looked for him, Graham's job as a busboy made him quite invisible and able to overhear members' conversations.

"Here, busboy. Here, busboy," a woman called out. "Busboy, my coffee is cold. Give me a refill."

"Certainly, I would be happy to," said Graham.

Before he returned to the kitchen, Graham heard the woman say to her companion, "My goodness. Did you hear that? That busboy has diction like an educated white person" (Graham, 1995, p. 12).

In real life, Lawrence Graham is a Harvard Law School graduate, has a job as an associate in a New York law firm, and makes $105,000 a year. Although he is ready to move up the social ladder, Graham, who is African American, received no invitations to join a country club, as his white associates did. So to find out what goes on in country clubs that do not admit African Americans, he got in the only way he could, as a busboy making $7 a hour.

Graham's example points out how people often make judgments about others on the basis of physical appearance and accompanying stereotypes, which are both major topics of social psychology.

Social psychology is a broad field whose goals are to understand and explain how our thoughts, feelings, perceptions, and behaviors are influenced by the presence of, or interactions with, others.

One relatively new, rapidly growing, and important subarea of social psychology is social cognition.

Social cognition is a subarea of social psychology that focuses on cognitive processes—for example, how we perceive, store, and retrieve information about social interactions and events. It rose to prominence in the 1980s (Hamilton et al., 1994).

Social psychologists study how we form impressions and perceive others, how we form attitudes and stereotypes, how we evaluate social interactions, and why racism exists—all of which are involved in Lawrence Graham's story.

Another major topic of social psychology is how people behave in groups.

Behavior in Groups

Why did they follow him to their deaths?

David Koresh, a 34-year-old high school drop-out, rock musician, polygamist, and preacher, built his church on a simple message: "If the Bible is true, then I'm Christ." This message drew more than a hundred people to join him at an armed fortress near Waco, Texas, where they waited for the end of the world.

Koresh's followers would do anything for him. For example, he taught that all the women in the world belonged to him. At one point, Koresh had 18 "wives"; some were only 12 years old. One of the young girls said, "You're going to marry this guy and he's God, and someday he will be resurrected as a perfect human being." Koresh fathered numerous children.

Koresh laid down strict rules for his followers. They were not allowed beer, meat, air conditioning, or MTV, had to turn over all their money and possessions to him, and were not allowed to marry. Sometimes Koresh enforced his rules with beatings and other punishment.

Agents of the Bureau of Alcohol, Tobacco, and Firearms became concerned about Koresh's increasing stash of weapons. After negotiations failed, they fired tear gas into the Koresh compound. A fire started. Fueled by kerosene in the compound and 30-mile-an-hour winds, the fire swept through the buildings. After the fire was put out, agents sifted through the burnt rubble and found the bodies of Koresh and 85 other adults and children (Gibbs, 1993b; Kantrowitz et al., 1993). Why 85 adults and children stayed with Koresh and burned to death is one of the topics we'll discuss when we examine behavior in groups.

What's Coming

We'll discuss how we perceive people, how we explain the causes of our behaviors, why we develop attitudes, and how we respond to persuasion. We'll also explore a variety of social influences and group behaviors, such as how we respond to group pressures, what motivates us to help others, and why we are aggressive.

We'll begin with Graham's story, which raises the question of how we form impressions of others.

A. Perceiving Others

Person Perception

How do you form first impressions?

As you compare the photo of Lawrence Graham on the left with that on the right, notice that your first impressions automatically change. In the left photo, your first impression is that Graham is a busboy or waiter. In the right photo, your first impression is that Graham is a confident businessman or professional. Your first impressions were formed in seconds, required little conscious deliberation, and were biased or distorted by your past experiences. For instance, if you were once a busperson, you might feel sympathetic toward Graham. This example illustrates some of the different factors that go into person perception.

Person perception refers to the process by which we form impressions of, and make judgments about, the traits and characteristics of others.

> Am I different because I'm carrying a tray?

As you looked at each photo of Graham and formed a first impression, four things were simultaneously influencing your judgment (Wyer & Lambert, 1994).

1 Physical appearance. Your initial impressions and judgments of Graham are heavily influenced and biased by physical appearance. When Graham is dressed as a busboy he makes a very different impression than when he is dressed as a professional.

2 Need to explain. You don't just look at or observe Graham, but rather you try to explain why he looks, dresses, or behaves in a certain way. You might explain that Graham-as-busboy is working his way through college, while Graham-as-professional is starting his career.

> Am I different because I'm wearing a suit?

3 Influence on behavior. Your first impressions of Graham will influence how you would interact with him. For example, if your first impression of Graham is as a $7-an-hour busboy, you would interact very differently than if your impression of him was as a $100,000-a-year professional working for a large corporation.

4 Effects of race. Researchers have found that members of one race generally recognize faces of their own race more accurately than faces of other races (Ng & Lindsay, 1994). This means that we may perceive faces that are racially different from our own in a biased or distorted way because they do not appear as distinctly as faces from our own race. For this reason, your first impressions of Graham will depend on your race and racial attitudes.

Although person perception occurs quickly, it may result in a strong impression that guides and directs our future interactions with that person (Park et al., 1994). One of the factors that plays a major role in person perception is physical appearance.

Physical Appearance

What makes a face attractive?

Greta Garbo (photo on the right) was a great film star of the 1930s and was considered to have one of the most beautiful faces ever. To determine what makes Garbo's face so attractive, researchers created faces by combining and averaging physical features taken from 4–32 different faces. They found that a face created by averaging 32 faces was judged as more attractive than a face created by averaging 16 or fewer faces. Researchers concluded that we judge those faces as most attractive that come closest to the average or prototypical face found in the general population, which is approximated by averaging features from 32 faces (Langlois et al., 1994; Rhodes & Tremewan, 1996). One reason social psychologists study physical appearance is that physical attractiveness influences person perception and first impressions.

One of the most widely cited early conclusions from research on physical attractiveness is the phrase "What is beautiful is good" (Dion et al., 1972). This phrase means that physically attractive people were found to create more favorable impressions than did less attractive people. For example, physically attractive people are considered to be more responsive, interesting, sociable, intelligent, kind, outgoing, and poised and are more likely to be recommended for job promotions (Kalick et al., 1998; Longo & Ashmore, 1995). One reason physical attractiveness may have such a strong influence on first impressions is that we interpret an attractive face as implying desirable personal qualities, such as intelligence and the ability to be a good partner, mentor, friend, or colleague (Cunningham et al., 1995).

> Is it true that a beautiful face is an average of many faces?

Besides an attractive face, certain *psychological characteristics* make a person more or less attractive and desirable as a friend or mate. For instance, women rated men as more physically and sexually attractive if they were also willing to be helpful and considerate of others (Jensen-Campbell et al., 1995). Thus, physical appearance plays an important role in creating positive first impressions. As the relationship progresses, and the individual's personality traits become apparent, those first impressions will be confirmed or revised.

One reason first impressions occur so quickly and automatically is that we may be using information based on various physical and psychological stereotypes.

Is your first impression wrong?

Harry Duh was born in Taiwan and grew up in predominantly white Tallmadge, Ohio. As part of a class project, Harry dressed up as what he called an "Asian nerd" (as in left photo). When he dressed that way, both Caucasians and fellow Asian students reacted very similarly with teasing and jeering behind his back. Bookstore cashiers explained the cost of his purchases in an extremely patronizing voice. In gym class he was mocked for trying to lift weights. Harry says that part of the negative reaction was because of his "nerd dress," but a part was because he was Asian (Myers, 1992). Thus, in forming impressions, perceiving, and reacting to Harry, fellow students apparently used

What's your first impression of us?

information from two negative stereotypes—nerd stereotype and Asian stereotype.

Stereotypes are widely held beliefs that people have certain traits because they belong to a particular group. Stereotypes are often inaccurate and frequently portray the members of less powerful, less controlling groups more negatively than members of more powerful or controlling groups.

When Harry returned to school dressed in a more fashionable hairstyle and clothes (as in right photo), students no longer teased or laughed at him. Harry's experience clearly demonstrates that students formed impressions based on stored social information, specifically stereotypes, which can bias and distort their person perceptions, especially first impressions (Kawakami et al., 1998).

DEVELOPMENT OF STEREOTYPES

How are they formed?

Psychologists believe that we develop stereotypes when parents, peers, coworkers, teachers, and others reward us with social approval for holding certain attitudes and beliefs. There are also cultural pressures to adopt certain values and beliefs about members of different groups. For example, in the weight-conscious culture of the United States, there is an emphasis on being thin (Module 15), so we might expect a negative stereotype to apply to women who are overweight (Sands et al., 1997).

Why do you think I wasn't hired?

To test this idea, researchers asked subjects to watch videotapes of job applicants and decide if they would hire them. The applicants were professional male and female actors made up to appear normal weight or overweight (about 28–35 pounds heavier). When asked to make hiring decisions, subjects showed a significant bias against hiring overweight applicants, especially overweight women (Pingitore et al., 1994). This bias against hiring overweight women is an example of a negative stereotype, which is often accompanied by prejudice and discrimination.

Prejudice refers to an unfair, biased, or intolerant attitude toward another group of people.

An example of prejudice is believing that overweight women are not as intelligent, competent, or capable as women of normal weight.

Discrimination refers to specific unfair behaviors exhibited toward members of a group.

An employer's bias against hiring overweight applicants would be an example of discrimination.

The history of the United States provides many examples of racist and sexist cultural stereotypes, such as beliefs that women are not smart enough to vote and that African Americans are inferior to whites (Swim et al., 1995). When we apply stereotypes to all members of a different group from our own, we usually use extreme stereotypes (they're all smart, dumb, lazy, hard-workers), which can be either positive or negative. One reason we frequently use stereotypes to make judgments about people is that stereotypes save us thinking time.

FUNCTIONS OF STEREOTYPES

What are their two functions?

Social cognitive psychologists suggest that, just as we have developed physical tools, such as hammers and saws, to help us build things more efficiently, we have also developed cognitive tools, such as stereotypes, to help us think and make decisions more efficiently. For example, instead of having to analyze in detail the person in the right photo, you can simply assign the person to a social group, such as teenage-punker, and use the information that you have stored in that stereotype. A stereotype for teenage-punker might include: disregards standard social customs and fashions, is independent, dislikes authority, goes to rave parties, experiments with drugs, and so on. From this example, you can see that stereotypes are used frequently because they serve at least two major functions (Macrae et al., 1994).

Why don't adults like me?

Source of information. A stereotype is like an information file stored in your brain. As soon as you assign someone to a stereotype, you mentally open that file and use the stored information to make judgments.

Thought-saving device. Stereotypes are ways to conserve time and energy when making decisions in social situations. By using stereotypes, you make quick (and sometimes inaccurate) decisions and thus save time and energy by not having to analyze an overwhelming amount of personal and social information.

However, a major problem with stereotypes is that they are, once formed, very difficult to change. One reason we don't easily change stereotypes is that we are often unaware of using them. Another reason we hold on to stereotypes is that we usually dismiss information that does not fit our stereotypes (Greenwald & Banaji, 1995). This means that biased stereotypes live on and on and lead to inaccurate judgments and decisions.

Some social psychologists describe stereotypes as representing hundreds of information files or categories, called schemas, that influence what we see and think.

A. Perceiving Others

Schemas

When do schemas act like filters?

In 1975, Fran Conley reached her goal of becoming a board-certified neurosurgeon. At the time, she was one of only two female board-certified neurosurgeons in the United States. Yet despite her exceptional accomplishments, Dr. Conley has had to put up with sexist attitudes from male colleagues. For example, as a young neurosurgeon, she was repeatedly propositioned by fellow doctors in front of others, primarily for effect. Dr. Conley admits that she tolerated this kind of behavior because she wanted to advance in her profession and be accepted by her colleagues. She believed that once she became a full professor and had sufficient status in her profession, the sexist treatment would cease. She was mistaken.

Even after Dr. Conley had achieved the status of a full professor at Stanford Medical Center (right photo), the sexism continued. For instance, whenever Dr. Conley disagreed with male colleagues, they would jokingly attribute her lack of agreement to a difficult menstrual period. But disagreements between male colleagues were viewed as honest differences of opinion (Libman, 1991; Manning, 1998). One reason male colleagues responded to Dr. Conley in sexist ways is that they had developed sexist schemas.

Schemas are mental categories that, like computer files, contain knowledge about people, events, and concepts. Because schemas influence what we attend to and how we interpret things, schemas can bias and distort our thoughts, perceptions, and behaviors.

Dr. Conley's experiences with her medical colleagues illustrate that their sexist schemas served at least three functions (Leyens & Fiske, 1994).

Functions. Schemas provided male colleagues with *information* about social stimuli, such as because Dr. Conley was a woman, she was inferior and less intelligent than men. Schemas influenced what male colleagues would pay *attention* to, such as noticing when Dr. Conley disagreed with a male colleague. Schemas influenced how male colleagues *responded* to women, such as by propositioning Dr. Conley. Thus, schemas are cognitive structures that influence and guide many of our behaviors.

Kinds of Schemas

We've just met but I feel like I already know you.

Schemas, which are like hundreds of different information files in your brain, are generally divided into four types: person, role, event, and self schemas.

Person schemas include our judgments about the traits that we and others possess.

For example, when meeting someone new, we may rely on person schemas to provide general information about that person. Person schemas that contain general information about people who have membership in groups are *stereotypes.*

Role schemas are based on the jobs people perform or the social positions they hold.

The reason we often ask, "What do you do?" is so we can use our role schemas to provide information about the person. Role schemas encourage us to develop beliefs and expectations about people so that we can sort them into cognitive pigeonholes.

Event schemas, also called scripts, contain behaviors that we associate with familiar activities, events, or procedures.

I'm going to celebrate till I drop.

For example, the script for graduation is to laugh, shout, and celebrate getting your degree. In contrast, the script for a college class is to be silent, pay attention, and take notes. Event schemas help us know what to expect and provide guidelines on how to behave in different kinds of situations.

Self schemas contain personal information about ourselves, and this information influences, modifies, and distorts what we perceive and remember and how we behave.

What's interesting about our self schemas is that they generally overemphasize our good points, and that explains why criticism hurts our feelings. We usually pay close attention to feedback that supports our self schemas and disregard information that doesn't (Taylor & Armor, 1996). Because we especially look for information to support them, schemas, once formed, are difficult to change.

Advantages and Disadvantages

No matter what you say, I'm a good student.

There are two *disadvantages* of schemas. The first is that schemas may restrict and distort what we attend to and remember and thus cause us to overlook important information (Devine et al., 1994). For example, if your self schema is that of being a very good student, you may not pay attention to suggestions from parents, teachers, or friends that may make you an even better student.

The second disadvantage of schemas is that they are highly resistant to change because we generally select and attend to information that supports our schemas and deny any information that is inconsistent with them (Vonk, 1995). For example, you might pay attention to and agree with positive written comments on a class paper and reject or rationalize any critical but constructive suggestions to improve it.

There are several *advantages* of schemas: they are efficient mental shortcuts for analyzing and responding to all kinds of social situations; they help us fill in missing information; they provide guidelines for appropriate behavior in various situations; and they help us explain why people behave the way they do. Explaining social behavior is one of the most intriguing areas of social cognition, and it's our next topic.

Definition

What is unusual about this umpire?

After 13 seasons and 2,000 games in the minor leagues, this umpire was passed over for promotion to the major leagues and released. An evaluation report by the Office for Umpire Development claimed that this umpire's work had "deteriorated in areas of enthusiasm and execution," even though earlier in the season the rating had been "better than average." What is unusual about this umpire is that she is a woman. Pam Postema (right photo) claims the reason that she was passed over for promotion and released was that she was a woman and there are no female umpires in major league baseball. She filed a sex discrimination suit against professional baseball

> Because I'm a woman, I wasn't promoted.

because, as Pam says, "Baseball wasn't ready for a woman umpire no matter how good she was" (Reed & Stambler, 1992).

Most sports fans would have an explanation as to why Pam Postema was not promoted to be an umpire in major baseball leagues. These kinds of explanations are called attributions.

Attributions are things we point to as the causes of events, other people's behaviors, and our own behaviors.

If you had to explain why there are no female umpires in the major baseball leagues, you would choose between internal and external attributions.

Internal versus External

A famous social psychologist, Fritz Heider (1958), believed that we all function to some extent like social psychologists as we try to explain everyday behaviors. Heider was the first to distinguish between internal and external causes or attributions for behaviors.

Internal attributions are explanations of behavior based on the internal characteristics or dispositions of the person performing the behavior. They are sometimes referred to as dispositional attributions.

For example, if you used internal attributions to explain why Postema was not made a major league umpire, you would point to her personal characteristics or dispositions, such as saying that she was not a good judge of balls and strikes.

External attributions are explanations of behavior based on the external circumstances or situations. They are sometimes called situational attributions.

If you used external attributions to explain why Postema was not promoted, you would point to external circumstances, such as saying that major baseball leagues are run by men, and they do not want a woman umpire.

Using internal, or dispositional, attributions to explain Postema's lack of promotion results in very different reasons compared with external, or situational, attributions (Wann & Dolan, 1994). Using internal attributions says she is not capable of being a major league umpire; using external attributions says that although she is capable, the league discriminated against her because she is a woman.

Thus, deciding between internal and external attributions can be very important. Social psychologists have studied how people make this distinction.

Kelley's Model of Covariation

How do we decide whether Pam was passed over for promotion because of dispositional or situational factors? To answer this question, social psychologist Harold Kelley (1967) developed the covariation model.

The *covariation model,* developed by Harold Kelley, says that, in making attributions, we should look for factors that are present when the behavior occurs and factors that are absent when the behavior does not occur.

Kelley proposed that, in explaining someone's behavior, we should look for information about three factors: consensus, consistency, and distinctiveness.

Consensus means determining whether other people engage in the same behavior in the same situation.

Consistency means determining whether the person engages in this behavior every time he or she is in a particular situation.

Distinctiveness means determining how differently the person behaves in one situation when compared to other situations.

In the examples on the left, we have applied the three factors in Kelley's covariation model to Pam Postema's situation. Notice that

1. HIGH CONSISTENCY
Pam performs about the same every time.

2. LOW DISTINCTIVENESS
Pam makes good decisions in calling strikes but not in calling base runners out.

3. LOW CONSENSUS
Pam does not show the same skills as other umpires.

INTERNAL ATTRIBUTION
Pam's lack of promotion is due to her poor umpiring skills.

1. HIGH CONSISTENCY
Pam performs about the same every time.

2. HIGH DISTINCTIVENESS
Pam makes good decisions in all aspects of the game.

3. HIGH CONSENSUS
Pam shows the same skills as other umpires.

EXTERNAL ATTRIBUTION
Pam's lack of promotion is due to discrimination by the league.

high consistency, low distinctiveness, and low consensus result in an internal, or dispositional, attribution (fired because she's a poor umpire). But high consistency, high distinctiveness, and high consensus result in an external or situational attribution (fired because of sexual discrimination). Thus, Kelley's covariation model helps us determine if Postema's firing was due to internal or external attributions (Smith, 1994). However, if we don't follow Kelley's model, which demands considerable time and effort, we make errors in attributing causes.

B. Attributions

Biases and Errors

Why do we make the wrong attributions?

Most people have heard the phrase *glass ceiling*, which refers to a real but invisible barrier that keeps women and people of color from reaching the top positions in a business or organization. Evidence that there is a very thick glass ceiling came from a recent survey of *Fortune* magazine's top 1,000 companies. In these companies, 97% of the senior managers are white and 95% are male (Michaelson, 1995). One person who is trying to break the glass ceiling is Mary Contreras-Sweet (right photo), who was born in Guadalajara, Mexico, and now lives in Los Angeles. Through perseverance, hard work, and a winning personality, she broke through the glass ceiling at age 30 by becoming vice-president for public affairs at 7-Up/RC Bottling Company of Southern California. Since then she has been appointed a member of the Federal Glass Ceiling Commission, which was charged with finding ways to help individuals break through the ceiling.

One difficulty in breaking through the glass ceiling involves decisions about attribution. Do women and people of color fail to be appointed to senior level positions because they lack skills and intel-

Let me tell you how I broke through the glass ceiling.

ligence, which is an internal or dispositional attribution; or because they face discrimination from senior-level white males, which is an external or situational attribution? Although Kelley's covariation model would help decide this issue, many people do not invest the required time and effort but instead use the cognitive miser model (Taylor, 1981).

The *cognitive miser model* says that, in making attributions, people feel they must conserve time and effort by taking cognitive shortcuts.

We have already discussed several cognitive shortcuts that we use in selecting, gathering, remembering, and using information—for example, relying on stereotypes and schemas. Besides these, researchers have identified a number of other cognitive shortcuts that we frequently use in making attributions (Wilson et al., 1997). Although these cognitive shortcuts save mental time and effort, they may result in biased or incorrect attributions. We'll discuss three of the most common biases in making attributions: the fundamental attribution error, the actor-observer effect, and self-serving bias.

Fundamental Attribution Error

If you believe that women and people of color cannot break through the glass ceiling because they lack the skills and intelligence to do so, you may be making the fundamental attribution error.

The *fundamental attribution error* refers to our tendency, when we look for causes of a person's behavior, to focus on the person's disposition or personality traits and overlook how the situation influenced the person's behavior.

When you explain someone's behavior, you may be wrong.

An example of the fundamental attribution error would be to conclude that women and people of color cannot break through the glass ceiling because of personal or dispositional factors, such as a lack of assertiveness or intelligence. This may not be the real reason, however. Because 97% of senior management in *Fortune*'s 1,000 top companies are white and 95% are male, another possible reason that women and people of color have difficulty breaking through the glass ceiling may be due to biased or discriminatory hiring practices.

Actor-Observer Effect

John angrily explains that he got to his car to put more money in the meter just as the police officer was driving away. John adds that he's very responsible and the ticket was bad luck because he was only 45 seconds late. John says the reason he got the ticket was because the police officer was just being mean. John's explanation is a good example of the actor-observer effect.

The *actor-observer effect* refers to the tendency, when you are behaving (or acting), to attribute your own behavior to situational factors. However, when you are observing others, you attribute another's behavior to his or her personality traits or disposition.

In the parking ticket example, John, the actor, attributes his getting the ticket to situational factors—bad luck—rather than to his being late. In addition, John, the observer, explains that the police officer ticketed him because of a dispositional or personality factor—the officer was mean. The actor-observer error is very common and can be checked by imagining yourself in the position of the person you are observing (Wilson et al., 1997).

Self-Serving Bias

When we look for the causes of our own behaviors, such as why we received a good or bad grade on a test, we may make errors because of the self-serving bias (Sedikides et al., 1998).

The *self-serving bias* refers to explaining our successes by attributing them to our dispositions or personality traits and explaining our failures by attributing them to the situations.

I didn't do well on this exam because the text was confusing.

The self-serving bias can be considered another part of the actor-observer effect. According to the self-serving bias, if you get an A on an exam, you tend to attribute your success to your personality traits or disposition, such as intelligence and preserverance. However, if you get a D on an exam, you tend to attribute your failure to the situation, such as a difficult test or unfair questions. Thus, according to the self-serving bias, we try to keep ourselves in the best possible light by making different and even opposite attributions, depending on whether we have performed well or poorly.

Although our attributions can be a problem when they are biased, they can also be an advantage when they help us change our behaviors, as we'll discuss next.

C. Research Focus: Attributions & Grades
Can Changing Attributions Change Grades?

What problems do freshmen face?

Perhaps 20% of the students I counsel tell me about getting poor grades in their freshman year, and their reasons are very similar. Either they didn't develop good study habits in high school so they weren't academically prepared for college or they spent too much time partying or dealing with stressful personal, social, or financial difficulties. What is interesting is that some of the freshmen who got poor grades their first year were able to bounce

I'm having problems with my grades and wonder if I should drop out.

back academically their second year, while others became discouraged and dropped out of college. Researchers discovered many differences in students' attributions—that is, how students explained why they bounced back or dropped out. Because one goal of psychology is to apply scientific findings to real-world problems, researchers used findings on attributions to develop a program for improving grades and decreasing dropouts (Wilson & Linville, 1982). Here's what actually happened.

1 Kinds of Attributions

In explaining why a freshman is having academic problems, researchers may point to personal or dispositional attributions, such as the lack of necessary academic skills. Or researchers may point to external or situational attributions, such as pressures to party rather than study. Once a freshman has developed a pattern of getting poor grades, another question is whether the causes are permanent or temporary. For example, if freshmen attributed their academic problems to relatively permanent conditions, such as poor abilities, they would have little motivation and would expect little improvement. In addition, poor academic performance would make new students worried and anxious, which in turn would interfere with their ability to study.

However, if freshmen attributed their academic problems to temporary conditions, such as poor study habits, they could expect to improve if they developed better study skills. Researchers thought that if they could change students' attributions about poor academic performance and help them realize that it was a temporary rather than a permanent state, students could improve their grades.

2 Method: Changing Attributions

I did terribly my freshman year but I got my act together and didn't drop out.

Researchers recruited freshmen who were having academic problems, such as scoring poorly on exams, not keeping up with assignments, and considering dropping out of college. These students were randomly divided into two different groups.

Students in the *experimental group* (attributions group) were given a number of procedures that changed their attributions about poor academic performance from a permanent cause to only a temporary condition. For example, students in the experimental group read a booklet about previous freshmen who had similar academic problems but showed improvement later in college. These subjects watched videotapes of previous students who described very convincingly how their grade point averages had risen after their freshman year. Next, these subjects were asked to write down all the reasons they could think of why grade point averages might increase after the freshman year.

The other group of freshmen with academic problems did not receive any of this information and served as a *control group*.

3 Results and Conclusions

Researchers found that by changing students' attributions for poor academic performance from permanent to temporary had two significant positive effects.

Change in Grade Point Average after Program

Control

Attributions

−.50   0.00   +.50

First, in the graph above, notice that freshmen who were told how to attribute their academic problems to temporary conditions (attributions group) had a significant improvement in grade point averages one year after the completion of this program.

Second, as shown in the graph below, only 5% of freshmen who changed their attributions for poor academic performance from permanent to temporary dropped out of college, while 25% of those in the control group dropped out.

Dropout Rate from College

Control

Attributions

5%   15%   25%

On the basis of these data, researchers reached two important conclusions. First, it is possible to change students' attributions and expectations about academic performance. Second, changing students' attributions and expectations actually improved academic performance and reduced dropout rate. This study illustrates how social psychologists used the concept of attribution to solve a real-world problem (Wilson & Linville, 1982).

Next, we'll discuss one of the most active areas of social cognition—forming and changing attitudes.

D. Attitudes

Definition

Can your attitudes get you fired?

We often remark that a certain person has a great attitude or a bad attitude or should change his or her attitude. The media regularly reports on people's attitudes toward a wide range of topics, such as illegal drug usage, assisted suicide, sexual harassment, skinheads, or fat-free potato chips. All this talk about attitude demonstrates that it is not only a very popular term but also one of the most important terms in social psychology (Petty et al., 1997).

An example of how important an attitude can be comes from a letter received by an airport sales agent named Terri. The letter was brief and to the point: "Terri . . . it is our decision to terminate your employment as an airport sales agent . . . for insubordination." Terri's insubordination was that she had refused to wear makeup (lipstick, eyeliner) as specified in Continental Airlines' new 45-page appearance code manual. Terri had never worn makeup in her 11 years in the airline industry, and no one had ever complained before. Her attitude was that she was doing a good job without wearing makeup, so why should she start now? Terri (right photo) stuck to her attitude and was fired. However, several weeks later, Continental announced that it had changed its mind, apologized to Terri, and allowed her to keep her job without having to wear makeup (Mehren, 1991).

Terri's story introduces the concept of *attitude,* which in the 1930s was called the single most indispensable term in social psychology (Allport, 1935).

Can they fire me because of my attitude toward wearing makeup?

An *attitude* is any belief or opinion that includes an evaluation of some object, person, or event along a continuum from negative to positive and that predisposes us to act in a certain way toward that object, person, or event.

In a very real sense, as demonstrated by Terri's experience, our attitudes can have a significant impact on our behaviors. Because attitudes are so important in influencing behaviors, attitude research has become very big business. For example, billions of dollars are spent each year in measuring or trying to change buyers' attitudes toward consumer products and in measuring and trying to change attitudes of voters toward candidates (Bassili, 1995; Dinh et al., 1995).

Although there are many definitions of attitude, they all share the following features (Ostrom et al., 1994):

■ An attitude is *evaluative:* it involves likes and dislikes. An attitude is like a point on a thermometer that ranges from very negative to very positive. For example, Terri makes a negative evaluation of using makeup, which means she has developed a negative attitude toward cosmetics.

■ The evaluation is always *targeted* toward some object, person, or event. Terri's negative attitude is targeted against a specific event, wearing makeup.

■ An attitude *predisposes* us to behave in a certain way. This means that we approach some objects, people, and events and avoid others because of corresponding positive or negative attitudes. Terri's attitude toward wearing makeup predisposed her to fight against wearing it, even to the point of losing her job.

Just as attitudes have the three general features discussed above, they also have the following three components.

Components

How many components?

If you closely examined how Terri's attitude toward wearing makeup affects her thoughts, feelings, and behaviors, you will discover that an attitude has three components: cognitive, affective, and behavioral (Eagly et al., 1994).

Cognitive Component

One reason Terri doesn't approve of wearing makeup is that some cosmetics are tested on animals, which she believes is a cruel practice.

Terri's belief that animals should not be used for cosmetic testing is an example of the cognitive component of attitudes. Thus, the *cognitive component* of our attitudes involves both thoughts and beliefs, which can strongly influence how we behave. For example, one reason vegetarians do not eat meat is based on the cognitive component of their attitude, namely, their firm belief that eating meat is immoral (Rozin et al., 1997).

Affective Component

Another reason Terri doesn't approve of using makeup is that when she does, she feels uncomfortable because she doesn't like what she sees in the mirror. Terri's strong negative feeling about how she looks in makeup is an example of the affective component of attitudes. Thus, the affective component of attitudes involves emotional feelings, which also influence our behaviors. For example, we in the United States do not eat dogs because we are emotionally attached to our pets. But in some parts of Asia, dog meat is considered a delicacy.

Behavioral Component

Terri's negative attitude toward cosmetics predisposed or influenced her behavior; although she refused to wear makeup, she also fought to save her job. Terri's strong actions—refusing to wear makeup and fighting to save her job—are examples of the *behavioral component* of attitudes. Thus, attitudes influence how we behave, and how we behave can also influence the development of attitudes.

Attitudes not only influence our behavior but also have other important functions, which we'll discuss next.

Functions of Attitudes

What if attitudes collide?

Shannon Faulkner (right photo, front) had an attitude about going to college that set off an enormous personal and legal struggle. In 1993, she applied to and was accepted at the Citadel, a military college in Charleston, South Carolina. But almost immediately, she was rejected because officials discovered that Shannon was a woman (she had eliminated all references to gender on her application). During the next two years, there was a battle of attitudes between the Citadel, which wanted to continue its 150-year-old tradition as a male-only college, and Shannon, who wanted to be given the same opportunities as males. She challenged the Citadel's all-male attitude and policy on legal grounds: since the Citadel received 28% of its financial support from the state's tax dollars, it should be open to all the state's residents, male or female.

Why are they harassing me?

Shannon's attitude—that she be allowed to attend the Citadel—elicited death threats, hate mail, harassing phone calls, and hissing in restaurants. However, in August of 1995, the court ruled that the Citadel had to admit Shannon, and she was escorted into the Citadel by her parents and federal marshals.

But her first week at the Citadel, which is called hell week because of the terrible harassment new cadets must endure, was doubly hell for Shannon. Not a single male cadet, new or old, would speak to her or offer any support (Reed & Esselman, 1995).

Shannon's struggle to become the first female cadet at the all-male Citadel resulted in a fierce battle between opposing attitudes. We'll use Shannon's experience to illustrate three general functions of attitudes: how they affect our predispositions, interpretations, and evaluations (Ostrom et al., 1994).

1 Predispose

Shannon had heard about the Citadel in her senior year of high school and said, "There was just something inside of me that wanted to do this" (Baum, 1994, p. 4). As Shannon's battle dragged on for two years, she explained, "It really has been a long struggle. When I started this lawsuit, I was told I would *never* enter the Citadel" (Reed & Esselman, 1995, p. 44). However, Shannon's attitude that women must be given the same opportunities as men predisposed her to behave in a certain way.

The *predisposing function* of attitudes means that they guide or influence us to behave in specific ways.

Shannon's attitude predisposed her to apply to the Citadel, so that she could obtain the same education and profit from the same network as males.

Because attitudes predispose us to behave in specific ways, attitudes are often used to predict behavior. A meta-analysis of 88 studies on how attitudes predispose behavior reported that attitudes significantly and substantially predicted future behaviors (Kraus, 1995). The fact that attitudes can and do predispose us to behave in certain ways is the primary reason that politicians survey voters' attitudes and manufacturers measure consumers' attitudes.

Although attitudes predispose us to behave in specific ways, they do not force us to do so, which explains why voters don't always vote as they say or consumers don't always buy what they say they like (Petty et al., 1997).

2 Interpret

New cadets' first week at the Citadel is called hell week because they endure constant harassment—for example, being yelled at for almost everything or being punished by having to take scalding showers until they throw up (Peyser et al., 1995). One reason cadets endure such harassment is that their attitudes influence how they interpret this cruel treatment.

The *interpreting function* of attitudes means that they provide convenient guidelines for interpreting and categorizing objects and events and deciding whether to approach or avoid them.

Cadets with very positive attitudes toward the Citadel's proud traditions will interpret hell week's harassment as one way to prove themselves. In contrast, cadets with less positive attitudes may question and rebel against such cruel harassment. Although Shannon had fought hard to enter the Citadel, she decided to drop out during hell week, as did 24 male cadets.

3 Evaluate

During the two years Shannon fought for admission to the Citadel, garbage was heaped on her car, hate mail called her every ugly name, and she was jeered and hissed at in restaurants. One reason that Shannon put up with this harassment was because attitudes help us evaluate situations and stand up for our beliefs.

The *evaluative function* of attitudes means that they help us stand up for those beliefs and values that we consider very important to ourselves.

For example, Shannon's strong attitude that women should have equal opportunities for education, especially in publicly supported institutions, helped her endure two years of harassment and struggle.

The evaluative function of attitudes explains why people with strong attitudes about equal rights, the homeless, religion, freedom, abortion, gays, and politics often endure great personal hardships in standing up and fighting for their beliefs.

Although Shannon dropped out of the Citadel in 1995, four more women entered the Citadel in 1996. Although the Citadel promised to halt harassment, two of the four women dropped out because of excessive harassment (having their clothes set on fire, made to drink iced tea till they vomited). The Citadel officially punished 10 cadets for excessive hazing (Gleick, 1997). One reason male cadets continue to excessively harass female cadets is that the Citadel knowingly or unknowingly has fostered negative attitudes toward women cadets. Researchers have found that strong negative attitudes are very difficult to change (Petty et al., 1997). Changing attitudes is our next topic.

D. Attitudes

Attitude Change

What made a skinhead reform?

At one time, Gregory Withrow (right photo) was an out-and-out hatemonger who belonged to the White Aryan Resistance, the Ku Klux Klan, the skinheads, and the American Nazi Party. His goal was "the complete and total extermination of all nonwhites from the face of the American continent." He preached hatred and bashed and robbed Japanese tourists in San Francisco. Then he met Sylvia, who completely rejected Gregory's white supremacist notions. As Gregory grew to love Sylvia, he found himself caught between her

I was a racist and a skinhead until I met Sylvia.

disapproval of his Nazi values and his years of preaching hate. Gregory finally resolved his personal dilemma by renouncing his previous white supremacist values and abandoning the hate organizations. He now speaks against hate and racism (Wride, 1989).

Social psychologists are interested in the process of changing attitudes, such as Gregory's radical change from preaching hate and racism to denouncing these beliefs. We'll discuss two popular theories that explain why people change their attitudes: the theory of cognitive dissonance and self-perception theory (Petty et al., 1997).

Cognitive Dissonance

After meeting Sylvia, Gregory's life became one big conflict. He had spent most of his adult life practicing racism and hate, but now he was in love with Sylvia, who was tolerant and peaceloving. Because Gregory's hateful beliefs clashed with Sylvia's nonhateful attitudes, he found himself in the middle of a very troubling inconsistency, which Leon Festinger (1957) called cognitive dissonance.

Cognitive dissonance refers to a state of unpleasant psychological tension that motivates us to reduce our cognitive inconsistencies by making our beliefs more consistent with each other.

There are two main ways to reduce cognitive dissonance—that is, to make our beliefs and attitudes consistent with our behavior (Aronson, 1997).

Adding or changing beliefs. We can reduce cognitive dissonance by adding new beliefs or changing old beliefs and making them consistent with our behavior. In Gregory's case, cognitive dissonance was created by the conflict between Sylvia's nonviolent values and his own racist and hate-filled beliefs. To decrease his cognitive dissonance, Gregory renounced his hateful beliefs so that his attitudes became consistent with his behavior, which was loving Sylvia and her nonviolent ways (Gibbons et al., 1997).

I changed my racist beliefs and attitudes in order to resolve my _____ dissonance.

Counterattitudinal behavior. Another way we can reduce cognitive dissonance is by engaging in opposite or counterattitudinal behavior (Leippe & Eisenstadt, 1994).

Counterattitudinal behavior involves taking a public position that runs counter to your private attitude.

A classic study by Festinger & Carlsmith (1959) illustrates how counterattitudinal behavior works. In this study, subjects were asked to do an extremely boring task, such as turning pegs in a board. At the end of the task, the experimenter asked the subjects to help out by telling the next group of subjects how interesting the task was. Subjects were asked to lie about the task and say it was interesting, which is engaging in counterattitudinal behavior. For saying the task was interesting, some subjects received $1 and some received $20. Sometime later, the original subjects were asked how much they had liked the boring task. A curious finding emerged. Subjects paid just $1 had a more favorable attitude to the boring task than those who were paid $20. That's because subjects paid $20 felt they were paid well for lying. Subjects paid $1 had no good reason for lying, and so, to resolve the cognitive dissonance between what they'd said (it was interesting) and what they felt (it was boring), they convinced themselves that the task was somewhat interesting. This shows that engaging in opposite or counterattitudinal behaviors can change attitudes.

Now, we'll consider a different explanation for the results of this experiment.

Self-Perception Theory

Perhaps subjects in the previous experiment came to believe their own lies (task was interesting) after engaging in counterattitudinal behavior not to reduce cognitive dissonance but because of changing their own self-perceptions.

Self-perception theory says that we first observe or perceive our own behavior and then, as a result, we change our attitudes.

Daryl Bem (1967), who developed self-perception theory, would explain that subjects paid only $1 for lying would recall their behavior and conclude that they would never have lied for only $1, so the task must have actually been interesting.

At first glance, cognitive dissonance theory and self-perception theory seem to be similar, since they both indicate that if we say something it must be true. However, each theory points to different reasons. According to *cognitive dissonance theory*, the belief "if I said it, it must be true" occurs because we are trying to reduce the inconsistency in our beliefs and behaviors. In comparison, according to *self-perception theory*, concluding that "if I said it, it must be true" simply reflects another way of explaining our own behaviors.

Self-perception theory also challenges the traditional assumption that attitudes give rise to behavior. According to self-perception theory, behaviors give rise to attitudes. For example, after Gregory began speaking out against racism, his attitudes changed radically. Researchers have shown that behavior can influence attitudes (Leippe & Eisenstadt, 1994).

I changed my attitudes after speaking against racism, which is an example of engaging in _____ behavior.

We may change our own attitudes in response to cognitive dissonance or self-perception. However, others are continually trying to change our attitudes through various forms of persuasion, our next topic.

Persuasion

How to persuade people?

Political candidates spend much of their time, energy, and money trying to persuade people to vote for them. As we examine what politicians do and say, you'll discover that there are different methods of persuasion.

If you were to run for a campus office, you would need to decide whether to use an intellectual or emotional appeal, how to appear honest, and what arguments to use. We'll begin with choosing between two different routes—central or peripheral (Dalto et al., 1994; Petty & Cacioppo, 1986).

Central Route

If the audience is interested in and will think about the real issues, a politician should seek votes using the central route.

> I think logical arguments and hard facts work best.

The *central route for persuasion* presents information with strong arguments, analyses, facts, and logic.

A political candidate using the central route for persuasion must present clear and detailed information about his or her views and accomplishments and about opponents' records. In addition, the candidate should appear *credible* by demonstrating knowledge and commitment to the issues and be perceived as *honest* (Priester & Petty, 1995).

Politicians should choose the central route when they are trying to persuade voters who have a high need for cognition—that is, a high need to know the facts and issues (Cacioppo & Petty, 1982). The central route of persuasion works with people who think about and analyze the issues.

However, not all voters can be persuaded by the central route. For some, a peripheral route for persuasion proves the better method.

Peripheral Route

If the audience is interested in the candidate's personality or image, a politician should seek votes using the peripheral route.

> I think emotional and personal appeals work best.

The *peripheral route for persuasion* emphasizes emotional appeal, focuses on personal traits, and generates positive feelings.

The peripheral route assumes that not all voters will spend the time and energy to digest or discuss the issues. Instead, some audiences are more interested in the excitement a candidate can generate by an *energetic* and *enthusiastic delivery*. For this audience, politicians should choose the peripheral route for seeking votes (Priester & Petty, 1995). This route includes bands, banners, parties, and personal appearances, which build an inviting and exciting image and create a positive attitude toward the candidate. If audiences like the candidate's image, they will more likely agree with the candidate's views (Carlson, 1990).

The peripheral route is more concerned with style and image, and the central route is more concerned with substance and ideas. Researchers generally find that the central route produces more enduring results, while the peripheral route produces more transient results (Mackie & Skelly, 1994). Whether the central or peripheral route is used, a number of specific elements are important in persuasion.

Elements of Persuasion

Figuring out which elements are important in persuading people was begun in the 1950s by the Yale Communication Program, which is still considered one of the best models. This communication program identified a number of important elements in persuasion, including the source, message, and audience (Mackie & Skelly, 1994; Petty et al., 1997).

Source. One element in persuading someone to adopt your point of view involves the *source of the message:* we are more likely to believe sources who appear honest, trustworthy, have expertise and credibility, are attractive, or appear similar to us (Priester & Petty, 1995). For example, national newscasters, such as ABC's Peter Jennings, receive multi-million-dollar contracts because they appear attractive, honest, and credible. Can you name one national newscaster who is not physically attractive?

> It's important for a newscaster to be honest and trustworthy.

Message. Another element of persuasion involves the *content of the message.* If the persuader is using the *central route,* the messages will contain convincing and understandable facts. If the facts are complicated, a written message is better than a spoken one (Chaiken & Eagly, 1976).

If the persuader is using the *peripheral route,* the messages will be designed to arouse emotion, sentiment, and loyalty. One type of message that uses the peripheral route is the *fear appeal.* Could we, for example, change people's attitudes toward smoking by showing them blackened lungs? Researchers find that fearful messages are more effective if the audience is already fearful and the message is relevant to their lives (Baron et al., 1994).

Some messages are better presented as *one-sided*—that is, you present only the message that you want accepted. Other messages are better presented as *two-sided*—that is, you include both the message and rebuttals against potential disagreements. Thus, a good persuader will pick the best route (central or peripheral) and kind of message (one- or two-sided).

Audience. Other elements of being an effective persuader involves knowing the *characteristics of the audience.* For example, audiences who are interested in facts are best persuaded using the central route, while audiences interested in personal traits are best persuaded using the peripheral route. If the audience is leaning toward the persuader, a one-sided message is best; if an audience is leaning away from the persuader, a two-sided message is best.

Thus persuasion is a complicated process that involves the persuader's traits, a central or peripheral route, and the audience's characteristics (Tykocinski et al., 1994).

Besides being influenced by the source's traits and the message's route, we are also influenced by social forces, which we'll discuss next.

E. Social & Group Influences

At the beginning of this module, we told you about David Koresh. He was a 34-year-old high school dropout, rock musician, polygamist, and preacher, whose teaching attracted more than a hundred people to join him at an armed fortress near Waco, Texas.

Koresh's followers would do anything for him. He taught that all the women in the world belonged to him, and every one of the women followers was only too happy to be his "wife." At one point, Koresh had 18 "wives," some as young as 12 years old.

Koresh (top photo) laid down strict rules for his followers. They were not allowed beer, meat, air conditioning, or MTV; they had to turn over all their money and possessions to him; and they were not allowed to marry. Koresh enforced his rules with beatings and other punishment.

Concerned about Koresh's increasing stash of weapons, agents of the Bureau of Alcohol, Tobacco and Firearms assaulted the Koresh compound but were held off by returning gunfire. However, on April 19, 1993, after 51 days of unsuccessful negotiations,

the Bureau moved up armored vehicles, punched holes in the Waco compound, and fired tear gas. Somehow, a fire started and was fueled by kerosene stores and 30-mile-per-hour winds. Within minutes the compound was a blazing inferno (left photo). Agents sifting through the rubble after the fire was put out found the bodies of Koresh and 85 other adults and children (Gibbs, 1993; Kantrowitz et al., 1993).

What happened to Koresh and his followers is an extreme example of social and group influences. However, some of the reasons these people followed Koresh even to their deaths are similar to the reasons we obey people in authority and conform to group and social pressures. We'll examine why people conform and obey.

Conformity

The followers of David Koresh worked in the commune, recognized his leadership, and followed his teaching, all examples of conformity.

Conformity refers to any behavior you perform because of group pressure, even though that pressure might not involve direct requests.

For example, you may conform by wearing clothes that are in style, using similar slang phrases, and buying the latest and

most popular products. One of the best examples of conformity in the United States occurred in the late 1990s, when a large percentage of students as well as of the general population began carrying small bottles of drinking water wherever they went. One reason many conformed was because of social pressures—seeing others carrying bottles of water. We'll begin our discussion of conformity with a classic study in social psychology.

ASCH'S EXPERIMENT

Remember that a classic experiment is one that changes the way we think about something—in this case, how social pressures influence conformity. We describe the classic experiment of Solomon Asch (1958), who studied how group pressures influenced conformity. Imagine that you are a subject in Asch's study and guess how you might behave.

Procedure

You are seated at a round table with five others and have been told that you are taking part in a visual perception experiment. Your group is shown a straight line and then is instructed to look at three more lines of different lengths and pick out the line equal in length to the original one. The three choices are different enough that it is not hard to pick out the correct one. Each person at the round table identifies his or her choice out loud, with you answering next to last. When you are ready to answer, you will have heard four others state their opinions. What you do not know is that these four other people are the experimenter's accomplices. On certain trials, they will answer correctly, making you feel your choice is right. On other trials, they will deliberately answer incorrectly, much to your surprise. In these cases you will have heard four identical incorrect answers before it is your turn to answer. You will almost certainly feel some group pressure to conform to the others' opinion. Will you give in?

Is this line similar in length to lines 1, 2, or 3?

1 2 3

These are the kinds of lines used in Asch's study on conformity.

Results

Out of 50 subjects in Asch's experiment, 75% conformed on some of the trials, but no one conformed on all the trials; 25% never conformed. These data indicate that the desire to have your attitudes and behaviors match those of others in a group can be a powerful force. Although Asch's original results are rather dramatic, they have not always been replicated. Researchers have concluded that group conformity is unpredictable and dependent upon the personality and culture of the group (Mackie & Skelly, 1994). Asch's study is considered a classic because it showed how group pressures can influence conformity. Salespeople use a kind of conformity called compliance.

Compliance

Were the subjects just pretending?

One interpretation of Asch's data is that subjects were not really changing their beliefs but rather just pretending to go along with the group. For example, when subjects in Asch's experiment privately recorded their answers, conforming drastically declined. This decline indicated that subjects were conforming but not really changing their beliefs, which is one kind of compliance.

Compliance is a kind of conformity in which we give in to social pressure in our public responses but do not change our private beliefs.

For example, you may conform to your instructor's suggestions on rewriting a paper although you do not agree with the suggestions. In this case, you would be complying with someone in authority.

One particular technique of compliance is used by many salespeople. Those in sales soon learn that if they can get the customer to comply with a small request (get a foot in the door), the customer is more likely to comply with a later request to buy the product.

The *foot-in-the-door technique* relies on the increased probability of compliance to a second request if a person complies with a small, first request.

The request may be sales-related, as we've said, or may be in social contact, as in asking a friend for a favor. A review of 15 years of research on the foot-in-the-door technique indicates that it is a small but repeatable finding (Beaman et al., 1983).

Next we'll examine the kind of compliance that we call obedience.

Obedience

Do you run red lights?

When it comes to signs, laws, rules, and regulations, such as speed limits, traffic lights, smoking restrictions, parental requests, instructors' assignments, and doctors' orders, people differ in what they choose to obey.

Obedience refers to behavior performed in response to an order given by someone in a position of power or authority.

For example, a big traffic problem in California is drivers who run red lights and thus cause accidents. To increase obedience, police are installing cameras that automatically take photos of drivers who run red lights. These drivers receive tickets in the mail. Here's a case of increasing obedience through punishment. Sometimes it's for the general good to obey orders, rules and regulations. But what if the orders or rules are cruel or immoral?

MILGRAM'S EXPERIMENT

Stanley Milgram's (1963) experiment on obedience is a classic experiment in social psychology because it was the first to study whether people would obey commands that were clearly inhumane and immoral. As we describe this famous experiment, imagine being the "teacher" and consider whether you would have obeyed the experimenter's commands.

Procedure

Imagine that you have volunteered for a study on the effects of punishment on learning. After arriving in the laboratory at Yale University, you are selected to be the "teacher" and another volunteer is to be the "learner." What you don't know is that the learner is actually an accomplice of the experimenter. You watch as the learner is strapped into a chair and has electrodes placed on his wrists. The electrodes are attached to a shock generator in the next room. You and the researcher then leave the learner's room and go into an adjoining room.

The researcher gives you a list of questions to ask the learner over an intercom, and the learner is to signal his answer on a panel of lights in front of you. For each wrong answer, you are to shock the learner, and you are to increase the intensity of the shock by 15 volts for each succeeding wrong answer. In front of you is the shock machine, with 30 separate switches that indicate increasing intensities. The first switch is marked "15 volts. Slight shock," and the last switch is marked "XXX 450 volts. Danger: Severe shock." You begin to ask the learner questions, and as he misses them, you administer stronger and stronger shocks.

> Whenever you make a mistake, you'll receive an electric shock.

Shock Controller

Slight shock — MAXIMUM XXX 450 volts

Results

After receiving shocks of increasing intensity, the learner pounds on the wall when given 300 volts. After 315 volts, the learner pounds on the wall again and then stops answering your questions. Since you don't know that this is all an act and that the learner is not actually being shocked, you plead with the researcher to stop the experiment.

But the researcher tells you to continue asking questions and says that, if the learner fails to respond, you should treat it as a wrong answer and deliver the next level of shock. Would you continue to follow the researcher's orders? How much higher would you increase the shock intensity? Even though the learner has stopped answering, would you continue until delivering the **XXX 450 volts**?

What the subjects (teachers) did in this experiment was quite unexpected.

Milgram's Results

How many obeyed? When Stanley Milgram conducted these studies on obedience in the early 1960s, they demonstrated that people will obey inhumane orders simply because they are told to do so. This kind of unthinking obedience to immoral commands was something that neither psychiatrists nor members of the general population had predicted.

0.1% When psychiatrists were asked to predict how many people would deliver the full range of shocks, including the last 450 volts, they estimated that only 0.1% of the population would do so, while 65% actually did.

2% When members of the general public were asked the same question, they predicted that only 2% would deliver the 450 volts.

65% To the surprise and dismay of many, including Milgram, 65% of the subjects delivered the full range of shocks, including the final **XXX 450 volts**. Milgram (1974) repeated variations of this experiment many times and obtained similar results. Additionally, Milgram's experiment was repeated in various parts of the world with similar results (Meeus & Raaijmakers, 1989).

The results of these experiments helped answer a question people had asked since World War II: Why had Germans obeyed Hitler's commands? And why did the followers of Koresh obey his rigid rules and even commit mass suicide by being burnt alive? According to Milgram's experiments, social situations that involve power and authority greatly increase obedience to the point that a large percentage of people will obey orders, even if they are clearly unreasonable and inhumane.

Percentage of Subjects Who Obeyed Experimenter's Commands

0 20 40 60 80 100

Slight
Moderate
Strong
Very strong
Intense — Learner pounded on the wall at this point.
Extreme intensity — Learner pounded on the wall again at this point; after this, he gave no further answers.
Danger: severe shock
XXX 450 volts — 65% of the subjects in Milgram's study obeyed the experimenter's command to deliver the maximum 450-volt shock to the learner.
Labels on the shock controller

Why Do People Obey?

Psychologists have suggested several reasons why about 65% of the subjects in Milgram's experiment agreed to deliver the maximum shock to learners. Perhaps the major reason is that people have learned to follow the orders of *authority figures*, whether they are religious leaders, army commanders, doctors, scientists, or parents. However, people are more likely to obey authority figures when they are present. In one of his followup studies, Milgram (1974) found that when subjects received their instructions over the telephone, they were more likely to defy authority than when they received their instructions in person. This also explains why patients don't follow doctors' orders once they leave their offices.

People also obey because they have *learned to follow orders* in their daily lives, whether in traffic, on the job, or in personal interactions. However, people are more likely to obey if an authority figure is present (police officer, boss, or parent). What Milgram's study showed was that blind obedience to unreasonable authority or inhumane orders is more likely than we think.

Were Milgram's Experiments Ethical?

Although the Milgram experiments provided important information about obedience, it is unlikely that, for a number of reasons, they could be conducted today. As we discussed in Module 2, all experiments today, especially those with the potential for causing psychological or physical harm, are carefully screened by research committees, a practice that did not exist at the time of Milgram's research. Currently, committees must determine whether proposed experiments on animals or humans have the potential for psychological or physical harm and whether these potentially damaging effects can be eliminated or counteracted. When there is a possibility of an experiment causing *psychological harm*, the researchers must propose ways to eliminate or counteract the potential harmful effects. This is usually done by thoroughly debriefing the subjects.

Debriefing occurs after an experimental procedure and involves explaining the purpose and method of the experiment, asking the subjects about their feelings of being in the experiment, and helping the subjects deal with possible doubts or guilt arising from their behaviors in the experiment.

After the Milgram experiments, the subjects were debriefed. For example, subjects were told that, contrary to what they believed, no shock was actually delivered to the learner. The subjects were also given the opportunity to discuss their feelings about the experiment and their own actions during it. In addition, some of the subjects were sent questionnaires or were interviewed a year later by a psychiatrist to determine whether there were any long-lasting harmful effects of having been a teacher. Although Milgram's subjects were debriefed, critics doubted that the question of whether enormous psychological harm had been done to the subjects was successfully resolved. Because the potential for psychological harm to the subjects was so great in Milgram's studies, researchers seriously doubt if such studies could be approved under current ethical standards for conducting safe research.

Next, we turn to another interesting question: Why do people help?

Helping: Prosocial Behavior

Would you help an accident victim?

About 60 people had gathered around a serious car crash in a downtown area. They were talking about the accident and pointing at the victims, but no one was helping. One of the victims was a woman, obviously pregnant and unconscious. One person in the crowd, Ken Von, came forward and tried to save the woman with cardiopulmonary and mouth-to-mouth resuscitation that he had learned by watching television. He kept her alive until paramedics arrived (*San Diego Tribune,* September 9, 1983).

Ken's quick action is an example of helping, or prosocial behavior.

Prosocial behavior, which is also called helping, is any behavior that benefits others or has positive social consequences.

In our society, professionals, such as paramedics, are trained and paid to provide help. However, in Ken's case, he was the only one of

I donated most of my life savings for student scholarships.

60 onlookers who came forward to help the unconscious traffic victim. Ken's helping may be described as altruistic, since he expected no external reward.

Altruism is one form of helping or doing something, often at a cost or risk, for reasons other than the expectation of a material or social reward.

Altruistic people often do things that touch our hearts. Consider 87-year-old Osceola McCarty, who handwashed clothes most of her life for grateful clients. When she finally retired at age 86, she donated most of her life savings, an amazing $150,000, to the University of Southern Mississippi to finance scholarships for the area's African American students. "I want them to have an education," said McCarty, who never married and has no children of her own. "I had to work hard all my life. They can have the chance that I didn't have" (Plummer & Ridenhur, 1995, p. 40). As these examples show, some people help in emergencies, and others help by donating time or money.

Why People Help

Would you help?

Why did Osceola McCarty, who spent her life washing clothes, donate most of her hard-earned life savings to finance scholarships instead of using her savings to make her retirement more comfortable? Researchers suggest at least three different motivations—empathy, personal distress, and norms and values—to explain why people, like McCarty, are altruistic and help others without thought of rewards (Batson, 1998; Schroeder et al., 1995):

■ We may help because we feel *empathy*—that is, we identify with what the victim must be going through. Osceola McCarty may have donated her life savings for scholarships because she felt empathy for other African American students.

■ We may help because we feel *personal distress*—that is, we have feelings of fear, alarm, or disgust from seeing a victim in need. Osceola said that she didn't want other African American young people to have to go through the hard times that she had faced.

■ We may help because of our *norms* and *values*—that is, we may feel morally bound or socially responsible to help those in need.

Researchers have combined these three motivations along with several other ideas to construct two different theories of why people come out of a crowd and help perfect strangers. We can use these two theories to explain why Ken Von was the only person in a crowd of 60 spectators to help a pregnant woman who was seriously injured in a car accident.

DECISION-STAGE MODEL

Ken may have decided to help after going through five stages, which involved making five different decisions.

The *decision-stage model of helping* says that you go through five stages in deciding to help: (1) you notice the situation; (2) you interpret it as one in which help is needed; (3) you assume personal responsibility; (4) you choose a form of assistance; and (5) you carry out that assistance.

According to the decision-stage model, Ken helped because he went through all five stages. Most onlookers stopped at stage 3 and decided it was not their responsibility; so they did not help. This model explains that people may recognize a situation as an emergency (stages 1 and 2) yet fail to help because they do not take personal responsibility for the situation (Latané & Darley, 1970).

AROUSAL-COST-REWARD MODEL

Ken also may have helped the pregnant woman because he thought about the costs and rewards.

The *arousal-cost-reward model of helping* says that we make decisions to help by calculating the costs and rewards of helping.

For example, seeing an accident may cause you to be unpleasantly and emotionally *aroused,* which you wish to reduce. In deciding how to reduce these unpleasant feelings, you calculate the *costs* and *rewards* of helping. For example, those who decided not to help may have felt that the costs of helping, such as getting involved in a potentially dangerous situation, outweighed the rewards (Piliavin et al., 1982).

According to these two models, Ken experienced five stages (five decisions) and then decided to help, or Ken possibly considered the costs and rewards of reducing his unpleasant emotional feelings and then decided to help. Although the arousal-cost-reward model and the decision-stage model focus on different factors, they are not mutually exclusive.

Next, we'll explain how social forces influence people in groups.

E. Social & Group Influences

Group Dynamics

What happens in groups?

When you're with family, friends, or coworkers, you may or may not be aware of the numerous group influences that can greatly change how you think, feel, and behave.

Groups are collections of two or more people who interact, share some common idea, goal, or purpose, and influence how their members think and behave.

To illustrate the powerful influences of groups, we'll describe the case of Dennis Jay, who almost died in a drunken coma and later heard that his fraternity brothers had lied about the initiation that had almost killed him.

Group Cohesion and Norms

As a pledge at a fraternity initiation party, Dennis Jay and 19 others were forced to drink from a "beer bong," a funnel into which beer was poured; the beer ran down a plastic hose placed in the mouth (photo below). The rule was that once you threw up you could stop drinking from the beer bong. Because he did not throw up, Jay was given straight shots of whiskey until he fell on his face. By the time his frat brothers got Jay to the hospital 30 minutes later, he was in a coma and barely breathing. His blood alcohol content was 0.48, and a level of 0.50 is usually fatal (legally drunk in many states is 0.08).

> My fraternity brothers lied about why I was in a coma.

At first, Jay refused to describe what happened because he wanted to be loyal to his fraternity. Then he heard that the fraternity brothers had lied about Jay and said that he had stumbled drunk into their frat house and that they had brought him to the emergency ward just to help out. The fraternity brothers' lies made Jay angry, and he finally told the truth about the incident (Grogan et al., 1993).

Why would a group of fraternity members make up a story about what happened to Jay, who was one of their pledges? Rather than answering this question by saying the members lacked consciences, social psychologists would point to the powerful influence of group membership and of two group forces: group cohesion and group norms.

Group cohesion is group togetherness, which is determined by how much group members perceive that they share common attributes.

One reason many groups have some form of initiation rites and rituals is to have all members share a common experience and thus increase group cohesion.

Group norms are the formal or informal rules about how group members should behave.

Apparently, the fraternity members made up a story about what happened to Jay in order to protect their group. For his part, Jay initially did not describe what had happened, also apparently to protect a group that he wanted to join. Thus, group norms, written or unwritten, can exert powerful influences, both good and bad, on group members' behaviors.

Does the fact that Jay was willing to endure the drinking initiation mean that we have a need to join groups?

Why Do We Form Groups?

In his hierarchy of human motivation, humanistic psychologist Abraham Maslow identified *the need for love and belonging* as fundamental to human happiness (Maslow, 1954). One way to satisfy this need is through membership in a group that helps people develop a sense of identity. For instance, in high school and college, students join various groups to meet others of similar interests, form friendships, and get social support. Our need for belonging carries into adulthood as we join community and business organizations. Maslow's theory provides *motivational reasons* for forming groups: they satisfy our need to belong.

At about the same time that Maslow published his work on the hierarchy of motivation, Leon Festinger's (1954) social comparison theory offered another reason for joining groups.

Social comparison theory says that we are driven to compare ourselves to others who are similar to us, so that we can measure the correctness of our attitudes and beliefs. According to Festinger, this drive motivates us to join groups.

Festinger's theory provides *cognitive reasons* for forming groups: they help us create our social reality by allowing us to compare our social selves with others like us.

An additional reason for forming groups is that we can accomplish things in groups that we simply cannot do alone. In fact, groups can be so important that members are willing to make considerable sacrifices for the group in terms of time, effort, and money, as occurs in volunteer groups.

Many students form study groups because they want academic help, social support, and motivation. However, there are two kinds of study groups, each with different goals: task-oriented and socially oriented groups.

In a *task-oriented group*, members have specific duties to complete.

In task-oriented groups, especially if there is high cohesiveness (togetherness), students will perform much better than those in groups that have less cohesiveness or are more socially oriented (Mullen & Cooper, 1994).

In a *socially oriented group*, the members are primarily concerned about fostering and maintaining social relationships among the members of the group.

A socially oriented study group may be fun but provides little academic support.

A group can strongly influence its members' behavior. As we see next, even the presence of strangers can influence our behaviors.

How do you behave in a crowd?

The presence of strangers, such as a crowd, may cause you to behave very differently than if you were alone.

A *crowd* is a large group of persons, most of whom are unacquainted.

Being in a crowd can increase or decrease certain behaviors, can lead to antisocial behaviors, such as riots, or may result in your refusing to help someone in need. We'll examine how crowds influence our behaviors.

Facilitation and Inhibition

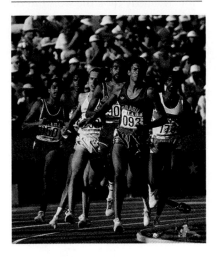

If a runner has a history of successful competition, he may turn in a better performance in front of a large crowd as a result of social facilitation.

Social facilitation is an increase in performance in the presence of a crowd.

In contrast, if a runner has a spotty history in competition, he may turn in a worse performance in front of a large crowd because of social inhibition.

Social inhibition is a decrease in performance in the presence of a crowd.

Whether we show facilitation or inhibition depends partly on our previous experience. Generally, the presence of others will facilitate well-learned, simple, or reflexive responses but will inhibit new, unusual, or complex responses. Researchers also report that, during championship games, supporters of a home team develop enormous expectations about their team's winning. Because of these expectations, the home team feels great pressure not to let their fans down and thus may play more poorly than they ordinarily would (Baumeister, 1995; Schlenker et al., 1995a). This is an interesting case of social inhibition, sometimes called choking, in front of the home crowd.

Deindividuation in Crowds

During the Los Angeles riots of 1992, people were arrested for looting, setting fires, and beating others. Such behaviors may not have occurred if these people had not been in a crowd. Individuals in a crowd are more likely to commit antisocial acts because they cannot easily be identified; this tendency is called deindividuation.

Deindividuation refers to the increased tendency for subjects to behave irrationally or perform antisocial behaviors when there is less chance of being personally identified.

For example, researchers found that drivers are more likely to honk their horns long and hard if they have little chance of being identified (Ellison et al., 1995).

One researcher thinks that deindividuation occurs because being in a crowd reduces guilt and self-awareness so that people are less controlled by internal standards and more willing to engage in deviant or antisocial roles (Zimbardo, 1970). Researchers report some support for deindividuation but emphasize that just being in a rowdy situation can turn people into potential mobsters (Postmes & Spears, 1998).

The Bystander Effect

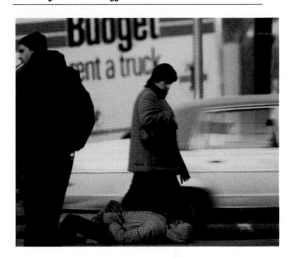

As a person lies unconscious on a city sidewalk, dozens or hundreds of people may walk by without helping. There are several reasons no one stops to help, including fear of the person's reactions, inexperience with providing help, and the bystander effect.

The *bystander effect* says that an individual may feel inhibited from taking some action because of the presence of others.

Data from over 50 studies indicate that 75% of people offer assistance when alone, but fewer than 53% do so when in a group (Latané & Nida, 1981). There are two explanations for the bystander effect.

The *informational influence theory* says that we use the reactions of others to judge the seriousness of the situation.

If other bystanders are taking no action, we conclude that no emergency exists and do nothing to offer help or aid.

The *diffusion of responsibility theory* says that, in the presence of others, individuals feel less personal responsibility and are less likely to take action in a situation where help is required (Latané, 1981).

Researchers report a significant negative correlation between helping and increased population density in small, medium, and large cities in the United States (Levine et al., 1994). Thus, an individual may feel less responsibility to offer help or aid the more crowded a city becomes.

The presence of others also influences how we make decisions, which we'll examine next.

E. Social & Group Influences

Group Decisions

All of us have been in groups—families, fraternities, sororities, and various social or business clubs. What you may not realize is that being in a group creates social pressures that influence how how you think and make decisions. We'll discuss two interesting factors in making decisions: group polarization and groupthink.

Group Polarization

Imagine that a young lawyer is trying to decide between two job offers. The first offer is from a large, well-established firm that promises more security, financial opportunities, and prestige. However, it has a poor record as an equal employer of women and currently has no women partners. The second offer is from a small, recently established firm that can promise little security or prestige. However, this firm is doing well and has an excellent record in promoting women as partners. Which offer should she accept? Using dilemmas such as this, a researcher compared the recommendations from individuals in a group with those made by the group after it had engaged in discussion (Gigone & Hastie, 1997; Pruitt, 1971). Group discussions change individuals' judgements, such as when a group urges a more risky recommendation than do individuals. This phenomenon became known as the *risky shift.*

Researchers later discovered that the direction of a group's risky shift depends on how conservative or liberal the group was to begin with. If a group's members are initially more conservative, group discussion will shift its recommendation to an even more conservative one. If a group's members are initially more liberal, group discussion will shift its recommendation to an even more liberal one.

The group's shift to a more extreme position is called *polarization.*

Group Polarization

Before group discussion, individual views are generally positive.

After group discussion, individual views shift to more positive views.

Group polarization is a phenomenon in which group discussion reinforces the majority's point of view and shifts that view to a more extreme position.

Whether this polarization is in a liberal or conservative direction depends on the initial leanings of the group's members. Researchers also found that the more the group repeated each others' arguments, the more polarized the group became (Brauer et al., 1995). Thus, repetition of the same arguments resulted in stronger formation of attitudes and more group polarization.

Groupthink

In the early 1960s, President John F. Kennedy took the world to the brink of nuclear war when he ordered the invasion of Cuba. This invasion, which occurred at the Bay of Pigs, was a terrible decision and a well-remembered failure. Researchers have analyzed group decision-making processes involved in bad decisions, such as the Bay of Pigs, escalation of war in Vietnam, the Watergate cover-up, and the more recent Challenger disaster, as well as flawed group decisions in business and other organizations. One reason that groups made bad decisions in the above examples was due to something called groupthink (Granstrom & Stiwne, 1998; Janis, 1982, 1989).

Groupthink

What's most important is that we stick together.

Groupthink occurs when group discussions emphasize sticking together and agreement over the use of critical thinking to make the best decisions.

According to psychologist Irving Janis (1982, 1989), groupthink has a number of clearly defined characteristics: discussions are limited, few alternatives are presented, and there is increased pressure to conform. For example, the group usually has a member that Janis calls a *mindguard,* whose job is to discourage ideas that might be a threat to the group's unity. In addition, groupthink results in viewing the world in very simple terms: there is the *ingroup,* which includes only the immediate members of the group, versus the *outgroup,* which includes everyone who is not a part of the group. When a group adopts the ingroup-outgroup attitude and mentality, the result is that it strengthens groupthink by emphasizing the protection of the group's members over making the best decisions.

Psychologists suggest several ways to avoid groupthink. The first is to allow the group's members the freedom to express differing opinions without being criticized or being considered a threat to the group. A second is to make sure that communication and gathering of information are kept open and unbiased within the group.

When studying group decisions, researchers also found that the more socially focused a group becomes, the poorer the decisions it makes; the more task oriented a group becomes, the better its decisions (Mullen et al., 1994). Additionally, if being in a group makes its members anxious, their performance and decisions will worsen (Camacho & Paulus, 1995). Thus, the best decisions would come from groups whose members feel free to express opinions, value gathering information, are task oriented, and are not made anxious by being in groups (Kramer et al., 1997; Rowatt et al., 1997).

After the Concept Review, we'll discuss a potentially very disruptive social behavior—aggression.

CONCEPT REVIEW

1. A broad field that studies how our thoughts, feelings, perceptions, and behaviors are influenced by interactions with others is called (a)_____. A major branch of this field that studies how people perceive, store, and retrieve information about social interactions is called (b)_____.

2. Making judgments about the traits of others through social interactions and gaining knowledge from our social perceptions is called _____.

3. Widely held beliefs that people have certain traits because they belong to a particular group are known as (a)_____. An unfair, biased, or intolerant attitude toward another group of people is called (b)_____. Specific unfair behaviors exhibited toward members of a group are known as (c)_____.

4. Cognitive structures that represent an organized collection of knowledge about people, events, and concepts are called _____. They influence what we perceive and remember and how we behave.

5. The process by which we look for causes to explain a person's behavior is known as (a)_____. If we attribute behavior to the internal characteristics of a person, we are attributing the behavior to the person's (b)_____. If we attribute behavior to the external circumstances or context of that behavior, we are attributing the behavior to the (c)_____.

6. If we attribute the cause of a behavior to a person's disposition and overlook the demands of the environment or situation, we are committing the (a)_____ error. If we attribute our own behavior to situational factors but the behaviors of others to their disposition, we are committing the (b)_____ error. If we attribute success to our disposition and failure to the situation, we are using the (c)_____ bias.

7. Beliefs or opinions that include a positive or negative evaluation of some target (object, person, or event) and that predispose us to act in a certain way toward the target are called _____.

8. There are two different theories about why we change our attitudes. One theory says that experiencing cognitive inconsistencies produces psychological tension that we try to reduce by making our beliefs more consistent. This is called (a)_____ theory. If we take a public position that is counter to our private attitude, we are engaging in (b)_____ behavior.

9. Another theory of attitude change says that we first observe our own behaviors, which in turn causes us to change our attitudes. This is called _____ theory.

10. If a politician tries to get votes by presenting information with strong arguments, analyses, facts, and logic, he or she is using the (a)_____ route of persuasion. If a politician seeks votes by emphasizing emotional appeals, focusing on personal accomplishments, and generating positive feelings, he or she is using the (b)_____ route of persuasion.

11. Persuasion involves at least three elements: we are likely to believe a (a)_____ who appears honest and trustworthy; if we disagree with the message, it is better if the persuader presents a (b)_____ message; if the (c)_____ is less interested in issues, the peripheral route is more effective.

12. Any behavior we perform because of social influences or group pressure, even if that pressure involves no direct requests, is called (a)_____. A kind of conformity in which we give in to social pressure in our public responses but do not change our private beliefs is called (b)_____. Any behavior performed in response to an order given by someone in a position of authority is called (c)_____.

13. An increase in performance in the presence of a crowd is called social (a)_____; a decrease in performance in the presence of a crowd is called social (b)_____. An increased tendency for individuals to behave irrationally or perform antisocial behaviors if there is less chance of being personally identified is called (c)_____. Being socially inhibited to take some action, such as helping, because of the presence of others is called the (d)_____ effect.

14. A collection of two or more people who interact and share some common attribute or attributes is called a (a)_____. Togetherness, which is determined by how much group members perceive that they share common attributes, is called group (b)_____.

15. The phenomenon by which group discussion reinforces the majority's point of view and shifts that view to a more extreme position is called group (a)_____. Emphasizing group cohesion and agreement over critical thinking and making the best decisions is called (b)_____.

Answers: *1. (a) social psychology, (b) social cognition; 2. person perception; 3. (a) stereotypes, (b) prejudice, (c) discrimination; 4. schemas; 5. (a) attribution, (b) disposition, (c) situation; 6. (a) fundamental attribution, (b) actor-observer, (c) self-serving; 7. attitudes; 8. (a) cognitive dissonance, (b) counter-attitudinal; 9. self-perception; 10. (a) central, (b) peripheral; 11. (a) source, (b) two-sided, (c) audience; 12. (a) conformity, (b) compliance, (c) obedience; 13. (a) facilitation, (b) inhibition, (c) deindividuation, (d) bystander; 14. (a) group, (b) cohesion; 15. (a) polarization, (b) groupthink.*

F. Aggression

Definition

How much violence?

With frightening regularity, the media reports drive-by shootings, spouse and child abuse, violence and shootings in schools, revenge-shooting by angry workers, and other forms of violence and aggression (Stanton et al., 1997).

Aggressive behavior is any act that is intended to do physical or psychological harm.

As the right graph shows, about 48% of homes in the United States have guns compared to about 1% of the homes in Japan. In 1994, there were 32 gun murders in Japan compared to 15,456 in the United States (Kristof, 1996). Experts predict that by the year 2003, and possibly sooner, guns will surpass traffic accidents as the leading cause of injuries and death in the United States (Squitieri, 1994). Although gun restrictions do not keep guns out of the hands of criminals, gun control does cut

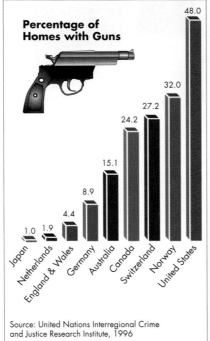

Percentage of Homes with Guns

Japan	1.0
Netherlands	1.9
England & Wales	4.4
Germany	8.9
Australia	15.1
Canada	24.2
Switzerland	27.2
Norway	32.0
United States	48.0

Source: United Nations Interregional Crime and Justice Research Institute, 1996

down on murders within families and gun crimes by teenagers, which account for a high percentage of violent deaths (Kristof, 1996).

At a recent annual convention, the American Psychological Association brought together a group of researchers to discuss the causes of aggression. These expert psychologists discussed a number of factors that contribute to aggression, including genes, neurotransmitters in the brain, personality characteristics, social feedback, exposure to violence in neighborhoods and in the media, and family environment (Azar, 1994c). Based on their findings, psychologists have developed the following model of aggression that involves the interaction of a number of factors.

Model of aggressive behavior. One model of why we act aggressively assumes that we go through the following series of steps: (1) A person encounters a provoking or dangerous situation. (2) The person's initial emotional response is to feel threatened or bad. (3) The person's initial behavioral response is either to fight or to flee. (4) The person chooses between fighting or fleeing on the basis of the interaction between three major factors that differ for each person: predisposing biological factors (genetic predispositions or brain neurotransmitters), social learning factors, and environmental or situational factors (Berkowitz, 1994).

According to this model, one person may flee the provoking situation while another may stay and fight, depending on the interaction of biological, social, and situational factors. To help you understand these factors, we'll discuss each one in more detail.

Biological Factors

What regulates aggression in animals?

You can clearly see how biological factors regulate aggression when you watch the behavior of animals. Ethologists, who study animal behavior in natural settings, report numerous examples of social signals that animals have evolved to stop fights and avoid injury. For example, the photo below shows an interaction between two wolves: one wolf makes a submissive gesture, rolling on its back, which stops the dominant wolf from attacking. Many dominant and submissive gestures observed in animals are programmed innate biological responses that regulate and control aggression.

Violent humans. There is growing evidence that biological factors also influence aggression in humans. For example, from twin and adoption studies, researchers estimate that up to 50% of human aggression is regulated by genetic factors (Miles & Carey, 1997). One way that genetic factors can influence aggression is through the regulation of neurotransmitters, especially serotonin, in the brain.

More than 30 years ago, a Dutch schoolteacher noted that there was a pattern of violence among his male relatives, and he concluded that they must be suffering from an inherited mental disability. Current researchers studied the relatives of this particular family and identified five males who shared a number of symptoms, including mild mental retardation and outbursts of violent behavior (impulsive aggression, arson, and attempted rape). All five males shared a defective gene that caused an overproduction of neurotransmitters, including serotonin (Brunner et al., 1993). Researchers suggested that this genetic defect, which causes too much serotonin, may have been the basis for the violent outbursts displayed by certain members of this family.

Mutant mice. Evidence supporting the involvement of serotonin in aggression comes from studies on mice whose genes have been altered so that they lack serotonin receptors in their brains.

Piece of Genetic Code

These mutant mice attack intruder mice faster and with more intensity, indicating that serotonin is involved in aggression (Shih, 1996). Thus, both human and mice studies suggest that biological factors, such as genetic influences on levels of serotonin as well as other neurotransmitters (nitric oxide), are involved in aggressive behavior (Cadoret et al., 1997). However, at this point, researchers caution against using biological factors alone to label, prosecute, or imprison individuals for aggressive acts, since the influence of environmental factors on aggression account for at least 50% (Berman et al., 1997).

Compared with animals, whose aggressive behaviors are largely controlled by biological factors, human aggression results from an interaction between three factors—biological, social, and environmental.

Social Cognitive and Personality Factors

How does a child learn to be a bully?

Although biological factors may predispose a person to be aggressive, whether or not the person actually engages in aggressive behaviors also depends on his or her learning experiences and personality traits. One theory that explains how people learn to perform aggressive behaviors is Bandura's (1989a) social cognitive theory.

I like to bully kids and make them do things.

Social cognitive theory says that much of human behavior, including aggressive behavior, may be learned and maintained through observation, imitation, and self-reinforcement.

Support for social cognitive theory comes from both laboratory and naturalistic studies. A classic laboratory study by Bandura (1965) found that children who observed a model's aggressive behaviors later performed similar aggressive behaviors (Module 10). In a more naturalistic study, researchers reported that children who were exposed to aggressive models of parents, such as parents' using physical punishment, showed increased aggression with their peers (Eron et al., 1987). These studies indicate that the individuals most likely to behave aggressively and violently are ones who have learned through observing and imitating adult role models (Eron, 1990).

Personality traits. Besides imitating aggressive adults, individuals who develop into bullies are usually physically strong males with the following personality traits: they are impulsive, have little empathy, and like to dominate (Olweus, 1995).

Because aggressive adults were usually aggressive children, researchers suggest that bullies result from an interaction among three factors: genetic factors that predispose individuals to become bullies, social cognitive factors that involve imitation and modeling of aggressive adults, and the personality factors stated above. Together, these three factors increase the chances that a child bully will turn into an adult bully (Elkins et al., 1997).

Sources of aggressive role models for children to observe and imitate come from television and hundreds of video games.

Television. After watching about 2,500 hours of television (no sports or newscasts), researchers concluded that the majority of programs on cable and network television contain violence, that 73% of aggressive actions go unpunished, and that 53% of all violent portrayals show no painful or negative consequences. Researchers concluded that

televised violence poses substantial risks to an audience of children and adults by showing role models whose aggressive actions go unpunished and by not showing the negative consequences of aggressive actions (Wilson, 1996).

Besides biological and social cognitive factors, there are also environmental factors in aggression, many of which cause frustration.

Environmental Factors

How do you deal with frustration?

In 1998, a new term of violence was identified: road rage. This is the angry response of a driver frustrated by another's annoying driving habits to the point of aggressively pursuing, ramming, fighting, and even shooting the other driver. Road rage is an extreme example of a common environmental situation in which our goals are blocked and we feel frustrated. Another cause of frustration is hot weather (above 90° F), when incidences of violence significantly increase (Anderson et al., 1997). The idea that frustration plays a major role in aggression was proposed more than 60 years ago by a group of researchers at Yale University (Dollard et al., 1939).

The *frustration-aggression hypothesis* says that when our goals are blocked, we become frustrated and respond with anger and aggression.

However, researchers soon discovered that although frustration may lead to aggression, the link between the two is not absolute. Leonard Berkowitz (1989) reviewed the research on the frustration-aggression hypothesis and concluded the following.

■ Frustration doesn't always lead to aggression.

■ Social rules may inhibit aggression.

■ Frustration may result in behaviors other than aggression.

■ Cognitive factors can override aggression.

Thus, Berkowitz (1993) modified the original hypothesis.

I'll get you for cutting me off you dumb . . . !

The *modified frustration-aggression hypothesis* says that although frustration may lead to aggression, a number of situational and cognitive factors may override the aggressive response.

Although our daily lives are often filled with frustrations, we usually find ways to control our frustrations and don't express them in anger, violence, or road rage. However, a child may be more likely to react to frustration with violence if he or she has observed and imitated the aggressive behaviors of adults, whether it be real, on television, or in video games. For these children, frustration may trigger violent behavior that they have already observed, modeled, and practiced (Osofsky, 1995).

Three factors. We have discussed three factors—biological, social cognitive, and environmental—that combine and interact to result in aggressive behavior. Formerly, psychologists focused on social cognitive and environmental factors in aggression. However, recent studies indicate that biological factors, which may account for as much as 50% of aggressive behavior, need to be given equal consideration (Miles & Carey, 1997).

One terrifying and degrading form of aggression is sexual aggression, which we'll examine next.

F. Aggression

Sexual Harassment and Aggression

Why do men rape?

According to a very reliable 1995 National Crime Victimization Survey, which pooled 100,000 U.S. citizens aged 12 or older, the annual number of rapes and sexual assaults was 354,670. About 51% of rape victims were under 18 years old, and of those, 85% were raped by either a relative or an acquaintance. However, only about a third of rape victims report their attacks to the police.

In the United States, a woman is raped about every 3 minutes.

National surveys of 3,000 male and 3,000 female college students report that date rape is also relatively common. About 27% of the college females had experienced either rape or attempted rape, and about 8% of the college males reported committing or attempting rape (Kalof, 1993; Koss et al., 1987).

Most researchers agree that the primary motivation for rape is not sexual but rather a combination of aggression, power, and control (Polaschek et al., 1997). For example, in interviews with ten convicted rapists, nine stated that sex was of secondary importance in motivating their assaults. Rather, these rapists stressed that either anger or the need to dominate was the most important factor to them (Levine & Koenig, 1980).

Another form of aggression occurs during sexual harassment. Researchers found that sexual harassment is widespread and was reported by 42% of women and 15% of men in occupational settings and by 73% of women and 22% of men during medical training. Although sexual harassment produces psychological and physical effects in 90% of the victims, only about 1 to 7% of victims file formal complaints (Charney & Russell, 1994).

Here, we'll focus on rape and sexual assault and begin by describing the more common types of rapists, their behavioral patterns, and their motivations.

Characteristics and Kinds of Rapists

Psychologists have identified several developmental factors that are associated with men who rape: they often come from broken homes, did not have a loving caregiver, were sexually or physically abused, were neglected, and spent time in penal institutions (Polaschek et al., 1997). However, these factors alone do not produce rapists; other men who have suffered similar development problems do not become rapists. At present, there is no generally accepted theory of what turns men into rapists.

The most common rapist is a man who wants to possess his victim.

Researchers have interviewed rapists to understand the motivation behind their sexual aggression. Rapists reported different degrees and combinations of anger, sexual violence, power, and control. Here are descriptions of four types of rapists (Knight, 1992).

■ The *power rapist,* who commits 70% of all rapes, is not out to hurt physically but to possess. His acts are premeditated and are often preceded by rape fantasies. He may carry a weapon, not to hurt but to intimidate the victim.

■ The *sadistic rapist* accounts for fewer than 5% of rapes, but he is the most dangerous because for him sexuality and aggression have become fused, and using physical force is arousing and exciting.

■ For the *anger rapist,* rape is an impulsive, savage attack of uncontrolled physical violence. The act is of short duration, accompanied by abusive language, and the victim usually suffers extensive physical trauma, such as broken bones and bruises.

■ The *acquaintance or date rapist* knows his victim and uses varying amounts of verbal or physical coercion to force his partner to engage in sexual activities.

These examples indicate that men rape for a number of or combination of reasons, such as to exercise power and control, express anger, and become sexually aroused.

Other factors that contribute to rape are the false beliefs, called rape myths, that some men hold about women.

Rape Myths

One consistent finding about rapists is that they hold negative and demeaning attitudes toward women. For example, here are some of their negative attitudes:

■ Healthy women cannot be raped against their will.

■ Women often falsely accuse men of rape.

■ Rape is primarily a sex crime committed by sex-crazed maniacs.

■ Only bad girls get raped.

■ If a girl engages in necking or petting and lets things get out of hand, it is her own fault if her partner forces sex on her.

Some men mistakenly believe that only bad women get raped.

These kinds of statements are called rape myths (Foubert & Marriott, 1997).

Rape myths are misinformed, false beliefs about women, and these myths are frequently held by rapists.

Men who believe in rape myths tend to have a more traditional view of sex roles and hold more negative attitudes toward women. Although researchers have found that acceptance of rape myths is more common among men who have raped, rape myths are also held by men in general. For example, one survey of male college students reported that from 17% to 75% of the students agreed with one or more of nine rape myths (Giacopassi & Dull, 1986). This association between rape myths and rapists illustrates how negative beliefs and attitudes can contribute to sexual aggression (Johnson et al., 1997).

In the United States, it is estimated that during their lifetime 20–30% of women will be victims of some type of sexual aggression. Researchers are currently starting a number of rape prevention programs to both prevent rape and stop the perpetuation of rape myths (Ullman, 1997). We'll discuss ways to prevent rape in the upcoming Application section.

Next, we'll discuss how cultures differ in their attitudes toward assisted suicide, heart transplants, and women's rights.

G. Cultural Diversity: National Attitudes & Behaviors

United States: Assisted Suicide

How do Americans view assisted suicide?

One reason that the concept of attitude has been so dominant in social psychology is that our attitudes push or predispose us to act in certain ways. This means that if you can change people's attitudes, you can often change their behaviors. As we discussed earlier, people may change their attitudes to reduce their psychological distress from holding conflicting beliefs, a process called reducing cognitive dissonance. People may also change their attitudes by engaging in public behaviors that are opposite to their private attitudes, a process called counterattitudinal behavior. Attitudes can also be changed by persuasion.

In some cases, changing attitudes are accompanied by social, moral, and political consequences. For example, since the early 1990s, Dr. Jack Kevorkian has helped 47 people, who were in great physical pain from incurable diseases, to take their own lives, which is

called assisted suicide. Some people who oppose Dr. Kevorkian's work in promoting assisted suicide have used emotional appeals—peripheral approach—to turn people's attitudes against Dr. Kevorkian, such as labeling him "Dr. Death." Some respected doctors who are in favor of assisted suicide have used intellectual appeals by writing articles in professional journals—central approach—in which they explain why they are in favor of assisted suicide and have unofficially helped their patients to die (Clay, 1997).

Most recently, people in Oregon have changed their attitudes and their behaviors by voting to allow assisted suicide under very controlled conditions. As of this writing, four people in Oregon have used assisted suicide (McMahon, 1998). The debate over assisted suicide illustrates the important role of attitudes in influencing our behaviors.

A debate over attitudes and behaviors is also going on in Japan.

Japan: Organ Transplants

How do Japanese view heart transplants?

Miss Wakana Kume, who lives in Japan, was going to die unless she received a liver transplant. However, since 1968, it has been illegal in Japan to transplant organs from donors who are brain-dead. Like all Japanese, Miss Kume grew up with the attitude that brain-dead was not really dead, so she was very reluctant to get a transplant from a brain-dead donor. But because of the seriousness of her condition, Miss Kume flew to Australia, where she underwent a liver transplant. In a very real sense, Miss Kume engaged in counterattitudinal behavior by doing a behavior opposite of what she believed—getting a transplanted organ. Since her life-saving transplant, Miss Kume has changed her attitude toward transplant organs and now approves of them. This is a real example of changing attitudes by engaging in counterattitudinal behavior.

The reason there were about 24,000 organ transplants in the United States in 1997 but none in Japan is that cultures have different definitions of death. In the United States, death is defined as brain death—when a person's brain no longer shows electrical activity, even though the heart is still beating. In Japan, however, death is defined only as the moment when a person's heart stops beating; and donor organs can be removed only after the heart stops. But to be useful, donor organs must be removed when a person's heart is still beating. Currently, the Japanese are debating changing their definition of death to include brain death, which goes against a long cultural tradition. If brain death is legalized in Japan, organ transplants will be possible, provided that the Japanese change their attitudes toward death and accept organ transplants (WuDunn, 1997).

A debate over attitudes and behaviors is also going on in Egypt.

Egypt: Women's Rights

How do Egyptians view women?

Since the early 1900s, Egyptian women have been fighting for their sexual, political, and legal rights in a society that is dominated by Muslim religious principles, which grant women few rights. For example, while women are supposed to wear veils to preserve their dignity, a husband may strike his wife as long as he doesn't hit her in the face and hits lightly. Many women are not given birth certificates, which means that they cannot vote, get a passport, or go to court. Although female circumcision is illegal in Egypt, virtually all women in certain areas have been circumcised (Module 15). There are no public hot lines to help battered women and no

statistics on rape, although both are common in certain areas. Although Egyptian women are currently fighting for equal rights, such as not wearing veils in public (below photo), they are having limited success because these traditional attitudes are backed by powerful social forces, including political, cultural, and religious institutions (Lief, 1994). In getting Egyptians to change their attitudes toward women, the persuaders will need to use some of the methods that we have discussed, such as using trustworthy and honest sources, presenting one- or two-sided arguments, and, depending on the audience, using either the central or peripheral approach.

Next, we'll examine programs psychologists have developed to change attitudes toward aggression.

H. Application: Controlling Aggression

Case Study

How can we curb violence?

The discovery that about half the contribution to aggressiveness comes from genetic factors and about half from the environment explains what happened in this family of six children. One, called Monster Kody Scott, became a gang member and shot his first victim at age 11. He continued to engage in violent behavior until he was arrested, convicted, and sentenced to jail for robbery. When he wrote his autobiography from his prison cell, he blamed his problems and violent behavior on his parents' poverty and destitution and on his own gang's history of engaging in violent fights. But as it turned out, Monster Kody Scott had three brothers and two sisters who grew up in the same poverty and destitution and were surrounded by the same kind of gang violence. Only Scott, however, became a gang member with a history of violence; the other five are leading law-abiding, productive lives (Azar & Sleek, 1994).

The reason only one of the six children became an aggressive adult illustrates how the development of aggressive behavior depends on the interaction of biological, social cognitive, and environmental factors. Because biological and environmental factors are sometimes difficult to change, some recent programs focus on social cognitive factors to reduce and control aggression.

Controlling Aggression in Children

What if children act out?

Almost all children show occasional outbursts of anger and aggression. But if the outbursts become frequent and intense, young children may develop a pattern of using aggressive behaviors to deal with problems. If this aggressive pattern of behavior is not treated early, it may persist into adulthood and become very difficult to change (Lochman & Lenhart, 1993). Additionally, aggressive children are at risk for developing later problems, such as substance abuse, criminality, and various mental health disorders (Coie et al., 1992). Researchers have discovered that aggressive children have a number of cognitive-behavioral deficits that make them perceive, remember, and react to a world that appears more hostile than it really is. We'll first discuss these cognitive-behavioral deficits and then a program to decrease aggressive behavior.

COGNITIVE-BEHAVIORAL DEFICITS

Parents, teachers, and peers need to realize that an aggressive child or teenager does not perceive the world, take feedback, or act like regular nonaggressive children. Here are some of the ways that aggressive children differ.

An aggressive child does not accurately perceive or recall social cues. For example, the aggressive child selectively attends to aggressive or hostile actions and overlooks positive social cues. When an aggressive child is asked to recall what happened that day, the child tends to remember all the hostile actions rather than any positive or friendly cues.

An aggressive child does not make accurate explanations or attributions of the situation. For instance, aggressive children tend to attribute hostile actions to other children when, in fact, other children are not behaving in an aggressive or hostile way.

An aggressive child does not have many adaptive solutions to problems. This means that aggressive children tend to use hostile and aggressive actions to solve many of their problems rather than using nonhostile or verbal solutions.

An aggressive child is reinforced for aggressive behaviors rather than for positive social behaviors. That's because aggressive children use hostile actions to get their ways, and thus these aggressive behaviors are reinforced. In addition, aggressive children have poor social skills, which means they rarely try to solve problems with positive social skills, such as discussion.

Because of these cognitive-behavioral deficits, aggressive children perceive a more hostile world and respond with more aggressive behaviors (Patterson, 1994). One successful program teaches children to control their anger so that stressful situations do not trigger their aggressiveness.

You know I've got a quick temper so don't make me angry!

PROGRAM TO CONTROL AGGRESSION

Aggressive children often have a bad temper or are quick to anger, which triggers their aggressive behavior. One group of researchers has developed a program to control anger and keep children from becoming aggressive (Lochman & Lenhart, 1993).

1 Aggressive children do not know how to stop themselves from thinking in aggressive ways or to overcome their belief that other children, not they themselves, are acting aggressively. A child with a bad temper would be taught specific rules. For example, no matter how angry the child gets, he or she must not hit, yell, or kick. The child receives special reinforcement for obeying these rules.

2 The child learns to use self-statements to inhibit impulsive behavior. These include "Count to ten before acting," "I'll be sorry later," and "I can stop myself."

3 The child learns to use alternate, nonaggressive solutions when frustrated. These might be hand clapping, scribbling on a sheet of paper, or tensing and relaxing muscles.

4 The child learns through observation and imitation of students who had bad tempers but have used this program to control their temper.

This and similar kinds of anger control programs have been shown to be effective in reducing aggression. For example, after being in this or similar programs, children showed significant reductions in aggression (as rated by their parents) and in disruptive and aggressive classroom behaviors, as well as increases in self-reported self-esteem (Kaiser & Hester, 1997; Lochman & Lenhart, 1993; Lore & Schultz, 1993).

Now, we'll examine methods of controlling aggression in adults.

Controlling Aggression in Adults

What should I do?

You've probably known people who get mad, rant and rave, and then take their anger out on whoever happens to be near. Then, after their violent outbursts, they may apologize, say they're sorry, or explain that they have to let out their angry feelings or they'll explode. Is it true that "letting it all out" is a good way to deal with anger?

CATHARSIS

A popular idea for reducing and controlling aggression involves the idea of cartharsis.

Catharsis refers to a psychological process through which anger or aggressive energy is released by expressing or letting out powerful negative emotions.

According to the concept of catharsis, a good way to deal with anger or aggression is to "let off steam" or "get it off your chest," which means expressing strong negative emotions, such as through yelling, arguing, or hitting or kicking some object.

When I get angry, I like to let it all out!

Sigmund Freud used the term *catharsis* to mean that engaging in aggressive behavior can get rid of pent-up emotions and thus be helpful for reducing aggression. However, most research does not support Freud's conclusion about the usefulness of catharsis. For example, researchers measured the levels of aggression in fans before and after a football game. On the basis of catharsis, we would predict that the losing fans who showed the most aggression during the game should have the lowest levels after the game. Instead, researchers found that both losing and winning fans showed increased levels of aggression at the end of the game (Goldstein, 1989).

Another drawback to the use of catharsis is that, as researchers report, it is difficult to find appropriate people on whom to vent cathartic aggression, since these people feel obliged to respond with aggression (Tavris, 1982). Thus, venting aggression may actually trigger aggression (Lippa, 1994). Generally, the notion that catharsis is a method for reducing aggression by letting out strong aggressive emotions has received little scientific support (Deaux et al., 1993).

COGNITIVE-BEHAVIORAL PROGRAM

A more successful method than catharsis for dealing with anger involves a program that combines cognitive-behavioral methods and learning new social skills.

Let's consider Margaret's problem. She is very good at selling computer software, but she becomes angry at clients and at herself if she loses a sale. She has developed a pattern of taking out her anger on her husband. As a result, their marriage is in trouble.

Researchers have developed an anger-control program for people like Margaret, whose quick tempers lead to problems (Adler & Denmark, 1995). These researchers use a program that combines cognitive relaxation and social skills training. We'll follow Margaret through this program to show its main features.

During the first two weeks of this program, Margaret practices progressive relaxation and monitors when, where, and why she becomes angry. During the next six sessions, she imagines events that make her angry, such as losing a sale, and then reduces her anger by relaxing. She is then told to continue monitoring events that make her angry outside the sessions and to reduce her anger by relaxing rather than taking it out on her husband. In addition, she is taught to minimize interpersonal anger by developing better listening and communications skills—for example, learning how to ask questions, seek clarifications, and check for understanding.

The researchers found that five weeks after finishing this program clients report significant reductions both in suppressing anger and in coping better with potentially angering situations.

Controlling Sexual Aggression

What's the biggest problem?

One of the biggest problems women seem to have is saying "No!" to unwanted male sexual advances and really meaning it. Researchers found that about 39% of college women offered only token resistance, such as, saying "No," but later changed their minds because they actually wanted to have sex (Shotland & Hunter, 1995). This kind of token resistance gives males the impression that women can be manipulated to have sex, even if they initially say, "No." Thus, one common method men use to obtain unwanted sex is to just do it, even if the woman has said no. For this reason, researchers counsel women to use a strategy of increasing forcefulness, going from direct refusal to vehement verbal refusal and, if necessary, physical force. However, when women were presented with sexual situations and asked whether they could refuse comfortably, only 60% said they could. This means that 40% of respondents would seem to be at risk for sexual aggression on dates. The researchers suggest

How do I say "NO" and really mean "NO!"?

that women take assertiveness training if they foresee having a problem saying no (Muehlenhard & Linton, 1987).

Not being able to say "No!" and back it up is one of the risk factors associated with date rape. According to researchers, one way to avoid sexual aggression on a date is to know all the risk factors. These factors include heavy use of alcohol or other drugs and letting the man be in total control, such as initiating the date, paying all the expenses, driving, and "parking."

One of the problems in avoiding date rape is that men who are guilty of this act do not fit the stranger-in-the-dark-alley stereotype. Women are less likely to recognize what is happening and more likely to blame themselves or be blamed by others for arousing the man. To prevent sexual aggression, the researchers suggest that women avoid the risk factors associated with date rape, learn to recognize the cues very early, and clearly and forcefully put an early stop to unwanted sexual advances (Shotland & Hunter, 1995; Ullman, 1997).

A. PERCEIVING OTHERS

1. How our thoughts, feelings, perceptions, and behaviors are influenced by interactions with others is studied in the field of (a)_____ psychology. A branch of this field studies how people perceive, store, and retrieve information about social interactions; this branch is called social (b)_____.

2. Making judgments about the traits of others through social interactions and gaining knowledge from our social perceptions is part of person (a)_____. This process is aided by a wealth of social information that is stored in our memories. However, some memories can bias our perceptions. Widely held beliefs that people have certain traits because they belong to a particular group are called (b)_____. Those that are negative are often accompanied by an unfair, biased, or intolerant attitude toward another group of people, called (c)_____, and by specific unfair behaviors exhibited toward members of a group, called (d)_____.

3. Cognitive structures that represent an organized collection of knowledge about people, events, and concepts are called _____. They help us select and interpret relevant information from a tremendous amount of incoming social information and provide guidelines for how we should behave in different situations.

4. There are different kinds of schemas: those that include our judgments about the traits that we and others possess are called (a)_____ schemas; those that are based on the jobs people perform or the social positions they hold are called (b)_____ schemas; those that contain behaviors that we associate with familiar activities, events, or procedures are called (c)_____ schemas, or scripts.

B. ATTRIBUTIONS

5. The factors or events that we point to as causes or explanations for people's behavior are called (a)_____. If we attribute behavior to the internal characteristics of the person performing the behavior, we are using (b)_____ explanations; if we attribute behavior to the circumstances or context of that behavior, we are using (c)_____ explanations.

6. Harold Kelley proposed that in deciding between dispositional and situational explanations, we should look for factors that change along with the behavior we are trying to explain; this is called the _____ model. To decide between dispositional and situational explanations, we should look for consensus, consistency, and distinctiveness.

7. An error that we make by attributing the cause of a behavior to a person's disposition and overlooking the demands of the environment or situation is the (a)_____ attribution error. If we attribute our own behavior to situational factors but others' behaviors to their dispositions, we fall prey to the (b)_____ effect. If we attribute success to our disposition and failure to the situation, we use the (c)_____ bias.

C. RESEARCH FOCUS: ATTRIBUTIONS & GRADES

Dropout Rate from College

(bar graph: Percent Leaving School; bars labeled Control (~25) and Change (~5))

8. Researchers found that freshmen who were encouraged to attribute their academic problems to _____ conditions, such as poor study habits, showed a significant improvement in grade point average and were less likely to drop out than were students who continued to attribute their poor performance to permanent factors.

D. ATTITUDES

9. Beliefs or opinions that include a positive or negative evaluation of an object, person, or event and that predispose us to act in a certain way are called (a)_____. General attitudes are convenient guidelines for interpreting and categorizing objects and events and deciding whether to approach or avoid them. Attitudes have three components: beliefs and ideas make up the (b)_____ component; emotions and feelings make up the (c)_____ component; and predispositions make up the (d)_____ component.

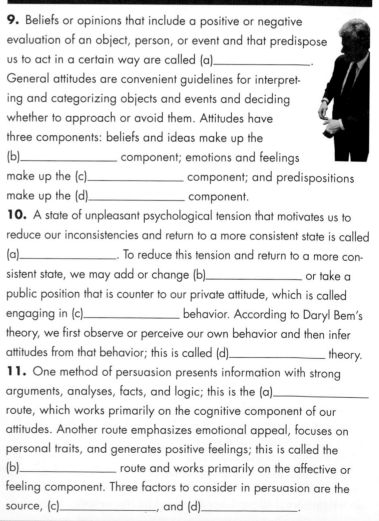

10. A state of unpleasant psychological tension that motivates us to reduce our inconsistencies and return to a more consistent state is called (a)_____. To reduce this tension and return to a more consistent state, we may add or change (b)_____ or take a public position that is counter to our private attitude, which is called engaging in (c)_____ behavior. According to Daryl Bem's theory, we first observe or perceive our own behavior and then infer attitudes from that behavior; this is called (d)_____ theory.

11. One method of persuasion presents information with strong arguments, analyses, facts, and logic; this is the (a)_____ route, which works primarily on the cognitive component of our attitudes. Another route emphasizes emotional appeal, focuses on personal traits, and generates positive feelings; this is called the (b)_____ route and works primarily on the affective or feeling component. Three factors to consider in persuasion are the source, (c)_____, and (d)_____.

E. SOCIAL & GROUP INFLUENCES

12. If you perform a behavior because of group pressure, you are exhibiting (a)_____. Giving in to social pressure in your public responses but not changing your private beliefs is called (b)_____. A sales technique that relies on the increased probability of meeting a second request if you comply with a small, first request is called the (c)_____ technique. Performing a behavior in response to an order given by someone in a position of authority is called (d)_____.

13. Any behavior that benefits others or has positive social consequences is called (a)_____ behavior. A form of helping that involves doing something, often at a cost or risk, for reasons other than the expectation of a material or social reward is called (b)_____. Two different models explain how we make our decisions to help. The model that frames our decision as a five-stage process is called the (c)_____ model. According to another model, we make decisions to help by calculating the costs and rewards of helping; this is called the (d)_____ model.

14. A collection of two or more people who interact and share some common attribute or attributes is called a (a)_____. How much group members perceive that they share common attributes determines group (b)_____. The formal or informal rules about how group members should behave are called group (c)_____. According to Leon Festinger's (d)_____ theory, we compare ourselves to others who are similar to us so that we can measure the correctness of our attitudes and beliefs.

15. If the presence of a crowd increases performance, it is called social (a)_____; if it decreases performance, it is called social (b)_____. If people in a crowd take on antisocial roles because they cannot be identified easily, it is called (c)_____. If an individual in a crowd is inhibited from helping someone in need, it is called the (d)_____ effect.

16. The effect in which a group discussion reinforces the majority's point of view and shifts that view to a more extreme position is called (a)_____. The phenomenon in which group discussions tend to emphasize cohesion and agreement over critical thinking and making the best decisions is called (b)_____.

F. AGGRESSION

17. Three major factors influence aggression. The finding that aggressive male relatives all shared the same gene supports the influence of (a)_____ factors. The finding that people can learn aggressive behavior through observation, imitation, and self-reinforcement support the influence of (b)_____ factors. The finding that frustration may lead to or trigger aggression supports the influence of (c)_____ factors.

18. The primary motivation for rape is not sexual but a combination of (a)_____, _____ and _____. Men who rape have been classified into four types: power, sadistic, anger, and acquaintance/date rapists. The misinformed beliefs that are frequently held by rapists and that are contributing factors to rape are called (b)_____.

G. CULTURAL DIVERSITY: NATIONAL ATTITUDES & BEHAVIORS

19. National attitudes are important because they push or predispose citizens to (a)_____ in certain ways. For example, people in Oregon changed their attitudes toward assisted suicide and then (b)_____ to legalize it. Because of Japan's attitude toward brain death, they do not approve of (c)_____. One reason Egyptian women are having such difficulty changing (d)_____ toward them is that these discriminatory policies are backed by social, political, and religious forces.

H. APPLICATION: CONTROLLING AGGRESSION

20. An aggressive child perceives and reacts to a world that appears more hostile than normal because this child has a number of (a)_____ deficits. One program to decrease aggressive behavior teaches children how to control their (b)_____. Freud theorized that one way to control aggression in adults was to release emotional tension. This process, known as (c)_____, is supposed to get rid of pent-up anger, but there is little experimental support for this idea. A proven method to decrease anger involves a combination of cognitive, relaxation, and social skills training.

Answers: *1. (a) social, (b) cognition; 2. (a) perception, (b) stereotypes, (c) prejudice, (d) discrimination; 3. schemas; 4. (a) person, (b) role, (c) event; 5. (a) attributions, (b) internal (dispositional), (c) external (situational); 6. covariation model; 7. (a) fundamental, (b) actor-observer, (c) self-serving; 8. temporary; 9. (a) attitudes, (b) cognitive, (c) affective, (d) behavioral; 10. (a) cognitive dissonance, (b) beliefs, (c) counterattitudinal, (d) self-perception; 11. (a) central, (b) peripheral, (c) message, (d) audience; 12. (a) conformity, (b) compliance, (c) foot-in-the-door, (d) obedience; 13. (a) prosocial or helping, (b) altruism, (c) decision stage, (d) arousal-cost-reward model; 14. (a) group, (b) cohesion, (c) norms, (d) social comparison; 15. (a) facilitation, (b) inhibition, (c) deindividuation, (d) bystander; 16. (a) group polarization, (b) groupthink; 17. (a) biological, (b) social learning, (c) environmental; 18. (a) power, aggression, control, (b) rape myths; 19. (a) behave, (b) voted, (c) organ transplants, (d) attitudes; 20. (a) cognitive-behavioral, (b) anger, (c) catharsis.*

CRITICAL THINKING

Newspaper Article

QUESTIONS

TEEN PREGNANCIES FORCE TOWN TO GROW UP

by Sheryl Stolberg

1. What kind of attribution does the author seem to make about the rate of teen pregnancy in Tipton?

After 20 years of practicing obstetrics and gynecology in Indianapolis, 52-year-old physician William Stone was eager to set up shop in a community where he might make a difference. He chose Tipton, a small town in Indiana, and what a difference the doctor has made.

The first thing he noticed were the teenagers. Girls, some as young as 14, growing babies in their bellies. And not the stereotypical troubled teens, but girls from good families, girls in the National Honor Society at school.

In his first year of practice, Stone delivered infants to 16 teenagers. He did a little checking and discovered that unwed teens accounted for 11.8% of births in Tipton County—a rate slightly higher than both Indiana's and the nation's.

2. How did the adult's attitude toward the teens change after the doctor pointed out their teen pregnancy problem?

So it was that in August 1994, the doctor boldly informed his new hometown that it had a teen pregnancy problem. It was a declaration that opened a Pandora's box of questions about teenage sexuality, unwed motherhood, and, most important, the values that parents impart to children.

Listen to the troubled voices of Tipton and one can hear the voices of a troubled America. Adults preach abstinence but secretly expect their kids to have sex—and then worry that they are creating a self-fulfilling prophecy. A local minister wonders aloud whatever happened to shame.

3. What group norms do the people of Tipton share?

In a community that prides itself on neighbor helping neighbor, people are now chiding themselves for coddling teen mothers. Educators fret over whether they have made it too easy for pregnant girls to get a diploma. Some are suggesting that teen fathers be banned from school sports.

4. How might Tipton teens experience cognitive dissonance?

At Tipton High School, the administration has cracked down on necking in the hallways. The quarterback got his girlfriend pregnant—and married her. His teammates think that's cool.

"I don't know of a society in the history of the world that has simultaneously stretched out marriage so long and has successfully preached abstinence before marriage," said William Galston, who heads the "religious and public values" task force of the National Campaign to Prevent Teen Pregnancy.

5. What are some possible solutions to Tipton's teen pregnancy problem?

"My guess," he said, "is that most people in their heart of hearts, wish that teens would abstain. But they are not sure that they will and are not sure what the best response is to the fact that many of them won't."

Source: *Los Angeles Times,* November 29, 1996.

Study Questions

A. Perceiving Others—Mark says that he doesn't make snap judgments but waits until he knows people. Do you think Mark does what he claims? (See answer in Critical Thinking Appendix.)

B. Attributions—What should you be aware of when you try to explain the behaviors of your friend or mate? (See answer in Critical Thinking Appendix.)

C. Research Focus: Attributions & Grades—As a senior in college, what advice would you give to your younger brother or sister who is an incoming freshman?

D. Attitudes—You are trying to persuade your loved one to be more neat and tidy around the house. How would you do this?

E. Social & Group Influences—A family of five is trying to decide where to go on vacation. What problems might arise?

F. Aggression—One of your friends says, "Getting angry and being aggressive is just part of human nature." What would you reply? (See answer in Critical Thinking Appendix.)

G. Cultural Diversity: National Attitudes & Behaviors—In changing national attitudes, do you think the central or peripheral route of persuasion is more effective?

H. Application: Controlling Aggression—Why do you think that about four million women each year are victims of domestic violence initiated by their spouses?

Web Sites & Learning Activities

● BROOKS/COLE ONLINE PSYCHOLOGY STUDY CENTER

http://psychstudy.brookscole.com/student/plotnik/quiz/ch25frm.html

This site gives students a chance to review material by taking quizzes and doing exercises and activities for this module.

● THE CENTER FOR THE STUDY OF GROUP PROCESSES

http://www.uiowa.edu/~grpproc/

This site offers information and resources for the study of how people behave in groups.

● CULTIC STUDIES

http://www.csj.org/

This organization researches and educates on the ways cults use psychological manipulation. Their home page describes cults and what it takes to get free of them.

● INTERNATIONAL ASSOCIATION FOR CROSS-CULTURAL PSYCHOLOGY

http://www.fit.edu/CampusLife/clubs-org/iaccp

This home page includes the organization's publications, conference proceedings, a listing of graduate programs in cross-cultural psychology, and links.

● RACISM AND PREJUDICE: PSYCHOLOGICAL PERSPECTIVES

http://www.bhs.mq.edu.au/aps/publications/racism/contents.html

Here is a full-length paper on the psychology of racism, including issues of language, politics, stereotypes, and the media.

Welcome to the WEB

● NATIONAL CONSORTIUM ON VIOLENCE RESEARCH

http://www.ncovr.heinz.cmu.edu/ncovr/index.asp

This organization is dedicated to advancing scientific knowledge of the causes of violence in society.

● PEACENET

http://www.igc.org/igc/peacenet/index.html

This massive site includes information on conflicts around the world, news alerts, and ways to work for peace.

Activities

● *Integrator Online™ for Introductory Psychology* CD-ROM, Plotnik, Module 25

● Study Guide to accompany *Introduction to Psychology,* 5th edition, Module 25 (choice of PC or Mac computer version or hard copy).

● *PsychNow!* CD-ROM
    Social Psychology
        Helping Others; Attribution; Social Influence; Attitudes and Prejudice; Aggression; Environmental Psychology; Gender and Stereotyping

---

Answers to questions on page 608

1. The author focuses on external attributions, such as social policies and delayed marriage.
2. It changed from resignation and acceptance to concern and introspection.
3. Adults seem to share the belief that teen sex is bad. However, many of the teens do not seem to share this value.
4. The community disapproves of teen sex, but parents seem to expect that young people will have sex.
5. There are many possible solutions. They include trying to change the norms of the teens to make sex less acceptable and providing contraception for those who are sexually active.

Appendix A

STATISTICS IN PSYCHOLOGY

Descriptive Statistics

Do numbers speak for themselves?

Suppose you are curious about how many people are capable of being hypnotized. You read up on how to induce hypnosis and put together a list of five things that people under hypnosis have been known to do, such as feeling no pain when a finger is pricked, being unable to bend an arm when told that the arm will remain stiff, and acting like a young child when told to regress to infancy.

You next persuade 20 people to participate in a little test. You attempt to hypnotize them and then ask them to do each of the things on your list. Of your 20 subjects, 2 follow none of your suggestions, 4 follow only one, 7 go along with two suggestions, 4 go along with three, 2 go along with as many as four, and only 1 follows all five.

The next day, a friend asks you how your study worked out. How would you make generalizations about your findings?

To answer this type of question, psychologists rely on *statistics*. Although you often hear that numbers "speak for themselves," this is not really true. Numbers must be sorted, organized, and presented in a meaningful fashion before they tell us much.

Statistics are the tools researchers use to analyze and summarize large amounts of data.

If the very word *statistics* brings to mind complex formulas you think you could never master, you may be surprised to realize how much you already use statistics in your everyday life. When you hear that a ball player has a batting average of .250 and you know this means he has gotten one hit in every four times at the plate, you are using statistics. When you understand that a rise in the median income means that people, on average, are earning more money, you are understanding statistics. When you know that scoring in the 90th percentile on a final exam means you did better than nine out of ten of your classmates, you are showing a grasp of statistics—specifically, descriptive statistics.

Descriptive statistics are numbers used to present a collection of data in a brief yet meaningful form.

One important part of descriptive statistics is presenting distributions of measurements and scores.

FREQUENCY DISTRIBUTIONS

Individual differences show up in everything that can be measured. There are no measurements—whether of height, heart rate, memory capability, shyness, or political opinion—that do not show individual variation.

The *frequency distribution* is the range of scores we get and the frequency of each one when we measure a sample of people regarding some trait.

Frequency distributions are often presented in graphic form so their patterns can be seen at a glance. We'll discuss two of these distributions, normal and skewed.

What is a normal distribution?

For many traits in a large population, the frequency distribution has a characteristic pattern. For instance, if you measured the height of 500 students chosen at random from your school, you would find a few very short people and a few very tall people, while the height of the majority of students would be somewhere in the middle. Height, like weight, IQ, years of education, and many other characteristics, has what is known as a **normal distribution.** When graphed, a normal distribution produces a normal curve.

A **normal curve** is a graph of a frequency distribution in which the curve tapers off equally on either side of a central high point.

This characteristic bell shape (Figure A.1) shows that most of the measurements fall near the center, with as many falling to one side as to the other. When you measure a trait that is distributed normally throughout a population, your measurements should produce an approximately normal curve, provided that your sample is large enough.

What is a skewed distribution?

Not all traits are distributed normally.

Skewed distributions are distributions in which more data fall toward one side of the scale than toward the other.

When plotted on a graph, skewed distributions do not have a symmetrical shape. Instead, they have a "tail" on one end, which shows that relatively fewer frequencies occur on that side of the horizontal scale. When the

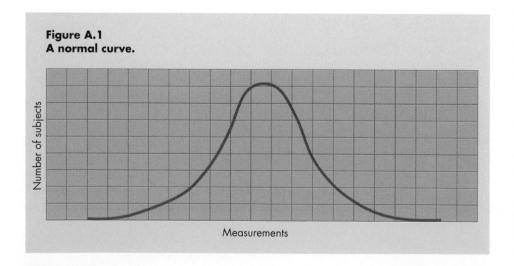

Figure A.1
A normal curve.

Number of subjects

Measurements

tail is on the right, as in Figure A.2, we say the distribution is skewed to the right, or has a *positive skew* (there are fewer frequencies at the higher end of the horizontal scale). When the tail is on the left, as in Figure A.3, we say the distribution is skewed to the left, or has a *negative skew* (there are fewer frequencies at the lower end of the horizontal scale).

The data you collected about susceptibility to hypnosis present a skewed distribution. If you plotted them on a graph, with score along the horizontal axis and number of people along the vertical one, the curve would be skewed to the right. This would show at a glance that more people in the sample fell at the low end of your hypnotic susceptibility scale than fell at the high end.

In fact, your sample is fairly representative of the general population. About twice as many people are poor hypnotic subjects as are excellent ones. But note that to be assured of obtaining the true distribution in a large population, you would usually have to test quite a large representative sample.

MEASURES OF CENTRAL TENDENCY

Suppose you want to summarize in a few words the average height of people, the typical susceptibility to hypnosis, or the most common performance on an IQ test. For this you would need another kind of descriptive statistic, called a **measure of central tendency.** There are three measures of central tendency: the mean, the median, and the mode. Each is a slightly different way of describing what is "typical" within a given distribution.

The *mean* is the arithmetic average of all the individual measurements in a distribution.

Suppose that ten students in a seminar took an exam. Their scores were 98, 96, 92, 88, 88, 86, 82, 80, 78, and 72. You would find the mean by adding all the scores and dividing the sum by the total number of scores. In this case, the sum of all the scores is 860; dividing this by 10 gives a mean of 86.

The *median* is the score above and below which half the scores in the distribution fall.

If you took our ten test results and arranged them in order from highest to lowest, the median would be the point right in the middle, between the fifth and sixth scores on the list. That would be 87.

The *mode* is the most frequent measurement in a distribution.

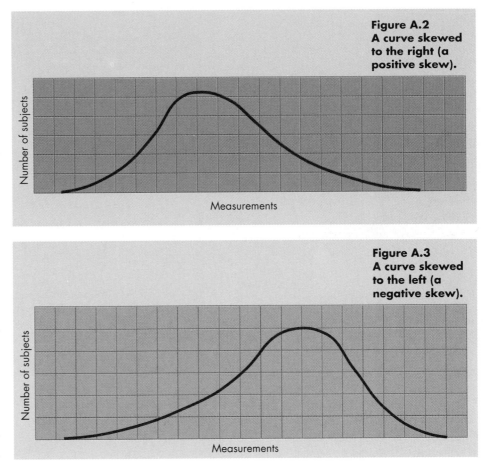

**Figure A.2
A curve skewed to the right (a positive skew).**

**Figure A.3
A curve skewed to the left (a negative skew).**

In this group of scores, the mode, the score that occurs most often, is 88.

In the example just given, the mean, median, and mode are very close together, but this is not always true. In some distributions, particularly those that are strongly skewed, these three measures of central tendency may be quite far apart. In such cases, all three of the measures may be needed to give a complete understanding of what is typical.

For instance, look at the graph in Figure A.4, which shows the distribution of income in an imaginary company. The mean income of its 50 employees is $30,600 a year. But look at the distribution. The president of the company earns $140,000, three other executives earn $80,000, and another four earn $60,000 a year. There are also six lower-level managers at $40,000, six salespeople at $30,000, and ten foremen at $25,000. The rest of the employees, the 20 people who keep the company records and run the machines, earn only $12,000 each. Thus, the mean of $30,600 does not really give an accurate indication of a typical income of an employee at this firm.

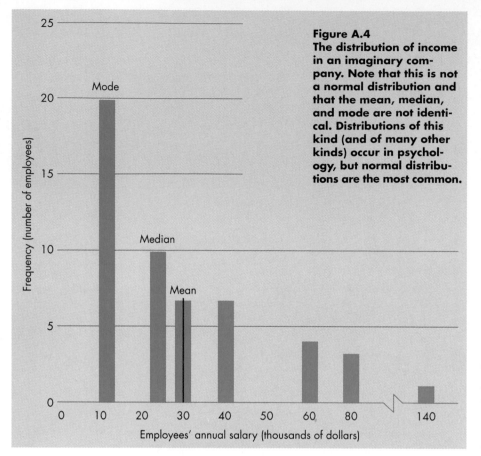

Figure A.4
The distribution of income in an imaginary company. Note that this is not a normal distribution and that the mean, median, and mode are not identical. Distributions of this kind (and of many other kinds) occur in psychology, but normal distributions are the most common.

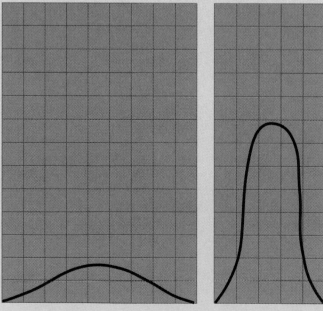

Figure A.5
At left, a distribution with a great deal of variability. At right, a distribution with little variability.

A better measure of central tendency in this instance is probably the median, or $25,000. It tells us that half the people at the company earn no more than this amount. Also revealing is the mode, or most common salary; it is only $12,000 a year. As you can see, the mean, median, and mode can provide us with very different figures.

MEASURES OF VARIABILITY

If you get an A in a course and are told that the grades ranged from A to F, you will feel a greater sense of accomplishment than if the grades ranged only from A to B. Why this difference in how you perceive a grade? The answer is that it is often important to take into account the extent to which scores in a distribution are spread out. In other words, it is often informative to have a measure of variability.

A *measure of variability* is an indication of how much scores vary from one another.

On a graph, scores that vary greatly produce a wide, flat curve; scores that vary little produce a curve that is narrow and steep. Figure A.5 illustrates these two patterns.

One measure of variability is the range.

The *range* consists of the two most extreme scores at either end of a distribution.

Another measure is the standard deviation.

The *standard deviation* shows how widely all the scores in a distribution are scattered above and below the mean.

If scores cluster closely around the mean, the standard deviation will be small; if scores are dispersed widely from the mean, the standard deviation will be large. Thus, the standard deviation is an indication of how representative the mean is. If the standard deviation is small, we know that the mean is representative of most scores in the distribution. Conversely, if the standard deviation is large, we know that many scores are quite far from the mean.

Figure A.6 shows that the standard deviation divides a normal curve into several portions, each of which has a certain percentage of the total distribution. As you can see, 68.2% of all scores fall somewhere between the mean and one standard deviation to either side of it. If you move two standard deviations to either side of the mean, you will take in 95.4% of all the scores in the distribution. Finally, 99.8% of all the scores will fall between the mean and three standard

Finding the standard deviation of a distribution is not difficult, although it is tedious without the aid of a calculator. To compute the standard deviation, follow these five steps:

1. Determine the mean of all the measurements in the distribution.
2. Subtract the mean from each measurement and square the difference. (Squaring the difference eliminates the negative signs that result when dealing with measurements that fall below the mean.)
3. Add the squares together.
4. Divide the sum of the squares by the number of measurements.
5. Take the square root of the value you obtained in step 4. This figure is the standard deviation.

deviations from it. Only a scant 0.2% fall beyond three standard deviations.

Knowing the mean and the standard deviation of any normal distribution allows you to determine just how "average" any given score is.

For instance, suppose you take a difficult test consisting of 100 questions and receive a score of 80. How well did you perform? If you learn that the mean is 60 and the standard deviation is 8, you know that your score of 80 is very good indeed. The overwhelming majority of people—95.4%—scored no better than 76, or two standard deviations above the mean. Thus, relative to what most others have done, an 80 is excellent. By the same token, a 40 is not very good at all; 95.4% of people scored 44 or higher on this test. Thus, if you received a 40 you are near the bottom of the distribution and had better start studying much harder.

Inferential Statistics

Can scientists be 100% certain?

In the mid-1970s, many Americans were puzzled to learn that a distinguished panel of scientists could not determine with absolute certainty whether the artificial sweetener called cyclamate posed a risk of cancer. The scientists announced that, after months of research, costing millions of dollars, they could be only 95% sure that cyclamate was safe. Why this remaining margin of doubt? Why can't a team of

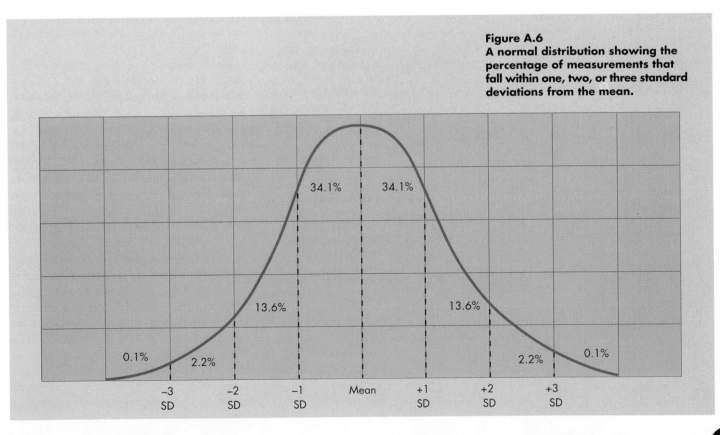

Figure A.6
A normal distribution showing the percentage of measurements that fall within one, two, or three standard deviations from the mean.

highly skilled researchers, backed by government funds, manage to tell us absolutely if a substance is hazardous to our health?

CHANCE AND RELIABILITY

No one can totally eliminate the influence of chance on scientific findings. Even when you randomly select groups of subjects, there is always the possibility that, just by chance, those groups will differ slightly in ways that affect your experiment. This is why scientists must rely on statistics to tell them the likelihood that a certain set of results could have happened purely by chance. If this likelihood is small—5% or less—the researchers are justified in rejecting the chance explanation and in concluding instead that their findings are probably reliable. *Reliable* means that the investigators would probably obtain similar results if they repeated their study over and over with different groups of subjects.

Determining the reliability of experimental findings is a major way in which psychologists use inferential statistics.

Inferential statistics are a set of procedures for determining what conclusions can be legitimately inferred from a set of data.

These procedures include what are called *tests of statistical significance.* Tests of statistical significance were used to determine the 95% certainty of the finding that cyclamate is safe to eat. Different tests of statistical significance are needed for different kinds of data.

TESTS OF STATISTICAL SIGNIFICANCE

Suppose you are an educational psychologist who has put together a special program to raise the IQ levels of children with learning disabilities. You expose one group of children with learning deficits to the special program and another group, with equal learning deficits, to the standard curriculum. At the end of a year, you give all the subjects an IQ test. Those in the special program score an average of ten points higher than those in the standard curriculum. Is this enough of a difference to reject the chance explanation and conclude that the program was a success? The procedure most frequently used to answer questions like this is a test of statistical significance called the *t* test.

What is a t test?

The *t* test is an estimate of reliability that takes into account both the size of the mean difference and the variability in distributions. The *greater* the mean difference and the *less* the variability, the less the likelihood that the results happened purely by chance.

Imagine that the results of your experiment looked like the ones in Figure A.7. The mean IQs of the two groups differ by ten points: 75 for the experimental subjects and 65 for the controls. But look at the variability in the two distributions: there is almost none. All the children in the experimental group received a score within five points of 75; all the children in the control group received a score within five points of 65. It seems that some genuine effect is at work here. The IQ patterns in the two groups are distinctly different and are not the kinds of differences usually caused by chance.

Unfortunately, the results of most experiments are not this clear-cut. Far more often, the distributions look more like those in Figure A.8. In this figure, you can see that the mean difference in scores is still ten points, but now there is a sizable amount of variability in the two groups. In fact, some of the experimental subjects are doing no better than some of the controls, while some of the controls are

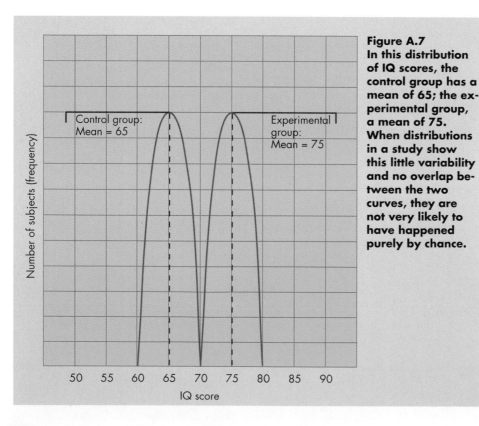

Figure A.7
In this distribution of IQ scores, the control group has a mean of 65; the experimental group, a mean of 75. When distributions in a study show this little variability and no overlap between the two curves, they are not very likely to have happened purely by chance.

Control group: Mean = 65

Experimental group: Mean = 75

Number of subjects (frequency)

50 55 60 65 70 75 80 85 90

IQ score

scoring higher than some of those in the experimental program. Is a mean difference of ten points in this case large enough to be considered reliable?

When should you use a t test?

The *t* test also considers how many subjects are included in the study. You should not put much faith in a comparison of educational programs that tries out each approach on only two or three children. There is too great a likelihood that such samples are not representative of the larger population from which they are drawn. Let's say that, in the hypothetical experiment we have been describing, you included 100 randomly selected children in each of the two groups. It is much less likely that samples of this size would be biased enough to distort the research's findings.

To learn the steps involved in actually performing the *t* test, please read the accompanying box.

ANALYSIS OF VARIANCE

Not all data lend themselves to a *t* test, however. Often researchers want to compare the mean scores of more than two groups, or they want to make comparisons among groups that are classified in more than one way. (For instance, does age or sex have an effect on how much children benefit from our special educational program?) In such cases another test of statistical significance is needed. This test is

Figure A.8
This set of distibutions is much more likely than the one in Figure A.7. The mean is still 65 for the control group and 75 for the experimental group. But now the variability of the distributions is substantially greater. There is also substantial overlap between the two curves. Is the mean difference in this case statistically significant? A *t*-test can provide the answer.

called an ***analysis of variance,*** or ***ANOVA*** for short. An analysis of variance is rather like a more complex *t* test. To learn more about the ANOVA technique, consult any introductory statistics text.

How to Perform the t Test

The *t* test is an estimate of how reliable the difference between two means is. To determine the likelihood that the outcome occurred by chance, you first need to know the size of the mean difference (mean 1 minus mean 2). In general, the larger the mean difference, the less likely that it happened by chance alone. You also need to know the variance within each group.

The *variance* is a measure of the variability within the two distributions.

In general, the lower the variance, the less likely that chance alone caused the results. Finally, you need to know how many subjects are in the random samples. In general, the larger the samples, the less the likelihood of a purely chance explanation.

To calculate the *t* test just follow these steps:

1. Determine the mean of the scores for each group and subtract one from the other.
2. Go back to the box on standard deviation and work through that calculation for each of your distributions, stopping at step 4. This gives you the variance of each distribution.
3. Add the two variances.
4. Add the total number of subjects minus 2 (in our example 200 − 2 = 198).
5. Divide the summed variances by the number obtained in step 4 and take the square root.
6. Divide the mean difference between the two groups by the square root from step 5.

If the samples add up to more than 50 individuals, any value of *t* over 2 is statistically reliable more than 95% of the time.

CHI-SQUARE

Sometimes the data psychologists collect do not consist of sets of scores with means or averages. Instead, the researchers have recorded who does what, or who falls into which of several categories. For instance, psychologists have found that chess players are more apt to be introverts than they are to be extroverts. Is this just a chance association? To answer such questions, statisticians often use the *chi (ky) square,* a test of statistical significance.

Suppose you are a psychologist and you want to study the usefulness of fear tactics in changing people's behavior. You randomly select 200 habitual smokers who are willing to participate in an experiment. You expose half to a 20-minute talk on the known health hazards of smoking, complete with graphic illustrations of diseased lungs and hearts. You expose the rest to a 20-minute talk on the history of tobacco. After the talks, the members of each group are given the opportunity to sign up for a free "quit smoking" clinic. Some people from each group sign up for the clinic; some do not. The easiest way to present their choices is with a 2 × 2 table, like the one set up in Table A.1.

Table A.2 shows how the distribution worked out in your study. Of the 100 subjects in your experimental group (the ones exposed to the fear tactic), 60 signed up for the quit-smoking clinic and 40 did not. Of the 100 subjects in the control group, 40 signed up for the free clinic and 60 did not. Is this difference in the distribution of choices statistically significant? The chi-square can be used to estimate the reliability of this difference.

The *chi-square* is a test of statistical significance that compares the actual observed distribution of people (or events) among various categories with the distribution expected purely on the basis of chance.

If people had made their decisions purely by chance—for instance, by the toss of a coin—the same number of people would be expected to sign up for the clinic in each of the two groups. The accompanying box gives a step-by-step description of how to do the chi-square calculation.

Table A.1: The Format of a 2 × 2 Table

Talk heard	Signed up for clinic	Didn't sign up	Row total
Fear tactics			100
No fear tactics			100
Column totals			200 (grand total)

Table A.2: Study Results in Our Example

Talk heard	Signed up for clinic	Didn't sign up	Row total
Fear tactics	60	40	100
No fear tactics	40	60	100
Column totals	100	100	200 (grand total)

How to Calculate Chi-Square

Chi-square (χ^2) is an estimate of how sure we can be that a distribution of events or of people did not happen just by chance. In our example, chi-square calculates the *expected* number of people that a chance distribution would place in each of the categories represented by the four cells in the table. This expected number is then compared with the actual *observed* number of people in each of these categories, shown by cells (the data presented in Table A.2). If the difference between the expected and observed numbers is large enough, the distribution is not likely to have happened by chance alone.

Here are the steps in making the chi-square calculation:

1. Figure out how many people, by chance alone, would be likely to fall into the upper-left cell. To do this, multiply the first row total by the first column total (100 × 100) and divide by the grand total (200). The expected number is 50.

2. Subtract the expected number (50) from the observed number in the upper-left cell (60). The difference is 10 (60 − 50 = 10). Square the difference to eliminate negative signs (10 × 10 = 100) and divide the result by the expected number: 100 ÷ 50 = 2.

3. Repeat steps 1 and 2 for each of the four cells. In this example, the expected values are the same for each cell, but that won't always be true.

4. Add the four values you get from calculating the difference between the expected and observed number for each cell. This is the chi-square.

The reliability of the chi-square value must be looked up in a table. In this example, the fear-tactic subjects signed up for the clinic so much more often than the control subjects did that this distribution could have occurred by chance only two times in a hundred.

SUMMARY TEST

DESCRIPTIVE STATISTICS

1. The tools that researchers use to analyze and summarize large amounts of data are called (a)_____. Numbers that are used to present a collection of data in a brief yet meaningful form are (b)_____ statistics, which are often used to present distributions of measurements and scores. The range of scores and the frequency of each one is called the (c)_____; this is often presented in graphic form so the patterns can be seen at a glance.

2. When graphed, a normal distribution produces a curve that tapers off equally on either side from a central high point; this is called a (a)_____ curve. This curve has the characteristic shape of a (b)_____ and shows that most of the measurements fall near the center, with as many falling to one side as to the other. However, not all traits are distributed normally. If more data fall toward one side of the scale than toward the other, it is called a (c)_____ distribution. Such distributions do not have symmetrical shapes when plotted; instead, they have a "tail" on one end. When there are fewer frequencies at the higher end of the horizontal scale (the tail is on the right), we say the distribution is skewed to the right or has a (d)_____ skew. When there are fewer frequencies at the lower end of the horizontal scale (the tail is on the left), we say the distribution is skewed to the left or has a (e)_____ skew.

3. Ways of describing what is "typical" within a given distribution are called measures of (a)_____. The arithmetic average of all the individual measurements in a distribution is the (b)_____. The score above and below which half the scores in the distribution fall is the (c)_____. The measurement that occurs most often in a distribution is the (d)_____.

4. The extent to which scores in a distribution are spread out—in other words, how much scores vary from one another—is the measure of (a)_____. The two most extreme scores at either end of a distribution indicate the range. The measure of variability that shows how widely all the scores in a distribution are scattered above and below the mean is called the (b)_____.

INFERENTIAL STATISTICS

5. Because the influence of chance on scientific findings cannot be completely avoided, procedures are necessary to determine what conclusions can be properly inferred from a set of data; these procedures are called (a)_____ statistics. If the likelihood that the results could have occurred purely by chance is small, researchers can reject the chance explanation and conclude that their findings are probably (b)_____; that is, they would probably obtain similar results if they repeated the study over and over with different groups.

6. Different kinds of data require different tests of statistical significance. An estimate of reliability that takes the size of the mean difference and the variability in distributions into account is called the (a)_____; it estimates how reliable the difference between two means is. In general, the larger the difference between (b)_____, the less likely that it happened by chance alone.

7. A measure of the variability within two distributions is called the (a)_____. In general, the lower the variance, the less likely that chance alone caused the results. An analysis of variance, or (b)_____ test, is similar to, but more complex than, the *t* test.

8. How sure we can be that a distribution of events or of people did not happen just by chance is measured by another test of statistical significance, called the _____.

Answers: *1. (a) statistics, (b) descriptive, (c) frequency distribution; 2. (a) normal, (b) bell, (c) skewed, (d) positive, (e) negative; 3. (a) central tendency, (b) mean, (c) median, (d) mode; 4. (a) variability, (b) standard deviation; 5. (a) inferential, (b) reliable; 6. (a) t test, (b) mean difference; 7. (a) variance, (b) ANOVA; 8. chi-square.*

CRITICAL THINKING STUDY QUESTIONS WITH ANSWERS

Why Answer the Critical Thinking Study Questions?

As you read and study a module, you will learn new concepts, terms, and theories. We hope you will think about how you can apply these concepts to your own lives and to the problems and events in your own environment. To give you some practice, we have included answers to some of the Critical Thinking study questions that appear at the end of each module. Other kinds of questions may have a single correct answer, but study questions are open to a variety of interpretations. Answering them will help you learn to think about and discuss issues in greater depth.

Just as you must put extra effort into acquiring any complex skill, from tennis to algebra, you will have to exert yourself mentally to answer the study questions. To make the task easier, we have provided possible answers for selected questions. The first study question in each module is discussed in considerable detail to give you a strategy for answering other questions. Remember that our answers are only suggestions; you may think of other, equally good responses. If you use our answers as examples when you answer study questions on your own, you will acquire the very important skill of knowing how to apply concepts, terms, and theories to significant questions that often have no single correct answer. In fact, you will discover that many of the issues you face in the real world are very similar to the ones included here. When you have practiced answering our study questions, you will be better equipped to respond to related questions in your own life.

In this appendix we answer three to four study questions from each module. We always include a detailed response to the first question in each module and then suggest briefer answers to the following questions. As a result, you have an opportunity both to study a model for answering questions and to practice answering them more fully on your own.

At first you may find it difficult to answer study questions by yourself, but with practice you'll get the knack and actually find it fun to apply the concepts that you have learned. Remember, the more you stretch your mind by answering study questions, the bigger and stronger your mind will become. Unlike a balloon that bursts when expanded too far, your mind loves to be stretched and will never explode.

Rod Plotnik
Katie Townsend-Merino

Module 1
DISCOVERING PSYCHOLOGY

A. Definition & Goals

STUDY QUESTION: How would you rank the four goals of psychology in terms of importance?

1. *Need to Know:* What specific information do I need to answer this question?

I need to know the four goals of psychology: **describe, explain, predict, and control.**

2. *Defining Terms:* Do I need to use my own words to define or review any terms?

I need to define each of the four goals.

Describe: Psychologists want to describe in detail the particular behavior. What is the organism doing?

Explain: Psychologists want to explain why organisms behave in a particular way. What causes this behavior to occur?

Predict: Psychologists want to make predictions about how organisms will behave in the future. If I know something about the causes of a particular behavior, I can predict who will demonstrate that behavior.

Control: Psychologists want to control the behavior of an organism. This may allow for positive change in an individual's behavior.

3. *Identify Key Words:* Which words in the question hold the key to the best answer?

The key terms are "rank" and "importance." Both are dependent on the nature of a *particular* question. For example, if you are trying to understand what *causes* schizophrenia, the goals **describe** and **explain** would be ranked 1 and 2. However, if you want to *treat* or *prevent* schizophrenia, the goals **predict** and **control** would be ranked 1 and 2. Keep in mind, though, that it is impossible to predict and control without first describing and explaining!

D. Cultural Diversity: Early Discrimination

STUDY QUESTION: Why would discriminatory practices exist in psychology, an area devoted to studying human behavior?

Possible Answer: In our culture people can be privileged in a number of ways. Privilege by race (White), gender (male), and class (upper) are among the most common types of special status. Historically, advantaged groups have had a difficult time seeing that status differences are real, or they have attributed them to differences in abilities. The founders of psychology were themselves privileged and saw no harm in their beliefs regarding women and minorities. For example, being Black and female in the early days of psychology meant that you were doubly disadvantaged. Disadvantages took a number of forms: difficulties for a minority member in obtaining an education, problems finding work in academia, and being unemployable as a clinical psychologist.

H. Application: Study Skills

STUDY QUESTION: What changes would you make to study most efficiently?

Possible Answer: There is no simple relationship between the amount of time spent studying and the grades one receives. Study time is judged by its *quality* rather than its *quantity*.

In-class time must not be wasted. To make the most of it, I must keep my attention focused. I will ask myself questions during class, or I will participate in discussion when the opportunity arises. Note-taking in my own words demands more attention than direct dictation.

Good planning is the key to using study time efficiently. My plan will include specific goal setting, a realistic time schedule, and self-reinforcement. Such planning is *present-oriented* because it emphasizes getting down to work right away on tasks that will result in my meeting short-term goals. When I think, "How will I ever graduate?!" I'm looking beyond the here and now to do some rather destructive "global worrying."

When learning, I will focus on specific material and concepts, dividing the course into manageable chunks. I will do the self-tests that are contained in the text.

Module 2
PSYCHOLOGY & SCIENCE

A. Methods for Answering Questions

STUDY QUESTION: Which method would you use to find out if caffeine improves memory?

1. *Need to Know:* What specific information do I need to answer this question?

I need to know the methods for answering questions: **survey, case study,** and **experiment.**

I need to know the **advantages** and **disadvantages** of each method.

2. *Defining Terms:* Do I need to use my own words to define or review any terms? Do I know the advantages and disadvantages of each?

I need to define each of the methods and list the advantages and disadvantages.

Survey: This is a way to get information by asking people directly to respond to a set of questions. This can be done in person, over the phone, or through the mail. An advantage is that you can easily get a lot of information relatively quickly, but it may be biased in accord with the beliefs and truthfulness of the respondents.

Case study: This is a way to get information by studying a particular individual in depth. You get a lot of information about one person, but this information may not apply to anyone else.

Experiment: This is a way to get information in a controlled environment so you can systematically manipulate treatments and measure their effects on behavior. You can identify cause-and-effect relationships, but information gained in a controlled environment may not apply in the real world.

3. *Identify Key Words:* Which words in the question hold the key to the best answer?

The key terms are "caffeine" and "improves memory." Although you might get interesting stories using the survey approach, your data would not be particularly valuable: it would be distorted by error and bias. That is, the placebo effect might be strong in this case. If you used the case-study method, you would learn a lot about the relationship between one individual's memory response and caffeine. But you would not know whether that information applied to anyone else. The best method of assessing cause-and-effect relationships ("Does caffeine cause memory improvement?") is to do an experiment. You could have two groups of students tested on the same material. Before the test, one group would drink a cup of caffeinated coffee and the other would drink one cup of decaffeinated coffee. You would then compare their test performances. This method would provide the most accurate answer to this question.

D. Cultural Diversity: Use of Placebos

STUDY QUESTION: Why do Americans think it strange that Asians use rhino horn as medicine?

Possible Answer: Belief is the most important factor in generating the placebo effect. In some Asian cultures there is a strong belief that rhino horn is an aphrodisiac and a potent medicine. Therefore, there is a high incidence of rhino horn treatments available in those countries. In the United States, we hold no beliefs about the medicinal value of rhino horn and recognize it as a placebo. Therefore, we regard those who use rhino horn as strange! But Americans do not regard taking Vitamin C as unusual, because we believe it has medicinal value.

F. Decisions about Doing Research

STUDY QUESTION: Which research techniques and settings would you use to study mental problems in the homeless?

Possible Answer: To decide on the best way of answering this question, let's look at each of the methods at our disposal and assess their utility.

Questionnaires and interviews. We could interview people who live in homeless shelters or on the street about their mental conditions. We could also talk to people who work with the homeless, asking their opinions about mental illness and the homeless.

Standardized tests. We could administer tests designed to detect different kinds of mental illness to homeless individuals. This might give us information about the prevalence and type of mental illness in that population.

Laboratory experiment: behaviors. It would be impossible to do a true experiment on this question. You cannot randomly assign someone to homelessness or mental illness. It would be difficult to get homeless people to a laboratory setting. You could possibly assess the effects of treatments for mental illness on the homeless.

Laboratory experiment: physiological and genetic techniques. Again, it may be difficult to get homeless individuals to a laboratory. If you could, you might be able to compare brain structure and function in the mentally ill and the non-mentally ill homeless.

Module 3
BRAIN'S BUILDING BLOCKS

A. Overview: Human Brain

STUDY QUESTION: Why is it really smart to drive a car only if it is equipped with driver- and passenger-side airbags?

1. *Need to Know:* What specific information do I need to answer this question?

I need to know the advantages of airbags and to relate them to the information regarding the brain provided in this module.

2. *Defining Terms:* Do I need to use my own words to define or review any terms?

I need to know that airbags reduce the incidence of head injury in auto accidents.

3. *Identify Key Words:* Which words in the question hold the key to the best answer?

The key terms are "really smart to drive only." In the context of the current module, we should focus on the fact that airbags can help prevent head injuries during auto accidents. Severe blows to the head during a traffic accident can damage neurons in the brain and spine. Because mature primate brains are capable of very little growth of new neurons, such damage is usually permanent.

This is very serious, because the brain controls almost all of our most important functions. So airbags are advantageous because they might help prevent irreversible damage to the brain.

D. Sending Information

STUDY QUESTION: How are the structure and function of the axon like those of a battery?

Possible Answer: Both batteries and neurons must generate electrical impulses. They both achieve this by transforming chemical energy into electrical energy. Like batteries, neurons get their potential to generate electrical impulses from an imbalance between positive and negative charges. When the barrier between these charges is removed, positive and negative charges are attracted to each other like opposite poles of magnets. In a battery, a built-up charge is released when a connection is made between the negative and positive terminals. In the axon, the barrier between positive and negative ions is broken when the axon membrane becomes permeable.

Once the charge has been spent, both batteries and neurons must be recharged. For the neuron, this involves pumping the positively charged sodium ions back outside the axon membrane, which returns to its semipermeable state.

H. Cultural Diversity: Plants, Drugs, & Transmitters

STUDY QUESTION: What are the different ways that drugs can affect neurotransmitters?

Possible Answer: Some of the ways drugs can affect neurotransmitters are by blocking reuptake, blocking receptors, and mimicking neurotransmitters. A drug like cocaine blocks the process of reuptake, so that the neurotransmitter stays in the synapse and continues to activate the receiving neuron. Other drugs block the receptors on the receiving neuron by occupying the receptor sites, which prevents the neurotransmitter from relaying its message. Finally, some drugs, such as mescaline, actually mimic one of the brain's natural neurotransmitters. These drugs bind to receptor sites, thereby activating neurons.

Module 4
INCREDIBLE NERVOUS SYSTEM

A. Genes & Evolution

STUDY QUESTION: If a species of humans with 5-pound brains was discovered, would their behavior differ from ours?

1. Need to Know: What specific information do I need to answer this question?

I need to know how much an average human brain weighs. Furthermore, I must know how much our ancestors' brains weighed on average.

2. Identify Key Words: Which words in the question hold the key to the best answer?

The key terms are "would their behavior differ from ours?" In the context of the current module, we see that our brain has already tripled in size since the time of our earliest known ancestors. It is believed that these early humans did not make tools, make fire, or use language. Later, humans with a brain twice as large as our earliest ancestors' walked upright and made precise tools. By the time the human brain was as large as ours today, our ancestors were growing crops, living in communities, developing language, and painting representations of animals and humans. It seems that large changes in brain size are associated with large changes in human capabilities and behaviors. If we had 5-pound brains, our behavior would probably be very different. *How* different is impossible to predict. Much science fiction has been written on this topic.

B. Studying the Living Brain

STUDY QUESTION: How would you know if a professional boxer had brain damage?

Possible Answer: If the behavior or capabilities of this boxer have changed in ways that make us suspect brain damage, we could examine the brain using one or more imaging techniques.

Computerized axial tomography—CAT scan. We could take a sophisticated x-ray of the patient's brain to check for possible abnormalities. This would give us video images that represented slices of the brain. In this way, we could penetrate brain tissue to search for possible causes of the changes in the boxer's behavior.

Magnetic resonance imaging—MRI. We could penetrate farther into the boxer's brain with a device that sends nonharmful magnetic fields and radio frequencies through it. This gives us more detailed and clearer pictures and, unlike the CAT scan, does not expose the patient to radiation.

Positron emission tomography—PET scan. PET scans allow us to analyze brain function by providing a video image whose colors correspond to various levels of brain activity and abnormality. In our diagnosis of the boxer, we could compare these images to PET scans of age- and gender-matched controls to see if there are any *functional* differences.

H. Cultural Diversity: Brain Size & Racial Myths

STUDY QUESTION: Why is there a continuing interest in whether a bigger brain is more intelligent?

Possible Answer: Scientists might hope for a relationship between brain size and intelligence for a number of reasons. First of all, brain size is measurable, and thus we would have another quantifiable indicator of intelligence, of which there are precious few. Second, individuals' brain sizes can be quite easily compared. Group comparisons of intelligence have always intrigued science, though their usefulness to society has been questioned.

Other reasons have more to do with historical sociology than psychology. For example, Marx might have said that finding consistent differences in brain size that correlate with intelligence would be of interest to the ruling class, as a means of maintaining the status quo. An individual's ticket to aristocracy would be an MRI.

Finally, racism and sexism may play a part in the continuing interest in establishing differences. If such a measure were found to be reliably true, some would argue that, because their brains are somewhat smaller, women cannot be regarded as men's equal in intelligence.

Module 5
SENSATION

A. Eye: Vision

STUDY QUESTION: What kinds of problems in the visual system could result in some forms of blindness?

1. Need to Know: What specific information do I need to answer this question?

I need to know: the structure and function of the parts of the eye; how light gets to the retina; how the light is transformed into a neural message; and the pathway that the neural message takes to the brain.

2. Identify Key Words: Which words in the question hold the key to the best answer?

The key terms are "problems in the visual system" and "result in . . . blindness." In order to effectively answer this question, we need to examine the entire process of normal vision and to imagine all the possible ways that this process could be interrupted.

Let's examine the structure and function of the eye. First, we see that if the cornea or lens is damaged or occluded, the light waves cannot reach the retina, and vision cannot occur. If the retina or any of its cells are damaged, the light waves cannot be transformed into neural messages that are sent to the brain; in other words, there can be no vision.

Second, if any part of the optic nerve is damaged, the neural messages cannot be sent to the brain. Damage to the part of the thalamus responsible for sending messages about vision to the occipital lobe would also cause blindness.

Finally, if an individual sustains damage to the primary visual cortex or the association cortex, either total or partial blindness would occur.

B. Ear: Audition

STUDY QUESTION: What kinds of problems in the auditory system could result in some form of deafness?

Possible Answer: If we examine the structure of the auditory system, we can see where problems could occur that would result in some form of deafness. First, if the tympanic membrane lost flexibility (as sometimes occurs in children with frequent ear infections), the vibrations could lose strength and fail to be transmitted to the ossicles, which would prevent those sound vibrations from reaching the cochlea. Second, if any of the ossicles became calcified or fused together, sound vibrations would again be stopped before reaching the cochlea. These types of damage result in conduction deafness.

In the event of damage to any part of the cochlea, particularly the hair cells, the vibrations would not be changed into nerve impulses that are sent to the brain. Consequently, no sound would be heard. If there is any damage to the auditory nerve, the primary auditory cortex, or the auditory association areas, various types of nerve deafness will occur.

D. Chemical Senses

STUDY QUESTION: How might a master chef's chemical senses differ from your own?

Possible Answer: It makes sense that a master chef would have a particularly acute sense of taste. The number of taste buds on the human tongue varies widely from individual to individual. Very likely, the tongue of a master chef would have more taste buds than the average person's. Also, because flavor is actually the combination of taste and smell, a master chef might have a very sensitive sense of smell (olfaction). It's reasonable to guess that a master chef could distinguish very subtle differences in flavor that the average person could not.

Module 6
PERCEPTION

A. Perceptual Thresholds

STUDY QUESTION: How does Weber's law apply to how old you perceive someone to be?

1. *Need to Know:* What specific information do I need to answer this question?

I need to know what Weber's law states and what a "just noticeable difference" is.

2. *Defining Terms:* Do I need to use my own words to define or review any terms?

I need to define *just noticeable difference* and Weber's law.

Just noticeable difference (JND): The smallest increase or decrease in the intensity of a stimulus that a person can manage to detect.

Weber's law: This law states that the amount of increase in a stimulus needed to provide a just noticeable difference grows with the intensity of the stimulus.

3. *Identify Key Words:* Which words in the question hold the key to the best answer?

The key term is "how old you perceive someone to be." When people are babies, just a few months make a huge difference in how old we perceive them to be. As humans age, the increase in time before someone looks older becomes longer; it may even be many years. For example, it might take five or more years before someone of 60 looks older to us, while if we saw a child at three it might take only six months before the child looks different. This follows directly from Weber's law. If the person's age is the stimulus, Weber's law says that the change in the person's age that we are able to notice increases with increase in intensity of the stimulus—that is, as the person gets older.

B. Sensation versus Perception

STUDY QUESTION: What would your life be like if your brain could receive sensations but could not assemble them into perceptions?

Possible Answer: Sensations are just the bits of information that we first become aware of from an outside stimulus. The receptors have transformed the stimulus into a neural impulse that the brain can understand. However, without perception, those neural impulses have *no meaning*. For example, if you had no ability to form visual perceptions, you would be aware that something was out there in the environment, but you would not be able to know or to tell anyone what it was.

If you lost *all* your perceptual abilities, you would be extremely disadvantaged; in fact, the world would cease to have meaning. You would be unable to form a relationship with the world.

H. Cultural Diversity: Different Perceptions

STUDY QUESTION: When foreigners visit the United States, what do you think they perceive differently?

Possible Answer: It is very difficult to answer this question because the way we perceive our own world is invisible to us. However what is normal in one culture may be abnormal in another. For example, it may seem weird to us that women in India cover their heads. But, to Indians, it is the custom. So to answer this question, we have to step outside ourselves and our culture.

The new visitor might notice that American teenagers are more heavily monitored by their parents than are teenagers in Europe. It is normal in many European countries for adolescents of 16 to smoke, drink, and dance the night away (with no curfew) at the local discos.

Module 7
CONSCIOUSNESS, SLEEP, & DREAMS

A. Continuum of Consciousness

STUDY QUESTION: How many different states of consciousness have you been in today?

1. *Need to Know:* What specific information do I need to answer this question?

I need to know what the different states of consciousness are.

The states of consciousness include controlled processes, automatic processes, daydreaming, altered states of consciousness, sleep and dreams, the unconscious, and unconsciousness.

2. *Defining Terms:* Do I need to use my own words to define or review any terms?

I need to define each of the states of consciousness.

Controlled processes: These activities require our full awareness and concentration to complete. Usually we cannot perform other tasks at the same time.

Automatic processes: These tasks (eating, driving, listening to the radio) are performed on autopilot and can be done in conjunction with other activities.

Daydreaming: This occurs with very low levels of awareness and often *during* automatic processes. In this state, we are fantasizing or imagining while we are awake.

Altered states of consciousness: We experience these states under the influence of an external source or technique, such as meditation, psychoactive drugs, sleep deprivation, or hypnosis.

Sleep and dreams: During **sleep,** we go through five different stages of awareness and consciousness. When we **dream,** we experience visual and auditory images, both in black-and-white and in color.

The unconscious: Freud's theory of the unconscious says that when we experience something threatening (sexual or aggressive events or thoughts), we put these in a place in our mind that cannot be accessed during ordinary recall. The updated theory of the **cognitive unconscious** says that a mental structure of which we are unaware influences our conscious behaviors and thoughts.

Unconsciousness: This refers to a state in which we are completely unaware and unresponsive, most often as a result of a head injury, disease, or surgical anesthesia.

3. *Identify Key Words:* Which words in the question hold the key to the best answer?

The key terms are "How many . . . states . . . have you been in today?" Simply review what you have learned about the different states and apply it to what you have experienced so far today.

D. Research Focus: Circadian Preference

STUDY QUESTION: What kind of problems might arise if a morning person married an evening person?

Possible Answer: The lifestyles of these two people are likely to be quite different. The morning person would wake up early and get a number of things accomplished in the morning. She or he would eat a large breakfast before beginning the day. The evening partner would probably be annoyed by all this early activity. She or he would wake up later, skip breakfast (or eat lightly), and not feel like beginning the day's activities until the afternoon or evening. During the evening, when the night owl still had energy to spare, the early bird would be wound down and ready for bed. This couple would need to understand that their differences in this regard are innate and that

one style is not superior to the other. They would need to compromise and have realistic expectations (which is difficult for any of us!).

F. Cultural Diversity: Incidence of SAD

STUDY QUESTION: What cultural values might New York residents have that contribute to their incidence of SAD?

Possible Answer: This question is difficult to answer for those of us who have never been to New York. The answer given here is based purely on film and TV portrayals of New Yorkers, which are probably full of stereotypes.

Icelanders appear to have lower expectations of the good life than do New Yorkers. When New Yorkers' expectations are not met, depression may be one outcome. Also, the text reports that Icelanders tend not to complain. In New York, complaining is more socially acceptable and, in fact, may be a lifestyle itself. Complaining may cause New Yorkers to dwell on problems that might trigger SAD. Further, if New Yorkers have fewer support systems than do Icelanders, that would also contribute to the higher incidence of SAD. (It also seems possible that there could be fewer people who are susceptible to SAD in Iceland—from an evolutionary perspective. New York is a city of immigrants from all over the world.)

Module 8
HYPNOSIS & DRUGS

A. Hypnosis

STUDY QUESTION: A student has great test anxiety, which is interfering with his success in college. Would hypnosis help?

1. *Need to Know:* What specific information do I need to answer this question?

I need to know what type of hypnotic tool I could use and whether hypnosis helps with relaxation.

I could give the student a posthypnotic suggestion to be relaxed during test taking.

2. *Identify Key Words:* Which words in the question hold the key to the best answer?

The key terms are "would hypnosis help [with test anxiety]?" I know from the text that I can give a posthypnotic suggestion, and the text further reports that hypnosis appears to relieve tension. So, in this case hypnosis might be worth a try—if my student is susceptible.

F. Alcohol

STUDY QUESTION: If researchers know who has an increased risk for alcoholism, at what age should such a person be told?

Possible Answer: Before we tell people that they are at increased risk for any condition, we must have clear evidence that a risk exists. What is the evidence that we can confidently predict increased risk for alcoholism when someone is still in childhood?

Environmental and genetic risk factors can be reliably identified in childhood. For example, an adoption study has shown that babies born to alcoholic parents are three or four times more likely to become alcoholics than are babies born to nonalcoholics. There are also some environmental risk factors associated with growing up in a home in which the parents are alcoholic: specifically, children can learn to turn to alcohol as a way of coping with problems. In addition, they may learn different norms regarding how much alcohol consumption is appropriate, or where and when it is appropriate to consume alcohol.

What are the possible benefits of telling children that they are at risk? It might act as an early warning, alerting children that they should exercise extreme caution when consuming alcohol. This might reduce the likelihood that they will become alcoholics.

Are there any reasons why we shouldn't tell children that they are at risk? We should bear in mind that children of different ages have different levels of comprehension. Our warning would be lost on young children, who could not understand the notion of a risk much later in their lives. Adolescents might benefit from the warning, but we would have to be careful not to make the risk seem thrilling. Telling some people that they are at risk for something actually increases the likelihood that they will bring it on; the warning becomes a self-fulfilling prophecy. We would also have to be careful to accompany our warning with clear advice on how the risk can be lowered.

Given all this, we can state the following guidelines about informing children of their risk for alcoholism. Don't bring up the idea before the child is old enough to understand the notion of long-term risk. If talking with adolescents, don't make the notion of risk sound attractive to thrill seekers. Finally, be sure to accompany the warning with clear advice regarding how the risk can be reduced.

H. Marijuana

STUDY QUESTION: A regular user of marijuana says that he can drive just fine after smoking. Would you ride with him?

Possible Answer: Only if I was driving. Otherwise, *no way!*

This person is overlooking a number of factors. The most obvious is that marijuana acts as a depressant: it decreases reaction time, judgment, and the use of peripheral vision. In addition, larger dosages can produce time and perceptual distortions and hallucinations, none of which are conducive to the safe operation of heavy machinery, such as a car.

Module 9
CLASSICAL CONDITIONING

A. Three Kinds of Learning

STUDY QUESTION: Can you recall situations in which you have experienced each of the three kinds of learning?

1. *Need to Know:* What specific information do I need to answer this question?

I need to know what the three types of learning are.

They are classical conditioning, operant conditioning, and cognitive learning.

2. *Defining Terms:* Do I need to use my own words to define or review any terms?

Classical conditioning: This kind of learning involves *involuntary* responses. A neutral stimulus is paired with an unconditioned stimulus, so that the response that occurred to the unconditioned stimulus now occurs to what was the neutral stimulus (which is now called the conditioned stimulus).

Operant conditioning: This kind of learning involves *voluntary* behavior. The responses that follow a behavior will either increase or decrease the likelihood of that behavior's recurrence.

Cognitive learning: This kind of learning involves our mental processes. A behavior can be learned through observation or imitation.

3. *Identify Key Words:* Which words in the question hold the key to the best answer?

The key terms are "you have experienced." Since we all have learned something in these three ways, you just need to come up with a personal example for each learning method.

B. Procedure: Classical Conditioning

STUDY QUESTION: How do you explain why your heart pounds when you hear the words "There will be a test next time"?

Possible Answer: In this example, the pounding heart would be considered a *conditioned response.* (In fact, it's a *conditioned emotional response.*) The heart is stimulated to beat faster by the sympathetic nervous system when danger is perceived. In this case, the teacher's words are perceived to be anxiety provoking (or "dangerous") because of learning that has taken place via classical conditioning.

The words "There will be a test next time" constitute the conditioned stimulus. We know this is a conditioned stimulus because words are not inherently dangerous. Also, someone who has never taken a test and, therefore, has had no opportunity to be conditioned would not experience the same change in heart rate.

H. Application: Conditioned Fear & Nausea

STUDY QUESTION: How would systematic desensitization be used to help reduce a student's test anxiety?

Possible Answer: I would use the three steps of the systematic desensitization procedure to help reduce the test anxiety in a student. (To avoid the complication of saying "he or she," I'll assume, arbitrarily, that the student is female.) First, she must learn how to relax intentionally. I would teach her to tense and relax all the muscles in her body from her toes to her head. The student must practice this for 15–20 minutes every day for several weeks before we could proceed. The second step would be for this student to make up a list of 7–12 stressful situations associated with test taking and to rank them from least to most stressful. Finally, my student friend would put herself in a deeply relaxed state and vividly imagine the least stressful situation. At the first sign of stress, I would stop her and have her put herself in a deeply relaxed state again. She would then begin imagining the situation again until she could continue without becoming stressed. When she had mastered that stressful situation, we would move up the hierarchy to the next stressful scenario. In this way, she would move all the way up her hierarchy until she could actually take a test with reduced anxiety.

Module 10
OPERANT & COGNITIVE APPROACHES

A. Operant Conditioning

STUDY QUESTION: How do you explain why your significant other sulks every time something is wrong even though you've told him or her that it bugs you?

1. Need to Know: What specific information do I need to answer this question?

I need to know why people persist in a particular behavior.

BICOC: behavior is contingent on consequences. This is the essence of operant conditioning.

2. Defining Terms: Do I need to use my own words to define or review any terms?

BICOC: This means that someone performs or does not perform a specific behavior because of the consequences that will follow. If the consequence is a reinforcer, the person will likely repeat the behavior. If the consequence is a punisher, the person will not repeat that behavior.

Operant conditioning: This kind of learning involves voluntary behavior. The responses that follow a behavior will either increase or decrease the likelihood of that behavior's recurrence.

3. Identify Key Words: Which words in the question hold the key to the best answer?

The key terms are "explain why [the person] sulks." From understanding the concepts involved, it is clear that whatever I am doing when my partner sulks is reinforcing that behavior. I need to change my behavior before my partner's behavior will change.

B. Reinforcers

STUDY QUESTION: How would you use operant conditioning to change a rude friend into a more likable and friendly person?

Possible Answer: This question asks me to design a program that **shapes** my friend toward a desired **goal**, that of polite behavior. In order to do this operantly, I must find a relevant reinforcer for my friend. If my friend does not like people very much, that might be difficult. However, I'll assume that anyone likes the company of another as long as it is pleasant and the attention the person receives is positive.

This means that the reinforcer in this case will be that positive attention my friend receives from others. One way to accomplish this is to enlist the help of my other friends. I'll tell them to give this positive attention in the form of smiles, compliments, and general concerned attention whenever my friend exhibits the desired behaviors.

If I'm going to shape my friend, then I will have to move him or her gradually away from rude behavior toward more polite, likable behavior. I cannot simply wait for the desired final behavior before giving any reinforcement. In the beginning of the program, my other friends must be instructed to provide reinforcement whenever my problematic friend is in their company and not being rude. This might mean reinforcing him or her for just standing quietly.

From there, my friends must become more particular in the criteria they use for giving reinforcement. They will wait until the friend does or says something that is polite or pleasant. For example, if the friend asks someone how she is today, the person must respond very positively and ask after his or her welfare as well. If the friend offers to get someone a cup of coffee or help carry something, that must be reinforced strongly as well.

If this program works, my friend will learn that rude behavior gets him or her ignored, whereas polite, considerate behavior leads to social rewards in the form of pleasant attention from others. This program won't be easy to put into practice, because rude behavior is hard to ignore, and it makes people less interested in persevering to find polite behavior in the person. Still, people can be shaped by the social reinforcement they receive.

H. Cultural Diversity: East Meets West

STUDY QUESTION: Why do the same principles of learning work in very different cultures?

Possible Answer: Actually, this shows that learning principles come close to being laws of human nature, just like the laws of physics or chemistry. There is no reason why these principles *should* be different in other cultures. What is learned varies—for example, using a fork and knife or using chopsticks. It is also true that what an individual perceives as a reinforcer or punisher varies between cultures. However, once we know what is reinforcing to an individual, we can use that reinforcer to increase the likelihood that a response will occur again. Social mores are culturally dependent; the principles of learning are not.

Module 11
TYPES OF MEMORY

A. Three Types of Memory

STUDY QUESTION: Why does seeing an ambulance speed by remind you of your father's heart attack and his trip to the hospital?

1. Need to Know: What specific information do I need to answer this question?

I need to know what processes are involved in memory formation and retrieval.

The basic process is sensory memory to short-term memory to long-term memory.

2. Defining Terms: Do I need to use my own words to define or review any terms?

Sensory memory. Visual images are stored here for a quarter of a second or more, and auditory images last for about two seconds.

Short-term memory. If we attend to information, we can hold it for about 30 seconds in the working memory.

Long-term memory. Unlimited amounts of information can be held here for an unlimited amount of time. This information can go back and forth between long-term memory and short-term memory.

3. Identify Key Words: Which words in the question hold the key to the best answer?

The key terms are "why does seeing an ambulance remind you?"

The visual and probably also auditory image of the ambulance was put into my short-term memory and, while exploring ambulance-related thoughts from my long-term memory, I stumbled upon an emotional memory related to my father's heart attack.

F. Encoding: Transferring

STUDY QUESTION: Why is it important that teachers make learning interesting and meaningful?

Possible Answer: Most of what you learn and need to remember from teachers requires that you use **effortful encoding.** You have to work hard to transfer information from short-term to long-term memory either by using **maintenance rehearsal** or by making new associations. We know from research that simple maintenance rehearsal results in reduced retention and retrieval. When teachers make material *interesting* to you, you pay attention, which in itself makes it more likely you will remember—because the information got through the first process in memory. When teachers make the material *meaningful,* it means something to you individually, and you can connect this information to other information in your memory. By **making associations** between this new learning and previous learning, you will process this meaningful information at the deepest **level of processing.** Thus, you will have the best retention and recall for information learned in this manner.

H. Cultural Diversity: Oral versus Written

STUDY QUESTION: How might playing video games affect a child's encoding process?

Possible Answer: The text points out that we in the United States spend most of our time encoding information with words—by reading and writing—and that we excel at retrieving information in that form. But individuals in cultures with a strong oral tradition excel at retrieval of information that they have heard. This suggests that using a particular form of encoding over a period of time may improve your recall for information encoded in that way. Video games are organized around visual images. Children who play them get a lot of practice at encoding visual-spatial images. It seems likely that children who play video games would have better recall for visual-spatial information than do children (or adults) who do not play video games.

Module *12*
REMEMBERING & FORGETTING

A. Organization of Memories

STUDY QUESTION: How would your memory be affected if you accidentally took a drug that prevented the formation of any new nodes?

1. *Need to Know:* What specific information do I need to answer this question?

I need to know what a node is and how it relates to memory formation.

2. *Defining Terms:* Do I need to use my own words to define or review any terms?

Node: A node is a memory file in which information is organized around a specific topic.

Memory process and nodes: Nodes are linked to one another in a hierarchy.

3. *Identify Key Words:* Which words in the question hold the key to the best answer?

The key terms are "memory be affected" and "stopped the formation of any new nodes." Probably the nature of the memory damage would be related to the age at which I took this drug. Presuming I'm an adult when this happens, I would appear normal much of the time because I would already have had time to form many hundreds (thousands) of nodes. But I would be unable to learn any new concepts. I would have to try and fit any new information into an already existing node. This would greatly impair the sophistication of my network hierarchy.

D. Biological Bases of Memory

STUDY QUESTION: If a virus suddenly destroyed your hippocampus, what effect would it have on your performance in college?

Possible Answer: The hippocampus is crucial for transferring semantic information and episodic information from short-term to long-term memory. However, it is not involved in the processing of procedural information—for example, motor skills.

Therefore, my performance in English would be impaired because I would not be able to encode details from what I read into long-term memory. Thus, it would be impossible for me to discuss a novel I read because I could not remember its plot. I would also have great difficulty in mathematics. The rules for solving quadratic equations or finding the area under a curve wouldn't be in long-term memory when I needed them.

My physical education class would be a slightly different story. I would not lose my motor skills, so if I had been a talented athlete before losing my hippocampus, I would still be one after losing it. My coordination would not be affected. However, if I had played a sport in which there were any rule changes after my hippocampus had been destroyed, I would have to be reminded of them all the time because I would not be able to encode them.

H. Application: Eyewitness Testimony

STUDY QUESTION: If you were on a jury, what concerns would you have when listening to eyewitness testimony?

Possible Answer: Most jurors regard eyewitness testimony as a very important form of evidence, yet it is prone to biases and errors. If I were on a jury, I would listen carefully to the way the lawyers phrased their questions to the witnesses because, as the textbook points out, this phrasing can influence the witnesses' testimony.

I would remember that witnesses are often not completely sure of the accuracy of their accounts. This makes them susceptible to influence. So if the lawyer used an especially strong verb, such as "smashed," to describe a collision, the witness might tend to give a higher estimate of the vehicle's speed. The lawyer can also introduce potentially false information as background to a question, so that the witness will verify that information at a later time.

Witnesses are often trying to recall events they experienced under considerable emotional duress. Thus, encoding the information must have been difficult in the first place. Now, under more duress on the witness stand, the person is expected to recall with accuracy something that occurred as an emotional blur perhaps six months or a year ago.

Finally, I would try hard to remember that there is no correlation between the accuracy of an eyewitness's testimony and the person's confidence in that accuracy. So when a lawyer asks a witness if she is sure she is right, the fact that the witness answers yes does not verify the accuracy of the testimony.

Module 13
INTELLIGENCE

A. Defining Intelligence

STUDY QUESTION: How intelligent was Ray Kroc, who never finished high school but started the world-famous McDonald's hamburger chain?

1. Need to Know: What specific information do I need to answer this question?

I need to know the different ways intelligence is defined.

Intelligence has been defined in three ways: using a two-factor approach; using Gardner's theory of multiple intelligences; and using Sternberg's triarchic theory.

2. Defining Terms: Do I need to use my own words to define or review any terms?

Two-factor theory: This theory of intelligence says that there is a general factor, *g*, that represents a person's ability to perform complex mental functions. Standard IQ tests are presumed to measure *g*.

A second factor, *s*, measures specific mental skills such as mathematical skills and verbal skills.

Theory of multiple intelligences: This theory concludes that there are seven kinds of intelligence: verbal, musical, logical-mathematical, spatial, body movement, understanding oneself, and understanding others.

Triarchic Theory: This theory concludes that there are three kinds of intelligence: analytical and logical thinking; the ability to deal creatively with new situations and learn from experience; and the ability to use practical skills to adjust to one's sociocultural environment.

3. Identify Key Words: Which words in the question hold the key to the best answer?

The key terms are "how intelligent was Ray Kroc?" The answer to this question lies in the way we define intelligence. We could try comparing Ray Kroc to Albert Einstein using each approach.

Two-factor approach: There are two basic tenets to this approach. First, intelligence can be quantified in the form of tests, most notably the IQ test. Second, there is a general trait called intelligence, *g*, that is supplemented by a few specific abilities, *s*. In this approach, if Albert Einstein scored higher on an IQ test than Ray Kroc, he would be considered more intelligent.

Multiple-intelligence approach: Gardner also considers intelligence to be quantifiable, but not into one composite score. Instead, he considers intelligence to be multidimensional: there are many different kinds of intelligence. It may be that Ray Kroc would have scored very high on measures of insight about others and verbal skills, whereas Einstein would have scored higher on math skills. Using this approach, we would not talk about one person being more intelligent than another; rather (provided some skills were demonstrated), we'd say the individuals had different kinds of intelligence.

Triarchic approach: According to this approach, intelligence should not be defined by how much you know, but by how you came to know it. In other words, *thinking skills*—logic, problem-solving, and practicality—are the hallmark of intelligence. It could be assumed that both Kroc and Einstein had impressive problem-solving skills, though some might want to debate which man was working on the more complex problems. Certainly, it is hard to build a business empire without some ability to think practically. Einstein's thinking could stay at a very abstract level, which does not necessitate practicality. Again, this approach does not make comparisons between people in terms of a global trait called intelligence. Rather, the emphasis is on the way the person thinks.

D. Potential Problems of IQ Testing

STUDY QUESTION: Should we use IQ scores to assign the growing number of students from different cultures to grade levels?

Possible Answer: First of all, unless IQ tests were also being used to assess nonminority students' grade levels (which they are not), the possibility should not even be considered. However, for the sake of discussion, let's assume that IQ tests are used to place children into grade levels. Given that, the question is whether IQ tests are a good means of deciding at which grade level a child should be placed.

Experience (for example, the story of Larry described in the text) leads us to predict that if IQ tests were used as the sole criterion for placement, minority students would be overrepresented at the lower levels and underrepresented at the upper levels. This would mean that, at each grade level, the average age of minority children would be higher than that of nonminority children. This is due, in no small part, to the **cultural bias** in most IQ tests.

The problem, then, is that IQ tests are not valid criteria for placement; rather, they are *discriminatory*. The conclusion would be to avoid the use of IQ tests as the sole criterion for placement. Perhaps the best strategy is to use a number of criteria, including past academic performance and the child's behaviors both in and out of the classroom.

H. Application: Intervention Programs

STUDY QUESTION: Since the Head Start program fails to raise IQ scores over the long run, should its financial support be reduced?

Possible Answer: This is another question that probes the value of IQ scores in decision-making—in this case, in evaluating the efficacy of the intervention program Head Start.

It is true that Head Start has not yielded long-term changes in children's IQs. However, research quite clearly indicates other very tangible benefits of the program. The text cites research demonstrating that the Head Start children were less likely to repeat classes and less likely to show antisocial or delinquent behavior. People who had been in the Head Start program were more likely to be holding jobs.

Research has also shown that the program has benefited other family members. Mothers of children who had been in the program reported fewer psychological symptoms, greater feelings of mastery, and greater current life satisfaction.

Given all the problems in assessing what an IQ score really means, it should not be used as the sole measure of a program's success. The Head Start program should not be dropped.

Module *14*
THOUGHT & LANGUAGE

A. Forming Concepts

STUDY QUESTION: Why is it difficult to explain to your younger sister or brother that a whale is a mammal and not a fish?

1. Need to Know: What specific information do I need to answer this question?

I need to know how people form concepts like "fish" and "mammal."

The two theories of concept formation are **definition theory** and **prototype theory.**

2. Defining Terms: Do I need to use my own words to define or review any terms?

Definition theory: This theory suggests that we make a concept by listing all the properties that define it.

Prototype theory: This theory says we form a concept by forming a prototype, which is a mental picture of an average example of the thing we are defining.

3. Identify Key Words: Which words in the question hold the key to the best answer?

The key terms are "difficult to explain . . . that a whale is a mammal and not a fish." The answer to this question lies in the way we form concepts. Let's look at the two different approaches in terms of whales.

Definition theory helps us understand why your younger sister (provided she is quite young) might have difficulty understanding that a whale is not a fish. The problem is that a whale and a fish share many common **defining properties:** they both swim in water; they both have similar shapes; they have similar tails; and so on. In fact, the property that defines a whale as a mammal—the fact that it gives birth to its young—is not readily apparent to a young child.

You might have more success taking a **prototype** approach. With this approach, you would show the child a picture of a typical whale—one that was an average of most whale types. Perhaps a killer whale would be a good prototype. This would lead the child to the rather straightforward and often-correct conclusion that whales are larger than fish. The disadvantage, of course, is that you haven't really taught the child what a mammal is.

F. Reason, Thought, & Language

STUDY QUESTION: What problems might result when heads of governments speak through translators?

Possible Answer: The text explores the different ways a person can think depending on which language the person is using. This reminds us that there is more to language than mere words; language is inextricably tied to culture. Not only are there words that exist in one language but not in another; there are also *ideas* that are not shared across cultures. This means that *literal translations* often lack clarity and, in fact, can be misunderstood.

To be a translator is difficult, therefore, when words and concepts encountered in one language do not have equivalents in another. For example, to call someone "a character" in English does not translate well into French. The French might use a word like "type" (pronounced "teep") to describe an unusual or eccentric person. In English we would use "type" to describe certain personalities, like "the nervous type" or "the outgoing type."

We can see how potentially dangerous translation can become when applied to something as important as diplomatic relations and communication. Translators must have a very good working knowledge of the nuances of both languages and the way words are used in each cultural context.

H. Cultural Diversity: Power of Words

STUDY QUESTION: What kinds of social problems can arise from finding differences between male and female brains?

Possible Answer: In an ideal world, the fact that there are gender differences in the brain should not cause any social dissension. Historically, though, we have seen that differences (for example, in skin color, genitalia, presumed brain size, IQ) have been used to imply that one is better than another. So, instead of a "different but equal" philosophy, we see attitudes that "mine is better than yours" or "you can't play with me."

One problem is that when most people hear about gender differences, they assume that all males are different from all females, when, in fact, there is a huge overlap. For example, there is a gender difference in height, but this *doesn't* mean that all males are taller than all females. These false beliefs may translate into social policy that would unfairly discriminate against people because of their gender and not because of their individual abilities. A woman who is applying to be an air traffic controller might be told, "Well, women have a smaller amount of brain area devoted to visual-spatial skills than men do, so we don't want to hire you."

These findings may be used to enforce a difference in status between men and women in our social structure.

Module *15*
MOTIVATION

A. Theories of Motivation

STUDY QUESTION: Which theory best explains why students work hard to get good grades?

1. *Need to Know:* What specific information do I need to answer this question?

I need to know the various theories regarding human motivation.

The four theories of motivation are **instinct theory, drive-reduction theory, incentive theory,** and **cognitive theory.**

2. *Defining Terms:* Do I need to use my own words to define or review any terms?

Instinct theory: This theory suggests that there are innate, inborn forces that cause us to behave in certain ways or inborn forces that cause a particular behavior when faced with a specific environmental condition.

Drive-reduction theory: This theory states that a biological need produces a drive to fill that need. To bring our body back to homeostasis, we are motivated to produce a particular need-reducing behavior.

Incentive theory: This theory suggests that we are motivated to behave in certain ways by external and environmental factors (rewards, money, and other reinforcers).

Cognitive theory: This theory proposes that our beliefs can influence our behavior and that our motivation is intrinsic: we engage in particular behaviors because we find them personally rewarding or because they fulfill our beliefs and expectations.

3. *Identify Key Words:* Which words in the question hold the key to the best answer?

The key terms are "which theory *best explains?*" I need to evaluate each of the theories in terms of its account of why students work hard to get good grades. Then I can decide which is the best explanation.

Instinct theory: It is unlikely that a student's hard work is purely instinctual: we are not born with the biological determination to study and attain good grades. You might want to say that a desire for survival motivates students, but it would be much easier to argue that notion from a cognitive, rather than instinctual, point of view.

Drive-reduction theory: This approach is also too biological to explain something as cognitively based as studying in college. Some students might tell you that if they don't get good grades, their parents will stop sending them money and so they will go hungry! Nevertheless, the brain does not monitor *homeostasis* in terms of grade maintenance, and so if students are driven, it is not likely to be because of biological necessity.

Incentive theory: Now we come to a perspective that will help us explain the hard work of college students. People with college degrees tend to have higher salaries than those without such degrees, and money can be translated into other material incentives, such as clothes, a nice apartment, and a Ford Explorer. Beyond material incentives, there are also social incentives, such as praise and status. Just having a college degree confers status in our culture.

Cognitive theory: The focus here is on intrinsic motivators. In a humanistic sense, students might think that they have the potential to excel academically, and they believe that the best way to reach that potential is by getting good grades. In those terms, they get considerable satisfaction from their success. This means that some

students do not need praise or encouragement from others, nor do they need the promise of a big salary at the end of their studies. Their motivation is self-determined and independent of these external factors. If these students decide to go into academic life, they are well advised to be motivated by cognitive, rather than external, factors.

B. Biological & Social Needs

STUDY QUESTION: How would your needs change if you won a $20 million lottery?

Possible Answer: We have all heard the cliché "Money can't buy happiness." Money can help us satisfy some, but not all, of our needs. After winning a lottery, I should be able to look after most *biological needs*, unless I become ill or am physically threatened (for instance, kidnapped for ransom). Money can also help with the attainment of *social needs*, to the extent that it allows the person to meet others, be generous, and just plain have fun.

However, money might be less helpful in my attempt to satisfy my need to achieve. Getting $1 million per year would eliminate the need to work for a living, but many people satisfy most of their achievement needs at work. I could travel the world; I could have servants, expensive cars, and wild parties; but boredom might set in anyway because I would not be *achieving* anything through all this. Such lack of self-actualization might explain why people's lives don't change as much as they expect when they win large sums of money.

Another problem in terms of social needs is that an abrupt change in financial status might bring about an unwelcome change in my friendship network. I might like to continue as always with my friends, but they now perceive me to be rich and, therefore, different from them.

H. Application: Eating Problems & Treatment

STUDY QUESTION: Would you believe an ad that promised you could "lose weight easily and quickly without dieting or exercise by practicing self-hypnosis?"

Possible Answer: A good starting question would be, "What is the physiological basis for weight loss via hypnosis?" Since the only known means of losing weight are reducing consumption of certain foods or increasing metabolism, usually by exercise, it is hard to imagine that a hypnosis program could work without at least one of those components.

Another question, therefore, would be, "What is the content of the hypnotic suggestion?" A strong hunch would be that it would involve repressing urges to eat by becoming desensitized to external food cues. That might be all right, depending on the answers to the next questions.

"How quickly will I lose weight with this program, and what long-term coping strategies does it include?" If the hypnosis provides little more than the means to survive a crash diet, it isn't a good idea. Staying within healthy weight limits involves controlling aspects of one's *lifestyle*. Self-hypnosis can play a part in this, especially with confidence building and relaxation (since some people eat more when anxious), but people should probably be skeptical of "lose-weight-quick" schemes that rely on self-hypnosis. In fact, any plan to lose weight quickly should be given careful scrutiny.

Appendix B

Module 16
EMOTION

A. Peripheral Theories

STUDY QUESTION: Does someone with many facial expressions experience more emotions than someone with few facial expressions?

1. Need to Know: What specific information do I need to answer this question?

I need to know what facial expressions have to do with emotions. Specifically, what is facial feedback theory?

2. Defining Terms: Do I need to use my own words to define or review any terms?

Facial feedback theory: This theory suggests that sensations or feedback from the movement of the facial muscles are interpreted as emotions.

3. Identify Key Words: Which words in the question hold the key to the best answer?

The key terms are "experience a greater number of emotions." The answer to this question lies in the validity of facial feedback theory.

At first glance, the answer would seem to be yes. If facial feedback theory is correct, the individual with few expressions is having fewer emotions than is the individual with a lot of facial expressions. But the text reports that facial feedback theory has not been demonstrated to be correct. A relationship has, however, been found between facial expression and the *intensity* of our subjective emotional experience. So, the person with a lot of facial expressions would be having more *intense* experiences than would someone with fewer expressions, but not *more* emotions.

D. Function of Emotions

STUDY QUESTION: Why might people who are madly in love have difficulty making the right decisions?

Possible Answer: When individuals are madly in love, they are in a state of high physiological arousal. According to the Yerkes-Dodson law, high levels of arousal improve our performance on easy tasks but impair performance on difficult tasks. When we are making an important decision (which is certainly a difficult task), it's best to be in a relaxed state of low arousal. If we are in a heightened state of arousal, the decision that we make at this time—for example, "Should I marry this person?"—might not be the best one for us.

H. Application: Lie Detection

STUDY QUESTION: Would it be fair to use lie detector tests to identify students who are suspected of cheating on exams?

Possible Answer: Let's start with the assumption that your students did not, in fact, cheat on the exams. Can you prove their innocence via the polygraph? Putting the question another way, could an innocent person fail a lie detector test?

The answer to this question appears to be yes. The text points out that such tests lead to false conclusions from 5% to 75% of the time. There are many reasons for this. The most important follows from the fundamental assumptions of the lie detector test—that lying is accompanied by guilt, and guilt yields arousal.

No one has doubted that a polygraph can detect physiological arousal. The problem is in the interpretation of that arousal. Your students might respond with arousal to a critical question about the exam because they know that they are under suspicion and the exam is very relevant to that suspicion. Perhaps they saw someone who seemed to be cheating during the exam, and the mention of that makes them anxious. In short, there are many reasons why the students might show a positive response to the critical question.

It would be extremely unfair to use the lie detector to assess guilt (or innocence) of cheating.

Module 17
INFANCY & CHILDHOOD

A. Prenatal Influences

STUDY QUESTION: A pregnant woman asks, "Why do I have to worry about ingesting chemicals, since my unborn child has a separate blood supply?"

1. Need to Know: What specific information do I need to answer this question?

I need to know whether fetuses in fact have their own blood supply.

2. Identify Key Words: Which words in the question hold the key to the best answer?

The key terms are "separate blood supply." To answer this question, I must establish whether the blood supplies of mother and fetus are shared.

This pregnant woman is wrong. The blood supplies of mother and fetus are connected via the **placenta**, which is the life-support system for the fetus. In fact, the chemicals that this woman injects might very well be **teratogens**—agents that can cause birth defects. Here is some evidence that the mother's bloodstream can supply teratogens to the fetus.

Heavy maternal drinking during pregnancy results in **fetal alcohol syndrome,** which is characterized by a number of physical and psychological defects. Mothers who smoke heavily during pregnancy have a higher rate of stillbirths and premature births and have babies with significantly lower birth weight. Finally, pregnant women who are cocaine and heroine addicts experience problems such as the premature birth, lower birth weight, and smaller head circumference of babies. These babies are also born with dependencies on the drugs and must go through drug withdrawal after birth.

D. Research Focus: Temperament

STUDY QUESTION: Marcie and Jeff love their 6-month-old son but find that he is easily irritated and frightened. What should they do?

Possible Answer: Marcie and Jeff should be told that, for reasons that have nothing to do with parenting, children differ in the early emotional patterns they display. Their son would fit into a category called **inhibited children.** Inhibited children show reluctance, anxiety, and fear when approaching a strange child, exploring new objects, playing with peers, or speaking to adults.

Once they know they have not done anything wrong, Marcie and Jeff can be told that there are things they can do that might reduce their son's relatively high fear response. They need to be caring and supportive and to consistently help their child with minor stressors. Marcie and Jeff should also avoid becoming too anxious, overprotective, or angry at their child's fearfulness. If they can provide their infant son with the love and support he needs, this inhibited baby will have a better chance of becoming less and less fearful as he approaches adolescence. Parents can help their shy or fearful child become more expressive and outgoing.

F. Social Development

STUDY QUESTION: How would Freud's and Erikson's theories apply to a 3-year-old child whose parents are getting divorced?

Possible Answer: Let's consider Freud's and Erikson's approaches in turn.

Freud. Freud would probably say that the parents' separation will cause more problems when the child approaches puberty than at age 3. The child had both parents around when he or she was going through some of the early stages that Freud considered vital—breast feeding and toilet training. The next critical stage will be near puberty, when the child begins to develop subconscious sexual urges. Freud believed that, for a boy, these subconscious urges are directed at the mother, and that the father is then seen as a rival. (For a girl, the parents' roles are reversed.) All of this arouses subconscious guilt in the child. With one of the parents missing, this process will be disrupted. (This Oedipal analysis is presented later in the text.)

Erikson. In Erikson's view, this 3-year-old is making a transition between stages 2 and 3 in terms of psychosocial development. This means that the child might be working to establish autonomy over shame and initiative over guilt. The parents can play an important role in the resolution of both these conflicts. If they encourage the child to try things on his or her own—for example, getting dressed in the morning—the child is more likely to develop autonomy. If they also encourage the child to take on appropriate challenges—for example, building things or cleaning up his or her room—the child will develop initiative.

The problem is that both these processes require parental presence. The parents must take the time to encourage and praise the child when he or she shows autonomy and initiative. Unfortunately, divorce often becomes the focus of the parents' attention. In addition, the child might feel partly to blame for the parents' difficulties, which makes shame and guilt more likely.

Module 18
ADOLESCENCE & ADULTHOOD

A. Puberty & Sexual Behavior

STUDY QUESTION: How are the sexual concerns of adolescents and senior adults similar but also different?

1. Need to Know: What specific information do I need to answer this question?

I need to know what the sexual concerns of adolescents and senior adults are.

2. Identify Key Words: Which words in the question hold the key to the best answer?

The key terms are "similar but also different." To answer this question, I need to examine the sexual concerns of people in these age groups.

One of the biggest concerns for teenagers is whether to become sexually active. And there is considerable peer pressure for them to do so. Once they have decided to be sexually active, avoiding pregnancy and sexually transmitted diseases is of great concern. Many teens are not viewed as sexually active by adults, in the same way that senior adults are not viewed as sexually active. Senior adults are often confused by the physical changes in their bodies (just like teens!) that make sex different than it once was. Seniors have to fight the stereotype that they are asexual: research indicates that many senior couples are happier with their sex lives now than when they were individuals in the singles scene.

C. Personality & Social Changes

STUDY QUESTION: If you become a parent, what special concerns might you have when your own children go through adolescence?

Possible Answer: According to the text, one of the primary tasks an adolescent has is to develop a **self-identity** and **self-esteem**. This also corresponds to Erikson's **stage 5: identity versus role confusion.** Erikson suggests that if teens do not develop a purposeful life, they will experience **identity confusion** and they will be unstable or socially withdrawn. So I would be concerned about their successful development of self-identity.

A parent might not only want teenagers to be happy with their self-identity but also hope that they will find productive work that they love and form deep and lasting relationships with their family and friends. Safety is another concern: can the teenagers explore their developing selves without getting AIDS, having bad experiences with drugs, or becoming enmeshed in unhealthy relationships with other people?

H. Application: Suicide

STUDY QUESTION: If your grandmother had incurable cancer and unbearable pain and asked you to help her commit suicide, would you help her?

Possible Answer: Here is what I would do for my grandmother. Other people might have different responses.

I would not get angry with her or say that her desire to end her life was silly or selfish. Instead, I would say that her wishes were perfectly understandable. Then I would suggest that we find a hospice facility willing to do its utmost to reduce her pain and allow her to retain her dignity.

If, in the hospice, she found that the pain was still intolerable, I would have to face the moral dilemma of whether to help her commit suicide. Probably, I would first try to convince her caregivers to let her end her life peacefully and with dignity. I could not actively kill my grandma but, if it came to it, I would help her to do what it takes to commit suicide—to gather pills, and so on.

Appendix B

Module 19
FREUDIAN & HUMANISTIC THEORIES

A. Freud's Psychodynamic Theory

STUDY QUESTION: According to Freud, why do some students plan to study on the weekend but end up partying?

1. Need to Know: What specific information do I need to answer this question?

I need to know what Freud's psychodynamic theory of personality is.

It is a theory about our personality development that emphasizes early childhood experiences, the importance of repressed thoughts that we can't access, and conflicts between our conscious and our unconscious desires. These conflicts are used to explain why we do things that we don't intend.

2. Defining Terms: Do I need to use my own words to define or review any terms?

Conscious thoughts: These are wishes and desires that we can express at any time.

Unconscious thoughts: These are our wishes and desires that are repressed because of their disturbing content. We cannot access them.

3. Identify Key Words: Which words in the question hold the key to the best answer?

The key terms are "plan to study . . . but end up partying." This question asks us to explain why we do things we don't intend to do.

Our conscious desire is to study. But every weekend we end up partying and don't understand why. Freud would say that we had an unconscious desire to seek pleasure (remember Module 17?) in the form of partying. We aren't aware that we desire to party every weekend (this wish is repressed), because to recognize that we'd rather party than graduate from college threatens our sense of who we are. The unconscious desire is winning over our conscious desire.

F. Cultural Diversity: Achievement

STUDY QUESTION: If you were the principal of a grade school, what might you do to improve overall student performance?

Possible Answer: The experiences of Indochinese immigrants outlined in the text suggest that you must pay attention to particular **primary values** in order to improve overall student performance at your school. These primary values include mutual respect, cooperation, a love of learning, a commitment to accomplishment and achievement, and the belief that you cannot let fate or luck control your life. Instead, students must believe that they are the masters of their own destiny.

Parental involvement appears to be vital. Over half the Indochinese parents read aloud to their children. Parents at your school should be encouraged to make homework a family activity. This doesn't mean that parents do their children's homework. Instead, it means that, each night, every family member has something to do that enhances his or her learning. This makes it clear that all family members are committed to accomplishment and achievement. Students should be expected to do more homework than the national average, perhaps as much as three hours per night, to the

exclusion of television. You should also encourage strong family ties, so that parents and children feel mutual respect and obligation, and family members strive to maintain cooperation and harmony.

All of this would be very difficult to achieve because, as principal, you are going beyond the principles of pedagogy; you are attempting to make changes to our culture by borrowing from the strengths of another.

H. Application: Assessment—Projective Tests

STUDY QUESTION: How useful would projective tests be in identifying students who are most likely to cheat on exams?

Possible Answer: Strong proponents of projective tests might claim that they have this type of predictive power. Others would suggest that projective tests can provide insights into general personality traits or more global behavioral tendencies but they could not be used to predict a behavior as specific as cheating on exams. Still others would argue that projective tests are too open to interpretation by the clinician to be predictive of anything.

If projective tests were to be used in this way, many different testings would have to be conducted with a variety of projective tests. If a student showed consistent trends indicative of extreme mark anxiety, external pressure, poor moral development, or perhaps an animosity toward the instructor or toward authority in general, we could perhaps infer that this student would be more likely to cheat than would students who do not show these tendencies. Of course, the problem comes in ascertaining these tendencies from the open-ended responses of the student.

Module 20
SOCIAL LEARNING & TRAITS

A. Social Cognitive Theory

STUDY QUESTION: Why do some students invest thousands of dollars and 4–6 years of hard work to obtain a college degree?

1. Need to Know: What specific information do I need to answer this question?

I need to know what social cognitive theory says about our behaviors—in this case, going to college.

Social cognitive theory suggests that our beliefs and feelings influence our behavior. What beliefs (cognitive factors) might be related to our behavior of going to college?

2. Defining Terms: Do I need to use my own words to define or review any terms?

Cognitive factors: Four cognitive factors are important, according to social cognitive theory. Specifically, there are three important beliefs: locus of control, self-efficacy, and delay of gratification.

3. Identify Key Words: Which words in the question hold the key to the best answer?

The key term is "why?" We are asked to examine what motivates a person to go to college, from a social cognitive perspective. Let's look at the relevant cognitive factors.

One important belief that would help explain students' desire to attain a university degree is their **locus of control**. Most people who put out considerable effort and resources to attain a goal believe that its attainment is within their control. In other words, they have an *internal locus of control.*

Students' sense of **self-efficacy** refers to their beliefs regarding how capable they are of achieving their goals. Individuals who have a history of success in similar tasks, who feel they are as good as or better than others, and who have received positive feedback about their capabilities will have a high sense of self-efficacy. Students generally come to university with a fairly high sense of self-efficacy, since they were successful in high school. However, university presents new challenges that might make immediate success difficult. The danger, therefore, is that students' self-efficacy will drop dramatically in their first year. This can start a damaging cycle for them, in which they do not succeed because they feel they can't. In turn, their lack of success reinforces their low self-efficacy.

Students who invest all this money and effort must be willing to **delay gratification** for long periods of time. While some of their friends have full-time jobs that allow them to buy new cars and stereos, students live in residence halls or noisy apartments and drive beaters. To be successful students, they must persist at a number of difficult tasks for the promise of future reward.

B. Trait Theory

STUDY QUESTION: Would knowing about the Big Five traits help you write an ad to find the perfect roommate or life mate?

Possible Answer: This question is as concerned with attraction and compatibility as it is with trait theory. The literature on attraction makes it quite clear that similarity is a stronger unifying force than is dissimilarity, or complementary differences. Given that, it would be reasonable to assume that you are better advised to look for a roommate or a life partner who is similar to you.

Remember also that the definition of personality includes behavioral tendencies. Indeed, personality theorists assume that it is our personalities that predispose us to act in certain ways. This means that compatible personalities will engage in similar behaviors, such as keeping the apartment tidy, going to bed at similar times, and respecting other people's privacy. Similarity in these behaviors reduces the likelihood of conflict.

Knowing how you measure in the Big Five traits—openness, conscientiousness, extraversion, agreeableness, and neuroticism—might help you in finding someone who is more similar than different to share your apartment. Of course, this assumes that you can measure these traits in ways that will predict behavior in this particular situation (living together). To do this with some reliability, you must have made observations in related contexts.

It seems unlikely that you could find a life partner from a simple ad in the paper using the Big Five traits. You could find someone who appears to be very similar to you on a paper-and-pencil test but have no interpersonal or sexual attraction to that person.

F. Cultural Diversity: Resolving Conflicts

STUDY QUESTION: What could happen when United States officials negotiate public trade agreements with Japanese officials?

Possible Answer: Interpersonal conflict is associated with opposing interests or disagreements in which one person's goal interferes with that of another person. Trade conflicts between countries are very similar to interpersonal conflicts. The research has indicated that, in general, citizens of the United States tend to resolve conflicts by being independent, assertive, and competitive in achieving their personal goals. Citizens of Japan, in general, place a higher priority on group goals than on personal goals and often avoid discussion of the conflict. This contrast between the **collectivist culture** of Japan and the **individualistic culture** of the United States can make negotiating trade agreements very difficult.

It is possible that, because of this difference, the U.S. could appear to bully Japan into agreement by engaging in public discussion of the conflict and using persuasive, assertive negotiating techniques. The research with students suggests that the Japanese might back away from, or cut off, discussion of topics that cause serious conflict. Presumably, women and men who are trained in cross-cultural differences are advising politicians on matters such as these.

Module 21
HEALTH, STRESS, & COPING

A. Appraisal

STUDY QUESTION: Sue says that some situations always cause her stress, but John says it is how she thinks about them. Who's right?

1. *Need to Know:* What specific information do I need to answer this question?

I need to know what the research indicates about how situations cause stress.

2. *Identify Key Words:* Which words in the question hold the key to the best answer?

The key terms are "some situations always cause her stress" and "how she thinks about them." The question is asking if the way we think about situations can change the amount of stress we feel in reaction to the situation.

According to the text, any situation (even a nonthreatening one) can cause stress through a process called **primary appraisal**. This is our first evaluation of the situation and how it relates to us. We may appraise the situation in one of three ways: as *irrelevant*, which means that the situation doesn't affect us at all; as *positive,* meaning that the situation will benefit us in some way; or as **stressful**, meaning that it overtaxes our resources. This would indicate that John is right and that how we appraise, or think about, the situation greatly affects whether or not we feel stressed.

The text also reports that in an experimental setting, the type of appraisal that individuals gave a stressful situation (whether they were told to view an industrial accident film objectively, or to think about how they would feel) changed the physiological reaction to the stress. Subjects who were told to think about how they would feel in an industrial accident demonstrated higher physiological stress responses. This also supports John's position that how Sue thinks about a situation causes (or increases) her stress.

F. Research Focus: Coping with Trauma

STUDY QUESTION: What can you learn from how burn victims cope with stress that would apply to dealing with stress in your own life?

Possible Answer: Research on burn victims helps us understand what factors contribute to successfully coping with major trauma in life. High self-esteem was the most important personality trait in long-term coping with burn aftereffects. Also, patients with a strong social support network of family and friends were better able to adjust to their burn injuries than those lacking social support.

In terms of our own lives, this research indicates that we should cultivate warm and lasting friendships and that family members should support one another. Additionally, if we do not have high self-esteem, it would be wise to find and become involved in activities that increase our esteem levels. If these factors can help victims of burn trauma cope, they must also be powerful enough to help the rest of us.

H. Application: Stress Management Program

STUDY QUESTION: Why is it better to cope with stress by changing three things—thoughts, behaviors, and physiological responses—rather than just one?

Possible Answer: Our thoughts, behaviors, and physiological reactions all contribute to our feelings of stress. So it makes sense that the *best* way to reduce or manage stress is by changing all three factors. We can make our acid stomach better by popping antacids, thereby reducing the physiological reaction, but this is only temporary and doesn't change our reactions to stress.

Changing our thoughts means, for example, appraising events as a challenge rather than a threat and substituting positive self-statements when we notice ourselves making negative self-statements. Changing our behaviors means taking a problem-solving approach (taking action) rather than using emotion-focused temporary solutions to our stressors. Finally, changing our physiological reaction to stress means learning how to relax. Relaxation methods can include biofeedback, progressive relaxation, or meditation. Successful long-term stress management involves changing all three of the factors affecting our stress levels.

Module 22
DISORDERS I: DEFINITION & ANXIETY DISORDERS

A. Three Approaches

STUDY QUESTION: The night before a big exam, John gets drunk to relax. However, the next day he has a terrible hangover and does poorly on the exam. Is his behavior abnormal?

1. Need to Know: What specific information do I need to answer this question?

I need to know how *abnormal* is defined.

Abnormality can be defined by three different methods: statistical frequency, deviation from the social norm, and maladaptive behavior.

2. Defining Terms: Do I need to use my own words to define or review any terms?

Statistical frequency: This method defines behavior as abnormal if it occurs rarely in the population as a whole.

Deviation from social norm: Behavior is considered abnormal if it differs greatly from the prevailing social standards.

Maladaptive behavior: Behavior is regarded as abnormal if it interferes with an individual's ability to function in society and as a person.

3. Identify Key Words: Which words in the question hold the key to the best answer?

The key words are "is his behavior abnormal?" If we look at John's behavior in the context of each method of defining what is abnormal, we will be able to answer the question.

If we use the statistical frequency approach and compare John's behavior to the general population of college students, his behavior would probably be considered abnormal. Most college students do not get so drunk before an exam that they are hung over.

On the basis of deviation from social norms, we would call John's behavior abnormal. It is not socially acceptable to drink so much that it interferes with your ability to take a test. However, it is probably more acceptable among young college students than in the population at large.

On the basis of the maladaptive behavior approach, we would say that if this is an isolated incident, John's behavior is not abnormal and will not greatly interfere with his responsibilities. However, if this behavior were to increase in frequency, it would interfere with his ability to function as a person and in society and would thus be considered abnormal.

B. Assessing Mental Disorders

STUDY QUESTION: Why must mental health professionals spend so much time and effort in assessing their client's symptoms?

Possible Answer: There are a number of reasons why a detailed and usable diagnosis of mental disorders is essential to the understanding of mental health and the treatment of those disorders. Here are some of them.

Human behavior covers an extremely broad range. Because people are capable of so many different behaviors, it can be difficult to determine which are normal and which are abnormal. It might be that a behavior is infrequent and unusual but not maladaptive. Also, the possible range of abnormal behaviors is very broad, and it takes a great deal of time and experience to put names to each type.

The consequences of diagnosis are considerable. Passing diagnosis on a person carries considerable implications for that person. It could mean the difference between a prison term and psychiatric treatment, for example, or the difference between getting a job and being passed over. For this reason, the classification system must be detailed enough to gain diagnosticians' confidence. Also, diagnoses of mental disorders often carry a social stigma. This stigma can be reduced if the language is carefully chosen; for example, "antisocial personality disorder" sounds less condemning than "psychopath."

Treatment depends upon classification. As with any intervention, the type of treatment is determined by the diagnosis.

H. Application: Treating Phobias

STUDY QUESTION: If you were very shy and uncomfortable about meeting strangers and talking to groups, what could you do about this problem?

Possible Answer: A number of cognitive-behavioral programs could help me. These programs use four components that I can try on my own. First, I would try to understand and believe that, since social fears are learned, they can be unlearned; after reading all the modules so far, this is easy to believe. I need to understand that I avoid meeting people and talking to groups of people in order to avoid the thoughts and physiological arousal that I experience in these situations.

Second, I would learn and substitute new social skills. I would carefully watch individuals who successfully meet others, so as to learn what the appropriate behaviors are. I would begin to write down my thoughts when I think about a group social situation or when I am in one. Then I would write a list of positive and healthy thoughts that I can use instead.

Third, I would begin to imagine myself successfully meeting others and talking to groups of strangers, until I am comfortable with these thoughts. Then I would begin actually to participate in these social situations.

Finally, I would continue doing homework by imagining these situations and also actually participate in group situations. If I was unable to treat myself to my satisfaction, I would get a referral to a therapist.

Module 23
DISORDERS II: MOOD DISORDER & SCHIZOPHRENIA

A. Mood Disorders

STUDY QUESTION: A student is brought into the health clinic for being depressed and having attempted suicide. What will be her treatment program?

1. *Need to Know:* What specific information do I need to answer this question?

I need to know what treatments are usually given for severe depression.

According to the text, the usual treatment consists of antidepressant drug therapy and/or psychotherapy.

2. *Identify Key Words:* Which words in the question hold the key to the best answer?

The key terms are "what will be her treatment program?" The treatment options for major depression that are discussed in this section are antidepressant drug therapy and psychotherapy.

Generally, someone who has just attempted suicide is hospitalized for two reasons. First, constant monitoring will ensure the safety of the individual while he or she is deeply depressed. Second, this student will immediately begin a regimen of antidepressant drugs, as well as intensive psychotherapy. After the individual is no longer a suicide risk and if the depression has remitted somewhat, he or she will be released. It is important to continue the drug treatment and/or psychotherapy in order to prevent relapse.

B. Electroconvulsive Therapy

STUDY QUESTION: How would you compare the effectiveness and side effects of electroconvulsive therapy with those of antidepressant drugs?

Possible Answer: The text notes that about half of those patients for whom antidepressant drugs were initially prescribed quit because of the negative side effects. So there are obviously some significant side effects. Of those who remain on the drugs, about 30% show no benefit from the treatment; they still have major depression.

The question for those with unremitting depression is, "Are the side effects and risks of ECT worth the benefits?" One of the side effects of ECT is significant memory impairment. Consequently, ECT should not be undertaken without first attempting to treat the depression with several different antidepressants under the direction of qualified therapists. However, the effectiveness rate of ECT is 60%–80%. This is very high, considering that only the most depressed people ever get ECT. It may be that ECT is worth the risks when all else fails.

H. Application: Dealing with Mild Depression

STUDY QUESTION: When some people get depressed, why do they prefer to spread their gloom, rather than do something to get over it?

Possible Answer: The essential problem is that those who are mildly depressed are used to this condition and often do not know that help is available. What's more, the state of depression leaves a person without the motivation or energy to do anything. Taken together, these problems mean that depressed people are unlikely to get unsolicited help or to help themselves. So where does the impetus to get help come from?

People with mild depression get caught in a cycle that cuts off social contact. It usually begins with deficiencies in social behavior, such as overdependence or general mistrust of others. Not surprisingly, people react negatively to depressed individuals, who interpret this to mean that they are right about themselves: they are worthless. In addition, friends tend to withdraw social support. This deepens the person's depressed state, which makes it less likely that the person will try to do anything to remedy the situation. Often, it takes a persistent, true friend to start the change, by getting the depressed person to seek professional help.

Module 24
THERAPIES

A. Historical Background

STUDY QUESTION: Should our major cities spend more money to develop care and treatment programs for the homeless?

1. *Need to Know:* What specific information do I need to answer this question?

I need to know why the homeless would need care and treatment programs.

According to the text, one of the results of deinstitutionalization has been that many former mental patients are no longer able to get the care and medication that they need. It is estimated that 25–50% of the current homeless population have serious mental disorders.

2. *Identify Key Words:* Which words in the question hold the key to the best answer?

The key terms are "should our major cities spend more money?" This is a question of personal values. What do I think government should do?

Many homeless individuals are actually very ill and are untreated. In some cases, good treatment might be able to rehabilitate an individual as a functioning member of society. In other cases, even though treatment would improve the quality of an individual's life, he or she would never become an independent, functioning member of society. I think that it is important to deliver humane psychological and medical care and housing to individuals in *both* cases. How we choose to spend our money reflects what we value.

D. Behavior Therapy

STUDY QUESTION: Susan complains of having terrible test anxiety. What would a behavior therapist do to help her?

Possible Answer: A behavior therapist would look at **behaviors** that are causing Susan's problems, with the hope of replacing these with new **target behaviors**. The therapist would also look at **stimuli** that might be eliciting these unwanted responses, with the hope of desensitizing Susan so that the stimuli no longer bring on the unwanted response. For example, Susan might feel her heart pound before an exam. She might shake and feel nauseated. She might avoid studying because it is associated with the test; she goes jogging or hits the fridge instead. The therapist would like Susan to remain relaxed when she thinks about her exam and when she approaches the exam room. This will allow her to concentrate when she studies and when she takes the exam. After identifying which behaviors to change and which new ones to replace them with, the therapist could use **desensitization** to help Susan overcome her test anxiety. The steps of systematic desensitization include relaxation, stimulus hierarchy, and desensitization training. Susan and the therapist together would design a stimulus hierarchy. The therapist would slowly take Susan through each step, making sure that she is fully relaxed and comfortable before proceeding to the next level of the hierarchy. This might take weeks, but the end result would be a reduction in Susan's test anxiety.

H. Application: Cognitive-Behavior Techniques

STUDY QUESTION: Frank has very little self-confidence and self-esteem. What is one way that he could work on raising them?

Possible Answer: There are a few cognitive-behavior techniques that can be practiced without the assistance of a therapist. Two very good strategies are called **thought stopping** and **thought substitution**.

Thought stopping has two basic components. In the first step, Frank must close his eyes each time he has a thought that is self-deprecating, silently yell "Stop!" and then silently count to ten. In the second step, Frank uses a collection of five photographs that he has pulled from albums. These photos show Frank having a good time with friends. On the back of each photo, he has written positive self-statements—for example, "I am a good person with good friends" or "My life is under my control. " He thinks about each picture for a moment, then turns over the photo, and repeats the sentence to himself. The entire process takes from one to two minutes.

Frank can follow up on this by making plans to improve his self-confidence. He can engage in activities for which he has some ability. Also, he can make a list of the irrational thoughts that have accompanied these activities—for example, "I can never do well" or "People will hate me if I don't do well. " These can be replaced with positive statements like those on the back of his photos. He must also be willing to reinforce himself when he succeeds. This can take the form of self-praise or tangible reinforcers—things he likes to eat and do.

Module 25
SOCIAL PSYCHOLOGY

A. Perceiving Others

STUDY QUESTION: Mark says that he doesn't make snap judgments but waits until he knows people. Do you think Mark does what he claims?

1. *Need to Know:* What specific information do I need to answer this question?

I need to know how we normally form first impressions.

Normally, our first impression of an individual is shaped by the person's physical appearance; our need to explain why the individual looks, dresses, or behaves as he or she does, and the person's race. Our first impression is formed in seconds, and it influences how we interact with that person.

2. *Identify Key Words:* Which words in the question hold the key to the best answer?

The key terms are "do you think Mark does what he says?" The question is asking whether or not anyone can stop making first impressions.

Mark might reserve judgment about people until he gets to know them better. If so, he's in a very small minority. Most of us do form judgments about others on meeting them. Let's look at some of the reasons why we form these first impressions.

As the text points out, making judgments about others has *social consequences:* the behavior we exhibit toward another person is guided by our impressions of that person. It is very difficult to treat someone in an entirely neutral way; our behavior can be placed on a continuum of friendliness, or of patience, tolerance, and so on. In order for Mark to reserve judgment, he must treat everyone *the same way* until he makes a judgment that helps dictate how he will treat the person. While this is possible, it is not the way most people operate.

Another factor is that, in order to avoid forming first impressions, Mark will have to either ignore some very salient social data or store it in memory without acting upon it. He must remain totally uninfluenced by appearance, accent, nonverbal behavior, and the first things a person says to him. Again, if Mark can do this, he has set himself apart from most of us, who pay quite close attention to these things.

In summary, Mark will have to control powerful motivational and cognitive factors in order to avoid these snap judgments. It's unlikely that he does so. Perhaps a more realistic goal is to admit to making first impressions but to allow for changes in them as you get to know a person better.

B. Attributions

STUDY QUESTION: What should you be aware of when you try to explain the behaviors of your friend or your mate?

Possible Answer: This question requires a knowledge of biases and errors in attribution. Let's look at each of the three discussed in the text and see how they can be avoided.

Fundamental attribution error. According to fundamental attribution error, we place inordinate weight on dispositional factors when making attributions. This means that we fail to appreciate the power that a situation can exert on behavior. For example, when someone does poorly on a test, we think the person isn't very smart, rather than thinking that the person might have been prevented from studying by a family crisis. To avoid this error, we must force ourselves to look at the situations in which people find themselves and acknowledge that they can have a strong influence on behavior.

Actor-observer effect. The actor-observer effect describes our tendency to attribute our own behavior to the situation and other people's behavior to their dispositions. We have eliminated some fundamental attribution error by gaining an appreciation of how the situation can influence our own behavior, but we still are insensitive to the effect the situation can have on the behavior of others. To avoid this effect requires that we show *empathy* for other people when they are in situations that bring out behavior that is less than their best. It also requires that we realize how favorable situations can sometimes make other people look better than they really are.

Self-serving bias. As its name implies, self-serving bias applies to our explanations of our own behavior. This isn't directly relevant to explanations of your friend's behavior, but it is worth reviewing as an addendum to the question.

We attribute our successes to our dispositions and our failures to the situation. In so doing, we protect our self-esteem. Though this protection has benefits as a short-term strategy, it does little to help us reduce the likelihood of failure in the future. If we were to be truly honest with ourselves, we would admit that some of our success is due to good fortune and the hard work of others, both of which are situational factors. Also, we would acknowledge that some of our failures could have been avoided if we had worked harder or if we had the talent to do better.

On the other hand, this honesty is not necessarily the best way to improve ourselves. A large body of research indicates that attributing all our outcomes to our own effort is most likely to result in self-improvement and high motivation.

F. Aggression

STUDY QUESTION: One of your friends says, "Getting angry and being aggressive is just a part of human nature." What would you reply?

Possible Answer: The key phrase in my friend's sentence is "human nature." This term implies that being aggressive is inborn and that nothing can be done to change aggressive behavior. Although there is research suggesting that some aggressive behavior is related to neurotransmitter levels, and thus is inborn, much more evidence points to external contributors to aggressive behavior, such as social learning and environmental factors. If all anger (an emotion that probably is inborn) were expressed aggressively, there would be even more worldwide cross-cultural aggression than we see now.

I would further suggest to my friend that his belief is more likely to cause his own anger to be expressed as aggression. Research has shown that cognitive factors can override aggression and also indicates that social rules can inhibit aggression. If we have rules that say aggressive behavior is unacceptable, we are less likely to experience aggression.

Glossary

ability tests Achievement tests, which measure what we have learned; aptitude tests, which measure our potential for learning or acquiring a specific skill; and intelligence tests, which measure our general potential to solve problems, think abstractly, and profit from experience.

absolute threshold The intensity level of a stimulus such that a person has a 50% chance of detecting it.

accommodation The process by which a person changes old methods to deal with or adjust to new situations.

achievement need The desire to set challenging goals and to persist in pursuing those goals in the face of obstacles, frustrations, and setbacks.

Acquired Immune Deficiency Syndrome *See* AIDS.

action potential A tiny electric current that is generated when the positive sodium ions rush inside the axon. The enormous increase of sodium ions inside the axon causes the inside of the axon to reverse its charge: the inside becomes positive, while the outside becomes negative.

activation-synthesis theory of dreams The idea that dreaming represents the random and meaningless activity of nerve cells in the brain. According to this theory, the pons, an area in the brain, sends millions of random nerve impulses to the cortex; in turn, the cortex tries to make sense of these signals by creating the feelings, imagined movements, perceptions, changing scenes, and meaningless images that we define as dreams.

actor-observer effect Our tendency, when we are behaving (or acting), to attribute our own behavior to situational factors but, when we are observing, to attribute another person's behavior to his or her personality traits or disposition.

acupuncture An ancient Chinese procedure for relief of pain, in which a trained practitioner inserts thin needles into various points on the body's surface, often far from the site of the pain, and then manually twirls or electrically stimulates the needles.

adaptation The decreasing response of the sensory organs as they are exposed to a continuous level of stimulation.

adaptation-level theory The idea that we quickly become accustomed to receiving some good fortune (money, job, car, degree); we take the good fortune for granted within a short period of time; and, as a result, the initial impact of our good fortune fades and contributes less to our long-term level of happiness.

adaptive theory A theory suggesting that sleep evolved as a survival mechanism, since it prevented early humans and animals from wasting energy and exposing themselves to the dangers of nocturnal predators.

adaptive value The usefulness of certain abilities or traits that have evolved in animals or humans that tend to increase their chances of survival, such as the ability to find food, acquire mates, and avoid illness and injury.

addiction A behavioral pattern of drug abuse that is marked by an overwhelming and compulsive desire to obtain and use the drug. Even after stopping, the addict has a tendency to relapse and begin using the drug again.

adolescence A developmental period, lasting from about the ages of 12 to 18, that marks the end of childhood and the beginning of adulthood; it is a transitional period of considerable biological, cognitive, social, and personality changes.

adolescent egocentric thinking Difficulties in separating one's own thoughts and feelings from those of others.

adrenal glands Structures in the endocrine system. The adrenal cortex (outer part) secretes hormones that regulate sugar and salt balances and help the body resist stress; they are also responsible for the growth of pubic hair, a secondary sexual characteristic. The adrenal medulla (inner part) secretes two hormones that arouse the body to deal with stress and emergencies: epinephrine (adrenaline) and norepinephrine (noradrenaline).

affective-primacy theory The idea that, in some situations, we feel an emotion before we have time to interpret or appraise the situation.

afferent neurons Neurons that carry information from the senses to the spinal cord; also called sensory neurons.

afterimage A visual image that continues after the original stimulus is removed.

age regression In hypnosis, the suggestion that subjects regress, or return, to an earlier time in their lives—for example, to early childhood.

aggressive behavior Any act intended to do physical or psychological harm.

aging by chance theory The idea that our bodies age because of naturally occurring problems or breakdowns in the body's cells, which become less able to repair themselves.

aging by design theory The idea that our bodies age because preset biological clocks determine the number of times cells can divide and multiply; after that limit is reached, cells begin to die and aging occurs.

agoraphobia An anxiety about being in places or situations from which escape might be difficult or embarrassing if a panic attack or panic-like symptoms (sudden dizziness or onset of diarrhea) were to occur.

AIDS (Acquired Immune Deficiency Syndrome) A life-threatening condition that, by the latest definition, is present when the individual is HIV positive and has a level of T-cells (CD4 immune cells) of no more than 200 per cubic milliliter of blood (one-fifth of the level of a healthy person) or has developed one or more of 26 specified illnesses (including recurrent pneumonia and skin cancer).

alarm stage In the general adaptation syndrome, our initial reaction to stress, marked by activation of the fight-flight response, which causes physiological arousal.

alcohol (ethyl alcohol) A psychoactive drug classified as a depressant; it depresses activity of the central nervous system. Alcohol causes friendliness and loss of inhibitions at low doses; impairs drinkers' social judgment and understanding at medium doses; and seriously impairs motor coordination, cognitive abilities, decision making, and speech at higher doses. Very high doses may result in coma and death.

alcoholism A problem involving addiction to alcohol. An alcoholic is a person who has drunk heavily for a long period of time, is addicted to and has an intense craving for alcohol, and, as a result, has problems in two or three major life areas (social, personal, and financial areas, for example).

algorithms Rules that, if followed correctly, will eventually lead to the solution of a problem.

all-or-none law The fact that, once a nerve impulse starts in a small segment at the very beginning of the axon, it will continue at the same speed, segment by segment, to the very end of the axon.

alpha stage In sleep, a stage marked by feelings of being relaxed and drowsy, usually with the eyes closed. Alpha waves have low amplitude and high frequency (8–12 cycles per second).

altered state of consciousness An awareness differing from normal consciousness; such awareness may be produced by using any number of procedures, such as meditation, psychoactive drugs, hypnosis, or sleep deprivation.

altered state theory of hypnosis The idea that hypnosis is not a trancelike state but rather an altered state of consciousness, during which a person experiences different sensations and feelings. No physiological measures have been found to indicate that a person is in a trance. For another view of hypnosis, see the sociocognitive theory of hypnosis.

altruism Helping or doing something, often at a cost or risk, for reasons other than the expectation of a material or social reward.

Alzheimer's disease A disorder that usually begins after people reach age 50 and is always fatal; it results from widespread damage to the brain, including the hippocampus, and produces deterioration in personality, emotions, cognitive processes, and memory.

Ames room A viewing environment, designed by Albert Ames, that demonstrates how our perception of size may be distorted by manipulating our depth cues.

amnesia Memory loss that may occur after damage to the brain (temporary or permanent), following drug use, or after severe psychological stress.

amniocentesis A medical test performed between weeks 14 and 20 of pregnancy. A long needle is inserted through the mother's abdominal muscles into the amniotic fluid surrounding the fetus. By withdrawing and analyzing fetal cells in the fluid, doctors can identify a number of genetic problems.

amygdala A structure in the limbic system that is located in the tip of the temporal lobe and is involved in forming, recognizing, and remembering emotional experiences and facial expressions.

anal stage Freud's second psychosexual stage, lasting from the age of about $1\frac{1}{2}$ to 3. In this stage, the infant's pleasure seeking is centered on the anus and its functions of elimination.

analogy A strategy for finding a similarity between a new situation and an old, familiar situation.

androgens Male sex hormones.

anencephaly The condition of being born with little or no brain. If some brain or nervous tissue is present, it is totally exposed and often damaged because the top of the skull is missing. Survival is usually limited to days; the longest has been 2 months.

animal model An approach to studying some human problem, situation, or disease by observing, testing, and measuring animals' behavioral, physiological, or neurological changes under conditions that closely approximate it.

anorexia nervosa A serious eating disorder characterized by refusing to eat and not maintaining weight at 85% of what is expected, having an intense fear of gaining weight or becoming fat, and missing at least three consecutive menstrual cycles. Anorexics also have a disturbed body image: they see themselves as fat even though they are very thin.

anterior pituitary The front part of the pituitary gland, a key component of the endocrine system. It regulates growth through the secretion of growth hormone and produces hormones that control the adrenal cortex, pancreas, thyroid, and gonads.

anticipatory nausea Feelings of nausea that are elicited by stimuli associated with nausea-inducing chemotherapy treatments. Patients experience nausea after treatment but also in anticipation of their treatment. Researchers believe that anticipatory nausea occurs through classical conditioning.

antidepressant drugs Drugs used to combat depression. They act by increasing levels of a specific group of neurotransmitters (monoamines, such as serotonin) that is believed to be involved in the regulation of emotions and moods.

antipsychotic drugs *See* neuroleptic drugs.

antisocial personality disorder A pattern of disregarding or violating the rights of others without feeling guilt or remorse. It is found in 3% of the population, predominantly in males.

anxiety An unpleasant state that is associated with feelings of uneasiness, apprehension, and heightened physiological arousal, such as increased heart rate and blood pressure. According to Freud, it arises when there is an unconscious conflict between the id's and superego's desires regarding how to satisfy the need; the ego, caught in the middle, reacts by creating a feeling of anxiety. More modern theories of anxiety are based on conditioned emotional responses and observational learning.

apparent motion An illusion that a stimulus or object is moving in space when, in fact, it is stationary. This illusion is created by rapidly showing a series of stationary images, each of which has a slightly different position or posture than the one before.

approach-approach conflict Having to choose between two situations that both have pleasurable consequences.

approach-avoidance conflict The conflict that arises in a single situation that has both pleasurable and disagreeable aspects.

approaches to understanding behavior Distinctive psychological viewpoints that may involve different methods or techniques—for example, the psychobiological, cognitive, behavioral, psychoanalytic, humanistic, and cross-cultural approaches.

arousal-cost-reward model of helping The idea that we make decisions to help by calculating the costs and rewards of helping.

assimilation The process by which a child uses old methods or experiences to deal with new situations and then incorporates the new information into his or her existing knowledge.

atmospheric perspective In three-dimensional vision, a monocular depth cue that comes into play in the presence of dust, smog, or water vapor. Hazy objects are interpreted as being farther away.

attachment A close fundamental emotional bond that develops between the infant and his or her parent or caregiver.

attention-deficit/hyperactivity disorder (ADHD) A condition diagnosed on the basis of the occurrence of certain behavioral problems, rather than medical tests. A child must have six or more symptoms of inattention (such as making careless mistakes in schoolwork) and six or more symptoms of hyperactivity (such as fidgeting or talking excessively). These symptoms should have been present from an early age, persisted for at least six months, and contributed to maladaptive development.

attitude Any belief or opinion that includes a positive or negative evaluation of some object, person, or event and that predisposes us to act in a certain way toward that object, person, or event.

attributions Our explanations of the causes of events, other people's behaviors, and our own behaviors.

atypical neuroleptic drugs Neuroleptics that somewhat lower levels of dopamine but, more importantly, reduce levels of other neurotransmitters, especially serotonin. One group of these drugs is the benzamides, such as clozapine. These drugs primarily reduce positive symptoms and may slightly improve negative symptoms.

auditory association area An area directly below the primary auditory cortex that receives and transforms meaningless auditory sensations into perceptions, or meaningful sounds, such as melodies or words.

auditory canal A long tube in the ear that funnels sound waves down its length so that the waves strike a thin, taut membrane—the eardrum, or tympanic membrane.

auditory nerve A band of fibers that carries impulses (electrical signals) from the cochlea to the brain, resulting in the perception of sounds.

authoritarian parents Parents who attempt to shape, control, and evaluate the behavior and attitudes of their children in accordance with a set standard of conduct, usually an absolute standard that comes from religious or respected authorities.

authoritative parents Parents who attempt to direct their children's activities in a rational and intelligent way. They are supporting, loving, and committed, encourage verbal give-and-take, and discuss their rules and policies with their children.

autism A condition marked by especially abnormal or impaired development in social interactions, spoken language, and sensory-motor systems. Autistics characteristically have few activities or interests and spend long periods repeating the same ritualistic physical behaviors. Signs of autism begin in a child's first three years.

automatic encoding The transfer of information from short-term into long-term memory without any effort and usually without any awareness.

automatic processes Activities that require little awareness, take minimal attention, and do not interfere with other ongoing activities.

autonomic nervous system That portion of the peripheral nervous system that regulates heart rate, breathing, blood pressure, digestion, hormone secretion, and other functions, as well as maintaining the body in a state of optimal balance, or homeostasis. It usually functions without conscious effort, which means that only a few of its responses, such as breathing, can also be controlled voluntarily. Its two subdivisions are the sympathetic division and the parasympathetic division.

availability heuristic A rule of thumb by which we rely on information that is more prominent or easily recalled and overlook other information that is available but less prominent or notable.

avoidance-avoidance conflict Having to choose between two situations that both have disagreeable consequences.

axon A single threadlike structure within the neuron. It extends from, and carries signals away from, the cell body to neighboring neurons, organs, or muscles.

axon membrane The axon wall, which contains chemical gates that may be opened or closed to control the inward and outward flow of electrically charged particles called ions.

babbling The first stage in acquiring language, in which infants, at an age of about 6 months, begin to make one syllable sounds such as "deedeedee" or "bababa." Many of these sounds are common across languages.

Bandura's social cognitive theory A personality theory that assumes that personality development, growth, and change are influenced by four distinctively human cognitive processes: highly developed language ability, observational learning, purposeful behavior, and self-analysis. Bandura emphasizes the importance of learning through observation, imitation, and self-reward in the development of social skills, interactions, and behaviors. He contends that we can learn new social skills without performing any observable behaviors or receiving any external rewards. *See also* social cognitive theory.

Glossary

Barnum principle A technique used in horoscopes and elsewhere, in which a number of traits are listed in such a general way that almost everyone who reads them thinks that these traits apply specifically to him or her. This technique was named after circus owner P. T. Barnum.

basal ganglia A group of structures in the center of the brain that are involved in regulating movements. To function properly, neurons in the basal ganglia must have a sufficient supply of the neurotransmitter dopamine.

basic rules of grammar Rules for combining nouns, verbs, and adjectives into meaningful sentences.

basilar membrane A membrane within the cochlea that contains the auditory receptors, or hair cells.

Beck's cognitive theory of depression The idea that when we are depressed, automatic, negative thoughts that we rarely notice occur continually throughout the day. These negative thoughts distort how we perceive and interpret the world and thus influence our behaviors and feelings, which in turn contribute to our feeling depressed.

Beck's cognitive therapy *See* cognitive therapy.

behavior modification A treatment or therapy that changes or modifies problems or undesirable behaviors by using learning principles based on operant conditioning, classical conditioning, and social cognitive learning.

behavior therapy A form of psychotherapy in which disruptive behaviors are changed and human functioning is improved on the basis of principles of classical and operant conditioning. It focuses on changing particular behaviors rather than on the underlying mental events or possible unconscious factors. Sometimes called behavior modification or cognitive-behavior therapy.

behavioral approach A psychological viewpoint that analyzes how organisms learn new behaviors or modify existing ones, depending on whether events in their environments reward or punish these behaviors. Historically, as founded by John B. Watson, the behavioral approach emphasized the objective, scientific analysis of observable behaviors. *See also* Skinner and Bandura.

behavioral genetics The study of how inherited or genetic factors influence and interact with psychological factors to shape our personality, intelligence, emotions, and motivation and also how we behave, adapt, and adjust to our environment.

benzodiazepines Minor tranquilizers (Librium, Valium, Xanax, Dalmane, Halcion) that reduce anxiety and stress. They are frequently prescribed for short-term (3–4 weeks) treatment of insomnia. Side effects associated with high doses or prolonged usage include daytime drowsiness, loss of memory, tolerance, and dependency.

Binet-Simon Intelligence Scale The world's first standardized intelligence test, containing items arranged in order of increasing difficulty. The items measured vocabulary, memory, common knowledge, and other cognitive abilities.

binocular depth cues In three-dimensional vision, depth cues that depend upon the movement of both eyes (*bi* means two; *ocular* means eye).

biofeedback A training procedure through which a person is made aware of his or her physiological responses, such as muscle activity, heart rate, blood pressure, or temperature, and then tries to increase or decrease these physiological responses.

biological approach A psychological viewpoint that examines how our genes, hormones, and nervous systems interact with our environments to influence learning, personality, memory, motivation, emotions, coping techniques, and other traits and abilities.

biological clocks The body's internal timing devices that are genetically set to regulate various physiological responses for certain periods of time.

biological factors Innate tendencies or predispositions that may either facilitate or inhibit certain kinds of learning.

biological hunger factors Physiological changes in blood chemistry and signals from digestive organs that provide feedback to the brain, which, in turn, triggers us to eat or stop eating.

biological needs Physiological requirements that are critical to our survival and physical well-being.

biological psychology *See* psychobiology.

biological sex factors The action of sex hormones, which is involved in secondary sexual characteristics (facial hair, breasts), sexual motivation (more so in animals than in humans), and the development of ova and sperm.

biological theory of depression The idea that underlying genetic, neurological, or physiological factors may predispose a person to developing a mood disorder.

BioPsychoSocial model The representation of adolescent development as a process that occurs simultaneously on many levels and includes sexual, cognitive, social, and personality changes that interact and influence each other.

bipolar I disorder A mood disorder characterized by fluctuations between episodes of depression and mania. A manic episode goes on for at least a week, during which a person is unusually euphoric, cheerful, and high and has at least three of the following symptoms: has great self-esteem, has little need of sleep, speaks rapidly and frequently, has racing thoughts, is easily distracted, and pursues pleasurable activities. Formerly called manic-depressive illness.

bisexual orientation A pattern of sexual arousal by persons of either sex.

brightness constancy Our tendency to perceive brightness as remaining the same in changing illumination.

Broca's aphasia An inability to speak in fluent sentences while retaining the ability to understand written or spoken words. It is caused by damage to Broca's area.

Broca's area An area usually located in the left frontal lobe that is necessary for combining sounds into words and arranging words into meaningful sentences. *See* Broca's aphasia.

bulimia nervosa An eating disorder characterized by a minimum of two binge-eating episodes per week for at least three months; fear of not being able to stop eating; regularly engaging in vomiting, use of laxatives, or rigorous dieting and fasting; and excessive concern about body shape and weight.

burnout Feelings of doing poorly at one's job, physically wearing out, and becoming emotionally exhausted due to intense involvement with people who demand too much of one's time and energy and provide too little reward or satisfaction.

bystander effect The phenomenon in which an individual feels inhibited from taking some action because of the presence of others.

caffeine A mild stimulant that produces dilation of blood vessels, increased secretion of stomach acid, and moderate physiological arousal. Psychological effects include a feeling of alertness, decreased fatigue and drowsiness, and improved reaction times. Caffeine, which is present in coffee, tea, chocolate, and other foods, can be addictive, especially in higher doses.

care orientation Making moral decisions based on issues of caring, on avoiding hurt, on how things affect interpersonal relationships, and on concern for others.

case study An in-depth analysis of the thoughts, feelings, beliefs, experiences, behaviors, or problems of an individual. This research method offers little opportunity to control or manipulate situations or variables.

CAT scan *See* computerized axial tomography.

catatonic schizophrenia A subcategory of schizophrenia characterized by periods of wild excitement or periods of rigid, prolonged immobility; sometimes the person assumes the same frozen posture for hours on end.

catharsis A psychological process through which anger or aggressive energy is released by expressing or letting out powerful negative emotions. Freud's view that catharsis can be helpful in reducing aggression is not supported by most research.

cell body For neurons, a relatively large, egg-shaped structure that provides fuel, manufactures chemicals, and maintains the entire neuron in working order; also called the soma.

central cues Hunger cues associated with the activity of chemicals and neurotransmitters in different areas of the brain.

central nervous system Neurons located in the brain and spinal cord. From the bottom of the brain emerges the spinal cord, which is made up of neurons and bundles of axons and dendrites that carry information back and forth between the brain and the body. Neurons in the central nervous system normally have almost no capacity to regrow or regenerate if damaged or diseased.

central route for persuasion Presenting information with strong arguments, analyses, facts, and logic.

cephalocaudal principle The rule that parts of the body closer to the infant's head develop before parts closer to the feet.

cerebellum A region of the hindbrain that is involved in coordinating movements but not in initiating voluntary movements. It is also involved in cognitive functions, such as short-term memory, following rules, and carrying out plans. Surprising new evidence suggests the cerebellum is also involved in learning to perform timed motor responses, such as those required in playing games or sports.

challenge appraisal Our conclusion that we have the potential for gain or personal growth in a particular situation but that we also need to mobilize our physical energy and psychological resources to meet the challenging situation.

chi-square A test of statistical significance that compares the actual observed distribution of people (or events) among various categories with the distribution expected purely on the basis of chance.

child abuse and neglect Inadequate care or acts by the parent(s) (physical or emotional abuse) that put a child in danger, cause physical harm or injury, or involve sexual molestation.

Chomsky's theory of language The idea that all languages share a common universal grammar and that children inherit a mental program to learn this universal grammar. This theory includes the concepts of deep structure and surface structure and of transformational rules to convert from one to the other.

chromosome A hairlike structure that contains tightly coiled strands of deoxyribonucleic acid (DNA). Each cell of the human body (except for the sperm and egg) contains 46 chromosomes, arranged in 23 pairs.

chunking Combining separate items of information into a larger unit, or chunk, and then remembering chunks of information rather than individual items. A technique of memory enhancement.

circadian rhythm A biological clock that is genetically programmed to regulate physiological responses within a time period of 24 or 25 hours (about a day); one example is the sleep-wake cycle.

clairvoyance The ability to perceive events or objects that are out of sight.

classical conditioning A kind of learning in which a neutral stimulus acquires the ability to produce a response that was originally produced by a different stimulus.

client-centered therapy An approach developed by Carl Rogers that assumes that each person has an actualizing tendency—that is, a tendency to develop his or her own potential; the therapist's task is to show compassion and positive regard in helping the client reach his or her potential. Also called person-centered therapy.

clinical assessment A systematic evaluation of an individual's various psychological, biological, and social factors, as well as the identification of past and present problems, stressors, and other cognitive and behavioral symptoms.

clinical diagnosis A process of determining how closely an individual's specific symptoms match those that define a particular mental disorder.

clinical interview In assessment, a method of gathering information about relevant aspects of a person's past as well as current behaviors, attitudes, emotions, and details of present difficulties or problems. Some clinical interviews are unstructured, which means that they have no set questions; others are structured, which means that they follow a standard format of asking the same questions.

clinical psychologist An individual who has a Ph.D, has specialized in the clinical subarea, and has spent an additional year in a supervised therapy setting to gain experience in diagnosing and treating a wide range of abnormal behaviors. To train as a clinical psychologist usually requires 4–6 years of work after obtaining a college degree.

closure rule A perceptual rule stating that, in organizing stimuli, we tend to fill in any missing parts of a figure and see the figure as complete.

cocaine A stimulant produced from the leaves of the coca plant. Its physiological and behavioral effects are very similar to those of amphetamine: it produces increased heart rate and blood pressure, enhanced mood, alertness, increased activity, decreased appetite, and diminished fatigue. At higher doses, it can produce anxiety, emotional instability, and suspiciousness.

cochlea A coiled, fluid-filled structure in the inner ear that contains the receptors for hearing. Its function is transduction—transforming vibrations into nerve impulses that are sent to the brain for processing into auditory information.

cochlear implant A miniature electronic device that is surgically implanted into the cochlea to restore hearing in those with neural deafness. It converts sound waves to electrical signals, which are fed into the auditory nerve and hence reach the brain for processing.

cognitive appraisal theory The idea that our interpretation or appraisal of a situation is often the primary cause of emotions.

cognitive approach *See* cognitive psychology.

cognitive-behavior therapy A treatment for phobias and other mental disorders based on a combination of two methods: changing negative, unhealthy, or distorted thoughts and beliefs by substituting positive, healthy, and realistic ones; and changing limiting or disruptive behaviors by learning and practicing new skills to improve functioning. Sometimes called behavior therapy.

cognitive-behavioral approach The view that mental disorders result from deficits in cognitive processes, such as thoughts and beliefs, and from behavioral problems, such as deficits in skills and abilities. In this approach, mental disorders are treated by changing the person's maladaptive thoughts and behaviors.

cognitive development How a person perceives, thinks, and gains an understanding of his or her world through the interaction and influence of genetic and learned factors.

cognitive developmental theory The idea that, as they develop mental skills and interact with their environments, children learn one set of rules for male behavior and another set of rules for female behavior.

cognitive dissonance A state of unpleasant psychological tension that motivates us to reduce our cognitive inconsistencies by making our beliefs more consistent with one another.

cognitive factors According to social cognitive theory, factors that include our beliefs, expectations, values, intentions, and social roles—all of which help to shape our personalities.

cognitive factors in motivation The influence of individuals' evaluations or perceptions of a situation on their willingness to work.

cognitive interview A technique for questioning eyewitnesses and others by having them imagine and reconstruct the details of an event, report everything they remember without holding anything back, and narrate the event from different viewpoints.

cognitive learning A kind of learning that involves mental processes, such as attention and memory; may proceed through observation or imitation; and may not involve any external rewards or require the person to perform any observable behaviors.

cognitive map A mental representation of the layout of an environment and its features.

cognitive miser model The idea that, in making attributions, people feel they must conserve time and effort by taking cognitive shortcuts.

cognitive perspective The theory that an organism learns a predictable relationship between two stimuli such that the occurrence of one stimulus (neutral stimulus) predicts the occurrence of another (unconditioned stimulus). In other words, classical conditioning occurs because the organism learns what to expect. Formerly called information theory.

cognitive psychology The study of how we process, store, retrieve, and use information and how cognitive processes influence what we attend to, perceive, learn, remember, believe, feel, and do.

cognitive therapy An approach to therapy that focuses on the role of thoughts in our emotions and actions. The widely used version developed by Aaron Beck assumes that we have automatic negative thoughts that we typically say to ourselves without much notice. By continuously repeating these automatic negative thoughts, we color and distort how we perceive and interpret the world and influence how we behave and feel. The goal of the therapy is to change these automatic negative thoughts.

cognitive unconscious Mental structures and processes that, although we are unaware of them, automatically and effortlessly influence our conscious thoughts and behaviors.

Glossary

collective unconscious According to Jung, ancient memory traces and symbols that are passed on by birth and are shared by all people in all cultures.

collectivistic culture A culture that places a high priority on group goals and norms over personal goals and values. Individuals in these cultures work to control their behaviors and maintain harmonious relationships with others.

color blindness Inability to distinguish between two or more shades in the color spectrum. There are several kinds of color blindness. *See* monochromats and dichromats.

color constancy Our tendency to perceive colors as remaining stable despite differences in lighting.

commitment In Sternberg's triangular theory of love, the component of love associated with making a pledge to nourish the feelings of love and to actively maintain the relationship.

common factors A basic set of procedures and experiences shared by different therapies that account for those therapies' comparable effectiveness despite their different fundamental principles and techniques. Common factors include the growth of a supportive and trusting relationship between therapist and client and the accompanying development of an accepting atmosphere in which the client feels willing to admit problems and is motivated to work on changing.

communication The ability to use sounds, smells, or gestures to exchange information.

community mental health centers Government-sponsored centers that offer low-cost or free mental health care to members of the surrounding community, especially the underprivileged. The services may include psychotherapy, support groups, or telephone crisis counseling.

companionate love A condition associated with trusting and tender feelings for someone whose life is closely bound up with one's own.

compliance A kind of conformity in which we give in to social pressure in our public responses but do not change our private beliefs.

computerized axial tomography (CAT scan) A technique used to study the structure of the living brain. Low levels of X rays are passed through the brain. A computer measures the amount of radiation absorbed by the brain cells, which depends on their density, and produces a relatively good image of the brain.

concept A way to group objects, events, or characteristics on the basis of some common property they all share.

conception The process in which one of the millions of sperm penetrates the ovum's outside membrane; also called fertilization. After penetration, the outside membrane changes and becomes impenetrable to the millions of remaining sperm.

concrete operations stage The third of Piaget's cognitive stages, lasting from about the age of 7 to 11 years. During this stage, children can perform a number of logical mental operations on concrete objects that are physically present.

conditional positive regard Positive regard that depends on our behaving in certain ways—for example, living up to or meeting others' standards.

conditioned emotional response The feeling of some positive or negative emotion, such as happiness, fear, or anxiety, when experiencing a stimulus that previously accompanied a pleasant or painful event. This is an example of classical conditioning.

conditioned response (CR) A response elicited by the conditioned stimulus; it is similar to the unconditioned response but not identical in magnitude or amount.

conditioned stimulus (CS) A formerly neutral stimulus that has acquired the ability to elicit a response previously elicited by the unconditioned stimulus.

conduct disorder A repetitive and persistent pattern of aggressive behavior that has been going on for at least a year and that violates the established social rules or the rights of others. Problems may include threatening to harm people, abusing or killing animals, destroying property, being deceitful, or stealing.

conduction deafness Deafness caused by wax in the auditory canal, injury to the tympanic membrane, or malfunction of the ossicles.

cones Photoreceptors that contain three chemicals called opsins, which are activated in bright light and allow us to see color. Unlike rods, cones are wired individually to neighboring cells; this one-on-one system of relaying information allows us to see fine details.

conflict The feeling we experience when we must decide between two or more incompatible choices.

conformity Any behavior you perform because of group pressure, even though that pressure might not involve direct requests.

conscious thoughts Wishes, desires, or thoughts that we are aware of, or can recall, at any given moment.

consciousness An individual's different levels of awareness of his or her thoughts and feelings. Creating images in the mind, following thought processes, and having unique emotional experiences are all part of consciousness.

consensus In making attributions, determining whether other people engage in the same behavior in the same situation.

consistency In making attributions, determining whether an individual engages in a certain behavior every time he or she is in a particular situation.

contiguity theory The view that classical conditioning occurs because two stimuli (the neutral stimulus and the unconditioned stimulus) are paired close together in time (are contiguous). Eventually, as a result of this contiguous pairing, the neutral stimulus becomes the conditioned stimulus, which elicits the conditioned response.

continuity rule A perceptual rule stating that, in organizing stimuli, we tend to favor smooth or continuous paths when interpreting a series of points or lines.

continuous reinforcement The simplest reinforcement schedule, in which every occurrence of the operant response results in delivery of the reinforcer.

continuum of consciousness The wide range of human experiences, from being acutely aware and alert to being totally unaware and unresponsive.

control group In an experiment, subjects who undergo all the same procedures as the experimental subjects do, except that the control subjects do not receive the treatment.

Control Question Technique A lie detection procedure in which the examiner asks two kinds of questions: neutral questions that elicit little emotional response; and critical questions that are designed to elicit greater emotional responses. The person answers only "Yes" or "No" to the questions and, if guilty, is expected to show a greater emotional response to the critical questions than to the neutral questions.

controlled processes Activities that require full awareness, alertness, and concentration to reach some goal. Because of the strongly focused attention they require, controlled processes often interfere with other ongoing activities.

conventional level Kohlberg's intermediate level of moral reasoning. It consists of two stages: At stage 3, moral decisions are guided most by conforming to the standards of others we value; at stage 4, moral reasoning is determined most by conforming to the laws of society.

convergence In three-dimensional vision, a binocular cue for depth perception based on signals sent from the muscles that turn the eyes. To focus on near or approaching objects, these muscles turn the eyes inward, toward the nose. The brain uses the signals sent by these muscles to determine the distance of the object.

convergent thinking Beginning with a problem and coming up with a single correct solution.

conversion disorder A type of somatoform disorder characterized by unexplained and significant physical symptoms—headaches, nausea, dizziness, loss of sensation, paralysis—that suggest a real neurological or medical problem but for which no physical or organic cause can be identified. Anxiety or emotional distress is apparently converted to symptoms that disrupt physical functioning.

cornea The rounded, transparent covering over the front of the eye. As the light waves pass through the cornea, its curved surface bends, or focuses, the waves into a narrower beam.

corpus callosum A wide band of fibers that connects the left and right hemispheres of the brain. It has 200 million nerve fibers that allow information to pass back and forth between the hemispheres.

correlation An association or relationship between the occurrence of two or more events.

correlation coefficient A number that indicates the strength of a relationship between two or more events: the closer the number is to −1.00 or +1.00, the greater is the strength of the relationship.

cortex A thin layer of cells that essentially covers the entire surface of the forebrain. The cortex consists of the frontal, parietal, occipital, and temporal lobes, whose control centers allow us to carry out hundreds of cognitive, emotional, sensory, and motor functions.

counseling psychologist An individual who has a Ph.D in psychology or education and whose training included work in a counseling setting. Counseling psychologists generally have a less extensive research background than clinical psychologists and work in real-world settings, such as schools, industry, and private practice. Whereas clinical psychologists treat mental disorders, counseling psychologists deal largely with problems of living. To train as a counseling psychologist generally takes 4–6 years after obtaining a bachelor's degree.

counterattitudinal behavior Taking a public position that runs counter to your private attitude.

covariation model A model developed by Harold Kelley that may be used in deciding between internal and external attributions. The model says that, in determining attributions, we should look for factors that are present when the behavior occurs and factors that are absent when the behavior does not occur.

creative individual Someone who regularly solves problems, fashions products, or defines new questions that make an impact on his or her society.

creative thinking A combination of flexibility in thinking and reorganization of understanding to produce innovative ideas and solutions.

critical language period A period of time from infancy to adolescence when language is easiest to learn; in the period after adolescence through adulthood, language is more difficult to learn.

critical period In imprinting, a relatively brief time during which learning is most likely to occur. Also called the sensitive period.

cross-cultural approach A psychological viewpoint that studies the influence of cultural and ethnic similarities and differences on psychological and social functioning.

cross-sectional method A research design in which several groups of different-aged individuals are studied at the same time.

crowd A large group of persons, most of whom are unacquainted.

cultural bias In testing, the situation in which the wording of the questions and the experiences on which they are based are more familiar to members of some social groups than to others.

cultural-familial retardation Mental retardation that results from greatly impoverished environments, with no evidence of genetic or brain damage.

cultural influences Pervasive pressures that encourage members of a particular society or ethnic group to conform to shared behaviors, values, and beliefs.

culture-free test Test that does not contain vocabulary, experiences, or social situations greatly different from the cultural experiences of the individual taking the test.

cumulative record A continuous written record that shows an organism's responses and reinforcements.

curare A drug that enters the bloodstream, reaches the muscles, and blocks receptors on the muscles. As a result, acetylcholine, the neurotransmitter that normally activates muscles, is blocked, and the muscles are paralyzed.

DARE (Drug Abuse Resistance Program, sometimes referred to as D.A.R.E.) A program taught in the classroom by trained, uniformed police officers. It is based on the idea of using social influence and role playing to discourage adolescents from starting drug use and to encourage them to refuse drugs in the future.

daydreaming An activity that requires a low level of awareness, often occurs during automatic processes, and involves fantasizing or dreaming while awake.

debriefing A procedure administered to subjects after an experiment to minimize any potential negative effects. It includes explaining the purpose and method of the experiment, asking the subjects their feelings about having been in the experiment, and helping the subjects deal with possible doubts or guilt arising from their behaviors in the experiments.

decibel A unit to measure loudness. Our threshold for hearing ranges from 0 decibels, which is absolutely no sound, to 140 decibels, which can produce pain and permanent hearing loss.

decision-stage model of helping The idea that we go through five stages in deciding to help: (1) we notice the situation; (2) we interpret it as one in which help is needed; (3) we assume personal responsibility; (4) we choose a form of assistance; and (5) we carry out that assistance.

declarative memory Memories of facts or events, such as scenes, stories, words, conversations, faces, or daily events. We are aware of these kinds of memories and can retrieve them.

deductive reasoning Reasoning from the general to the particular: deriving a conclusion about particulars that is based on a general assumption that one knows or believes to be true.

deep structure According to Chomsky, a sentence's underlying meaning that is not spoken but is present in the mind of the listener.

defense mechanisms Freudian processes that operate at unconscious levels to help the ego reduce anxiety through self-deception.

deficiency needs Physiological needs (food, sleep) and psychological needs (safety, belongingness, and esteem) that we try to fulfill if they are not met.

definition theory The idea that we form a concept of an object, event, animal, person, or characteristic by making a mental list of the actual or essential properties that define it.

deindividuation The increased tendency for subjects to behave irrationally or perform antisocial behaviors when there is less chance of being personally identified.

deinstitutionalization The release of mental patients from mental hospitals and their return to the community to develop more independent and fulfilling lives.

delay of gratification Voluntarily postponing an immediate reward to persist in completing a task for the promise of a future reward.

dendrites Branchlike extensions that arise from the cell body; they receive signals from other neurons, muscles, or sense organs and pass them to the cell body.

denial Refusal to recognize some anxiety-provoking event or piece of information.

dependency A change in the nervous system such that a person addicted to a drug now needs to take it to prevent the occurrence of painful symptoms.

dependent personality disorder A pattern of being submissive and clingy because of an excessive need to be taken care of. It is found in 2% of the population.

dependent variable In an experiment, one or more of the subjects' behaviors that are used to measure the potential effects of the treatment or independent variable.

depth perception In visual perception, the ability of the eye and brain to add a third dimension, depth, to visual perceptions, even though the images projected on our retina have only two dimensions, height and width.

descriptive statistics Numbers used to present a collection of data in brief yet meaningful form.

designer drugs Manufactured or synthetic drugs designed to resemble already existing illegal psychoactive drugs and to produce or mimic their psychoactive effects.

developmental norms The average ages at which children perform various skills or exhibit particular abilities or behaviors.

developmental psychologists Psychologists who study a person's biological, emotional, cognitive, personal, and social development across the life span, from infancy through late adulthood.

developmental psychology The study of moral, social, emotional, and cognitive development throughout a person's entire life.

***Diagnostic and Statistical Manual of Mental Disorders–IV* (DSM-IV)** The 1994 edition of the American Psychiatric Association's uniform diagnostic system for assessing specific symptoms and matching them to almost 300 different mental disorders. The DSM-IV has five major dimensions, or axes.

diathesis stress theory of schizophrenia The idea that some people have a genetic predisposition (a diathesis) that interacts with life stressors to result in the onset and development of schizophrenia.

dichromats People who have trouble distinguishing red from green because their eyes have just two kinds of cones. This is an inherited condition, found mostly in males, that results in seeing mostly shades of green, but it differs in severity.

diffusion of responsibility theory The idea that, in the presence of others, individuals feel less personal responsibility and are less likely to take action in a situation where help is required.

direction of a sound The brain determines the direction of a sound by calculating the slight difference in time that it takes sound waves to reach the two ears, which are about six inches apart.

discrimination In classical conditioning, the tendency for some stimuli but not others to elicit a conditioned response. In operant conditioning, the tendency for a response to be emitted in the presence of a stimulus that is reinforced but not in the presence of unreinforced stimuli. In social psychology, specific unfair behaviors exhibited toward members of a group.

discriminative stimulus In conditioning, a cue that behavior will be enforced.

disgust A universal facial expression—closing the eyes, narrowing the nostrils, curling the lips downward, and sometimes sticking out the tongue—that indicates the rejection of an item of food.

disorganized schizophrenia A subcategory of schizophrenia marked by bizarre ideas, often about one's body (bones melting), confused speech, childish behavior (giggling for no apparent reason, making faces at people), great emotional swings (fits of laughing or crying), and often extreme neglect of personal appearance and hygiene.

displacement Transferring feelings from their true source to another source that is safer and more socially acceptable.

display rules Specific cultural norms that regulate when, where, and how much emotion we should or should not express in different situations.

dispositional attributions See internal attributions.

dissociative amnesia A dissociative disorder characterized by inability to recall important personal information or events and usually associated with stressful or traumatic events. The importance of the information forgotten or the duration of the memory lapse is too great to be explained by normal forgetfulness.

dissociative disorder A disorder characterized by a disruption, split, or breakdown in a person's normally integrated and functioning consciousness, memory, sense of identity, or perception.

dissociative fugue A disturbance in which an individual suddenly and unexpectedly travels away from home or place of work and is unable to recall his or her past. The person may not remember his or her identity or may be confused about his or her new, assumed identity.

dissociative identity disorder The presence in a single individual of two or more distinct identities or personality states, each with its own pattern of perceiving, thinking about, and relating to the world. Different personality states may take control of the individual's thoughts and behaviors at different times. Formerly called multiple personality disorder.

distinctiveness In making attributions, determining how differently the person behaves in one situation in comparison with other situations.

divergent thinking Beginning with a problem and coming up with many different solutions.

dopamine theory The idea that, in schizophrenia, the dopamine neurotransmitter system is somehow overactive and gives rise to a wide range of symptoms.

double-blind design An experimental design in which neither the researchers nor the subjects know which group is receiving which treatment. This design makes it possible to separate the effects of medical treatment from the participants' beliefs or expectations about the treatment.

double standard for sexual behavior A set of beliefs, values, and expectations that subtly encourages sexual activity in males but discourages the same behavior in females.

Down syndrome A genetic disorder that results from an extra 21st chromosome and causes abnormal physical traits (a fold of skin at the corner of each eye, a wide tongue, heart defects) and abnormal brain development, resulting in degrees of mental retardation.

dream interpretation A Freudian technique of dream analysis, based on the assumption that dreams contain underlying, hidden meanings and symbols that provide clues to unconscious thoughts and desires. Freud distinguished between a dream's manifest content—the plot of the dream at the surface level—and its latent content—the hidden or disguised meaning of the plot's events.

dreaming A unique state of consciousness in which we are asleep but we experience a variety of images, often in color. People blind from birth have only auditory or tactile dreams, while sighted people have dreams with astonishing visual, auditory, and tactile images.

drive A state of tension, produced by a need, that motivates the organism to act to reduce that tension.

drive-reduction theory The idea that a need results in a drive, which is a state of tension that motivates the organism to act to reduce the tension and return the body to homeostasis.

Drug Abuse Resistance Program See DARE.

DSM-IV See Diagnostic and Statistical Manual of Mental Disorders–IV.

dyslexia Reading, spelling, and writing difficulties that may include reversing or skipping letters and numbers. This condition affects 1–2% of children and is now regarded as a neurological disorder rather than a reading problem.

dysthymic disorder A mood disorder characterized by feeling chronically but not continuously depressed for a period of two years. While depressed, a person experiences at least two of the following symptoms: poor appetite, insomnia, fatigue, low self-esteem, poor concentration, and feelings of hopelessness.

eardrum See tympanic membrane.

echoic memory A form of sensory memory that holds auditory information for one or two seconds.

eclectic approach An approach to therapy in which the psychotherapist combines techniques and ideas from many different schools of thought.

ecological psychology An approach to measuring intelligence by observing how people solve problems in their usual settings.

ECT See electroconvulsive therapy.

efferent neurons Neurons that carry information away from the spinal cord to produce responses in various muscles and organs throughout the body. Also called motor neurons.

effortful encoding The transfer of information from short-term into long-term memory either by working hard to repeat or rehearse the information or by making associations between new and old information.

ego Freud's second division of the mind, which develops from the id during infancy; its goal is to find safe and socially acceptable ways of satisfying the id's desires and to negotiate between the id's wants and the superego's prohibitions.

egocentric thinking Seeing and thinking of the world only from your own viewpoint and having difficulty appreciating someone else's viewpoint. See also adolescent egocentric thinking.

eidetic imagery The ability to examine a picture or page for 10–30 seconds and then retain a detailed visual image of the material for several minutes. Eidetic memory is found in a small percentage of children and almost always disappears around adolescence.

elaborative rehearsal Making meaningful associations between information to be learned and information already learned. An effective strategy for encoding information into long-term memory.

Electra complex See Oedipus complex.

electroconvulsive therapy (ECT) A treatment for depression in which electrodes are placed on the skull and a mild electrical current is administered. As it passes through the brain, the current causes a seizure. Usual treatment consists of 10–12 ECT sessions, at the rate of about three per week.

embryonic stage The second stage of the prenatal period, spanning the 2–8 weeks that follow conception; during this stage, cells divide and begin to differentiate into bone, muscle, and body organs.

EMDR See Eye Movement Desensitization and Reprocessing.

emotion A response consisting of four components: interpreting or appraising a stimulus (event, object, or thought) in terms of one's well-being; having a subjective feeling, such as happiness or sadness; experiencing physiological responses, such as changes in heart rate or breathing; and possibly showing overt behaviors, such as smiling or crying.

emotion-focused coping Making some effort to deal with the emotional distress caused by a harm/loss or threat appraisal. These efforts include seeking support and sympathy, avoiding or denying the situation, or redirecting our attention.

emotional development The process in which we learn to produce facial expressions and experience associated emotional feelings, as a result of the interaction between our biological capacity to produce emotional expressions (nature) and the positive or negative feedback we receive from our environment (nurture).

encoding Placing or storing information—such as images, events, or sounds (music, noise, speech)—in memory by making mental representations.

end bulbs Bulblike swellings at the extreme ends of axons' branches that store chemicals called neurotransmitters, which are used to communicate with neighboring cells.

endocrine system Numerous glands, located throughout the body, that secrete various chemicals called hormones, which affect organs, muscles, and other glands in the body.

endorphins Chemicals produced by the brain and secreted in response to injury or severe physical or psychological stress. Their powerful pain-reducing properties are similar to those of morphine.

environmental language factors Interactions that children have with parents, peers, teachers, and others whose feedback rewards and encourages language development; these interactions also provide opportunities for children to observe, imitate, and practice language skills.

episodic memory A type of declarative memory, consisting of knowledge about one's personal experiences (episodes) or activities, such as naming or describing favorite restaurants, movies, songs, habits, or hobbies.

ESP *See* extrasensory perception.

estrogen One of the major female hormones. At puberty, estrogen levels increase eightfold and stimulate the development of both primary and secondary sexual characteristics.

ethologists Behavioral biologists who observe and study animal behavior in the animal's natural environment or under relatively naturalistic conditions.

evaluative function The role of our attitudes in helping us to stand up for those beliefs and values that we consider very important to ourselves.

evening persons People who prefer to get up late, go to bed late, and engage in afternoon or evening activities. *See* morning persons.

event schemas Social schemas containing behaviors that we associate with familiar activities, events, or procedures. Also called scripts.

evolution *See* theory of evolution.

evolutionary theory (of gender differences) The idea in sociobiology, which emphasizes genetic and biological forces, that current behavioral and cognitive differences between men and women can be traced back to different survival problems faced by early women and men and the different behaviors they adapted to survive.

exhaustion stage The third stage in the general adaptation syndrome. In reaction to long-term, continuous stress, there is actual breakdown in internal organs or weakening of the infection-fighting immune system.

experiment A method for identifying cause-and-effect relationships by following a set of rules and guidelines that minimize the possibility of error, bias, and chance occurrences. *See also* laboratory experiment.

experimental group In an experiment, the subjects who receive the treatment.

experimental psychology The study of sensation, perception, learning, human performance, motivation, and emotion in carefully controlled laboratory conditions, with both animal and human subjects.

exposure therapy A treatment for anxiety in which the person is gradually exposed to the real anxiety-producing situations or objects that he or she is attempting to avoid; exposure treatment is continued until the anxiety decreases.

external attributions Explanations of behavior based on the external circumstances or situations. Also called situational attributions.

external ear An oval-shaped structure that protrudes from the side of the head. Its function is to pick up sound waves and send them along the auditory canal.

extinction In classical conditioning, the reduction in a response when the conditioned stimulus is no longer followed by the unconditioned stimulus. As a result, the conditioned stimulus tends to no longer elicit the conditioned response. In operant conditioning, reduction in the operant response when it is no longer followed by the reinforcer.

extrasensory perception (ESP) A group of psychic experiences that involve perceiving or sending information (images) outside normal sensory processes or channels. ESP includes four general abilities—telepathy, precognition, clairvoyance, and psychokinesis.

extrinsic motivation Engaging in certain activities or behaviors that either reduce biological needs or help us to obtain incentives or external rewards.

Eye Movement Desensitization and Reprocessing (EMDR) A new technique in which the client focuses on a traumatic memory while visually following the back-and-forth movement of a therapist's hand or pen. One memory may trigger another, which the client focuses on while again visually following the back-and-forth movement. The process usually continues throughout a 90-minute session, during which the traumatic memories are said to be reprocessed by eye movements that help replace traumatic memories with pleasant ones.

eyewitness testimony Recollection or recognition of a suspect observed during a possibly disruptive emotional situation that may have interfered with accurate remembering.

facial expressions Social signals that accompany emotions and express the state of our personal feelings; they provide social signals that elicit a variety of responses from those around us.

facial feedback theory The idea that sensations or feedback from the movement of facial muscles and skin are interpreted by your brain as emotional feelings.

factor analysis A complicated statistical method that finds relationships among different or diverse items and allows them to be grouped together.

farsightedness A visual acuity problem that may result when the eyeball is too short, so that objects are focused at a point slightly behind the retina. The result is that distant objects are clear, but near objects are blurry.

FAS *See* fetal alcohol syndrome.

fat cells Cells that store body fat. The number of fat cells in the body is primarily determined by heredity. They do not normally multiply except when we become obese. Fat cells shrink as we give up fat and lose weight and greatly enlarge as we store fat and gain weight.

fear A realistic response to a threatening situation.

fear of failure A tendency to avoid failure by choosing easy, nonchallenging tasks where failure is unlikely or difficult.

female circumcision The practice of cutting away the female's external genitalia, usually including her clitoris and surrounding skin (labia minora). The remaining edges are sewn together, which leaves only a small opening for urination and menstruation.

female hypothalamus Because of neural programming in the womb, the hypothalamus, a structure in the brain that controls the endocrine system, functions differently in the male and female. The female hypothalamus triggers a cyclical release of estrogens from the ovaries. The increased estrogen level is responsible for female secondary sexual characteristics, such as pubic hair, breast development, and widening of the hips. The cyclic release of hormones (estrogen and progesterone) also regulates the menstrual cycle.

female secondary sexual characteristics Sexual characteristics whose development in the female is triggered by the increased secretion of estrogen during puberty; they include the growth of pubic hair, development of breasts, and widening of hips.

fertilization *See* conception.

fertilized egg A single cell that results after a sperm has entered or fertilized an egg, or ovum. A fertilized egg contains the equivalent of a million pages of chemically coded instructions for the development of the body and brain.

fetal alcohol syndrome (FAS) A condition caused by heavy maternal drinking during pregnancy. It results in a combination of physical changes, such as short stature, flattened nose, and short eye openings, and psychological defects, such as degrees of mental retardation and hyperactivity.

fetal stage The third stage in prenatal development, beginning two months after conception and lasting until birth.

fight-flight response A state of increased physiological arousal that (a) directs great sources of energy to the muscles and brain, (b) can be triggered by either physical stimuli that threaten our survival or psychological situations that are novel, threatening, or challenging, and (c) involves numerous physiological responses that arouse and prepare the body for action—fight or flight. Caused by the activation of the sympathetic nervous system, it helps us to cope with, and survive, threatening situations.

Glossary

figure-ground rule A perceptual rule stating that, in organizing stimuli, we tend to automatically distinguish between a figure and a ground: the figure, with more detail, stands out against the background, which has less detail.

five-factor model An approach to personality in which all traits are organized under five categories—openness, conscientiousness, extraversion, agreeableness, and neuroticism—that are used to describe differences in personality.

fixation A Freudian process through which an individual may be locked into any one of the three psychosexual stages—oral, anal, or phallic—because his or her wishes were either overgratified or undergratified in that stage.

fixed action pattern An innate biological force that predisposes an organism to behave in a fixed way in the presence of a specific environmental condition. Previously called instinct.

fixed-interval schedule In conditioning, a schedule in which a reinforcer occurs following a subject's first response after a fixed interval of time.

fixed-ratio schedule In conditioning, a schedule in which a reinforcer occurs only after a fixed number of responses by the subject.

flashbulb memories Vivid recollections, usually in great detail, of dramatic or emotionally charged incidents, which are encoded effortlessly and may last for long periods of time.

flavor What we experience when we combine the sensations of taste and smell.

foot-in-the-door technique A method of persuasion that relies on the increased probability of compliance to a second request if a person complies with a small, first request.

forebrain The largest part of the brain, consisting of left and right hemispheres, which are connected by a wide band of fibers, the corpus callosum. The hemispheres are responsible for a vast array of responses, including learning and memory, speaking and language, emotional responses, experiencing sensations, initiating voluntary movements, planning, and making decisions.

forgetting Inability to retrieve, recall, or recognize information that was stored or is still stored in long-term memory.

forgetting curve A graph measuring the amount of previously learned information that subjects can recall or recognize across time.

formal operations stage Piaget's fourth cognitive stage, lasting from about 12 years of age through adulthood. During this stage, adolescents and adults develop the ability to think about abstract or hypothetical concepts, to consider an issue from another person's viewpoint, and to solve cognitive problems in a logical manner.

fragile X syndrome A defect in the X chromosome that can result in physical changes such as a relatively large head with protruding ears, as well as mild to profound levels of mental retardation.

fraternal twins Twins who develop from separate eggs and share 50% of their genes.

free association A Freudian technique in which clients are encouraged to talk about any thoughts or images that enter their heads; the assumption is that this kind of free-flowing, uncensored talking will provide clues to unconscious material.

frequency distribution The range of scores we get and the frequency of each one, when we measure a sample of people (or objects) regarding some trait.

frequency theory In explaining pitch perception, the idea that, for low-frequency sound waves (1000 cycles or less), the rate at which nerve impulses reach the brain determines how low a sound is. A rate of 50 impulses per second would be interpreted as a lower sound than a rate of 200 impulses per second.

Freud's psychodynamic theory of personality A personality theory that emphasizes the importance of early childhood experiences; repressed thoughts that we cannot voluntarily access; and the conflicts between conscious and unconscious forces that influence our thoughts and behaviors. *See also* psychoanalytic approach.

Freud's theory of dreams A theory that says we have a "censor" that protects us from realizing threatening and unconscious desires or wishes, especially those involving sex or aggression, by transforming them into harmless symbols that appear in our dreams and do not disturb our sleep or conscious thoughts.

Freud's theory of the unconscious The idea that, when faced with very threatening—especially sexual or aggressive—wishes or desires, we automatically defend our self-esteem by placing these psychologically dangerous thoughts into a mental place, the unconscious, that is sealed off from voluntary recall.

Freudian slips Mistakes or slips of the tongue that we make in everyday speech; such mistakes are thought to reflect unconscious thoughts or wishes.

frontal lobe An area in the front part of the brain that includes a huge area of cortex. The frontal lobe is involved in many functions: performing voluntary motor movements, interpreting and performing emotional behaviors, behaving normally in social situations, maintaining a healthy personality, paying attention to things in the environment, making decisions, and carrying out plans.

frontal lobotomy A surgical procedure in which about one-third of the front part of the frontal lobe is separated from the rest of the brain.

frustration The feeling that results when our attempts to reach some goal are blocked.

frustration-aggression hypothesis The idea that, when our goals are blocked, we become frustrated and respond with anger and aggression. *See also* modified frustration-aggression hypothesis.

functional fixedness A mental set characterized by the inability to see an object as having a function different from its usual one.

functionalism An early school of psychological thought that emphasized the function rather than the structure of consciousness and was interested in how our minds adapt to our changing environment.

fundamental attribution error Our tendency, when we look for causes of a person's behavior, to focus on the person's disposition or personality traits and overlook how the situation influenced the person's behavior.

galvanic skin response Changes in sweating of the fingers (or palms) that accompany emotional experiences and are independent of perspiration under normal temperatures.

Ganzfeld procedure A controlled method for eliminating trickery, error, and bias while testing telepathic communication between two people.

Gardner's multiple-intelligence theory The idea that, instead of one kind of general intelligence, there are at least seven different kinds: verbal intelligence, musical intelligence, logical-mathematical intelligence, spatial intelligence, body movement intelligence, intelligence to understand oneself, and intelligence to understand others.

GAS *See* general adaptation syndrome.

gate control theory The idea that nonpainful nerve impulses compete with pain impulses as they enter the spinal cord, creating a neural gate through which only the nonpainful impulses pass; the pain impulses do not reach the brain. Thus, feelings of pain may be reduced by rubbing an injured area or becoming absorbed in other activities.

gender identity The individual's subjective experience and feelings of being either a male or a female; formerly called sexual identity.

gender identity disorder Commonly referred to as transsexualism, it is an individual's strong desire or feeling of wanting to be the opposite sex, discomfort with being one's assigned sex, and the wish to live as a member of the other sex.

gender roles Traditional or stereotypic behaviors, attitudes, and personality traits that parents, peers, and society designate as masculine or feminine. Gender roles affect how we think and behave; formerly called sex roles.

gender schemas Sets of information and rules organized around how either a male or a female should think and behave.

gene A specific segment on the strand of DNA (the chromosome) that contains instructions for making proteins, the chemical building blocks from which all the parts of the brain and body are constructed.

general adaptation syndrome (GAS) According to Selye, a series of three stages—alarm, resistance, and exhaustion—that correspond to the three different reactions of the body to stressful situations and that gradually increase the chances of developing psychosomatic symptoms.

generalization In classical conditioning, the tendency for a stimulus that is similar to the original conditioned stimulus to elicit a response that is similar to the conditioned response.

Usually, the more similar the new stimulus is to the original conditioned stimulus, the larger will be the conditioned response. In operant conditioning, the situation in which an animal or a person emits the same response to similar stimuli.

generalized anxiety disorder A psychological disorder primarily characterized by excessive and/or unrealistic worry or feelings of general apprehension about events or activities. These anxious feelings occur on a majority of days for a period of at least six months.

genetic hunger factors Inherited instructions found in our genes that influence our hunger; these instructions may determine our number of fat cells or our metabolic rate of burning off the body's fuel, for example, and push us toward being normal, overweight, or underweight.

genetic marker An identifiable gene or number of genes or a specific segment of a chromosome that is directly linked to some behavioral, physiological, or neurological trait or disease.

genetic sex factors Inherited instructions for the development of sexual organs, the secretion of sex hormones, and the wiring of the neural circuits that control sexual reflexes.

genital stage Freud's fifth, and final, psychosexual stage, lasting from puberty through adulthood. In this stage, the individual has renewed sexual desires that he or she seeks to fulfill through relationships with other people.

germinal stage The first stage of prenatal development, lasting two weeks from the moment of conception.

Gestalt approach An older theoretical approach that emphasized the idea that perception is more than the sum of its parts. In contrast to the structuralists, the Gestalt psychologists believed that perceptions are formed by the brain on the basis of a set of rules specifying how individual elements may be organized to form a meaningful pattern—that is, a perception.

gifted A term applied to an individual (usually to a child) who has above-average intelligence as well as some superior talent or skill. A moderately gifted child is usually defined by an IQ score between 130 and 150; a profoundly gifted child has an IQ score of 180 or above.

glial cells Cells in the nervous system that have at least three functions: they provide scaffolding to guide the growth of developing neurons and support mature neurons; they wrap themselves around neurons and form a kind of insulation to prevent interference from other electrical signals; and they release chemicals that influence a neuron's growth and function.

gonads Glands—the ovaries in females and the testes in males—that produce hormones to regulate sexual development, ovulation or sperm production, and the growth of sex organs. They are part of the endocrine system.

grammar A set of rules for combining words into phrases and sentences to express an infinite number of thoughts that can be understood by others.

group A collection of two or more people who interact and share some common attribute or purpose. A group also influences how its members think and behave.

group cohesion Group togetherness, which is determined by how much group members perceive that they share common attributes.

group norms Formal or informal rules about how group members should behave.

group polarization The phenomenon in which group discussion reinforces the majority's point of view and shifts that view to a more extreme position.

groupthink Poor group decision making that occurs when group discussions emphasize cohesion and agreement rather than critical thinking and the best possible outcome.

growth needs According to Maslow, higher-level needs that are not essential to existence, such as the desire for truth, goodness, beauty, and justice.

hair cells The auditory receptors. These miniature hair-shaped cells rise from the basilar membrane in the cochlea.

hallucinations Sensory experiences without any stimulation from the environment. Common symptoms of schizophrenia, hallucinations may be auditory, such as hearing voices; or they may include distorted perceptions, such as feeling that parts of one's body are too small or too large.

hallucinogens Psychoactive drugs that can produce hallucinations—strange perceptual, sensory, and cognitive experiences that the person sees or hears but knows are not occurring in reality. Such unreal experiences are called hallucinations.

happiness A mental state that includes three components: feeling positive emotions, being satisfied with one's life, and not experiencing negative emotions.

hardiness A combination of three personality traits—control, commitment, and challenge—that protect or buffer us from the potentially harmful effects of stressful situations and reduce our chances of developing psychosomatic illness.

harm/loss appraisal Our conclusion that we have already sustained some damage or injury in a particular situation.

hassles Small, irritating, frustrating events that we face daily and that we usually appraise as stressful experiences.

helping *See* prosocial behavior.

heritability A statistical measure that estimates the amount or proportion of some ability, characteristic, or trait that can be attributed to genetic factors.

heterosexual orientation A pattern of sexual arousal by persons of the opposite sex.

heuristics Rules of thumb that reduce the number of operations or allow us to take shortcuts in solving problems.

hierarchy of needs *See* Maslow's hierarchy of needs.

high need for achievement A tendency to persist longer at tasks; show better performance on tasks, activities, or exams; set challenging but realistic goals; compete with others to win; and be attracted to careers that require initiative.

hindbrain An area at the base of the brain that is involved in sleeping, waking, coordinating body movements, and regulating vital reflexes (heart rate, blood pressure, and respiration).

hippocampus A curved structure within the temporal lobe that is involved in transforming many kinds of fleeting memories into permanent storage. It forms part of the limbic system.

histrionic personality disorder A disorder characterized by excessive emotionality and attention seeking. It is found in 2% of the population.

HIV positive Having HIV antibodies, which implies infection by the human immunodeficiency virus (HIV).

holistic view The idea, emphasized in humanistic theories, that a person's personality is more than the sum of its individual parts; instead, the individual parts form a unique and total entity that functions as a unit.

homeostasis The tendency of the sympathetic and parasympathetic divisions of the autonomic nervous system to work together to maintain the body's level of arousal in balance for optimum functioning.

homosexual orientation A pattern of sexual arousal by persons of the same sex.

humanistic approach A psychological viewpoint emphasizing that each individual has great freedom in directing his or her future, considerable capacity for achieving personal growth, intrinsic worth, and enormous potential for self-fulfillment.

humanistic theories *See* humanistic approach.

hypnosis A situation or set of procedures in which a researcher, clinician, or hypnotist suggests to another person that he or she will experience various changes in sensation, perception, cognition, or control over motor behaviors.

hypnotic analgesia Reduction in pain reported by clients after undergoing hypnosis and receiving suggestions that reduced anxiety and promoted relaxation.

hypnotic induction Various methods of inducing hypnosis, such as asking subjects to close their eyes and go to sleep, having them fix their attention on an object (for example, a watch), and instructing them to go into deep relaxation.

hypothalamus A structure of the limbic system that is located near the bottom middle of the brain and regulates many motivational and emotional behaviors. It controls much of the endocrine system by regulating the pituitary gland.

hypothesis An educated guess about some phenomenon, stated in precise, concrete language so as to rule out any confusion or error in the meaning of its terms.

iconic memory A form of sensory memory that holds visual information for about a quarter of a second or more. (The word *icon* means "image.")

Glossary

id Freud's first division of the mind, which contains two biological drives—sex and aggression—that are the source of all psychic or mental energy; the id's goal is to pursue pleasure and satisfy the biological drives.

ideal self According to Rogers, the self that is based on our hopes and wishes and reflects how we would like to see ourselves; its complement is the real self.

ideal weight *See* optimum weight.

identical twins Twins who develop from a single egg and thus have exactly the same genes.

identity How we describe ourselves, including our values, goals, traits, interests, and motivations.

illusion Perception of an image so distorted that, in reality, it cannot and does not exist. An illusion is created when space, size, and depth cues are manipulated so that our brains can no longer correctly interpret them.

imagined perception In hypnosis, the subject's willingness, at the hypnotist's suggestion, to respond to nonexistent stimuli and imaginary perceptions. It can also include bizarre behaviors, such as imitating Elvis Presley in public.

immune system The body's defense and surveillance network of cells and chemicals that fight off bacteria, viruses, and other foreign or toxic substances.

implicit memory *See* procedural memory.

impossible figure A perceptual experience in which a drawing seems to defy basic geometric laws.

imprinting Inherited tendencies or responses that are displayed by newborn animals when they encounter certain stimuli in their environment.

incentives Environmental factors, such as external stimuli, reinforcers, or rewards, that motivate our behavior.

independent variable In an experiment, a treatment or something else that the researcher controls or manipulates.

individualistic culture A culture that places a high priority on attaining personal goals and striving for personal satisfaction, often by being competitive and assertive.

inductive reasoning Reasoning from particulars to the general: using particular experiences or observations to draw a broader conclusion.

inferential statistics A set of procedures for determining what conclusions can be legitimately inferred from a set of data.

informational influence theory The theory that we use the reactions of others to judge the seriousness of the situation.

inhibited children Kagan's term for children who show reluctance, anxiety, or fear (measured by motor activity, fretting, or crying) when approaching a strange child, exploring novel objects, playing with a peer, or talking to an unfamiliar adult. In addition, inhibited children show increased physiological arousal to novel or strange situations.

inhibited female orgasm A persistent delay or absence of orgasm after becoming aroused and excited.

innate language factors Genetically programmed physiological and neurological features of the brain and vocal apparatus that facilitate our making speech sounds and learning language skills.

insanity According to the legal definition, not knowing the difference between right and wrong.

insecure attachment An emotional bond characteristic of infants who avoid, or show ambivalence toward, their parents.

insight A mental process marked by the sudden and unexpected solution to a problem: a phenomenon often called the "ah-ha!" experience.

insight therapy An approach in which the therapist and client talk about the client's symptoms and problems, with the goal of identifying the cause of the problem. Once the client has an insight into the cause of the problem, possible solutions can be discussed with the therapist.

insomnia Difficulties in going to sleep or in staying asleep through the night. Associated daytime complaints include fatigue, impairment of concentration, memory difficulty, and lack of well-being. About 20–40% of adult Americans report bouts of insomnia.

instincts According to McDougal (1908), innate tendencies or biological forces that determine behavior; now used as a synonym for fixed action pattern.

intelligence quotient (IQ) A measure of intelligence computed by dividing a child's mental age, as measured in an intelligence test, by the child's chronological age and multiplying the result by 100.

interactive model of sexual orientation The theory that genetic and biological factors, such as genetic instructions and prenatal hormones, interact with psychological factors, such as the individual's attitudes, personality traits, and behaviors, to influence the development of sexual orientation.

interference The forgetting process in which the recall of some particular memory is blocked or prevented by new information that overwrites or interferes with it. *See also* proactive interference and retroactive interference.

internal attributions Explanations of behavior on the basis of the internal characteristics (or dispositions) of the person performing the behavior. Also referred to as dispositional attributions.

interneuron A relatively short neuron whose primary task is to make connections between other neurons.

interpersonal conflict A situation characterized by opposing interests or disagreements, in which one person interferes with a goal, a wish, or an expectation of another.

interposition In three-dimensional vision, a monocular depth cue that comes into play when objects overlap. The overlapping object appears closer, and the object that is overlapped appears to be farther away.

interpreting function The role played by our attitudes in providing convenient guidelines by means of which we can interpret and categorize objects and events and decide whether to approach or avoid them.

interval timing clock A sort of timing device, located in the basal ganglia of the brain, that gauges the passage of seconds, minutes, or hours and helps creatures know when to start or stop doing some activity.

intervention program A program for disadvantaged children that creates an environment offering increased opportunities for intellectual, social, and personality-emotional development while ensuring good physical health.

interview A technique for obtaining information by asking questions, ranging from open-ended to highly structured, about a subject's behaviors and attitudes, usually in a one-on-one situation.

intimacy In Sternberg's triangular theory of love, the component of love associated with feeling close and connected to someone; it develops through sharing and communicating.

intrinsic motivation Engaging in certain activities or behaviors because they are personally rewarding or because we are fulfilling our beliefs or expectations.

introspection A method of exploring conscious mental processes adopted by the structuralists: subjects were asked to look inward and report their sensations and perceptions.

intrusive thoughts Thoughts that we repeatedly experience, that are usually unwanted or disruptive, and that are very difficult to stop or eliminate.

Inuit beliefs about dreams The Inuit, or Eskimo people, like other isolated indigenous people, believe that dreams are ways to enter the spiritual world, where the souls of departed animals, supernaturals, and relatives are made known.

ions Electrically charged chemical particles, which obey the rule that opposite charges attract and like charges repel.

IQ *See* intelligence quotient.

iris A circular muscle that surrounds the pupil and controls the amount of light that enters the eye. In dim light, the iris relaxes, allowing more light to enter—the pupil dilates; in bright light, the iris constricts, allowing less light to enter—the pupil constricts. The iris muscle contains the pigment that gives the eye its characteristic color.

James-Lange theory The idea that our brains interpret specific physiological changes as feelings or emotions and that there is a different physiological pattern underlying each emotion.

jet lag A condition in which travelers' internal circadian rhythm is out of step, or synchrony, with the external clock time at their new location. They experience fatigue, disorientation, lack of concentration, and reduced cognitive skills. It takes about one day to reset the circadian clock for each hour of time change.

just noticeable difference (JND) The smallest increase or decrease in the intensity of a stimulus that a person can manage to detect.

justice orientation Making moral decisions based more on issues of law and equality and individual rights.

labeling A process of identifying differences among individuals and placing them into specific categories, which may have either positive or negative associations.

laboratory experiment A technique to gather information by studying behavior in a controlled environment that permits the careful manipulation of some treatment and the measurement of the treatment's effects on behavior.

laboratory setting An environment in which individuals may be studied under systematic and controlled conditions, thus eliminating many of the real-world influences.

language A form of communication in which we learn and use complex rules to form and manipulate symbols (words or gestures) that are used to generate an endless number of meaningful sentences.

language stages Four different periods in a child's acquisition of language and grammar—babbling, single words, two-word combinations, and sentences; in each subsequent stage, a child displays new and more complex language skills.

latency stage The fourth of Freud's psychosexual stages, lasting from the age of about 6 to puberty. In this stage, the child represses sexual thoughts and engages in nonsexual activities, such as developing social and intellectual skills.

law of effect The principle that behaviors followed by positive (pleasurable) consequences are strengthened (and thus will likely occur in the future), while behaviors followed by negative consequences are weakened.

learning A relatively permanent change in behavior (both unobservable mental events and observable responses) associated with specific stimuli and/or responses that change as a result of experience.

learning-performance distinction The idea that learning may occur but may not always be measured by, or immediately evident in, performance.

lens A transparent, oval structure in the eye whose curved surface functions to bend and focus light waves into an even narrower beam. The lens is attached to muscles that adjust the curve of the lens, which, in turn, adjusts the focusing.

levels-of-processing theory The theory that memory depends on how well information is encoded in the mind. Information is encoded at a shallow level if we simply pay attention to its basic features but is encoded at a deep level if we form new associations with existing information. According to the theory, poor memory corresponds to information encoded at a shallow level, and good memory to information encoded at deep levels.

lie detector tests *See* polygraph tests.

light and shadow A monocular depth cue: brightly lit objects appear closer, while objects in shadows appear farther away.

light therapy The use of bright, artificial light to reset circadian rhythms and so combat the insomnia and drowsiness that plague shift workers and jet-lag sufferers; it is also used to help people with sleeping disorders in which the body fails to stay in time with the external environment.

limbic system A group of about half a dozen interconnected structures in the core of the forebrain that are involved in many motivational behaviors, such as obtaining food, drink, and sex; organizing emotional behaviors such as fear, anger, and aggression; and with storing memories. It is sometimes referred to as our primitive, or animal, brain because the same structures are found in the brains of animals that are evolutionarily very old.

linear perspective In three-dimensional vision, a monocular depth cue associated with the convergence of parallel lines in the far distance.

linguistic relativity *See* theory of linguistic relativity.

lithium A naturally occurring mineral salt that is the most effective treatment for bipolar I disorder. It reduces or prevents manic episodes.

locus of control Our beliefs concerning how much control we have over situations or rewards. For each of us, these beliefs lie somewhere on a continuum between internal and external locus of control. We have an internal locus of control if we believe that we have control over situations and rewards and an external locus of control if we believe that we do not have control over situations and rewards and that events outside ourselves (fate) determine what happens.

long-term memory The process that can store almost unlimited amounts of information over long periods of time.

long-term potentiation (LTP) The increased sensitivity of a neuron to stimulation after it has been repeatedly stimulated. Neuroscientists believe that the LTP process may be the basis for learning and memory in animals and humans.

longitudinal method A research design in which the same group of individuals is studied repeatedly at many different points in time.

loudness Our subjective experience of a sound's intensity, which is determined by the height (amplitude) of the sound wave. The brain calculates loudness from the rate of nerve impulses that arrive in the auditory nerve.

LSD (lysergic acid diethylamide) A very potent hallucinogen. Very small doses can produce experiences such as visual hallucinations, perceptual distortions, increased sensory awareness, and emotional responses that may last 8–10 hours.

LTP *See* long-term potentiation.

magnetic resonance imaging (MRI scan) A technique for studying the structure of the living brain. Nonharmful radio frequencies are passed through the brain, and a computer measures their interaction with brain cells and transforms this interaction into an incredibly detailed image of the brain (or body).

maintenance rehearsal The practice of intentionally repeating or rehearsing information (rather than forming any new associations) so that it remains longer in short-term memory.

major depressive disorder A mood disorder marked by at least two weeks of continually being in a bad mood, having no interest in anything, and getting no pleasure from activities. In addition, a person must have at least four of the following symptoms: problems with eating, sleeping, thinking, concentrating, or making decisions; lacking energy, thinking about suicide, and feeling worthless or guilty. Also called unipolar depression.

major life events Potentially disturbing, troubling, or disruptive situations, both positive and negative, that we appraise as having a significant impact on our lives.

maladaptive behavior approach In defining abnormality, the idea that a behavior is psychologically damaging or abnormal if it interferes with the individual's ability to function in one's personal life or in society.

male hypothalamus Because of neural programming in the womb, the hypothalamus, a structure in the brain that controls the endocrine system, functions differently in the male and female. The male hypothalamus triggers a continuous release of androgens, such as testosterone, from the testes. The increased androgen level is responsible for male secondary sexual characteristics, such as facial and pubic hair, muscle growth, and lowered voice.

male secondary sexual characteristics Sexual characteristics whose development in the male is triggered by the increased secretion of testosterone during puberty; they include the growth of pubic hair, muscle development, and a change (deepening) of the voice.

marijuana A psychoactive drug whose primary active ingredient is THC (tetrahydrocannabinol), which is found in the leaves of the cannabis plant. Low doses produce mild euphoria; moderate doses produce perceptual and time distortions; and high doses may produce hallucinations, delusions, and distortions of body image.

Maslow's hierarchy of needs An ascending order, or hierarchy, in which biological needs are placed at the bottom and social needs at the top. As needs at lower levels are met, we advance to the next higher level. This hierarchy indicates that we satisfy our biological needs before we satisfy our social needs.

mass hysteria A condition experienced by a group of people who, through suggestion, observation, or other psychological processes, develop similar fears, delusions, abnormal behaviors, and in some cases, similar physical symptoms.

maturation The succession of developmental changes that are genetically or biologically programmed rather than acquired through learning or life experiences.

MDMA A stimulant and hallucinogen that appeared in the early 1980s. Users claim that this designer drug, whose street name is ecstasy, causes changes in visual perceptions, increases emotional awareness, feelings of intimacy, and ability to interact with others. Because it lowers inhibitions, some consider it an aphrodisiac.

mean The arithmetic average of all the individual measurements in a distribution.

measure of variability An indication of how much scores in a distribution vary from one another.

median The score above and below which half the scores in the distribution fall.

medical model approach The view that mental disorders are similar to physical diseases and that both have symptoms that can be diagnosed and treated. Just as doctors use drugs to treat physical diseases, psychiatrists use psychoactive drugs to treat mental disorders.

medical therapy Any approach that uses psychoactive drugs, such as tranquilizers and neuroleptics, to treat mental disorders by changing biological factors, such as the levels of neurotransmitters in the brain.

medulla An area in the hindbrain, located at the top of the spinal cord, that includes a group of cells that control vital reflexes, such as respiration, heart rate, and blood pressure.

melatonin A hormone secreted by the pineal gland, an oval group of cells in the center of the human brain. Melatonin secretion, controlled by the suprachiasmatic nucleus, increases with darkness and decreases with light; thus, it plays a role in the regulation of circadian rhythms and in promoting sleep.

memory The ability to retain information over time through the processes of encoding, storing, and retrieving. Memories are not copies but representations of the world that vary in accuracy and are subject to error and bias.

menarche The first menstrual period; it is a signal that ovulation may have occurred and that the girl may have the potential to conceive and bear a child.

Meniere's disease Sudden attacks of dizziness, nausea, vomiting, and head-splitting buzzing sounds that result from a malfunction of the semicircular canals in the vestibular system.

menopause A gradual stoppage in the secretion of the major female hormone (estrogen). This process, which occurs in women at about age 50 (range 35–60), results in the cessation of ovulation and the menstrual cycle.

mental age The estimation of a child's intellectual progress, which is calculated by comparing the child's score on an intelligence test to the scores of average children of the same age.

mental disorder A prolonged or recurring problem that seriously interferes with an individual's ability to live a satisfying personal life and function adequately in society.

mental retardation Substantial limitation in present functioning, characterized by significantly subaverage intellectual functioning along with related limitations in two of ten areas, including communication, self-care, home living, social skills, and safety.

mescaline The active ingredient in the peyote cactus. At high doses, mescaline produces physiological arousal and very clear, colorful, and vivid visual hallucinations. It primarily increases the activity of the neurotransmitters norepinephrine and dopamine. Mescaline does not impair the intellect or cloud consciousness.

meta-analysis A powerful statistical procedure that compares the results of dozens or hundreds of studies to determine the effectiveness of some variable or treatment examined in those studies (for example, a type of therapy).

metabolic rate The efficiency with which the body breaks food down into energy and the speed with which the body burns off that fuel. An inherited trait, it can be raised by exercise or smoking.

methamphetamine (D-methamphetamine) A stimulant similar to amphetamine in both its chemical makeup and its physical and psychological effects. It causes marked increases in blood pressure and heart rate and feelings of enhanced mood, alertness, and energy. Methamphetamine, whose street names are crystal and ice, produces an almost instantaneous high when smoked and is highly addictive.

method of loci A mnemonic device, or encoding technique, that improves encoding by creating visual associations between memorized places and new items to be memorized.

midbrain The smallest division of the brain; it makes connections with the hindbrain and forebrain and alerts the forebrain to incoming sensations.

middle ear A bony cavity that is sealed at each end by a membrane. The two membranes are connected by three small bones, collectively called ossicles. Because of their shapes, these bones are referred to as the hammer, anvil, and stirrup. The ossicles act like levers that greatly amplify vibrations from the eardrum and transmit them to the oval window and inner ear.

mind-body connection The ability of our thoughts, beliefs, and emotions to produce physiological changes that may be either beneficial or detrimental to our health and well-being.

mind-body question The debate about how complex mental activities, such as feeling, thinking, learning, imagining, and dreaming, can be generated by the brain's physical membranes, fluids, and chemicals.

mind-body therapy An approach to healing based on the finding that thoughts and emotions can change physiological and immune responses. It attempts to increase physical and mental well-being by means of mental strategies such as relaxation, meditation, and biofeedback, as well as social support groups.

Minnesota Multiphasic Personality Inventory-2 (MMPI-2) A true-false self-report questionnaire that consists of 567 statements describing a wide range of normal and abnormal behaviors. The purpose of MMPI-2 is to help distinguish normal from abnormal groups.

mnemonic methods Very effective ways to improve encoding and create better retrieval cues by forming vivid associations or images, which facilitate recall and decrease forgetting.

mode The most frequent measurement in a distribution.

modified frustration-aggression hypothesis The idea that although frustration may lead to aggression, a number of situational and cognitive factors may override the aggressive response.

monochromats Individuals who have total color blindness; their world looks like a black-and-white movie. This kind of color blindness is rare and results from individuals having only rods or only one kind of functioning cone instead of three.

monocular depth cues In three-dimensional vision, depth cues produced by signals from a single eye. They are most commonly determined by the way objects are arranged in the environment.

mood disorder A prolonged and disturbed emotional state that affects almost all of a person's thoughts and behaviors.

moral therapy The belief that mental patients could be helped to function better by providing humane treatment in a relaxed and decent environment; this approach was fundamental to the reform movement of the early 1800s.

morning persons People who prefer to get up early, go to bed early, and engage in morning activities. *See* evening persons.

morphemes The smallest meaningful combination of sounds in a language.

morphology A system that we use to group phonemes—consonants and vowels—into meaningful combinations of sounds and words.

motion parallax In three-dimensional vision, a monocular depth cue based on the speed of moving objects: objects that appear to be moving at high speed are interpreted as closer to us than those moving more slowly.

motion sickness Feelings of nausea and dizziness experienced in a moving vehicle when information from the vestibular system (that your head is bouncing around) conflicts with that reported by your eyes (that objects in the distance look fairly steady).

motivation Various physiological and psychological factors that cause us to act in a specific way at a particular time.

motor cortex A narrow strip of cortex that is located on the back edge of the frontal lobe and extends down its side. It is involved in the initiation of all voluntary movements. The right motor cortex controls muscles on the left side of the body and vice versa.

motor development The stages of motor skills that all infants pass through as they acquire the muscular control necessary for making coordinated movements.

motor neurons *See* efferent neurons.

MRI scan *See* magnetic resonance imaging.

multiple-intelligence theory *See* Gardner's multiple-intelligence theory.

myelin sheath A tubelike structure of fatty material that wraps around and insulates an axon, preventing interference from electrical signals generated in adjacent axons.

narcolepsy A relatively rare, chronic disorder in which the individual abruptly falls asleep at intervals throughout the day. Brief periods of REM sleep are accompanied by muscle paralysis (cataplexy), which may range from tilting of the head to buckling of the knees and falling. Narcolepsy has a genetic component that interferes with the neural mechanisms that control the sleep-wake cycle.

naturalistic setting A relatively normal environment in which researchers gather information by observing individuals' behaviors without attempting to change or control the situation.

nature-nurture question The debate concerning the relative contribution of genetic factors (nature) and environmental factors (nurture) to a person's intelligence, as well as to his or her biological, emotional, cognitive, personal, and social development.

nearsightedness A visual acuity problem that may result when the eyeball is too long, so that objects are focused at a point slightly in front of the retina. The result is that near objects are clear, but distant objects appear blurry.

need A biological state in which the organism lacks something essential for survival, such as food, water, or oxygen. The need produces a drive, which is a state of tension that motivates the organism to act to reduce that tension.

negative punishment Removal of a reinforcing stimulus (for example, taking away a child's allowance) after a response. This removal decreases the chances that the response will recur.

negative reinforcement The occurrence of an operant response that either stops or removes an aversive stimulus. Removal of the aversive stimulus increases the likelihood that the response will occur again.

negative symptoms of schizophrenia Symptoms that reflect a decrease in or loss of normal functions: decreased range and intensity of emotions, decreased ability to express thoughts, and decreased initiative to engage in goal-directed behaviors.

neglect syndrome The failure of a patient to see objects or parts of the body on the side opposite the brain damage when the damage is to an association area, usually in occipital and parietal lobes, and usually in the right hemisphere.

nerve impulse A series of separate action potentials that take place, segment by segment, as they move down the length of an axon.

nerves Stringlike bundles of axons and dendrites that are held together by connective tissue. Nerves in the peripheral nervous system have the ability to regrow, regenerate, or reattach if severed or damaged. They carry information from the senses, skin, muscles, and the body's organs to and from the spinal cord.

network hierarchy In the network theory of memory, the arrangement of nodes or categories so that concrete ideas are at the bottom of the hierarchy and are connected to more abstract ideas located above them. The most abstract ideas are at the top of the hierarchy.

network theory The theory that we store related ideas in separate memory categories, or files, called nodes. As we make associations between information, we create links among thousands of nodes, which make up a gigantic interconnected network for storing and retrieving information.

neural assemblies Groups of interconnected neurons whose activation allows information or stimuli to be recognized and held briefly and temporarily in short-term memory.

neural deafness Deafness caused by damage to the auditory receptors (hair cells), which prevents the triggering of impulses, or by damage to the auditory nerve, which prevents impulses from reaching the brain. *See also* cochlear implant.

neuroleptic drugs Drugs that change levels of neurotransmitters in the brain. They are used to treat serious mental disorders, such as schizophrenia. Also called antipsychotic drugs.

neurons Cells that have specialized extensions for the reception and transmission of electrical signals.

neuroses According to Freud, maladaptive thoughts and actions that arise from some unconscious thought or conflict and indicate feelings of anxiety.

neurotransmitters About a dozen different chemicals that are made by neurons and then used for communication between neurons during the performance of mental or physical activities.

neutral stimulus A stimulus that causes a sensory response, such as being seen, heard, or smelled, but does not produce the reflex being tested.

nicotine A stimulant; it first produces arousal but then produces calming. Present in cigarettes, nicotine increases both heart rate and blood pressure. It improves attention and concentration, may improve short-term memory, but may interfere with complex processing. Regular use of nicotine causes addiction, and stopping leads to withdrawal symptoms.

night terrors Sleep disruptions in children that occur during stage 3 or stage 4 (delta) sleep. They usually start with a piercing scream, after which the child wakes suddenly in a fearful state, with rapid breathing and increased heart rate. The next morning, the child has no memory of the frightening experience.

nightmares Dreams that contain frightening and anxiety-producing images. They usually involve great danger—being attacked, injured, or pursued. Upon awakening, the dreamer can usually describe the nightmare in considerable detail. Nightmares occur during REM sleep.

nodes Memory files that contain related information organized around a specific topic or category.

noncompliance In children, refusal to follow directions, carry out a request, or obey a command given by a parent or caregiver. Noncompliance is one of the most common complaints of parents in general and the most frequent problem of parents who bring their children to clinics for treatment of behavioral problems.

nonintellectual factors Factors such as attitude, experience, and emotional functions that may help or hinder an individual's performance on intelligence tests.

non-REM sleep Stages 1–4 of sleep, in which rapid eye movement does not occur; it makes up about 80% of sleep time.

normal aging A gradual and natural slowing of our physical and psychological processes from middle through late adulthood.

normal curve A graph of a frequency distribution in which the curve tapers off equally on either side of a central high point—in other words, a graph of a normal distribution.

normal distribution A bell-shaped frequency distribution curve: the scores are arranged symmetrically so that the vast majority fall in the middle range, with fewer scores near the two extreme ends of the curve.

obedience Behavior performed in response to an order given by someone in a position of authority.

obesity A body weight 30% or more above the ideal value.

object permanence The understanding that objects or events continue to exist even if they can no longer be heard, touched, or seen.

objective personality tests Tests consisting of specific written statements that require individuals to indicate—for example, by checking "true" or "false"—whether the statements do or do not apply to them; also called self-report questionnaires.

observational learning *See* social cognitive learning.

obsessive-compulsive disorder An anxiety disorder consisting of obsessions, which are persistent, recurring, irrational thoughts, impulses, or images that a person is unable to control and that interfere with normal functioning; and compulsions, which are irresistible impulses to perform over and over some senseless behavior or ritual (hand washing, checking things, counting, putting things in order).

obsessive-compulsive personality disorder A personality disorder characterized by an intense interest in being orderly, achieving perfection, and having control. It is found in 4% of the population.

occipital lobe A region at the very back of the brain that is involved in processing visual information, which includes seeing colors and perceiving and recognizing objects, animals, and people.

Oedipus complex According to Freud, a process in which a child competes with the parent of the same sex for the affections and pleasures of the parent of the opposite sex; called the Electra complex in girls.

olfaction The sense of smell. Its stimuli are various chemicals that are carried by the air.

olfactory cells The receptors for smell, located in the uppermost part of the nasal passages. As volatile molecules dissolve in the mucus covering the cells, they stimulate the receptors, which send nerve impulses to the brain.

operant conditioning A kind of learning in which the consequences—reward or punishment—that follow some behavior increase or decrease the likelihood of that behavior's occurrence in the future. Also called instrumental conditioning.

operant response A response that can be modified by its consequences. Operant responses offer a way of dividing ongoing behavior into meaningful and measurable units.

opiates Drugs derived from the opium poppy, including opium and morphine, which is chemically altered to make heroin. All opiates have three primary effects: analgesia (pain reduction); opiate euphoria, which is often described as a pleasurable state between waking and sleeping; and constipation. Continued usage of opiates results in tolerance, physical addiction, and an intense craving for the drug.

opponent-process theory A theory of color vision suggesting that ganglion cells in the retina and cells in the thalamus respond to two pairs of colors: red-green and blue-yellow. When these cells are excited, they respond to one color of the pair; when inhibited, they respond to the complementary pair.

optimal weight The body weight resulting from an almost perfect balance between how much food an organism eats and how much it needs to meet its body's energy needs; also called ideal weight.

optimism A relatively stable personality trait that leads one to believe and expect that good things will happen. It is one of the personality factors associated with lower stress levels and fewer chances of developing psychosomatic symptoms. *See* pessimism.

oral stage Freud's first psychosexual stage, which lasts for the first 18 months of life. In this stage, the infant's pleasure seeking is centered on the mouth.

organic causes Medical conditions or drug or medication problems that lead to sexual difficulties.

organic retardation Mental retardation that results from genetic problems or brain damage.

ossicles *See* middle ear.

outer ear Three structures important to the hearing process: the external ear, auditory canal, and tympanic membrane (eardrum).

overgeneralization A common error during language acquisition, in which children apply a grammatical rule to cases where it should not be used.

overweight A body weight 20–30% over the ideal value.

ovulation The release of an ovum or egg cell from a woman's ovaries.

pain Sensations caused by various stimuli that activate the pain receptors, free nerve endings. Nerve impulses from these pain receptors travel to the somatosensory and limbic areas of the brain, where they are transformed into pain sensations. Pain is essential for survival: it warns us to avoid or escape dangerous situations or stimuli and makes us take time to recover from injury.

pancreas An organ that regulates the level of sugar in the bloodstream by secreting insulin. It forms part of the endocrine system.

panic attack A period of intense fear or discomfort in which four or more of the following symptoms are present: pounding heart, sweating, trembling, shortness of breath, feelings of choking, chest pain, nausea, feeling dizzy, and fear of losing control or dying.

panic disorder A mental disorder characterized primarily by recurrent and unexpected panic attacks, plus continued worry about having another attack; such worry interferes with psychological functioning.

paranoid personality disorder A pattern of distrust and suspiciousness and perceiving others as having evil motives. It is found in 0.5–2.5% of the population.

paranoid schizophrenia A subcategory of schizophrenia characterized by auditory hallucinations or delusions, such as thoughts of being persecuted by others or delusions of grandeur.

paraphilias Repetitive or preferred sexual fantasies involving nonhuman objects, such as sexual attractions to particular articles of clothing (shoes, underwear); commonly called sexual deviations.

parasympathetic division The subdivision of the autonomic nervous system that decreases physiological arousal and helps return the body to a calmer, more relaxed state. It also stimulates digestion during eating.

parentese A way of speaking to young children in which the adult speaks in a voice that is slower and higher than normal, emphasizes and stretching out each word, uses very simple sentences, and repeats words and phrases. Formerly known as motherese.

parietal lobe An area of the cortex located directly behind the frontal lobe. Its functions include: processing sensory information from body parts, which includes touching, locating positions of limbs, and feeling temperature and pain; and carrying out several cognitive functions, such as attending to and perceiving objects.

Parkinson's disease A condition caused by the destruction of neurons that produce the neurotransmitter dopamine. Symptoms include tremors and shakes in the limbs, a slowing of voluntary movements, and feelings of depression. As the disease progresses, patients develop a peculiar shuffling walk and may suddenly freeze in space for minutes or hours at a time.

partial reinforcement A schedule of reinforcement in which the response is reinforced only some of the time.

passion In Sternberg's triangular theory of love, the component of love associated with feeling physically aroused and attracted to someone.

passionate love A condition that is associated with continuously thinking about the loved one and is accompanied by warm sexual feelings and powerful emotional reactions.

pathological aging Acceleration of the aging process, which may be caused by genetic defects, physiological problems, or diseases.

peg method A mnemonic device, or encoding technique, that creates associations between number-word rhymes and items to be memorized.

perception The experience of a meaningful pattern or image that the brain assembles from thousands of individual, meaningless sensations; a perception is normally changed, biased, colored, or distorted by a person's unique set of experiences.

perceptual constancy Our tendency to perceive sizes, colors, brightness, and shapes as remaining the same even though their physical characteristics are constantly changing.

perceptual sets Learned expectations that are based on our personal, social, or cultural experiences. These expectations automatically add information, meaning, or feelings to our perceptions and thus change or bias our perceptions.

perceptual speed The rate at which we can identify a particular sensory stimulus; this rate slows down noticeably after age 60.

peripheral cues Hunger cues associated with changes in blood chemistry or signals from digestive organs.

peripheral nervous system All the nerves that extend from the spinal cord and carry messages to and from various muscles, glands, and sense organs located throughout the body. It has two divisions: the somatic nervous system and the autonomic nervous system.

peripheral route for persuasion Approaches to persuasion that emphasize emotional appeal, focus on personal traits, and generates positive feelings.

peripheral theories of emotions Theories attributing our subjective feelings primarily to our body's physiological changes.

permissive parents Parents who are less controlling and behave with a nonpunishing and accepting attitude toward their children's impulses, desires, and actions. They consult with their children about policy decisions, make few demands, and tend to use reason rather than direct power.

person perception The process by which we form impressions of, and make judgments about, the traits and characteristics of others.

person schemas Social schemas including our judgments about the traits that we and others possess.

person-situation interaction The interaction between a person's traits and the effects of being in a particular situation, which, according to Mischel, determines the person's behavior.

personal factors According to social cognitive theory, factors that include our emotional makeup and our biological and genetic influences and that help to shape our personalities.

personality A combination of long-lasting and distinctive behaviors, thoughts, motives, and emotions that typify how we react and adapt to other people and situations. *See also* theory of personality.

personality development *See* social development.

personality disorder Any psychological disorder characterized by inflexible, long-standing, maladaptive traits that cause significantly impaired functioning or great distress in one's personal and social life.

personality psychology The study of personality development, personality change, assessment, and abnormal behaviors.

personality tests Tests used to measure a person's observable traits and behaviors and unobservable characteristics. In addition, some are used to identify personality problems and psychological disorders, as well as to predict how a person might behave in the future. Objective personality tests (self-report questionnaires), such as the MMPI, consist of specific statements or questions to which the person responds with specific answers; projective tests, such as the Rorschach inkblot test, have no set answers but consist of ambiguous stimuli that a person interprets or makes up stories about.

pessimism A relatively stable personality trait that leads one to believe and expect that bad things will happen. It is one of the personality factors associated with increased stress levels and chances of developing psychosomatic symptoms. *See* optimism.

PET scan *See* positron emission tomography.

phallic stage Freud's third psychosexual stage, lasting from the ages of about 3 to 6. In this stage, the infant's pleasure seeking is centered on the genitals.

phantom limb The experience of sensations and feelings coming from a limb that has been amputated. The sensations and feelings are extremely vivid, as if the amputated limb were still present.

phenomenological perspective The idea that our perspective of the world, whether or not it is accurate, becomes our reality. This idea is stressed in humanistic theories.

phenothiazines The first group of drugs to reduce schizophrenic symptoms, such as delusions and hallucinations. Discovered in the early 1950s, the phenothiazines operate by blocking or reducing the effects of the neurotransmitter dopamine.

phi movement The illusion that stationary lights are moving. The illusion of movement—today called apparent motion—is created by flashing closely positioned stationary lights at regular intervals.

phobia An anxiety disorder characterized by an intense and irrational fear that is out of all proportion to the danger elicited by the object or situation. In comparison, fear is a realistic response to a threatening situation.

phonemes The basic sounds of consonants and vowels.

phonology Rules specifying how we make the meaningful sounds used by a particular language.

photographic memory The ability to form sharp, detailed visual images after examining a picture or page for a short period of time and to recall the entire image at a later date. Photographic memory is similar to eidetic imagery but occurs in adults.

physiological psychology *See* psychobiology.

Piaget's cognitive stages Four different stages—the sensorimotor, preoperational, concrete operations, and formal operations stages—each of which is more advanced than the preceding stage because it involves new reasoning and thinking abilities.

pica A behavioral disorder in which individuals eat inedible objects or nonnutritive substances. Pica can lead to serious physical problems, including lead poisoning, intestinal blockage, and parasites, and is more often seen in individuals with mental retardation.

pitch Our subjective experience of how low or high a sound is. The brain calculates pitch from the speed (frequency) of the sound waves. The frequency of sound waves is measured in cycles, which refers to how many sound waves occur in one second.

pituitary gland A key component of the endocrine system, which hangs directly below the hypothalamus, to which it is connected by a narrow stalk. Its anterior section regulates growth and controls much of the endocrine system, while its posterior section regulates water and salt balance.

place theory The theory that the brain perceives the pitch of a sound by receiving information about where on the basilar membrane a given sound vibrates the most; it applies to medium and higher pitches.

placebo An intervention—taking a pill, receiving an injection, or undergoing an operation—that resembles medical therapy but that, in fact, has no medical effects.

placebo effect A change in the patient's illness that is attributable to an imagined treatment rather than to a medical treatment.

placenta An organ that connects the blood supply of the mother to that of the fetus. The placenta acts like a filter, allowing oxygen and nutrients to pass through while keeping out certain toxic or harmful substances.

pleasure principle The satisfaction of drives and avoidance of pain, without concern for moral restrictions or society's regulations; according to Freud, this is the id's operating principle.

polygraph tests Tests based on the theory that, if a person tells a lie, he or she will feel some emotion, such as guilt or fear. Feeling guilty or fearful will usually be accompanied by involuntary physiological responses, which are difficult to suppress or control and can be measured with a machine called a polygraph.

pons A bridge that connects the spinal cord with the brain and parts of the brain with one another. Cells in the pons manufacture chemicals involved in sleep.

positive punishment The presentation of an aversive stimulus (for example, spanking) after a response. The aversive stimulus decreases the chances that the response will recur.

positive regard Love, sympathy, warmth, acceptance, and respect, which we crave from family, friends, and people important to us.

positive reinforcement The presentation of a stimulus that increases the probability of a behavior's recurrence.

positive reinforcer A stimulus that increases the likelihood that a response will occur again.

positive symptoms of schizophrenia Symptoms that reflect a distortion of normal functions: distorted thinking results in delusions; distorted perceptions result in hallucinations; distorted language results in disorganized speech.

positron emission tomography (PET scan) A technique to measure the function of the living brain. A slightly radioactive solution is injected into the blood and the amount of radiation absorbed by the brain cells is measured. Very active brain cells—neurons—absorb more radioactive solution than less active ones. A computer transforms the different levels of absorption into colors that indicate activity of neurons. The colors red and yellow indicate maximum activity of neurons, while blue and green indicate minimal activity.

postconventional level Kohlberg's highest level of moral reasoning, at which moral decisions are made after carefully thinking about all the alternatives and striking a balance between human rights and laws of society.

posterior pituitary The rear part of the pituitary gland, a key component of the endocrine system. It regulates water and salt balance.

posthypnotic amnesia Inability to remember what happened during hypnosis, prompted by a specific suggestion from the hypnotist.

posthypnotic suggestion A suggestion given to the subject during hypnosis about performing a particular behavior, in response to a predetermined cue, when the subject comes out of hypnosis.

posttraumatic stress disorder A disabling condition that results from direct personal experience of an event that involves actual or threatened death or serious injury or from witnessing such an event or hearing that such an event has happened to a family member or close friend.

precognition The ability to foretell events.

preconventional level Kohlberg's lowest level of moral reasoning. It consists of two stages: At stage 1, moral decisions are based primarily on fear of punishment or the need to be obedient; at stage 2, moral reasoning is guided most by satisfaction of one's self-interest, which may involve making bargains.

predisposing function The role of our attitudes in guiding or influencing us to behave in specific ways.

prejudice An unfair, biased, or intolerant attitude toward another group of people.

premature ejaculation Persistent or recurrent absence of voluntary control over ejaculation, in that the male ejaculates with minimal sexual stimulation before, upon, or shortly after penetration and before he wishes to; also called rapid ejaculation.

prenatal period The period from conception to birth, which lasts about 266 days (about nine months). It is divided into three phases: the germinal, embryonic, and fetal period. During the prenatal period, a single cell will divide and grow to form 200 billion cells.

preoperational stage The second of Piaget's cognitive stages, lasting from the ages of about 2 to 7. During this stage, children learn to use symbols (such as words or mental images) to think about things that are not present and to help them solve simple problems.

preparedness The innate or biological tendency of animals and humans to recognize, attend to, and store certain cues over others, as well as to associate some combinations of conditioned and unconditioned stimuli more easily than others. Also called prepared learning.

primacy effect Better recall, or improvement in retention, of information presented at the beginning of a task.

primacy question The question of whether we can experience an emotion immediately, without any thinking, or whether we must engage in some kind of thinking before feeling.

primacy-recency effect Better recall of information presented at the beginning and end of a task.

primary appraisal Our initial, subjective evaluation of a situation, in which we balance the demands of a potentially stressful situation against our ability to meet them.

primary auditory cortex An area at the top edge of the temporal lobe that transforms nerve impulses (electrical signals) into basic auditory sensations, such as meaningless sounds and tones of varying pitch and loudness. Next, it sends impulses (sensations) to the auditory association areas.

primary reinforcer A stimulus, such as food, water, or sex, that is innately satisfying and requires no learning on the part of the subject to become pleasurable.

primary visual cortex A small area, located at the back of each occipital lobe, that receives electrical signals from receptors in the eyes and transforms these signals into meaningless, basic visual sensations, such as lights, lines, shadows, colors, and textures.

principle of bidirectionality The idea that a child's behaviors influence how his or her parents respond and, in turn, the parents' behaviors influence how the child responds.

proactive interference A forgetting process in which information that we learned earlier blocks or disrupts the retrieval of related information that was learned later.

problem-focused coping Solving a problem by seeking information, changing our own behavior, or taking whatever action is necessary.

problem solving Searching for some rule, plan, or strategy in order to reach a certain goal that is currently out of reach.

procedural memory Memories of performing motor or perceptual tasks (playing sports), carrying out habitual behaviors (brushing teeth), and responding to stimuli because of classical conditioning (fearing spiders). We cannot retrieve these memories and are not conscious of them.

processing speed The rate at which we encode information into long-term memory or recall or retrieve information from long-term memory; this rate slows down after age 60.

procrastination The tendency to always put off completing a task to the point of feeling anxious or uncomfortable about one's delay.

prodigy A child who shows unusual talent, ability, or genius at a very early age and does not have mental retardation. A small percentage of autistic children, who have some degree of mental retardation, may also show unusual artistic or mathematical abilities; they are called savants.

progressive relaxation An exercise in which the major muscle groups of the body are tensed and relaxed repeatedly until the individual can relax any group of muscles at will.

projection Unconsciously transferring unacceptable traits to others.

projective tests Tests in which the subject is presented with some type of ambiguous stimulus—such as a meaningless object or ambiguous photo—and then asked to make up a story about the stimulus. The assumption is that the person will project conscious or unconscious feelings, needs, and motives in his or her responses.

prosocial behavior Any behavior that benefits others or has positive social consequences. Also called helping.

prototype theory The idea that we form a concept by first constructing a prototype of an object—that is, a mental image based on its average characteristics. Once we have formed a set of prototypes, we identify new objects by matching them against our prototypes.

proximity rule A perceptual rule stating that, in organizing stimuli, objects that are physically close to one another will be grouped together.

proximodistal principle The rule that parts closer to the center of the infant's body develop before parts that are farther away.

psi The processing of information or transfer of energy by methods that have no known physical or biological mechanisms and that seem to stretch the laws of physics.

psilocybin A hallucinogen, the active ingredient in magic mushrooms. Low doses produce pleasant and relaxed feelings; medium doses produce distortions in the perception of time and space; and high doses produce distortions in perceptions and body image and sometimes hallucinations.

psychiatrist A medical doctor (M.D.) who has taken a psychiatric residency, which involves additional training in pharmacology, neurology, psychopathology, and therapeutic techniques. In diagnosing the possible causes of abnormal behaviors, psychiatrists focus on biological factors; they tend to view mental disorders as diseases and to treat them with drugs. Psychiatrists who receive additional training in psychoanalytic institutes are called psychoanalysts.

psychoactive drugs Chemicals that affect the nervous system and, as a result, may alter consciousness and awareness, influence sensations and perceptions, and modify moods and cognitive processes. Some are legal (coffee, alcohol, and tobacco) and some are illegal (marijuana, heroin, cocaine, and LSD).

psychoanalysis A form of psychotherapy based on the idea that each of us has an unconscious part that contains ideas, memories, desires, or thoughts, which have been hidden or repressed because they are psychologically dangerous or threatening to our self-concept. To protect our self-concept, we automatically build a mental barrier that we cannot voluntarily remove. But the presence of these thoughts and desires gives rise to unconscious conflicts, which, in turn, can result in psychological and physical symptoms and mental disorders.

psychoanalyst See psychiatrist.

psychoanalytic approach A psychological viewpoint that stresses the influence of unconscious fears, desires, and motivations on thoughts and behaviors and also the impact of childhood experiences on the development of later personality traits and psychological problems. As applied to mental disorders, this approach traces their origin to unconscious conflicts or problems with unresolved conflicts at one or more of Freud's psychosexual stages. Treatment of mental disorders, in this approach, centers on the therapist's helping the patient to identify and resolve his or her unconscious conflicts.

psychobiological approach See biological approach.

psychobiology The scientific study of the physical and chemical changes that occur during stress, learning, and emotions, as well as how our genetic makeup and nervous system interact with our environments and influence our behaviors.

psychodynamic psychotherapy An approach that shares many of the features of psychoanalysis—for example, discussing the client's feelings; breaking down the client's defenses and resistances; interpreting the client's behaviors; and working through transference problems. However, these therapies take a more directive role than do classical psychoanalysts and thus shorten the total time in therapy. See also short-term dynamic psychotherapy.

psychodynamic theory of personality See Freud's psychodynamic theory of personality.

psychoevolutionary theory of emotions The idea that we inherit the neural structure and physiology to express and experience emotions and that we evolved basic emotional patterns to adapt to our environment and solve patterns important for our survival.

psychokinesis The ability to exert mind over matter—for example, by moving objects without touching them.

psychological assessment The use of various tools—including psychological tests and interviews—to measure characteristics, traits, or abilities in order to understand behavior and predict future performance or behavior.

psychological causes Performance anxiety, sexual trauma, guilt, or failure to communicate, all of which may lead to sexual problems.

psychological sex factors Factors involved in the development of a gender identity, gender role, and sexual orientation, as well as in difficulties in sexual performance or enjoyment.

psychologist An individual who has completed four to five years of postgraduate education and has obtained a Ph.D in psychology; in some states, an individual with a master's degree.

psychology The systematic, scientific study of behaviors and mental processes.

psychometric approach An approach to the assessment of intelligence that measures or quantifies cognitive abilities or factors that are thought to be involved in intellectual performance.

psychometrics A subarea of psychology concerned with the development of tests to assess an individual's abilities, skills, intelligence, personality traits, and abnormal behaviors in a wide range of settings—school, the workplace, or a clinic.

psychoneuroimmunology The study of the relationship among the central nervous system, the endocrine system, and psychosocial factors such as cognitive reactions to stressful events, the individual's personality traits, and social influences.

psychosexual stages According to Freud, five developmental periods—the oral, anal, phallic, latency, and genital stages—each marked by potential conflict between parent and child. The conflicts arise as the child seeks pleasure from different bodily areas associated with sexual feelings (different erogenous zones). Freud emphasized that the child's first five years were most important in social and personality development.

psychosocial factors Underlying personality traits, amount of social support, and ability to deal with stressful life events—these factors are believed to combine and interact with predisposing biological factors to either increase or decrease a person's vulnerability to the development and maintenance of a mood disorder.

psychosocial hunger factors Learned associations between food and other stimuli, such as snacking while watching television; sociocultural influences, such as pressures to be thin; and various personality problems, such as depression, dislike of body image, or low self-esteem.

psychosocial stages According to Erikson, eight developmental periods during which an individual's primary goal is to satisfy desires associated with social needs: the eight periods are associated, respectively, with issues of trust, autonomy, initiative, industry, identity, intimacy, generativity, and ego integrity.

psychosomatic symptoms Real, physical, and often painful symptoms, such as headaches, muscle pain, and stomach problems, that are caused by psychosomatic factors, such as worry, tension, and anxiety.

psychotherapy Approaches to treating psychological problems that share three characteristics: verbal interaction between therapist and client(s); the development of a supportive relationship during which a client can bring up and discuss traumatic or bothersome experiences that may have led to current problems; and analysis of the client's experiences and/or suggested ways for the client to deal with or overcome his or her problems.

puberty A developmental period, corresponding to the ages of 9–17, when the individual experiences significant biological changes and, as a result, develops secondary sexual characteristics and reaches sexual maturity.

punishment A consequence that occurs after behavior and decreases the likelihood that that behavior will recur.

pupil The round opening at the front of the eye that allows light waves to pass through into the eye's interior.

quantum personality change A sudden and radical or dramatic shift in personality, belief, or values.

questionnaire A method for obtaining information by asking subjects to read a list of written questions and to check off, or rate their preference for, specific answers.

random selection A research design such that each subject in a sample population has an equal chance of being selected to participate in the experiment.

range The two most extreme scores at either end of a distribution.

rape myths Misinformed false beliefs about women that are frequently held by rapists, as well as by other men.

rationalizations Inventing acceptable excuses for behaviors that make us feel anxious.

reaction formation Turning unacceptable wishes into acceptable behaviors.

reaction range The extent to which traits, abilities, or IQ scores may increase or decrease as a result of interaction with environmental factors.

reaction time The rate at which we respond (see, hear, move) to some stimulus; this rate slows down noticeably after age 60.

real motion Our perception of any stimulus or object that actually moves in space; the opposite of apparent motion.

real self According to Rogers, the self that is based on our actual experiences and represents how

we really see ourselves; its complement is the ideal self.

reality principle A policy of satisfying a wish or desire only if a socially acceptable outlet is available; according to Freud, this is the ego's operating principle.

reasoning A mental process by which we apply knowledge to achieve goals that involve solving problems or making plans and decisions.

recall Retrieval of previously learned information without the aid of or with very few external cues.

recency effect Better recall, or improvement in retention, of information presented at the end of a task.

recognition The identification of previously learned information with the help of external cues.

reflex An unlearned, involuntary reaction to some stimulus. The neural connections of the network underlying a reflex are prewired by genetic instructions.

reinforcement A consequence that occurs after behavior and increases the likelihood that that behavior will recur.

relative size In three-dimensional vision, a monocular depth cue that results when we expect two objects to be the same size, and they are not. In that case, the larger of the objects will appear closer, and the smaller will appear to be farther away.

relaxation response A physiological response induced by sitting or lying in a comfortable position while repeating a meaningless sound over and over to drive out anxious thoughts.

reliability The extent to which a test is consistent: a person's score on a test at one point in time should be similar to the score obtained by the same person on a similar test at a later point in time.

REM (rapid eye movement) sleep The stage of sleep in which our eyes move rapidly back and forth behind closed eyelids. This stage makes up 20% of our sleep time; in a normal night, we experience 5–6 periods of REM sleep, each one lasting 15–45 minutes. REM brain waves, which have a high frequency and a low amplitude, look very similar to the beta waves that are recorded when we are wide awake and alert; the body's voluntary muscles, however, are paralyzed. Dreams usually occur during REM sleep.

REM behavior disorder A disorder, usually found in older people, in which the voluntary muscles are not paralyzed during REM sleep; sleepers can and do act out their dreams.

REM rebound The tendency of individuals to spend proportionately longer in the REM stage after they have been deprived of REM sleep on previous nights.

repair theory A theory of sleep suggesting that activities during the day deplete key factors in the brain or body that are replenished or repaired by sleep.

Glossary

repression According to Freud, a mental process that automatically hides emotionally threatening or anxiety-producing information in the unconscious. Repressed information cannot be retrieved voluntarily, but something may cause it to be released and to reenter the person's consciousness at a later time.

resiliency Various personal, family, or environmental factors that compensate for increased life stresses so that expected problems do not develop.

resistance In psychotherapy, especially psychoanalysis, the client's reluctance to work through or deal with feelings or to recognize unconscious conflicts and repressed thoughts.

resistance stage The second stage in the general adaptation syndrome. In reaction to continued stress, most physiological responses return to normal levels, but the body uses up great stores of energy.

resting state A condition in which the axon, like a battery, has a charge, or potential, because the axon membrane separates positive ions on the outside from negative ions on the inside.

reticular formation A column of brain cells that arouses and alerts the forebrain and prepares it to receive information from all the senses. It plays an important role in keeping the forebrain alert and producing a state of wakefulness. Animals or humans whose reticular formation is seriously damaged lapse into permanent unconsciousness or coma.

retina A thin film, located at the very back of the eyeball, that contains cells, called photoreceptors, that are extremely sensitive to light. The retina consists of three layers, the third and deepest of which contains two kinds of photoreceptors, rods and cones, that perform transduction—that is, they change light waves into nerve impulses.

retinal disparity A binocular depth cue that depends on the distance between the two eyes. Because of their different positions, the two eyes receive slightly different images. The difference between these images is the retinal disparity. The brain interprets large retinal disparity to mean a close object, and small retinal disparity to mean a distant object.

retrieval cues Mental reminders that we create by forming vivid mental images of information or associating new information with information that we already know. Forgetting can result from not taking the time to create effective retrieval cues.

retrieving The process of getting or recalling information that has been placed into short-term or long-term storage.

retroactive interference A forgetting process in which information that we learned later blocks or disrupts the retrieval of related information that was learned earlier.

reuptake The process by which some neurotransmitters, such as dopamine, are removed from the synapse by being transported back into the end bulbs.

rods Photoreceptors containing the chemical rhodopsin, which is activated by small amounts of light. Because rods are extremely light sensitive, they allow us to see in dim light but to see only black, white, and shades of gray.

Rogers' self-actualizing tendency An inborn tendency for us to develop all of our capacities in ways that best maintain and benefit our lives.

role schemas Social schemas based on the jobs people perform or the social positions they hold.

Rorschach inkblot test A projective test used to assess personality in which a person is shown a series of ten inkblots and then asked to describe what he or she sees in each.

rules of organization Rules identified by Gestalt psychologists that specify how our brains combine and organize individual pieces or elements into a meaningful whole—that is, a perception.

SAD *See* seasonal affective disorder.

savants Autistic individuals who show some incredible memory, music, or drawing talent. They represent about 10% of the total number of autistics.

Schachter-Singer cognitive theory The idea that cognitive factors, such as one's interpretation or appraisal of a situation, is the primary cause of emotions.

schedule of reinforcement In conditioning, a program or rule that determines how and when a response will be followed by a reinforcer.

schemas Mental categories that, like computer files, contain knowledge about people, events, and concepts. Because schemas influence which stimuli we attend to, how we interpret stimuli, and how we respond to stimuli, they can bias and distort our thoughts, perceptions, and behaviors. *See also:* event schemas; gender schemas; person schemas; role schemas; and self schemas.

schizophrenia A serious mental disturbance that lasts at least six months and includes at least two of the following symptoms: delusions, hallucinations, disorganized speech, grossly disorganized behavior, and decreased emotional expression. These symptoms interfere with personal or social functioning. *See also* Type I and Type II schizophrenia.

schizotypical personality disorder A disorder characterized by acute discomfort in close relationships, distortions in thinking, and eccentric behavior. It is found in 3–5% of the population.

scientific method A general approach to gathering information and answering questions so that errors and biases are minimized.

scripts *See* event schemas.

seasonal affective disorder (SAD) A pattern of depressive symptoms that cycle with the seasons, typically beginning in fall or winter. The depression is accompanied by feelings of lethargy, excessive sleepiness, overeating, weight gain, and craving for carbohydrates.

secondary appraisal Deciding what we can do to deal with a potentially stressful situation. We can choose some combination of problem-focused coping, which means doing something about the problem, and emotion-focused coping, which means dealing with our emotions.

secondary reinforcer Any stimulus that has acquired its reinforcing power through experience; secondary reinforcers are learned, for example, by being paired with primary reinforcers or other secondary reinforcers.

secure attachment An emotional bond characteristic of infants who use their parent as a safe home base from which they can wander off and explore their environments.

self How we see or describe ourselves; also called self concept. The self is made up of many self-perceptions, abilities, personality characteristics, and behaviors that are organized so as to be consistent with one another.

self-actualization Our inherent tendency to reach our true potentials. The concept of self-actualization, developed by Maslow, is central to humanistic theories. *See also* Rogers' self-actualizing tendency.

self-actualization theory *See* self theory.

self-concept *See* self.

self-efficacy Our personal beliefs regarding how capable we are of exercising control over events in our lives, such as completing specific tasks and behaviors.

self-esteem How much an individual likes himself or herself; it includes feelings of self-worth, attractiveness, and social competence.

self-fulfilling prophecy A situation in which a person has a strong belief or makes a statement (prophecy) about a future behavior and then acts, usually unknowingly, to fulfill or carry out that behavior.

self-handicapping A tendency to adopt tactics that are prone to failure and then to use those tactics as excuses for failures in performance, activities, or achieving goals.

self-identity *See* identity.

self-injurious behavior A behavior pattern in which an individual inflicts serious and sometimes life-threatening physical damage on his or her own body; this may take the form of body or head banging, biting, kicking, poking ears or eyes, pulling hair, or intense scratching.

self-perception theory The idea, developed by Daryl Bem, that we first observe or perceive our own behavior and then, as a result, change our attitudes.

self-report questionnaires *See* objective personality tests.

self schemas Social schemas containing personal information about ourselves. They can influence how we behave, as well as what we perceive and remember.

self-serving bias Attributing our successes to our dispositions or personality traits and our failures to the situations.

self theory Rogers' humanistic theory, based on two major assumptions: that personality development is guided by each person's unique self-actualization tendency; and that each of us has a personal need for positive regard.

semantic memory A type of declarative memory consisting of factual knowledge about the world, concepts, word definitions, and language rules.

semantics A set of rules specifying the meaning of words or phrases when they appear in various sentences or contexts.

sensation Our first awareness of some outside stimulus. The stimulus activates sensory receptors, which in turn produce electrical signals that are transformed by the brain into meaningless bits of information.

sensitive period *See* critical period.

sensorimotor stage The first of Piaget's cognitive stages, lasting from birth to about age 2. During this stage, infants interact with and learn about their environments by relating their sensory experiences (such as hearing and seeing) to their motor actions (mouthing and grasping).

sensory homunculus A drawing of the somatosensory cortex that shows the relationship between the size of each body part and the degree of its sensitivity to external stimulation. *Homunculus* means "little man."

sensory memory An initial memory process that receives and holds environmental information in its raw form for a brief period of time, from an instant to several seconds.

sensory neurons *See* afferent neurons.

sentence stage The fourth stage in acquiring language, which begins at about 4 years of age. Sentences range from three to eight words in length and indicate a growing knowledge of the rules of grammar.

separation anxiety An infant's distress—as indicated by loud protests, crying, and agitation—whenever his or her parents temporarily leave.

set point A certain level of body fat (adipose tissue) that our body strives to maintain constant throughout our lives; the set point is an inherited characteristic.

sex chromosome The sperm or the egg. Each contains only 23 chromosomes, on which are the genes bearing the instructions that determine the sex of the child.

sex (gender) differences in the brain Structural or functional differences in cognitive, behavioral, or brain processes that arise from being male or female.

sex hormones Chemicals, secreted by glands, that circulate in the bloodstream and influence the brain, other body organs, and behaviors. The major male sex hormones secreted by the testes are androgens, such as testosterone; the major female sex hormones secreted by the ovaries are estrogens.

sexual dysfunctions Problems of sexual arousal or orgasm that interfere with adequate functioning during sexual behavior.

sexual orientation A person's pattern of primary sexual arousal: by members of his or her own sex, the opposite sex, or both sexes; also called sexual preference.

shape constancy Our tendency to see an object as remaining the same shape when viewed at different angles—that is, despite considerable change in the shape of its image on the retina.

shaping In operant conditioning, a procedure in which an experimenter successively reinforces behaviors that lead up to or approximate the desired behavior.

short-term dynamic psychotherapy A shortened version of psychoanalysis. It retains the principles that symptoms are signs of more basic underlying problems, that transference needs to be worked out, and that clients' behaviors need to be interpreted. In contrast to traditional psychoanalysis, however, therapists take a more active and directive role in identifying and discussing the client's problems and suggesting solutions. *See also* psychodynamic psychotherapy.

short-term memory A process that can hold a limited amount of information—an average of seven items—for a short time (2–30 seconds), which can be lengthened if you rehearse the information. Sometimes called working memory.

shyness The tendency to feel tense, worried, or awkward in social situations.

similarity rule A perceptual rule stating that, in organizing stimuli, elements that appear similar are grouped together.

simplicity rule A perceptual rule stating that stimuli are organized in the simplest way possible.

single-word stage The second stage in acquiring language, which begins when the child is about 1 year old. Infants say single words that usually refer to what they can see, hear, or feel.

situational attributions *See* external attributions.

size constancy Our tendency to perceive objects as remaining the same size even when their images on the retina are continually growing or shrinking.

skewed distributions Distributions in which more data fall toward one side of the scale than toward the other.

Skinner, B. F. A psychologist who used the behavioral approach, stressing the study of observable behaviors, the importance of environmental reinforcers (reward and punishment), and the exclusion of mental processes. His "strict behaviorism" continues to have an impact on psychology.

sleep A condition in which we pass through five different stages, each with its own level of consciousness, awareness, responsiveness, and physiological arousal. In the deepest stage of sleep, we enter a state that borders on unconsciousness.

sleep apnea A condition characterized by a cycle in which a sleeper stops breathing for intervals of 10 seconds or longer, wakes up briefly, resumes breathing, and returns to sleep. This cycle can leave apnea sufferers exhausted during the day but oblivious to the cause of their tiredness. It is more common among habitual snorers.

sleepwalking Walking or carrying out behaviors while still asleep. Sleepwalkers generally are clumsy and have poor coordination but can avoid objects; they can engage in very limited conversations. Sleepwalking behaviors can include dressing, eating, performing bathroom functions, and even driving a car. Sleepwalking usually occurs in stage 3 or stage 4 (delta) sleep.

social cognition A subarea of social psychology that focuses on cognitive processes—for example, how we perceive, store, and retrieve information about social interactions and events. It rose to prominence in the 1980s.

social cognitive learning A form of learning that results from watching, imitating, and modeling and does not require the observer to perform any observable behavior or receive any observable reward. Formerly called observational learning.

social cognitive theory The theory that grew out of the research of a number of psychologists—Rotter, Bandura, and Mischel—that says that personality development is primarily shaped by three forces: environmental conditions, cognitive-personal factors, and behavior, which all interact to influence how we evaluate, interpret, organize, and apply information. *See also* Bandura's social cognitive theory; social learning theory.

social comparison theory The idea that we are driven to compare ourselves to others who are similar to us, so that we can measure the correctness of our attitudes and beliefs. According to Festinger, this drive motivates us to join groups.

social development How a person develops a sense of self or self-identity, develops relationships with others, and develops the skills useful in social interactions.

social facilitation An increase in performance in the presence of a crowd.

social inhibition A decrease in performance in the presence of a crowd.

social learning approach A theory that emphasizes the role of observation, exploration, and imitation in acquiring language skills.

social learning theory The idea that personality development is primarily shaped by environmental conditions (learning), cognitive-personal factors, and behavior, which all interact to influence how we evaluate, interpret, and organize information and apply that information to ourselves and others. As applied to gender roles, it says that mothers, fathers, teachers, grandparents, friends, and peers expect, respond to, and reward different behaviors in boys than in girls. In response to this differential treatment, boys learn a gender role that is different from girls'. As applied to aggression, it says that such behavior may be learned and maintained through observation, imitation, and self-reinforcement. *See also* social cognitive theory.

social needs Needs that are acquired through learning and experience.

social norms approach In defining abnormality, the idea that a behavior is considered abnormal if it deviates greatly from accepted social standards, values, or norms.

social phobias Irrational, marked, and continuous fear of performing in social situations. The individuals fear that they will humiliate or embarrass themselves.

social psychology A broad field whose goals are to understand and explain how our thoughts, feelings, perceptions, and behaviors are influenced by interactions with others. It includes the study of stereotypes, prejudices, attitudes, conformity, group behaviors, and aggression.

Glossary

social role theory The theory that emphasizes the importance of social and cultural influences on gender roles and states that gender differences between males and females arise from different divisions of labor.

social support A stress-reducing factor that includes three components: having a group or network of family or friends who provide strong social attachments; being able to exchange helpful resources among family or friends; and feeling, or making appraisals, that we have supportive relationships or behaviors.

socially oriented group A group in which members are primarily concerned about fostering and maintaining social relationships among the members of the group.

sociobiology theory *See* evolutionary theory.

sociocognitive theory of hypnosis The idea that the impressive effects of hypnosis are due to social influences and pressures as well as the subject's personal abilities. For another view, see the altered state theory of hypnosis.

sodium pump A chemical transport process that picks up any sodium ions that enter the axon's chemical gates and returns them back outside. In this way, the sodium pump is responsible for keeping the axon charged by returning and keeping sodium ions outside the axon membrane.

somatic nervous system A network of nerves that are connected either to sensory receptors or to muscles that you can move voluntarily, such as muscles in your limbs, back, neck, and chest. Nerves in the somatic nervous system usually contain two kinds of fibers: afferent, or sensory, fibers that carry information from sensory receptors in the skin, muscles, and other organs to the spinal cord and brain; and efferent, or motor, fibers that carry information from the brain and spinal cord to the muscles.

somatization disorder A somatoform disorder that begins before age 30, lasts several years, and is characterized by multiple symptoms—including pain, gastrointestinal, sexual, and neurological symptoms—that have no physical causes but are triggered by psychological problems or distress.

somatoform disorder A pattern of recurring, multiple, and significant bodily (somatic) complaints that extend over several years. The physical symptoms (pain, vomiting, paralysis, blindness) are not under voluntary control, have no known physical causes, and are believed to be caused by psychological factors.

somatosensory cortex A narrow strip of the cortex that is located at the front edge of the parietal lobe and extends down its side. It processes sensory information about touch, location of limbs, pain, and temperature. The right somatosensory cortex receives information from the left side of the body and vice versa.

sound waves The stimuli for hearing, or audition. Similar to ripples on a pond, sound waves travel through space with varying heights and speeds. Height, or amplitude, is the distance from the bottom to the top of a sound wave; speed, or frequency, is the number of sound waves that occur within one second.

source misattribution A memory error that results when a person has difficulty in deciding which of two or more sources a memory came from: Was the source something the person saw or imagined, or was it a suggestion?

specific phobias Unreasonable, marked, and persistent fears triggered by anticipation of, or exposure to, a specific object or situation (flying, heights, spiders, seeing blood); formerly called simple phobias.

split-brain operation A procedure for moderating severe, uncontrollable seizures by cutting the corpus callosum, a wide band of nerve fibers that connects the right and left hemispheres.

spontaneous recovery In classical conditioning, the temporary occurrence of the conditioned response to the presence of the conditioned stimulus. In operant conditioning, a temporary recovery in the rate of responding.

stage 1 In sleep, a stage lasting 1–7 minutes in which the individual gradually loses responsiveness to stimuli and experiences drifting thoughts and images. This stage marks the transition from wakefulness to sleep and is characterized by the presence of theta waves, which are lower in amplitude and lower in frequency (3–7 cycles per second) than alpha waves.

stage 2 In sleep, the stage that marks the beginning of what we know as sleep; subjects awakened in stage 2 report having been asleep. EEG tracings show high-frequency bursts of brain activity called sleep spindles.

stages 3 and 4 About 30–45 minutes after drifting off to sleep, we pass rapidly through stage 3 and enter stage 4 sleep, a stage characterized by delta waves, which are of very high amplitude and very low frequency (less than 4 cycles per second). Stage 4 is often considered the deepest stage of sleep, because it is the most difficult from which to be awakened. During stage 4, heart rate, respiration, temperature, and blood flow to the brain are reduced, and there is a marked secretion of growth hormone, which controls many aspects of metabolism, physical growth, and brain development. This stage is also called slow-wave or delta sleep.

stages of sleep Distinctive changes in the electrical activity of the brain and accompanying physiological responses of the body that occur as we pass through different stages of sleep. *See also* stage 1, stage 2, stages 3 and 4.

standard deviation A statistic indicating how widely all the scores in a distribution are scattered above and below the mean.

standardized test A technique to obtain information by administering a psychological test that has been standardized, which means that the test has been given to hundreds of people and shown to reliably measure thought patterns, personality traits, emotions, or behaviors.

state-dependent learning The idea that we recall information more easily when we are in the same physiological or emotional state or setting as when we originally encoded the information.

statistical frequency approach In defining abnormality, the idea that a behavior may be considered abnormal if it occurs rarely or infrequently in relation to the behaviors of the general population.

statistical procedures In experiments, procedures to determine whether differences observed in dependent variables (behaviors) are due to independent variables (treatment) or to error or chance occurrence.

statistics Tools researchers use to analyze and summarize large amounts of data.

stereotaxic procedure A method used for the introduction of material at a precise location within the brain. The patient's head is fixed in a holder, and a small hole is drilled through the skull. The holder has a syringe that can be precisely guided to a predetermined location in the brain.

stereotypes Widely held beliefs that people have certain traits because they belong to a particular group. Stereotypes are often inaccurate and frequently portray the members of less powerful, less controlling groups more negatively than members of more powerful or more controlling groups.

Sternberg's triangular theory of love The idea that love has three components: passion, intimacy, and commitment. *Passion* is feeling physically aroused and attracted to someone; *intimacy* is feeling close and connected to someone, through sharing and communicating; and *commitment* is pledging to nourish the feelings of love and actively maintain the relationship.

Sternberg's triarchic theory The idea that intelligence can be divided into three ways of gathering and processing information (*triarchic* means three): using analytical or logical thinking skills that are measured by traditional intelligence tests; using problem-solving skills that require creative thinking, the ability to deal with novel situations, and the ability to learn from experience; and using practical thinking skills that help a person adjust to, and cope with, his or her sociocultural environment.

stimulants Drugs, such as cocaine, amphetamines, caffeine, and nicotine, that increase activity in the nervous system and result in heightened alertness, arousal, and euphoria and decreased appetite and fatigue.

stimulus substitution The theory that, in classical conditioning, a neural bond or association is formed between the neutral stimulus and unconditioned stimulus. After repeated trials, the neutral stimulus becomes the conditioned stimulus, which, in turn, substitutes for the unconditioned stimulus. Thereafter, the conditioned stimulus elicits a response similar to that of the unconditioned stimulus.

storing The process of placing encoded information into relatively permanent mental storage for later recall.

stress The anxious or threatening feeling that comes when we interpret or appraise a situation as being more than our psychological resources can adequately handle.

stress management program A program to reduce anxiety, fear, and stressful experiences by using a variety of strategies to change three different aspects of our lives: thoughts (appraisals), behaviors, and physiological responses.

structuralism An early school of psychological thought that emphasized the study of the basic elements—primarily sensations and perceptions—that make up conscious mental experiences. Structuralists argued that we can understand how perceptions are formed by breaking them down into smaller and smaller elements. Then we can analyze how these basic elements are recombined to form a perception. They believed that a perception is simply the sum of its parts.

structured interviews A research technique in which each individual is asked the same set of relatively narrow and focused questions, so that the same information is obtained from everyone.

subgoals In problem solving, a strategy by which the overall problem is broken into separate parts that, when completed in order, will result in a solution.

sublimation A type of displacement in which threatening or forbidden desire, usually sexual, is redirected into socially acceptable forms.

subliminal messages Brief auditory or visual messages that are presented below the absolute threshold, so that their chance of perception is less than 50%.

subliminal stimulus A stimulus whose intensity is such that a person has a less than 50% chance of detecting it.

substance abuse A maladaptive pattern of frequent and continued usage of a substance—a drug or medicine—that results in significant problems, such as failing to meet major obligations and having multiple legal, social, family, health, work, or interpersonal difficulties. These problems must occur repeatedly during a single 12-month period to be classified as substance abuse.

superego Freud's third division of the mind, which develops from the ego during early childhood; its goal is to apply the moral values and standards of one's parents or caregivers and society in satisfying one's wishes.

superstitious behavior In operant conditioning, any behavior that increases in frequency because its occurrence is accidentally paired with the delivery of a reinforcer.

suprachiasmatic nucleus A sophisticated biological clock, located in the hypothalamus, that regulates a number of circadian rhythms, including the sleep-wake cycle. Suprachiasmatic cells are highly responsive to changes in light.

surface structure According to Chomsky, the actual wording of a sentence, as it is spoken.

survey A way to obtain information by asking many individuals—person to person, by telephone, or by mail—to answer a fixed set of questions about particular subjects.

sympathetic division The subdivision of the autonomic nervous system that is triggered by threatening or challenging physical or psychological stimuli, increasing the body's physiological arousal and preparing the body for action.

synapse An infinitely small space (20–30 billionths of a meter) between an end bulb and its adjacent body organ, muscle, or cell body; it is a space over which chemical messages are transmitted.

syntax *See* grammar.

systematic desensitization A technique of behavior therapy, based on classical conditioning, in which a person is gradually and progressively exposed to fearful or anxiety-evoking stimuli while practicing deep relaxation. Systematic desensitization is a form of counterconditioning because it replaces, or counters, fear and anxiety with relaxation.

t-test An estimate of reliability that takes into account both the size of the mean difference and the variability in distributions.

taijin kyofusho (TKS) A mental disorder found only in Asian cultures, particularly Japan. This social phobia is characterized by a morbid fear of offending others through awkward social or physical behavior, such as making eye-to-eye contact, blushing, giving off an offensive odor, having an unpleasant or tense facial expression, or having trembling hands.

tardive dyskinesia A condition characterized by the appearance of slow, involuntary, and uncontrollable rhythmic movements and rapid twitching of the mouth and lips, as well as unusual movements of the limbs. This condition is a side effect of the continued use of typical neuroleptics.

task-oriented group A group in which members have specific duties to complete.

taste-aversion learning The association of a particular sensory cue (smell, taste, sound, or sight) with an unpleasant response, such as nausea or vomiting, resulting in future avoidance of that particular sensory cue.

taste buds Onion-shaped structures on the tongue that contain the receptors for taste.

TAT *See* Thematic Apperception Test.

telegraphic speech A distinctive speech pattern observed during language acquisition in which the child omits articles, prepositions, and parts of verbs.

telepathy The ability to transfer thoughts to another person or to read the thoughts of others.

temperament An individual's distinctive pattern of attention, arousal, and reactivity to new or novel situations. This pattern appears early, is relatively stable and long-lasting, and is influenced in large part by genetic factors.

temporal lobe A segment of the brain located directly below the parietal lobe that is involved in hearing, speaking coherently, and understanding verbal and written material.

teratogen Any agent that can harm a developing fetus (causing deformities or brain damage). It might be a disease (such as genital herpes), a drug (such as alcohol), or another environmental agent (such as chemicals).

test anxiety A combination of physiological, emotional, and cognitive components that are caused by the stress of taking exams and that may interfere with a student's ability to think, reason, and plan.

testimonial A statement in support of a particular viewpoint based on personal experience.

testosterone The major male hormone, which stimulates the growth of genital organs and the development of secondary sexual characteristics.

texture gradient In three-dimensional vision, a monocular depth cue: areas with sharp, detailed texture are interpreted as being closer, and those with less sharpness and detail as more distant.

thalamus A structure of the limbic system that is located in the middle of the forebrain and is involved in receiving sensory information, doing some initial processing, and then relaying the sensory information to appropriate areas of the cortex, including the somatosensory cortex, primary auditory cortex, and primary visual cortex.

Thematic Apperception Test (TAT) A personality test in which subjects are asked to look at pictures of people in ambiguous situations and to make up stories about what the characters are thinking and feeling and what the outcome will be.

theory of evolution Darwin's theory that different species arose from a common ancestor and that those species survived that were best adapted to meet the demands of their environments.

theory of linguistic relativity Whorf's theory that the differences among languages result in differences in the ways people think and perceive the world.

theory of personality An organized attempt to describe and explain how personalities develop and why personalities differ.

theory theory The idea that children have innate abilities to make guesses about how things are, test their guesses through interactions with the environment, and change their guesses as they gather new or conflicting information.

thinking Mental processes by which we form concepts, solve problems, and engage in creative activities. Sometimes referred to as reasoning.

threat appraisal Our conclusion that harm or loss has not yet taken place in a particular situation but we anticipate it in the near future.

threshold A point above which a stimulus is perceived and below which it is not perceived. *See also* absolute threshold.

thyroid A gland located in the neck that regulates metabolism through secretion of hormones. It forms part of the endocrine system.

time-out In training children, a form of negative punishment in which reinforcing stimuli are removed after an undesirable response. This removal decreases the chances that the response will recur. In time-out, the child is told to sit quietly in the corner of a room or put in some other situation where there is no chance to obtain reinforcers or engage in pleasurable behaviors.

tip-of-the-tongue phenomenon The situation in which, despite making a great effort, we are temporarily unable to recall information that we absolutely know is in our memory.

Glossary

TKS *See* taijin kyofusho.

tolerance The reaction of the body and brain to regular drug use, whereby the person has to take larger doses of the drug to achieve the same behavioral effect.

touch The skin senses, which include temperature, pressure, and pain. Touch sensors change mechanical pressure or changes in temperature into nerve impulses that are sent to the brain for processing.

trait A relatively stable and enduring tendency to behave in a particular way.

trait theory An approach for analyzing the structure of personality by measuring, identifying, and classifying similarities and differences in personality characteristics or traits.

transcendental meditation (TM) A meditation exercise in which individuals assume a comfortable position, close their eyes, and repeat and concentrate on a sound to clear their head of all thoughts (worrisome and otherwise).

transduction The process by which a sense organ changes, or transforms, physical energy into electrical signals that become neural impulses, which may be sent to the brain for processing.

transference In psychotherapy, the process by which a client expresses strong emotions toward the therapist because the therapist substitutes for someone important in the client's life, such as the client's mother or father. Freud first developed this concept.

transformational rules According to Chomsky, procedures by which we convert our ideas from surface structures into deep structures and from deep structures back into surface structures.

transmitter A chemical messenger that transmits information between nerves and body organs, such as muscles and heart. *See also* neurotransmitters.

transsexualism *See* gender identity disorder.

triangular theory of love *See* Sternberg's triangular theory of love.

triarchic theory *See* Sternberg's triarchic theory.

trichromatic theory The idea that there are three different kinds of cones in the retina, and each cone contains one of three different light-sensitive chemicals, called opsins. Each opsin is most responsive to wavelengths that correspond to each of the three primary colors—blue, green, and red—from which all other colors can be mixed.

two-factor theory A theory of intelligence proposed by Spearman, according to which a general mental ability factor, *g,* represents a person's ability to perform complex mental work, such as abstract reasoning and problem solving, while many specific factors, *s,* represent a person's specific mental abilities, such as mathematical, mechanical, or verbal skills. Thus, *g* is constant across tests, while *s* may vary across tests.

two-word combinations The third stage in acquiring language, which begins at about 2 years of age. The infant says strings of two words that express various actions ("Me play," "See boy") or relationships ("Hit ball," "Milk gone").

tympanic membrane The thin, taut membrane, commonly called the eardrum, that is the boundary between the outer ear and middle ear. Struck by sound waves, it vibrates and passes the vibrations to the ossicles.

Type A behavior A combination of personality traits that may be a risk factor for coronary heart disease. According to the original (1970s) definition, these traits included an overly competitive and aggressive drive to achieve, a hostile attitude when frustrated, a habitual sense of time urgency, a rapid and explosive pattern of speaking, and workaholic tendencies; in contrast, type B behavior was easygoing, calm, relaxed, and patient. In the 1980s, the list of traits was reduced to being depressed, aggressively competitive, easily frustrated, anxious, and angry. In the 1990s, the list was reduced again, to frequent feelings of anger and hostility, which may or may not be publicly expressed. At this point, the association between Type A behavior and risk of coronary disease is much in doubt.

Type I schizophrenia A type of schizophrenia characterized by positive symptoms, such as hallucinations and delusions, which are distortions of normal functions. Individuals diagnosed with Type I schizophrenia have no intellectual impairment, good reaction to medication, and thus a good chance of recovery.

Type II schizophrenia A type of schizophrenia characterized by negative symptoms, such as dulled emotions and little inclination to speak, which are a loss of normal functions. Individuals diagnosed with Type II schizophrenia have intellectual impairment, poor reaction to medication, and thus a poor chance of recovery.

typical neuroleptic drugs Neuroleptics that primarily reduce the levels of the neurotransmitter dopamine. Two of the more common are phenothiazines (for example, Thorazine) and butrophenones (for example, haloperidol). These drugs primarily reduce positive symptoms but have little or no effects on negative symptoms.

unconditional positive regard The warmth, acceptance and love that others show us because we are valued human beings even though we may behave in ways that disappoint them by behaving in ways that differ from their standards and values or the way they think.

unconditioned response (UCR) An unlearned, innate, involuntary physiological reflex that is elicited by the unconditioned stimulus.

unconditioned stimulus (UCS) A stimulus that triggers or elicits some physiological response, such as salivation or eye blink.

unconscious *See* Freud's theory of the unconscious; cognitive unconscious.

unconscious forces Wishes, desires, or thoughts that, because of their disturbing or threatening content, we automatically repress and cannot voluntarily access.

unconscious motivation A Freudian concept that refers to the influence of repressed thoughts,

desires, or impulses on our conscious thoughts and behaviors.

unconsciousness Total loss of awareness and responsiveness to the environment. It may be due to disease, trauma, a blow to the head, or general medical anesthesia.

underachievers Individuals who score relatively high on tests of ability or intelligence but perform more poorly than their scores would predict.

unipolar depression *See* major depressive disorder.

universal emotional expressions A number of specific inherited facial patterns or expressions that signal specific feelings or emotional states, such as a smile signaling a happy state.

uplifts Small, pleasurable, happy, and satisfying experiences that we have in our daily lives.

validity The extent to which a test measures what it is supposed to measure.

variable-interval schedule A conditioning schedule such that the time between the response and the subsequent reinforcer is variable.

variable-ratio schedule A conditioning schedule in which the subject must make a different number of responses for the delivery of each reinforcer.

variance A measure of the variability within two distributions.

ventrolateral preoptic nucleus (VPN) A group of cells in the hypothalamus that acts like a master switch for sleep. Turned on, the VPN secretes a neurotransmitter (GABA) that turns off areas that keep the brain awake; turned off, certain brain areas become active and we wake up.

vertigo Feelings of dizziness and nausea resulting from malfunction of the semicircular canals in the vestibular system.

vestibular system Three semicircular canals in the inner ear that sense the position of the head, keep the head upright, and maintain balance. Fluid in the semicircular canals moves in response to movements of the head, and sensors (hair cells) in the canals respond to the movement of the fluid.

virtual reality A perceptual experience—of being inside an object, moving through an environment, or carrying out some action—that is, in fact, entirely simulated by a computer.

visible spectrum The one particular segment of electromagnetic energy that we can see because these waves are the right length to stimulate receptors in the eye.

visual acuity The ability to see fine details.

visual agnosia A condition caused by damage to the visual association area. An individual with visual agnosia is unable to recognize some object, person, or color and yet is able to see and even describe parts of some visual stimulus.

visual association area An area of the brain, located next to the primary visual cortex, that transforms basic sensations, such as lights, lines, colors, and textures, into complete, meaningful visual perceptions, such as persons, objects, or animals.

visual cliff A glass tabletop with a checkerboard pattern over part of its surface; the remaining surface consists of clear glass with a checkerboard pattern several feet below, creating the illusion of a clifflike drop to the floor.

VPN *See* ventrolateral preoptic nucleus.

vulnerability Psychological or environmental difficulties that make children more at risk for developing later personality, behavioral, or social problems.

Weber's law A psychophysics law stating that the increase in intensity of a stimulus needed to produce a just noticeable difference grows in proportion to the intensity of the initial stimulus.

Wechsler Adult Intelligence Scale (WAIS-III) and Wechsler Intelligence Scale for Children (WISC-III) Intelligence tests that are divided into various subtests. The verbal section contains a subtest of general information, a vocabulary subtest, and so forth. The performance section contains a subtest that involves arranging pictures in a meaningful order, one that requires assembling objects, and one that involves using codes. The verbal and performance scores are combined to give a single IQ score.

weight-regulating genes Genes that play a role in influencing appetite, body metabolism, and secretion of hormones (such as leptin) that regulate fat stores.

Wernicke's aphasia Difficulty in understanding spoken or written words and in putting words into meaningful sentences, as a result of injury to Wernicke's area in the brain.

Wernicke's area An area usually located in the left temporal lobe that plays a role in understanding speech and speaking in coherent sentences. *See* Wernicke's aphasia.

withdrawal symptoms Painful physical and psychological symptoms that occur when a drug-dependent person stops using a drug.

word An arbitrary pairing between a sound or symbol and a meaning.

working memory *See* short-term memory.

Yerkes-Dodson law The principle that performance on a task is an interaction between the level of physiological arousal and the difficulty of the task. For difficult tasks, low arousal results in better performance; for most tasks, moderate arousal helps performance; and for easy tasks, high arousal may facilitate performance.

zero correlation The absence of a relationship between the occurrence of one event and the occurrence of a second event.

zygote The cell that results when a zygote is fertilized. It contains 46 chromosomes, arranged in 23 pairs.

References

Abernethy, B., Neal, R. J., & Koning, P. (1994). Visual-perceptual and cognitive differences between expert, intermediate, and novice snooker players. *Applied Cognitive Psychology, 8,* 185–211.

Abramov, I., & Gordon, J. (1994). Color appearance: On seeing red—or yellow, or green, or blue. *Annual Review of Psychology, 45,* 451–485.

Abramowitz, J. S. (1997). Effectiveness of psychological and pharmacological treatments for obsessive-compulsive disorder: A quantitative review. *Journal of Consulting and Clinical Psychology, 65,* 44–52.

Abu-Lughod, L. (1986). *Veiled sentiments.* Berkeley: University of California Press.

Adams, C. (1991). Qualitative age differences in memory for text: A life-span developmental perspective. *Psychology and Aging, 6,* 323–336.

Adan, A. (1992). The influence of age, work schedule and personality on morningness dimensions. *International Journal of Psychophysiology, 12,* 95–99.

Adelmann, P. K., & Zajonc, R. B. (1989). Facial efference and the experience of emotion. *Annual Review of Psychology, 40,* 249–280.

Ader, R., & Cohen, N. (1975). Behaviorally conditioned immunosuppression. *Psychosomatic Medicine, 37,* 333–340.

Adler, J., & Rosenberg, D. (1994, December 19). The endless binge. *Newsweek.*

Adler, L. L., & Denmark, F. L. (1995). *Violence and the prevention of violence.* Westport, CT: Praeger.

Adler, T. (1993b, April). Sense of invulnerability doesn't drive teen risks. *APA Monitor.*

Adler, T. (1994). Comprehending those who can't relate. *Science News, 145,* 248–249.

Aghajanian, G. K. (1994). Serotonin and the action of LSD in the brain. *Psychiatric Annals, 24,* 137–141.

Ainsworth, M. D. S. (1979). Infant-mother attachment. *American Psychologist, 34,* 932–937.

Ainsworth, M. D. S. (1989). Attachments beyond infancy. *American Psychologist, 44,* 709–716.

Aitchison, K., & Kerwin, R. W. (1997). Cost-effectiveness of clozapine. *British Journal of Psychiatry, 171,* 125–130.

Alanen, P. P. (1997). A critical review of genetic studies of schizophrenia. I. Epidemiological and brain studies. *Acta Psychiatrica Scandinavica, 95,* 1–5.

Alcock, J. (1995, May/June). Why faith in anecdotal reports? *Skeptical Inquirer.*

Alexander, G. E., Furey, M. L., Grady, C. L., Pietrini, P., Brady, D. R., Mentis, M. J., & Schapiro, M. B. (1997). Association of premorbid intellectual function with cerebral metabolism in Alzheimer's Disease: Implications for the cognitive reserve hypothesis. *American Journal of Psychiatry, 154,* 165–172.

Ali, S. I., & Begum, S. (1994). Fabric softeners and softness perception. *Ergonomics, 37,* 801–806.

Alivisatos, B., & Petrides, M. (1997). Functional activation of the human brain during mental rotation. *Neuropsychologia, 35,* 111–118.

Allen, G., Buxton, R. B., Wong, E. C., & Courchesne, E. (1997). Attentional activation of the cerebellum independent of motor involvement. *Science, 275,* 1940–1943.

Allen, R. P., & Mirabile, J. (1997, June 18). Cited in E. Woo, How to get A's, not Zzzz. *Los Angeles Times.*

Allport, G. W. (1935). Attitudes. In C. Murchison (Ed.), *Handbook of social psychology* (Vol. 2). Worcester, MA: Clark University Press.

Allport, G. W., & Odbert, H. S. (1936). Trait-names: A psycho-lexical study. *Psychological Monographs, 47* (Whole No. 211).

Althof, S. E. (1995). Pharmacologic treatment of rapid ejaculation. *The Psychiatric Clinics of North America, 18,* 85–94.

Altman, L. K. (1997, January 19). With AIDS advance, more disappointment. *New York Times.*

Amabile, T. M. (1985). Motivation and creativity: Effects of motivational orientation on creative writers. *Journal of Personality and Social Psychology, 48,* 393–399.

American Association on Mental Retardation. (1993). *Mental retardation* (9th ed.). Annapolis Junction, MD: AAMR Publications.

American Psychiatric Association. (1952). *Diagnostic and statistical manual of mental disorders.* Washington, DC: Author.

American Psychiatric Association. (1968). *Diagnostic and statistical manual of mental disorders* (2nd ed.). Washington, DC: Author.

American Psychiatric Association. (1980). *Diagnostic and statistical manual of mental disorders* (3rd ed.). Washington, DC: Author.

American Psychiatric Association. (1994). *Diagnostic and statistical manual of mental disorders* (4th ed.). Washington, DC: Author.

American Psychological Association. (1992). Ethical principles of psychologists and code of conduct. *American Psychologist, 47,* 1597–1611.

American Psychological Association, Division of Psychological Hypnosis (1993). Hypnosis. *Psychologial Hypnosis 2*(3).

American Psychological Association. (1995). *How to choose a psychologist.* Washington, DC: Author.

Anastasi, A., & Urbina, S. (1997). *Psychological testing.* Upper Saddle River, NJ: Prentice Hall.

Anderson, C. A., Bushman, B. J., & Groom, R. W. (1997). Hot years and serious and deadly assault: Empirical tests of the heat hypothesis. *Journal of Personality and Social Psychology, 73,* 1213–1223.

Anderson, K. J. (1994). Impulsivity, caffeine, and task difficulty: A within-subjects test of the Yerkes-Dodson law. *Personality and Individual Differences, 16,* 813–819.

Andreasen, N. C. (1997a). The role of the thalamus in schizophrenia. *Canadian Journal of Psychiatry, 42,* 27–33.

Andreasen, N. C. (1997b). Linking mind and brain in the study of mental illnesses: A project for a scientific psychopathology. *Science, 275,* 1586–1593.

Andreasen, N. C., Nopoulos, P., Schultz, S., Miller, D., Gupta, S., Swayze, V., & Flaum, M. (1994). Positive and negative symptoms of schizophrenia: Past, present, and future. *Acta Psychiatrica Scandinavica, 90,* 510–519.

Angelo, B. (1991, November 4). Life at the end of the rainbow. *Time.*

Antonuccio, D. O., Thomas, M., & Danton, W. G. (1997). A cost-effective analysis of cognitive behavior therapy and fluoxetine (Prozac) in the treatment of depression. *Behavior Therapy, 28,* 187–210.

Archer, J. (1996). Sex differences in social behavior. *American Psychologist, 51,* 909–917.

Archer, J. (1997). On the origins of sex differences in social behavior: Darwinian and non-Darwinian accounts. *American Psychologist, 52,* 1383–1384.

Arena, J. G., Bruno, G. M., & Rozantine, G. S. (1997). A comparison of tension headache sufferers and nonpain controls on the state-trait anger expression inventory: An exploratory study with implications for applied psychophysiologists. *Applied Psychophysiology and Biofeedback, 22,* 209–214.

Arendt, J., & Deacon, S. (1997). Treatment of circadian rhythm disorders—melatonin. *Chronobiology International, 14,* 185–204.

Arkowitz, H. (1997). Integrative theories of therapy. In P. L. Wachtel & S. B. Messer, (Eds.), *Theories of psychotherapy: Origins and evolution.* Washington, D.C.: American Psychological Association.

Aronson, E. (1997). Back to future: Retrospective review of Leon Festinger's *A theory of cognitive dissonance. American Journal of Psychology, 110,* 127–157.

Asch, S. E. (1958). Effects of group pressure upon modification and distortion of judgments. In E. E. Maccoby, T. M. Newcomb, & E. L. Hartley (Eds.), *Readings in social psychology* (3rd ed.). New York: Holt, Rinehart & Winston.

Aserinsky, E., & Kleitman, N. (1953). Regularly occurring periods of eye motility, and concomitant phenomena during sleep. *Science, 118,* 273–274.

Ashton, H. (1994). The treatment of benzodiazepine dependence. *Addiction, 89,* 1535–1541.

Atkinson, J. W. (1964). *An introduction to motivation.* Princeton, NJ: Van Nostrand Reinhold.

Atkinson, J. W. (Ed.). (1958). *Motives in fantasy, action and society.* Princeton, NJ: Van Nostrand Reinhold.

Atkinson, J. W., & Birch, D. (1978). *Introduction to motivation.* New York: Van Nostrand.

Atkinson, J. W., & Raynor, J. O. (Eds.) (1974). *Motivation and achievement.* Washington, DC: V. H. Winston.

Atkinson, R. C., & Shiffrin, R. M. (1968). Human memory: A proposed system and its control processes. In K. W. Spence & J. T. Spence (Eds.), *The psychology of learning and motivation: Advances in research and theory* (Vol. 2). New York: Academic Press.

Atkinson, R. C., & Shiffrin, R. M. (1971). The control of short term memory. *Scientific American, 225,* 82–90.

Attias, J., Gordon, C., Ribak, J., Binah, O., & Arnon, R. (1987). Efficacy of transdermal scopolamine against seasickness: A 3-day study at sea. *Aviation, Space and Environmental Medicine, 58,* 60–62.

Audrain, J. E., Klesges, R. C., & Klesges, L. M. (1995). Relationship between obesity and the metabolic effects of smoking in women. *Health Psychology, 14,* 116–123.

Azar, B. (1994, October). Scientists eye complexities of aggression. *APA Monitor.*

Azar, B. (1994, November). Mixed messages fuel dieting dilemmas. *APA Monitor.*

Azar, B. (1997, August). When research is swept under the rug. *APA Monitor.*

Azar, B., & Sleek, S. (1994, October). Do roots of violence grow from nature or nurture? *APA Monitor.*

Baddeley, A. (1994). The magical number seven: Still magic after all these years? *Psychological Review, 101,* 353–356.

Bahrick, H. P., Bahrick, P. O., & Wittlinger, R. P. (1975). Fifty years of memory for names and faces. *Journal of Experimental Psychology: General, 104,* 54–75.

Bahrick, H. P., Hall, L. K., Berger, S. A. (1996). Accuracy and distortion in memory for high school girls. *Psychological Science, 7,* 265–271.

Bailey, J. M., & Zucker, H. J. (1995). Childhood sex-typed behavior and sexual orientation: A conceptual analysis and quantitative review. *Developmental Psychology, 31,* 43–55.

Baldwin, J. D., & Baldwin, J. I. (1997). Gender differences in sexual interest. *Archives of Sexual Behavior, 26,* 181–210.

Balint, K. (1995, March 4). La Jolla senior, 17, wins top U.S. science prize. *San Diego Union-Tribune.*

Ball, E. M. (1997). Sleep disorders in primary care. *Comprehensive Therapy, 23,* 25–30.

Balter, M. (1996). New clues to brain dopamine control, cocaine addiction. *Science, 271,* 909.

Balzar, J. (1997, March 8). A passion for canines, cold winds. *Los Angeles Times.*

Bandura, A. (1965). Influence of models' reinforcement contingencies on the acquisition of imitative responses. *Journal of Personality and Social Psychology, 1,* 589–596.

Bandura, A. (1986). *Social foundations of thought and action: A social cognitive theory.* Englewood Cliffs, NJ: Prentice-Hall.

Bandura, A. (1989a). Human agency in social cognitive theory. *American Psychologist, 44,* 1175–1184.

Bandura, A. (1989b). Social cognitive theory. In R. Vasta (Ed.), *Annals of child development* (Vol. 6). Greenwich, CT: JAI Press.

Bandura, A. (1989c). Regulation of cognitive processes through perceived self-efficacy. *Developmental Psychology, 25,* 729–735.

Bandura, A. (Ed.). 1995. *Self-efficacy in changing societies.* New York: Cambridge University Press.

Bandura, A., Blanchard, E. B., & Ritter, B. (1969). Relative efficacy of desensitization and modeling approaches for inducing behavioral, affective and attitudinal changes. *Journal of Personality and Social Psychology, 13,* 173–179.

Bandura, A., Ross, D., & Ross, S. A. (1963). Imitation of film-mediated aggressive models. *Journal of Abnormal and Social Psychology, 66,* 3–11.

Barinaga, M. (1992). The brain remaps its own contours. *Science, 258,* 216–218.

Barinaga, M. (1996). Backlash strikes at affirmative action programs. *Science, 271,* 1908–1910.

Barinaga, M. (1997a). A mitochondrial Alzheimer's gene? *Science, 276,* 682.

Barinaga, M. (1997b). Ban has mixed impact on Texas, California grad schools. *Science, 277,* 633–634.

Barkley, R. (1994, July 18). Cited in C. Wallis, Life in overdrive. *Time.*

Barkley, R. A. (1997). Behavioral inhibition, sustained attention, and executive functions: Constructing a unifying theory of ADHD. *Psychological Bulletin, 121,* 65–94.

Barling, J., Kelloway, E. K., & Cheung, D. (1996). Time management and achievement striving to predict car sales performance. *Journal of Applied Psychology, 81,* 821–826.

Barlow, D. H., & Durand, V. M. (1995). *Abnormal psychology: An integrative approach.* Pacific Grove, CA: Brooks/Cole.

Baron, R., Logan, H., Lilly, J., Inman, M., & Brennan, M. (1994). Negative emotion and message processing. *Journal of Experimental Social Psychology, 30,* 181–201.

Barrett, S. (1995, January–February). The dark side of Linus Pauling's legacy. *Skeptical Inquirer.*

Bartol, C. R., Bergen, G. T., Volckens, J. S., & Knoras, K. M. (1992). Women in small-town policing. *Criminal Justice and Behavior, 19,* 240–259.

Bartoshuk, L. M. (1997). Cited in K. Fackelmann, The bitter truth. *Science News, 152,* 24–25.

Bartoshuk, L. M., & Beauchamp, G. K. (1994). Chemical senses. *Annual Review of Psychology, 45,* 419–449.

Bashore, T. R., Osman, A., & Heffley, E. F., III. (1989). Mental slowing in elderly persons: A cognitive psychophysiological analysis. *Psychology and Aging, 4,* 235–244.

Bashore, T. R., & Rapp, P. E. (1993). Are there alternatives to traditional polygraph procedures? *Psychological Bulletin, 113,* 3–22.

Basil, R. (1989). Graphology and personality: Let the buyer beware. *Skeptical Inquirer, 13,* 241–248.

Bassili, J. N. (1995). Response latency and the accessibility of voting intentions: What contributes to accessibility and how it affects vote choice. *Personality and Social Psychology Bulletin, 21,* 686–695.

Bates, B. L. (1994). Individual differences in response to hypnosis. In J. W. Rhue, S. J. Lynn, & I. Kirsch (Eds.), *Handbook of clinical hypnosis.* Washington, DC: American Psychological Association.

Bateson, P. (1991). Is imprinting such a special case? In J. R. Krebs & G. Horn (Eds.), *Behavioural and neural aspects of learning and memory.* Oxford: Oxford University Press.

Batson, C. D. (1998). Who cares? When? Where? Why? How? *Contemporary Psychology, 43,* 108–109.

Bauer, P. J. (1996). What do infants recall of their lives? *American Psychologist, 51,* 29–41.

Baum, D. (1996). *Smoke and mirrors: The war on drugs and the politics of failure.* New York: Little, Brown.

Baum, G. (1994, February 13). Storming the Citadel. *Los Angeles Times.*

Baumeister, R. F. (1995). Disputing the effects of championship pressures and home audiences. *Journal of Personality and Social Psychology, 68,* 644–648.

Baumeister, R. F., & Leary, M. R. (1995). The need to belong: Desire for interpersonal attachments as a fundamental human motivation. *Psychological Bulletin, 117,* 497–529.

Baumrind, D. (1991). Effective parenting during the early adolescent transition. In P. A. Cowan & E. M. Hetherington (Eds.), *Advances in family research.* Hillsdale, NJ: Erlbaum.

Baumrind, D. (1993). The average expectable environment is not good enough: A response to Scarr. *Child Development, 64,* 1299–1317.

Baumrind, D. (1995). Commentary on sexual orientation: Research and social policy implications. *Developmental Psychology, 31,* 130–136.

Beaman, A. L., Cole, C. M., Preston, M., Lentz, B., & Steblay, N. M. (1983). Fifteen years of foot-in-the-door research. *Personality and Social Psychology Bulletin, 9,* 181–196.

Bear, M. F., Connors, B. W., & Paradiso, M. A. (1996). *Neuroscience: Exploring the brain.* Baltimore: Williams & Wilkins.

Beardsley, T. (1997, August). The machinery of thought. *Scientific American,* 78–83.

Bechara, A., Damasio, H., Tranel, D., Damasio, A. R. (1997). Deciding advantageously before knowing the advantageous strategy. *Science, 275,* 1293–1295.

Bechara, A., Tranel, D., Damasio, H., Adolphs, R., Rockland, C., & Damasio, A. R. (1995). Double dissociation of conditioning and declarative knowledge relative to the amygdala and hippocampus in humans. *Science, 269,* 1115–1120.

Beck, A. T. (1976). *Cognitive therapy and the emotional disorders.* New York: International Universities Press.

Beck, A. T. (1991). Cognitive therapy: A 30-year retrospective. *American Psychologist, 46,* 368–375.

Beck, A. T., Rush, A. J., Shaw, B. F., & Emery, G. (1979). *Cognitive therapy of depression.* New York: Guilford Press.

Beck, R., & Fernandez, E. (1998). Cognitive-behavioral therapy in the treatment of anger: A meta-analysis. *Cognitive Therapy and Research, 22,* 63–74.

Becker, J. V., & Kaplan, M. S. (1994). Sexual disorders. In V. B. Van Hasselt & M. Mersen (Eds.), *Advanced abnormal psychology.* New York: Plenum Press.

Bednekoff, P. A., Kamil, A. C., Balda, R. P. (1997). Clark's nutcracker (Aves: Corvidae) spatial memory; Interference effects on cache recovery performance? *Ethology, 103,* 554–565.

References

Begley, S. (1994, August 29). Why Johnny and Joanie can't read. *Newsweek*.

Begley, S. (1997, February 24). Mammogram war. *Newsweek*.

Begley, S. (1998, January 19). Aping language. *Newsweek*.

Begley, S. (1998, January 26). Is everybody crazy? *Newsweek*, 51–55.

Bell, A. P., Weinberg, M. S., & Hammersmith, S. K. (1981). *Sexual preference: Its development in men and women*. Bloomington: Indiana University Press.

Bell, S. M., McCallum, R. S., Bryles, J., Driesler, K., McDonald, J., Park, S. H., & Williams, A. (1994). Attributions for academic success and failure: An individual difference investigation of academic achievement and gender. *Journal of Psychoeducational Assessment, 13,* 4–13.

Belsky, J. (1993). Etiology of child maltreatment: A developmental-ecological analysis. *Psychological Bulletin, 114,* 413–434.

Bem, D. (1967). Self-perception: An alternative interpretation of cognitive dissonance phenomena. *Psychological Review, 74,* 183–200.

Bem, D. J., & Honorton, C. (1994). Does psi exist? Replicable evidence for an anomalous process of information transfer. *Psychological Bulletin, 115,* 4–18.

Bem, S. L. (1981). Gender schema theory: A cognitive account of sex-typing. *Psychological Review, 88,* 354–364.

Bem, S. L. (1985). Androgyny and gender schema theory: Conceptual and empirical integration. In T. B. Sonderegger (Ed.), *Nebraska symposium on motivation*. Lincoln: University of Nebraska Press.

Ben-Shakhar, G., Bar-Hillel, M., Bilu, Y., Ben-Abba, E., & Flug, A. (1986). Can graphology predict occupational success? Two empirical studies and some methodological ruminations. *Journal of Applied Psychology, 71,* 645–653.

Benes, F. M. (1997). The role of stress and dopamine—GABA interactions in the vulnerability for schizophrenia. *Journal of Psychiatric Research, 31,* 57–275.

Benson, H. (1975). *The relaxation response*. New York: Morrow.

Benson, H. (1997). Cited in W. Roush, Herbert Benson: Mind-body maverick pushes the envelope. *Science, 276,* 357–359.

Benson, H., Lehmann, J. W., Malhotra, M. S., Goldman, R. F., Hopkins, P. J., & Epstein, M. D. (1982). Body temperature changes during the practice of g Tum-mo yoga. *Nature, 295,* 234–235.

Benson, H., Malhotra, M. S., Goldman, R. F., Jacobs, G. D., & Hopkins, P. J. (1990). Three case reports of the metabolic and electroencephalographic changes during advanced Buddhist meditation techniques. *Behavioral Medicine, 16,* 90–95.

Berger, J., & Cunningham, C. (1994). Active intervention and conservation: Africa's pachyderm problem. *Science, 263,* 1241–1242.

Bergin, A. E., & Garfield, S. L. (1994). Overview, trends, and future issues. In A. E. Bergin & S. L. Garfield (Eds.), *Handbook of psychotherapy and behavior change* (4th ed.). New York: Wiley.

Berglas, S. (1989). Self-handicapping behavior and the self-defeating personality disorder. In R. C. Curtis (Ed.), *Self-defeating behaviors: Experimental research, clinical impressions, and practical implications*. New York: Plenum Press.

Berk, L. B., & Patrick, C. F. (1990). Epidemiologic aspects of toilet training. *Clinical Pediatrics, 29,* 278–282.

Berkowitz, L. (1989). Frustration-aggression hypothesis: Examination and reformulation. *Psychological Bulletin, 106,* 59–73.

Berkowitz, L. (1993). *Aggression: Its causes, consequences, and control*. New York: McGraw-Hill.

Berkowitz, L. (1994, October). Cited in B. Azar, Scientists eye complexities of aggression. *APA Monitor*.

Berman, A. L., & Jobes, D. A. (1994). Treatment of the suicidal adolescent. *Death Studies, 18,* 375–389.

Berman, A. L., & Jobes, D. A. (1995). Suicide prevention in adolescents (age 12–18). *Suicide and Life-Threatening Behavior, 25,* 143–154.

Berman, M. E., Tracy, J. I., & Coccaro, E. R. (1997). The serotonin hypothesis of aggression revisited. *Clinical Psychology Review, 17,* 651–665.

Bermond, B., Nieuwenhuyse, B., Fasotti, L., & Schuerman, J. (1991). Spinal cord lesions, peripheral feedback, and intensities of emotional feelings. *Cognition and Emotion, 5,* 201–220.

Bernstein, D. A. (1993, March). Excuses, excuses. *APS Observer*.

Bernstein, P. W. (1994, May 9). The words Nelson Mandela lives by. *U.S. News & World Report*.

Betancourt, H., & Lopez, S. R. (1993). The study of culture, ethnicity, and race in American psychology. *American Psychologist, 48,* 629–637.

Biederman, J., Faraone, S., Milberger, S., Guite, J., Mick, E., Chen, L., Mennin, D., Marrs, A., Ouellette, C., Moore, P., Spencer, T., Norman, D., Wilens, T., Kraus, I., & Perrin, J. (1996). A prospective 4-year follow-up study of attention- deficit hyperactivity and related disorders. *Archives of General Psychiatry, 53,* 437–446.

Biehl, M., Matsumoto, D., Ekman, P., Hearn, V., Heider, K., Kudoh, T., & Ton, V. (1997). Matsumoto and Ekman's Japanese and Caucasian facial expressions of emotion (JACFEE): Reliability data and cross-national differences. *Journal of Nonverbal Behavior, 21,* 3–21.

Billy, J. O. G., Tanfer, K., Grady, W. R., & Klepinger, D. H. (1993). The sexual behavior of females in the United States. *Family Planning Perspectives, 25,* 52–60.

Binet, A., & Simon, T. (1905). Methodes nouvelles pour le diagnostic du niveau intellectual des anormaux. *L'Annee Psychologique, 11,* 191–244.

Bisserbe, J. C., Lane, R. M., Flament, M. R., & Franco-Belgian OCD Study Group (1997). A double-blind comparison of sertraline and clomipramine in outpatients with obsessive-compulsive disorder. *European Psychiatry, 12,* 82–93.

Black, D. W., Baumgard, C. H., & Bell, S. E. (1995). A 16- to 45-year follow-up of 71 men with antisocial personality disorder. *Comprehensive Psychiatry, 36,* 130–140.

Blackmore, S. (1994). Psi in psychology. *Skeptical Inquirer, 18,* 351–356.

Blakely, M. R. (1994, May 15). A place of belonging. *Los Angeles Times Magazine*.

Blanchard, E. B., Andrasik, F., Guarnieri, P., Neff, D. F., & Rodichok, L. D. (1987). Two-, three-, and four-year follow-up on the self-regulatory treatment of chronic headache. *Journal of Consulting and Clinical Psychology, 55,* 257–259.

Blendon, R. J., Szalay, U. S., & Knox, R. A. (1992). Should physicians aid their patients in dying? The public perspective. *Journal of the New England Journal of Medicine, 267,* 2658–2662.

Bliwise, D. L. (1997). Sleep and aging. In M. R. Pressman & W. C. Orr (Eds.), *Understanding sleep: The evaluation and treatment of sleep disorders*. Washington, DC: American Psychological Association.

Block, J. (1995a). A contrarian view of the five-factor approach to personality description. *Psychological Bulletin, 117,* 187–215.

Block, J. (1995b). Going beyond the five factors given: Rejoinder to Costa & McCrae (1995) and Goldberg & Saucier (1995). *Psychological Bulletin, 117,* 226–229.

Block, J., & Robins, R. W. (1993). Longitudinal study of consistency and change in self-esteem from early adolescence to early adulthood. *Child Development, 64,* 909–923.

Block, R. I. (1996). Does heavy marijuana use impair human cognition and brain functioning? *Journal of the American Medical Association, 275,* 560–561.

Boddy, J. (1988). Spirits and selves in northern Sudan: The cultural therapeutics of possession and trance. *American Ethnologist, 15,* 4–27.

Boden, M. A. (1994). Précis of the creative mind: Myths and mechanisms. *Behavioral and Brain Sciences, 17,* 519–570.

Boivin, D. B., Czeisler, C. A., Kijk, D. J., Duffy, J. F., Folkard, S., Minors, D. S., Totterdell, P., & Waterhouse, J. M. (1997). Complex interaction of sleep-wake cycle and circadian phase modulates mood in healthy subjects. *Archives of General Psychiatry, 54,* 145–152.

Bondolfi, G., Dufour, H., Patris, M., May, J. P., Billeter, U., Eap, C. B., Baumann, P. (1998). Risperidone versus clozapine in treatment-resistant chronic schizophrenia: A randomized double-blind study. *American Journal of Psychiatry, 155,* 499–504.

Bonebakker, A. E., Jelicic, M., Passchier, J., & Bonke, B. (1996). Memory during general anesthesia: Practical and methodological aspects. *Consciousness and Cognition, 5,* 542–561.

Booth-Kewley, S., & Friedman, H. S. (1987). Psychological predictions of heart disease: A quantitative review. *Psychological Bulletin, 101,* 343–362.

Bootzin, R. R., & Rider, S. P. (1997). Behavioral techniques and biofeedback for insomnia. In M. R. Pressman & W. C. Roo (Eds.), *Understanding sleep: The evaluation and treatment of sleep disorders.* Washington, DC: American Psychological Association.

Born, J., Lange, T., Hansen, K., Molle, M., & Fehm, H. L. (1997). Effects of sleep and circadian rhythm on human circulating immune cells. *Journal of Immunology, 158,* 4454–4464.

Bouchard, T. J., Jr. (1994). Genes, environment, and personality. *Science, 264,* 1700–1701.

Bouchard, T. J., Jr. (1995). Breaking the last taboo. *Contemporary Psychology, 40,* 415–418.

Bouchard, T. J., Jr. (1997). IQ similarity in twins reared apart: Findings and responses to critics. In R. J. Sternberg & E. Grigorenko (Eds.), *Intelligence, heredity, and environment.* New York: Cambridge University Press.

Bouchard, T. J., Jr., Lykken, D. T., McGue, M., Segal, N. L., & Tellegen, A. (1990). Sources of human psychological differences: The Minnesota study of twins reared apart. *Science, 250,* 223–228.

Bower, B. (1991). Oedipus wrecked. *Science News, 140,* 248–250.

Bower, B. (1993a). Sudden recall. *Science News, 144,* 184–186.

Bower, B. (1993b). Flashbulb memories: Confident blunders. *Science News, 143,* 166–167.

Bower, B. (1994). Babies' brains charge up to speech sounds. *Science News, 146,* 71.

Bower, B. (1996). Creatures in the brain. *Science News, 149,* 234–235.

Bower, B. (1997a). Forbidden flavors. *Science News, 151,* 198–199.

Bower, B. (1997b). Thanks for the memories: Scientists evaluate interviewing tactics for boosting eyewitness recall. *Science News, 151,* 246–247.

Bower, F. (1997). The power of limited thinking. *Science News, 152,* 334–335.

Bowers, K., & Farvolden, P. (1996). Revisiting a century-old Freudian slip—From suggestion disavowed to the truth repressed. *Psychological Bulletin, 119,* 335–380.

Bowlby, J. (1969). *Attachment and loss: Vol. 1. Attachment.* New York: Basic Books.

Boykin, A. W. (1996, August). The case of African-American inner-city schools. In R. Serpell & B. Nsamenang (Convenors), *Basic education for the modern world: Alternatives to Western cultural hegemony.* Quebec City, Quebec, Canada: International Society for the Study of Behavioral Development.

Bradley, C. L. (1997). Generativity-stagnation: Development of a status model. *Developmental Review, 17,* 262–290.

Bradley, S. J., & Zucker, K. J. (1997). Gender identity disorder: A review of the past 10 years. *Journal of the American Academy of Child Adolescence Psychiatry, 36,* 87–880.

Bragg, R. (1995, July 16). In South Carolina, a mother's defense, and life, could hinge on 2 choices. *New York Times.*

Brainerd, C. J., & Poole, D. A. (1997). Long-term survival of children's false memories: A review. *Learning and Individual Differences, 9,* 125–151.

Brannon, L., & Feist, J. (1997). *Health psychology* (3rd ed.). Pacific Grove, CA: Brooks/Cole.

Brauer, M., Judd, C. M., & Gliner, M. D. (1995). The effects of repeated expressions on attitude polarization during group discussions. *Journal of Personality and Social Psychology, 68,* 1014–1029.

Brecher, E. M. (1972). *Licit and illicit drugs.* Boston: Little, Brown.

Brennan, J. (1997, September 28). This 1,800-pound bear is no 800-pound gorilla. *Los Angeles Times/Calendar.*

Brennan, P. A., & Raine, A. (1997). Biosocial bases of antisocial behavior: Psychophysiological, neurological, and cognitive factors. *Clinical Psychology Review, 17,* 589–604.

Breuer, J., & Freud, S. (1895; reprinted 1955). Studies on hysteria. In J. Strachey (Ed. and Trans.), *The standard edition of the complete psychological works of Sigmund Freud.* London: Hogarth.

Brewer, J. D. (1991). Hercules, Hippolyte, and the Amazons—or policewomen in the RUC. *British Journal of Sociology, 42,* 231–247.

Brickman, P., Coates, D., & Janoff-Bulman, R. (1978). Lottery winners and accident victims: Is happiness relative? *Journal of Personality and Social Psychology, 36,* 917–927.

Briere, J., & Conte, J. (1993). Self-reported amnesia for abuse in adults molested as children. *Journal of Traumatic Stress, 6,* 21–31.

Briggs, J. L. (1970). *Never in anger: Portrait of an Eskimo family.* Cambridge, MA: Harvard University Press.

Bristol, M. M., Cohen, D. J., Costello, E. J., Denckla, M., Eckberg, T. H., Kallen, R., Kraemer, H. C., Lord, C., Maurer, R., McIlvane, W. J., Minskew, N., Sigman, M., & Spence, M. A. (1996). State of the science in autism: Report to the National Institute of Health. *Journal of Autism and Developmental Disorders, 26,* 121–154.

Brody, J. E. (1996, April 16). Vitamin C by the numbers: 200 milligrams gets the nod. *San Diego Union-Tribune.*

Brody, J. E. (1998, January 6). Depression: 2 famous men tell their stories. *San Diego Union-Tribune.*

Brody, N. (1992). *Intelligence.* New York: Academic Press.

Brody, N. (1997). Intelligence, schooling, and society. *American Psychologist, 52,* 1046–1050.

Brooks, C. (1994, February 27). Breakdown into the shadows of mental illness. Special report. *San Diego Union-Tribune.*

Brooks, C. (1995a, June 5). Rod Steiger is powerful voice for mentally ill. *San Diego Union-Tribune.*

Brooks, C. (1995b, February 27). Shadowlands: Three profiled in mental illness series are striv-

ing to improve their conditions. *San Diego Union-Tribune.*

Brown, A. S. (1991). A review of the tip-of-the-tongue experience. *Psychological Bulletin, 109,* 204–223.

Brown, R., & Kulik, J. (1977). Flashbulb memories. *Cognition, 5,* 73–99.

Brown, S. L. (1994, December). Animals at play. *National Geographic.*

Brown, T. A., Barlow, D. H., & Liebowitz, M. R. (1994). The empirical basis of generalized anxiety disorder. *American Journal of Psychiatry, 151,* 1271–1280.

Brown, W. A. (1997, January). The placebo effect. *Scientific American,* 90–95.

Brownell, K. D., & Rodin, J. (1994). The dieting maelstrom. *American Psychologist, 49,* 781–791.

Brownlee, S. (1997, February 3). The case for frivolity. *U.S. News & World Report.*

Brownlee, S., & Schrof, J. M. (1997, March). The quality of mercy. *U.S. News & World Report.*

Brunner, H. G., Nelen, M., Breakefield, X. O., Ropers, H. H., & van Oost, B. A. (1993). Abnormal behavior associated with a point mutation in the structural gene for monoamine oxidase A. *Science, 262,* 578–580.

Brzezinski, A. (1997). Melatonin in humans. *New England Journal of Medicine, 336,* 186–195.

Buchanan, C., Eccles, J., & Becker, J. (1992). Are adolescents the victims of raging hormones? Evidence for activational effects of hormones on moods and behavior at adolescence. *Psychological Bulletin, 111,* 62–107.

Buck, K. J., Metten, P., Belknap, J. K., & Crabbe, J. C. (1997). Quantitative trait loci involved in genetic predisposition to acute alcohol withdrawal in mice. *Journal of Neuroscience, 17,* 3946–3955.

Buckley, P. (1989). Fifty years after Freud: Dora, the Rat Man, and the Wolf-Man. *American Journal of Psychiatry, 146,* 1394–1403.

Buckout, R. (1980). Nearly 2,000 witnesses can be wrong. *Bulletin of the Psychonomic Society, 16,* 307–310.

Bueler, R., Griffin, D., & Ross, M. (1994). Exploring the "planning fallacy": Why people underestimate their task completion times. *Journal of Personality and Social Psychology, 67,* 366–381.

Bugental, B. B., & Goodnow, J. J. (1998). Socialization processes. In W. Damon and N. Eisenberg (Eds.), *Handbook of child psychology* (5th ed.). New York: John Wiley & Sons.

Buitelaar, J. K., Jan van der Gaag, R., Swaab-Barneveld, H., & Kuiper, M. (1996). Pindolol and methlphenidate in children with attention-deficit hyperactivity disorder. Clinical efficacy and side effects. *Journal of Child Psychology and Psychiatry, 37,* 587–595.

Buonomano, D. V., & Merzenich, M. M. (1995). Temporal information transformed into a spatial code by a neural network with realistic properties. *Science, 267,* 1028–1030.

Burcham, B., Carlson, L., & Milich, R. (1993). Promising school-based practices for students with attention deficit disorder. *Exceptional Children, 60,* 174–180.

References

Burge, D., Hammen, C., Davila, J., Daley, S. E., Paley, B., Herzberg, D., & Lindberg, N. (1997). Attachment cognitions and college and work functioning two years later in late adolescent women. *Journal of Youth and Adolescence, 26,* 285–301.

Burnette, E. (1994, November). Psychology makes top 10% of country's hottest careers. *Monitor American Psychological Association.*

Burnham, D. (1993). Visual recognition of mother by young infants: Facilitation by speech. *Perception, 22,* 1133–1153.

Buss, D. (1996, August). Cited in B. Azar, Modern mating: Attraction or survival? *APA Monitor,* 31–32.

Buss, D. M. (1994a). *The evolution of desire.* New York: Basic Books.

Buss, D. M. (1994b). Mate preferences in 37 cultures. In W. J. Lonner & R. Malpass (Eds.), *Psychology and culture.* Boston: Allyn & Bacon.

Buss, D. M. (1995). Psychological sex differences. *American Psychologist, 50,* 164–168.

Buss, D. M., Abbott, M., Angleitner, A., Asherian, A., Biaggio, A., Blanco-VillaSenor, A., Bruchon-Schweitzer, M., Ch'u, H. Y., Czapinski, J., DeRaad, B., Ekehammar, B., Fioravanti, M., Georgas, J., Gjerde, P., Guttman, R., Hazan, F., Iwawaki, S., Janakiramaiah, H., Khosroshani, F., Kreitler, S., Lachenicht, L., Lee, M., Liik, K., Little, B., Lohamy, N., Makun, S., Mika, S., Moadel-Shahid, M., Moane, G., Montero, M., Mundy-Casde, A. C., Niit, T., Nsenduluka, E., Peltzer, K., Pienkowski, R., Pirttila-Backman, A., Ponce De Leon, J., Rousseau, J., Runco, M. A., Safir, M. P., Samuels, C., Sanitioso, R., Schweitzer, B., Serpell, R., Smid, N., Spencer, C., Tadinac, M., Todorova, E. N., Troland, K., Van den Brande, L., Van Heck, G., Van Langenhove, L., & Yang, K. S. (1990). International preferences in selecting mates. *Journal of Cross-Cultural Psychology, 21,* 5–47.

Buss, D. M., & Schmitt, D. P. (1993). Sexual strategies theory: An evolutionary perspective on human mating. *Psychological Review, 100,* 204–232.

Butcher, J. N., Dalhstrom, W. G., Graham, J. R., Tellegen, A. M., & Kaemmer, B. (1989). *MMPI-2: Manual for administration and scoring.* Minneapolis: University of Minnesota Press.

Butler, K. (1994, June 26). A house divided. *Los Angeles Times Magazine.*

Byerley, W., & Coon, H. (1995). Strategies to identify genes for schizophrenia. *American Psychiatric Press Review of Psychiatry* (Vol. 14). Washington, DC: American Psychiatric Press.

Byne, W. (1994). The biological evidence challenged. *Scientific American, 270,* 50–55.

Byne, W. (1997). Why we cannot conclude that sexual orientation is primarily a biological phenomenon. *Journal of Homosexuality, 34,* 73–80.

Byrd, K. R. (1994). The narrative reconstructions of incest survivors. *American Psychologist, 49,* 439–440.

Cabeza, R., & Nyberg, L. (1997). Imaging cognition: An empirical review of PET studies with normal subjects. *Journal of Cognitive Neuroscience, 9,* 1–26.

Cacioppo, J. T., Klein, D. J., Berntson, G. G., & Hatfield, E. (1993). The psychophysiology of emotion. In M. Lewis & J. M. Haviland (Eds.), *Handbook of emotions.* New York: Guilford Press.

Cacioppo, J. T., & Petty, R. E. (1982). The need for cognition. *Journal of Personality and Social Psychology, 42,* 116–131.

Cacioppo, J. T., Petty, R. E., Feinstein, J. A., & Jarvis, W. B. G. (1996). Dispositional differences in cognitive motivation: The life and times of individuals varying in need for cognition. *Psychological Bulletin, 119,* 197–253.

Cadoret, R. J., Leve, L. D., & Devor, E. (1997). Genetics of aggressive and violent behavior. *Psychiatric Clinics of North America, 20,* 301–322.

Cahill, L., Prins, B., Weber, M., & McGaugh, J. L. (1994). B-adrenergic activation and memory for emotional events. *Nature, 371,* 702–704.

Caldwell, J. C., Orubuloye, I. O., & Caldwell, P. (1997). Male and female circumcision in Africa from a regional to a specific Nigerian examination. *Social Science & Medicine, 44,* 1181–1193.

Calvo, M. G., & Carreiras, M. (1993). Selective influence of test anxiety on reading processes. *British Journal of Psychology, 84,* 375–388.

Camacho, L. M., & Paulus, P. B. (1995). The role of social anxiousness in group brainstorming. *Journal of Personality and Social Psychology, 68,* 1071–1080.

Cameron, J., & Pierce, D. (1994). Reinforcement, reward, and intrinsic motivation: A meta-analysis. *Review of Educational Research, 64,* 363–423.

Camp, G. C. (1994). A longitudinal study of correlates of creativity. *Creativity Research Journal, 7,* 125–144.

Campbell, R. A., & Ramey, C. T. (1990). The relationship between cognitive development, mental test performance, and academic achievement in high-risk students with and without early educational experience. *Intelligence, 14,* 293–308.

Cannon, T. D., Kaprio, J., Lonnqvist, J., Huttunen, M., & Koskenvuo, M. (1998). The genetic epidemiology of schizophrenia in a Finnish twin cohort. *Archives of General Psychiatry, 55,* 67–74.

Caplan, N., Choy, M. H., & Whitmore, J. K. (1992). Indochinese refugee families and academic achievement. *Scientific American, 266,* 36–42.

Caplan, P. (1994, June 5). Cited in A Japenga, DMS. *Los Angeles Times Magazine.*

Cardon, L. R., Smith, S. D., Fulker, D. W., Kimberling, W. J., Pennington, B. F., & DeFries, J. C. (1994). Quantitative trait locus for reading disability on chromosome 6. *Science, 266,* 276–279.

Carducci, B. J. (1998). *The psychology of personality.* Pacific Grove, CA: Brooks/Cole. *Psychology Today,* 34–40.

Carducci, B. J., & Zimbardo, P. G. (1995, November/ December). Are you shy? *Psychology Today,* 34–40.

Carey, K. B., & Correia, C. J. (1997). Drinking motives predict alcohol-related problems in college students. *Journal of Studies on Alcohol, 58,* 100–185.

Carlin, A. S., Hofman, H. G. & Weghorst, S. (1997). Virtual reality and tactile augmentation in the treatment of spider phobia: A case report. *Behavior Research and Therapy, 35,* 153–158.

Carlson, J. G., Chemtob, C. M., Rusnak, K., Hedlund, N. L., & Muraoka, M. Y. (1998). Eye movement desensitization and reprocessing (EDMR) treatment for combat-related posttraumatic stress disorder. *Journal of Traumatic Stress, 11,* 3–24.

Carlson, J. M. (1990). Subjective ideological similarity between candidates and supporters: A study of party elites. *Political Psychology, 11,* 485–492.

Carlson, N. R. (1998). *Physiology of behavior* (6th ed.). Boston: Allyn & Bacon.

Carskadon, M. A., & Taylor, J. F. (1997). Public policy and sleep disorders. In M. R. Pressman & W. C. Orr (Eds.), *Understanding sleep: The evaluation and treatment of sleep disorders.* Washington, DC: American Psychological Association.

Carton, J. S. (1996). The differential effects of tangible rewards and praise on intrinsic motivation: A comparison of cognitive evaluation theory and operant theory. *Behavior Analyst, 19,* 237–255.

Cartwright, R. (1988, July–August). Cited in *Psychology Today.*

Cartwright, R. D. (1993). Who needs their dreams? The usefulness of dreams in psychotherapy. *Journal of the American Academy of Psychoanalysis, 21,* 539–547.

Cattell, H., & Jolley, D. J. (1995). One hundred cases of suicide in elderly people. *British Journal of Psychiatry, 166,* 451–457.

Cattell, R. B. (1943). The description of personality: Basic traits resolved into clusters. *Journal of Abnormal and Social Psychology, 38,* 476–506.

Cauchon, D. (1995, December 6). Shock therapy. *USA Today.*

Cavett, D. (1992, August 3). Goodbye, darkness. *People.*

Ceci, S. J., & Bruck, M. (1995). *Jeopardy in the courtroom: A scientific analysis of children's testimony.* Washington, DC: American Psychological Association.

Ceci, S. J., & Huffman, M. L. C. (1997). How suggestible are preschool children? Cognitive and social factors. *Journal of the American Academy of Child and Adolescent Psychiatry, 36,* 948–958.

Ceci, S. J., Huffman, M. L. C., Smith, E., & Loftus, E. (1994). Repeatedly thinking about a non-event: Source misattributions among preschoolers. *Consciousness and Cognition, 3,* 388–407.

Ceci, S. J., Rosenblum, T., de Bruyn, E., & Lee, D. Y. (1997). A bio-ecological model of intellectual development: Moving beyond h². In R.

J. Sternberg & E. Grigorenko (Eds.), *Intelligence, heredity, and environment.* New York: Cambridge University Press.

Centers for Disease Control and Prevention. (1988). CDC recommendations for a plan for the prevention and containment of community clusters. *Monthly Morbidity and Mortality Weekly Reports,* Supplement 37, 1–12.

Centers for Disease Control and Prevention. (1992, December 18). 1993 revised classification system for HIV infection and expanded surveillance case definition for AIDS among adolescents and adults. *Morbidity and Mortality Weekly Report.*

Centers for Disease Control and Prevention. (1997). Update: Trends in AIDS incidence, deaths, and prevalence—United States, 1996. *Journal of the American Medical Association, 277,* 874–875.

Cerone, D. (1989, October 22). How to train an 1,800-pound star. *Los Angeles Times/Calendar.*

Cervone, D. (1997). Social-cognitive mechanisms and personality coherence: Self-knowledge, situational beliefs, and cross-situational coherence in perceived self-efficacy. *Psychological Science, 8,* 43–50.

Chaiken, S., & Eagly, A. H. (1976). Communication modality as a determinant of message persuasiveness and message comprehensibility. *Journal of Personality and Social Psychology, 34,* 605–614.

Chalmers, D. J. (1995, December). The puzzle of conscious experience. *Scientific American,* 80–86.

Charney, D. A., & Russell, R. C. (1994). An overview of sexual harassment. *American Journal of Psychiatry, 151,* 10–17.

Chasnoff, I. (1997, December). Cited in B. Azar, Researchers debunk myth of the "crack baby." *APA Monitor.*

Chaves, J. F. (1994). Hypnosis in pain management. In J. W. Rhue, S. J. Lynn, & I. Kirsch (Eds.), *Handbook of clinical hypnosis.* Washington, DC: American Psychological Association.

Chavez, S. (1994, January 3). Tough stand on attendance pays off at South Gate High. *Los Angeles Times.*

Chellappah, N. K., Viegnehas, H., Milgrom, P., & Lo, B. L. (1990). Prevalence of dental anxiety and fear in children in Singapore. *Community Dentistry Oral Epidemiology, 18,* 269–271.

Chen, G., Li, S., & Jiang, C. (1986). Clinical studies on neurophysiological and biochemical basis of acupuncture analgesia. *American Journal of Chinese Medicine, 14,* 86–95.

Chen, J., Chang, S., Duncan, S. A., Okano, H. J., Fishell, G., & Aderem, A. (1996). Disruption of the MacMARCKS gene prevents cranial neural tube closure and results in anencephaly. *Proceedings of the National Academy of Sciences, 93,* 6275–6279.

Chen, Y., Mestek, A., Liu, J., Hurley, J. A., & Yu, L. (1993). Molecular cloning and functional expression of a u-opioid receptor from rat brain. *Molecular Pharmacology, 44,* 8–12.

Chisholm, A. H. (1996). Fetal tisssue transplantation for the treatment of Parkinson's disease: A review of the literature. *Journal of Neuroscience Nursing, 28,* 329–338.

Chomsky, N. (1957). *Syntactic structures.* The Hague: Mouton.

Chuang, D. (1998). Cited in J. Travis, Stimulating clue hints how lithium works. *Science News, 153,* 165.

Chwalisz, K., Diener, E., & Gallagher, D. (1988). Autonomic arousal feedback and emotional experience: Evidence from the spinal cord injury. *Journal of Personality and Social Psychology, 54,* 820–828.

Cimons, M. (1997, September 19). New AIDS cases show decline in U.S. *Los Angeles Times,* A12.

Cirelli, C., Pompeiano, M., & Tononi, G. (1996). Neuronal gene expression in the waking state: A role for locus coeruleus. *Science, 274,* 1211–1215.

Clark, L. A., Watson, D., & Reynolds, S. (1995). Diagnosis and classification of psychopathology: Challenges to the current system and future directions. *Annual Review of Psychology, 46,* 121–153.

Clarke, A. M., & Clarke, A. D. B. (1989). The later cognitive effects on early intervention. *Intelligence, 13,* 289–297.

Clay, R. A. (1997, April). Is assisted suicide ever a rational choice? *APA Monitor.*

Clay, R. A. (1997, September). Meditation is becoming more mainstream. *APA Monitor.*

Coccaro, E. F., & Kavoussi, R. J. (1997). Fluoxetine and impulsive aggressive behavior in personality-disordered subjects. *Archives of General Psychiatry, 54,* 1081–1088.

Coe, W. C. (1994). Expectations and hypnotherapy. In J. W. Rhue, S. J. Lynn, & I. Kirsch (Eds.), *Handbook of clinical hypnosis.* Washington, DC: American Psychological Association.

Cohen, A. (1997, September 8). Battle of the binge. *Time.*

Cohen, B., & Murphy, G. L. (1984). Models of concepts. *Cognitive Science, 8,* 27–58.

Cohen, D. B. (1979). *Sleep and dreaming: Origins, nature and functions.* New York: Pergamon Press.

Cohen, J. (1994). New fight over fetal tissue grafts. *Science, 263,* 600–601.

Cohen, N. J. (1984). Preserved learning capacity in amnesia: Evidence for multiple memory systems. In L. R. Squire, & N. Butters (Eds.), *Neuropsychology of memory.* New York: Guilford Press.

Cohen, S. (1996). Psychological stress immunity, and upper respiratory infections. *Current Directions in Psychological Science, 5,* 86–89.

Cohen, S., Tyrrell, D. A. J., & Smith, A. P. (1997). Psychological stress in humans and susceptibility to the common cold. In T. W. Miller (Ed.). *Clinical disorders and stressful life events.* Madison, CT: International Universities Press.

Cohen, S., & Williamson, G. M. (1991). Stress and infectious disease in humans. *Psychological Bulletin, 109,* 5–24.

Coie, J. D., & Dodge, K. A. (1998). Aggression and antisocial behavior. In W. Damon & R. M. Lerner (Eds.), *Handbook of child psychology* (Vol. 1). New York: John Wiley & Sons.

Coie, J. D., Lochman, J. E., Terry, R., & Hyman, C. (1992). Predicting early adolescent disorder from childhood aggression and peer rejection. *Journal of Consulting and Clinical Psychology, 60,* 783–792.

Colangelo, N. (1997). The "termites" grow up and grow old. *Contemporary Psychology, 42,* 208–209.

Colapinto, J. (1996, May 30). Rock & roll heroin. *Rolling Stone.*

Cole, K. C. (1997, April 28). Upsetting our sense of self. *Los Angeles Times.*

Collings, S., & King, M. (1994). Ten-year follow-up of 50 patients with bulimia nervosa. *British Journal of Psychiatry, 164,* 80–87.

Collins, A. M., & Quillian, M. R. (1969). Retrieval time from semantic memory. *Journal of Verbal Learning and Verbal Behavior, 8,* 240–247.

Compas, B. E., Hinden, B. R., & Gerhardt, C. A. (1995). Adolescent development: Pathways and processes of risk and resilience. *Annual Review of Psychology, 46,* 265–293.

Connor, L. (1982). In A. J. Marsella & G. M. White (Eds.), *Cultural conceptions of mental health and therapy.* Boston: D. Reidel.

Conway, M. A., Anderson, S. J., Larsen, S. F., Donnelly, C. M., McDaniel, M. A., McClelland, A. G. R., Rawles, R. E., & Logie, R. H. (1994). The formation of flashbulb memories. *Memory and Cognition, 22,* 326–343.

Cook, E., Courchesne, R., Lord, C., Cox, N. J., Lincoln, A., Haas, R., Courchesne, E., & Leventhal, B. L. (1997). Evidence of linkage between the serotonin transporter and autistic disorder. *Molecular Psychiatry, 2,* 247–250.

Cookson, J. (1997). Lithium: Balancing risks and benefits. *British Journal of Psychiatry, 171,* 113–119.

Coren, S., & Ward, L. M. (1993). *Sensation and perception* (4th ed.). San Diego: Harcourt Brace Jovanovich.

Cork, L. C., Clarkson, T. B., Jacoby, R. O., Gaertner, D. J., Leary, S. L., Linn, J. M., Pakes, S. P., Ringler, D. H., Strandberg, J. D., & Swindle, D. (1997). The costs of animal research: Origins and options. *Science, 276,* 758–759.

Cosmides, L., & Tooby, J. (1994). Cited in B. Bower, Roots of reason. *Science News, 145,* 72–75.

Costa, P. T., Jr., & McCrae, R. R. (1995). Solid ground in the wetlands of personality: A reply to Block. *Psychological Bulletin, 117,* 216–220.

Costa, P. T., Jr., & McCrae, R. R. (1997). Longitudinal stability of adult personality. In R. Hogan, J. Johnson, & S. Briggs (Eds.), *Handbook of personality psychology.* New York: Academic Press.

Courchesne, E., Townsend, J., Akshoomoff, N. A., Saiton, O., Yeung-Courchesne, R., &

References

Lincoln, A. J., James, H. E., Haas, R. I. T., Schreibman, L., & Lau, L. (1994). Impairment in shifting attention in autistic and cerebellar patients. *Behavioral Neuroscience, 108,* 848–865.

Cowley, G. (1997, June 30). How to live to 100. *Newsweek.*

Cowley, G., Miller, S., Crandall, R., & Hager, M. (1995, February). RoboDocs and mouse-calls. *Newsweek.*

Coyne, J. C. (1994). Self-reported distress: Analog or ersatz depression? *Psychological Bulletin, 116,* 29–45.

Coyne, J. C., & Whiffen, V. E. (1995). Issues in personality as diathesis for depression: The case of sociotropy—dependency and autonomy—self-criticism. *Psychological Bulletin, 118,* 358–378.

Craik, F. I. M., & Lockhart, R. S. (1972). Levels of processing: A framework for memory research. *Journal of Verbal Learning and Verbal Behavior, 11,* 671–684.

Craik, F. I. M., & Tulving, E. (1975). Depth of processing and the retention of words in episodic memory. *Journal of Experimental Psychology: General, 104,* 268–294.

Cravatt, B. F., Prospero-Garcia, O., Siuzdak, G., Gilula, N. B., Henriksen, S. J., Boger, D. L., and Lerner, R. A. (1995). Chemical characterization of a family of brain lipids that induce sleep. *Science, 268,* 1506–1509.

Crawford, H. J., Gur, R. C., Skolnick, B., Gur, R. E., & Benson, D. M. (1993). Effects of hypnosis on regional cerebral blood flow during ischemic pain with and without suggested hypnotic analgesia. *International Journal of Psychophysiology, 15,* 181–195.

Creed, F. (1993). Stress and psychosomatic disorders. In L. Goldberger & S. Breznitz (Eds.), *Handbook of stress: Theoretical and clinical aspects* (2nd ed.). New York: Free Press.

Crews, F. (1996). The verdict on Freud. *Psychological Science, 7,* 63–68.

Crichton, S. (1995, February). Caught between east and west, Rushdie keeps on. *Newsweek.*

Crick, F. (1994). *The astonishing hypothesis.* New York: Scribner's.

Crick, F., & Koch, C. (1997). The problem of consciousness. *Scientific American,* Special Issue, 19–26.

Crisp, A. H. (1997). Anorexia nervosa as flight from growth: Assessment and treatment based on the model. In D. M. Garner & P. E. Garfinkel (Eds.) (1997), *Handbook of treatment for eating disorders* (2nd ed.). New York: Guilford Press.

Croce, C. M. (1996, April 5). Cited in F. Flam, Scientists identify gene that triggers smokers' lung cancer. *San Diego Union-Tribune.*

Cromer, A. (1993). *Uncommon sense: The heretical nature of science.* New York: Oxford University Press.

Cross, S. E., & Madson, L. (1997). Models of the self: Self-construals and gender. *Psychological Bulletin, 122,* 5–37.

Crow, T. J. (1985). The two syndrome concept: Origins and current status. *Schizophrenia Bulletin, 11,* 471–486.

Crowder, R. G. (1992). Eidetic imagery. In L. R. Squire (Ed.), *Encyclopedia of learning and memory.* New York: Macmillan.

Crowe, R. A. (1990). Astrology and the scientific method. *Psychological Reports, 67,* 163–191.

Cull, W. L., & Zechmeister, E. B. (1994). The learning ability paradox in adult metamemory research: Where are the metamemory differences between good and poor learners? *Memory & Cognition, 22,* 249–257.

Cull, W. L., & Zechmeister, E. B. (1994). The learning ability paradox in adult metamemory research: Where are the metamemory differences between good and poor learners? *Memory & Cognition, 22,* 249–257.

Culp, R. E., Culp, A. M., Osofsky, J. D., & Osofsky, H. J. (1991). Adolescent and older mothers' interaction patterns with their six-month-old infants. *Journal of Adolescence, 14,* 195–200.

Cunningham, M. R., Roberts, A. R., Barbee, A. P., Druen, P. B., & Wu, C. (1995). "Their ideas about beauty are, on the whole, the same as ours": Consistency and variability in the cross-cultural perception of female physical attractiveness. *Journal of Personality and Social Psychology, 68,* 261–279.

Czeisler, C. A. (1994). Cited in R. Nowak, Chronobiologists out of sync over light therapy patents. *Science, 263,* 1217–1218.

Czeisler, C. A., Shanahan, T. L., Klerman, E. B., Martens, H., Brotman, D. J., Emens, J. S., Klein, T., & Rizzo, J. F. (1995). Suppression of melatonin secretion in some blind patients by exposure to bright light. *New England Journal of Medicine, 332,* 6–11.

Dadds, M. R., Bovbjerg, D. H., Redd, W. H., & Cutmore, T. R. H. (1997). Imagery in human classical conditioning. *Psychological Bulletin, 122,* 80–103.

Dahmer, L. (1994). *A father's story.* New York: Morrow.

Dalgard, O. S., Bjork, S., Tambs, K. (1995). Social support, negative life events and mental health. *British Journal of Psychiatry, 166,* 29–34.

Dallos, P., & Evans, B. N. (1995). High-frequency motility of outer hair cells and the cochlear amplifier. *Science, 267,* 2006–2010.

Dalto, C. A., Ossoff, E. P., & Pollack, R. B. (1994). Processes underlying reactions to a campaign speech: Cognition, affect, and voter concern. *Journal of Social Behavior and Personality, 9,* 701–713.

Damasio, H., Brabowski, T., Frank, R., Galaburda, A. M., & Damasio, A. R. (1994). The return of Phineas Gage: Clues about the brain from the skull of a famous patient. *Science, 264,* 1102–1105.

Dandoy, A. C., & Goldstein, A. G. (1990). The use of cognitive appraisal to reduce stress reactions: A replication. *Journal of Social Behavior and Personality, 5,* 275–285.

Daniel, M. H. (1997). Intelligence testing. *American Psychologist, 52,* 1038–1045.

Daniszewski, J. (1997, June 25). Female circumcision ban nullified. *Los Angeles Times,* A4.

Darling, J. (1997, March 29). Drug war appears to make little dent in supply. *Los Angeles Times.*

Darwin, C. (1859). *The origin of species by means of natural selection or the preservation of favored races in the struggle for life.* London: John Murray.

Darwin, C. (1872; reprinted 1965). *The expression of the emotions in man and animals.* Chicago: University of Chicago Press.

Davidson, J. R. T. (1994). International advances in the treatment of social phobia. *Journal of Clinical Psychiatry, 55,* 123–129.

Davidson, J. R. T., Tupler, L. A., & Potts, N. L. S. (1994). Treatment of social phobia with clonazepam and placebo. *Journal of Clinical Psychopharmacology, 13,* 423–428.

Davidson, L., & McGlashan, T. H. (1997). The varied outcomes of schizophrenia. *Canadian Journal of Psychiatry, 42,* 34–43.

Davies, I. R. L., & Corbett, G. G. (1997). A cross-cultural study of colour grouping: Evidence for weak linguistic relativity. *British Journal of Psychology, 88,* 493–517.

Davison, G. C., & Neale, J. M. (1990). *Abnormal psychology* (3rd ed.). New York: Wiley.

Dawes, R. M. (1994). *House of cards.* New York: Free Press.

Dawson, D. D. (1996). Cited in B. Bower, Alcoholics synonymous. *Science News, 151,* 62–63.

de Rivera, J. (1997). The construction of false memory syndrome: The experience of retractors. *Psychological Inquiry, 8,* 271–292.

Deaconson, R. F., O'Hair, D. P., Levy, M. R., Lee, M. B. F., Schuenerman, A. L., & Condon, R. E. (1988). Sleep deprivation and resident performance. *Journal of the American Medical Association, 260,* 1721–1727.

DeAngelis, T. (1966, March). Women's contributions large; recognition isn't. *Monitor American Psychological Association.*

DeAngelis, T. (1994, February). People's drug of choice offers potent side effects. *APA Monitor.*

Deater-Deckard, K., & Dodge, K. A. (1997). Externalizing behavior problems and discipline revisited: Nonlinear effects and variation by culture, context, and gender. *Psychological Inquiry, 8,* 161–175.

Deaux, K., Dane, F. C., Wrightsman, L. S., & Sigelman, C. K. (1993). *Social psychology* (6th ed.). Pacific Grove, CA: Brooks/Cole.

DeCarvalho, R. J. (1990). A history of the "Third Force" in psychology. *Journal of Humanistic Psychology, 30,* 22–44.

deCharms, R. (1980). The origins of competence and achievement motivation in personal causation. In L. J. Fyans, Jr. (Ed.), *Achievement motivation.* New York: Plenum Press.

Deci, E. L., & Ryan, R. M. (1985). *Intrinsic motivation and self-determination in human behavior.* New York: Plenum Press.

DeCurtis, A. (1994, June 2). Kurt Cobain, 1967–1994. *Rolling Stone.*

Dehaene-Lambertz, G., & Dehaene, S. (1994). Cited in B. Bower, Babies' brains charge up to speech sounds. *Science News, 146,* 71.

Della Selva, P. C. (1996). *Intensive short-term dynamic psychotherapy: Theory and technique.* New York: Wiley.

Dement, W. C., & Kleitman, N. (1957). The relation of eye movements during sleep to dream activity: An objective method for the study of dreaming. *Journal of Experimental Psychology, 53,* 339–346.

Dennerstein, L., Dudley, E., & Burger, H. (1997). Well-being and the menopausal transition. *Journal of Psychosomatic Obstetrics and Gynecology, 18,* 95–101.

Deregowski, J. B. (1980). *Illusions, patterns and pictures: A crosscultural perspective.* Orlando, FL: Academic Press.

DeRubeis, R. J., & Crits-Christoph, P. (1998). Empirically supported individual and group psychological treatments for adult mental disorders. *Journal of Consulting and Clinical Psychology, 66,* 37–52.

Detterman, D. K., & Thompson, L. A. (1997). What is so special about special education? *American Psychologist, 52,* 1082–1090.

Deutsch, G., & Halsey, J. H., Jr. (1991). Cortical blood flow indicates frontal asymmetries dominate in males but not in females during task performance. *Journal of Cerebral Blood Flow and Metabolism, 11,* S787.

Devine, P. G., Hamilton, D. L., & Ostrom, T. M. (Eds.) (1994). *Social cognition: Impact on social psychology.* New York: Academic Press.

Diamond, J. (1994, November). Race without color. *Discover.*

Diener, E., & Diener, C. (1996). Most people are happy. *Psychological Science, 7,* 181–185.

Digman, J. M. (1997). Higher-order factors of the Big Five. *Journal of Personality and Social Psychology, 73,* 1246–1256.

Dimberg, U., & Ohman, A. (1996). Behold the wrath: Psychophysiologial responses to facial stimuli. *Motivation and Emotion, 20,* 149–182.

Dinh, K. T., Sarason, I. G., Peterson, A. V., & Onstad, L. E. (1995). Children's perceptions of smokers and nonsmokers: A longitudinal study. *Health Psychology, 14,* 32–40.

Dion, K. K., Berscheid, E., & Walster, E. (1972). What is beautiful is good. *Journal of Personality and Social Psychology, 24,* 285–290.

Docherty, J. P., & Streeter, M. J. (1995). Advances in psychotherapy research. *Current Opinion in Psychiatry, 8,* 145–149.

Dodes, J. E. (1997, January–February). The mysterious placebo. *Skeptical Inquirer.*

Dolan, M. (1995, February 11). When the mind's eye blinks. *Los Angeles Times.*

Dolan, M. (1995, August 1). Justices rule for adoptive parents of San Diego boy. *Los Angeles Times.*

Dollard, J., Doob, L. W., Miller, N. E., Mower, O. H., & Sears, R. R. (1939). *Frustration and aggression.* New Haven, CT: Yale University Press.

Domino, G. (1994). Assessment of creativity with the ACL: An empirical comparison of four scales. *Creativity Research Journal, 7,* 21–33.

Domjan, M. (1998). *The principles of learning and behavior* (4th ed.). Pacific Grove, CA: Brooks/Cole.

Domjan, M., & Purdy, J. E. (1995). Animal research in psychology. *American Psychologist, 50,* 496–503.

Doupe, A. J. (1996). Plasticity of a different feather. *Science, 274,* 1851–1853.

Dowd, E. T. (1994). Cognitive-developmental hypnotherapy. In J. W. Rhue, S. J. Lynn, & I. Kirsch (Eds.), *Handbook of clinical hypnosis.* Washington, DC: American Psychological Association.

Downey, K. K., Stelson, F. W., Pomerleau, O. F., & Giordani, B. (1997). Adult attention deficit hyperactivity disorder: Psychological test profiles in a clinical population. *Journal of Nervous and Mental Disease, 185,* 32–38.

Doyle, R. P. (1994). *Books challenged or banned in 1993–1994.* Chicago: American Library Association.

Drevets, W. C., Price, J. L., Simpson, J. R., Jr., Todd, R. D., Reich, T., Vannier, M., & Raiche, M. E. (1997). Subgenual prefrontal cortex abnormalities in mood disorders. *Nature, 386,* 824–827.

Drewnowski, A. (1997). Cited in K. Fackelmann, The bitter truth. *Science News, 152,* 24–25.

Driver, J., & Baylis, G. C. (1996). Edge-assignment and figure-ground segmentation in short-term visual matching. *Cognitive Psychology 31,* 248–306.

Dunnerstein, L., Dudley, E., & Burger, H. Well-being and the menopausal transition. *Journal of Psychosomatic Obstetrics and Gynecology, 18,* 95–101.

DuPaul, G. J., & Eckert, T. L. (1997). The effects of school-based interventions for attention deficit hyperactivity disorder: A meta-analysis. *School Psychology Review, 26,* 5–27.

Durso, F. T., Rea, C. B., & Dayton, T. (1994). Graph-theoretic confirmation of restructuring during insight. *Psychological Science, 5,* 94–98.

Dykman, B. M., Abramson, L. Y., Alloy, L. B., & Hartlage, S. (1989). Processing of ambiguous and unambiguous feedback by depressed and nondepressed college students: Schematic biases and their implications for depressive realism. *Journal of Personality and Social Psychology, 56,* 431–445.

Eagly, A. H. (1995a). The science and politics of comparing women and men. *American Psychologist, 50,* 145–158.

Eagly, A. H. (1995b). Reflections on the commenters' views. *American Psychologist, 50,* 169–171.

Eagly, A. H. (1997). Sex differences in social behavior: Comparing social role theory and evolutionary psychology. *American Psychologist, 52,* 1303–1382.

Eagly, A. H., Ashmore, R. D., Makhijani, M. G., & Longo, C. C. (1991). What is beautiful is good, but...: A meta-analytic review of research on the physical attractiveness stereotype. *Psychological Bulletin, 110,* 109–128.

Eagly, A. H., Mladinic, A., & Otto, S. (1994). Cognitive and affective bases of attitudes toward social groups and social policies. *Journal of Experimental Social Psychology, 30,* 113–137.

Eaton, M. J., & Dembo, M. H. (1997). Differences in the motivational beliefs of Asian American and non-Asian students. *Journal of Educational Psychology, 89,* 433–440.

Eaves, L., Silberg, J., Hewitt, J. K., Meyer, J., Rutter, M., Simonoff, E., Neale, M., & Pickles, A. (1993). Genes, personality, and psychopathology: A latent class analysis of liability to symptoms of attention-deficit hyperactivity disorder in twins. In R. Pomin & G. E. McClearn (Eds.), *Nature, nurture and psychology.* Washington, DC: American Psychological Association.

Ebbinghaus, H. (1885; reprinted 1913). *Memory: A contribution to experimental psychology* (H. A. Ruger & C. E. Bussenius, Trans.). New York: Teachers College Press.

Eberhardt, J. L., & Randall, J. L. (1997). The essential notion of race. *Psychological Science, 8,* 198–203.

Eckensberger, L. H. (1994). Moral development and its measurement across cultures. In W. J. Lonner & R. Malpass (Eds.), *Psychology and culture.* Boston: Allyn & Bacon.

Eddings, J. (1994, December 26). Atlanta's new top cop makes her mark. *U.S. News & World Report.*

Edwards, R. (1995, January). Is hyperactivity label applied too frequently? *APA Monitor.*

Egan, T. (1998, June 14). From adolescent angst to shooting up schools. *New York Times.*

Eibl-Eibesfeldt, I. (1973). The expressive behavior of the deaf-and-blind-born. In M. von Cranach & I. Vine (Eds.), *Social communication and movement.* San Diego, CA: Academic Press.

Eich, E. (1995). Searching for mood-dependent memory. *Psychological Science, 6,* 67–75.

Eich, E., Macaulay, D., Loewenstein, R. J., & Dihle, P. H. (1997). Memory, amnesia, and dissociative identity disorder. *Psychological Science, 8,* 417–422.

Eichenbaum, H. (1993). Thinking about brain cell assemblies? *Science, 261,* 993–994.

Eichenbaum, H. (1997a). Declarative memory: Insights from cognitive neurobiology. *Annual Review of Psychology, 48,* 547–572.

Eichenbaum, H. (1997b). How does the brain organize memories? *Science, 277,* 330–332.

Eisen, M. R. (1994). Psychoanalytic and psychodynamic models of hypnoanalysis. In J. W. Rhue, S. J. Lynn, & I. Kirsch (Eds.), *Handbook of clinical hypnosis.* Washington, DC: American Psychological Association.

Eisenberger, R., & Armeli, S. (1997). Can salient reward increase creative performance without reducing intrinsic creative interest? *Journal of Personality and Social Psychology, 72,* 652–663.

Eisenberger, R., & Cameron, J. (1996). Detrimental effects of reward: Reality or myth? *American Psychologist, 51,* 1153–1166.

Ekman, P. (1993). Facial expression and emotion. *American Psychologist, 48,* 384–392.

Ekman, P. (1994). Strong evidence for universals in facial expressions: A reply to Russell's mistaken critique. *Psychological Bulletin, 115,* 268–287.

Ekman, P., & Davidson, R. J. (1993). Voluntary smiling changes regional brain activity. *Psychological Science, 4,* 342–345.

Ekman, P., & Friesen, W. V. (1969). The repertoire of nonverbal behavior: Categories, origins, usage, and coding. *Semiotica, 1,* 49–98.

Elias, M. (1989, August 9). With guidance, a child can control negative traits. *USA Today.*

Elkin, I., Shea, M. T., Watkins, J. T., Imber, S. D., Sotsky, S. M., Collins, J. F., Glass, D. R., Pilkonis, P. A., Leber, W. R., Docherty, J. P., Fiester, S. J., & Parloff, M. B. (1989). NIMH treatment of depression collaborative research program: 1. General effectiveness of treatments. *Archives of General Psychiatry, 46,* 971–982.

Elkind, D. (1978). Understanding the young adolescent. *Adolescence, 13,* 127–134.

Elkins, I. J., Iacono, W. G., Doyle, A. E., & McGue, M. (1997). Characteristics associated with the persistence of antisocial behavior: Results from recent longitudinal research. *Aggression and Violent Behavior, 2,* 101–124.

Ellason, J. W., & Ross, C. A. (1997). Two-year follow-up of inpatients with dissociative identity disorder. *American Journal of Psychiatry, 154,* 832–839.

Elliott, D. (1995, March 20). The fat of the land. *Newsweek.*

Ellis, A. (1997). Extending the goals of behavior therapy and of cognitive behavior therapy. *Behavior Therapy, 28,* 333–339.

Ellison, P. A., Govern, J. M., Petri, H. L., & Figler, M. H. (1995). Anonymity and aggressive driving behavior. *Journal of Social Behavior and Personality, 10,* 265–272.

Ellsworth, P. C. (1994a). William James and emotion: Is a century of fame worth a century of misunderstanding? *Psychological Review, 101,* 222–229.

Ellsworth, P. C. (1994b). Sense, culture, and sensibility. In S. Kitayama & H. R. Markus (Eds.), *Emotion and culture.* Washington, DC: American Psychological Association.

Elmer-Dewitt, P. (1997, January 6). Turning the tide. *Time.*

Emery, R. E., & Laumann-Billings, L. (1998). An overview of the nature, causes, and consequences of abusive family relationships. *American Psychologist, 53,* 121–135.

Emmelkamp, P. M. G., & van Oppen, P. (1994). Anxiety disorders. In V. B. Van Hasselt & M. Hersen (Eds.), *Advanced abnormal psychology.* New York: Plenum Press.

Endler, N. S., Kantor, L., & Parker, J. D. A. (1994). State-trait coping, state-trait anxiety and academic performance. *Personality and Individual Differences, 16,* 663–670.

Ennett, S. T., Rosenbaum, D. P., Flewelling, R. L., Bieler, G. S., Ringwalt, C. L., & Bailey, S. L. (1994). Long-term evaluation of drug abuse resistance education. *Addictive Behaviors, 19,* 113–125.

Epstein, L. H., Valoski, A. M., Vara, L. S., McCurley, J., Wisniewski, L., Kalarchian, M. A., Klein, K. R., & Shrager, L. R. (1995). Effects of decreasing sedentary behavior and increasing activity on weight change in obese children. *Health Psychology, 14,* 109–115.

Erickson, J. S. (1994). The use of hypnosis in anesthesia: A master class commentary. *International Journal of Clinical and Experimental Hypnosis, 42,* 8–12.

Erickson, M. H. (1980/1941). Hypnosis: A general review. In E. L. Rossie (Ed.), *The collected papers of Milton H. Erickson on hypnosis* (Vol. 30). New York: Irvington.

Erikson, E. H. (1963). *Childhood and society.* New York: Norton.

Erikson, E. H. (1982). *The life cycle completed: Review.* New York: Norton.

Eron, L. D. (1990). Understanding aggression. *Bulletin of the International Society for Research on Aggression, 12,* 5–9.

Eron, L. D., Huesmann, L. R., Dubow, E., Romanoff, R., & Yarmel, P. W. (1987). Aggression and its correlates over 22 years. In D. H. Crowell, I. M. Evans, & C. R. O'Donnell (Eds.), *Childhood aggression and violence: Sources of influence, prevention, and control.* New York: Plenum Press.

Espy, K. A., Riese, M. L., & Francis, D. J. (1997). Neurobehavior in preterm neonates exposed to cocaine, alcohol, and tobacco. *Infant Behavior and Development, 20,* 297–309.

Evans, J. (1993). The cognitive psychology of reasoning: An introduction. Quarterly *Journal of Experimental Psychology, 46A,* 561–567.

Everson, C. A. (1997). Sleep deprivation and the immune system. In M. R. Pressman & W. C. Orr (Eds.), *Understanding sleep: The evaluation and treatment of sleep disorders.* Washington, DC: American Psychological Association.

Everson, H. T., Smodlaka, I., & Tobias, S. (1994). Exploring the relationship of test anxiety and meta-cognition on reading test performance: A cognitive analysis. *Anxiety, Stress, and Coping, 7,* 85–96.

Eysenck, H. J. (1994). The outcome problem in psychotherapy: What have we learned? *Behaviour Research and Therapy, 32,* 477–495.

Fackelmann, K. A. (1993). Marijuana and the brain. *Science News, 143,* 88–94.

Fackelmann, K. A. (1995a). Forever smart: Does estrogen enhance memory? *Science News, 147,* 74–75.

Fackelmann, K. A. (1995b). Staying alive: Scientists study people who outwit the AIDS virus. *Science News, 147,* 172–174.

Fackelmann, K. A. (1997a). Marijuana on trial. *Science News, 151,* 178–179.

Fackelmann, K. A. (1997b). The bitter truth. *Science News, 152,* 24–25.

Fahy, T. A. (1988). The diagnosis of multiple personality disorder: A critical review. *British Journal of Psychiatry, 153,* 597–606.

Fairburn, C. G., Welch, S. L., Doll, H. A., Davies, B. A., & O'Connor, M. E. (1997). Risk factors for bulimia nervosa. *Archives of General Psychiatry, 54,* 509–517.

Farb, P., & Armelagos, G. (1980). *Consuming passions.* Boston: Houghton Mifflin.

Fava, M., & Kaji, J. (1994). Continuation and maintenance treatments of major depressive disorder. *Psychiatric Annals, 24,* 281–290.

Favell, J. E., Azrin, N. H., Baumeister, A. A., Carr, E. G., Dorsey, M. F., Forehand, R., Foxx, R. M., Lovaas, O. I., Rincover, A., Risley, T. R., Romanczyk, R. G., Russo, D. C., Schroeder, S. R., & Solnick, J. V. (1982). The treatment of self-injurious behavior. *Behavior Therapy, 13,* 529–554.

Fechner, G. T. (1860). *Elemente der psychophysik* (Vol. 1). Leipzig: Brietkopf and Marterl. H. E. Alder, D. H. Howes, & E. G. Boring (Trans.). New York: Holt, Rinehart & Winston.

Feder, L. (1987). The cold reading of writing. *Skeptical Inquirer, 11,* 346–348.

Federman, D. D. (1994). Life without estrogen. *New England Journal of Medicine, 331,* 1088–1089.

Feingold, B. R. (1975). Hyperkinesis and learning disabilities linked to artificial food flavors and colors. *American Journal of Nursing, 75,* 797–803.

Fenly, L. (1996, August 4). Computer technology can virtually wipe out phobias. *San Diego Union-Tribune,* E-1.

Fernald, A. (1992). Human maternal vocalizations to infants as biologically relevant signals: An evolutionary perspective. In J. H. Barkow, L. Cosmides, & Tooby (Eds.), *The adapted mind: Evolutionary psychology and the generation of culture.* New York: Oxford University Press.

Ferrari, J. R. (1994). Dysfunctional procrastination and its relationship with self-esteem, interpersonal dependency, and self-defeating behaviors. *Personality and Individual Differences, 17,* 673–679.

Ferrari, J. R., McCown, W., & Johnson, J. (1997). *Procrastination and task avoidance: Theory, research, and treatment.* New York: Plenum.

Ferster, D., & Spruston, N. (1995). Cracking the neuronal code. *Science, 270,* 756–757.

Feske, U., & Goldstein, A. J. (1997). Eye movement desensitization and reprocessing treatment for panic disorder: A controlled outcome and partial dismantling study. *Journal of Consulting and Clinical Psychology, 65,* 1026–1035.

Festinger, L. (1954). A theory of social comparison processes. *Human Relations, 7,* 117–140.

Festinger, L. (1957). *A theory of cognitive dissonance.* Palo Alto, CA: Stanford University Press.

Festinger, L., & Carlsmith, J. M. (1959). Cognitive consequences of forced compliance. *Journal of Abnormal and Social Psychology, 58,* 203–210.

Fiez, J. A., & Petersen, S. E. (1993). PET as part of an interdisciplinary approach to understanding processes involved in reading. *Psychological Science, 4,* 287–293.

Finch, C. E., & Tanzi, R. E. (1997). Genetics of aging. *Science, 278,* 407–411.

Fineman, M., & Pyes, C. (1996, June 6). Cocaine traffic to U.S. finds holes in high-tech "fence." *Los Angeles Times.*

Finke, R. A. (1993). Mental imagery and creative discovery. In B. Roskos-Ewoldsen, M. J. Intons-Peterson, & R. E. Anderson (Eds.), *Imagery, creativity, and discovery: A cognitive perspective.* Amsterdam: North Holland.

Finn, J. D., & Rock, D. A. (1997). Academic success among students at risk for school failure. *Journal of Applied Psychology, 82,* 221–234.

Firestein, S., Breer, H., & Greer, C. A. (1996). Olfaction: What's new in the nose. *Journal of Neurobiology, 30,* 1–2.

Fisch, G. S., Simensen, R., Tarleton, J., Chalifoux, M., Holden, J. J. A., Carpenter, N., Howard-Peebles, P. N., & Maddalena, A. (1996). Longitudinal study of cognitive abilities and adaptive behavior levels in fragile X males: A prospective multicenter analysis. *American Journal of Medical Genetics, 64,* 356–361.

Fischbach, G. D. (1992). Mind and brain. *Scientific American, 267,* 48–57.

Fisher, C. B., & Fryberg, D. (1994). Participant partners. *American Psychologist, 49,* 417–427.

Fisher, L. (1995, October 16). Tested by fire. *People.*

Fisher, R. P., & Geiselman, R. E. (1992). *Memory-enhancing techniques for investigative interviewing.* Springfield, IL: Charles C. Thomas.

Fisher, R. P., & McCauley, M. R. (1994). Improving eyewitness memory with the cognitive interview. In D. Ross, J. Read, & M. Toglia (Eds.), *Eyewitness memory: Current trends and developments.* New York: Springer-Verlag.

Fishman, D. B., & Franks, C. M. (1997). The conceptual evolution of behavior therapy. In P. L. Wachtel & S. B. Messer (Eds.), *Theories of psychotherapy: Origins and evolution.* Washington, DC: American Psychological Association.

Fishman, S. (1988). *A bomb in the brain.* New York: Scribner's.

Fisk, J. E., & Pidgeon, N. (1997). The conjunction fallacy: The case for the existence of competing heuristic strategies. *British Journal of Psychology, 88,* 1–27.

FitzGerald, G. J. (1993). The reproductive behavior of the stickleback. *Scientific American, 268,* 80–85.

Flavell, J. H. (1996). Piaget's legacy. *Psychological Science, 7,* 200–203.

Fleischhacker, W. W., Hummer, M., Kurz, M., Kurzthaler, I., Lieberman, J. A., Pollack, S., Safferman, A. Z., & Kane, J. J. (1994). Clozapine dose in the United States and Europe: Implications for therapeutic and adverse effects. *Journal of Clinical Psychiatry, 55,* 78–80.

Fletcher, C. (1995). *Breaking and entering: Women cops talk about life in the ultimate men's club.* New York: HarperCollins.

Flett, G. L., Vredenburg, K., & Krames, L. (1997). The continuity of depression in clinical and nonclinical samples. *Psychological Bulletin, 121,* 395–416.

Flor, H., Elbert, T., Knecht, S., Wienbruch, C., Pantev, C., Birbaumer, N., Larbig, W., & Taub, E. (1995). Phantom-limb pain as a perceptual correlate of cortical reorganization following arm amputation. *Nature, 375,* 482–483.

Floyd, M., & Scogin, F. (1997). Effects of memory training on the subjective memory functioning and mental health of older adults: A meta-analysis. *Psychology and Aging, 12,* 150–161.

Foa, E. B., & Meadows, E. A. (1997). Psychosocial treatments for posttraumatic stress disorder: A critical review. *Annual Review of Psychology, 48,* 449–480.

Ford, J. G. (1991). Rogers's theory of personality: Review and perspectives. *Journal of Social Behavior and Personality, 6,* 19–44.

Foster, G. D., Wadden, T. A., Vogt, R. A., & Brewer, G. (1997). What is reasonable weight loss? Patients' expectations and evaluations of obesity treatment outcomes. *Journal of Consulting and Clinical Psychology, 65,* 79–85.

Foubert, J. D., & Marriott, K. A. (1997). Effects of a sexual assault peer education program on men's belief in rape myths. *Sex Roles, 36,* 259–268.

Foulks, E. G. (1992). Reflections on dream material from arctic native people. *Journal of the American Academy of Psychoanalysis, 20,* 193–203.

Fowers, B. J., & Richardson, F. C. (1996). Why is multiculturalism good? *American Psychologist, 51,* 609–621.

Fox, C. (1997, December). Starved out. *Life.*

Foxx, R. M. (1996). Twenty years of applied behavior analysis in treating the most severe problem behavior: Lessons learned. *Behavior Analyst, 19,* 225–235.

Franklin, A. (1995, June). Cited in E. Burnette, Black males retrieve a noble heritage. *APA Monitor.*

Franks, C. M. (1994). Behavioral model. In V. B. Van Hasselt & M. Hersen (Eds.), *Advanced abnormal psychology.* New York: Plenum Press.

Fredrickson, M., Hursti, T., Salmi, P., Borjeson, S., Furst, C. J., Peterson, C., & Steineck, G. (1993). Conditioned nausea after cancer chemotherapy and autonomic nervous system conditionability. *Scandinavian Journal of Psychology, 34,* 318–317.

Freed, C. R., Breeze, R. E., Rosenberg, N. L., Schneck, S. A., Kriek, E., Qi, J., Lone, T., Zhang, Y., Snyder, J. A., Wells, T. H., Ramig, L. O., Thompson, L., Mazziotta, J. C., Huang, S. C., Grafton, S. T., Brooks, D., Sawle, G., Schroter, G., & Ansari, A. A. (1992). Survival of implanted fetal dopamine cells and neurologic improvement 12 to 46 months after transplantation for Parkinson disease. *New England Journal of Medicine, 327,* 1549–1555.

Freedman, R. R. (1991). Physiological mechanisms of temperature biofeedback. *Biofeedback and Self-Regulation, 16,* 95–115.

Freiberg, P. (1998, February). We know how to stop the spread of AIDS: So why can't we? *APA Monitor, 32.*

Freud, S. (1891; reprinted 1966). Hypnosis. In J. Strachey (Ed. and Trans.), *The standard edition of the complete psychological works of Sigmund Freud* (Vol. 1). London: Hogarth.

Freud, S. (1900; reprinted 1980). *The interpretation of dreams* (J. Strachey, Ed. and Trans.). New York: Avon.

Freud, S. (1901; reprinted 1960). The psychopathology of everyday life. In J. Strachey (Ed. and Trans.), *The standard edition of the complete psychological works of Sigmund Freud* (Vol. 6). London: Hogarth.

Freud, S. (1905; reprinted 1953). Three essays on the theory of sexuality. In J. Strachey (Ed. and Trans.), *The standard edition of the complete psychological works of Sigmund Freud* (Vol. 7). London: Hogarth.

Freud, S. (1909; reprinted 1949). Notes upon a case of obsessional neurosis. In *Collected papers* (Vol. 3), (Alix and James Strachey, Trans.). London: Hogarth.

Freud, S. (1924). *A general introduction to psychoanalysis.* New York: Boni & Liveright.

Freud, S. (1940; reprinted 1961). An outline of psychoanalysis. In J. Strachey (Ed. and Trans.), *The standard edition of the complete psychological works of Sigmund Freud* (Vol. 23). London: Hogarth.

Freyd, J. J. (1991, August). *Memory repression, dissociative states, and other cognitive control processes involved in adult sequelae of childhood trauma.* Paper presented at the Second Annual Conference of Psychodynamics–Cognitive Science Interface, University of California, San Francisco.

Freyd, J. J. (1994). Circling creativity. *Psychological Science, 5,* 122–126.

Fricke, D. (1994, June 2). Heart-shaped noise: The music and the legacy. *Rolling Stone.*

Friedman, H. S., Hawley, P. H., & Tucker, J. S. (1994). Personality, health and longevity. Current Directions in *Psychological Science, 3,* 37–41.

Friedman, M., & Rosenman, R. (1974). *Type A behavior and your heart.* New York: Knopf.

Friedman, S., & Stevenson, M. (1980). Perception of movements in pictures. In M. Hagen (Ed.), *Perception of pictures, Vol. 1: Alberti's window: The projective model of pictorial information.* Orlando, FL: Academic Press.

Friend, T. (1996, August 21). Teens and drugs. *USA Today.*

Friend, T. (1997, February 5). Heroin spreads across the USA. *USA Today.*

Friend, T. (1997, December 9). The race to save the wild tiger from extinction. *USA Today.*

Frijda, N. H. (1986). *The emotions.* Cambridge, England: Cambridge University Press.

Frijda, N. H., & Mesquita, B. (1994). The social roles and functions of emotions. In S. Kitayama & H. R. Markus (Eds.), *Emotion and culture.* Washington, DC: American Psychological Association.

Friman, P. C., Allen, K. D., Kerwin, L. E., & Larzelere, R. (1993). Changes in modern psychology. *American Psychologist, 48,* 658–644.

Fritz, S. (1995, June). Found: Wonders in a secret cave. *Popular Science.*

Fucci, D., Harris, D., Petrosino, L., & Banks, M. (1993). Effects of preference for rock music on magnitude-production scaling behavior in young adults: A validation. *Perceptual and Motor Skills, 77,* 811–815.

Furumoto, L. (1989). The new history of psychology. In I. S. Cohen (Ed.), *The G. Stanley Hall lecture series* (Vol. 9). Washington, DC: American Psychological Association.

Furumoto, L., & Scarborough, E. (1986). Placing women in the history of psychology. *American Psychologist, 41,* 35–42.

Gabrieli, J. D. E., Brewer, J. B., Desmond, J. E., & Glover, G. H. (1997). Separate neural bases of two fundamental memory processes in the human medial temporal lobe. *Science, 276,* 264–266.

Gabrieli, J. D. E., Fleischman, D. A., Keane, M. M., Reminger, S. L., & Morrell, F. (1995). Double dissociation between memory systems underlying explicit and implicit memory in the human brain. *Psychological Science, 6,* 76–82.

Gage, F. (1997). Cited in B. Bower, Enriched mice show adult neuron boost. *Science News, 151,* 206.

Galaburda, A. M., Menard, M. T., & Rosen, G. D. (1994). Evidence for aberrant auditory anatomy in developmental dyslexia. *Proceedings of the National Academy of Science, 91,* 8010–8013.

Gallup, G. H., Jr., & Newport, F. (1991). Belief in paranormal phenomena among adult Americans. *Skeptical Inquirer, 15,* 137–146.

Galton, F. (1888). Head growth in students at the University of Cambridge. *Nature, 38,* 14–15.

Gambrill, E. D. (1994). Concepts and methods of behavioral treatment. In D. K. Granvold (Ed.), *Concepts and methods of cognitive treatment.* Pacific Grove, CA: Brooks/Cole.

Gannon, P. J., Holloway, R. L., Broadfield, D. C., & Braun, A. R. (1998). Asymmetry of chimpanzee planum temporale: Humanlike pattern of Wernicke's brain language area homolog. *Science, 279,* 220–222.

Gannon, R. (1995, March). Why we throw up. *Popular Science,* 97–101.

Garcia, J., Ervin, F. R., & Koelling, R. A. (1966). Learning with prolonged delay of reinforcement. *Psychonomic Science, 5,* 121–122.

Garcia, J., Hankins, W. G., & Rusinak, K. W. (1974). Behavioral regulation of the milieu interne in man and rat. *Science, 185,* 824–831.

Gardner, B. T., & Gardner, R. A. (1975). Evidence for sentence constituents in the early utterances of child and chimpanzee. *Journal of Experimental Psychology: General, 104,* 244–267.

Gardner, H. (1976). *The shattered mind.* New York: Vintage Books.

Gardner, H. (1993). *Creating minds.* New York: Basic Books.

Gardner, H. (1995, November). Reflections on multiple intelligences. *Phi Delta Kappan.*

Gardner, H. (1997). Six afterthoughts: Comments on "Varieties of intellectual talent." *Journal of Creative Behavior, 31,* 120–124.

Gardner, H., Hatch, T., & Torff, B. (1997). A third perspective: The symbol systems approach. In R. J. Sternberg & E. Grigorenko (Eds.), *Intelligence, heredity, and environment.* New York: Cambridge University Press.

Gardner, M. (1995, November/December). Waking up from Freud's theory of dreams. *Skeptical Inquirer,* 10–12.

Gardner, M. (1996, January/February). Post-Freudian dream theory. *Skeptical Inquirer,* 7–9.

Garfield, S. L., & Bergin, A. E. (1994). Introduction and historical overview. In A. E. Bergin & S. L. Garfield (Eds.), *Handbook of psychotherapy and behavior change* (4th ed.). New York: Wiley.

Garfinkel, P. E., & Walsh, B. T. (1997). Drug therapies. In D. M. Garner & P. E. Garfinkel (Eds.), *Handbook of treatment for eating disorders* (2nd ed.). New York: Guilford Press.

Garland, A. R., & Zigler, E. (1993). Adolescent suicide prevention. *American Psychologist, 48,* 169–182.

Garner, D. M., & Garfinkel, P. E. (Eds.) (1997). *Handbook of treatment for eating disorders* (2nd ed.). New York: Guilford Press.

Gazzaniga, M. S. (1983). Right hemisphere language following brain bisection. *American Psychologist, 39,* 525–537.

Gazzaniga, M. S. (1994). *Nature's mind.* New York: Basic Books.

Gazzaniga, M. S. (1996). Cited in B. Bower, Whole-brain interpreter. *Science News, 149,* 124–125.

Gazzaniga, M. S. (1997). Brain, drugs, and society. *Science, 275,* 459.

Gazzaniga, M. S., Bogen, J. E., & Sperry, R. W. (1962). Some functional effects of sectioning the cerebral commissures in man. *Proceedings of the National Academy of Science, 48,* 1765–1769.

Geiger, R. (1994, October). What the experts say. *Parenting.*

Geller, L. (1982). The failure of self-actualization theory: A critique of Carl Rogers and Abraham Maslow. *Journal of Humanistic Psychology, 22,* 56–73.

George, K. I. (1995, December 6). Driver gets children to mind pizzas and Qs. *USA Today.*

George, M. S., Ketter, T. A., Parekh, P. T., Herscovitch, P., and Post, R. M. (1996). Gender differences in regional cerebral blood-flow during transient self-induced sadness or happiness. *Biological Psychiatry, 40,* 859–871.

Gerber, L. (1996, June 22). After 16 years, he's cleared. *San Diego Union-Tribune.*

Gergen, K. J., Gulerce, A., Lock, A., & Girishwar, M. (1996). Psychological science in cultural context. *American Psychologist, 51,* 496–503.

Gerlach, J., & Peacock, L. (1994). Motor and mental side effects of clozapine. *Journal of Clinical Psychiatry, 55,* 107–109.

Gershoff-Stowe, L., Thal, J. J., Smith, L. B., & Namy, L. L. (1997). Categorization and its developmental relation to early language. *Child Development, 68,* 843–859.

Giacopassi, D. J., & Dull, R. T. (1986). Gender and racial differences in the acceptance of rape myths within a college population. *Sex Roles, 15,* 63–75.

Gibbon, J. (1996). Cited in V. Morell, Setting a biological stopwatch. *Science, 271,* 905–906.

Gibbons, A. (1991). Deja vu all over again: Chimp-language wars. *Science, 251,* 1561–1562.

Gibbons, F. X., Eggleston, T. J., & Benthin, A. C. (1997). Cognitive reactions to smoking relapse: The reciprocal relation between dissonance and self-esteem. *Journal of Personality and Social Psychology, 72,* 184–195.

Gibbs, N. (1993a, July 19). In whose best interest? *Time.*

Gibbs, N. (1993b, May 3). Tragedy in Waco. *Time.*

Gibbs, W. W. (1996, August). Gaining on fat. *Scientific American,* 88–94.

Gibson, E. J., & Walk, R. (1960). The visual "cliff." *Scientific American, 202,* 64–71.

Giedd, J. N., Castellanos, F. X., Casey, B. J., Kozuch, P., King, A. C., Hamburger, S. D., & Rapoport, J. L. (1994). Quantitative morphology of the corpus callosum in attention deficit hyperactivity disorder. *American Journal of Psychiatry, 151,* 665–669.

Giedd, J. N., Castellanos, F. X., Rapoport, J. L. (1995). Corpus callosum morphology in ADHD: Dr. Giedd and colleagues reply. *American Journal of Psychiatry, 152,* 1105–1106.

Gigone, D., & Hastie, R. (1997). Proper analysis of the accuracy of group judgments. *Psychological Bulletin, 121,* 149–167.

Gilbert, P. L., Harris, J. H., McAdams, L. A., & Jeste, D. V. (1995). Neuroleptic withdrawal in schizophrenic patients. *Archives of General Psychiatry, 52,* 173–188.

Gilligan, C. (1982). *In a different voice: Psychological theory and women's development.* Cambridge, MA: Harvard University Press.

Gladue, B. A. (1994). The biopsychology of sexual orientation. *Current Directions in Psychological Science, 3,* 150–154.

Glanzer, M., & Cunitz, A. R. (1966). Two storage mechanisms in free recall. *Journal of Verbal Learning and Verbal Behavior, 5,* 351–360.

Gleick, E. (1997, January 27). And then there were two. . . . *Time,* 38–39.

Gleick, E., Alexander, B., Eskin, L., Pick, G., Skolnik, S., Dodd, J., & Sugden, J. (1994, December 12). The final victim. *People.*

Glenberg, A. M., Sanocki, T., Epstein, W., & Morris, C. (1987). Enhancing calibration of comprehension. *Journal of Experimental Psychology: General, 116,* 119–136.

Gold, P. E., & McGaugh, J. L. (1975). A single-trace, two-process view of memory storage processes. In D. Deutsch & J. A. Deutsch (Eds.), *Short-term memory.* New York: Academic Press.

Gold, S. N., Hughes, D., Hohnecker, L. (1994). Degrees of repression of sexual abuse memories. *American Psychologist, 49,* 441–442.

Goldberger, L., & Breznitz, S. (Eds.) (1993). *Handbook of stress: Theoretical and clinical aspects* (2nd ed.). New York: Free Press.

Goldfried, M. R., & Davison, G. C. (1976). *Clinical behavior therapy.* New York: Holt, Rinehart & Winston.

Goldman, D. (1996). High anxiety. *Science, 274,* 1483.

Goldsborough, J. O. (1997, July 3). Harvesting the (sour) fruits of the U.C. regents' labors. *San Diego Union-Tribune.*

Goldsmith, H. H., Buss, K. A., & Lemery, K. S. (1997). Toddler and childhood temperament: Expanded content, stronger genetic evidence, new evidence for the importance of environment. *Developmental Psychology, 33,* 891–905.

Goldstein, A. P. (1989). Aggression reduction: Some vital steps. In J. Groebel & R. A. Hinde (Eds.), *Aggression and war: Their biological and social bases.* Cambridge, England: Cambridge University Press.

Goleman, D. (1996, July 16). Forget money; Nothing can buy happiness, some researchers say. *New York Times.*

Goleman, D., & Gurin, J. (1993). *Mind/body medicine: How to use your mind for better health.* New York: Consumer Reports.

Goodman, G. S., & Quas, J. A. (1997). Trauma and memory: Individual differences in children's recounting of a stressful experience. In N. L. Stein, P. A. Ornstein, B. Tversky, & C. Brainerd (Eds.), *Memory for everyday and emotional events.* Mahwah, NJ: Lawrence Erlbaum.

Goodwin, F. K., & Jamison, K. R. (1990). *Manic-depressive illness.* New York: Oxford University Press.

Gopnik, A., & Meltzoff, A. N. (1997). *Words, thoughts, and theories.* Cambridge: The MIT Press.

Gore, R. (1997, February). The first steps. *National Geographic,* 72–99.

Gottesman, I. I. (1997). Twins: En route to QTLs for cognition. *Science, 276,* 1522–1523.

Gottesmann, I. I. (1991). *Schizophrenia genesis: The origins of madness.* New York: W. H. Freeman.

Gottlieb, G., Wahlsten, D., & Lickliter, R. (1998). The significance of biology for human development: A developmental psychobiological systems view. In W. Damon & R. M. Lerner (Eds.), *Handbook of child psychology* (Vol. 1). New York: John Wiley & Sons.

Gottman, J. (1995). *Why marriages succeed or fail.* New York: Simon & Schuster.

Gottman, J. (1995, February). Cited in R. Edwards, New tools help gauge marital success. *APA Monitor.*

Gottman, J. M. (1998). Psychology and the study of marital processes. *Annual Review of Psychology, 49,* 169–197.

Gottman, J. M., Coan, J., Carrere, S., & Swanson, C. (1998). Predicting marital happiness and stability from newlywed interactions. *Journal of Marriage and the Family, 60,* 5–22.

Gould, L. (1995, April 23). Ticket to trouble. *New York Times Magazine.*

Gould, R. A. (1969). Subsistence behaviour among the Western Desert Aborigines of Australia. *Oceania, 39,* 253–274.

Gould, R. A., Otto, M. W., Pollack, M. H., & Yap, L. (1997). Cognitive behavioral and

pharmacological treatment of generalized anxiety disorder: A preliminary meta-analysis. *Behavior Therapy, 28,* 285–305.

Gould, S. J. (1981). *The mismeasure of man.* New York: Norton.

Gould, S. J. (1994, November). *The geometer of race.* Discover.

Gould, S. J. (1996). *The mismeasure of man.* (Revised and expanded). New York: W.W. Norton.

Graber, J. A., Brooks-Gunn, J., & Warren, M. P. (1995). The antecedents of menarcheal age: Heredity, family environment, and stressful life events. *Child Development, 66,* 346–359.

Grabowska, A., & Nowicka, A. (1996). Visual-spatial frequency model of cerebral asymmetry: A critical survey of behavioral and electrophysiological studies. *Psychological Bulletin, 120,* 434–449.

Graham, L. O. (1995). *Member of the club.* New York: HarperCollins.

Granhag, P. A. (1997). Realism is eyewitness confidence as a function of type of event witnessed and repeated recall. *Journal of Applied Psychology, 82,* 599–613.

Granstrom, K., & Stiwne, D. (1998). A bipolar model of groupthink: An expansion of Janis's concept. *Small Group Research, 29,* 32–56.

Granvold, D. K. (Ed.). (1994). *Cognitive and behavioral treatment.* Pacific Grove, CA: Brooks/Cole.

Gray, R. (1996). Cited in B. Bower, Clues to nicotine's memory, plaque impact. *Science News, 150,* 263.

Graziano, W. B., & Eisenberg, N. H. (1997). Agreeableness: A dimension of personality. In R. Hogan, J. Johnson, & S. Briggs (Eds.), *Handbook of personality psychology.* New York: Academic Press.

Green, L., Fry, A. R., & Myerson, J. (1994). Discounting of delayed rewards: A life-span comparison. *Psychological Science, 5,* 33–36.

Greenberg, J. (1978). The Americanization of Roseto. *Science News, 113,* 378–382.

Greenberg, L., Elliott, R., & Lietaer, G. (1994). Research on experiential psychotherapies. In A. E. Bergin & S. L. Garfield (Eds.), *Handbook of psychotherapy and behavior change* (4th ed.). New York: Wiley.

Greenberg, L. S., & Rice, L. N. (1997). Humanistic approaches to psychotherapy. In P. L. Wachtel & S. B. Messer (Eds.), *Theories of psychotherapy: Origins and evolution.* Washington, DC: American Psychological Association.

Greene, B., & Winfrey, O. (1996). *Make the connection.* New York: Hyperion.

Greene, R. L., & Clopton, J. R. (1994). Minnesota Multiphasic Personality Inventory–2. In M. E. Maruish (Ed.), *The use of psychological testing for treatment planning and outcome assessment: Introduction.* Hillsdale, NJ: Lawrence Erlbaum.

Greenfield, P. M. (1997). You can't take it with you. *American Psychologist, 52,* 1115–1124.

Greeno, J. G. (1989). A perspective on thinking. *American Psychologist, 44,* 134–141.

Greenwald, A. G., & Banaji, M. R. (1995). Implicit social cognition: Attitudes, self-esteem, and stereotypes. *Psychological Review, 102,* 4–27.

Greenwald, A. G., Draine, S. C., & Abrams, R. L. (1996). Three cognitive markers of unconscious semantic activation. *Science, 273,* 1699–1702.

Greenwald, A. G., Spangenberg, E. R., Pratkanis, A. R., & Eskenazi, J. (1991). Double-blind tests of subliminal self-help audiotapes. *Psychological Science, 2,* 119–122.

Gregory, R. L. (1974). Recovery from blindness: A case study. In R. L. Gregory (Ed.), *Concepts and mechanisms of perception.* London: Gerald Duckworth.

Grimaldi, J. V. (1986, April 16). "The mole" evicted from sewer. *San Diego Tribune.*

Grinspoon, L., Bakalar, J. B., Zimmer, L., & Morgan, J. P. (1997). Marijuana addiction. *Science, 277,* 751–752.

Grogan, B., Shaw, B., Ridenhour, R., Fine, A., & Eftimiades, M. (1993, May). Their brothers' keepers? *People.*

Grunbaum, A. (1993). *Validation in the clinical theory of psychoanalysis.* Madison, CT: International Universities Press.

Guastello, S. J., Guastello, D. D., & Craft, L. L. (1989). Assessment of the Barnum effect in computer based test interpretations. *Journal of Psychology, 12,* 477–484.

Gudjonsson, G. H. (1997). Accusations by adults of childhood sexual abuse: A survey of the members of the British False Memory Society (BFMS). *Applied Cognitive Psychology, 11,* 3–18.

Guerin, D. W., Gottfried, A. W., & Thomas, C. W. (1997). Difficult temperament and behaviour problems: A longitudinal study from 1.5 to 12 years. *International Journal of Behavioral Development, 21,* 71–90.

Guida, F. V., & Ludlow, L. H. (1989). A cross-cultural study of test anxiety. *Journal of Cross-Cultural Psychology, 20,* 178–190.

Guilford, J. P. (1967). *The nature of human intelligence.* New York: McGraw-Hill.

Guinness book of records, The. (1995). New York: Bantam.

Gullette, E. C. D., Blumenthal, J. A., Babyak, M., Jiang, W., Waugh, R. B., Frid, D. J., O'Connor, C. M., Morris, J. J., & Krantz, D. S. (1997). Effects of mental stress on myocardial ischemia during daily life. *Journal of American Medical Association, 277,* 1521– 1526.

Gur, R. C., Mozley, L. H., Mozley, P. D., Risnick, S. M., Karp, J. S., Alavi, A., Arnold, S. E., & Gur, R. E. (1995). Sex differences in regional cerebral glucose metabolism during a resting state. *Science, 267,* 528–531.

Gur, R. E., Cowell, P., Turetsky, B. I., Gallacher, F., Cannon, T., Bilker, W., & Gur, R. C. (1997). A follow-up magnetic resonance imaging study of schizophrenia. *Archives of General Psychiatry, 55,* 145–152.

Gura, T. (1997). Obesity sheds its secrets. *Science, 275,* 751–753.

Gureje, O., Simon, G. E., Ustun, T. B., & Goldberg, D. P. (1997). Somatization in cross-cultural perspective: A World Health Organization study in primary care. *American Journal of Psychiatry, 154,* 989–995.

References

Gurman, E. B. (1994). Debriefing for all concerned: Ethical treatment of human subjects. *Psychological Science, 5,* 139.

Gustavson, C. R., Kelly, D. J., Sweeney, M., & Garcia, J. (1976). Prey-lithium aversion I: Coyotes and wolves. *Behavioral Biology, 17,* 61–72.

Guthrie, J. P., Ash, R. A., & Bendapudi, V. (1995). Additional validity evidence for a measure of morningness. *Journal of Applied Psychology, 80,* 186–190.

Guthrie, R. V. (1976). *Even the rat was white.* New York: Harper & Row.

Gutkin, A. J., Holborn, S. W., Walker, J. R., & Anderson, B. A. (1994). Cost-effectiveness of home relaxation training for tension headaches. *Journal of Behavior Therapy and Experimental Psychiatry, 25,* 69–74.

Gwyer, P., & Clifford, B. R. (1997). The effects of the cognitive interview on recall, identification, confidence, and the confidence/accuracy relationship. *Applied Cognitive Psychology, 11,* 121–145.

Haber, N. R. (1980, November). Eidetic images are not just imaginary. *Psychology Today.*

Hager, M. (1997, February 24). Beyond the mammogram. *Newsweek.*

Haidt, J., Koller, S. H., & Dias, M. G. (1993). Affect, culture, and morality, or is it wrong to eat your dog? *Journal of Personality and Social Psychology, 65,* 613–628.

Haidt, J., McCauley, C., & Rozin, P. (1994). Individual differences in sensitivity to disgust: A scale sampling seven domains of disgust elicitors. *Personality and Individual Differences, 16,* 701–713.

Haier, R. (1996, October 17). Cited in J. Marquis, A real brain teaser. *Los Angeles Times.*

Haier, R. J., Chueh, D., Touchette, P., Lott, I., Buchsbaum, M. S., MacMillan, D., Sandman, C., LaCasse, L., & Sosa, E. (1995). Brain size and glucose metabolic rate in mental retardation and Down syndrome. *Intelligence, 20,* 199–210.

Haith, M. M., & Benson, J. B. (1998). Infant cognition. In W. Damon & R. M. Lerner (Eds.), *Handbook of child psychology* (Vol. 1). New York: John Wiley & Sons.

Hall, C. I. (1997). Cultural malpractice. *American Psychologist, 52,* 642–651.

Halpern, D. F. (1992). *Sex differences in cognitive abilities* (2nd ed.). Hillsdale, NJ: Lawrence Erlbaum.

Halpern, D. F. (1998). Teaching critical thinking for transfer across domains. *American Psychologist, 53,* 449–455.

Hamer, D. H., Hu, S., Maagnuson, V. L., Hu, H., & Pattatucci, A. M. L. (1993). Male sexual orientation and genetic evidence: Response. *Science, 262,* 2,065.

Hamilton, D. L., Devine, P. G., & Ostrom, T. M. (1994). Social cognition and classic issues in social psychology. In P. G. Devine, D. L. Hamilton, & T. M. Ostrom (Eds.), *Social cognition: Impact on psychology.* New York: Academic Press.

Hammer, D. (1995). Cited in C. Holden, More on genes and homosexuality. *Science, 268,* 1571.

Hammer, R. P., Egilmez, Y., & Emmett-Oglesby, M. W. (1997). Neural mechanisms of tolerance to the effects of cocaine. *Behavioural Brain Research, 84,* 225–239.

Hancock, L. (1996, March 18). Mother's little helper. *Newsweek.*

Hancock, L. Rosenberg, D., Springen, K., King, P., Rogers, P., Brant, M., Kalb, C., & Gegax, T. T. (1995, March 6). Breaking point. *Newsweek.*

Hanson, G., & Venturelli, P. J. (1998). *Drugs and society* (5th ed.). Boston: Jones and Bartlett.

Happé, F. & Frith, U. (1996). The neuropsychology of autism. *Brain, 119,* 1377–1400.

Hardin, C., & Banaji, M. R. (1993). The influence of language on thought. *Social Cognition, 11,* 277–308.

Harding, C. M., & Hall, G. M. (1997). Long-term outcome studies of schizophrenia: Do females continue to display better outcome as expected? *International Review of Psychiatry, 9,* 409–418.

Hardy, J. B., Welcher, D. W., Mellits, E. D., & Kagan, J. (1976). Pitfalls in the measurement of intelligence: Are standardized intelligence tests valid for measuring the intellectual potential of urban children? *Journal of Psychology, 94,* 43–51.

Harmon, A. (1995, October 1). High-tech hidden persuaders. *Los Angeles Times.*

Harriott, J., & Ferrari, J. R. (1996). Prevalence of procrastination among samples of adults. *Psychological Reports, 78,* 611–616.

Harris, B. (1979). Whatever happened to little Albert? *American Psychologist, 34,* 151–160.

Harris, G., Thomas, A., & Booth, D. A. (1990). Development of salt taste in infancy. *Developmental Psychology, 26,* 534–538.

Harris, J. L., Salus, D., Rerecich, R., & Larsen, D. (1996). Distinguishing detection from identification in subliminal auditory perception: A review and critique of Merikle's study. *Journal of General Psychology, 123,* 41–50.

Hart, F., & Risley, T. (1996). Cited in B. Bower, Talkative parents make kids smarter. *Science News, 150,* 100.

Harter, S. (1990). Self and identity development. In S. S. Feldman & G. R. Elliott (Eds.), *At the threshold: The developing adolescent.* Cambridge, MA: Harvard University Press.

Hartlage, S., Alloy, B., Vazquez, C., & Dykman, B. (1993). Automatic and effortful processing in depression. *Psychological Bulletin, 113,* 247–278.

Harvey, J. (1997, December). Cited in B. Azar, Researchers debunk myth of the "crack baby." *APA Monitor.*

Hasselt, V. B., & Hersen, M. (Eds.) (1994). *Advanced abnormal psychology.* New York: Plenum.

Hatfield, E., & Rapson, R. L. (1995). *A world of passion: Cross-cultural perspective on love and sex.* New York: Allyn & Bacon.

Hayamizu, T. (1997). Between intrinsic and extrinsic motivation: Examination of reasons for academic study based on the theory of internalization. *Japanese Psychological Research, 39,* 98–108.

Hayes, B. K., & Delamothe, K. (1997). Cognitive interviewing procedures and suggestibility in children's recall. *Journal of Applied Psychology, 82,* 562–577.

Hayes, J. A., & Mitchell, J. C. (1994). Mental health professionals' skepticism about multiple personality disorder. *Professional Psychology: Research and Practice, 25,* 410–425.

Hayes, K. J., & Hayes, C. H. (1951). The intellectual development of a home-raised chimpanzee. *Proceedings of the American Philosophical Society, 95,* 105–109.

Hayes, S. C., Munt, E. D., Korn, Z., Wulfert, E., Rosenfarb, I., & Zettle, R. D. (1986). The effect of feedback and self-reinforcement instructions on studying performance. *Psychological Record, 36,* 27–37.

Heatherton, T. F., Mahamedi, F., Striepe, M., Gield, A. E., & Keel, P. (1997). A 10-year longitudinal study of body weight, dieting, and eating disorder symptoms. *Journal of Abnormal Psychology, 106,* 117–125.

Heatherton, T. F., & Weinberger, J. L. (Eds.) (1994). *Can personality change?* Washington, DC: American Psychological Association.

Heider, F. (1958). *The psychology of interpersonal relations.* New York: Wiley.

Helgeson, V. S. (1994). Prototypes and dimensions of masculinity and feminity. *Sex Roles, 31,* 653–682.

Hellige, J. B. (1993). Unity of thought and action: Varieties of interaction between the left and right cerebral hemispheres. Current Directions in *Psychological Science, 2,* 21–30.

Helmers, K. H., Krantz, D. S., Merz, C. N. B., Klein, J., Kop, W. J., Gottdiener, J. S., & Rozanski, A. (1995). Defensive hostility: Relationship to multiple markers of cardiac ischemia in patients with coronary disease. *Health Psychology, 14,* 202–209.

Helson, R. (1993). Comparing longitudinal studies of adult development: Toward a paradigm of tension between stability and change. In D. C. Funder, R. D. Parke, C. Tomlinson-Keasey, & K. Widaman (Eds.), *Studying lives through time.* Washington, DC: American Psychological Association.

Helson, R. (1996). In search of the creative personality. *Creativity Research Journal, 9,* 295–306.

Helwig, C. C. (1997). Making moral cognition respectable (again): A retrospective review of Lawrence Kohlberg. *Contemporary Psychology, 42,* 191–195.

Helzer, J. E., & Canino, G. J. (Eds.) (1992). *Alcoholism in North America, Europe, and Asia.* New York: Oxford University Press.

Hendin, H. (1994). *Suicide in America.* New York: Norton.

Hendy, H. (1984). Effects of pets on the sociability and health activities of nursing home residents. In R. K. Anderson, B. J. Hart, & L. A. Hart (Eds.), *The pet connection.* Minneapolis:

Center to Study Human-Animal Relationships and Environments, University of Minnesota.

Henker, B., & Whalen, C. K. (1989). Hyperactivity and attention deficits. *American Psychologist, 44,* 216–233.

Henry, W. A., III. (1994, June 27). Pride and prejudice. *Time.*

Henry, W. P., Strupp, H. H., Schacht, T. E., & Gaston, L. (1994). Psychodynamic approaches. In A. E. Bergin & S. L. Garfield (Eds.), *Handbook of psychotherapy and behavior change* (4th ed.). New York: Wiley.

Herkenham, M. (1996, December 16). Cited in D. Ferrell, Scientists unlocking secrets of marijuana's effects. *Los Angeles Times.*

Herman, L. (1989, April). Cited in S. Chollar, Conversations with the dolphins. *Psychology Today.*

Herman, L. (1993, March 22). Cited in S. Linden, Can animals think? *Time.*

Herman, W. E. (1990). Fear of failure as a distinctive personality trait measure of test anxiety. *Journal of Research and Development in Education, 23,* 180–185.

Hernstein, R. J., & Murray, C. (1994). *The bell curve.* New York: Free Press.

Herzog, H. (1993). Animal rights and wrongs. *Science, 262,* 1906–1908.

Hewitt, J. K. (1997). The genetics of obesity: What have genetic studies told us about the environment? *Behavior Genetics, 27,* 353–358.

Hickey, E. W. (1991). *Serial murderers and their victims.* Pacific Grove, CA: Brooks/Cole.

Higgins, E. T. (1997). Beyond pleasure and pain. *American Psychologist, 52,* 1280–1300.

Hilgard, E. R. (1977). *Divided consciousness: Multiple controls in human thought and action.* New York: Wiley.

Hilgard, E. R. (1979). Divided consciousness in hypnosis: The implications of the hidden observer. In E. Fromm & R. E. Shor (Eds.), *Hypnosis: Developments in research and new perspectives* (2nd ed.). New York: Aldine.

Hill, A. B., Kemp-Wheeler, S. M., & Jones, S. A. (1987). Subclinical and clinical depression: Are analogue studies justifiable? *Personality and Individual Differences, 8,* 113–120.

Hill, A., Niven, C. A., & Knussen, C. (1996). Pain memories in phantom limbs: A case study. *Pain, 66,* 381–384.

Hill, C. E., Diemer, R. A., & Heaton, K. J. (1997). Dream interpretation sessions: Who volunteers, who benefits, and what volunteer clients view as most and least helpful. *Journal of Counseling Psychology, 44,* 53–62.

Hill, P. (1995, June). Cited in E. Burnette, Black males retrieve a noble heritage. *APA Monitor.*

Hilts, P. H. (1995). *Memory's ghost: The strange tale of Mr. M and the nature of memory.* New York: Simon & Schuster.

Hirsch, B. J. (1997). Where are the interventions? *Contemporary Psychology, 42,* 1113–1114.

Hirshkowitz, M., Moore, C. A., & Minhoto, G. (1997). The basics of sleep. In M. R. Pressman & W. C. Orr (Eds.), *Understanding sleep: The evaluation and treatment of sleep disorders.*

Washington, DC: American Psychological Association.

Hobson, J. A. (1988). *The dreaming brain.* New York: Basic Books.

Hobson, J. A., & McCarley, R. W. (1977). The brain as a dream state generator: An activation-synthesis hypothesis of the dream process. *American Journal of Psychiatry, 134,* 1335–1348.

Hoch, T. A., Babbitt, R. L., Coe, D. A., Krell, D. M., & Hackbert, L. (1994). Contingency contacting. *Behavior Modification, 18,* 106–128.

Hocker, J. L., & Wilmot, W. W. (1991). *Interpersonal conflict.* Dubuque, IA: William C. Brown.

Hodgson, R. (1994). Treatment of alcohol problems. *Addiction, 89,* 1529–1534.

Hoffman, C., Lau, I., & Johnson, D. R. (1986). The linguistic relativity of person cognition: An English-Chinese comparison. *Journal of Personality and Social Psychology, 51,* 1097–1105.

Hofmann, A. (1983). *LSD: My problem child.* Los Angeles: J. P. Tarcher.

Hogan, J., & Ones, D. S. (1997). Conscientiousness and integrity at work. In R. Hogan, J. Johnson, & S. Briggs (Eds.), *Handbook of personality psychology.* New York: Academic Press.

Hokanson, J. E., & Butler, A. C. (1992). Cluster analysis of depressed college students' social behaviors. *Journal of Personality and Social Psychology, 62,* 273–280.

Holahan, C. K., & Sears, R. R. (1995). *The gifted group in later maturity.* Stanford, CA: Stanford University Press.

Holden, C. (1985). A guarded endorsement for shock therapy. *Science, 228,* 1510–1511.

Holden, C. (1995). Sex and the granular layer. *Science, 268,* 807.

Holden, C. (1996). Researchers find feminization a two-edged sword. *Science, 271,* 1919–1920.

Holden, C. (1997). Thumbs up for acupuncture. *Science, 278,* 1231.

Hollis, K. L. (1997). Contemporary research on Pavlovian conditioning. *American Psychologist, 52,* 956–965.

Hollon, S. D., & Beck, A. T. (1994). Cognitive and cognitive behavioral therapies. In A. E. Bergin & S. L. Garfield (Eds.), *Handbook of psychotherapy and behavior change* (4th ed.). New York: Wiley.

Holmes, C., & Lovestone, S. (1997). The molecular genetics on mood disorders. *Current Opinion in Psychiatry, 10,* 79–83.

Holmes, T. H., & Rahe, R. H. (1967). The social readjustment rating scale. *Journal of Psychosomatic Research, 11,* 203–218.

Holt, R. R. (1993). Occupational stress. In L. Goldberger & S. Breznitz (Eds.), *Handbook of stress: Theoretical and clinical aspects* (2nd ed.). New York: Free Press.

Honts, C. R. (1994). Psychophysiological detection of deception. *Current Directions in Psychological Science, 3,* 77–82.

Honts, C. R., Raskin, D. C., & Kircher, J. C. (1994). Mental and physical countermeasures

reduce the accuracy of polygraph tests. *Journal of Applied Psychology, 79,* 252–259.

Hoptman, M. J., & Davidson, R. J. (1994). How and why do the two cerebral hemispheres interact? *Psychological Bulletin, 116,* 195–219.

Horgan, J. (1996, December). Why Freud isn't dead. *Scientific American,* 106–111.

Hotz, R. (1997, October 27). Chemical in pot cuts severe pain, study says. *Los Angeles Times.*

Howard, K. I., Krause, M. S., Saunders, S. M., & Kopta, S. M. (1997). Trials and tribulations in the meta-analysis of treatment differences: Comment on Wampold et al. (1997). *Psychological Bulletin, 122,* 221–225.

Howard, K. I., Moras, K., Brill, P. L., Martinovich, Z., & Lutz, W. (1996). Evaluation of psychotherapy: Efficacy, effectiveness, and patient progress. *American Psychologist, 51,* 1059–1064.

Howe, M. L., & Courage, M. L. (1997). The emergence and early development of autobiographical memory. *Psychological Review, 104,* 499–525.

Howe, T. (1997, June). Cited in T. DeAngelis, Abused children have more conflicts with friends. *APA Monitor.*

Howieson, D. B., & Lezak, M. D. (1997). The neuropsychological evaluation. In S. C. Yodofsky & R. E. Hales (Eds.), *The American Psychiatric Press textbook of neuropsychiatry* (3rd ed.). Washington, DC: American Psychiatric Press.

Howlett, D. (1997, September 10). Easy-to-concoct drug often makes users turn violent. *USA Today.*

Howlin, P. (1997). Prognosis in autism: Do specialist treatments affect long-term outcome? *European Child & Adolescent Psychiatry, 6,* 55–72.

Hsu, D. T. (1996). Acupuncture: A review. *Regional Anesthesia, 21,* 361–370.

Hubel, D. H., & Wiesel, T. N. (1979). Brain mechanisms of vision. *Scientific American, 241,* 150–162.

Huff, R. (1995, February 11). Cited in M. Dolan, When the mind's eye blinks. *Los Angeles Times.*

Hughes, J., Smith, T. W., Kosterlitz, H. W., Fothergill, L. A., Morgan, B. A., & Morris, H. R. (1975). Identification of two related pentapeptides from the brain with potent opiate agonist activity. *Nature, 258,* 577–579.

Hughes, R. J., & Badia, P. (1997). Sleep-promoting and hypothermic effects of daytime melatonin administration in humans. *Sleep, 20,* 124–131.

Hull, C. L. (1952). A behavior system: An introduction to behavior theory concerning the individual organism. New Haven, CT: Yale University Press.

Hultquist, C. M., Meyers, A. W., Whelan, J. P., Klesges, R. C., Preacher-Ryan, H., & DeBon, M. W. (1995). The effect of smoking and light activity on metabolism in men. *Health Psychology, 14,* 124–131.

Hunt, M. (1993). *The story of psychology.* New York: Doubleday.

Hyde, J. A. (1994). Can meta-analysis make feminist transformations in psychology? *Psychology of Women Quarterly, 18,* 451–462.

Hyde, J. S., Fennema, E., & Lamon, S. J. (1990). Gender differences in mathematics performance: A meta-analysis. *Psychological Bulletin, 107,* 139–155.

Hyde, J. S., & Linn, M. C. (1988). Are there sex differences in verbal abilities? A meta-analysis. *Psychological Bulletin, 104,* 53–69.

Hyde, J. S., & Plant, E. A. (1995). The magnitude of psychological gender differences: Another side to the story. *American Psychologist, 50,* 159–161.

Hyman, R. (1994). Anomaly or artifact? Comments on Bem and Honorton. *Psychological Bulletin, 115,* 19–24.

Hyman, R. (1996a, March/April). Evaluation of the military's twenty-year program on psychic spying. *Skeptical Inquirer.*

Hyman, R. (1996b, March/April). The evidence for psychic functioning: Claims vs. reality. *Skeptical Inquirer.*

Iacono, W. G., & Lykken, D. T. (1997). The validity of the lie detector: Two surveys of scientific opinion. *Journal of Applied Psychology, 82,* 426–433.

Ingram, R. E., Partridge, S., Scott, W., & Bernet, C. Z. (1994). Schema specificity in subclinical syndrome depression: Distinctions between automatically versus effortfully encoded state and traits depressive information. *Cognitive Therapy and Research, 18,* 195–209.

Irwin, M., Mascovich, A., Gillin, J. C., Willoughby, R., Pike, J., & Smith, T. L. (1994). Partial sleep deprivation reduces natural killer cell activity in humans. *Psychosomatic Medicine, 56,* 493–498.

Ito, T. A., Miller, N., & Pollock, V. E. (1996). Alcohol and aggression: A meta-analysis on the moderating effects of inhibitory cues, triggering events, and self-focused attention. *Psychological Bulletin, 120,* 60–82.

Iwata, B. A., Pace, G. M., Dorsey, M. F., Zarcone, J. R., Vollmer, T. R., Smith, R. G., Rodgers, T. A., Lerman, D. C., Shore, B. A., Mazaleski, J. L., Goh, H. L., Cowdery, G. E., Kalsher, M. J., McCosh, K. C., & Kimberly, D. W. (1994). The functions of self-injurious behavior: An experimental-epidemiological analysis. *Journal of Applied Behavior Analysis, 27,* 215–240.

Izard, C. E. (1990). Facial expressions and the regulation of emotions. *Journal of Personality and Social Psychology, 58,* 487–498.

Izard, C. E. (1993). Four systems for emotion activation: Cognitive and noncognitive processes. *Psychological Review, 100,* 68–90.

Izard, C. E. (1994). Innate and universal facial expressions: Evidence from developmental and cross-cultural research. *Psychological Bulletin, 115,* 288–299.

Izquierdo, I., & Medina, J. H. (1997). The biochemistry of memory formation and its regulation by hormones and neuromodulators. *Psychobiology, 25,* 1–9.

Jackendoff, R. (1994). *Patterns in the mind. Language and human nature.* New York: Basic Books.

Jacklin, C. N. (1989). Female or male: Issues of gender. *American Psychologist, 44,* 127–133.

Jackson, R. L. (1994, May 4). A false sense of sincerity: Some cases belie polygraph results. *Los Angeles Times.*

Jackson, T., Towson, S., & Narduzzi, K. (1997). Predictors of shyness: A test of variables associated with self-presentational models. *Social Behavior and Personality, 25,* 149–154.

Jacobs, B. (1993, January 19). In M. Elias, Brain power a case of "use it or lose it." *USA Today.*

Jacobson, N. S., & Christensen, A. (1996). Studying the effectiveness of psychotherapy: How well can clinical trials do the job? *American Psychologist, 51,* 1031–1039.

James, W. (1884; reprinted 1969). What is an emotion? In *William James: Collected essays and reviews.* New York: Russell & Russell.

James, W. (1890). *The principles of psychology.* New York: Dover.

Jamison, K. R. (1995). Manic-depressive illness and creativity. *Scientific American, 272,* 62–67.

Jan, J. E., Espezel, H., & Appelton, R. E. (1994). The treatment of sleep disorders with melatonin. *Developmental Medicine and Child Neurology, 36,* 97–107.

Janca, A., Isaac, M., Bennett, L. A., & Tacchini, G. (1995). Somatoform disorders in different cultures: A mail questionnaire survey. *Social Psychiatry and Psychiatric Epidemiology, 30,* 44–48.

Janis, I. L. (1982). *Groupthink* (2nd ed.). Boston: Houghton Mifflin.

Janis, I. L. (1989). *Crucial decisions: Leadership in policymaking and crisis management.* New York: Free Press.

Jansen, A. S. P., Nguyen, X. V., Karpitskiy, V., Mettenleiter, T. C., & Loewy, A. D. (1995). Central command neurons of the sympathetic nervous system: Basis of the fight-or-flight response. *Science, 270,* 644–646.

Janus, S. S., & Janus, C. L. (1993). *The Janus report on sexual behavior.* New York: John Wiley & Sons.

Japenga, A. (1994, June 5). Rewriting the dictionary of madness. *Los Angeles Times Magazine.*

Jensen, P. S., & Hoagwood, K. (1997). The book of names: DSM-IV in context. *Development and Psychopathology, 9,* 231–249.

Jensen-Campbell, L. A., Graziano, W. G., & West, S. G. (1995). Dominance, prosocial orientation, and female preferences: Do nice guys really finish last? *Journal of Personality and Social Psychology, 68,* 427–440.

Johanson, D. C. (1996, March). Face-to-face with Lucy's family. *National Geographic,* 96–117.

John, O. P. (1990). The "big five" factor taxonomy: Dimensions of personality in the natural language and in questionnaires. In L. A. Previn (Ed.), *Handbook of personality.* New York: Guilford Press.

Johnson, B. E., Kuck, D. L., & Schander, P. R. (1997). Rape myth acceptance and sociodemographic characteristics: A multidimensional analysis. *Sex Roles, 36,* 693–707.

Johnson, C. R., Hunt, F. M., & Siebert, J. J. (1994). Discrimination training in the treatment of pica and food scavenging. *Behavior Modification, 18,* 214–229.

Johnson, J. A. (1997). Units of analysis for the description and explanation of personality. In R. Hogan, J. Johnson, and S. Briggs (Eds.), *Handbook of personality psychology.* New York: Academic Press.

Johnson, L. C., Slye, E. S., & Dement, W. (1965). Electroencephalographic and autonomic during and after prolonged sleep deprivation. *Psychosomatic Medicine, 27,* 415–423.

Johnson, S. L., & Roberts, J. E. (1995). Life events and bipolar disorder: Implications from biological theories. *Psychological Bulletin, 117,* 434–449.

Johnston, D. (1997). A missing link? LTP and learning. *Science, 278,* 401–403.

Jones, D. R., Levy, R. A., Gardner, L., Marsh, R. W., & Patterson, J. C. (1985). Self-control of psychophysiologic response to motion stress: Using biofeedback to treat airsickness. *Aviation, Space and Environmental Medicine, 56,* 1152–1157.

Jones, E. (1953). *The life and work of Sigmund Freud* (3 vols.). New York: Basic Books.

Jones, E., & Berglas, S. (1978). Control of attributions about the self through self-handicapping strategies: The appeal of alcohol and the role of underachievement. *Personality and Social Psychology Bulletin, 4,* 200–206.

Jones, K. L., & Smith, D. W. (1973). Recognition of the fetal alcohol syndrome in early infancy. *Lancet, 2,* 999–1001.

Jorgensen, R. S., Johnson, B. T., Kolodziej, M. E., & Schreer, G. D. (1996). Elevated blood pressure and personality: A meta-analytic review. *Psychological Bulletin, 120,* 293–320.

Jusczyk, P. W., & Hohne, E. A. (1997). Infants' memory for spoken words. *Science, 277,* 1984–1986.

Just, M. A., Carpenter, P. A., Keller, T. A., Eddy, W. F., & Thulborn, K. R. (1996). Brain activation modulated by sentence comprehension. *Science, 274,* 114–116.

Kagan, J. (1998). Biology and the child. In W. Damon & R. M. Lerner (Eds.), *Handbook of child psychology* (Vol. 1). New York: John Wiley & Sons.

Kagan, J., Reznick, J. S., & Snidman, N. (1988). Biological bases of childhood shyness. *Science, 240,* 167–171.

Kagan, J., & Snidman, N. (1991). Temperamental factors in human development. *American Psychologist, 46,* 856–862.

Kaiser, A. P., & Hester, P. P. (1997). Prevention of conduct disorder through early intervention: A social-communicative perspective. *Behavioral Disorders, 22,* 117–130.

Kaiser, J. (1997). A new way to resist AIDS? *Science, 275,* 1258.

Kalafat, J. (1997, March 10). Cited in S. Nazario, Schools struggle to teach lessons in life and death. *Los Angeles Times.*

Kalick, S. M., Zebrowitz, L. A., Langlois, J. H., & Johnson, R. M. (1998). Does human facial attractiveness honestly advertise health? *Psychological Science, 9,* 8–13.

Kalof, L. (1993). Rape-supportive attitudes and sexual victimization experiences of sorority and nonsorority women. *Sex Roles, 29,* 767–780.

Kandel, E., & Abel, T. (1995). Neuropeptides, adenylyl cyclase, and memory storage. *Science, 268,* 825–826.

Kane, J. M. (1997). Update of treatment strategies. *International Review of Psychiatry, 9,* 419–427.

Kanner, A. D., & Feldman, S. S. (1991). Control over uplifts and hassles and its relationship to adaptational outcomes. *Journal of Behavioral Medicine, 14,* 187–201.

Kantrowitz, B., Carroll, G., Annin, P., Barrett, T., Cohn, B., & Liu, M. (1993, May 3). The killing ground. *Newsweek.*

Kao, G., & Tienda, M. (1995). Optimism and achievement: The educational performance of immigrant youth. *Social Science Quarterly, 76,* 1–19.

Kaplan, D. M. (1972). On shyness. *International Journal of Psycho-Analysis. 53,* 439–453.

Kaplan, H. B., & Damphousse, K. R. (1997). Reciprocal relationships between life events and psychological distress. *Stress Medicine, 13,* 75–90.

Kaplan, P. S. (1998). *The human odyssey: Life-span development* (3rd ed.). Pacific Grove, CA: Brooks/Cole.

Kaplan, R. M., & Saccuzzo, D. P. (1997). *Psychological testing: Principles, applications, and issues* (4th ed.). Pacific Grove, CA: Brooks/Cole.

Kareken, D. A., Gur, R. C., Mozley, D., Mozley, L. H., Saykin, A. J., Shtasel, D. L., & Gur, R. E. (1995). Cognitive functioning and neuroanatomic volume measures in schizophrenia. *Neuropsychology, 9,* 211–219.

Karney, B. R., & Bradbury, T. N. (1995). The longitudinal course of marital quality and stability: A review of theory, method, and research. *Psychological Bulletin, 118,* 3–34.

Kassebaum, N. L. (1994). Head start: Only the best for America's children. *American Psychologist, 49,* 123–126.

Katz, J. (1992). Psychophysiological contributions to phantom limbs. *Canadian Journal of Psychiatry, 37,* 282–298.

Kaufman, A. S., Reynolds, C. R., & McLean, J. E. (1989). Age and WAIS-R intelligence in a national sample of adults in the 20 to 74 age range: A cross-sectional analysis with educational level controlled. *Intelligence, 13,* 235–253.

Kaufman, J., & Zigler, E. (1989). The intergenerational transmission of child abuse. In C. Cicchetti & V. Carlson (Eds.), *Child maltreatment: Theory and research on the causes and consequences of child abuse and neglect.* Cambridge, England: Cambridge University Press.

Kavoussi, R. J., Liu, J., & Coccaro, E. F. (1994). An open trial of sertraline in personality disordered patients with impulsive aggression. *Journal of Clinical Psychiatry, 55,* 137–141.

Kawachi, I., Sparrow, D., Vokonas, P. S., & Weiss, S. T. (1994). Symptoms of anxiety and risk of coronary heart disease. *Circulation, 90,* 2225–2229.

Kawakami, K., Dion, K. L., & Dovidio, J. F. (1998). Racial prejudice and stereotype activation. *Personality and Social Psychology Bulletin, 24,* 407–416.

Kay, S. A. (1997). PAS, present, and future: Clues to the origins of circadian clocks. *Science, 276,* 753–754.

Kearins, J. M. (1981). Visual spatial memory in Australian Aboriginal children of desert regions. *Cognitive Psychology, 13,* 434–460.

Keefe, F. J., & Lefebure, J. C. (1997). Introduction to the featured section: Pain—From mechanisms to management. *Health Psychology, 16,* 307–309.

Keenan, K., & Shaw, D. (1997). Developmental and social influences on young girl's early problem behavior. *Psychological Bulletin, 121,* 95–113.

Keiser, R. E., & Prather, E. N. (1990). What is the TAT? A review of ten years of research. *Journal of Personality Assessment, 55,* 800–803.

Kelley, H. H. (1967). Attribution theory in social psychology. In D. Levine (Ed.), *Nebraska symposium on motivation* (Vol. 15). Lincoln: University of Nebraska Press.

Kelly, A. E., & Kahn, J. H. (1994). Effects of suppression of personal intrusive thoughts. *Journal of Personality and Social Psychology, 66,* 998–1006.

Kendall-Tackett, K., Williams, M., & Finkelhor, D. (1993). Impact of sexual abuse on children: A review and synthesis of recent empirical studies. *Psychological Bulletin, 113,* 164–180.

Kennedy, S. H., Javanmard, M., & Vaccarino, F. J. (1997). A review of functional neuroimaging in mood disorders: Positron emission tomography and depression. *Canadian Journal of Psychiatry, 42,* 467–475.

Kenrick, D. T., & Funder, D. C. (1988). Profiting from controversy. *American Psychologist, 43,* 23–34.

Kernis, M. H., Cornell, D. P., Sun, C., Berry, A., & Harlow, T. (1993). There's more to self-esteem than whether it is high or low: The importance of stability of self-esteem. *Journal of Personality and Social Psychology, 65,* 1190–1204.

Kessler, R. C. (1997). The effects of stressful life events on depression. *Annual Review of Psychology, 48,* 191–214.

Kessler, R. C., McGonagle, K. A., Zhao, S., Nelson, C. B., Higher, M., Eshleman, S., Wittchen, H., & Kendler, K. S. (1994). Lifetime and 12-month prevalence of DSM-III-R psychiatric disorders in the United States. *Archives of General Psychiatry, 51,* 8–19.

Khantzian, E. J., & Mack, J. E. (1994). How AA works and why it's important for clinicians to understand. *Journal of Substance Abuse Treatment, 11,* 77–92.

Kiecolt-Glaser, J. K., & Glaser, R. (1989). Psychoneuroimmunology: Past, present, and future. *Health Psychology, 8,* 677–682.

Kihlstrom, J. F. (1993). The continuum of consciousness. *Consciousness and Cognition, 2,* 334–354.

Kihlstrom, J. F., Glisky, M. L., & Angiulo, M. J. (1994). Dissociative tendencies and dissociative disorders. *Journal of Abnormal Psychology, 103,* 117–124.

Kihlstrom, J. R. (1996). Perception without awareness of what is perceived, learning without awareness of what is learned. In M. Velmans (Ed.), *The science of consciousness.* New York: Routledge.

Kimura, D. (1992). Sex differences in the brain. *Scientific American, 267,* 119–125.

King, A. (1992). Comparison of self-questioning, summarizing, and notetaking-review as strategies for learning from lectures. *American Educational Research Journal, 29,* 303–323.

King, D. P., Zhao, Y., Sangoram, A. M., Wilsbacher, L. D., Tanaka, M., Antoch, M. P., Steeves, T. D. L., Vitaterna, M. H., Kornhauser, J. M., Lowrey, P. L., Turek, F. W., Takahashi, J. S. (1997). Positional cloning of the mouse circadian clock gene. *Cell, 89,* 641–653.

King, F. A., Yarbrough, C. J., Anderson, D. C., Gordon, T. P., & Gould, K. G. (1988). Primates. *Science, 240,* 1475–1482.

Kinsbourne, M. (1994). Sugar and the hyperactive child. *New England Journal of Medicine, 330,* 355–356.

Kinsey, A. C., Pomeroy, W. B., & Martin, C. E. (1948). *Sexual behavior in the human male.* Philadelphia: Saunders.

Kirk, M. S. (1972, March). Head-hunters in today's world. *National Geographic.*

Kirmayer, L. J. (1991). The place of culture in psychiatric nosology: Taijin kyofusho and DSM-III-R. *Journal of Nervous and Mental Disease, 179,* 19–28.

Kirmayer, L. J., Robbins, J. M., & Paris, J. (1994). Somatoform disorders: Personality and social matrix of somatic distress. *Journal of Abnormal Psychology, 103,* 125–136.

Kirsch, I. (1994). Cognitive-behavioral hypnotherapy. In J. W. Rhue, S. J. Lynn, & I. Kirsch (Eds.), *Handbook of clinical hypnosis.* Washington, DC: American Psychological Association.

Kirsch, I. (1997). Suggestibility or hypnosis: What do our scales really measure. *International Journal of Clinical and Experimental Hypnosis, 45,* 212–225.

Kirsch, I., & Lynn, S. J. (1995). The altered state of hypnosis. *American Psychologist, 50,* 846–858.

Kirsner, D. (1990). Is there a future for American psychoanalysis? *Psychoanalytic Review, 77,* 175–200.

Kitayama, S., & Markus, H. R. (Eds.) (1994). *Emotion and culture.* Washington, DC: American Psychological Association.

Kitto, J., Lok, D., & Rudowicz, E. (1994). Measuring creative thinking: An activity-based approach. *Creativity Research Journal, 7,* 59–69.

Kleijn, W. C., van der Ploeg, H. M., & Topman, R. M. (1994). Cognition, study habits, test anxiety, and academic performance. *Psychological Reports, 75,* 1219–1226.

Kleinknecht, R. A. (1994). Acquisition of blood, injury, and needle fears and phobias. *Behavior Research and Therapy, 32,* 817–823.

Kleinknecht, R. A., Dinnel, D. L., & Kleinknecht, E. E. (1997). Cultural factors in social anxiety: A comparison of social phobia symptoms and *taijin kyofusho. Journal of Anxiety Disorders, 11,* 157–177.

Kleinman, A., & Cohen, A. (1997, March). Psychiatry's global challenge. *Scientific American,* 86–89.

Klich, L. Z., & Davidson, G. R. (1983). A cultural difference in visual memory: On le voit, on ne le voit plus. *International Journal of Psychology, 18,* 189–201.

Klingberg, G., & Hwang, C. P. (1994). Children's dental fear picture test (CDFP): A projective test for the assessment of child dental fear. *Journal of Dentistry for Children, 62,* 89–96.

Klinger, E. (1987, October). The power of daydreams. *Psychology Today.*

Knight, R. A. (1992, July). Cited in N. Youngstrom, Rapist studies reveal complex mental map. *APA Monitor.*

Knowlton, B. J., Mangels, J. A., & Squire, L. R. (1996). A neostriatal habit learning system in humans. *Science, 273,* 1399–1402.

Knutson, J. R. (1995). Psychological characteristics of maltreated children: Putative risk factors and consequences. *Annual Review of Psychology, 46,* 401–431.

Kobasa, S. C. (1982). Commitment and coping in stress resistance among lawyers. *Journal of Personality and Social Psychology, 42,* 707–717.

Kobasa, S. C., Maddi, S. R., & Kahn, S. (1982). Hardiness and health: A prospective study. *Journal of Personality and Social Psychology, 42,* 168–177.

Kobasa, S. C., Maddi, S. R., & Puccetti, M. C. (1982). Personality and exercise as buffers in the stress-illness relationship. *Journal of Behavioral Medicine, 5,* 391–404.

Koch, P. B. (1993). Promoting healthy sexual development during early adolescence. In R. M. Lerner (Ed.), *Early adolescence: Perspectives on research, policy, and intervention.* Hillsdale, NJ: Lawrence Erlbaum.

Koegel, L. K., Valdez-Menchacha, M. C., & Koegel, R. L. (1994). Autism: Social communication difficulties and related behaviors. In V. B. Van Hasselt & M. Hersen (Eds.), *Advanced abnormal psychology.* New York: Plenum.

Kohlberg, L. (1984). *The psychology of moral development: Essays on moral development* (Vol. 11). San Francisco: Harper & Row.

Kohler, T., & Troester, U. (1991). Changes in the palmar sweat index during mental arithmetic. *Biological Psychology, 32,* 143–154.

Köhler, W. (1917; reprinted 1925). *The mentality of apes* (E. Winter, Trans.). New York: Harcourt Brace & World.

Kohyama, J., Shimohira, M., & Iwakawa, Y. (1997). Maturation of motility and motor inhibition in rapid-eye-movement sleep. *Journal of Pediatrics, 130,* 117–122.

Kolko, D. (1995, April). Cited in T. DeAngelis, Research documents trauma of abuse. *APA Monitor.*

Kondo, D. S. (1997). Strategies for coping with test anxiety. *Anxiety, Stress, and Coping, 10,* 203–215.

Koopman, J. M. (1995, February 20). Cited in M. Cimons & T. H. Maugh, II, New strategies fuel optimism in AIDS fight. *Los Angeles Times.*

Kordower, J. H., Rosenstein, J. M., Collier T. J., Burke, M. A., Chen, E., Li, J. M., Martel, L., Levey, A. E., Mufson, E. J., Freeman, T. B., & Olanow, W. (1996). Functional fetal nigral grafts in a patient with Parkinson's disease: Chemoanatomic, ultrastructural, and metabolic studies. *Journal of Comparative Neurology, 370,* 203–230.

Koss, M. P., Gidycz, C. A., & Wisniewski, N. (1987). The scope of rape: Incidence and prevalence of sexual aggression and victimization in a national sample of higher education students. *Journal of Consulting and Clinical Psychology, 55,* 162–170.

Kosslyn, S. M. (1995). Introduction. In M. S. Gazzaniga (Ed.), *The cognitive neurosciences.* Cambridge, MA: MIT Press.

Kowalski, R. M. (1996). Complaints and complaining: Functions, antecedents, and consequences. *Psychological Bulletin, 119,* 179–196.

Kramer, M. W., Kuo, C. L., & Dailey, J. C. (1997). The impact of brainstorming techniques on subsequent group processes: Beyond generating ideas. *Small Group Research, 28,* 218–242.

Kraus, S. J. (1995). Attitudes and the prediction of behavior: A meta-analysis of the empirical literature. *Personality and Social Psychology Bulletin, 21,* 58–75.

Kristof, N. D. (1996, March 10). Guns: One nation bars, the other requires. *New York Times,* E-3.

Krueger, J., & Heckhausen, J. (1993). Personality development across the adult life span: Subjective conceptions vs cross-sectional contrasts. *Journal of Gerontology: Psychological Sciences, 48,* P100–P108.

Kua, E. H., Chew, P. H., & Ko, S. M. (1993). Spirit possession and healing among Chinese psychiatric patients. *Acta Psychiatrica Scandinavica, 88,* 447–450.

Kubovy, M., & Wagemans, J. (1995). Grouping by proximity and multistability in dot lattices: A quantitative Gestalt theory. *Psychological Science, 6,* 225–234.

Kuch, K., Cox, B. J., Evans, R., & Shulman, I. (1994). Phobias, panic, and pain in 55 survivors of road vehicle accidents. *Journal of Anxiety Disorders, 8,* 181–187.

Kuffer, D. J., & Reynolds, C. R. (1997). Management of insomnia. *New England Journal of Medicine, 336,* 341–346.

Kuhl, P. K., Andruski, J. E., Christovich, I. A., Christovich, L. A., Kolzhevnikova, E. V., Ryskina, V. L., Stolyarova, E. I., Sundberg, U., & Lacerda, F. (1997). Cross-language analysis of phonetic units in language addressed to infants. *Science, 277,* 684–687.

Kurahashi, T., & Menini, A. (1997). Mechanism of odorant adaptation in the olfactory receptor cell. *Nature, 385,* 725–729.

Kurten, B. (1993). *Our earliest ancestors.* New York: Columbia University Press.

Kurtz, E. (1979). *Not-God: A history of Alcoholics Anonymous.* Center City, MN: Hazelden.

Kurtz, P. (1995, May/June). Is John Beloff an absolute paranormalist? *Skeptical Inquirer.*

Laan, E., & van Lunsen, R. H. W. (1997). Hormones and sexuality in postmenopausal women: A psychophysiologial study. *Journal of Psychosomatic Obstetrics and Gynecology, 18,* 126–133.

LaBar, K. S., & LeDoux, J. E. (1996). Partial disruption of fear conditioning in rats with unilateral amygdala damage: Correspondence with unilateral temporal lobectomy in humans. *Behavioral Neuroscience, 110,* 991–997.

Labouvie-Vief, G. (1996). Emotion, thought, and gender. In C. Magai & S. H. McFadden (Eds.), *Handbook of emotion, adult development, and aging.* San Diego: Academic Press.

Lach, J. (1997, Spring/Summer). Cultivating the mind. *Newsweek.* Special Issue.

LaFee, S. (1996, September 11). Fragile lives. *San Diego Union-Tribune.*

Laird, J. D. (1974). Self-attribution of emotion: The effects of expressive behavior on the quality of emotional experience. *Journal of Personality and Social Psychology, 29,* 475–486.

Lamb, N. (1990). *Guide to teaching string* (5th ed.). Dubuque, IA: William C. Brown.

Lambert, M. J., & Bergin, A. E. (1994). The effectiveness of psychotherapy. In A. E. Bergin & S. L. Garfield (Eds.), *Handbook of psychotherapy and behavior change* (4th ed.). New York: Wiley.

Lane, H. (1997, July). Cited in R. A. Clay, Do hearing devices impair deaf children? *APA Monitor.*

Lane, R. D., Reiman, E. M., Ahern, G. L., Schwartz, G. E., & Davidson, R. J. (1997). Neuroanatomical correlates of happiness, sadness, and disgust. *American Journal of Psychiatry, 154,* 926–933.

Lang, P. J. (1995). The emotion probe. *American Psychologist, 50,* 372–385.

Langlois, J. H., Roggman, L. A. & Musselman, L. (1994). What is average and what is not average about attractive faces? *Psychological Science, 5,* 214–220.

Lanzetta, J. T., Cartwright-Smith, J., & Kleck, R. E. (1976). Effects of nonverbal discrimination on emotional experience and autonomic arousal. *Journal of Personality and Social Psychology, 33,* 354–370.

Larkin, K. T., & Edens, J. L. (1994). Behavior therapy. In V. B. Van Hasselt & M. Hersen (Eds.), *Advanced abnormal psychology.* New York: Plenum Press.

Latané, B. (1981). The psychology of social impact. *American Psychologist, 36,* 343–356.

Latané, B., & Darley, J. M. (1970). *The unresponsive bystander: Why doesn't he help?* New York: Appleton-Century-Crofts.

Latané, B., & Nida, S. (1981). Ten years of research on group size and helping. *Psychological Bulletin, 89,* 308–324.

Laumann, E., Michael, R. T., Gagnon, J. H., & Kolata, G. (1994). *The social organization of sexuality.* Chicago: University of Chicago Press.

Lawrie, S. M., & Abukmeil, S. S. (1998). Brain abnormality in schizophrenia. *British Journal of Psychiatry, 172,* 110–120.

Lazarus, R. S. (1990). Psychological stress in the workplace. *Journal of Social Behavior and Personality, 6,* 1–13.

Lazarus, R. S. (1991). Cognition and motivation in emotion. *American Psychologist, 46,* 352–367.

Lazarus, R. S. (1993). Why we should think of stress as a subset of emotion. In L. Goldberger & S. Breznitz (Eds.), *Handbook of stress: Theoretical and clinical aspects* (2nd ed.). New York: Free Press.

Leafgren, A. (1989). Health and wellness programs. In M. L. Upcraft & J. N. Gardner (Eds.), *The freshman year experience.* San Francisco: Jossey-Bass.

Leary, M. R., Tambor, E. S., Terdal, S. K., & Downs, D. L. (1995). Self-esteem as an interpersonal monitor: The sociometer hypothesis. *Journal of Personality and Social Psychology, 68,* 518–530.

Leavy, J. (1996, March 18). With Ritalin, the son also rises. *Newsweek.*

LeDoux, J. (1996). *The emotional brain: The mysterious underpinnings of emotional life.* New York: Simon & Schuster.

Lee, C., & Bobko, P. (1994). Self-efficacy beliefs: Comparison of five measures. *Journal of Applied Psychology, 79,* 364–369.

Leedham, B., Meyerowitz, B. E., Muirhead, J., & Frist, W. H. (1995). Positive expectations predict health after heart transplantation. *Health Psychology, 14,* 74–79.

Lehrer, P. M., Carr, R., Sargunaraj, D., & Woolfolk, R. L. (1994). Stress management techniques: Are they all equivalent, or do they have specific effects? *Biofeedback and Self-Regulation, 19,* 353–401.

Leibel, R. L., Rosenbaum, M., & Hirsch, J. (1995). Changes in energy expenditure resulting from altered body weight. *New England Journal of Medicine, 332,* 621–628.

Leiblum, S. R. (1990). Sexuality and the midlife woman. *Psychology of Women Quarterly, 14,* 495–508.

Leigh, B. C., Morrison, D. M., Trocki, K., & Temple, M. T. (1994). Sexual behavior of American adolescents: *Results from a U.S. National Survey. Journal of Adolescent Health, 15,* 117–125.

Leippe, M. R., & Eisenstadt, D. (1994). Generalization of dissonance reduction: Decreasing prejudice through induced compliance. *Journal of Personality and Social Psychology, 67,* 395–413.

Leland, J. (1994, February 14). Homophobia, *Newsweek.*

Lendon, C. L., Ashall, F., & Goate, A. M. (1997). Exploring the etiology of Alzheimer disease using molecular genetics. *Journal of the American Medical Association, 277,* 825–831.

Leo, J. (1987, January 12). Exploring the traits of twins. *Time.*

Lepore, S. J., Mata Allen, K. A., & Evans, G. W. (1993). Social support lowers cardiovascular reactivity to an acute stressor. *Psychosomatic Medicine, 55,* 518–524.

Lerner, R. M., & Galambos, N. L. (1998). Adolescent development: Challenges and opportunities for research, programs, and policies. *Annual Review of Psychology, 49,* 413–446.

Leshner, A. I. (1997). Drug abuse and addiction treatment research. *Archives General Psychiatry, 54,* 691–693.

Lester, B. (1997, December). Cited in B. Azar, Researchers debunk myth of the "crack baby." *APA Monitor.*

Leung, P. W. L., Luk, S. L., Ho, T. P., Taylor, E., Mak, R. L., & Bacon-Shone, J. (1996). The diagnosis and prevalence of hyperactivity in Chinese schoolboys. *British Journal of Psychiatry, 168,* 486–496.

LeVay, S., & Hamer, D. H. (1994). Evidence for a biological influence in male homosexuality. *Scientific American, 270,* 44–49.

Levenson, R. W., Carstensen, L. L., & Gottman, J. M. (1994). The influence of age and gender on affect, physiology, and their interrelations: A study of long-term marriages. *Journal of Personality and Social Psychology, 67,* 56–68.

Levin, R. (1994). Sleep and dreaming characteristics of frequent nightmare subjects in a university population. *Dreaming, 4,* 127–137.

Levine, R. V., Martinez, T. S., Brase, G., & Sorenson, K. (1994). Helping in 36 U.S. cities. *Journal of Personality and Social Psychology, 67,* 69–82.

Levine, S., & Koenig, J. (Eds.) (1980). *Why men rape: Interviews with convicted rapists.* Toronto: Macmillan.

Levitt, S., & Wagner, J. (1994, January 21). Weight and see. *People.*

Levy, D. (1997). *Tools of critical thinking.* New York: Allyn & Bacon.

Levy, J. (1985, May). Right brain, left brain: Fact and fiction. *Psychology Today.*

Levy, J., & Trevarthen, C. (1976). Metacontrol of hemispheric function in human split-brain patients. *Journal of Experimental Psychology: Human Perception and Performance, 2,* 299–312.

Levy, J., Trevarthen, C., & Sperry, R. W. (1972). Perception of bilateral chimeric figures following hemispheric deconnection. *Brain, 95,* 61–68.

Lewin, R. (1993). *The origin of modern humans.* New York: Scientific American Library.

Lewinsohn, P. M., Rohde, P., & Seeley, J. R. (1994). Psychosocial risk factors for future adolescent suicide attempts. *Journal of Consulting and Clinical Psychology, 62,* 297–305.

Lewis, C. E. (1991). Neurochemical mechanisms of chronic antisocial behavior (psychopathy). *Journal of Nervous and Mental Disease, 179,* 720–727.

Leyens, J. P., & Fiske, S. T. (1994). Impression formation: From recitals to Symphonie Fantastique. In P. G. Devine, D. L. Hamilton, & T. M. Ostrom (Eds.), *Social cognition: Impact on social psychology.* New York: Academic Press.

Libman, J. (1991, June 7). Sudden end to a trailblazing career. *Los Angeles Times,* E-1.

Liddle, P. F. (1997). Dynamic neuroimaging with PET, SPET, or fMRI. *International Review of Psychiatry, 9,* 331–337.

Lie, R. T., Wilcox, A. J., & Skjaerven, R. (1994). A population-based study of the risk of recurrence of birth defects. *New England Journal of Medicine, 331,* 1–4.

Lieberman, D. A. (1993). *Learning* (2nd ed.). Pacific Grove, CA: Brooks/Cole.

Liebert, R. M., & Spiegler, M. D. (1994). *Personality: Strategies and issues* (7th ed.). Pacific Grove: Brooks/Cole.

Lief, H. I. & Fetkewicz, J. (1995). Retractors of false memories: The evolution of pseudo-memories. *Journal of Psychiatry & Law, 23,* 411–436.

Lief, L. (1994, August 29/September 5). An old oasis of tolerance runs dry. *U.S. News & World Report.*

Lilienfeld, S. O. (1993). Do "honesty" tests really measure honesty? *Skeptical Inquirer, 18,* 32–41.

Lilly, J. C. (1972). *The center of the cyclone.* New York: Bantam.

Lin, J. G. (1996). A concept in analgesic mechanisms of acupuncture. *Chinese Medical Journal, 109,* 179–192.

Linden, E. (1993, March 22). Can animals think? *Time.*

Lindenberger, U., & Baltes, P. B. (1997). Intellectual functioning in old and very old age: Cross-sectional results from the Berlin aging study. *Psychology and Aging, 12,* 410–432.

Lipkin, R. (1995). Additional genes may affect color vision. *Science News, 147,* 100.

Lippa, R. A. (1994). *Introduction to social psychology* (2nd ed.). Pacific Grove, CA: Brooks/Cole.

Lipton, S. D. (1983). A critique of so-called standard psychoanalyric technique. *Contemporary Psychoanalysis, 19,* 35–52.

Liska, K. (1994). *Drugs & the human body* (4th ed.). New York: Macmillan.

Liu, W., & McGucken, E. (1997, March). Cited in: Stover, D. *Popular Science.*

Liu, W., & McGucken, E. (1997, August). Cited in M. Shaffer, Restoring sight. *Popular Science.*

Lochman, J. E., & Lenhart, L. A. (1993). Anger coping intervention for aggressive children: Conceptual models and outcomes effects. *Clinical Psychology Review, 13,* 785–805.

Locke, E. A., Latham, G. P. (1994). Goal setting theory. In H. F. O'Neil Jr., & M. Drillings (Eds.), *Motivation: Theory and research.* Hillsdale, NJ: Lawrence Erlbaum.

References

Locker, D., Shapiro, D., & Liddell, A. (1997). Overlap between dental anxiety and blood-injury fears: Psychological characteristics and response to dental treatment. *Behaviour Research and Therapy, 35,* 583–590.

Loehlin, J. C. (1992). *Genes and environment in personality.* Newbury Park, CA: Sage.

Loftus, E. F. (1975). Leading questions and the eyewitness report. *Cognitive Psychology, 7,* 560–572.

Loftus, E. F. (1979). The malleability of memory. *American Scientist, 67,* 312–320.

Loftus, E. F. (1993a). Psychologists in the eyewitness world. *American Psychologist, 48,* 518–537.

Loftus, E. F. (1993b). The reality of repressed memories. *American Psychologist, 48,* 518–537.

Loftus, E. F. (1994). The repressed memory controversy. *American Psychologist, 49,* 443–445.

Loftus, E. F. (1997a). Creating false memories. *Scientific American,* September, 70–75.

Loftus, E. F. (1997b). Repressed memory accusations: Devastated families and devastated patients. *Applied Cognitive Psychology, 11,* 25–30.

Loftus, E. F., & Hoffman, H. G. (1989). Misinformation and memory: The creation of new memories. *Journal of Experimental Psychology: General, 118,* 100–104.

Loftus, E. F., Miller, D. G., & Burns, H. J. (1978). Semantic integration of verbal information into a visual memory. *Journal of Experimental Psychology: Human Learning and Memory, 4,* 19–31.

Loftus, E. F., Polonsky, S., & Fullilove, M. T. (1994). Memories of childhood sexual abuse. *Psychology of Women Quarterly, 18,* 67–84.

Logue, A. W., Ophir, I., & Strauss, K. E. (1981). The acquisition of taste aversions in humans. *Behavior Research and Therapy, 19,* 319–335.

Long, J. D., Gaynor, P., Erwin, A., Williams, R. L. (1994). The relationship of self-management to academic motivation, study efficiency, academic satisfaction, and grade point average among prospective education majors. *Psychology, A Journal of Human Behavior, 31,* 22–30.

Longo, L. C., & Ashmore, R. D. (1995). The looks-personality relationship: Global self-orientations as shared precursors of subjective physical attractiveness and self-ascribed traits. *Journal of Applied Social Psychology, 25,* 371–398.

Lore, R. K., & Schultz, L. A. (1993). Control of human aggression. *American Psychologist, 48,* 16–25.

Lorenz, K. (1952). King Solomon's ring. New York: Crowell.

Lovaas, O. I. (1987). Behavioral treatment and normal educational and intellectual functioning in young autistic children. *Journal of Consulting and Clinical Psychology, 55,* 3–9.

Lovaas, O. I. (1993). The development of a treatment-research project for developmentally disabled autistic children. *Journal of Applied Behavior Analysis, 26,* 617–630.

Lovaas, O. I., & Buch, G. (1997). Intensive behavioral intervention with young children. In N. N. Singh (Ed.), *Prevention and treatment of severe behavior problems.* Pacific Grove, CA: Brooks/Cole.

Lowry, J. L., & Ross, M. J. (1997). Expectations of psychotherapy duration: How long should psychotherapy last? *Psychotherapy, 34,* 272–277.

Lubart, T. I. (1994). Creativity. In R. J. Sternberg (Ed.)., *Thinking and problem solving.* San Diego, CA: Academic Press.

Ludwig, A. M. (1995). *The price of greatness: Resolving the creative and madness controversy.* New York: Guilford Press.

Luna, T. D., French, J., & Mitcha, J. I. (1997). A study of USAF air traffic controller shiftwork: Sleep, fatigue, activity, and mood analyses. *Aviation, Space, and Environmental Medicine, 68,* 18–23.

Luo, L., & Shih, J. B. (1997). Sources of happiness: A qualitative approach. *Journal of Social Psychology, 137,* 181–187.

Lupart, J. L., & Pyryt, M. C. (1996). "Hidden gifted" students: Underachiever prevalence and profile. *Journal for the Education of the Gifted, 20,* 36–53.

Lutz, J., Means, L. W., & Long, T. E. (1994). Where did I park? A naturalistic study of spatial memory. *Applied Cognitive Psychology, 8,* 439–451.

Lykken, D. & Tellegen, A. (1996). Happiness is a stochastic phenomenon. *Psychological Science, 7,* 186–189.

Lynn, S. J. (1997). Automaticity and hypnosis: A sociocognitive account. *International Journal of Clinical and Experimental Hypnosis, 45,* 239–250.

Maccoby, E. E. (1984). Socialization and developmental change. *Child Development, 55,* 317–328.

MacCoun, R. J. (1993). Drugs and the law: A psychological analysis of drug prohibition. *Psychological Bulletin, 113,* 497–512.

Macfarlane, A. J. (1975). Olfaction in the development of social preferences in the human neonate. *CIBA Foundation Symposium, 33,* 103–117.

Mackie, D. M., & Skelly, J. J. (1994). The social cognition analysis of social influence: Contributions to the understanding of persuasion and conformity. In P. G. Devine, D. L. Hamilton, & T. M. Ostrom (Eds.), *Social cognition: Impact on social psychology.* New York: Academic Press.

Macmillan, M. (1997). *Freud evaluated.* Cambridge, MA: MIT Press.

MacQueen, G., Marshall, J., Perdue, M., Siegel, S., & Biennenstock, J. (1989). Pavlovian conditioning of rat mucosal mast cells to secrete rat mast cell protease II. *Science, 243,* 83–85.

Macrae, C. N., Bodenhausen, G. V., & Milne, A. B. (1998). Saying no to unwanted thoughts: Self-focus and the regulation of mental life. *Journal of Personality and Social Psychology, 74,* 578–589.

Macrae, C. N., Milne, A. B., & Bodenhausen, G. V. (1994). Stereotypes as energy-saving devices: A peek inside the cognitive toolbox. *Journal of Personality and Social Psychology, 66,* 37–47.

Madon, S., Jussim, L., & Eccles, J. (1997). In search of the powerful self-fulfilling prophecy. *Journal of Personality and Social Psychology, 72,* 791–809.

Madsen, K. B. (1973). Theories of motivation. In B. B. Wollman (Ed.), *Handbook of general psychology.* Englewood Cliffs, NJ: Prentice-Hall.

Magidoff, R. (1955). *Yehudi Menuhin.* London: Robert Hale.

Magnuson, A., & Stefansson, J. G. (1993). Prevalence of seasonal affective disorder in Iceland. *Archives of General Psychiatry, 50,* 941–946.

Mah, Z., & Bryant, H. E. (1997). The role of past mammography and future intentions in screening mammography usage. *International Society for Preventive Oncology, 21,* 213–220.

Maier, S. R., Watkins, L. R., & Fleshner, M. (1994). Psychoneuroimmunology. *American Psychologist, 49,* 1004–1007.

Maj, M., Pirozzi, R., Magliano, L., & Bartoli, L. (1997). Long-term outcome of lithium prophylaxis in bipolar disorder: A 5-year prospective study of 402 patients at a lithium clinic. *American Journal of Psychiatry, 155,* 30–55.

Maldonado, P. E., Godecke, I., Gray, C. M., & Bonhoffer, T. (1997). Orientation selectivity in pinwheel centers in cat straite cortex. *Science, 276,* 1551–1555.

Manderscheid, R. W., & Sonnenschein, M. A. (1992). *Mental health, United States, 1992.* Washington, DC: U.S. Department of Health and Human Services.

Mann, A. (1998, April 6). Cross-gender sex pill. *Time.*

Manning, A. (1996 September 17). Caught dirty-handed: Many fail to wash when they should. *USA Today.*

Manning, A. (1998, February 23). Operating with sexism. *USA Today,* D-1.

Mannuzza, S., Klein, R. G., Bessler, A., Malloy, P., & LaPadula, M. (1993). Adult outcome of hyperactive boys. *Archives of General Psychiatry, 50,* 565–576.

Manuel, L. L., Retzlaff, P., & Sheehan, E. (1993). Policewomen personality. *Journal of Social Behavior and Personality, 8,* 149–153.

Maquet, P. (1997). Positron emission tomography studies of sleep and sleep disorders. *Journal of Neurology, 244* (supplement 1), S23–S28.

Maratsos, M., & Matheny, L. (1994). Language specificity and elasticity: Brain and clinical syndrome studies. *Annual Review of Psychology, 45,* 487–516.

Marecek, J. (1995). Gender, politics, and psychology's ways of knowing. *American Psychologist, 50,* 162–163.

Marin, R., & Miller, S. (1997, April 14). Ellen steps out. *Newsweek.*

Markman, H. J. (1995, February). Quoted in R. Edwards, New tools help gauge marital success. *APA Monitor.*

Marks, I. (1994). Behavior therapy as an aid to self-care. *Current Directions in Psychological Science, 3,* 19–22.

Marshall, E. (1995). Dispute splits schizophrenia study. *Science, 268,* 792–794.

Marta, E. (1997). Parent-adolescent interactions and psychosocial risk in adolescents: An analysis of communication, support, and gender. *Journal of Adolescence, 20,* 471–487.

Martin, A., Wiggs, C. L., Ungerfelder, L. G., & Haxby, J. V. (1996). Neural correlates of category-specific knowledge. *Nature, 379,* 649–652.

Martin, G. L. (1982). Thought-stopping and stimulus control to decrease persistent disturbing thoughts. *Journal of Behavior Therapy and Experimental Psychiatry, 13,* 215–220.

Martin, L. (1986). Eskimo words for snow: A case study in the genesis and decay of an anthropological example. *American Anthropologist, 88,* 418–423.

Martin, R. P., Wisenbaker, J., & Baker, J. (1997). Gender differences in temperament at six months and five years. *Infant Behavior and Development, 20,* 339–347.

Martin, S. (1995, January). Field's status unaltered by the influx of women. *APA Monitor.*

Maruish, M. E. (Ed.). (1994). *The use of psychological testing for treatment planning and outcome assessment: Introduction.* Hillsdale, NJ: Lawrence Erlbaum.

Masling, J. M. (1997). On the nature and utility of projective tests and objective tests. *Journal of Personality Assessment, 69,* 357–370.

Maslow, A. H. (1968). *Toward a psychology of being* (2nd ed.). New York: Van Nostrand.

Maslow, A. H. (1970). *Motivation and personality.* New York: Harper & Row.

Maslow, A. H. (1971). *The farther reaches of human nature.* New York: Viking Press.

Masten, A. S., & Coatsworth, J. D. (1998). The development of competence in favorable and unfavorable environments. *American Psychologist, 53,* 205–220.

Masters, W. H., & Johnson, V. E. (1966). *Human sexual response.* Boston: Little, Brown.

Masters, W. H., & Johnson, V. E. (1970). *Human sexual inadequacy.* Boston: Little, Brown.

Masters, W. H., & Johnson, V. E. (1981). Sex and the aging process. *Journal of the American Geriatrics Society, 19,* 385–389.

Mathews, R. C. (1997). Commentaries. *Psychonomic Bulletin & Review, 4,* 38–42.

Mathews, T., Reiss, S., & Artholet, J. (1990, February 19). The threat of a white backlash. *Newsweek.*

Matson, J. L., & Ollendick, T. H. (1977). Issues in toilet training normal children. *Behavior Therapy, 8,* 549–553.

Matsuda, L. A., Lolait, S. J., Brownstein, M. J., Young, A. C., & Bonner, T. I. (1990). Structure of a cannabinoid receptor and functional expression of the cloned cDNA. *Nature, 346,* 561–564.

Matsumoto, D., & Ekman, P. (1989). American-Japanese cultural differences in intensity ratings of facial expressions of emotion. *Motivation and Emotion, 13,* 143–157.

Matt, G. E., & Navarro, A. M. (1997). What meta-analyses have and have not taught us about psychotherapy effects: A review of future directions. *Clinical Psychology Review, 17,* 1–32.

Matthews, K. A., & Haynes, S. G. (1986). Type A behavior pattern and coronary disease risk. *American Journal of Epidemiology, 123,* 923–960.

Matthias, R. E., Lubben, J. E., Atchison, K. A., & Schweitzer, S. T. (1997). Sexual activity and satisfaction among very old adults: Results from a community-dwelling medicare population survey. *Gerontologist, 37,* 6–14.

Mattson, S., Riley, E. P., Gramling, L., Delis, D. C., & Jones, K. L. (1998). Neuropsychological comparison of alcohol-exposed children with or without physical features of fetal alcohol syndrome. Neuropsychology, *12,* 146–153.

Maugh, T. H. (1997, July 11). Heroin use soars in state, study says. *Los Angeles Times.*

Maugh, T. H., II (1998, February 21). Study's advice to husbands: Accept wife's influence. *Los Angeles Times.*

Mayberg, H. S., Mahurin, R. K., & Brannan, S. K. (1997). Neuropsychiatric aspects of mood and affective disorders. In S. C. Yudofsky & R. E. Hales (Eds.), *American Psychiatric Press textbook of neuropsychiatry* (3rd ed.). Washington, DC: American Psychiatric Press.

Mayer, J. D., & Salovey, P. (1997). What is emotional intelligence? In P. Salovey & D. Sluyter (Eds.), *Emotional development and emotional intelligence: Implications for educators.* New York: Basic Books.

Mayes, A. R., & Downes, J. J. (1997). What do theories of the functional deficit(s) underlying amnesia have to explain? *Memory, 5,* 3–36.

Mays, V. M., Rubin, J., Sabourin, M., & Walker, L. (1996). Moving toward a global psychology. *American Psychologist, 51,* 485–487.

Mazzoni, G., & Cornoldi, C. (1993). Strategies in study time allocation: Why is study time sometimes not effective? *Journal of Experimental Psychology: General, 122,* 47–60.

McAninch, W. (1995, July 16). Cited in R. Bragg, In South Carolina, a mother's defense, and life, could hinge on 2 choices. *New York Times.*

McCall, R. B. (1994). Academic underachievers. *Current Directions in Psychological Science, 3,* 15–19.

McCarry, J. (1996, May). Peru begins again. *National Geographic.*

McClearn, G. E., Johansson, B., Berg, S., Pedersen, N. L., Ahern, F., Petrill, S. A., & Plomin, R. (1997). Substantial genetic influence on cognitive abilities in twins 80 or more years old. *Science, 276,* 1560–1563.

McClelland, D. C. (1985). *Human motivation.* Glenview, IL: Scott, Foresman.

McClelland, D. C., Atkinson, J. W., Clark, R. W., & Lowell, E. L. (1953). *The achievement motive.* New York: Appleton-Century-Crofts.

McConnell, J. V., Cutler, R. L., & McNeil, E. B. (1958). Subliminal stimulation: An overview. *American Psychologist, 13,* 229–242.

McCrae, R. R., & Costa, P. T., Jr. (1990). *Personality in adulthood.* New York: Guilford Press.

McCrae, R. R., & Costa, P. T., Jr. (1994). The stability of personality: Observations and evaluations. *Current Directions in Psychological Science, 3,* 173–175.

McCrae, R. R., & Costa, P. T., Jr. (1997). Personality trait structure as a human universal. *American Psychologist, 52,* 509–516.

McDaniel, M. A., & Einstein, G. O. (1986). Bizarre imagery as an effective memory aid: The importance of distinctiveness. *Journal of Experimental Psychology: Learning, Memory and Cognition, 12,* 54–65.

McDonald, H. E., & Hirt, E. R. (1997). When expectancy meets desire: Motivational effects in reconstructive memory. *Journal of Personality and Social Psychology, 72,* 5–23.

McDougall, W. (1908). *Social psychology.* New York: Putnam.

McDougle, C. J. (1997). Update on pharmacologic management of OCD: Agents and augmentation. *Journal of Clinical Psychiatry, 58* (supplement 12), 11–17.

McDowell, D. M., & Kleber, H. D. (1994). MDMA: Its history and pharmacology. *Psychiatric Annals, 24,* 127–130.

McDowell, J. (1992, February 17). Are women better cops? *Time.*

McEachin, J. J., Smith, T., & Lovaas, O. I. (1993). Long-term outcome for children with autism who received early intensive behavioral interventions. *American Journal on Mental Retardation, 97,* 359–372.

McElrath, D. (1997). The Minnesota model. *Journal of Psychoactive Drugs, 29,* 141–144.

McGaugh, J. L. (1990). Significance and remembrance: The role of neuromodulatory systems. *Psychological Science, 1,* 15–25.

McGinnis, J. M., & Foege, W. H. (1993). Actual causes of death in the United States. *Journal of the American Medical Association, 270,* 2207–2212.

McGrady, A. V., Bush, E. G., & Grubb, B. P. (1997). Outcome of biofeedback-assisted relaxation for neurocardiogenic syncope and headache: A clinical replication series. *Applied Psychophysiology and Biofeedback, 22,* 63–72.

McGue, M., Bouchard, T. J., Jr., Iacono, W. G., & Lykken, D. T. (1993). Behavioral genetics of cognitive ability: A life-span perspective. In R. Plomin & G. E. McClearn (Eds.), *Nature, nurture, and psychology.* Washington, DC: American Psychological Association.

McGue, M., & Christensen, K. (1997). Genetic and environmental contributions to depression symptomatology: Evidence from Danish twins 75 years of age and older. *Journal of Abnormal Psychology, 106,* 439–448.

McGuire, P. K. (1993, September 29). Cited in D. Goleman, Thinking, not hearing voices. *San Diego Union-Tribune.*

McIntosh, D. N. (1996). Facial feedback hypothesis: Evidence, implications, and directions. *Motivation and Emotion, 20,* 121–147.

McKenna, K. (1994, November 13). *He just did it.* Los Angeles Times Calendar.

McLellan, A. T., Grossman, D. S., Blaine, J. D., & Haverkos, H. W. (1993). Acupuncture treatment for drug abuse: A technical review.

Journal of Substance Abuse Treatment, 10, 569–576.

McMahon, P. (1998, July 14). Law has changed how Oregonians die. *USA Today,* 3A.

Meck, W. (1996). Cited in V. Morell, Setting a biological stopwatch. *Science, 271,* 905–906.

Meeus, W., & Raaijmakers, Q. (1989). Obedience to authority in Milgram-type studies: A research review. *Zeitschrift für Sozialpsychologie, 20,* 70–85.

Megargee (1997). Internal inhibitions and controls. In R. Hogan, J. Johnson, & S. Briggs (Eds.), *Handbook of personality psychology.* New York: Academic Press.

Mehren, E. (1991, May 27). Grounded for cosmetic reasons. *Los Angeles Times,* E-1.

Meichenbaum, D., & Fitzpatrick, D. (1993). A constructivist narrative perspective on stress and coping: Stress inoculation applications. In L. Goldberger & S. Breznitz (Eds.), *Handbook of stress: Theoretical and clinical aspects* (2nd ed.). New York: Free Press.

Meissner, J. S., Blanchard, E. B., Malamood, H. S. (1997). Comparison of treatment outcome measures for irritable bowel syndrome. *Applied Psychophysiology and Biofeedback, 22,* 55–62.

Melzack, R. (1989). Phantom limbs, the self and the brain. *Canadian Psychology, 30,* 1–16.

Melzack, R. (1997). Phantom limbs. *Scientific American.* Special Issue, 84–91.

Melzack, R., & Wall, P. D. (1983). *The challenge of pain.* New York: Basic Books.

Menzies, R. G., & Clarke, J. C. (1995). The etiology of phobias: A nonassociative account. *Clinical Psychology Review, 15,* 23–48.

Merzenich, M. M., Jenkins, W. M., Johnston, P., Schreiner, C., Miller, S. L., & Tallal, P. (1996). Temporal processing deficits of language-learning impaired children ameliorated by training. *Science, 271,* 77–81.

Mesirow, K. H. (1984). *Report on animal research survey.* Paper presented at the American Psychological Association, Toronto.

Messer, S. B., & Wachtel, P. L. (1997). The contemporary psychotherapeutic landscape: Issues and prospects. In P. L. Wachtel & S. B. Messer (Eds.), *Theories of psychotherapy: Origins and evolution.* Washington, DC: American Psychological Association.

Mestel, R. (1993, July 31). Cannibis: The brain's other supplier. *New Scientist.*

Meyers, S. A., & Berscheid, E. (1997). The language of love: The difference a preposition makes. *Personality and Social Psychology Bulletin, 23,* 347–362.

Michaelson, J. (1995, July 16). Front and center. *Los Angeles Times.*

Middlebrooks, J. C., Clock, A. E., Xu, L., & Green, D. M. (1994). A panoramic code for sound location by cortical neurons. *Science, 264,* 842–884.

Mignot, E. (1997). Behavioral genetics '97: Genetics of narcolepsy and other sleep disorders. *American Journal of Human Genetics, 60,* 1289–1302.

Miles, D. R., & Carey, G. (1997). Genetic and environmental architecture of human aggression.

Journal of Personality and Social Psychology, 72, 207–217.

Milgram, N. A., Dangour, W., & Raviv, A. (1992). Situational and personal determinants of academic procrastination. *Journal of General Psychology, 119,* 123–133.

Milgram, S. (1963). Behavioral study of obedience. *Journal of Abnormal and Social Psychology, 67,* 371–378.

Milgram, S. (1974). *Obedience to authority.* New York: Harper & Row.

Milgrom, P., Mancl, L., Kng, B., & Weinstein, P. (1995). Origins of childhood dental fear. *Behaviour Research and Therapy, 33,* 313–319.

Milgrom, P., Quang, J. Z., & Tay, K. M. (1994). Cross-cultural validity of a parent's version of the Dental Fear Survey Schedule for children in Chinese. *Behavior Research and Therapy, 32,* 131–135.

Milgrom, P., Vigehesa, H., & Weinstein, P. (1992). Adolescent dental fear and control: Prevalence and theoretical implications. *Behavior Research and Therapy, 30,* 367–373.

Millan, M. J. (1986). Multiple opioid systems and pain. *Pain, 27,* 303–347.

Miller, D. D., Perry, P. J., Cadoret, R. J., & Andreasen, N. C. (1994). Clozapine's effect on negative symptoms in treatment-refractory schizophrenics. *Comprehensive Psychiatry, 35,* 8–15.

Miller, F. G., Quill, T. E., Brody, H., Fletcher, J. C., Gostin, L. O., & Meier, D. E. (1994). Regulating physician-assisted death. *New England Journal of Medicine, 331,* 119–122.

Miller, G. (1956). The magical number seven, plus or minus two: Some limits on our capacity for information processing. *Psychological Review, 48,* 337–442.

Miller, I. J., Jr. (1993, February 10). Cited in J. Williams, Survival of the sweetest. *San Diego Union-Tribune.*

Miller, J. (1995, April). Cited in T. DeAngelis, Research documents trauma of abuse. *APA Monitor.*

Miller, M. A., & Rahe, R. H. (1997). Life changes scaling for the 1990s. *Journal of Psychosomatic Research, 43,* 279–292.

Miller, N. S., & Gold, M. S. (1994). LSD and Ecstasy: Pharmacology, phenomenology, and treatment. *Psychiatric Annals, 24,* 131–133.

Miller, P. H. (1993). *Theories of developmental psychology* (3rd ed.). New York: Freeman.

Miller, R. W., & C'deBaca, J. (1994). Quantum change: Toward a psychology of transformation. In T. F. Heatherton & J. L. Weinberger (Eds.), *Can personality change?* Washington, DC: American Psychological Association.

Miller, T. Q., Turner, C. W., Tindale, R. S., Posavac, E. J., & Dugoni, B. L. (1991). Reasons for the trend toward null findings in research on Type A behavior. *Psychological Bulletin, 110,* 469–485.

Miller, W. R., & Brown, S. A. (1997). Why psychologists should treat alcohol and drug problems. *American Psychologist, 52,* 1269–1279.

Millon, T. (1981). *Disorders of personality.* New York: Wiley.

Milstein, M. (1993, October 27). A dizzying dilemma. *San Diego Union-Tribune.*

Miltner, W., Matjek, M., Braun, C., Diekmann, H., & Brody, S. (1994). Emotional qualities of odors and their influence on the startle reflex in humans. *Psychophysiology, 31,* 107–110.

Mindell, J. A. (1997). Children and sleep. In M. R. Pressman & W. C. Orr (Eds.), *Understanding sleep: The evaluation and treatment of sleep disorders.* Washington, DC: American Psychological Association.

Minshew, N. J., Goldstein, G., & Siegel, D. J. (1995). Speech and language in high-functioning autistic individuals. *Neuropsychology, 9,* 255–261.

Minton, L. (1995, May 8). Fresh voices. *Parade.*

Mirsky, A. F., & Quinn, O. W. (1988). The Genain quadruplets. *Schizophrenia Bulletin, 14,* 595–612.

Mischel, W. (1990). Personality dispositions revisited and revised: A view after three decades. In L. A. Previn (Ed.), *Handbook of Personality.* New York: Guilford Press.

Mischel, W., & Peake, P. K. (1982). Beyond deja vu in the search for cross-situational consistency. *Psychological Review, 89,* 730–755.

Mischel, W., & Shoda, Y. (1995). A cognitive-affective system theory of personality: Reconceptualizing situations, dispositions, dynamics, and invariance of personality structure. *Psychological Review, 102,* 246–268.

Mischel, W., Shoda, Y., & Rodriguez, M. L. (1989). Delay of gratification in children. *Science, 244,* 933–937.

Mitchell, S. (1996, September). Cited in T. DeAngelis, Psychoanalysis adapts to the 1990s. *APA Monitor.*

Miyashita, Y. (1995). How the brain creates imagery: Projection to primary visual cortex. *Science, 268,* 1719–1720.

Mizes, J. S. (1994). Eating disorders. In V. B. Van Hasselt & M. Hersen (Eds.), *Advanced abnormal psychology.* New York: Plenum Press.

Mohr, D. C. (1995). Negative outcome in psychotherapy: A critical review. *Clinical Psychology: Science and Practice, 2,* 1–27.

Moldin, S. O., Reich, T., & Rice, J. P. (1991). Current perspectives on the genetics of unipolar depression. *Behavior Genetics, 21,* 211–242.

Moncrieff, J. (1997). Lithium: Evidence reconsidered. *British Journal of Psychiatry, 171,* 113–119.

Mondain, M., Sillon, M., Vieu, A., Lanvin, M., Reuillard-Artieres, F., Tobey, E., & Uziel, A. (1997). Speech perception skills and speech production intelligibility in French children with prelingual deafness and cochlear implants. *Archives of Otolaryngology, Head and Neck Surgery, 123,* 181–184.

Money, J. (1987). Sin, sickness or status? *American Psychologist, 42,* 384–399.

Montgomery, G. H., & Bovbjerg, D. H. (1997). The development of anticipatory nausea in patients receiving adjuvant chemotherapy for breast cancer. *Physiology & Behavior, 61,* 737–741.

Montgomery, G., & Kirsch, I. (1996). Mechanisms of placebo pain reduction: An empirical investigation. *Psychological Science, 7,* 174–176.

Moore, R. Y. (1997). Circadian rhythms: Basic neurobiology and clinical applications. *Annual Review of Medicine, 48,* 253–266.

Morash, M., & Greene, J. R. (1986). Evaluating women on patrol: A critique of contemporary wisdom. *Evaluation Review, 10,* 230–255.

Morell, V. (1996). Life at the top: Animals pay the high price for dominance. *Science, 271,* 292.

Morey, L. C. (1997). Personality diagnosis and personality disorders. In R. Hogan, J. Johnson, S. Briggs (Eds.), *Handbook of personality psychology.* New York: Academic Press.

Morgan, D. (1995, July 11). Cited in C. Sullivan, Mother called fit for trial in sons' deaths. *San Diego Union-Tribune.*

Morgan, M. (1985). Self-monitoring of attained subgoals in private study. *Journal of Educational Psychology, 77,* 623–630.

Morganthau, T. (1995, February 13). What color is black? *Newsweek.*

Morrison, A. (1993). Cited in H. Herzog, Animal rights and wrongs. *Science, 262,* 1906–1908.

Morrison-Bogorad, M., Phelps, C., & Buckoltz, N. (1997). Alzheimer's disease research comes of age. *Journal of the American Medical Association, 277,* 837–840.

Morrissey, J., Calloway, M., Johnsen, M., & Ullman, M. (1997). Service System performance and integration: A baseline profile of the ACCESS demonstrations sites. *Psychiatric Services, 48,* 374–380.

Mortensen, M. E., Sever, L. E., & Oakley, G. P. (1991). Teratology and the epidemiology of birth defects. In S. G. Gabbe, J. R. Niebyl, & J. L. Simpson (Eds.), *Obstetrics: Normal and problem pregnancies.* New York: Churchill Livingstone.

Moscovitch, M. (1997). Cited in C. Holden, A special place for faces in the brain. *Science, 278,* 41.

Moss, D. (1993, August 3). A painful parting in Michigan. *USA Today.*

Muehlenhard, C. L., & Linton, M. A. (1987). Date rape and sexual aggression in dating situations: Incidence and risk factors. *Journal of Counseling Psychology, 34,* 186–196.

Mullen, B., Anthony, T., Salas, E., & Driskell, J. E. (1994). Group cohesiveness and quality of decision making: An integration of tests of the groupthink hypothesis. *Small Group Research, 25,* 189–204.

Mullen, B., & Cooper, C. (1994). The relation between group cohesiveness and performance: An integration. *Psychological Bulletin, 115,* 210–227.

Mullen, M. K. (1994). Earliest recollections of childhood: A demographic analysis. *Cognition, 52,* 55–79.

Mumford, D., Rose, A. S., & Goslin, D. A. (1995). *An evaluation of remote viewing: Research and applications.* Washington, DC: The American Institutes for Research.

Mundy, C. (1994, June 2). The lost boy. *Rolling Stone.*

Munk, M. H. J., Roelfsema, P. R., Konig, P., Engel, A. K., & Singer, W. (1996). Role of reticular activation in the modulation of intracortical synchronization. *Science, 272,* 271–277.

Murberg, M. (Ed.). (1994). *Catecholamine function in post-traumatic stress disorder: Emerging data on child sexual abuse.* Beverly Hills, CA: Sage.

Murphy, G. G., & Glanzman, D. L. (1997). Mediation of classical conditioning in *Aplysia californica* by long-term potentiation of sensori-motor synapses. *Science, 278,* 467–471.

Murphy, K. (1996, November 19). Seattle dares to seek DARE alternatives. *Los Angeles Times.*

Murphy, K. R. (1993). *Honesty in the workplace.* Pacific Grove, CA: Brooks/Cole.

Murray, B. (1997, May). Is it a rise in ADHD, or in students' false claims? *APA Monitor.*

Murray, H. (1938). *Explorations in personality.* New York: Oxford University Press.

Murray, H. (1943). *Thematic apperception test manual.* Cambridge, MA: Harvard University Press.

Musto, D. F. (1991). Opium, cocaine and marijuana in American history. *Scientific American, 265,* 40–47.

Musto, D. F. (1996, April). Alcohol in American history. *Scientific American,* 78–83.

Mydans, S. (1997, February 2). Legal euthanasia: Australia faces a grim reality. *New York Times International.*

Myers, D. G., & Diener, E. (1996, May). The pursuit of happiness. *Scientific American,* 70–72.

Myers, L. (1992, March 12). Nerd-for-a-day is harassed, teased, shunned. *San Diego Union-Tribune,* A-3.

Myrtek, M. (1995). Type A behavior pattern, personality factors, disease, and physiological reactivity: A meta-analytic update. *Personality and Individual Differences, 18,* 491–502.

Nagarahole, E. L. (1994, March 28). Tigers on the brink. *Time.*

NAMHC (National Advisory Mental Health Council). (1996). Basic behavioral science research for mental health: Perception, attention, learning, and memory. *American Psychologist, 51,* 133–142.

Nash, J. M. (1997, February 3). Fertile minds. *Time.*

Nash, M. (1987). What, if anything, is regressed about hypnotic age regression? A review of the empirical literature. *Psychological Bulletin, 102,* 42–52.

Nathans, J., Piantanida, T. P., Eddy, R. L., Shows, T. B., & Hogness, D. S. (1986). Molecular genetics of inherited variation in human color vision. *Science, 232,* 203–210.

National Advisory Mental Health Council. (1995). Basic behavioral science research for mental health: A national investment. *American Psychologist, 50,* 838–845.

National Center for Health Statistics. (1997). Update: Prevalence of overweight among children, adolescents, and adults—United States, 1988–1994. *Journal of the American Medical Association, 277,* 1111.

National Task Force on the Prevention and Treatment of Obesity. (1994). Weight cycling. *Journal of the American Medical Association, 272,* 1196–1202.

Nazario, S. (1993, July 5). Force to be reckoned with. *Los Angeles Times.*

Nazario, S. (1997, March 10). Schools struggle to teach lessons in life and death. *Los Angeles Times.*

NCSDR (National Commission on Sleep Disorders Research) (1993). *Wake up America: A national sleep alert.* Washington, DC: Department of Health and Human Services.

Neath, I. (1998). *Human memory.* Pacific Grove, CA: Brooks/Cole.

Neher, A. (1991). Maslow's theory of motivation: A critique. *Journal of Humanistic Psychology, 31,* 89–112.

Neisser, U. (1997). Never a dull moment. *American Psychologist, 52,* 79–81.

Neisser, U., Boodoo, G., Bourchard, T. J. Jr., Boykin, A. W., Brody N., Ceci, S. J., Halpern, D. R., Loehlin, J. C., Perloff, R., Sternberg, R. J., & Urbina, S. (1996). Intelligence: Knowns and unknowns. *American Psychologist, 51,* 77–101.

Neitz, J., Neitz, M., Kainz, P. M. (1996). Visual pigment gene structure and the severity of color vision defects. *Science, 274,* 801–803.

Neitz, M., & Neitz, J. (1995). Numbers and ratios of visual pigment genes for normal red-green color vision. *Science, 267,* 1013–1016.

Nelson, R. J., Demas, G. E., Huang, P. L., Fishman, M. C., Dawson, V. L., Dawson, T. M., & Snyder, S. H. (1995). Behavioural abnormalities in male mice lacking neuronal nitric oxide synthase. *Nature, 378,* 383–386.

Nelson, T. O. (1993). Judgments of learning and the allocation of study time. *Journal of Experimental Psychology: General, 122,* 269–273.

Nelson, T. O. (1996). Consciousness and metacognition. *American Psychologist, 51,* 102–116.

Nemeroff, C. B. (1998, June). The neurobiology of depression. *Scientific American,* 42–49.

Neugarten, B. (1994, May). Cited in B. Azar, Women are barraged by media on "the change." *APA Monitor.*

Neverlien, P. O., & Johnsen, T. B. (1991). Optimism-pessimism dimension and dental anxiety in children aged 10–12. *Community Dentistry Oral Epidemiology, 19,* 342–346.

Newman, L. S., Duff, K. J., & Baumeister, R. F. (1997). A new look at defensive projection: Through suppression, accessibility, and biased person perception. *Journal of Personality and Social Psychology, 72,* 980–1001.

Ng, W., & Lindsay, R. C. L. (1994). Cross-race facial recognition. *Journal of Cross-Cultural Psychology, 25,* 217–232.

NICHD. (1997). The effects of infant child care on infant-mother attachment security: Results of the NICHD study of early child care. *Child Development, 68,* 860–879.

Nichelli, P., Grafman, J., Pietrini, P., Alway, D., Carton, J. C., & Miletich. (1994). Brain activity in chess playing. *Nature, 369,* 191.

Niedenthal, P. M. (1992). Affect and social perception: On the psychological validity of rose-colored glasses. In R. Bornstein & T. Pittman (Eds.), *Perception without awareness.* New York: Guilford.

Niedenthal, P. M., & Setterlund, M. C. (1994). Emotion congruence in perception. *Personality and Social Psychology Bulletin, 20,* 401–411.

NIH Consensus Development Panel on cochlear implants in adults and children. (1995). Cochlear implants in adults and children. *Journal of the American Medical Association, 274,* 1955–1961.

Nishizawa, S., Benkelfat, C., Young, S. N., Leyton, M., Mezengeza, S., de Montigny, C., Plier, P., & Diksic, M. (1997). Differences between males and females in rates of serotonin synthesis in human brain. *Proceedings of the National Academy of Science, 94,* 5308–5313.

Noah, T. (1997, March 3). OK, OK, cigarettes do kill. *U.S. News & World Report.*

Nobler, M. S., & Sackeim, H. A. (1998). Mechanisms of action of electroconvulsive therapy: *Functional brain imaging studies. Psychiatric Annals, 28,* 23–29.

Noriyuki, D. (1996, February). Breaking down the walls. *Los Angeles Times,* E-1.

Norman, D. A. (1982). *Learning and memory.* New York: Freeman.

Nottebohm, F. (1989). From bird song to neurogenesis. *Scientific American, 260,* 74–79.

Nousaine, T. (1996, July). Hear today, gone tomorrow. *Stereo Review,* 71–73.

Novy, D. M., Nelson, D. V., Francis, D. J., & Turk, D. C. (1995). Perspectives of chronic pain: An evaluative comparison of restrictive and comprehensive models. *Psychological Bulletin, 118,* 238–247.

Nowak, R. (1994). Chronobiologists out of sync over light therapy patents. *Science, 263,* 1217–1218.

Nurius, P. S., & Berlin, S. S. (1994). Treatment of negative self-concept and depression. In D. K. Granvold (Ed.), *Cognitive and behavioral treatment: Methods and applications.* Pacific Grove, CA: Brooks/Cole.

Oakes, L. M., Coppage, D. J., & Dingel, A. (1997). By land or by sea: The role of perceptual similarity in infant's categorization of animals. *Developmental Psychology, 33,* 396–407.

Ohbuchi, K., & Takahashi, Y. (1994). Cultural styles of conflict management in Japanese and Americans: Passivity, covertness, and effectiveness of strategies. *Journal of Applied Social Psychology, 24,* 1345–1366.

Ojemann, J. G., Buckner, R. L., Corbetta, M., & Raichle, M. E. (1997). Imaging studies of memory and attention. *Neurosurgery Clinics of North America, 8,* 307–319.

Olanow, C. W., Kordower, J. H., & Freeman, T. B. (1996). Fetal nigral transplantation as a therapy for Parkinson's disease. *Trends in Neurosciences, 19,* 102–109.

O'Leary, A., Brown, S., & Suarez-Al-Adam, M. (1997). Stress and immune function. In T. W. Miller (Ed.), *Clinical disorders and stressful life events.* Madison, CT: International Universities Press.

Olmos, D. R. (1997, January 7). Seeing the light. *Los Angeles Times.*

Olson, L., Cheng, H., & Cao, Y. (1997, January). Cited in J. Goldberg, Mending spinal cords. *Discover.*

Olweus, O. (1995). Bullying or peer abuse at school: Facts and intervention. *Current Directions in Psychological Science, 4,* 196–200.

O'Neil, H. R., Jr., & Drillings, M. (Eds.) (1994). *Motivation: Theory and research.* Hillsdale, NJ: Lawrence Erlbaum.

Orne, M. T., & Evans, F. J. (1965). Social control in the psychological experiment: Antisocial behavior and hypnosis. *Journal of Personality and Social Psychology, 1,* 189–200.

Ornish, D. (1998). *Love & survival.* New York: HarperCollins.

Ortony, A., Clore, G., & Collins, A. (1988). *The cognitive structure of emotions.* New York: Cambridge University Press.

Osofsky, J. D. (1995). The effects of exposure to violence on young children. *American Psychologist, 50,* 782–788.

Ost, L., Helstrom, K., & Kaver, A. (1992). One versus five sessions of exposure in the treatment of injection phobia. *Behavior Therapy, 23,* 263–282.

Ostrom, T. M., Skowronski, J. J., & Nowak, A. (1994). The cognitive foundation of attitudes: It's a wonderful construct. In P. G. Devine, D. L. Hamilton, & T. M. Ostrom (Eds.), *Social cognition: Impact on social psychology.* New York: Academic Press.

Page, A. C. (1994). Blood-injury phobia. *Clinical Psychology Review, 14,* 443–461.

Page, A. C., Bennett, K. S., Carter, O., Smith, M., & Woodmore, K. (1997). The blood-injection symptoms scale (BISS) assessing a structure of phobic symptoms elicited by blood and injections. *Behaviour Research and Therapy, 35,* 457–464.

Paikoff, R. L., & Brooks-Gunn, J. (1991). Do parent-child relationships change during puberty? *Psychological Bulletin, 110,* 47–66.

Painter, K. (1997, August 15–17). Doctors have prenatal test for 450 genetic diseases. *USA Today.*

Pappas, G. D., Lazorthes, Y., Bes, J. C., Tafani, M., & Winnie, A. P. (1997). Relief of intractable cancer pain by human chromaffic cell transplants: Experience at two medical centers. *Neurological Research, 19,* 71–77.

Park, B., DeKay, M. L., & Kraus, S. (1994). Aggregating social behavior in person models: Perceiver-induced consistency. *Journal of Personality and Social Psychology, 66,* 437–459.

Parks, G. (1997). *Half past autumn.* New York: Bulfinch Press & Little, Brown & Company.

Patterson, D. R., Everett, J. J., Bombadier, C. H., Questad, K. A., Lee, V. K., & Marvin, J. A. (1993). Psychological effects of severe burn injuries. *Psychological Bulletin, 113,* 362–378.

Patterson, G. R. (1994, October). Cited in B. Azar & S. Sleek, Do roots of violence grow from nature or nurture? *APA Monitor.*

Patton, G. C., Harris, R., Carlin, J. B., Hibbert, M. E., Coffey, C., Schwartz, M., & Bowes, G. (1997). Adolescent suicidal behaviours: A population-based study of risk. *Psychological Medicine, 27,* 715–724.

Paul, S. M., Extein, I., Calil, H. M., Potter, W. Z., Chodoff, P., & Goodwin, F. K. (1981). Use of ECT with treatment-resistant depressed patients at the National Institute of Mental Health. *American Journal of Psychiatry, 138,* 486–489.

Paulesu, E., Frith, C. D., & Frackowiak, R. S. J. (1993). The neural correlates of the verbal component of working memory. *Nature, 362,* 342–345.

Paulhus, D. L., Fridhandler, B., & Hayes, S. (1997). Psychological defense. In R. Hogan, J. Johnson, & S. Briggs (Eds.), *Handbook of personality psychology.* New York: Academic Press.

Payne, D. G., Toglia, M. P., & Anastasi, J. S. (1994). Recognition performance level and the magnitude of the misinformation effect in eyewitness memory. *Psychonomic Bulletin and Review, 1,* 376–382.

Payte, J. T. (1997). Methadone maintenance treatment: The first thirty years. *Journal of Psychoactive Drugs, 29,* 149–153.

Peele, S. (1997). Utilizing culture and behaviour in epidemiological models of alcohol consumption and consequences of western nations. *Alcohol & Alcoholism, 32,* 51–64.

Pelham, W. E., Bender, M. E., Caddell, J., Booth, S., & Moorer, S. H. (1985). Methylphenidate and children with attention deficit disorder. *Archives of General Psychiatry, 42,* 948–952.

Pennebaker, J. W., Colder, M., & Sharp, L. (1990). Accelerating the coping process. *Journal of Personality and Social Psychology, 58,* 528–537.

Pennebaker, J. W., & Memon, A. (1996). Recovered memories in context: Thoughts and elaborations on Bowers and Farvolden, 1996). *Psychological Bulletin, 119,* 381–385.

Perry, C. (1997). Admissibility and per se exclusion of hypnotically elicited recall in American courts of law. *International Journal of Clinical and Experimental Hypnosis, 45,* 266–279.

Perry, T. (1995, May 28). Woman's work. *Los Angeles Times.*

Persons, J. B. (1997). Dissemination of effective methods: Behavior therapy's next challenge. *Behavior Therapy, 28,* 465–471.

Pert, C. B., Snowman, A. M., & Snyder, S. H. (1974). Localization of opiate receptor binding in presynaptic membranes of rat brain. *Brain Research, 70,* 184–188.

Peters, J. (1997, May 12). After sudden defeat, it's Kasparov who's blue. *Los Angeles Times.*

Peterson, K. S. (1997, July 22). Helping procrastinators get to it. *USA Today.*

Peterson, L., & Brown, D. (1994). Integrating child injury and abuse-neglect research: Common histories, etiologies, and solutions. *Psychological Bulletin, 116,* 293–315.

Peterson, L. R., & Peterson, M. J. (1950). Short-term retention of individual verbal terms. *Journal of Experimental Psychology, 58,* 193–198.

Peterson, M. A., & Gibson, B. S. (1994). Must figure-ground organization precede object recognition? *Psychological Science, 5,* 253–259.

Petitto, L. A. (1997, December 11). Cited in R. L. Hotz, The brain: Designed to speak the mind. *Los Angeles Times.*

Petitto, L. A., & Marentette, P. F. (1991). Babbling in the manual mode: Evidence for the ontogeny of language. *Science, 251,* 1493–1496.

Petrill, S. A. (1998). Molarity versus modularity of cognitive functioning? A behavioral genetic perspective. *Current Directions in Psychological Science, 6,* 96–99.

Petty, R. E., & Cacioppo, J. T. (1986). *Attitudes and persuasion: Classic and contemporary approaches.* Dubuque, IA: William C. Brown.

Petty, R. E., Wegener, D. T., & Fabrigar, L. R. (1997). Attitudes and attitude change. *Annual Review of Psychology, 46,* 609–647.

Peyser, M., Biddle, N. A., Brant, M., Wingert, P., Hackworth, D. H., & O'Shea, M. (1995, August 28). Sounding retreat. *Newsweek.*

Pezdek, K. (1995, February 11). Cited in M. Dolan, When the mind's eye blinks. *Los Angeles Times.*

Piaget, J. (1929). *The child's conception of the world.* New York: Harcourt Brace.

Pich, E. M., Pagliusi, S. R., Tessari, M., Talabot-Ayer, D., van Huijsduijnen, R. H., & Chiamulera, C. (1997). Common neural substrates for the addictive properties of nicotine and cocaine. *Science, 275,* 83–86.

Piliavin, J. A., Dovidio, J. F., Gaertner, S. L., & Clark, R. D. (1982). Responsive bystanders: The process of intervention. In V. J. Derlega & J. Grzelak (Eds.), *Cooperation and helping behavior.* Orlando, FL: Academic Press.

Pillard, R. C., & Bailey, M. J. (1995). A biologic perspective on sexual orientation. *The Psychiatric Clinics of North America, 18,* 71–84.

Pillemer, D. B. (1984). Flashbulb memories of the assassination attempt on President Reagan. *Cognition, 16,* 63–80.

Pines, A. M. (1993). Burnout. In L. Goldberger & S. Breznitz (Eds.), *Handbook of stress: Theoretical and clinical aspects* (2nd ed.). New York: Free Press.

Pingitore, R., Dugoni, B. L., Tindale, R. S., & Spring. B. (1994). Bias against overweight job applicants in a simulated employment interview. *Journal of Applied Psychology, 79,* 909–917.

Pinker, S. (1994). *The language instinct.* New York: William Morrow.

Pinker, S. (1995). Introduction. In M. S. Gazzaniga (Ed.), *The cognitive neurosciences.* Cambridge, MA: MIT Press.

Piomelli, D. (1997). Cited in J. Travis, Brain doubles up on marijuana-like agents. *Science News, 152,* 118.

Pitman, R. (1994, August 4). Cited in N. Wartik, The amazingly simply inexplicable therapy that just might work. *Los Angeles Times Magazine.*

Plazzi, B., Corsini, R., Provini, R., Pierangeli, G., Martinelli, P., Montagna, P., Lugaresi, E., & Cortelli, P. (1997). REM sleep behavior disorders in multiple system atrophy. *Neurology, 48,* 1094–1097.

Plomin, R. (1997, May). Cited in B. Azar, Nature, nurture: not mutually exclusive. *APA Monitor.*

Plomin, R., Owen, M. J., & McGuffin, P. (1994). The genetic basis of complex human behaviors. *Science, 264,* 1733–1739.

Plomin, R., & Petrill, S. A. (1997). Genetics and intelligence: What's new? *Intelligence, 24,* 53–77.

Plomin, R., & Rutter, M. (1998). Child development, molecular genetics and what to do with genes once they are found. *Child Development, 69,* 68–71.

Plug, C., & Ross, H. E. (1994). The natural mood illusion: A multifactor angular account. *Perception, 23,* 321–333.

Plummer, W., & Ridenhour, R. (1995, August 28). Saving grace. *People.*

Plutchik, R. (1993). Emotions and their vicissitudes: Emotions and psychopathology. In M. Lewis & J. M. HaViland (Eds.), *Handbook of emotions.* New York: Guilford Press.

Polaschek, D. L. L., Ward, T., & Hudson, S. M. (1997). Rape and rapists: Theory and treatment. *Clinical Psychology Review, 17,* 117–144.

Pollack, M. H., & Otto, M. W. (1997). Long-term course and outcome of panic disorder. *Journal of Clinical Psychiatry, 58* (supplement 2), 57–60.

Polymeropoulos, M. H., Higgins, J. J., Golbe, L. I., Johnson, W. G., Ide, S. E., Iorio, G. D., Sanges, G., Stenroos, E. S., Pho, L. T., Schaffer, A. A., Lazzarini, A. M., Nussbaum, A. L., Duvoisin, R. C. (1996). Mapping of a gene for Parkinson's disease to chromosome 4q21–q23. *Science, 274,* 1197–1198.

Pomerleau, A., Bolduc, D., Malcuit, G., & Cossette, L. (1990). Pink or blue: Environmental gender stereotypes in the first two years of life. *Sex Roles, 22,* 359–367.

Ponsi, M. (1997). Interaction and transference. *International Journal of Psycho-Analysis, 78,* 243–263.

Porkka-Heiskanen, T., Strecker, R. E., Thakkar, M., Bjorkum, A. A., Greene, R. W., McCarley, R. W. (1997). Adenosine: A mediator of the sleep-inducing effects of prolonged wakefulness. *Science, 276,* 1265–1268.

Portillo, E., Jr. (1994, June 17). Minority graduates choose to succeed. *San Diego Union-Tribune.*

Portin, P., & Alanen, Y. O. (1997). A critical review of genetic studies of schizophrenia. II. Molecular genetic studies. *Acta Psychiatrica Scandinavica, 95,* 73–80.

Portman, K., & Radanov, B. P. (1997). Dental anxiety and illness behaviour. *Psychotherapy and Psychosomatics, 66,* 141–144.

Posner, M. I. (1997). Introduction: Neuroimaging of cognitive processes. *Cognitive Psychology, 33,* 2–4.

Posner, M. I., & Dehaene, S. (1994). Attentional networks. *Trends in Neuroscience, 17,* 75–79.

Post, R. (1994). Creativity and psychopathology: A study of 291 world-famous men. *British Journal of Psychiatry, 165,* 22–34.

Postmes, T., & Spears, R. (1998). Deindividuation and antinormative behavior: A meta-analysis. *Psychological Bulletin, 13,* 238–259.

Poulton, R., Thomson, W. M., Davies, S., Kruger E., Brown, R. H., & Silva, P. (1997). Good teeth, bad teeth, and fear of the dentist. *Behaviour Research and Therapy, 35,* 327–334.

Powell, D. H., & Whitla, D. K. (1994). Normal cognitive aging: Toward empirical perspectives. *Current Directions in Psychological Science, 3,* 27–31.

Pratkanis, A. R. (1992). The cargo cult science of subliminal persuasion. *Skeptical Inquirer, 16,* 260–286.

Prescott, C. A., Hewitt, J. K., Truett, K. R., Heath, A. C., Neale, M. C., & Eaves, L. J. (1994). Genetic and environmental influences on alcohol-related problems in a volunteer sample of older twins. *Journal of Studies on Alcohol, 55,* 184–202.

Pressley, M., Yokoi, L., van Meter, P., Van Etten, S., & Freebern, G. (1997). Some of the reasons why preparing for exams is so hard: What can be done to make it easier? *Educational Psychology Review, 9,* 1–38.

Pressman, M. R., & Orr, W. C. (Eds.) (1997). *Understanding sleep: The evaluation and treatment of sleep disorders.* Washington, DC: American Psychological Association.

Priest, R. G., Terzano, M. G., & Boyer, P. (1997). Efficacy of zolpidem in insomnia. *European Psychiatry, 12* (Supplement), 5s–14s.

Priester, J. R., & Petty, R. E. (1995). Source attributions and persuasion: Perceived honesty as a determinant of message scrutiny. *Personality and Social Psychology Bulletin, 21,* 637–654.

Prince, A., & Smolensky, P. (1997). Optimality: From neural networks to universal grammar. *Science, 75,* 1604–1610.

Prince, S. E., & Jacobson, N. S. (1997). A review and evaluation of marital and family therapies for affective disorders. *Journal of Marital and Family Therapy, 21,* 377–402.

Project Match Research Group. (1997). Matching alcoholism treatments to client heterogeneity: Project MATCH posttreatment drinking outcomes. *Journal of Studies on Alcohol, 58,* 7–29.

Pruitt, D. G. (1971). Choice shifts in group discussion: An introductory review. *Journal of Personality and Social Psychology, 20,* 339–360.

Pullum, G. K. (1991). *The great Eskimo vocabulary hoax.* Chicago: University of Chicago Press.

Putnam, P. (1995, April). Cited in T. DeAngelis, Research documents trauma of abuse. *APA Monitor.*

Quadrel, M. J., Fischhoff, B., & Davis, W. (1993). Adolescent (in)vulnerability. *American Psychologist, 48,* 102–116.

Rabheru, K., & Persad, E. (1997). A review of continuation and maintenance electroconvulsive therapy. *Canadian Journal of Psychiatry, 42,* 476–484.

Rabkin, J. G., & Ferrando, S. (1997). A "second life" agenda. *Archives of General Psychiatry, 54,* 1049–1053.

Rabkin, S. W., Boyko, E., Shane, F., & Kaufert, J. (1984). A randomized trial comparing smoking cessation programs utilizing behavior modification, health education or hypnosis. *Addictive Behaviors, 9,* 157–173.

Raichle, M. E. (1994). Visualizing the mind. *Scientific American, 270,* 58–64.

Rainville, P., Duncan, G. H., Price, D. D., Carrier, B., & Bushnell, M. C. (1997). Pain affect encoded in human anterior cingulate but not somatosensory cortex. *Science, 277,* 968–971.

Rajkowska, G., Selemon, L. D., & Goldman-Rakic, P. S. (1997). Neuronal and glial somal size in the prefrontal cortex. *Archives of General Psychiatry, 55,* 215–224.

Rakic, P. (1985). Limits of neurogenesis in primates. *Science, 227,* 1054–1055.

Raloff, J. (1995). Languishing languages: Cultures at risk. *Science News, 147,* 117.

Raloff, J. (1997). FDA can regulate tobacco as a device. *Science News, 151,* 268.

Ralph, M. R., Foster, R. G., Davis, F. C., & Menaker, M. (1990). Transplanted suprachiasmatic nucleus determines circadian period. *Science, 247,* 975–978.

Ralston, J. (1989, April). Cited in S. Chollar, Conversations with the dolphins. *Psychology Today.*

Ramachandran, V. S., & Anstis, S. M. (1986). The perception of apparent motion. *Scientific American, 254,* 102–109.

Ramey, C. T., MacPhee, D., & Yeates, K. O. (1982). Preventing developmental retardation: A general system model. In D. K. Detterman & R. J. Sternberg (Eds.), *How and how much can intelligence be increased?* Norwood, NJ: Ablex Publishing.

Ransdell, E., & Eddings, J. (1994, May 9). The man of the moment. *U.S. News & World Report.*

Rao, S. C., Rainer, G., & Miller, E. K. (1997). Integration of what and where in the primate prefrontal cortex. *Science, 276,* 821–824.

Rapoport, J. L. (1988). The neurobiology of obsessive-compulsive disorder. *Journal of the American Medical Association, 260,* 2888–2890.

Rapoport, J. L., Buchsbaum, M. S., Weingartner, H., Zahn, T. P., Ludlow, C., & Mikkelsen, E. J. (1980). Dextroamphetamine: Its cognitive and behavioral effects in normal and hyperactive boys and normal men. *Archives of General Psychiatry, 37,* 933–942.

Rapport, M. D. (1994). Attention-deficit hyperactivity disorder. In V. B. Van Hasselt & M. Hersen (Eds.), *Advanced abnormal psychology.* New York: Plenum Press.

Rapport, M. D., Denney, C., DuPaul, G. J., & Bardner, M. J. (1994). Attention deficit disorder and methylphenidate; Normalization rates, clinical effectiveness, and response prediction in 76 children. *Journal of the American Academy of Child and Adolescent Psychiatry, 33,* 882–893.

Rauch, S. L., & Renshaw, P. F. (1995). Clinical neuroimaging in psychiatry. *Harvard Review of Psychiatry, 2,* 297–312.

Ray, W. J. (1997). EEG concomitants of hypnotic susceptibility. *International Journal of Clinical and Experimental Hypnosis, 45,* 301–313.

Rechtschaffen, A. (1997, August). Cited in T. Geier, What is sleep for? *U.S. News & World Report.*

Redelmeier, D. A., & Tibshirani, R. J. (1997). Association between cellular-telephone calls and motor vehicle collisions. *New England Journal of Medicine, 336,* 453–458.

Reed, C. F. (1996). The immediacy of the moon illusion. *Perception, 25,* 1295–1300.

Reed, M. K. (1994). Social skills training to reduce depression in adolescents. *Adolescence, 29,* 293–302.

Reed, S., & Breu, G. (1995, June 6). The wild ones. *People.*

Reed, S., & Esselman, M. (1995, August 28). Catching hell. *People.*

Reed, S., & Free, C. (1995, October 16). The big payoff. *People.*

Reed, S., & Stambler, L. (1992, May 25). The umpire strikes back. *People,* 87–88.

Reeve, C. (1998). *Still me.* New York: Random House.

Register, A. C., Beckham, J. C., May, J. G., & Gustafson, D. J. (1991). Stress inoculation bibliotherapy in the treatment of test anxiety. *Journal of Counseling Psychology, 38,* 115–119.

Reid, J. B., Taplin, P. S., & Lorber, R. (1981). A social interactional approach to the treatment of abusive families. In R. B. Stuart (Ed.), *Violent behavior: Social learning approaches to prediction, management and treatment.* New York: Brunner/Mazel.

Reiman, E. M., Lane, R. D., Ahern, G. L., Schwartz, G. E., Davidson, R. J., Friston, K. J., Yun, L. S., & Cen, K. (1997). Neuroanatomical correlates of externally and internally generated human emotion. *American Journal of Psychiatry, 154,* 918–925.

Relman, A. S. (Ed.). (1982). *Marijuana and health.* Washington, DC: National Academy Press.

Renfrey, G., & Spates, C. R. (1994). Eye movement desensitization: A partial dismantling study. *Journal of Behavior Therapy and Experimental Psychiatry, 25,* 231–239.

Reppert, S. (1997). Cited in M. Barinaga, How jet-lag hormone does double duty in the brain. *Science, 277,* 480.

Rescorla, R. A. (1966). Predictability and number of pairings in Pavlovian fear conditioning. *Psychonomic Science, 4,* 383–384.

Rescorla, R. A. (1987). A Pavlovian analysis of goal-directed behavior. *American Psychologist, 42,* 119–129.

Rescorla, R. A. (1988). Pavlovian conditioning. *American Psychologist, 43,* 151–160.

Research Triangle Institute. (1994). *Past and future directions of the D.A.R.E. program: An evaluation review.* National Institute of Justice.

Resnick, M., Bearman, P. S., Blum, R. W., Bauman, K. E., Harris, K. H., Jones, J.,

Tabor, J., Beuhring, T., Sieving, R. E., Shew, M., Ireland, M., Bearinger, L. H., & Udry, J. R. (1997). Protecting adolescents from harm. *Journal of the American Medical Association, 278,* 823–832.

Rey, G. (1983). Concepts and stereotypes. *Cognition, 15,* 237–262.

Reyna, V. F., & Lloyd, F. (1997). Theories of false memory in children and adults. *Learning and Individual Differences, 9,* 95–123.

Reyneri, A. (1984). The nose knows, but science doesn't. *Science.*

Reynes, R. L. (1996). The dream, communication, and attunement. *Psychotherapy, 33,* 479–483.

Reynolds, A. J. (1994). Effects of a preschool plus follow-on intervention for children at risk. *Developmental Psychology, 30,* 787–804.

Rhodes, G., & Tremewan, T. (1996). Averageness, exaggeration, and facial attractiveness. *Psychological Science, 7,* 105–110.

Rhue, J. W., Lynn, S. J., & Kirsch, I. (Eds.) (1994). *Handbook of clinical hypnosis.* Washington, DC: American Psychological Association.

Richardson, G. (1997, December). Cited in B. Azar, Researchers debunk myth of the "crack baby." *APA Monitor.*

Richardson, G. E., & Day, N. L. (1994). Detrimental effects of prenatal cocaine exposure: Illusion or reality. *Journal of the American Academy of Child and Adolescent Psychiatry, 33,* 28–34.

Richardson, L. (1994, June 7). OK, so I'll never be a waif. *Los Angeles Times.*

Richmond, R. L., Kehoe, L., & de Almeida Neto, A. C. (1997). Effectiveness of a 24-hour transdermal nicotine patch in conjunction with a cognitive behavioural programme: One year outcome. *Addiction, 92,* 27–31.

Richter, P. (1997, April 17). Pentagon to OK peyote for religious rites. *Los Angeles Times.*

Richters, J. M. A. (1997). Menopause in different cultures. *Journal of Psychosomatic Obstetrics and Gynecology, 18,* 73–80.

Rieke, M. L., & Gaustello, S. J. (1995). Unresolved issues in honesty and integrity testing. *American Psychologist, 50,* 458–459.

Rieker, P. P., & Carmen, E. H. (1986). The victim-to-patient process: The discomfirmation and transformation of abuse. *American Journal of Orthopsychiatry, 56,* 360–370.

Risold, P. Y., & Swanson, L. W. (1996). Structural evidence for functional domains in the rat hippocampus. *Science, 272,* 1484–1486.

Rivas-Vazquez, R. A., & Blais, M. A. (1997). Selective serotonin reuptake inhibitors and atypical antidepressants: A review and update for psychologists. *Professional Psychology: Research and Practice, 28,* 526–536.

Rivers, P. C. (1994). *Alcohol and human behavior.* Englewood Cliffs, NJ: Wiley.

Roan, S. (1997, March 26). Faint chances. *Los Angeles Times.*

Roan, S. (1997, June 11). A losing gamble. *Los Angeles Times.*

Roberts, M. J. (1993). Human reasoning: Deduction rules or mental models, or both.

Quarterly *Journal of Experimental Psychology, 46A*, 569–589.

Roberts, S. B. (1997). Cited in J. Raloff, Getting older—and a little rounder? *Science News, 152,* 282.

Robins, L. N., & Regier, D. A. (Eds.) (1991). *Psychiatric disorders in America.* New York: Free Press.

Robins, L. N., Tipp, J., Przybeck, T. (1991). Antisocial personality. In L. N. Robins, & D. A. Regier (Eds.), *Psychiatric disorders in America.* New York: Free Press.

Robinson, R. G. (1995). Mapping brain activity associated with emotion. *American Journal of Psychiatry, 152,* 327–329.

Robinson-Riegler, B., & McDaniel, M. A. (1994). Further constraints on the bizarreness effect: Elaboration at encoding. *Memory and Cognition, 22,* 702–712.

Rock, I., & Palmer, S. (1990). The legacy of Gestalt psychology. *Scientific American, 263,* 84–90.

Rodgers, J. E. (1982). The malleable memory of eyewitnesses. *Science.*

Rodriguez-Tome, H., Bariaud, F., Cohen-Zardi, M. F., Delmas, C., Jeanvoine, F., & Szylagyi, P. (1993). The effects of pubertal changes on body image and relations with peers of the opposite sex in adolescence. *Journal of Adolescence, 16,* 421–438.

Rogers, C. R. (1951). *Client-centered therapy: Its current practice, implications, and theory.* Boston: Houghton Mifflin.

Rogers, C. R. (1980). *A way of being.* Boston: Houghton Mifflin.

Rogers, C. R. (1986). Client-centered therapy. In I. L. Kutash & A. Wolf (Eds.), *Psychotherapists' casebook.* San Francisco: Jossey-Bass.

Rogers, C. R. (1989). Cited in N. J. Raskin & C. R. Rogers, Person-centered therapy. In R. J. Corsini & D. Wedding (Eds.), *Current psychotherapies* (4th ed.). Itasca, IL: F. E. Peacock.

Rogoff, B., & Chavajay, P. (1995). What's become of research on the cultural basis of cognitive development? *American Psychologist, 50,* 859–877.

Rokicki, L. A., Holroyd, K. A., France, C. R., Lipchik, G. L., France, J. L., & Kvaal, S. A. (1997). Change mechanisms associated with combined relaxation/EMG biofeedback training for chronic tension headache. *Applied Psychophysiology and Biofeedback, 22,* 21–41.

Romney, D. M., & Bynner, J. M. (1997). A re-examination of the relationship between shyness, attributional style, and depression. *Journal of Genetic Psychology, 158,* 261–270.

Rorer, L. G. (1990). Personality assessment: A conceptual survey. In L. A. Pervin (Ed.), *Handbook of personality: Theory and research.* New York: Guilford Press.

Rorschach, R. (1921; reprinted 1942). *Psychodiagnostics.* Bern: Hans Huber.

Rortvedt, A. K., & Miltenberger, R. G. (1994). Analysis of a high-probability instructional sequence and time-out in the treatment of child noncompliance. *Journal of Applied Behavior Analysis, 27,* 327–330.

Rosch, E. (1978). Principles of categorization. In E. Rosch & B. B. Lloyd (Eds.), *Cognition and categorization.* Hillsdale, NJ: Lawrence Erlbaum.

Rosch, P. J. (1994). Does stress cause hypertension? *Stress Medicine, 10,* 141–143.

Rose, F. D., Attree, E. A., & Johnson, D. A. (1996). Virtual reality: An assistive technology in neurological rehabilitation. *Current Opinion in Neurology, 9,* 461–467.

Rosenberg, H. (1993). Prediction of controlled drinking by alcoholics and problem drinkers. *Psychological Bulletin, 113,* 129–139.

Rosenberg, K. P. (1994). Notes and comments: Biology and homosexuality. *Journal of Sex and Marital Therapy, 20,* 147–150.

Rosenfeld, J. P. (1995). Alternative views of Bashore and Rapp's (1993) alternatives to traditional polygraphy: A critique. *Psychological Bulletin, 117,* 159–166.

Rosenfeld, J. V. (1996). Minimally invasive neurosurgery. *Australian Journal of Surgery, 66,* 553–559.

Rosenthal, M. S. (1994). The 1993 distinguished lecturer in substance abuse. *Journal of Substance Abuse Treatment, 11,* 3–7.

Rosenthal, N. E. (1993). Diagnosis and treatment of seasonal affective disorder. *Journal of the American Medical Association, 270,* 2717–2720.

Rosenthal, R. H. (1993). Relationships of the type A behavior pattern with coronary heart disease. In L. Goldberger & S. Breznitz (Eds.), *Handbook of stress: Theoretical and clinical aspects* (2nd ed.). New York: Free Press.

Rosenthal, R. (1994). Science and ethics in conducting, analyzing, and reporting psychological research. *Psychological Science, 5,* 127–134.

Rosenthal, S. L., Burklow, K. A., Lewis, L. M., Succop, P. A., & Biro, F. M. (1997). Heterosexual romantic relationships and sexual behaviors of young adolescent girls. *Journal of Adolescent Health, 21,* 238–243.

Rosenzweig, M. R. (1992). Psychological science around the world. *American Psychologist, 47,* 718–722.

Ross, B. M., & Millsom, C. (1970). Repeated memory of oral prose in Ghana and New York. *International Journal of Psychology, 5,* 173–181.

Ross, P. E. (1991). Hard words. *Scientific American, 264,* 138–147.

Rossi, A. S. (Ed.). (1994). *Sexuality across the life course.* Chicago: University of Chicago Press.

Rostan, S. M. (1994). Problem finding, problem solving, and cognitive controls: An empirical investigation of critically acclaimed productivity. *Creativity Research Journal, 7,* 79–110.

Rothbart, M. K., & Bates, J. E. (1998). Temperament. In W. Damon & R. M. Lerner (Eds.), *Handbook of child psychology* (Vol. 1). New York: John Wiley & Sons.

Rothenberg, S. A. (1997). Introduction to sleep disorders. In M. R. Pressman & W. C. Orr (Eds.), *Understanding sleep: The evaluation and treatment of sleep disorders.* Washington, DC: American Psychological Association.

Rotter, J. B. (1966). Generalized expectancies for internal versus external locus of control of reinforcement. *Psychological Monographs: General and Applied, 80* (Whole No. 609).

Rotter, J. B. (1990). Internal versus external control of reinforcement: A case history of a variable. *American Psychologist, 45,* 489–493.

Routh, D. K. (1994). *The founding of clinical psychology (1896) and some important early developments: Introduction.* New York: Plenum Publishing.

Rowatt, W. C., Nesselroade, K. P., Jr., Beggan, J. K., & Allison, S. T. (1997). Perceptions of brainstorming in groups: The quality-over-quantity hypothesis. *Journal of Creative Behavior, 31,* 131–151.

Rowe, D. C. (1997). Genetics, temperament, and personality. In R. Hogan, J. Johnson, & S. Briggs (Eds.), *Handbook of personality psychology.* New York: Academic Press.

Roy-Byrne, P. P., & Fann, J. R. (1997). Psychopharmacologic treatments for patients with neuropsychiatric disorders. In S. C. Yudofsky & R. E. Hales, (Eds.). *American Psychiatric Press textbook of neuropsychiatry* (3rd ed.). Washington, DC: American Psychiatric Press.

Rozin, P. (1986). One-trial acquired likes and dislikes in humans: Disgust as a U.S. food predominance, and negative learning predominance. *Learning and Motivation, 17,* 180–189.

Rozin, P., Markwith, M., & Stoess, C. (1997). Moralization and becoming a vegetarian. *Psychological Science, 8,* 67–73.

Rubin, D. C., & Kozin, M. (1984). Vivid memories. *Cognition, 16,* 81–95.

Ruble, D. N., & Martin, C. L. (1998). Gender development. In W. Damon & R. M. Lerner (Eds.), *Handbook of child psychology* (Vol. 1). New York: John Wiley & Sons.

Ruegg, R., & Frances, A. (1995). New research in personality disorders. *Journal of Personality Disorders, 9,* 1–48.

Rugg, M. (1995). La difference vive. *Nature, 373,* 561–562.

Rushdie, S. (1988). *The satanic verses.* New York: Viking-Penguin.

Saarni, C., Mumme, D. L., & Campos, J. J. (1998). Emotional development: Action, communication, and understanding. In W. Damon & N. Eisenberg (Eds.), *Handbook of Child Psychology* (5th ed.). New York: John Wiley & Sons.

Sackeim, H. A., & Stern, Y. (1997). Neuropsychiatric aspects of memory and amnesia. In S. C. Yudofsky & R. E. Hales, (Eds.). *The American Psychiatric Press textbook of neuropsychiatry* (3rd ed.). Washington, DC: American Psychiatric Press.

Sacks, O. (1995). *An anthropologist on Mars.* New York: Alfred A. Knopf.

Saffran, J. R., Aslin, R. N., & Newport, E. L. (1996). Statistical learning by 8-month-old infants. *Science, 274,* 1926–1928.

Salgado, J. F. (1997). The five-factor model of personality and job performance in the European Community. *Journal of Applied Psychology, 82,* 30–43.

References

Siliciano, R. (1997). Cited in M. Balter, HIV survives drug onslaught by hiding out in T cells. *Science, 278,* 1227.

Silver, W. (1997, July 8). Cited in S. L. Jones, High schoolers learn that smell is a matter of taste. *San Diego Union-Tribune.*

Simonton, D. K. (1994). *Greatness.* New York: Guilford Press.

Sinclair, R. C., Hoffman, C., Mark, M. J., Martin, L. L., & Pickering, T. L. (1994). Construct accessibility and the misattribution of arousal: Schachter and Singer revisited. *Psychological Science 5,* 15–25.

Singelis, T., Choo, P., & Hatfield, E. (1995). Love schemas and romantic love. *Journal of Social Behavior and Personality, 10,* 15–36.

Singer, M. T., & Lalich, J. (1997). *Crazy therapies: What are they? Do they work?* San Francisco: Jossey-Bass.

Skaar, K. L., Tsho, J. Y., McClure, J. B., Cinciripini, P. M., Friedman, K., Wetter, D. W., & Gritz, E. R. (1997). Smoking cessation 1: An overview of research. *Behavioral Medicine, 23,* 5–13.

Skerrett, P. J. (1994, October). Turning back the clock. *Popular Science.*

Skinner, B. F. (1938). *The behavior of organisms.* New York: Appleton-Century-Crofts.

Skinner, B. F. (1953). *Science and human behavior.* New York: Macmillan.

Skinner, B. F. (1957). *Verbal behavior.* New York: Appleton-Century-Crofts.

Skinner, B. F. (1989). The origin of cognitive thought. *American Psychologist, 44,* 13–18.

Sleek, S. (1994, December). Psychology takes the fear out of flying. *APA Monitor.*

Sleek, S. (1995, June). Unlocking the restrictions on drinking. *APA Monitor.*

Sloan, R. P., Shapiro, P. A., Bagiella, E., Boni, S. M., Paik, M., Bigger, J. T., Jr., Steinman, R. C., & Gorman, J. M. (1994). Effect of mental stress throughout the day on cardiac autonomic control. *Biological Psychology, 37,* 89–99.

Sloman, S. A. (1996). The empirical case for two systems of reasoning. *Psychological Bulletin, 119,* 3–22.

Slone, K. C. (1985). *They're rarely too young . . . and never too old "to twinkle"!* Ann Arbor, MI: Shar Publications.

Slutske, W. S., Heath, A. C., Dinwiddie, S. H., Madden, P. A. F., Bucholz, K. K., Dunne, M. P., Statham, D. J., & Martin, N. G. (1997). Modeling genetic and environmental influences in the etiology of conduct disorder: A study of 2,682 adult twin pairs. *Journal of Abnormal Psychology, 106,* 266–279.

Small, G. W., Propper, M. W., Randolph, E. T., & Spencer, E. (1991). Mass hysteria among student performers: Social relationship as a symptom predictor. *American Journal of Psychiatry, 148,* 1200–1205.

Smith, C. A., & Ellsworth, P. C. (1985). Patterns of cognitive appraisal in emotion. *Journal of Personality and Social Psychology, 48,* 813–838.

Smith, D. (1982). Trends in counseling and psychotherapy. *American Psychologist, 37,* 802–809.

Smith, E. E., & Jonides, J. (1997). Working memory: A view from neuroimaging. *Cognitive Psychology, 33,* 5–42.

Smith, E. R. (1994). Social cognition contributions to attribution theory and research. In P. G. Devine, D. L. Hamilton, & T. M. Ostrom (Eds.), *Social cognition: Impact on social psychology.* New York: Academic Press.

Smith, J. C., & Seidel, J. M. (1982). The factor structure of self-reported physical stress reactions. *Biofeedback and Self-Regulation, 7,* 35–47.

Smith, L. (1993, July 13). Men in the making. *Los Angeles Times.*

Smith, P. B., Dugan, S., & Trompenaars, F. (1997). Locus of control and affectivity by gender and occupational status: A 14-nation study. *Sex Roles, 36,* 51–77.

Snow, R. E., & Jackson, D. N., III. (1994). Individual differences in conation: Selected constructs and measures. In H. F. O'Neil, Jr., & M. Drillings (Eds.), *Motivation: Theory and research.* Hillsdale, NJ: Lawrence Erlbaum.

Snyder, C. R., Shenkel, R. J., & Lowery, C. R. (1977). Acceptance of personality interpretations: The "Barnum effect" and beyond. *Journal of Consulting and Clinical Psychology, 45,* 104–114.

Sobin, C., Sackeim, H. A., Prudic, J., Devanant, D. P., Moody, B. J., & McElhiney, M. C. (1995). Predictors of retrograde amnesia following ECT. *American Journal of Psychiatry, 152,* 995–1001.

Socolar, R., & Stein, R. E. K. (1995). Spanking infants and toddlers: Maternal belief and practice. *Pediatrics, 95,* 105–111.

Solomon, D. A., Keller, M. B., Leon, A. C., Mueller, T. I., Shea, M. R., Warshaw, M., Maser, J. D., Coryell, W., & Endicott, J. (1997). Recovery from major depression. *Archives of General Psychiatry, 54,* 1001–1006.

Somers, V. K., Phil, D., Dyken, M. E., Mark, A. L., & Abboud, F. M. (1993). Sympathetic-nerve activity during sleep in normal subjects. *New England Journal of Medicine, 328,* 303–307.

Sorbi, M. J., Maassen, G. H., & Spierings, E. L. H. (1996). A time series analysis of daily hassles and mood changes in the 3 days before the migraine attack. *Behavioral Medicine, 22,* 103–113.

Sozzi, G., Veronese, M. L., Negrini, M. J., Baffa, R., Cohicelli, M. G., Inoue, H., Tornielli, S., Pilotti, S., DeGregorio, L., & Pastorino, U. (1996). The FHIT gene 3p14.2 is abnormal in lung cancer. *Cell,* 17–26.

Spangler, D. L., Simons, A. D., Monroe, S. M., & Thase, M. E. (1997). Response to cognitive-behavioral therapy in depression: Effects on pretreatment cognitive dysfunction and life stress. *Journal of Consulting and Clinical Psychology, 65,* 568–575.

Spanos, N. P. (1994). Multiple identity enactments and multiple personality disorder: A sociocognitive perspective. *Psychological Bulletin, 116,* 143–165.

Spanos, N. P. (1996). *Multiple identities and false memories: A sociocognitive perspective.* Washington, DC: American Psychological Association.

Spearman, C. (1904). "General intelligence" objectively determined and measured. *American Journal of Psychology, 15,* 201–293.

Spelke, E. S., Breinlinger, K., Jacobson, K., & Phillips, A. (1993). Gestalt relations and object perception: A developmental study. *Perception, 22,* 1483–1501.

Sperling, G. A. (1960). The information available in brief visual presentations. *Psychological Monographs, 74* (Whole No. 498).

Sperry, R. W. (1974). Lateral specialization in the surgically separated hemisphere. In R. O. Schmitt and F. G. Worden (Eds.), *The neurosciences: Third study program.* Cambridge, MA: MIT Press.

Sperry, R. W. (1993, August). Cited in T. Deangelis, Sperry plumbs science for values and solutions. *APA Monitor.*

Spiegel, D. A., & Bruce, T. J. (1997). Benzodiazepines and exposure-based cognitive behavior therapies for panic disorder: Conclusions from combined treatment trials. *American Journal of Psychiatry, 154,* 773–781.

Spitz, H. H. (1997). Some questions about the results of the Abecedarian early intervention project cited by the APA task force on intelligence. *American Psychologist, 52,* 72.

Spitzer, R. L., Gibbon, M., Skodol, A. E., Williams, J. B. W., & First, M. B. (Eds.) (1994). *DSM-IV casebook.* Washington, DC: American Psychiatric Association.

Spohr, M. L., Willms, J., & Steinhausen, H. C. (1993). Prenatal alcohol exposure and long-term developmental consequences. *Lancet, 341,* 907–910.

Springer, S. P., & Deutsch, G. (1997). *Left brain, right brain* (5th ed.). New York: W. H. Freeman.

Squire, L. R. (1994). Declarative and nondeclarative memory: Multiple brain systems supporting learning and memory. In D. L. Schachter & E. Tulving (Eds.), *Memory systems 1994.* Cambridge, MA: MIT Press.

Squire, L. R., & Knowlton, B. J. (1995). Memory, hippocampus, and brain systems. In M. S. Gazzaniga (Ed.), *The cognitive neurosciences.* Cambridge, MA: MIT Press.

Squire, L. R., & Slater, P. C. (1983). Electroconvulsive therapy and complaints of memory dysfunction: A prospective three-year follow-up study. *British Journal of Psychiatry, 142,* 1–8.

Squire, L. R., & Zola-Morgan, S. (1991). The medial temporal lobe memory system. *Science, 253,* 1380–1386.

Squitieri, T. (1994, January 28–30). Guns soon to be No. 1 cause of injury deaths. *USA Today.*

Stahl, S. M. (1996). *Essential psychopharmacology.* New York: Cambridge University Press.

Stanley, M. A., & Turner, S. M. (1995). Current status of pharmacological and behavioral treatment of obsessive-compulsive disorder. *Behavior Therapy, 26,* 163–186.

Stanton, B., Baldwin, R. M., & Rachuba, L. (1997). A quarter century of violence in the United States. *Psychiatric Clinics of North America, 20,* 269–282.

Stanton, B., Fang, X., Li, X., Feigelman, S., Galbraith, J., & Rocardo, I. (1997). Evolution of risk behaviors over 2 years among a cohort of urban African American adolescents. *Archives of Pediatrics and Adolescent Medicine, 151,* 398–406.

Stanton, M. D., & Shadish, W. R. (1997). Outcome, attrition, and family-couples treatment for drug abuse: A meta-analysis and review of the controlled, comparative studies. *Psychological Bulletin, 122,* 170–191.

Steele, C. (1995, December 11). Cited in E. Woo, Can racial stereotypes psych out students? *Los Angeles Times,* A1.

Stein, J. (1997, March 12). A child's heavy burden. *Los Angeles Times.*

Stein, N. L., Ornstein, P. A., Tversky, B., & Brainerd, C. (Eds.) (1997). *Memory for everyday and emotional events.* Mahwah, NJ: Lawrence Erlbaum.

Steiner, R. (1989). Live TV special explores, tests psychic powers. *Skeptical Inquirer, 14,* 2–6.

Steptoe, A., & Wardle, J. (1988). Emotional fainting and the psychophysiologic response to blood and injury: Autonomic mechanisms and coping strategies. *Psychosomatic Medicine, 50,* 402–417.

Steriade, M. (1966). Arousal: Revisiting the reticular activating system. *Science, 72,* 225–226.

Stern, G. S., McCants, T. R., & Pettine, P. W. (1982). Stress and illness: Controllable and uncontrollable life events' relative contributions. *Personality and Social Psychology Bulletin, 8,* 140–143.

Stern, R. M., & Koch, K. L. (1966). Motion sickness and differential susceptibility. *Current Directions in Psychological Science, 5,* 115–119.

Sternberg, R. J. (1985). Human intelligence: The model is the message. *Science, 230,* 1111–1118.

Sternberg, R. J. (1986). A triangular theory of love. *Psychological Review, 93,* 119–135.

Sternberg, R. J. (1988). Triangulating love. In R. J. Sternberg & M. L. Barnes (Eds.), *The psychology of love.* New Haven, CT: Yale University Press.

Sternberg, R. J. (1995). For whom the Bell Curve tolls: A review of *The Bell Curve. Psychological Science, 6,* 257–261.

Sternberg, R. J. (1997a). The concept of intelligence and its role in lifelong learning and success. *American Psychologist, 52,* 1030–1037.

Sternberg, R. J. (1997b). Intelligence and lifelong learning. *American Psychologist, 52,* 1034–1039.

Sternberg, R. J., & Grigorenko, E. (Eds.) (1997). *Intelligence, heredity, and environment.* New York: Cambridge.

Sternberg, R. J., & Lubart, T. I. (1996). Investing in creativity. *American Psychologist, 51,* 677–688.

Sternberg, R. J., & Soriano, L. J. (1984). Styles of conflict resolution. *Journal of Personality and Social Psychology, 47,* 115–126.

Sternberg, R. J., & Wagner, R. K. (1993). The g-ocentric view of intelligence and job performance is wrong. *Current Directions in Psychological Science, 2,* 1–5.

Stevens, J. E. (1994, February 27). Tribeswomen disfigure themselves in name of tourism. *San Diego Union-Tribune.*

Stolberg, S. (1993, July 14). Long-term study gives grim picture of heroin addiction. *Los Angeles Times.*

Stolberg, S. (1994, August 29). Study shows drug abuse programs are cost-effective. *Los Angeles Times.*

Stone, B. (1997, June 2). Zapping the eye. *Newsweek,* 80–81.

Strain, E. C., Mumford, G. K., Silverman, K., & Griffiths, R. R. (1994). Caffeine dependence syndrome. *Journal of the American Medical Association, 272,* 1043–1048.

Straker, G. (1994). Integrating African and Western healing practices in South Africa. *American Journal of Psychotherapy, 48,* 455–467.

Strassman, R. J. (1995). Hallucinogenic drugs in psychiatric research and treatment: Perspectives and prospects. *Journal of Nervous and Mental Diseases, 183,* 127–138.

Strauss, C. C. (1994). Anxiety disorders. In V. B. Van Hasselt & M. Hersen (Eds.), *Advanced abnormal psychology.* New York: Plenum Press.

Strauss, N. (1994, June 2). Kurt Cobain 1967–1994. *Rolling Stone.*

Streissguth, A. P., Aase, J. M., Clarren, S. K., Randels, S. P., LaDue, R. A., & Smith, D. F. (1991). Fetal alcohol syndrome in adolescents and adults. *Journal of the American Medical Association, 265,* 1961–1967.

Stritzke, W. G. K., Lang, A. R., & Patrick, C. J. (1996). Beyond stress and arousal: A reconceptualization of alcohol—Emotion relations with reference to psychophysiological methods. *Psychological Bulletin, 120,* 376–395.

Stromeyer, C. F., III. (1970, November). Eidetikers. *Psychology Today.*

Stromswold, K. (1995). The cognitive and neural bases of language acquisition. In M. S. Gazzaniga (Ed.), *The cognitive neurosciences.* Cambridge, MA: MIT Press.

Stumpf, D. A., Cranford, R. E., Elias, S., Fost, N. C., McQuillen, M. P., Myer, E., Poland, R., & Queenam, J. T. (1990). The infant with anencephaly. *New England Journal of Medicine, 322,* 669–674.

Suddath, R. L., Christison, G. W., Torrey, E. F., Casanova, M. R., & Weinberger, D. R. (1990). Anatomical abnormalities in the brains of monozygotic twins discordant for schizophrenia. *New England Journal of Medicine, 322,* 789–794.

Sullivan, R. M., Taborsky-Barba, S., Mendoza, R., Itano, A., Leon, M., Cotman, C. W., Payne, T. R., & Lott, I. (1991). Olfactory classical conditioning in neonates. *Pediatrics, 87,* 511–518.

Sussman, N., & Ginsberg, D. (1998). Rethinking side effects of the selective serotonin reuptake inhibitors: Sexual dysfunction and weight gain. *Psychiatric Annals, 28,* 89–97.

Suzuki, L. A., & Valencia, R. R. (1997). Race—Ethnicity and measured intelligence: Educational implications. *American Psychologist, 5,* 1103–1114.

Svensen, S., & White, K. (1994). A content analysis of horoscopes. *Genetic, Social and General Psychology Monographs, 12,* 5–38.

Swanson, J. M., McBurnett, K., Wigal, T., Pfiffner, L. J., Lerner, M. A., Williams, L., Christian, D. L., Tamm, L., Willcutt, E., Crowley, K., Clevenger, W., Khouzam, N., Woo, C., Crinella, F. M., & Fisher, T. D. (1993). Effect of stimulant medication on children with attention deficit disorder: A "review of reviews." *Exceptional Children, 60,* 154–162.

Swayze, V. W., II. (1995). Frontal leukotomy and related psychosurgical procedures in the era before antipsychotics (1935–1954): A historical overview. *American Journal of Psychiatry, 152,* 505–515.

Sweet, R. A., Mulsant, B. H., Gupta, B., Rifai, A. H., Pasternak, R. E., McEachran, A., Zubenko, G. S. (1995). Duration of neuroleptic treatment and prevalence of tardive dyskinesia in late life. *Archives of General Psychiatry, 52,* 478–486.

Swim, J. K., Aikin, K. J., Hall, W. S., & Hunter, B. A. (1995). Sexism and racism: Old-fashioned and modern principles. *Journal of Personality and Social Psychology, 68,* 199–214.

Szyfelbein, S. K., Osgood, P. F., & Carr, D. B. (1985). The assessment of pain and plasma B-endorphin immunoactivity in burned children. *Pain, 22,* 173–182.

Taddese, A., Nah, S. Y., & McCleskey, E. W. (1995). Selective opiod inhibition of small nociceptive neurons. *Science, 270,* 1366–1369.

Talbot, J. D., Marrett, S., Evans, A. C., Meyer, E., Bushnell, M. C., & Duncan, G. H. (1991). Multiple representations of pain in human cerebral cortex. *Science, 251,* 1355–1358.

Tallal, P. (1995, August 29). Cited in S. Begley, Why Johnny and Joanie can't read. *Newsweek.*

Tallal, P., Miller, S. L., Bedi, G., Byma, G., Wang, Z., Nagarajan, S. S., Shreiner, C., Jenkins, W. M., & Merzeich, M. M. (1996). Language comprehension in language-learning impaired children impaired with acoustically modified speech. *Science, 271,* 81–84.

Tamis-LeMonda, C. S., Bornstein, M. H., Baumwell, L., Dakmast, A. M. (1996). Responsive parenting in the second year: Specific influences on children's language and play. *Early Development and Parenting, 5,* 173–183.

Tamminga, C. A. (1997). The promise of new drugs for schizophrenia treatment. *Canadian Journal of Psychiatry, 42,* 264–273.

Tang, S. W. (1998, January 9). Cited in S. Emmons, Emotions at face value. *Los Angeles Times.*

Tankova, I., Adan, A., & Buela-Casal, G. (1994). Circadian typology and individual differences. A review. *Personality and Individual Differences, 16,* 671–684.

Tannen, D. (1990). *You just don't understand: Women and men in conversation.* New York: William Morrow.

Tannen, D. (1994). *Talking from 9 to 5.* New York: William Morrow.

Tanofsky, M. B., Wilfley, D. E., Spurrell, E. B., Welch, R., & Brownell, K. D. (1997). Comparison of men and women with binge

Handbook of child psychology (Vol. 1). New York: John Wiley & Sons.

Wells, G. L., Luus, E., & Windschitl, P. D. (1994). Maximizing the utility of eyewitness identification evidence. *Current Directions in Psychological Science, 3,* 194–197.

Werle, M. A., Murphy, T. B., & Budd, K. S. (1993). Treating chronic food refusal in young children: Home-based parent training. *Journal of Applied Behavior Analysis, 26,* 421–433.

Werner, E. E. (1989). Children of the garden island. *Scientific American, 260,* 106–111.

Werner, E. E. (1995). Resilience in development. *Current Directions in Psychological Science, 4,* 81–85.

Werner, E. E., & Smith, R. S. (1982). *Vulnerable but invincible.* New York: McGraw-Hill.

Wertz, F. J. (1998). The role of the humanistic movement in the history of psychology. *Journal of Humanistic Psychology, 38,* 42–70.

West, R. L. (1996). An application of prefrontal cortex function theory to cognitive aging. *Psychological Bulletin, 120,* 272–292.

Westen, D. (1990). Psychoanalytic approaches to personality. In L. A. Previn (Ed.), *Handbook of personality.* New York: Guilford Press.

Westen, D. (1998). Unconscious thought, feeling, and motivation: The end of a century-long debate. In R. F. Bornstein & J. M. Masling (Eds.), *Empirical perspectives on the psychoanalytic unconscious.* Washington, DC: American Psychological Association.

Wheeler, M. A., Stuss, D. T., & Tulving, E. (1997). Toward a theory of episodic memory: The frontal lobes and autonoetic consciousness. *Psychological Bulletin, 121,* 331–354.

Whitaker-Azmitia, P. (1997, December). Cited in B. Azar, Researchers debunk myth of the "crack baby." *APA Monitor.*

Whitbourne, S. K., Zuschlag, M. K., Elliot, L. B., & Waterman, A. S. (1992). Psychosocial development in adulthood: A 22-year sequential study. *Journal of Personality and Social Psychology, 63,* 260–271.

Whorf, B. L. (1940). In J. B. Carroll (Ed.), *Language, thought, and reality: Selected writing of Benjamin Lee Whorf.* Cambridge, MA: MIT Press.

Whorf, B. L. (1956). *Language, thought, and reality.* New York: Wiley.

Wickelgren, I. (1997a). Getting a grasp on working memory. *Science, 275,* 1580–1582.

Wickelgren, I. (1997b). Marjuana: Harder than thought? *Science, 276,* 1967–1968.

Wickett, J. C., Vernon, P. A., Lee, D. H. (1994). In vivo brain size, head perimeter, and intelligence in a sample of healthy adult females. *Personality and Individual Differences, 16,* 831–838.

Widiger, T. A., & Costa, P. T., Jr. (1994). Personality and personality disorders. *Journal of Abnormal Psychology, 103,* 78–91.

Widman, M., Platt, J. J., Lidz, V., Mathis, D. A., & Metzger, D. S. (1997). Patterns of service use and treatment involvement. *Journal of Substance Abuse Treatment, 14,* 29–35.

Wiebe, D. J. (1991). Hardiness and stress moderation: A test of proposed mechanisms. *Journal of Personality and Social Psychology, 60,* 89–99.

Wiebe, D. J., & Smith, T. W. (1997). Personality and health: Progress and problems in psychosomatics. In R. Hogan, J. Johnson, & S. Briggs (Eds.), *Handbook of Personal Psychology.* New York: Academic Press.

Wierson, M., & Forehand, R. (1994). Parent behavioral training for child noncompliance: Rationale, concepts, and effectiveness. *Current Directions in Psychological Science, 3,* 146–150.

Wiggins, J. S. (1997). In defense of traits. In R. Hogan, J. Johnson, & S. Briggs (Eds.), *Handbook of personality psychology.* New York: Academic Press.

Wilcoxon, H. C., Dragoin, W. B., & Kral, P. A. (1971). Illness-induced aversions in rat and quail: Relative salience of visual and gustatory cues. *Science, 171,* 826–828.

Wilde, M. C., & Cinciripini, P. M. (1994). Biological model. In V. B. Van Hasselt & M. Hersen (Eds.), *Advanced abnormal psychology.* New York: Plenum Press.

Wilens, T. E., Biederman, J., Mick, E., Farone, S., & Spencer, T. (1997). Attention deficit hyperactivity disorder (ADHD) is associated with early onset substance use disorders. *Journal of Nervous and Mental Disease, 185,* 475–482.

Wilfley, D. E., & Cohen, L. R. (1997). Psychological treatment of bulimia nervosa and binge eating disorder. *Psychopharmacology Bulletin, 33,* 437–454.

Wilhelm, F. H., & Roth, W. T. (1997). Clinical characteristics of flight phobia. *Journal of Anxiety Disorders, 11,* 241–261.

Willett, W. C. (1994). Diet and health: What should we eat? *Science, 264,* 532–537.

Williams, B. K., & Knight, S. M. (1994). *Healthy for life.* Pacific Grove, CA: Brooks/Cole.

Williams, D. (1992). *Nobody nowhere.* New York: Times Books.

Williams, D. (1994). *Somebody somewhere.* New York: Times Books.

Williams, D. E., Kirkpatrick-Sanchez, S., & Iwata, B. A. (1993). A comparison of shock intensity in the treatment of longstanding and severe self-injurious behavior. *Research in Development Disabilities, 14,* 207–219.

Williams, J. (1994, February 10). Survival of the sweetest. *San Diego Union-Tribune.*

Williams, J. E., & Best, D. L. (1990). *Measuring sex stereotypes* (Vol. 6, rev. ed.). Newbury Park, CA: Sage Publications.

Williams, M. A., & Gross, A. M. (1994). Behavior therapy. In V. B. Hasselt & M. Hersen (Eds.), *Advanced abnormal psychology.* New York: Plenum.

Williams, P. (1997, December 7). Town wants to move on, but past won't be ignored. *San Diego Union-Tribune.*

Wilson, B. (1996, February 7). Cited in G. Braxton, TV violence poses risk to viewers, study says. *Los Angeles Times,* F-1.

Wilson, D., Killen, J. D., Hayward, C., Robinson, T. N., Hammer, L. D., Kraemer, H. C., Varady, A., & Taylor, C. B. (1994). Timing and rate of sexual maturation and the onset of cigarette and alcohol use among teenage girls. *Archives of Pediatric and Adolescent Medicine, 148,* 789–795.

Wilson, G. T. (1994). Behavioral treatment of obesity: Thirty years and counting. *Advances in Behavior, Research and Therapy, 16,* 31–75.

Wilson, K. G., Hayes, S. C., & Gifford, E. V. (1997). Cognition in behavior therapy: Agreements and differences. *Journal of Behavior Therapy and Experimental Psychiatry, 28,* 53–63.

Wilson, S. A., Becker, L. A., & Tinker, R. H. (1997). Fifteen month follow-up of eye movement desensitization and reprocessing (EMDR) treatment for posttraumatic stress disorder and psychological trauma. *Journal of Consulting and Clinical Psychology, 65,* 1047–1056.

Wilson, S. R., Levine, K. J., Cruz, M. G., & Rao, N. (1997). Attribution complexity and actor-observer bias. *Journal of Social Behavior and Personality, 12,* 709–726.

Wilson, T. D., & Linville, P. W. (1982). Improving the academic performance of college freshmen: Attribution therapy revisited. *Journal of Personality and Social Psychology, 42,* 367–376.

Wincze, J. P., & Carey, M. P. (1991). *Sexual dysfunction: A guide for assessment and treatment.* New York: Guilford Press.

Wink, P., & Helson, R. (1996). Personality change in women and their partners. *Journal of Personality and Social Psychology.*

Winkler, J., Suhr, S. T., Gage, F. H., Thai, L. J., & Fisher, L. J. (1995). Essential role of neocortical acetylcholine in spatial memory. *Nature, 375,* 484–487.

Winn, P. (1995). The lateral hypothalamus and motivated behavior: An old syndrome reassessed and a new perspective gained. *Current Directions in Psychological Science, 4,* 182–187.

Winner, E. (1997). Exceptionally high intelligence and schooling. *American Psychologist, 52,* 1070–1081.

Winograd, E., & Neisser, V. (Eds.) (1992). *Studies of "flashbulb" memories.* New York: Cambridge Press.

Winograd, E., & Soloway, R. M. (1986). On forgetting the locations of things stored in special places. *Journal of Experimental Psychology: General, 115,* 366–372.

Winter, K. A., & Kuiper, N. A. (1997). Individual differences in the experience of emotions. *Clinical Psychology Review, 17,* 791–821.

Witelson, S. F., Glezor, I. I., & Kigar, D. L. (1995). Women have greater density of neurons in posterior temporal cortex. *Journal of Neuroscience, 15,* 3418–3428.

Witkin, G. (1995, November 13). A new drug gallops through the West. *U.S. News & World Report.*

Witkin, G., Tharp, M., Schrof, J. M., Toch, T., & Scattarella, C. (1998, June 1). Again. *U.S. News & World Report,* 16–18.

Wittman, J. (1994, January 5). Nausea, euphoria alternate marks of chemotherapy. *San Diego Union-Tribune.*

Wolf, T. H. (1973). *Alfred Binet*. Chicago: University of Chicago Press.

Wolitzky, D. L., & Eagle, M. N. (1997). Psychoanalytic theories of psychotherapy. In P. L. Wachtel & S. B. Messer (Eds.), *Theories of psychotherapy: Origins and evolution*. Washington, DC: American Psychological Association.

Wolpe, J. (1958). *Psychotherapy by reciprocal inhibition*. Stanford, CA: Stanford University Press.

Wolpe, J. (1990). *The practice of behavior therapy* (4th ed.). London: Pergamon Press.

Wolpe, J., & Lazarus, A. A. (1966). *Behavior therapy techniques*. London: Pergamon Press.

Wolpe, J., & Plaud, J. J. (1997). Pavlov's contributions to behavior therapy. *American Psychologist, 52*, 966–972.

Wolraich, M. L., Lindgren, S. D., Stumbo, P. L., Stegink, L. D., Appelbaum, M. J., & Kiritsy, M. C. (1994). Effects of diets high in sucrose or aspartame on the behavior and cognitive performance of children. *New England Journal of Medicine, 330*, 301–308.

Wong, J. (1994, February 26). Obesity weighing in as life-style for modern Chinese. *San Diego Union-Tribune*.

Wood, W., Christensen, P. N., Hebl, M. R., & Rothgerber, H. (1997). Conformity to sex-typed norms, affect and the self-concept. *Journal of Personality and Social Psychology, 73*, 523–535.

Woody, E. Z. (1997). Have the hypnotic susceptibility scales outlived their usefulness? *International Journal of Clinical and Experimental Hypnosis, 45*, 226–238.

Wool, C. A., & Barsky, A. J. (1994). So women somatize more than men? *Psychosomatics, 35*, 445–452.

World Health Organization. (1993). *International classification of disease and related health problems* (10th rev.). Geneva: Author.

Wride, N. (1989, June 14). Odyssey of a skinhead. *Los Angeles Times*.

Wright, D. B., & Gaskell, G. D. (1995). Flashbulb memories: Conceptual and methodological issues. *Memory, 3*, 67–80.

Wu, K. K., & Lam, D. J. (1993). The relationship between daily stress and health: Replicating and extending previous findings. *Psychology and Health, 8*, 329–344.

WuDunn, S. (1997, May 11). In Japan, use of dead has the living uneasy. *New York Times*, 1.

Wyer, R. S., Jr., & Lambert, A. J. (1994). The role of trait constructs in person perception: An historical perspective. In P. G. Devine, D. L. Hamilton, & T. M. Ostrom (Eds.), *Social cognition: Impact on social psychology*. New York: Academic Press.

Yamashita, I. (1993). *Taijin-kyofu or delusional social phobia*. Sapporo, Japan: Hokkaido University Press.

Yapko, M. D. (1994). Suggestibility and repressed memories of abuse: A survey of psychotherapists' beliefs. *American Journal of Clinical Hypnosis, 36*, 163–171.

Ybarra, M. J. (1991, September 13). The psychic and the skeptic. *Los Angeles Times*.

Yerkes, R. M. (1921). *Psychological examining in the United States Army*. Washington, DC: (Memoir No. 15). National Academy of Sciences, No. 15.

Yoffe, E. (1997, October). How quickly we forget. *U.S. News & World Report*.

Young, N. K. (1997). Effects of alcohol and other drugs on children. *Journal of Psychoactive Drugs, 29*, 23–42.

Yule, W., & Fernando, P. (1980). Blood phobia: beware. *Behavior Research and Therapy, 18*, 587–590.

Zajonc, R. B. (1984). On the primacy of affect. *American Psychologist, 39*, 117–123.

Zald, D. H., & Pardo, J. (1997). Emotion, olfaction, and the human amygdala: Amygdala activation during aversive olfactory stimulation. *Proceedings of the National Academy of Science, 94*, 4119–4124.

Zane, J. P. (1996, April 15). Time wasted, money lost. *San Diego Union-Tribune*.

Zaragoza, M. S., & Lane, S. M. (1994). Source misattributions and the suggestibility of eyewitness memory. *Journal of Experimental Psychology: Learning Memory, and Cognition, 20*, 934–935.

Zeifman, D., & Hazan, C. (1997). Cited in B. Bower, The ties that bond. *Science News, 152*, 94–95.

Zeiler, M. D. (1996). On books: Whither behaviorism? *Behavior Analyst, 19*, 301–309.

Zeki, S. (1993). *A vision of the brain*. Cambridge, MA: Blackwell Scientific.

Zener, K. (1937). The significance of behavior accompanying conditioned salivary secretion for theories of the conditioned response. *American Journal of Psychology, 50*, 384–403.

Zeng, R. G., & Shannon, R. V. (1994). Loudness-coding mechanisms inferred from electric stimulation of the human auditory system. *Science, 264*, 564–566.

Zigler, E. (1994). Reshaping early childhood intervention to be a more effective weapon against poverty. *American Journal of Community Psychology, 22*, 37–47.

Zigler, E. (1995, January). Cited in B. Azar, DNA-environment mix forms intellectual fate. *APA Monitor*.

Zigler, E., & Seitz, V. (1982). Social policy and intelligence. In R. J. Sternberg (Ed.), *Handbook of human intelligence*. Cambridge, England: Cambridge University Press.

Zigler, E., & Styfco, S. J. (Eds.) (1993). *Head Start and beyond*. New Haven, CT: Yale University Press.

Zigler, E., & Styfco, S. J. (1994). Head start: Criticisms in a constructive context. *American Psychologist, 49*, 127–132.

Zimbardo, P. G. (1970). The human choice: Individuation, reason and order versus deindividuation, impulse and chaos. In W. J. Arnold & D. Levine (Eds.), *Nebraska symposium on motivation*. Lincoln: University of Nebraska Press.

Zimmer, C. (1993, June). Making senses. *Discover*.

Zimmer, L., & Morgan, J. P. (1997). *Marijuana myths, marijuana fact: A review of scientific evidence*. New York: Lindesmith Center.

Zimmerman, M. A., Copeland, L. A., Shope, J. T., & Gielman, T. E. (1997). A longitudinal study of self-esteem: Implications for adolescent development. *Journal of Youth and Adolescence, 26*, 117–141.

Zucker, K. J. (1990). Gender identity disorders in children: Clinical descriptions and natural history. In R. Blanchard & B. W. Steiner (Eds.), *Clinical management of gender identity disorders in children and adults*. Washington, DC: American Psychiatric Press.

Zuckerman, M., Klorman, R., Larrance, D. T., & Speigel, N. H. (1981). Facial, autonomic, and subjective components of emotion: The facial feedback hypothesis versus the externalizer-internalizer distinction. *Journal of Personality and Social Psychology, 41*, 929–944.

Photo Credits

This page constitutes an extension of the copyright page. We have made every effort to trace the ownership of all copyrighted material and to secure permission from copyright holders. In the event of any question arising as to the use of any material, we will be pleased to make the necessary corrections in future printings. Thanks are due to the following authors, publishers, and agents for permission to use the material indicated.

Front Matter

ix: (below) John Karapelou/© 1993 The Walt Disney Co. Reprinted with permission of *Discover Magazine;* x: (top right) Craig McClain; xi: (top right) © George Frey; xiii: (bottom right) © Michael Nichols/Magnum Photos; xiv: (top left) PhotoDisc, Inc.; xv: (above) PhotoDisc., Inc.; xv: (below) © Werner Bokeberg/The Image Bank; altered by Doug Stern/ *U.S. News & World Report;* xvi: PhotoDisc, Inc.; xvii: (bottom left) PhotoDisc, Inc.; xix: (top left) PhotoDisc, Inc.; xxi: (left C) *People Weekly* © 1992 Taro Yamasaki; xxi: (right G) David Longstrength/AP/Wide World Photos; xxii: (left) Tomas Muscionico/Contact Press Images; xxii: (right) © Alan Weiner/Gamma Liaison Network; xxiv: PhotoDisc, Inc.; xxv: (above) © Kevin O'Farrell Concepts; xxv: (center far right) Craig McClain; xxvi: (center far left) © John Harding; xxvi: (center far right) AP by Al Francis/Wide World Photos; xxvii: (top left) © Warren Bolster/Tony Stone Images; xxvii: (center far right) Digital Stock Corporation; xxvii: (center near right) © Topham/OB/The Image Works; xxviii: Photo by Dr. John W. Lehman, courtesy of Dr. Herbert Bensen, Mind/Body Medical Institute; xxxi: *People Weekly* © 1992 Taro Yamasaki.

Module 1

2: (left A) Courtesy of Doubleday/AB/Times Books/Random House, by permission of Donna Williams; 2: (left B) Courtesy of Eric Courchesne and Rachel Yeung Courchesne, Children's Hospital Research Center, San Diego; 2: (left D) Courtesy, Margaret Clapp Library Archives, Wellesley College, photo by Patridge; 2: (right G) © Doug Menuez/Saba Press Photos, Inc.; 2: (right H) © Hangarter/The Picture Cube; 4: Courtesy of Doubleday/AB/Times Books/Random House, by permission of Donna Williams; 5: (left 1) Courtesy of Eric Courchesne and Rachel Yeung Courchesne, Children's Hospital Research Center, San Diego; 5: (right 5) Reprinted with permission of Times Books; 6: Courtesy of Eric Courchesne and Rachel Yeung Courchesne, Children's Hospital Research Center, San Diego; 10: Reprinted with permission of Times Books; 11: (above) © Ira Wyman/Sygma; 13: (center near left) © Tony Freeman/Photo Edit; 13: (above) Archives of the History of American Psychology, University of Akron, Akron, Ohio; 14: (above) Courtesy, Margaret Clapp Library Archives, Wellesley College, photo by Patridge; 14: (center far left) Robert Guthrie Collection; 14: (center far right) The Institute of Texan Cultures, University of Texas, San Antonio; 15: (left 1) Courtesy of Doubleday/AB/Times Books/Random House, by permission of Donna Williams; 15: (left 2) Courtesy of Eric Courchesne and Rachel Yeung Courchesne, Children's Hospital Research Center, San Diego; 15: (right 11) © Tony Freeman/Photo Edit; 15: (left 7) Reprinted with permission of Times Books; 18: (left) © Tony Freeman/Photo Edit; 18: (center) © Lori Adamski Peek/Tony Stone Images; 19: (left) © Doug Menuez/Saba Press Photos, Inc.; 19: (right) © 1988 Joel Gordon; 20: (below) © Hangarter/The Picture Cube; 22: (left A) Courtesy of Doubleday/AB/Times Books/Random House, by permission of Donna Williams; 22: (left B) Courtesy of Eric Courchesne and Rachel Yeung Courchesne, Children's Hospital Research Center, San Diego; 22: (right D) Courtesy, Margaret Clapp Library Archives, Wellesley College, photo by Patridge; 23: (bottom left) © Doug Menuez/Saba Press Photos, Inc.; 23: (right) © Hangarter/The Picture Cube.

Module 2

26: (left A) © Jose Azel/Aurora Quanta Productions; 26: (left D) © Joe McDonald/Animals, Animals; 26: (right I) Craig McClain; 27: (above) © Jose Azel/Aurora Quanta Productions; 27: (below) © Joe McDonald/Animals, Animals; 28: © Jose Azel/Aurora Quanta Productions; 31: (far left) © Joe McDonald/Animals, Animals; 31: © Peter Weimann/Animals, Animals; 31: © Belinda Wright/DRK Photo; 32: © Jose Azel/Aurora Quanta Productions; 33: © Edward Thomas/Leo DeWys; 34: (bottom left) *People Weekly* © 1995/Alan S. Weiner; 34: (bottom right) John Sholtis, The Rockefeller University, New York. Copyright © 1995 Amgen, Inc.; 35: © Michael McLoughlin; 36: (above & below) © Jose Azel/Aurora Quanta Productions; 38: (left 2) © Joe McDonald/Animals, Animals; 38: © Michael McLoughlin; 39: © Michael McLoughlin; 40: (center) Craig McClain; 40: (bottom left) Craig McClain; 41: Courtesy of the Foundation for Biomedical Research; 42: (left A) © Jose Azel/Aurora Quanta Productions; 42: (left D) © Joe McDonald/Animals, Animals; 43: Craig McClain; 44: PhotoDisc, Inc.

Module 3

46: (left-C) *People Weekly* © 1992 Taro Yamasaki; 46: (right-G) David Longstrength/AP/Wide World Photos; 47: © Melchior Digiacomo; 48: (right E) Courtesy of Miles Herkenham, Ph.D., Section of Functional Neuroanatomy, NIMH; 50: © Melchior Digiacomo; 51: *People Weekly* © 1992 Taro Yamasaki; 55: (below) Courtesy of Johns Hopkins University, Office of Public Affairs; 55: (above) Courtesy of Miles Herkenham, Ph.D., Section of Functional Neuroanatomy, NIMH; 58: (above) David Longstrength/AP/Wide World Photos; 59: (right) © Borys Malkin/Anthro-Photo; 59: (below) © G.I. Bernard/Animals, Animals/Earth Sciences; 61: (below) From "Survival of Implanted Fetal Dopamine Cells and Neurologic Improvement 12 to 46 months after Transplantation for Parkinson's Disease," by C.R. Freed, et al., 1992, New England Journal of Medicine, 327: 1549–1555. Copyright © 1992 by the Massachusetts Medical Society. Courtesy of Dr. Curt R. Freed; 62: *People Weekly* © 1992 Taro Yamasaki; 63: (above) David Longstrength/AP/Wide World Photos; 64: (above) © Gabe Palmer/The Stock Market.

Module 4

66: (left B) Courtesy of J.A. Fiez, Dept of Neurology, Washington University School of Medicine; 66: (right E) © Paul Berger/Tony Stone Images; 67: Patrick Farrell/Miami Herald photo; 67: (top right) © Peter A. Simon/Phototake, NYC; 67: (bottom right) By courtesy and kind permission of Cynthia de Gruchy; 68: By courtesy and kind permission of Cynthia de Gruchy; 69: (center far right) Craig McClain; 69: (above) © Kevin O'Farrell Concepts; 70: (center far right) Digital Stock Corporation; 70: (bottom right) Craig McClain; 70: (bottom left) Digital Stock Corporation; 71: (top left) Courtesy of Dr. Marcus Raichle, University of Washington; 71: (center near left) Courtesy of Dr. Marcus Raichle, University of Washington; 71: (bottom right) Digital Stock Corporation; 72: (bottom left) © Dana Fineman/Sygma; 72: (bottom right) © David Stewart/Tony Stone Images; 74: (top right) Patrick Farrell/Miami Herald photo; 74: (top left) © CNRI/Phototake NYC; 75: (left) Courtesy of Dr. Hanna Damasio, Human Neuroanatomy & Neuroimaging Laboratory, Dept of Neurology, University of Iowa College of Medicine. Published in 1994 in *Science, 264,* p 1104. Copyright © 1994 by the American Association for the Advancement in Science. Reprinted with permission of author and publisher; 76: (below) Courtesy of J.A. Fiez, Dept of Neurology, Washington University School of Medicine; 80: (top left) © Paul Berger/Tony Stone Images; 80: (right) © Topham/OB/The Image Works; 80: (bottom left) Tomas del Amo/Aristock; 81: (top far right) © David Stewart/Tony Stone Images; 83: (left 2) Digital Stock Corporation; 83: (center 5) © David Stewart/Tony Stone Images; 85: (above right) © Myrleen Ferguson/Photo Edit; 85: (below right) © Stewart Cohen/Tony Stone Images; 88: (left B) Courtesy of Dr. Marcus Raichle, University of Washington; 89: (left E) © Paul Berger/Tony Stone Images.

Module 5

92: (right F) © Danielle Pellegrini/Photo Researchers, Inc.; 93: (bottom near left) PhotoDisc, Inc.; 98: (top right) Digital Stock Corporation; 99: (below) Courtesy of Graham-Field, Inc.; 99: (above) Normal and altered reproduction of Vincent van Gogh self portrait reprinted by permission of Los Angeles Times Syndicate, originally appearing in *Popular Science,* July 1995 issue, "Color for the Color Blind: Self Portrait of Van Gogh"; 100: (top & center left) © Stanley Rowin/The Picture Cube; 100: (center near left) © Tony Freeman/Photo Edit; 101: (aircraft) Corbis Collection; 101: (autodrill) PhotoDisc, Inc.; 101: (couple) PhotoDisc, Inc.; 101: (sunset) PhotoDisc, Inc.; 104: (left) © M.P. Kahl/DRK Photo; 104: (bottom right) © Tony Freeman/Photo Edit; 105: (left) © David Hamilton/The Image Bank; 106: (left) PhotoDisc, Inc.; 107: (below) © 1989 Jonathan Levine; 108: (top left) © 1986 Steven Green-Armytage/The Stock Market; 110: (right)

© Danielle Pellegrini/Photo Researchers, Inc.; **110:** (above) © Burt Glinn/Magnum Photos; **110:** (center far left) © Malcolm S. Kirk; **110:** (center) © Guy Mary-Rousseliere; **110:** (below) © Malcolm S. Kirk; **112:** (above) Digital Stock Corporation; **113:** (right) © Leonard FreedMagnum Photos; **113:** (above) © P.R. Miller/Focus on Sports; **115:** (below) © James M. Kubus, Greensburg, PA; **117:** (left F) © Danielle Pellegrini/Photo Researchers, Inc.

Module 6

120: (left A) © Al Francekevich/The Stock Market; **120:** (left E) © Peter Turner/The Image Bank; **120:** (right H) Digital Stock Corporation; **120:** (right J) Courtesy of Colors Magazine; **121:** (right) © Howard Sochurek/The Stock Market; **122:** (right) © Howard Sochurek/The Stock Market; **123:** (left) © Al Francekevich/The Stock Market; **123:** (below) © Pat Bruno/Positive Images; **124:** (bottom left) Custom Medical Stock Photo; **126:** Painting by Richard Haas, photo © Bill Horsman; **127:** (above) Painting by Richard Haas, photo © Bill Horsman; **128:** (right) © Pat Bruno/Positive Images; **129:** (right) Random House photo by Charlotte Green; **130:** (top left) © Peter Turner/The Image Bank; **130:** (above) Photo Courtesy of Nikon Inc., photography © Jerry Friedman; **130:** (bottom left) © Bob Daemmrich/Stock, Boston; **130:** (center near right) Digital Stock Corporation; **131:** (top left) © Stephen Firsch/Stock, Boston; **131:** (bottom left) © Garry Gay/The Image Bank; **131:** (top right) © Gamma Press Images/Gamma-Liaison Network; **131:** (bottom right) Jackie Estrada; **132:** (left) © Robert P. Comport/Animals, Animals/Earth Sciences; **132:** (right) © John Elk/Stock, Boston; **133:** (top left) © Baron Wolman/Woodfin Camp & Associates; **133:** (center near and far right) Craig McClain; **134:** (left 4) Painting by Richard Haas, photo © Bill Horsman; **134:** (left 3) Custom Medical Stock Photo; **134:** (right 13) © Garry Gay/The Image Bank; **135:** (above) PhotoDisc, Inc.; **136:** (center near right) Digital Stock Corporation; **136:** (center far left) © Ken Novak/Tony Stone Images; **136:** (center near left) © Norvia Behling/Animals, Animals; **136:** (below) © Cannon-Bonventr K/AnthroPhoto; **137:** (left) Digital Stock Corporation; **137:** (center) Digital Stock Corporation; **137:** (right) © 1991 Jim Amentler; **138:** (below) © Dana Fineman/Sygma; **139:** (above) Corel Gallery; **140:** (left) © Jeffry W. Meyers/Stock, Boston; **140:** (center) © Globus Brothers/The Stock Market; **141:** (left to right) Marilyn Monroe © Doc Alain/Retna, Inc., Julie Roberts © Bill Davila/Retna, Inc., Howard Stern © Allen Tannenbaum/Sygma. Photos illustration by Doug Stern. *U.S. News & World Report.* Reproduced by permission; **141:** (center far left) Courtesy of Colors Magazine; **141:** (center near right) Courtesy of Colors Magazine; **141:** (above) © Rick Friedman/Black Star; **141:** (left to right) Marilyn Monroe © Doc Alain/Retna, Inc., Julie Roberts © Bill Davila/Retna, Inc., Howard Stern © Allen Tannenbaum/Sygma. Photos illustration by Doug Stern. *U. S. News & World Report.* Reproduced by permission; **141:** (left to right) Marilyn Monroe © Doc Alain/Retna, Inc., Julie Roberts © Bill Davila/ Retna, Inc.,

Howard Stern © Allen Tannenbaum/ Sygma. Photos illustration by Doug Stern. *U.S. News & World Report.* Reproduced by permission; **142:** (left A) © Al Francekevich/The Stock Market; **142:** (right E) © Peter Turner/The Image Bank; **143:** (right J) Courtesy of Colors Magazine.

Module 7

146: (right H) © Paul Buddle; **146:** (left A) © Allsport; **147:** (left) © Murrae Haynes/Mercury Pictures; **147:** (right) © Alan Hobson/Science Source/Photo Researchers; **148:** (near right) © David Stewart/Tony Stone Images; **148:** (far left) © Allsport; **148:** (near left) © Tony Freeman/Photo Edit; **148:** Craig McClain; **149:** (top left) © Robert E. Daemmrich/Tony Stone Images; **149:** (center) © Cesar Paredes/The Stock Market; **149:** (right) Neil Leifer/Sports Illustrated, © Time Warner; **150:** (left) © Tom Ives; **153:** (left) © Alan Hobson/ Science Source/Photo Researchers, Inc.; **158:** (left 1) © Allsport; **159:** Digital Stock Corporation; **160:** (above) © Linda Troeller; **161:** (below) Craig McClain; **162:** (left) © Paul Buddle; **162:** (center) © Carol Ford/Tony Stone Images; **163:** (right) © Dan McCoy/Rainbow; **163:** (center) © Louis Psihoyos/Matrix; **164:** (left A) © Allsport; **165:** (right H) © Paul Buddle.

Module 8

168: (left A) Craig McClain; **168:** (right I) Courtesy of D.A.R.E. America; **169:** (left) Craig McClain; **170:** (center) Craig McClain; **171:** Craig McClain; **172:** (center far right) © Michael Salas/The Image Bank; **172:** (center near right) © Myrleen Ferguson/Photo Edit; **173:** Courtesy, Rainbow Babies and Children's Hospital, University Hospitals of Cleveland, Dr. Howard Hall. Photo © Joe Glick; **174:** (above) © James Porto; **178:** (top left) Craig McClain; **180:** (far right) © Joy Spurr/Bruce Coleman Inc.; **182:** (center) Craig McClain; **182:** (above) Courtesy, Joseph E. Seagram's and Sons, Inc.; **183:** (above) © Andrew Lichtenstein/Sygma; **184:** (left 1) Craig McClain; **184:** (right 10) Craig McClain; **184:** (left 2) Craig McClain; **184:** (left 4) © James Porto; **185:** (left) © Richard Kalvar/Magnum Photos; **185:** (above) © Pat Bruno/Positive Images; **186:** (left) © Brooks Kraft/Sygma; **187:** (below) Courtesy of D.A.R.E. America; **188:** (left) © Pat Bruno/Positive Images; **188:** (bottom right) PhotoDisc, Inc.; **189:** (below) © Pat Bruno/Positive Images; **190:** (left A) Craig McClain; **191:** (right I) Courtesy of D.A.R.E. America.

Module 9

194: (right F) Digital Stock Corp.; **195:** (below) Digital Stock Corporation; **196:** (right) Craig McClain; **200:** (bottom left) © Janice Fullman/The Picture Cube; **200:** (bottom right) Courtesy of Professor Stuart Ellins, California State University, San Bernardino, CA.; **200:** (center) PhotoDisc, Inc.; **201:** (center far left) © Runk/Schoenberger/Grant Heilman Photography; **201:** (bottom left) © Michael Stuckey/Comstock; **201:** (center near left) Courtesy, Wurlitzer; **201:** (top right) © Fred Chase/Impact Visuals; **201:** (bottom right) © Tony

Freemann/Photo Edit; **202:** PhotoDisc, Inc.; **204:** (child) Digital Stock Corporation; **204:** (rat) PhotoDisc, Inc.; **204:** (rabbit) PhotoDisc, Inc.; **205:** (top left) © Schmid-Langsfeld/The Image Bank; **206:** (below) Digital Stock Corporation; **207:** (above) Digital Stock Corporation; **209:** (child) Digital Stock Corporation; **209:** (rat) PhotoDisc, Inc.

Module 10

212: (right F) Photo by Ron Garrison, © Zoological Society of San Diego; **212:** (left D) © Stephen Kraseman/DRK Photo; **212:** (right H) © Hiroji Kubota/Magnum Photos; **212:** (left B) PhotoDisc, Inc.; **213:** (left) © George Frey; **213:** (right) Vince Compagnore/Los Angeles Times Photo; **214:** (right) © PhotoDisc, Inc.; **216:** (left) © Peter Southwick/Stock, Boston; **217:** (bottom left) © George Frey; **217:** (top left) © George Frey; **217:** (child) Digital Stock Corporation; **217:** (rat) PhotoDisc, Inc.; **217:** (center far left) PhotoDisc, Inc.; **218:** (center far right) PhotoDisc, Inc.; **218:** (right) © Hangarter/The Picture Cube; **219:** (left) PhotoDisc, Inc.; **220:** (above) © 1971 Time Inc. Reprinted by permission; **221:** (top left) © Andy Sacks/Tony Stone Images; **221:** (top right) © Michael P. Gadomski/Photo Researchers, Inc.; **221:** (bottom left) © Vince Cavataio/Allsport Photographic Ltd./USA; **221:** (bottom right) © Norman Mosallem/Tony Stone Images; **222:** (left) © Stephen Kraseman/DRK Photo; **222:** (center) © George Frey; **222:** (top right) © George Frey; **222:** (center near right) PhotoDisc, Inc.; **223:** (above) Vince Compagnore/Los Angeles Times Photo; **223:** (spider) PhotoDisc, Inc.; **223:** (rat) PhotoDisc, Inc.; **224:** (center) Craig McClain; **225:** (left) © Barry Lewis/Network/Saba; **226:** (left) From *The Mentality of Apes,* by Wolfgang Koehler, Routledge & Kegan Paul. Reproduced by permission of International Thomason Publishing Services, Ltd; **226:** (center far left) Craig McClain; **226:** (center near right) PhotoDisc, Inc.; **226:** (bottom far right) PhotoDisc, Inc.; **227:** right #11 Craig McClain; **227:** (left 8) © Stephen Kraseman/DRK Photo; **227:** (left 6) PhotoDisc, Inc.; **227:** (left 4) PhotoDisc, Inc.; **228:** (right) Photo by Ron Garrison, © Zoological Society of San Diego; **228:** (above) Mitsuaki Iwago/National Geographic Society; **228:** (left) PhotoDisc, Inc.; **229:** (left) Arthur C. Smith, III/Grant Heilman Photography; **229:** (top right) Kennan Ward Photography/Corbis Collection; **231:** © Hiroji Kubota/Magnum Photos; **233:** (left) © Dan McCoy/Rainbow; **233:** (bottom right) © 1998 Danny Gonzalez; **234:** (below) © Stephen Kraseman/DRK Photo; **234:** (right B) PhotoDisc, Inc.; **235:** (right H) © Hiroji Kubota/Magnum Photos; **235:** (left F) Photo by Ron Garrison, © Zoological Society of San Diego.

Module 11

238: (left B) © Marshall Cavendish Picture Library; **238:** (right H) Bob Carey/Los Angeles Times Photo; **238:** (right E) © Bob Martin/Allsport; **239:** (top right) AP by Al Francis/Wide World Photos; **239:** (center far right) © John Harding; **239:** (top left) Chris Assaf/© *The Washington Post;* **240:** (left) PhotoDisc, Inc.; **241:** (center) © Marshall Cavendish Picture Library; **242:** (above) PhotoDisc, Inc.; **243:**

Photo Credits

Chris Assaf/© *The Washington Post;* **244:** (bottom near left) PhotoDisc, Inc.; **244:** (center near right) PhotoDisc, Inc.; **244:** (center far left) PhotoDisc, Inc.; **245:** (center right) PhotoDisc, Inc.; **245:** (center far left) PhotoDisc, Inc.; **245:** (center near left) PhotoDisc, Inc.; **245:** (bottom left) PhotoDisc, Inc.; **246:** (center far left) Digital Stock Corporation; **246:** (center near right) PhotoDisc, Inc.; **247:** (above) © Bob Martin/Allsport; **250:** (top right) AP by Al Francis/Wide World Photos; **250:** (top left) © John Harding; **252:** (left 5) Chris Assaf © *The Washington Post;* **252:** (left 7) PhotoDisc, Inc.; **253:** Bob Carey/Los Angeles Times Photo; **254:** (left) AP/Wide World Photos; **254:** (right) Courtesy of Prof. Ralph Norman Haber; **256:** (left B) © Marshall Cavendish Picture Library; **257:** Bob Carey/Los Angeles Times Photo.

Module 12

260: (right H) [left side]) UPI/Corbis-Bettmann; **260:** (right H [right side]) UPI/Corbis-Bettmann; **260:** (right F) © Tad Janocinski/The Image Bank; **260:** (left B) PhotoDisc, Inc.; **260:** (left D) Photo-Disc, Inc.; **264:** © Laura Dwight; **264:** (bottom left) PhotoDisc, Inc.; **264:** (bottom right) Photo-Disc, Inc.; **265:** (center near right) PhotoDisc, Inc.; **265:** (bottom right) PhotoDisc, Inc.; **267:** (below) © Topham/OB/The Image Works; **267:** (center far left) PhotoDisc, Inc.; **268:** (center far right) Photo-Disc, Inc.; **268:** (center near left) PhotoDisc, Inc.; **268:** (bottom near right) PhotoDisc, Inc.; **269:** (above) © Gary MacDonald; **269:** (center) PhotoDisc, Inc.; **270:** (left 4) PhotoDisc, Inc.; **270:** (right 7) PhotoDisc, Inc.; **270:** (left 6) Photo-Disc, Inc.; **272:** (right) PhotoDisc, Inc.; **272:** (left) © Tad Janocinski/The Image Bank; **274:** (below) UPI/Corbis-Bettmann; **274:** (center far right) UPI/Corbis-Bettmann; **276:** (right D) PhotoDisc, Inc.; **276:** (left B) PhotoDisc, Inc.; **277:** (right H [left side]) UPI/Corbis-Bettmann; **277:** (right H [right side]) UPI/Corbis-Bettmann; **277:** (left F) © Tad Janocinski/The Image Bank; **278:** *People Weekly* © 1996 Adolphe Pierre-Louis.

Module 13

280: (right F) Corbis-UPI/Bettmann; **280:** (left D) © Rick Smolan/Stock, Boston; **280:** (right G) Courtesy of Richard Haier, PhD., University of California, Irvine; **280:** (right H) © 1991 Ira Block/The Image Bank; **281:** (top left) © 1995 Ken Heinen; **281:** (top right) © Rob Nelson; **281:** (below) © Myrleen Ferguson/Photo Edit; **282:** (far left) © Martin Simon/SABA Press Photos; **282:** (near left) © Kevin Levine/Allsport; **283:** (top right) PhotoDisc, Inc.; **283:** (center) PhotoDisc, Inc.; **283:** (right bottom) PhotoDisc, Inc.; **285:** (center) Corbis-Bettmann; **285:** (bottom far left) PhotoDisc, Inc.; **285:** (center far right) PhotoDisc, Inc.; **286:** (left) Courtesy, John Fitzgerald Kennedy Library/Museum, # C283-51-63; **286:** (center) Deborah Feingold, courtesy of *Parade Magazine* and Marilyn vos Savant; **286:** (right) Corbis-UPI/Bettmann; **288:** (left) Courtesy of Marian Burke; **288:** (right) Deborah Feingold, courtesy of *Parade Magazine* and Marilyn vos Savant; **289:** (left) PhotoDisc, Inc.; **289:** (left) PhotoDisc, Inc.; **289:** (below) Deborah Feingold,

courtesy of *Parade Magazine* and Marilyn vos Savant; **291:** (center) © Rick Smolan/Stock, Boston; **291:** (below) PhotoDisc, Inc.; **292:** (right) © Rob Nelson; **292:** (left) © Martin Simon/SABA Press Photos; **292:** (center) © Myrleen Ferguson/Photo Edit; **293:** (above) © Anne Rippy/The Image Bank; **293:** (left) PhotoDisc, Inc.; **293:** (right) PhotoDisc, Inc.; **294:** © Anthony Barboza; **294:** © Anthony Barboza; **294:** © Anthony Barboza; **294:** © Anthony Barboza; **295:** (left 3) PhotoDisc, Inc.; **295:** (left 4) PhotoDisc, Inc.; **296:** Corbis-UPI/Bettmann; **297:** (below) Courtesy of Dr. Richard Haier, University of California, Irvine; **297:** (above) Courtesy of J.A. Fiez, Dept of Neurology, Washington University School of Medicine; **298:** © 1991 Ira Block/The Image Bank; **299:** (right) © Jacques Chenet/Woodfin Camp & Associates; **299:** (left) PhotoDisc, Inc.; **301:** (right G) Courtesy of Dr. Richard Haier, University of California, Irvine; **301:** (left D) © Rick Smolan/Stock, Boston; **301:** (right F) Corbis-UPI/Bettmann; **302:** (above) Courtesy of Dr. Richard Haier, University of California, Irvine.

Module 14

304: (left B) Craig McClain; **304:** (right H) Shaywitz, et al., 1995 NMR Research/Yale Medical School; **304:** (right I) © Ronald H. Cohn/The Gorilla Foundation, Woodside, California 94062; **304:** (left C) Courtesy of and by permission of John Johnson, Ltd. on behalf of Steven Wilshire; **304:** (right E) Digital Stock; **305:** (above) © 1994 Paul Morse, *Los Angeles Times.* Reprinted by permission; **305:** (left) © Charles Allen/The Image Bank; **306:** (left top) PhotoDisc, Inc.; **306:** (left center) PhotoDisc, Inc.; **306:** (left bottom) Photo-Disc, Inc.; **306:** (right top) PhotoDisc, Inc.; **306:** (right center) PhotoDisc, Inc.; **306:** (right bottom) PhotoDisc, Inc.; **306:** (below) © Animals, Animals; **307:** (above) PhotoDisc, Inc.; **307:** (right top) Photo-Disc, Inc.; **307:** (right center) PhotoDisc, Inc.; **307:** (right bottom) PhotoDisc, Inc.; **308:** (below) © Bill Gillette/Gamma Liaison Network; **308:** (above) © Richard Pohle/Sipa Press; **309:** (center) Craig McClain; **310:** © 1994 Paul Morse, *Los Angeles Times.* Reprinted by permission; **310:** (right) © 1994 Gordon Parks; **311:** (left) Courtesy of and by permission of John Johnson, Ltd. on behalf of Steven Wilshire; **314:** (center far left) © Romilly Lockyer/The Image Bank; **314:** (right) © Al Hamdan/The Image Bank; **314:** (above) Digital Stock; **315:** (left) © Laura Dwight; **315:** © Frank Bates/The Image Bank; **316:** (above) Digital Stock Corporation; **316:** (below) PhotoDisc, Inc.; **316:** (center) Courtesy of Robert Zatorre, and Denise Klein, McGill University; **317:** (left 4) Craig McClain; **317:** (right 8) © Romilly Lockyer/The Image Bank; **317:** (right 9) Digital Stock Corporation; **318:** PhotoDisc, Inc.; **319:** (left) © P H Cornut/Tony Stone Images; **319:** (right) Photo-Disc, Inc.; **320:** © Brian Vander Brug; **321:** (below) Shaywitz, et al., 1995 NMR Research/Yale Medical School; **321:** (above) © Damian Walker/Camera Press/Retna, Ltd; **322:** (below) By Ed Kashi © 1989; **322:** (below) By Ed Kashi © 1989; **322:** (above) Author's collection; **323:** (below) © Michael Nichols/Magnum Photos; **323:** (above) ©

Ronald H. Cohn/The Gorilla Foundation, Woodside, California 94062; **323:** (center) Courtesy of Lanuage Research Center, Georgia State University, Dr. Duane Rumbaugh, © 1991 Public Sphere; **324:** (right C) Courtesy of and by permission of John Johnson, Ltd. on behalf of Steven Wilshire; **324:** (left B) Craig McClain; **325:** (right H) Shaywitz, et al., 1995 NMR Research/Yale Medical School; **325:** (left E) Digital Stock Corporation; **325:** (right I) © Michael Nichols/Magnum Photos; **326:** Digital Stock Corporation.

Module 15

328: (right E) © Mariella Furrer/Saba Press Photos; **328:** (right A) © Richard Sjoberg; **328:** (right H) UPI/Corbis-Bettmann; **328:** (right F) PhotoDisc, Inc.; **329:** (left) © Jay Mather/Sygma; **329:** (right) Union-Tribune/John McCutchen; **330:** (left) John Dominis, LIFE Magazine © Time, Inc.; **330:** (right) © Michael Melford/The Image Bank; **331:** (left) © Richard Sjoberg; **331:** (right) © Mike Malyszko/Stock, Boston; **332:** (above) WIlliam Campbell/Time Magazine; **332:** (center far left) PhotoDisc, Inc.; **332:** (below) PhotoDisc, Inc.; **334:** (center) Les Stone/Sygma; **334:** (above) PhotoDisc, Inc.; **335:** (above) © Kim Newton/Woodfin Camp & Associates; **336:** (below) Courtesy of Jeffrey M. Friedman, Rockefeller University; **336:** (above) © Bob Sacha; **337:** (center) © FoodPix; **337:** (above) © FoodPix; **338:** (left) © George B. Shaller/Bruce Coleman, Inc.; **340:** (bottom left) © Tony Freeman/Photo Edit; **340:** (right) PhotoDisc, Inc.; **341:** (left) PhotoDisc, Inc.; **342:** PhotoDisc, Inc.; **343:** Red Morgan/Time Magazine; **345:** (above) © Dave Black; **346:** (above) © 1995 Gina Ferazzi, *Los Angeles Times.* Reprinted by permission; **346:** (below) © Mariella Furrer/Saba Press Photos; **347:** (left 1) © Michael Melford/The Image Bank; **347:** (left 4) © Mike Malyszko/Stock, Boston; **348:** (above) Union-Tribune/John McCutchen; **348:** (bottom right) © Dave Black; **348:** (bottom left) Reprinted by permission of the publishers from The Thematic Apperception Test, by Henry A. Murray, Cambridge, Mass.: Harvard University Press © 1971 by Henry A. Murray; **350:** (left) Photo by Dr. Alfred McLaren. Reprinted with permission from *Science News,* the weekly newsmagazine of science, copyright 1995 by Science Service, Inc.; **350:** (right) PhotoDisc, Inc.; **350:** (below) PhotoDisc, Inc.; **351:** © Jason Goltz; **352:** (top right) Corbis-UPI/Bettmann; **352:** (top left) Corbis-UPI/Bettmann; **352:** (bottom left) AP/Wide World Photos; **352:** (bottom right) © L. Schwartzwald/Sygma; **353:** (above) © Jim McHugh/Outline Press Syndicate; **353:** (center) © Nina Berman/Sipa Press Photos; **354:** (left C) Courtesy of Jeffrey M. Friedman, Rockefeller University; **354:** (left A) © Richard Sjoberg; **354:** (right H) Corbis-UPI/Bettmann; **355:** (left E) © Mariella Furrer/Saba Press Photos; **355:** (left F) PhotoDisc, Inc.

Module 16

358: (right E) *Idaho Statesman/* © Tom Shanahan; **358:** (left B) PhotoDisc, Inc.; **358:** (left C) Digital Stock Corporation; **359:** (left) © Warren Bolster/Tony Stone Images; **360:** (below) PhotoDisc, Inc.; **361:** (below) PhotoDisc, Inc.; **362:** (center, top left) PhotoDisc, Inc.; **362:** (right, bottom left) PhotoDisc, Inc.; **363:** PhotoDisc, Inc.; **364:** (top) Digital Stock Corporation; **364:** (top center) Digital Stock Corporation; **364:** (center) Digital Stock Corporation; **364:** (center bottom) Digital Stock Corporation; **365:** (center) © Topham/OB/ The Image Works; **365:** (above) Digital Stock Corporation; **366:** (above) *Idaho Statesman/* © Tom Shanahan; **366:** (bottom left) *Idaho Statesman/* © Tom Shanahan; **366:** (right) PhotoDisc, Inc.; **367:** (center-anger) © Topham/OB/The Image Works; **367:** (below-digust) © Burt Glinn/Magnum Photos; **367:** (above-surprise) PhotoDisc, Inc.; **367:** (center-sadness) © Ray Ellis/Photo Researchers, Inc.; **367:** (bottom-happy) PhotoDisc, Inc.; **368:** (left 1) © Warren Bolster/Tony Stone Images; **368:** (right 7) © Topham/OB/The Image Works; **368:** (right 6) Digital Stock Corporation; **370:** (above) Agence France Presse [AFP]/Archive Photos; **370:** (below) Photo below by Joel Reicherter; reprinted by permission and courtesy of the photographer; **371:** (below) Agence France Presse [AFP]/Archive Photos; **372:** (right C) Digital Stock Corporation; **373:** (left E) *Idaho Statesman/* © Tom Shanahan; **374:** Photo below by Joel Reicherter; reprinted by permission and courtesy of the photographer.

Module 17

376: (right F) PhotoDisc, Inc.; **376:** (right G) © Steven Winn/AnthroPhoto; **376:** (left C) © Melchior Digiacomo; **376:** (right H) Private Collection; **377:** (left) Lennox McLendon/AP/Wide World Photos; **377:** (right) © Melchior Digiacomo; **378:** (above) UPI/Corbis-Bettmann; **379:** (above) © Francis Leroy/BioCosmos/Science Photo Library/ Photo Researchers, Inc.; **379:** (below) © Petit Format/Science Source/Photo Researchers, Inc.; **380:** (above) Lennart Nilsson, *The Incredible Machine,* National Geographic Society, by permission of Bokforlaget Bonnier Alba AB; **381:** (right) © George Steinmetz; **381:** (center) PhotoDisc, Inc.; **382:** (center far left) PhotoDisc, Inc.; **382:** (bottom left) PhotoDisc, Inc.; **382:** (right) PhotoDisc, Inc.; **383:** (center far right) © Laura Dwight; **383:** (below) © Elyse Lewin/The Image Bank; **383:** (above) © Laura Dwight; **384:** (right) *People Weekly* © 1995 Taro Yamaski; **384:** (center near left) © David M. Grossman/Photo Researchers, Inc.; **384:** (below) PhotoDisc, Inc.; **385:** (above) Lennox McLendon/AP/Wide World Photos; **385:** (below) © Melchior Digiacomo; **386:** (above) © Joseph Nettis/Stock, Boston; **386:** (below) © Brad Martin/The Image Bank; **387:** (below) © Joseph Nettis/Stock, Boston; **387:** (above) © Brad Martin/ The Image Bank; **388:** (above) PhotoDisc, Inc.; **388:** (center) PhotoDisc, Inc.; **389:** (left) © Doug Goodman/Monkmeyer Press Photo; **389:** (left) © Doug Goodman/Monkmeyer Press Photo; **389:** (right) Craig McClain; **389:** (right) Craig McClain; **389:** (right) Craig McClain; **390:** (right) PhotoDisc, Inc.; **390:** (below) PhotoDisc, Inc.; **390:** (center far left) Craig McClain; **390:** (center far left) Craig McClain; **391:** © Yves DeBraine/ Black Star; **392:** PhotoDisc, Inc.; **393:** PhotoDisc, Inc.; **394:** (below) © Mike Teruya/Free Spirit Photography; **394:** (above) PhotoDisc, Inc.; **395:** (right 10) PhotoDisc, Inc.; **396:** (above) © Jon Feingersh/

The Stock Market; **396:** (left) © Bob Daemmrich/ Stock, Boston; **396:** (right) © Charles Gupton/ Stock, Boston; **397:** (center) © Gabe Palmer/The Stock Market; **397:** (below) © Cliff Feulner/ The Image Bank; **397:** (top left) PhotoDisc, Inc.; **397:** (top left) PhotoDisc, Inc.; **398:** (bottom right) "On Credit Page", 2nd column Olivero Toscani for BENETTON; **398:** (top left) PhotoDisc, Inc.; **398:** (center far right) PhotoDisc, Inc.; **399:** (above) © Steven Winn/AnthroPhoto; **399:** (below) © Lila Abu Lughod/AnthroPhoto; **400:** (above) UPI/ Corbis-Bettmann; **400:** (right) © Christopher Little/ Outline; **401:** Private Collection; **402:** (right C) © Melchior Digiacomo; **403:** (right H) Private Collection; **403:** (right G) © Steven Winn/AnthroPhoto; **403:** (left F) PhotoDisc, Inc.

Module 18

406: (left C) Tammy Lechner/Los Angeles Times Photo; **406:** (right G) © David J. Sams/Stock, Boston; **406:** (left A) PhotoDisc, Inc.; **406:** (right E) PhotoDisc, Inc.; **406:** (right F) © Roger Wood/ Corbis-Bettmann; **406:** (right H) PhotoDisc, Inc.; **406:** (left D) PhotoDisc, Inc.; **407:** (right) H. Armstrong Roberts; **407:** (left) Tammy Lechner/ Los Angeles Times Photo; **408:** © David Michael Kennedy; **409:** (below) PhotoDisc, Inc.; **410:** (above) Tammy Lechner/Los Angeles Times Photo; **410:** (right) PhotoDisc, Inc.; **411:** (left) PhotoDisc, Inc.; **411:** (below) PhotoDisc, Inc.; **411:** (right) Photo-Disc, Inc.; **413:** © David Michael Kennedy; **414:** (above) PhotoDisc, Inc.; **414:** (left) Photo-Disc, Inc.; **414:** (right) PhotoDisc, Inc.; **415:** (below) © Tom McCarthy/The Picture Cube; **415:** (above) PhotoDisc, Inc.; **415:** (right) PhotoDisc, Inc.; **416:** (center) Tammy Lechner/Los Angeles Times Photo; **416:** (below) © David Michael Kennedy; **417:** (center) © Bob Grant/Archive Photos; **417:** (below) © All Action/LGI Photo Agency; **417:** (above) H. Armstrong Roberts; **418:** (above) © 1995 Dave Garley, *Los Angeles Times.* Reprinted by permission; **418:** (right) PhotoDisc, Inc.; **418:** (left) PhotoDisc, Inc.; **419:** (above) H. Armstrong Roberts; **420:** PhotoDisc, Inc.; **421:** (right 10) Tammy Lechner/Los Angeles Times Photo; **421:** (left 3) PhotoDisc, Inc.; **421:** (right 9) PhotoDisc, Inc.; **421:** (right 11) PhotoDisc, Inc.; **422:** (right) Photo-Disc, Inc.; **422:** (left) PhotoDisc, Inc.; **422:** (above) PhotoDisc, Inc.; **423:** Corbis-Bettmann; **424:** (below) © Werner Bokeberg/The Image Bank; altered by Doug Stern/ *U.S. News & World Report,* **424:** (above) © David J. Sams/Stock, Boston; **425:** (left) PhotoDisc, Inc.; **425:** (right) PhotoDisc, Inc.; **426:** PhotoDisc, Inc.; **427:** PhotoDisc, Inc.; **428:** (left A) PhotoDisc, Inc.; **428:** (right C) © David Michael Kennedy; **428:** (right D) PhotoDisc, Inc.; **429:** (right E) PhotoDisc, Inc.; **429:** (right G) © David J. Sams/Stock, Boston; **429:** PhotoDisc, Inc.

Module 19

432: (right F) © Jason Goltz; **432:** (right E) © Robert Durell; **432:** (right G) © Walter Wick/ Telegraph Colour Library/FPG International; **433:** (right) © Fox/Shooting Star; **433:** (left) © Sin/ Doralba Picerno/LGI Photo Agency; **436:** (above) © Frank Micelotta/Outline Press; **438:** © Mike Hashimoto/NGI/LGI Photo Agency; **440:** (center)

Courtesy, Adler School of Professional Psychology. Reproduced by permission of Kurt Adler; **440:** (left) National Library of Medicine, Bethesda, MD; **440:** Courtesy, Association for the Advancement of Psychoanalysis; **442:** (above) © Fox/Shooting Star; **442:** (below) © Photo 3045 Pool: by J.O. Alber/ Gamma Liaison Network; **443:** (below) © Bob Adelman/Magnum Photos; **443:** J. Howard Miller/ National Archives/Corbis-Bettmann; **444:** (below) © Francois Lochon/Gamma-Liaison Network; **444:** (center) © Nancy Moran/Sygma; **444:** (above) © Laura Dwight/Corbis-Bettmann; **445:** (below) © Harry Benson; **445:** (center) © David Michael Kennedy; **445:** (above) © Jose Azel/Woodfin Camp & Associates; **446:** © Robert Durell; **447:** (right 10) © Jose Azel/Woodfin Camp & Associates; **448:** © Jason Goltz; **449:** © Walter Wick/Telegraph Colour Library/FPG International; **450:** (above) © Mike Hashimoto/NGI/LGI Photo Agency; **450:** (right) Reprinted by permission of the publishers from The Thematic Apperception Test, by Henry A. Murray, Cambridge, Mass.: Harvard University Press © 1971 by Henry A. Murray; **451:** (right) Reprinted by permission of the publishers from The Thematic Apperception Test, by Henry A. Murray, Cambridge, Mass.: Harvard University Press © 1971 by Henry A. Murray; **453:** (left F) © Jason Goltz; **453:** (left E) © Robert Durell; **453:** (right G) © Walter Wick/Telegraph Colour Library/FPG International; **454:** Los Angeles Times Photos/Rick Meyer.

Module 20

456: (left C) © Michael Nichols/Magnum Photos; **456:** (left A) *People Weekly* © 1998 Photo by Frank Veronsky; **456:** (right H) PhotoDisc, Inc.; **456:** (right H) PhotoDisc, Inc.; **457:** (right) © Alan Weiner/Gamma Liaison Network; **457:** (left) © Tomas Muscionico/Contact Press Images; **458:** (bottom left) IDAF/Sipa Press; **458:** (above) © Nils Jorgensen/RDR Productions/Rex Features, London; **458:** (bottom right) © David Turnley, Detroit Free Press/Black Star; **458:** (center far left) © Tomas Muscionico/Contact Press Images; **459:** (below) PhotoDisc, Inc.; **459:** (above) © Peter Turnley/Black Star; **460:** (left) PhotoDisc, Inc.; **460:** (right) PhotoDisc, Inc.; **461:** *People Weekly* © 1998 Photo by Frank Veronsky; **462:** (left) © Alan Weiner/Gamma Liaison Network; **462:** (right) PhotoDisc, Inc.; **462:** (right) PhotoDisc, Inc.; **462:** PhotoDisc, Inc.; **462:** PhotoDisc, Inc.; **462:** (right) PhotoDisc, Inc.; **463:** (below) © Photo Edit; **463:** (above) PhotoDisc, Inc.; **463:** (above) PhotoDisc, Inc.; **463:** (above) PhotoDisc, Inc.; **463:** PhotoDisc, Inc.; **463:** PhotoDisc, Inc.; **464:** (center) © Eugenie Aderbari/RDR Productions/Rex Features/London; **464:** (above) © Ernie McCreight/ Rex Features, Ltd; **466:** (above) © Michael Nichols/ Magnum Photos; **466:** (center) © Michael Nichols/ Magnum Photos; **466:** (left) PhotoDisc, Inc.; **466:** (right) PhotoDisc, Inc.; **467:** (left) © Michael Nichols/Magnum Photos; **467:** (center) © Michael Nichols/Magnum Photos; **467:** (right) PhotoDisc, Inc.; **468:** (center) © Eugenie Aderbari/RDR Productions/Rex Features/ London; **469:** (left 5) PhotoDisc, Inc.; **469:** (left 4) PhotoDisc, Inc.; **469:** (right 9) PhotoDisc, Inc.; **469:** (right 10)

PhotoDisc, Inc.; **471:** (left) PhotoDisc, Inc.; **471:** (below) PhotoDisc, Inc.; **472:** (above) © Photo 3045 Pool: by J.O. Alber/Gamma Liaison Network; **473:** (top left) © Nils Jorgensen/RDR Productions/Rex Features, London; **473:** (top right) PhotoDisc, Inc.; **473:** (right center) PhotoDisc, Inc.; **473:** (bottom right) © Michael Nichols/Magnum Photos; **473:** (bottom left) PhotoDisc, Inc.; **474:** (left) PhotoDisc, Inc.; **474:** (right) PhotoDisc, Inc.; **474:** (bottom right) PhotoDisc, Inc.; **475:** (right center) PhotoDisc, Inc.; **475:** (bottom right) PhotoDisc, Inc.; **475:** (left) PhotoDisc, Inc.; **478:** Adapted from "Companies Using Personality Tests for Making Hire That Fit," by Carol Smith, *Los Angeles Times,* February 9, 1997 p. D5. Copyright © 1997 by *Los Angeles Times.* Adapted by permission of the publisher; **478:** (above) PhotoDisc, Inc.

Module 21

480: (right G) Photo by Dr. John W. Lehman, courtesy of Dr. Herbert Bensen, Mind/Body Medical Institute; **480:** (right E) PhotoDisc, Inc.; **480:** (right F) © Ann States/Saba; **480:** (left A) PhotoDisc, Inc.; **480:** (left D) PhotoDisc, Inc.; **481:** (right) Arlene Gottfried, Life Magazine © Time Inc.; **481:** © Craig McClain; **482:** PhotoDisc, Inc.; **482:** PhotoDisc, Inc.; **482:** PhotoDisc, Inc.; **483:** PhotoDisc, Inc.; **484:** (right) © Paul Berger/Tony Stone Images; **484:** (above) PhotoDisc, Inc.; **484:** (center) PhotoDisc, Inc.; **486:** PhotoDisc, Inc.; **487:** (center) PhotoDisc, Inc.; **488:** (left) © Lennart Nilsson, *The Incredible Machine,* National Geographic Society; **488:** (above) Digital Stock Corporation; **489:** PhotoDisc, Inc.; **490:** (left) © Photo Edit; **490:** (above) Arlene Gottfried, Life Magazine © Time Inc.; **490:** (center) © L.D. Gordon/The Image Bank; **491:** (above) © David Liam Kyle/Sportslight; **491:** (below) © 1991 David Turnley, Detroit Free Press/Black Star; **491:** (center) PhotoDisc, Inc.; **493:** (center) Arlene Gottfried, Life Magazine © Time Inc.; **493:** (above) PhotoDisc, Inc.; **494:** (above) © Chuck Fishman/Contact Press Images; **495:** PhotoDisc, Inc.; **495:** PhotoDisc, Inc.; **497:** PhotoDisc, Inc.; **498:** (right 13) © Chuck Fishman/Contact Press Images; **498:** (right 12) © Craig McClain; **498:** (left 9) © L.D. Gordon/The Image Bank; **498:** (right 10) PhotoDisc, Inc.; **498:** (right 14) PhotoDisc, Inc.; **499:** PhotoDisc, Inc.; **500:** © Ann States/Saba; **501:** Photo by Dr. John W. Lehman, courtesy of Dr. Herbert Bensen, Mind/Body Medical Institute; **502:** PhotoDisc, Inc.; **502:** PhotoDisc, Inc.; **502:** PhotoDisc, Inc.; **503:** (above) PhotoDisc, Inc.; **503:** PhotoDisc, Inc.; **505:** (left E) PhotoDisc, Inc.; **505:** (left F) © Ann States/Saba; **505:** (right H) PhotoDisc, Inc.; **506:** Los Angeles Times Photo/Gina Ferazzi.

Module 22

508: (right F) © David Young-Wolff/Photo Edit; **508:** (right E) © Marvin Mattelson; **508:** (left B) Ruth Fremson/AP/Wide World Photos; **508:** (left A) *San Diego Union Tribune*/Rick McCarthy; **509:** (left) Reuters/Corbis-Bettmann; **509:** (right) © Elizabeth Roll; **510:** (above) © Henrik Drescher; **510:** (center) © Henrik Drescher; **511:** © Henrik Drescher; **511:** (above) *San Diego Union Tribune*/Rick McCarthy; **511:** (center) *San Diego Union Tribune*/Rick McCarthy; **512:** (right) William Cambell/Time Magazine; **512:** (left) © Tim Kimzey/Union Daily Times/Sipa Press; **512:** (below) Tim Kimzey/AP/Wide World Photos; **513:** (above) Ruth Fremson/AP/Wide World Photos; **513:** (below) William Cambell/Time Magazine; **514:** Tim Kimzey/AP/Wide World Photos; **515:** (right) Reuters/Corbis-Bettmann; **515:** (left) © Elizabeth Roll; **518:** © Elizabeth Roll; **520:** (above) © Marvin Mattelson; **521:** (left 4) Tim Kimzey/AP/Wide World Photos; **521:** (left 3) *San Diego Union Tribune*/Rick McCarthy; **522:** (center) © David Young-Wolff/Photo Edit; **524:** (above) © Elizabeth Roll; **524:** (below) © Elizabeth Roll; **526:** (left B) Ruth Fremson/AP/Wide World Photos; **526:** (left A) *San Diego Union Tribune*/Rick McCarthy; **527:** (left E) © Marvin Mattelson; **528:** Los Angeles Times Photo/Perry C. Riddle.

Module 23

530: (left A) *San Diego Union-Tribune*/Robert Gauthier; **530:** (right E) Craig McClain; **531:** (left) *San Diego Union-Tribune*/Robert Gauthier; **531:** (right) *San Diego Union-Tribune*/Robert Gauthier; **532:** (center) *San Diego Union-Tribune*/Robert Gauthier; **532:** (left) *San Diego Union-Tribune*/John Gastaldo; **533:** (below) © 1997 Time Inc., Reprinted by permission; **533:** (above) *San Diego Union-Tribune*/Robert Gauthier; **534:** (above) *San Diego Union-Tribune*/John Gastaldo; **534:** (below) *San Diego Union-Tribune*/Robert Gauthier; **535:** (above) Courtesy of CNBC; **536:** (below) Reuters/Corbis-Bettmann; **538:** *San Diego Union-Tribune*/Robert Gauthier; **539:** *San Diego Union-Tribune*/Robert Gauthier; **539:** (left) Courtesy of Edna Morlok; **540:** (below) *San Diego Union-Tribune*/Robert Gauthier*;* **540:** (left) Courtesy of Drs. E. Fuller Torrey & Daniel R. Weinberger, NIMH, Neuroscience Center, Washington D.C; **541:** (above) *San Diego Union-Tribune*/Robert Gauthier; **541:** (below) *San Diego Union-Tribune*/Jim Baird; **543:** (right 10) *San Diego Union-Tribune*/Robert Gauthier; **545:** Craig McClain; **547:** (center near left) Digital Stock Corporation; **551:** (left E) Craig McClain.

Module 24

554: (right F) © Roger Dashow/AnthroPhoto; **554:** (left A) National Library of Medicine; **555:** (left) Mary Evans/Sigmund Freud Copyrights/Sulloway; **555:** (right) Digital Stock Corporation; **555:** (right) PhotoDisc, Inc.; **556:** (bottom left) National Library of Medicine, # A-13394; **556:** (center near left) National Library of Medicine, neg. 93072; **556:** (right) Photo by Ken Smith of painting in Harrisburg State Hospital/LLR Collection; **557:** © Bernard Gotfryd/Woodfin Camp & Associates; **558:** (right) PhotoDisc, Inc.; **561:** (below) Mary Evans/Sigmund Freud Copyrights/Sulloway; **566:** Digital Stock Corporation; **566:** PhotoDisc, Inc.; **567:** © Elizabeth Roll; **572:** © Roger Dashow/AnthroPhoto; **574:** (above) PhotoDisc, Inc.; **574:** (below) PhotoDisc, Inc.; **575:** © Paul Buddle; **576:** (left A) National Library of Medicine; **577:** (right F) © Roger Dashow/AnthroPhoto.

Module 25

580: (left B) PhotoDisc, Inc.; **580:** (right H) PhotoDisc, Inc.; **580:** (left A) © James Wilson/Woodfin Camp & Associates; **580:** (left D) © Wade Spees; **580:** (left C) PhotoDisc, Inc.; **581:** (right) Channel 9 Australia/Gamma Liaison Network; **581:** (left) © Ted Hardin; **582:** (below) The Kobal Collection; **582:** (left) © Ted Hardin; **582:** (right) © Ted Hardin; **583:** (center near left) PhotoDisc, Inc.; **583:** (center near right) PhotoDisc, Inc.; **583:** (above) Craig McClain; **584:** (center far left) PhotoDisc, Inc.; **584:** (center near right) PhotoDisc, Inc.; **584:** (below) PhotoDisc, Inc.; **584:** (above) © James Wilson/Woodfin Camp & Associates; **585:** (above) © Robert Johnson/Gamma-Liaison Network; **585:** (right) PhotoDisc, Inc.; **586:** (center near left) PhotoDisc, Inc.; **586:** (center far right) PhotoDisc, Inc.; **586:** (above) Vince Campagnore/Los Angeles Times Photo; **587:** (above) PhotoDisc, Inc.; **587:** (below) PhotoDisc, Inc.; **588:** (above) Paula Scully/AP/Wide World Photos; **588:** (right) Paula Scully/AP/Wide World Photos; **588:** (left) PhotoDisc, Inc.; **589:** © Wade Spees; **590:** Photo by A. L. Wendrof, courtesy of the Anti Defamation League of B'nai B'rith, San Francisco and Gregory Withrow; **591:** (below) © 1997 Gregory Pace/Sygma; **591:** (center) Wesley Hitt/AP/Wide World Photos; **591:** (center) Wesley Hitt/AP/Wide World Photos; **592:** (above) Channel 9 Australia/Gamma Liaison Network; **592:** (center) Dallas Morning News/Gamma Liaison Network; **593:** PhotoDisc, Inc.; **595:** (above) Alan Weiner/New York Times Photo; **596:** People Weekly © 1993 Taro Yamasaki; **597:** (right) © Dan Miller/Woodfin Camp & Associates; **597:** (center) Reuters/Corbis-Bettmann; **597:** (left) © Bill Ross/Woodfin Camp & Associates; **598:** (left) PhotoDisc, Inc.; **598:** (right) PhotoDisc, Inc.; **599:** (right 10) Wesley Hitt/AP/Wide World Photos; **599:** (left 1) © Ted Hardin; **599:** (right 13) © Bill Ross/Woodfin Camp & Associates; **599:** (left 4) PhotoDisc, Inc.; **599:** (left 8) Photo by A. L. Wendrof, courtesy of the Anti Defamation League of B'nai B'rith, San Francisco and Gregory Withrow; **599:** (right 15) PhotoDisc, Inc.; **599:** (left 6) PhotoDisc, Inc.; **600:** (right) © Zig Leszcynski/Animals, Animals; **601:** (below) PhotoDisc, Inc.; **601:** (above) PhotoDisc, Inc.; **602:** (above) PhotoDisc, Inc.; **602:** (center) PhotoDisc, Inc.; **603:** (below) © Thomas Hartwell/Saba Press Photos; **604:** PhotoDisc, Inc.; **605:** PhotoDisc, Inc.; **606:** (left A) © James Wilson/Woodfin Camp & Associates; **606:** (right D) Wesley Hitt/AP/Wide World Photos; **606:** (left B) PhotoDisc, Inc.; **607:** (right H) PhotoDisc, Inc.; **608:** (above) PhotoDisc, Inc.

Figure Credits

This page constitutes an extension of the copyright page. We have made every effort to trace the ownership of all copyrighted material and to secure permission from copyright holders. In the event of any question arising as to the use of any material, we will be pleased to make the necessary corrections in future printings. Thanks are due to the following authors, publishers, and agents for permission to use the material indicated.

Module 1

6: Graph data from "Changes in the Palmar Sweat Index During Mental Arithmetic," by T. Kohler and U. Troester, 1991, *Biological Psychology, 32,* 143–154; **7:** Graph data from "Isolating Gender Differences in Test Anxiety: A Confirmatory Factor Analysis of the Test Anxiety Inventory," by Howard T. Everson, Roger E. Millsap, & Caroline M. Rodriguez, 1991, *Educational and Psychological Measurement, 51,* p. 247; **8:** Data from "The Relationship of Self-Management to Academic Motivation, Study Efficiency, Academic Satisfaction, and Grade Point Average Among Prospective Education Majors," by J. D. Long, P. Gaynor, A. Erwin and R. L. Williams, 1994, *Psychology: A Journal of Human Behavior, 31,* 22–30; **16:** Graph data from "Comparison of Self-Questioning, Summarizing, and Notetaking-Review as Strategies for Learning from Lectures," by A. King, 1992, *American Educational Research Journal, 29,* 303–23; **17:** Data from "Psychological Science Around the World," by M. R. Rosenzweig, 1992, *American Psychologist, 47,* 718–22; **21:** Excuses list from "Excuses, Excuses," by D. A. Bernstein, 1993, *APS Observer,* March, 1993 p. 4. Copyright © 1993 by the American Psychological Society. Reprinted by permission of the author; **24:** Adapted from "When Research is Swept Under the Rug," by Beth Azar. *APA Monitor,* August 1997, Vol. 28 (8). Copyright © by the American Psychological Association. Adapted by permission.

Module 2

30: Data from "Aspartame, Behavior, and Cognitive Function in Children with Attention Deficit Disorder," by B.A Shaywitz, C. M. Sullivan, G. Anderson, S. M. Gillespie, B. Sullivan & S. E. Shaywitz, *Pediatrics, 93,* 70–5; **33:** Data from reports by Long Beach, California Unified School District in years 1993–1994 versus 1994–1995; **37:** Data from "Methylphenidate and Children with Attention Deficit Disorder," by W. E. Pelham, M. E. Bender, J. Caddell, S. Booth, S. H. Moorer, 1985, *Archives of General Psychiatry, 42,* 948–52; **39:** Data from information in *Newsweek,* March 15, 1996, p. 52, from the Drug Enforcement Administration; **44:** Adapted from "Frequent Sexual Activity May Help Men Live Longer, Study Finds" by Lawrence K. Altman, 1997, New York Times News Service. Copyright © 1997 by *The New York Times Company.* Adapted by permission.

Module 3

64: Adapted from "Upsetting Our Sense of Self," by K. C. Cole, *Los Angeles Times,* April 28, 1997, p. A1. Copyright © 1997 by the *Los Angeles Times.* Adapted by permission of the publisher.

Module 4

68: Chromosome drawing (right) redrawn by permission from an illustration on page 126 by Michael Goodman in "DNA's New Twists," by John Rennie, *Scientific American,* March, 1993. Copyright © 1993 by Scientific American, Inc. All rights reserved; **79:** From "Language Specificity and Elasticity: Brain and Clinical Syndrome Studies," by M. Maratsos and L. Matheny, 1994, *Annual Review of Psychology, 45,* 487–516; **84:** Figures (left) adapted from "Sex Differences in the Brain," by D. Kimura, 1992, *Scientific American, 267,* 119–125; **90:** Adapted from "Reseachers Monkey Around with Origins of the Mind," by Lauren Neergaard, May 11, 1998. Copyright © 1998 by the Associated Press. Adapted by permission.

Module 5

92: John Karapelou/© 1993 The Walt Disney Co. Reprinted with permission of *Discover Magazine;* **93:** Adapted from an article in the *Los Angeles Times,* October 30, 1992; **98:** Adapted from an article in the *San Diego Union-Tribune,* April 3, 1984; **114:** John Karapelou/ © 1993 The Walt Disney Co. Reprinted with permission of *Discover Magazine;* **114:** Illustration by K. Daniel Clark from "Newsfronts—Science & Technology," by Dawn Stover, *Popular Science,* August 1997 p. 29. Reprinted by permission; **117:** John Karapelou/© 1993 The Walt Disney Co. Reprinted with permission of *Discover Magazine;* **118:** Adapted from "Tinnitus Study Offers Hope for Treatment" by Thomas H. Maugh II, *Los Angeles Times,* January 22, 1998, p. A1. Copyright © 1998 by the *Los Angeles Times.* Adapted by permission of the publisher.

Module 6

135: Bar graph (right) based on data from "Emotion Congruence in Perception," by P. M. Niedenthal and M. C. Sutterlund, *Personality and Social Psychology, 20,* 401–411; **139:** Bar graph (left) data adapted from "Does PSI Exist? Replicable Evidence for an Anomalous Process of Information Transfer," by D. J. Bem and C. Honorton, 1994, *Psychological Bulletin, 115,* 4–18; **144:** Adapted from "Predictably, Psychics Botch '97 Forecasts." Copyright © 1998 by the Associated Press. Adapted by permission.

Module 7

147: Adapted from an article in *Newsweek,* June 5, 1989; **155:** Temperature graph adapted from *Wide Awake at 3am by Choice or Chance?* by R. M. Coleman. Copyright © 1986 by Richard M. Coleman. Used with permission of W. H. Freeman and Company; **155:** Adapted from "Circadian Typology and Individual Differences," by I. Tankova, A. Adan & G. Buela-Casal, 1994, *Personality and Individual Differences, 16,* 671–684; **159:** Data [for Florida and New York] from "Diagnosis and Treatment of Seasonal Affective Disorder," by N. E. Rosenthan, 1993, *Journal of the American Medical Association, 270,* 2717–2720. Data [for Iceland] from "Prevalence of Seasonal Affective Disorder in Iceland," by A. Magnusson and J. F. Stefansson, 1993, *Archives of General Psychiatry, 50,* 941–946; **166:** Adapted from "Sorry, Freud, Dreams Aren't Conflict Resolvers," by Nicholas Wade. Copyright © 1998 by the New York Times Co. Adapted by permission.

Module 8

170: Bar graph data from "Individual Differences in Response to Hypnosis," by B. L. Bates, 1994. In J. W. Rhue, S. J. Lynn & I. Kirsch (Eds.), *Handbook of Clinical Hypnosis.* American Psychological Association; **173:** Bar graph on left Adapted from "Effects of Hypnosis on Regional Cerebral Blood Flow During Ischemic Pain wtih and without Suggested Hypnotic Analgesia," by H. J. Crawford, R. C. Gur, B. Skolnick, R. E. Gur & D. M. Benson, *International Journal of Psychophysiology, 15,* 181–195; **173:** Bar graph on right Adapted from "A Randomized Trial Comparing Smoking Cessation Programs Utilizing Behavior Modification, Health, Education or Hypnosis," by S. W. Rabkin, E. Boyko, F. Shane & J. Kaufert, 1984, *Addictive Behaviors, 9,* 157–173; **178:** Bar graph data from "Actual Causes of Death in the United States," by J. M. McGinnis and W. H. Foege, 1993, *Journal of the American Medical Association, 270,* 2207–2212; **188:** Adapted from "How AA Works and Why It's Important for Clinicians to Understand," by E. J. Khantzian and J. E. Mack, 1994, *Journal of Substance Abuse Treatment, 11,* 77–92; **192:** From "The Facts About Women, Alcohol," by Marilyn Elias, *USA Today,* January 5, 1998. Copyright © 1998 by *USA Today.* Adapted by permission.

Module 9

195: Adapted from "Cross-cultural Validity of a Parent's Version of the Dental Fear Survey Schedule for Children in Chinese," by P. Milgrom, J. Z Quang, K. M. Tay, 1994, *Behavior Research and Therapy, 32,* 131–135; **196:** Bar graph data from "Pitch Discrimination in the Dog," by H. M. Anrep, 1920, *Journal of Physiology, 53,* 367–385; **206:** Adapted from "Emotional Fainting and the Psychophysiologic Response to Blood and Injury: Autonomic Mechanisms and Coping Strategies," by A. Steptoe and J. Wardle, 1988, *Psychosomatic Medicine, 50,* 402–417; **210:** Adapted from "Study: Olestra Chips Score Well in Digestive Test," by Nanci Hellmich, *USA Today,* January 14, 1998. Copyright © 1998 by *USA Today.* Adapted by permission.

Figure Credits

Module 10

214: Graph on right based on *Behavior of Organisms,* by B. F. Skinner, 1938. Appleton-Century-Crofts; **215:** Skinner box illustration from *Introduction to Psychology* by E. Bruce Goldstein. Copyright © 1995 by Brooks/Cole Publishing Company; **216:** Adapted from "Treating Chronic Food Refusal in Young Children: Home-Based Parent Training," by M. A. Werle, T. B. Murphy & K. S. Budd, 1993, *Journal of Applied Behavior Analysis, 26,* 421–433. Adapted by permission of the author; **219:** Bar graph data from "A Comparison of Shock Intensity in the Treatment of Longstanding and Severe Self-Injurious Behaviors," by D. E. Williams, S. Kirkpatrick-Sanchez & B. A. Iwata, 1993, *Research in Development Disabilities, 14,* 207–219; **220:** Reinforcement diagram from *Psychology: Themes and Variations,* by Wayne Weiten, 2nd ed., figure 6.13. Copyright © 1992 by Wadsworth, Inc. Reproduced by permission; **220:** Skinner box illustration from *Introduction to Psychology* by E. Bruce Goldstein. Copyright © 1995 by Brooks/Cole Publishing Company; **223:** Skinner box illustration from *Introduction to Psychology* by E. Bruce Goldstein. Copyright © 1995 by Brooks/Cole Publishing Company; **224:** Bar graph data from "Influence of Models' Reinforcement Contingenices on the Acquisition of Imitative Responses," by A. Bandura, 1965, *Journal of Personality and Social Psychology, 1,* 589–596; **225:** Bar graph data from " Relative Efficacy of Densensitization and Modeling Approaches for Inducing Behavior, Affective and Attitudinal Changes" by A. Bandura, E. B. Blanchard & B. Ritter, 1969, *Journal of Personality and Social Psychology, 13,* 173–179; **227:** Skinner box illustration from *Introduction to Psychology* by E. Bruce Goldstein. Copyright © 1995 by Brooks/Cole Publishing Company; **230:** Graph from "Analysis of a High-Probability Instructional Sequence and Time-Out in the Treatment of Child Noncompliance," by A. K. Rortvedt and R. G. Miltenberger, 1994, *Journal of Applied Behavior Analysis, 27,* 327–330, figure 1a. Copyright © 1993 Society for the Experimental Analysis of Behavior. Reprinted by permission of the author; **232:** Bar graph data from "Behavioral Treatment and Normal Educational and Intellectual Functioning in Young Autistic Children," by O. I. Lovaas, 1987, *Journal of Consulting and Clinical Psychology, 55,* 3–9; **236:** Adapted from and reprinted with permission of Knight-Ridder/Tribune Information Services.

Module 11

241: Bar graph data from "The Information Available in Brief Visual Presentations," by G. A. Sperling, 1960, *Psychological Monographs, 74* (Whole No. 498); **242:** Graph data from "Short-Term Retention of Individual Verbal Items," by L. R. Peterson and M. J. Peterson, 1950, *Journal of Experimental Psychology, 58,* 193–198; **244:** Bar graph data from "Accuracy and Distortion in Memory for High School Girls," by H. P. Bahrick, L. K. Hall & S. A. Berger, 1996, *Psychological Science, 7,* 265–271; **245:** Graph data from "Two Storage Mechanisms in Free Recall," by M. Glanzer and A. R. Cunitz, 1966, *Journal of Verbal Learning and Verbal Behavior, 5,* 351–360; **247:** Bar graph data from "B-Adrenergic Activation and Memory for Emotional Events," by L. Cahill, B. Prins, M. Webert & J. McGaugh, 1994, *Nature, 371,* 702–704; **249:** Bar graph data from "Depth of Processing and the Retention of Words in Episodic Memory," by E. I. M. Craik and E. Tulving, 1975, *Journal of Experimental Psychology, General, 104,* 268–294; **251:** Bar graph data from "Repressed Memory Accusations: Devastated Families and Devastated Patients," by E. F. Loftus, 1997, *Applied Cognitive Psychology, 11,* 25–30; **253:** Excerpt from *Remembering: A Study in Experimental and Social Psychology,* by F. C. Bartlett, p. 65, 1932. Cambridge University Press. Copyright © 1932. Reprinted with the permission of Cambridge University Press; **253:** Bar graph data from "Repeated Memory of Oral Prose in Ghana and New York," by B. M. Ross and C. Millson, 1970, *International Journal of Psychology, 5,* 173–181; **255:** Adapted from "Vivid Memories," by D. C. Rubin and M. Kozin, 1984, *Cognition, 16,* 81–95. Copyright © 1984 by Elsevier Science Publishers BV. Adapted by permission; **258:** Adapted from "Boomer Brain Meltdown," by Anita Manning, *USA Today,* January 6, 1998, p. 1A. Copyright © 1998 by *USA Today.* Adapted by permission.

Module 12

261: Adapted from "Nearly 2,000 Witnesses Can Be Wrong," by R. Buckout, 1980, *Bulletin of the Psychonomic Society, 16,* 307–310; **262:** Based on *Learning and Memory,* by D. A. Norman, 1982. W. H. Freeman & Company; **263:** Based on "Retrieval Time from Semantic Memory," by A. M. Collins and M. R. Quillian, 1969, *Verbal Learning and Verbal Behavior, 8,* 240–247; **264:** Graph (bottom) data from "Fifty Years of Memory for Names and Faces," by H. P. Bahrick, P. O. Bahrick & R. P. Wittlinger, 1975, *Journal of Experimental Psychology: General, 104,* 54–75; **272:** Bar graph data from "Visual Spatial Memory in Australian Aboriginal Children of Desert Regions," by J. M. Kearins, 1981, *Cognitive Psychology, 13,* 434–460; **273:** Bar graph data from "Repeatedly Thinking About a Non-Event: Source Misattributions Among Pre-Schoolers," by S. J. Ceci, M. L. C. Huffman, E. Smith & E. Loftus, 1994, *Consciousness and Cognition, 3,* 388–407; **278:** Adapted from "Second Time Around," by Michael Haederle, *Los Angeles Times,* May 23, 1996 p. E1. Copyright © 1996 by *Los Angeles Times.* Adapted by permission of the publisher.

Module 13

287: Graphs : Adapted from "Age and WAIS-R A Cross-Sectional Analysis with Educational Level Controlled," by A. S. Kaufman, C. R. Reynolds & J. E. McLean, 1989, *Intelligence, 13,* pp. 246, 247. Copyright © 1989 by Ablex Publishing Company. Adapted by permission; **292:** Adapted from "Familial Studies of Intelligence: A Review," by T. J. Bouchard and M. McGue, 1981, *Science, 212,* 1055–1059. Copyright © 1981 by the American Association for the Advancement of Science. Adapted by permission of the author; **294:** Graph reprinted with permission of The Free Press, an imprint of Simon & Schuster Inc. from *The Bell Curve: Intelligence and Class Structure in American Life,* by Richard Hernstein and Charles Murray, 1994, p. 279. Copyright © 1994 Richard J. Hernstein and Charles Murray; **299:** Adapted from "Young Children Grow Up: The Effects of the Perry Preschool Program on Youth Through Age 15," by L. J. Schweinhart and D. P. Weikart, 1980, *Monographs of the High/Scope Educational Research Foundation,* 1980, No. 7. Courtesy of L. J. Schweinhart; **302:** Adapted from "A Real Brain Teaser," by Julie Marquis, *Los Angeles Times,* October 17, 1996 p. B2. Copyright © 1996 by *Los Angeles Times.* Adapted by permission of the publisher.

Module 14

309: Top left and p. 317: Adapted from *Conceptional Blockbusting: A Guide to Better Ideas,* by James L. Adams, pp. 17–18. Copyright © 1974 by James L. Adams. Used with permission of W. H. Freeman & Co., Publishers; **311:** Bar graph data from "Creativity and Psychopathology: A Study of 291 World-Famous Men," by F. Post, 1994, *British Journal of Psychiatry, 165,* 22–34; **326:** Adapted from "The Language of Learning," by Robert Lee Hotz, 1997, *Los Angeles Times,* Sept. 18. 1997, p. B2. Copyright © 1997 by the *Los Angeles Times.* Adapted by permission of the publisher.

Module 15

342: Bar graph data from *The Social Organization of Sexuality,* by E. Laumann, R. T. Michael, J. H. Gagnon & G. Kolata, 1994. University of Chicago Press; **351:** Math scores data from National Educational Longitudinal Study of 1988, National Opinon Research Center, University of Chicago; **356:** Adapted from "Childhood Obesity: A Lurking Health Risk" by Julie Marquis, *Los Angeles Times,* December 14, 1997 p. A1. Copyright © 1997 by the *Los Angeles Times.* Adapted by permission of the publisher.

Module 16

369: Based on "Brain Activity During Transient Sadness and Happiness in Healthy Women," by M. S. George, T. A. Ketter, P. P. Parekh, B. Horwitz, P. Herscovitch & R. M. Post, 1995, *American Journal of Psychiatry, 152,* 341–357; **370:** (Center) Reprinted from an illustration by John Tom Seetin and photograph by Gary Moo Young in "Working Knowlege," *Scientific American, 277 (6),* December, 1997, p. 132. Reprinted by permission of Scientific American and the illustrator. All rights reserved;

371: Bar graph data from "Detection of Deception: Polygraph and Integrity Tests," by L. Saxe, 1994, *Current Directions in Psychological Science, 3,* 69–73; **374:** Adapted from "Supreme Court Weighs Polygraph's Legal Admissibility," and "Supreme Court Bars Use of Polygraph Test as Defense," by D. G. Savage, *Los Angeles Times,* November 4, 1997 p. A14, and April 1, p. A11. Copyright © 1997 & 1998 by the *Los Angeles Times.* Adapted by permission of the publisher.

Module 17

380: Graph adapted from a figure in *The Developing Human: Clinically Oriented Embryology, 4th ed.,* by Keith L. Moore. W.B. Saunders Co., Copyright © 1988 by Keith L. Moore. Adapted by permission of the author; **387:** Data from "Temperamental Factors in Human Development," by J. Kagan and N. Snidman, *American Psychologist, 46,* 856–862; **387:** Data from "Biology and the Child," by J. Kagan, 1998. In W. Damon and R. M. Lerner (Eds.), *Handbook of Child Psychology, Vol. 1.* John Wiley & Sons, Inc.; **404:** Adapted from "An Angry Child Can Change" by Michael Ryan, *Parade,* April 14, 1996, pp. 20–21. Copyright © 1996 by *Parade.* Reprinted by permission of *Parade* and Scovil, Chichak & Galen Literary Agency on behalf of the author.

Module 18

407: Adapted from the *Los Angeles Times,* December 22, 1991, pp. E1, E12; **407:** Adapted from *Midterm Report,* by D. Wallechinsky, 1986. Viking Press; **409:** Bar graph data from "Sexual Behavior of American Adolescents: Results from a U. S. National Survey," by B. C. Leigh, D. M. Morrison, K. Trocki & M. T. Temple, 1994, *Journal of Adolescent Health, 15,* 117–125; **410:** Adapted from the *Los Angeles Times,* December 22, 1991, p. E13; **411:** Adapted from article in *San Diego Union-Tribune,* October 23, 1993, p. E4; **411:** Adapted from an article in the *Los Angeles Times,* May 2, 1994, p. E3; **413:** From *Parade Magazine,* July 14, 1991, pp. 6–7. Reprinted with permission from *Parade.* Copyright © 1991; **420:** List and page lists on p. 423 adapted from "Preferences in Human Mate Selection," by D. M. Buss and M. Barnes, 1986, *Journal of Personality and Social Psychology, 7,* 3–15. American Psychological Association; **423:** List [bottom] adapted from "International Preferences in Selecting Mates," by D. M. Buss, M. Abbott, A. Angleitner, A. Asherian, A. Biaggio, A. Blanoco-Villasenor, A. Bruchon-Scwietzer, H. Y. Ch'U, J. Czapinski, B. Deraad, B. Ekehammar, N. E. Lohamy, M. Fioravanti, J. Georgas, P. Gjerde, R. Guttmann, E. Hazan, S. Iwawaki, H. Jankiramaiah, F. Khosroshani, D. Kreitler, L. Lachenicht, M. Lee, K. Kiik, B. Little, S. Mika, M. Moadel-Shahid, G. Moane, M. Montero, A. C. Mundy-Castle, T. Niit, E. Nsenduluka, R. Pienkowski, A. M. Pirttila-Backman, J. P. De Leon, J. Rousseau, M. A. Runco, M. P. Safir, C. Samuels, R. Sanitioso, R. Serpell, N. Smid, C. Spencer, M. Tadinac, E. N. Tordorova, Z. K. Troland, L. Van Den Brande, G. Van Heck, L. Van Langenhove & K. S. Yang, 1990, Journal of Cross-Cultural Personality, 21, 5–47; **423:** Lists [center] adapted from "Mate Preferences in 37 Cultures," by D. M. Buss, 1994. In W. J. Lonner & R. Malpass (Eds.), *Psychology and Culture.* Allyn and Bacon; **426:** Center text adapted from *People Magazine,* May 21, 1990, pp. 56–59; **430:** Adapted from "Adulthood? Later, Dude!" by D. James Romero, *Los Angeles Times,* March 21, 1997. Copyright © 1997 by the *Los Angeles Times.* Adapted by permission of the publisher.

Module 19

454: Adapted from "Friends, Others Offer Complex View of Rathbun," by Robert J. Lopez and Eric Slater, *Los Angeles Times,* December 11, 1995, p. B1. Copyright © 1995 by *Los Angeles Times.* Adapted by permission of the publisher.

Module 20

465: Temperament survey data from "Personality Stability and Its Contribution to Successful Aging," by P. T. Costa, E. J. Metter & R. R. McCrae, 1994, *Journal of Geriatric Psychiatry, 27,* 41–59; **465:** Dependency scale data from "Personality Change in Women and Their Partners," by P. Wink and R. Helson, in press, *Journal of Personality and Social Psychology;* **465:** Excerpt from "Ok, so I'll Never Be a Waif," by L. Richardson, *Los Angeles Times,* June 7, 1994. Copyright © 1994 by the *Los Angeles Times.* Reprinted by permission; **467:** Bar graph data from "Genes, Environment, and Personality," by T. J. Bouchard, 1994, *Science, 264,* 1700–1701. American Association for the Advancement of Science; **468:** Bar graph data from "Genes, Environment, and Personality," by T. J. Bouchard, 1994, *Science, 264,* 1700–1701. American Association for the Advancement of Science; **471:** Bar graph data from "Cultural Styles of Conflict Management in Japanese and Americans: Passivity, Covertness and Effectiveness of Strategies," by K. Ohbushi and Y. Takahaski, 1994, *Journal of Applied Social Psychology, 24,* 1345–1366; **478:** Adapted from "Companies Using Personality Tests for Making Hire That Fit," by Carol Smith, *Los Angeles Times,* February 9, 1997 p. D5. Copyright © 1997 by *Los Angeles Times.* Adapted by permission of the publisher.

Module 21

481: Text about Sandra Sullivan, adapted from an article by Sasha Nyary, *Life Magazine,* April, 1992 pp. 62–65; **483:** Bar graph data from "The Use of Cognitive Appraisal to Reduce Stress Reactions: A Replication," by A. C. Dandoy and A. G. Goldstein, 1990, *Journal of Social Behavior and Personality, 5,* 272–285; **483:** Situation list data from *USA Today,* August 19, 1987, p. 4D; **486:** Adapted from "The Factor Structure of Self-Reported Physical Stress Reactions," by J. C. Smith and J. M. Seidel, 1982, *Biofeedback and Self-Regulation, 7,* 35–47; **488:** Bar graph data from "Psychological Stress and Susceptibility to the Common Cold," by S. Cohen, D. A. J. Tyrrell & A. P. Smith, *New England Journal of Medicine, 325,* 606–612; **490:** Scale: Reprinted with permission from *Journal of Psychosomatic Research, 11,* 213–218, by T. H. Holmes and R. H. Rahe in "The Social Readjustment Rating Scale," 1967, Pergamon Press, Ltd., Oxford, London; **490:** Text about Sandra Sullivan, adapted from an article by Sasha Nyary, *Life Magazine,* April, 1992 pp. 62–65; **494:** Graph adapted from "Hardiness and Stress Moderation: A Test of Proposed Mechanisms," by D. J. Wiebe, 1991, *Journal of Personality and Social Psychology,* 60, pp. 89–99, p. 94. American Psychological Association; **495:** Bar graph data from "Stress and Illness: Controllable and Uncontrollable Life Events' Relative Contributions," by G. S. Stern, T. R. McCants & P. W. Pettine, *Personality and Social Psychology Bulletin, 8,* 140–143; **497:** Probability graph data from "Social Support, Negative Life Events and Mental Health," by O. S. Dalgard, S. Bjork & K. Tambs, 1995, *British Journal of Psychiatry, 166,* 29–34; **497:** Change in blood pressure data from "Social Support Lowers Cardiovascular Reactivity to an Acute Stressor," by S. J. Lepore, K. A. Mata Allen & G. W. Evans, 1993, *Psychosomatic Medicine, 55,* 518–524; **501:** Graph data from "Body Temperature Changes During the Practice of g Tummo-Yoga," by H. Bensen, J. W. Lehmann, M. S. Malhotra, R. F. Goldman, P. J. Hopkins & M. D. Epstein, 1982, *Nature, 295,* 234–235; **506:** Adapted from "The Diagnosis," by Mary Herczog, *Los Angeles Times,* December 8, 1997, p. S1. Copyright © 1997 by the *Los Angeles Times.* Adapted by permission of the publisher.

Module 22

514: Pages 514–515: Syndrome titles from *Diagnostic and Statistical Manual of Mental Disorders,* Fourth Edition. Copyright © 1994 American Psychiatric Association; **514:** Pages 514–520: Disorder definitions are based on descriptions in *DSM-IV,* American Psychiatric Association, 1994; **516:** Bar graph data from "Lifetime and 12-month Prevalence of DSM-III-R Psychiatric Disorders in the United States," by R. C. Kessler, K. A. McGonagle, S. Zhao, C. B. Nelson, M. Hughes, S. Eshleman, H. Wittchen & K. S. Kendler, 1994, *Archives of General Psychiatry, 51,* 8–19; **518:** Bar graph data from "Panic and Phobia" by W. W. Eaton, A. Dryman & M. M. Weissman, 1991. In L. N. Robins & D. A. Regier (Eds.), *Psychiatric Disorders in America: The Epidemiological Catchment Area Study.* Free Press; **519:** Bar graph data from "Current Status of Pharmacological and Behavioral Treatment of Obseesive-Cumpulsive Disorder," by G. B. Stanley and S. M. Turner, 1995, *Behavior Therapy, 26,* 163–186; **522:** Bar graph (upper) data from "The Place of Culture in Psychiatric Nosology: Taijin Kyofusho and DSM-III-R," by L. J. Kirmayer, 1991, *Journal of Nervous and Mental Disease, 179,* 19–28; **522:** Bar graph (lower) data from "Social

Figure Credits

Phobia Syndrome in Japan," by T. Takahashi, 1989, *Comprehensive Psychiatry, 30,* 45–52; **525:** Graphs adapted from "International Advances in the Treatment of Social Phobia," by J. R. T. Davidson, 1994, *Journal of Clinical Psychiatry, 55,* 123–129; **528:** Adapted from "Prisoners of Love" by Pamela Warrick, *Los Angeles Times,* January 23, 1997, p. E1. Copyright © 1997 by the *Los Angeles Times.* Adapted by permission of the publisher.

Module 23

531: Adapted from "Breakdown into the Shadows of Mental Illness," by C. Brooks, *San Diego Union-Tribune,* February 27, 1994, p. 4; **531:** Adapted from "Shadowland: Three Profiled in Mental Illness Series Are Striving to Improve Their Condition" by C. Brooks, *San Diego Union-Tribune,* February 27, 1995; **533:** Bar graph data from "Current Perspectives on the Genetics of Unipolar Depression," by S. O. Moldin, T. Reich & J. P. Rice, 1991, *Behavior Genetics, 21,* 211–242; **535:** ECT treatment graph adapted from "Use of ECT with Treatment-Resistant Depressed Patients at the National Institute of Mental Health," by S. M. Paul, I. Extein, H. M. Calil, W. Z. Potter, P. Chodiff & F. K. Goodwin, 1981, *American Journal of Psychiatry, 138,* 486–489; **535:** Bar graph data from "Use of ECT in the United States in 1975, 1980 and 1986," by J. W. Thompson, R. D. Weiner & C. P. Myers, 1994, *American Journal of Psychiatry, 151,* 1657–1661. 1995 data from "Shock Therapy," by D. Cauchon, *USA Today,* December 6, 1995; **537:** Graph data from "An Open Trial of Sertraline in Personality Disordered Patients with Impulsive Aggression," by R. J. Kavoussi, J. Liu & E. F. Caccaro, 1994, *Journal of Clinical Psychiatry, 55,* 137–141; **539:** Bar graph data from *Schizophrenia Genesis: The Origins of Madness,* by I. I. Gottesmann, 1991. W. H. Freeman & Company; with additional data from

"The Epidemiology of Schizophrenia in a Finnish Twin Cohort," by T. D. Cannon, J. Kaprio, J. Lonnqvist, M. Huttunen & M. Koskenvuo, 1998, *Archives of General Psychiatry, 55,* 67–74; **542:** Data from "Duration of Neuroleptic Treatment and Prevalence of Tardive Dyskinesia in Late Life," by R. A. Sweet, B. H. Mulsant, B. Gupta, A. H. Rifai, R. E. Pasternak, A. McEachran & G. S. Zubenko, 1995, *Archives of General Psychiatry, 52,* 478–486; **545:** Bar graph data from "The Diagnosis of Multiple Personality Disorder: A Critical Review," by T. A. Fahy, 1988, *British Journal of Psychiatry, 153,* 597–606; and "Multiple Identity Enactments and Multiple Personality Disorder: A Sociocognitive Perspective," by N. P. Spanos, 1994, *Psychological Bulletin, 116,* 1434–1465; **546:** Bar graph data from "Lifetime and 12-month Prevalence of DSM-III-R Psychiatric Disorders in the United States," by R. C. Kessler, K. A. McGonagle, S. Zhao, C. B. Nelson, M. Higher, S. Eshleman, H. Wittchen & K. S. Kendler, 1994, *Archives of General Psychiatry, 51,* 8–19; **552:** Adapted from "Recovered" by Shari Roan, *Los Angeles Times,* January 30, 1996, p. E1. Copyright © 1996 by the *Los Angeles Times.* Reprinted by permission of the *Los Angeles Times.*

Module 24

557: Graph data from the National Institute of Mental Health; **560: Therapy Session** Adapted from "A Critique of So-Called Standard Psychoanalytic Technique," by S. D. Lipton, 1983, *Contemporary Psychoanalysis, 19,* 35–52; **563:** Bar graph adapted from "Trends in Counseling and Psychotherapy," by D. Smith, 1982, *American Psychologist, 37,* 802–809. Copyright © 1982 by the American Psychological Association. Adapted by permission; **564: Therapy Session:** Adapted from "Person-Centered Therapy," by N. J. Raskin and C. R. Rogers, 1989. In R. J. Corsini and D. Wedding (Eds.), *Current Psychotherapies,* 4th ed. F. E. Peacock;

565: Therapy Session: Adapted from *Cognitive Therapy of Depression,* by A. T. Beck, A. J. Rush, B. F. Shaw & G. Emery, 1979, pp. 145–146. Guilford Press; **566: Therapy Session:** Adapted from *Clinical Behavior Therapy,* by M. R. Goldfried and G. C. Davison, 1976. Holt, Rinehart & Winston; **571:** Bar graph adapted from "Trends in Counseling and Psychotherapy," by D. Smith, 1982, *American Psychologist, 37,* 802–809. Copyright © 1982 by the American Psychological Association. Adapted by permission; **573:** Bar graph data from "Eye Movement Desensitation: A Partial Dismantling Study," by G. Renfrey and C. R. Spates, 1994, *Journal of Behavior Therapy and Experimental Psychiatry, 25,* 231–239; **578:** Adapted from "Virtual Therapy" by Jane E. Stevens, *Los Angeles Times,* Feb 28, 1995. Copyright © 1995 by the *Los Angeles Times.* Adapted by permission.

Module 25

587: Bar graphs adapted from "Improving the Academic Performance of College Freshmen," by T. D. Wilson and P. W. Linville, 1982, *Journal of Personality and Social Psychology, 42,* 367–376, Copyright © 1982 by the American Psychological Association. Adapted by permission of the author; **592:** Based on "Effects of Group Pressure Upon Modification and Distortion of Judgements," by Solomon Asch, 1958. In E. Maccoby, T. M. Newcomb & E. L. Hartley (Eds.), Readings in Social Psychology (3rd Ed.). Holt, Rinehart & Winston; **594:** Bar graph adapted from "Behavioral Study of Obedience," by S. Milgram, 1963, *Journal of Abnormal and Social Psychology, 67,* 371–378; **608:** Adapted from "Teen Pregnancies Force Town to Grow Up" by Sheryl Stolberg, *Los Angeles Times,* November 29, 1996. Copyright © 1996 the *Los Angeles Times.* Adapted by permission.

Name Index

Subject Index

Subject Index

explanations for, 202
of immune system, 489
operant conditioning vs., 217
procedure for, 197–198
review and study questions on, 203, 210
summary test on, 208–209
systematic desensitization and, 207
Web sites on, 211
Client-centered therapy, 564, 570, 622
Clinical assessment, 512–513, 622
Clinical diagnosis, 514–516, 622
Clinical interview, 512, 622–623
Clinical psychologists, 17, 557, 558, 623
Clinical scales, 474
Clinical syndromes, 514–515
Clomipramine, 519
Cloning, 64
Closure rule, 127, 623
Clozapine, 541, 542
Cocaine, 59, 177, 623
Cochlea, 102–103, 623
Cochlear implants, 115, 623
Coffee, 178
Cognition, 311
Cognitive appraisal theory, 360, 362–363, 623
Cognitive approach, 5, 7, 305, 310, 623
Cognitive-behavioral approach, 510, 568, 623
Cognitive-behavioral deficits, 604
Cognitive-behavior therapy, 559, 568, 574–575, 623
 for controlling aggression, 605
 for insomnia, 162, 575
 for substance abusers, 189
 for treating phobias, 524
Cognitive component of attitudes, 588
Cognitive development, 623
 in adolescents, 410–414
 in children, 388–391, 398
Cognitive developmental theory, 396, 623
Cognitive dissonance, 590, 623
Cognitive factors, 623
 aggressive behavior and, 601
 human motivation and, 350
 personality development and, 458, 459, 473
Cognitive factors in motivation, 350, 623
Cognitive interview, 275, 623
Cognitive learning, 196, 213, 223–226, 623
 behavior modification and, 232
 cultural diversity and, 231
 insight and, 226
 observational learning and, 224
 review and study questions on, 227, 236
 social cognitive theory and, 225

three viewpoints on, 223
Web sites on, 237
Cognitive map, 223, 623
Cognitive miser model, 586, 623
Cognitive neuroscience, 71, 223
Cognitive perspective theory, 202, 623
Cognitive processes. *See also* Thinking
 aging and, 415
 brain anatomy and, 76, 77
 creativity and, 311
 motivation and, 350
 test anxiety and, 7
Cognitive psychology, 19, 623
Cognitive rules, 397
Cognitive stage theory, 388–391, 410
Cognitive theory
 of depression, 548
 of emotion, 362
 of human motivation, 331
Cognitive therapy, 565, 570, 623
Cognitive unconscious, 149, 441, 623
Collective unconscious, 440, 623
Collectivistic culture, 471, 623
Color blindness, 99, 624
Color constancy, 128, 624
Color vision, 98–99
Commitment, 419, 624
Common factors, 571, 624
Communication, 322, 624. *See also* Language
 adolescent-parent, 414
 animal, 322–323
Community mental health centers, 557, 624
Companionate love, 419, 624
Compensatory factors, 401
Compliance, 593, 624
Compromise, 492
Computerized axial tomography (CAT) scan, 624
Conception, 379, 624
Concepts, 306, 624
 forming, 306–307
 functions of, 307
Concrete operations stage, 390, 624
Conditional positive regard, 445, 624
Conditioned emotional response, 201, 493, 624
Conditioned nausea, 568
Conditioned reflex, 196, 197
Conditioned response (CR), 197, 198, 217, 624
Conditioned stimulus (CS), 197, 198, 624
Conduct disorder, 523, 624
Conduction deafness, 115, 624
Cones (eye), 96, 624
Conflict
 defined, 492, 624
 interpersonal, 471

marital, 420, 422
parent-child, 438, 439
stress and, 492
styles of dealing with, 492
unconscious, 493
Conflict resolution
 cultural differences in, 471
 psychosexual stages and, 438
 in relationships, 420, 422
Conformity, 592, 624
Consciousness, 146–167. *See also* Dreams; Sleep
 altered states of, 148, 171
 biological clocks and, 150–151, 155
 continuum of, 148–149
 defined, 148, 624
 research on, 147, 149
 review and study questions on, 158, 166
 seasonal affective disorder and, 159
 stages of sleep and, 152–154
 summary test on, 164–165
 Web sites on, 166
Conscious thoughts, 434, 472, 624
Consensus, 585, 624
Consequences, in operant conditioning, 217, 218
Conservation, 389, 390
Consistency, 585, 624
Constancy, perceptual, 128
Contemporary Hypnosis, 171
Content scales, 474
Contiguity theory, 202, 624
Continuity rule, 127, 624
Continuous reinforcement, 220, 624
Continuum of consciousness, 148–149, 624
Control
 of behavior, 4, 16
 locus of, 459, 473, 495
 of situations, 499
Control group, 37, 587, 624
Controlled processes, 148, 625
Controlling behavior, 4, 16
Control Question Technique, 370–371, 625
Conventional level, 412, 625
Convergence, 129, 625
Convergent thinking, 310, 625
Conversion disorder, 520, 625
Coping
 with anxiety, 493
 appraisal and, 494, 499
 strategies for, 499, 503
 with trauma, 500
Cornea, 95, 625
Corpus callosum, 86, 625
Correlation, 32–33, 85, 625
Correlation coefficient, 32, 625
Cortex, 74, 161, 268, 625
Counseling psychologists, 558, 625
Counterattitudinal behavior, 590, 625
Covariation model, 585, 625

Creative individuals, 305, 310, 625
Creative thinking, 310–311, 625
Crisis management, 427
Critical language period, 316, 625
Critical period, 228, 625
Cross-cultural approach, 5, 11, 625
Cross-sectional method, 386, 625
Crowds, 597, 625
Cultural bias, 291, 625
Cultural diversity
 achievement and, 448
 alcoholism and, 185
 conflict resolution and, 471
 dental fears and, 205
 discrimination and, 14
 drugs and, 59
 emotional expressions and, 364, 367
 gender roles and, 399, 546
 intelligence and, 296
 language and, 319, 321
 learning principles and, 231
 memory and, 253, 272
 mental disorders and, 522, 546
 perception and, 136–137
 placebo use and, 31
 psychotherapy and, 572
 relationships and, 423
 seasonal affective disorder and, 159
 taste and, 110
Cultural-familial retardation, 288, 625
Cultural influences, 136, 625
Cultural values, 412
Culture-free tests, 291
Cumulative record, 220, 625
Curare, 59, 625

D

DARE (Drug Abuse Resistance Program), 187, 625–626
Date rapist, 602, 605
Daydreaming, 148, 626
Deafness, 101, 115
Debriefing, 40, 594, 626
Deceptive techniques, 40
Decibels, 101, 626
Decisions, group, 598
Decision-stage model of helping, 595, 626
Declarative memory, 246, 626
Deductive reasoning, 318, 626
Deep structures, 313, 626
Defense mechanisms, 437, 449, 493, 626
Deficiency needs, 443, 626
Definition theory, 306, 626
Deindividuation, 597, 626
Deinstitutionalization, 557, 626
Delay of gratification, 460, 473, 626
Dendrites, 50, 87, 626
Denial, 437, 626
Dental fears, 173, 205
Dependency, 174, 626
Dependent personality disorder, 536, 626

Hollywood love, 419
Homeostasis, 81, 330, 632
Homo erectus, 69
Homo sapiens, 69
Homosexual orientation, 341, 343, 632
Honesty tests, 474
Hormones, 82, 247, 255, 258, 339
Horoscopes, 475
Hotline services, 427
Humanistic approach, 5, 10, 632
Humanistic theories, 442–446, 458, 472
　characteristics unique to, 442
　criticisms of, 446
　Maslow's hierarchy of needs, 332–333, 443
　practical application of, 446
　Rogers' self theory, 444–445
　self-actualization and, 443, 444, 445
Hunger, 334–337
　biological factors in, 334, 335
　genetic factors in, 334, 336
　psychosocial factors in, 334, 337
Hypnosis, 169, 170–173, 632
　behaviors under, 172
　procedure for inducing, 170
　repressed memories and, 251
　review and study questions on, 184, 192
　susceptibility to, 170
　theories of, 171
　uses for, 173
Hypnotherapy, 173
Hypnotic analgesia, 172, 632
Hypnotic induction, 170, 632
Hypothalamus, 80, 82, 335, 339, 408, 484, 485, 632
Hypothesis, 36, 632
Hysteria, 520

I

Icelanders, 159
Iconic memory, 241, 632
Id, 9, 436, 472, 632
Ideal self, 444, 632
Ideal weight, 334
Identical twins, 292, 632
Identity, 416, 632
Identity confusion, 417
Identity vs. role confusion stage, 393, 417
Illusions, perceptual, 132–133, 632
Imaginary audience, 411
Imaginary exposure, 525
Imagined perception, 172, 632
Imitation, 225
Immediate reinforcement, 215
Immigrants
　achievement motivation among, 351, 448
　intelligence tests and, 296
Immune system, 488–489, 632
Implicit memory. *See* Procedural memory

Impossible figure, 132, 633
Imprinting, 228, 633
Incentives, 331, 633
Independent variable, 36, 633
Individualistic culture, 471, 633
Individual psychology, 440
Inductive reasoning, 318, 633
Industrial psychologists, 17
Industry vs. inferiority stage, 393
Infants. *See also* Children
　attachment behavior in, 385
　cognitive development in, 388–391
　emotional development in, 384–385
　fearfulness in, 386–387
　genetic development in, 382
　language used with, 326
　motor development in, 383
　review and study questions on, 395, 404
　sensory development in, 382
　sleep needs of, 156
　social and personality development in, 392–394, 396–398
　speech recognition in, 229
　temperament in, 384, 386–387
　universal emotions in, 364
Infatuated love, 419
Inferential statistics, 613–616, 633
Informational influence theory, 597, 633
Ingroup, 598
Inhibited children, 386–387, 633
Inhibited female orgasm, 344, 633
Inhibitory transmitters, 54
Initial state, 308
Initiative vs. guilt stage, 393
Innate intelligence, 296
Innate language factors, 316, 633
Innate program, 313
Inner ear, 102–103
Insanity, 509, 633
Insecure attachment, 385, 633
Insight, 226, 309, 633
Insight therapies, 559, 560–565, 633
　client-centered therapy, 564
　cognitive therapy, 565
　psychoanalysis, 560–563
Insomnia, 162, 568, 575, 633
Instincts, 330, 633
Instrumental conditioning. *See* Operant conditioning
Integration, 492
Integrity tests, 474
Integrity vs. despair stage, 417
Intelligence, 280–303
　brain size and, 85, 284
　creativity and, 310–311
　cultural factors and, 291, 296
　defining, 282–283
　emotion and, 302
　environmental factors and, 281, 292–294, 298–299
　genetic factors and, 281, 292–294
　measuring, 284–291, 297

PET scans and, 297, 302
　review and study questions on, 295, 302
　summary test on, 300–301
　theories of, 282–283
　Web sites on, 303
Intelligence quotient (IQ), 633
　computing, 285
　creativity and, 311
　distribution of, 288–289
　general intelligence (*g*) factor and, 282
　historical origins of, 285
　intervention programs and, 298–299
　nature-nurture question and, 292–294
　racial and cultural biases in, 290–291, 294, 296
　tests for measuring, 286–287
　twin studies and, 281
Intelligence tests
　examples of, 286
　historical origins of, 285
　immigration and, 296
　problems with, 290–291, 294, 296
　uses for, 288–289
　validity and reliability of, 287
Interactive model of sexual orientation, 341, 633
Interference, 242, 265, 266, 267, 271, 633
Internal attributions, 585, 633
Internal locus of control, 459, 495
International Classification of Disease and Related Health Problems (ICD-10), 546
Interneurons, 56, 633
Interpersonal conflict, 471, 633
Interposition, 130, 633
Interpretation of Dreams, The (Freud), 160
Interpreting function of attitudes, 589, 633
Interval timing clock, 150, 633
Intervention programs, 298–299, 633
Interviews, 34, 633
　clinical, 512
　cognitive, 275
　structured, 470
Intestines, 335, 485
Intimacy, 417, 419, 633
Intimacy vs. isolation stage, 417
Intrinsic motivation, 331, 350, 633
Introspection, 12, 633
Intrusive thoughts, 574, 633
Inuit people, 161, 319, 634
In vivo exposure, 525, 567
Involuntary response, 217
Ions, 52, 634
IQ. *See* Intelligence quotient
Iris, 95, 634
Irrational thoughts, 575
Isolation, 417

J

James-Lange theory of emotion, 360, 634
Japan
　conflict resolution in, 471
　organ transplants in, 603
　social phobias in, 522
Jet lag, 151, 634
Job discrimination, 584, 586
Job performance, 289
Journal of Black Psychology, 14
Journal of Cross-Cultural Psychology, 11
Journal of Humanistic Psychology, 10
Justice orientation, 412, 634
Just noticeable difference (JND), 123, 634

K

Kohlberg's theory of moral reasoning, 412

L

Labeling, 516, 634
Laboratory experiment, 34, 634
Laboratory setting, 35, 634
Language, 312–323. *See also* Speech
　in animals, 322–323
　Chomsky's theory of, 313
　cultural differences and, 319, 321
　defined, 305, 312, 634
　dyslexia and, 320
　factors in learning, 316
　gender differences and, 321
　personality development and, 459
　review and study questions on, 317, 326
　rules of, 312–313
　stages in acquiring, 314–315, 634
　summary test on, 324–325
　thought and, 318–319
　understanding, 313
　verbal retrieval cues and, 272
　Web sites on, 327
Latency stage, 392, 439, 634
Lateral hypothalamus, 335
Laws
　all-or-none, 52, 619
　of effect, 196, 214, 634
　Weber's, 123, 651
　Yerkes-Dodson, 365, 652
L-dopa, 60
Learned associations, 337
Learning. *See also* Memory
　biological factors in, 228–229
　classical, 196, 197–207
　cognitive, 196, 213, 223–226
　cultural diversity and, 231
　defined, 195, 634
　imprinted, 228
　insight, 226
　language, 316, 326
　observational, 224, 459
　operant, 196, 213, 214–222, 232–233

review and study questions on, 347, 356
sexual behavior and, 338–345
social cognitive learning and, 225
social needs and, 332
summary test on, 354–355
theories of, 330–331
unconscious, 434
values and, 448
Web sites on, 357
Motivational therapy, 189
Motor cortex, 76, 637
Motor development, 383, 398, 637
Motor disorders, 538
Motor homunculus, 76
Motor neurons, 56
MRI scans, 70, 547, 635
Müller-Lyer illusion, 133
Multiple-intelligence theory, 283, 637
Multiple personality disorder, 545
Muscle tension, 485
Myelin sheath, 50, 53, 637

N

Narcolepsy, 163, 176, 637
Narcotics, 179
Narcotics Anonymous (NA), 189
National attitudes, 603
National Center for Health Statistics, 337
National Center on Addiction and Substance Abuse, 187
National Committee to Prevent Child Abuse, 400
National Enquirer, 144
National Institute of Mental Health, 41, 535
National Institute on Alcohol Abuse and Alcoholism (NIAAA), 192
National Institutes on Drug Abuse, 186
Naturalistic setting, 35, 637
Nature-nurture question, 292–294, 377, 637
Nearsightedness, 95, 637
Needs
defined, 330, 637
hierarchy of, 332–333, 443, 472
satisfying, 332
types of, 332, 443
Negative correlation coefficient, 32
Negative emotion, 491, 495
Negative punishment, 219, 230, 233, 637
Negative reinforcement, 218, 637
Negative reinforcers, 218
Negative self-concept, 444
Negative self-statements, 502
Negative skews, 611
Negative symptoms of schizophrenia, 541, 637
Negative thoughts, 549
Neglect syndrome, 79, 637
Neo-Freudians, 440

Nerve fibers, 96
Nerve impulse, 52, 637
Nerves, 51, 637
Nervous system. *See also* Brain
autonomic, 72, 81
central, 51, 72
effects of drugs on, 175, 176–182, 186
major divisions of, 72
parasympathetic, 72, 81, 484
peripheral, 51, 72
phantom limbs and, 58
reflex responses and, 56
review and study questions on, 57, 64
sleep deprivation and, 157
somatic, 72
structure and function of, 51–56
summary test on, 62–63
sympathetic, 72, 81, 484, 485
Web sites on, 65
Network hierarchy, 263, 637
Network theory of memory, 262, 637
Neural assemblies, 269, 637
Neural deafness, 115, 637
Neural impulses, 96
Neuroleptic drugs, 541–542, 637
Neurological factors
mood disorders and, 533
personality disorders and, 537
schizophrenia and, 540
Neurological tests, 512
Neurons, 48, 637
communication between, 54–55
damage to, 49, 50
fetal tissue transplants and, 60–61
nerves vs., 51
reflex responses and, 56
regrowth of, 51
structure and function of, 50
Neuropeptide Y, 335
Neuroses, 514, 561, 637
Neurotransmitters, 54–55, 637
drug effects and, 55, 59, 175
sleep-related, 157
Neutral stimulus, 197, 198, 637
Newborns, 382–383, 398. *See also* Infants
emotional expression in, 384
New England Journal of Medicine, 427
New York Times, 85
Nicotine, 178, 637
Nightmares, 163, 638
Night terrors, 163, 637–638
Nitric oxide, 55
Nodes, 262, 263, 638
Noncompliance, 230, 568, 638
Nonintellectual factors, 291, 638
Non-REM sleep, 152, 638
Nonshared environmental factors, 467
Norepinephrine, 335
Normal aging, 424, 638

Normal curve, 610, 638
Normal distribution, 288–289, 610, 638
No-single-category babies, 384
Note-taking strategies, 16, 21

O

Obedience, 593, 638
Obesity, 334, 356, 638
Objective personality tests, 474–475, 638
Object permanence, 389, 638
Observational learning, 224, 459, 493
Obsessive-compulsive disorders, 519, 638
Obsessive-compulsive personality disorder, 536, 638
Occipital lobe, 74, 79, 97, 638
OCEAN model of personality traits, 463, 468, 473
Oedipus complex, 439, 638
Olfaction, 107, 638
Olfactory cells, 107, 638
One Flew Over the Cuckoo's Nest (film), 535
Operant conditioning, 196, 213, 214–222, 232–233. *See also* Classical conditioning
behavior modification and, 232
biofeedback as, 233
classical conditioning vs., 217
concepts associated with, 222
defined, 638
discovery of, 214
examples of, 216
language acquisition and, 316
noncompliance and, 230
principles and procedures, 215
punishment and, 218, 219, 230, 233
reinforcers and, 218–219
review and study questions on, 227, 236
schedules of reinforcement and, 220–221
summary test on, 234–235
Web sites on, 237
Operant response, 214, 215, 638
Operations state, 308
Opiates, 179, 638
Opium, 179
Opponent-process theory, 99, 638
Optic nerve, 96, 97
Optimal weight, 334, 638
Optimism, 495, 638
Oral stage, 392, 439, 638
Oral tradition, 253
Organic causes, 344, 638
Organic mental disorders, 514
Organic retardation, 288, 638
Orgasmic dysfunctions, 344
Origin of Species, The (Darwin), 69
Ossicles, 102
Outer ear, 102, 639

Outgroup, 598
Overgeneralization, 315, 548, 565, 639
Overweight, 334, 356, 639
Ovulation, 379, 639

P

Pacinian corpuscle, 108
Pain, 112–113, 639
hypnotic analgesia and, 172, 173
perception of, 111, 205
placebo effect and, 111
Palmar sweating, 6
Pancreas, 82, 639
Panic attack, 517, 639
Panic disorder, 517, 639
Paradoxical sleep, 153
Paranoid personality disorder, 536, 639
Paranoid schizophrenia, 538, 546, 639
Paraphilias, 344, 639
Parasympathetic nervous system, 72, 81, 484, 501, 639
Parentese, 314, 326, 639
Parenting
child abuse and, 400–401, 568
immigrant values and, 448
noncompliance and, 230
styles of, 413
Parietal lobe, 74, 77, 639
Parkinson's disease, 60, 639
Partial reinforcement, 220–221, 639
Passion, 419, 639
Passionate love, 419, 639
Passive strategy, 471
Pathological aging, 424, 639
Peer pressure, 329, 348
Peg method, 271, 639
Perception, 120–145
beliefs and, 30
constancy of, 128
creating, 140–141
cultural diversity and, 136–137
defined, 93, 124, 639
depth, 129–131
disorders of, 538
emotional states and, 135
extrasensory, 138–139
first impressions and, 141, 581, 582
illusions and, 132–133
imagined, 172
motion, 137, 140
organizational rules of, 126–127
pain, 111, 205
phi movement, 13, 140
review and study questions on, 134, 144
sensation vs., 124–125
subliminal, 135
summary test on, 142–143
thresholds of, 122–123
virtual reality and, 141
Web sites on, 145

Psychopathology. *See also* Mental disorders
  creativity and, 311
  psychotherapy and, 537
Psychopaths, 536–537
Psychoses, 514
Psychosexual stages, 392, 393, 438–439, 472, 643
Psychosocial factors, 643
  diagnosis of mental disorders and, 515
  hunger motivation and, 334, 337
  mood disorders and, 533
  personality disorders and, 537
Psychosocial hunger factors, 334, 643
Psychosocial stages, 393, 417, 440, 643
Psychosomatic symptoms, 486–487, 489, 568, 643
Psychotherapy, 554–579
  behavior therapy, 566–568
  careers in, 17
  cognitive-behavior techniques, 574–575
  common factors in, 571
  cultural diversity and, 572
  defined, 556, 643
  for depression, 534
  effectiveness of, 559, 571
  evaluation of approaches to, 570
  Eye-Movement Desensitization and Reprocessing, 573
  historical background of, 556–557
  hypnosis and, 173
  insight therapies, 560–565
  repressed memories and, 250–251
  review and study questions on, 569, 578
  summary test on, 576–577
  typical questions about, 558–559
  virtual reality and, 578
  Web sites on, 579
Puberty, 408, 643
Punishment
  defined, 218, 643
  positive vs. negative, 219, 233
  spanking as form of, 233, 236
  time-out as form of, 230
Pupil (eye), 95, 485, 643
Purposeful behavior, 459

Q

Quantum personality change, 470, 643
Questionnaires, 34, 155, 474, 643

R

Racial issues
  brain size and, 85
  first impressions and, 141
  intelligence testing and, 290, 294, 296
  person perception and, 581, 582
Random selection, 36, 643

Range, 612, 643
Rape myths, 602, 643
Rapid ejaculation, 344
Rapid eye movement. *See* REM sleep
Rapists, 602
Ratio IQ, 285
Rationalization, 437, 643
Rational thoughts, 575
Rat Man case study, 561, 562
Reaction formation, 437, 643
Reaction range, 293, 643
Reaction time, 415, 643
Reading, and dyslexia, 320
Real (in vivo) exposure, 525, 567
Reality principle, 436, 643–644
Real motion, 140, 643
Real self, 444, 643
Reasoning, 318, 644
Recall, 261, 644
Recency effect, 245, 644
Receptors, 54
Recognition, 261, 644
Reflection, 564
Reflexes, 56, 644
Rehearsal, 243
  elaborative, 249
  maintenance, 242, 249
Reinforcement, 218, 644
  continuous, 220
  immediate, 215, 217
  partial, 220–221
  positive vs. negative, 218, 219
  schedules of, 220–221
Reinforcers, 215, 216, 218–219
Relapse prevention, 189
Relationships
  cultural influences on, 423
  long-term, 422
  love and, 419–420
  perfect-partner schema and, 420
  success vs. failure in, 420, 422
Relative size, 130, 644
Relaxation response, 503, 644
Relaxation techniques, 503
Reliability, 287, 451, 475, 614, 644
REM behavior disorder, 153, 644
REM rebound, 153, 644
REM sleep, 153, 644
  discovery of, 147
  dreaming and, 147, 153, 160, 161, 166
  EMDR and, 573
Repair theory, 156, 644
Repressed memories, 239, 250–251, 265
Repression, 250, 265, 437, 644
Research, 27–45
  animals used in, 41
  areas of specialization in, 18–19
  case studies used for, 28, 30
  concerns of research subjects, 40
  controversy in, 24, 39
  correlation in, 32–33
  experiments used for, 28, 36–37
  methods of, 28

note-taking strategies and, 16
placebo use in, 31
review and study questions on, 38, 44
settings for, 35
summary test on, 42–43
surveys used for, 28, 29
techniques for, 34
Web sites on, 45
Resiliency, 394, 644
Resistance, 562, 644
Resistance stage, 487, 644
Respiration, 485
Responses
  in classical conditioning, 197, 198, 217
  in operant conditioning, 214, 215, 217
Resting state, 53, 644
Reticular formation, 157, 644
Retina, 95, 96, 114, 644
Retinal disparity, 129, 644
Retrieval cues, 265, 267, 271, 272, 644
Retrieving information, 239, 244, 644
Retroactive interference, 266, 644
Reuptake, 59, 175, 644
Review and study questions. *See also* Summary tests
  on adolescence, 421, 430
  on adulthood, 421, 430
  on the brain, 57, 64, 83, 90
  on childhood development, 395, 404
  on classical conditioning, 203, 210
  on cognitive learning, 227, 236
  on consciousness, 158, 166
  on drugs, 184, 192
  on emotions, 374
  on hypnosis, 184, 192
  on intelligence, 295, 302
  on language, 317, 326
  on learning, 203, 210, 227, 236
  on memory, 252, 258, 270, 278
  on mental disorders, 521, 528, 543, 552
  on motivation, 347, 356
  on the nervous system, 57, 64
  on operant conditioning, 227, 236
  on perception, 134, 144
  on personality, 447, 454, 469, 478
  on psychotherapy, 569, 578
  on research, 38, 44
  on the senses, 109, 118
  on sleep, 158, 166
  on social psychology, 599, 608
  on stress, 498, 506
  on thinking, 317, 326
Rewards. *See also* Reinforcement
  for goal achievement, 21
  intrinsic motivation and, 350
  voluntary delay of, 460
Rhino horn, 31
Rhodopsin, 96

Right hemisphere of the brain, 87
Risk factors, 427
Risky shift, 598
Ritalin, 30, 36–37, 39
Roc (TV series), 433, 442
Rods (eye), 96, 644
Rogers' self theory, 444–445
Role schemas, 584, 644
Romantic love, 419, 528
Rorschach inkblot test, 450, 644–645
Rules of organization, 127, 645

S

Sadistic rapist, 602
Sadness, 367, 369
Safety needs, 333
Salivation, 201
Satanic Verses, The (Rushdie), 321
Savants, 7, 311, 645
Schachter-Singer cognitive theory, 362, 645
Schedules of reinforcement, 220–221, 645
Schemas, 420, 584, 645
Schizophrenia, 538–542, 645
  case study of, 531, 538
  causes of, 539–540
  symptoms of, 514, 538, 541
  treatments for, 541–542, 552
Schizotypal personality disorder, 536, 645
School psychologists, 17
Scientific method, 36–37, 645
Seasonal affective disorder (SAD), 159, 532, 645
Secondary appraisal, 499, 645
Secondary reinforcers, 219, 645
Secure attachment, 385, 645
Seizures, 86
Selective attention, 548, 565
Selective serotonin reuptake inhibitors, 534
Self, 444, 645
  clones and, 64
  real vs. ideal, 444
Self-actualization, 333, 442, 443, 444, 472, 645
Self-actualization theory, 444, 472
Self-actualizing tendency, 444, 644
Self-analysis, 459
Self-concept, 444
Self-efficacy, 460, 473, 645
Self-esteem, 416, 645
Self-fulfilling prophecy, 30, 135, 645
Self-handicapping, 349, 645
Self-identity, 416
Self-injurious behavior, 219, 645
Self-management practices, 8
Self-monitoring, 574
Self-perception theory, 590, 645
Self-report questionnaires, 474, 475, 645
Self schemas, 584, 645
Self-serving bias, 586, 645

I'd like to ask you a small favor. I have worked very hard to make this book readable and stimulating and would like to know if I have succeeded. Would you take a few minutes to fill out this form and tell me your reactions to this textbook? I will use your comments, suggestions, and criticisms to improve the next edition of *Introduction to Psychology, 5th Edition.*

School: _____

Instructor's name: _____

1. What did you like most about *Introduction to Psychology*? _____

   _____

   _____

2. What did you like least about the book? _____

   _____

3. Were all the modules assigned for you to read?   Yes _____   No _____

   If not, which ones were omitted? _____

4. Did you use the Concept Review sections? Yes _____   No _____   Did you find them useful? Yes _____   No _____

5. How interesting and informative did you find the Cultural Diversity sections, which told you about behaviors in other cultures?

   _____

   _____

6. Did you use the Summary Test sections?   Yes _____   No _____

   Did you find them useful?   Yes _____   No _____

7. How interesting and informative did you find the Research Focus? _____

   _____

   _____

8. Did you purchase the *Study Guide*?   Yes _____   No _____

   If so, in electronic _____ or print _____ format?

9. Do you own a computer?   Yes _____   No _____

   If so, what type? _____

10. Do you use the Internet?   Yes _____   No _____

    If so, do you use it at school _____, at home _____, or both?

11. Did you go to the Psychology Study Center Web site?   Yes _____   No _____

    If so, did you use the quizzes or other activities?   Yes _____   No _____

12. In the space below (or in a separate letter) please make any other comments that you have about the book. (For example, did you like the way that photos and figures were integrated with the text?) I would really like to hear from you.

   _____

   _____

Many thanks for taking the time to fill out this survey.

Best wishes,
Rod Plotnik

Optional:

Your name: _____ Date: _____

May Brooks/Cole • Wadsworth quote you, either in promotion for *Introduction to Psychology,
5th Edition* or in future publishing ventures?

Yes: _____ No: _____

Sincerely,

Rod Plotnik

Also available to accompany your textbook!

World Wide Web Psychology Study Center

Featuring a full range of web-based services: **http://psychstudy.brookscole.com**

When you purchase Rod Plotnik's *Introduction to Psychology, Fifth Edition*, you can visit the Brooks/Cole • Wadsworth Psychology Study Center any time, any day, 24 hours a day! Inside the center, you can take practice quizzes for every module of your text. You'll find these online quizzes a great way to get ready for tests, because they not only give you a running score, but they offer page references to help you brush up on areas in which you need more study. In addition, you'll find fun and interactive Activities, links to psychology-related sites on the Web, Hot Topics that discuss psychology topics in the news, and more.

Available at your campus bookstore or from the publisher

Study Guide, **by Matthew Enos**
ISBN: 0-534-36145-5
Get the grade you want in your introductory psychology course!
You'll find a wide range of study aids including:
- short summaries and outlines of modules
- multiple-choice, matching, and true-false questions and answers
- Integrated language enrichment tools in each module that provide grammar and vocabulary assistance.

PsychNow!™ Interactive Experiences in Psychology
CD-ROM
ISBN: 0-314-07220-9
A dynamic, multimedia experience! Stunning graphics and animations, interesting video clips, and interactive exercises bring the theories of psychology to life. *PsychNow!* contains 39 fully interactive modules designed to pique your curiosity and enhance your understanding of core concepts.

Integrator Online™ for Introductory Psychology
CD-ROM by Arthur J. Kohn and Wendy Kohn
ISBN: 0-534-35746-6
Psychology comes to life with *Integrator Online!* Now studying for tests or exploring psychology concepts can be fun and interactive! *Integrator Online* is directly correlated to every module of your textbook. With a click of the mouse, you can reinforce your learning or explore independently by calling up animations, video clips, interactive experiments, transparencies, study pages, and quizzes.

Psychology Resources on the World Wide Web
by Edward Kardas
ISBN: 0-534-35941-8
A concise guide to psychology-related resources on the World Wide Web! Organized by topic, this handy guide will serve as a directory when you conduct research via the Internet. Up-to-date and comprehensive, this book is organized to match the organization of your textbook and includes a chapter on how to perform research on the Web.

www.wadsworth.com

ISBN 0-534-36319-9

90000

9 780534 363192